CULINARY FUNDAMENTALS

JOHNSON & WALES UNIVERSITY
College of Culinary Arts

America's Career University®

Acknowledgement of Rights: Portions of this textbook were derived from *Culinary Essentials*
© 2002, published by Glencoe/McGraw-Hill, a division of the McGraw-Hill Companies.

ISBN 0-9742491-0-6

Printed in Thailand

5 4 3 2 1

CONTENTS

Subject

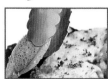

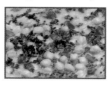

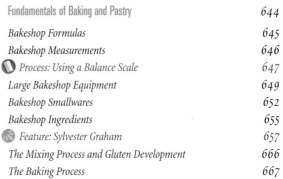

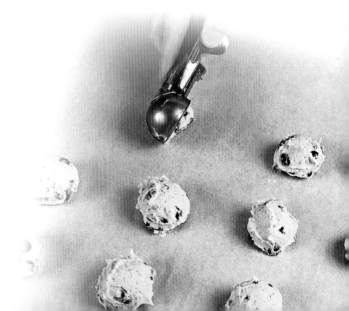

Recipes

MESSAGE FROM THE PRESIDENT

Dear Student:

The College of Culinary Arts of Johnson & Wales University is committed to your success as a future foodservice professional. The revised curriculum of the College of Culinary Arts is a reflection of this commitment. This carefully designed, flexible curriculum provides you with an exciting challenge to learn and excel in your chosen career.

Our unique "upside-down" curriculum ensures your immediate, hands-on involvement within your chosen profession. Opportunities for practical and cooperative education complement your laboratory and related classroom studies and provide valuable on-the-job experiences to build confidence in your skills.

Clearly, your formal education in the culinary arts is only the beginning of your lifelong study. This education, however, is the foundation on which your success will be built, a foundation established by Culinary Fundamentals. From this text, you will learn that foodservice is a multifaceted field that is constantly growing and changing to respond to the needs and desires of the customer. In studying the fundamentals of food, you will learn the behind-the-scenes facts and theories of food preparation and presentation. These fundamentals will prepare you to explore, discover, and create your own food frontiers.

The faculty and staff of the College of Culinary Arts have spent thousands of hours and dedicated years of their own knowledge and experience to the development of this curriculum. Culinary Fundamentals will serve not only as a learning tool but also as a resource and guide that reflects the knowledge of true culinary professionals. I invite you to take advantage of their combined wisdom. Within these covers, you will discover a truly enjoyable learning experience.

John A. Yena

University President

FOREWORD

Welcome to Johnson & Wales University. Thank you for choosing us as your educational resource. The education you will receive at the College of Culinary Arts will prepare you for a career working with food as a living and for a life colored by all the exciting possibilities awaiting the twenty-first century food professional.

As we prepare our students for industry, we incorporate many tools to ensure a quality educational experience. These tools are like the instruments of a great orchestra working together to make beautiful music. One important "instrument" for us is this textbook. Culinary Fundamentals provides you with the essential elements of our great profession and contains the collective knowledge of talented professionals, faculty, and administrators who have worked tirelessly to make this world-class resource. Whether you become a chef at a fine-dining restaurant, a manager of a prestigious hotel, the owner of your own business, or any other position in our ever-growing industry, I ask that you absorb its contents, analyze its application and practice its instructions. Make this book what it is intended to be—a lifelong "instrument" in the orchestra of your life and profession.

A special thank you to Associate Dean Paul McVety and the culinary leaders, faculty, and curriculum committee who have worked together as a team to achieve a common goal. These individuals have devoted their time, talent, knowledge, and expertise to provide you with the most current information and valuable skills necessary to maintain the most sophisticated approach to our profession. Take full advantage of the many tools, resources, and opportunities that will be afforded to you.

Thank you for trusting Johnson & Wales University to work with you in building the foundation for your future success.

Dean Karl Guggenmos, M.B.A., C.E.C., A.A.C.

Certified German Master Chef

Dean, College of Culinary Arts

ACKNOWLEDGEMENTS

Professionals who truly love educating students have written Culinary Fundamentals. I wish to thank all the faculty, administration, students, and friends from the University for their support and participation in this tremendous undertaking.

Paul McVety
Associate Dean
Project Manager

A special thanks to John Chiaro, Ed Korry, Dr. Robert Nograd, and Dr. Bradley Ware for their tireless efforts and dedication in producing this textbook.

Educational Task Force

Paul McVety	Project Manager
John Chiaro	Associate Project Manager
Dr. Robert Nograd	Associate Project Manager
Dr. Bradley Ware	Associate Project Manager

Reading and reviewing text

Amy Felder	Suzanne Vieira
Paula Figoni	Gary Welling
Steven Kalble	
Ed Korry	
Susan Marshall	

Reviewing and testing recipes

Allison Acquisto	Peter Kelly
Claudia Berube	Linda Kender
Martha Crawford	Maureen Pothier
Elaine Cwynar	Adam Sacks
Amy Felder	Cynthia Salvato

DEDICATION

This book is dedicated to Chef Robert Nograd, Dean Emeritus and former Corporate Executive Chef for Johnson & Wales University, whose contributions to Johnson & Wales and the culinary profession span the last 45 years.

Chef Nograd is a concentration camp survivor who vowed that he would never know the pain of hunger or thirst again. He dedicated himself to his profession throughout his extraordinary journey—never losing his thirst for knowledge or his hunger to become a world-class master chef.

His commitment to educating others in his art and in his craft as well as his quest to leave a legacy for future culinarians have resulted in a life spent teaching and learning, never content to settle for the status quo. In so doing, he has left an indelible mark on the lives of many past, present, and future chefs.

It is because of his personal generosity and willingness to share his knowledge, his countless contributions to culinary education, and his inspiration to culinarians around the globe that we dedicate this book to Robert Nograd, C.M.C.

With profound respect,

The faculty, students, and alumni of Johnson & Wales University

Photographs

Frank Andreozzi	Scott Parker
Tom Choice	Brook Redican
John Dion	Robert Ross
Ciril Hitz	Adam Sacks
Steve Kalble	Stephen Scaife
Juergen Knorr	Jeanette Scarcella
Ed Korry	Gerhard Schmid
Barbara Kuck	Louis Serra
Joseph Leonardi	Mark Soliday
Karen Lucier	Stephen Spencer
Diane Madsen	Adela Tancayo-Sannella
Susan Marshall	Segundo Torres
Sean O'Hara	Gary Welling
George O'Palenick	

Photographer

Ron Manville

Formatting the text and recipes

Debra Bettencourt

Karin Lucier

Storeroom

Martha Charles	Robert Lucier
Reginald Dow	David Petrone
Jack Flanagan	Rick Quarry
Erik Goellner	Cassandra Shores
Cristina Hernandez	Gil Stansfield

Student Reviewers

Jennifer Behrens

Morissa Silfen

Lindsay VanHouten

Curriculum and Recipe Contributors

College of Culinary Arts Directors

Pam Peters	Providence Campus
Wanda Cropper	Charleston Campus
Peter Lehmuller	Norfolk Campus
Mike Moskwa	North Miami Campus
Bruce Ozga	Denver Campus

Department Chair International Baking & Pastry Institute

Martha Crawford

ACKNOWLEDGEMENTS

College of Culinary Arts Faculty

Sadruddin Abdullah
Allison Acquisto
Jeff Adel
Frank Andreozzi
Charles Armstrong
Diane Aghapour
Max Ariza
Jeff Alexander
John Aukstolis
Adrian Barber
Ed Batten
Susan Batten
Donato Becce
Alan Bergman
Claudia Berube
Donna Blanchard
Patricia Blenkiron
Dedra Blount
Drue Brandenburg
Timothy Brown
Wayne Bryan
Julian Buckner
Frances Burnett
Joseph Boches
Victor Calise
Carl Calvert
Brian Campbell
Mary Campbell
Tim Campbell
Tim Cameron
John Chiaro
Thomas Choice
Elena Clement
Charles Collins
Jerry Comar
Cynthia Coston
Elaine Cwynar
David Dawson
Mark Denittis
Marc DeMarchena
Richard DeMaria

Jean-Luc Derron
Birch De Vault
Jean Jacques Dietrich
Kevin Duffy
Roger Dywer
Mary Ann Eaton
Valerie Ellsworth
Amy Felder
Paula Figoni
Christian Finck
Eric Frauwirth
James Fuchs
Hilmar Geiger
Marcella Giannasio
Russ Green
Armin Gronert
Kim Gibbs-O'Hayer
Frederick Haddad
Stephanie Hardwick
Christina Harvey
Kathy Hawkins
James Hensley
Peter Henkel
Judith Hestnes
Gilles Hezard
Rainer Hienerwadel
Ciril Hitz
Jeffrey Howard
Andrew Hoxie
Miles Huff
Helene Houde-Trzcinski
Jeremy Houghton
Steven Johansson
John Kacala
Peter Kelly
Linda Kender
Kerstin Kleber
Juergen Knorr
Ed Korry
Maria Kramer
Jean-Louis Lagalle

Lawrence LaCastra
Jerry Lanuzza
Ron Lavallee
Dean Lavornia
Alan Lazar
Joseph Leonardi
Alex Leuzzi
Hector Lipa
Robert Lothrop
Robert Lucier
Diane Madsen
Ann Marie
Michael Marra
Susan Marshall
Marcel Massenet
Kim Montello
Mary Etta Moorachian
Carrie Moranha
Michael Moskwa
Francis Mullaney
Maureen Nixon
Steve Nogle
Raymond Olobri
Sean O'Hara
George O'Palenick
Scott Parker
Yves Payraudeau
Shane Pearson
Harry Peemoeller
Robert Pekar
David Petrone
Linda Pettine
Daniel Polasek
Maureen Pothier
Felicia Pritchett
Thomas J. Provost
CharLee Puckett
Margaret Rauch
Patrick Reed
Lloyd Regier
Joseph Peter Reinhart

David Ricci
Rand Robison
Ronda Robotham
Robert Ross
Janet Rouslin
Adam Sacks
Steve Sadowski
Cynthia Salvato
Stephen Scaife
Gerhard Schmid
Robin Schmitz
Mark Segobiano
Louis Serra
Victor Smurro
Mark Soliday
Heath Stone
Karl Stybe
Adela Tancayo-Sannella
Frank Terranova
Fred Tiess
Todd Tonova
Jorge de la Torre
Segundo Torres
Lynn Tripp
Martin Tuck
Alan Vaccaro
Peter Vaillancourt
Suzanne Vieira
Jean-Michel Vienne
Chris Wagner
Bradley Ware
Dieter Wenninger
Robert Weill
Gary Welling
Susan Wigley
Patricia Wilson
Kenneth Wollenberg
Robert Zielinski
Russ Zito

Equipment Vendors

Advance Tabco
American Metal Craft, Inc.
Anne Noble
Ateco
Baxter
Boydis Coffee Company
Candlelamp Company
Carlisle FoodService Products
Carpigiani
Cleveland Range
CookShack
Demarle, Inc. USA

Detecto
Dexter-Russell, Inc.
Dinex International
Enodis Corporation
Erika Record LLC
F. Dick Corporation
Garland Commercial Industries, Inc.
Hatco Corporation
Hobart Corporation
InterMetro Industries, Inc.
JB Prince Company
John Boos & Co.

Kemper Bakery Systems
Lincoln Foodservice Products
Matfer Group
McCormick & Co., Inc.
Misono
Morton International Inc.
Oneida Ltd.
Robot Coupe USA
Scandicraft
Sid Wainer & Son Specialty Produce-
    Specialty Foods
SYSCO Corporation

Tablecraft Products Company
Taylor Precision Instruments
The Vollrath Company, L.L.C.
Town Food Service Equipment
    Company
Traulsen & Co., Inc.
Update International
Varimixer
Vita-Mix Corporation
Vulcan-Hart Company
Waring
Winston Industries, LLC

Beverage Vendors

Anne Noble
Banfi
Baronne Philippine de Rothschild
Bernkasteler Lay
Bridgeview Vineyards
Buzzard's Bay Brewing
Caliterra Reserva
Carlo Pelligrino
Cas Solar Plata
Castello Banfi
Chateau St. Michelle
Coors
Cragganmore

Cune
Dalwhinnie
d'Arenberg Wines
Delamain
Dinkel Acker
Feudi di San Gregorio
Firestone
Fortant de France
Franziskaner
Gallo Vineyards
George Killian
Glenkinchie
Harpoon

Hennessy
Johnnie Walker
Joseph Phelps Vineyards
Kobrand
Lagavulin
Louis Jadot
Luis Pato
Lungarotti
Marc Bredif
Marienhof
Melini
Muscadet de Sevre et Maine
Pesquera de Duero

Quinta Do Vale Meão
Ribera del Duero
Robert Mondavi
Rodney Strong
Sakonnet
SCAA
Shenandoah School Road Vineyards
Sierra Nevada
St. Francis
Stellenbosch
The British Beer and Pub Association

1 Cooking: A Journey

The history of cooking, which began in the Stone Age, is still evolving today. Since ancient times and the development of civilization, the culinary arts and tastes in food have mirrored the achievements and interactions of societies. Only 400 years old, the fascinating story of modern cookery is one of tradition and innovation, classic dishes and food trends. It is one of great chefs who possess a masterful command of technique and an often visionary creativity. Since extensive knowledge and appreciation of the culinary past is a distinguishing mark of the professional chef, an understanding of this rich heritage is a requirement for every serious student of the culinary arts.

8000 B.C.
People in the Near East begin to cultivate crops.

A.D. 14
The first known cookbook, "De Re Coquinaria by Apicius," is published.

1533
Grande cuisine is introduced to the French court by chefs of Catherine de Medici.

1833
Grande cuisine is detailed in Marie-Antoine Carême's "L'art de la Cuisine Française."

1890s
Escoffier opens the Savoy Hotel and develops the modern brigade system.

1970s
Paul Bocuse inspires a fresh "nouvelle" look at French cuisine.

1977
Through the efforts of Dr. Minor, Chef Szathmary, and Lt. Gen. McLaughlin, the U.S. government recognizes chefs as professionals.

Through Time

KEY TERMS

grande cuisine

regional cuisine

nouvelle cuisine

cuisine minceur

fusion cuisine

The Stone Age

Millions of years ago, the diet of the earliest humans consisted primarily of foods such as fruits, leaves, and grains that were easy to gather and required no preparation before eating. During the Stone Age—the Paleolithic period, or Old Stone Age (beginning as early as 750,000 B.C.), and the Neolithic period, or New Stone Age (beginning around 8000 B.C.)— humans began to make and use stone tools and acquire a larger variety of foods in new ways.

Paleolithic Tools and Foods

Although few traces of human activity during the Paleolithic period have survived, a variety of stone tools has been found. Some of the oldest known stone implements come from East Africa and date as far back as 600,000 B.C. Paleolithic tools include axes and blades for cutting and chopping. Caves in Western Europe, which depict scenes of food gathering and hunting, provide other clues about prehistoric life.

In order to survive during the Paleolithic period, humans hunted wild animals, birds, and fish and collected nuts, fruits, and berries. Artifacts found at Vestonice show that people ate mammoth, reindeer, horse, fox, wolf, and tortoise. Other evidence from this period indicates that food sources included fish, fowl, and water lilies.

The Neolithic Food Revolution

One of the most significant changes in human food habits occurred around 8000 B.C., when people in the Near East began to grow food rather than gather it. This led to a more settled and sedentary existence. For example, humans started raising cereal crops such as rye and wheat and keeping livestock, including pigs, cows, goats, and sheep. Archaeologists have discovered millstones in these areas, an indication that Neolithic peoples were grinding wheat and other grains to make flour for bread.

Changes in cooking methods also may have taken place at this time. Cooking techniques in the Paleolithic period already included broiling or roasting food over an open flame or glowing hot coals and braising food in clay cylinders laid on top of hot ashes in a pit. People now began cooking foods in water brought to a boil in earthenware pottery. They also built the first closed ovens for baking.

Early Civilizations

Advances in food production and preparation in early civilizations had a broad reach. Agriculture and the domestication of animals spread from Mesopotamia in southwestern Asia through the Middle East north into Turkey and Greece and west across Egypt and North Africa. People in northern Europe began to farm sometime after 3000 B.C. Farming practices advanced with the invention of the plow around 3550 B.C., and food production increased.

In the Bronze Age, which began around 3000 B.C. in Mediterranean areas, people began to cook using liquid in pots of copper and bronze. New tools and utensils also became available, making daily life easier.

Mesopotamia and Ancient Egypt

The early civilizations of Mesopotamia and Egypt shared some food habits and traditions. Although beef, lamb, pork, deer, fowl (excluding chicken), fish, turtles, vegetables, and fruits were all part of the Mesopotamian diet, grains were a staple food. Besides cooking cereals in water as a porridge and using ground grain to make bread, the Mesopotamians favored beer as a beverage for festive occasions. Inscriptions on Egyptian tombs—"Give me bread when I am hungry. Give me beer when I am thirsty"—bear witness to the heavy use of grain in the ancient Egyptian diet.

Both the Mesopotamians and the Egyptians developed a system of writing early on and thus had the means to record recipes. The first known recipes come from Mesopotamia and date to the second millennium B.C. Although no formal cookbooks from either civilization exist to shed light on food preparation, Egyptian tomb paintings and hieroglyphics reveal that food was an integral part of Egyptian social and religious ceremonies. Excavated tombs have yielded remnants of foods such as figs and bread, which were typical funerary offerings. Barley, wheat, preserved meats, beer, and wine also have been found in Egyptian tombs, some from as early as 2613 to 2181 B.C. Ancient Egyptian food preparation methods such as open-hearth baking of unleavened bread and salt preservation of meats and fish are still common today. The Egyptians also dried and smoked foods and stored fruits in honey and fish in oil to preserve them.

Hebrew Dietary Traditions

Food also had religious associations for the ancient Hebrews. According to the Torah, or Hebrew Bible, Moses announced rules for Hebrews about the consumption of food. Today, Jews around the world continue to observe the dietary rules set in ancient times.

Hebrew dietary laws cover a broad spectrum of foods, but the most important rules deal with the use of food from animals. The laws cover which animals can be eaten and which cannot, methods of slaughter, permitted animal parts, preparation of meat, the combination of meat and other foods, and examination of foods. Followers of the Jewish faith believe that the laws express the will of God and reflect the Hebrews' covenant, or formal agreement, with God. Observation of the dietary rules that reflect this covenant set the Hebrews apart from others.

The Classical Period

By the time of the Greeks and Romans, cooking and eating had an objective beyond survival and ceremony—pleasure. Although a few staples (bread, wine, oil), "humble" vegetables (leeks, onions, garlic, cabbage), and simple delicacies such as figs and honey formed the basis of the average person's diet, upper-class Greeks and Romans sampled and enjoyed a variety of foods in a banquet setting.

Food and the Greeks

Greek writers such as Plato (fourth century B.C.) and Athenaeus (third century A.D.) tell us that Greek cooks practiced the culinary arts with considerable care and refinement and that diners thoroughly enjoyed the fruits of their labors. The Greeks made cheeses, baked bread, and produced wine. They became skilled in the use of seasonings and spices, made sauces using oil and cheese, and cultivated olives. Meat, such as rabbit, gained popularity and was commonly grilled.

Influenced in large part by the ideas of the great physician and teacher Hippocrates (ca. 460–377 B.C.), the Greeks, and later the Romans, focused on eating a healthful diet. Consuming food items for both medicinal and nutritional purposes, they viewed cooking methods, combinations of foods, drink, and seasonings as contributors to overall well-being.

The Greeks introduced a tradition of lavish dinner parties or banquets, which were often followed by a symposium, the ritual consumption of wine. Although the Greeks kept food and wine separate, the Romans did not. Instead, wine was consumed during the banquet and was considered simply a beverage. Greek dinner parties customarily seated five guests, and Roman parties usually accommodated nine. A full dinner often required as many as a dozen cooks, each responsible for a specific task.

Roman Cooking

The cookbook of Marcus Apicius (first century A.D.), one of the first written works on food, offers a wealth of information about Roman cooking. Apicius outlined some of the basic characteristics of Roman cookery, including grinding meats with mortar and pestle, spit roasting, pungent seasonings, high regard for rabbit, and frequent use of saffron, honey, and garum (a fermented liquid made from fish viscera, which was the base of almost every sauce).

In the typical Roman kitchen, the master cook supervised food preparation from a platform at the rear of the room. Square hearth fires stood in the middle. Kitchen equipment featured pots made of bronze, brass, clay, or silver, as well as stone ovens fired with wood.

Formal dining developed further during the Roman Empire. A Roman banquet usually featured three courses: the appetizer (eggs, salads, oysters), the main course, and a final course of fruit. Historical research suggests that formal dining followed rules of etiquette. Guests were greeted at the door and provided with a change of robes and sandals. After entering the host's home, the guests washed their hands and feet and were adorned with a garland of flowers, which was believed to repel the ill effects of alcohol consumption.

The Middle Ages and the Renaissance

Roman traditions continued to dominate cooking and dining practices during the Middle Ages. Another important tradition that began in this period was the formation of culinary guilds, which gave chefs a sense of community. During the Renaissance, advances in the culinary arts helped set the stage for the development of modern cookery.

Medieval Ways

Culinary staples during the Middle Ages included leeks, carrots, and turnips, following the model of the Roman diet. Contact with Germanic tribes in the later Roman Empire had resulted in wider use of animal products, especially pork, milk, and butter. By the medieval period, the meat supply also included game, some cattle, and an abundance of fish. Garum was widely used as a seasoning over mashed boiled meats and fish. The Roman cooking techniques of chopping, mashing, and heavy seasoning of foods continued through the Middle Ages. In the late Middle Ages, many spices and other foods such as sugar, fruits, and nuts came to European kitchens from distant places by way of the Crusaders and merchants from Venice, who developed a monopoly on trade in the Middle East.

Medieval kitchens typically stood apart from the main house to reduce the risk of fire. The traditional kitchen was crowded, noisy, hot, and smoky. Vents in the ceiling allowed the release of smoke and heat from the roasting spits and simmering iron kettles. Cooks kept food cold in cellars or along the floor of the kitchen.

Kitchen equipment included iron pots as well as various hooks, spoons, and knives. The cauldron, an iron vessel hanging from a metal arm over hot coals, was the main cooking pot. The chimney hearth accommodated three cauldrons. The cauldron on the left side of the hearth was used for roasting, and the others were used for boiling. Breads and pies were baked in an oven on the side of the chimney.

The medieval kitchen produced the first master chef—Guillaume Tirel, better known as Taillevent. Taillevent, who served as cook to the French king Charles VI, published *Le Viandier de Taillevent*, the forerunner of other European cookbooks.

Renaissance Developments

The late 1300s marked the beginning of the Renaissance, an era of revival in the arts and sciences that spread across Europe from south to north. Italy dominated the culinary scene in the 1400s. By the end of the century, it had shifted to Spain, whose explorations and conquests in the Americas introduced new foods and methods of food preparation to Europe. Christopher Columbus and Hernán Cortés as well as other explorers and conquistadors returned to Europe with tomatoes, chili peppers, potatoes, avocados, corn, vanilla beans, and cacao, the main ingredient of chocolate. These food items had a lasting impact on European cuisine.

In the period prior to 1400, European cooking assimilated elements of Arab cuisine, such as the use of citrus juices, almonds, rose water, and certain spices, as a result of Spanish and Sicilian contact with Muslims. Muslims' own eating habits are strictly prescribed by their religion, which recognizes eating as a form of worship. Islamic dietary laws differentiate between permitted foods (*halal*) and prohibited foods (*haram*). *Haram* includes all swine and improperly slaughtered animals.

By the late 1500s, France had become Europe's culinary center, thanks in part to Italian noblewoman Catherine de Medici's marriage to the future French king Henry II in 1533, a union that brought Italian chefs and culinary expertise to the French court. Cultural trends in France and France's wealth and power also fostered the development of the culinary arts and gastronomy.

The Birth of Grande Cuisine

Over the next several hundred years, French cooking changed, incorporating new ingredients, seasonings, procedures, and styles of presentation. The result of these changes was grande cuisine, an elaborate cuisine consisting of many courses and following strict cooking rules. Three chefs were instrumental in the development and refinement of grande cuisine—La Varenne, Carême, and Escoffier.

La Varenne

Modern cooking began in 1651 with the publication of *Le Cuisinier François* by François Pierre de la Varenne (1615–1678). This 30-volume work fully documented the development of French cooking from the beginning of the Middle Ages and detailed Italian influences on French cuisine. *Le Cuisinier François* also reflected contemporary chefs' interest in detail, balance, and harmony in cooking and ingredients. La Varenne described the reduction of cooking juices to concentrate their flavor, for instance, and the use of nuts, truffles, and mushrooms. La Varenne's cookbook also contained the first published reference to the use of roux. With its emphasis on the natural flavors of food and other recommendations, *Le Cuisinier François* changed culinary arts forever.

Over the next 100 years, chefs employed by royalty and working in the households of nobility built on the foundation laid by La Varenne, who is recognized as the founder of classical French cuisine. They created their own recipes, following rigorous cooking principles, and presented elaborate meals with multiple courses featuring rich new dishes named for royalty and nobility. Their culinary efforts were the beginning of grande cuisine.

Carême

After the French Revolution, noble families and households disbanded, leaving chefs without a livelihood. To survive, many chefs looked for work in public houses. They prepared food and sold it to whoever could pay, thus establishing the first modern restaurants. Now new dishes bore the names of chefs. Restaurants on the grand boulevards of Paris catered to the wealthy upper class and offered a version of grande cuisine once served only to nobles and royals.

Grande cuisine, or haute cuisine, reached its height under the influence of Marie-Antoine Carême (1784–1833). A chef to royalty throughout Europe, Carême systematized French cooking by identifying the basic, or mother, sauces (also known as leading sauces); compound sauces; classical garnishes; and standard terminology for recipes. Carême documented his style of grande cuisine in *L'Art de la Cuisine Française*.

Escoffier

In the nineteenth century, Georges Auguste Escoffier (1847–1935), chef at some of Europe's finest hotels, including the Ritz in Paris and the Savoy in London, refined grande cuisine by modifying many of Carême's recipes and classifications. In particular, Escoffier simplified Carême's complex system of sauces to the five basic sauces (espagnole, béchamel, velouté, hollandaise, and tomato) and their compounds. He was also known for creating the French brigade system, which streamlined culinary operations. Since it observes the basic principles of classical French cooking without complicated procedures and display, Escoffier's grande cuisine is sometimes called *cuisine classique,* or classic cuisine.

Escoffier's *Le Guide Culinaire,* first published in 1903, remains a classic reference today, with its emphasis on the use of quality ingredients and the importance of an in-depth understanding of cooking technique. *Le Guide Culinaire* contains thousands of recipes, including many named for Escoffier's greatest patrons, as well as traditional garnishes for hundreds of dishes.

American Cookery

While grande cuisine was taking shape in France, American cuisine was only in its infancy. European settlers in the Americas brought familiar cooking methods and some staple foods from the Old World with them and combined these with culinary techniques and ingredients they found in the New World. From the start, American cookery has been a mosaic of ingredients and techniques from a variety of cultures.

Native American Food Patterns

When Columbus arrived in the Americas in the late 1400s, most Native Americans followed traditional practices. Their main crops were maize (corn), beans, and squash, but other valuable crops included potatoes, sweet potatoes, and manioc, or cassava. Domesticated animals were not a large source of food. However, in addition to cultivating crops, indigenous Americans fished, hunted, and collected foods. They devised storage pits for grains, nuts, and other foods, used a variety of cooking techniques, including roasting and boiling in pots, and preserved some foods by drying and smoking.

Colonial Food Habits

European settlers learned a great deal from indigenous peoples about growing and preparing foods native to the New World. Native Americans taught newcomers from Europe the most efficient ways to cook outdoors and how to prepare beans and corn. Corn breads, succotash, and various soups and stews became part of the colonial cooking repertoire. For their part, Europeans changed the food supply in the Americas, introducing livestock such as pigs, cattle, and sheep, and plant foods such as rice, wheat, barley, and broadbeans from Europe.

Soon colonists were comfortable preparing a variety of foods using a blend of Native American and European techniques. Their food choices established the basic American eating pattern still evident today: a meat entrée accompanied by vegetables, grains, legumes, and dairy products. The beverage of choice was cider, beer, rum, or wine, which colonists enjoyed both at home and at the newly opened inns and taverns. In the early nineteenth century, Americans began to dine at such eating establishments as Durgin-Park's Market Dining Room in Boston, which is still in operation today near Boston's famed Faneuil Hall Marketplace. Durgin-Park's offerings, then as now, were regional specialties, including chowder, broiled lobster, venison, New England boiled dinner, apple pandowdy, Indian pudding, and pies.

Regional Cuisine

During the vast land expansion of the nineteenth century, the American diet began to show variety from one geographic region to the next. Each part of the country developed its own *regional cuisine*—foods, ingredients, and cooking methods characteristic of that particular geographic region. Several factors contributed to the development of regional cuisines, including availability of local ingredients and the influence of cultural groups. Figure 1-1 on page 9 shows some of the culinary differences between regions of the United States.

Changes in Food Production, Service, and Consumption

The nineteenth century was a time of great change in the United States. The Industrial Revolution introduced machines that transformed farming and manufacturing. Large numbers of people moved to the cities. Many of these people were immigrants, or newcomers to America. These developments brought changes in food production and service as well as in eating habits.

New ideas and technology in the 1800s had a great impact on agriculture, industry, and cities. Improved tools; new farming methods such as fertilization; and the development of various farm machines, including tractors, combines, and cultivators, increased the supply of food. At the same time, the need for farm workers decreased. A manufacturing boom in the cities attracted people from rural areas and other countries.

Transportation also improved in the 1800s. Railroads could now ship fresh food to cities on the East Coast and across the country, allowing people in cities who could not grow their own food to purchase food delivered to the city by train. With the availability of fresh food, more restaurants began to open in big cities, such as Ye Olde Union Oyster Bar in Boston. It opened for business in 1826, one year before the publication of Robert Roberts's *House Servant's Directory*. This cookbook, the first written by an African American, appeared in Boston in 1827. Roberts, who had served as a butler to Governor Christopher Gore, wanted to encourage house servants to become caterers and managers, not subservient workers.

Food service benefited from the many technological advances of the nineteenth century. The invention of the icebox; the mechanization of canning; the development of pasteurization, electric ovens, and kitchen equipment; and the improvement of gas stoves and ranges all helped fuel the growth of food service. Prior to the mid-nineteenth century, most commercial kitchens had no refrigeration, running water, electricity, or gas.

Immigration in the nineteenth century changed American cities and cuisine. Nearly 5 million immigrants arrived in the United States in the period between 1830 and 1860. Most were from Germany, Great Britain, and Ireland. Two waves of immigration after 1860 brought people from Scandinavian countries and from Italy, Austria, Hungary, Russia, Greece, Poland, Portugal, and Spain. Asian immigrants also began to make a home in America's big cities. Ethnic communities spread across America, and ethnic dishes began to find a place in American cuisine.

FIGURE 1-1

Cooking: A Journey Through Time

9

Regional Cuisine

NORTHEAST

Foods and Preparations	*Influences*
New England boiled dinner, meat pie, fish stews and soups, clam chowder, clambakes, codcakes, salt cod, chorizo and peppers, baked beans, succotash, Indian pudding, Southern Italian specialties, brown bread, maple syrup, cider, fruit pies and desserts, cream dishes, light seasonings	*Native American, English, French Canadian, Italian, Portuguese*

MID-ATLANTIC

Foods and Preparations	*Influences*
Schnitzel, scrapple, sausages, apple butter, sauerkraut, slaw, pretzels, bagels, waffles, pork, dairy products, stronger seasonings	*Dutch, German*

MIDWEST

Foods and Preparations	*Influences*
Jerky, country hams, sausages, gravies, beef stews and pot pies, meatloaf, fish boils, corn roasts, freshwater fish, cheese, potatoes, root vegetables, fondue, rye and pumpernickel breads, wild rice, pancakes, strudel, applesauce, apple juice, sauerkraut, nut candies, poppy seed cake, lager beer, mild seasonings	*Native American, Polish, Hungarian, Czech, German, Scandinavian*

SOUTH

Foods and Preparations	*Influences*
Brunswick stew, country hams, redeye gravy, corn breads, biscuits, spoon bread, barbecued pork and beef, chitterlings, jambalaya, fried chicken, crab cakes, crab boils, shrimp boils, crawfish boils, catfish, butter bean custard, peanut soup, peach pie, key lime pie, greens with fatback or salt pork, hoppin' John, fried okra and okra stews, hominy, grits, gumbos, sweet potato pie, nut cakes, pies, brittles, rice, hot and spicy seasonings	*Scots-Irish, English, Welsh, French, Creole, Cajun, African*

WEST

Foods and Preparations	*Influences*
Barbecue, corn dishes, Tex-Mex food, California cuisine, chorizo, chili con carne, citrus fruits, guacamole, poi, olives, tuna, crab, sourdough bread, mesclun, steaks, game, grilled lamb, Basque potatoes, cioppino, teriyaki, luau pork, clam hash, salmon chowder, sashimi, trout, fry bread, Asian noodle dishes, stir-fried dishes, tortillas, tacos, quesadillas, chimichangas, turkey and chicken mole, pineapple, sugarcane, chilies prepared or used variously, hot and spicy seasonings	*Spanish, Mexican, Native American, Chinese, Japanese, Southeast Asian, Hawaiian, Pacific Island*

Traditional New England Clambake

The New England clambake is a prime example of regional cuisine. The clambake is a Native American tradition that European settlers adopted and adapted. Native Americans steamed shellfish by placing them over hot stones and covering them with seaweed. Today a clambake often includes corn, potatoes, onions, and lobster or chicken in addition to clams. Though not particularly complicated, preparation and actual cooking take time. The first step is to dig a deep pit in the sand and line it with dry stones. (Wet stones may explode during heating.) Then build a wood fire on top of the stones, leaving it to burn for several hours. While the fire is burning, prepare the food items. Put lobsters or chicken halves on ice. Wash the clams. Soak ears of corn (still in the husk but with silk removed) in cold water. If using onions, peel and trim them.

Wash and oil the potatoes. When the fire has burned down and the stones are hot, place the food on top of the stones. The usual order is potatoes, corn, onions, chicken or lobsters, and clams. Then cover with a layer of wet seaweed, which will provide both steam and aromatics. Put a tarpaulin over everything, and let the food cook. The different foods will determine cooking times. Check the clams after about a half hour. When the clams are open and the lobsters are red, the food is ready. Lemon and melted butter are traditional accompaniments. As an alternative, shown in the photo, the New England clambake can be cooked in a metal steamer or pot placed on a fire grate over the fire. The ingredients would be the same; only the cooking method would change.

Evolution in European Cuisine

As American cooking was beginning to absorb elements of other cuisines, a new cuisine was evolving in Europe. French chef Fernand B. Point (1897–1955) brought Escoffier's French classic cuisine into the twentieth century by merging it with aspects of regional French cooking to produce what is known as *nouvelle cuisine,* or "new cooking." Nouvelle cuisine moved away from the rich sauces, intricate garnishes, and traditional accompaniments of classic French cuisine to lighter, fresher food, preserving natural flavors and served in smaller portions. Point emphasized procedure and wanted food to be at once elegant and simple. He trained a number of chefs, including Paul Bocuse and Roger Verge, who, along with Michel Guérard and others, carried nouvelle cuisine into the 1960s and 1970s.

Guérard introduced *cuisine minceur* (or "cookery of slimness") in the 1970s, a cooking technique that reduced calories without sacrificing flavor. He used herbs instead of fats such as butter and oil to flavor foods. Guérard also eliminated sugar—except for the natural ones contained in fruits—as well as starches and cream from his list of ingredients. Steaming, baking, and poaching were his main cooking methods, and he added miniature or julienne vegetables to his artfully arranged serving plates.

Emergence of Modern American Cuisine

The evolution of European cuisine laid the groundwork for modern American cuisine. American chefs of the 1970s adapted nouvelle cuisine and cuisine minceur in their kitchens. The 1971 opening of Alice Waters's Chez Panisse in Berkeley, California, raised the status of American chefs and drastically altered the cuisine of U.S. restaurants. Following Guérard's lead, Waters offered delicious lowfat meals that centered around local seasonal ingredients, fresh vegetables, fish, poultry, and lean meats. Like Guérard, Waters shunned frying and instead steamed or grilled her entrées. She won national acclaim and inspired many chefs, especially women, who before then had been reluctant to enter this predominately male field. Among her protégées are Lydia Shire (Boston's Biba), Anne Rosenzweig (New York's Arcadia), Joyce Goldstein (San Francisco's Square One), and Mary Sue Milliken and Susan Feniger (L.A.'s City Restaurant). Other well-known American chefs of the 1970s and 1980s include Jeremiah Tower and Paul Prudhomme. Tower, once a chef at Chez Panisse before opening his own restaurant (San Francisco's Stars), is known for his use of fresh California ingredients, such as Monterey Bay prawns and San Francisco almonds, walnuts, and mountain pears. Prudhomme, who opened K-Paul's Louisiana Kitchen in New Orleans in 1979, started the U.S. craze for blackened fish and Cajun cuisine.

The 1980s also introduced a new cooking style, *fusion cuisine*, which combines culinary elements from the United States, France, Spain, Italy, China, and Thailand. It was inspired by the ever-increasing number of people living or traveling abroad. Washington, D.C.'s Cities, which featured cuisine from a different international city every month, and New York's Quilted Giraffe, which featured such diverse offerings as tuna wasabi pizza, duck confit, and Japanese tasting menus called kaiseki, are examples of fusion cuisine.

The proliferation of new restaurants in the United States at the end of the twentieth century catapulted chefs toward celebrity status. The popularity of cooking shows in the 1960s and food magazines, including "Food & Wine" and "Bon Appétit," in the 1980s contributed to this trend.

Media and Celebrity Chefs

Television brought American chefs to the attention of the public beginning in the 1960s. Julia Child pioneered the professional cooking show when she appeared on public television in 1963 to expound on the pleasures of French cooking and demonstrate its techniques. Child studied culinary arts at the Cordon Bleu cooking school in Paris and then privately with chefs Max Bugnard, Claude Thilmond, and Pierre Mangelatte. After publishing *Mastering the Art of French Cooking* in 1961 with coauthors Simone Beck and Louisette Bertholle, Child was invited to appear on a public television program to promote the new book. Her famous television series, "The French Chef," was launched, and the marriage between mass media and cooking began.

Other media pioneers in the culinary arts include the following:

- James Beard, often called the Father of American Cooking
- "Galloping Gourmet" Graham Kerr, who helped make fine cuisine accessible to an American audience
- Joyce Chen, a restaurateur and writer, who was the first Asian chef to have a television show in the United States
- Martin Yan, another Asian chef, who hosted the long-running cooking show "Yan Can Cook" and was a distinguished visiting chef at Johnson & Wales
- Paul Prudhomme, whose shows, including "A Fork in the Road," were based on his cookbooks
- Emeril Lagasse, a Johnson & Wales graduate and celebrity chef with an extremely faithful following

American Culinary Leaders

The media frenzy continued during the 1980s, when American chefs capitalized on mass media, writing hundreds of cookbooks that documented the many different movements occurring in the foodservice industry. Among the topics of such books as *New Recipes from Moosewood Restaurant* by the Moosewood Collective and *Lord Krishna's Cuisine: The Art of Indian Vegetarian Cooking* by Yamuna Devi were American regional and vegetarian cuisine, the infusion of world cuisines, and comfort foods. American chefs continue to lead the way in innovative cookery. Each adds to the mosaic that is American cuisine.

Foodservice has a rich heritage that dates back thousands of years. Around 3000 B.C., grain traders traveling to different regions needed food, beverages, and shelter on their journeys. Inns and lodges were created to accommodate these travelers. As cooking evolved, so did positions in foodservice. The brigade system was established by Escoffier, a great chef of the early twentieth century, who assigned specific tasks to certain positions. Today, positions are available in production, management, and other related fields.

A.D. 1782
The first modern restaurant opens, run by Antoine Beauvilliers. It has regular hours, private tables, and a menu listing available dishes.

1803
The first restaurant guides are written and published.

late 19th century
The French brigade system is developed by Escoffier while working at the Savoy Hotel. This system allows dishes to be prepared more efficiently, decreasing patrons' waiting time. Also during this time, chefs begin to become entrepreneurs, rather than working as servants.

1963
Julia Child hosts the first televised cooking show.

1972
Leslie Revsin becomes the first female chef to take charge of a famous hotel kitchen.

The Foodservice Industry

The foodservice industry employs 11.6 million people in the United States, ranging from short order cooks to general managers in fine-dining restaurants, making it one of the largest employment sectors in the nation. In 2000, chefs, cooks, and food preparation workers held more than 2.8 million jobs. Job openings are expected to increase through 2010. Driving the industry's growth are increases in household income and work hours— changes that cause people to dine out more frequently. In addition to new jobs created by industry growth, retiring foodservice personnel will create additional job openings.

Careers in food service include jobs in production, service, and management. Most positions depend on providing a service, such as cooking food or waiting on customers. The kitchen staff responsible for production includes chefs and cooks who may specialize in particular types of food production. In serving food, the servers directly influence the experience and satisfaction of guests. Management carries the responsibility of overseeing operations, recruiting and training staff, and guiding the direction of the foodservice facility.

Opportunities in Production, Service, and Management

Historically, large hotels have used a *brigade* system, which divides responsibilities into special tasks assigned to each member of the staff. Today, however, most establishments use a variation of the classical brigade system. For example, many foodservice operations employ prep cooks who are responsible for preparing ingredients. Other opportunities include line or station cooks who work on the production line. The sous chef reports to the executive chef, supervises other cooks, and fills in for the executive chef when necessary. There is also a service brigade system to manage the responsibilities of the dining room staff. Figure 2-1 and Figure 2-2 on page 16 describe each position in the brigade and in management. Figure 2-3 on page 17 provides information on other related foodservice opportunities.

Hospitality Industry

The hospitality industry was created to provide travelers with food, beverages, and shelter. Fueled by the rapid growth of travel and tourism, this industry boasts an extensive network of businesses that stretches around the world, employing millions of people and serving billions.

Because people who are away from home depend on foodservice for snacks, meals, and beverages, this service is a critical part of the hospitality industry. According to a recent Travel Industry Association of America report, more than 67 million tourists dined out when they traveled, and dining out was the most popular activity planned after arriving at their destination.

FIGURE 2-1

GARDE-MANGER, PANTRY CHEF

Is responsible for cold food items (salads, dressings, cold meat and cheese platters, cold meats and sauces)

SAUCIER, SAUCE CHEF

Prepares sautéed foods and their sauces

POISSONIER, FISH CHEF

Is responsible for all types of fish and their sauces

GRILLARDIN, GRILL CHEF

Produces all grilled foods

FRITURIER, FRY CHEF

Cooks fried foods

ROTISSEUR, ROAST CHEF

Roasts, braises, and stews foods and produces their sauces

ENTREMETIER, VEGETABLE CHEF

Cooks hot appetizers, soups, egg dishes, pasta, and vegetables

TOURNANT, SWING CHEF

Works every station in absence of the regular chef

PATISSIER, PASTRY CHEF

Produces all baked goods, desserts, and pastries

BOUCHER, BUTCHER

Butchers all meats and poultry

COMMUNARD

Prepares the staff's food

ABOYEUR, EXPEDITER/ANNOUNCER

Takes the order and gives it to the correct chef

COMMIS

Works as an apprentice under a particular station chef

SOMMELIER, WINE STEWARD

In charge of all aspects of wine service

MAÎTRE D'HÔTEL

In charge of all front-of-house operations

CHEF DE SALE, DINING ROOM MANAGER

Is responsible for service in the dining room

CHEF DE RANG, CAPTAIN

Explains the menu to the guests, takes the order, prepares food tableside

COMMIS DE RANG, FRONT WAITER

Serves food and beverages to guests

COMMIS DE SUITE, BACK WAITER

Places and picks up orders from the kitchen

COMMIS DE BARRASSEUR, BUSSER

Clears and grooms the table

FIGURE 2-2

GENERAL MANAGER

Oversees hiring and training of personnel; orders and purchases supplies and equipment, including equipment maintenance; coordinates the establishment's foodservice activities; may devise marketing strategy and/or promotional campaigns; depending on the type of establishment involved, may also work with budgets or participate in food preparation or packaging

FOOD AND BEVERAGE MANAGER

Acts as liaison to the sales department to enhance profitability; directs management and operation of establishment; oversees budgets

EXECUTIVE CHEF

Manages all kitchen operations, including the supervision of food preparation and presentation; ensures that the work environment is safe and sanitary; plans menus; devises budgets; trains employees in necessary cooking methods

RESTAURANT MANAGER

Oversees entire restaurant, including its day-to-day operations such as record keeping, payroll, advertising, and hiring; supervises kitchen manager and dining room supervisor; may perform other roles, especially if staffing or budget is limited

KITCHEN MANAGER

Is the "executive chef" for most chain restaurants; orders ingredients and makes sure that they are correctly prepared; supervises non-production kitchen staff, such as purchasing staff; may not have the authority to determine the culinary direction of operation

FOODSERVICE DIRECTOR, OR BANQUET MANAGER

Supervises banquet operations in hotels, banquet facilities, hospitals, and universities; coordinates events that require food and servers; in large operations, manages all self-service or full-service dining operations; works closely with executive chef to ensure high-quality foodservice

CATERING DIRECTOR

Coordinates and plans menus for multifunction foodservice operations; reports to foodservice director or general manager

PURCHASING DIRECTOR

Oversees the buying of goods; evaluates pricing to determine best cost and value; orders appropriate quantities; works with executive chef, food and beverage director, and department heads

FIGURE 2-3

FOODSERVICE CONSULTANT

Advises and directs foodservice managers or owners about business and marketing decisions; may assist with facility site selection and planning, restaurant concept, menu design and selection, equipment evaluation and planning, and interior design and layout; may provide advice about budgeting and pricing strategies

FOOD WRITER

Writes and/or edits information about food, beverages, and the foodservice industry; jobs include book authors, magazine and newspaper journalists, broadcasters, and reviewers

FOOD PHOTOGRAPHER

Photographs food for magazines, advertising, marketing, menus, and other printed and electronic materials

FOOD STYLIST

Arranges and styles food before it is photographed, filmed, or taped

NUTRITIONIST

Promotes good nutrition through healthy eating and behaviors and encourages dietary modification to treat or prevent illness; directs food programs; supervises meal preparation

RESEARCH CHEF/CULINOLOGIST

Works in a lab or test kitchen to create new food products; may develop packaged food products and final menu items

PERSONAL CHEF

Works directly for individuals or families who have little time to prepare meals for themselves; plans menus, shops for food items, and prepares food (usually in the client's home)

ATHLETIC TEAM CHEF

Plans menus and prepares food (or supervises its preparation) for an athletic team; usually works with a nutritionist and athletes to meet individual dietary needs

TEACHER

Teaches courses at a culinary school or university; usually requires many years of experience, certification, and advanced degrees in foodservice education

SALES REPRESENTATIVE

Represents a supplier or manufacturer; assists chefs in selecting food and equipment that will best meet the foodservice operation's needs and budget

Where Are the Opportunities?

Opportunities for employment are plentiful in the foodservice industry, which offers hundreds of jobs in a variety of settings, ranging from entry-level positions that require little or no experience to positions that require years of work experience and education. Food service takes place in two settings: commercial and noncommercial.

Commercial operations *Commercial operations,* such as fast-food chains and fine-dining restaurants, are in business to be profitable. To stay in business, they must be cost-effective, earning more than enough to cover daily expenses.

Noncommercial operations *Noncommercial operations,* such as government facilities, schools, hospitals, and armed forces, aim to cover daily expenses, such as wages and food costs. These facilities are not in business to make money but to provide a service for their customers, who may be employees, students, patients, or military personnel.

Restaurants

Except for the U.S. government, foodservice operations provide work for more people than any other employer in the nation at about 11.6 million people, or 9% of employed workers in the United States. Because more people are eating out, dining establishments are multiplying across the nation to meet the demand. There are now operations suiting virtually any occasion, budget, or taste.

Fine-dining restaurants A fine-dining restaurant offers excellent food, fine wines, and skilled service from professional servers. More complex food preparation results in relatively high menu prices. Meals are served in several courses at a relaxed pace and usually last about two hours. Most job opportunities in fine dining require both training and work experience. Many fine-dining restaurants are independently owned.

Dinner-house restaurants Dinner-house restaurants provide moderately priced, easily prepared meals. Some dinner-house restaurants have added ethnic dishes to their menus in response to the growing multicultural market. Most serve alcoholic beverages. Dinner houses are usually part of a national chain or a franchise, but they can be independently operated.

Family restaurants Family restaurants offer customers a relaxed atmosphere. These operations feature moderate prices, home-style cooking, and child-friendly menus. Some family restaurants also serve alcoholic beverages.

Quick-service restaurants Quick-service restaurants provide a limited, fairly consistent selection of food at reasonable prices. The menu is usually à la carte, with items priced either individually or as combination meals. Customers place their orders and pay at the counter or the drive-thru window. These restaurants form the largest segment of the foodservice industry.

Hotels, Resorts, and Spas

An essential service in a lodging facility is providing customers with food and beverages. In addition, independent health spas and spas located in hotels and resorts offer their customers services for stress management, weight reduction, fitness, and other health enhancement programs. These personal services are usually accompanied by nutritious and appealing cuisine. Hotels, resorts, and spas offer employment opportunities for chefs, dietitians, and service staff.

Private Clubs

Private clubs are members-only facilities with a variety of foodservice options. Private club dining facilities typically offer high quality dining and service, and their job opportunities are similar to those at hotels, resorts, and spas.

Caterers

On-site catering operations employ managers, chefs, cooks, servers, and bus persons

Locations that offer food service total 858,000 nationwide, a 75% increase in the past 30 years. The number of restaurants is expected to reach one million by 2010. Currently, consumers spend 46% of their food dollars at restaurants, a number that is expected to reach 53% by 2010.

who provide food service to groups at the caterer's location for events such as business meetings, weddings, or other special occasions. Schools, hospitals, nursing homes, and government facilities frequently offer on-site catering. Many restaurants also cater on-site. Sometimes caterers or restaurants expand their business to the retail market. For example, Marie Callender® and Bob Evans® have developed and marketed frozen food products that are distributed to supermarkets nationwide.

Off-site catering operations prepare food at a centralized kitchen (commissary) and then deliver the food to the customer's location. Catering companies have a distinct advantage over restaurants because they know in advance how many guests will attend a particular function and thus the amount of food and preparation required. Having this knowledge also allows the caterer to staff the appropriate number of chefs, cooks, and servers.

Contract Dining

In recent years businesses have employed *outside contractors,* independent businesses that contract to provide a specific service, such as food service, for an organization's employees, customers, or patients. The outside contractor provides a professional staff to run the operation, freeing the business to focus on its main operation. Contract dining may take place in a variety of places such as executive dining rooms, schools, and hospitals.

Executive dining rooms Many businesses enhance productivity by offering on-site dining rooms or dining services for their executives and other industry professionals. Operated exclusively by outside contractors, executive dining rooms usually have a sophisticated, professional business atmosphere.

School facilities The National School Lunch Program, run by the U.S. Department of Agriculture, provides food for elementary and secondary school lunches. The meals are subject to Federal Dietary Guidelines. Many of these schools hire outside contractors to run their lunch programs. In response to student input, some cafeterias have been replaced by food courts and snack bars that offer a variety of foods. College and university foodservice

operations have added ethnic dishes and foods that meet special nutritional needs. Alternatives to the traditional board plan provide the flexibility students desire. Reduced board plans with fewer meals, debit cards or cash credits for à la carte food purchases, and quick-service chains or franchises located on campus offer many choices.

Recreational and sports facilities Recreational venues that provide food service include zoos, amusement parks, sports stadiums, museums, convention centers, and cruise lines. Food, once considered a sideline, has now become an important feature at recreational sites. Many sports and recreational facilities hire outside contractors to manage and operate food service for their patrons. In addition to the hot dogs, hamburgers, snack foods, and beverages that are standard fare, visitors can purchase salads, bratwurst, sushi, pizza, shrimp, and burritos.

Hospitals Hospital foodservice departments supply meals and snacks for the medical and administrative staff as well as for patients. Because of the importance of nutrition and special dietary needs, hospital foodservice directors and chefs work closely with a registered dietitian when creating menu items. In some hospitals, patients can select menu items and phone in their orders, and employees can select foods from a take-out menu, an on-site convenience store, or a café.

Nursing homes/Assisted living Nursing homes face the challenge of providing nutritious foods for patients, many with digestive problems. A registered dietitian usually assists with menu planning. Nursing homes also face rising food and labor costs. Solutions include the cook-chill system (cooking and chilling large amounts of food to be reheated later) and sous vide (packaging raw or slightly cooked foods in airtight pouches that are cooked, refrigerated, and frozen). Nursing homes also hire outside contractors to manage foodservice operations. Assisted living establishments often employ experienced chefs, who work with registered dietitians to meet the nutrition needs of their clients.

Small Business Opportunities

An entrepreneur is a self-motivated person who creates and operates a business. Entrepreneurs take personal and financial risks when launching a small business, but the rewards of being one's own boss can be tremendously gratifying. There are many opportunities for ownership in the foodservice industry.

Chain restaurants A *chain restaurant* is one in which the atmosphere, service, menu, and quality of food are all established by a parent company. The parent company may choose to enter into a partnership in which, for a fee, they allow an individual unit owner to market products and services under the company name. This individually owned unit is called a franchise, and its owner a franchisee. The parent company is referred to as the franchiser. Franchisees may use company marketing and promotion tools, but they must also follow the procedures established by the franchiser.

Independent restaurants An *independent restaurant* is not affiliated with a theme or brand. Therefore, the owner is freer to make important and often creative decisions about the design, concept, direction, and menu selection of the restaurant.

Caterers Business opportunities for caterers range from intimate gatherings to large extravagant parties. The capital investment needed to operate a catering business is far less than that of a restaurant.

Retail outlets Many department stores continue their tradition of offering full-service dining rooms for customers' convenience, more recently adding cafés and coffee bars. Discount stores also provide this service by leasing space to quick-service food operations. Convenience stores and supermarkets have expanded their ready-to-eat food products to include salads, pizza, soups, and baked goods, and some provide outlets for quick-service restaurants.

Fine Dining at Delmonico's

In 1863 French chef Charles Ranhofer (1836–1899) began his reign at Delmonico's in New York City, a restaurant that would set the standard for gourmet food. Ranhofer quickly became the first world-renowned chef of an American restaurant. Under his direction the classic American Delmonico steak, a tender strip of boneless top loin, was created. Ranhofer also is credited with creating baked Alaska, ice cream covered with meringue and quickly baked in an oven. His other creations include lobster Newburg and eggs Benedict. Ranhofer's famous 1894 cookbook, The Epicurean, included more than 3,500 recipes. The subtitle of his book read: The Complete Treatise of Analytical and Practical Studies on the Culinary Art, Including Table and Wine Service, How to Prepare and Cook Dishes . . . etc. and a Selection of Interesting Bills of Fare of Delmonico's, from 1862 to 1894, Making a Franco-American Culinary Encyclopedia.

Seeking Employment

As in most professional careers, finding a good position requires skills such as research, writing, and interviewing.

Employment Resources

Finding a job through the classified ads is less promising when compared with other, more efficient methods, such as networking and professional affiliations.

Networking *Networking* makes use of personal connections to achieve career goals. Seeking job information from family and friends provides better information about jobs than classified ads. Networking is the most direct way to find a job. Networking possibilities exist with friends, classmates, employers, and coworkers. See Figure 2-4.

Lifelong Career Services

Unique to Johnson & Wales University, the Career Management Program provides an outstanding opportunity for students to gain an advantage in today's competitive job market. Offered by the Career Development Office, the program includes intensive instruction in a variety of job search skills, including résumé preparation, interviewing techniques, and portfolio development. In addition, all students graduating with an associate's degree or bachelor's degree take comprehensive courses designed to assist them with career planning and the employment search process.

Watch for these and other career development opportunities at Johnson & Wales throughout the year:

- *The Part-Time Job Fair*
- *The Summer Work Experience Program (SWEP)*
- *The Seasonal Job Fair*
- *The Business Expo*
- *Career Conference*
- *On-Campus Recruiting Program*

FIGURE 2-4

Networking Rules

Be courteous and respectful to others.

Do not pressure people for information.

Follow up on job leads.

Let anyone supplying a lead know how it affected your job search.

Remember that your behavior and appearance reflect on those who made the recommendation.

Treat job leads as gifts—if possible, return the favor in some way.

Share the information with your network.

Professional organizations, whose members are professionals and, in some cases, students in the industry, provide excellent networking opportunities as well as job postings. Some organizations sponsor after-work networking meetings, which are usually casual gatherings to talk about industry trends and opportunities.

> See Chapter 3: Foodservice Professionalism for more information about professional organizations.

Lifelong Alumni Career Services at Johnson & Wales Johnson & Wales boasts a network of more than 50,000 alumni. The university is committed to staying involved with its former students and assisting alumni throughout their careers. Career development services, such as résumé writing assistance, are available. Contact the The office of Alumi Relations 1 (888) JWU-ALUM for more information.

Trade Publications

Trade publications are a valuable source of information about the foodservice industry and specific employers. Some may also provide information about jobs and educational opportunities. See Figure 2-5 on page 21.

Employment Agencies

Employment agencies assist people with their job searches and put businesses in touch with potential employees. Employment agencies maintain lists of job openings and collect information from job seekers. Most employment agencies charge fees for their services, paid for by either the person hired for the position or the business that sought the agency's help.

Computers and the Internet

Thousands of employment resources are available on the Internet, and personal computers have simplified the communication and record-keeping processes for job seekers. Use computers to:

- keep a job folder that includes information such as a résumé, copies of cover letters, reference lists, job leads, and to-do lists.

Trade Publications

FOODSERVICE DIRECTOR

A monthly publication for foodservice professionals at noncommercial locations such as schools, hospitals, and military installations

NATION'S RESTAURANT NEWS

The weekly tabloid of the restaurant industry

QSR: THE MAGAZINE OF QUICK-SERVICE RESTAURANT SUCCESS

Bimonthly publication aimed specifically at quick-service managers and employees

RESTAURANT BUSINESS

Semimonthly magazine for executives in public and institutional foodservice management, operations, and purchasing

RESTAURANT HOSPITALITY

Monthly publication for restaurant executives and managers; discusses the foodservice industry and related news and legislation

RESTAURANTS & INSTITUTIONS

Biweekly publication focusing on industry trends and consumer research

RESTAURANTS USA

The official monthly publication of the National Restaurant Association

---

- maintain a telephone and e-mail contact list of people in the industry.
- schedule appointments and interviews.
- keep a résumé updated.
- customize résumés for particular positions.
- e-mail résumés, cover letters, and references. (Make sure that the employer will accept applications by e-mail.)

Connect to the Internet to network, contact professional organizations, read on-line publications, and keep current on industry news and trends. Register and post résumés with on-line employment agencies and job banks, and research a foodservice organization and its staff prior to an interview.

Applying for a Job

After identifying several good job leads, rank the potential jobs in order of preference, and apply for your first choice first. If possible, get a written copy of the job notice. This will include the specific information about how to apply. For example, some employers may require that an application be completed and returned by a particular date. Others may prefer that potential employees begin the application process with a telephone call. Most employers request a résumé. A *résumé* is a summary that includes your career objective, work experience, job qualifications, education, and training. Some employers also ask for a list of *references,* the names of people who can confirm job skills or who can inform a potential employer about personal qualities such as integrity, honesty, and work ethic.

The Application Form

When picking up an application form from the employer's place of business, be aware that the employer starts making judgments even before an application is turned in. Never appear in a potential workplace unless well groomed with neat and appropriate clothing.

Sometimes application forms are filled out later in the job-seeking process. Most employers, however, request them as the first step. Some require that the application be filled out at the business location, so bring information such as social security number, driver's license, and the names, addresses, and phone numbers of previous employers and references.

Application forms vary, but most ask for similar kinds of information. When completing an application, print neatly, using blue or black ink. Use cursive handwriting for only the signature. If the application form is not printed on special paper, consider making a copy of it in case a mistake is made. Read the instructions for completing each blank before responding. Use a liquid correction product, or draw a line through any errors. Do not leave any part of the application blank unless asked to do so. If a question does not apply, write "N/A" for "not applicable" in the space provided. Always enter truthful information. Submitting false information is illegal.

Responding by Telephone

Sometimes a job lead may provide a phone number to call for information. When making the call, explain that it is in response to a job opening. The person who answers the phone should direct the call to the contact person or explain how to proceed with the application process. If connected with a contact person, give your name and state the job for which you would like to apply. When referred by someone and given permission to use his or her name, mention that name when inquiring about the position.

The contact person will explain the application process, which may include sending a letter of application and a résumé. The contact person may offer to mail an application or set up an appointment for an interview.

Be prepared to answer a few basic questions regarding experience and education. Have a copy of your résumé available. Write down the contact person's name and information about the application process and/or the job. Repeat the information to ensure its accuracy.

Ask questions about the application process, but refrain from asking specific questions about the position at this point. Reserve those questions for the interview. Be sure to thank the contact person for his or her time.

Responding in Writing

Written responses to a job lead include letters of request and cover letters. A *letter of request* asks for an application form or requests an interview. A letter of request should include a brief summary of your education, experience, and qualifications for the job.

A *cover letter* accompanies and introduces the résumé. It should include a brief introduction describing your interest in and qualifications for the job without repeating the résumé.

Although cover letters should be brief (never more than one page), they should always include an explanation of how the job came to your attention; a brief statement formally applying for the job; basic qualifications, such as education and experience; a request for an interview; contact information (include phone number and e-mail address); and your signature.

Carefully proofread any written communication prepared for a potential employer. Sign the letter in blue or black ink, make a copy of anything sent to a potential employer, and use the correct postage.

Preparing a Résumé

Résumés should emphasize work experience, skills, education, and training that best represents one's capabilities. A résumé is a marketing tool: It must successfully sell a product (you) to a buyer (an employer). When preparing a résumé, always be truthful and accurate, keep the résumé to one page, and stress only relevant work experience, skills, education, and training. Include any foodservice experience. Write a career objective. Use correct spelling and grammar, and do not use decorative graphics and pictures. Include up-to-date contact information.

In an effort to simplify the hiring process, many large employers are utilizing computer software to help them screen job applicants and select the best potential job candidates. Employers can now electronically scan and search résumés or perform on-line searches of résumés looking for keywords. *Keywords* are significant words such as *foodservice, restaurant,* and *baking* that indicate a match of background and experience with the job requirements. Résumés should contain appropriate keywords.

A good place to look for essential keywords is in the job posting. The description of the job opening usually indicates the qualities and skills desired in an ideal job candidate. Computer-generated résumés can easily be customized by making slight keyword changes to emphasize skills specific to each job posting.

Hard copy résumé A hard copy résumé is printed on paper and hand-delivered or mailed to a prospective employer. Use quality paper, and avoid using bright or distracting colors.

On-line résumé An on-line résumé is sent electronically to a prospective employer through e-mail or the Internet.

Some on-line job search firms have standard résumé forms that applicants must use to provide information about background and skills. Many employers prefer electronic copies of résumés. Special care should be taken when preparing an electronic version of a résumé.

- Never use a colored background or colored type.
- Use standard fonts, such as Arial, Times, or Courier.
- Use a 10- to 14-point font size.
- Avoid underlining, shading, and italics. Bold fonts, bullets, and asterisks can be used.
- Your name should always be on the first line of the résumé.

The Interview Process

The job interview is the first, and possibly only, chance to convince an employer that you are the best candidate for the job. Employers evaluate candidates on appearance, attitude, and answers to questions, as well as verbal and nonverbal communication skills.

Before the Interview

Thorough preparation for an interview will bring a feeling of confidence. Being prepared, positive, and relaxed is the best way to reduce tension. Reread the job posting, and review the qualities and skills that are needed. Learn as much as possible about the organization, its competitors, and the interviewer. Look for information in trade publications, local newspapers, professional organizations, and on the Internet. Make a list of questions the interviewer may ask, and rehearse your answers. Print copies of your résumé and references to take to the interview. Prepare necessary questions to gain information about the organization, its policies, the work environment, and the job responsibilities.

An employer's first impression will be based on your appearance. Clothes should be appropriate, professional, clean, pressed, and in good condition. Make sure that you are well groomed and well rested. Wear a minimum of jewelry, and never wear perfume or cologne.

On the day of the interview, allow extra time to get to the establishment; arrive a few minutes early. Always be polite and respectful when meeting people. The interviewer may check with these people to get their impression of you.

During the Interview

A candidate who is well prepared, positive, and relaxed will perform well during the interview. Remember to smile and be positive throughout the interview. Shake hands firmly, and remain standing until asked to be seated. Maintain eye contact throughout the interview. This shows confidence and interest in what the interviewer is saying.

In addition, speak clearly and use correct grammar and good office manners. For example, sit up straight, do not cross your legs, do not chew gum, and avoid nervous gestures such as tapping. Do not smoke, even if the interviewer smokes or offers a cigarette.

Do not interrupt the interviewer. Answer questions thoughtfully and completely. If a question is confusing, ask for clarification. Ask questions. Usually the last question an interviewer asks is "Do you have any questions?" Always be prepared to ask one final question. Do not discuss money unless the interviewer brings up the subject first. However, it is appropriate to discuss benefits.

At the end of the interview, thank the interviewer for his or her time. A professional attitude will be remembered and may make your interview stand out from the others. Interviews normally end in one of the following ways:

- The interviewer may say that you will be contacted later. If he or she does not specify a time period, ask, "When may I expect a call?" or "When will a decision be made?"
- If asked to contact the employer later, note the telephone number, the preferred time to call, and the contact person.
- The job may be offered. If unsure about the job, ask the interviewer for time to think about the offer. Most employers will grant the request. If given this option, be sure to follow up with your decision promptly.
- The job may not be offered. Normally, this decision is communicated later by telephone or letter. If turned down for the job following the interview, accept the decision gracefully, and keep a professional attitude.

After the Interview

Immediately following the interview, make notes about the job, the organization, and the interviewer. Consider the impression made and what can be done to improve your interview skills next time. Write down the positive things said during the interview. Note any key information, such as employer expectations and job responsibilities. List any unanswered questions about the job.

Within a day of the interview, send a letter to the interviewer thanking him or her for the interview. Do this even if turned down for the job. Closely proofread your writing, and check the spelling of the person's name and the correct address.

If asked to contact the employer, do so at the specified time. Send or deliver any materials or information that the interviewer requested, such as additional references. If the employer promised to call by a certain date and that date passes, telephone the employer and politely request information about the status of the position.

Responding to a Job Offer

When receiving an offer of employment, you have three options:

- **Accept the offer.** The employer will give information on the start date, including any employee orientation or training sessions before formally beginning the job. The employer may set up another meeting during which specific details about pay, benefits, schedules, and other job expectations will be provided.
- **Ask for time to consider the offer.** Ask the employer any unanswered questions that might affect your decision. Come to an agreement with the employer about when he or she needs to know a decision.
- **Turn down the job offer.** Feel free to say so if you do not intend to take the position. A detailed explanation for the decision is not necessary.

Successful Career Moves

There are a variety of reasons why someone might choose to leave a job. Some reasons are personal (for example, health problems or relocation). Most people decide to leave a job because it will be a successful career move. Here are some other reasons why people decide to leave:

- A better paying or more satisfying job is found elsewhere.
- A desire to further expand their skills and responsibilities is present, but no opportunity exists in the current organization.
- Poor performance reviews cause fear that they will not be promoted or will be let go.
- Job responsibilities or duties do not match their initial expectations.

Whatever the reason, avoid making a hasty decision to leave a job, especially if another one has not been secured. Always give an employer adequate *notice* in writing, informing him or her of your intention to leave the job on a specific date. A notice of two to three weeks is usually appropriate. Review the organization's written policies to see whether there is a required notice period.

Building a Career Portfolio

Just as an artist's portfolio represents his or her best work, your career portfolio should include a representative sample of the skills and talents you have to offer. A portfolio is a collection of one's accomplishments in the foodservice industry that can be shown to a prospective employer to document credentials.

It is a good idea to start compiling a portfolio even before your first job. A portfolio for a foodservice professional could include:

- a printed copy and a computer disk of résumés and reference lists.
- letters of reference from employers, professors, and personal friends who are working professionals in food service.
- employer evaluations and performance reviews (include volunteer work evaluations).
- photographs of recognition.
- awards or honors received at work or school, such as certificates or ribbons.
- articles written as biographical sketches or about personal foodservice projects.
- certificates showing completion of or participation in a professional conference, seminar, or workshop.
- university transcripts, grades, and other papers attesting to academic performance.
- attendance records.
- copies of materials, such as menus, advertisements, or manuals, created for an employer or for a volunteer organization.
- menus that reflect personal expertise.
- documentation of licenses or certifications received.

Keep in mind that a portfolio is a work in progress added to over time with each new experience.

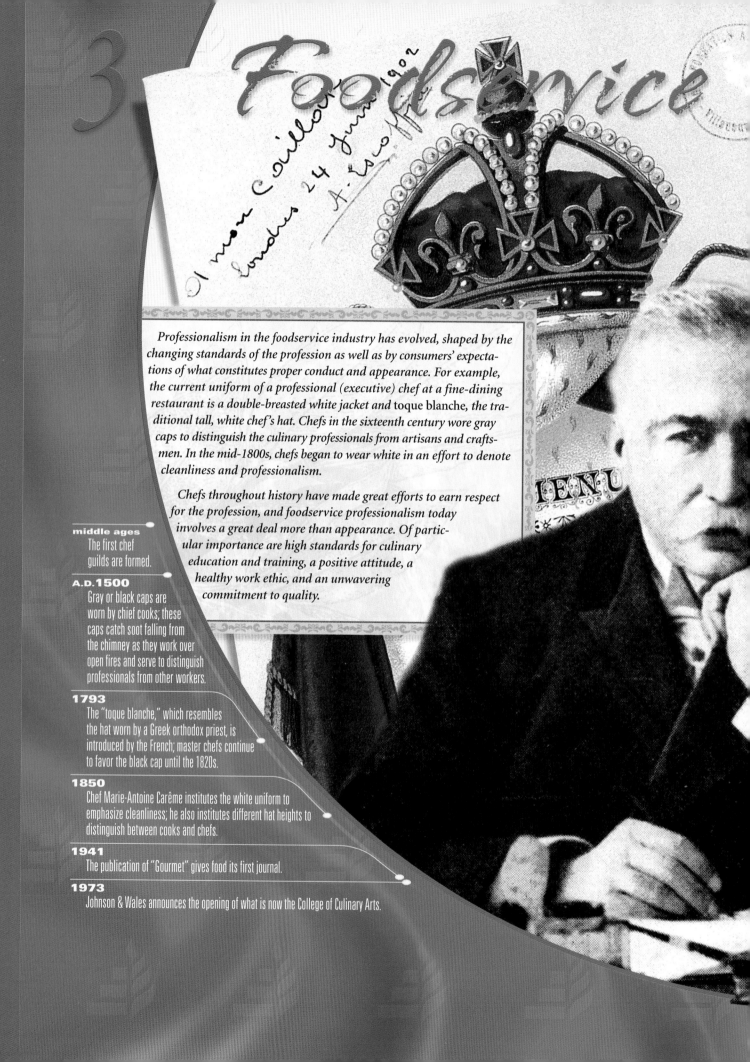

3 Foodservice

Professionalism in the foodservice industry has evolved, shaped by the changing standards of the profession as well as by consumers' expectations of what constitutes proper conduct and appearance. For example, the current uniform of a professional (executive) chef at a fine-dining restaurant is a double-breasted white jacket and toque blanche, *the traditional tall, white chef's hat. Chefs in the sixteenth century wore gray caps to distinguish the culinary professionals from artisans and craftsmen. In the mid-1800s, chefs began to wear white in an effort to denote cleanliness and professionalism.*

Chefs throughout history have made great efforts to earn respect for the profession, and foodservice professionalism today involves a great deal more than appearance. Of particular importance are high standards for culinary education and training, a positive attitude, a healthy work ethic, and an unwavering commitment to quality.

middle ages
The first chef guilds are formed.

A.D. 1500
Gray or black caps are worn by chief cooks; these caps catch soot falling from the chimney as they work over open fires and serve to distinguish professionals from other workers.

1793
The "toque blanche," which resembles the hat worn by a Greek orthodox priest, is introduced by the French; master chefs continue to favor the black cap until the 1820s.

1850
Chef Marie-Antoine Carême institutes the white uniform to emphasize cleanliness; he also institutes different hat heights to distinguish between cooks and chefs.

1941
The publication of "Gourmet" gives food its first journal.

1973
Johnson & Wales announces the opening of what is now the College of Culinary Arts.

Professionalism

ES MENUS

Jour

JANU

KEY TERMS

apprentice

discrimination

sexual harassment

dues

traditional food banks

Prepared and Perishable Food Programs (PPFPs)

Saumon f
* Jambor
r fines he

à l'Ecossaise * Réjane
il * Bisque d'Ecrevisses
Soupe aux Huitres

/ * Merlan Richelieu
d'écrevisses
in
ricaine

La bonne cuisine est la base du véritable bonheur

A. Escoffier

Mai 1911

olonaise
' au Currie
usaine
arrons
i

Learning the Trade

Chefs learn the trade through formal education and on-the-job training. Experience, post-secondary education, continuing education opportunities, and certificate programs are hallmarks of professionalism in the industry.

Getting an Education

Many career chefs began their education by enrolling in an associate's or bachelor's degree program, such as the ones offered at Johnson & Wales University. Although it may be possible to advance through the ranks in the industry without formal study, a person with education and training is likely to advance more rapidly. Students seeking formal education demonstrate the desire for excellence and consequently are well on their way to building solid careers in the foodservice industry.

Associate's Degree

Many colleges and universities offer associate's degrees in the culinary field. Johnson & Wales University offers associate's degree programs in culinary arts and in baking and pastry arts. A good associate program offers more than classroom learning. It provides hands-on experience so that students can apply classroom techniques in the kitchen or other foodservice areas.

Bachelor's Degree

Bachelor's degree programs prepare students for supervisory and management positions in the foodservice industry. They provide in-depth training in one or more areas. Johnson & Wales University offers bachelor's degrees in the following areas:

- Culinary arts
- Baking and pastry arts
- Culinary nutrition
- Food service management
- Food marketing
- Food service entrepreneurship

While pursuing a bachelor's degree, students also participate in cooperative education or work experience programs. These programs match students with a company whose business is related to their interests. Johnson & Wales students gain both national and international experience through cooperative education, internship, externship, and term-abroad programs. The Ritz Carlton, Foxwoods Resort Casino, Charlie Trotter's, and Emeril's are just a few of the many co-op sites available to students. Internship and externship sites include the Radisson Airport Hotel, Johnson & Wales Inn, the Bay Harbor Inn and Suites, Adam's Mark Hotel, and Compass Group. Opportunities abroad are available in both Europe and Asia. Experience outside the classroom educates students about the industry and enhances their visibility to potential employers.

Certification

Achieving certification, or proof of expertise, is an important way to document professional accomplishments and uphold the standards of professionalism in the foodservice industry. If the certification comes from a respected organization or association, such as the American Culinary Federation, Research Chefs Association, Retailer's Bakery Association, or American Dietetic Association, the accomplishment is a well-recognized designation of specialized culinary expertise. See Figure 3-1.

FIGURE 3-1

American Culinary Federation Certification Levels

CERTIFIED MASTER CHEF/MASTER PASTRY CHEF

The highest degree of professional knowledge and skill; requires theoretical and practical examination of knowledge and skills

CERTIFIED CULINARY EDUCATOR

For chefs who are working as teachers in a nontraditional learning environment; requires extensive post-secondary teacher education in addition to a minimum number of contact hours of teaching experience; must possess culinary experience/expertise of a certified sous chef

CERTIFIED SECONDARY CULINARY EDUCATOR

For chefs working in accredited secondary or vocational institutes with experience in the development, implementation, administration, and evolution of curriculum

CERTIFIED EXECUTIVE CHEF

For full-time chefs who are department heads and supervise a minimum of five full-time people

CERTIFIED EXECUTIVE PASTRY CHEF

For pastry chefs who are department heads, usually reporting to the executive chef or the management of the foodservice establishment

PERSONAL CERTIFIED EXECUTIVE CHEF

For expert chefs who possess at least seven years' experience; work for a variety of clientele planning and developing menus and preparing meals

CERTIFIED CHEF DE CUISINE

For chefs who are supervisors of food production; must supervise a minimum of three full-time people

CERTIFIED SOUS CHEF

For chefs who supervise a shift, station, or stations; must supervise a minimum of two full-time people; typical job titles include sous chef, banquet chef, chef garde-manger, and first cook

CERTIFIED WORKING PASTRY CHEF

For pastry chefs responsible for a pastry section or a shift

PERSONAL CERTIFIED CHEF

For chefs with 3 years' experience; cook, serve, and sort foods as needed

CERTIFIED CULINARIAN/PASTRY CULINARIAN

For people positioned in a station at a foodservice operation who prepare and cook meats, vegetables, soups, sauces, and other food items; for people in a pastry station who prepare and bake pies, cookies, cakes, breads, rolls, or other baked goods and desserts

Continuing Education

As in most professional careers, learning continues even after a degree or certification is achieved. To maintain respect as a skilled professional and to attain success, chefs are committed to lifelong learning.

Many colleges and universities offer continuing education courses for working professionals in the foodservice industry who want to supplement their education or change a career focus. Some continuing education courses can be applied toward completion of an associate's or bachelor's degree.

Advanced Degrees

The educational experience gained from attaining a bachelor's degree can provide the appropriate background for an advanced degree. The Alan Shawn Feinstein Graduate School at Johnson & Wales University offers an M.B.A. in Hospitality and Tourism and in Global Business Leadership with majors in Marketing, Finance, Event Leadership, and Tourism Planning.

Research and Reading

Self-guided research and reading should become standard practice for professionals in the foodservice industry in order to keep up with industry trends and standards. The Internet and local libraries are excellent sources for information on the industry. Consider subscribing to foodservice trade publications for articles on specific areas of expertise.

Seminars, Workshops, and Conferences

Research, reading, and continuing education training are good sources of news about seminars, workshops, and conferences that can provide in-depth, comprehensive training. These sessions are valuable in keeping abreast of the latest methods, developments, and practices in the foodservice industry. Chefs take advantage of these opportunities to broaden their knowledge about important issues and trends in the industry.

Internships

Internships provide on-the-job training for college students and entry-level workers. Normally, classroom instruction and job training are combined in internship programs. Internships are a valuable way for students to gain hands-on, practical experience. At Johnson & Wales University, students are assigned a one-term internship at one of the university's practicum properties.

Work Experience

From entry-level workers in fast-food restaurants to chefs at fine-dining restaurants, nothing strengthens professional development like on-the-job experience. Solid work experience enhances marketability and chances for advancement.

Apprenticeships

An *apprentice* works under the guidance of a skilled chef in order to learn a particular skill. An apprenticeship can be an excellent way to gain one-on-one training in a particular culinary skill. Instruction usually involves a combination of hands-on experience and classroom learning.

The tradition of apprenticing originated in France. It has a long history in Europe, and the practice continues today. Apprenticeships offer young people hands-on education from master chefs. Apprentices work long hours over a period of years to master and progress in culinary skills.

Professional organizations and industry associations, such as the American Culinary Federation, now sponsor apprenticeships throughout the United States.

On-the-Job Training

Employees never underestimate the value of on-the-job training to both improve their culinary skills and enhance their chances for career advancement. Some large hotels and restaurants offer no-cost, specialized training programs for their employees. These programs provide employees with opportunities for advancement within the organization.

Strategies for Success

To attain on-the-job success, be loyal and trustworthy to an employer and an organization. Listen to coworkers, show them respect, and be a team player. Remain calm and level-headed in stressful situations; maintain a positive attitude and a sense of humor. Respect diversity among coworkers and customers, and demonstrate a willingness to take on new responsibilities.

Professionalism in the Foodservice Industry

The jobs of executive chef, chef de cuisine, and sous chef are now recognized by the U.S. Department of Labor as professional occupations that require substantial educational preparation (usually at the university, junior college, or technical institute level). For many years, chefs did not hold this professional status.

Looking and Acting Like a Professional

To earn respect from customers and coworkers, behave professionally on the job via appearance, actions, and words. Cordial relationships with customers and coworkers are enhanced by a clear, friendly manner of speaking and by active listening.

Developing a Healthy Work Ethic

A healthy work ethic demonstrates commitment to the job and to the foodservice team. Several important elements come together to form a strong work ethic.

Responsibility

Responsibility is understanding what a particular situation demands and knowing how to respond appropriately, including showing up for the job on time and ready to work, becoming familiar with the tasks of a position, and carrying those tasks out correctly and with a positive attitude. Responsibility is a key characteristic of professionalism.

Responsibility to customers Responsibility to customers includes preparing and serving quality food. Ensure that the food and service meets or exceeds expectations and that the food is safe and nutritious. Be vigilant about food allergies because some allergies can be fatal, and respect special dietary needs and preferences, such as those for vegetarians and members of certain religions.

Responsibility to employers Contribute to the success of the organization by arriving on time, working a full shift, carrying out assigned tasks properly, and taking on extra work if necessary. Avoid working unsafely and putting yourself and others at both physical and financial risk.

Responsibility to coworkers and fellow students Carry out your tasks completely. Never rely on others to do work that is your responsibility. Support the efforts of coworkers and fellow students, perform assigned duties so that the whole team succeeds, and encourage others to be positive and professional.

Responsibility to oneself Accept responsibility for personal actions. Take constructive criticism with an open mind, and do not compromise personal standards or ethics. One's appearance and behavior should always reflect professionalism. Most employers and schools have a zero-tolerance policy for drugs and alcohol use. Johnson & Wales strictly enforces its policy, which prohibits the unlawful possession or use of narcotics, drugs, other controlled substances, or alcohol.

Commitment to Quality and Excellence

To build a strong professional work ethic, it is essential to demonstrate a high level of commitment to oneself, the employing organization, and the foodservice industry. Commitment is the characteristic that distinguishes valuable employees. A strong work ethic requires a commitment to quality and excellence.

Quality Commitment to quality involves striving to meet high standards, using excellent ingredients, and preparing and serving food in the most pleasing manner.

Excellence Excellence involves striving to do one's best at all times and making the most of opportunities for continuing education and career development.

Commitment to the Environment

To ensure quality food, a commitment to the environment is essential. The amount of energy used and the waste produced by the industry is staggering. More than one quarter of food in the United States, about 96 billion pounds per year, is wasted, and the United States spends about $1 billion each year disposing of food waste.

Impact of foodservice on the environment Restaurants are one of the largest consumers of energy, and they generate enormous amounts of food waste each year. Restaurants and other foodservice organizations that practice conservation efforts can minimize their environmental impact and make significant inroads toward saving precious environmental resources.

Recycling The goal of recycling is to reduce the vast amount of waste disposed of in landfills. Restaurants should follow locally recommended and/or enforced recycling guidelines.

Some restaurants have reduced their disposal costs by reducing the amount of money they spend on garbage collection.

Waste disposal Nearly all restaurants use large quantities of cooking oil, and much of it remains as waste after use. Dumping used oil in a sink can be dangerous to the environment. Store used cooking oil safely in closed containers, and have it collected by grease recycling or rendering companies.

Energy conservation According to the Environmental Protection Agency (EPA), saving on energy operating costs can increase restaurant profits. Turn off appliances and lights when not in use. Switch to energy-efficient lighting—fluorescent bulbs last longer and use less energy. Conserve water and lower utility costs by reducing unnecessary wastewater.

Working in a Culturally Diverse Environment

Today's workplace reflects the nation's growing number of ethnic citizens. Not only are customers likely to be culturally diverse, but coworkers may also come from diverse cultural backgrounds. This cultural diversity is likely due to the fact that most chefs promote workplace tolerance and respect for diversity and require these qualities from all workers.

According to the National Restaurant Association (NRA), the restaurant industry employs more minority managers—13% African Americans and 12% Hispanics—than any other industry, and this figure is expected to increase in the next decade. The number of ethnic workers also is expected to increase.

Avoiding Discrimination and Sexual Harassment

Employers have a responsibility to protect their employees from *discrimination,* which is unfair treatment on the basis of age, gender, race, ethnicity, religion, physical appearance, disability, or other attributes. There are a number of laws and regulations that protect workers from discrimination, including the Equal Pay Act of 1963, Title VII of the Civil Rights Act of 1964, the Age Discrimination in Employment Act of 1967, Sections 501 and 505 of the Rehabilitation Act of 1973, the Civil Service Reform Act of 1978, and

the Civil Rights Act of 1991. Contact the U.S. Equal Employment Opportunity Commission (EEOC) for more information on discriminatory practices.

Gender discrimination, which includes sexual harassment and pregnancy-based discrimination, is prohibited in the workplace. *Sexual harassment,* which is any unwelcome behavior of a sexual nature, is also prohibited in the workplace. It can include direct requests for sexual favors as well as workplace conditions that create a hostile environment for persons of either gender, including same-sex harassment. Pregnancy-based discrimination laws protect workers by requiring that pregnancy, childbirth, and related medical conditions be treated in the same way as other temporary illnesses or conditions.

The Americans with Disabilities Act (ADA)

The Americans with Disabilities Act of 1990 (ADA) guarantees equal opportunity for individuals with disabilities in public accommodations, employment, transportation, state and local government services, and telecommunications. It promotes the education, rehabilitation, and employment of individuals with disabilities so that they can lead more productive lives and so that others can benefit from their skills and talents. The ADA also prohibits employment discrimination against qualified individuals with disabilities.

The Act prohibits discrimination in all employment practices, including job application procedures, hiring, firing, advancement, compensation, and training, as well as other terms, conditions, and privileges of employment. It applies to recruitment, advertising, tenure, layoff, leave, fringe benefits, and employment-related activities. For more information, contact the ADA, or visit the U.S. Department of Justice's ADA Web site.

Professional Organizations

Professional organizations are made up of people already employed in a particular field. Participation in a professional organization has many benefits, including

- professional development and continuing education.
- awards and peer recognition.
- networking arrangements and professional camaraderie.
- education about industry trends.
- job postings and placement.
- scholarships and grants.
- publishing and research opportunities.
- processes to establish and raise professional standards.
- certification education and programs.

Annual dues, or regular fees, are usually required for membership in a professional organization. Often employers pay the dues for their senior employees.

The Nature of Professional Organizations

Employees and employers alike should not underestimate the value of participation in a professional organization. Employers benefit because their workers are more in touch with what is happening in the foodservice industry and can receive training and information about a variety of job skills. Important advantages for employees are career enhancement and development.

Professional organizations are known for having both novice members and members who are professional experts with a thorough knowledge of specialized areas of the foodservice industry. They offer student chapters, usually with reduced dues (for example, the Junior Chapter of the American Culinary Federation, or the Junior Chapter of the International Food Service Executives Association) and engage in philanthropic and community service activities.

Professional organizations and trade publications There are many professional organizations in the foodservice industry. Depending on specific areas of interest and expertise, consider joining any one of the well-respected organizations. See Figure 3-2.

Many professional organizations publish trade magazines and newsletters for distribution to members only. Other trade publications are available to the general public by subscription, and some can be found on the Internet or in public libraries. These publications contain helpful articles on all aspects of the foodservice industry and may list employment opportunities. Reading these publications regularly can help foodservice professionals stay current on industry trends and best practices.

FIGURE 3-2

Professional Organizations

AMERICAN CULINARY FEDERATION
10 San Bartola Drive   www.acfchefs.org
St. Augustine, FL 32086
(904) 824-4468
(800) 624-9458

AMERICAN DIETETIC ASSOCIATION
216 W. Jackson Blvd.   www.eatright.org
Chicago, IL 60606-6995
(312) 899-0040

INTERNATIONAL ASSOCIATION OF CULINARY PROFESSIONALS
304 W. Liberty St.   www.iacp.com
Suite 201
Louisville, KY 40202
(502) 581-9786

INTERNATIONAL ASSOCIATION OF WOMEN CHEFS AND RESTAURATEURS
304 W. Liberty St.   www.chefnet.com/wcr
Suite 201
Louisville, KY 40202
(502) 581-0300

NATIONAL BAR AND RESTAURANT ASSOCIATION
307 West Jackson Ave.   www.bar-restaurant.com
Oxford, MS 38655
(866) 368-3753

NATIONAL RESTAURANT ASSOCIATION
1200 Seventeenth St. NW   www.restaurant.org
Washington, DC 20036
(202) 331-5900/(800) 424-5156

NATIONAL SOCIETY FOR HEALTHCARE FOOD SERVICE MANAGEMENT
204 E St. NE   www.hfm.org
Washington, DC 20002
(202) 546-7236

RESEARCH CHEFS ASSOCIATION
5775 Peachtree-Dunwoody Rd.   www.researchchef.org
Suite 500 G
Atlanta, GA 30342
(404) 252-3663

RETAILER'S BAKERY ASSOCIATION
14239 Park Center Drive   www.rbanet.com
Laurel, MD 20707-5261
(301) 725-2187/(800) 638-0924

SOCIETY OF FOODSERVICE MANAGEMENT
304 W. Liberty St.   www.sfm-online.org
Suite 201
Louisville, KY 40202
(502) 583-3783

Social Involvement

Americans waste an enormous amount of food each year. The foodservice industry supports a growing national movement that limits environmental impact and makes a substantial difference in the lives of hungry people in the United States. Johnson & Wales is committed to helping people in need by reducing hunger in the United States. This principle is reflected in the university's dedication to service learning. An integral part of a student's education involves learning how chefs can take leadership roles in helping reduce hunger. Faculty and students are encouraged to offer their time and talents in support of community endeavors, such as those sponsored by soup kitchens, and are actively involved in food donation and waste reduction programs.

Involvement in Local Community Activities

Donating surplus food to people in need is one way chefs make use of excess food to help solve a growing national problem. There are two types of food donation programs. *Traditional food banks* distribute large quantities of nonperishable food that is dried, canned, or packaged. *Prepared and Perishable Food Programs (PPFPs),* also called food recovery programs or surplus food distribution programs, redistribute small quantities of freshly prepared foods and perishables. PPFPs are an increasingly common way for foodservice organizations and chefs to get involved in helping people in need.

The Good Samaritan law, enacted in 1996, protects restaurants and stores from liability for food they donate in good faith to food banks or other food programs. All prepared food items are still subject to state requirements for safe handling and sanitation. The law states, "Immunity from liability for food donors—a person, including but not limited to a farmer, processor, distributor, wholesaler, or retailer of food, who in good faith donates food which appears to be fit for human consumption at the time it is donated to a bona fide or non-profit organization for the use or distribution to the needy shall not be liable for civil damages or criminal penalties for any injury or illness resulting from the nature, age, condition, or packaging of the donated food unless the injury or illness is a direct result of the intentional misconduct or recklessness of the donor."

Ambassadors of Good Will in the Community

Despite our general prosperity, millions of people go hungry every day in the United States. Foodservice professionals and their establishments have taken leadership roles in reducing hunger in their communities. Education and skills can be put to good use by helping others in a variety of ways.

- Donate excess food to a local food bank.
- Volunteer to work at a food bank or other programs that support people who are hungry.
- Support programs that provide urban garden space where residents can grow their own food.
- Volunteer to teach a class about nutrition and healthful eating.

Hunger Relief Programs

In addition to many excellent local hunger relief programs, several national organizations offer programs that help feed people who are hungry, raise money, provide relief, and offer nutrition education. See Figure 3-3.

FIGURE 3-3

Relief Programs

SHARE OUR STRENGTH

Activities

Mobilizes culinary professionals to organize events, host dinners, and teach cooking and nutrition to low-income families. Members serve as anti-hunger advocates.

Contact Information

733 15th St. NW, Suite 640
Washington, DC 20005
(800) 969-4767
www.strength.org

AMERICAN CULINARY FEDERATION CHEF AND CHILD FOUNDATION

Activities

Focuses on the nutritional development of children in the United States. Provides nutrition education, children's disaster relief, and local grants to feed hungry children. Raises funds for local agencies that provide dietary assistance and nutrition education.

Contact Information

c/o the American Culinary Federation, 10 San Bartola Rd.
St. Augustine, FL 32086
(904) 824-4468
www.acfchefs.org

AMERICA'S SECOND HARVEST

Activities

Through a network of more than 200 food banks and food-rescue programs, provides emergency food assistance. The nation's largest domestic hunger relief organization.

Contact Information

35 E. Wacker Dr., #2000
Chicago, IL 60601
(800) 771-2303
www.secondharvest.org

KIDS CAFÉ

Activities

One of the nation's largest free meal service programs for children. Provides free prepared food and nutrition education to hungry children. A program of America's Second Harvest.

Contact Information

35 E. Wacker Dr., #2000
Chicago, IL 60601
(800) 771-2303
www.secondharvest.org/childhunger/ kidscafe.html

4 Food Safety

Serving safe food is a top priority for foodservice professionals. Food safety started becoming an issue in the United States during the industrial revolution. As problems arose, safeguards were established. In 1902, the Department of Agriculture set up a "Poison Squad," a group of volunteers who tested the safety of U.S. foods. The Food and Drug Administration (1906), in addition to the Food, Drug, and Cosmetic Act (1938) and the HACCP system developed in the 1960s, are geared toward food safety.

Contamination

Foodborne illnesses are diseases caused by microorganisms, such as bacteria and viruses, transmitted to people through food. Although the number of foodborne illnesses is growing each year, they can be minimized. Foodservice professionals who follow industry standards for safety can reduce the threat of these serious diseases.

Contamination occurs when harmful substances such as microorganisms adulterate food, making it unfit for consumption. Biological, chemical, and physical hazards can contaminate food. Contamination can happen by either direct contamination or cross-contamination.

Direct contamination *Direct contamination* occurs when raw foods or the plants or animals from which they come are exposed to toxins in their natural environment or habitat. For example, grains or vegetables may become contaminated in the soil in which they were grown, or fish may become contaminated in the waters in which they live.

Cross-contamination Foods may also become adulterated by cross-contamination. *Cross-contamination* involves the transference of microorganisms or other harmful bacteria from one source to another through physical contact. Cross-contamination is usually caused by people, but rodents and insects can also transfer contaminants to food.

Cleaning and sanitizing Direct and cross-contamination can be prevented to some degree by maintaining a clean and sanitary environment. *Cleaning* removes all visible dirt and grime but does not kill microorganisms. *Sanitizing* reduces the number of pathogenic microorganisms to a safe level through the use of chemicals and/or moist heat. Therefore, to ensure food safety, both procedures must be conducted in foodservice establishments.

Foodservice Hazards

Foodservice hazards can be biological, chemical, or physical in nature, any of which can result in contaminated food. These hazards are mostly the result of improper foodhandling and safety practices, resulting in unsatisfied customers; fines, summonses, and lawsuits; injuries, medical bills, and increased absenteeism; and an increase in food cost because of spoilage.

Biological Biological hazards include bacteria, viruses, parasites, and fungi—all microorganisms. Some foodborne bacterial illnesses include *Salmonella* spp., *Listeria monocytogenes*, *Shigella* spp., *Campylobacter jejuni*, and *Clostridium botulinum*.

Chemical Chemical contamination results from not following proper food safety procedures. These types of hazards include cleaning supplies, polishes, pesticides, soap residue, fertilizers, lead, mercury, and copper. Antimony, cyanide, lead, and zinc poisoning can result from chemical contamination as well.

Physical Physical hazards that pose a risk are hair (human and rodent), dirt, metal shavings, stones, insects and insect parts, glass, and shards of bone. These hazards may cause injury or discomfort to the consumer.

Foodborne Illness

Microorganisms can grow in and on food when it is not handled or cooked properly or as a result of cross-contamination, poor personal hygiene, and illness. In addition, chemical spills or residue and physical hazards can come in contact with food, causing contamination and resulting in foodborne illnesses.

Some parts of the population are at greater risk for contracting foodborne illnesses when contaminated food is consumed. Children, the elderly, pregnant women, and those who are chronically ill or who have weakened immune systems are at highest risk for contracting foodborne illnesses. Establishments must prescribe and follow strict procedures for handling food safely.

Potentially Hazardous Foods

Some foods are considered *potentially hazardous foods* because they present more of a risk for harboring microorganisms that cause foodborne illnesses. These foods are typically high in protein and moisture and low in pH levels—the amount of acid or alkaline in a substance. Dairy products, eggs, meats, poultry, fish, and shellfish all are vulnerable to contamination, but so are cooked rice and pasta, beans, potatoes, sliced melons, and garlic and oil mixtures. Particular attention and precautions must be taken when receiving, storing, preparing, cooking, holding, serving, cooling, and reheating any of these items.

Foodborne Illness Outbreaks

A foodborne illness outbreak occurs when two or more people become ill after eating the same food. Symptoms of foodborne illness may vary from person to person but typically include nausea, vomiting, abdominal pain, diarrhea, dizziness, fever, headache, chills, dry mouth, and prostration. These symptoms can appear within hours to several days after consuming the infected food. An outbreak of foodborne illness must be reported to the Department of Health, which will in turn investigate the outbreak in an effort to determine the cause.

Food Safety and Irradiation

Food irradiation is a process in which food products are exposed to a controlled amount of radiant energy to kill harmful bacteria such as E. coli O157:H7, Campylobacter jejuni, and Salmonella. The process also can control insects and parasites, reduce spoilage, and inhibit ripening and sprouting.

The Food and Drug Administration (FDA) has evaluated the safety of this technology over the last 40 years and has found irradiation to be safe under a variety of conditions and has approved its use for many foods. Scientific studies have shown that irradiation does not significantly reduce nutritional quality or significantly change food taste, texture, or appearance. Irradiated foods do not become radioactive. Irradiation can produce changes in food, similar to changes caused by cooking, but in smaller amounts.

Irradiation works as follows:

- Food is packed in containers and moved by conveyor belt into a shielded room. There the food is exposed briefly to a radiant-energy source. The amount of energy depends on the food.

- Energy waves passing through the food break molecular bonds in the DNA of bacteria, other pathogens, and insects. These organisms die or, unable to reproduce, their numbers decrease. Food is left virtually unchanged, but the number of harmful bacteria, parasites, and fungi is reduced and may be eliminated.

The FDA currently requires that irradiated foods include labeling with either the statement "treated with radiation" or "treated by irradiation" and the international radura symbol.

Biological Hazards

Disease-causing microorganisms, such as bacteria, viruses, parasites, and fungi, are biological hazards that result in foodborne illnesses. See Figure 4-1 on pages 36–38.

Bacteria

Bacteria—tiny, single-celled microorganisms that are in the air and water, on the ground, on food, in our bodies, and on our skin—are the leading cause of foodborne illness. There are four different categories of bacteria:

- **Harmless**—Most bacteria are harmless, living in the intestines and aiding in digestion. They also provide nutrients to some extent.
- **Beneficial**—Beneficial bacteria are used in food production to make such products as cheese, yogurt, and sauerkraut.
- **Undesirable (putrefactive)**—Undesirable, or *putrefactive,* bacteria cause food only to spoil, producing off-flavors, odors, slimy surfaces, and discoloration.
- **Pathogens**—*Pathogens* are the disease-causing bacteria responsible for 95% of all food-borne illnesses, although only 1% of bacteria are considered pathogens. Because they cannot be detected by sight or smell, they are especially dangerous.

These bacteria, which include *Salmonella, Staphylococcus aureus, Listeria monocytogenes,* and *Clostridium botulinum,* grow by multiplying, doubling as often as every 20 minutes. In a period of six hours, one bacterium can split and multiply to numbers in the billions. However, in order to grow, bacteria require the right environment. If just one of these criteria—food, oxygen, moisture, pH level, temperature, and time—is not properly met, bacteria cannot grow. See growth requirements on page 38.

Bacteria cannot move by themselves. They must be moved from one place to another by hands, coughing, sneezing, foods, equipment, utensils, air, water, insects, or rodents.

Pathogens can cause foodborne illness in three ways: infection, intoxication, and toxin-mediated infection.

Infection *Infection* occurs when pathogens grow in the intestines of a person who has consumed contaminated food. Listeriosis is an example of infection.

Intoxication *Intoxication* results when the pathogen produces toxins that cannot be seen, smelled, or tasted. It is not the toxin-producing bacteria that are fatal, but the toxins they produce. Handling food properly is the only way to prevent intoxication. Heat does not destroy the toxins. Botulism is an example of intoxication.

Toxin-mediated infection *Toxin-mediated infection* occurs when someone eats food contaminated with pathogens. These pathogens then establish colonies in the consumer, producing toxins. This type of infection is dangerous for children, the elderly, and those with weakened immune systems. *Clostridium perfringens* and *Escherichia coli* are examples.

Viruses

Viruses, the smallest known form of life, also are responsible for foodborne illnesses, but unlike bacteria, viruses require a host, such as an animal, plant, or human, in order to grow.

Hepatitis A results in inflammation of the liver. The virus can be transmitted to food by people or by food that comes into contact with contaminated water. Hepatitis A can be prevented by following effective hand-washing procedures and by getting immunized for hepatitis A.

They can be transmitted from person to person through poor hygiene, such as not washing hands, from people to food-contact surfaces, and from people to food. Viruses can be present on any foods, but salads, sandwiches, milk, baked goods, raw fish and shellfish, and other unheated food products are especially susceptible to viruses. Hepatitis A, the Norwalk virus, and rotavirus are examples.

Parasites

Parasites, such as protozoa, roundworms, and flatworms, are tiny organisms that must live in or on a host to survive. Often found in poultry, fish, and meats, parasites enter the animal through contaminated feed and then settle in the intestines and grow. Common foodborne parasitic illnesses include trichinosis, caused by undercooked infected pork or game, and anisakiasis, the result of roundworms in raw or undercooked fish. Parasitic illnesses can be prevented in several ways:

- Utilize proper cooking and freezing techniques.
- Use only sanitary water supplies.
- Avoid cross-contamination.
- Make sure that all employees utilize proper hand-washing procedures.

Fungi

Fungi are microorganisms found in plants, animals, soil, water, and the air. They can be tiny, single-celled plants or large, multi-celled organisms such as giant mushrooms. Fungi also are present in some foods. Molds and yeast are two forms of fungi.

FIGURE 4-1

Foodborne Illnesses

SALMONELLOSIS—BACTERIA

Symptoms

Cramps, nausea, headache, fever, diarrhea, vomiting

Foods Involved

Poultry and poultry products such as eggs, meat and meat products, fish, dairy products, protein foods, fresh produce

Preventive Measures

Keep foods refrigerated; avoid cross-contamination; cook poultry to a minimum of 165°F (74°C) for at least 15 seconds and other foods to minimum internal temperatures; cool cooked meats and meat products within 6 hours; avoid food and surface contamination by following good personal hygiene practices; avoid pooling eggs.

CAMPYLOBACTER JEJUNI—BACTERIA

Symptoms

Nausea, vomiting, fever, diarrhea, abdominal pain, headache, muscle pain

Foods Involved

Meats and poultry, unpasteurized milk and dairy products

Preventive Measures

Pasteurize milk; use only treated water; cook all foods to safe internal temperatures; avoid cross-contamination.

SHIGELLOSIS—BACTERIA

Symptoms

Abdominal pain, nausea, diarrhea, vomiting, fever, chills, dehydration

Foods Involved

Protein salads, lettuce, raw vegetables, poultry, shrimp, milk and milk products

Preventive Measures

Use only sanitary food and water sources; avoid cross-contamination; practice good personal hygiene; cool foods rapidly; control flies.

LISTERIOSIS—BACTERIA

Symptoms

Headache, fever, chills, nausea, vomiting, diarrhea, backache, meningitis, encephalitis

Foods Involved

Ice cream, frozen yogurt, unpasteurized milk and cheese, raw vegetables, poultry, meat, seafood

Preventive Measures

Avoid cross-contamination; properly clean and sanitize work areas; ensure that all milk and dairy products are pasteurized; cook all foods to safe internal temperatures.

BOTULISM—BACTERIA

Symptoms

Constipation, diarrhea, vomiting, fatigue, vertigo, double vision, dry mouth, paralysis, death

Foods Involved

Underprocessed foods, canned low-acid foods, sautéed onions in butter sauce, baked potatoes, untreated garlic and oil products

Preventive Measures

Do not use home-canned products; cool leftovers rapidly; use proper time and temperature control for large, bulky, and sous vide items; refrigerate garlic-and-oil mixtures; sauté onions to order.

E. COLI—BACTERIA

Symptoms

Severe abdominal cramps, diarrhea, vomiting, mild fever, kidney failure

Foods Involved

Raw ground beef, undercooked meat, roast beef, dry salami, unpasteurized milk and apple cider or juice, commercial mayonnaise, lettuce, melons, fish from contaminated waters

Preventive Measures

Avoid cross-contamination; thoroughly cook ground beef to a minimum of 155°F (68°C) for 15 seconds; practice good personal hygiene.

STAPHYLOCOCCUS AUREUS—BACTERIA

Symptoms

Nausea, retching, cramps, diarrhea, headache

Foods Involved

Meats, poultry, protein foods, sandwiches, dairy products, eggs, salad dressings, reheated foods

Preventive Measures

Practice good personal hygiene, especially proper handwashing procedures; do not allow employees with skin infections to handle or prepare foods; rapidly cool prepared foods; refrigerate foods properly.

CLOSTRIDIUM PERFRINGENS—BACTERIA

Symptoms

Abdominal pain, diarrhea, nausea, dehydration

Foods Involved

Meat, poultry, gravy, stew, meat pies, beans, leftovers

Preventive Measures

Use proper time and temperature control to cool and reheat cooked foods.

BACILLUS CEREUS—BACTERIA

Symptoms

Nausea, vomiting, cramps, diarrhea

Foods Involved

Rice products, potatoes, pasta, sauces, puddings, soups, casseroles, salads, fish, milk

Preventive Measures

Use proper time and temperature control and quick-chilling methods to cool foods; cook foods adequately.

VIBRIO PARAHAEMOLYTICUS AND VIBRIO VULNIFICUS—BACTERIA

Symptoms

Diarrhea, cramps, nausea, vomiting, headache, chills, fever, blisters

Foods Involved

Oysters, shrimp, lobsters, clams, scallops, mussels

Preventive Measures

Avoid cross-contamination; do not eat raw or undercooked seafood, especially oysters; purchase seafood from approved sources only.

HEPATITIS A—VIRUS

Symptoms

Fatigue, discomfort, fever, headache, nausea, loss of appetite, vomiting, jaundice

Foods Involved

Water, ice, salads, cold cuts, sandwiches, shellfish, fruit, fruit juices, milk and milk products, vegetables

Preventive Measures

Use only sanitary water sources; ensure that all shellfish comes from approved sources; practice good personal hygiene; avoid cross-contamination; clean and sanitize all equipment and food-contact areas.

NORWALK VIRUS—VIRUS

Symptoms

Cramps, nausea, headache, fever, vomiting

Foods Involved

Water, raw vegetables, fresh fruit, salads, shellfish

Preventive Measures

Use only sanitary, chlorinated water sources; ensure that all shellfish comes from approved sources; practice good personal hygiene; avoid cross-contamination; cook all foods to safe internal temperatures.

ROTAVIRUS—VIRUS

Symptoms

Abdominal pain, diarrhea, vomiting, mild fever

Foods Involved

Water, ice, salads, fruit, and ready-to-eat foods

Preventive Measures

Cook all foods to safe internal temperatures; practice good personal hygiene; use only sanitary, chlorinated water.

ANISAKIASIS—PARASITE

Symptoms

Tingling in throat, abdominal pain, coughing up worms, cramping, vomiting, nausea

Foods Involved

Fish, seafood

Preventive Measures

Ensure that all seafood comes from certified sources only; do not eat raw or partially cooked fish or shellfish; freeze fish properly; fish meant to be eaten raw must be frozen at –4°F (–20°C) or lower for 7 days in a freezer or at –31°F (–35°C) or lower for 15 hours in a blast chiller.

CYCLOSPORIASIS—PARASITE

Symptoms

Watery diarrhea, loss of appetite and weight, cramps, gas, bloating, nausea, vomiting, fatigue, muscle aches

Foods Involved

Fish, raw milk and produce, water

Preventive Measures

Use only sanitary water; practice good personal hygiene; wash produce thoroughly.

GIARDIASIS—PARASITE

Symptoms

Cramps, nausea, intestinal gas, fatigue, loss of weight

Foods Involved

Water, ice, salads

Preventive Measures

Practice good personal hygiene; use only sanitary, chlorinated water; carefully wash raw produce.

TRICHINOSIS—PARASITE

Symptoms

Abdominal pain, nausea, diarrhea, fever, swelling around eyes, thirst, sweating, chills, fatigue, hemorrhaging

Foods Involved

Pork, nonpork sausages, wild game

Preventive Measures

Freeze pork products that are less than 6 inches thick at 5°F (–15°C) for 30 days or 30°F (–1°C) for 12 days; cook pork and other meats to safe internal temperatures; properly wash, rinse, and sanitize any equipment used to prepare raw pork and other meats.

CIGUATERA TOXIN—SEAFOOD TOXIN

Symptoms

Nausea, vomiting, dizziness, itching, hot/cold flashes, temporary blindness

Foods Involved

Reef fish such as grouper, snapper, amberjack, barracuda

Preventive Measures

Purchase seafood only from approved sources that can guarantee that it comes from safe waters.

SCOMBROID TOXIN—SEAFOOD TOXIN

Symptoms

Nausea, diarrhea, cramps, dizziness, headache, flushing, sweating, facial rash, hives, edema

Foods Involved

Mahi mahi, tuna, sardines, bluefish, mackerel

Preventive Measures

Purchase fish only from approved sources that use strict time and temperature controls; receive fish at 41°F (5°C) or lower (note that a scombroid intoxication can still occur if proper temperature control was not maintained during harvesting or before arrival); do not use fish that have been thawed and refrozen.

SHELLFISH TOXIN—SEAFOOD TOXIN

Symptoms

Respiratory failure, death

Foods Involved

Mussels, clams, scallops, cockles

Preventive Measures

Purchase fish only from approved sources that use strict time and temperature controls.

Molds Molds often can be found growing on bread or cheese. See Figure 4-2. They can grow in any environment. The algaelike spores produced by molds can be seen with the naked eye. Molds mostly affect the appearance and flavor of foods through discoloration, odor, and off-flavors. The exception to this is mycotoxin, which produces toxins that can cause foodborne illness. Heating mold cells and spores can destroy the mold but not toxins. Therefore, unless the mold is a natural part of the product, such as mold on blue cheese, discard foods that contain mold.

Yeast Yeast is most often associated with bread and the baking process, whereby yeast is beneficial. However, yeast can cause spoilage when present in other foods. To survive, yeasts require water and a starch or sugar. Because carbon dioxide and alcohol are by-products of yeast, some foods spoiled by yeast smell of alcohol. Others appear slimy or have a pink discoloration. Discard any foods spoiled by yeast.

Growth Requirements

All microorganisms require a certain environment to survive and thrive. Viruses need a living cell in order to reproduce. They are not affected by factors such as oxygen, moisture, or pH levels. Heat will destroy viruses. Parasites depend on the host to survive and can be destroyed either by heating the food to high temperatures or by freezing the food for several days. Fungi can grow in any environment, but they are destroyed by heat. Bacteria, however, need food, oxygen, moisture, a balanced pH level, temperature, and time to grow.

Food Food provides energy for bacteria to grow, which is why potentially hazardous foods are the ideal environment for bacterial growth.

Oxygen Bacteria can be *aerobic,* requiring oxygen to survive; *anaerobic,* having the ability to survive without oxygen, as in canned foods; or *facultative,* surviving with or without oxygen. Most bacteria are facultative.

Moisture Bacteria cannot survive without moisture. This moisture is referred to as *water activity (a_w).* The amount of water activity in food is measured on a scale of 0 to 1.0. (Distilled water has a water activity of

FIGURE 4-2

Mold is most often seen growing on bread.

1.0.) At .85 a$_w$, bacteria can grow. Dry foods and those high in salt or sugar do not support bacterial growth. See Figure 4-3.

pH level A balanced, or neutral, pH environment supports bacterial growth. The pH scale ranges from 0 to 14.0—0 to 7.0 is acidic; 7.0 to 14.0 is alkaline; 7.0 is neutral. Bacteria grow well in substances with a pH level between 4.6 and 7.5. Growth is unlikely at a pH level of 4.6 or lower. Therefore, highly acidic foods such as lemon juice, tomatoes, and vinegar do not actively promote the growth of bacteria.

Temperature Of all the bacterial growth requirements, temperature is the easiest to control. Bacteria thrive in the ***temperature danger zone,*** or TDZ (41°F–140°F/ 5°C–60°C), but they are destroyed when exposed to high heat for a specified amount of time. Freezing does not destroy bacteria; it only slows its growth.

Time Bacteria require time to adjust to their new environment. This duration is called the ***lag phase,*** and it typically lasts anywhere from one to four hours. The lag phase allows foodhandlers to quickly and safely work with food. After the lag phase is the ***log phase,*** a period of accelerated bacterial growth. This phase continues until overcrowding is reached and competition exists among bacteria for food and space. At this point in time, the bacteria population comes to a ***stationary growth phase,*** in which bacteria are growing and dying at the same rate. When more bacteria are dying than growing, a population decline called the ***death phase*** has been reached.

Time and Temperature Abuse

Most foodborne illnesses are the result of time and temperature abuse by kitchen staff. Foods that remain in the temperature danger zone (41°F–140°F/5°C–60°C) allow for the growth of bacteria that cause foodborne illnesses. Therefore, it is vital that staff minimize the time that food is kept in the temperature danger zone. Potentially hazardous foods must be thrown away after four hours if they are held within the temperature danger zone. Typically, the four-hour time zone begins when food is received. However, food can be time and temperature abused before arriving at its destination. For example, food can be contaminated at the point of production. Every time the food is within the temperature danger zone, the four-hour time zone decreases—it does not begin again. To prevent time and temperature abuse, adhere to safety guidelines. See Figure 4-4 on page 40.

Thermometers Both bimetallic stem and digital thermometers are used in the foodservice industry to measure the

FIGURE 4-3

Water activities (a$_w$) of some common foods

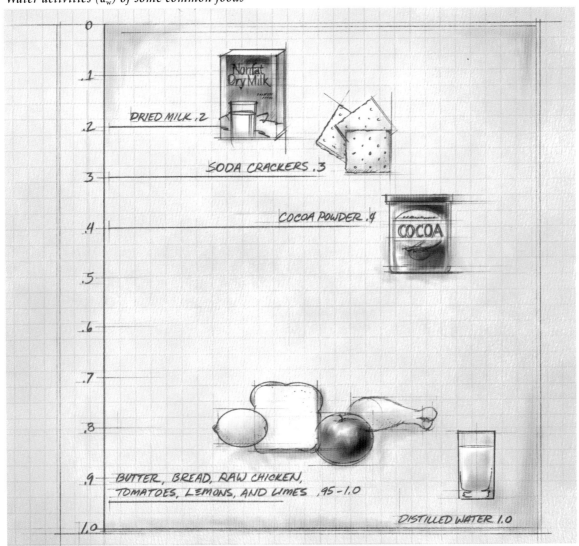

DRIED MILK .2

SODA CRACKERS .3

COCOA POWDER .4

BUTTER, BREAD, RAW CHICKEN, TOMATOES, LEMONS, AND LIMES .95–1.0

DISTILLED WATER 1.0

source: ServSafe®

internal temperature of food. See Figure 4-5. When using a thermometer, place it in the thickest part of the food, and take at least two readings in different places.

Thermometers should be thoroughly cleaned, sanitized, and air-dried after each use to avoid the risk of cross-contamination. Thermometers should be calibrated and accurate to within +/–2°F or +/–1°C, after an extreme temperature change.

Personal Hygiene

Microorganisms on equipment, hand tools, smallwares, and cooking surfaces can come into contact with the hands of kitchen staff and be transported from hands to food, contaminating the food. To avoid contamination, practice good personal hygiene, including bathing, proper hand washing, wearing foodservice gloves, and maintaining good personal health.

Bathing Foodservice employees should shower or bathe before arriving at work. Fingernails should be neat, clean, and short.

Washing hands Because the transmission of microorganisms occurs mostly by hands, it is vital that foodservice employees wash hands frequently—after eating, drinking, smoking, chewing gum, and using the restroom; touching the face, hair, or skin; and coughing, sneezing, or wiping the nose. Hands also should be washed before and after handling raw food, between performing tasks, before using preparation equipment, and after removing trash or clearing tables.

Clothes Clothes should be cleaned daily before coming to work. If possible, change into the establishment's uniform after arriving at work. This helps lower the risk of cross-contamination.

Jewelry Jewelry can harbor harmful microorganisms and poses a physical hazard as well. Foodhandlers should remove all jewelry, except for plain wedding bands, prior to starting their shift.

Hair and facial hair Hair should be cleaned daily prior to arriving at work. Dirty hair can be a breeding ground for pathogens, risking cross-contamination. Hair also should be held back in a hair restraint in an effort to keep employees from touching their hair and then touching food. Hair restraints also keep hair from falling into food. Men with long beards should wear beard restraints for the same reasons.

FIGURE 4-4

Safe Internal Cooking Temperatures

PRODUCT	TEMPERATURE
Injected meats, including brined ham and flavor-injected roasts	155°F (68°C) for 15 seconds
Poultry, stuffed meats and pasta, casseroles, stuffings, and other dishes combining raw and cooked foods	165°F (74°C) for 15 seconds
Beef, pork, veal, and lamb roasts	145°F (63°C) for 4 minutes
Beef, pork, veal, and lamb steaks/chops	145°F (63°C) for 15 seconds
Hamburger, ground pork, sausages, flaked fish	155°F (68°C) for 15 seconds
Fish	145°F (63°C) for 15 seconds
Fresh eggs for immediate service	145°F (63°C) for 15 seconds
Any potentially hazardous foods cooked in a microwave	165°F (74°C) and then let food stand for 2 minutes

FIGURE 4-5
Bimetallic stem and digital thermometers

Practicing the Proper Hand-Washing Procedure

Proper hand washing is key to preventing the transmission of microorganisms to food.

Follow these steps when washing hands:

1 Wet hands and forearms with hot water.

2 Apply enough soap to build up a good lather.

3 Rub hands and arms for at least 20 seconds.

4 Clean fingernails with a brush.

5 Rinse off soap thoroughly under running hot water.

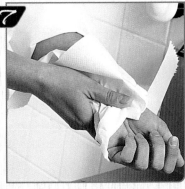

6 Turn off the water faucet using a paper towel.

7 Dry hands and arms using a separate paper towel.

Chemical Hazards

Chemical hazards—chemical substances such as cleaning supplies, polishes, pesticides, food additives, and toxic metals from worn cookware—can cause food contamination when they come into contact with food. When using such chemicals, follow manufacturer directions. Chemical hazards are a common cause of foodborne illness. Any chemical that is known to have chronic or acute effects on health or that is flammable or unstable is considered a hazardous chemical.

Cleaning Products and MSDS

A variety of cleaning products and sanitizers are commonly used in food service. Material Safety Data Sheets (MSDS)—sheets that list a material's chemical and common names as well as its possible hazards and ways to avoid these hazards—must be kept on file for each cleaning product, and the products should be used and stored properly. Cleaning products and sanitizers should never be used around or near food. They should always be kept in their original containers and properly labeled. Never reuse chemical containers or packages for storage; discard all packaging when the product is gone.

Detergents Detergents are used to clean walls, floors, prep surfaces, equipment, and utensils and to cut through grease.

Hygiene detergents These detergents are made specifically to clean, deodorize, and disinfect floors, walls, and tabletops.

Degreasers Degreasers are solvents used on range hoods, oven doors, and backsplashes to remove grease.

Abrasive cleaners Abrasives are used to clean difficult-to-remove soil on floors and burned-on food from pots and pans.

Acid cleaners Acid cleaners remove mineral deposits in dishwashers and steam tables and should always be used with care.

Kitchen Cleanliness

Keeping the kitchen clean and sanitary decreases the risk of contamination. Always clean as work is performed, and follow up by sanitizing. Clean all pots, pans, dishes, and food-contact surfaces before preparing another food product or if hand tools become contaminated.

Some commercial kitchens use designated color-coded cutting boards, knives, cloths, and containers for each particular type of food product to further prevent the risk of contamination. Some kitchens even color-code sanitation equipment. For example, green may be the designated color for vegetables and fruits. This means that all utensils, including knives, tongs, and cutting boards, as well as cleaning equipment that comes into contact with produce, are green. Red is typically the color designated for raw meat, brown for cooked meat, yellow for poultry, blue for raw fish and seafood, and white for dairy. See Figure 4-6.

Pesticides often are used in food storage and preparation areas to control pests, but if they are not used properly, chemical contamination may occur. Only a trained Pest Control Operator (PCO) should apply pesticides. Before pesticides are applied, all foods should be properly stored and wrapped. Store pesticides away from food and in a locked or secure area, and clearly label the containers to avoid any confusion.

FIGURE 4-6

Color-coded cutting boards, knives, and other kitchen equipment are used to prevent the risk of contamination.

Physical Hazards

Physical hazards are foreign particles such as glass chips, metal shavings, tooth picks, dirt, stones, hair, jewelry, fingernail polish chips, and bone shards that can contaminate food. Most physical hazards are the direct result of poor food handling and can cause injury or discomfort to the consumer.

Avoiding Physical Hazards

The easiest way to avoid physical hazards is by practicing proper food handling procedures. These procedures include:

- carefully inspecting foods upon receiving them
- avoiding physical contamination during the flow of food

Hazard Analysis Critical Control Point (HACCP)

The Hazard Analysis Critical Control Point (HACCP) system is used to monitor the flow of food through a foodservice operation. HACCP allows operators to identify potential hazards and correct them before they become a problem.

The HACCP System

The HACCP system was developed by the Pillsbury Company for the National Aeronautics and Space Administration (NASA) in the early 1960s in an effort to ensure safe food in outer space. The system was so successful that many parts of it were adopted by the foodservice industry and used as a system of self-inspection even though local health departments regularly inspect foodservice operations.

HACCP ensures food safety by combining food-handling procedures, monitoring techniques, and record keeping. The system focuses on the flow of food through the foodservice facility at critical control points, helping employees identify foods and procedures that are likely to cause foodborne illness, develop facility procedures that will reduce the risk of foodborne illness, monitor procedures in order to keep food safe, and make sure that the food is served properly.

Establishing a HACCP Plan

In establishing a HACCP plan, a foodservice operation may rely on research, food regulations, and past experience. A good HACCP plan should have standards that are measurable and observable, such as temperature and time.

The establishment then determines the steps that will be followed in measuring and observing the set standards for each critical control point. The procedures must be documented in a log and followed by all employees.

The Seven Steps of HACCP

A typical HACCP system has seven steps: analyzing hazards, determining critical control points, establishing critical limits, monitoring the system, taking corrective action, verifying procedures, and record keeping.

Analyze hazards The first step of HACCP is to identify and analyze potential food hazards. Check the flow of food to identify where potential hazards—biological, chemical, and physical—may occur.

Determine critical control points A *critical control point (CCP)* is the last point in the flow of food where potential food hazards can be prevented or eliminated by a foodhandler before the food is served to a consumer.

Establish critical limits For each critical control point identified, establish standards that each food item must meet to be considered safe. For example, cook meat to the safe internal temperature before service.

Monitor the system Foodservice operators and employees are responsible for monitoring the systems in place and creating checks and balances to ensure that potential problems are eliminated. This allows them to ensure that proper procedures are followed in the flow of food, such as that of monitoring internal temperatures of food.

Take corrective action Taking corrective action involves enacting predetermined steps if a critical limit is not met. For example, if the temperature of beef stew on a steam table has fallen below 140°F (60°C), the corrective action to take is that of reheating the stew to a temperature of 165°F (74°C) and replacing the food on the steam table.

Verify procedures An important aspect of HACCP is that of determining whether the set procedures are working. To do this, critical control points, such as cooking, holding and cooling food, and critical limits must be checked to ensure that they are adequate. Follow-up must be conducted on all corrective action taken to ensure the reduction of foodborne illness. Furthermore, check that established procedures are being followed by all employees.

Establish record keeping Record keeping is an important part of maintaining an effective self-inspection system. Record-keeping systems, which are simple and easy to maintain, include flowcharts, policy and procedure manuals, written records, and temperature readings. Logs are usually completed at the end of each shift or meal period.

The Flow of Food

The flow of food is the process by which food items move through a foodservice operation, beginning with receiving and ending with reheating. See Figure 4-7.

Receiving and Storing Food

The flow of food begins when food items are received. Safety and sanitation procedures begin here, too. All food items must be carefully inspected for damage and to ensure that the food has been maintained at the proper temperatures during transit. Potential problems that could be encountered in receiving include thawed and refrozen foods, insect infestation, damaged foods or containers, repacked or mishandled items, and foods shipped at incorrect temperatures. Products that do not meet food safety standards should be rejected.

Storing food, whether dry, refrigerated, or frozen, is another control point at which improper handling can result in contamination. All foods should be stored properly, in the appropriate location, to prevent contamination, spoilage, and the growth of harmful bacteria. Storage areas should always be kept clean and dry, and the temperature should be monitored.

Dry storage Foods that have a long shelf life are placed in dry storage. Flour, salt, dried beans, and canned foods are examples. The ideal temperature in a dry storage area is 50°F–70°F (10°C–21°C) with 50%–60% humidity. All stored food products should be kept at least six inches off the floor and six inches away from the wall.

Refrigerated storage Food products that need refrigeration should be kept at or below 41°F (5°C). Clearly label and date all containers, and use the *First In, First Out (FIFO)* inventory program, moving older items to the front and storing fresher items behind them. Cooked foods should be stored above raw ingredients to prevent cross-contamination. Drip pans should be placed under raw ingredients to catch any spills. When thawing frozen foods, always place them below prepared foods, and leave space for air to circulate around food. Also check unit and food temperatures.

Frozen storage Frozen foods should be stored between 0°F and 10°F (–18°C and –12°C). Label and date all containers, and ensure that wrappings are airtight to prevent freezer burn. Other guidelines include:

- Check unit and food temperatures.
- Defrost the freezer on a regular basis.
- Use cold curtains to maintain temperature control.
- Use FIFO.
- Open the freezer only when absolutely necessary.

Preparation and Cooking

After properly receiving and storing foods, the flow of food moves to preparation and cooking. Wash all fresh fruits and vegetables before preparation, and never prepare fruits and vegetables on the same cutting boards used to prepare uncooked meats. Each type of food product prepared is susceptible to a different kind of contamination. Designated color-coded cutting boards, knives, and cloths can cut down on the risk of cross-contamination.

When preparing and cooking foods, use clean, sanitized cutting boards, knives, and utensils. Remove refrigerated food products as needed. Wash, rinsed, and sanitize the areas each time a different food product is prepared, and prepare or cook foods immediately.

Always use the recommended utensils, such as tongs or spatulas, when handling ready-to-eat food. Ready-to-eat foods can be defined as follows:

- raw, washed, or cut fruits and vegetables
- food that is ready for consumption (no further washing or cooking is required)
- unpacked, potentially hazardous food that has been cooked according to the required time and temperature specifications

Wear gloves to create a barrier between hands and food when nothing else (tongs, deli tissue, and so on) is being used. See Figure 4-9 on page 46. Before putting on gloves, wash hands thoroughly with soap and water following proper hand-washing procedures. The type of single-use gloves

---

FIGURE 4-7

The Flow of Food

1. **RECEIVING (CP):**
   Receive and store chicken breasts quickly. Check for signs of deterioration or contamination. Chicken must be at 41°F (5°C) or lower at time of receiving.

2. **STORING (CP):**
   Store the chicken breasts at 41°F (5°C) or lower.

3. **PREPARING (CP):**
   If preparing stuffed chicken breasts, minimize the time they spend in the temperature danger zone.

4. **COOKING (CCP):**
   Cook the stuffed chicken breasts to an internal temperature of 165°F (74°C) for 15 seconds.

5. **HOLDING (CCP):**
   Hold the stuffed chicken breasts at 140°F (60°C) or higher.

6. **COOLING (CCP):**
   Cool the stuffed chicken breasts to 70°F (21°C) within two hours and from 70°F (21°C) to 41°F (5°C) or lower within an additional four hours.

7. **REHEATING (CCP):**
   Reheat the stuffed chicken breasts at 165°F (74°C) for 15 seconds within two hours.

FIGURE 4-8

An ice bath may be used to cool smaller portions.

worn in food service depends on the task to be accomplished and includes:

- nitrile powder-free gloves
- plastic disposable gloves
- powder-free gloves
- uniseal gloves
- vinyl gloves

Although latex gloves are also available, they should be used sparingly because of the prevalence of allergic reactions to latex. As of July of 2001, the state of Rhode Island and Johnson & Wales University prohibited the use of natural rubber latex gloves in any foodservice establishment.

Foodservice gloves should be changed when they become damaged or torn, after handling any raw food, or when an interruption of the job occurs.

Keep cold ingredients properly chilled in the refrigerator until they are needed, and cook protein ingredients before mixing them with other food products. Always follow recipe directions when preparing foods, and cook to the minimum internal temperature. See Figure 4-4 on page 40.

Certain foods, such as poultry and meat, must be cooked at specific temperatures in order to keep them safe. In addition, boil leftover sauces and gravies before serving, thoroughly cook any battered or breaded foods, and never mix leftover food with freshly prepared foods.

Holding Food Safely

Foods may be cooked and served immediately or prepared ahead of time and held for service. Because foods are extremely susceptible to microorganism growth during holding, it is vital to follow proper procedures. Keep foods covered to reduce contamination, and take the internal temperature regularly, a minimum of every two hours. Cooked foods should be held at 140°F (60°C) or higher. If the temperature drops below 140°F (60°C), reheat the food to 165°F (74°C) for 15 seconds within two hours, and hold again at 140°F (60°C) or higher. If the temperature drops below 140°F (60°C) for a second time, discard the food. Hot foods should also be stirred regularly to distribute the heat throughout the food.

Cold food should be held at 41°F (5°C) or lower. Except for fruits and vegetables, do not store cold food directly on ice. Instead, place it in a container, such as a hotel pan. Use self-draining drip pans for displays.

Serving Food Safely

Microorganisms are easily spread, so never touch ready-to-eat food or the surfaces of glasses, dinnerware, or flatware with bare hands when serving food. Hold dishes by the bottom or an edge, cups by their handles, glassware by the lower third, and flatware by the handles.

Plates of food should never overlap when dishes are served to guests. Instead, use a tray to carry the plates. When serving beverages, use scoops, not bare hands, to pick up ice.

Cooling Food Safely

The FDA recommends using a two-stage method for cooling food safely. Cool cooked foods to 70°F (21°C) within two hours, and then cool the food down to 41°F (5°C) or lower within four hours. However, food also may be cooled using a one-stage method, dropping the temperature to 41°F (5°C) or lower within four hours.

Foods can be cooled using any of the following methods:

- **The Rapid Kool™**—The Rapid Kool™ is a container of water that can be frozen and placed directly in stock to accelerate cooling.
- **Ice-water bath**—An ice-water bath allows smaller portions of stock to be placed in ice water in a sink or large pot. See Figure 4-8.

FIGURE 4-9

Single-use gloves are used when handling raw food.

- **Blast chiller**—Blast chillers are units used to cool food, moving it through the temperature danger zone in less than two hours. After food is chilled in a blast chiller, it can be safely refrigerated.
- **Ice or cold paddles**—Ice or cold paddles are directly added to the product to reduce the temperature. The paddles, which are hollow, are filled with ice and are then used to stir the product.
- **Metal cooling pins**—Metal cooling pins inserted into a food item cool food by transferring heat from the food to cold air.

Reheating Food Safely

When reheating foods, the internal temperature must reach 165°F (74°C) for 15 seconds within two hours after being removed from the refrigerator.

Disposal of Food

Cleaning and sanitizing are key to the proper disposal of food. Dishes, flatware, smallwares, hand tools, and equipment must be cleaned and sanitized. To do this, remove leftover food by scraping it into a garbage can. Rinse items over the disposal before washing. Dishes, flatware, small-wares, and hand tools can be washed either manually or mechanically. Chemical sanitizers are used in sinks and dishwashers to prevent bacteria growth.

Manual dishwashing A commercial sink with three compartments is used for manual dishwashing. See Figure 4-10. To wash items by hand, scrape, prerinse, and then wash items in at least 110°F (43°C) water and detergent. Follow up by rinsing with clear water at a temperature of at least 110°F (43°C). Change the water as needed to keep it clear and hot. Sanitize items for 30 seconds in water of at least 171°F (77°C) or follow the manufacturer's suggested water temperature if using chemical sanitizers. Each chemical sanitizer has different levels of concentration and temperature requirements, i.e., chlorine above 75°F (24°C) or below 115°F (46°C).

Mechanical dishwashing Commercial dishwashers include single-compartment, multicompartment, carousel, recirculating, and conveyor machines. When using a dishwasher, scrape and rinse soiled dishes, and presoak flatware. Clean utensils by following manual dishwashing procedures. Prerinse dishes to remove all visible food and soil, and then load the dishwasher. Always run the dishwasher through a full cycle, and check its cleanliness throughout the workday.

Drying and storing items After cleaning and sanitizing either manually or mechanically, allow the items to air dry. Do not touch the surfaces that will come in contact with food, and wash your hands before storing the items.

FIGURE 4-10

A three-compartment sink, such as the one shown here, is used to manually wash dishware.

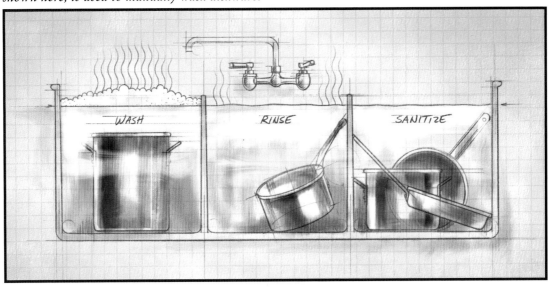

Workplace Safety

Kitchen staff are particularly at risk for injuries that result from workplace accidents because of fatigue, poor kitchen design, and insufficient training. Yet despite the frequency of workplace accidents, they can be controlled. The Occupational Safety and Health Administration (OSHA) plays a large role in keeping the workplace safe by enforcing workplace standards outlined in the Occupational Safety and Health Act. Employers are required to post OSHA safety and health information in their facilities, and employees are required to follow OSHA regulations.

In addition, the Environmental Protection Agency (EPA) requires foodservice operations to track how they handle and dispose of hazardous materials such as cleaning products and pesticides.

Personal Protective Clothing

Personal protective clothing, such as uniforms, aprons, and gloves, keep foodservice workers safe from injury. Personal protective clothing should be kept clean to avoid contamination.

Proper uniforms Uniforms should be neat and clean before each shift begins. Change into uniforms at work, if possible, thereby reducing the risk of cross-contamination. Uniforms should be kept in clean lockers.

Proper shoes Protective shoes will vary throughout foodservice operations, but all should be sturdy, slip-resistant, and closed-toe.

Protective gloves and mitts According to the Bureau of Labor Statistics, most hand injuries recorded in food service are cut, puncture, and burn injuries, which could have been prevented if the proper protective gloves or mitts were worn. This type of protective clothing also guards hands against the effects of chemical compounds. There are a number of different protective gloves and mitts from which to choose, including:

- stainless-steel mesh—worn when there is potential for cuts, such as when cutting meat or shucking oysters
- knife glove—used to protect hands from cuts and amputation when cutting a variety of food products
- cut-resistant—as with knife gloves, used to protect hands from cuts and amputation
- terrycloth heat resistant—worn to protect hands whenever a potential hazard of a burn or scald is present

Personal Injuries

Employees have a responsibility for preventing slips and falls, cuts, burns and scalds, and other personal injuries that can occur in the kitchen. The guidelines that follow can help minimize such workplace injuries.

Slips and Falls

Although most slips and falls can be avoided, they are a common work-related injury. Prevent such accidents by performing tasks carefully and keeping walking areas uncluttered and free of spills, especially around exits, aisles, and stairs.

When working in the kitchen, walk; do not run. Wipe up spills immediately, and use slip-resistant floor mats. Many falls occur on wet floors slick with water and cleaning products, so use care when walking through the kitchen. Also use "Caution" or "Wet floor" signs after mopping or cleaning to warn others to be careful. Never use a chair or box for climbing; use safe ladders or stools. Always close drawers and doors, and use a cart when moving heavy objects.

Cuts

The risk of being cut in a commercial kitchen is high but can be minimized by following safety guidelines. Unplug appliances before cleaning them, and wear protective gloves and cuff guards when cleaning slicers.

Knives are the most common cause of cuts in a commercial kitchen. Always use knives for their intended purpose. Never use them to open plastic overwrap or boxes. Knives should be carried at the side of the body with the blade tip pointed toward the floor and the sharp edge facing back. Look where hands are placed when reaching for a knife, and never wave hands when holding a knife.

Use a firm grip on the handle when holding a knife, and cut away from the body, not toward your body. If the knife is dropped, do not try to catch it.

In addition, never leave a knife handle hanging over the edge of the work surface. Keep knife handles and hands dry when using knives, and keep knives sharp. Dull knives require applying more pressure, possibly causing slipping.

Wash sharp tools separately from other utensils; never leave knives in the sink. Throw away broken knives or knives with loose blades, and store knives in a knife kit or a rack.

Burns and Scalds

Another risk of working in commercial kitchens is that of burns and scalds. To prevent these accidents, remove lids by tilting them away from the body to let steam escape. Use dry potholders or oven mitts; wet cloth forms steam when it touches hot pots and pans. The handles of pots and pans should be turned away from the front of the range, thus preventing spills that could cause burns. Use caution when filtering or changing shortening in fryers, and wear gloves and aprons because splatters can cause serious injury.

Back Injuries and Strains

Back injuries from improper lifting and bending are one of the most common workplace injuries, accounting for more than 20%–25% of all workers' compensation claims. When lifting heavy items, use rollers under the objects, or ask for help. If lifting heavy objects, by yourself, follow these guidelines:

Lifting Guidelines

Bend at your knees.

Keep your back straight.

Keep your feet close to the object.

Center your body over the load.

Lift straight up without jerking.

Do not twist your body when you pick up or move the object.

Set the load down slowly, keeping your back straight.

Cleaning Kitchen Equipment

When cleaning any piece of kitchen equipment, turn switches to the "off" position, unplug the machine from its power source, and follow the manufacturer's instruction manual and the food establishment's cleaning directions.

Maintenance and Repairs

Maintaining and repairing equipment require compliance with OSHA's lockout/tagout procedure. This means that all necessary switches on electrical equipment must be locked out and tagged when they are malfunctioning, thus preventing the equipment from being used while it is being repaired.

Fire Safety

Fires cause substantial property and equipment damage, injuries, and death. Flames and high heat sources in the commercial kitchen associated with the foodservice industry increase the probability of fires.

Equipment

Foodservice operations rely on a variety of fire extinguishers and hood and sprinkler systems as standard fire safety equipment.

- **Fire extinguishers**—Fire extinguishers are the most common type of fire protection equipment used in foodservice operations. The type, number, and location of fire extinguishers needed in a commercial kitchen may vary, but each workstation must have a working fire extinguisher within reach. Fire extinguishers use several types of chemicals to fight different kinds of fires; use the appropriate class of extinguisher to fight a fire properly. Classes include class A (wood, paper, cloth, plastic), class B (grease, oil, chemicals), class C (electrical cords, switches, wiring), class D (combustible switches, wiring, metals, iron), and class K (fires in cooking appliances involving vegetable or animal oils or fats).
- **Hood and sprinkler systems**—Hood and sprinkler systems are standard equipment in commercial kitchens. A properly ventilated hood system will remove excess smoke, heat, and vapors caused by fire, and sprinkler systems aid in extinguishing flames. Hoods and ducts should be cleaned regularly, and products and supplies should be stored properly.

Emergency Procedures

Every foodservice establishment has fire emergency procedures with which each employee must be familiar. Fire exit signs must be posted in plain view above exits, and a meeting place should be designated outside so that a head count can be conducted. Employees should also know how to direct customers out of the building and keep them calm during emergencies. If a fire is discovered, regardless of its size, call the fire department immediately. Then quickly and calmly assist customers and co-workers in exiting the building.

First Aid

The definition of first aid is assisting an injured person until professional medical help can be provided. This involves

- *checking the scene and staying calm.*
- *keeping the victim comfortable and calm.*
- *calling the local emergency number for professional medical help.*
- *caring for the victim by administering first aid according to the first-aid manual.*
- *keeping people who are not needed away from the victim.*
- *completing an accident report by writing the victim's name, the date and time of the accident, the type of injury or illness, the treatment, and how long it took for assistance to arrive.*

The American Red Cross (ARC) offers courses that teach hands-on practical information about first aid in the workplace, and foodservice workers are encouraged to take an ARC first-aid course. Contact your local chapter of the ARC for additional information.

First Aid for Burns

Any degree of burn requires immediate treatment. See Figure 4-11. Call the local emergency number for medical assistance, but until help arrives, follow these general guidelines:

- Remove the person from the source of the heat.
- Cool the burned skin to stop the burning. Do this by applying cold water over the affected area. Use water from a faucet or soaked towels. Do not use ice or ice water.
- Never apply ointments, sprays, antiseptics, or remedies unless instructed to do so by a medical professional.
- Bandage the burn as directed in the first-aid manual.
- Minimize the risk of shock. Keep the victim from getting chilled or overheated. Have the victim rest.

FIGURE 4-11

Types and Characteristics of Burns

FIRST-DEGREE BURNS

The skin becomes red, sensitive, and sometimes swollen. These are the least severe of all burns.

SECOND-DEGREE BURNS

These burns cause deeper, painful damage, and blisters form on the skin. The blisters ooze and are painful.

THIRD-DEGREE BURNS

The skin may be white and soft or black, charred, and leathery. The burned area has no feeling. Sometimes third-degree burns are not painful because the nerves in the skin have been destroyed. These are the worst kinds of burns. Third-degree burns require immediate medical attention at a hospital.

First Aid for Wounds

There are four types of open wounds or cuts that foodservice employees are susceptible to: abrasions, lacerations, avulsions, and punctures. Each requires immediate medical attention.

Abrasions An *abrasion* is a scrape and is considered a minor cut.

Lacerations A *laceration* is a cut or tear in the skin that can be quite deep. A knife wound is a type of laceration.

Avulsions An *avulsion* occurs when a portion of the skin is partially or completely torn off.

Punctures Puncture wounds occur when the skin is pierced with a pointed object, such as an ice pick, making a deep hole in the skin.

For a minor cut, the first-aid provider should follow these guidelines:

1. Put on disposable gloves to protect against infection.
2. Clean the cut with soap, and rinse it under water.
3. Place a bandage over the cut. Use sterile gauze if possible.
4. Apply direct pressure over the sterile gauze or bandage to stop any bleeding from the cut.
5. If bleeding does not stop, elevate the limb above the heart to reduce the amount of blood going to the cut area.
6. Follow instructions in the first-aid manual.

To administer emergency relief for lacerations, avulsions, and punctures, the first-aid provider should follow these guidelines:

1. Put on disposable gloves to protect against infection.
2. Control the bleeding by applying pressure, using sterile gauze or a clean cloth towel. Do not waste time washing the wound first. Elevate the area while applying pressure.
3. Cover the wound with clean bandages. Continue to apply pressure.
4. Wash your hands thoroughly after treating the wound.

First Aid for Choking

In case of a choking incidence, the Heimlich maneuver may need to be performed. To do this:

1. Stand behind the victim. Wrap your arms around his or her waist.
2. Locate the victim's navel.
3. Make a fist with one hand. Place the thumb side of your fist against the middle of the abdomen. Position your hand just above the navel and below the bottom of the breastbone.
4. Place your other hand on top of your fist.
5. Press your hands into the victim's abdomen. Use quick inward and upward thrusts. Each thrust should be a separate and distinct action.
6. Repeat this motion as many times as it takes to dislodge the object or food from the victim's throat. Note that a conscious victim can become unconscious during this maneuver if the object is not dislodged.

This maneuver should be used only on someone who is conscious and choking. If the person can cough or speak, or is unconscious, do not perform this maneuver; doing so can cause physical injury. The Heimlich maneuver also should never be performed on a pregnant woman. Doing so could harm the baby.

Cardiopulmonary Resuscitation (CPR)

Unresponsive victims—those who are unconscious because of choking, cardiac arrest, stroke, or heart attack—will need cardiopulmonary resuscitation (CPR) performed until emergency help arrives. CPR helps keep oxygen flowing to the brain and heart, improving the chances of survival. It is advisable for foodservice workers to learn CPR. Contact your local chapter of the American Heart Association or the American Red Cross for additional information.

Sickness in the Workplace or Classroom

Employees in food service must maintain their health and be free of illnesses in order to come to work or attend classes. Employees who are ill can transmit harmful microorganisms to other foodservice employees or to the food they are preparing or serving.

If an employee or student exhibits any of the symptoms listed below, he or she should not report to work or attend classes but instead should inform the supervisor or instructor of the condition. See Figure 4-12.

Should the employee or student become sick while at work or in class, he or she should inform the supervisor or instructor and then leave immediately, reporting to a doctor or university health service. Any surfaces that the ill employee came into contact with should be cleaned and sanitized to prevent cross-contamination.

Any medications that must be taken while ill should be stored with the employee's or student's personal belongings to ensure that they do not get mixed in with food. Cuts, sores, wounds, or infections must be covered with a clean, dry bandage. If the bandage is on the hand, gloves or a finger cot should be worn at all times while at work. Employees with these types of injuries may need to be reassigned to another duty.

FIGURE 4-12

Reporting Agreement

I AGREE TO REPORT TO UNIVERSITY HEALTH SERVICES:

FUTURE SYMPTOMS and PUSTULAR LESIONS:

1. *Diarrhea*
2. *Fever*
3. *Vomiting*
4. *Jaundice*
5. *Lesions containing pus on the hand, wrist, or an exposed body part (such as boils and infected wounds, however small)*

The success of a foodservice establishment is the result of serving a consistently good product, meeting customer expectations, and using proper cost controls. There are two areas of control on which managers must focus: sales and cost. Sales is the amount of money brought into the foodservice operation by customers paying for goods and services. Cost is the amount of money paid out by the foodservice operation to produce food and to serve its customers. Each is important to the profitability of a foodservice operation.

Cost Controls

There are four major areas of cost that foodservice operations must manage: food, beverage, labor, and overhead. Well-run foodservice operations that use cost-saving tools and techniques to control these costs are often profitable and have high customer satisfaction.

Types of Costs

Food cost is the total dollar amount spent by the foodservice operation to purchase food and beverages needed to prepare menu items intended for sale. Food cost includes all produce, meats, poultry, seafood, grocery, and baking goods needed to prepare a recipe. Beverage items may also be included in food cost when the beverage is an ingredient in the recipe, such as wine used for cooking. The amount of money spent to purchase these products may vary from one type of foodservice operation to the next, depending on the characteristics of the market segment being served. Food cost typically ranges from 20%–35% of the money earned through food sales.

Beverage cost is the total dollar amount spent by the foodservice operation to purchase all the ingredients needed to produce a beverage item. Beverage cost may include alcoholic beverages, nonalcoholic beverages, and food items needed to produce the beverage recipe. Beverage costs typically represent 15%–20% of money earned through beverage sales. When food cost and beverage costs are combined, they are called the *cost of sales.* Cost of sales is the total amount spent to purchase all food and beverage products needed to produce total sales.

Labor cost is the cost of paying employees wages, salaries, and benefits. Labor cost normally represents 25%–35% of the total sales earned by the foodservice operation. *Overhead costs* include all other expenses needed to operate a foodservice operation. Examples of overhead costs include utilities, linens, mortgage, paper goods, glassware, and many others. Overhead costs often represent about 15%–25% of the total sales. The combination of labor and overhead costs are *operating expenses.*

A foodservice operation must serve enough customers and bring in enough sales to pay these major areas of costs. If sales are greater than costs, the foodservice operation has a profit. If sales are less than costs, the foodservice operation sees a loss.

Managing Food Costs

The most important cost-control tool used in a commercial kitchen is a standardized recipe. A *standardized recipe* is a written formula customized to meet the needs of a foodservice operation. The standardized recipe describes the quality and quantity of ingredients, as well as the method of preparation, cooking techniques, and temperatures required to make a menu item. See Figure 5-1 on page 54. Using the standardized recipe as a tool allows a foodservice operation to create a consistent product. Before standardized recipes are used, they are tested repeatedly for consistency and quantity. They are also tested to ensure that directions are easy to follow and that the ingredients are listed accurately.

> **For the sake of clarity, recipe conversion examples are in U.S. Standard measurements. These examples also apply to metric measurements. See the appendix for metric conversions.**

FIGURE 5-1

The standardized recipe is an important cost-control tool.

Roast Leg of Lamb with Tarragon
Gigot d'Agneau Rôti à l'Estragon

 Yield: 10 servings
Portion size: 5 ounces

Ingredients	Amount
Leg of lamb, *boneless*	5 lbs. (80 oz.)
Salt	TT
Black pepper, *ground*	TT
Tarragon, *ground*	1/2 tsp.
Oil, *heated*	3 oz.
Lamb demi-glace, *seasoned*	1 qt.
Cornstarch, *diluted with 1 1/2 oz. cold lamb stock*	1 oz.
Tarragon leaves	2 Tbsp.
Garlic, *peeled and left whole*	1/2 head
Fresh tarragon	5 stems
Mirepoix	
Onions, *peeled, diced 1/2"*	8 oz.
Carrots, *washed and peeled, diced 1/2"*	8 oz.
Celery, *cleaned, washed, diced 1/2"*	8 oz.

Method of Preparation
1. Gather all the ingredients and equipment.
2. Season the lamb with salt, pepper, and ground tarragon. Truss leg with butcher's twine.
3. Sear and brown lamb in hot oil, and place on mirepoix and garlic in roasting pan. Roast in a ... the internal temperature reaches 145°F (63°C). Baste with demi-

The quantities of ingredients in a standardized recipe are stated in an edible portion form. *Edible portion* means that the quantities of ingredients are in their ready-to-use state. If a standardized recipe calls for eight ounces of carrots, it means eight ounces of peeled, trimmed, usable carrots. By using the standard quantity and quality of ingredients, the standardized recipe yields a consistent amount of product, called *standard yield.* The product is then divided into *standard portions,* the amount of food that is served for each order.

Portion control is an essential component of controlling food costs, and it is also important for customer satisfaction. Serving too much food in each portion reduces profits, but serving too little may drive away customers. A set method of preparation helps the kitchen staff consistently prepare a known quantity and quality of the food item. By using standards in the food production cycle, the foodservice operation can serve a consistent product that allows for customer satisfaction and profitability.

In baking, a standardized recipe is referred to as a *formula.* Although formulas and recipes are similar, there are significant differences. In recipes, ingredients are listed in order of use followed by the procedures. In formulas, precise measures of ingredients are listed in order by decreasing weight and are often seen as percentages, often called a baker's percentage. The *baker's percentage* includes the percentage of each ingredient in relationship to the weight of the flour in the final baked

product. Baker's percentages make it easy to increase or decrease the quantity of individual ingredients.

> See Chapter 29: Fundamentals of Baking and Pastry for more information on formulas and baker's percentages.

Benefits of Standardized Recipes

The benefits of standardized recipes include consistency, cost control, quality control, and truth-in-menu advertising.

Consistency A key reason to use standardized recipes is that customers equate consistency with quality. See Figure 5-2. When customers order a menu item, they expect that the item they order today will be the same quality and quantity as the one they enjoyed last week. Many successful foodservice operations have stuck to a simple, well-defined menu that is consistently executed.

Cost control Cost control is another benefit of using standardized recipes. By specifying the specific ingredients and portion size of a recipe, foodservice operators are able to forecast the costs and profits associated with a menu item. Adding more or using less of an ingredient than the standardized recipe specifies can increase costs, distort inventory, and displease customers.

Quality control Quality control is achieved through standardized recipes by carefully specifying the quality and quantity of ingredients used. The quality of the ingredients used is closely related to the market position of the foodservice operation. The

key is to maintain consistent quality so that the customers get what they expect.

Truth in menu Properly informing customers of the ingredients used, preparation and cooking methods, and portion size is important to customer satisfaction and operational success. The National Restaurant Associations (NRA) *Accuracy in Menu* paper identifies guidelines that foodservice operators may use in menu planning and preparation.

> **Truth in menu includes proper identification of an item's quantity, quality, weight, and product ingredients, to name a few. Adherence to ingredient specifications in a standardized recipe ensures that what is supposed to be in the recipe is, in fact, in the recipe. Customers can then make informed decisions. People with food allergies, in particular, need to know what is in their food. This can be a life-threatening issue. Failing to properly inform someone who asks about a specific ingredient can also have serious financial implications.**

FIGURE 5-2

Standardized recipes ensure consistent results.

Recipe Conversion

Changing a recipe to produce a new amount or yield is called recipe conversion.

Before the yield of a standardized recipe can be changed, a conversion factor has to be established. The **conversion factor** is the number that results from dividing the desired yield (the quantity of portions needed) by the existing standard yield. The conversion factor is obtained by this calculation:

Formulas
Desired yield ÷ Standard yield = Conversion factor

Increasing the desired yield of a recipe yields a conversion factor greater than one. Using the standardized recipe found in Figure 5-1, the standardized recipe for roast leg of lamb yields 10 portions. If the desired yield is 30 portions, the conversion factor is calculated as follows:

Formulas
Desired yield (30) ÷ Standard yield (10) = Conversion factor (3)

The conversion factor is 3. Each ingredient quantity is multiplied by the conversion factor to obtain the new quantity needed to produce the desired yield. For example, if the recipe calls for 5 pounds of lamb, the recipe would be converted as follows:

5 lbs. lamb × 3 = 15 lbs. lamb

Decreasing a recipe results in a conversion factor of less than one. Using the recipe in Figure 5-1, to decrease the desired yield to 5, if the existing yield is 10, the same formula is used:

Formulas
Desired yield (5) ÷ Standard yield (10) = Conversion factor (0.5)

The conversion factor is 0.5. Each ingredient quantity is multiplied by the conversion factor to obtain the new quantity of ingredients needed to produce the desired yield. For example, if a recipe calls for 5 pounds of lamb, the recipe would be converted as follows:

5 lbs. lamb × 0.5 = 2.5 lbs. lamb

Recipe conversion is a skill used daily in the commercial kitchen. Accuracy and consistency in making conversions is important for maintaining quality.

Considerations When Converting Recipes

Mathematical recipe conversions do not take into account adjustments that must be made to certain ingredients, equipment, cooking temperatures, trim, and shrinkage that may occur when altering standardized recipes. When such adjustments are needed, they should be noted on the recipe.

Adjustments to Ingredients
Ingredients such as spices are often stated on standardized recipes as to taste, pinch, dash, as needed, and so on. Expertise must be used to carefully adjust the quantities of these ingredients to maintain a consistent product.

Adjustments to Equipment
Recipes usually indicate the size of equipment needed to prepare the food product. If a recipe is increased or decreased, the size of the equipment can become a factor. The wrong equipment can affect the outcome of a recipe. Always use the proper equipment to accommodate the recipe conversion.

■ *See Chapter 7: Equipment for more information on equipment.*

Cooking Temperatures
Cooking temperatures can be affected by a change in equipment. The use of a convection oven as opposed to the conventional oven called for in the recipe will require a change in cooking time because convection ovens cook more quickly than conventional ovens.

Trim and Shrinkage
Trim is the percentage of food lost during the preparation of the food product. *Shrinkage* is the percentage of food lost during cooking. The amount of trim and shrinkage affects not only the edible yield of the product but also the portion cost. Knowing how much trim and shrinkage loss can be expected allows for the correct amount of ingredients to be used per portion. For example, corned beef generally shrinks almost 50% when it is cooked, so this must be considered when it is purchased. If 10 pounds of cooked corned beef is needed to make sandwiches, 20 pounds of corned beef must be used to prepare the forecasted portions.

Edible portion is the amount of food product that is servable after preparing the ingredient for use. Waste, including peelings, stems, and trim, and shrinkage in cooking are factors that affect product yield. The percentage of a food product that is left after trim and/or shrinkage is called the *edible yield percentage.* Yield tests or cooking loss tests are often performed to determine how much product will be lost through preparation or cooking.

Yield Test
Yield tests are performed on food products that are prepared for use or service in their raw form. For example, the outermost leaves of a head of lettuce are trimmed and discarded when cleaning the lettuce. Another example would be the cutting and trimming of individual filets from tenderloin of beef.

Follow these steps to conduct a yield test:

1. Weigh the product before trimming to determine the AP weight. *AP weight* is the weight of the product when purchased.

2. Trim and prepare the product for use. Weigh the by-product material that was trimmed from the purchased product. This number is called the *trim loss.*

3. Weigh the usable product. This number is the *edible yield,* the weight of the product in its edible portion form.

4. Divide the edible yield weight by the AP weight. The result is in the edible yield percentage.

To follow the yield test procedure for a one-pound bag of carrots, the carrots would first be weighed in the as-purchased form (16 oz.). After peeling and trimming the carrots, the usable product is weighed (12.8 oz.). The trim loss would be the difference between the AP weight and the yield weight (3.2 oz.). Then the edible yield weight (12.8 oz.) is divided by the AP weight (16 oz.). The edible yield percentage would be 80% (0.8). Because each foodservice operation has its own standards for how workers should trim products, edible yield percentages may differ.

Formulas

AP weight (16 oz.) − Edible yield weight (12.8 oz.) = Trim loss (3.2 oz.)

Formulas

Edible yield weight (12.8 oz.) ÷ AP weight (16 oz.) = Edible yield percentage (.8 or 80%)

Cooking Loss Test

A cooking loss test is performed on products that must be cooked before the edible yield weight is determined. To determine how cooking affects yield percentage, follow these steps:

1. Weigh the product before trimming to determine the AP weight, or as-purchased weight.
2. Trim and prepare for cooking.
3. Determine precooked weight.
4. Cook, following methods of preparation on the standardized recipe.
5. Trim after cooking.
6. Weigh edible portion.
7. Divide the edible portion weight by the AP weight. The result is the edible yield percentage.

To follow the cooking loss test procedure for a 5-pound leg of lamb, weigh the leg of lamb in its as-purchased form (80 oz.). Then prepare and trim the leg of lamb to ready it for the cooking process, and weigh it again (75 oz.). After it is cooked, trim and prepare the lamb for service, and weigh it in its edible portion form (50 oz.).

FIGURE 5-3

A recipe costing form helps determine and control costs.

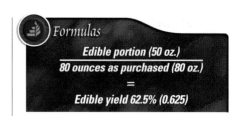
Formulas

$$\frac{\text{Edible portion (50 oz.)}}{\text{80 ounces as purchased (80 oz.)}}$$

=

Edible yield 62.5% (0.625)

Using the recipe in Figure 5-1 on page 54, a yield test would be performed on the onions, carrots, and celery to determine the yield percentage, and a cooking loss test would be performed on the leg of lamb.

Knowing the edible yield percentage of a product not only aids the chef in using the proper quantity of ingredients to prepare a standardized recipe but also can help the foodservice professional order the correct quantity of foods to meet production needs.

Recipe Costing

When costing a standardized recipe, the following items must be understood and provided in order for kitchen staff to do their jobs well. See Figure 5-3.

- **Recipe name**—The name of the recipe should be the same as that listed on the menu.
- **Standard yield**—The standard yield is the number of servings that one preparation of the recipe yields.
- **Standard portion**—Standard portion is the standard amount of the food item that is served to each customer, usually stated in ounces or count.

Standard Recipe Cost Card

Standard Portion: 5 ounces

Recipe Name: Roast Leg of Lamb with Tarragon

Standard Yield: 10

Recipe		Edible Yield %	As Purchased		Ingredient	Invoice		Recipe		Individual Ingredient Cost
Quantity	Unit	%	Quantity	Unit		Cost	Unit	Cost	Unit	
3.13	lb.	62.5%	5.00	lb	Lamb, boneless	$4.25	lb.	$4.250	lb.	$21.25
	to taste	100.0%	0.00	to taste	Salt	$4.95	25 lbs.		to taste	$0.00
	to taste	100.0%	0.00	to taste	Black pepper	$18.50	18 oz.		to taste	$0.00
0.50	tsp.	100.0%	0.50	tsp.	Tarragon	$11.50	3.5 oz.	$0.077	tsp.	$0.04
3.00	oz.	100.0%	3.00	oz.	Oil	$19.75	gal.	$0.154	oz.	$0.46
1.00	qt.	100.0%	1.00	qt.	Demi-glace	$32.00	gal.	$0.250	qt.	$0.25
1.00	oz.	100.0%	1.00	oz.	Cornstarch	$17.50	24-16 oz.	$0.046	oz.	$0.05
2.00	Tbsp.	100.0%	2.00	Tbsp.	Tarragon leaves	$11.50	3.5 oz.	$0.077	Tbsp.	$0.15
0.50	head	100.0%	0.50	head	Garlic	$8.35	5 lbs.	$0.334	head	$0.17
5.00	stems	100.0%	5.00	stems	Fresh tarragon				stems	$0.00
8.00	oz.	88.0%	9.09	oz.	Onions	$11.50	3.5 oz.	$0.013	oz.	$0.12
8.00	oz.	80.0%	10.00	oz.	Carrots	$10.75	50 lbs.	$0.024	oz.	$0.24
8.00	oz.	65.0%	12.31	oz.	Celery	$9.75	25 lbs.	$0.081	oz.	$1.00
						$7.80	6 lbs.			

Total Ingredient Cost:		$23.73
Q Factor %:	3.0%	$0.71
Recipe Cost:		$24.44
Portion Cost:		$2.44
Red Potatoes:		$0.42
Green Beans:		$0.65
Total Plate Cost:		$3.51
Desired Cost %:		25.0%
Preliminary Selling Price:		$14.04

- **Ingredient**—This section of the recipe cost card specifies the ingredients and the proper amount of ingredients needed to produce the standard yield.
- **Edible yield percentage**—This represents the part of the purchased product that is usable after trimming or cooking.
- **Invoice cost per unit**—This is the purchase cost and unit of purchase of each ingredient in the recipe. This price can be obtained from regularly used purveyors or from the most recent *invoice,* or bill, for purchased products.

Determining the Portion Cost

Calculating the Ingredient Cost

The first step in calculating a recipe's portion cost is to transfer all ingredients and quantities to the costing form. See Figure 5-3 on page 56. The costing process can then begin.

Individual ingredient cost It is important to determine the cost of each ingredient in the recipe. This step helps identify the excessive cost of an ingredient and where a less-expensive ingredient may be substituted without affecting quality. In order to achieve the standard yield, the quantity of ingredients must be measured in edible portion form. If the ingredient is not purchased in the edible portion form, an edible yield percentage must be applied to that ingredient. Therefore, it is important for the foodservice professional to understand edible yield percentages. Refer back to yield and cooking loss tests.

As-purchased quantity As standardized recipes list the quantity of ingredients in the edible portion form, the foodservice professional costing the recipe must be able to determine how much of the product is needed to yield that quantity. In Figure 5-3, ingredients such as salt and pepper are already in their usable form, so they have an edible yield percentage of 100%.

Ingredients that are not purchased in the edible form must have the edible yield percentage applied to determine how much product would actually be needed to yield the quantity listed. For example, the recipe for leg of lamb calls for 8 ounces of washed and peeled carrots. To determine how many ounces of carrots must be used to yield 8 ounces of usable carrots, a yield test may be performed on the carrots. Using the

edible yield percentage of 80% previously determined, the 8 ounces of edible weight would be divided by the edible yield percentage to determine the as-purchased weight. The as-purchased quantity is the weight of the unprepared product that would be used to yield the quantity of edible product.

Formulas

8 oz. ÷ 80% (0.8) = 10 oz. of as-purchased carrots

This formula indicates that 10 ounces of carrots in their as-purchased form would need to be used to yield 8 ounces of usable carrots. Therefore, the 10 ounces of as-purchased carrots should be used when calculating the ingredient cost for carrots.

Again looking at Figure 5-1 on page 54, the recipe requires a 5-pound leg of lamb to achieve ten 5-ounce servings. The professional writing this recipe has already taken into consideration that the lamb is going to lose almost 2 pounds through the cooking process. To confirm this, multiply the standard yield by the standard portion.

Formulas

Standard yield	×	Standard portion	=	Amount needed
Example: 10 portions	×	5 oz. each	=	50 oz.

This formula informs us that 50 ounces of edible product is needed to serve 10 portions. However, the standardized recipe calls for 5 pounds of lamb, which is equal to 80 ounces. It has been estimated that approximately 30 ounces (almost 2 pounds) will be lost during the cooking process, which results in a 62.5% edible yield percent.

Changing the invoice cost per unit to the recipe cost per unit The *invoice cost per unit* is the cost to purchase an ingredient in the specified unit in which it is purchased. The *recipe cost per unit* is how much one recipe unit of the ingredient costs. For example, lamb is purchased at $4.25 per pound. The recipe unit is a pound, so in this case the invoice cost per unit and the recipe cost per unit are the same. If 5 pounds are needed, calculate as follows:

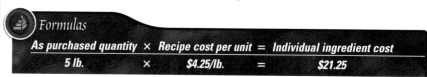

Formulas

As purchased quantity	×	Recipe cost per unit	=	Individual ingredient cost
5 lb.	×	$4.25/lb.	=	$21.25

To calculate the ingredient cost of carrots, the foodservice professional would first need to calculate the recipe unit cost, which is an ounce. If carrots are purchased at $9.75 for a 25-pound bag, and there are 400 ounces in a 25-pound bag (25 lb. × 16 oz.), the cost per ounce for carrots would be:

Formulas

Invoice cost per unit	÷	Ounce in purchase unit	=	Recipe cost per unit
$9.75/25 lb.	÷	400 oz.	=	$0.024/oz.

It was previously determined that 10 ounces of as-purchased carrots would be needed to yield 8 ounces of edible carrots.

To complete the individual ingredient cost for carrots:

Formulas

As-purchased quantity	×	Cost per unit	=	Individual ingredient cost
10 oz.	×	$0.024/oz.	=	$0.24

Total Ingredient Cost

After all the individual ingredient costs have been determined (illustrated in the formula above), they are totaled. The total ingredient cost for the leg of lamb is $23.73.

Q Factor

A **Q factor** (questionable cost) is a cost that covers all ingredients that have a measure but are insignificant in cost, such as salt, and ingredients that are regularly adjusted, such as flour as needed. A Q factor is usually applied as a percentage of the total ingredient cost to achieve the recipe cost. In Figure 5-3 on page 56, a 3% Q factor is applied, and would be calculated as follows:

Formulas

Total ingredient cost	×	Q factor %	=	Q factor amount
$23.73	×	3.0%	=	$0.71

Recipe Cost

The **recipe cost** is the total cost to prepare the recipe, after having calculated the measurable ingredients and estimated the cost of the immeasurable ingredients by using a Q factor. The Q factor amount is added to the total ingredient cost to determine the recipe cost as follows:

Formulas

Total ingredient cost	+	Q factor amount	=	Recipe cost
$23.73	+	$0.71	=	$24.44

Portion Cost

The **portion cost** is the cost of one portion of the standardized recipe. The recipe cost is divided by the standard yield (number of portions) to determine the cost per portion as follows:

Formulas

Recipe cost	÷	Standard yield	=	Portion cost
$24.44	÷	10	=	$2.44

Plate Cost

Often the portion costs of several recipes need to be determined so that they may be added together to determine the **plate cost** of a menu item. If a portion of lamb is served with 5 ounces of roasted red potatoes ($0.42 per portion) and 4 ounces of green beans ($0.65 per portion), the two additional portion costs would be added to the entrée to determine the cost of the plate as follows:

Formulas

Lamb	+	Potatoes	+	Green beans	=	Plate cost
$2.44	+	$0.42	+	$0.65	=	$3.51

Preliminary Selling Price

The **preliminary selling price** is the lowest suggested selling price to list on the menu. There are two basic mathematical approaches to setting the preliminary selling price: the desired cost percentage and the pricing factor.

Desired cost percentage One method to determine the preliminary selling price is to divide the plate cost by the food cost percentage the restaurant is trying to achieve. If a restaurant's goal was 25% food cost, the formula would be as follows:

Formulas

Plate cost	÷	Food cost %	=	Preliminary selling price
$3.51	÷	25%	=	$14.04

Pricing factor The second method to calculate the preliminary selling price is to use the pricing factor. Again using the food cost percentage goal of 25%, the formula to calculate the pricing factor, thus the preliminary selling price, is as follows:

Formulas

100%	÷	Food cost %	=	Pricing factor
100%	÷	25%	=	4

Plate cost	×	Pricing factor	=	Preliminary selling price
$3.51	×	4	=	$14.04

Both processes will provide the same preliminary selling price. It is rare that the preliminary selling price is the selling price found on the menu. The foodservice professional would use his or her expertise to adjust (mark up) the preliminary selling price to meet the financial demands of the foodservice operation, taking into consideration the foodservice concept, clientele, and competition. When setting the menu selling price, there are three areas of importance: to make certain that all costs are covered; to determine that the price is fair and reasonable to the business in terms of profit; and to know that the price is fair and reasonable to the customer.

See Chapter 6: Menu Development for more information about menu design.

Controlling Costs

After the menu has been developed and selling prices have been determined, control tools must be used to realize a profit. These begin with purchasing and continue through to the production and sales processes.

Purchasing

Depending on the size and type of the operation, purchasing food may be the responsibility of the chef, a food steward, or a designated purchasing agent. By giving responsibility and control of purchasing to one person quantity control is assured, ingredient quality is consistent, and food is purchased at the appropriate cost.

It is important to set purchasing procedures to define who has purchasing authority, identify which purveyors are preferred for what items, provide standards on how often orders should be made, and offer specific criteria on what should be ordered. Large multiunit operations will usually have employees dedicated to purchasing activities so that they can leverage *economies of scale,* or price breaks, for purchasing in larger quantities.

Product Specifications

Decisions related to food quality are based on the menu and customer expectations. The most efficient way to ensure consistency and quality is through the use of standardized recipes and carefully creating a description of the ingredients the recipe requires in terms of standard product specifications. *Product specifications* describe the quality and quantity of each standardized recipe ingredient. A well-written standardized recipe will specify the exact quality, such as a grade for fruits and vegetables, or the classification of prime or choice for beefsteaks, and quantity of the ingredients to be used. Menu items based on clear specifications are prepared at a consistent level of quality within cost parameters determined by the foodservice operation. Chefs have ultimate control, but controlling costs and quality of products is a shared responsibility of all kitchen personnel.

Types of Purchased Products

Not all purchased products are food, but all are essential to a commercial kitchen. Foodservice operators purchase four types of products: perishable, semiperishable, nonperishable, and nonedibles.

Perishable Perishable products are generally fresh foods that have a relatively short shelf life. The quality of these items, such as fresh fruits, vegetables, meat, poultry, and seafood, tends to diminish in a relatively short period of time. These items must be ordered frequently and in quantities that can be used quickly so that the ingredients are at their peak of freshness and waste is minimized.

Semiperishable Semiperishable products are those that often have been treated with preservatives (usually smoked or salted) to extend shelf life. These products include processed meats, smoked fish, and pickled vegetables.

Nonperishable Nonperishable items have a long shelf life—they do not decompose rapidly when stored in their original packages at room temperature. The quality of these items remains intact when stored for up to one year. Examples of nonperishable items include canned fruits and vegetables; bags of rice, sugar, and flour; and condiments such as catsup, steak sauce, and mustard.

Nonedibles Nonedibles are nonfood products and include such items as aluminum foil and plastic wrap, paper goods, and cleaning supplies.

Determining Purchase Quantities

The quantity of the item purchased depends on several factors:

- Type of product being ordered
- Storage constraints
- Number of times a menu item will be sold in a particular timeframe
- Discounts on volume purchases
- Available seasonal specials

Purveyor Relationships

The relationship between foodservice operations and purveyors is based on mutual trust and performance. Foodservice operations should show integrity when interacting with purveyors, and they should be able to trust purveyors to consistently deliver products of the desired quality at a reasonable cost. Proper cost control measures add integrity to the relationship of trust between the buyer and the purveyor.

Methods of Purchasing

There are two primary methods of purchasing products for a foodservice operation: open market and single-source buying. The **open market** allows foodservice operators to obtain bids from various purveyors. Purveyors compete with one another to offer the specified quality and quantity of product at the lowest price and best service to the foodservice operation.

Depending on the volume of sales a restaurant produces, the effort required to purchase items on a competitive basis is sometimes more than the cost benefit received. If hours must be spent seeking and responding to bids for only a small cost savings, it is wiser to use single-source buying. In **single-source buying**, operators can purchase products from a single purveyor, negotiating price for volume-based

discounts. This makes single-source buying attractive for items that are consistently purchased in large volumes.

After the purchasing method is determined, a purchase order is prepared. A **purchase order** is a form that communicates to the purveyor the items to be purchased. See Figure 5-4. A purchase order lists the products that were ordered and specifies the type and amount of the products. In addition, a formal purchase order includes the unit price of the product and the total cost of items to be purchased.

❧ **FIGURE 5-4**

A purchase order lists the items to be purchased.

Receiving Goods

Receiving refers to the process by which product is accepted from the purveyor. An invoice is the bill that normally accompanies the delivery. Receiving standards ensure the correct quantity and quality of product ordered. A good receiving system ensures that the correct items and the proper quantity of items has been received and the product has been handled properly during shipping. Receiving is the first opportunity the restaurant has to control costs.

■ *See Chapter 4: Food Safety for more information on receiving.*

Receiving Tools and Equipment

The following tools and equipment make receiving more efficient:

- Heavy-duty gloves with nonslip fingertips
- Scales that are of the proper size to weigh food when received
- A calculator to check total costs or weights

- Cutting devices for opening containers, packages, and boxes
- Hand trucks to move cases from receiving to the storage area
- Thermometers to make sure that refrigerated and frozen goods are received at the right temperature
- Business forms, such as purchase orders and invoices

■ *See Chapter 7: Equipment for more information.*

Physical Inspection of Goods

All products received should be visually inspected to ensure that they are of good quality; that is, fresh, undamaged, and free from product tampering or mishandling, improper storage, and pest or rodent infestation. Weigh the products to make sure that their weights match those that were ordered. Check the products against the invoice. Report any discrepancies immediately.

Checking Purchase Order to Invoice

After the physical inspection of products is complete and the invoice quantities are confirmed, make sure that the items received are the ones that were ordered by checking the invoice against the purchase order. The purveyor supplies an invoice, and it should match the purchase order. The purpose of this step is to ensure that the items on the invoice are in fact the items that were ordered.

Storing and Issuing Controls

When food items are received, items are moved to the proper storage facility until needed for production. If a product's bar code sticker can be scanned, do so on receipt to help track the item through the inventory system. See Figure 5-5.

❧ **FIGURE 5-5**

Bar codes help track items through the inventory system.

Storeroom Controls

When storing goods, keep them in the proper environment to maximize the shelf life of the product and ensure its continued quality. Moving received products through proper inventory rotation is an important component of food storage, accomplished by using the FIFO method.

■ *See Chapter 4: Food Safety for more information on FIFO.*

Inventory Control

Inventory control is an essential component for business success. When a customer orders a particular item from the menu, the item should be available. Running out of a popular menu item can alienate a loyal patron. Food inventory is also a large expense for a foodservice operation. Managing inventory helps the establishment manage its capital assets efficiently. It is not cost efficient to hold excessive inventory.

Physical Inventory

A physical inventory is an actual count of items on hand. If a foodservice operation uses physical inventories as a control tool, an inventory may be performed daily (for alcoholic beverages) or weekly (for high-cost ingredients). Performing a physical inventory can assist in the control of theft and pilferage and in the decision-making process for determining how much to order. Performing periodic physical inventories at specific intervals allows the calculation of food and beverage costs (cost of sales) for that time period.

Parstock The amount of a product kept on hand from one delivery date to the next is called the *parstock.* Product shortages, bad weather, or delivery delays can affect delivery intervals, so plan for sufficient parstock to account for such unforeseen events. Having a parstock quantity assigned to each product assists the purchaser in determining how much to purchase. It lessens the decision-making time for determining how much to buy. The purchaser simply compares the inventory on hand with the parstock quantity; the difference between the two quantities determines the quantity to be ordered. This is often referred to as the periodic ordering method. The *periodic ordering method* of inventory control is used to establish how much product will be used in a given time period. The amount of the product on hand will be reviewed to determine what will be needed and how much parstock of the product should be available. A formula is used to determine how much to order:

Formulas

Parstock + Production needs − Stock on hand = Order amount

Perpetual inventory *Perpetual inventory* is a continuously updated, documented record of food items on hand. A perpetual inventory is often stored on a computer and, at preestablished levels, products are automatically reordered. Perpetual inventory systems are often difficult to use in foodservice operations because thousands of different items must be tracked and many of them are perishable.

The use of computers in inventory control can help in the purchasing process. Through the use of computers, foodservice operators can establish desired minimum and maximum inventory levels. When the inventory reaches the preestablished minimum level, an order is generated to increase the inventory to the maximum level. Computers can even be programmed with ordering parameters and tied in to point-of-sale cash registers so that inventory can be adjusted downward whenever a specific menu item is sold. When inventory levels reach parstock levels, the computer automatically generates a purchase order for the item needed. When the item is received, it is added to inventory by scanning the product bar code in the receiving area.

Issuing Controls

Unfortunately, food pilferage occurs in the foodservice industry. Operators can take precautions to prevent pilferage whenever possible by building controls into the operation to make sure that pilferage does not occur. Two ways to achieve this is through requisitions and security.

Using *requisitions,* an internal invoice that allows management to track the release of inventory from storage, helps control the internal flow of items. This ensures that only authorized staff sign the requisition. By limiting access, pilferage is decreased.

Physical security of inventory can be accomplished by locking storage areas to limit access to unauthorized employees. Procedures should be established and followed. Employee theft should result in immediate termination. Managers should monitor sales patterns and inventory levels to uncover any aberrations that might indicate a pilferage problem, and video cameras can be used to monitor storage areas.

Production Controls

When products leave the storage areas, they move to the kitchen for production. Production includes the preparation, production, and distribution of food products to the dining room. Managers often use *daily production report* forms to help control and manage costs and show how much product was prepared, how much was sold, and how much was unused. Not all leftover products can be reused, so minimizing them is important to cost savings. For example, by tracking daily the number of items left unused, the operation may adjust its preparation to better meet, rather than exceed, sales needs.

Sales Controls

Sales is the final information-gathering area of control that is necessary to complete the cost-control system. The recording of sales information begins when the customer places an order with the foodserver and the items are entered on a guest check or into the cash register system. The customer is served, completes his or her meal, and pays the guest check. The daily sales information is tallied within the cash register system and is printed out for analysis. With this information, managers can determine how well the foodservice operation performed; adjustments, if any, can be made; and the cycle of cost control can continue.

6 Menu

DELAVAN HOUSE.

DINNER BILL OF FARE.

SUNDAY, January 13th, 1867.

SOUP.
Mock Turtle.

FISH.
Boiled Striped Bass, Anchovy Sauce.   Baked Cod, Wine Sauce.

BOILED.
Westphalia Ham.   Pickled Tongue.   Turkey, Oyster Sauce.
Corned Beef and Savoy Cabbage.   Leg of Mutton, Capre Sauce.

ROAST.
Chicken.   Veal.   Lamb.   Mutton.   Turkey, Giblet Sa
Spare Rib of Pork.   Rib Beef.   Ham, Champagne S
Saddle South Down Mutton, Cranberry Sauce.
Roast Tame Duck, Apple Sauce.

COLD DISHES.
Westphalia Ham.   Lobsters.   Pressed
ne.

ENTREES.
Mushroom Sauce.
y Sauce.

e Hens, Larde
ddle of Venison C

RELISHES
Cele

s.

A.D. 1541
First known written bill of fare
used by Duke Henry of Brunswick.

1750
American colonist Thomas Pepper provides
first "table d'hôte" menu at his tavern.

1765
M. Boulanger displays the first "à la carte" menu
on posters at his Paris restaurant.

1831
The Delmonico brothers pioneer the wine menu at their New York restaurant.

1990
The Nutrition Labeling and Education Act requires that menu nutritional claims be documented.

The first known written menu appeared at an elaborate banquet in 1541. Duke Henry of Brunswick glanced at a sheet of paper beside his plate. When asked about its contents, the Duke explained that the chef had written a list of dishes he would serve and the order of their presentation. By referring to the list, the Duke could be sure to leave room for what he liked best. Soon other hosts and their chefs adopted the idea, creating large bills of fare to sit at the end of the banquet table. Over time, the bill of fare became smaller, and the custom of providing an individual menu to each guest was born.

Development

The Menu

A menu *is a list of dishes offered or served at each meal. A menu also is called a bill of fare. The menu, however, is much more than just a list of choices that customers must consider before placing an order. The menu impacts every phase of a foodservice operation, including the type of customer the establishment will attract. It affects the kitchen layout and type of equipment required, the number of workers needed and the skills they must possess, and the type and quantity of supplies the foodservice operation will order. A well-planned menu can increase sales by offering guests an appealing variety of choices as it facilitates peak efficiency and cost-effectiveness behind the scenes.*

Menu Types

Menus are classified according to the way food and beverages are priced and ordered and the regularity with which a food is offered. The most common pricing structures for sales menus include *à la carte*, semi-*à la carte, prix fixe*, and *table d'hôte*. Many menus combine elements of one or more pricing structures. In addition, the menu can be either a fixed or a cycle menu. Restaurant menus also may combine fixed and cycle elements, offering a repeating cycle of daily specials in addition to a fixed listing of basic offerings.

À la carte The *à la carte* menu prices and serves each item separately. The customer chooses and pays for the exact dishes or beverages he or she orders.

The à la Carte Menu

The à la carte menu dates back to 1765 at the small Paris shop of an unemployed chef named Boulanger. In Boulanger's day only inns, hostelries, and caterers could legally provide meals to guests. Because Boulanger was not a member of the caterer's guild, he was able to sell only drinks and broths. Boulanger challenged the letter of the law, and in time offered more substantial dishes, which he listed on a slate or poster along with the prices. Boulanger set out tables and chairs for his customers and created a model for what would later become the modern restaurant.

Semi-à la carte The **semi-*à la carte*** menu prices and serves some items together and other items separately. See Figure 6-1. For example, entrées often are priced with a salad and side dish, but appetizers, soups, desserts, and beverages are priced separately. Because the semi-*à la carte* menu typically includes the most popular accompaniments as part of the entrée price, customers often believe that this menu offers good value.

Prix fixe The term ***prix fixe*** is French for "fixed price." The *prix fixe* menu charges a set price for the entire meal. See Figure 6-2. Regardless of what the guest chooses from each course, the price is the same. A supplement may be charged for a small selection of items containing costly ingredients.

Table d'hôte The *table d'hôte* menu is similar to the *prix fixe* menu in that it offers a complete meal for a set price. However, the degree to which a guest may choose individual dishes may be more limited on the *table d'hôte* menu than on the *prix fixe* menu.

Fixed menu The ***fixed menu*** offers the same dishes every day for an extended period of time. Restaurants that serve a different clientele every day or offer a wide variety of selections may choose a fixed menu. Hotels, fast-food operations, ethnic restaurants, and most commercial restaurants typically use a fixed menu.

Cycle menu The ***cycle menu*** changes daily for a set period and then repeats. See Figure 6-3. The cycle menu is most common in institutions that serve the same people day after day, such as schools, hospitals, and military foodservice facilities.

Table d'hôte

The term table d'hôte means "host's table" in French. Originally, the phrase referred to the manner in which innkeepers served meals to their guests. Guests ate together at a communal table, sharing whatever dishes the innkeeper (the "host") had prepared. The ancient table d'hôte menu offered no real choices to guests, other than whether to accept or decline a dish. It also punished those who ate slowly or politely. Regular customers claimed the best seats near the center of the table, where the food was placed, and followed the practice of "first come, first served." A traditional table d'hôte menu is still offered in some small hotels and inns.

❧ **FIGURE 6-1**
Restaurants often use a semi-à la carte format for the dinner menu.

❧ **FIGURE 6-2**
Elegant upscale restaurants sometimes use a prix fixe menu.

❧ **FIGURE 6-3**
Some cycle menus, such as this one, repeat every other week. Monthly and weekly cycle menus are also common.

Who Plans the Menu?

When developing a menu, it is a good idea to utilize the expertise of a variety of people. Successful menu development takes time. Depending on the foodservice operation, menus may be planned by the executive chef working in combination with management staff such as the food and beverage director. In chain operations, the corporate chef is involved in menu planning. For institutions such as schools, hospitals, and retirement facilities, a registered dietitian (R.D.) also may collaborate in menu planning.

Factors to Consider When Planning the Menu

There are a multitude of factors to consider when planning a menu. In commercial foodservice operations, profit is a driving factor; in noncommercial operations, the facility must be able to bring in enough money to pay for the costs in order for the facility to remain operational. Successful menu planning has occurred when the needs of both the foodservice operation and the target market are met.

Target market The *target market* is the group of people a foodservice operation will serve or attract. The menu is a foodservice operation's primary marketing tool, so the menu must appeal to the needs and lifestyles of the target market. For example, a fast-food or take-out restaurant serves people who want an inexpensive, easily transported meal in a hurry. Since parents often take children to fast-food restaurants, the menu needs to appeal to the tastes of both parents and children. An upscale restaurant usually draws customers who are interested in a leisurely meal served by experienced servers. These customers are attracted to the quality of the food and often the originality of its preparation.

Type of food The dishes listed on the menu should appeal directly to the target market. An establishment that seeks to attract a clientele of people in their retirement years may offer foods that meet the nutritional requirements and preferences of this age group. On the other hand, an upscale restaurant that sees itself as a pacesetter will have a menu that reflects the latest in food trends and presentations, and an ethnic restaurant will offer foods that are representative of a particular culture, region, or country.

Price structure There are several ways to establish menu prices. Restaurants with a past history of successful performance may use the *price factor method.* To apply the price factor method, the chef must first determine the food cost of the items being served and the desired food cost percent the restaurant wants to achieve. The food cost of all items served on a plate can be calculated using a standard recipe costing sheet.

The desired food cost percent is a goal, a forecast that the restaurant strives to achieve. It represents the percent of sales that is used to purchase the products needed to produce the menu item. Most successful food operations work within a range of 25%–35% food cost. After the desired food cost percent and the food cost of the menu item have been determined, a factor is established to help set menu prices.

To use the factor method, first determine the desired food cost percent and the total cost of the menu item.

Formulas

$$\frac{100\% \text{ divided by the desired food cost \%}} {} = \text{Price factor}$$

If the desired food cost percent is 25%:
100% divided by 25% = 4.0

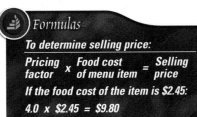

Formulas

To determine selling price:

$$\text{Pricing factor} \times \text{Food cost of menu item} = \text{Selling price}$$

If the food cost of the item is $2.45:
4.0 × $2.45 = $9.80

The selling price of the menu item would be $9.80.

The pricing factor method is the first step in determining the selling price. The pricing factor method helps determine the lowest selling price of an item if the operation wishes to achieve its desired food cost percent. Most managers adjust this selling price using additional considerations as described in other methods that follow.

Another method for determining menu price is the *competitors' pricing method.* With this method the restaurant establishes its menu prices in relation to those of its competitors. To appear more upscale, a restaurant may charge slightly more than the competition. To attract customers who might be lured by a bargain, a restaurant may charge slightly less than the competition.

Although the competitors' pricing method can be used by a start-up restaurant, it carries some risks. Overhead, labor, and food costs can differ from restaurant to restaurant, making it difficult to determine whether charging the same as a competitor will provide sufficient funds to cover expenses and supply a reasonable profit.

The *psychological pricing method* helps restaurants refine their menu prices. After a reasonable price is determined using other pricing methods, the restaurant considers psychological factors before setting the asking price. For instance, a customer may be more willing to pay $13.95 for an entrée than $14.00. To allow for future price increases, starting a menu item with a price at the low end of a dollar figure gives the restaurant more room to raise the price before entering the next dollar category. This may be important because of customer reaction to price increases. A price change from $13.95 to $14.25 may sound like more than one from $14.25 to $14.95, even though the second example actually is a greater increase than the first.

Equipment analysis Menus must be planned with restaurant equipment in mind. Both the types and the capacity of the equipment must be considered. If a restaurant has limited broiler space, then the number of broiled offerings on the menu should be limited. Care also must be taken to spread the workload across equipment. It is not cost-efficient to run a heated oven partially full while the fryer runs nonstop.

Skill level of employees Menu planners must consider the skill level of employees when determining what to offer. A kitchen staff without baking experience will be unable to meet the demand for home-baked desserts or breads. The menu also should strive to equalize the workload between members of the kitchen staff. Distributing the workload throughout the day helps control the demands on kitchen staff during peak times. Offering some items that can be partially made ahead of time balances the workload.

Geography Geography affects the menu through product availability and customer expectations. Restaurants usually can obtain fresh seafood more easily and affordably near the coastline than farther inland, so it makes sense to offer more fresh seafood products in coastal restaurants. Regional expectations also affect menu offerings. A menu found in the South may include biscuits or grits as a side dish, but a menu in the Pacific Northwest would be unlikely to feature these items.

Religious and cultural background
Menu planners might consider customers' religious and cultural backgrounds when planning what to offer. Members of some religious groups do not eat certain foods, such as pork or shellfish. Some vegetarians avoid all meat, including fish. Others eat fish or shellfish, but no other animals. Vegans avoid all animal products, including eggs and milk. Most restaurant menus offer sufficient choices so that even those who follow restricted diets can find appropriate selections. Foodservice operations that offer fewer options, such as those in schools, hospitals, camps, military institutions, the workplace, and retirement facilities, should be especially careful to consider the religious and cultural backgrounds of their guests when planning menus.

Nutritional concerns Lifestyles dictate a need for a variety of healthful food choices, and this is reflected on the menus of most restaurants and foodservice operations. More than ever, fruits, vegetables, grains, fish, and legumes are common menu offerings. Although a restaurant cannot force its customers to choose nutritious meals, offering a variety of choices that reflect the nutritional and cultural considerations of guests enables the establishment to meet the needs of a greater customer base. A primary concern when planning a menu for a hospital, retirement facility, camp, or school is nutrition.

■ *See Chapter 9: Nutrition for more information.*

Age and health issues The body's need for calories and nutrients changes over time. Young children, adolescents, and older people all have different nutritional needs. People with certain health conditions and those who are recovering from illness also have special dietary considerations. The foodservice operation whose primary mission is to serve a special population must take extra care to meet the daily nutritional needs of its guests. Many people must follow a low-fat diet because of heart disease, cancer, weight control, or other health concerns. High-fiber, low-fat foods with plenty of fruits, vegetables, whole-grain breads and cereals, and lean meat and fish are important offerings for those on special diets. People with diabetes also may require special diets because the disease affects the body's ability to convert blood sugar to energy. Diabetics must balance food, portion sizes, exercise, and sometimes medication to maintain a healthy lifestyle. Food allergies can cause some people to have severe reactions to particular foods they eat. Detailed menu descriptions can provide information about ingredients in each dish. In addition, staff should know the contents of menu offerings so that they can respond to guests' questions about potential food allergens.

Menu Components

After the needs of the guests and the foodservice operation have been considered, additional principles are used to plan successful menus. See Figure 6-4.

Variety
Variety adds interest to the menu and whets the appetite. Variety can be achieved in a number of different ways.

Serving temperature One of the easiest ways to provide variety is through differences in the serving temperature of foods, such as a meal containing warm bread, a cold salad, and a hot entrée. The number of hot and cold items on a menu may change from season to season, with a summer menu including more cold offerings than its winter counterpart. Regional differences, affected by climate, also may affect the proportion of hot and cold menu items.

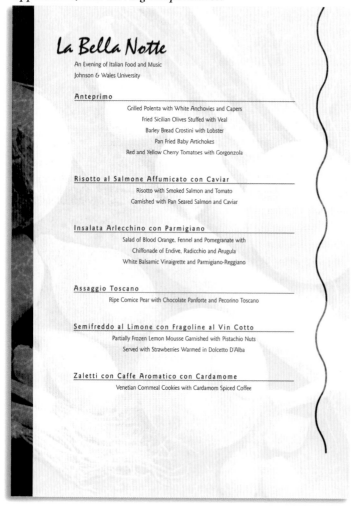

Figure 6-4

A well-planned menu demonstrates good composition by providing variety and balance in food choices, cooking technique, texture, appearance, and serving temperatures.

La Bella Notte
An Evening of Italian Food and Music
Johnson & Wales University

Anteprimo
Grilled Polenta with White Anchovies and Capers
Fried Sicilian Olives Stuffed with Veal
Barley Bread Crostini with Lobster
Pan Fried Baby Artichokes
Red and Yellow Cherry Tomatoes with Gorgonzola

Risotto al Salmone Affumicato con Caviar
Risotto with Smoked Salmon and Tomato
Garnished with Pan Seared Salmon and Caviar

Insalata Arlecchino con Parmigiano
Salad of Blood Orange, Fennel and Pomegranate with
Chiffonade of Endive, Radicchio and Arugula
White Balsamic Vinaigrette and Parmigiano-Reggiano

Assaggio Toscano
Ripe Comice Pear with Chocolate Panforte and Pecorino Toscano

Semifreddo al Limone con Fragoline al Vin Cotto
Partially Frozen Lemon Mousse Garnished with Pistachio Nuts
Served with Strawberries Warmed in Dolcetto D'Alba

Zaletti con Caffe Aromatico con Cardamome
Venetian Cornmeal Cookies with Cardamom Spiced Coffee

Cooking techniques Varying food preparation is another way of providing variety. A restaurant that specializes in fish and shellfish can offer entrées that are roasted, broiled, or fried. Appetizers might include sushi and steamed shellfish.

Texture Texture includes the way a food feels in the mouth, as well as whether the food is soft or firm. Food textures can be liquid, soft, solid, chewy, and crispy. A food's richness also can be related to texture. A menu consisting of a cream soup, followed by a salad with creamy dressing and an entrée with a heavy sauce lacks variety in texture. Even though some guests may select dishes with similar textures, the food service should offer a variety of dishes with a range of different textures.

Height The appearance of foods offers another type of variety. A plate on which everything is one height lacks appeal. The dramatic effect offered by a tall food presentation is diminished if everything else on the plate is vertical.

Taste Avoid offering too many foods that contain the same ingredients or the same intensity of flavor. A menu with half the items containing garlic lacks variety, as does one that offers only bland dishes. Cheese should not be the dominant flavor in an appetizer if the main dish is pasta stuffed with cheese. Unless planning a menu for a specialty restaurant, such as a steak house, seafood restaurant, or pasta house, offer a wide variety of meat, fish, and nonmeat choices for the main course. In addition, pairing sweet with tart or mellow with strong can heighten the guest's appreciation for the taste of a dish.

Shapes Varying the shape of foods on a plate can offer diversity. Serving vegetables such as long, thin asparagus spears or carrots sliced into thin disks is an excellent way to introduce different shapes and contrasting colors to a plate.

Balance

A menu can achieve balance by offering an appropriate range of food items within each menu classification. Appetizers, entrées, and desserts could include both hot and cold items. Unless a concept is designed around a specific theme, such as Mediterranean seafood, Southwestern steak house, or Indian vegetarian, offerings

should be varied to include selections from meat, fish, cheese-based, starch, and vegetable categories. The number of items within each category should also be balanced. In most cases, it would be inappropriate to offer seventeen appetizers, ten entrees, and three desserts. Balance in cooking techniques also provides interest and minimizes the chance of overloading particular work stations.

Composition

It is important to consider the composition of each plate when deciding on menu items. Composition refers to a plate's visual and sensory appeal. Generally, an odd number of foods on a plate is more visually appealing than an even number. One side or section of a plate should not overwhelm another. Food should be served in appropriate portion sizes. Keep in mind that a plate overladen with food looks heavy and unappealing and a plate with too much open space can look sparse. Plates with all soft food or food with little variation in color lack interest and appeal.

> *See Chapter 10: Sensory Perception for more information on presentation.*

Descriptive Copy

Descriptive copy is menu text that describes each menu item. See Figure 6-5 on page 68. Descriptive copy may include information about the method of preparation, primary and secondary considerations, portion size, geographical origin of the recipe or the ingredients, or an explanation of accompaniments or garnishes. Descriptive copy makes use of correct food terminology such as toasted, whipped, grilled, glazed, and sautéed. Adjectives used in descriptive copy should reflect the concept and theme. Words such as magnificent, colossal, and thick and juicy may be appropriate for a casual concept and less appropriate for fine dining.

Truth in Menu

Federal law requires that certain menu statements be accurate. Menu information about items such as quantity, quality, price, brand names, product identification, origin, merchandising terms, preservation methods, food preparation, and verbal and visual presentation must be accurate. See Figure 6-6 on page 68 for guidelines.

Menu Labeling Regulations

In 1990, Congress passed labeling regulations under the Nutrition Labeling and Education Act (NLEA) stating that claims about the health benefits or nutrient content in packaged food must be substantiated with scientific evidence. In 1997, the FDA extended this regulation to foodservice establishments.

If a foodservice establishment makes a health benefit or nutrient claim, it needs to supply proof to customers if asked. If no such claims are made, the regulations do not apply.

Menu Classifications

The menu is divided into categories or classifications of food items, each with its own heading. The number of menu classifications or headings is dependent on the type of restaurant. Usually menu classifications are listed in the order in which the food items are consumed. Standard menu classifications include: appetizers, soups, salads, hot entrées, cold entrées, sandwiches, accompaniments, desserts, and beverages.

Appetizers Appetizers are meant to stimulate the palate before the main part of the meal. They are generally served in small portions and can be hot or cold. They include meat, fish, shellfish, fruits, vegetables, or combinations of these items.

Soups Some menus group soups and appetizers together under the same menu heading. Soups, which can be cold or hot, fall into four categories: clear soups, thin soups, thick soups, and specialty soups.

Salads Salads can be offered as a first course, as accompaniments to a main course, or as a cold entrée. A first course salad may take the place of an appetizer or soup and may contain grilled vegetables, fruit, fish, meat, or seafood. The accompanying salad, generally served right before the entrée, is a light salad of mixed greens. In the European tradition, however, green salads usually come after the entrée and before the dessert. The main course salad can be a cold entrée, such as chicken salad, lobster salad, or a mixture of greens with grilled meats or vegetables. Main course salads also can be a combination of hot and cold items, such as a grilled chicken Caesar salad.

FIGURE 6-5

Descriptive Copy

ELEGANT FINE DINING (SIMPLE, TO THE POINT)

Grilled beef tenderloin with cabernet sauvignon reduction and black truffle butter

ELEGANT FINE DINING (MORE VERBOSE)

Addieville East Farm wild pheasant consommé baked in a Westport Macomber turnip "bowl" garnished with pheasant quenelles and a julienne of shiitake mushrooms and golden chanterelles

CASUAL DINNER HOUSE

A full one and one-half pound rack of mouth-watering baby back ribs, coated with our own barbecue sauce and served with house baked beans, creamy coleslaw, and buttery jalapeño cornbread

FIGURE 6-6

Truth-in-Menu Guidelines

Guideline	Examples
1. Brand names must be represented accurately.	Examples of brand name products include Hunt's® ketchup, Hellmann's® mayonnaise, Green Giant® frozen vegetables, and Butterball® turkey.
2. Dietary and nutritional claims must be exact.	To protect customers from potential health hazards, health claims and nutritional information must be correct. For example, low-sodium or fat-free foods must be correctly prepared to ensure the protection of customers. Nutritional claims must be supported with statistical data.
3. Description of food preservation methods must be accurate.	The preservation of foods is as follows: frozen; chilled; dehydrated; dried, such as by sun or smoking; bottled; and canned. If used, the terms must be accurate. For example, fish cannot be listed as "fresh" on the menu if it has been frozen.
4. Quantity must be correct.	Whenever a menu indicates that the appetizer consists of a certain number of items, that number must be served. Weights given for steaks or other cuts of meat should be identified on the menu as weight prior to cooking.
5. Origin of ingredients must be truthful.	If Dover sole is on the menu, the fish must originate in Dover. Pancakes with Vermont maple syrup must be served with syrup from Vermont, not New Hampshire.
6. Quality or grade must be exact.	The quality or grade listed for dairy products, meat, poultry, and vegetables or fruits must be correct. If you state that a cut of meat is "primesirloin," it must be exactly that. You cannot use choice meat and label it "prime" on the menu.
7. Cooking techniques must be accurately described.	Where a cooking technique is given on the menu, i.e. broiled the chef must prepare the food item using the described technique.
8. Pictures must be precise.	Apple pie à la mode must be apple pie with ice cream. Pictured portion sizes should be the same as an actual serving.
9. Food product descriptions must be accurate.	A menu that describes shrimp salad as being made with jumbo shrimp should not arrive to the guest with medium-sized shrimp. The product description is incorrect.
10. Pricing structure must be clearly stated.	The menu must make known if the price includes a cover charge, gratuity, or service charge. Any supplement charged for side items with more costly ingredients should be listed.
11. Menus must indicate if substitutions are made.	Substituting one item for another is a common practice because of delivery problems, availability, or price. Examples of substitutions include maple syrup and maple-flavored syrup, and capon and chicken.
12. Merchandising terms must be accurate.	Foodservice establishments may exaggerate in their advertising of food items as long as they are not misleading customers. Saying, "We are the best in town," or "We serve only the finest beef," is acceptable, but implying that the beef is prime when it is not is misleading.

Hot entrées Hot entrées are the largest menu classification. The ingredients and manner of preparation for hot entrées vary greatly. Hot entrées may include meat such as beef, lamb, pork, and veal, as well as poultry, fish, and shellfish. Casserole items and vegetarian dishes are common hot entrées found in many restaurants.

Cold entrées Cold entrées can include sliced meats, main course salads, or cold fruit and vegetable plates. An assortment of fruits and cheeses may be offered as a cold entrée.

Sandwiches Hot and cold sandwiches, such as grilled chicken and tuna salad, sometimes appear only on the lunch menu. The sandwich section of a menu may list a choice of breads, spreads, and condiments appropriate for the sandwich offerings.

Accompaniments Vegetables, pasta, rice, and potatoes are some of the accompaniments that may appear on the menu. Accompaniments should complement the list of entrées.

Desserts Guests often decide to order dessert after they have eaten their meals. For this reason, desserts may be listed on a separate dessert menu or shown on a dessert tray. Ice cream, sorbet, fruits, and an assortment of tarts, cakes, and other pastries are popular desserts.

Beverages Beverages include hot and cold drinks, such as juices, specialty waters, soft drinks, milk, coffee, and tea. Separate wine and bar menus are standard in most restaurants, though some establishments include these beverages on the same menu.

Menu Style and Design

The menu's primary goal is to convey information and make a sale. In doing so, the menu must create a favorable impression. The menu's style and design must be chosen to present information in a clear and understandable format. It also must present an image consistent with the establishment's own vision. Details such as the cover design, color, style of lettering, type of paper, and choice of language influence the message a restaurant presents to its customers.

The Printed Menu

The most common menu form is the printed menu. The guest reads the printed menu and reviews clip-ons fastened to it. *Clip-ons* draw attention to new products and seasonal offerings. They also may highlight daily specials, specialty drinks, or desserts. Ready access to a computer and printer enables a foodservice operation to publish its menu or clip-ons daily.

Some restaurants supplement the printed menu with a spoken menu, whereby the server presents daily specials or explains the menu. A spoken menu allows a server to establish a rapport with the customer. Some guests view the spoken menu as a sign of well-trained servers. Others believe that the spoken menu makes it difficult to make a decision or carefully consider all the menu choices.

Table Tents

Like clip-ons, table tents list specials, seasonal offerings, specialty drinks, desserts, and new products. *Table tents* are folded cards placed on the diner's table or inserted into a stand that sits on the table. Sometimes a photograph illustrates each item listed on the table tent.

Menu Board

A *menu board* contains a handwritten menu printed on a chalkboard, white board, or easel. See Figure 6-7. A menu board is easily updated to reflect daily menu changes. It presents a casual, informal message suited to delicatessens and casual dining establishments, as well as the upscale restaurant that wants to emphasize its freshness and creativity.

✤ FIGURE 6-7
A menu board allows for quick changes to menu items and prices.

7 Equipment

30,000 B.C.
Europeans cook food on hot stones in the dirt.

12,000 B.C.
Japanese make clay cooking pots.

A.D. 1803
A Maryland farmer patents the first icebox.

1828
E. Hoyt gains a patent on the wood cookstove.

1879
William W. Goodwin & Company manufactures gas stoves.

Since the discovery of fire some 800,000 years ago, cooking equipment has evolved from simple clay pots to the sophisticated tools used today. Europeans dug a hole in the ground, lined it with hot stones, and cooked the food in direct contact with the stones. Later, a hole lined with clay was used for cooking. By about 12,000 B.C., potters in present-day Japan were making clay cooking pots and storage containers. At the same time, people in Egypt used grinding stones to pound the seeds of wild grasses into flour. By the fourth century B.C., artisans in Asia and Sumeria had invented a way to cast bronze, opening the path to even more functional cooking tools.

KEY TERMS:
work station
work section
cooking line
freezer burn
mise en place
vertical cutter mixer
salamander
steam-jacketed kettle
trunnion kettle
rotisserie
steam table
bain marie
holding cabinet
chafing dishes
blast chiller

Equipment Layout

A well-designed commercial kitchen promotes the best performance of kitchen personnel and equipment. Good design creates an efficient work flow and can reduce wasted motion during food preparation and production. Kitchen space is usually limited, so designers must carefully consider each task that takes place in the kitchen.

The layout of the commercial kitchen is influenced by several factors.

- Type and size of the foodservice establishment
- Amount of available space
- Menu
- Number of meals to be served
- Size of the kitchen staff
- Organization and placement of the kitchen staff

Work Stations and Work Sections

Commercial kitchens are organized into work stations and work sections. Organizing the kitchen in this way streamlines the work flow and helps reduce the amount of time it takes to prepare and serve food.

Work stations A ***work station*** contains all the tools and equipment needed to prepare a certain dish or type of food. For example, if a restaurant offers onion rings on the menu, they are prepared at the fry station. The fry station contains a deep fryer, tongs, and fry baskets. It may also contain a holding station with heat lamps to keep foods hot. Each work station also contains storage and a power source. The menu and the size of the establishment impact the size of each work station.

Work sections Related work stations are organized into ***work sections*** that may share equipment or perform similar tasks. A hot foods section, for example, might contain a fry station and a sauté station, along with other stations that prepare hot foods. Grouping work stations into work sections allows a foodservice operation to assign staff to cover more than one station if neither station requires the full-time services of one person or if the kitchen is short-staffed. See Figure 7-1.

FIGURE 7-1

Work Stations and Work Sections

GARDE-MANGER SECTION

This section consists of the cold platter station, the salad station, and the sandwich station.

HOT FOODS SECTION

The hot foods section contains the broiler/grill station, the fry station, the griddle station, and the sauté station. It also includes the baking and steam stations.

SHORT-ORDER SECTION

The broiler/grill station, griddle station, and fry station make up the short-order section.

BEVERAGE SECTION

The cold beverage and hot beverage stations are the mainstays of this section.

BAKERY SECTION

This section includes the mixing station, the baking and cooling station, and the dessert preparation station.

The Cooking Line

The organization of work stations and work sections directs the *cooking line,* or arrangement of kitchen equipment. See Figure 7-2. This arrangement also affects which storage areas and additional equipment can be located above, below, or across from the main equipment.

Single, straight-line arrangement The single, straight-line arrangement, commonly used in larger kitchens, places equipment in a straight line, either along a wall or as an island.

L-shaped arrangement The L-shaped arrangement separates equipment into two major areas. The vertical section of the line may be used for preparation, and the horizontal leg may contain the equipment used for production and service.

U-shaped arrangement Foodservice operations with limited space and kitchen staff sometimes prefer the U-shaped arrangement, also common in the bar and dishwashing areas.

Parallel, back-to-back arrangement The parallel, back-to-back arrangement is comprised of two parallel lines of equipment, placed back to back. Sometimes a wall divides the lines. Hotels and ships favor this arrangement.

Parallel, face-to-face arrangement The parallel, face-to-face arrangement faces two straight lines of equipment toward each other. A work aisle separates the parallel equipment lines. Larger kitchens that require constant communication between stations sometimes choose this arrangement.

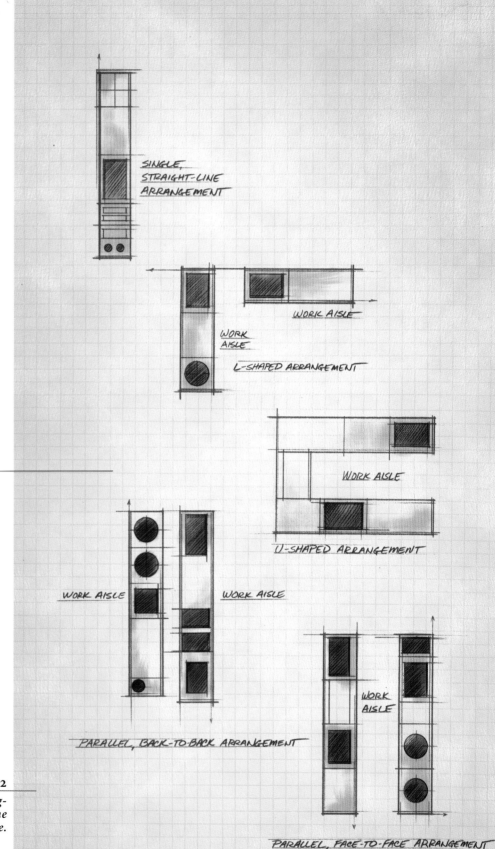

FIGURE 7-2
Typical configurations of the cooking line.

Receiving and Storage Equipment

The commercial kitchen is designed to facilitate the flow of food, beginning with its receipt. As soon as products are received, they must be properly stored.

Receiving Equipment

Receiving equipment allows food items to be checked for quantity and quality of goods received. The type of receiving equipment varies, often depending on the size of the foodservice operation.

Scales Platform and countertop scales are used to check weights of boxes and bags. To check weights on portion control cuts or individually quick frozen cuts of meat, use a portion scale.

Thermometers To ensure food safety, receiving foods at the proper temperature is critical. The two most commonly used thermometers are bimetallic stemmed and digital. Bimetallic stemmed thermometers have a sharp probe at the end that reads the temperature and presents it on an indicator head. Digital thermometers also have a metal probe that measures temperature, but the readout is presented digitally.

Dollies Dollies are wheeled frames that enable the quick and efficient movement of large, heavy, or bulky items from receiving to storage areas.

Storage Equipment

The choice of storage equipment depends on the type of food to be stored, its quantity, available storage space, and the type of foodservice operation. Proper storage is necessary to prevent food from spoiling or causing foodborne illness. Choosing the right storage containers also helps minimize product lost to waste or spoilage. Follow the FIFO rule. Mark products with the delivery date, and then use them in the order in which they are received. Move older items to the front of the storage area for easy access, and place newer items in back.

Refrigerators and freezers Refrigerators and freezers are designed to hold fresh and frozen foods at proper temperatures. See Figure 7-3. There are three basic types of commercial refrigerators: walk-in, roll-in, and reach-in units. Walk-in refrigerators are room-sized refrigerators, usually with shelves along the walls. Roll-in refrigerators are designed to use racks of sheet pans that can be rolled up a ramp and into the unit. Reach-in refrigerators are upright, typically two- to three-door units with sliding shelves.

Some commercial kitchens use half-size refrigerators called lowboys to store items that are frequently used. Lowboy refrigerators are small reach-in refrigerators that may serve as a counter and fit under a counter in a work station.

Freezers are walk-ins, roll-ins, or reach-ins capable of storing foods for extended periods of time at 0°F (–18°C) or lower. Wrapping foods tightly will help prevent *freezer burn,* light-colored spots that indicate surface drying has occurred. Date all frozen foods, and follow the FIFO rule.

Storage bins Storage bins are useful for holding dry ingredients such as flour, sugar, beans, and rice. These covered bins are usually made from heavy plastic or polyurethane. Wheels make them transportable between work stations.

Storage containers Storage containers come in a variety of shapes and sizes and are useful for holding smaller quantities of foods. Glass is easily broken and aluminum reacts with acidic foods such as tomatoes, so storage containers are often made from durable plastic. Plastic storage containers have airtight lids and may be constructed to allow stacking for efficient space utilization. Large containers with handles are well suited for storing stocks and other liquids. To minimize exposure to air, store food in the smallest container possible. Choose opaque containers to protect light-sensitive foods. List contents and the storage date on a label affixed to the container.

Rolling racks Rolling racks on wheels enable trays or shelves filled with food or food products to be wheeled from place to place.

Shelving Shelving makes the best use of storage space. Storage shelves are often stainless steel wire grates. Adjustable shelves accommodate a variety of sizes and shapes of stored products.

Storage equipment, like all kitchen equipment and machinery, needs periodic cleaning and maintenance. Put cold foods in alternate cold storage, and disconnect power before cleaning refrigerators. Wash the interiors of walk-in and roll-in refrigerators with a detergent solution. Keep the outside clean by wiping daily with a damp cloth. To clean shelving units and storage bins, remove all food products, and then use hot, soapy water to wash the shelves. Rinse, sanitize, and dry the shelves and bins before returning foods to them.

FIGURE 7-3
Commercial refrigerators

ROLL-IN

WALK-IN

REACH-IN

LOWBOY

(a)

Kitchen Equipment

Proper equipment and knowledge of how to use it enables the preparation of high-quality food efficiently and safely. The right equipment can make the job much easier. Knowing how to clean and maintain equipment will maximize the life of the product and ensure that it runs properly.

Heat Sources for Cooking

The cooking process begins with heat, which is transferred to foods in three ways: conduction, convection, and radiation. Conduction involves a direct transfer of heat from, for example, a burner to a skillet to the food in the skillet. Convection involves a transfer of heat through liquids or gases. This process can occur naturally, as when a pot of liquid is heated over a gas burner and a cycle of current moves throughout the liquid to distribute the heat. Convection can also occur mechanically, through stirring or a convection fan. Radiation involves a transfer of energy from waves of heat or light, such as infrared or microwaves. When coals are glowing beneath a food, infrared heating is taking place.

Few methods of heat transfer are independent. For example, when a steak is grilled, conduction heat causes grill marks to appear on the surface of the meat because of direct contact with the hot surface of the grill, but the radiant heat from the grill actually cooks the meat.

(b)

Mise en Place

Mise en place is a French term that means "put in place." It includes all the pre-preparation tasks for a dish or meal. Assembling ingredients, equipment, tools, and serving pieces are facets of mise en place. Mise en place recognizes that all tasks cannot be performed at the last minute and plans accordingly. In addition to gathering and organizing equipment and ingredients, mise en place can include the preparation of stocks, sauces, and batters, as well as tasks such as cutting meat, fish, vegetables, and fruit.

Work simplification techniques are used to perform mise en place most efficiently. Evaluate all aspects of the foodservice operation, including food preparation and cooking techniques, cooking times, energy use, and allocation of personnel to find the most efficient means of performing kitchen tasks.

(c)

Preparation Equipment

Preparation equipment streamlines the time required to mix, chop, grind, grate, and slice large volumes of food before cooking. A large variety of specialized equipment exists. See the Preparation Equipment chart on the following page.

Cooking Equipment

Commercial kitchens use a variety of ranges, broilers, ovens, and other equipment to cook food quickly and efficiently. Using equipment properly requires training. The pieces of cooking equipment shown on pages 76–78 are among the most important for foodservice operations.

(d)

Preparation Equipment

a Food chopper

A food chopper, also called a buffalo chopper, is a general chopping device useful for chopping vegetables such as celery or grinding bread crumbs. The length of time the food stays in the chopper determines the size of the pieces. Some food choppers have slicer or meat grinder attachments.

b Meat grinder

A meat grinder can be an attachment to a mixer or food chopper or a free-standing unit. Meat is ground as it passes through a faceplate or die. Dies of varying sizes allow meat to be ground to specifications.

c Vertical cutter mixer

A vertical cutter mixer (VCM) is used to produce large volumes of food quickly. The VCM operates like a high-powered food blender or food processor. It is used to chop, grind, purée, knead, or liquefy large quantities of food for doughs, sauces, and other applications.

d Bench mixer

A bench mixer is used primarily for whipping, mixing, and kneading. A removable stainless steel bowl in the base of the mixer holds the ingredients. The mixer has three basic parts: the motor and control box, the carriage that holds the bowl and raises or lowers it to the attachments, and the frame. The three most common attachments are the whipping attachment for whipping eggs and cream, the paddle for all-purpose mixing, and the dough hook for kneading doughs. Alternate attachments can be used to slice, dice, shred, grind, or grate foods. Bench mixers are available with capacities from 5–20 quarts. Some large floor mixers can hold more than 100 quarts.

e Food processor

Food processors are used to grind, purée, emulsify, crush, and knead foods. The food processor has a removable work bowl and an S-shaped blade. By inserting specialty disks, the food processor can be used to slice, julienne, and shred food.

f Blender

The blender has a stainless steel blade that blends and mixes ingredients in a tall, narrow thermoplastic or stainless steel food container. Although similar in operation to a food processor, the blender excels in processing liquids and liquefying foods, as well as in crushing ice.

g Commercial juicer

A commercial juicer squeezes juice and automatically separates the pulp from the juice. Commercial juicers have stainless steel blades and removable bowls. Two types of juicers are typically used: reamers and extractors. Reamers are used to remove juice from citrus fruits; extractors liquefy fruits and vegetables.

h Table-mounted can opener

The table-mounted can opener attaches to the edge of a table, enabling large institutional-sized cans to be opened. To prevent contamination, clean and sanitize the can opener daily. Check blades for wear, and replace them immediately to keep metal shavings from falling into the food during opening.

i Work tables

Work tables can be made from either stainless steel or butcher block. Most food preparation tasks are well-suited for the stainless steel work table. Butcher block work tables are sometimes preferred in the baking station.

Cooking Equipment

a Open-burner range

An open-burner range is a stove top commonly equipped with four to six individual burner units. The open-burner range can have either electric element burners or gas flames. Each burner has its own heat source and control, which allows for an efficient use of heat. A major disadvantage to the open-burner range is that each burner can accommodate only one pot.

b Flat-top range

The flat-top range, also called the French-top range, has a solid plate of metal that conceals individual burners below. A metal top covers the burners, so the flat-top range takes longer to heat and provides a less intense heat than the open-burner range. On the other hand, a flat-top range supports very heavy weights and provides a large surface area upon which to cook.

c Deep-fat fryer

Three types of deep-fat fryers are generally used in a commercial kitchen: standard deep-fat fryers, automatic fryers, and pressure fryers. A standard deep-fat fryer is used to fry food in hot oil at a thermostatically controlled temperature, which allows even cooking and quick heat recovery after each batch. Automatic or computerized fryers control the movement of food baskets into and out of fat to eliminate the chance of over- or undercooking food. Pressure fryers cook foods quickly because the covered fry kettles keep food under pressure. Filtering allows extended use of oil. Both gas and electric deep-fat fryers are available.

d Griddle

Also used by upscale restaurants with à la carte menus, a griddle is similar to a flat-top range, but the metal plate surface is thinner, enabling foods to cook directly on the griddle surface. A griddle can be part of the range top or a separate unit. Short-order and fast-food operations use griddles to cook items such as pancakes, hamburgers, and eggs.

e Broiler or grill

Both broilers and grills cook food with intense, direct heat. The broiler supplies heat from above, and the grill supplies heat from below. Grills use gas, electricity, or charcoal as the heat source. Wood also can be used as a fuel source for heat in a grill. Certain types of wood give flavor to the food being cooked. Burning hickory or mesquite wood in a grill imparts a smoky flavor to food.

f Salamander/cheese melter

A salamander is a small broiler with an overhead heat source used to brown, glaze, or melt the surface of foods. Salamanders are available in electric and gas models and are often attached to open-burner ranges.

g Tilting skillet

Because the tilting skillet can perform the functions of a griddle, fry pan, brazier, stockpot, steam table, and steamer, it is considered to be among the most useful pieces in the commercial kitchen. The tilting skillet is shaped like a large flat-bottomed shallow pan with a lid. It has a lever or other tilting mechanism that allows liquid to be drained off or the cooking surface tilted for convenient removal of foods.

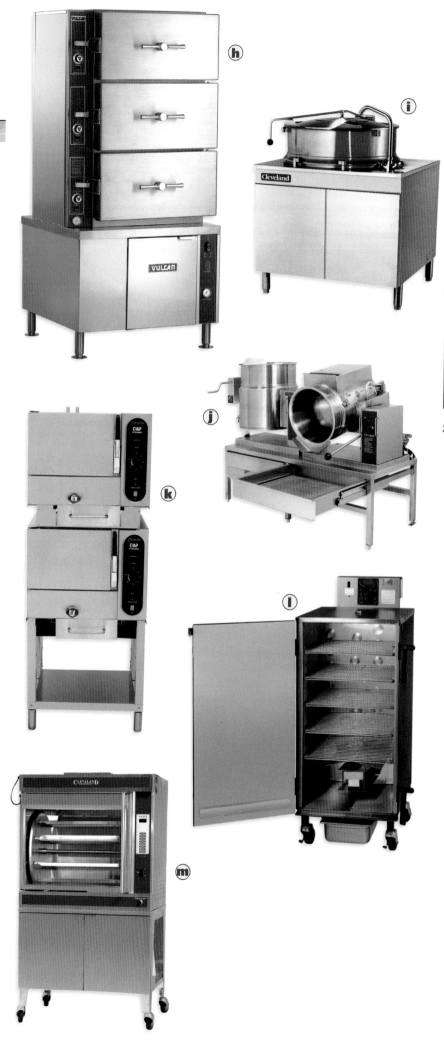

Cooking Equipment *(continued)*

h Pressure steamer

A pressure steamer cooks by applying steam under pressure directly to the food. Food is placed in perforated hotel pans and put into the cooker compartments. A locked door limits access to the contents of the pressure steamer until the cooking is completed and the pressure returns to zero.

i Steam-jacketed kettle

A steam-jacketed kettle is a double-walled stainless steel kettle that allows steam pressure to build between the kettle walls. Unlike in steamers, the steam makes no contact with the food. By controlling the amount of steam entering the chamber, an even temperature can be achieved for quick boiling or slow simmering. This double-boiler effect makes the steam-jacketed kettle an excellent choice for simmering sauces and soups. The cover allows meats to be braised or large quantities of water to boil in a short time.

j Trunnion kettle

The trunnion kettle is a specially designed steam-jacketed kettle made to be emptied easily. Heat in the trunnion kettle is regulated by controlling the flow of steam. Pushing a lever or turning a wheel tilts the kettle for pouring.

k Pressureless or convection steamer

A convection steamer does not operate under pressure. Instead, jets of steam are channeled toward the food to speed the heat transfer. The door of the steamer can be opened at any point during cooking.

l Smoker

A smoker uses either cool or hot temperatures to smoke meats and other foods. Woods such as hickory, mesquite, apple, or cherry can be placed in the smoker to contribute a distinctive flavor to the food. The device used to produce the smoke usually consists of some sort of heating element capable of heating small blocks or chips of wood so that they smoke but do not ignite.

m Rotisserie

A rotisserie is a special type of broiler that cooks meat or other foods as they turn slowly on a spit in front of an electric or gas-powered heating element. Rotisseries can be closed or open and come in a range of sizes, with the largest holding up to 70 chickens.

Cooking Equipment (continued)

n Conventional oven

A conventional oven cooks food by heating air in an enclosed space. The most common conventional oven is part of the range unit. Stack ovens contain shelves stacked one above the other.

o Convection oven

The convection oven contains a blower fan that evenly distributes hot air throughout the oven, enabling foods to cook more quickly and at lower temperatures than in a conventional oven. Foods can be more closely spaced in a convection oven than in a conventional one because the blower distributes air around pans or food items that might interfere with the flow of heat.

p Deck oven

The deck oven, also called a stack oven, has separate oven units arranged one on top of the other. Pans are placed directly on the base or deck of each oven unit, rather than on wire shelves. Each deck has its own temperature controls. Deck ovens are useful for baking, roasting, and braising.

q Roll-in rack oven

A roll-in rack oven works like a convection oven. It has a large door that allows a cart loaded with food trays to be rolled directly into the oven. The heat source is usually gas or electric.

r FlashBake™ oven

The FlashBake™ oven uses a combination of infrared light and intense visible light to cook a variety of foods. Intense heat cooks the food quickly without the loss of flavor or moisture. The FlashBake™ oven requires no preheating or venting.

s Microwave oven

The microwave oven uses electricity to generate microwaves, which cook, reheat, and defrost foods quickly. Unless it is fitted with a special element, the microwave does not brown food, so its foodservice use is primarily to reheat food or thaw small amounts of frozen food.

> If a recipe does not specify convection baking temperature, a good rule of thumb is to reduce conventional oven cooking time by about 30% and oven temperature by about 25°F–50°F (-4°C–10°C).

Cleaning Cooking Equipment

Regular and thorough cleaning of cooking equipment is essential to ensure optimal performance and food safety. When cleaning equipment, follow the manufacturer's directions found in the instruction manual for each product. The general guidelines below also apply.

Flat-top range Use a scraper to loosen burned-on food. Clean the surface with a damp, soapy cloth. Rinse with clear water, and wipe the surface dry.

Open-burner range Remove the grids and drip pans, and soak them in hot, soapy water. Wash the remainder of the range with a damp, soapy cloth, and then rinse and dry well. Replace the grids and drip pans and, if applicable, check that the pilot light is burning. The flame on a gas range pilot light should look blue, not yellow.

Griddle Use a special griddle cloth or stone to clean the griddle. To avoid scratching the surface, polish the griddle top in the same direction as the grain of the metal, rather than with a circular motion. Wash other areas of the griddle with warm, soapy water, and then rinse and dry. To recondition the surface, apply a thin layer of canola or salad oil, and then heat the griddle to 400°F (204°C). Wipe off the oil, and repeat the process until the surface of the griddle is smooth and shiny.

Broiler Remove the grids, and soak them in hot, soapy water. With a wire brush, scrape off caked-on food. Rinse and dry the grids, and then lightly coat them with non-edible oil. Clean the inside of the broiler by scraping away grease and burned food. Wash drip pans in hot, soapy water, and empty the grease trap. Before replacing the grease trap, wash it well. Add a small amount of water to the trap before using the broiler again. The water in the trap will force the dripping fat to float to the surface instead of burning on the bottom of the trap.

Conventional and convection ovens Allow the oven to cool completely before cleaning. Remove the shelves, and clean them in hot, soapy water. Rinse with clear water, and allow the shelves to air dry. With a soft cloth and warm, soapy water, wash the inside of the oven. Towel dry. Wipe the exterior surface with warm, soapy water. After rinsing with clear water, polish the surface with a soft cloth.

Microwave oven Wipe the oven inside and out with a soft cloth dipped in warm, soapy water. Rinse with clear water, and wipe dry. Check the door seal for a close fit. Do not use the microwave if the door is damaged or loose.

Cleaning Equipment

Cleaning equipment is used to clean and sanitize cookware, dishes, and flatware.

Commercial sinks A commercial sink must suit the size and operation of the enterprise. The most common type is the three-compartment sink, used to wash, rinse, and sanitize dishes.

Garbage disposal Garbage disposals, mounted on sink drains, grind and dispose of food scraps. The food scraps are ground into a semi-liquid with cold water from the sink that runs into the disposal while it operates. Although the garbage disposal cannot replace a kitchen trash receptacle, it is an appropriate way to discard food scraped from plates or left over from food preparation.

Commercial dishwashers Large commercial kitchens often use a multi-tank dishwasher. The dishwashing process begins with the removal of food scraps from dirty dishes. The dishes are then placed in racks on a conveyor belt and rinsed. After the dishes are manually loaded into one end of the dishwasher, they travel through a series of tanks to complete the dishwasher's prewash, wash, rinse, sanitize, and dry cycles. Commercial dishwashers sanitize dishes either with very hot water (180°F/82°C) or with an application of chemicals during the final rinse cycle.

Pot-washing machine A pot-washing machine is a specialty dishwasher designed to clean greasy pots, pans, and large utensils.

Holding Equipment

Holding equipment allows prepared foods or ingredients to be held at the proper temperature. Some of the equipment is designed to keep foods hot; others maintain the temperature of cold foods. Proper temperatures are key to ensuring food safety and quality.

Hot Holding Equipment

To prevent the growth of bacteria, hot holding equipment is designed to keep foods at a temperature of at least 140°F (60°C). At this temperature, the texture and color of certain foods can deteriorate quickly. For best taste and appearance, hold foods for only a short time. See the Hot Holding Equipment chart on page 81.

Cold Holding Equipment

Cold holding equipment holds foods under refrigeration at 41°F (5°C) or lower. Some cold holding equipment, such as refrigerated work tables, also may be used in the kitchen preparation area. Other pieces, such as the portable salad bar, may be used in the buffet line.

Portable salad bar The portable salad bar (photo shown above) is a refrigerated unit that holds pans or bowls of lettuce, other vegetables, salad dressings, and other salad bar items. Because refrigeration or ice maintains the temperature of the food items, salad bar selections can be safely held for extended service.

Sandwich unit The sandwich unit is a refrigerated freestanding unit designed to hold pans filled with meats, cheese, vegetables, and condiments (photo shown right). A cutting board or other work surface may extend from the front of the sandwich unit. Refrigeration holds pans and their contents at the proper temperature so that sandwich-making items can be safely held during extended preparation times.

Hot Holding Equipment

(a) Steam table

A steam table uses steaming hot water to hold hot food for service. Graduated dials allow the temperature of the water to be regulated. Foods should be cooked completely or preheated before being placed on the steam table. The steam table is designed with separators that allow foods to be placed in various-sized hotel pan inserts.

(b) Bain marie

A bain marie is a water bath that is especially useful for holding sauces and soups at the proper temperature. Hot food is placed in a bain-marie insert, which is then placed in a bain marie filled with hot water. A bain marie is also used to melt ingredients such as chocolate. For this reason, some foodservice operations use the bain marie primarily in the production area, rather than in service.

(c) Overhead warmers

Overhead warmers keep food that is ready for service hot until the servers pick it up for delivery to the customer. Overhead warmers make it possible for quick-service operations to prepare some items ahead so that workers can quickly fill customer orders. Because overhead warmers quickly dry out foods, food should be held under an overhead warmer for only a very brief time.

(d) Holding cabinets

A holding cabinet is a large, wheeled, metal container that holds sheet pans of food. The cabinet holds the food in an airtight environment under controlled temperature and humidity. Holding cabinets are designed to optimize food quality at temperatures of 140°F (60°C) or higher.

(e) Heated carving stations

Heated carving stations are used to hold large cuts of roast beef, turkey, ham, or other meat at the proper temperature for carving. Infrared lights supply the heat from above. A special cutting board serves as the base of the carving station. Some carving stations have a heated base or a holding cabinet in addition to overhead lamps.

Service Equipment

Service equipment includes any tool, appliance, or apparatus used to serve the customer. Foodservice operations use service equipment in the dining room or buffet line at catered functions.

Service Equipment

(a) Insulated carriers

An insulated carrier is a special box designed to maintain the temperature of the food it holds. Hotel pans or sheet pans fit inside the carrier. An insulated carrier with a spigot can be filled with warm or cold beverages. Wheels or handles allow insulated carriers to be moved from place to place.

(b) Chafing dishes

Chafing dishes hold hotel pans filled with food. During service the chafing dish functions as a bain marie, holding the hotel pan above another pan filled with hot water. Available in a variety of sizes, chafing dishes are most often made from stainless steel. Chafing dishes are designed to keep hot food hot and should not be used to reheat food.

(c) Canned fuel

Canned fuel supplies the energy needed to keep food warm in chafing dishes. Ignited containers of canned fuel are placed beneath the chafing dish to keep the contents warm.

(d) Coffee system

A coffee system brews coffee and keeps it warm for service. It contains a water tank, thermostat, warming plate, and coffee server. Many also have a hot water spigot, which supplies plain hot water for making tea or hot chocolate.

(e) Airpot brewing systems

Airpot brewers brew coffee or other hot beverages in a tall container with a plastic lid and pump dispenser. Liquids stay hot for up to 10 hours in the airpot.

(f) Utility carts

Utility carts are useful for displaying or holding food, busing tables, or transporting heavy items from place to place. Wheels facilitate easy movement, and handles allow the cart to be pushed or pulled. Utility carts are typically made of heavy-duty plastic or stainless steel.

(g) Hotel pans

Hotel pans are stainless steel pans, available in a variety of sizes, used to cook, serve, and store food. Standard-sized hotel pans fit in steam tables and other holding equipment. See Figure 7-4 on page 83.

FIGURE 7-4

HOTEL PAN SIZE	CAPACITY	HOTEL PAN SIZE	CAPACITY
Full size 20 3/4" × 12 3/4"	2 1/2" deep = 8.3 quarts 4" deep = 13 quarts 6" deep = 20 quarts	One-third size = 6 7/8" × 12 3/4"	2 1/2" deep = 2.6 quarts 4" deep = 4.1 quarts 6" deep = 6.1 quarts
Half size long 20 3/4" × 6 7/16"	2" deep = 3.7 quarts 4" deep = 5.7 quarts	One-fourth size = 6 3/8" × 10 3/8"	2 1/2" deep = 1.8 quarts 4" deep = 3 quarts 6" deep = 4.5 quarts
Two-third size 13 3/4" × 12 3/4"	2 1/2" deep = 5.6 quarts 4" deep = 9.3 quarts 6" deep = 14 quarts	One-sixth size = 6 7/8" × 6"	2 1/2" deep = 1.2 quarts 4" deep = 1.8 quarts 6" deep = 2.7 quarts
Half size 10 3/8" × 12 3/4"	2" deep = 4 quarts 4" deep = 6.7 quarts 6" deep = 10 quarts	One-ninth size = 6 7/8" × 4 1/4"	2 1/2" deep = 6 quarts 4" deep = 1.1 quarts

Cooling Equipment

Hot foods must be cooled quickly to move them out of the temperature danger zone. Standard refrigerators and freezers are designed to hold foods that are already cool; they cannot cool prepared foods quickly enough to comply with recommendations for safe food handling. The thicker and denser the preparation, the longer it takes to cool down. To rapidly cool prepared food, a variety of methods can be employed.

■ *See Chapter 4: Food Safety for more information on cooling procedures.*

Blast chiller A *blast chiller* is a special refrigeration unit designed to quickly chill prepared foods by drawing hot air away from the food and/or forcing cold air across it. Even foods just removed from the range or oven can be put into a blast chiller. The blast chiller immediately stops the cooking process and begins to bring the food temperature down. By reducing the amount of time that food spends in the temperature danger zone, a blast chiller slows bacterial growth, extending the shelf life of prepared foods. A blast chiller rapidly chills even deep pans of cooked foods, including casseroles, meats, and other slow-to-cool items. After they are properly chilled, foods can be moved from the blast chiller to the refrigerator or freezer for longer storage. Some blast chillers also convert to refrigeration-storage mode after the blast chill cycle completes.

Ice bath Another way to quickly cool prepared foods is in an ice bath. Metal containers of hot food are placed in the ice bath, and the surrounding ice water quickly chills the food. An ice bath is a viable solution for rapidly chilling small quantities of food.

Cold paddles Stirring hot stock, sauce, or soups with cold paddles is another way to accomplish rapid chilling of a small quantity of food. The cold paddles are filled with water and frozen. After the paddles are solidly frozen, use them to stir the prepared food, drawing heat from it. Cold paddles are often used in combination with the ice bath. Cold paddles can be refilled and refrozen following each use after they have been washed, rinsed, and sanitized.

8

Knives, Hand Tools, and Smallwares

Knives are among the oldest known tools made by humans. Early people sharpened pieces of stone, such as flint, into knives for cutting and chopping. They also used bone, shell, and the volcanic glass called obsidian to create cutting blades. By about 1500 B.C., people were using knife blades forged from bronze. Other cooking and serving implements developed later. The earliest spoons were shaped from clay or carved from bone or wood. The earliest forks had only a single prong, but by the Middle Ages, serving forks were two-pronged, often with handles made of precious metal or stone.

12,000 B.C.
Egyptians make knives with flint blades.

6500 B.C.
The first known butcher shop provides meat cuts in Jordan.

2500 B.C.
Craft workers in the Near East produce iron, a harder and more functional metal than bronze.

A.D. 1860
Mass production of cast-iron kitchen gadgets begins.

1938
A DuPont chemist develops Teflon, a nonstick coating for pans.

Knife Construction

The knife is the most valuable tool in the commercial kitchen. An understanding of how cutlery is constructed aids in the selection of appropriate knives and the care required to maintain them. See Figure 8-1.

Blade The blade of a professional knife is a single piece of metal that has been cut, stamped, or forged into shape. Most professional knife blades are made from high-carbon stainless steel—an alloy of iron, carbon, chromium, and other metals. The metal combines the best features of stainless steel and carbon steel, resulting in a blade that can be easily sharpened but is resistant to rust and discoloration.

Before the development of high-carbon stainless steel, most professional knives were made of carbon steel. Although carbon steel knives are still available today, they are not as desirable as those made from high-carbon stainless steel. Carbon steel blades rust easily and can impart a metallic flavor to food. The edge wears down quickly, as well.

Some knives are made from stainless steel, which is an alloy of chromium and carbon steel. Stainless steel knives are extremely durable. They do not rust, discolor, or contribute off-flavors to food, and they hold their edge longer than carbon steel knives do. However, because the metal is very hard, these knives are difficult to sharpen.

Tang The *tang* is the portion of the blade that extends into the knife's handle. A full tang that runs through the entire length of the knife handle contributes strength and durability to the knife. For this reason, knives meant for heavy use, such as French knives and cleavers, should have a full tang. Paring knives, utility knives, or other knives used for lighter work may have a partial tang.

Handle The knife handle can be made from hardwoods, such as walnut or rosewood, or other materials, such as plastic or vinyl. When choosing a knife, consider the feel and fit of the handle. Knives are held for long periods of time, so the handle must fit comfortably in the hand. A handle that is either too small or too large can be uncomfortable to hold.

Rivet Metal *rivets* hold the tang in the handle. Rivets should lie smooth and flat against the handle to prevent rubbing and irritation against the hand. They should also be flush with the surface so that there are no crevices in which dirt or microorganisms can collect.

Bolster The shank, or *bolster,* is the metal point on the knife where the blade and handle meet. Although not all knives have a bolster, those that do are very strong and durable. The bolster also helps block food particles from entering the space between the tang and the knife handle.

FIGURE 8-1

A knife is constructed of the elements shown below.

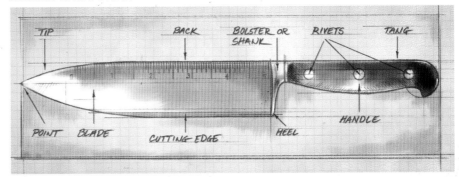

Types of Knives

The choice of knife depends on the type of food being prepared and the specific cutting or chopping task required. Although there are a number of specialty knives, the following list includes the basic types used by professionals.

Types of Knives

a) French knife
The French knife, or chef's knife, is the most frequent knife choice. This all-purpose knife comes in lengths from 8 to 14 inches (200 to 350 mm), the longest knives being best suited for heavy cutting and chopping. The blade of the French knife is wide at the heel and tapered at the point.

b) Utility knife
Smaller and lighter than other knives, this knife is intended for light cutting assignments. The blade is 5 to 7 inches long (127 to 178 mm).

c) Boning knife
The boning knife is a thin, angled knife with a blade that may be from 5 to 7 inches (130 to 180 mm) in length. As its name indicates, the boning knife is used for separating bones from meat. It is available with either a rigid or flexible blade. Choose a rigid blade for heavier work and a flexible blade for lighter tasks.

d) Fillet knife
The fillet knife is used primarily to fillet fish. The 8- to 9-inch (200- to 230-mm) blade comes in both rigid and flexible styles.

e) Paring knife
The paring knife has a pointed, rigid, 2- to 4-inch (50- to 100-mm) blade. It is used for paring or trimming vegetables and fruits.

f) Tourné knife
The tourné knife is similar to the paring knife but with a curved blade that resembles a bird's beak. Use a tourné knife to trim potatoes and other vegetables into football-shaped pieces.

g) Slicer
The slicer is used for carving and slicing cooked meats. It has a long, thin blade with either a rounded or pointed tip. Slicers come in rigid or flexible blade styles, and some have serrated, or saw-toothed, edges. The serrated slicer smoothly slices coarse foods, such as bread or pastry items.

h) Butcher knife
The butcher knife has a broad, rigid blade that measures 6–14 inches (150–350 mm), with a tip that curves up at a 25° angle. Use the butcher knife for cutting and trimming meat and poultry.

Knife Skills

Using a knife properly is one of the culinary professional's most important tasks. Good technique not only improves the appearance of food items but also speeds preparation times and reduces fatigue.

Grip A good grip provides control over the knife, increases cutting efficiency, minimizes hand fatigue, and lessens the chance of an accident. The size of the knife, the task at hand, and personal comfort determine how best to grip the knife. No matter which gripping style is used, avoid placing the index finger on the top of the blade. See Figure 8-2 and Figure 8-3.

Control Knife movement must be controlled in order to make safe, even cuts. Guide the knife with one hand while holding the food firmly in place with the other hand. Allow the sharp edge of the blade to do the work, rather than forcing the blade through the food. A sharp knife provides the surest cuts and is the safest to use. Smooth, even strokes work best.

The hand holding the food is referred to as the guiding hand. To protect the guiding hand from cuts, curl the fingertips back. The knife blade rests against the second knuckle of the index finger, which acts as a guide for the cut. See Figure 8-4.

FIGURE 8-2

Grip the knife by placing four fingers on the bottom of the handle and the thumb against the other side of the handle.

FIGURE 8-3

Grip the knife by placing three fingers on the bottom of the handle, the index finger flat against the blade on one side, and the thumb on the opposite side. Although this grip may be uncomfortable for some, it offers maximum control and stability.

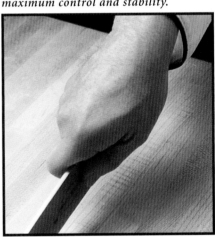

FIGURE 8-4

To make slices of equal width, adjust the index finger while working, moving the thumb and fingertips down the length of the food.

Knife Cuts

A knife is used to cut food into uniform shapes or sizes. Food that has been cut into equal pieces looks more attractive and cooks more evenly.

Basic Peeling Techniques

For best appearance, texture, and flavor, many kinds of vegetables and fruits must be peeled before cuts are made. Before peeling, thoroughly wash vegetables and fruits to remove dirt and other contaminants. To maintain highest quality, wash and peel vegetables and fruits as close as possible to the time they are used.

Using a Vegetable Peeler

Use a swivel-bladed vegetable peeler to remove the skin from thin-skinned vegetables and fruits. Asparagus, carrots, parsnips, and potatoes are examples of thin-skinned foods that are best peeled with a vegetable peeler. A vegetable peeler shaves off only a thin layer of skin without removing too much of the edible flesh. An added advantage of the swivel-bladed peeler is its ability to remove the peel with either an upward or downward stroke. See Figure 8-5. Remove the stem with a French knife. See Figure 8-6.

Using a Paring Knife

A paring knife can be used in much the same way as a vegetable peeler to shave the peel from thin-skinned vegetables and fruits. Hold the paring knife at a 20° angle to the food surface, and shave the skin from the fruit or vegetable. Thick-skinned vegetables and fruits should be peeled with a paring knife rather than shaved with a peeler. See Figure 8-7.

Using a French Knife

Use a French knife to remove the peel from large vegetables and fruits or from those with very thick skins. The French knife works well for removing the peel, core, stems, or seeds from vegetables and fruits such as winter squash, pineapple, and grapefruit. Before beginning to peel, cut off the top and bottom of the fruit or vegetable to create a flat, stable end. When peeling, follow the contours of the fruit or vegetable. See Figure 8-8.

Coarse Chopping

Coarse chopping is the process of cutting food into imprecise but relatively uniform pieces. Use a coarse chopping technique for mirepoix or whenever the recipe calls for fruits, vegetables, or other cut foods with no specific shape. Coarse chopping is especially appropriate when cut foods will be puréed or removed from the dish before presentation. See Figure 8-9.

Mincing

Mincing is the process of cutting food into very fine pieces. Herbs and some vegetables, such as shallots and garlic, lend themselves to mincing. Using a French knife, begin by coarsely chopping the food. Then use the guiding hand to hold the tip of the knife against the cutting board. Quickly rock the knife up and down, keeping the blade tip stationary. Gradually move the knife blade back and forth across the food. Continue mincing until the food reaches the desired fineness. See Figure 8-10.

FIGURE 8-5

A swivel peeler is ideal for removing thin peels and minimizing waste. Peeling over a paper towel helps keep the work area clean.

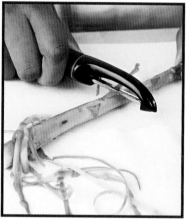

FIGURE 8-6

The hard woody stems of asparagus need to be cut from the stalk before cooking.

FIGURE 8-7

Hold the fruit or vegetable in the guiding hand and the paring knife in the cutting hand. Use the thumb on the guiding hand to control the movement of the fruit or vegetable as the knife is held in position.

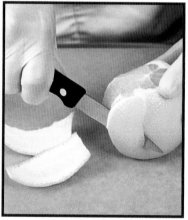

FIGURE 8-8

Use a French knife to peel extremely thick-skinned vegetables and fruits, such as a pineapple.

FIGURE 8-9

Coarse chopping is useful when the final appearance of the cut ingredients does not matter.

FIGURE 8-10

Mincing creates a very fine cut.

Vegetable Cuts

Vegetable cuts influence the appearance and the even cooking of foods. Cuts can enhance the natural shape of a vegetable, maximize the release of flavor to a dish, or create an impressive presentation. See Figure 8-11 for standardized dimensions of each cut.

FIGURE 8-11

scale in inches

1 2 3 4 5

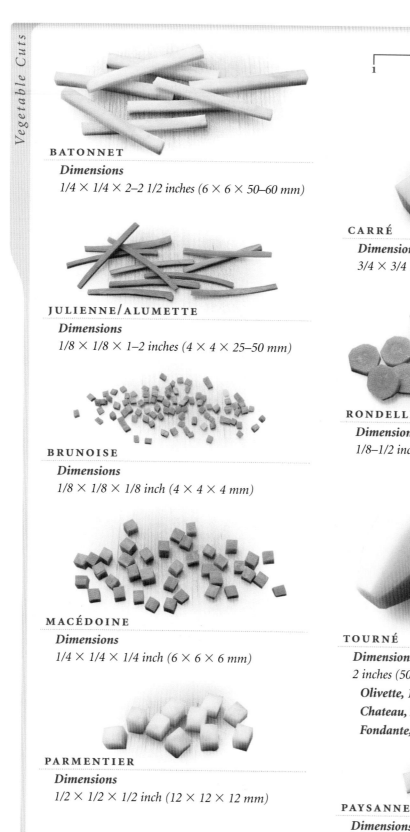

BATONNET

Dimensions

1/4 × 1/4 × 2–2 1/2 inches (6 × 6 × 50–60 mm)

JULIENNE/ALUMETTE

Dimensions

1/8 × 1/8 × 1–2 inches (4 × 4 × 25–50 mm)

BRUNOISE

Dimensions

1/8 × 1/8 × 1/8 inch (4 × 4 × 4 mm)

MACÉDOINE

Dimensions

1/4 × 1/4 × 1/4 inch (6 × 6 × 6 mm)

PARMENTIER

Dimensions

1/2 × 1/2 × 1/2 inch (12 × 12 × 12 mm)

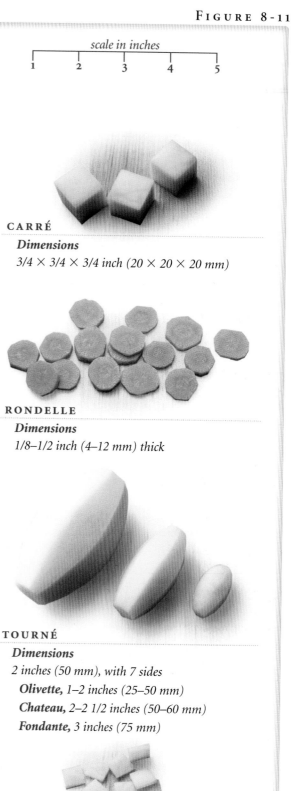

CARRÉ

Dimensions

3/4 × 3/4 × 3/4 inch (20 × 20 × 20 mm)

RONDELLE

Dimensions

1/8–1/2 inch (4–12 mm) thick

TOURNÉ

Dimensions

2 inches (50 mm), with 7 sides

Olivette, *1–2 inches (25–50 mm)*

Chateau, *2–2 1/2 inches (50–60 mm)*

Fondante, *3 inches (75 mm)*

PAYSANNE

Dimensions

1/2 × 1/2 × 1/8 inch (12 × 12 × 4 mm)

Making Chiffonade Cuts

Chiffonade cuts are fine strips or ribbons of leafy vegetables.

To make a chiffonade cut:

1 Wash the vegetable leaves, and discard the stems as necessary. Remove the core from vegetables such as cabbage or Belgian endive.

2 Stack several leaves on top of one another, and then roll them into a cylinder. This step is unnecessary for vegetables with firm heads, such as cabbage.

3 Use a French knife to slice through the layers, making very fine parallel cuts.

Chiffonade The *chiffonade* cut creates fine ribbons or strips of leafy herbs or vegetables. The resulting shreds often are used as a garnish or in salad such as coleslaw.

Rondelle A *rondelle* is a round cut made to a cylindrical vegetable, such as a carrot or cucumber. Make a rondelle by cutting perpendicular to the vegetable, thus creating a disk-shaped slice. See Figure 8-12.

• A variation on the straight rondelle is the diagonal or bias-cut. By cutting the vegetable on the diagonal, an oval or elongated slice is created. The more elongated the cut is, the faster the cooking time is. See Figure 8-13.

FIGURE 8-12

A rondelle cut made perpendicular to a cylindrical vegetable produces a disk-shaped slice.

FIGURE 8-13

Angling the knife against the vegetable surface will create a diagonal cut.

Oblique or roll cut The oblique or roll cut creates a wedge-shaped piece with two diagonally cut sides. It is most often used with long, cylindrical vegetables, such as carrots or parsnips.

Julienne A *julienne* is a 1/8-inch (4-mm) thick, matchstick-shaped cut about 1–2 inches (25–50 mm) long.

Batonnet A *batonnet* is a long, rectangular cut similar to the julienne, but the cut

Making Oblique or Roll Cuts

Oblique or roll cuts are used with most long, cylindrical vegetables.

To make an oblique or roll cut:

1 *Wash and peel the vegetable.*

2  *Place on the cutting board, and make a diagonal cut.*

3 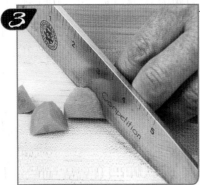 *Roll the vegetable to make each subsequent cut.*

Cutting Julienne and Brunoise

Before cutting a brunoise dice, the vegetable must first be cut into a julienne or matchstick shape.

To do this, follow these steps:

1 *Wash and peel the vegetable.*

2  *On a cutting board, use a French knife to trim the food, squaring the sides and ends. Save the trimmings for another use.*

3  *Evenly slice through the trimmed food to create slices 1/8 inch (4 mm) thick.*

4 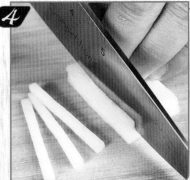 *Stack a few slices, and cut to create 1/8-inch (4-mm) matchsticks.*

5  *Evenly stack the matchsticks, and cut across the stack to make 1/8 inch (4 mm) thick dice.*

sticks are slightly wider and longer (1/4 × 1/4 × 2–2 1/2 inches/6 × 6 × 50–60 mm). To make a batonnet cut, follow the same procedure as for julienne, increasing the dimensions of the cut food.

Dicing Dicing produces cubes between 1/8- and 3/4-inch (4- to 20-mm) square. To make the cubes, begin by cutting the foods into julienne or batonnet.

- The *paysanne* cut is similar to a dice, but instead of a true cube, the cut produces a square slice that is 1/2 × 1/2 × 1/8 inch (12 × 12 × 4 mm). To cut paysanne, cut 1/2-inch (12-mm) sticks into 1/8-inch (4-mm) slices.
- The *brunoise* is a very fine dice cut, producing a 1/8-inch square (4-mm) cube.
- The *macédoine* is a 1/4-inch square (6-mm) dice cut.
- The *parmentier* is a 1/2-inch square (12-mm) dice cut.
- The *carré* is the largest dice cut, 3/4-inch square (20-mm).

Additional Preparation Techniques

A variety of special techniques are used to cut tomatoes, onions, and other vegetables.

Tomato concassée *Tomato concassée* describes a tomato that has been peeled, seeded, and diced or chopped.

The French verb *concasser* refers to the act of chopping or pounding. Tomatoes are not the only food that the French prepare *concassée*. Herbs, meat, and even crushed ice is *concassée* with a meat cleaver, chopper, or French knife.

Peeling and dicing an onion Diced onions are one of the most frequently used ingredients in the commercial kitchen. For best taste and texture, dice onions as close to the time of use as possible.

Gaufrette A *gaufrette,* or waffle cut, is made with a *mandoline,* a specialized cutting tool that can quickly and precisely slice or julienne vegetables and fruits. Cuts such as the gaufrette can be accomplished only with a tool such as the mandoline.

Fanning Fanning is a decorative cut used on raw and cooked foods, such as pickles, avocados, and strawberries. The cut is used to spread vegetables and fruits into a fan shape.

Fluting Fluting is a decorative cut used to prepare vegetables such as mushrooms for garnish or for use in a prepared dish.

Tourné *Tourné* is a cut used to trim and shape vegetables, such as potatoes, beets, or carrots. The verb *tourner* means "to turn" in French. The final shape resembles a football or barrel, with the food's cut ends narrower than its center. The cut food has seven sides and blunt ends.

Until the late 1500s, Europeans used knives not only to cut their food but also to spear and hold the food while eating. Individuals carried their knives with them, strapped to the belt, and the color of the knife handle reflected the season or holiday. Round-ended knives emerged around 1630, supposedly to discourage the habit of picking one's teeth with the sharp tip of the knife.

PROCESS

Preparing Tomato Concassée

Another important procedure is preparing a tomato concassée.

To prepare tomato concassée:

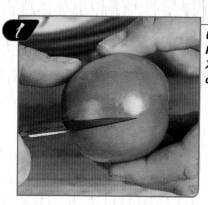

1 Use a paring knife to mark an X on the bottom of the tomato.

2 Blanch the tomato in boiling water.

3 After 10–20 seconds, remove the tomato from the boiling water, using a skimmer, spider, or slotted spoon. Place the tomato immediately in ice water.

4 Remove the tomato from the ice water. Use a paring knife to peel away the skin and cut out the core.

5 Cut the peeled tomato in half horizontally, and gently squeeze to remove the seeds and juice.

6 Dice or chop the tomato into the desired size.

Knives, Hand Tools, and Smallwares

93

 **PROCESS**

Peeling and Dicing Onions

Onions are a common ingredient in a commercial kitchen, therefore it is important to learn the proper peeling and dicing procedures.

To peel and dice an onion:

1 Use a pairing knife to remove the root end from the onion.

Peel away the outer skin, and trim underlying layers if necessary. Cut a thin slice from the stem end to remove the peel.

Using a French knife, cut the onion in half from the root end to the stem end.

Place the onion half cut side down on the cutting board. Make parallel vertical cuts through the onion, beginning each cut at the stem end. Do not cut completely through to the root end.

Turn the onion, and make perpendicular cuts at regular intervals through all of its layers. Begin the cuts at the stem end, and work toward the root end.

Keeping the tip of the knife on the cutting board, rock the knife up and down over the cut onions to make a smaller dice.

Making a Gaufrette Cut

Gaufrettes, or waffle cuts, are another common vegetable cut.

To make gaufrette cuts using a mandoline, follow these steps:

1 Select the ridged blade on the mandoline, and set to the desired thickness.

2

Hold the mandoline with one hand and the food with the other, then slide the food across the blade to make grooves. The cut vegetable should look like this.

3
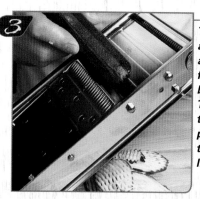
Turn the food to a 60°–90° angle and slide the food across the blade again. This will create the crosshatch pattern and cut the first waffle-like slice.

4

Turn the food back to its original position and start the process again. Continue until the desired number of slices is cut.

Making a Fan Cut

The decorative fanning procedure adds elegance to any vegetable tray.

To make a fan cut:

1 Using one hand to guide, grasp the food by the stem end.

2

With a paring knife, make parallel lengthwise slices in the food, beginning at the stem end. Do not cut entirely through to the stem.

3 Spread the slices into a fan shape.

Fluting a Mushroom

Another important decorative technique is fluting.

To flute a mushroom:

1 Hold the mushroom in the guiding hand, between the thumb and forefinger. Angle the sharp edge of a paring knife against the center of the mushroom cap.

2 Using the thumb of the cutting hand as a brace against the mushroom, cut thin slivers from the mushroom cap. Use the guiding hand to rotate the mushroom away from the cutting hand.

3 Continue the cuts until the entire mushroom cap is fluted.

4 Trim off the stem and mushroom slivers.

Making a Tourné Cut

Tourné, or turned, vegetables can be cut into olivette, chateau, or fondante. The same process can be used for most root vegetables.

To tourné a potato, follow these steps:

1 Wash and peel the potatoes.

2 Cut the potato just slightly larger than the desired length of the finished product. A large potato may have to be cut in half.

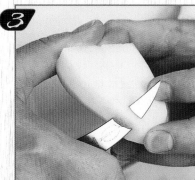

3 Grip the potato firmly, and begin shaping the potato with a tourné knife.

4 Continue turning the potato to cut even sides.

5 The finished tourné potato should be evenly shaped with seven sides and flat edges.

Knife Safety and Care

Good knives are an investment. With proper use and care, quality knives will last for many years. Maintain knives in good condition by keeping them clean and sharp.

Knife Use Guidelines

Knives can be dangerous if mishandled or used improperly. Follow the safety guidelines in Figure 8-14.

Sharpening Knives

Use a sharpening stone, or **whetstone,** to sharpen knives. The stone can be dry or wet with water or mineral oil. As the edge of the blade is passed over the whetstone, the grit in the stone sharpens the cutting edge. A whetstone can be made of either silicon carbide or stone and may have up to three sides, which range from coarse to fine grain. Begin by sharpening against the coarsest stone and end with the finest stone, taking only about 10 strokes against the coarsest stone before moving on to the next.

Trueing Knives

In a process called **trueing,** a steel is used to keep the knife blade straight and to smooth out any irregularities. Trueing does not sharpen the blade, but it does help maintain the edge between sharpenings.

Sanitizing Knives

Wash, rinse, and sanitize knives after every cutting task to avoid cross-contamination and to destroy harmful microorganisms. Do not leave a knife in a water-filled sink. Someone could reach into the sink without seeing the knife and be cut.

Storing Knives

Storing knives properly will protect both the knives and the people who work around them. A slotted knife holder or a magnetized bar hung on the wall are two convenient storage solutions. A custom-built drawer with a slot for each knife is another storage option. A knife kit is a safe, convenient, and portable storage unit. Individual slots hold knives safely in the kit. Vinyl cases are easy to clean and sanitize.

FIGURE 8-15
Always carry a knife by the handle, blade pointed down.

FIGURE 8-14

Safety Guidelines

Always use the appropriate knife for the cutting task.

Never use a knife for a task for which it was not designed. Opening cans and prying open lids are not tasks meant for knives.

Always use a sharp knife. Dull knives require more force, creating a situation in which the knife might slip and cause an injury.

Always use a cutting board with a knife. Marble and metal surfaces dull the blade and may cause damage to the knife.

Never let the knife blade or its handle hang over the edge of a cutting board or work table. Someone might be injured by bumping into the knife, or the knife might fall and be damaged.

When carrying a knife, hold it by the handle with the point of the blade pointed straight down. See Figure 8-15.

Never try to catch a falling knife. Step away from the knife, and let it fall.

To hand a knife to someone else, lay the knife down on the work surface, or hold the knife by the dull side of the blade while carefully extending the handle toward the other person.

Do not leave a knife in a water-filled sink. Someone could reach into the sink without seeing the knife and get cut.

Always wash, rinse, sanitize, and air-dry knives before putting them away.

Do not clean knives in the dishwasher. They pose a risk to the person loading and unloading the dishwasher, and the blades could be dented or damaged through contact with other utensils. Also, wooden handles cannot stand the intense heat and prolonged exposure to water.

Dry the blade by carefully wiping from its dull side.

Sharpening a Knife

A whetstone may be used to sharpen a knife, but it must be oiled to be effective and avoid damaging the stone.

To use a whetstone to sharpen knives:

1 Moisten the stone by applying honing oil or dipping it into the oil reservoir. Lock into place. Start using the coarsest grade and then proceed to the finest grade.

2 With the cutting hand, hold the knife at a 20° angle with the heel of the blade against the stone. Use three fingers on the guiding hand to apply pressure.

3 Maintain a 20° angle, and gently push the blade from heel to tip across the stone. The guiding hand should continue to apply even pressure on the blade.

4 Continue to move the knife smoothly and evenly across the stone, all the way to the tip of the blade.

5 Gently bring the knife off the stone. Repeat the process 3–10 times as necessary.

6 Turn the knife over, and repeat the process, pulling the knife toward you as you move it across the stone.

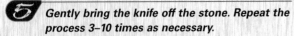

7 Rotate the stones to the finer grits, maintaining the same 20° angle and pressure throughout. Finish with a sharpening steel, and then wash, sanitize, and air-dry the knife before using.

Trueing a Knife

Trueing a knife with a steel maintains the edge between sharpenings.

Follow these steps to use a steel:

1 Rest the heel of the blade at a 20° angle against the inner side of the steel at its tip. The steel should be held slightly above waist height, a comfortable distance away from the body, on a 0° to 45° angle.

2 Draw the blade downward along the entire length of the steel, maintaining the knife's 20° angle.

3 Complete the movement with the tip of the blade just above the base of the steel.

4 True the opposite side of the blade by repeating steps 1–3, but this time pass the blade over the outer side of the steel.

5 Repeat these steps about 3–5 times on each side of the blade.

6 Wipe the blade to remove any metal particles.

Hand Tools

Handheld tools used in the preparation, cooking, baking, and service of food are known as hand tools. Most hand tools are made from stainless steel, aluminum, or plastic. Durability, ease of use and cleaning, characteristics of heat transfer, and price determine the material from which each hand tool is made. See the chart that follows for some of the most frequently used hand tools in the commercial kitchen.

Selecting Appropriate Tools

To withstand the heavy use of a busy commercial kitchen, foodservice tools must meet high standards for quality and durability. Choose tools that are well constructed, safe to operate, and comfortable to hold. NSF International, formerly known as the National Sanitation Foundation, performs rigorous tests on tools and equipment used in the foodservice industry. Many states require that all tools and equipment used in foodservice operations be NSF-certified.

NSF standards NSF tests tools and equipment according to a set of design, construction, and installation criteria. NSF standards reflect the following requirements:

- Tools, equipment, and their coatings must be nontoxic, with no ill effect on the taste, odor, or color of food with which they come into contact.
- All surfaces that come into contact with food must be smooth and free from cracks, crevices, rivet heads, and bolts.
- External corners and angles of tools and equipment must be smooth and sealed. Internal corners and edges must be rounded and smooth.
- Coatings and exposed surfaces of equipment and tools must resist chipping and cracking.
- Waste must be easily removed from equipment, tools, and their surfaces.
- Tools and equipment must be easy to clean.

Hand Tools

ⓐ Apple corer/slicer
An apple or fruit corer/slicer quickly and cleanly removes the core in one long round piece from the fruit's center. The handle fits easily into the palm of the hand. It is important to choose handles with nonskid grips because a good grip is necessary to guide the corer through the apple. A serrated ring forms the tip. The tip is inserted through the fruit's center. A deep, open groove under the ringed tip holds the core as it is pulled from the fruit's center.

ⓑ Bench scraper
The bench scraper, also called a dough knife, has a sturdy handle and a stainless steel blade that is used to scrape work surfaces and cut dough into equal-sized pieces.

ⓒ Box grater
The box grater has four sides and is made of stainless steel. Each side contains a sharp cutting surface. The size and distance between each raised, open, cutting circle determines the function of each side. Two sides are used for grating; two sides are used for shredding.

ⓓ Butter curler
Butter can be cut with a butter curler, which is used to produce butter garnishes. Butter is placed in cold water, and the butter curler is placed in warm water. As the warm curler moves through the cold butter, curls or butter balls are formed cleanly.

ⓔ Cheese slicers
Cheese slicers are special knives with a handle on each side of the blade, allowing one to safely push down into firm cheeses using both hands.

f Chef's fork

This double-tine fork is larger than a regular serving fork. Chef's forks test for doneness in vegetables or meats that have been braised. A chef's fork also may be used for carving. When used in this way, the chef's fork steadies the meat while it is being carved.

g Chinois or China cap

The chinois or China cap is a cone-shaped metal strainer used to strain stocks or sauces. Sometimes a pestle is used to press soft foods through the chinois.

h Colander

Colanders are used to drain cooking liquids from pasta or vegetables. Colanders also can be used to rinse beans and rice before cooking or to wash and rinse fruits, vegetables, or salad greens. A colander can have a raised, sturdy base, allowing it to be set in a sink without contaminating the food. A metal colander can be set as an insert into a pan for boiling. Perforations, or circular holes, allow the water or other cooking liquid to drain.

i Corkscrews

Corkscrews are used to remove corks from wine bottles. There are a number of corkscrews used in food service, including the ah-so, butterfly, screw pull, and waiter's friend.

j Cutting boards

Cutting boards are used to cut, chop, or slice fruits, vegetables, meat, or pastry dough. Cutting boards can be made from plastic or hardwood, such as maple, and should be free of any surface imperfection.

k Egg slicer/wedger

Egg slicers evenly and uniformly slice hard-boiled eggs. These uniform disks are used in salads and sandwiches. To create oval-shaped disks, position the egg lengthwise; place eggs horizontally to create circular disks. Stainless steel wires do the cutting. Use an egg wedger to cut hard-boiled eggs into sections.

l Food mill

The food mill is used to purée and strain food. Place food in the mill, and turn the handle, forcing the food through a disk. Use a variety of disks to control the degree of coarseness or fineness of strained food.

m Food molds

Food molds are used to make gelatins, custards, and puddings more visually appealing. The liquids for these desserts are poured into the molds and require refrigeration to set. To remove the mold, fit a plate over the open end of the mold. Gently invert both mold and plate, and lift the mold away.

n Fruit corer

The fruit corer is used to core and remove stems from fruit.

o Funnel

Funnels are used to transport liquids from larger containers to smaller containers with narrower openings. Funnels are open-ended and wider at the top, narrowing to a small opening at the tip.

p Kitchen shears

Kitchen shears with curved, razor-sharp blades are used to make a variety of kitchen cuts. These shears can cut anything from fresh herbs to poultry pieces, so it is important to clean and sanitize them to avoid cross-contamination.

q Mandoline

The mandoline is used for slicing vegetables and fruits into thin slices, strips, or waffle cuts.

r Meat mallet/tenderizer

Meat mallets are used to tenderize meat. A long handle is topped with a hammerlike head, each side of which has a different surface. The different surfaces can create various types of impact on meat. The meat is tenderized by breaking up and bruising the muscle fiber.

s Parisienne scoop

The Parisienne scoop, also called a melon baller, is used to scoop out small balls of cheese, butter, potatoes, and melons.

t Pasta machine

A pasta machine is used to roll and cut fresh dough for pasta.

u Pastry bags and tips

Pastry bags and tips are made from plastic, canvas, and nylon. Interchangeable tips create different styles for piping creams, meringues, icings, and puréed foods and can be used to dress up deviled eggs or to shape potatoes. Pastry bags and tips are used in bakeshops and regular kitchens.

v Pie marker

A pie marker is a circular tool that partitions pie into uniform servings or wedges. The tool is placed over the pie and gently pressed on the top, marking the pie in pieces.

w Pizza cutter

A razor-sharp circular wheel attaches to a longer handle to roll-cut pizzas.

x Ricer

To create smooth texture in mashed or puréed potatoes, use a potato ricer. Place boiled potatoes in a chamber, and use the top handle to force the potato through a perforated bottom.

y Rolling pins

Rolling pins are used to roll and stretch the dough used in baking and for pasta. Rolling pins made from hard, tightly grained wood do not absorb fats and flavors. There are two styles of rolling pins. A long, cylindrical piece of wood is characteristic of the French-style rolling pin. The palms of the hand move the pin to roll over the dough. A second style of rolling pin is the rod-and-bearing pin. A metal rod runs lengthwise through a wooden shaft. The bearings in the metal rod make rolling the pin easy. Rolling pins made from wood should not be washed with soap and water. Instead, dry thoroughly with a towel, and store in a clean, dry place.

z Rubber, straight, and offset spatulas

A rubber spatula has a wide, flexible rubber or plastic tip useful for scraping food from bowls, pots, and pans or for folding whipped cream or egg whites into batters. A straight spatula, also called a palette knife, has a long, flexible metal blade with a rounded end. It is useful for spreading icing, soft cheese, butter, or mayonnaise. An offset spatula, also called a turner, has a wide, bent stainless steel blade and is designed to lift and turn food that must cook on both sides.

Knives, Hand Tools, and Smallwares

101

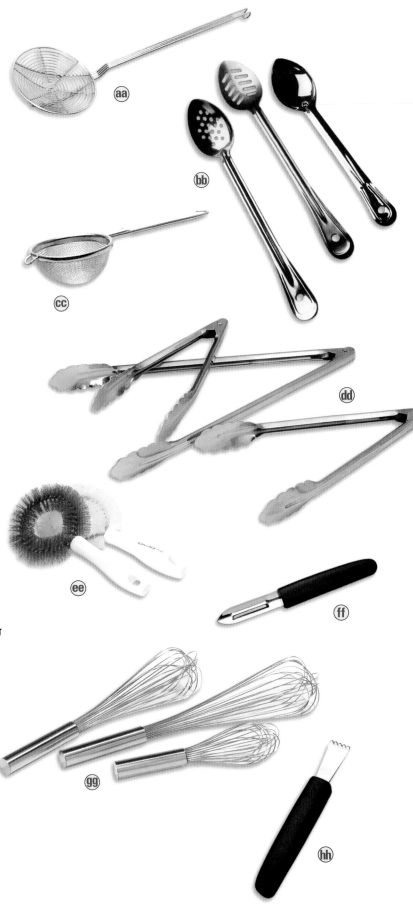

aa Skimmer/spider

A skimmer, with its flat, perforated surface, is designed for removing solids from stocks and soups and for skimming surface impurities from liquids. A spider is a long-handled skimmer used for the same purpose.

bb Solid, perforated, and slotted spoons

Large solid spoons are used for serving and for basting meats, poultry, and other foods to be kept moist while roasting. Slotted spoons lift and drain foods cooked in liquid. The design of the perforated spoon makes it perfect for skimming or removing fat from cooking liquids, soups, and sauces.

cc Strainer

Made from a fine or a coarse mesh, strainers can be used for a variety of purposes, such as draining pastas, vegetables, or stocks. Strainers can also be used to smooth cream soups or decorate cakes by dusting powered sugar.

dd Tongs

Tongs have long handles and a spring action. Some tongs lock to secure the hold on large items. Scalloped edges help grasp and lift steaks, chicken breasts, or other sliced meats or vegetables.

ee Vegetable brush

The short, stiff bristles of a vegetable brush make it ideal for cleaning raw vegetables.

ff Vegetable peeler

Vegetable peelers remove thin layers of skin without removing too much of the edible flesh. Chocolate curls and carrot curls for garnishing desserts and other dishes can be made with a vegetable peeler.

gg Whisk

Whisks are made from stainless steel wires formed in an elongated pear shape extending into a long handle. They are used to beat eggs, delicately mix sauces, or whip dressings. Whisks with thin wires draw air in and should be used to make foams. Those with thicker wires should be used to make sauces.

hh Zester

The zester is used to remove the outer skin from citrus fruits, such as lemons, limes, and oranges.

Smallwares

A variety of smallwares, *small, nonmechanical kitchen equipment that includes measuring equipment, pots, and pans, is used to accomplish food preparation and cooking tasks in commercial kitchens.*

Measuring Equipment

Accurate measurements are essential for success in a commercial kitchen. Consistency in measuring is key to controlling cost and portion sizes and creating tasteful and reliable finished products. Measurements are determined in different ways and are dependent on the types of ingredients and the measurement system specified in the recipe. Measuring equipment is used to measure weight, volume, and temperature. The commercial kitchen must have measuring devices suitable for measuring large quantities of both liquid and dry ingredients. Depending on the operation, the kitchen may need equipment to measure volume and weight in either U.S. or metric systems and to measure temperature in both Fahrenheit and Celsius.

(a)

Measuring Equipment

(a) Portion scale

A portion scale is a spring scale used to determine the weight of an ingredient or portion of food. Resetting the scale to zero allows the user to measure individual ingredients as they are combined.

(b) Electronic scale

An electronic, or digital, scale weighs items placed on its tray. The weight is displayed as a digital readout, so the electronic scale makes more precise measurements than does a portion scale.

(c) Balance scale

A balance scale is chosen most often for weighing flour, sugar, and other baking ingredients. Bakers place the ingredients in the pan on one side of the scale and put standard weights on the other side of the scale. The ingredients weigh the same as the weights when the two sides are balanced.

(d) Dry measures

Dry ingredients can be measured in measuring cups or containers without pour spouts. This allows dry ingredients to be scooped into the dry measure and leveled with a knife or metal spatula for accurate volume measurement. Dry measures often come in sets with 1/4-cup, 1/3-cup, 1/2-cup, and 1-cup measures.

(b)

(c)

(d)

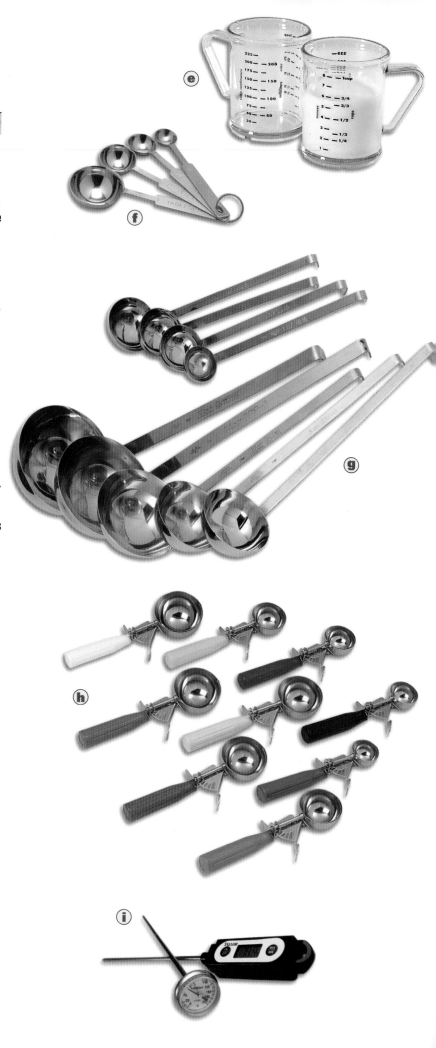

Measuring Equipment *continued*

(e) Liquid measures

A volume of liquid is measured in either plastic or metal containers. Glass measures are not recommended for foodservice operations because of the risk of breakage. A lip or spout on the liquid measure helps prevent spills and makes pouring easier. Liquid measures come in a variety of sizes, such as pint, quart, half-gallon, and gallon.

(f) Measuring spoons

Measuring spoons measure the volume of small amounts of either liquid or dry ingredients. Measuring spoons usually come in sets of 1/4-teaspoon, 1/2-teaspoon, 1-teaspoon, and 1-tablespoon measures. Stainless steel measuring spoons resist warping and hold up well under heavy use.

(g) Ladle

A ladle is used to divide liquids such as sauces, soups, and batters into portions. The long handle allows one to reach to the bottom of a deep pot or pan. The ladle's capacity is marked on the handle.

(h) Scoops

Scoops are used to portion foods such as ice cream, rice, stuffing or mashed potatoes. The bowls of the scoops come in different sizes coded by numbers. Color coding can help identify scoop size and use.

(i) Thermometers

Use instant-read thermometers to determine the internal temperatures of cooked or refrigerated foods and foods being held for service.

Selecting Cookware

The commercial kitchen uses a wide array of cookware. Cookware includes pots, pans, and baking dishes made from a variety of heat-conducting materials, including stainless steel, aluminum, copper, cast iron, or ceramic.

Cookware

(a) Stockpot
The stockpot, or marmite, is a tall, straight pot with loop handles. The stockpot is taller than it is wide, making it useful for simmering or boiling large amounts of liquids, such as stocks and soups. A spigot on the bottom of some stockpots allows liquid to be drained off without lifting the pot.

(b) Saucepot
The saucepot is similar to a stockpot but not as tall. Like the stockpot, the saucepot is meant for range cooking and is well suited to braising, stewing, blanching, poaching, or boiling.

(c) Saucepan
The saucepan, or russe, has a long handle and straight sides. Saucepans come in a variety of sizes and in either shallow- or high-sided versions. They can be used for stewing, blanching, poaching, and boiling.

(d) Roasting pan
The roasting pan, or rotissoire, is a rectangular pan with rounded corners that is used for roasting meat and poultry. The roasting pan may have a lift-out rack that fits in the bottom of the pan, allowing fat and juices to drain away from the food.

(e) Sauté pan
The sauté pan, or sautoir, is a straight-sided shallow pan with a long handle, used to sauté or fry foods.

(f) Sauté pan
The sauteuse is a sauté pan with sloped sides. The sloping sides allow food items to be flipped without the aid of a spatula.

(g) Braising pan
The braising pan, or braisière, is a shallow, heavy-duty pan with loop handles and a tight-fitting lid. It is suited to browning, braising, and stewing meat and poultry.

(h) Fish poacher
The fish poacher, also called a salmon kettle, is a long, deep cooking vessel used for poaching fish in a minimal amount of liquid. A two-handled perforated rack that fits inside the fish poacher allows the whole fish to be easily lowered into and raised from the poacher.

ⓘ Omelette pan
The omelette pan is a shallow skillet with sloped sides. It is designed for cooking omelettes and eggs.

ⓙ Crêpe pan
The crêpe pan is a very shallow skillet with very short, slightly angled sides.

ⓚ Wok
The wok is used for fast, Asian-style range top cooking. The sides of the pan slope, giving height to the pan. The wok's curved bottom requires only a small amount of oil when cooking. Food cooked in a wok generally is cut into small pieces. The size of the food pieces combined with the continuous tossing of the ingredients allow the food to cook quickly.

ⓛ Cast-iron skillet
The cast-iron skillet is a heavy frying pan that can sustain very high heat. A cast-iron skillet is appropriate for frying foods that require steady, even heat.

ⓜ Hotel pans
Hotel pans are rectangular pans used for holding cooked foods in steam tables and for storing foods under refrigeration. Hotel pans also can be used in steamers or in food preparation. Hotel pans come in a variety of sizes and in both shallow- and deep-sided versions.

ⓝ Sheet pans
Sheet pans are rectangular, shallow-sided pans suitable for baking a variety of foods, such as chicken breasts, meatloaf, sheet cakes, and rolls. Sheet pans are available in full and half sizes.

ⓞ Stainless steel mixing bowls
Stainless steel mixing bowls are used for combining, mixing, and whipping ingredients. The bowls come in a variety of sizes to accommodate the needs of the commercial kitchen.

Cookware and Heat Transfer

Size, shape, and quality are all important aspects of cookware. However, *heat transfer,* or the efficiency with which heat passes from one object to another, is a critical factor to consider when choosing cookware. The type of material used and its gauge, or thickness, determines how well the cookware conducts heat. Cookware that heats up too quickly or has hot spots may cause food to burn or cook unevenly. No single cookware material suits every purpose, so different types of cookware should be used according to the nature of the cooking task. See Figure 8-16.

FIGURE 8-16

Different cookware is used to meet various needs.

Aluminum The most commonly used material for commercial cookware is aluminum. Aluminum is lightweight, inexpensive, rust free, and a good conductor of heat. However, aluminum is relatively soft and easily dented. In addition, aluminum reacts chemically with acidic foods. Light-colored soups, sauces, and gravies cooked in aluminum can discolor if stainless steel utensils scrape against the surface of the cookware, releasing microscopic amounts of aluminum. Avoiding the use of metal utensils when cooking with aluminum will prevent this problem. Anodized aluminum has a corrosion-resistant surface that resists sticking and discoloration from chemical reactions.

Stainless steel Stainless steel offers the benefit of a rust-free, nonreactive, and dent-resistant surface. However, stainless steel is a poor and uneven conductor of heat. To improve heat transfer, stainless steel pots may be clad across the bottom with copper or aluminum. Some top-quality stainless steel cookware contains an aluminum core that extends across the bottom and up the sides, between the inner and outer stainless steel surfaces. Aluminum-core stainless steel cookware offers the best of both stainless steel and aluminum by joining rapid and uniform heat conduction traits with the superior surface characteristics of stainless steel.

Copper Copper is an excellent heat conductor. Copper cookware heats quickly, conducts heat evenly, and cools rapidly. Although copper cookware effectively uses heat, copper can produce dangerous results when cooking with acidic foods. Copper reacts with foods that have a pH of 6.0 and below. Upon contact with the food, corrosion occurs. Copper, acting as a contaminant, is released onto or into the foods it touches. The toxic compound formed is a source of metal poisoning. Fruits, fruit juices, salad dressings, tomatoes, vinegar, sauerkraut, and carbonated beverages should not be cooked, served, or mixed in copper cookware or bowls. Copper bowls can be used to beat egg whites or foods high in sugar because they are alkaline and will not produce the toxic chemical reaction. Utensils with copper bottoms on the outside and stainless steel, aluminum, or porcelain interiors maximize heat conductivity and keep foods safe.

Cleaning and Sanitizing Smallwares

When cleaning smallwares, remove food scraps, and then wash, rinse, sanitize, and air-dry after each use.

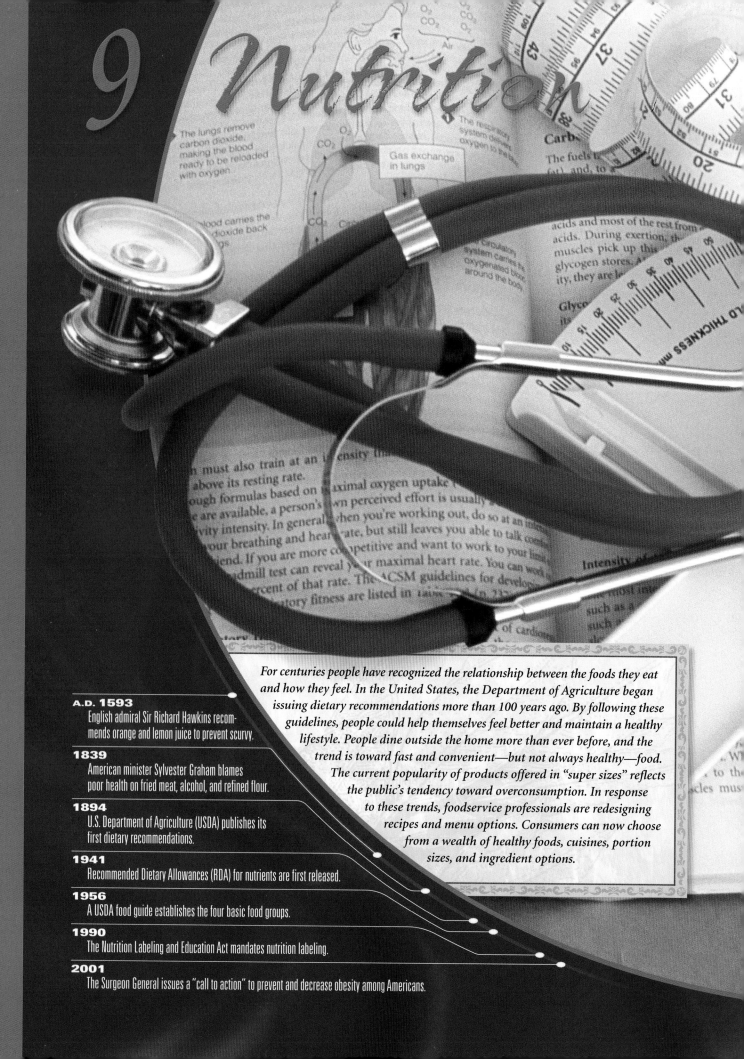

9 Nutrition

For centuries people have recognized the relationship between the foods they eat and how they feel. In the United States, the Department of Agriculture began issuing dietary recommendations more than 100 years ago. By following these guidelines, people could help themselves feel better and maintain a healthy lifestyle. People dine outside the home more than ever before, and the trend is toward fast and convenient—but not always healthy—food. The current popularity of products offered in "super sizes" reflects the public's tendency toward overconsumption. In response to these trends, foodservice professionals are redesigning recipes and menu options. Consumers can now choose from a wealth of healthy foods, cuisines, portion sizes, and ingredient options.

A.D. 1593
English admiral Sir Richard Hawkins recommends orange and lemon juice to prevent scurvy.

1839
American minister Sylvester Graham blames poor health on fried meat, alcohol, and refined flour.

1894
U.S. Department of Agriculture (USDA) publishes its first dietary recommendations.

1941
Recommended Dietary Allowances (RDA) for nutrients are first released.

1956
A USDA food guide establishes the four basic food groups.

1990
The Nutrition Labeling and Education Act mandates nutrition labeling.

2001
The Surgeon General issues a "call to action" to prevent and decrease obesity among Americans.

Nutrition in the Foodservice Industry

Dining out and dining by takeout have become an essential part of the contemporary American lifestyle. A rise in the number of dual-income households has left people with little time to prepare meals at home and an increased amount of money to use for purchasing foodservice-prepared meals. According to the National Restaurant Association (NRA), Americans today eat out about four times each week. On a typical day, four out of ten adults eat one or more meals in a restaurant. Foodservice workers are faced with the challenges of meeting consumers' food choice demands while providing healthy, nourishing foods. Today's consumers are increasingly aware of the relationship between the food they eat and health, and many are taking action to improve their eating habits. According to a 2002 survey by the American Dietetic Association, 75% of consumers carefully select foods to achieve balanced nutrition. Nearly 38% of Americans have significantly adjusted their eating patterns within the last two years to achieve a healthier diet.

Cultural Issues

The place and circumstances in which individuals are raised strongly affect the food choices they make. A person's cultural background often influences the foods to which he or she is exposed, the way that food is served, and the way that food is eaten. For example, Latinos may enjoy a diet high in plant-based foods such as maize and potatoes, and people of Asian descent may choose grains such as rice. Cultural groups help determine a person's eating habits and patterns, but each person also develops his or her own food preferences. Regardless of culture, people can make sound choices to achieve a nutritious diet.

Food has long been associated with family and cultural traditions. Families pass down their food habits, patterns, and traditions through their children. The children then modify what they have learned as they become adults, but their cultural identity remains at their inner core.

Religious Beliefs

Religious beliefs can also affect the food choices people make, and foodservice professionals should be aware of customers' dietary restrictions and sensitive to customers' food choice requirements, particularly during religious holy days. For example, both Jewish and Islamic dietary laws forbid the eating of pork and require that acceptable meats be slaughtered according to their respective dietary law. Jewish dietary laws also forbid the consumption of shellfish and require that meat and dairy foods not be eaten at the same meal. Many Seventh-Day Adventists and Hindus avoid all meat and poultry. Most devout Buddhists do not consume any animal products at all. People from a variety of religious groups avoid alcohol. Some religious groups also prohibit the drinking of coffee and tea.

Vegetarianism

People follow a vegetarian diet for a wide variety of reasons. Those reasons may be based on religion, ethics, health, and concerns about animal welfare. According to the Vegetarian Resource Group, 2.5% of the American population are vegetarians. *Vegetarians* do not eat meat but may consume some animal products. They rely on plant-based foods, such as legumes, nuts, seeds, grains, fruits, and vegetables.

Vegans are strict vegetarians who consume no meat or animal products (including fish, eggs, and dairy products). The vegetarian diet is typically lower in fat, saturated fat, and cholesterol than the usual American diet. A vegetarian diet can be nutritionally complete, provided that vegetarians include a variety of foods and combine plant-based food sources to obtain complete protein. However, because vitamin B12 is supplied only by animal sources, vegans should eat foods fortified with this vitamin or take a vitamin B12 supplement.

In addition to vegans, there are several major categories of vegetarians:

- *Ovo vegetarians* eat eggs but not meat, poultry, fish, or dairy.
- *Lacto vegetarians* eat dairy products but not eggs, meat, poultry, or fish.
- *Lacto-ovo vegetarians* eat dairy and egg products but not meat, poultry, or fish.
- *Pesco vegetarians* eat fish but no other meat or poultry.
- *Pollo vegetarians* eat poultry but no other meat or fish.

Customer Demands

Surveys conducted by the National Restaurant Association (NRA) and the American Dietetic Association (ADA) confirm that increasing numbers of consumers are making choices out of concern for their health and nutrition. Nearly all restaurants today allow customers to substitute menu items and request alternative preparations. Consumers are more aware of the health benefits associated with reducing calories, restricting saturated fat and cholesterol, and increasing their consumption of fruits, vegetables, legumes, and other complex carbohydrates. Even so, most customers continue to base most of their restaurant food choices on taste more than on any other factor.

Dining Trends

Meeting consumers' ever-changing tastes and preferences has always been a challenge for foodservice professionals. Dining trends must be carefully considered when creating recipes, planning menus, and purchasing foods. Today, as consumers become more nutritionally aware, their attitudes about food and healthy eating have established several trends that directly impact the foodservice industry.

- Eating light: Many restaurants offer diners a selection of portion sizes, and many offer low-fat menu items and ingredient substitutions. Asian vegetable salad, jícama salad, quinoa and tabouli salads, tricolored lentil salad, and salads that incorporate vegetables, grains, legumes, pasta, rice, and other light dining options have become popular.
- Choosing meatless meals even if not a vegetarian: Restaurants offer more meatless selections, which are often lower in fat than meat-based menu items.
- Incorporating more fresh fruits and vegetables in the menu: This includes fruit as part of the entrée. Restaurants commonly offer a selection of fresh fruits and vegetables and make them available as menu substitution items.
- Increasing consumption of seafood and leaner meats: Health-conscious consumers are requesting low-fat entrée options, such as seafood and lean meats, prepared in ways that add flavor without adding extra calories.
- Choosing healthy beverage options: Juice bars are rising in popularity, offering healthier alternatives to sodas and coffee. Restaurants also routinely offer juices and specialty waters in addition to the more traditional beverages.
- Substituting healthful fats: Many restaurants, even some fast-food chains, have switched to using healthier fats, such as olive oil, and are reducing the levels of trans-fatty acids in their cooking.
- Following a restricted diet: Menu options, such as low-salt and low-sugar foods, are created for those with dietary restrictions.

In addition, the growing market of senior citizens and families with children has had a direct impact on the foodservice industry. Both of these groups traditionally care about healthy food choices. For example, portion size is a concern, and restaurants that cater to seniors or young children offer reduced portions at lower prices.

The trend toward super-sized portions is becoming popular. Some value-conscious consumers think that they will get a better bargain by ordering larger-sized portions. In addition, a 2001 National Restaurant Association survey found that 70% of customers aged 18 to 24 prefer ordering larger portions so that they can take leftovers home.

According to the U.S. Department of Agriculture (USDA), one serving equals:

- 1 slice of whole-grain bread
- 1/2 cup of cooked rice or pasta
- 1/2 cup of mashed potatoes
- 3–4 small crackers
- 1 small pancake or waffle
- 2 medium-sized cookies
- 1/2 cup vegetables, cooked or raw
- 4 leaves of lettuce
- 1 small baked potato
- 3/4 cup vegetable juice
- 1 medium apple
- 1/2 grapefruit or mango
- 1/2 cup berries
- 1 cup yogurt or milk
- 1 1/2 ounces of cheddar cheese
- 1 chicken breast
- 1 medium pork chop
- 1/4 pound hamburger patty

Health

Nutrition plays a role in providing immunity against many diseases. Poor nutritional choices can be a contributing risk factor for chronic diseases such as heart disease, cancer, Type II diabetes, and obesity. Controlling diet can be significant in minimizing the risk of certain diseases or in combating harmful effects of those diseases.

Throughout much of recent history, scientists have studied the relationship between diet and health. In the 1960s, research demonstrated the relationship between excess consumption of fats, particularly saturated fats, and heart disease and stroke. University of Minnesota professor Ancel Keyes began studying the diets of people on the island of Crete and in Greece and southern Italy at that time. At those sites, despite limited medical resources, the rates of chronic disease were among the lowest in the world and life expectancy was among the highest. The Mediterranean Diet, as Keyes called it, consisted of grains, vegetables, dried beans, olive oil, cheese, fish, and small amounts of poultry. Today, scientists continue to study closely the relationship between a variety of health problems and the foods people consume in an effort to fight disease.

Heart disease Coronary heart disease is the number one killer in the United States. Stroke is the third leading cause of death and the leading cause of serious disability in this country. Genetics may play a role in determining someone's risk factors for developing various diseases. For example, those with a family history of arteriosclerosis, the accumulation of fatty plaque on artery walls, are at a higher risk for developing heart disease than those without this genetic background.

Consuming a diet high in fats and calories, for example, can be a risk factor for developing heart disease. Making wiser choices such as reducing saturated fats and adding fruits, vegetables, and fiber can help reduce some of the risk. Foodservice professionals can provide heart-healthy menu options in several ways:

- Offer entrées that are based on complex carbohydrates and legumes, such as dry beans and whole grains.
- Provide moderate portions of lean meats and fish.
- Use olive oil instead of butter and skim milk instead of whole or low-fat milk.
- Use seasonings other than salt to flavor foods.

Cancer Cancer is the second leading cause of death in the United States. One of every four deaths is from cancer. According to the American Cancer Society, scientists estimate that about one-third of today's cancer deaths are in some way related to nutrition, obesity, or physical inactivity. Hundreds of thousands of research dollars are spent each year studying the possible risks associated with long- and short-term exposure to carcinogens such as pesticides as well as the possible risks of foods containing hormones, antibiotics, and preservatives.

In addition, some scientists believe that various substances in food may promote cancer and other substances in food may be more protective against cancer. Fat, alcohol, excess calories, and low intakes of fruits and vegetables have been related to an increased risk of certain kinds of cancers, whereas foods rich in antioxidants, such as most vegetables and fruits, may help prevent some forms of cancer. *Antioxidants* are chemical substances, such as beta-carotene, vitamin E, and vitamin C, that prevent or repair damage to cells caused by exposure to oxidizing agents—automobile and factory emissions, smoke, ozone, and oxygen.

Diabetes Although the exact cause of diabetes is unknown, being overweight can significantly increase one's risk of developing Type II diabetes. Diabetes is a chronic disease in which the body fails to produce sufficient insulin or does not properly utilize the available insulin. Type I diabetes occurs when a person fails to produce sufficient insulin, elevating the blood glucose level. Type I diabetes, also called insulin-dependent diabetes mellitus or juvenile diabetes, develops most often in children and young adults. Type II diabetes, called noninsulin-dependent diabetes mellitus or adult-onset diabetes, usually develops in adults. With Type II diabetes, the body is insulin resistant—it fails to make enough insulin or use it properly, and insulin levels and blood glucose levels rise too high. Over the past few years there has been an alarming increase in Type II diabetes in children and adolescents.

Diabetes affects 17 million people, or 6.2% of the population in the United States. About 90%–95% of people with diabetes have Type II.

Obesity and lack of exercise appear to be related to the development of Type II diabetes. Diet is important to controlling both Type I and Type II diabetes. People with Type I diabetes should eat at regular intervals and consume consistent amounts of food. Consistency helps keep blood glucose levels from being too high or too low throughout the day. People with Type II diabetes should concentrate on eating a well-balanced diet that is low in fat. Consuming complex carbohydrates and high-fiber foods also may help regulate blood glucose levels.

Weight Management

Being overweight or obese substantially increases the risk of cardiovascular disease and premature death. One way to determine whether you have a healthy body weight is to calculate your *body mass index (BMI).* BMI is a measure of a person's weight in relation to height. In general, a person's BMI correlates with body fatness and can be a useful method for evaluating health risks from being either underweight or overweight. The National Institutes for Health and World Health Organization set the definition of overweight as a person who has a BMI of 25 or higher. A BMI below 18.5 indicates that a person is underweight.

Cutting back on calories and increasing exercise are two ways to reduce weight. The number of calories required to maintain a particular weight depends on many factors, such as a person's body type, metabolism, age, and sex. For example, an adult female who is 5′0″ tall might require 1,200 calories/day, but another female of the same age who is 5′9″ tall might require 2,400 calories/day just to maintain her current weight.

Reducing daily caloric intake by 500 calories may result in a loss of about one pound per week. For weight loss, many dietitians recommend a diet that incorporates plenty of fruits, vegetables, and whole grains while reducing total fat consumption. Controlling portion sizes is a good way to reduce total calorie intake. Very low calorie diets rarely achieve lasting results and can be dangerous.

Foodservice professionals have a role in helping their customers reduce their overall intake and still enjoy flavorful meals. Some restaurants help their customers make informed food choices by providing clear and accurate nutritional information, offering reduced portion sizes, and allowing substitutions. Restaurants can also offer a variety of colorful, appetizing wholesome foods and limit the use of processed foods and foods with hydrogenated and partially hydrogenated oils. Moreover, restaurants can reduce added fats, such as the saturated fats common in rich sauces.

Obesity According to the Centers for Disease Control and Prevention, a record 64.5% of all adults in the United States are overweight, and 30% of them can be considered obese. Fifteen percent of children over age 6 are overweight, nearly double the number from a decade ago. People are overweight if they have a body mass index (BMI) of 25 or more, obese if their BMI is 30 or more, and severely obese if it is 40 or more.

The rise in obesity can be attributed to several factors—overconsumption of high-fat foods is just one. In particular, studies show that more people, especially children, are leading unhealthy, sedentary lifestyles. For example, the American Academy of Pediatrics reports that in 1999, the percentage of children involved in daily physical activity dropped to just 20%, down from 80% in 1969. Consumer-driven trends toward fast food, super-sized meals and poor dietary choices such as fried foods have added to the problem. Despite the evidence that following healthy lifestyle patterns is beneficial, being overweight or obese is the second leading cause of preventable premature death. According to the Centers for Disease Control and Prevention, adult obesity has increased by 60% since 1991.

Food Allergies

A *food allergy* is a reaction by the body's immune system to proteins found in some foods. The body reacts by releasing antibodies, antihistamines, or other defensive agents. Hives, headache, breathing difficulties, gastrointestinal distress, and nasal congestion are symptoms of allergic reactions. Some reactions can be life-threatening.

People can be allergic to almost any food; however, the following eight foods account for about 90% of all food allergies, and the first three cause approximately 75% of all food allergies.

1. Eggs
2. Peanuts
3. Milk
4. Seafood
5. Shellfish
6. Tree nuts (such as walnuts and cashews)
7. Soy
8. Gluten

Food Intolerances

Problems from exposure to foods can sometimes result in a *food intolerance.* A food intolerance does not involve an allergic reaction, but people who eat certain foods may suffer adverse effects such as lactose intolerance. Food labels and accurate menu descriptions can help protect people from reactions to known problem foods. Foodservice professionals should know the ingredients of the dishes they serve in case a customer has any concerns about ingredients. Those working in food preparation should take precautions against cross-contamination. For example, a pan that held peanut oil should be thoroughly washed before it is used to prepare a dish in which peanut oil is not a stated ingredient.

Opportunities

Consumer demands control the choices available today in the foodservice industry. Foodservice professionals must learn the fundamentals of nutrition and its relationship to health. The chef plays an integral role alongside the nutrition expert in producing meals that are flavorful, attractive, and nutritionally well balanced. In addition, the foodservice industry has the opportunity to market and promote healthy menu items in an effort to raise consumer awareness. Health-conscious consumers are learning that the flavor is not always in the fat—it also may be found in interesting combinations of herbs and spices or flavor systems.

Nutrients

Although some people say they "live to eat," the notion that we all must eat to live is quite true. To survive, the body requires fuel in the form of energy derived originally from the sun's rays. The sun's energy is captured in the tissues of the plants we eat, such as vegetables, fruits, and grains. The flesh of animals we eat also has compounds containing energy transformed from solar energy.

Chemical Compounds

The body requires chemical compounds called **nutrients** to survive. There are three classes of macronutrients and three classes of micronutrients.

Macronutrients
1. Carbohydrates
2. Proteins
3. Fats (lipids)

Micronutrients
1. Vitamins
2. Minerals
3. Water

Food Energy

Food energy is measured in units of heat called **calories.** One calorie is equivalent to the amount of heat required to raise the temperature of 1 kg of water by 1°C. Three of the six classes of nutrients supply energy and calories to the body. They are carbohydrate, protein, and fat.

- One gram of carbohydrate supplies 4 calories/gram.
- One gram of protein supplies 4 calories/gram.
- One gram of fat supplies 9 calories/gram.

FIGURE 9-1

Sources of Nutrients

SOURCES OF VITAMIN A (CAROTENOIDS)
- *Orange vegetables such as carrots, sweet potatoes, pumpkins*
- *Dark-green leafy vegetables such as spinach, collards, turnip greens*
- *Orange fruits such as mangoes, cantaloupes, apricots, red grapefruits*
- *Tomatoes*

SOURCES OF VITAMIN C
- *Citrus fruits such as lemons, limes, grapefruits, oranges, kiwis, strawberries, cantaloupes*
- *Broccoli, peppers, tomatoes, cabbage, potatoes*
- *Leafy greens such as romaine lettuce, turnip greens, spinach*

SOURCES OF FOLATE
- *Cooked dry beans and peas, peanuts*
- *Oranges, orange juice*
- *Dark-green leafy vegetables such as spinach and mustard greens, romaine lettuce*
- *Green peas*

SOURCES OF POTASSIUM
- *Baked white or sweet potatoes, cooked greens (such as spinach), winter (orange) squash*
- *Bananas, plantains, dried fruits such as apricots and prunes, oranges*
- *Cooked dry beans and lentils*

Vitamins, minerals, and water do not supply calories or energy.

Fruits and vegetables are excellent sources of a wide variety of nutrients. Some may provide vitamin A (carotenoids), vitamin C, folate, fiber, energy, and potassium. See Figure 9-1.

Carbohydrates

Carbohydrates are compounds composed of *glucose* units, which are found only in plant foods and milk sugars. All carbohydrates contain the same chemical elements: carbon, hydrogen, and oxygen. Carbohydrates are ideal sources of energy for the body, and experts recommend that about 50%–60% of a person's daily calorie intake comes from carbohydrates. The body breaks down carbohydrates into glucose. Glucose is the only sugar that all plants and animals use for energy. Plants can store extra glucose as starch, and animals can store extra glucose as glycogen.

Complex Carbohydrates
Complex carbohydrates are composed of starch and fiber units, and they help maintain the digestive system's function. Digestive enzymes in the body slowly break down these carbohydrate strands into smaller glucose molecules. Complex carbohydrates contain many other nutrients that the body needs, such as vitamins and minerals, therefore experts urge people to make most of their carbohydrate choices from foods containing complex carbohydrates. See Figure 9-2 on page 114.

Complex carbohydrates such as whole wheat flour and oat bran can add structure and texture to foods. Other complex carbohydrates, such as applesauce, can retain moisture in a baked product. Caramelization occurs when sugars are heated above their melting point, and the sugar units are broken down. Bread browning in the oven is an example of this process.

Starches Starch is a polysaccharide, a compound made up of many long strands of sugar units linked together. See Figure 9-3 on page 114. Plants store starch in their seeds and roots. Starch is found in whole grains, pasta, and vegetables such as potatoes, corn, and legumes. During the digestive process, the body breaks down the starch into smaller glucose units.

Fiber Fiber is found in complex carbohydrates. Some fiber molecules are not digestible because the human body does not have the enzymes to break them down. There are two types of fiber: *soluble fiber,* which dissolves in water to form a gel, and *insoluble fiber,* which absorbs water. Insoluble fiber, such as that found in brown rice and whole wheat, helps maintain a healthy digestive tract. Fiber also may help reduce the risk of colon cancer by binding or diluting cancer-causing materials in the colon, helping expel them from the digestive tract. Soluble fiber is found in foods such as oat bran, beans, peas, and certain fruits. Soluble fiber has been shown to help reduce blood cholesterol levels by binding to cholesterol and removing it from the body, which may reduce the risk of heart disease. Without soluble fiber, cholesterol is reabsorbed into the bloodstream. Food with soluble fiber slows down the digestive process. Fiber remains longer in the stomach and helps a person feel full longer. Therefore, eating more fiber can help in weight control by making a person feel full, lessening the desire for calorie-dense fats and sweets. See Figure 9-4 on page 115 for examples of foods that are good sources of fiber.

Simple Carbohydrates

Simple carbohydrates are sugars found in milk, honey, fruit, maple syrup, refined table sugar, and raw or unrefined sugar. Simple carbohydrates can help retain moisture, and simple carbohydrates such as the sugar in custard help delay protein coagulation. Other simple carbohydrates add texture and sensory appeal, aid in caramelization, and act as leavening agents. In addition, simple carbohydrates can help preserve foods and stabilize egg foams.

Simple sugars are often referred to as concentrated sweets. Natural sugars are in foods such as fruits, vegetables, and milk. Simple carbohydrates can be formed from monosaccharides or disaccharides.

Monosaccharides Monosaccharides are composed of a single sugar carbohydrate unit. See Figure 9-5 on page 115. Three monosaccharide sugars are glucose, fructose, and galactose. Glucose and fructose occur in all fruits and vegetables. Glucose is the main component of corn syrup, a common ingredient used in baked goods. High-fructose corn syrup can be artificially

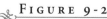

FIGURE 9-2

For maximum health benefit, choose vegetables, fruits, and complex carbohydrates, such as whole-grain breads, cereals, and legumes.

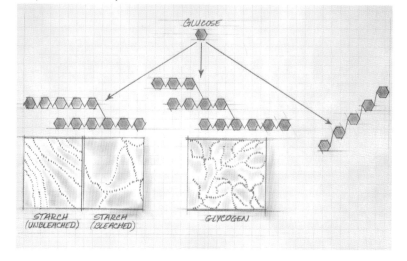

FIGURE 9-3

A polysaccharide is composed of many long branches of sugar units that are linked together. Poly- *means "many."*

manufactured by a process that changes glucose to fructose. High-fructose corn syrup is often used in soft drinks. Galactose is not found alone in natural foods but is a part of lactose (milk sugar).

Disaccharides Disaccharides are two or more monosaccharides linked together. See Figure 9-5. Sucrose, lactose, and maltose are three important disaccharides. Sucrose, which is created from one molecule of glucose and one of fructose, is table sugar. Lactose, or milk sugar, is made up of glucose and galactose. It is found naturally in milk and in whey, which is a by-product of cheese. Maltose is made up of two molecules of glucose and is a component of corn syrup.

Although fruits and vegetables contain fructose and glucose, eating whole foods differs greatly from consuming refined sugar and honey. Fruits and vegetables are packed with fiber, vitamins, and minerals. They also supply large volumes of water, another important nutrient the body needs.

Dietary Trends

According to the USDA, Americans now consume 50% more grain products and 25% more fruits and vegetables than they did in 1970. Restaurant industry data confirms consumer interest in incorporating more fresh fruits, vegetables, and whole grains in the average diet. Main-dish salads with a variety of vegetables are popular entrées for lunch and dinner and are found at all levels of restaurant service, from quick-serve to fine dining. Appearing more frequently on menus are nutritious, fiber-rich dishes using grains such as rice or risotto, polenta, couscous, quinoa, and bulgur. Tasty and innovative side dish preparations made from fresh vegetables are integral accompaniments to fine-dining entrées. Leafy green vegetables such as red chard, kale, beet greens, and collards are gaining in popularity. In addition to soups, pilafs, and sauces, greens are commonly served as sides or as beds for meat and fish entrees. In recent years, carbohydrate-rich meatless meals such as grain, pasta, and legume dishes are increasingly being added to menus—a trend favored even by those who do not consider themselves vegetarians.

FIGURE 9-4

Fruits, vegetables, legumes, and whole grains are the best sources of dietary fiber.

FIGURE 9-5

When more than two mono-saccharides join, a disaccharide is formed. Mono- means "one," and di- means "two."

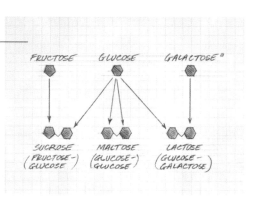

115

Nutrition

Proteins

Proteins for the human body are supplied by plants, such as nuts and seeds, and animal foods, such as meat and eggs. The body also makes its own protein. Protein contains nitrogen in addition to the chemical elements of carbon, oxygen, and hydrogen. The human body uses protein to build, maintain, and repair body tissues. Proteins help the body fight disease and are essential for healthy muscles, skin, bones, eyes, and hair. Current recommendations suggest that 12%–15% of a person's daily calories should come from protein.

Proteins help tenderize foods and help retain their moisture. Proteins such as beaten egg whites function as leavening agents, and proteins such as the gluten in flour add structure. In addition, protein aids in the browning process and produces gels and foams.

Amino Acids

Amino acids are the building blocks of proteins. About 20 amino acids make up all the proteins in the human body and in food. All amino acids contain the chemical elements of carbon, nitrogen, hydrogen, and oxygen, but not all amino acids have the same structure. The body has the ability to make about half of the necessary amino acids, but it must obtain the other amino acids, called essential amino acids, from food sources.

Complete Versus Incomplete Proteins

Proteins that supply all of the essential amino acids are called *complete proteins.* Animal proteins, such as meat, fish, poultry, cheese, eggs, and milk are complete proteins. Most plant proteins, such as those found in bread and cereals, legumes, nuts, and vegetables, are missing one or more of the essential amino acids and are called *incomplete proteins.* The body is able to combine amino acids from separate foods to create *complementary proteins.* For example, legumes provide certain types of amino acids that grains do not have. Eating legumes and grains either together or at different meals on the same day will help the body obtain all the essential amino acids it needs. Figure 9-6 shows some complementary protein combinations.

Dietary Trends

Most Americans do not have trouble obtaining enough protein in their diets. According to the USDA, Americans eat, on average, 190 pounds (86.36 kg) of meat (red meat, poultry, and fish) each year. Although overall meat consumption has risen since 1970, the choice of meat has changed. In 1970 red meat accounted for 74% of all meat consumed. Today beef, pork, lamb, and veal make up only 58% of the total meat supply. Consumers choose chicken and turkey for 34% of their meat. Fish and shellfish account for 8% of total meat consumption. Dairy products are significant protein sources, as well. Although Americans drink far less milk than they did in 1970, they consume 2.5 times as much cheese.

The recommended dietary allowance of protein for adults is 0.8 grams of protein per kilogram of body weight per day. It is recommended that adults choose to supplement their diet with one of the following:

- 2–3 servings (4–6 ounces/113–170 g) of cooked dry beans and peas, lean beef or other lean meat, skinless poultry, fish and shellfish, and eggs and organ meats.
- 2–3 servings of low-fat or fat-free milk, yogurt, or cheese.
- A variety of foods to provide small amounts of protein from other sources.

Fats/Lipids

Fats and oils belong to a class of chemical compounds called *lipids.* Both plant and animal foods contain fat. Fat plays an important role in the body by storing energy, cushioning vital organs, and insulating the body from extremes in temperature. Fat also acts as a carrier of fat-soluble vitamins A, D, E, and K and provides the essential fatty acids the body needs. Fats create feelings of fullness, or *satiety,* because the stomach digests fat more slowly than carbohydrates or protein. Fats provide a rich mouth feel to foods, make baked products tender, and conduct heat during cooking.

Fats are classified by the chemical structure of their carbon, oxygen, and hydrogen bonds. Fatty acids are long carbon chains that are either saturated, monounsaturated, or polyunsaturated. The more hydrogen atoms linked to carbons, the more saturated

FIGURE 9-6

Complementary Proteins

Combine foods from two or more of the groups shown below to obtain complete protein.

GRAINS
barley
bulgur
cornmeal
oats
pasta
rice
whole-grain breads

LEGUMES
beans
lentils
peas
peanuts
soy products

SEEDS AND NUTS
cashews
nut butter
sesame seeds
sunflower seeds
walnuts

the fatty acid will be. The degree of saturation affects the temperature needed to melt the fat. Saturation, therefore, affects a fat's hardness. For example, lard is saturated, and corn oil is unsaturated.

Saturated Fats

Saturated fats have all their carbon atoms linked, with each link holding onto a hydrogen atom. See Figure 9-7. These fats are solid at room temperature. Saturated fats are found in animal products including lard, butter, whole and reduced-fat milk and cheese, and meats. Tropical oils, such as coconut, palm, and palm kernel oils, are also saturated fats. A diet high in saturated fats has been linked to increased risk for cardiovascular disease and cancer.

Monounsaturated Fats

Monounsaturated fats have a missing hydrogen link in their chain. See Figure 9-7. These fats are liquid at room temperature. Olive, canola, and peanut oils are monounsaturated fats. Recent research indicates that olive oil may actually lower the risk of heart disease by increasing the levels of beneficial blood lipids and lowering the levels of harmful blood lipids. The popular Mediterranean Diet uses olive oil rather than animal fats such as butter, cream, and lard.

Polyunsaturated Fats

Polyunsaturated fats have more than one missing hydrogen link in their chain. See Figure 9-7. These fats are liquid at room temperature. Safflower, sunflower, corn, soy bean, and cottonseed oils are polyunsaturated fats. Some examples of these fats are found in seeds, nuts, and fish.

Hydrogenation *Hydrogenation* is a manufacturing process by which the fatty acid chains in polyunsaturated vegetable oil are altered to extend the oil's freshness, raise its smoking point, and change it from a liquid to a solid. Many food product manufacturers use hydrogenated fats because they keep foods fresher longer. Fast-food restaurants use hydrogenated vegetable oils for frying, and consumers tend to prefer softer, spreadable margarines to butter. Most margarines are hydrogenated, so they have a longer shelf life than butter; however, hydrogenated fats have none of the health benefits that come from eating polyunsaturated oils. Hydrogenated and partially hydrogenated

FIGURE 9-7

Carbon atoms link to form fatty acids.

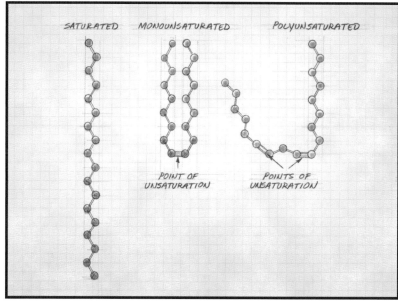

oils are more saturated than the oils from which they are made.

When polyunsaturated oils are hydrogenated and hardened, some of the fatty acids are altered into unusual shapes and become **trans-fatty acids.** Researchers have found a strong correlation between a diet rich in trans-fatty acids and cardiovascular disease. Fast foods, potato chips, hard margarines, doughnuts, peanut butter, and many other sources of commercially processed food products have trans-fatty acids.

It can be difficult to determine how much trans-fatty acid a person is eating because food labels can be deceiving. Trans-fatty acids are counted as polyunsaturated fats and not saturated fats. Foods fried in vegetable oil may actually be prepared in hydrogenated oil and contain high levels of trans-fatty acids.

Cholesterol

Cholesterol is a waxy substance found in both animals and humans. Although it is a necessary substance in the body, too much cholesterol can create problems that can lead to cardiovascular disease. Dietary cholesterol is found in meat, organ meats, egg yolks, dairy products, and all animal products.

High-density lipoproteins (HDL) carry lipids to and from the body's cells. HDL, sometimes called the "good cholesterol," carries excess cholesterol in the blood to the liver, from where it leaves the

body. High concentrations of HDL are associated with a low risk of heart attack.

Low-density lipoproteins (LDL) carry excess cholesterol to tissues, where it slowly builds up as a thick, hard deposit called plaque. If too much LDL cholesterol circulates in the blood, plaque can slowly build up in the walls of the arteries that circulate through the heart and brain, which can eventually impede the flow of blood. Research indicates that elevated levels of LDL increase the risk of heart attack, a quality that gives LDL its nickname: "bad cholesterol."

Eating foods that are high in saturated fat or trans-fatty acids can cause two problems:
- Increase in LDL levels
- Decrease in HDL levels

It is best to eat foods that are high in monounsaturated fats, a diet that will help lower LDL cholesterol levels and increase HDL cholesterol levels.

Essential Fatty Acids

A diet that includes a group of polyunsaturated fats known as omega-6 fatty acids and omega-3 fatty acids has been linked to low death rate from heart disease because of these acids' cell-protecting qualities. Vegetable oils, nuts, seeds, and whole grains provide omega-6 fatty acids. These fatty acids contain linoleic acid, which plays a key role in cell membrane structure and body function.

Omega-3 fatty acids are found in fish and oils. These fatty acids are important

FIGURE 9-8

Sources of Omega-6 and Omega-3		
SOURCES OF OMEGA-6 FATTY ACIDS	SOURCES OF OMEGA-3 FATTY ACIDS	EPA AND DHA:
Linoleic Acid:	*Linolenic Acid:*	*human breast milk*
leafy vegetables	*canola oil*	*shellfish*
seeds	*soy bean oil*	*mackerel*
nuts	*walnut oil*	*salmon*
grains	*wheat germ*	*bluefish*
corn oil	*margarine/short-*	*mullet*
safflower oil	*ening from*	*sablefish*
soy bean oil	*soy bean and*	*menhaden*
cottonseed oil	*canola oil*	*anchovy*
sunflower oil	*butternuts*	*herring*
	walnuts	*lake trout*
	soy bean kernels	*sardines*
	soy beans	*tuna*

to brain development and vision, and research suggests that omega-3 fatty acids help lower the risk of heart attacks. The linolenic acid of the omega-3 fatty acid family and two types of omega-3 fatty acids, EPA and DHA, are found in high concentrations in cold-water fish, such as salmon, mackerel, tuna, sardines, and lake trout. Experts say that a balanced diet that includes fish two or three times a week as well as some vegetable oils will provide an adequate supply of omega-6 and omega-3 fatty acids. See Figure 9-8 for sources of omega-6 and omega-3 fatty acids.

Reducing Fat

As a nutrient, fat helps the body perform many important functions. Although monounsaturated fats, especially olive oil, are considered healthier than other fats, most nutrition experts recommend limiting fat to no more than 30% of daily calorie needs. By reducing fat in recipes, this goal can be achieved.

Reduce total fat Reducing a recipe's total fat and oil can often be accomplished with little effect on taste. However, remember that taste remains the first concern of most diners. Experiment with recipes, gradually reducing the amount of fat or oil over time.

Use lean cuts of meat Foodservice operations concerned with fat content in their food choose lean cuts of meat and trim the fat from them to reduce fat in meat dishes. Skin is removed from poultry, and meats are cooked in nonstick or cast-iron pans to minimize the need for added fat. Meat or poultry stock can be chilled until the fat becomes solid. Then the fat can be spooned off before the stock is used.

Reduce saturated fat Many restaurants substitute olive oil, peanut oil, or other vegetable oils for saturated animal fats. Chefs also experiment with replacing part of the butter in a recipe with oil or substituting yogurt for sour cream.

Replacing Fat

Foodservice professionals know that customers respond best to a variety of food colors, shapes, and textures that add interest and visual appeal to the meal. In addition, these professionals make their food creations healthier by replacing fat with healthier alternatives. For example, part of the whole eggs in a recipe is sometimes replaced with egg whites. High-quality, reduced-fat dairy products are also used, such as reduced-fat cream cheese in place of full-fat products, and part of the fat in baking is replaced with puréed fruits. In addition, the following methods are used to limit fat, but not flavor.

Offer plant-based foods To appeal to vegetarians and others who want low-fat, high-fiber meals, many restaurants offer menu entrées that are based on pasta, rice, grains, and legumes, such as risotto cakes, black bean chili, vegetable lasagna, and couscous with lentils, as alternatives to meats. Some also increase the serving size of fruit and vegetable side dishes.

Change cooking techniques As alternatives to deep-frying or pan-frying, many foodservice operations use roasting, steaming, baking, and other cooking techniques that require little or no added fat.

Use seasonings and flavorings Fresh herbs, spices, and wine are often used instead of butter or margarine to flavor foods. A popular technique is using low-fat marinades to tenderize and add flavor to meats, poultry, and seafood and substituting a salsa for a high-fat, cream-based sauce.

Use special equipment The use of nonstick pans and cast-iron cookware allows food to brown with minimal fat.

Reduce portion size Ideal portion sizes for meat, poultry, and seafood are 3–4 oz. (85–113 g), pre-cooked weight. Increase the portion size for vegetables, grains, beans, and pastas. See Figure 9-9 on page 119.

Dietary Trends

Interest in reducing saturated fat and cholesterol and increasing monounsaturated and polyunsaturated fats in the diet have changed consumer behavior and increased the foodservice industry's responsibility to provide a variety of healthy foods. For example, olive oil's healthful qualities, full flavor, and versatility in cooking have made it a new favorite with chefs. Concerns about cholesterol have also resulted in the production of leaner animals and the increased popularity of menu selections such as fish, poultry, and vegetarian options as alternatives to red meat. The proportion of saturated fat in the diet contributed by meat, poultry, and fish has declined by more than 10% since 1970. In addition, concerns about the fat content of whole milk has made its popularity fall from a high of 81% of all beverage milk sales in 1970 to only about 35% today. In response to these dietary trends, chefs are creating nutritious, wholesome food choices.

Restaurants today commonly offer reduced portion sizes for those concerned with getting too much protein in their diets. Health-conscious consumers wary of "hidden fats," such as those in cheese or cream sauces and au gratin dishes, will ask that sauces be served on the side. Most restaurants are ready to accommodate these special requests.

FIGURE 9-9
Decreasing the portion size of the protein and increasing the vegetable and carbohydrate helps limit fat.

Vitamins

Vitamins are organic compounds that work in conjunction with enzymes and hormones in the body to regulate bodily functions and maintain health. Vitamins themselves supply no energy but are needed in small amounts so that the body can use other sources of energy. Vitamins may be either fat-soluble or water-soluble.

Fat-Soluble Vitamins

Vitamin-rich foods are often those that are the most colorful, such as ripe red strawberries and vibrant green fresh broccoli. Thus, foods rich in vitamins offer all of the colors needed to make a dish visually appealing. Vitamins A, D, E, and K are fat-soluble vitamins. Occurring in the fats and oils of foods, these vitamins are absorbed by the body and stored in the liver. The body can function effectively even without daily consumption of each fat-soluble vitamin. See Figure 9-10.

Water-Soluble Vitamins

Vitamin C and all the B vitamins are water-soluble vitamins; that is, they dissolve in water. The body easily absorbs water-soluble vitamins and efficiently excretes the surplus intake of them in urine. Water-soluble vitamins are not stored for long in the tissues, therefore they rarely reach toxic levels; therefore, they must be consumed daily. To avoid losing or destroying the water-soluble vitamins in foods, preparers must take special precautions. See Figure 9-11 on page 120.

Minerals

Minerals are naturally occurring substances that the body requires in very small amounts. Although minerals, like vitamins, supply no energy, they regulate certain body processes and make up an essential part of the body's bones and teeth. Minerals are divided into two categories: major minerals and trace minerals. Major minerals are those present in the body in amounts greater than five grams. Calcium and potassium are major minerals. Trace minerals are those present in the body in amounts less than five grams. Iron, zinc, and copper are trace minerals. See Figure 9-12 and Figure 9-13 on pages 121 and 122.

FIGURE 9-10

Fat-Soluble Vitamins

VITAMIN A

Function in the Body
Keeps skin and hair healthy and strengthens immune system; protects eyes and facilitates night vision

Food Sources
Dark-green, leafy vegetables such as spinach; yellow-orange fruits and vegetables including carrots, pumpkin, and apricots; dairy products; liver; egg yolks

VITAMIN D

Function in the Body
Helps the body absorb and regulate calcium and phosphorus for strong bones, teeth, and muscles

Food Sources
Fortified milk; fatty fish such as salmon; liver; egg yolks; exposure to sunlight causes the body to produce vitamin D

VITAMIN E

Function in the Body
Protects other nutrients; helps create muscles and red blood cells

Food Sources
Dark-green, leafy vegetables such as spinach; vegetable oils; nuts and seeds; whole grains; wheat germ

VITAMIN K

Function in the Body
Assists in blood clotting

Food Sources
Egg yolks; dark-green, leafy vegetables such as spinach; liver; wheat germ and wheat bran

Phytochemicals

Phytochemicals are nonnutritive chemicals made by plants. A diet that is high in fruits, vegetables, legumes, and grains contains phytochemicals that may help guard against cardiovascular disease, hypertension, diabetes, and cancer.

Scientists have identified more than 900 different phytochemicals in plants. See the chart on page 123 for information about some of the most widely studied phytochemicals and the foods that contain them.

Water

Water makes up about 60% of an adult's body weight and is essential for sustaining life. In fact, dehydration is a serious condition, and people can survive for only a few days without water. Water cleans toxins from the body, cushions and lubricates joints, regulates body temperature, and transports nutrients throughout the body. In recent years, offering bottled specialty waters has become a dining trend in response to the belief that the more water one drinks, the healthier one is.

Dietary Trends

Sales of bottled water, including mineral, sparkling, and flavored waters, have skyrocketed in recent years. Twenty years ago, there was little demand for bottled water in the United States. Now it is a significant beverage category in all types of foodservice operations. Health-conscious consumers believe that drinking plenty of water will improve their skin and resistance to disease and help maintain bowel regularity. Most adults lose about 34 fluid ounces (1 l) of water a day from body processes such as sweating and other functions. For this and other reasons, the rise of interest in fitness and aerobic activities has also fueled the rise in bottled water sales.

FIGURE 9-11

Water-Soluble Vitamins

THIAMIN (VITAMIN B1)

Function in the Body	Food Sources
Helps the body use carbohydrates for energy; promotes normal appetite	Dry beans; pork and other meats; whole and fortified grains

RIBOFLAVIN (VITAMIN B2)

Function in the Body	Food Sources
Keeps skin and eyes healthy; helps the body use carbohydrates, fats, and proteins for energy	Dairy products; meat, poultry, and fish; whole and fortified grains; eggs

NIACIN (VITAMIN B3)

Function in the Body	Food Sources
Helps the skin and nervous system stay healthy; enables normal digestion; helps the body use nutrients for energy	Meat, poultry, fish, liver, and shellfish; dry beans; nuts; whole and fortified grains

VITAMIN B6

Function in the Body	Food Sources
Assists the body in building red blood cells; helps the body use carbohydrates and proteins; keeps the nervous system healthy	Meat, poultry, fish, liver, and shellfish; dry beans; potatoes, whole grains; some fruits and vegetables

VITAMIN B12

Function in the Body	Food Sources
Aids the body in building red blood cells; keeps nervous system healthy; helps the body use carbohydrates, fats, and proteins	Eggs; meat, poultry, and fish; dairy products; shellfish; some fortified foods

FOLATE (FOLIC ACID)

Function in the Body	Food Sources
Assists in the synthesis of new DNA; assists the body in building new cells and tissue; helps the body use proteins	Dark-green, leafy vegetables; dry beans; orange juice; seeds; whole and fortified grains; fruits; peanuts

VITAMIN C (ASCORBIC ACID)

Function in the Body	Food Sources
Strengthens the immune system; keeps teeth, gums, blood vessels, and bones healthy; helps heal wounds and absorb iron	Citrus fruits such as oranges and grapefruit; kiwi, cabbage, strawberries, broccoli, tomatoes, cantaloupe, green peppers, and potatoes

BIOTIN

Function in the Body	Food Sources
Helps the body use carbohydrates, fats, and proteins	Many foods, including dark green, leafy vegetables; liver; egg yolks; whole grains

PANTOTHENIC ACID

Function in the Body	Food Sources
Assists the body in using carbohydrates, fats, and proteins for energy; promotes growth; helps the body produce cholesterol	Many foods, including dry beans; meat, poultry, and fish; eggs; milk; whole grains; fruits and vegetables

FIGURE 9-12

CALCIUM

Function in the Body

Builds and renews bones and teeth; essential for muscle contraction and heart function; aids in blood clotting

Food Sources

Dairy products; dry beans; fortified juices and cereals; dark-green, leafy vegetables such as kale; turnips; canned sardines and salmon

MAGNESIUM

Function in the Body

Assists nervous system and helps muscles work; builds and renews bones

Food Sources

Whole grains; dry beans; dark-green, leafy vegetables; nuts and seeds; fish and shellfish

PHOSPHORUS

Function in the Body

Aids bones and teeth; helps the body maintain the proper balance of cell fluids; builds and renews tissues; assists the body extract energy from nutrients

Food Sources

Dairy products; nuts; dry beans; whole grains; poultry, meat, and fish; egg yolks

POTASSIUM

Function in the Body

Maintains a healthy blood pressure and heartbeat and fluid balance in the body

Food Sources

Fruits such as bananas, oranges, and cantaloupes; meats, poultry, and fish; dry beans; vegetables; dairy products; potatoes

SODIUM

Function in the Body

Aids in regulating blood pressure; maintains fluid balance in the body

Food Sources

Salt and foods that contain salt; soy sauce; MSG; processed foods; deli meats; naturally occurring table salt

FIGURE 9-13

CHLORIDE

Function in the Body

Works with sodium to balance fluids in the body

Food Sources

Salt and foods that contain salt; soy sauce; meats; milk

IRON

Function in the Body

Assists cells in using oxygen; helps the blood carry oxygen

Food Sources

Meat, fish, and shellish; dry beans; egg yolks; dried fruit; whole and fortified grains; dark-green, leafy vegetables

IODINE

Function in the Body

Aids the regulation of the metabolic rate

Food Sources

Iodized salt; saltwater fish and shellfish; bread

ZINC

Function in the Body

Assists in growth and maintenance of tissues; helps heal wounds and form blood; helps metabolize carbohydrates, fats, and proteins; affects taste and smell

Food Sources

Whole grains; poultry, fish, and shellfish; legumes; dairy products; eggs

COPPER

Function in the Body	*Food Sources*
Assists iron in building red blood cells; keeps nervous system, bones, and blood vessels healthy	Meat, fish, and shellfish; whole grains; nuts and seeds; dry beans

FLUORIDE

Function in the Body	*Food Sources*
Strengthens teeth and prevents tooth decay	Fish and shellfish; often added to drinking water

SELENIUM

Function in the Body	*Food Sources*
Helps heart function normally	Fish, shellfish, and liver; eggs; whole grains

Alcohol

Throughout the ages, the simple act of pairing alcohol with food has been strongly linked to traditions, ceremony, and community. Raising a glass and offering a toast is a ritual repeated daily throughout the world, symbolizing friendship and camaraderie.

Research suggests that moderate drinking (no more than one drink per day for women and no more than two drinks per day for men) can be beneficial by reducing cholesterol and thus lowering the risk of heart attack, stroke, and the blockage of arteries in the legs.

In particular, wine may contain phyto-chemicals that act as antioxidants, helping protect the cardiovascular system and prevent heart disease. The so-called French paradox may indicate the protective proper-ties of wine: Although people in France and the United States share many of the same risk factors, including a high-fat diet, scientists in the early 1990s discovered that France's heart attack rate was one-third that of the United States. The French practice of drinking wine with meals was identified as a key factor in the discrepancy.

Most experts recommend that those who drink do so in moderation. They also suggest drinking with meals to slow the absorption of alcohol. Doctors often recommend that people avoid alcohol if they

- have a strong family history of alcoholism.
- are pregnant or trying to conceive.
- have certain medical conditions including ulcers, liver disease, and some kinds of heart problems.

Some vitamins, such as vitamins A, C, and E, are classified as antioxidants. Antioxidants help protect healthy cells from damage by free radicals. Free radicals form as a result of normal body functions, such as breathing and physical activity, and as a result of smoking or exposure to other environmental hazards. They can weaken and damage healthy cells, making the body more susceptible to heart disease and certain types of cancers. Foods rich in beta-carotene and vitamins B, C, and E are good sources of antioxidants. These include a range of colorful fruits and vegetables. The Food and Drug Administration (FDA) believes that diets high in these foods reduce the risk of several types of cancer.

CRUCIFEROUS VEGETABLES *Cruciferous vegetables such as cauliflower, broccoli, cabbage, and brussels sprouts are rich in the phytochemicals known as isothiocyanates and indoles. These phytochemicals may activate the production of enzymes that stop carcinogens from damaging DNA.*

ALLIUM VEGETABLES *Allium vegetables such as onions, garlic, leeks, and shallots contain the phytochemical allyl sulfide. Allyl sulfide may slow the production of enzymes that cause carcinogens while increasing the production of enzymes that destroy carcinogens.*

BERRIES *Berries such as cranberries, blackberries, and strawberries contain the phytochemical ellagic acid. Ellagic acid may deactivate carcinogens and prevent other chemicals from causing mutations in bacteria.*

HOT PEPPERS AND SPICES *Hot peppers and spices made from them contain the phytochemical capsaicin. Capsaicin may reduce the blood clotting that can cause heart disease, and it may prevent carcinogens from binding to DNA.*

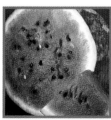

TOMATOES AND WATERMELON *The phytochemical lycopene is found in tomatoes and watermelon. Lycopene may function as an antioxidant, reducing the risk of cancer and heart disease.*

Managing Nutrients in Food Preparation

The nutritional value of food varies according to how the food is handled. Improper preparation, cooking, and storage not only make foods taste unpleasant but also cause nutrient loss.

Time

Foods lose nutrients as they age, therefore it is important to use both fresh and frozen foods as soon as possible.

- Use fresh produce and meats within three or four days.
- Use fresh ground meats within one to two days.
- Refrigerate or use cut fruits and vegetables soon after slicing or cutting. Do not leave cut fruits and vegetables at room temperature for long before serving.

Water

Water-soluble vitamins, such as vitamins B and C, as well as other nutrients, can *leach,* or dissolve in water. Take these precautions to limit water-related damage.

- Limit the amount of time vegetables rest in water before or after cooking.
- Thoroughly wash produce, but do not soak it in water for longer than necessary.
- Steam rather than boil fresh produce.

Cooking

High temperatures and prolonged cooking can destroy vitamins in foods. It is important to follow temperature recommendations for cooking foods and reduce exposure to heat by cooking in small batches. In addition, avoid overcooking foods, especially vegetables.

Healthful Cooking Techniques

Tasty, healthful food choices that fit specific dietary needs can be provided by cooking with less fat and sodium. Using fresh, high-quality foods will also provide customers with flavorful, healthy choices.

Certain cooking techniques are more effective than others in retaining the nutritive value of foods and minimizing the use of added fats. Steaming, grilling, poaching, stir-frying, sautéing, and roasting/baking are healthful cooking techniques.

Steaming Steaming can take place in commercial steamers, steam-jacketed kettles, in pots with special steamer inserts, and in bamboo or metal steamers. Steaming offers advantages over boiling, during which vitamins quickly seep into the cooking liquid. Even when part of the liquid is incorporated into a sauce or soup, valuable nutrients are usually lost during boiling. Steaming helps preserve these nutrients.

Grilling Grilling on a gridlike surface over a heat source creates tender foods with a charbroiled flavor. Grilling requires little or no added fats to develop flavor.

Poaching Poaching in 160°F–185°F (71°C–85°C) liquid minimizes the effects of nutrient leaching. No fat is added, and the cooking liquid can be incorporated into a sauce or soup.

Stir-frying Stir-frying creates crisp, colorful vegetables by quick-cooking foods in a minimal amount of oil. Nutrient loss is minimized by the quick application of heat.

Sautéing Like stir-frying, sautéing offers the advantage of quick cooking with little fat. Using a non-stick or well-seasoned pan, or adding a small amount of vegetable oil pan spray can also help reduce the need for added fat. Nutrients are preserved because cooking time is relatively short.

Roasting/Baking Roasting or baking requires the addition of little or no fat to develop tender, full-flavored foods. Roasting minimizes nutrient loss because little water is added during cooking. Roasting vegetables develops full flavor while preserving nutritional values.

Storage

Storage exposes food to the effects of water, light, air, and time and results in the loss of nutrients. To maintain food safety and conserve nutrients, follow food storage recommendations for the length of time food can safely be stored as well as the best method for storing each type of food product.

▌ *See Chapter 4: Food Safety for more information.*

Temperature The destruction of nutrients occurs more rapidly at high temperatures. One way to slow the process that destroys a food's nutrients is to plunge cooked vegetables into cold water to halt the cooking process. After the food has been shocked in cold water, drain it promptly to prevent nutrients from leaching into the water. Store foods covered in the refrigerator to slow the loss of nutritional value. Chilling fresh produce helps slow the ripening process, which leads to the destruction of nutrients.

Batching *Batch cooking* is the process of preparing small amounts of food several times throughout the time food is served. This process decreases the quantity of food that must be kept warm, lessening food storage problems and the resulting loss of quality and nutrients. Batch cooking allows the kitchen to offer freshly prepared meals at the peak of quality.

Holding Prolonged exposure to heat and water hastens nutrient loss. To preserve food nutrient content, limit the time foods are held in a steam table.

Guidelines for Meal Planning

Most experts agree that to please a variety of palates, meal and menu planning should take into account a variety of foods. In general, colorful foods and a variety of textures will enhance the dining experience and provide healthful meal choices for customers.

In addition, numerous guidelines and recommendations are available to help consumers make healthful food choices and create well-balanced meals. For example, the Food and Nutrition Board of the National Academy of Sciences develops the Recommended Dietary Allowances (RDA) for essential nutrients, including protein, vitamins, and minerals. The RDA specifies the level of nutrients necessary to prevent deficiency diseases. For 50 years the RDA has provided nutrient intake standards for the United States.

Today the RDA is being replaced by a new set of standards called the Dietary Reference Intakes (DRI). The DRI suggests dietary nutrient intakes for healthy people on the basis of age and gender. The DRI also establishes an upper limit of safety for nutrients.

The Food Guide Pyramid

Figuring out how to get the appropriate nutrients and the right amount of nutrients can be difficult. Updated in 1990, the USDA's Food Guide Pyramid outlines what people should consume each day on the basis of dietary guidelines. A person's age and sex determines the amount of food needed to get the recommended nutrients. Although there has been considerable debate about the merits of the Food Guide Pyramid, the number one factor driving consumers' food choices continues to be taste. See Figure 9-14 on page 126.

The Pyramid separates foods into six major groups:

1. Bread, Cereal, Rice, and Pasta Group (especially whole grain)
2. Vegetable Group
3. Fruit Group
4. Milk Group (includes milk, yogurt, and cheese—preferably fat-free or low-fat)
5. Meat and Beans Group (includes meat—preferably lean or low-fat—poultry, fish, dry beans, eggs, and nuts)
6. Fat Group (includes oils and sweets)

The USDA and the U.S. Department of Health and Human Services publish the *Dietary Guidelines for Americans*, on which the Pyramid is based. The Guidelines identify healthy eating plans that focus on moderation and variety.

AIM FOR FITNESS

- Aim for a healthy weight.
- Be physically active each day.

FIGURE 9-14

Food Guide Pyramid: A Guide to Daily Food Choices

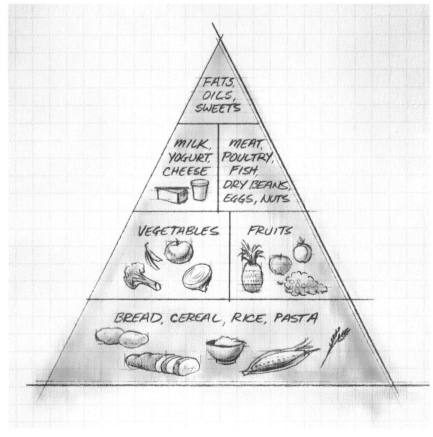

BUILD A HEALTHY BASE
- Let the Pyramid guide your food choices.
- Choose a variety of grains daily, especially whole grains.
- Choose a variety of fruits and vegetables daily.
- Keep food safe to eat.

CHOOSE SENSIBLY
- Choose a diet that is low in saturated fat and cholesterol and moderate in total fat.
- Choose beverages and foods to moderate your intake of sugars.
- Choose and prepare foods with less salt.
- If you drink alcoholic beverages, do so in moderation.

Food Pyramid Alternatives
Healthy foods and dietary patterns in cultures throughout the world have inspired several alternatives to the USDA's Food Guide Pyramid. For example, the Mediterranean Diet Pyramid is one of several guides created by the Oldways Preservation and Exchange Trust, working jointly with the Harvard School of Public Health. This diet is based on traditional diets from cultures, particularly those bordering the Mediterranean Sea, that have historically enjoyed good health. The Mediterranean Diet Pyramid emphasizes a diet that is primarily plant-based and low in saturated and trans-fats. Fish is recommended over poultry, eggs, or red meat, and olive oil is the principal fat. Wine is consumed with meals. See Figure 9-15 on page 127.

The Asian Diet Pyramid, also created by the Oldways Preservation and Exchange Trust, emphasizes plant-based foods, including rice and other grains, nuts, seeds, beans, soy foods, vegetable and nut oils, fruits, and vegetables. This diet is low in saturated and total fat. Fish is consumed in moderate amounts, and red meat is used sparingly. Black and green tea are common beverages, and wine and beer are used in moderation. See Figure 9-16 on page 127.

Oldways created the Latin American Diet Pyramid to reflect a healthy, traditional Latino diet. This diet emphasizes plant-based foods, especially maize and potatoes, as well as breads and grains, rice, cornbread, tortillas, bean, nuts, seeds, fruits, and vegetables. Fats come primarily from nuts and certain vegetables. Poultry and fish are consumed weekly, and red meat is eaten only a few times a month. Chilies are eaten at almost every meal, and chocolate is eaten daily. See Figure 9-17 on page 127.

The Oldways Vegetarian Diet Pyramid represents a traditional healthy vegetarian diet that is based on cuisines throughout the world. The guide recommends multiple daily servings of fruits and vegetables, whole grains, and legumes. Daily servings of soy milks, dairy products, plant oils, nuts, seeds, and egg whites are also recommended. See Figure 9-18 on page 127.

Dr. Meir Stampfer and Dr. Walter Willet of the Harvard School of Public Health have suggested that the USDA Food Guide Pyramid be revised to reflect more recent research findings. The Harvard group points out that current guidelines promote an overconsumption of carbohydrates and underestimate the health benefits of unsaturated fats in the diet. They have proposed the Harvard Healthy Eating Pyramid, which limits servings of dairy products and includes more servings of fruits and vegetables. See Figure 9-19 on page 127.

Nutrition Labels

The Nutrition Labeling and Education Act of 1990 requires most foods to include nutrition labels indicating the serving size, number of calories per serving, number of calories from fat per serving, and the labeled product's nutrients. Product nutrients are measured in grams and as a percentage of daily values. *Daily values* are the amount of nutrients a person needs every day on the basis of a 2,000-calorie diet. Each person's caloric needs differ, therefore the daily values provide only a guide. For reference, labels also show the recommended daily values of several important nutrients and list the number of calories per gram of fat, protein, and carbohydrate. See Figure 9-20 on page 128 for hints on how to read a Nutrition Facts panel.

Food Safety and Additives
Concern about food safety and additives influences the dietary choices of some individuals.

Organics To avoid the possible health effects of chemicals or other processes used to grow and produce foods, some people choose foods that have been organically grown. Organic food is produced by farmers in an effort to protect the quality

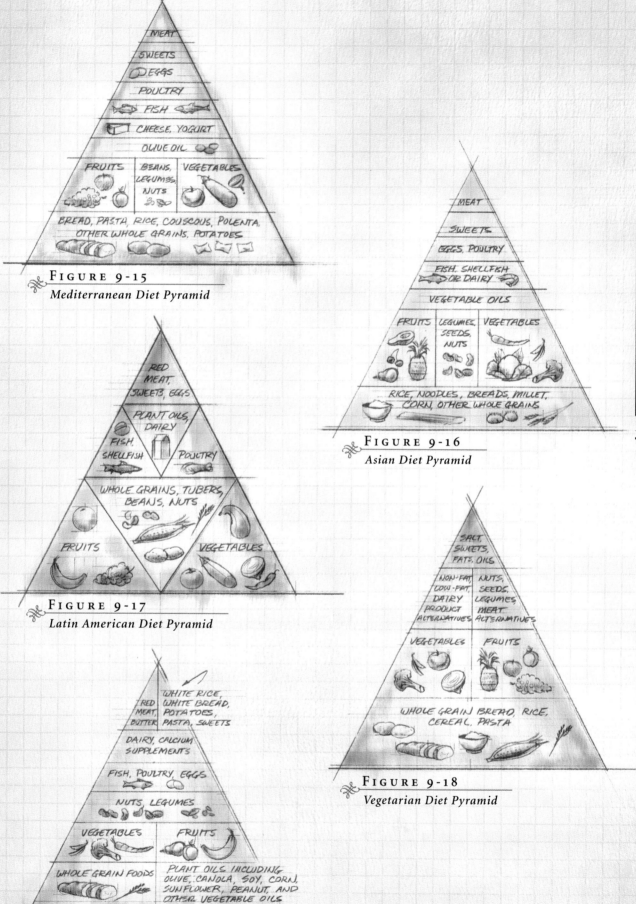

FIGURE 9-15
Mediterranean Diet Pyramid

MEAT
SWEETS
EGGS
POULTRY
FISH
CHEESE, YOGURT
OLIVE OIL
FRUITS | BEANS, LEGUMES, NUTS | VEGETABLES
BREAD, PASTA, RICE, COUSCOUS, POLENTA, OTHER WHOLE GRAINS, POTATOES

FIGURE 9-16
Asian Diet Pyramid

MEAT
SWEETS
EGGS, POULTRY
FISH, SHELLFISH OR DAIRY
VEGETABLE OILS
FRUITS | LEGUMES, SEEDS, NUTS | VEGETABLES
RICE, NOODLES, BREADS, MILLET, CORN, OTHER WHOLE GRAINS

FIGURE 9-17
Latin American Diet Pyramid

RED MEAT, SWEETS, EGGS
PLANT OILS, DAIRY
FISH, SHELLFISH | POULTRY
WHOLE GRAINS, TUBERS, BEANS, NUTS
FRUITS | VEGETABLES

FIGURE 9-18
Vegetarian Diet Pyramid

SALT, SWEETS, FATS, OILS
NON-FAT, LOW-FAT, DAIRY PRODUCT ALTERNATIVES | NUTS, SEEDS, LEGUMES, MEAT ALTERNATIVES
VEGETABLES | FRUITS
WHOLE GRAIN BREAD, RICE, CEREAL, PASTA

FIGURE 9-19
Harvard Healthy Eating Pyramid

RED MEAT, BUTTER | WHITE RICE, WHITE BREAD, POTATOES, PASTA, SWEETS
DAIRY, CALCIUM SUPPLEMENTS
FISH, POULTRY, EGGS
NUTS, LEGUMES
VEGETABLES | FRUITS
WHOLE GRAIN FOODS | PLANT OILS INCLUDING OLIVE, CANOLA, SOY, CORN, SUNFLOWER, PEANUT, AND OTHER VEGETABLE OILS
DAILY EXERCISE, WEIGHT CONTROL

FIGURE 9-20

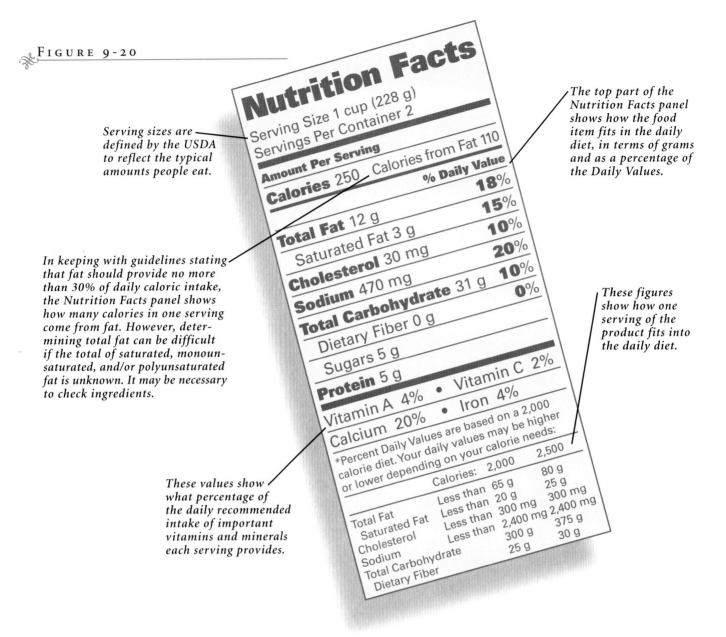

Nutrition Facts

Serving Size 1 cup (228 g)
Servings Per Container 2

Amount Per Serving

Calories 250   Calories from Fat 110

	% Daily Value
Total Fat 12 g	**18%**
Saturated Fat 3 g	**15%**
Cholesterol 30 mg	**10%**
Sodium 470 mg	**20%**
Total Carbohydrate 31 g	**10%**
Dietary Fiber 0 g	**0%**
Sugars 5 g	
Protein 5 g	

Vitamin A 4%	•	Vitamin C 2%
Calcium 20%	•	Iron 4%

*Percent Daily Values are based on a 2,000 calorie diet. Your daily values may be higher or lower depending on your calorie needs:

		Calories:	2,000	2,500
Total Fat	Less than		65 g	80 g
Saturated Fat	Less than		20 g	25 g
Cholesterol	Less than		300 mg	300 mg
Sodium	Less than		2,400 mg	2,400 mg
Total Carbohydrate			300 g	375 g
Dietary Fiber			25 g	30 g

Serving sizes are defined by the USDA to reflect the typical amounts people eat.

In keeping with guidelines stating that fat should provide no more than 30% of daily caloric intake, the Nutrition Facts panel shows how many calories in one serving come from fat. However, determining total fat can be difficult if the total of saturated, monounsaturated, and/or polyunsaturated fat is unknown. It may be necessary to check ingredients.

These values show what percentage of the daily recommended intake of important vitamins and minerals each serving provides.

The top part of the Nutrition Facts panel shows how the food item fits in the daily diet, in terms of grams and as a percentage of the Daily Values.

These figures show how one serving of the product fits into the daily diet.

---

of the environment. They do this by using renewable resources and conserving both soil and water. Organic meat, poultry, eggs, and dairy products come from animals that are given no antibiotics or growth hormones. Organic food is produced without using most conventional pesticides; fertilizers made with synthetic ingredients or sewage sludge; bioengineering; or ionizing radiation.

Genetically modified foods *Genetically modified organisms (GMO)* are foods that have undergone a modification of genes in the laboratory in order to enhance specific traits, such as improved nutritional content or resistance to spoilage or insect damage. Some people argue that scientists do not yet know enough about the long-term effects of genetically modified foods to make decisions about their safety. Currently a food manufacturer is not

bound by law to label whether the food has been genetically modified or not.

Additives *Additives* are substances placed in foods to improve characteristics such as flavor, texture, and appearance or to extend shelf life. Mindful of safety and effectiveness, the FDA regulates what additives can be added to foods. It also determines whether the additives offer benefits that outweigh any known risks. A list of approved food additives can be found on the FDA's GRAS list (Generally Recognized As Safe).

Irradiation *Irradiation* is a process involving the application of ionizing radiation to foods in order to kill insects, bacteria, and fungi or to slow the ripening or sprouting process. Many favor the use of irradiation because it could limit or eliminate the use of pesticides and protect consumers from foodborne illnesses. Others

fear irradiation, believing that irradiated foods will not be safe to eat or that the radioactive substances used to perform the procedure could pose a danger to workers and the environment.

Functional foods *Functional foods* are those foods that provide health benefits beyond their basic nutrients. At their most basic level, fruits and vegetables are natural examples of functional foods because they contain phytochemicals. Orange juice fortified with calcium and cereal fortified with soy protein are other examples of functional foods. Some functional foods are sold as dietary supplements. For example, juices fortified with the herb echinacea may be marketed as an aid for boosting the immune system.

Recipe Modification

To meet the demands of health-conscious consumers, foodservice professionals should be able to modify recipes. Recipes can be modified to reduce, replace, or eliminate ingredients from the original recipe.

Steps in Recipe Modification

People consume food because it tastes and looks good, not necessarily because it is healthy. Therefore recipe modification should take into account the taste, texture, appearance, and nutrition of the dish. Foodservice professionals can follow these four steps to modify a recipe:

1. Identify the ingredients that need adjustment. An adjustment could be an increase or a decrease in quantity or a substitution of one ingredient for another. Concentrate on increasing complex carbohydrates and dietary fiber while reducing total fat, saturated fat, cholesterol, sodium, and protein.

2. Determine the function or purpose of the ingredient in the recipe. Each ingredient in a recipe contributes to the final product. An ingredient may add flavor, bind substances together, provide color, or tenderize. See Figure 9-21 for a list of nutrients and their functions in recipes.

3. Modify ingredients as appropriate. This could involve increasing or decreasing the amount of a particular ingredient or substituting a new ingredient for the original. An ingredient replacement must give results similar to those of the original. Modifying the method used for preparation or cooking could also be part of the process.

4. Analyze the recipe for sensory desirability. Ideally, the modification should create a new dish with plenty of visually appealing color as well as the taste, texture, aroma, and mouth feel of the original. Using ingredients such as fresh herbs, spices, wine, or lemon may help maintain the sensory appeal of a dish while limiting its fat, salt, or sodium.

FIGURE 9-21

Functions of Nutrients in Food and Recipes

FAT

Function	Example
Sensory	Butter
Tenderizer	Marbling in meat
Heat conductor	Oil in sautéing
Starch separation	Butter in roux
Sealing	Basting with fat
Lubrication	Coating pans with fat

PROTEIN

Function	Example
Thickening/gels	Egg protein in custard; raft in consommé
Moisture retention	Increases shelf life
Structure	Gluten in flour
Maillard browning	Browning meat
Leavening	Beaten egg white
Tenderizing	Enzymes

COMPLEX CARBOHYDRATES

Function	Example
Thickening	Flour in roux, water-soluble fiber, oat bran
Structure	Flour in cake and bread
Texture	Vegetables in recipes, water-insoluble fiber skins, seeds
Moisture retention	Applesauce in baking
Maillard browning	Toast

SALT

Function	Example
Flavor enhancer	Tomato juice
Preservation	Bacon
Leavening	Bread
Lowers freezing point	Frozen desserts
Slows down protein coagulation	Custards

SIMPLE CARBOHYDRATES

Function	Example
Sensory	Sugar in candy
Moisture retention	Quick breads
Caramelization	Butterscotch candy
Delays protein coagulation	Sugar in custard
Leavening	Creaming sugar and butter in cakes, food for yeast
Texture	Cake
Preservation	Dehydrates
Stabilizing egg foams	Meringues

EGGS

Function	Example
Binder	Meatballs
Thickener	Custard
Coating	Egg wash
Color	Yellow cake
Flavor	Egg noodles
Leavening	Egg foams
Emulsification	Hollandaise sauce

10 Sensory Perception

Early humans used their sensory organs to assist in their survival. Olfactory receptors in the nose sniffed out appealing smells and warned of rotten or contaminated food. Taste buds helped distinguish between safe foods and foods that were poisonous. Today, eating food is also a pleasurable experience. Food is chosen as much for its pleasing sensory qualities as for health and nutrition.

KEY TERMS

sensory perception
sensory evaluation
umami
common chemical sense
top notes
middle notes
base notes
background notes
aftertaste
volatile

The Sensory Properties of Food

Sensory perception is the ability of the sensory organs to detect and evaluate sensory stimuli such as odors, tastes, textures, sights, and sounds, all of which are active during eating. These organs have special receptors that detect stimuli. When a receptor like a taste cell on a taste bud is stimulated, it produces an electrical signal. Nerve impulses carry many such signals to the brain, where the information is processed. The brain determines whether a taste is sweet or salty, or whether it is pleasant or unpleasant. Food presents many sensory stimuli, therefore an understanding of sensory perception is important to the chef.

Sensory evaluation, or analysis, requires systematic tasting of food to determine its objective qualities and consumer appeal. Whereas culinary skills require an ability to synthesize or create flavors, sensory evaluation involves analysis by taking apart and examining the components of flavor. Successful sensory evaluation helps chefs realize when a food combination is likely to produce a pleasant eating experience.

Color and Appearance of Food

A food's appearance is usually the first indicator of how it will taste. The brighter and more colorful the food, the more visual its appeal. The brain processes information about flavor and texture on the basis of appearance and makes decisions about likes and dislikes. This evaluation happens because humans have a highly developed sense of sight. In fact, human sight is so perceptive that the brain sometimes ignores competing messages from other senses. For example, lemon candy is expected to be yellow. If it were made colorless, many would have difficulty identifying the flavor as lemon. If it were purple, some would mistakenly identify it as grape.

Color and appearance are important to food evaluation. Therefore, care should be taken in how food is presented. Factors that affect the perception of a food's color and appearance include its chemical and physical properties, the quality of light that is illuminating the food, and the food's surroundings.

Chemical properties All food—all matter—is made up of chemicals. Chlorophyll, for example, is the chemical that gives green vegetables their color. It is logical to expect two products to look different when they are made from different chemicals or varying amounts of the same chemical. Cake made from egg whites will be whiter than cake made from whole eggs because egg whites do not contain yellow carotenoids. Fresh spinach looks greener than old spinach because it contains more chlorophyll.

Preparation also affects the chemical properties of food. The longer green vegetables are cooked, the duller and more olive-green they become. This occurs because heat chemically alters the chlorophyll in green vegetables. Likewise, the longer a cake is baked in the oven, the darker it becomes. The change in color is visible proof that chemical changes occur during baking.

Physical properties The physical process of food preparation also influences appearance. The more mayonnaise or hollandaise is whisked, the lighter in color it becomes. Whisking breaks the liquid oil or butter into smaller and smaller droplets and whips air into the sauce. Small oil droplets and air bubbles scatter light more completely than large droplets do, so the sauce has a whiter appearance.

Raw spinach and other greens are composed of plant cells that contain a large amount of liquid surrounded by air pockets. When these greens are cooked, air escapes, and the air pockets fill with liquid. Light reflects off liquid differently than it does off air, so the cooked vegetables will have a translucent quality. Greens served during the short time after air leaves the cells but before they fill with water are the brightest and most attractive.

Quality of light Different types of lighting can affect the perception of color. Greens viewed under incandescent lighting, such as that in a dining room, appear more yellow than when seen under fluorescent lighting, such as that in a kitchen.

Food surroundings The interaction of the plate as a background with the surrounding food and garnishes can sometimes cause optical illusions. White cake served on a dark plate or sauce appears whiter than if it were served on a white plate. This is because the dark plate or sauce provides a contrast that tricks the brain into thinking the cake is whiter than it is.

Flavor of Food

Ask consumers why they like or dislike a particular food, and they will mention flavor, or the way the food tastes. Appearance may provide the first impression of a food, but flavor provides a lasting impression.

Flavor is the blend of taste, aroma, and feeling factor sensations. These three sensations occur when food molecules (chemicals) stimulate receptors in the mouth and nose. It is because of their chemical nature that these senses are considered chemical senses. Although together they constitute flavor, each sense system is distinctly different in that each one is stimulated by different chemicals and detected by different receptors. Yet the perception of these sensations happens at once, while the appearance, texture, and temperature are evaluated and as the food is enjoyed. This is one explanation for the complexity of sensory perception. This also explains why evaluating food objectively takes deliberate practice.

The three components of flavor are perceived by three separate systems, therefore each continues to function even when the other systems no longer work well or at all. For example, persons who have lost their sense of smell can still perceive the tastes and feeling factors of foods.

The term *taste* is often used interchangeably with *flavor*, but taste also refers specifically to one component of flavor—the perception of dissolved substances by the taste buds. To avoid confusion, this component of flavor is often referred to as a basic taste.

An evolutionary advantage to having well-developed senses is to better detect danger. Many poisonous foods are bitter or otherwise unpleasant, and many healthful foods, such as ripe fruit, are sweet or otherwise pleasant.

Basic Tastes

There are four basic tastes: sweet, sour, salty, and bitter. Sugars are the most well-known stimuli that produce sweetness, but certain other chemicals do as well. For example, high-intensity sweeteners, like saccharin and aspartame, taste sweet although they are not sugars. The sweet taste of shrimp and other seafood is from a naturally occurring amino acid called glycine. Acids in foods, such as citric acid in lemons and acetic acid in vinegar, produce a sour taste. Salts, such as sodium chloride (table salt), produce a salty taste. A heterogeneous mix of chemicals, including caffeine, quinine, and many poisonous substances, creates a bitter taste.

Taste buds are located primarily on the tongue, but others are scattered throughout the mouth. Each taste bud contains about 40 to 60 taste cells, clustered in visible bumps called papillae. Taste cells are the receptors of the basic tastes—sweet, sour, salty, and bitter. Taste chemicals—the acids, sweeteners, salts, and bitter components—alter the chemistry of taste cells, triggering a signal that travels through nerve fibers to the brain, where the information is processed.

Saliva plays an important role in taste perception. Saliva, which is composed mostly of water, transports the taste chemicals to the taste cells on the taste buds. Without saliva, we would not be able to experience the basic tastes.

The Japanese and some Americans include a fifth basic taste called **umami,** which is roughly translated as "savoriness" or being full of flavor. Umami is triggered by glutamate, a naturally occurring amino acid first extracted from dried seaweed as monosodium glutamate (MSG). MSG is a popular flavor enhancer used in Asian cooking. Glutamate is also found in mushrooms, asparagus, ripe tomatoes, aged cheeses, and many other foods.

See Chapter 12: Seasoning and Flavoring Food for more information on monosodium glutamate (MSG).

Aroma

The perception of aroma—smell—is much more complex than the perception of the basic tastes and is not as well understood. Although humans can identify only a few basic tastes, they can sense many hundreds, even thousands, of distinct aromas.

Each aroma is highly complex. For example, the aroma of fresh coffee consists of more than 800 separate chemicals. The chemicals in food evaporate or escape and, together, bombard the aroma receptors, called olfactory cells, at the top of the nasal cavity. Smells are perceived as they evaporate through the nose or up the back of the throat as food is chewed and swallowed. From there, nerve fibers transport signals from the olfactory cells to the brain, where the information is processed. Aroma is often thought of as the most important component of flavor. Without aroma, it would be difficult to distinguish between certain foods, such as orange juice and tangerine juice.

Aroma is a large component of flavor. When nasal passages are blocked from a cold, it is common to say that we cannot taste. In fact, in this case we can perceive the basic tastes but are unable to smell. The part of the brain in which information about aromas is received and processed is wired to the part of the brain responsible for memories and emotions. Not surprisingly, aromas often trigger memories or strong emotions. One successful way to entice customers is to have the smell of barbecued chicken or cinnamon buns, for example, wafting through the air, drawing customers to these familiar foods.

Feeling Factors

Just below the skin of the mouth and nose is a series of raw nerve endings. These nerve endings make up a sensory system sometimes called the *common chemical sense,* or the trigeminal nerve system. This system is distinct from basic tastes and aroma. These nerve endings perceive the feeling factors associated with foods. Feeling factors, sometimes called chemical irritation, trigeminal factors, or simply pungency, include the cooling sensation of menthol in mint and the burning sensation of capsaicin, the active ingredient in hot peppers. Other examples of feeling factors include the effervescence of carbon dioxide in carbonated beverages, the sting of alcohol, and the pungency of piperine in black pepper.

Factors Affecting Flavors

The perception of flavor is affected by many factors. For example, two vinaigrettes could have the same amount of acid yet could taste different from each other for a variety of reasons.

Type of ingredient Different ingredients contain different chemical components that can affect the strength and quality of the flavor they produce. In a vinaigrette, the type of acid used will affect the perception of sourness. Vinegar contains twice as much acid as lemon juice, for example. Not surprisingly, a vinaigrette made from vinegar tastes more sour than one made from lemon juice. Additionally, vinegar contains acetic acid, whereas lemon juice contains citric acid. Acetic acid, even when used in the same amount as citric acid, will have a different sourness to it. The saltiness of sea salt, a heterogeneous mix of various salts, has a different intensity and quality than the saltiness of kosher salt, which is essentially sodium chloride.

Product temperature Products that are warmed typically have a stronger taste and aroma than products that are chilled. There are two exceptions to this, however. First, flavor strength diminishes above a certain temperature, possibly because the flavor molecules are moving too rapidly to be received by our sensory receptors. Second, saltiness is perceived as stronger at lower temperatures. Product temperature affects flavor perception, so be sure to complete the final seasoning of food at its serving temperature. Season hot foods when they are hot, and cold foods when they are cold.

Thickness or consistency Thick soups, sauces, and vinaigrettes seem to have less flavor because the flavor molecules of thick foods take longer to dissolve in saliva and to evaporate. Two hollandaise sauces can contain the same ingredients in the same proportions, but if one is whisked more vigorously, it will be thicker and will therefore have a milder taste.

Presence of other tastes, aromas, and feeling factors Sometimes combining tastes, aromas, and feeling factors in food can suppress the perception of specific flavors. Adding a little sugar to vinaigrette makes the vinaigrette taste less sour, even if it contains the same amount of acid. Acids can make foods taste less sweet, and salt can make foods less bitter. Sugar, salt, and monosodium glutamate (MSG) can even affect the perception of aroma. Often a small amount of sugar increases the aroma of fruit, and a small amount of salt or MSG increases the aroma of chicken stock. Some common food pairings seem intuitive—the saltiness of pretzels or peanuts moderates the bitterness of beer; sweet desserts pair well with coffee, as the bitterness of coffee reduces the sweetness of the dessert.

Amount of oil and fat Many taste and odor chemicals are dissolved in the fats and oils in food and are slowly released to evaporate or to dissolve in saliva. As they are slowly released, they provide a balanced and sustained flavor profile. If the amount of fat in food is reduced, flavors are typically released more quickly. The result is often an initial rush of flavor, with little staying power.

Factors Affecting the Ability to Perceive Flavors

Supertasters Supertasters have significantly more than the average number of **fungiform papillae**—the rounded structures on the tongue that house the taste buds. French physiologist and author Jean-Anthalme-Brillat-Savarin first identified this phenomenon in 1826, but it was not until late in the twentieth century that Yale University psychologist Linda Bartoshuk confirmed the existence of supertasters. Her research indicates that about 25% of the U.S. population are supertasters, 50% are normal tasters, and 25% are nontasters. Nontasters are referred to as such simply because they have fewer taste buds.

Most supertasters tend to be intensely sensitive to bitter sensations. The sensitivity to sweet, sour, and salty sensations has not been proven as yet. Supertasting seems to be a genetic trait. Experts believe that supertasters often have more restricted diets than nontasters because they frequently reject bitter-tasting foods such as green tea or coffee. More important, supertasters are affected by likes and dislikes of food learned at home, such as Brussels sprouts and soy products.

Genetics and gender The number of taste receptor cells varies widely. Some people have as many as 10,000 taste buds, and others have as few as 500. This disparity is partly because of genetics. Just as we are born at different weights and with different colors of hair, so too are we born with different numbers of taste buds. In addition, about two-thirds of supertasters are female.

Age The number of taste buds decreases with age, resulting in a progressive loss of taste. This loss becomes measurable at about age 60. People compensate for any loss of taste by increasing a food's flavor intensity, particularly sweetness, saltiness, and aroma.

Disease, malnutrition, and medical treatments More than two million Americans have a significant loss of the sense of smell. This loss may be caused by disease, malnutrition, or medical treatments. People with Alzheimer's disease, for example, have a significantly reduced ability to detect odors; however, their ability to detect the basic tastes remains intact.

Emotional condition Stress, fatigue, or social deprivation can reduce the perception of flavor. This may be related to a reduced output of saliva that occurs under these conditions.

Focus Food is a mix of sensory characteristics. If the focus of the taster concentrates on only one characteristic of the food, such as color, then other characteristics, such as aroma or texture, may be overlooked.

Adaptation The brain processes information about changes from the senses but ignores information that indicates there is no change. Thus, the first bite of a dish is perceived to its fullest. Subsequent bites are not so easily tasted or smelled. Taste boredom can be defeated by orchestrating contrasting flavors and textures to further stimulate the senses.

Flavor Profiles

A flavor profile is a description of a product's flavor from the time it is first smelled until after it is swallowed. Flavor profiles consist of complex blends of basic tastes, aromas, and feeling factors. Often, countries and cultures rely on specific combinations of foods, seasonings, and spices to lend a distinct flavor profile to their cuisine. For example, many East Indian dishes are seasoned with curries.

| See Chapter 12: Seasoning and Flavoring Food for more information on international flavor profiles.

Time is an important factor in flavor profiles. Some flavors, such as the aroma of fresh lemon, are perceived immediately. These light aromas are called *top notes.* Top notes come from molecules that evaporate easily because they are small and light. They provide instant impact. When a product is described as low in flavor, it may lack top notes.

Middle notes follow top notes in a flavor profile. Middle notes are usually large and heavy, produced by slowly evaporating molecules, therefore they provide a satisfying staying power to flavor. Cream flavors from dairy products and the flavors of caramelized sugar are examples of middle notes.

Base notes (background notes) consist mostly of the largest, heaviest molecules, which do not evaporate. Basic tastes, especially sweetness, saltiness, and sourness, and many feeling factors are part of a flavor's base notes. They provide lasting richness. If a product is thin, weak in flavor, and lacking in staying power, it is probably deficient in middle and base notes.

Aftertaste, or finish, is the final flavor that remains in the mouth after food is swallowed. Aftertaste lingers from one bite to the next, and it is the final chance for food to leave a lasting positive impression. The bitterness of chocolate and the pungency from ginger and black pepper are examples of aftertastes.

The most satisfying flavor experiences combine a mixture of taste, aroma, and feeling factors that provide a full flavor profile of top notes, middle notes, base notes, and aftertastes.

Texture of Food

Like flavor, texture is complex. It consists of many different characteristics that occur simultaneously. Sometimes, one textural characteristic predominates, but more often, many textures exist in a given food. For instance, cooked rice can be described as rough or smooth, sticky or slick, hard or soft, moist or dry, chewy or crumbly, and more.

The first impression of texture comes from appearance. Foods can look rough or smooth, soft or hard. However, texture is truly evaluated by touch and by how food responds when touched or when heated by the warmth of the mouth. Food may react differently to the pressure of the hand than to being bitten and chewed. When evaluating the texture of food products, ask the following questions:

- How does the food feel against the soft tissue in the mouth? Is it rough or smooth?
- How does the food react to a force such as squeezing, pulling, biting, or chewing? If it resists force, it may be hard, firm, or thick. If it bounces back, then it is considered rubbery or springy. Should it shatter into pieces, it may be either crumbly or brittle.
- How does the food react to the warmth of your mouth? Gelatins, fats, ice cream, and chocolate are all foods that respond to body heat.
- How much remains to coat the mouth and throat after swallowing? Shortenings, especially those with high melting points, tend to leave a waxy coating in the mouth, whereas oils tend to leave a slick, greasy coating.
- How does the food sound when chewed? Potato chips are not actually crispy unless you hear the crispiness. Similarly, tortilla chips are not crunchy without the sound of crunching. Scientists have determined that the difference between crispiness and crunchiness depends on how long and how high-pitched the sound is during chewing. Crunchy products sound louder longer, and crispy products sound higher pitched for a shorter time.

The Role of the Chef

Regardless of a taster's current abilities, the single most important way of improving the ability to taste is through experience, paying attention to the details of food while eating. With keen awareness, the taster will be able to

- *identify and correct flavor imbalances.*
- *detect off-flavors, such as burnt or spoiled food, before they reach the customer.*
- *create interesting new flavor combinations.*
- *plan food presentation to highlight the most appealing aspects of the dish.*

Shared terminology is useful when referring to the flavor of food. Food manufacturers have standardized terminology to simplify understanding, as with coffee. See Figure 10-1.

Seasoning and Flavoring

When seasoning and flavoring food, the most important flavors in the dish are always the flavors of the main ingredients themselves. Roast beef should taste like roast beef, not the seasonings. Added seasonings and flavorings should emphasize the main flavors rather than disguise them. Too much seasoning or flavoring deadens the taste buds, numbing them to further taste perception.

- Season liquid foods at the end of the cooking process. Just about every recipe will advise adjusting seasonings to taste as one of the final instructions. Taste, then evaluate the flavor to decide whether salt or perhaps a bit of lemon juice or other seasoning will improve the flavor.
- When cooking larger pieces of food, add salt or other seasonings at the start of the cooking process so that the food can absorb them.
- Taste after each addition of seasonings.
- Be sparing with seasonings when preparing something that will be concentrated during cooking. It is always possible to add more seasoning later, if needed, but it is difficult to correct overseasoning.

FIGURE 10-1

Off-Flavors Found in Coffee

SOAPY; WET WOOL; WET DOG

Cause
Chemical changes to oils in coffee

ACRID; KEROSENE

Cause
Chemical changes to acids in coffee

GREEN; HAY; WET PAPER

Cause
Loss of organic material

BURNT; CHARRED; CEREAL-LIKE

Cause
Improper roasting

YEASTY; MILDEWY

Cause
Absorbed moldy or musty odor

- No amount of added seasoning or flavoring can rescue poorly prepared food. The purpose of seasonings and flavorings is to heighten and add extra interest to the main ingredients, not to serve as the main flavor or to cover up natural flavors.
- Most flavorings benefit from being added early in the cooking process to release their flavors and blend with the main ingredients. Whole spices take the longest to disperse; ground spices release flavor quickly and do not require as much cooking time.
- A few flavorings (such as fresh herbs, sherry, and flamed brandy) and condiments (such as prepared mustard and Worcestershire sauce) can be added at the end of cooking.
- Overcooking results in loss of flavor. Most flavors are *volatile,* meaning that they evaporate when heated. The longer a food has cooked, the more flavor has evaporated.

See Chapter 12: Seasoning and Flavoring Food for more information on the process of enhancing foods and on the types of seasonings and flavorings available.

Presentation

Chef Escoffier (1846–1935) once said, "The art of cooking, which in many ways is similar to that of fashion design, will evolve as society evolves. . . . Only basic rules remain unalterable."

The art of presenting food elegantly has always been highly regarded. However, styles of presentation have changed over the years. In previous times banquets featured an entire suckling pig as the main dish and table centerpiece. Today the main pork dish might be presented not as a centerpiece but rather as individually plated slices of tenderloin lying amidst a fruit sauce and garnished vegetables.

The challenge of good food presentation is to arrange or plate the food in an interesting way that pleases the eye as well as the palate. Sometimes this means presenting food simply, letting the natural colors and textures take center stage. See Figure 10-2 on page 136. In other cases presentations can be intricate, such as spun sugar covering a fruit dessert, brightly colored and surrounded with crème anglaise.

Even before beginning to cook, plan the way the food will be presented. Determine how the food will look on the plate; what the focus of the presentation will be; and how the guest's visual, textural, and flavor interest will be engaged throughout the meal. This is done by presenting contrasts within each of the following design components.

Color and Appearance

The colors in the presented food should be vibrant and contrasting. Incorporate other colors to create diversity. For example, a grilled steak, roasted potatoes, and broccolini show a range of colors on the plate. The colors used in a presentation should be not only planned conceptually but also followed through in the cooking process.

Color also can be attained by carefully choosing the plate on which the food will be served. The china may add color and design, but it should not have such a striking appearance that it detracts from the food presentation.

The overall food presentation should be neat, revealing that care was taken in the planning and assembly of the plate. Avoid placing food on the rim of the plate, even when garnishing. The rim of the plate is a neutral zone, acting both as a frame for the presentation of the food and an area for the service staff to pick up the plate. Neither food nor the garnish should touch the rim of the plate.

The appearance of the food should create excitement in the guest, developing a high level of perceived value. Avoid overcrowding the plate with food, but make sure that there is enough food to satisfy the guest.

Height

Often one of the most difficult elements to achieve in plate presentation is that of varying food heights. Achieving this requires careful planning.

An effective presentation may incorporate mashed potatoes that have been neatly piped onto the plate in a circular pinnacle using a piping bag fitted with a star tip. A grilled steak placed with the left end of the meat leaning slightly on the front side of the mashed potatoes adds height. An ear of corn cut on a mild diagonal in half, seasoned and buttered, and stood on each cut end provides additional height and visual interest. If another contrast is

❧ **FIGURE 10-2**
The best presentations focus attention on the food itself.

desired, a dollop of red onion chutney could be added to the presentation to accompany the meat. If added texture is needed, a bit of potato, cut into a paille, could be fried and placed on top of the mashed potatoes.

Shape

Vary the shape of foods in every presentation. Serving meatloaf in the form of a round patty with sautéed peas and parisienne potatoes would create a dull presentation because all the shapes are round. Serving the meatloaf as a slice with snow peas and diced, roasted potatoes would create a better variation of shape.

Some foods work well when molded or cut into attractive shapes with metal rings, cutters, or other forms. These shapes can add height to the plate while providing a neat, clean appearance.

Texture

Include a variety of textures in each plate composition by carefully choosing foods that have soft, hard, chewy, crunchy, creamy, or meaty textures. Food textures

often play as important a role in likes and dislikes of foods as taste does. When the plate of food is first presented, the guest looks at the food and unconsciously compares the different textures in each element on the basis of knowledge provided by previous dining experiences. This informal audit influences whether the guest will enjoy the food, even before taking a bite.

Flavor

Each element of food in a plate presentation should contribute a variety of basic tastes and aromas to the overall flavor of the food. Flavors and seasonings used should be varied and should complement one another. In planning, consider not only the flavor of the raw ingredients but also the preparation and cooking method used.

Temperature

Foods should be served at the appropriate temperature. Hot foods, such as soup, should be served hot on hot dishware (see Figure 10-3 on page 137), and cold foods, such as fresh vegetable salads, should be served cold on cold dishware.

Garnishing

A garnish is an optional, decorative, edible accompaniment that is placed on food to improve its visual appeal. See Figure 10-4. In most instances, it should be the same temperature as the food on which it is served.

When the elements of color and appearance, height, shape, texture, flavor, and temperature have all been achieved in the presentation, then a garnish may not be needed. If the dish is still lacking visual appeal, then those elements should be reexamined and organized before any garnishing takes place. Garnishing should not be used to fix a poorly planned presentation but to heighten the appeal of the dish. As a rule, garnishes should be kept to a minimum. They should be attractive and simple.

Guidelines for Presenting Foods

All foods look best when they are properly prepared. A medium-rare grilled steak should have a surface that glistens, with well-defined hatch marks from the grill. The inside should be an inviting, tender pink, and the steak should be served while it is still hot with the appropriate accompaniments.

How foods are cut can also increase their visual appeal, reflecting an attention to detail. Meats, fish, poultry, seafood, vegetables, and starches should all be cut neatly in uniform pieces appropriate to the cooking method used. This helps control the cooking process so that the food is not overcooked or undercooked. It is also useful in determining portion sizes.

The food on a plate should look like one meal—there should be some logic and consistency to the food items being served together. Elaborate arrangements in the center of the plate can be very effective; however, if overdone, they can present the customer with the challenge of how to eat the food. Many restaurants still use the classical approach to plating whereby the entrée (meat or fish item) is placed in front of the guest and the accoutrements are placed in the back.

Not to be overlooked, inspection of the serving plate is the final step of presentation. Before the plate leaves the kitchen, ensure that there are no stray streaks of sauce or specks of food.

FIGURE 10-3

Hot foods should be served on hot dishware.

FIGURE 10-4

Shown is a dish displaying complementary colors and varying height, shapes, and textures.

11 Cooking Techniques

5000–3500 B.C.
Containers, including metal pots, are used to boil and bake food in pits.

prior to A.D. 1400
Boiling and braising meat become popular as tenderizing techniques.

1500–1700
The art of cooking develops.

mid-1800s
Classical cooking techniques are recorded.

Cooking and the development of cooking techniques began some 750,000 years ago, when humans learned to use the heat energy from fire to prepare food. These Stone Age peoples very likely used simple cooking methods, such as roasting over an open fire or hot coals. Eventually, people baked food in clay pots that were placed on top of hot ashes or they added to food liquid and boiled it in containers that were then placed in pits. By the Middle Ages, people were roasting meat on spits, simmering soups, and stewing foods in pots hung over the kitchen fire. Ovens built next to the fireplace allowed people to roast meat and bake bread. Over the next centuries, stoves with a variety of heat sources—wood, coal, gas, and, finally, electricity—revolutionized cooking.

Heat Transfer

Cooking transfers energy from a heat source to food. Success in cooking will depend in part on understanding the different methods of heat transfer. There are three ways to transfer heat to and through food: conduction, convection, and radiation. See Figure 11-1.

Conduction

Heat transfer by *conduction* takes place in two ways: direct physical contact with another item, and inwardly as heat moves through one part of food to another part of the same food.

When items touch, heat moves from one item to the other. In a filled stockpot on a range, for instance, heat moves from the burner to the stockpot. Then the metal of the stockpot conducts heat to the food. Because this type of conduction requires direct contact, it is a fairly slow means of heat transfer. Some materials conduct heat more rapidly than others. Aluminum and copper conduct heat faster than stainless steel. Glass and porcelain conduct heat more slowly. Liquids (water) transfer heat more rapidly than gases (air).

The inward transfer of heat warms food from the outside inward, as when the interior of a roast cooks not because of contact with a hot item but from the contact with the hot exterior of the roast.

Convection

In *convection,* heat spreads through air or water. Convection can be natural or mechanical.

Natural convection This kind of convection occurs naturally. Warm liquids and gases tend to rise, and cooler liquids and gases fall. This continuous, natural movement distributes heat. Such natural circulation of heat takes place in an oven, a pot of liquid, or a deep-fryer. When a pot of

FIGURE 11-1

Cooking transfers heat to food in three different ways: conduction, convection, and radiation (infrared or microwave.)

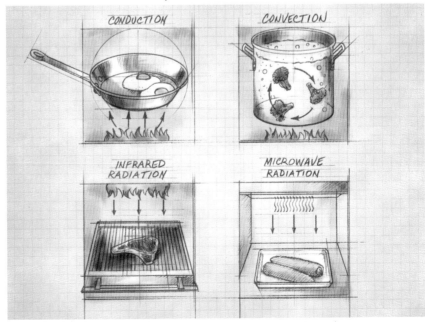

CONDUCTION   CONVECTION

INFRARED RADIATION   MICROWAVE RADIATION

water is placed on an electric burner or gas flame, for instance, the liquid at the bottom of the pot becomes warm and rises to the top. The cooler liquid at the top of the pot falls to the bottom. Then it heats and rises. This natural process creates a circular motion that spreads heat throughout the liquid. Natural circulation of heat is much slower in thick liquids because the hot liquid often does not rise quickly enough from the heat source. The result is burning on the bottom of the pot. Stirring is a safeguard against burning when heating thick liquids. Trunion kettles or steam kettles are used to minimize burning when thick liquids are made in large quantities. Stirring also helps foods heat faster and more evenly.

Mechanical convection This kind of convection involves outside forces. Fans in convection ovens and convection steamers make air or water circulate faster. The increased circulation helps distribute heat more quickly and evenly.

Radiation

Radiation transfers energy to food by waves. When the waves come into contact with the food, they change into heat energy. There are various types of radiation, but only two—infrared and microwave—have kitchen uses.

Infrared Infrared cooking occurs when a heated electric or ceramic element reaches a high temperature and gives off waves. The waves travel at the speed of light in all directions. The food cooks as it absorbs the waves. Heat transfer through infrared radiation takes place in broilers and toasters. Special infrared ovens also can cook food very rapidly.

Microwave Microwave cooking is the fastest type of heat transfer. A special oven generates microwaves. These invisible waves of energy enter the food and cause the water molecules in the food to move around. The molecules rub against one another, creating friction and producing heat. The heat then spreads through the food by conduction and cooks it.

How Cooking Alters Food

What is cooking? Cooking is producing safe, palatable, tasteful, digestible food by using heat energy. Cooking affects the nutritive value, texture, color, aroma, and flavor of food. Understanding how cooking changes food helps achieve the desired results during the cooking process.

All foods contain proteins, fats, carbohydrates (starches and sugars), and water, as well as vitamins, minerals, pigments, and flavor elements. Pigments are the matter in the cells and tissue of animals and plants that provide color. The application of heat energy produces specific changes in a food's nutrients and other components. The degree of change will vary with the cooking technique used, the cooking temperature, and the cooking time.

Nutritive Value

The application of heat in cooking causes all food to lose nutrients. The length of time food is cooked and the cooking technique used are significant factors in how much nutritive value the food retains. The nutritive value of raw food diminishes the longer it cooks, and certain cooking methods may accelerate the loss. Blanching green beans by boiling, for instance, not only destroys nutrients by means of heat but dilutes them into the cooking medium as well. When pouring off the cooking liquid, valuable nutrients are discarded. Steaming is a more effective method for maintaining nutrients in vegetables. Although the exposure to heat causes some nutritive loss, vegetables do not lose nutrients through dilution in the medium.

Texture

Foods change texture during cooking because of the loss of moisture, the softening of tissue, and the coagulation of proteins. All foods contain water and are subject to moisture loss during cooking. As vegetables and fruits cook, for instance, the water molecules in the produce begin to move rapidly. Then the water turns into steam and escapes into the air. At the same time, the fiber that gives structure and firmness to the produce becomes more soluble in water, causing the food to soften.

Protein Coagulation

When heat is applied to a food, its proteins **coagulate,** or change to a solid state from a liquid or semiliquid state. The longer proteins cook, the firmer and drier they become. Consider, for example, the textural difference between a medium-rare steak and one that is cooked well done. Observe the different textures of a soft-cooked egg and a hard-cooked egg. In each case, the proteins in the food that cooks longer become more solid. The loss of moisture causes proteins to shrink during heating. Excessive heat can cause meat proteins to toughen. Following coagulation, proteins will eventually begin to break down. The tenderizing of tough meats that occurs during the stewing and braising processes is a good example of this denaturation of proteins.

Color

As heat cooks the food, chemical changes occur within the food's surface, and the food's sugars react with protein to cause Maillard browning. Though technically not proper, this process is sometimes referred to as *caramelization* as the resulting color mimics that of caramelized sugar.

The cooking process also affects the color of food. Generally, the longer a food cooks, the more its color will change. As meat cooks for extended periods, for example, it loses moisture and *myoglobin,* the primary substance that gives meat its red color. A rare steak maintains this original red color inside because of its short cooking time. A medium-rare steak, by contrast, will be pink inside because it cooks longer. A well-done steak will be brownish-gray in color.

The color of produce also changes with cooking. Naturally occurring pigments give vegetables and fruits their unique coloration. See Figure 11-2. Pigmentation varies from food to food, and cooking techniques affect pigments in different ways.

Certain ingredients that are sometimes used in vegetable cookery, such as wine, lemon juice, vinegar, and salt, also can change the color of produce.

> *See Chapter 27: Vegetables and Legumes for more information on how cooking changes the color of vegetables.*

Aroma

The aroma of food also changes during cooking. As food cooks, volatile components are released that produce distinctive aromas. The aroma created from cooking various foods can be as pleasing as the flavor and presentation of the final plated item.

Flavor

The cooking process also can alter the flavor of food. The same food, cooked in different ways can produce distinctively different flavors. Cooking methods that use liquid instead of fat help extract the unique flavor elements of a food. Slow roasting produces rich flavors in certain foods and deep-fat frying produces a unique flavor that is enhanced by the crispness of the item. Adding seasonings and flavorings at different stages in the cooking process is another way to effect the flavor of food. Like color, methods that enhance flavor increase the appeal of food.

FIGURE 11-2

Foods that contain chlorophyll, such as spinach, broccoli, and peas, have a distinctive green color. Red betalains dominate in beets. Carotenoids are orange-red pigments characteristic of produce such as carrots, winter squash, red peppers, tomatoes, peaches, and citrus fruits. Anthoxanthins give produce such as potatoes, cauliflower, parsnips, onions, and apples their pale yellow color. Red cabbage, eggplant, berries, grapes, and cherries get their purple or red color from anthocyanins.

Types of Cooking Methods

All cooking involves heating food. However, each technique uses a different method to transfer heat to food and has different results. Cooking techniques can be classified as dry, moist, or a combination of both. See Figure 11-3. This classification is based on the medium used for cooking—air, fat, water, or steam.

Dry Cooking

The dry technique transfers heat by hot metal, hot air, hot fat, or radiation. This cooking technique uses no moisture. Any moisture that exudes from the food *evaporates,* or escapes into the air. Baking is an example of dry cooking.

Moist Cooking

The moist technique uses liquid other than oil to transfer heat. The liquid medium may be water, stock, or steam. Simmering is a good example of moist cooking.

Combination Cooking

The combination cooking technique uses both moist and dry cooking methods, beginning with one technique and finishing with the other. Braising is an example of the combination technique.

FIGURE 11-3

Cooking Techniques

Technique	Medium	Method
BAKE/CUIRE AU FOUR	Air	Dry
ROAST/RÔTIR	Air	Dry
SAUTÉ/SAUTER	Fat	Dry
STIR-FRY	Fat	Dry
SHALLOW-FRY	Fat	Dry
DEEP-FRY/FRIRE	Fat	Dry
GRILL/GRILLER	Air	Dry
BROIL/GRILLER	Air	Dry
POACH/POCHER	Water or other liquid	Moist
SIMMER/MIJOTER	Water or other liquid	Moist
BOIL/BOUILLIR	Water or other liquid	Moist
BLANCH/BLANCHIR	Water or other liquid, steam	Moist
STEAM/CUISSON À LA VAPEUR	Steam	Moist
BRAISE/BRAISER	Fat, then liquid	Combination
STEW/ÉTUVER	Fat, then liquid	Combination

Dry Cooking Techniques

In dry cooking techniques, food is cooked by applying heat directly to it or by surrounding it with hot air or hot fat. Descriptions of specific dry cooking methods follow. As for other types of cooking methods, mise en place (ingredients, equipment, tools, and serving pieces) and guidelines for testing for doneness in each case will depend on the food item and recipe used for each specific method. As a rule, the cooking process is not complete until the food has been tasted, the flavor evaluated, and the seasonings adjusted as needed.

Baking

Baking is the method of using dry, hot air to cook food in a closed environment. Heat surrounds the food by radiation and convection and then spreads through it by conduction. The cooking medium contains no perceptible fat or liquid, and the moisture that the food releases in the form of steam evaporates in the heat of the oven or through vents. When food is covered during baking, the cover is often removed toward the end of the process to facilitate browning. Baking is complete when the food is cooked to desired doneness and proper color is achieved.

Mise en place Ingredients for baking vary with the food and recipe. Prepare the food as required. After washing and cutting vegetables, marinate them, toss them with oil, or rub them with butter before baking. Have seasonings at hand to add before and after baking. Peel, core, or pit fruit, and add sugar or other flavorings as directed. Have pastry dough prepared if it is needed for wrapping fruit. Fish may require marination or seasoning with lemon, butter, salt, and pepper. If stuffing fish or mixing it with other ingredients, have those items prepared. Assemble the necessary finishing ingredients, such as herbs, sauces, or seasoned butters. A roasting pan, baking pan, or other piece of cookware is essential. For breads and pastry items, follow the formula for preparation.

Method The baking process is simple. Place the food in a pan that will allow air to circulate, and bake in a preheated oven set to the proper temperature until the desired degree of doneness is achieved.

Testing for Doneness When testing for doneness, vegetables and fruit should be baked until they are just tender, and, for hot holding, should reach 140°F (60°C) or higher. Fish is done when the flesh is beginning to flake and appears opaque. If fish is baked with the bone,

the flesh will separate from the bone when done. Fish should reach an internal temperature of 145°F (63°C) or higher for 15 seconds. If fish is stuffed or mixed with other ingredients, it must reach 165°F (74°C) or higher for 15 seconds. Always follow suggested cooking times. When done, baked foods such as bread and pastry goods will be lightly browned.

Checking the internal temperature of food is the most reliable way to determine whether it is fully cooked and safe to eat. Always use a thermometer to find out whether the food has reached the minimum internal temperature required. This standard is the lowest temperature at which cooking destroys microorganisms that can cause illness. The minimum internal temperature varies from one food to another.

Roasting

Essentially the same as baking, roasting also uses dry heat in a closed environment, usually an oven. Roasting typically applies to meat, poultry, or game. Unlike foods that are baked, however, meat, poultry, or game usually cooks on a rack or bed of mirepoix inside a pan. This arrangement allows the hot air to circulate around the food. It also keeps the food from cooking in its own juices and fat. As in baking, convection transfers heat to the surface of the food, and conduction enables heat to spread through the food. In general, roasting takes longer than baking.

Mise en place Prepare meat, poultry, or game as required. Have available desired seasonings, flavorings, mirepoix (onion, carrots, celery), and brown stock for gravy or jus. Obtain a roasting pan that has low sides and is just large enough to hold the food; a rack, bones, or mirepoix to elevate the food; and a meat thermometer to determine doneness.

Method Roasting, like baking, is a relatively simple process. Place meat, poultry, or game on a rack or bed of mirepoix in a

PROCESS

Baking

Whether baking meat, fish, vegetables, fruit, bread, or pastry, the basic procedure is the same.

To bake an item, follow these steps:

1 Complete mise en place.

2 Preheat the oven to the proper temperature.

3 Place the food in a baking pan appropriate for the food item. Often, lean meat is wrapped with fat, such as bacon, to help meat retain its moisture and add flavor.

4 Place the baking pan of food in the oven, usually on the center rack.

5 Bake until the food item is lightly browned and cooked throughout.

6 Remove from the oven, and hold for service.

roasting pan. Cook it in a preheated oven set to the proper temperature until the desired degree of doneness is achieved. Though most foods can be roasted at temperatures between 325°F–425°F (163°C–218°C), the specific temperature used to roast may be dependent on the type of food being roasted, the size of the food, and the desired result. Roasted meats need to rest several minutes before slicing to allow the meat fibers to relax and keep the juices in the roast.

Before putting the food into the oven, it is common to sear the outside of the meat, poultry, or game. Searing results in a more flavorful roast with a crisp, well-browned exterior. Very large items are usually not seared prior to roasting because the length of time required to cook the item is sufficient to produce a well-browned exterior. Food can be seared manually on the range or in a hot oven.

- *Manual searing*—Add a small amount of oil or fat to cookware, and heat it on a range. Then place the food in the cookware, and let it brown on one side. Turn the food until all surfaces are brown. When searing is complete, transfer the food to a roasting pan, and place it in the oven to finish cooking by roasting.

- *Oven searing*—Place the food in a roasting pan in an oven preheated to 450°F–500°F (232°C–260°C). Cook for approximately 15–20 minutes, or until the outside has begun to turn a golden brown. This method, often preferred to manual searing because it requires fewer steps, sears the roast by means of hot air. As soon as the searing process is done, reduce the oven temperature to 325°F–350°F (163°C–177°C) so that the food cooks slowly and evenly.

Barding and larding Before cooking, either barding or larding could be performed to ensure that lean meats retain their flavor and moisture during roasting. *Barding* involves wrapping lean meat with fat, commonly bacon or fatback, before roasting it. Remove the fat a few minutes before taking the meat out of the oven to allow the surface of the meat to brown. *Larding* is inserting long, thin strips of fat, and sometimes vegetables, into the center of the meat to add moisture and, sometimes, visual appeal.

Roasting

Roasting is a simple cooking method that will bring out the rich flavor of meat, poultry, or game.

To roast an item, follow these steps:

1 Complete mise en place.

2 Preheat the oven to the proper temperature.

3 Select a roasting pan that is large enough to hold the food without overcrowding.

4
If necessary, sear the food following either the manual or oven-searing procedure. (see page 144)

5 Lower the heat and roast the item uncovered and elevated on a rack, on bones, or on a base of mirepoix until the desired color and internal temperature are reached.

6
If the food item is large, add mirepoix about 45 minutes to 1 hour before the item has finished cooking.

7
Baste often to keep the product moist and to add flavor.

8 When determining doneness, remember to consider carryover cooking. (see page 146)

9 Let the roasted food rest before carving.

10
Prepare gravy (or jus) by deglazing the roasting pan with wine, stock, or demi-glace to release the flavors created during roasting. Thicken if desired, and then strain.

FIGURE 11-4

Internal Temperature of Meats

GROUND TURKEY OR CHICKEN
155°F (69°C)

WHOLE POULTRY
165°F (74°C)

POULTRY BREASTS, ROASTS
165°F (74°C)

POULTRY THIGHS, WINGS
165°F (74°C)

GROUND BEEF, PORK, VEAL, OR LAMB
155°F (69°C)

FRESH BEEF, VEAL, OR LAMB
145°F (63°C)

FRESH PORK
145°F (63°C)

HAM
145°F (63°C)

Open-spit roasting Roasting food, especially meats, over an open fire is called *open-spit roasting.* To do this, place the food on a metal rod or a long skewer, and turn it slowly over the heat source. A drip pan placed under the meat will catch the food's juices.

Barbecue (slow roasting) *Barbecue* involves roasting food slowly using dry heat generated by burning wood or hot wood coals. The traditional method cooks food in a pit or a wood-burning oven. Today, however, special cookers or smoke ovens can produce results similar to those of the traditional roasting pit.

Testing for doneness When testing for doneness, always use a meat thermometer to check the internal temperature of the food. See Figure 11-4.

Carryover cooking Be sure to take carryover cooking into consideration during the cooking process. *Carryover cooking* is the continued cooking that occurs even after a large food item is removed from the oven. A large food item, such as a roasted top round of beef, will continue to cook because the outside of the food is hotter than the inside. The cooking will continue until the heat spreads through the food and the temperature throughout is stable. Generally, a large piece of meat will continue to cook for 5–15 minutes after removal from the oven.

Sautéing

Sautéing is a dry cooking method that cooks food quickly in a sauté pan with a small amount of fat. With the help of the fat, conduction conveys heat from the pan to the food. Heat then spreads through the food by conduction. Sautéing is best suited to delicate foods that cook relatively quickly, such as scallops, fillets of fish, tender cuts of meat, vegetables, and fruit. It is customary to serve sautéed foods with a sauce.

Mise en place Because sautéing is a quick cooking method, it is important to have all the necessary ingredients, equipment, and tools ready. Prepare food as required. Have clarified butter or oil at hand. Avoid whole butter, because the milk solids in it burn easily at the high heat used in sautéing. Choose a sauté pan that will accommodate the food without crowding and will allow you to toss or flip smaller pieces easily if desired.

Preparing food for sautéing Before sautéing, cut vegetables and fruit as required. Bone meat and fish as needed. Trim excess fat from meat. Use a mallet to lightly pound or flatten each piece of meat, taking care not to tear the flesh. If desired prepare food for sautéing by *dredging.* To dredge a food item, dip it into seasoned flour, coating it evenly on all surfaces. Shake off the excess to achieve a thin coating.

When dredging, keep the following in mind:

- Avoid dredging foods in advance. Dredging should be performed immediately before sautéing or before dipping in other liquid.
- Dredging before dipping in egg or other liquid helps creates a dry surface to which liquid can adhere when using the standard breading procedure (see page 152)
- Do not stack or overlap dredged foods, as this will result in the dry, floured surface becoming pasty.

Dredging a food item before sautéing helps brown it evenly and prevents its sticking during cooking.

Method To sauté, preheat the sauté pan before adding butter, oil, or other fat. Add just enough fat to coat the bottom of the sauté pan. When the fat nears the smoking point, add the food. If the fat is too cold, the food will absorb the fat, and the result will be a poor-quality product. A high temperature results in proper coloration of the food. Also, do not overcrowd the pan. Too much food in the pan will lower the temperature, inhibiting browning and causing the food to emit natural juices. After the initial searing, lower the heat to allow for even cooking. Turning the food occasionally or flipping the sauté pan to toss the food also helps it cook evenly.

See Chapter 12: Seasoning and Flavoring Food for specific information or smoking points.

Testing for doneness Brown vegetables only as the recipe requires. Remove when cooked or heated through. Remove meat or fish when browned and cooked through. Small or thin pieces will cook quickly over high heat. After larger or thicker pieces of meat are seared over high heat, they may require additional cooking over lower heat.

Deglazing Sauces accompany many sautéed foods. These sauces often incorporate the liquid produced by deglazing the sauté pan after removing the sautéed food and draining off any fat. To *deglaze,* swirl a liquid such as wine or stock in the sauté pan to dissolve the cooked particles of food sticking to the bottom. The deglazing liquid can be used to make a sauce, or can be added to a prepared sauce to augment its color and flavor.

PROCESS

Sautéing

Use sautéing to cook delicate foods or to reheat partially cooked foods. High heat and minimal fat are key to successful sautéing.

To sauté an item, follow these steps:

1 Complete mise en place.

2 Heat the sauté pan over medium-high heat.

3 Add fat to the sauté pan, and continue to heat until the fat is hot but not yet smoking.

4 Add the food to the sauté pan, presentation side down first, if applicable.

5 Cook until the food reaches desired, even browning.

6 Turn the food over, and brown the other side.

7 To make a pan sauce, remove the food, and pour off the excess fat from the sauté pan, or add butter as needed. Add aromatics and/or garnishing ingredients that require cooking.

8 Return the sauté pan to the heat, and deglaze with wine or stock. Reduce liquid as desired.

9 Add any prepared sauce, such as demi-glace, and/or garnishing ingredients if desired, and simmer.

10 To enrich the sauce, monte au beurre (blend in small pieces of butter) if desired.

Cooking Techniques

147

Stir-Frying

Stir-frying is a quick dry technique in which stirring and tossing keep food in constant motion over high heat. A small amount of fat facilitates cooking.

To stir fry an item, follow these steps:

1 Complete proper mise en place.

2 Heat the wok over high heat.

3 Add a small amount of oil to the wok, and continue to heat until the oil is hot and just beginning to smoke.

4 If stir-frying meats, add them to the wok first. All meats should be thinly sliced.

5 Stir-fry. Use a spatula or similar tool to keep food in constant motion, using the entire cooking surface of the wok. Remove meat from the wok if desired.

6 Add remaining food items in proper sequence (longest cooking time first). Stir-fry using as much cooking surface as needed. Return meat back to the wok.

7 Add delicate items such as snow peas toward the end of the stir-frying process.

8 Add any liquids or thickening agents as required, and cook to proper doneness.

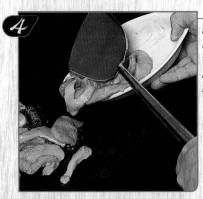

Thickening pan juice á la minute In many classical sauté recipes, demi-glace is added to the sauté pan after it has been deglazed. This allows the natural flavor of the sautéed food to influence the flavor of the sauce. Pan juices also may be thickened á la minute.

Because the á la minute process is so quick, flour-based thickeners, such as roux, should be avoided. Alcohol may be used to deglaze the sauté pan, and then a more neutral liquid such as chicken stock, veal stock, or fish stock is added. The mixture is allowed to reduce slightly, and then it may be thickened using butter, compound butter, or a flavorless thickener, such as cornstarch and water.

> See Chapter 15: Stocks, Sauces, and Soups for information on creating sauces.

Stir-Frying

Stir-frying, an Asian dry cooking method similar to sautéing, uses a large pan with sloping sides known as a wok. Like sautéing, stir-frying involves cooking small pieces of food over high heat, using a minimal amount of fat. Due to the size, metallic composition, and shape of the wok, the potential heat intensity and cooking surface area are much greater than in a sauté pan. This requires a constant, brisk movement of the food and results in shorter cooking times than those for sautéed foods. Unlike sautéing, in which it is usual to move the pan to flip or toss the food, stir-frying involves the use of a spatula or similar tool to stir and turn food in the hot fat. Vegetables and tender, boneless meats are common stir-fry food items.

Mise en place Stir-frying demands that all ingredients, equipment, and tools be ready for use. Cut or slice vegetables as required. Cut meat, poultry, or seafood into dice, chunks, or strips as needed for easy frying. Gather seasonings (salt, ginger root, garlic, scallions, soy sauce). Have wok and appropriate smallwares available. Also have finishing ingredients such as seasonings, liquids (stock, water), and cornstarch at hand.

Use of marinades For increased tenderness and flavor, marinate meats, tofu, and other stir-fry items. Soy sauce, sherry or shaoxing wine, and cornstarch may be used to create a basic marinade for beef, for

 PROCESS

Shallow-Frying

Shallow-frying requires more fat than sautéing but less fat than deep-frying. The amount of fat needed for this cooking method depends on the food to be cooked.

To shallow-fry a food item, follow these steps:

1 **Complete mise en place.**

2 **Heat the fat in the sauté or frying pan to 350°F–375°F (177°C–191°C).**

3  **Place the food in the pan in a single layer, and cook until evenly golden brown on one side.**

4  **Turn the food, and cook until evenly brown on both sides. For thicker items, check the internal temperature, and finish cooking in the oven if necessary.**

5 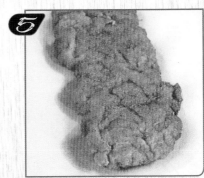 **Remove the food from the sauté or frying pan, and drain on absorbent paper.**

6 **Season and serve immediately.**

7 **If necessary, hold elevated and uncovered in the pan at the proper temperature.**

 PROCESS

Deep-Frying

Deep-frying is a versatile cooking method that is suited to a variety of foods. Proper deep-frying results in food with a crisp exterior and a moist interior.

Use these steps as a guide when deep-frying:

1 Complete mise en place, including breading.

2  Place the food in a fry basket. Avoid overcrowding and stacking.

3  Lower the fry basket in the fat, making sure that the food is completely submerged.

4 Turn the food to brown evenly or use the double basket method of frying, if necessary.

5  When the food is golden brown on all sides and cooked, remove it from the fat, and drain.

6 Place the food on absorbent paper, and season if necessary.

7 Serve immediately or hold uncovered at the proper temperature.

example. Marination times for stir-fry can be as short as 30 minutes.

> *See Chapter 12: Seasoning and Flavoring Food for more information on marinades.*

Method Preheat a wok over high heat. Then add and heat a small quantity of oil. Flavor the oil with seasonings such as ginger root, garlic, or scallions. If using meat, poultry, or seafood, cook it before other ingredients. Stir-fry in batches if necessary to avoid overloading the wok, adding a little oil with each batch. Allow the main food items to brown slightly before stirring and tossing with a spatula. Add soy sauce or other liquid seasonings to the main food items at this point, but only sparingly, so that the main items do not begin to simmer or stew in the liquid. If the recipe requires, remove the main item from the wok when almost done, and set it aside. Add a small amount of oil and additional seasonings to the wok before adding vegetables. Vegetables with the longest cooking time should be added first, ending with those that cook fastest. Return the main food items to the wok to reheat when the vegetables are lightly cooked but still crisp. Season and serve immediately.

Finishing with liquids, sauces, or seasonings If adding a broth, cook vegetables in the liquid until almost done, then return the meat to the wok, and toss to reheat and combine with the vegetables. Stir in cornstarch and water to thicken the liquid into a sauce if desired. Soy sauce, sesame oil, and other seasonings are common finishing ingredients.

Shallow-Frying

Sometimes referred to as pan-frying, *shallow-frying* is a dry cooking method that transfers heat to food with the help of a moderate amount of fat. In addition to using more fat than sautéing, shallow-frying requires longer cooking times and lower heat than either sautéing or stir-frying. It is an appropriate cooking method for larger pieces of food, including chops, chicken, fish, and potatoes.

Mise en place Preparation for shallow-frying is much the same as that for sautéing. Have all ingredients ready. Season, dredge, or bread the food as required. Have sufficient fat at hand for frying multiple batches if needed. A sauté pan or frying pan, tongs or a spatula, and absorbent paper for draining the food are standard equipment and tools for this cooking method.

Method First add fat to the sauté or frying pan and heat to a temperature of 350°F–375°F (177°C–191°C). Use enough fat to cover one-half to three-quarters of the food in the pan. The fat should not smoke, but it should sizzle when you add the food. The food will absorb too much fat if the fat is not hot enough. If the fat is too hot, the surface of the food will burn before it cooks on the inside. Use a tong or spatula to turn the food when it has browned as desired on one side. When the food is well browned and cooked, remove it from the pan, and drain it on absorbent paper. Skim the fat if frying multiple batches. Serve immediately, or hold briefly under a heat lamp.

Testing for doneness Some foods fried according to this method will be done when turned once and are golden brown on both sides. Larger pieces of food may require more than one turn per side or further cooking uncovered in the oven after browning by the shallow-frying method. Use a food thermometer to determine doneness.

Deep-Frying

Deep-frying cooks food by complete submersion in hot fat. It is common to dredge or bread foods or dip them in batter before frying. These coatings help preserve moisture in the food and prevent excessive absorption of fat during frying. They also give foods flavor, color, and a crisp texture. Deep-frying is a relatively quick cooking method carried out at high temperatures, therefore it is best suited to tender foods. Deep-frying is a popular method for cooking potatoes, onions, young chicken, and lean fish or shellfish.

Mise en place Prepare foods as required. Cut foods that will be fried at the same time into uniform pieces. Blanch slow-cooking vegetables. Potatoes should be blanched in 325°F (163°C) fat until tender before being deep-fried at 375°F (191°C) to achieve maximum crispness. Set up the breading station or prepare batter as needed. A deep pan or deep-fryer is necessary, as is a good-quality fat with a high smoke point. Have seasonings ready for use after deep-frying.

Deep-Frying with Batter

Batter keeps food moist on the inside and protects it from excessive greasiness.

To deep-fry battered food:

1 Dredge food in seasoned flour, then dip it into batter.

2 Place food into hot fat using tongs or another suitable utensil. Avoid dropping the food directly into the fryer. It may fall to the bottom of the fryer and stick.

3 Turn the food to brown evenly, if necessary.

4 When the food is golden brown on all sides and cooked, remove it from the fat, and drain.

5 Place the food on absorbent paper, and season if necessary.

6 Serve immediately or hold uncovered at the proper temperature.

Standard Breading Procedure

Breading adds flavor and texture and aids in the coloration of deep-fried foods.

The steps in the standard breading procedure are as follows:

1 Set up a breading station (seasoned flour, egg wash, crumbs).

2 Dredge the dried food item in seasoned flour. Shake off any excess flour.

3 Keeping one hand dry, dip the food into egg wash, coating it completely. Let any excess liquid pour off.

4 Place the food into the crumbs and cover to coat it evenly. Shake off any excess crumbs.

Dredging Dredging is common before deep-frying. Prepare the food by coating with seasoned flour or finely ground crumbs.

Standard breading procedure Breading is the process of coating food with bread crumbs or other crumbs in preparation for frying. The most widely used breading method, known as the *standard breading procedure,* involves a sequence of steps in which food is covered alternately with wet and dry ingredients. Set up shallow containers of the wet and dry ingredients for the procedure, and dry the food to be breaded. Then, dredge the food in seasoned, dry flour. Next, dip the flour-covered food into an egg wash, or mixture of beaten eggs and a liquid such as milk or water. Finally, cover the egg-coated food with dry crumbs. Ground nuts, crushed cereal or crackers, cornmeal, and shredded coconut are some alternatives to bread crumbs. Deep-fry the coated food as soon as possible. When conducting this, keep one hand dry to prevent mixing egg wash and bread crumbs while working.

Batters Battering foods is another way to prepare them for deep-frying. A *batter* is a semiliquid mixture that combines a liquid such as milk, water, or beer with a starch, usually flour. Eggs are another common batter ingredient. The addition of a leavening agent such as beaten egg whites, baking powder, or the carbonation from beer produces a light batter. The procedure for using batters is simple: pat the food dry, dredge it in flour if desired, dip it in the batter, and deep-fry. Always deep-fry foods immediately after dipping them in batter.

Method The proper fat temperature is critical in deep-frying. Preheat the fryer to 350°F–375°F (177°C–191°C). Fat in this temperature range will seal the surface of the food so that it does not become greasy while still allowing the food to cook fully. When the fat is hot, add the food to the fryer and allow it to float freely, or place the food in a basket and submerge. Use tongs to turn the food as needed. Remove when golden brown and fully cooked. Drain on an absorbent surface. Season, if desired, on the draining surface, not over the fat. Deep-fried foods are best when served immediately; however, if holding is necessary, store the fried food in a hot oven. When doing so, follow these guidelines to maintain the food's crisp texture:

- Never cover a container of fried foods.
- Arrange the fried foods in a single layer; stacking foods causes the fried coating to become soggy because moisture cannot escape.

Although a deep pan is traditional for this method of frying, most deep-frying in the foodservice industry today takes place in commercial fryers equipped with wire baskets for submerging food in hot fat. Commercial fryers have some advantages. Like all cooking methods, deep-frying must take into account *recovery time,* or the time it takes for the fat to return to the required cooking temperature after the food has been submerged. Commercial fryers generally have a much shorter recovery time. In addition, the design of commercial equipment helps maximize the life of the frying fat.

Use the double-basket method for foods that float as they cook. When placing a second basket on top of the basket containing the food, the second basket keeps the food submerged, ensuring that it cooks fully. The double-basket method also helps food cook evenly.

Testing for doneness Determining when deep-fried foods are done can be difficult. Color is one sign: foods should be golden brown on all sides. Browning, however, is not a guarantee that the food is fully cooked on the inside. Temperature and timing also help determine doneness. An instant-read thermometer should be used to check the internal temperature of large food items, such as fried chicken. The internal temperature should reach 165°F–170°F (74°C–77°C). Removing smaller pieces of the food from the fat and cutting them open is another method for testing doneness.

Grilling

Grilling uses radiant heat from below to cook food on an open grid. In commercial kitchens, gas or electric grills are common heat sources for grilling. Some commercial kitchens have charcoal or wood-fired grills,

PROCESS

Grilling

Grilling is a favorite method for tender foods that cook relatively quickly.

Follow these steps for grilling meat, poultry, or fish.

 Complete mise en place.

 Clean and heat the grill.

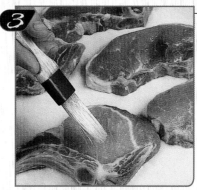
Season the food to be grilled, and brush with oil, if necessary, to prevent sticking.

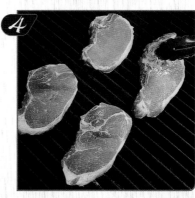
Place the food on the grill, presentation side down.

To make cross-hatch marks after the first grill marks appear, move the food to a new spot on the grill, rotating the food 90 degrees.

When the food shows cross-hatch marks, turn it over, and finish cooking to desired doneness.

which give a smoky flavor to foods. Meat, poultry, seafood, vegetables, and fruits are all suitable for grilling.

Mise en place Cut vegetables and fruits into desired shapes and sizes. Season, marinate, coat, or prepare as the recipe indicates. Prepare tender, well-marbled cuts of meat by trimming off connective tissue and excessive fat. Trimming fat will help prevent flare-ups during grilling. Marinate or season the food, as required. Have butter, oil, or barbecue sauce ready for basting, if needed. Have compound butters or sauces available if desired for service. Tongs are useful for turning meat, poultry, and fish. Use skewers to grill vegetables and fruits. Bamboo or wooden skewers should be soaked in water before using.

Using marinades Marinades add distinctive flavors to all kinds of grilled food. Marinades suitable for grilling include both simple mixtures of oil, herbs, and seasonings and more involved cooked blends of wine and other ingredients. A coating of sugar, honey, and spices or macerating with liqueurs or fruit juice gives grilled fruit extra flavor. Allow sufficient time for marination. Be sure to cover food completely, or turn as needed to promote even distribution of flavor. Marinated foods should be kept refrigerated.

| See Chapter 12: Seasoning and Flavoring Food for more information on marinades.

Method Properly grilling foods involves preheating the grill while performing mise en place. Lightly brush the food with oil, as required, before placing it on the grill. Coat fruit with sugar or honey to aid caramelization. Once on the grill, the food should remain in the same position until it displays distinct grill marks on its underside. When the grill marks are created as desired, use tongs to turn the food. It is best to turn food only once during cooking. Cook food to completion on the other side, adjusting the food's position on the grill or the grate's distance from the heat source as needed.

Creating grill marks Place the food on the grill presentation side down. Cook until grill marks develop where the food makes contact with the grill. To make cross-hatch markings, lift and turn the food 90 degrees after one set of grill marks has developed,

and cook until cross-hatch marks appear. Then turn the food over, and finish cooking.

Testing for doneness Grill meat to the requested degree of doneness. Rare, medium-rare, medium, and medium-well are common orders for grilled meats. See Figure 11-5. Internal temperature as determined by using a food thermometer, checking food color, and pressing food with a finger for resistance will help tell when meat is done as desired. Cook poultry until well done, using internal temperature, touch, looseness of joints, and juice color as a gauge of doneness. Look for the following signs of doneness in fish: light charring and coloring on exterior and opaque, firm flesh that separates easily from the bone and has begun to flake. Fish should be cooked to an internal temperature of 145°F (63°C). Vegetables and fruits should be tender and lightly charred.

Griddling

Griddling is similar to sautéing in heat transfer (conduction). Griddling, however, involves cooking on a solid metal surface called a griddle over a gas or electric heat source. Griddles are usually flat, although some have a grooved design for cooking meats that simulate the look and flavor of grilling. Griddling is a common method for preparing breakfast and luncheon items such as pancakes, eggs, meat, and sandwiches. When cooking some foods, it is common to add a small amount of fat to the hot griddle to prevent sticking. Cooking temperatures for griddling are more consistent and adjustable and generally lower than those for sautéing, around 350°F (177°C).

Broiling

Although similar to grilling in some ways, *broiling* differs in that it uses radiant heat from above, not below, to cook food. Tender meats, poultry, fish, and selected vegetables lend themselves to this dry cooking technique. Commercial kitchens usually have either a grill or a broiler. Broilers have a gas or electric heat source and thus, unlike grills, do not offer the possibility of adding extra flavor to food by burning charcoal or wood. Full heat is customary for broiling, and temperatures are higher than for grilling. Infrared broilers can reach temperatures that exceed 1,500°F (816°C). The procedure for broiling is much the same as that for grilling. Place the food on a preheated metal

rack under the heat source. The hot rack will make grill marks on the food. To avoid grill marks, you may broil the food on a heat-proof platter. As in grilling, it is usual to turn broiled foods over just once to cook on both sides.

FIGURE 11-5

When grilling meat, do not rely on timing alone to determine the degree of doneness. Also take into account resistance, color, and internal temperature.

RARE

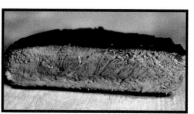

MEDIUM RARE

MEDIUM

MEDIUM WELL

WELL

FIGURE 11-6

Small bubbles may appear on the surface of the cooking liquid during poaching.

Moist Cooking Techniques

In moist techniques, food is cooked by submerging or partially submerging it in hot water or other liquid or by surrounding it with steam. Procedures for specific moist cooking methods follow. As with the other cooking methods, mise en place (ingredients, equipment, tools, and serving pieces) and guidelines for testing for doneness will depend on the food being prepared and the recipe used each specific method. It is important to remember that for most methods the cooking process is not complete until the food has been tasted, its flavor evaluated, and seasonings adjusted as needed.

Poaching

Poaching cooks food gently in a small amount of flavorful liquid. Convection transfers heat from the liquid to the food. Poaching is an excellent technique for cooking delicate foods such as fish, eggs, and fruit. Food can be poached on the range or in the oven.

Mise en place Prepare food as required. Have cooking liquid available. Stock, court bouillon, or broth will enhance the flavor of the food being poached. Choose a pot suited to the quantity and type of food being cooked. Have ready a rack for immersing the food and any desired sauce or sauce ingredients.

Method Heat the poaching liquid to a simmer. Submerge the food in the hot liquid by dropping it slowly or lowering it in a rack. Reduce the heat so that the surface of the liquid moves just slightly during the cooking process. Slight bubbling may occur at the higher temperature ranges of the poaching process. See Figure 11-6. Maintain a cooking temperature of 160°F–185°F (71°C–85°C). When the cooking process is complete, remove the food from the liquid. Keep the food moist and warm until it is served. Incorporate the poaching liquid in a sauce as desired.

Testing for doneness Monitoring internal temperature, firmness, and texture are the best ways to determine doneness.

Simmering

Like poaching, *simmering* cooks food by means of mild convection and usually in a flavorful liquid. Simmering, however, occurs at a slightly higher temperature than poaching, with more consistent bubbling on the surface of the cooking liquid. Although it produces more bubbles than poaching, simmering is a less turbulent technique than boiling, and offers the following advantages:

- Less moisture loss and shrinkage of the food
- Less evaporation and better control over any evaporation that does occur
- Less breakup of delicately textured foods such as fish

Simmering is the most commonly used moist cooking method. Simmering also can have the effect of reducing a liquid, such as a sauce to achieve a more concentrated flavor. It is also a viable blanching, or precooking, method for foods with fragile textures and little connective tissue.

Mise en place Prepare food according to the recipe. Select a cooking liquid, such as stock or broth, that will augment the food's flavor. Have an appropriate pot available.

Method Simmering is similar to poaching. First, bring the liquid to a boil. Add the food to the liquid, and completely submerge it. Adjust the heat to maintain a cooking temperature of 185°F–200°F (85°C–93°C). Steam bubbles that rise slowly to the surface of the liquid are evidence of a good simmer. See Figure 11-7 on page 156. Remove the food when fully cooked. Keep moist and warm until it is served.

Testing for doneness In general, simmer foods until moist and tender. The size of the food will determine how long it should cook.

FIGURE 11-7

Simmering should show some bubbling action near the surface of the cooking liquid.

Boiling

Boiling also transfers heat from liquid to food by convection but usually with a greater quantity of liquid and with greater agitation than in poaching or simmering. In boiling, liquid rises to the boiling point and remains at that temperature throughout cooking. The extremely rapid and bubbling convection movement of boiling makes it an appropriate cooking method for only a few vegetables and starches. Although the high temperature of this moist technique cooks foods quickly, the very brisk circular motion of the liquid can damage delicate foods. Boiling is an effective method for cooking pasta, for instance, because pasta keeps its shape well while cooking. See Figure 11-8. Boiling also prevents pasta from sticking as it cooks. By contrast, rapidly boiling liquid can tear a tender piece of fish apart, and the high temperature of the liquid makes proteins in meat, fish, and eggs tough and unpalatable.

Mise en place Prepare food items as specified in the recipe. Have the appropriate cooking liquid (water, stock, court bouillon) ready. Select a saucepan or stockpot that will accommodate both the food and ample liquid. Have slotted spoon, spider, or colander available as needed.

FIGURE 11-8

Agitated bubbling is characteristic of the boiling process.

Assemble and prepare finishing ingredients and seasonings.

Method Bring the cooking liquid to the boiling point—212°F (100°C) at sea level. Add the food to the boiling liquid, and completely submerge it. Return the liquid to a boil. The liquid should continue to move rapidly, and large bubbles should rise and break the surface. Stir the contents of the pot occasionally to prevent sticking and to ensure even cooking. When the food is done, remove it from the liquid, or drain. Serve immediately or hold at the proper temperature.

> Be aware that it takes longer to boil foods at higher altitudes. As altitude, or the height above sea level, increases, the boiling point of water decreases. Water boils at around 203°F (95°C) at 5,000 feet (1,500 m) above sea level, for instance. Because the temperature of boiling water at 5,000 feet (1,500 m) is lower than that of boiling water at sea level, food will need more time to cook in the water at the higher altitude.

Testing for doneness Cook food to desired doneness or tenderness. When cooking pasta, test by removing a piece from the water and biting o3r pinching it. It should be firm to the tooth, or bite, or what is referred to as *al dente*.

> See Chapter 26: Pasta and Grains for more information on cooking pasta.

Blanching

Using boiling to cook food briefly and partially as a first step to other processes is *blanching*. Sautéing blanched food before serving is one way to complete the cooking process. Blanching can be used to loosen skins of vegetables and fruits (a process known as *monder*), soften herbs, remove undesirable odors or flavors, or set the texture and color of foods. Although blanching usually takes place in water, hot fat is a blanching medium for some foods, especially potatoes.

Mise en place Prepare food as required. Have the cooking liquid and a stockpot or saucepan at hand. A slotted spoon or spider should be available for removing the food. Cold water or an ice bath should be ready for quickly cooling the blanched items.

Method Blanching is usually a two-step process:

1. Completely submerge the food in boiling liquid, and lightly cook it.
2. Remove the blanched food from the liquid, and immediately plunge it into cold water or an ice bath. This step, known as shocking, stops the cooking process.

Testing for doneness Cooking times for blanching are very brief. Cook food only until *al dente*. Also blanch to preserve the color and texture of the food.

Steaming

Steaming is the method of cooking foods in a closed environment, such as a covered pot or pan, filled with steam. As liquid heats in the covered pot or pan, it turns into vapor. The food does not touch the liquid but rests above it in a rack or a basket. Convection transfers heat from the steam to the food. Steam conveys much more heat than does boiling liquid; thus steaming generally cooks foods faster than other moist cooking methods do. Steaming is widely used for cooking vegetables because it is quick and gentle, and helps preserve nutrients. Steamed fish and shellfish are also popular.

Mise en place Prepare food as required. Cut vegetables into uniform pieces. Have water, court bouillon, or other cooking liquid ready as appropriate. Assemble seasonings (salt, pepper, herbs, spices) as desired. Prepare steamer, pot or pan with lid, or parchment or foil, as required. Also have a rack, bamboo, or basket at hand if needed.

Method The traditional method of steaming involves placing a rack or stainless steel steamer basket in a pot or pan containing a small amount of water or a flavorful liquid. (Pacific Rim cookery uses a bamboo steamer, which sits on top of the pot or wok.) The rack or basket should just clear the surface of the liquid so that the steam can circulate around the food. Cover the pan, and bring the liquid to a boil. When the liquid boils and begins to vaporize, place the food in a single layer on the rack or in the basket. Cook covered to desired doneness.

Pressureless steaming The steam trapped in a pressureless steamer creates a certain amount of pressure that helps accelerate the cooking process. At normal pressure, steam is 212°F (100°C), the same as boiling water. Although slower than pressurized steaming, pressureless steaming cooks food faster than do other moist cooking methods.

Pressurized steaming Pressure steamers hold steam under pressure, increasing its temperature beyond 212°F (100°C) and cooking food very rapidly. When cooking carrots at a pressure of 5 psi (pounds per square inch), for example, the temperature of the steam rises to 227°F (108°C). At 15 psi, the steam temperature will rise to 250°F (121°C).

Steaming en papillote Cooking *en papillote* is an application of steaming. *En papillote* cookery involves sealing a food, often seafood, with aromatics and liquid in nonporous (parchment) paper and baking the packet in a hot oven. See Figure 11-9. As the heat in the packet increases, the moisture in the food begins to turn to steam. The steam is not able to escape the tightly sealed edges of the packet and thus remains inside it, cooking the food.

Testing for doneness It is important to keep the steaming chamber closed to maintain vaporization, however this makes it a bit more difficult to monitor doneness when steaming. For this purpose, commercial steamers are equipped with timers. Recipes designed specifically for steaming usually include appropriate cooking times. However, many of the same methods used to determine doneness in other cooking techniques apply to steaming.

FIGURE 11-9

The presentation of food cooked en papillote can be quite dramatic, with steam escaping from the packet as it is cut open.

Steaming

Steamers are standard equipment in commercial kitchens. Because they create a more controlled environment than is possible in a pot or pan, steamers, whether pressureless or pressurized, cook food more quickly.

To steam food, follow these steps:

1 Complete mise en place.

2 Preheat the steamer (pressureless or pressurized).

3 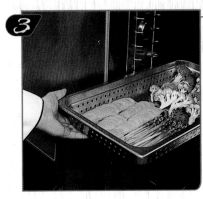 Place food in a perforated pan and insert into the steam chamber.

4 Close the door of the steamer, making sure that it locks.

5  Set desired cooking time, keeping in mind that a steamer cooks food more quickly than does steaming in a covered pot or pan.

6  Remove food from the steamer when cooked to desired doneness, being careful to allow steam to escape before reaching into the hot steam chamber.

7 Season and serve immediately, conduct the final cooking process, if any, or shock for later preparation.

Braising

Braising is a combination cooking technique used to cook tougher cuts of meat and vegetables such as cabbage and celery.

To braise food, follow these steps:

 1 Complete mise en place.

2 Sear and brown the food in a pan with hot oil.

3 Remove the food when properly browned and add the mirepoix. Cook until desired doneness is achieved. Tomato product often is added to help tenderize the food and add both color and flavor to the braise.

4 Deglaze the pan with wine or stock.

5 Add stock or demi-glace to the pan and bring to a simmer. Add just enough liquid to cover the food by one- to two-thirds. Adjust the seasonings according to the recipe.

6 Return the food to the pan and cover with a lid if desired. Place the pan in a moderate oven or finish cooking on the range. Turn and baste often during the cooking process.

7 Braised foods are done when they are fork-tender.

8 Strain the braising liquid and use as a sauce. Thicken and/or adjust the seasonings as necessary.

Combination Cooking Techniques

Combination techniques involve both a dry cooking method and a moist cooking method. The usual sequence is to use dry heat to brown food by searing and then to simmer or steam the food in a liquid until done. During the dry cooking method, heat moves from the pan to the food by conduction. During the moist cooking method, heat travels by conduction from the liquid to the food and from the air by convection in the form of steam. The dry technique elicits flavor and develops color, and the moist technique completely cooks and tenderizes the food. The two main combination techniques are braising and stewing.

Braising

Braising is cooking food in a small amount of seasoned and flavored liquid over low heat, usually after an initial browning. Foods ideal for braising include tough cuts of meat, mature birds, and vegetables such as cabbage, celery, lettuces, and leeks. Braising is a long, slow process. It produces a very flavorful liquid medium, because the flavors extracted from the food become concentrated during cooking. This cooking liquid accompanies the braised food as a sauce.

Mise en place Prepare food as required. Cut vegetables, meat, and poultry in large pieces, or leave whole. Truss, or tie, large pieces of meat or whole poultry to ensure retention of moisture, even cooking, and a more appealing presentation. Have available fat for searing, liquid for cooking, mirepoix, seasonings, and flavorings as needed, and thickening agents for making a sauce as an accompaniment. Ready a heavy-bottom braising pan with a cover.

■ *See Chapter 23: Poultry for more information on trussing.*

Method Place food in a preheated pot or pan on the range, and sear and brown on all sides in a small amount of fat. Dredge meat or poultry before browning if desired. Then remove the food and sauté mirepoix and/or aromatic vegetables. Add tomato product to help tenderize the main food item and add color and flavor. Deglaze the pan with wine or stock. After deglazing, add stock or sauce to the pan, and return the seared food to the pan. Use only enough liquid to cover one- to two-thirds of the food. Add other ingredients, such as vegetables and seasonings, as desired. Cook over low heat on the range, or place the pan in the oven and cook the food slowly at 325°F–350°F (163°C–177°C). Oven-braising results in more uniform cooking because heat surrounds the pan and food. It also requires less attention because the temperature remains stable and it reduces the chance of scorching. Covering the pan in either location is optional however, in preparations of fish or vegetables to which little liquid is added, covering is essential to trap steam and allow the food to cook with adequate moisture. Some chefs cover foods through most of the braising process then remove the cover to complete cooking and concentrate the pan juices.

Testing for doneness Properly braised meat, fish, and poultry should be fork-tender but should not break apart. When a braising fork is inserted into the food, it should enter with little resistance and it should be easily withdrawn. Vegetables should be tender and moist. Though timing by itself is usually insufficient to determine doneness, it is easier to use timing as a guide when braising fish and vegetables.

Using the cooking liquid It is customary to use the cooking liquid as a sauce for braised foods. When braising is complete, remove the main food items, and strain the liquid into a saucepan. Reduce the liquid by simmering, or add roux, cornstarch, or arrowroot to thicken the liquid. Taste, and then season as needed with salt, pepper, and other spices.

Stewing

Similar to braising, *stewing* is a combination cooking method for cooking smaller pieces of food in liquid after browning or blanching. Meats, poultry, and the same kinds of vegetables that are suited to braising also lend themselves to stewing. In contrast to braising, liquid completely covers the food during stewing, resulting in a shorter cooking process. Like braising, stewing produces a very flavorful liquid because the extracted flavors of the stewed food become concentrated during the cooking process. Stewed foods are usually served with their cooking liquid, which is seasoned and often thickened.

Mise en place Trim fat from meat. Cut meat and vegetables into bite-sized pieces. Have fat for searing or sautéing available if needed. Prepare cooking liquid, seasonings, and any ingredients needed for thickening the cooking liquid. Choose a heavy pot or pan.

Method Stewing is very similar to braising. Steps for making the two main types of stew—brown stews and white stews—differ slightly, however. The basic steps for stewing are as follows, with variations noted for brown and white stews:

1. First, sear, sauté, blanch, or sweat the food. For a brown stew, sear the meat in fat over high heat. For the white stew known as a fricasse, sauté the meat in a small quantity of fat over low heat so that it does not brown; for a blanquette, also a white stew, blanch and then rinse the meat before further cooking. Sauté or sweat vegetables for stewing.

2. Cover the food completely with liquid, and simmer. (Only partially cover vegetables if they are the main food item for stewing.)

3. Cover and cook on the range or in a 325°F–350°F (163°C–177°C) oven until tender. If meat is the main item, add a bouquet garni (and a tomato product if making a brown stew) before covering.

4. During the cooking process, add vegetables to the main food item if desired. Time so that they will be done when the main food item is fully cooked.

Testing for doneness Stewed foods should be moist and tender when done. Test meat by piercing with a fork or by removing a portion and cutting with a fork.

Sweating

Sweating uses the natural moisture that exudes from the food during the cooking process as the cooking medium, allowing food to cook slowly without browning. To sweat food, cook it over low heat in a covered pan. This allows the food to release moisture and soften. Sweating helps vegetables develop their natural sweetness. As it draws out flavor without browning, sweating is an appropriate choice for cooking vegetables for soup or other dishes that will be combined with other ingredients.

Mise en place Prepare food as required. Have oil or fat available. A pan or pot with a tight-fitting lid is essential.

Method Add fat as required to the pan or pot, and heat. Place vegetables or other food items in the pan or pot, and cover. Cook the food slowly over low heat allowing it to release its juices and simmer. Shake the pan or pot or stir occasionally to prevent sticking and to promote even cooking.

Testing for doneness Food will soften as it exudes moisture and cooks in its juices. Cook until food reaches desired tenderness.

Yankee Pot Roast

INGREDIENTS

	U.S. Standard	Metric
Beef, chuck	3 1/2 lbs.	1.6 kg
Oil	as needed	as needed
MIREPOIX		
Onions, peeled, 1/2" (1.27 cm) rough-cut	6 oz.	170 g
Celery, trimmed, 1/2" (1.27 cm) rough-cut	4 oz.	115 g
Carrots, peeled, 1/2" (1.27 cm) rough-cut	4 oz.	115 g
Garlic, cloves, peeled and crushed	4 each	4 each
Red wine, dry	4 oz.	120 ml
Tomato, purée	1 1/2 oz.	45 ml
Marjoram, dried	1/2 tsp.	2.5 ml
Thyme, dried	1/2 tsp.	2.5 ml
Basil, dried	1/2 tsp.	2.5 ml
Spanish paprika	1/2 tsp.	2.5 ml
Brown beef stock	1 pt.	500 ml
Demi-glace	1 pt.	500 ml
Salt	TT	TT
Black pepper	TT	TT

METHOD OF PREPARATION

1. Gather all the ingredients and equipment.

2. Preheat the oven to 325°F (163°C).

3. Trim the beef of excess fat and silverskin; *truss.*

4. Place a thin layer of oil in an appropriately sized *rondeau,* and heat to smoking. Add the meat, and sear until well browned on all sides.

5. Remove the meat, and add the mirepoix and garlic cloves to the rondeau; sauté until lightly browned.

6. Add the red wine, and deglaze. Lower the heat; add the tomato purée, herbs, and paprika. Continue to cook for 2 more minutes.

7. Add the stock and demi-glace, and bring mixture to a boil. Season lightly with salt and pepper. Final seasoning will be done when finishing sauce.

8. Return the meat to the pot, cover tightly, and cook in preheated oven until fork-tender.

9. Remove the meat from the braising liquid. Hold tightly covered in a hotel pan (add a bit of the braising liquid to keep beef moist) at 140°F (60°C) or higher until service.

10. Strain the braising liquid into a saucepan. Reduce liquid until proper flavor and consistency is achieved, or thicken with roux or cornstarch. *Dépouille,* taste, and adjust seasonings as needed. Hold at 140°F (60°C) or higher in a bain-marie until service.

11. For service, remove trussing from beef, and slice thinly against the grain. Shingle three slices on a preheated dinner plate, and *nappé* with sauce.

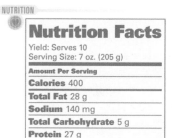

Crabmeat Benedict

INGREDIENTS	U.S. Standard	Metric
Butter	5 oz.	140 g
Crabmeat, cleaned and meat shredded	10 oz.	285 g
English muffins, lightly toasted, warm	10 each	10 each
Poached eggs	20 each	20 each
Hollandaise sauce, heated to 140°F (60°C)	20 oz.	570 g

METHOD OF PREPARATION

1. Gather all the ingredients and equipment.

2. In a sauté pan, melt the butter; add the crabmeat and sauté until heated throughout.

3. To serve, place muffin halves toasted side up on a preheated plate. Top each with a 1-oz. (28-g) portion of crabmeat. Place one poached egg on each, and *nappé* with sauce.

Steamed Asparagus with Lemon and Parmesan

INGREDIENTS

INGREDIENTS	U.S. Standard	Metric
Asparagus, washed	3 lbs.	1.4 kg
Leeks, green tops, cut into twelve 6–8″ (15.24–20.32 cm) strips (save white section for other uses)	as needed	as needed
Salt	as needed	as needed
Butter, melted	2 oz.	55 g
Parmesan cheese, grated	2 oz.	55 g
Lemon, washed, cut into 6 wedges	2 each	2 each

METHOD OF PREPARATION

1. Gather all the ingredients and equipment.

2. Preheat the steamer.

3. Trim away the tough ends from the bottom of the asparagus, and then trim stalks all to the same size. Peel if desired.

4. Blanch the leek strips until pliable; shock, and drain.

5. Divide the asparagus into 10 equal portions, and tie each portion into a bundle with a leek strip.

6. Lay the bundles in a perforated hotel pan. When ready for service, steam the asparagus until tender yet crisp. Remove from steamer and sprinkle lightly with salt.

7. Drizzle each bundle with 1 tsp. (5 g) each of butter and Parmesan cheese.

8. Arrange a lemon wedge alongside. Serve immediately.

Chef's Notes

Because asparagus contains chlorophyll, the color will dull quickly if exposed to an acid. Therefore, to prevent color loss, the lemon is served on the side.

COOKING TECHNIQUES

Steaming (Traditional):
1. Place a rack over a pot of water.
2. Prevent steam vapors from escaping.
3. Shock or cook the food product throughout.

NUTRITION

Nutrition Facts

Yield: Serves 10
Serving Size: 5 oz. (140 g)

Amount Per Serving

Calories 140

Total Fat 7 g

Sodium 170 mg

Total Carbohydrate 16 g

Protein 7 g

Wiener Schnitzel

INGREDIENTS

	U.S. Standard	Metric
Veal cutlets, 5 oz. (140 g) each	10 each	10 each
Salt	TT	TT
White pepper, ground	TT	TT
Milk	6 oz.	180 ml
Flour, seasoned	as needed	as needed
Eggs, large, lightly beaten	4 each	4 each
White bread crumbs, fresh	1 lb.	454 g
Butter, clarified	8 oz.	225 g
Vegetable oil	6 oz.	180 ml
Lemons	3 each	3 each
Anchovies, drained of oil	10 each	10 each
Capers, drained and rinsed	2 oz.	55 g
Parsley, washed, squeezed dry, and chopped	1/2 oz.	15 g

METHOD OF PREPARATION

1. Gather all the ingredients and equipment.

2. Pound each veal cutlet lightly with a meat mallet to tenderize. Season with salt and pepper.

3. *Dredge* cutlets in milk, and then lightly coat with flour, shaking off any excess. Dip in egg, and then coat with bread crumbs. Lay the breaded cutlets out on a parchment-lined sheet pan. Refrigerate at 41°F (5°C) or lower until needed.

4. Combine the clarified butter and oil to make a *fortified butter.* Heat sauté pan with enough fortified butter to shallow-fry the cutlets. Fry the veal until golden brown and crisp on both sides, turning once. Remove and drain on a rack, and then transfer to a sheet pan lined with plenty of absorbent paper. Hold at 140°F (60°C) or higher.

5. Trim ends off lemon, and cut into 10 round slices; remove seeds.

6. To serve, place a cutlet on a preheated dinner plate, and garnish with a lemon slice, an anchovy, a sprinkle of capers, and parsley.

COOKING TECHNIQUES

Shallow-Frying:

1. Heat the cooking medium to the proper temperature.
2. Cook the food product throughout.
3. Season, and serve hot.

GLOSSARY

Dredge: to coat with flour

Fortified butter: clarified butter to which another fat has been added

NUTRITION

Nutrition Facts

Yield: Serves 10
Serving Size: 5 oz. (140 g)

Amount Per Serving

Calories 390

Total Fat 27 g

Sodium 330 mg

Total Carbohydrate 5 g

Protein 31 g

Spaghetti Aglio e Olio

INGREDIENTS

Ingredients	U.S. Standard	Metric
Olive oil	3 oz.	90 ml
Garlic, peeled, minced	6 cloves	6 cloves
Crushed red pepper	1/2 tsp.	2.5 ml
Black olives, pitted, sliced	4 oz.	115 g
Spaghetti	1 1/2 lbs.	680 g
Salt	TT	TT
Black pepper, ground	TT	TT
Parmesan cheese, shredded	4 oz.	115 g
Parsley, flat leaf, washed, squeezed dry, chopped	1/2 oz.	15 g

METHOD OF PREPARATION

1. Gather all the ingredients and equipment.
2. Heat the olive oil in a sauté pan over medium heat. Add the garlic, and sauté until fragrant, but not browned.
3. Remove pan from heat, allow to cool slightly, and then add the crushed red pepper and the olives; set aside until service.
4. Bring a large pot of salted water to a boil.
5. When ready for service, place the spaghetti in the boiling water, stir, and cook until al dente. Strain but do not rinse.
6. While the spaghetti is cooking, gently reheat the garlic, oil, and olive mixture.
7. Toss the spaghetti into the hot garlic/olive mixture, mix well, taste, and season with salt and pepper.
8. Serve immediately on preheated dinner plates with the Parmesan cheese and parsley sprinkled over the top, or hold briefly at 140°F (60°C) or higher.

Sautéing:
1. Heat the sauté pan to the appropriate temperature.
2. Evenly brown the food product.
3. For a sauce, pour off any excess oil, reheat, and deglaze.

Boiling (At sea level):
1. Bring the cooking liquid to a rapid boil.
2. Stir the contents, and cook the food product throughout.
3. Serve hot.

NUTRITION

Nutrition Facts

Yield: Serves 10
Serving Size: 5 oz. (140 g)

Amount Per Serving

Calories 400

Total Fat 15 g

Sodium 300 mg

Total Carbohydrate 57 g

Protein 10 g

Cooking Techniques

165

Old-Fashioned Beef Stew

INGREDIENTS

	U.S. Standard	Metric
Vegetable oil	as needed	as needed
Beef, bottom round, cut into 1" (2.54 cm) pieces	2 lbs.	910 g
Onions, peeled, cut parmentier	1/2 lb.	225 g
Carrots, washed, peeled, rewashed, cut parmentier	6 oz.	170 g
Celery, washed, trimmed, cut parmentier	6 oz.	170 g
Tomatoes, canned, crushed	1 pt.	500 ml
Brown sauce	5 1/2 c.	1.3 l
Brown beef stock	2/3 c.	175 ml
Thyme leaves, dried	1/2 tsp.	2.5 ml
Bay leaf	1 each	1 each
Potatoes, washed, peeled, cut parmentier	1/2 lb.	225 g
Butter, clarified	as needed	as needed
Mushrooms, cultivated, cleaned, sliced	3 oz.	85 g
Peas, frozen	3 oz.	85 g
Salt	TT	TT
Black pepper, freshly ground	TT	TT
Parsley, washed, squeezed dry, chopped	as needed	as needed

METHOD OF PREPARATION

1. Gather all the equipment and ingredients.

2. Heat a thin layer of oil in a rondeau until smoking. Sear the beef cubes until well browned on all sides. Do not crowd the pan; sear in batches, if necessary.

3. Remove the meat and reserve. In same pan, sweat the onions until they are translucent, then add the carrots and celery.

4. Add the crushed tomatoes, brown sauce, brown beef stock, thyme, and bay leaf. Bring to a boil, and dépouille.

5. Add the meat back to the rondeau, cover, and allow stew to simmer gently until the meat is fork-tender, approximately 2 hours; dépouille as necessary.

6. In the meantime, place the potatoes in a saucepan, and cover with cold, salted water. Bring to a boil, and then turn down to a simmer, and cook until potatoes are tender. Strain and shock. When stew is all cooked, add the potatoes (just long enough to heat them through).

7. Heat an appropriate amount of clarified butter in a sauté pan, and sauté the mushrooms. Add the peas, and heat through; add mushrooms and peas to stew.

8. Taste stew, and adjust seasoning. Hold stew covered at 140°F (60°C) or higher.

9. Serve stew garnished with chopped parsley.

Nutrition Facts

Yield: Serves 10
Serving Size: 13 oz. (370 g)

Amount Per Serving

Calories 340

Total Fat 21 g

Sodium 810 mg

Total Carbohydrate 18 g

Protein 22 g

Roast Leg of Lamb with Tarragon

INGREDIENTS	U.S. Standard	Metric
Leg of lamb, boneless	5 lbs.	2.3 kg
Garlic, peeled, sliced fine	6 cloves	6 cloves
Salt	TT	TT
Black pepper, ground	TT	TT
Dried tarragon, crumbled fine	1 tsp.	5 ml
Vegetable oil	3 oz.	90 ml
MIREPOIX		
Onions, peeled	8 oz.	225 g
Carrots, washed, peeled	8 oz.	225 g
Celery, trimmed, washed	8 oz.	225 g
Red wine, dry	6 oz.	180 ml
Lamb stock	24 oz.	720 ml
Lamb demi-glace, seasoned	8 oz.	240 ml
Fresh tarragon leaves, washed, dried, chopped	3 Tbsp.	45 ml
Fresh tarragon, sprigs (optional for garnish)	10 each	10 each

METHOD OF PREPARATION

1. Gather all the ingredients and equipment.

2. Preheat the oven to 350°F (177°C).

3. Using a paring knife, make random slits all over the lamb, and push the garlic slices into the slits. Season the lamb with salt, pepper, and dried tarragon. Truss leg with butcher's twine.

4. Heat the oil to smoking in a large sauté pan, and *sear* the lamb, browning well on all sides. Place lamb on a rack in a roasting pan, and roast in preheated oven for 15 minutes. Remove from oven, sprinkle mirepoix around lamb on the roasting rack, and then return it to the oven. Continue to roast until the lamb reaches an internal temperature of 140°F (60°C). Place lamb on a sheet pan, uncovered (reserve roasting pan with mirepoix), and hold the lamb at 140°F (60°C) or higher, to allow it to rest and carry over to a final internal temperature of 145°F (63°C) before serving.

5. Place the roasting pan with the mirepoix on the stove top, and deglaze with the wine and lamb stock.

6. Add the demi-glace, bring to a boil, turn down to a simmer, and allow sauce to reduce until desired flavor and texture is achieved.

7. Strain and dépouille. Add the chopped tarragon. Taste, and season with salt and pepper as needed. Hold at 140°F (60°C) or higher.

8. To serve, remove the trussing from the lamb, slice thinly on a bias, and serve two to three slices per portion, shingled out on preheated dinner plate. *Nappé* with sauce, and garnish with a tarragon sprig.

COOKING TECHNIQUES

Roasting:
1. Sear the food product, and brown evenly.
2. Elevate the food product in a roasting pan.
3. Determine doneness, and consider carryover cooking.
4. Let the food product rest before carving.

Simmering:
1. Place the prepared product in an appropriately sized pot.
2. Bring the product to a boil, and then reduce the heat to allow the product to barely boil.
3. Cook until desired doneness is achieved.

GLOSSARY

Mirepoix: carrots, onion, celery, and sometimes leeks—rough-cut

Sear: to brown quickly

Nappé: coated or to coat

NUTRITION

Nutrition Facts
Yield: Serves 10
Serving Size: 8 oz. (225 g)

Amount Per Serving

Calories 450

Total Fat 28 g

Sodium 140 mg

Total Carbohydrate 7 g

Protein 42 g

Baked Meatloaf

INGREDIENTS

Ingredients	U.S. Standard	Metric
Ground beef	2 lbs.	910 g
Bread crumbs	1 cup	240 ml
Tomato sauce	8 oz.	240 ml
Eggs	2 each	2 each
Celery, *diced brunoise*	4 oz.	115 g
Onion, *diced brunoise*	6 oz.	170 g
Garlic, *peeled and finely chopped*	4 cloves	4 cloves
Salt	2 tsp.	10 ml
Black pepper	1 tsp.	5 ml
Worcestershire sauce	3 Tbsp.	45 ml
Bacon strips *(optional)*	4–6 each	4–6 each

METHOD OF PREPARATION

1. Gather all the ingredients and equipment.

2. Combine all ingredients except the bacon in a large bowl and mix well.

3. Make a small patty from the mixture, and fry it until it is fully cooked. Taste the patty, and adjust the seasonings in the mixture as needed.

4. Form into one loaf in a loaf pan (or divide into two pans if desired). Make sure that the loaves are as smooth and even as possible.

5. Lay the bacon slices over the top of the loaf, if desired.

6. Bake in a preheated 350°F (177°C) oven until an internal temperature of 155°F (68°C) is reached.

COOKING TECHNIQUES

Baking:
1. Preheat the oven.
2. Place the food product on the appropriate rack.

NUTRITION

Nutrition Facts
Yield: Serves 10
Serving Size: 6 oz. (170 g)

Amount Per Serving

Calories 340

Total Fat 20 g

Sodium 740 mg

Total Carbohydrate 13 g

Protein 27 g

Chinese Chicken and Vegetable Stir-Fry

INGREDIENTS

INGREDIENTS	U.S. Standard	Metric
Soy sauce	6 oz.	180 ml
Sherry wine	3 oz.	90 ml
Cornstarch	3 Tbsp.	45 g
Ginger, fresh, grated	2 Tbsp.	30 g
Garlic, peeled, finely chopped	3 cloves	3 cloves
Chicken breast, boneless, skinless, cut into 2" (5.08 cm) long strips	2 lbs.	910 g
Oil, peanut or soy	4 oz.	120 ml
Carrots, peeled, washed, sliced thinly on the bias	8 oz.	225 g
Broccoli, florets	8 oz.	225 g
Mushrooms, wiped clean, sliced 1/4" (6 mm)	8 oz.	225 g
Scallions, trimmed, sliced thinly on the bias	6 each	6 each
Snow peas, ends trimmed, strings removed	4 oz.	115 g
Baby corn, cut 1/2" (1.27 cm) lengthwise	4 oz.	115 g

Cooking Techniques

169

METHOD OF PREPARATION

1. Gather all the ingredients and equipment.

2. Combine the soy sauce, sherry, cornstarch, ginger, and garlic in a bowl, and stir to dissolve the cornstarch. Add the chicken, toss to coat, cover, and hold at 41°F (5°C) or lower for 2 hours. Drain the chicken, reserve marinade for sauce.

3. Heat a wok or heavy-bottom sauté pan over medium-high heat; add 2 oz. (60 ml) oil, and heat to smoking point. Add the chicken, and stir-fry until cooked, about 3 minutes. Transfer the chicken to a hotel pan, and keep warm.

4. Reheat the wok over medium-high heat; add 1 oz. (30 ml) of oil and heat to smoking point. Add the carrots and broccoli, and stir-fry until crisp/tender, about 1 minute. Transfer the vegetables to the hotel pan with the chicken and set aside.

5. Reheat the wok over medium-high heat, and add the remaining 1 oz. (30 ml) of oil. When oil is hot, add the mushrooms and scallions, and stir-fry for 1 minute. Add the snow peas, and stir-fry for another minute. Add the reserved chicken, carrots, and broccoli, along with the corn. Raise heat to high, and add the reserved marinade. Stir-fry until the sauce thickens and all ingredients are heated through.

6. Serve immediately on preheated dinner plates.

Lentil Soup with Spinach

Ingredients

Ingredients	U.S. Standard	Metric
Olive oil	2 oz.	60 ml
Onion, *peeled, diced brunoise*	4 oz.	115 g
Celery, *trimmed, washed, diced brunoise*	3 oz.	85 g
Carrots, *peeled, washed, diced brunoise*	3 oz.	85 g
Garlic, *peeled, finely minced*	2 cloves	2 cloves
Crushed red pepper	1/4 tsp.	1.25 ml
Lentils	12 oz.	340 g
Chicken or vegetable stock	2 1/2 qts.	2.4 l
Tomato, *crushed*	3 oz.	85 g
Baby spinach or spinach leaves, *washed, cut chiffonade*	4 oz.	115 g
Salt	TT	TT
Black pepper, *ground*	TT	TT
Olive oil, *extra virgin*	as needed	as needed
Pecorino Romano cheese, *grated*	as needed	as needed

Method of Preparation

1. Gather all the ingredients and equipment.

2. Heat the olive oil in a small stockpot. Add onion, celery, and carrots. Cook until onion is translucent.

3. Add garlic and crushed red pepper, and sauté 3 minutes longer. Do not let garlic brown.

4. Add lentils, stock, and tomato. Bring to a boil, lower heat, and simmer for about 1 hour or until lentils are tender. Dépouille as needed.

5. Add the chiffonade of spinach to the soup. Simmer for a few minutes, just to wilt spinach. Taste, and season with salt and pepper as needed.

6. Serve in preheated soup cups or bowls. Drizzle with a little extra virgin olive oil, and sprinkle lightly with grated cheese.

COOKING TECHNIQUES

Simmering:
1. Place the prepared product in an appropriately sized pot.
2. Bring the product to a boil, and then reduce the heat to allow the product to barely boil.
3. Cook until desired doneness is achieved.

Sautéing:
1. Heat the sauté pan to the appropriate temperature.
2. Evenly brown the food product.
3. For a sauce, pour off any excess oil, reheat, and deglaze.

GLOSSARY

Brunoise: 1/8″ (3 mm) dice

Chiffonade: ribbons of leafy greens

NUTRITION

Nutrition Facts

Yield: Serves 10
Serving Size: 8 oz. (225 g)

Amount Per Serving

Calories 230	
Total Fat 15 g	
Sodium 270 mg	
Total Carbohydrate 13 g	
Protein 11 g	

Beer-Battered Fish Fillets

INGREDIENTS	U.S. Standard	Metric
Cod fillets, boneless, cut into 5-oz. (140-g) portions	3 1/2 lbs.	1.6 kg
BEER BATTER		
Flour, all-purpose	3/4 lb.	340 g
Beer	12 oz.	360 ml
Salt	1/4 tsp.	1.25 ml
White pepper, ground	1/4 tsp.	1.25 ml
Eggs, separated	3 each	3 each
Flour, seasoned	as needed	as needed
Lemons, washed, cut into wedges	2 each	2 each
Parsley, washed, squeezed dry, chopped	1/2 oz.	15 g
Tartar sauce (for recipe, see Fried Fisherman's Platter)	1 pt.	500 ml

METHOD OF PREPARATION

1. Gather all the ingredients and equipment.

2. Preheat deep-fat fryer to 350°F (177°C).

3. Combine the flour, beer, salt, pepper, and egg yolks. Blend until smooth.

4. Whip the egg whites to a soft peak in a stainless bowl.

5. Fold the whipped egg whites into the batter.

6. *Dredge* the fillets in the seasoned flour, dip them in the batter, and place them into the deep-fat fryer. Fry until golden brown and cooked to an internal temperature of 145°F (63°C).

7. Remove and drain on absorbent paper.

8. Serve immediately on a preheated dinner plate with tartar sauce. Garnish with lemon wedges and parsley.

COOKING TECHNIQUES

Deep-Frying:

1. Heat the frying liquid to the proper temperature.
2. Submerge the food product completely.
3. Fry the product until it is cooked throughout.

GLOSSARY

Dredge: to coat with flour

NUTRITION

Nutrition Facts

Yield: Serves 10
Serving Size: 10 oz. (285 g)
without tartar sauce

Amount Per Serving

Calories 380

Total Fat 11 g

Sodium 160 mg

Total Carbohydrate 30 g

Protein 36 g

Sautéed Chicken Breast with Mushroom and Sage

INGREDIENTS

	U.S. Standard	Metric
Chicken breasts, whole, boneless, skinless	5 each	5 each
Butter, clarified	as needed	as needed
Flour, seasoned	4 oz.	115 g
Shallot, diced brunoise	2 oz.	55 g
Garlic, peeled, finely minced	4 cloves	4 cloves
White wine	8 oz.	240 ml
Mushrooms, cultivated, wiped clean, sliced 1/4" (6 mm)	1 lb.	454 g
Shiitake mushrooms, caps only, wiped clean, sliced 1/4" (6 mm)	1 lb.	454 g
Brown chicken stock	16 oz.	500 ml
Butter, cut into pieces, room temperature	3 oz.	85 g
Sage, fresh, washed, leaves stripped, chopped	2 Tbsp.	30 ml
Salt	TT	TT
Black pepper, ground	TT	TT

COOKING TECHNIQUES

⚙ Sautéing:
1. Heat the sauté pan to the appropriate temperature.
2. Evenly brown the food product.
3. For a sauce, pour off any excess oil, reheat, and deglaze.

NUTRITION

Nutrition Facts
Yield: Serves 10
Serving Size: 8 oz. (225 g)

Amount Per Serving

Calories 320

Total Fat 12 g

Sodium 150 mg

Total Carbohydrate 15 g

Protein 32 g

METHOD OF PREPARATION

1. Gather all the ingredients and equipment.

2. Separate chicken breast into halves. Trim away cartilage and fat. Place one breast between two sheets of plastic wrap and pound gently to flatten to about 3/4–1" (1.9–2.54 cm) thickness. Repeat with remaining breasts.

3. Heat a thin layer of clarified butter in a large sauté pan over medium heat.

4. Dredge the chicken in the seasoned flour and shake off the excess. Place the chicken, presentation side down, in the hot butter, and cook until the first side turns golden brown. Turn over, and cook the other side. Cook to an internal temperature of 165°F (74°C). Do not crowd the pan when sautéing.

5. Remove chicken and hold uncovered at 140°F (60°C) or higher.

6. Pour excess fat from the sauté pan, and add the shallots and garlic. Sauté until shallots are softened.

7. Deglaze with the wine and allow wine to reduce by one-half.

8. Add both mushrooms. Lower heat, and allow mushrooms to cook in the reduced wine and release their juices. Turn heat to high to reduce and evaporate the liquids, and then sauté the mushrooms until they turn golden brown.

9. Add the chicken stock, and reduce liquid by one-third.

10. Remove pan from heat; add the butter and swirl into the sauce to emulsify.

11. Add the sage. Taste, and season with salt and pepper as needed.

12. To serve, place a half chicken breast per portion on a preheated dinner plate, and nappé with mushroom sage sauce. Serve immediately.

Grilled Maple-Brined Pork Chops with Sautéed Apple

INGREDIENTS	U.S. Standard	Metric
Pork chops, cut 1 1/4″(3.18 cm) thick	10 each	10 each
BRINE		
Water	16 oz.	500 ml
Apple cider	16 oz.	500 ml
Maple syrup	4 oz.	120 ml
Thyme, fresh springs, broken into 1/2″ (1.27 cm) pieces	1/2 oz.	15 g
Sugar	1 1/2 oz.	40 g
Salt, kosher	2 1/2 oz.	75 g
Shallots, peeled, sliced	4 each	4 each
Garlic, peeled, sliced	4 each	4 each
Soy sauce	2 oz.	60 ml
Black peppercorns, whole, cracked	1 tsp.	5 ml
Bay leaves	2 each	2 each
Black pepper, ground	TT	TT
Butter, clarified	1 oz.	28 g
Maple syrup	1 oz.	30 ml
Apples, Granny Smith, cored, cut into 12 wedges	3 each	3 each
Salt	TT	TT
Thyme, fresh sprigs (for garnish)	20 each	20 each

METHOD OF PREPARATION

1. Gather all the ingredients and equipment.
2. Trim the pork chops of excess fat.
3. Combine all of the ingredients for the brine in a nonreactive container that will also hold the pork chops comfortably. Stir well until the sugar and salt have dissolved.
4. Add the pork chops to the brine, and allow brining for 2 hours at 41°F (5°C) or lower.
5. Preheat the grill.
6. Remove the pork chops from the brine, and discard the brining liquid. Pat the chops dry. Alternately, if time allows, place the chops on a roasting rack, hold at 41°F (5°C) or lower, and allow to air dry before grilling.
7. Season chops with pepper (they do not need salt, as it was contained in the brine).
8. Grill the chops to an internal temperature of 145°F (63°C) or to customer preference. Hold briefly at 140°F (60°C) or higher.
9. Heat the clarified butter and maple syrup in a sauté pan, add the apples, and sauté until the apples just soften. Season with salt to taste.
10. Serve one chop per portion on a preheated dinner plate. Garnish with three apple slices and thyme sprigs.

Chef's Notes

A brine is traditionally used as a preservative. In this case, however, the brine is being used as a way to introduce moisture into an otherwise dry product. Pork lacks fat marbling through the meat, which means that when cooked, there is no fat rendering within the meat to keep the pork moist. When pork is put into a brine prior to exposure to high, dry temperatures such as grilling, broiling, or roasting, osmosis and diffusion take place, which in turn allow the protein cells to retain moisture during the dry cooking process. This process is often used with white meat poultry as well.

COOKING TECHNIQUES

Grilling/Broiling:
1. Clean and heat the grill or broiler.
2. To prevent sticking, brush the food product with oil.

GLOSSARY

Osmosis: the spreading of fluid through a membrane until there is an equal concentration of fluid on both sides of the membrane

Diffuse: to spread and disseminate

NUTRITION

Nutrition Facts

Yield: Serves 10
Serving Size: 6 oz. (170 g)

Amount Per Serving

Calories 270

Total Fat 16 g

Sodium 75 mg

Total Carbohydrate 12 g

Protein 20 g

A.D. 1200
The spice trade between Europe and the East is reestablished after the Dark Ages.

1600
The British East India Company is chartered by Queen Elizabeth I to develop the spice trade.

1799
The Dutch East India Company dissolves, and the British take control of the spice trade.

1799
The United States enters the spice trade.

Seasonings and flavorings have historically changed the world: The spice industry, dating back thousands of years, has inspired explorers and travelers, opened passageways, started wars, initiated commerce, expanded knowledge, and led to the discovery of a new world.

Spices and herbs have been used since ancient times for medicinal and cosmetic purposes and as flavoring for foods. From the very beginning, spices and herbs had remarkable value, and they continue to impact modern foodways.

Flavoring Food

Seasonings and Flavorings

Seasonings and flavorings are incorporated into the cooking process to enhance and heighten the flavor of the base ingredients.

Seasonings include fresh or dried herbs, such as basil, oregano, and rosemary; spices, such as allspice and cinnamon; and salt-and-pepper products that have the ability to complement or enhance food without changing its natural flavor. These added seasonings should not dominate the final flavor of the food. Instead, they should allow a balance between the flavors.

Flavorings are any additional elements added to foods that transform or strengthen natural flavors. These elements have distinct flavors of their own and will affect the final outcome of the food being prepared. There are a number of flavorings used in cooking and baking, including oil-based emulsions, such as spice-scented oils, and alcohol-based extracts infused with natural ingredients such as almond, lemon zest, mint leaves, and vanilla beans. Nuts, fruits, and seasonings are used to produce emulsions and extracts. Use extracts in small quantities so as not to overpower the base food. Adjust by adding more; removing strong flavors is much more difficult.

Flavor enhancers, another type of flavoring, have little flavor of their own. Instead, they increase taste perception without changing the natural flavor of the food. Monosodium glutamate (MSG) and 5 ribonucleotide are examples of flavor enhancers used to strengthen and intensify the natural ingredients in foods.

Salt

The mineral sodium chloride (NaCl), or salt, is universally the most common seasoning used on food, and it comes in a wide variety of forms. See Figure 12-1 on page 176. Salt heightens flavor, allowing the natural base ingredients to be enhanced. Careful addition is important—the taste of saltiness cannot be removed, nor does it burn off during the cooking process. Salt has a stronger taste on cooler foods than on hot foods.

Table salt Table salt is the most common type of salt used in food preparation. Its fine granules contain additives—iodine and anti-caking agents—to keep the salt free flowing.

Rock salt Rock salt is available in edible and nonedible forms. Often used as a non-food grade salt, it is used primarily in ice cream making or other freezing techniques and as a cooking bed for shelled mollusks and bivalves.

Sea salt Sea salt is derived from the evaporation of seawater. This type of salt is often preferred because of its strong, intense, and distinctive flavor. Sea salt comes in fine and coarse crystals.

Kosher salt Kosher salt is a type of purified rock salt void of additives and iodine and often used interchangeably with table salt. Available in coarse form, it is used in the koshering of, or extracting blood from, meat, and is only considered a kosher product if marked with the kashrut insignia.

Pickling salt Pickling salt is a finely crystallized salt void of additives. It blends easily with the pickling solution.

Specialty salts Designer salts, including *la fleur de sel* ("the flower of the salt"), are available through specialty food purveyors. There are several varieties of specialty salt.

- **Hawaiian salt** This is an unrefined sea salt, pink to brown in color, and rich in iron oxide.
- **French sea salt** *(sel marin/la fleur de sel)* Many French salts are commercially available, and range in texture, from dry to moist; color, from white to gray; and crystal size, from coarse to fine. This salt comes from natural seawater that is pooled in basins and then evaporated. Unrefined, it is loaded with minerals that occur naturally in seawater.
- **Danish smoked salt** Made in the Viking tradition, seawater is evaporated producing a salt that is cooked over a fire composed of juniper, oak, and other hard woods. The salt is darker and has a distinctive smoky flavor.
- **Peruvian pink salt** This salt comes from an underground ocean that feeds springs high in the Andes mountains. The salt owes its color to the rose quartz that lines the sides of wells.
- **Hawaiian red alae salt** When the seawater evaporates, a salt is produced which is combined with Hawaiian red clay. This gives the salt a burnt red or sepia color and adds minerals.

Pepper

Pepper is the most widely used spice in the world. It is grown tropically and presents itself as a cluster of berries on a perennial climbing vine. After the berries have been dried, they are used to season foods during the cooking process or are ground and sprinkled on prepared foods. Pepper is available whole, cracked, and ground (from coarse to fine). See Figure 12-2. Green, red, and black pepper can be ground in dry form in a pepper mill and mixed for a unique taste. Whole black peppercorns are

FIGURE 12-1
Salt varieties

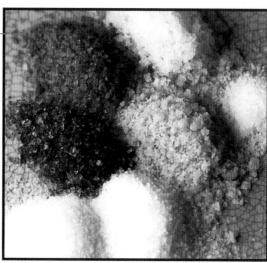

used in slow, moist cooking in which the flavors can dissipate over time and in court bouillons, marinades, and pickles. Ground pepper seasons food immediately upon use and is used in most savory dishes and some sweet dishes. Select specific textures of pepper to best complement the food to which it is added.

Black Pepper

Black pepper comes from unripe berries of the pepper plant. These berries are allowed to ferment for a short period and are then scattered on mats and left in the sun to dry, wrinkle, and deepen in color. Black pepper varieties include:

- **Lampong/lompong black peppercorns** These peppercorns from Indonesia are delicately pungent and aromatic.
- **Malabar black peppercorns** Malabar black peppercorns are aromatic and have a deep full-bodied flavor. They are native to India.

- **Sarawak black peppercorns** These peppercorns have a fruitier bouquet and are not as pungent as some of the other black peppercorns. They are indigenous to Malaysia.
- **Tellicherry black peppercorns** Considered the world's finest black pepper, tellicherry peppercorns are bold and pungent in aroma and flavor. They are grown in southwest India.

White Pepper

White pepper is produced from the same pepper plant as black pepper. The white version comes from the kernel of ripe berries and is usually ground; freshly ground is most preferable. Choose white pepper for light sauces and mixtures to keep food monochromatic in appearance.

Green Peppercorns

Green peppercorns are the unripened berries of the pepper plant. After the berries have been picked, they are pickled

FIGURE 12-2
Pepper comes in many different forms: whole, cracked, and crushed, or ground.

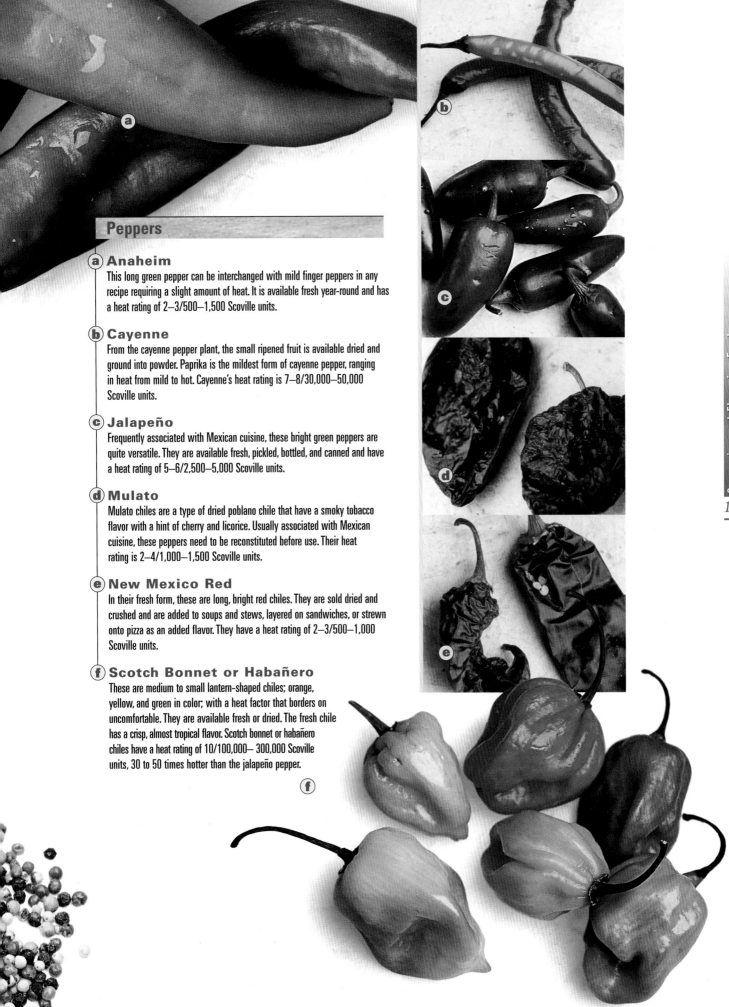

Peppers

a Anaheim

This long green pepper can be interchanged with mild finger peppers in any recipe requiring a slight amount of heat. It is available fresh year-round and has a heat rating of 2–3/500–1,500 Scoville units.

b Cayenne

From the cayenne pepper plant, the small ripened fruit is available dried and ground into powder. Paprika is the mildest form of cayenne pepper, ranging in heat from mild to hot. Cayenne's heat rating is 7–8/30,000–50,000 Scoville units.

c Jalapeño

Frequently associated with Mexican cuisine, these bright green peppers are quite versatile. They are available fresh, pickled, bottled, and canned and have a heat rating of 5–6/2,500–5,000 Scoville units.

d Mulato

Mulato chiles are a type of dried poblano chile that have a smoky tobacco flavor with a hint of cherry and licorice. Usually associated with Mexican cuisine, these peppers need to be reconstituted before use. Their heat rating is 2–4/1,000–1,500 Scoville units.

e New Mexico Red

In their fresh form, these are long, bright red chiles. They are sold dried and crushed and are added to soups and stews, layered on sandwiches, or strewn onto pizza as an added flavor. They have a heat rating of 2–3/500–1,000 Scoville units.

f Scotch Bonnet or Habañero

These are medium to small lantern-shaped chiles; orange, yellow, and green in color; with a heat factor that borders on uncomfortable. They are available fresh or dried. The fresh chile has a crisp, almost tropical flavor. Scotch bonnet or habañero chiles have a heat rating of 10/100,000– 300,000 Scoville units, 30 to 50 times hotter than the jalapeño pepper.

in brine or vinegar or freeze-dried. Green peppercorns should always be rinsed thoroughly prior to use. Often used to complement Thai cuisine, green peppercorns also pair well with veal, game, poultry, beef, and both light and dark sauces.

Pink Peppercorns

Pink peppercorns are not related to the same pepper plant (*Piper nigrum*) that produces black, white, and green peppercorns. Pink peppercorns are delicate, dried berries from the baies rose plant; therefore, they are not true peppercorns. They do not have the same pungency as white or black peppercorns; they are added primarily for visual appeal to traditional dried pepper berries to form what is commonly called peppercorn melange. Pink peppercorns can also be pickled.

Chile Peppers and Their Derivatives

Chile peppers fall under the botanical name of capsicum and are produced from annual or perennial shrublike plants that are part of the nightshade family. The nonaromatic pods of these plants range in heat and flavors from mild to fiery hot. The smaller the pepper, the hotter the taste, as the smaller pods have the capsaicin-laden seeds closer to the flesh. The heat, therefore, is far more intense. Chiles are rated on a temperature scale from 1–10, the least amount of heat to the hottest, or on the Scoville Unit Scale, which rates the heat from 0–300,000 units. Chiles are available fresh or dried, whole, crushed either with or without seeds, or ground into fine powders.

Adding chiles or their by-products to food creates intricate and interesting flavors, making the final flavors complex and distinctive. The current popularity of ethnic food and the awareness of chile varieties, which number more than 150, have made chiles far more available for purchase.

> When handling hot peppers, always wear disposable vinyl gloves for seeding and deveining. The sensation of heat remains on hands, fingers, and fingernails long after coming in contact with the fiery capsaicin and will cause painful distress to the eyes or to delicate facial areas.

Lemon

Small amounts of the juice of a lemon, as well as the *zest,* or colored rind, are used as a food flavoring. The bitter white **pith** below the colored rind should be avoided. Products made from lemon, such as lemon oil, pure lemon extract, and liqueur di limone, should be used in small quantities so as not to overwhelm the food to which it is being added. The juice and zest of the lemon contain the best natural flavor.

Sugar

Sugar used as a flavoring can bring out the deeper flavor of a primary food, especially in foods that are sour, unripe, or lacking flavor. A touch of sugar added to the water when cooking tender young vegetables will bring out their innate sweetness.

Extracts and Essences

Extracts, such as vanilla, are concentrated substances made by infusing alcohol with natural ingredients such as almond, mint, lemon zest, or vanilla beans. See Figure 12-3.

> See Chapter 29: *Fundamentals of Baking and Pastry for more information.*

Essences are significantly reduced liquids with a dominant prevailing flavor. Neutral liquids like water, vegetable or fruit juices, light stocks, or wine are simmered with the addition of a primary food until the strength of that food becomes the dominant flavor. If mushrooms are the primary food, the concentration of that liquid produces a mushroom essence. Essences can be made from seeds, fruits, herbs, spices, nuts, and flowers. Essences include orange, cinnamon, lemon, tarragon, chervil, tomato, fish, and game carcass.

FIGURE 12-3

Vanilla is an example of an extract.

Monosodium Glutamate

Monosodium glutamate (MSG) is the sodium salt of glutamic acid which occurs naturally in a number of foods. MSG is a flavor enhancer, derived from natural foods, with no distinct flavor of its own. It acts only as a boost to food. It also has been associated with the Japanese term *umami,* the fifth taste, distinctly different from the other four basic tastes.

> See Chapter 10: *Sensory Perception for more information on umami and the basic tastes.*

Monosodium glutamate has been responsible for allergic reactions such as headache, chest pain, and numbness in people with an allergy to MSG. Most often, the symptoms disappear quickly; in some cases, the symptoms are long lasting and can cause more severe complications.

When to Season

Seasoning is done at different times during the cooking process. When roasting meat, season prior to cooking. When cooking a liquid, such as soup, season at the end of cooking. Prior to the end of the cooking process, taste the food and adjust the seasonings. Overseasoning destroys the natural flavor of food and can cause an imbalance, offsetting the flavors.

When to Flavor

Flavoring can be achieved during any part of the cooking process, depending on the ingredient being used. When cooking food for a long period, add most fresh herbs at the end of the cooking process. Heat will dissipate the volatile oils contained in fresh herbs, causing them to quickly evaporate. Likewise, ground spices release their flavor quickly, so add them to foods near the end of cooking. Whole spices, however, need more time to release their flavor, so add them at the beginning of cooking. When adding ground spices to uncooked foods, allow the mixture to set for several hours so that it develops flavor.

Herbs and Spices

Herbs and spices are used to enhance the flavor of foods and, as such, are considered flavorings.

Herbs come from a large group of annual or perennial aromatic plants, the leaves, stems, buds, or flowers of which are used whole, ground, or chopped to add flavor to other food. They can be purchased fresh or dried.

Spices are the berries, fruits, flowers, bark, seeds, and roots of plants or trees grown in tropical regions. They are available mostly in dried form and can be purchased whole or ground.

The addition of herbs and spices to food can create new tastes and flavors without the addition of added fat or calories.

Herbs

Herbs are available in a variety of forms and flavors to accentuate the flavor of food. See the chart on pages 180–181.

Using Herbs

Although the preference is to use fresh herbs, that is not always a viable choice. Dried herbs often are used because they are readily available; procurement is an issue in making the choice. If purchasing dried herbs, keep the quantities relevant to usage; after they have been opened, they do not have a long shelf life.

Dried herbs have a more concentrated flavor than do fresh herbs, so when adding dried herbs to food, always cut the amount by either a third or a half. For example, if a tomato-based recipe calls for the use of one tablespoon of chopped fresh oregano, when using the dried version, start out by only adding one teaspoon of the oregano. Make adjustments by adding more oregano during cooking, if necessary.

Storing Herbs

Proper storage and handling is essential in maintaining the full flavor of herbs. Fresh herbs should be checked for insects and bad spots prior to refrigeration. To maintain freshness, keep them loosely wrapped in a damp cloth or paper towel and at a cool temperature (35°F–45°F/2°C–7°C). Dried herbs should be stored in airtight containers away from sunlight, moisture, and excessive heat.

Herbs

(a) Basil
Basil, a fragrant, leafy plant easily grown for culinary consumption, is a member of the mint family and is available in many varieties. Some varieties contain a hint of cloves, mint, or licorice. It is available fresh, dried, and crushed and can be used in sauces, especially those of the tomato family; soups; salads; and casseroles and to flavor meats, cheese, and traditional pesto.

(b) Bay leaf
Bay leaf is an herb that comes from an aromatic, ever-green, shrublike tree. The fresh leaves of the plant are leathery and dark green; the dried versions are pale. The leaves are sold whole and dried. They have a strong, herbaceous flavor. Use sparingly in soups, stews, stocks, chowders, roasting meats, fish preparations, marinades, and vegetables. The leaves are removed prior to serving. (Photo shown below.)

(c) Chervil
Chervil is parsley-like in appearance, slightly peppery in flavor, and available fresh, dried, crushed, or ground. Use in vegetable soups, stews, salads, sauces, and fish-based dishes; add to baked goods (mostly ethnic types); and sprinkle over roasted meat before serving.

(d) Chives
Chives are the long, green, stemlike leaves of the onion family, producing flowers and buds, both of which are edible and mildly onion-flavored. Chives are available fresh, frozen, or dried. Pair with just about any savory food. Use to flavor breads, soups, stews, sauces, dips, and soft cheese.

(e) Cilantro
Cilantro is the green leaves of the coriander plant. Parsley-like in appear-ance, it is often referred to as Mexican or Asian (Chinese) parsley. The distinct flavor of cilantro is not at all like that of parsley. It is available fresh, dried, or frozen; fresh cilantro is complete with stems, whereas the dried and frozen varieties are chopped. Use mostly in Mexican, Indian, and Asian foods.

(f) Dill
Dill is a feathery-leafed herb with a strong, distinct flavor and is available fresh, whole, dried, and chopped. Use to season fish and in pickling; add to soups, sauces, casseroles, specialty breads, butter, and soft cheese.

(g) Garlic chive
Garlic chive, often thought of as the Asian relative to the traditional chive, is a flat-leafed, garlic-flavored herb. Use fresh in salads, salad dressings, or stir-fries and as a substitute for the common green onion or traditional chive.

(h) Lemon grass
Lemon grass is a tough, elongated Asian grass with a bul-blike base, purchased in fresh stalk form, but also available dried, chopped, dried in strips, or finely ground to powder. The flavor of fresh lemon grass is lemonlike; the dried versions are not as strong. Use in soups, stews, curries, rice, stir-fries, and spiced dishes. (Photo shown above.)

(i) Marjoram
Marjoram, a perennial plant related to the mint family, looks and tastes like a mild version of oregano and is available fresh, dried, chopped, or ground. Use in stews, casseroles, sauces, soups, gravies, pâtés, and sausages; and sprinkle on meat, fish, lamb, and poultry dishes.

j Mint

Mint is a leafy, intrusive perennial herb with an array of flavors and intensity—spearmint, peppermint, apple mint, and chocolate mint are a few varieties. Suppliers often handle only the more common fresh varieties, peppermint and spearmint, and various dried versions. Use to season stews, sauces, casseroles, desserts, dips (savory and sweet), lamb, peas, and pastries and to flavor beverages (juices, fruit punch, bourbon-laced mint juleps, and tea).

k Oregano

Oregano is closely associated with wild marjoram. This aromatic green, bushy perennial has a distinct peppery flavor and is often associated with Italian cuisine. It is available fresh, dried, chopped, or ground and can be used in soups, stews, sauces, and egg dishes and to flavor meat, poultry, and fish.

l Parsley

Parsley is a biennial plant; two of the more common varieties are flat-leaf and curly parsley. Parsley pairs well with most foods and can be used as a garnish. Available fresh, chopped, or dried, it can be used in soups, stews, sauces, casseroles, salads, dips, and dressings.

m Rosemary

Rosemary, an evergreen shrub of the mint family, has needlelike leaves and a strong, distinct flavor. The fresh form is preferred; however, it is available dried, chopped, or ground. Pair with chicken and meats; use with soups, sauces, stews, casseroles, lamb, and breads; and infuse in olive oil and vinegar.

n Sage

Sage is a deeply fragrant perennial with a range of varieties and a musty, pungent flavor. It is available fresh, dried, chopped, or ground. Use with stuffing and savory dishes and to neutralize fatty meats and fowl. Add to soups, stews, sausage, salads (finely chopped and sprinkled lightly), and pork dishes.

o Savory

Savory has a spicy taste that can overwhelm food's natural flavor if overused. It is available fresh, dried, chopped, or ground. Use in meat and fish dishes; sprinkle on eggs; and add to stuffings, broad beans, soups, and stews.

p Tarragon

Tarragon is a lanky, aromatic perennial, common to France and Russia. French tarragon has a delicate, anise-like flavor; the Russian version is slightly bitter. Tarragon is available fresh or as dried, chopped leaves. Use to flavor vinegars, salad dressings, mustards, marinades, soups, and sauces. Pair with fish, veal, eggs, and chicken.

q Thyme

Thyme is an aromatic, perennial shrublike herb, having many varieties (some with a hint of lemon). It is available fresh, dried, chopped, or ground. Pair with other herbs, and use in soups, stews, casseroles, and savory baked goods, as well as meat, poultry, and fish.

Spices

Spices add flavor to appetizers, soups, salads, entrées, accompaniments, and desserts. See the chart on pages 183–185. Spices can be added directly to foods during the cooking process or infused into hot foods in a sachet. Toasting certain spices intensifies the flavor of food. See Figure 12-4.

> *See Chapter 11: Cooking Techniques for more information on making a sachet.*

Using Spices

The pairing of flavors is a learned skill. Some spice and food combinations are well suited, and well documented to be used together. These include basil and tomato, rosemary and lamb, sage and poultry stuffing, dill and salmon, cloves and pumpkin, and nutmeg and spinach.

Storing Spices

Whole spices keep their flavors much longer than do their ground versions. Spices should be kept in airtight containers away from sunlight, moisture, and excessive heat. Stale spices can be quickly identified; they will often fade, lose their pungent aroma, and develop a bitter, almost musty flavor. They should be discarded and replaced.

Spice Blends and Mixes

Spice blends and mixes are a combination of aromatic ingredients—spices, herbs, and sometimes dried vegetables.

Baharat Baharat is a hot spice mixture from the Arabian Gulf regions, usually associated with foods of the Middle East. The ingredients include ground chile, paprika, black peppercorns, coriander seeds, cumin seeds, cloves, nutmeg, cardamom seeds, and cinnamon. The proportion of ingredients used varies, depending on the recipe of the originating region. The baharat spice mixture can vary from subtle to fiery hot. Use on meat and vegetables.

Cajun seasoning Cajun seasoning is a Cajun- and Creole-influenced spice, usually found as a prepared spice. Ingredients include cumin, paprika, garlic, onion, black pepper, mustard powder, salt, oregano, cayenne, and thyme. Variations may substitute basil, sage, or fennel for any of the green herbs. Rub into fish, shellfish, meat, and chicken prior to grilling or roasting. Add to jambalayas and seafood gumbos.

FIGURE 12-4

Toasting cumin seeds in a sauté pan

Barbecue spice Barbecue spice is made of paprika, salt, celery seed, chili pepper, cumin, coriander, garlic, cloves, black pepper, and red pepper. Rub into meats and poultry, add to salad dressings, and use in egg and cheese dishes such as quiche, omelettes, and savory custards.

Crab boil/shrimp boil Crab boil/shrimp boil is a commercial spice blend. Used in the boiling of crab, shrimp, and other crustaceans to add flavor, the common ingredients are black peppercorns, mustard seeds, bay leaves, chile or chile flakes, and allspice. Other sweet spices can be substituted for the allspice.

Curry powder Curry powder, a mixture of dry ingredients, varies according to regional location, recipe, or commercially prepared product. Ingredients usually include red chiles, coriander seeds, cumin seeds, mustard seeds, fenugreek seeds, curry leaves, black peppercorns, turmeric, and ground ginger. Curry powder is used in many global recipes and can range in heat, color, and intensity of flavor. Add to fish, meat, vegetable dishes, soups, stews, sauces, salad dressings, and baked goods.

Five-spice powder Five-spice powder is used primarily throughout the southern part of China and Vietnam. The five base ingredients are star anise (the dominant flavor), Sichuan peppers, cinnamon (or cassia), fennel seeds, and cloves. It may sometimes include licorice root, cardamom, or ground ginger. Use to season cooked meats and to flavor marinades and sauces.

Garam masala Garam masala is an Indian spice mixture or paste that differs between regions. Aromatic and flavorful, this spice mixture is a combination of roasted and freshly ground spices. The main ingredients include cardamom, cinnamon, nutmeg, cloves, peppercorn, coriander, fennel seeds, and turmeric. The North Indian version includes cumin, ginger, garlic, and additional spices. Its South Indian counterpart includes mustard seed, asafoetida, tamarind, and a mixing agent—vinegar, coconut milk, or water—to form a pastelike consistency.

Pickling spice Pickling spice is used to infuse flavor when pickling meat, vegetables, and fruits; is often added to chutneys; and is used to poach fish. Typical ingredients for pickling spice include chiles, peppercorns, mustard seeds, whole allspice, mace, whole cloves, cardamom pods or seeds, broken cinnamon quills, dried ginger, and coriander seeds.

Pie spice Pie spice is a combination of sweet spices that is added to pie fillings prior to baking. The ingredients in pie spice usually include cinnamon, cloves, nutmeg, and ginger.

Spices

(a) Allspice

Allspice, the dried unripe berry from the Jamaican pepper tree, has a clovelike flavor, is available whole or ground into powder, and can be used to flavor pickles, meats, consommés, casseroles, and sauces. Ground allspice is used mostly in baked goods, pâtés, puddings, meats, sausages, relishes, and sauces.

(b) Anise seeds

Anise seeds are small dried seeds with a strong licorice-like aroma and flavor. Use sparingly to avoid the overwhelming licorice flavor. Anise seeds are available whole or finely ground and can be used in baked goods and confectioneries and with savory foods such as fish and vegetables.

(c) Cardamom

Cardamom is the aromatic pod from the perennial cardamom plant with a flavor similar to ginger and pine. It is available in pod, seed, or ground form. Use in sweet and savory foods, yogurt, curries, and baked goods.

(d) Cayenne

Cayenne is the ground powder of dried hot red cayenne peppers. This distinctively hot and spicy chile is not related to the black pepper family and is considered a spice in its ground form. Use cayenne with meat, fish, crustaceans, egg dishes, salads, sauces, and pickles.

(e) Celery seeds

Celery seeds are tiny and celery flavored. They are available whole or ground, or as a mix combined with salt for flavoring foods. Whole seeds are used in coleslaw, sauces, and dressings for flavor and visual interest. Ground seeds are used to flavor soups, fish stews, casseroles, sauces, and salad dressings.

(f) Chiles

Chiles are a variety of peppers that range in size, color, shape, flavor, and heat—from mild and sweet to fiery hot. They are available fresh, dried, canned, or bottled. Use as a flavoring or as a vegetable. (Photo shown above.)

(g) Chili powder

Chili powder is a mixture of ground dry red chiles and additional spices and herbs—cumin, garlic, and dried onion. Use to flavor chili (meat, vegetarian, or bean), sauces, egg dishes, sausages, and ground meats.

(h) Cinnamon

Cinnamon is the sticklike quills or inner bark of the cinnamon tree. Use in baking, and add to beverages and sweet and savory foods, curries, stuffings, pickles, desserts, sweet potatoes, and preserves.

(i) Cumin

Cumin seeds, the dried ripened fruit of a European spice shrub, are deep and complex in flavor. They are available whole or ground and are used in Middle Eastern, Indian, and Mexican cuisine and spicy chili, and with chicken, fish, curries, couscous, sausages, and hard cheese.

j Dill seeds

Dill seeds are the small, dark seeds of the dill plant. Their distinctively sharp odor and flavor add complexity to soups, stews, casseroles, sauces, cabbage, salads, and fish.

k Fennel seeds

Fennel seeds are the seeds of a parsley family member. The fennel plant is used as a vegetable, and the seeds are considered the spice. Both parts are mildly licorice-like in flavor. Whole seeds are used in tomato-based sauces, dressings, and sausages and in baked goods such as breads, rolls, biscuits, and crackers.

l Ginger

Ginger is a sweet-fiery flavored root often associated with Asian cuisine. Fresh ginger is available peeled and sliced, pickled or liberally coated in sugar crystals. Fresh ginger is added to fish and poultry and to almost any Chinese or Japanese dish. Ground ginger has a more global appeal, especially for baked goods.

m Mace

Mace is the fibrous growth that forms around the shell of nutmeg. Mace is available dried and has a flavor similar to that of nutmeg, but not as strong. Use to flavor soups, sauces, stuffings, cakes, and preserves.

n Mustard seeds

Mustard seeds are tiny round seeds, white, brown, and black in color, and nonaromatic. They range in flavor from mildly tangy to hot and spicy and are available whole, ground, or processed into a paste. The whole seeds are usually used in sauces, marinades, pickling liquids, dressings, and other condiment mixtures.

o Nutmeg

Nutmeg is a medium-large aromatic orb that is most fragrant and flavorful when freshly grated. It is also available whole or ground into powder. Pair with other sweet-pungent spices like cinnamon, cloves, ginger, and cardamom. Use in soups, sauces, custards, baked goods, desserts, and savory dishes.

p Paprika

Paprika, the mildest form of cayenne pepper, is available in ground form. Varieties of paprika range from mild to very hot and spicy. Use to season tomato dishes, salad dressings, soups, sauces, meats, shellfish, poultry, and fish, and as a decorative color accent on potato salads, coleslaw, and deviled eggs.

q Pepper and peppercorns

Pepper and peppercorns are available in black, white, green, and pink varieties. For specific information on pepper and peppercorns, see pages 176–178.

r Saffron

Saffron comes from the crocus plant. Usually sold in thread form, it is packaged in small glass bottles and tins. A mainstay in Spanish cuisine, this spice is added to paella, the traditional fish and shellfish-based stew laden with rice. Saffron is used to flavor rice dishes, bouillabaisse, lobster, and shrimp. Saffron is the most expensive spice in the world.

International Flavor Profiles

Flavors and foods are determined primarily by what is available within a region in addition to tradition and the recipes passed down through the ages, as shown below.

Key flavors of southern France—Aioli (traditional garlic-flavored mayonnaise with a hint of lemon), olives, pistou (basil paste, basil pesto), tapenade (olive paste), and herbes de Provence are the key flavors of this region.

Key flavors of southern Italy—Olive oil, garlic, anchovy, and tomato make up the favored four. These ingredients make some of the finest tomato-based sauces in the world.

Key flavors of Southeast Asia (Indonesia, Malaysia and Singapore)—Rice, fiery sauces and dips, soy beans, bitter gourds, tuberous roots, and the spices from neighboring countries influence the interesting cuisine that is grounded in its Chinese roots.

Key flavors of the Caribbean—Allspice, cassava, peanuts, breadfruit, plantains, fiery sauces, and coconut are typical flavors found in Caribbean dishes.

Key flavors of the Middle East (Syria, Iran/Ancient Persia, Iraq/Chaldea, Saudi Arabia, Egypt, Lebanon, Jordan, and Palestine)—Dried pulses, including garbanzo beans/chick peas and lentils; fresh herbs such as parsley, cilantro, and mint; spices such as sumac, cumin, coriander, Syrian allspice, cinnamon, and cayenne; olives; olive oil; rice; cracked wheat; lemon juice; yogurt; the paste of ground sesame seeds (tahini); and flavored waters such as rose water and orange blossom water are typical flavors of the Middle East region. Use in a variety of dishes, including desserts and puddings.

Key flavors of Spain—Olive oil, garlic, tomatoes, green peppers, olives, and peanuts are classic components of traditional Spanish cuisine. Use in sauces for fish, vegetables, and meat or as flavor enhancers for one-dish meals, soups, and sauces.

Key flavors of North Africa—Cinnamon, ginger, coriander, harissa, and fruits are key flavors that influence the dishes found in North Africa.

Key flavors of Greece—Greece is known for its use of olive oil, lemon, tomato, cinnamon, grape leaves, eggplant, feta cheese, and Kasseri, a soft mozzarella-like cheese, in its dishes.

Condiments

Condiments are flavored sauces served as accompaniments to food. Their primary purpose is to complement and visually enhance the food being served. With the current interest in ethnic cuisine and gourmet foods, there is a variety of commercially prepared condiment products and recipes available. These products and recipes vary in flavor and texture and range from sweet to sour, or mild to fiery hot.

Store unopened condiments in cool and dry areas at temperatures of 50°F–70°F (10°C–21°C). Opened condiments should always be stored closed and refrigerated. Prepared condiments that are canned, such as ketchup, mustard, barbecue sauce, and relishes, should be transferred from their cans to airtight plastic containers with tight-fitting lids. Any condiment transferred from its original packaging should be labeled, dated, and refrigerated.

Condiments

ⓐ Barbecue sauce

Barbecue sauce is a tomato-based sauce usually containing sugar, vinegar, and an array of spices. It can range from sweet and spicy to savory and ultra hot. Use as a basting sauce for meats and poultry and in place of the more subtle tomato ketchup.

ⓑ Chutney

Chutneys were originally East Indian saucelike relishes made from fruits and vegetables, laced with prominent spices, and served with curry to balance the hot flavor. Adapted and adopted by the British, these sauces were then made into a milder relish form. Today, chutneys are served on and with all kinds of foods—from cheese quesadillas to skewered grilled shrimp. Chutneys can be cooked or uncooked; their texture can be thin to chunky; and their ingredients can be as varied as the spices added.

ⓒ Hot sauce/pepper sauce

Hot sauce/pepper sauce is a product developed from fiery hot red chiles, vinegar, and salt. The trademarked name Tabasco™ has become synonymous with pepper sauce and often is asked for by name. Use sparingly to give an intense flavor to a base sauce or independently to give hot flavor to a more subtle food. Hot pepper sauces vary dramatically in heat and flavor.

ⓓ Ketchup (catsup)

Ketchup, a derivation from French and Italian tomato sauces, is made with the added ingredients of vinegar, salt, sugar, and spices. Use as a topping on sandwiches, such as hamburgers and hot dogs, and as a flavor boost to fried potatoes, scrambled eggs, and meat loaf.

ⓔ Prepared mustard

Prepared or blended mustards fall into two categories: those that have a smooth consistency and those that maintain a coarse appearance. Smooth types consist of completely crushed and pulverized seeds. Those with a grainy or coarse consistency contain whole or partially ground mustard seeds. Some varieties of mustards have been infused with herbs or laden with honey. Use as a topping or as an ingredient in other sauces. (Photo not shown.)

Condiments *continued*

f Relish

Relishes are coarsely chopped or ground pickled ingredients. The most common flavors are sweet and dill. Use as a topping for other foods or as a flavor enhancer to sauces and dressings.

g Salsa

Salsa can consist of a base of tomatoes, tomatillos, corn, black beans, or fruit and the addition of onions and cilantro. There are typically two types of salsa: cooked and fresh. Ingredients are as varied as the recipes and prepared products now available. Serve as an accompaniment to tacos, burritos, fish entrées, and quesadillas.

h Soy sauce

Soy sauce is made from naturally fermented soy beans, yeast, wheat, and salt. Almost all soy sauce is liquid and dark in color, ranging from a pale brown tone to almost midnight black. Some variations are thick to almost pastelike. With the current interest in salt-reduced diets, there is a variety of salt-reduced versions available. Add soy sauce to rice, vegetables, meat, fish, and casseroles.

i Specialty vinegar

Vinegar is fermented liquid, usually a diluted form, from cider, wine, beer, or any crop that contains sugar (apples, grapes, grain, and so on). This acetic acid gets its name from the French vin aigre (sour wine) and can be used in many foods and recipes. Some familiar types of specialty vinegars include balsamic, black, champagne, cider, fruit flavored, herb infused, malt, seasoned rice, sherry, and wine.

j Wasabi

Wasabi is grown in Japan and is often referred to as Japanese horseradish. This edible green root is served in a pasty mound as an accompaniment to sushi, sashimi, and grilled meats and chicken. Although it does contain an intense bite, it is not related to the western version of grated root horseradish.

k Worcestershire sauce

Worcestershire sauce, trademarked since 1838, is a dark liquid condiment containing a base of malt vinegar, molasses, sugar, onions, garlic, tamarind, anchovies, and an array of spices. Use on meats, either cooked or uncooked, and add to soups, stews, marinades, sauces, and mixed drinks.

Asian Condiments

Asian condiments are those associated with Asian cuisine. They include dried mushrooms, hot mustard, oyster sauce, and plum sauce.

Asian Condiments

a Dried mushrooms
Cloud ear, black mushrooms, and shiitake are the most common dried mushrooms used in Asian cuisine. All need to be reconstituted and cooked before use. They are strong in flavor and add a complexity to the foods cooked with them.

b Dried shrimp
This shrimp is tiny, dried, and preserved salty. Add to Asian dishes as a flavoring only; it is not a food ingredient.

c Fish sauce
Fish sauce is a liquid seasoning made from water, anchovy extracts, and salt. The finer-quality products are more golden in color and contain a transparent luster. Fish sauce is used as a marinade in stir-fries.

d Hoisin sauce
Frequently called Asian ketchup, this sauce is sweet and pungent. Pair with vegetables, meats, seafood, and poultry, especially duck.

e Hot Asian mustard
This pungent condiment is made from mustard flour—finely ground mustard seed and flour—and water. It often comes in dry powdered form. Water is then added to the desired heat and consistency.

f Pickled ginger
Pink in color, this pickled version of sliced ginger is served with sushi and almost always used as a garnish in other Asian dishes.

g Plum sauce
Often thought of as the sweet-and-sour sauce for egg rolls and fried wontons, plum sauce can be made in a variety of flavors and degrees of sweetness. The more traditional homemade versions are on the savory side and consistently used as a sauce.

Prepared Mustards

Prepared mustards are condiments made from white (yellow), black, or brown mustard seed.

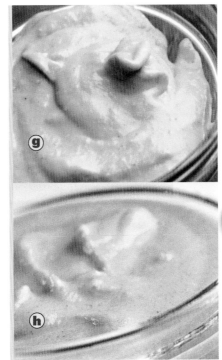

Prepared Mustards

ⓐ American-style

This is a smooth, bright yellow prepared mustard made from light-colored mustard seeds, sugar, vinegar, and turmeric. Mildly flavored, American-style mustard is often used as a sandwich topping or condiment specifically for hot dogs and corned beef, and paired with ketchup on hamburgers.

ⓑ Dijon style

A French prepared mustard coming from the Dijon region of the country, this mustard is made from brown or black mustard seeds, salt, a variety of spices, and the addition of unfermented grape juice or white wine.

ⓒ English

English mustard is a smooth medium-toned mustard made from brown, yellow, or white mustard seeds, turmeric, and wheat flour. It is hot flavored, and available prepared or in powdered form. It traditionally accompanies cheese sandwiches and those served at teatime.

ⓓ French

There are two versions of this French mustard: Bordeaux and Meaux. Bordeaux is made from brown or black mustard seeds, vinegar, sugar, and herbs (usually tarragon). It has a dark color, is mild in flavor, and is dominantly herb-flavored. Meaux is made from a combination of yellow, brown, and black mustard seeds. This mustard is grainy in texture and much spicier than the Bordeaux version.

ⓔ German

German mustard is a mixture of black mustard flour, vinegar, herbs, assorted spices, and a touch of caraway seed. Sometimes caramel coloring is added. A sweet-and-sour mustard, it is often served with cold meats and sausage.

ⓕ Grainy (coarse-grained)

A variation on the traditional versions, grainy mustard contains whole seeds along with partially ground ones, creating a grainy texture. (Photo shown below.)

ⓖ Hot

This is a variation on traditional versions, with the addition of chile peppers, horseradish, an assortment of spices, and vinegar.

ⓗ Oriental (Asian)

Oriental mustard is a smooth, hot paste prepared from mustard flour and water. It is used to enliven fried foods.

ⓘ Sweet

Sweet mustard is prepared with a large proportion of honey or brown sugar, making it sweet yet pungent. Use with smoked meats and as a topping on sandwiches. (Photo shown above.)

Hot Sauces

a) Harissa
Harissa tunisan is made from chiles, oil, cumin, fresh garlic, coriander, mint, and caraway seeds. Use with couscous and dried meats and to flavor soups and stews.

b) Nam prik
Nam prik is a traditional Thai sauce made by pounding together salted fish, chiles, soy sauce, garlic, fish sauce, lime juice, and sugar. It sometimes contains coconut milk. Use in rice dishes, with meat and poultry, and on noodles.

c) Sambal
Sambal is a spicy southeast Asian and Indonesian condiment with a number of variations. The one common ingredient is the chile. Other ingredients include lime juice, soy sauce, sugar, tamarind, garlic, onion, oil, and vinegar. The texture can vary from a paste to a relish.

d) Tabasco™ sauce
The Louisiana trademarked sauce is a spicy liquid made from a base of fiery hot peppers, vinegar, and salt. Tabasco™ scores 9,000–12,000 units on the Scoville scale. Add to soups, stews, and vegetables.

Hot Sauces

Hot sauces are used as a seasoning and fall into the condiment category. See the chart above. Many commercially prepared products are available for purchase. Some sauces are more like a relish or paste, the common ingredient being hot peppers.

Pickles

Pickles are made from fresh vegetables that are fermented, or have undergone chemical changes in their natural composition. Fermenting solutions, often called brines or vinegars, are flavored and seasoned with herbs and spices to impart flavor to the base vegetable. Common pickling spices include chiles, peppercorns, mustard seeds, whole allspice, mace, whole cloves, cardamom pods or seeds, broken cinnamon quills, and coriander seeds.

Pickled foods have always had a measure of popularity; with today's interest in ethnic foods and global commerce, this interest has soared. Cucumbers, peppers, carrots, cabbage, and a mix of assorted crisp vegetables are the favored choices in pickling. Fruits and fruit rinds can also be pickled and are usually referred to as spiced.

Cucumber Varieties

Pickling cucumbers are different from slicing cucumbers in that they are small, have sharp spines, and are bitter to taste. Varieties include dill and cornichon.

Dill pickles Dill pickles are available in a variety of shapes and sizes and fall into four categories:
- fermented in brine or vinegar
- unfermented, packed in brine and vinegar
- sour, fermented initially in salt, and then packed in a vinegar solution laden with spices, garlic, and usually dill
- sweet (really sweet-and-sour), initially packed in a brine and then drained and packed in a sweet sugar solution that is combined with vinegar

Half-sour The half-sour cucumber variety is considered the new crisp dill. This pickle is slightly tart, crisp, and can be served with a variety of sandwiches, such as corned beef and pastrami.

Cornichon The cornichon is a tiny, French, pickled gherkin, often served with meat pâté or as an accompaniment to smoked meats.

Pickled Vegetables

Vegetables are often preserved in a solution of vinegar flavored with spices, herbs, sugar, and salt (or a mixture thereof), and served as a part of the appetizer plate called mezze (mahza, maza, or mezah) in Middle Eastern cuisine. These spicy, crisp pickled vegetables often are flavored with curry.

Capers

Grown in Mediterranean regions, these almost round flower buds are usually sold bottled and pickled in vinegar. Opened jars should be kept tightly closed and refrigerated for up to several months. Capers are used in sauces, salad dressings, and seafood and can be combined with butter to flavor an assortment of cooked vegetables.

Cabbage Varieties

Pickling green cabbage can result in sauerkraut and kimchee, depending on how it is processed and on the ingredients used. Both ethnic varieties are prepared by a fermentation process.

Sauerkraut Sauerkraut is made from shredded cabbage that has been fermented by a process of dry salting. Sometimes spices are added. It can be used as a side dish or an accompaniment.

Kimchee Kimchee, most well known as Korea's fiery Napa cabbage condiment, is often made with other staple vegetables, such as cucumber and white radish. Regardless of the base vegetable, kimchee is layered in huge pottery crocks with fiery hot chiles, garlic, ginger, and green onions.

Table Olives

Olives are the fruit of small evergreen trees of the same name. Indigenous for over a thousand years in the Mediterranean regions, these stoned morsels remain a versatile product. See the chart below.

Raw green (unripened) and black (ripened) olives are bitter and must be processed and pickled (or cured) prior to eating. Methods for curing and preserving vary from region to region but historically include aging in baths of brine, water, or oil. Unripened olives can also be processed in an alkaline solution that cuts down the time factor. Mission olives from California are the product of this process. The olives are bathed in lye, which causes oxidization and deepens their color to black.

Olives

(a) Gaeta
This is an Italian black olive with a nutty flavor. Gaeta olives are either dry-cured, shown at right, or brine cured, making them smooth and shiny.

(b) Kalamata, or calamata
Often referred to as Greek olives, these olives are purple in color and brine-cured. They are very flavorful olives and can be found with or without stones. They are either packed in a vinegar-based liquid or in oil.

(c) Mission olives
These unripened green olives, bathed in lye changing their color to black, are from the Mission areas in California.

(d) Niçoise
Niçoise olives are red-brown in color, rather small, slightly sour, and lightly to moderately salted. They are not pitted.

(e) Picholine
Picholine olives have a tangy, almost fruity flavor.

(f) Spanish
Spanish olives are large, fleshy green olives, available stuffed or in their natural form.

(f)

Marinades

Marinades are seasoned prepared liquids or solutions for soaking a main ingredient, such as meats, poultry, game, fish, shellfish, or vegetables, providing them with added flavor and tenderization. In some cases, marinades also can serve as preservatives.

Components

There are two types of marinades. The first type includes only raw products. The second type uses products that have been cooked. Marinades contain liquids that have acid components, or they can have a neutral base. Oil is another option.

Acids such as wine, lemon juice, vinegar, or vegetable juices can be used as a fat-free base. The acidity also causes the deterioration of tough connective tissue in meats, thus causing tenderization.

Regardless of the type of marinade used, herbs, aromatics, and spices are often included. If using acidic ingredients, marinate in stainless steel or a nonporous ceramic or plastic container such as polycarbonate. The marinating food product should be tightly covered and refrigerated throughout the process. If the primary ingredient is not totally immersed in the marinade, it should be turned frequently to ensure consistent flavor and tenderization throughout.

Fats and Oils

Fats and oils belong to a family of compounds known as lipids. Fat refers to a lipid that is solid at room temperature and derived from an animal source. Oil generally refers to a lipid that is liquid at room temperature and is made from a vegetable or plant source.

Cholesterol is an animal fat not found in vegetable oil products but present in all meat and animal products. Fats and oils have the same chemical framework. They are composed of glycerol and three types of fatty acids: monounsaturated, polyunsaturated, and saturated.

Monounsaturated Monounsaturated fats are liquid at room temperature and therefore have a tendency to become rancid quickly when exposed to oxygen. Fats in this category include olive oil, canola oil, and peanut oil.

Polyunsaturated Polyunsaturated fats are usually liquid at room temperature; they also have a tendency to become rancid quickly when exposed to oxygen. Safflower, sunflower, corn, soy bean, and cottonseed oils are polyunsaturated fats.

Saturated Saturated fats are solid at room temperature. Tropical oils, such as coconut, palm, and palm kernel, are the exception to this rule; although they are liquid at room temperature, they are saturated fats.

Hydrogenation

Antioxidants, one of which is vitamin E, are often added to fats to extend their shelf life. Another way of protecting monounsaturated and polyunsaturated fats from oxidative rancidity is hydrogenation. *Hydrogenation* is a manufacturing process by which the fatty acids in polyunsaturated vegetable oil are altered to extend the oil's freshness, raise its smoking point, and change it from a liquid to a solid. Margarine is an example of a substance that is made by hydrogenating vegetable oil.

Margarine must include 80% oil, have at least 15,000 added IUs of vitamin A, and be an aqueous solution, such as one made of milk products and water. Ingredients such as salt and vitamins and those that enhance taste, texture, or stability may also be added. Because it is made from vegetable oils, margarine also contains vitamin E. Margarine products that have less than 80% oil are frequently called "spreads" or lowfat, reduced-fat, or fat-free margarine.

Prime sources of monounsaturated fats include olive oil and canola oil. Most other vegetable and plant-based oils (with the exception of the tropicals) and fish are good sources of polyunsaturated fats. Hydrogenated oils, coconut oil, palm oil, palm kernel oil, and animal fat are all saturated fats.

Smoking Point

Fats and oils are often chosen on the basis of personal taste, saturation level, and smoking point. The *smoking point* is the maximum temperature to which the fat or oil can be taken before it begins to burn, tainting the flavor and changing the color. See Figure 12-5. The smoking point of fat or oil will determine the type of cooking method used—methods with high heat require fats or oils that can withstand the temperatures. The smoking point of a fat or oil is lowered with each repeated use.

Economic Aspects

The cost of a fat or oil depends on the original cost of the product from which the fat or oil is taken; on processing, supply, and demand; and on the cost of comparable food values. For example, margarine is less expensive than butter, and lard is slightly less expensive than hydrogenated fats. Olive oil is generally more expensive than other vegetable oils, and many imported olive oils cost more than those produced in this country.

Product Selection

There are hundreds of products available for use in the kitchen or dining room. Some are as ancient as lard and others as new as canola oil blends. Select the product by comparing color, melting point, plasticity, smoking point, stability, emulsification value, shortening value, and flavor. See Figure 12-6 on page 194.

Animal Fats

Lard is obtained from the fatty tissue of pigs and varies in composition and characteristics according to the type of feed given the pig and the part of the animal from which the lard is obtained. Lard from pigs fed on soy beans or peanuts is much softer than lard from corn-fed animals, and lard made from fat near the organs is firmer than that made from the fat of other parts of the animal. *Prime steam lard* comes from the fat that is stripped from the internal organs of the animal at the time of slaughter. *Dry-rendered leaf lard* is made from the internal fat. It is firmer than other lards and slightly grainy because of the slow chilling it undergoes after being heated during processing.

Suet, another type of animal fat, is obtained from the area around the kidneys and loins of beef and sheep. It is harder than fats from other parts of the animals. Suet is marketed as oleo stearin or oleo. Suet is used in the production of baked goods and crackers.

Shortenings

Vegetable shortening is a lipid used for frying or baking. In baking, the effect of shortening is a crisp product that does not rise significantly. Because hydrogenated vegetable shortenings hold most of the air incorporated in mixing, they are preferred for cakes. High-ratio cake shortenings are made by adding 2%–5% monoglycerides and diglycerides to hydrogenated shortenings to improve their baking and emulsifying properties.

Fat Compounds

Fat compounds are produced by combining 20% rendered animal fats and 80% hydrogenated vegetable oils. A fat compound may also be any mixture of animal fats. Fat compounds are no longer widely used because of the increased public demand for unsaturated and cholesterol-free fats and oils.

Fat Substitutes

The demand for low-fat and nonfat products has spurred the use of fat substitutes, each of which is limited in its use, function, and appeal. Fat substitutes may be carbohydrate-based, such as fruit purées and pastes, gels (made from starch), gums, maltodextrin (made from corn), or oatrim (made from oats); fat-based, such as olestra and salatrim; or protein-based, such as microparticulated proteins from milk or egg whites.

Fat substitutes may be used as ingredients or can be found in prepared products such as cake mixes, candy, salad dressings, dips, cheese, potato chips, crackers, spreads, and ice cream.

FIGURE 12-5

Smoking Point	Type of Oil or Fat	Temperature
	Whole butter	Above 250°F (121°C)
	Clarified butter	Above 330°F (166°C)
	Vegetable oils	An average of 450°F (232°C) or above, with the exception of extra-virgin olive oil, which has a smoking point closer to 420°F (216°C)
	Vegetable shortenings	An average of 370°F (188°C) or above
	Lard	An average of 375°F (191°C)

FIGURE 12-6

BUTTER-FLAVORED VEGETABLE OIL

A blended oil often flavored with artificial butter flavoring; use for griddling, baked goods, and coating production line breads; polyunsaturate

CANOLA

A derivative product from rapeseeds, low in saturated fat, high in monounsaturated fat; contains omega-3 fatty acids; use in cooking and baking

COCONUT

High in saturated fat; an ingredient in blended oils and shortenings; almost colorless and tasteless; use for commercial baked goods

CORN

A by-product of the manufacturing of starch, cornmeal, syrup, and hominy; light amber in tone and clear-colored when fresh; inexpensive product with a high smoking point; use on salads; polyunsaturate

COTTONSEED

High in polyunsaturates; colorless and tasteless; can become rancid quickly; use in salad dressings

GRAPESEED

Processed from grape seeds; exhibits a fairly deep color (yellow or green) and flavor; use in salad dressings and for cooking; polyunsaturate

INFUSED OILS

Contain added ingredients that change or alter the flavor of the oil, including basil, roasted garlic, lemon, chile, roasted pepper, rosemary, and so on; can become rancid quickly; outbreaks of botulism have occurred because of time and temperature abuse; use during the cooking process, add to foods as a base for salad dressings, marinades, or sauces, or dip breads into it

OLIVE

Ranges in color from very pale yellow to green; quality can be compromised by region of growth, weather conditions, ripeness, care in collection, and the extraction process; high in monounsaturated fats; use as a base in salad dressings, in cooking and baking, and as an ingredient in sauces, such as pesto

PEANUT

Colorful, flavorful; high smoking point; use in Asian cuisine and for frying; foods cooked with peanut oil can cause severe and potentially toxic reactions in those with nut allergies; monounsaturate

SAFFLOWER

High in polyunsaturates; high smoking point; prone to rancidity; use in salad dressing and mayonnaise

SALAD

A highly refined blend of vegetable oils, light in color and taste; use in salad dressings and in the preparation of mayonnaise; polyunsaturate

SESAME SEED

Processed from the tiny roasted seeds with a deep color and nutty flavor; use in ethnic cuisine, such as Asian and Middle Eastern; drizzle on top of prepared foods to add a complexity to the flavor of the food; combine with soy bean or canola oil (rapeseed) for frying; polyunsaturate

SOY BEAN

Yellow to clear in color; quality affected by climate conditions, soil, and processing; use as a salad dressing; polyunsaturate

VEGETABLE

The generic name for oils extracted from vegetable or plant-related matter; some types of these oils include corn, soy bean, safflower, and cottonseed; polyunsaturate

WALNUT

Highly perishable and expensive; purchase in small quantities to avoid waste; use as a base in salad dressings, over noodles, and during the cooking process; monounsaturate

Cooking and Flavoring with Alcohol

Alcohol, such as wine, beer, liqueurs, and ciders, can be used to cook and flavor a variety of food. Using alcohol in food usually falls into two separate categories: foods that are cooked and foods that are not cooked. Alcohol is also a component of some marinades.

Cooked Dishes

Alcohol can be used a number of ways in cooking and in baking. Brandies are used in pâtés and terrines, flambéed meats, and desserts. Wine, ciders, and beer are often used with foods that are cooked because of their low proof of alcohol. The alcohol is usually added prior to cooking to give the food a distinct flavor. Wines also are used in marinades, consommés, and court bouillon and as poaching liquids. Chicken, beef, and veal dishes use wine as an important ingredient. Beer is a major component in soups, chicken and beef dishes, and batters. Traditionally in Normandy, cider is used in chicken, fish, and rabbit entrées.

Uncooked Dishes

Flavored liqueurs or spirits may be added to uncooked foods such as icings, mousses, beverages, fruit salads, and sweet sauces. Liqueurs or spirits are added to food to enhance flavor.

Marinades

Alcohol can be used as a preservative when added to a marinade. Asian cooking often uses sherry in fish and meat preparations. Fish, fruits, and some vegetables benefit from the addition of dry white wine as a marinade. Red wine can also be used as a marinade for fish and meat preparations.

Nuts and Seeds

A variety of nuts and seeds can be added to foods to enhance natural flavor, add color, and create texture. They also provide nutritional density to foods. Nuts are available shelled, unshelled, roasted, toasted, blanched, chopped (finely or coarsely), slivered, sliced, or processed into nut butters. The toasting and roasting of nuts brings out their own natural flavors. Nuts can be used in savory or sweet dishes and are a bakery staple. When purchasing nut products, save on food costs by ordering broken pieces to use as chopped nuts in recipes or formulas.

Seeds can also be used to add flavor and textures to food or to garnish a dish; the size and shape of the seeds create visual interest. Some seeds, such as cumin, coriander, celery, and fennel, are considered spices and are used during the cooking process rather than as a garnish. Poppy and sesame seeds, both white and black, are often used for baked goods but can be incorporated into savory dishes.

Storing Nuts and Seeds

Both nuts and seeds should be stored in airtight containers with limited exposure to light. Since nuts and seeds are prone to rancidity and pest infestation, purchase in quantities appropriate to usage. When purchasing nuts, make sure that they come from a current crop yield. Nuts that have not been shelled will keep longer than those removed from their shells or those that have been roasted.

Nuts

There are many nuts to choose from. See the chart on pages 197–199. Keep in mind that any dishes containing nuts or nut oils should be specified on the menu to avoid potential health risks. Nuts and nut oil can be highly toxic to those who are allergic to nuts.

Nut Butters

Nut butters are made from whole nuts, making a smooth spread that can be used in doughs, frostings, fillings, and ice cream. The benefit of adding nut butters to baked goods is longevity of shelflife and improved flavor, richness, and taste.

Nut butters are sometimes used as a substitute for oil and fat because they are plant based and do not contain any cholesterol. Varieties of nut butters include roasted almond, peanut, pecan, filbert, and walnut. Nut butters are available in pails, cans, or jars.

Nuts

ⓐ Almonds

Almonds are tear-shaped single nuts with a medium brown covering. The flavor ranges from sweet to bitter. Sweet almonds are added to foods; bitter almonds are used as a source for almond extracts and flavorings. Almonds can be purchased whole in shells or out of shells, skinned, sliced, chopped, or as a paste.

ⓑ Brazils

Brazils are the seeds of enormous hardwood trees. The nuts are encased in a hard outer shelled orb, containing orange-like segments which are the individual nuts. They are harvested only after the woody-shelled orbs fall to the ground. The whole nuts may be purchased in the shell or shelled and can range in size from medium to large. The larger nuts are most often used in confectioneries and baked goods.

ⓒ Cashews

The cashew is the edible kidney-shaped seed of a tropical evergreen tree. Cashews, always hulled, are available either salted or unsalted. For cooking, it is preferable to use unsalted cashews; the salted ones tend to contain too much salt.

ⓓ Chestnuts

Chestnuts contain more starch and less fat than most nuts. Large, rounded, and glistening brown, these nuts are often roasted whole. Chestnuts can be purchased fresh, dried, or canned. The naturally sweet, meaty nut pairs well with sweets and savory foods such as soups, purées, stuffings, and butters. Chestnuts can be toasted, steamed, or boiled prior to peeling, but they are always cooked.

ⓔ Hazelnuts/filberts

These two names, used interchangeably, refer to nuts that are found in the wild (hazelnuts) or cultivated from the European species (filberts). The largest commercial producer of hazelnuts is Turkey. Most often used in baked goods, desserts, and confectioneries, these nuts are also added to savory foods. Shelled filberts (hazelnuts) tend to be more shelf-stable than many other nuts.

ⓕ Macadamias

Macadamias are creamy white nuts encased in a hard shell that must be removed by a machine. They are sold shelled and usually vacuum packed in small glass jars. Macadamia nuts are high in fat and flavor. Combine with chocolate, coconut, and fruits that are fresh or dried.

ⓖ Peanuts

Peanuts, also called groundnuts, are members of the legume or pea family. High in protein, vitamins, and minerals, these nuts are considered highly nutritious. Unshelled in their fibrous coverings, peanuts keep well in cool, dark environments for several months; shelled, they are not as shelf-stable and should be kept in cool areas or in the refrigerator. Well-known by-products include peanut oil and peanut butter. Peanuts are sold in the shell, shelled, raw, roasted, salted, unsalted, or sugar-coated. Use as a flavor boost for subtle foods and to thicken sauces. Add to confectioneries, ice creams, puddings, baked goods, entrées, and side dishes.

Roasting Chestnuts

Chestnuts have a naturally sweet flavor that pairs well with soups, stuffings, purées, and butters.

A popular way to prepare chestnuts is roasting. To do this:

(h)

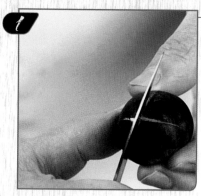

1 Cut a cross into the rounded side of each chestnut.

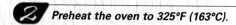

2 Preheat the oven to 325°F (163°C).

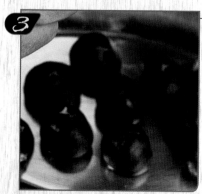

3 Arrange the chestnuts, cut side up, in a shallow baking pan.

4 Place the baking pan in the preheated oven, and roast the chestnuts for approximately 20 minutes.

5 Remove the baking pan from the oven. Peel the chestnuts when just cool enough to handle.

Nuts *continued*

(h) Pecans
These can be used in sweet or savory dishes and are often added to cakes, cookies, candies, breadings for fish and chicken, and peppered in stuffings.

(i) Pine nuts (pignoli)
Pine nuts are the tender kernels of pine cones; they have a soft shell and no skin and are high in oil. Pine nuts are fairly perishable and should be kept tightly covered in a cool, dark pantry, refrigerator, or freezer. Use in baked goods, desserts, confectioneries, and savory dishes. Add to stuffings and pesto.

(j) Pistachios
Pistachios are usually green in color but can range from yellow to creamy beige. They are available in the shell or shelled, salted or unsalted. The naturally beige shell is sometimes dyed red with no benefit or purpose. Use in baked goods, desserts and ice cream, or salt and eat as a snack food.

(k) Walnuts
Walnuts are the edible fruits of the walnut tree. The most common species is the Persian walnut, also known as the English walnut. Walnuts are graded by size: small, medium, and large. They are available in the shell, shelled, halved, or chopped. Use in baked goods, desserts, and confectioneries. Add to savory foods and condiment products.

Seeds

Like nuts, seeds can be added to many dishes to enhance a food's natural flavor, nutritive value, or visual appeal.

Seeds

(a) Poppy seeds
Common poppy seeds are the small, round, gray to blue-black seeds of the poppy plant. The Indian version is a tiny off-white seed and is usually used as a thickener and in baked goods.

(b) Pumpkin seeds
These are the seeds entangled in the fibrous strands of the interior of a pumpkin. They are available in their shells, shelled, salted, unsalted, roasted, or raw. Use as a garnish and in Mexican cuisine, and make into roasted pumpkin seed oil.

(c) Sesame seeds
These tiny flat seeds, either white, yellow, or black, come from an annual herb. The seeds have more flavor if toasted and can be used whole, pressed into oil, or pulverized into a flavorful paste called tahini. Many ethnic foods are enhanced by the tiny seeds. They can be sprinkled on baked goods, rice dishes, and salads; used as a coating; mashed into dressings; mixed with salt and other spices to form a seasoning mix; made into halvah; or used as a garnish for visual interest to a plated dish.

(d) Sunflower seeds
The seeds of the sunflower are grown primarily to be pressed into oil. Sunflower seeds are also a popular snack food when toasted and salted. Native to North America, this member of the daisy family is prized in Russia, where the seeds are used in sweets.

Dairy products and eggs have long been favored for their contributions to the human diet. Cave paintings made in the Libyan Sahara in 5000 B.C. show people milking animals and making cheese. Goats and sheep provided the first dairy products for humans. Later, cows supplied dairy products for much of the world. Although eggs did not become important food sources until later, both the Greeks and the Romans were using eggs in the kitchen by 25 B.C.

Before the use of refrigeration and pasteurization, milk spoiled rapidly. However, humans quickly learned that they could preserve milk by making butter and cheese. By the first century A.D., the Romans were master cheese makers, using a cheese press to extract excess liquid from the curd. Over the years, people have experimented with many variations in milk- and cheese-making processes. As a result, a great diversity of cheeses is available today.

1500 B.C.
Aryan invaders introduce ghee, or clarified butter, to India.

A.D. 1856
Louis Pasteur begins experiments that lead to pasteurization.

1877
The first commercial milking machines appear.

1948
Ultra high temperature pasteurization of milk begins.

1988
Lowfat and skim milk sales exceed whole milk sales.

and Eggs

Milk

Milk is a dairy product that is valued as a nutritious beverage, an ingredient in cooking, and the foundation of other dairy products, including butter, cheese, and yogurt.

The composition of milk varies, depending on the type of animal, the breed, the animal's diet, the season, and even the time of day the animal is milked. Unless qualified, milk in this book refers to cow's milk. Cow's milk is composed primarily of water (88%). It contains about 3.5% milkfat and about 8.5% milk solids in the form of proteins (primarily casein), lactose (milk sugar), minerals, and vitamins. Milk provides a rich source of calcium, as well as vitamins A, D, E, K, C, and B. Most milk is fortified with additional vitamin D. To replace the vitamin A drawn off with the removal of milkfat, lowfat and skim milk products are fortified with vitamin A.

A government grading system classifies milk as Grade A, B, or C on the basis of the milk's bacterial count. Grade A milk is the highest grade.

Casein is the primary protein in milk. It causes milk to clump and curdle in the presence of acid, too much salt, or too-high heat. When milk is heated, a skin can form on top. The skin is actually coagulated protein and fat. Milk also can coagulate, or become firm, and then burn on the bottom of a pan. Continuous stirring, heavy cookware, moderate heat, and minimal cook times help limit coagulation.

Milk Processing Methods

Milk provides a favorable host for the growth of bacteria, many of which can cause serious illness. Because of this, almost all milk is treated to kill bacteria and increase its keeping qualities and shelf life.

Pasteurization In the 1860s, French chemist Louis Pasteur discovered a way to use heat to prevent spoilage of beer and wine without destroying their flavor. *Pasteurization* applies the same theory to the treatment of milk. Law requires all Grade A milk to be pasteurized. In fact, nearly all milk sold commercially in Western countries is pasteurized. The most common pasteurization technique heats milk to 161°F (72°C) for 15 seconds and then rapidly cools the milk to 45°F (7°C). Pasteurization kills most bacteria and extends the keeping qualities of milk by killing naturally occurring enzymes that cause milk to spoil. Pasteurized milk, properly refrigerated, stays fresh for about one week.

Ultrapasteurization Often used to extend the shelf life of cream, *ultrapasteurization* subjects dairy products to much higher temperatures for shorter periods, destroying nearly all bacteria. Unopened, refrigerated ultrapasteurized milk and cream stays fresh for 60–90 days. Once opened, the product stays fresh about as long as conventionally pasteurized milk products.

Ultra high temperature processing
Ultra high temperature (UHT) processing combines the process of ultra-pasteurization with specialized packaging. Holding the milk for 2–6 seconds at 280°F–300°F (138°C–149°C) sterilizes it. Hermetically sealed sterile containers block out bacteria, gases, and light. Unopened UHT milk can safely be stored without refrigeration for up to 3 months. After it is opened, handle UHT milk in the same way as conventionally pasteurized milk products.

Homogenization In untreated milk, milkfat particles float to the top, creating a layer of cream. This happens because the fat globules, which are lighter than the surrounding water, are too large to stay suspended in the emulsion. To prevent the separation of milkfat, most commercially sold milk is homogenized. *Homogenization* breaks down fat globules by forcing the warm milk through a very fine nozzle. This process reduces the fat particles to one-tenth their original size, thus allowing the milkfat to stay suspended in liquid.

Certification *Certified milk* has met strict sanitary conditions. Veterinarians examine the herd to make sure that all the cows are disease-free. Doctors review the health of dairy workers. Rigid inspections ensure that milking equipment is sanitary. Some states allow certification of raw milk as well as pasteurized products.

Removal of milkfat Removing milkfat fills the demand for variety in milk and cream products. To remove milkfat, milk is processed in a separator, a type of centrifuge. The milk spins at high speeds, causing the lighter milk to collect at the outer wall of the separator, while the denser cream collects in the center, where it is piped off. Modern separators can produce a range of milk products, from whole milk to lowfat or reduced fat to skim. See Figure 13-1 for a description of milk products. See Figure 13-2 for information about cream varieties and Figures 13-3, 13-4, and 13-5 on page 203 for examples of whipping cream.

FIGURE 13-1

Milk Products

LIQUID WHOLE MILK
Contains not less than 3.25% milkfat and 8.25% milk solids. Vitamins A and D are optional additions, as are flavoring ingredients, such as chocolate.

LIQUID LOWFAT OR REDUCED-FAT MILK
Milk with some fat removed. Contains between 0.5% and 2% milkfat and not less than 8.25% milk solids. Common lowfat milk includes 1% milk; reduced-fat milk includes 2% milk. Lowfat and reduced-fat milks must contain added vitamin A; vitamin D is optional.

LIQUID SKIM MILK
Also called fat-free or nonfat milk; all or most fat removed. Less than 0.5% milkfat and not less than 8.25% milk solids. Vitamin A must be added. Vitamin D is optional.

EVAPORATED MILK
Canned concentrated milk, formed from evaporating about 60% of the water from whole or skim milk; cooked flavor and darker color than regular milk; condensed whole milk contains at least 6.5% milkfat and 16.5% milk solids.

SWEETENED CONDENSED MILK
Whole milk with 60% of its water removed and a large quantity of sugar added. Pasteurized; usually sold in cans. Sweetened condensed milk is not an acceptable substitute for whole or evaporated milk.

DRY MILK POWDER
Milk with nearly all moisture removed. Often made from skim milk, although whole milk powder is also available. Dry milk can be used to enrich baked goods or can be reconstituted in water.

FIGURE 13-2

Varieties of Cream

HALF AND HALF
A mixture of milk and cream; contains at least 10.5% milkfat but no more than 18% milkfat; used in baking and as an enrichment; served with coffee and cereal.

LIGHT CREAM
Also called coffee cream or table cream; contains between 18% and 30% milkfat; used in baking and as an enrichment; served with coffee and cereal.

LIGHT WHIPPING CREAM
Also called whipping cream; contains between 30% and 36% milkfat; can be whipped or used in making sauces, ice cream, and other desserts.

HEAVY WHIPPING CREAM
Also called heavy cream; contains at least 36% milkfat; whips well; used as a topping, for thickening, and as enrichment for sauces and desserts.

Receiving and Storing Milk, Cream, and Cultured Dairy Products

Proper temperature is key to maintaining the wholesomeness of dairy products. Receive fresh milk, cream, and cultured dairy products, such as yogurt and sour cream, at 41°F (5°C) or lower. Inspect canned milk products, such as *evaporated milk* and *sweetened condensed milk,* to look for dents, rust, bulges, and signs of leakage. Examine packages of dry milk for leakage, lumps, evidence of exposure to excess moisture, and signs of insects and rodents.

Label and date fluid milk, cream, and cultured dairy products, and then refrigerate them at 41°F (5°C) or lower. To minimize absorption of odors, store fresh dairy products in closed containers, away from other foods. Stored in this way, fresh milk products will keep for about one week. Freezing is not recommended.

Store canned milk products at least 6 inches off the floor and 6 inches away from the wall at 50°F–70°F (10°C–21°C). Inspect cans regularly for signs of spoilage. Unopened canned milk products keep for about a year at room temperature. Dry milk powder can be stored for several months, provided that it is kept in tightly closed containers in cool, dry storage.

Foodborne Illness and Dairy Products

Bacteria grow well in dairy foods because of the high protein and moisture content. Unpasteurized dairy products are particularly vulnerable. Pasteurization destroys *Mycobacterium tuberculosis* and many other disease-causing microorganisms found in milk. However, pasteurized milk is not sterile and contains a small number of bacteria. Other organisms can infect milk after pasteurization. Improperly stored and handled milk products can harbor *Staphylococcus, Salmonella, E. coli,* and *Listeria.*

Other Milks

All female mammals produce milk to feed their young, so it is not surprising that humans take milk from a variety of species. People in parts of Africa and the Middle East prize camel milk. Some groups in northern Scandinavia and Russia take milk from reindeer. Although cow's milk is the most common, people in many parts of the world use milk from sheep, water buffalo, and goats.

Soy milk Soy milk has a unique odor and flavor. In many Western countries, soy milk's taste and odor are removed, and it is often flavored with fruits. People who have lactose intolerance, choose to avoid animal fats, or cannot drink dairy milk may choose soy milk. Although it cannot always substitute for dairy milk, soy milk is used for milkshakes, custards, and sauces.

Almond milk The use of almonds in milk dates back to early Arabic and medieval European times. Today almond milk, made with blanched almonds, sugar, and distilled water, is used in the sweet, jellied *blancmange* and in savory drinks such as orgeat.

Rice milk Rice milk—rice steeped in cow's milk and mixed with breadcrumbs, sugar, and fennel—was given to nursing babies in Elizabethan England. Today rice milk is used to make desserts such as rice pudding and rice porridge. To make rice milk, mix blanched, cooked rice with boiled milk. Add sugar when making a dessert such as rice pudding.

Sheep's milk Sheep's milk has a higher fat (6.7%) and protein (5.8%) content than cow's milk does. People drink sheep's milk and make yogurt and cheese from it. True Roquefort cheese is made from sheep's milk. Feta is traditionally made with sheep's milk or a mixture of sheep's and goat's milk.

Water buffalo's milk Water buffalo's milk has a high percentage of fat (7.2%) and a protein count comparable to that of cow's milk (3.8%). Provolone was first made with water buffalo's milk. Today the best quality mozzarella comes from the milk of the water buffalo.

Goat's milk Goat's milk contains a similar amount of fat and protein as cow's milk, but the smaller fat globules in goat's milk stay suspended, making homogenization unnecessary. Cheese made from goat's milk is referred to as *chèvre* (the French word for "goat") and is noted for its sharp, tangy flavor.

FIGURE 13-3
Soft peaks of heavy whipping cream form when the cream is whipped to between one-half and three-quarter volume.

FIGURE 13-4
Firm peaks of heavy whipping cream are whipped to maximum volume and used for decorations such as rosettes.

FIGURE 13-5
Overwhipped cream loses its sheen, becomes grainy, and starts to curdle.

Fermented Dairy Products

Fermented dairy products, also called cultured dairy products, result from the addition of a starter bacterial culture to fluid dairy products. Under the right temperature conditions, these lactic-acid-producing bacteria reproduce rapidly, causing milk or cream to ferment. The fermentation process gives dairy products a tangy flavor and thicker consistency.

Cultured Products

Buttermilk, yogurt, sour cream, and crème fraîche are the most common cultured dairy products.

Buttermilk Traditionally, buttermilk was a by-product of the butter-making process. Today people make buttermilk by introducing starter cultures from bacterial strains into skim or lowfat milk and then holding the milk at a controlled temperature for 12–14 hours. Buttermilk adds a distinctive, tart taste to baked goods and other dishes. Some people enjoy buttermilk as a beverage.

Yogurt Yogurt adds a tangy flavor to sauces or other dishes and provides a lowfat substitute for sour cream. Yogurt is made by the same process as that for buttermilk but with different bacterial strains. This causes the milk to ferment and coagulate into a custardlike consistency. Some commercial yogurt contains live active bacteria. Medical research shows that yogurt with live active cultures helps the body produce lactase, an enzyme that breaks down lactose. This aids digestion, especially in those who have difficulty digesting milk products because of lactose intolerance. Research also suggests that eating yogurt with live active cultures speeds recovery from some forms of intestinal illness.

Sour cream Sour cream is made using the same process and bacteria as those for buttermilk, but it typically uses cream with 18% milkfat as its base. Sour cream is smooth, thick, and tangy.

Crème fraîche Commercial *crème fraîche* is cultured, heavy cream that resembles a thinner, richer version of sour cream. Widely available in Europe, crème fraîche is expensive in the United States. Crème fraîche is made by heating 1 quart (1 L) of heavy cream to 100°F (38°C), adding 3 ounces (100 ml) of buttermilk, and putting the mixture in a warm place until thickened, about 6–24 hours.

Making Emmental Cheese

Emmental gets its name from the Emme valley near Bern, Switzerland, the place where Emmental cheese was first made. Although the Swiss in Emme began making cheese in the Middle Ages, they did not produce giant wheels of Emmental until the sixteenth century.

It takes a day's milk production from 80 cows to make one wheel of Emmental. The cheese maker begins by heating unpasteurized milk to 90°F (32°C) and then adding rennet and special bacteria. As the milk begins to curdle, proteins coagulate. When the curds reach the desired consistency, they are cut into tiny pieces and then heated again. After about two hours, the whey is pumped out, and the cheese is pressed into huge molds.

The next day the wheel of cheese enters a saltwater bath, where it will stay for about two days, absorbing salt as it releases liquid. The rind, which will maintain the cheese's flavor over time, begins to form. Removed from the saltwater bath, the wheel spends the next two weeks in a cool salt cellar. Then the cheese maker moves the wheel to a warmer fermentation cellar, where the cheese will spend the next six to eight weeks. Bacteria within the cheese cause carbon dioxide to build up inside the wheel. As the gas bubbles burst, large, glossy holes in the cheese remain.

Next, the Emmental wheel goes into cool storage, where it will ripen and develop its characteristic nutty flavor. In the storage cellar, cheese makers turn the cheese and clear away mold from the rind, ensuring that the cheese will ripen from the inside out. Finally, after nearly five months, the cheese is ready. Emmental reaches full maturity when it is 10 months old.

Cheeses

Cheese results from an interaction between milk and bacteria or an enzyme called rennet. The milk proteins (casein) coagulate, forming the solid curds, which then are drained from the liquid whey. Further processing, which may include pressing; salting; adding special bacteria, yeast, or mold; aging; and curing, creates the variety of cheeses available today.

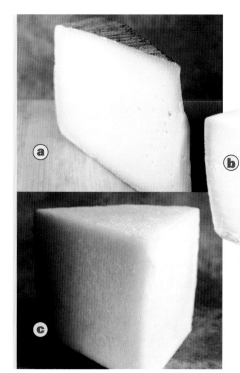

Hard Cheeses

Hard cheeses have been aged to reduce moisture content to about 30%. Hard cheeses often are used for grating. Maximum flavor comes from freshly grated cheese.

ⓐ Asiago

Asiago is an Italian cow's milk cheese with a tangy, nutty flavor and a texture that varies depending on the age of the cheese. Asiago is white to pale yellow and melts easily.

ⓑ Parmigiano-Reggiano (Parmesan)

True Parmigiano-Reggiano is a cow's milk cheese from an area in Italy near Parma. It has a sharp, spicy taste and a very hard, dry texture and is nearly always used for grating or shaving. Parmesan produced in the United States and elsewhere does not match the flavor of the original. Parmigiano-Reggiano is used in gratins and pastas and as a topping for salads and other dishes.

ⓒ Pecorino Romano

Made in central and southern Italy from sheep's milk, Pecorino Romano has a robust and piquant flavor and is noticeably salty. It can be served as a table cheese or grated for cooking.

Firm Cheeses

Firm cheeses have a moisture content of 30%—40%, giving them a firm, solid texture. Their flavors can range from mild to quite sharp, depending on age.

(a) Cheddar

With origins in Great Britain, cheddar is now the most popular cheese in the world. This cow's milk cheese ranges from mild to sharp in flavor and has a dense texture. Orange cheddars owe their color to vegetable dye. Uncolored cheddars are pale yellow. Colby is a popular mild American cheddar. Use cheddar in grilling and cooking, as well as on sandwiches and snack trays.

(b) Emmental

Emmental is the original cow's milk Swiss cheese with very large holes caused by gases that form during ripening. It has a mild, nutty taste and comes in 200-pound wheels enclosed in rind. Emmental is the classic choice for fondue, but it also is used in sandwiches and snack and dessert trays.

(c) Gruyère

Another Swiss cow's milk cheese, Gruyère, has a mild, nutty taste, moist texture, and small holes. Because Gruyère melts easily, it is suitable for cooking. It also can be served as an appetizer and as a dessert cheese.

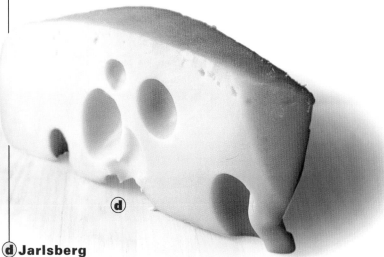

(d)

(d) Jarlsberg

Although Jarlsberg is a cow's milk cheese from Norway, its taste, fat content, and appearance are similar to the Swiss Emmental. Use Jarlsberg on cheese boards, in sandwiches, and in cooking.

(e) Monterey Jack

Monterey Jack is a rich cow's milk cheese from California. It ranges from mild and pale to a sharp and pungent yellow cheese. Monterey Jack sometimes contains peppers or herbs for flavor. It melts well, making it an appropriate choice for cooking.

(f) Provolone

Provolone is a cow's milk cheese from southern Italy. It has a pale yellow color and a flavor that ranges from mild to sharp, depending on age. Provolone also comes smoked and in a variety of shapes, including cones, rounds, and cylinders. Use provolone in cooking, as well as in sandwiches or as an appetizer.

(g) Swiss

Swiss cheese is a domestically produced product made in the style of the classic Swiss cheese, Emmental.

Semisoft Cheeses

Semisoft cheeses have a moisture content of 40%–50%. Their texture is smooth and sliceable but not spreadable. Semisoft cheeses can be classified into two groups: the smooth, buttery cheeses and the veined cheeses, which owe their distinctive appearance and taste to the veins of mold running through them.

ⓐ Bel Paese
Bel Paese is an Italian cow's milk cheese with a smooth, creamy texture and mild flavor. Its name means "beautiful country." Use Bel Paese in cooking and as an appetizer.

ⓑ Doux de Montagne
Doux de Montagne is a cow's milk cheese produced in the French Pyrenees. It has a creamy, slightly sweet flavor. Doux de Montagne often is served as an appetizer.

ⓒ Fontina
Fontina is a nutty, rich cow's milk cheese from Italy. It has a slightly elastic touch and a few small holes. The French make their own version, called Fontal. Use fontina on dessert trays and in cooking.

ⓓ Gorgonzola
Gorgonzola is a blue-veined cow's milk cheese from Italy. It has a distinct aroma and a tangy, pungent flavor that is sharper in mature cheeses. Its texture is smoother than that of other blue-veined cheeses, such as Roquefort or Stilton. Gorgonzola is used in sauces, on cheese trays, with fruit, and in mixed salads.

ⓔ Gouda
Gouda is a Dutch cow's milk cheese with a pale yellow color and a mellow, buttery flavor. Mature Gouda has a firmer texture and a more pronounced flavor. Gouda often is packaged in red or yellow wax-covered wheels. Use Gouda in cooking and serve it as an appetizer, with fruit, and on dessert trays.

ⓕ Havarti
Havarti is a cow's milk cheese from Denmark. This pale creamy cheese is filled with many small irregular holes. It has a mild, buttery taste and sometimes is flavored with caraway seeds. Havarti makes a fine addition to a snack tray or sandwich.

ⓖ Muenster
Cow's milk Muenster originated in France. European Muensters are yellow with small holes, red or orange rind, and a flavor that is much bolder than their mild American counterparts. Domestic Muenster is a very pale yellow with an orange rind. Muenster is used for snacking and sandwiches.

ⓗ Port du Salut
Both the French and the Danish produce a version of Port du Salut, also called Port Salut. Both are creamy cow's milk cheeses with a flavor that ranges from mild to sharp. Port du Salut is used on dessert trays, with fruit or breakfast, and in cooking such dishes as croque monsieur.

ⓘ Roquefort
Made from sheep's milk, Roquefort is a crumbly blue-veined cheese with a pungent taste and strong aroma. Roquefort is aged for three months in the limestone caves of Mount Cambalou, where the humid air helps develop the cheese's characteristic blue veins. Use Roquefort in mixed salads, Roquefort dressing, cooking, and as an appetizer or dessert cheese.

ⓙ Stilton
Stilton is an English cow's milk blue-veined cheese. It has a crumbly texture, edible rind, and pungent tang. Traditional accompaniments to Stilton are fruit, walnuts, and port.

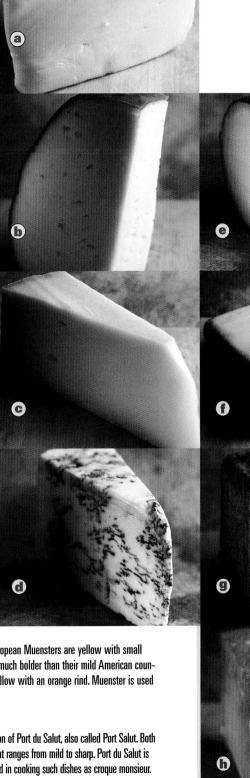

Fresh Soft Cheeses

Fresh soft cheeses are unripened cheeses with mild flavors and a moisture content of 40%—80%. The high moisture content gives these cheeses their soft texture and short shelf life.

a Boursin

Boursin is a French triple-crème cheese flavored with herbs, garlic, or pepper. Boursin serves as a spread for crackers and bread and sometimes is used in cooking.

b Chèvre frais

Chèvre frais is fresh goat cheese. It is soft and spreadable with a mild but characteristic goat cheese tang. Herb- and spice-flavored versions sometimes are available. Use chèvre frais in cooking, as a spread with crackers and raw vegetables, or on sandwiches.

c Cottage cheese

Cottage cheese gets its name from the fact that it was originally a home- or cottage-made cheese. Commercial cottage cheese is made from skim, lowfat, reduced-fat, or whole cow's milk and has a bland taste. It comes packed in tubs in small, medium, and large curd forms. Cottage cheese can be used in cooking and as an accompaniment to fruit or raw vegetables and salad.

d Farmer's cheese

Farmer's cheese, also known as baker's cheese, is a form of cottage cheese from which most of the water has been drained. Made from cow's milk, farmer's cheese has a mild taste with a slight tang. Farmer's cheese can be dry and crumbly or firm enough to be sliced. Serve it as is, or use it in cooking.

e Feta

Feta is a Greek cheese traditionally made from sheep's milk or a combination of sheep's and goat's milk. After the curd forms, it is salted, sliced, and packed in salt brine. Feta is a crumbly white cheese with a salty tang that grows stronger with age. Feta is used in cooked dishes and salads and as an accompaniment to olives and bread.

f Mascarpone

Mascarpone is an Italian cow's milk cream cheese with a rich, creamy taste and a silky, smooth texture. Use mascarpone in desserts such as tiramisu, in sauces, and as a spread. Mascarpone also can be served plain, with a sprinkle of cocoa or liqueur.

g Mozzarella

Mozzarella is the firmest of the fresh soft cheeses. Traditionally mozzarella is a small oval cheese made with water buffalo's milk, although cow's milk is now a common substitute. Fresh mozzarella is white and quite mild. It melts well in cooked dishes and often is served in salads with fresh tomatoes and olive oil and as a cold appetizer. Commercial mozzarella has a much firmer texture and a blander flavor. Use it shredded in cooked dishes and on pizza.

h Neufchâtel

Neufchâtel is a cow's milk cheese, similar to cream cheese, from the Neufchâtel region of Normandy. Neufchâtel has a soft rind, creamy texture, and slightly tart flavor that builds as the cheese ripens. Use it the same way as cream cheese.

i Ricotta

Ricotta is an Italian cheese made from the whey left after other cheeses, such as mozzarella and provolone, are made. Its uses are similar to those of cottage cheese, but its flavor is slightly sweeter. Ricotta has a smooth, slightly grainy texture. Use ricotta in baked goods and in pasta dishes such as lasagna. Italians also serve ricotta as a dessert cheese, sprinkled with sugar or salt, and as a filling for pastry.

Ripened Soft Cheeses

Ripened soft cheeses have rich flavors and a buttery smoothness. They are characterized by thin rinds and soft, creamy centers.

ⓐ Brie

Brie is a French cow's milk cheese with a white crusty rind and a buttery texture that oozes when the cheese is fully ripe. Brie has little flavor before it is ripe and stops ripening once cut. Overripe Brie develops a strong ammonia odor. Serve Brie when its center begins to bulge slightly. Include Brie on appetizer and dessert trays, in sauces, and in pastry. Brie should be served at room temperature.

ⓑ Camembert

Similar to Brie, Camembert is a cow's milk cheese that originated in the French village of Camembert. It has a slight tang but is generally milder than Brie. Its uses mirror those of Brie.

ⓒ St. André

St. André is a French triple-crème cheese with a white downy rind and a slightly sweet, buttery taste. It is most often served as a dessert cheese.

When a wine, spirit, cheese, or other food product's characteristics are uniquely tied to its location, French law allows products to carry the name of the place from which they originate. Strict laws regulate which products can share the name. In 1926 Roquefort became the first cheese to be granted the *appellation d'origine.* Since then no cheese makers outside a narrowly defined region can apply the name *Roquefort* to their products.

Specialty Cheeses

Specialty cheeses include pasteurized processed cheese and cold-pack cheese. See Figure 13-6.

Cold-pack cheese *Cold-pack cheese,* also called club cheese, is a mixture of one or more varieties of cheese, ground together. Packaged in tubs, cold-pack cheese is a spread for crackers.

Processed Cheese *Processed cheese* is a pasteurized product that combines melted ripened and fresh cheeses with flavorings and emulsifiers. The mix is poured into molds to solidify. Processing halts the ripening of the cheese, thus extending its shelf life. Processed cheese melts easily and is often used in sandwiches such as a grilled cheese. It costs less than regular cheese.

FIGURE 13-6

Specialty cheeses include cold-pack and processed cheeses.

Handling Cheese

Cheese requires special care to develop and maintain its distinctive characteristics and wholesomeness. Recommendations for ripening, storing, and serving cheese depend upon the type of cheese.

Ripening Cheese

Ripening is the stage in the cheese-making process in which added bacteria or molds begin to work on the fresh curds. Ripening develops the unique texture, aroma, and flavor that define a cheese. The length of the ripening phase and the conditions under which ripening occurs also contribute to the characteristics of a cheese. Some cheeses, such as cheddar and Roquefort, ripen from the inside out. Others, such as Brie and St. André, ripen from the outside in.

Uncut cheeses can continue to ripen after they leave the controlled cheese-making environment. Foodservice professionals determine when a cheese such as Brie reaches maturity and achieves its richest flavor.

Receiving Cheese

Receive cheese at 41°F (5°C) or lower. Inspect packaged cheeses for soiled wrappers, leakage, broken tubs or cartons, or an ammonia odor. Check expiration dates, and return damaged products for credit.

Storing Cheese

Refrigerate cheeses at 35°F–41°F (2°C–5°C). Store cheese in its original wrapping until it is ready to be used. After it is opened, tightly rewrap cheese in plastic wrap to keep it from absorbing odors, developing mold, and drying out.

Firm and hard cheeses generally keep for several weeks. Whole cheeses and large wedges maintain their freshness longer than shredded cheese. Soft and unripened cheeses stay fresh for 7–10 days. Although freezing is a safe way to extend the life of cheese, it changes the texture.

Serving Cheese

Cheeses are appropriate for breakfast, lunch, dinner, and snacks and are an alternative to sweet desserts. For peak flavor, serve ripened cheeses at room temperature. Remove them from the refrigerator 30–60 minutes before serving to allow them to reach proper serving temperature. Serve unripened, fresh cheeses chilled. Take them from the refrigerator just before serving.

When preparing cheese for a cheese board, follow these guidelines:

- Offer a selection of cheeses with contrasting flavors, colors, sizes, and textures.
- To prevent cheese from drying out, do not preslice it. Provide a separate knife for each cheese to keep flavors from mingling.
- Serve an assortment of small breads, crackers, or sliced fruit with the cheese board.

See Chapter 33: Principles of Dining Service for more about serving cheese.

Butter and Margarine

Butter is made from cream that has been churned, or agitated, until the fat solids separate out of the liquid, forming a solid mass. Butter is a water-in-oil emulsion with at least 80% milkfat. Butter also contains about 16% water and 2%–4% nonfat milk solids.

Butter is prized for the unmistakable flavor it contributes to cooked dishes and in baking. It has a low melting point (98°F/37°C), which contributes to its smooth, melt-in-your-mouth texture. Because of butter's relatively low smoking point (260°F/127°C), oil is sometimes added to butter to prevent burning when foods are fried and sautéed.

Butter Grades

Government regulations do not require the grading of butter, therefore butter manufacturers must pay for the service. Even so, most manufacturers choose grading. Federal graders judge butter by its flavor, texture, keeping qualities, color, and aroma. Graded butter carries the USDA shield on the package.

USDA Grade AA The highest grade, Grade AA butter is made from high-quality fresh, sweet cream. It has a smooth, creamy texture, a pleasant aroma, and a subtle, sweet flavor.

USDA Grade A Grade A butter is made from fresh cream and has a fairly smooth texture and a pleasant flavor.

USDA Grade B Grade B butter is wholesome, although its flavor is judged to be slightly acidic. It is used most often in manufactured foods.

Types of Butter

Sweet cream butter and cultured cream butter are two main types of butter. Most of the butter made in the United States is made with sweet cream and sold in salted and unsalted forms. Many European butters, or European-style butters made in the United States, are made from cream to which a lactic acid starter has been added. European-style butters usually have a slightly higher fat content than domestic butters, ranging from 82%–88% milkfat. Both U.S. and European butters usually are made from cow's milk, although they can be made from other milk-giving animals, such as goats and sheep.

Salted butter Salted butter contains up to 2.5% salt. Salting extends butter's shelf life but also can mask off-flavors or signs of rancidity. Some people prefer salted butter, both on the table and in general cooking. Adjust the quantity of added salt when preparing dishes with salted butter.

Unsalted butter Unsalted butter has a pure, clean taste. It usually is preferred for cooking and baking.

Whipped butter The light, fluffy texture of whipped butter results from the air that has been whipped into it. Whipped butter cannot be used interchangeably with salted or unsalted butter in cooking and baking.

PROCESS
Clarifying Butter

Because clarified butter has a higher smoking point than regular butter, it is used for many cooking tasks.

Follow these steps to make clarified butter:

Melt the butter in a heavy saucepan over medium heat. Cook until the foam rises to the surface.

Let the butter rest about 5 minutes, and then skim the foam from the surface.

Ladle the clarified butter into a container, being careful not to pick up the milk solids and water that have sunk to the bottom of the saucepan.

Clarified butter should be golden yellow and perfectly clear.

Clarifying Butter

Clarified butter, also called drawn butter or *ghee,* is pure butterfat, with all water and milk solids removed. One pound of butter yields three-quarters of a pound of clarified butter. Clarified butter does not burn as easily as regular butter, so it is preferred for making sauces, frying, and other cooking tasks.

Margarine

Margarine may contain vegetable oil and/or animal fat, along with flavorings, vitamins, salt, milk, whey, and emulsifiers. Margarine has an 80% fat content, but margarine spreads can have less. Margarine provides an alternative to butter in baking and cooking.

Receiving Butter and Margarine

Receive butter and margarine at 41°F (5°C) or lower. Look for the USDA grading stamp on butter and the expiration date on all products. Check for off-odors. Examine packaging for tears or signs of leakage.

Storing Butter and Margarine

Store butter and margarine tightly wrapped and away from foods with strong odors at 41°F (5°C) or lower. Freeze any product not intended to be used within a few weeks. Frozen butter and margarine keep for 2 months. Store up to a week's supply of butter or margarine in the refrigerator. To soften butter for the table, remove it from the refrigerator 15–30 minutes before serving.

Eggs

Eggs are among the most versatile and nutritious of foods. Alone or as a starring ingredient, eggs are appropriate for any meal. They contribute high-quality protein for a relatively low cost. In addition, eggs possess many qualities that make them indispensable in the kitchen. They add color, flavor, richness, and moisture to baked items and cooked dishes. They also can be used as a binder or thickening agent. Because of their ability to foam, eggs provide structure in baked goods. Eggs contain lecithin, a natural emulsifier, so eggs play a key role in dressings and sauces such as mayonnaise and hollandaise.

Composition of Eggs

Chicken eggs are the most popular, although duck, goose, turkey, quail, and ostrich eggs are sometimes available. Regardless of the bird, eggs are composed of three main parts: shell, yolk, and white. See Figure 13-7. For this discussion, *egg* means a chicken's egg.

Shell The shell acts as a protective vessel for its contents. Shells are composed of calcium carbonate and can be shades of white or brown, depending on the chicken's breed. The color has no relation to the quality or taste of the egg. A thin membrane lines the shell and forms an air pocket at the large end of the egg. Because eggshells are porous, eggs lose moisture and absorb flavor and odors over time, and the air pocket enlarges. Egg processors coat the shell with a thin film of mineral oil to extend the egg's shelf life.

White The egg white is composed of water and a protein called *albumin.* The white also contains minerals, including sulfur. The thinnest part of the white is close to the shell. The thickest part surrounds the yolk. When raw, the white is clear. The white coagulates when it is heated, turning white in color and firm. When a raw egg white is whipped, the protein and water molecules bond together, creating a stable foam.

Yolk The yolk contains fat, including lecithin, as well as protein, vitamins, and iron. The yolk makes up about one-third of the total weight of the egg but contains all the fat. It also contains all of an egg's cholesterol and most of its calories. The yolk is yellow, but the diet of the chicken determines the intensity of the color. The *chalaza* is a twisted white cord that holds the yolk in place. Yolks improve creaming and emulsification and act as thickeners in sauces. Because of their ability to hold air cells, whipped yolks create volume.

Forms of Eggs

Eggs come in fresh, frozen, and dried forms. Understanding the differences in egg products enables culinary professionals to choose the right one for the job.

Fresh Eggs

Fresh eggs are the same as shell eggs. They are chosen for a variety of cooking and baking tasks and for breakfast dishes such as fried and poached eggs. Fresh eggs come in a variety of sizes, from peewee to jumbo. Most standard recipes assume the use of large eggs. See Figure 13-8.

Frozen Eggs

Frozen eggs are high-quality fresh eggs that have been cracked, pasteurized, and bulk packaged. Thaw large containers of frozen eggs for several days in the refrigerator before using them in cooking and baking.

Pasteurization Pasteurization destroys harmful bacteria in eggs. Pasteurized egg products safely replace raw eggs in recipes for uncooked sauces, dressings, and drinks. Frozen, fluid, and dried eggs are pasteurized. Pasteurized fresh eggs are also available.

Whole eggs Frozen cracked and blended whole eggs can be thawed and used for baking and in cooked egg dishes.

Egg yolks Frozen egg yolks offer convenience and economy when only egg yolks are needed for a sauce, baked good, or prepared dish.

Egg whites Frozen egg products that contain only egg whites can be thawed and used in baking or cooking. Like frozen egg yolks, they offer convenience and minimal waste.

Dried Eggs

Dried eggs are made from fresh eggs that have been dehydrated to remove moisture. Dried egg products include whole-egg,

FIGURE 13-7
Composition of an egg

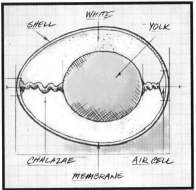

FIGURE 13-8
Egg sizes are based on the net weight per dozen eggs.

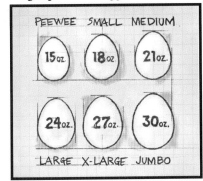

whites-only, and yolks-only products. Dried egg whites can be mixed with water and whipped to a foam. Because dried eggs are pasteurized, they can be used in products that will not be cooked or baked.

Egg Substitutes

Egg substitutes fill the need for egg products that may be acceptable for people on low-cholesterol diets. Some egg substitutes replace egg yolks with vegetable or milk products but leave the white. Other egg substitutes replace both the yolk and white with soy or milk proteins. When cooked, egg substitutes taste and react differently than real eggs do. Not all egg substitutes are interchangeable with real eggs in cooking and baking.

Testing for Freshness

Candling is one process used to determine the quality and freshness of an egg. Holding an egg up to a light, check the shell for cracks and tiny holes. Determine the location of the yolk. If the yolk is in the center, the air pocket is small, and the egg is fresh. Turn the egg. If the white holds the yolk in place, the egg is of good quality.

Water can also be used to test egg freshness. Dissolve 3.5 ounces (100 g) of salt in 1 quart (1 L) of water. Place the egg in the solution, and observe what happens. Fresh eggs sink to the bottom, but old eggs float. Although old, an egg that floats may still be safe to eat.

After the egg is cracked, check the odor. Old eggs smell slightly of sulfur. Look at the contents. Fresh eggs have round, firm yolks surrounded by a firm egg white with a more liquid white around the outside. Old eggs have flat yolks and thin, runny whites. A cloudy white is a sign that the egg is very fresh. Do NOT use an egg if the white appears pink or iridescent, as this is an indication of bacterial spoilage. Blood spots result from the rupture of a blood vessel in the yolk and do NOT indicate that the egg is unsafe.

The U.S. Department of Agriculture grades the quality of eggs on the basis of the appearance and characteristics of the yolk, white, and shell. See Figure 13-9.

Receiving Eggs

When fresh eggs are delivered, the air temperature of the truck must be 45°F (7°C) or lower. Eggs should be refrigerated immediately upon delivery. Frozen eggs should be received frozen. Examine eggs carefully. Check packaging for the USDA stamp to verify that the eggs came from USDA-approved processing plants. Check the packing date on fresh eggs. Eggs should be received within a few days from the packing date. Fresh eggs should be clean, dry, and uncracked.

Storing Eggs

Store fresh eggs in their original containers or in covered containers at 41°F (5°C) or lower. Keep frozen eggs between 0°F–10°F (−18°C–−12°C) and dried eggs tightly sealed in the refrigerator or freezer. Store eggs away from foods with strong odors and separated from raw foods. Thaw frozen egg products in the refrigerator. Refrigerated eggs stay fresh for several weeks. Remove eggs from the refrigerator immediately before use. Take out only as many eggs as needed.

Preparing and Cooking Eggs Safely

Eggs can harbor salmonella bacteria. Improperly stored, cooked, and served egg dishes can cause salmonella poisoning. Raw and undercooked eggs are especially risky. Follow these procedures to minimize the risk of foodborne disease.

- Keep fresh eggs refrigerated until immediately before use.
- Use only pasteurized eggs in recipes calling for uncooked eggs in ready-to-eat products such as egg nog, caesar salad, or hollandaise sauce.
- Discard eggs with broken or cracked shells.
- Carefully open eggs to keep pieces of shell from falling into liquid eggs.
- Wash hands, utensils, equipment, and work areas with hot, soapy water before and after contact with eggs.
- In general, cook fresh eggs to 145°F (63°C) or above for 15 seconds.
- Cook egg dishes, especially ones prepared in deep dishes such as casseroles, to an internal temperature of 165°F (74°C).

FIGURE 13-9

Egg Grades

AA GRADE EGGS

Characteristics
Yolk is firm and well-centered in the shell; yolk is round and high; white is clear and thick and does not spread out in the pan; shell is clean and well-shaped.

Uses
Poached, fried, hard- or soft-cooked

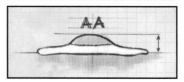

A GRADE EGGS

Characteristics
Egg spreads slightly when broken in the pan, but yolk is fairly firm; white is clear.

Uses
Hard- or soft-cooked

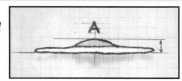

B GRADE EGGS

Characteristics
Egg spreads over a wide area when broken and does not hold its shape in the pan; yolk and white are less firm; shell may have an abnormal shape or show slight stains.

Uses
Scrambled eggs, omelettes; baking

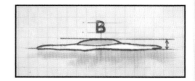

Handling Eggs

If fresh eggs are cracked and then prepared and served immediately, they should be cooked so that all parts of the food are heated to a temperature of 145°F (63°C) or above for 15 seconds. Foods made with raw fresh eggs that are not cracked and then prepared and served immediately should be cooked to heat all parts to 155°F (68°C) or above for 15 seconds. The photos that follow show how to incorporate eggs into foods.

Follow these steps to separate eggs:

Crack the egg in half, and allow the white to fall into a bowl.

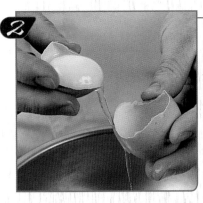

Transfer the egg yolk back and forth between shells until all of the egg white has been collected in the bowl.

Alternatively, eggs may be separated by cracking the eggs in half and allowing the yolk to remain cradled within your fingers as the white drops into a bowl below.

After separating the eggs, beat the egg whites in a clean metal bowl and use them immediately.

Follow these steps to beat egg whites:

Beat the egg whites slowly for about 30 seconds to introduce air into the whites.

Using your wrist or elbow, beat more vigorously until the egg whites increase about four to five times in volume. At this point, the egg whites most likely will be at the soft peak stage.

Soft peaks are formed when the whisk is lifted and the peaks of the beaten egg whites barely hold their shape and bend easily.

Stiff peaks are formed when the whisk is lifted and the peaks of the beaten egg whites hold their shape with just a slight bend. At this stage, egg whites may increase by up to seven times their original volume.

Dairy Products and Eggs

215

Continued on page 18

Handling Eggs Continued

Folding is the process of gently adding light, airy ingredients such as egg whites to heavier ingredients by using a smooth, circular movement.

Follow these steps to fold egg whites:

1 Mix about one-fourth of the foam mixture into the heavier mixture.

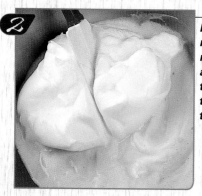

2 Put all the remaining foam mixture on top, and use a spatula to cut through the center of the mixture.

3 Lift half of the heavy mixture from the center of the bowl over the foam mixture, scraping along the sides of the bowl while folding.

4 Continue until the foam mixture is completely combined.

Tempering is the process of equalizing the temperatures of two liquids before combining them.

Follow these steps to temper egg yolks:

1 Slowly heat the egg yolks by gradually adding a small amount of hot liquid to the egg yolks, stirring constantly.

2 Continue adding hot liquid in a slow steady stream until the temperature of the yolk mixture is close to the temperature of the hot liquid.

3 Blend the yolk mixture into the hot liquid, stirring constantly. Do not allow the combined mixture to boil.

Mozzarella in Carrozza

INGREDIENTS	U.S. Standard	Metric
Eggs	10 each	10 each
Salt	TT	TT
Pepper	TT	TT
Mozzarella cheese, fresh	2 lbs.	910 g
French or Italian bread, stale	2 loaves	2 loaves
Skewers	10 each	10 each
Flour, all-purpose	as needed	as needed
Olive oil, extra virgin	1 1/2 c.	360 ml
Anchovy fillets, minced	10 each	10 each
Parsley, chopped	4 Tbsp.	60 g

METHOD OF PREPARATION

1. Gather all the ingredients and equipment.

2. Preheat the deep-fat fryer to 350°F (177°C). Or, mozzarella in carrozza may be deep-fried by using olive oil on the stove.

3. Beat eggs in a bowl, and season with salt and pepper. Transfer to a half hotel pan.

4. Cut mozzarella into 30 slices, each about 1/2″ (1.27 cm) thick.

5. Cut bread into 40 slices, each about 1/2″ (1.27 cm) thick, and remove from the crust. Trim the bread slices to about the same size as the cheese slices.

6. Thread 4 bread slices and 3 cheese slices onto the skewer, alternating so that you end and begin with a slice of bread.

7. Dredge the skewered bread and cheese in flour, and then dip each in beaten egg mixture, turning to coat all sides.

8. Deep-fry, turning often to lightly brown the batter.

9. Heat the extra virgin olive oil in a small saucepan. Add the anchovy fillets, and cook briefly until the oil is well flavored. Add chopped parsley, and cook 30 seconds longer.

10. Serve one skewer per person. Top each with a little anchovy oil, and remove the skewer before serving.

COOKING TECHNIQUES

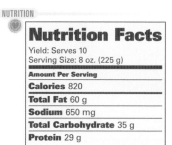

Deep-Frying:
1. *Heat the frying liquid to the proper temperature.*
2. *Submerge the food product completely.*
3. *Fry the product until it is cooked throughout.*

NUTRITION

Nutrition Facts

Yield: Serves 10
Serving Size: 8 oz. (225 g)

Amount Per Serving

Calories 820	
Total Fat 60 g	
Sodium 650 mg	
Total Carbohydrate 35 g	
Protein 29 g	

Scrambled Egg, Bacon, & Cheese Croissant

INGREDIENTS

	U.S. Standard	Metric
Croissants, split in half and toasted	10 each	10 each
Eggs, scrambled	10 servings	10 servings
Cheese, American or Swiss	10 1-oz. slices	10 slices
Bacon, crisply fried, halved, held at 140°F (60°C)	10 slices	10 slices

METHOD OF PREPARATION

1. Gather all the ingredients and equipment.

2. Fill the croissants with 4 oz. (115 g) of scrambled eggs, and top with one slice of cheese and two halves of bacon.

3. Serve immediately on a preheated plate, or hold at 140°F (60°C) or higher.

COOKING TECHNIQUES

Shallow-Frying:

1. Heat the cooking medium to the proper temperature.
2. Cook the food product throughout.
3. Season, and serve hot.

NUTRITION

Nutrition Facts

Yield: Serves 10
Serving Size: 1 each (205 g)

Amount Per Serving

Calories 550

Total Fat 36 g

Sodium 1180 mg

Total Carbohydrate 31 g

Protein 25 g

California-Style Ranch Eggs

INGREDIENTS

INGREDIENTS	U.S. Standard	Metric
MEXICAN TOMATO SAUCE		
Olive oil	1 oz.	30 ml
Onions, peeled, diced brunoise	8 oz.	225 g
Tomato juice	1 qt.	960 ml
Tomato purée	2 oz.	55 g
Jalapeño peppers, charred, peeled, seeded, minced	3 each	3 each
Cumin, ground	1 1/2 tsp.	8 ml
Oregano, ground	1/2 tsp.	2.5 ml
Corn tortillas	10 each	10 each
Avocados, ripe, washed, peeled, sliced thin lengthwise, drizzled with lemon juice	5 each	5 each
Eggs, poached	20 each	20 each
Monterey Jack cheese	10 oz.	285 g

METHOD OF PREPARATION

1. Gather all the ingredients and equipment.

2. In a medium-sized saucepan, heat the oil; add the onions, and sauté until they become translucent.

3. Add the remaining ingredients for the sauce, and bring the mixture to a boil. Reduce the heat, and simmer for 20–30 minutes or until the desired consistency is achieved. Remove from the heat, and hold at 140°F (60°C) or higher.

4. Preheat the oven to 350°F (177°C). Wrap the tortillas in aluminum foil, and warm them in the oven.

5. For service, place a corn tortilla in the center of a preheated plate. Arrange the slices of half an avocado around the outer edge of the tortilla. Place two poached eggs in the center, and *nappé* with sauce.

6. Sprinkle cheese over the dish, and place it in the oven until the cheese is melted. Serve immediately.

COOKING TECHNIQUES

Simmering and Poaching:
1. Heat the cooking liquid to the proper temperature.
2. Submerge the food product completely.
3. Keep the cooked product moist and warm.

Sautéing:
1. Heat the sauté pan to the appropriate temperature.
2. Evenly brown the food product.
3. For a sauce, pour off any excess oil, reheat, and deglaze.

GLOSSARY

Brunoise: 1/8″ (3 mm) dice

Nappé: coated or to coat

NUTRITION

Nutrition Facts

Yield: Serves 10
Serving Size: 1 each (416 g)

Amount Per Serving

Calories 580

Total Fat 41 g

Sodium 400 mg

Total Carbohydrate 28 g

Protein 28 g

Omelette Paysanne

INGREDIENTS

	U.S. Standard	Metric
Butter, clarified	7 oz.	197 g
Onions, peeled and diced brunoise	5 oz.	140 g
Ham, diced brunoise	10 oz.	285 g
Mushrooms, cleaned and sliced	5 oz.	140 g
Potatoes, washed, peeled, diced brunoise, steamed	10 oz.	285 g
Red bell pepper, washed, seeded, diced brunoise	5 oz.	140 g
Eggs, cracked and lightly beaten	30	30
Salt	TT	TT
White pepper, ground	TT	TT
Parsley, washed, squeezed dry, and chopped	1.5 oz.	40 g

METHOD OF PREPARATION

1. Gather all the ingredients and equipment.

2. Place 2 oz. (55 g) of butter in a saucepan, and sauté the onion until it is translucent. Add the ham, mushrooms, potatoes, and peppers, and sauté for another 5 minutes.

3. Season eggs with salt and pepper.

4. Heat an omelette pan, and add 1/2 oz. (15 g) of butter. When near the smoking point, add a 6-oz. (175-ml) ladle of the eggs to the pan.

5. Shake the pan, and mix the eggs until they begin to firm. Lift the eggs to allow liquid to run underneath.

6. Place 3 oz. (85 g) of the filling in the center of the eggs.

7. Roll the omelette in the pan. Turn out onto a preheated dinner plate.

8. Garnish with chopped parsley. Serve immediately.

Classic Swiss Cheese Fondue

INGREDIENTS

	U.S. Standard	Metric
Garlic cloves, peeled and cut in half	2 each	2 each
White wine, dry	1 qt.	960 ml
Gruyère cheese, grated	2 lbs.	910 g
Emmental cheese, grated	2 lbs.	910 g
Cornstarch	1 Tbsp.	15 ml
Kirschwasser	4 oz.	120 ml
Nutmeg, ground	pinch	pinch
White pepper, freshly ground	TT	TT
Crusty French bread, unsliced	2–3 loaves	2–3 loaves

METHOD OF PREPARATION

1. Gather all the ingredients and equipment.

2. Rub the inside of a fondue pot (or heavy saucepan) with the garlic cloves, and then add them to the pot.

3. Add the white wine, and bring to a simmer over medium heat. Add both cheeses, and stir constantly until the cheese is melted. Be very careful not to allow the cheese mixture to boil, or the cheese will break.

4. In a small bowl, blend the cornstarch and the Kirschwasser, and mix until smooth. Stir the mixture into the melted cheese.

5. Season with the nutmeg, and add pepper to taste.

6. Place the fondue over an alcohol burner to keep warm. Stir occasionally to keep uniformly warm; do not allow it to boil.

7. To serve: cut bread into 1–1 1/2″ (2.54–3.81 cm) cubes. Skewer bread cubes, and arrange the skewers around the fondue. Guests then dip the skewered bread cubes into the fondue.

Chef's Notes

A cheese crust will form on the bottom of the warm fondue pot. This is considered a treat and is divided among the guests.

COOKING TECHNIQUES

Simmering:

1. Place the prepared product in an appropriately sized pot.
2. Bring the product to a boil, and then reduce the heat to allow the product to barely boil.
3. Cook until desired doneness is achieved.

GLOSSARY

Kirschwasser: a clear, distilled cherry liqueur

NUTRITION

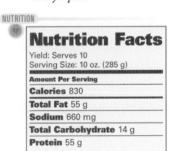

Nutrition Facts

Yield: Serves 10
Serving Size: 10 oz. (285 g)

Amount Per Serving

Calories 830

Total Fat 55 g

Sodium 660 mg

Total Carbohydrate 14 g

Protein 55 g

Quiche Lorraine

INGREDIENTS

	U.S. Standard	Metric
9″ (22.9 cm) single pie crust (see Basic Pie Dough recipe)	2 each	2 each
Butter, clarified	1 oz.	30 ml
Onion, minced	6 oz.	170 g
Canadian bacon, brunoise	24 oz.	680 g
Gruyère cheese, shredded	2 cups	110 g
Eggs, beaten	10 each	10 each
Light cream	1 qt.	960 ml
Salt	1/2 tsp.	2.5 ml
White pepper, ground	1/4 tsp.	1.25 ml
Nutmeg, ground	1/4 tsp.	1.25 ml

METHOD OF PREPARATION

1. Gather all the ingredients and equipment. Preheat oven to 425°F (218°C).

2. In a small sauté pan, heat the butter, and sauté the onions until translucent. Remove and place in medium-sized bowl. Combine the onions with the Canadian bacon and Gruyère cheese. Divide the mixture in two, and sprinkle the mixture into the bottom of the two pie shells.

3. In a medium-sized bowl, combine eggs, cream, salt, pepper, and nutmeg, and whisk gently to blend. Pour mixture over onions, bacon, and cheese in pie shells.

4. Bake 15 minutes at 425°F (218°C).

5. Reduce heat to 300°F (149°C), and bake an additional 30 minutes until the egg mixture is set.

6. Allow the quiche to cool on a wire rack 10 minutes before cutting and serving.

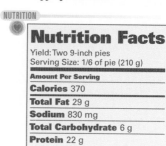

Eggs Benedict

INGREDIENTS

	U.S. Standard	Metric
Water	1/2 gal.	1.9 l
Salt	1/2 Tbsp.	8 ml
White vinegar	1 Tbsp.	15 ml
English muffins	5 each	5 each
Canadian bacon, 1/4" (6 mm) thick slices	10 slices	10 slices
Eggs	10 each	10 each
Hollandaise sauce	10 oz.	285 g

METHOD OF PREPARATION

1. Gather all ingredients.
2. Combine the water, salt, and vinegar in a pan, and bring to a low simmer.
3. Cut English muffins in half, and toast each half.
4. Heat the Canadian bacon by grilling or sautéing or on a griddle.
5. Top each muffin half with a slice of Canadian bacon, and keep warm.
6. Break each egg into a cup, and slide the eggs, one at a time, into the simmering water. Maintain a poaching temperature throughout the cooking process.
7. Cook the eggs approximately 3 minutes, and then remove them with a slotted spoon, blotting the eggs on paper towels to dry some of the liquid. Trim if desired.
8. Top each muffin half with a poached egg, and *nappé* with hollandaise.

COOKING TECHNIQUES

Simmering and Poaching:

1. Heat the cooking liquid to the proper temperature.
2. Submerge the food product completely.
3. Keep the cooked product moist and warm.

Sautéing:

1. Heat the sauté pan to the appropriate temperature.
2. Evenly brown the food product.
3. For a sauce, pour off any excess oil, reheat, and deglaze.

GLOSSARY

Nappé: coated or to coat

NUTRITION

Nutrition Facts

Yield: Serves 10
Serving Size: 1 each (130 g)

Amount Per Serving

Calories 280

Total Fat 18 g

Sodium 610 mg

Total Carbohydrate 14 g

Protein 16 g

14 Breakfast Cookery

A.D. 1364
Europeans make the 9:00 A.M. breakfast the main meal of the day.

1889
Aunt Jemima Pancake Flour becomes the first commercial ready-mix food.

1898
Charles Post invents Grape Nuts.

1945
U.S. food processors create frozen orange juice.

1973
McDonald's introduces the Egg McMuffin.

The notion of what constitutes a suitable breakfast varies from one time and culture to another. Before the eighteenth century, the French typically began the day with wine, a bowl of soup, and perhaps a bit of meat. The medieval English took ale, beer, or wine—not tea—with their breakfasts of bread, cold meats, fish, and cheese.

Although cooked porridge made from oats or other grains has a long culinary history, the cold cereal breakfast is a relatively modern invention. In the late 1800s, vegetarian Dr. John Kellogg developed flaked cereals to provide variety in his patients' diet. Today the Japanese breakfast typically consists of dried fish, pickles, or miso soup, and Europeans enjoy a *continental breakfast*—a quick meal consisting of coffee, a bread or pastry, and perhaps fruit.

KEY TERMS

continental breakfast
curdle
quiche
shirred eggs
curing
brining
smoking
Canadian bacon
hash
tempeh
seitan
quick breads
scones
crêpes

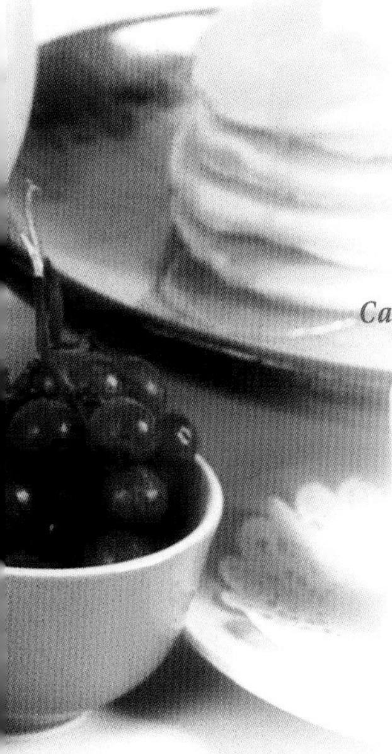

Egg Preparation

Eggs offer substantial protein and are among the most popular and versatile of breakfast foods. Eggs pair well with breakfast meats, quick breads, and lighter accompaniments such as fruit and toast.

Most egg dishes are quickly and easily prepared provided that a few basic procedures have been mastered. Dry cooking methods such as frying and baking as well as moist methods such as poaching and simmering are appropriate for egg cookery. Overcooking and high heat can leave eggs tough, rubbery, and discolored. Overcooked eggs also can develop an unpleasant flavor and odor. Long holding times have similar effects. Undercooked eggs present another set of problems, potentially carrying dangerous bacteria and the threat of foodborne illness.

Egg proteins coagulate, or become firm, with heat. Different parts of the egg coagulate at different temperatures, so a poached or fried egg may contain both a firm white and a runny yellow. As it coagulates, egg white turns from clear to white. As the yellow reaches the temperature of coagulation, it changes from liquid to semiliquid to solid. See Figure 14-1.

Overcooking egg mixtures that contain added milk or cream, such as those used for custard or scrambled eggs, causes egg solids to separate from the liquid, or curdle. A trickle of water running off a slice of quiche or a pool of water in a bowl of scrambled eggs is a sign of the effect of curdling.

FIGURE 14-1

Egg Coagulation

WHOLE EGGS, BEATEN
140°F–160°F (60°C–70°C)

WHITE
140°F–149°F (60°C–65°C)

YOLK
150°F–160°F (65°C–70°C)

CUSTARD (WHOLE EGGS PLUS MILK OR CREAM)
175°F–185°F (79°C–85°C)

Overcooking an egg results in an unappealing green ring around the yolk. Egg whites contain sulfur. Egg yolks contain iron. At high temperatures sulfur and iron can react, forming iron sulfide. Scrambled eggs can turn green when they are kept hot for an extended period of time. Avoid green eggs by not simmering hard-cooked eggs for an excessive period of time and by preparing scrambled eggs in small batches and serving them as soon as possible. Because the pH level of eggs changes as they age, fresher eggs are less likely to turn green than older eggs. Adding a small amount of an acid, such as lemon juice, helps keep scrambled eggs from turning green when hot holding in a steam table is necessary.

Fried Eggs

In the United States, fried eggs in all their forms rank first in popularity for breakfast egg dishes. For best appearance and flavor, use only the freshest eggs. A variety of fats are used for cooking fried eggs. Fats keep eggs from sticking and also add desirable flavor. Butter tastes best but costs the most. Margarine, oil, and rendered bacon fat are acceptable alternatives. The time and technique for cooking fried eggs vary according to the type of fried egg. See Figure 14-2.

Eggs are fried on a griddle or in a sauté pan. For pan-fried eggs, choose a pan that is just large enough to hold the eggs. An 8-inch diameter (20-centimeter) pan holds two eggs. To prevent eggs from sticking, use nonstick pans or set aside one set of well-seasoned pans for egg cookery.

Poached Eggs

Poached eggs cook with moist heat. The best poached eggs are well-rounded and free of ragged edges, with a firm but tender white and a warm, runny yolk. Use very fresh, cold eggs to create perfectly poached eggs. Adding about 2 tablespoons (30 milliliters) of vinegar for every quart (liter) of cooking water causes the protein to coagulate more quickly, which helps hold the egg white together.

Eggs can be poached in advance and held in ice water under refrigeration for up to one day. Just before serving, reheat the eggs to 165°F (74°C) in simmering water.

To prepare poached eggs, follow these steps:

1. In a shallow pan, bring vinegar and at least 3 inches (7.5 centimeters) of water to a simmer (160°F–185°F/71°C–85°C).
2. Carefully slip the eggs from a cup into the water. The eggs will sink to the bottom of the pan and then float up. See Figure 14-3 on page 277.
3. Cook the eggs for 3–4 minutes.
4. Use a slotted spoon or skimmer to remove the eggs from the water.
5. For immediate use, drain the eggs and trim off frayed edges.
6. For later service, plunge the eggs into ice water to stop the cooking.

FIGURE 14-2

Fried Eggs

SUNNY SIDE UP

Characteristics
The yolk is visible, highly mounded, and yellow. The yolk is intact, unless the customer requests otherwise.

Method
Cook on moderately high heat for about 4 minutes until the white is firm. Do not flip the egg during cooking.

BASTED

Characteristics
A basted egg has a thin veil of white covering the yolk.

Method
As the egg cooks, spoon cooking fat over the top. Alternatively, add 1–2 tsp. of water, and cover the pan to allow steam to cook the top of the egg.

OVER EASY

Characteristics
The egg is turned so that both sides cook directly in the pan. The yolk is still liquid when served.

Method
Cook about 3 minutes on the first side, and then flip the egg and cook about 1 minute on the other side.

OVER MEDIUM

Characteristics
The yolk is partly cooked.

Method
Cook until the yolk is partially set.

OVER HARD

Characteristics
The yolk is firm and fully cooked.

Method
Cook until the yolk is completely set but not rubbery.

FIGURE 14-3

Be careful to avoid damaging the poached egg while lifting it from the simmering water.

Scrambled Eggs

Usually made with whole eggs, scrambled eggs are fluffy and moist. Adding a small amount of milk or cream makes scrambled eggs puffier and enriches the flavor. To create scrambled eggs with no fat or cholesterol, scramble egg whites alone. To reduce the fat and cholesterol, remove some of the yolks. Because egg whites coagulate at lower temperatures than do yolks, use low heat and cook the eggs for a shorter period of time when scrambling egg whites.

Omelettes

Cooking an omelette begins the same way as cooking scrambled eggs. The difference begins when the eggs start to set in the pan. An omelette is folded or rolled and can be filled with or folded around a variety of ingredients, such as vegetables, meats, and cheese. Cook fillings that require more than just melting before adding them to the omelette.

Omelettes usually are cooked in single serving size, using two or three eggs. Use a seasoned omelette pan or nonstick sauté pan over moderately high heat.

French Omelette

The French omelette is rolled and tightly folded and has an oval, completely closed shape. See Figure 14-4. Its surface is

FIGURE 14-4

Place the French omelette with its seam side down.

PROCESS

Frying Eggs

When making fried eggs, always use very fresh eggs.

To prepare fried eggs over easy, follow these steps:

1 Heat a sauté pan over moderate heat, or heat a griddle to 325°F (165°C). Add a small amount of fat.

2 When the fat is hot, carefully slip the eggs from a cup into the pan.

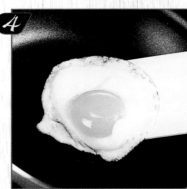

3 Reduce the heat. Cook the eggs for about 3 minutes on the first side.

4 Flip the eggs over gently, and cook an additional minute or two, until the whites are set.

5 The yolk should be warm but still liquid when cut open.

Scrambled Eggs

Light, fluffy scrambled eggs are a popular breakfast item.
To prepare scrambled eggs, follow these steps:

1 Break the eggs into a bowl, and whisk them until they are blended. Add the milk or cream, and blend well.

2 Heat a sauté pan over moderately high heat, or heat a griddle to 325°F (165°C). Add a small amount of fat.

3 When the fat is hot, add the eggs to the sauté pan. Reduce the heat. Stir slowly with a spatula, shifting uncooked egg to run underneath the cooked portion.

4 Cook the eggs until they are soft, shiny, and moist. Remove the pan from the heat. Scrambled eggs continue to cook a little after they are removed from the pan.

---

smooth and tender, and the interior is soft. The French omelette often is served plain, although fillings can be added during cooking or by making a slit in the top of the plated omelette and filling the omelette from the outside. To make a French omelette, shake the pan constantly and stir the egg mixture just until the eggs begin to set. Then roll the omelette to create its characteristic shape.

American Omelette

The American omelette is similar to the French, but the pan is not shaken while the eggs are stirred. The American omelette often is served folded loosely in half, rather than tightly rolled.

Soufflés

A typical savory soufflé consists of three elements:

- Base, usually a heavy béchamel sauce
- Flavor ingredient, such as cheese, vegetables, meat, or seafood
- Beaten egg whites

See Chapter 15: Stocks, Sauces, and Soups for more information on béchamel sauce.

Soufflés are not difficult to make, but they can collapse quickly after being removed from the oven. Good communication between the kitchen and server ensures prompt delivery to the table.

See Chapter 32: Desserts for more information on making soufflés.

Quiche

A *quiche* is an open tart filled with a baked egg custard to which other fillings have been added. The filling may contain one or more types of cheese, along with complementary meat, seafood, and/or vegetables. Use either puff pastry or pie dough for the quiche shell. As a quiche bakes, egg proteins in the custard coagulate, causing the filling to thicken. Overbaking causes the egg proteins to curdle, resulting in watery quiche.

Simmering Eggs in the Shell

Soft-, medium-, and hard-cooked eggs are cooked in the shell in hot water. Soft- and medium-cooked eggs are usually served in egg cups in the shell, often accompanied with toast points. Hard-cooked eggs may be shelled and eaten out of hand or used as a garnish or as the basis of other dishes.

Although eggs cooked in the shell are sometimes called boiled eggs, never boil them. Doing so can cause the eggs to toughen and discolor. Because the air sac is small in very fresh eggs, peeling can be difficult. Use eggs that are a few days old to make peeling easier. To prevent the shells from cracking as they cook, remove eggs from the refrigerator up to an hour before use. Cooking times vary according to the the size of the egg and the starting temperature of the egg. Thus, the suggested cooking times that follow are approximations. Calculate the cooking time from the point when the water returns to a simmer after the eggs are added.

Soft

Soft-cooked eggs have a coagulated but tender white and a runny yellow. See Figure 14-5.

To make soft-cooked eggs, follow this procedure:

1. Fill a saucepan with enough water to cover the eggs. Bring to a simmer.
2. Gently lower the eggs into the simmering water.
3. Simmer the eggs uncovered for 3 minutes.
4. Use a slotted spoon or spider to lift each egg from the water.
5. Drain the eggs, and serve them immediately.

Medium

Medium-cooked eggs have a tender, coagulated white and a yolk that is partially set but still semiliquid in the center. Prepare medium-cooked eggs using the same

FIGURE 14-5

The customer gently breaks and removes the shell from the top part of a soft-cooked egg and then eats the egg with a spoon.

Preparing the American Omelette

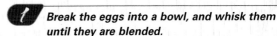
The American omelette is folded, not rolled.

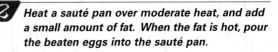
To prepare an American omelette, follow these steps:

1 Break the eggs into a bowl, and whisk them until they are blended.

2 Heat a sauté pan over moderate heat, and add a small amount of fat. When the fat is hot, pour the beaten eggs into the sauté pan.

3 When the eggs begin to set, lift the edges with a spatula to allow the uncooked portion to run underneath the cooked portion.

4 While the eggs are still soft, add the filling and then fold the omelette. Cook the omelette until lightly firm.

5 Slide the omelette out of the pan and onto a plate.

procedure as for soft-cooked eggs, simmering the eggs for 4–6 minutes.

Hard

Hard-cooked eggs have firm but not rubbery whites and fully cooked yolks that are free from discoloration or unpleasant odor. To prepare hard-cooked eggs, place the eggs in cold water, bring to a boil, lower the heat, and simmer for 10–12 minutes. Place hard-cooked eggs in ice water at the end of the cooking time. Peel the eggs when they are cool enough to handle, and then use them immediately or keep them covered and refrigerated for up to one week.

Baked Eggs

Baked or *shirred eggs* bake in individual ramekins or casserole dishes. See Figure 14-6. A ramekin is often lined with ham, bread, or vegetables and the egg topped with cheese, cream, or herbs.

To prepare shirred eggs:

1. Coat the ramekins with butter.
2. Line the ramekins, if desired, with flavoring ingredients. A small amount of cream may be added, if desired.
3. Crack one or more eggs into a cup, taking care to avoid breaking the yolk. Slide the eggs into the ramekins.
4. Sprinkle with salt and pepper.
5. Place the ramekins in a bain marie. Bake at 350°F (175°C) for 10–15 minutes or until the eggs fully set.

Egg Substitutes

For customers on restricted diets, use egg substitutes in some recipes calling for whole blended eggs, such as scrambled eggs and omelettes.

> *See Chapter 13: Dairy Products and Eggs for more information on egg substitutes.*

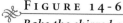

FIGURE 14-6

Bake the shirred egg until the white is fully set.

History of the Omelette

No one knows for sure who invented the first omelette. Linguists trace the French word omelette *back to Latin, the language of the Romans, and the word* lamella, *meaning "small thin plate," an apt description for a thin, unfolded omelette. Recipes by the Roman writer Apicius from 25 B.C. have convinced some culinary historians that the omelette originated with the Romans.*

Other historians theorize that the omelette might have been born even earlier, in ancient Persia. The contemporary Iranian version of an omelette is called the kookoo *or* kuku. *It consists of a mixture of chopped herbs in beaten eggs, fried in a round pan until firm and then sliced into wedges. Middle Easterners enjoy the* eggah, *a firm, flat, inch-thick (2 cm) egg cake, studded with cooked vegetables, meat, or noodles. Traditional Spanish cuisine offers the* tortilla *(unrelated to the Mexican tortilla), a thick, firm egg dish filled with potatoes. The Italians make the* frittata, *an open-faced, flat omelette, often containing hearty vegetables, which is fried and then finished under the broiler and served in cut wedges.*

French cookbooks from the 1600s contain recipes for what now is considered a classic French omelette. These seventeenth-century cookbooks also provide instructions for how to make the firmer, thicker, and perhaps older form of omelettes, fried on both sides and served flat and in slices, rather than rolled or folded.

Cooking Breakfast Meats

Breakfast meats, such as bacon, ham, sausage, and hash are frequent accompaniments to eggs. Breakfast meats supply protein, but because many have relatively high fat content, breakfast meats rarely serve as the primary focus of the breakfast meal.

Many breakfast meats are cured. Curing helps preserve the meat by removing moisture and limiting bacterial growth. Curing also stabilizes the meat's color and adds flavor. During salt curing, also called dry curing, the meat is rubbed with salt or a mixture of salt, sugar, nitrites, herbs, and spices. Country-style hams are salt-cured, as are Smithfield hams and prosciutto.

In quick curing, or brining, meats are injected with a salt-water solution that also may contain sugar, nitrites, herbs, and spices. Smoking improves preservation further and imparts a smoky wood flavor to meats. Cold smoking is used most often with meats that first have been salt-cured or brined. Cold smoking exposes meats to smoke at temperatures of 50°F–85°F (10°C–29°C), thus allowing the meat to remain uncooked. During hot smoking, meats cook fully while they absorb flavors. Many processed meats owe their smoky flavors to chemical smoke flavoring rather than exposure to a true smoking process.

Bacon

Bacon is one of the most popular breakfast meats. Both cured pork bacon and Canadian bacon are made from pork. See Figure 14-7 on page 232.

Cured Pork Bacon

Cured pork bacon is made from trimmed pork belly that has been brine-cured and cold-smoked. Bacon can be received in slab or sliced form, but presliced, uncooked bacon is most common. Commercial kitchens purchase presliced bacon according to the number of slices per pound or kilogram. The most common cut comes with 18–22 slices per pound (40–48 per kilogram).

Cured pork bacon can contain up to 70% fat, so count on considerable shrinkage during cooking. Use low heat to minimize loss.

To cook bacon, follow these steps:

1. Place single strips of bacon on a rack over a sheet pan or on a sheet pan lined with parchment paper.
2. Cook bacon at 300°F–350°F (150°C–175°C) until almost done.
3. Remove the sheet pan from the oven, being careful not to spill the grease.
4. On the griddle, use a flat weight to prevent curling, if desired, and cook the bacon until crisp.
5. Blot the bacon to remove excess grease, and then serve.

Canadian Bacon

Canadian bacon is made from boneless pork loin that has been trimmed and then brine-cured and smoked. Canadian bacon is much leaner than cured pork bacon and comes in pieces that can be sliced as needed. Although Canadian bacon costs more than cured pork bacon, the product provides more servings per pound because there is less waste. Canadian bacon comes precooked, so warm it in prepared dishes or brown it lightly on a griddle before serving.

Ham

Ham is a cured, processed pork product typically composed of meat from the pig's hind leg. Hams vary widely in quality and flavor and are available bone-in, partially boned, and boneless. Hams may come fully cooked, uncooked, or partially cooked. Boneless hams contain pieces of fresh ham that have been packed together in a casing and then cooked. See Figure 14-8 on page 232. The most common boneless hams are brined and smoked and can be sliced and served cold or warm. Commercial kitchens usually purchase fully cooked hams and slice them as needed. Warm the slices, or brown them on a griddle or under the broiler before serving.

Sausage

Breakfast sausage is usually made from fresh ground pork that has been seasoned and formed into patties or links. Sausage also comes in bulk form, which can be crumbled in cooked dishes, such as quiche or breakfast casseroles. Chicken and turkey sausage sometimes replace pork sausage on the breakfast menu. Fresh sausage must be kept refrigerated until preparation begins. It also must be thoroughly cooked. To prepare sausage in volume, first cook it in the oven and then finish the sausage to individual order on the griddle. The sausage can also be prepoached, drained, and then browned in the oven or on a griddle. Careful attention to cooking time and temperature will help prevent hard, shrunken sausage links and patties. Casings on link sausages help retain moisture and keep the sausage from becoming excessively dry.

Beef Hash

Hash is typically roast beef or corned beef, finely chopped and combined with cubed, cooked potatoes. Sometimes other vegetables are added, such as onion, celery, and green pepper, and then seasoned and fried or sautéed until lightly browned. An egg typically tops beef hash. Poach or fry the egg separately, or cook it atop the hash on the griddle or sauté pan.

Meat Substitutes

For customers on vegetarian or restricted diets, meat substitutes offer protein without the use of animal products. See Figure 14-9. Some meat substitutes are designed to have the taste and texture of meat.

Breakfast patties, links, and crumbled products replace sausage and other meats on the breakfast menu.

> See Chapter 23: Protein Alternatives for more information on meat substitutes.

Tempeh

Tempeh is made from whole soy beans that have been fermented and formed into a cake. It has a smoky, nutty flavor and a chewy consistency. Brown and serve tempeh alone, or add it to breakfast dishes in place of meat.

Seitan

Seitan is made from cooked wheat gluten and has a chewy, meatlike texture. Seitan has a mild taste that absorbs the flavors of foods to which it is added, making seitan a useful addition to cooked or baked breakfast dishes. Some ready-to-eat products incorporate seitan into sausage-style links or patties.

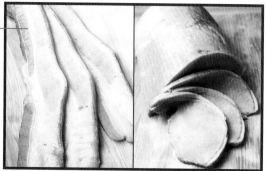

FIGURE 14-7
Cured pork bacon comes raw and must be fully cooked before serving. Precooked Canadian bacon requires only warming or browning.

FIGURE 14-8
Fully cooked boneless ham can be served cold or warm.

FIGURE 14-9
Commercially prepared vegetable-based breakfast links and patties offer alternatives to pork sausage.

Quick Breads

Quick breads are made from chemical leavening agents such as baking soda and baking powder. Because they require no yeast or fermentation, quick breads allow restaurants to offer homemade, fresh products with a minimal investment of time.

Breakfast menus feature a variety of quick breads to complement breakfast entrées or serve as the main focus of a continental breakfast. Biscuits are small, round quick breads, typically served with butter, jam, or honey at breakfast and dinner. Biscuits are made from a soft dough that is rolled, cut, and then baked. A good biscuit is light and tender with a somewhat flaky texture. Scones resemble biscuits but have a richer flavor, contributed by the addition of eggs, butter, and cream. Scones often contain raisins or currants.

Muffins and loaf breads are made from poured doughs and can add variety to the breakfast menu. Bran, blueberry, and cornmeal are three popular muffin types. Banana, lemon, and zucchini are perennial favorites among the seemingly limitless range of loaf-style quick breads. With the exception of cornmeal and bran muffins, most muffins and quick breads offer a cakelike texture and a sweet or fruity flavor.

▌ *See Chapter 31: Quick Breads, Cakes, and Cookies, for more information on quick breads.*

Pancakes

Pancakes belong to the category of quick breads called griddlecakes or griddle breads, which cook on a hot griddle or skillet rather than in the oven. Unlike biscuits, muffins, and most other quick breads, pancakes belong almost exclusively to the breakfast menu.

Because pancakes do not hold well for extended periods of time, they are best when prepared to order. However, pancake batters that are leavened with baking powder can be mixed and refrigerated for up to 12 hours. Pancake batters containing baking soda should not be blended until shortly before cooking, or the product will not rise satisfactorily. To save time with baking soda batters, assemble and mix dry ingredients ahead of time. Shortly before cooking, combine the premixed dry ingredients with the liquid ingredients. Packaged dry pancake mixes are widely available and can offer convenience and consistency for many operations.

Good pancakes are rich and moist with a light and tender texture. Typical accompaniments include butter, maple or flavored syrup, and fruit toppings. To avoid tough pancakes, do not overmix the batter. To keep pancakes from deflating during cooking, flip them no more than once.

To prepare pancakes, follow these steps:

1. Prepare the batter.
2. Heat a sauté pan over moderately high heat, or heat a griddle to 375°F (190°C). Add a small amount of clarified butter.
3. Ladle 1/4-cup portions of batter onto the griddle or pan, leaving room for pancakes to spread without touching.
4. Use an offset spatula to flip each pancake when bubbles appear on the top and the bottom is set and golden brown.
5. Cook the pancake until the second side is golden brown.

Crêpes

Crêpes, thin pancakes that are prepared from an egg-rich batter without chemical leavening, are filled and then rolled or folded. Then nappé with a sauce. Scrambled eggs, cheese, cooked vegetables, and seafood are typical savory fillings. Fruit-filled crêpes may appear on the breakfast or dessert menu.

▌ *See Chapter 32: Desserts for more information on making crêpes.*

Preparing Crêpes

Crêpes are prepared from an egg-rich batter and served rolled or folded with a sauce.

To prepare crêpes, follow these steps:

1 Heat a crêpe pan over moderately high heat. Add a small amount of clarified butter or oil. If the pan is seasoned properly, adding butter is not necessary.

2 Ladle a small amount of batter into the crêpe pan, and tilt the pan slightly so that the batter spreads evenly on the bottom.

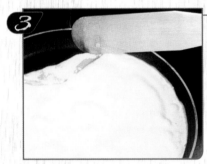

3 Cook the crêpe for 30 seconds or until the edges are brown and the bottom turns to a golden hue.

4 Flip the crêpe over, and cook for 1 more minute.

5 Cool the crêpes on a wire rack or on a sheet pan covered with parchment paper.

Waffles

Waffles are made with a thick but pourable batter and cooked on a waffle iron. Waffle batter contains more fat and less liquid than pancake batter does, and waffles develop a crisp outer shell as they cook. Separating egg whites from the yolks and then beating the egg whites and folding them into the batter creates an extra light batter. Waffles quickly lose their crispness when held, so cook waffles to order and serve them piping hot with butter and maple syrup, or sautéed fruit and whipped cream, or nuts.

To prepare waffles, follow these steps:

1. Mix the wet ingredients in one bowl and the dry ingredients in another bowl. Add the liquid ingredients to the dry ingredients, and stir just until the dry ingredients are moistened.
2. Whip the egg whites into soft peaks. Then add sugar, and beat until stiff peaks form.
3. Fold the egg whites into the batter.
4. Pour enough batter to almost cover the surface of a preheated and lightly oiled waffle iron. Close the lid of the waffle iron.
5. Cook 2–3 minutes or until the signal light on the waffle iron indicates that the waffle is done.

Corned Beef Hash

COOKING TECHNIQUES

Sautéing:

1. Heat the sauté pan to the appropriate temperature.
2. Evenly brown the food product.
3. For a sauce, pour off any excess oil, reheat, and deglaze.

Baking:

1. Preheat the oven.
2. Place the food product on the appropriate rack.

GLOSSARY

Brunoise: 1/8″ (3 mm) dice

NUTRITION

Nutrition Facts

Yield: Serves 10
Serving Size: 4.5 oz. (130 g)

Amount Per Serving	
Calories	230
Total Fat	16 g
Sodium	760 mg
Total Carbohydrate	11 g
Protein	10 g

INGREDIENTS

Ingredients	U.S. Standard	Metric
Butter, clarified	2 oz.	55 g
Onions, peeled and diced **brunoise**	6 1/2 oz.	205 g
Green bell peppers, washed, seeded, and diced brunoise	5 oz.	140 g
Corned beef, cooked, processed through food processor	1 lb.	454 g
Potatoes, washed, peeled, blanched, diced brunoise	8 oz.	225 g
Scallions, washed, trimmed, and diced brunoise	8 oz.	225 g
Parsley, washed, squeezed dry, and chopped	1/4 bunch	1/4 bunch
Thyme, dried	1/4 oz.	8 ml
Salt	TT	TT
Black pepper, freshly ground	TT	TT
Vegetable oil	as needed	as needed

METHOD OF PREPARATION

1. Gather all the ingredients and equipment.
2. In a sauté pan, heat the butter. Add the onions and peppers, and sauté until onions are translucent. Remove and place in a large bowl.
3. Add the beef, potatoes, scallions, parsley, and thyme to the onions and peppers and season to taste with salt and pepper. Mix well.
4. Place the hash in an oiled hotel pan, and bake at 325°F (163°C) until the potatoes are tender and the mixture is lightly browned.
5. Serve immediately, or hold at 140°F (60°C) or higher.

Buttermilk Waffles

COOKING TECHNIQUES

Baking:
1. Preheat the oven.
2. Place the food product on the appropriate rack.

NUTRITION

Nutrition Facts

Yield: Serves 10
Serving Size: 1 each (76 g)

Amount Per Serving

Calories 150

Total Fat 5 g

Sodium 310 mg

Total Carbohydrate 23 g

Protein 5 g

INGREDIENTS

Ingredients	U.S. Standard	Metric
Whole-wheat flour	3 1/4 oz.	100 g
All-purpose flour	6 1/2 oz.	185 g
Baking powder	1/2 oz.	15 g
Salt	1/2 tsp.	2.5 ml
Buttermilk	12 3/4 oz.	370 ml
Safflower oil	1 1/2 oz.	45 ml
Egg whites	3/4 oz.	25 ml

METHOD OF PREPARATION

1. Gather all the ingredients and equipment.

2. Preheat a waffle iron.

3. In a medium bowl, sift together the flours, baking powder, and salt.

4. Add the buttermilk and stir, but do not overmix. Add the oil.

5. Whip the egg whites to soft peaks, and gently fold them into the batter.

6. Ladle 2 1/2 ounces (75 ml) of batter onto a lightly oiled, hot waffle iron. Close, and bake until the steaming stops. Lift the waffle from the iron with a fork. Serve immediately, or hold at 140°F (60°C) or higher. Repeat the procedure until all of the batter is used.

French Toast

INGREDIENTS

INGREDIENTS	U.S. Standard	Metric
Eggs	6 oz.	180 ml
Milk	1 pt.	500 ml
Cinnamon	1 tsp.	5 ml
Salt	1/2 tsp.	2.5 ml
Sugar	1 oz.	28 g
Bread, thickly sliced, crust removed, cut in thirds	20 slices	20 slices
Butter, clarified	as needed	as needed
Maple syrup, heated	40 oz.	1.1 l

METHOD OF PREPARATION

1. Gather all the ingredients and equipment.

2. Preheat the griddle.

3. In a mixing bowl, whisk the eggs.

4. Add the milk, cinnamon, salt, and sugar, and mix well with a whisk. Hold at 41°F (5°C) or lower, or use immediately.

5. Place bread slices into egg mixture, and allow to soak for a minute.

6. Place soaked bread slices on a well-buttered griddle or into a large skillet, and brown on one side. Turn over and brown the other side.

7. To serve, place 2 bread slices on a plate. Top with butter and maple syrup, and hold at 140°F (60°C) or higher.

COOKING TECHNIQUES

Shallow-Frying:

1. Heat the cooking medium to the proper temperature.
2. Cook the food product throughout.
3. Season, and serve hot.

NUTRITION

Fresh Strawberry & Raspberry Crêpes

INGREDIENTS

	U.S. Standard	Metric
CRÊPES (TO MAKE 20)		
Flour, pastry	5.25 oz.	145 g
Sugar, granulated	1.5 oz.	40 g
Salt	pinch	pinch
Milk	13.5 oz.	400 ml
Eggs	9 oz.	270 ml
Oil, vegetable	1.5 oz.	45 ml
Vanilla extract	TT	TT
Oil, vegetable	as needed	as needed
FRESH FRUIT FILLING		
Strawberries, fresh, sliced	2 c.	350 g
Raspberries, fresh	2 c.	350 g
Sugar, granulated	1 oz.	28 g
Sugar, confectionary	1 c.	225 g

METHOD OF PREPARATION

1. Gather all the ingredients and equipment.

2. Place the pastry flour, granulated sugar, and salt in a bowl.

3. Slowly add the milk to the dry ingredients.

4. Add the eggs, 1.5 oz. (45 ml) oil, and vanilla extract. Combine well, and strain the mixture.

5. Let the mixture rest for 1 hour.

6. Combine strawberries and raspberries in a bowl.

7. Sprinkle granulated sugar over fruit, toss to mix, and refrigerate for 30 minutes to an hour.

8. To prepare crêpes, heat a non-stick crêpe/omelette pan; place a tablespoon (15 ml) of oil into the pan and roll to coat with oil; pour out excess. Add 1.5 oz. (45 ml) of batter to the hot pan and rotate pan continuously so that while the batter cooks it coats the bottom of the pan in a thin layer. Allow the crêpe to brown lightly on one side and turn to finish on the other side. Slide crêpe onto parchment paper and continue until all batter is used. Keep crêpes separated from one another with parchment paper.

9. Place 3 tablespoons (45 g) of berries at the end of each crêpe. Roll the crêpe around the berry filling.

10. To serve place 2 crêpes on a plate. Sprinkle confectionary sugar on top.

Fried Eggs

INGREDIENTS

	U.S. Standard	Metric
Butter, clarified	1 oz.	28 g
Eggs, large, broken into a cup	2 each	2 each

METHOD OF PREPARATION

1. Gather all the ingredients and equipment.

2. In a sauté pan, heat the butter.

3. When the butter is hot but not browning, slip the eggs into the pan, and cook to order: sunny side up, over easy, over medium, or as requested.

4. Serve immediately on preheated plates.

COOKING TECHNIQUES

Shallow-Frying:
1. Heat the cooking medium to the proper temperature.
2. Cook the food product throughout.
3. Season, and serve hot.

NUTRITION

Nutrition Facts
Yield: Serves 1
Serving Size: 2 each (128 g)

Amount Per Serving

Calories 400

Total Fat 38 g

Sodium 125 mg

Total Carbohydrate 1 g

Protein 13 g

Home Fries

COOKING TECHNIQUES

Boiling (At sea level):
1. Bring the cooking liquid to a rapid boil.
2. Stir the contents, and cook the food product throughout.
3. Serve hot.

Sautéing:
1. Heat the sauté pan to the appropriate temperature.
2. Evenly brown the food product.
3. For a sauce, pour off any excess oil, reheat, and deglaze.

GLOSSARY

Al dente: to the bite

NUTRITION

Nutrition Facts
Yield: Serves 10
Serving Size: 5 oz. (140 g)

Amount Per Serving

Calories 110

Total Fat .5 g

Sodium 510 mg

Total Carbohydrate 25 g

Protein 2 g

INGREDIENTS

	U.S. Standard	Metric
Potatoes, small, washed	3 lbs.	1.4 kg
Water, cold	to cover	to cover
Salt	1 tsp.	5 g
Lemon juice	1 oz.	30 ml
Butter, clarified	as needed	as needed
Salt	TT	TT
White pepper, ground	TT	TT
Parsley, washed, squeezed dry, and chopped	1 oz.	28 g

METHOD OF PREPARATION

1. Gather all the ingredients and equipment.

2. Place the potatoes in a saucepan and cover with cold water. Add the salt and lemon juice, and bring to a boil. Cook until *al dente*.

3. When done, drain and chill immediately.

4. Peel and slice the potatoes 1/4″ (6 mm) thick.

5. Coat the bottom of a large sauté pan with clarified butter. Add the potatoes, and sauté until golden brown.

6. Season to taste with salt and pepper; sprinkle with chopped parsley. Serve immediately.

Oatmeal

INGREDIENTS	U.S. Standard	Metric
Water	3 c.	720 ml
Milk	3 c.	720 ml
Butter	1 oz.	28 g
Salt	1/4 oz.	8 ml
Oatmeal, rolled oats	10 oz.	285 g
Sugar, optional	as needed	as needed

METHOD OF PREPARATION

1. Gather all the ingredients and equipment.

2. In a large saucepot, combine the water, milk, butter, and salt, and bring to a boil.

3. Add the oatmeal slowly, stirring continuously. Cook and stir for 10 to 15 minutes, or until the oatmeal is tender and the desired consistency is achieved.

4. Serve immediately in a preheated cereal bowl. Offer additional milk or sugar on the side, or hold at 140°F (60°C) or higher.

COOKING TECHNIQUES

Simmering:

1. Place the prepared product in an appropriately sized pot.
2. Bring the product to a boil, and then reduce the heat to allow the product to barely boil.
3. Cook until desired doneness is achieved.

NUTRITION

Nutrition Facts

Yield: Serves 10
Serving Size: 5 oz. (140 g)

Amount Per Serving

Calories 110

Total Fat 3.5 g

Sodium 280 mg

Total Carbohydrate 15 g

Protein 4 g

Pancakes with Maple Syrup

COOKING TECHNIQUES

Griddling:

1. Clean and heat the griddle.
2. To prevent sticking, coat the griddle with a thin layer of oil.
3. Place food product onto the griddle.
4. Cook the product, turning over when necessary, until desire doneness.

NUTRITION

Nutrition Facts

Yield: Serves 10
Serving Size: 2 each (200 g)

Amount Per Serving

Calories 490	
Total Fat 12 g	
Sodium 490 mg	
Total Carbohydrate 85 g	
Protein 10 g	

INGREDIENTS

Ingredients	U.S. Standard	Metric
Eggs	6 1/2 oz.	190 ml
Milk	19 oz.	570 ml
Vanilla extract	1 1/4 tsp.	6 ml
All-purpose flour	1 1/4 lbs.	570 g
Sugar	1 1/2 oz.	40 g
Baking powder	1 1/4 oz.	38 g
Butter, melted	3 1/4 oz.	90 g
Vegetable oil	as needed	as needed
Maple syrup, heated and held at 140°F (60°C)	as needed	as needed

METHOD OF PREPARATION

1. Gather all the ingredients and equipment.
2. Preheat the griddle to 325°F (163°C).
3. In a mixing bowl, beat the eggs.
4. Add the milk and vanilla to the beaten eggs, and mix well. Set aside.
5. Mix all of the dry ingredients together. Add the egg mixture, and whisk to a smooth batter.
6. Stir the butter into the mixture.
7. Let the batter rest for 1 hour before using.
8. To cook, pour approximately 2 oz. (60 ml) of batter on a seasoned, lightly oiled griddle.
9. Cook until bubbles appear on the top and the edges become dry.
10. Turn over, and bake the other side until done. Serve immediately, or hold at 140°F (60°C) or higher.
11. Serve with warm maple syrup.
12. Repeat the procedure until all of the batter is used. Hold any unused batter at 41°F (5°C) or lower.

A.D. 1375
Taillevent provides recipes for
17 sauces in Le Viandier.

1651
Stock is recognized as a basic cooking liquid in
La Varenne's cookbook "Le Cuisinier François."

early 1700s
Mirepoix is used to enrich stock.

1700s
Soup is featured on formal menus.

1869
Campbell Soup Co. opens first cannery in Camden, New Jersey.

1800s–1900s
Butter-based sauces characterize French haute cuisine.

Stocks, sauces, and soups are fundamental liquids with a close relationship to one another that is centuries old. The French word for stock is fond, *meaning "bottom, ground, or basis." Since the sixteenth century, stocks have served as the basic liquids for the preparation of sauces and soups. Soup has an equally long history. In parts of rural France,* la soupe *has been the name of the evening meal for centuries. From it comes the word* supper.

and Soups

What Are Stocks?

A *stock* is a gelatinous, flavorful liquid used in the preparation of sauces and soups. To produce a stock, bones, vegetables, herbs, and spices are simmered in a cooking liquid, such as water.

Slow, gentle simmering extracts flavor from the ingredients in the cooking liquid while allowing reduction to take place. Reduction occurs when a liquid simmers for increasing lengths of time, reducing the amount of water in the stock and concentrating the flavor.

Stocks can be purchased in a powdered or concentrated form called a base. When diluted with water, the base produces a stock that saves time, labor, and money. Bases can also be used to fortify the flavor of sauces and soups made from natural stocks. Although producing stocks in-house can be time consuming, well-prepared stocks form a foundation for fine cuisine.

See Chapter 7: Equipment for information on the type of equipment needed to make stocks.

Composition of Stocks

A stock is made from four ingredients: the nourishing element, mirepoix, bouquet garni, and liquid. The basic proportions of the main ingredients are
- 50% nourishing element (bones)
- 10% mirepoix
- Bouquet garni
- 100% liquid

Nourishing Element

The most important ingredient used to produce a stock is the **nourishing element,** which provides flavor, nutrients, and color. Some nourishing elements may add other benefits to the stock, as in the case of bones, which add gelatin.

Gelatin is an essential part of stock that is produced when connective tissues in meat break down during the simmering process. Gelatin gives stock its body. Evidence of a stock's gelatin content is clearest when the stock is chilled—if prepared correctly, stock will gel when chilled.

The nourishing element may include any one or a combination of the following ingredients:
- Fresh bones (beef, veal, lamb, chicken, fish, game)
- Meat trimmings from butchering
- Fish heads and trimmings from lean fish for fish stock
- Vegetables for vegetable stock

Making a Bouquet Garni

A bouquet garni is made by using any variety of aromatics, including thyme, bay leaves, cracked peppercorns, and parsley stems.

To make a bouquet garni, follow these steps:

1 Gather dried thyme, a bay leaf, cracked peppercorns, parsley stems, cheesecloth, and twine.

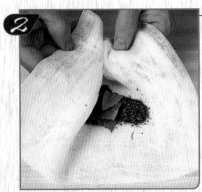

2 Wrap the ingredients in the cheesecloth, and tie the bundle with the twine.

3 A finished bouquet garni sachet should look like the one shown here.

Mirepoix

Mirepoix is a mixture of roughly chopped vegetables used to add flavor, nutrients, and color to a stock. It usually consists of onions, celery, carrots, and leeks. The ingredients and their proportions vary according to each recipe.

When preparing mirepoix, cut the ingredients into uniform pieces. Determine the size of the pieces by the cooking time. The longer the cooking time, the larger and thicker the pieces should be.

Bouquet Garni

A *bouquet garni* is a collection of aromatics. A standard bouquet garni consists of thyme, bay leaves, roughly cracked peppercorns, and parsley stems. Add or substitute other spices and herbs depending on the recipe.

The bouquet garni can be added directly to the simmering liquid, tied together in a sachet, or bundled in leek greens or celery stalks and suspended from the handle of the stockpot. Enclosing the aromatics in a sachet or bundle allows for easy removal when the stock is properly seasoned. Strain loose ingredients from the bouquet garni before using the stock in other foods.

Liquid

The largest portion of a stock is liquid. When all the ingredients for a stock are assembled, the ratio of liquid to the other ingredients should be about 2 to 1.

The liquid used to make a stock should be cold at the beginning of the cooking process to allow for the maximum extraction of flavor from the ingredients. Cold water helps eliminate impurities and blood in the bones. As the water heats, these substances coagulate and rise to the surface, where they can be skimmed. Using hot water at the outset will result in a cloudy stock because hot water speeds coagulation and prevents impurities from rising to the top.

The liquid most often used in preparing stock is water or remouillage. *Remouillage* is a weak stock made with solid ingredients left after straining a stock. After straining a stock, add water to the three remaining elements (bones, mirepoix, and bouquet garni), cook for about one-half of the original time, and then strain.

Remouillage naturally improves the taste of the new stock and reduces simmering time. It also can be used as a liquid for braising meats, preparing soups, or moistening stuffings.

Salt stocks only very lightly, if at all. Salt can aid in the extraction process or help extend a stock's holding period under refrigeration. However, added salt can become highly concentrated and overwhelm other flavors when reducing the stock or combining it with other ingredients.

French classical cooking is the foundation on which modern cooking is built, therefore French terms are often used in commercial kitchens around the world. It is important to acquire a knowledge of French culinary terminology. A vocabulary chart for French-English translations of terms for stock is listed below:

Vocabulary
French–English Translations

Fond de boeuf	**Beef stock**
Fond de veau	**Veal stock**
Fond de volaille	**Poultry stock**
Fond de légume	**Vegetable stock**
Fond d'agneau	**Lamb stock**
Fond de poisson	**Fish stock**
Fond de gibier	**Game stock**
Fond blanc	**White stock**
Fond brun	**Brown stock**

Production of Stocks

The five steps in producing a stock are cold liquid, natural clarification, skimming, maintaining a simmer, and straining.

Cold Liquid
To make stock, start with cold liquid to allow the solid ingredients to slowly release flavor and to help prevent cloudiness.

Natural Clarification
Muscles, blood, and many vegetable tissues in the nourishing element or mirepoix contain albumin. Albumin is a protein that is soluble only in cold water. After it has been released slowly into water, albumin can clarify the liquid naturally by coagulating with impurities. Gently simmering a stock instead of boiling it aids the albumin in the natural clarification process.

PROCESS

Bundling a Bouquet Garni

A bouquet garni can be bundled between celery stalks or leek leaves as an alternative to cheesecloth.

To bundle a bouquet garni in leek leaves, follow these steps:

1 Rinse leeks under running water to remove any dirt. Separate the leaves.

2 Place fresh thyme, parsley stems, cracked peppercorns, and bay leaf into leek leaves.

3 Top with additional leek leaves, and tie together with twine.

Skimming

During simmering, use the process of **dépouillage** to skim fat and impurities from the surface. This process is performed as the liquid simmers and the convection movement forces the fats and impurities to the surface. There they accumulate in a smaller area, making skimming easier. Remove the fat and impurities from the surface with a ladle. See Figure 15-1.

Maintaining Simmering Temperature

To allow the cooking liquid to properly clarify and fortify, simmer the stock by heating the liquid to a temperature between 185°F–200°F (85°C–93°C). This allows for slow convection movement to occur. Boiling the liquid forces the fat and impurities back into the body of the stock, so the process of *dépouillage* is not necessary. Cooking the stock at a temperature below the simmering point does not create a strong enough convection movement to push the impurities to the surface.

The following cooking times will allow a good amount of gelatin to be extracted from the bones:

Type of Bones	Cooking Time
Fish bones	30–45 minutes
Chicken bones	3–4 hours
Beef or veal bones	6–8 hours

Cooking Times

Straining Stocks

When the stock has simmered long enough for it to acquire the flavor, color, and body desired, it is ready to strain. Use a ladle to remove the stock from the stockpot into a *chinois* (China cap) lined with cheesecloth. If the stockpot has a spigot, release the stock slowly through the spigot.

Preparing White Stock

To make white stocks, start by simmering vegetables with the bones of chicken, beef, veal, or fish. Most white stocks are colorless, although those made from chicken may be pale yellow. To produce an especially clear stock, blanch the bones before cooking. Colored vegetables are often used when making white stocks; carrots may also be added for flavor, if desired.

Preparing Brown Stock

Brown stocks can be made from chicken, beef, veal, or game bones. Preparing a brown stock is different from preparing a white stock in that the bones and mirepoix are browned giving the stock its rich, brown color. A tomato product is added. The acidity of the tomato product aids in clarification. After the items have been browned, simmer the ingredients with water or *remouillage* and a bouquet garni.

Preparing Fish Stock

When making fish stocks, use the bones of only lean fish or shellfish. Preparing a fish stock is the same as preparing a white stock, except that fish stock simmers for less time. Use only light-colored ingredients, such as leeks, onions, and celery bottoms, in the mirepoix. Any other vegetable will discolor the stock. The cooking time for fish stock is abbreviated, therefore finely chop the mirepoix, add it soon after the stock begins to simmer, and keep it in the stockpot until the end of cooking. White wine or lemon is sometimes added to fish stock.

Preparing Vegetable Stock

Vegetable stocks are an important component of many recipes, as the demand for lighter, nonmeat-based dishes has grown. Vegetable stocks are made from vegetables, herbs, spices, and water. Bones or other meat products are not used in a vegetable stock.

Recipes for vegetable stocks require different kinds of vegetables in varying proportions. In an all-purpose vegetable stock, use neutral or mild-tasting vegetables, such as onions, celery, and mushrooms, in near-equal proportions. Avoid artichokes; green leafy vegetables such as spinach, parsnip, and kohlrabi; and cruciferous vegetables such as Brussels sprouts and cauliflower. Their strong flavors or odors can overpower a stock. Use potatoes, winter squash, and other high-starch vegetables only when the clarity of the stock is not important.

Simmer vegetable stocks for 30–45 minutes. This brief cooking time ensures that flavors are extracted but not lost. For a richer-flavored vegetable stock, sweat the vegetables in oil or butter before adding liquid.

> *See Chapter 11: Cooking Techniques for information on the technique of sweating.*

FIGURE 15-1

Careful skimming contributes to the clarity of the stock.

Preparing a White Stock

White stock is colorless, made by simmering vegetables with the bones of chicken, beef, veal, or fish. As an alternative to the method described below, it is acceptable to bring the liquid to a boil, reduce to a simmer, perform the process of depouillage, add the leeks and remaining mirepoix ingredients, and then simmer for the time required.

To prepare white stock, follow these steps:

1 Rinse bones with cold water to remove some of the impurities. Blanch chicken, beef, or veal bones, if desired. Do not blanch fish bones as they cook quickly.

2 Cover bones with cold water in a stockpot, and add leeks. Bring the liquid to a simmer. Impurities will rise to the surface.

3 Remove any impurities or fat from the surface with a ladle. Skim the surface as necessary during the cooking process to keep the stock clear, and continue simmering.

4 During the last 1 to 1 1/2 hours of cooking, add mirepoix and the sachet to the stockpot.

5 Maintain a simmer until the stock is finished.

6 Strain the stock through a chinois. The stock may be quickly chilled or put back on the range and simmered until the desired flavor is achieved.

Stocks, Sauces, and Soups

247

Preparing a Brown Stock

When making brown stock, the bones and mirepoix must be browned in a roasting pan before simmering in liquid. If desired, the mirepoix and a bouquet garni may be added to the stock after it comes to a boil.

To prepare a brown stock, follow these steps:

1 Arrange the bones in a single layer in a roasting pan. Brown the bones in a preheated oven set at 425°F (218°C).

2 Add tomato product to the bones, lower the temperature to 350°F (177°C), and roast an additional 5 minutes. Be careful not to burn the tomato.

3 Remove the bones from the oven, drain, and reserve the fat. Cover the bones with cold water, and add leeks. Bring the water to a boil, and then reduce to a simmer. Impurities will rise to the surface as the stock begins to simmer. Remove the impurities using the process of dépouillage.

4 Place the roasting pan on the range, add a small amount of reserved fat, and brown the mirepoix. Add it to the stockpot.

5 Place the roasting pan back on the range. Deglaze it using water or stock, and add the liquid to the stockpot.

6 Add the sachet to the stockpot, and simmer approximately six hours.

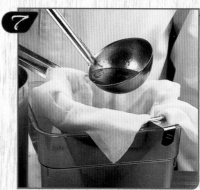

7 Strain the stock through a chinois; use cheesecloth if desired. Chill, or place the stock back on the range, and reduce until the desired flavor is achieved.

Preparing Glaces

A *glace* is a white or brown stock reduced 85%–90% through simmering. The end result is a concentrated liquid that is thick, syrupy, and highly flavored. The *glace* may also have a high sodium content caused by the extreme removal of water from the stock.

Types of *glaces* include the following:

Vocabulary
French–English Translations

Glace de viande	Meat glaze (often made from veal or beef stock)
Glace de veau	Veal glaze
Glace de boeuf	Beef glaze
Glace de volaille	Poultry glaze
Glace d'agneau	Lamb glaze
Glace de poisson	Fish glaze
Glace de gibier	Game glaze

Uses of *Glaces*

Glaces can be used in a variety of ways, but they should always be used in small amounts because they are so concentrated. *Glaces* can fortify a weak stock, sauce, soup, or other food item that lacks the desired flavor. *Glaces* also can make a light-bodied yet flavorful sauce and add shine to food items such as chateaubriand, tourné potatoes, or showpieces for food competitions.

Fumet

A *fumet* is a flavorful liquid made from vegetables, fowl, poultry, fish, or game that has been simmered in stock or wine and reduced by 50%. Fumets are used to make light-bodied sauces with deep flavor and to give additional body and richness to various stocks and sauces.

Essences (Extracts)

Essences are strongly reduced liquids. To make an essence, simmer neutral liquids, such as wine, stock, vegetable juices, or water, with a primary element, such as mushrooms, until the strength of the primary element dominates. Then strain the essence.

Essences may be used to fortify food with similar flavors, add a particular flavor to a food, or make a light-bodied sauce by incorporating essences with whole butter or flavored oil.

PROCESS

Preparing a Fish Stock

Fish stock is made with the bones of only lean fish or shellfish.

To prepare fish stock:

1 **Clean and remove all blood clots and gills from the head of the fish. Chop or split the bones, and wash thoroughly in cold water.**

2 **Cover the bones with cold water. Add a few lemon slices for additional flavor, if desired.**

3 **Bring the water to a simmer, and skim the surface to remove any impurities.**

4 **Add white mirepoix and bouquet garni, and simmer for 30–45 minutes.**

5 **Strain the stock through a chinois. The stock may be placed back on the range and simmered until the desired flavor is achieved.**

Court-Bouillon

A *court-bouillon,* or "short broth," is not a stock, but a flavored liquid customarily used to poach shellfish or fish. Its method of preparation, however, is similar to that of fish stock. To make a court-bouillon, simmer vegetables and seasonings in water with an acidic liquid such as wine, lemon juice, or vinegar. Although it is easy to make a court-bouillon when needed, it is customarily prepared ahead of time and labeled, dated, and refrigerated for later use.

Handling Stocks

Bacteria multiply rapidly in foods held within the temperature danger zone (41°F–140°F/5°C–60°C), so correct handling of stock is essential. Maintain a steady, slow simmer throughout the cooking process. Cooling, storing, and reheating stock at proper temperatures and by safe methods is equally important.

Cooling

Cool stock as quickly as possible after cooking. A cold-water bath is one safe and effective cooling method. See Figure 15-2. To quickly cool stock:

- In an empty sink, arrange a rack or several blocks as footing for the stockpot. Place the stockpot on top. To prevent spilling, check that the pot is balanced. This setup is known as venting. Venting allows cold water to flow around and under the stockpot.
- Run cold water into the sink to the level of the stock in the pot. Use an overflow pipe to maintain the water level and allow cold water to replace water that has been warmed by the stockpot.
- Keep the cold water running, and stir the stock from time to time so that cooled portions on the outer edge of the stockpot mix with warmer portions in the center.

Other effective cooling methods include
- **The Rapid Kool™**—The Rapid Kool™ is a container of water that can be frozen and placed directly in stock to accelerate cooling.
- **Ice-water bath**—An ice-water bath allows smaller portions of stock to be placed in ice water in a sink or large pot.
- **Blast chiller**—Blast chillers are small or large units used to cool food, moving it through the temperature danger zone

FIGURE 15-2

Cold water constantly circulates around a pot placed in a cold-water bath.

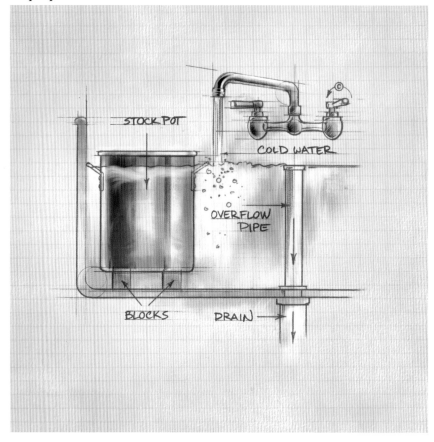

in less than two hours. After food is chilled in a blast chiller, it can be safely refrigerated.
- **Ice or cold paddles**—Ice or cold paddles are directly added to the product to reduce the temperature. The paddles, which are hollow, are filled with water that freezes and are then used to stir the product.

▌ *See Chapter 4: Food Safety for more information on cooling procedures.*

Storing

Hot stock raises the ambient temperature of the refrigerator, affecting the storage of food and making the cooling system work harder. Only after a stock has been cooled can it be safely stored in a tightly covered plastic container. Label the container with the stock name and date it was prepared.

Reheating

When stored stock is ready to be used, skim the layer of fat from its surface first. The fat will rise and solidify when stock is refrigerated, serving as a natural preservative, but it should be removed before reheating. As with other foods, make sure that the stock moves quickly through the temperature danger zone. The FDA recommends that a stock be reheated to an internal temperature of 165°F (74°C) within two hours.

> **To keep stock out of the temperature danger zone, the FDA recommends a two-stage cooling method: Cool the food from 140°F to 70°F (from 60° to 21°C) within two hours and from 70°F to below 41°F (from 21° to below 5°C) in an additional four hours, for a total of six hours. If these temperatures are not achieved within the allotted time, reheat the stock to 165°F (74°C) within two hours for 15 seconds.**

What Are Sauces?

A sauce is a flavored, thickened liquid served with entrées, accompaniments, and desserts. A good sauce complements the item being served, adding flavor, moistness, and intensity. Although a sauce should never detract from the flavor of the main item, a sauce's taste, aroma, and appearance should enhance the main item's appeal.

Components of a Sauce

Although some type of stock commonly serves as the base of a sauce, other liquids can be used. Most sauces are based on one of the following liquids: white stock, brown stock, tomato purée, milk, or clarified butter. Sauces derive their basic flavors from the liquid ingredient, but seasonings and flavorings contribute to a sauce's finished flavor. Adding one or more seasonings or flavorings can enhance or change a sauce's flavor. Ingredients such as salt, pepper, mustard, vinegar, spices, and herbs are often used.

A Short **History of Sauces**

Sauces have evolved as a result of social and geographical patterns, exploration, empire building, religion, and concepts of anatomy and medicine. The sauces the ancient Romans served were laden with salt. In fact, the word sauce *is derived from the Latin* salsus, *meaning "seasoned with salt." The Romans created an extremely salty all-purpose sauce called* garum, *or* liquamen, *from fish innards soaked in brine and fermented in wine or vinegar. Greek and Roman recipes for various foods, including sauces based on stock, were included in* De Re Coquinaria, *a "cookbook" compiled in the fourth or fifth century* A.D. *and attributed to Apicius.*

Salty sauces continued to be used well into the Middle Ages. Like the Greeks and Romans, medieval cooks also made use of verjus, *the juice of unripe or sour grapes. This highly acidic marinade ably tenderized tough meat. Soon, cooks were turning marinades into sauces as accompaniments to meat. In 1375, recipes for seventeen sauces, assembled by a cook by the name of Taillevent, were included in* Le Viandier, *the oldest known French cookbook. Some of Taillevent's sauces called for plain or toasted bread as a thickening agent.*

The Renaissance saw the introduction of flour as a thickener. By the 1500s, Italian chefs were creating flour-based sauces. This fundamental idea of modern sauce making may have come to France with Catherine de Medici, who married Henri II, future king of France, in 1553. Just less than a century later, the father of French cuisine, François Pierre La Varenne, introduced the world to roux in his culinary treatise Le Cuisinier français. *By the mid-1700s, the mother sauces and the compounds based on them were becoming an integral part of the culinary repertoire.*

Sauces are thicker than stocks. They are meant to hold onto or coat other foods. To achieve this effect, add a thickening agent in the proper ratio to the stock or other liquid ingredient. Starches are most frequently used to thicken sauces because starch granules easily absorb moisture and expand. Examples of starches as thickening agents in sauce making include flour, cornstarch, arrowroot, instant starches, bread crumbs, and vegetable purées.

Starches

A starch is a carbohydrate found naturally in fruits, seeds, roots, tubers, and the pith of stemmed plants. Wheat, corn, rice, potatoes, and arrowroot are some starches used as thickening agents.

Flour The most common flour in a commercial kitchen is wheat flour. As a thickening agent, flour is used in several ways.

- As is, flour is used to *singer,* a process in which a pan that may have been used to sauté an entrée, or the food itself, is dusted with flour. The fat in the pan absorbs the flour, instantly forming a thickening agent known as a roux.
- By combining equal parts of flour and whole butter a *beurre manié,* or uncooked thickening agent, is created. Soften the butter at room temperature before blending it with the flour. Then add the mixture to a hot sauce at the end of the cooking process. Do not bring it back to a simmer. *Beurre manié* is seldom used today because of the availability of cornstarch and arrowroot, which thicken liquids quickly and easily. The drawback to using a *beurre manié* is that although the final product may be the correct consistency, the flavor of the sauce or soup remains starchy because the flour has not been cooked properly.

Cornstarch Cornstarch is a dense, powdery flour made from the endosperm of corn. It has nearly twice the thickening power of flour and gives a sauce a translucent appearance.

Slurry, another uncooked thickening agent, is made by diluting a pure starch such as cornstarch or arrowroot in cold liquid. When combining the cold liquid and starch, the consistency of heavy cream is achieved. If slurry is not used immediately, stir it again to recombine. Slowly add the slurry to the simmering liquid, blending constantly with a whip. A simmering liquid will thicken quickly when a slurry is added.

To thicken a sauce using cornstarch:

1. Combine the cornstarch with an equal amount of cold liquid. When using an acidic liquid, increase the amount of cornstarch by 20%, or the liquid will not thicken.
2. Pour the diluted cornstarch into the boiling liquid.
3. Bring the boiling liquid down to a simmer.
4. Do not simmer for more than 10 minutes, or the cornstarch will begin to break down, resulting in the loss of thickening properties.

Arrowroot Arrowroot is a fine powder made from the dried, ground rootstalks of tropical plants. Its thickening power is about twice that of flour. The best of the purified starches, arrowroot is used like cornstarch. However, arrowroot imparts a more transparent appearance to a sauce and does not lose its thickening properties during the cooking process.

Vegetable purées A sauce is sometimes texturized by puréeing vegetables, mirepoix, or ground nuts and adding them to the sauce. In addition to texture, the sauce achieves a new flavor. An example of a vegetable purée is tomato sauce.

Handling Starches

When handling powdered starches, such as cornstarch or arrowroot, used for thickening, dilute them with a cool liquid, such as stock, water, or milk, before adding them to sauces or soups that need to be thickened.

Starches require heat to activate the thickening process. Some thickening agents need to be simmered longer than others for them to be effective. For example, cornstarch will thicken a hot liquid completely as soon as it comes back to a simmer, whereas roux (see below) requires 10–15 minutes of simmering to thicken fully.

Roux

Roux is a cooked thickening agent made by combining equal parts by weight of flour and a clarified fat or oil; use all-purpose flour and clarified butter or margarine for this purpose. To make a roux, add the flour to the warm clarified fat or oil in a pan, and whisk to incorporate. Cook over low to medium heat until desired color is achieved.

When cooked together, the main elements of a roux—flour and fat—form a paste. Cooking time determines whether the roux is white, blond, or brown. The longer a roux cooks, the darker its color and the less its thickening ability.

Fat A variety of cooking fats may be used to prepare roux. Each has its own effect on the consistency and flavor of the final product.

- **Clarified butter**—Clarified butter, or drawn butter, is used most often for roux. Clarified butter is pure butterfat; it is clear and, with the water and milk solids removed, it can be cooked at higher temperatures. Roux made from clarified butter has a different consistency from roux made from butter that still contains water and milk solids.
- **Butter-margarine blends**—For cost reasons a butter-margarine blend may be used instead of butter. The quality and flavor of such blends vary, however. A roux made with a blend of butter and margarine will not have the same flavor as one made exclusively of butter.
- **Animal fats**—When the flavors of poultry or meat are desired in a sauce, chicken fat, lard, and rendered fats from roasts are appropriate fats to use in roux. Pork drippings, for example, are essential to a pan gravy that accompanies a pork roast.
- **Vegetable oils**—Vegetable oils, either from specific plants or blends combining corn, safflower, and soy bean oils, offer variety, but they do not add flavor to a roux. In some cuisines vegetable oils are used to make dark roux.

Flour Wheat flour is standard in roux. The thickening power of the different wheat flours, however, varies with their starch content. Bread flour, for instance, contains less starch than cake flour. All-purpose flour falls somewhere between bread flour and cake flour as an effective thickening agent. Most sauce recipes call for bread flour or all-purpose flour.

Steps in Making Roux

The basic procedure for making roux is the same no matter what type of roux (white, blond, or brown) is being prepared. Use a heavy stainless steel pot, and stir frequently to prevent scorching or burning. Burning results in dark spots and an unpleasant odor and flavor. In addition, burnt roux will not thicken as desired. Avoid using aluminum cookware because it may make sauces gray-colored and metallic-tasting.

For white or blond roux, cook over medium heat for the recommended time. See Figure 15-3. Cook brown roux on low heat for the suggested time. White roux should be light beige, blond roux should appear golden with a light hazelnut odor, and brown roux may be light or deep brown. See Figure 15-4.

FIGURE 15-3

Types of Roux

ROUX BLANC

White roux
Cook for 3–5 minutes

ROUX BLOND

Blond roux
Cook for 5–6 minutes

ROUX BRUN

Brown roux
Cook 15–20 minutes (or mix fat with toasted flour and cook for 5–6 minutes)

FIGURE 15-4

White roux, blond roux, brown roux

PROCESS

Making Roux

Although most roux is made with clarified butter, any fat, such as vegetable oil or chicken fat, may be used. Cooking the roux helps remove any raw flour flavor. As a rule, the darker the roux becomes, the less thickening power it has.

To prepare a roux, follow these steps:

1 Heat clarified butter over low heat and add flour.

2 Blend into a smooth paste, adjusting the amount of flour needed to achieve proper consistency.

3 Cook, stirring constantly, until the proper color and flavor are achieved.

Stocks, Sauces, and Soups

253

Combining Roux and Liquid

After the cooked roux has reached the right consistency, combine it with liquid to thicken a sauce. Choose one of two approaches for combining roux and liquid: add roux to liquid (Method A), or add liquid to roux (Method B). See Figure 15-5.

The sauce is ready when it has reached the desired consistency and no longer has the starchiness of roux. The proportion of roux to liquid affects both thickening action and taste. For a sauce of medium consistency, use one pound (.5 g) of roux per gallon (3.75 l) of liquid.

Liaisons

Tempering is the process of equalizing the temperatures of two liquids before mixing them together. To temper, gradually add small quantities of the hot sauce or soup to the cool liquid, slowly raising the temperature until it is almost equal in both liquids. Then add the tempered liquid to the hot liquid, and continue to simmer it. Tempering prevents curdling of dairy products.

A *liaison,* which can consist of cream and egg yolks, is used to thicken sauces. Liaisons add luster, color, and flavor to the sauce.

To make a liaison, combine cream and egg yolks until smooth. Temper the liaison with hot liquid while whipping or blending the mixture of the two, until the temperature has equalized.

Add the tempered liaison to the sauce, and warm on the range over low heat. Stir the sauce until the desired consistency is achieved.

> To prevent a sauce or soup from curdling after the liaison has been added, do not allow the temperature of the product to exceed 185°F (85°C).

Emulsification

Emulsification is another method of thickening sauces. Emulsions are made by mixing two or more liquid ingredients that normally do not combine, with the aid of an emulsifying agent.

There are three types of emulsions:

- **Permanent**—A permanent emulsion usually lasts several days or more. Mayonnaise, an example of a permanent emulsion, contains an emulsifying agent, such as egg yolks.
- **Semipermanent**—A semipermanent emulsion lasts a shorter period of time than a permanent emulsion, usually several hours. Hollandaise sauce is an example of a semipermanent emulsion.
- **Temporary**—A temporary emulsion lasts the shortest period of time, usually only several minutes. A temporary emulsion is classified as such because it does *not* contain an emulsifying agent. Emulsion of the two liquid ingredients is achieved by briskly whisking them. During the whisking, the air bubbles incorporated into the liquid cling to each molecule of oil, allowing them to remain suspended temporarily. The air bubbles will dissipate after a few

minutes, however, and the liquid will need to be reblended to bring back the emulsion. An example of a temporary emulsion is a vinaigrette.

> Use caution when making hollandaise sauce because the eggs will begin to coagulate at a temperature above 140°F (60°C). Use only pasteurized eggs, and do not hold hollandaise sauce for more than 20 minutes at room temperature.

Reductions

Natural reduction is a method used to thicken sauces and enhance flavor. During this process water evaporates from the liquid (often stock) as it simmers. The result is a concentration of flavor and color. The sauce also thickens because as the water evaporates, the roux and other solids become concentrated.

Straining Sauces

Straining is a last step and adds to a sauce's smoothness. To strain, pour the sauce through a fine-mesh sieve or several layers of cheesecloth in a chinois. After straining the sauce, adjust the seasonings as needed.

Quality of a Sauce

Many factors contribute to the quality of a sauce. A good sauce is determined by its taste, color, luster, texture, opacity, and viscosity.

Taste The taste of the sauce should be distinct and well rounded, complementing the food it accompanies. Proper seasoning is an important element in developing a balanced flavor. Sauces containing thickeners should be free of any starchy taste.

Color The color of the sauce also should be distinct, and it should be natural. A cream sauce, for instance, should be white, not gray; and a velouté should be a pale ivory. Brown sauces should be rich and deep, and tomato sauces should be a robust red color.

Luster All sauces should have luster. The correct amount of fat in a sauce can contribute to the shine. Too much fat can detract from it.

FIGURE 15-5

Combining Roux and Liquid

METHOD A

- *Heat the cold liquid to a simmer.*
- *Add the hot roux slowly in small amounts, beating with a whisk to get rid of any lumps.*
- *Bring the liquid to a boil. Continue to beat constantly. Reduce to a simmer. Cook for at least 20 minutes, stirring occasionally.*

METHOD B

- *Cool the roux slightly.*
- *Add the hot liquid slowly, beating with a whisk to keep lumps from forming.*
- *Bring the liquid to a boil, beating constantly.*
- *Reduce to a simmer. Cook for at least 20 minutes, stirring occasionally.*

Texture Most sauces should have a smooth, creamy texture that is free of lumps or other particles.

Opacity A sauce should have the correct degree of opacity, which is often determined by the thickener used and the amount of reduction that has taken place. A good sauce should be opaque rather than transparent.

Viscosity The more a sauce is thickened, the more viscous it becomes. A sauce has an appropriate thickness, or viscosity, when it can lightly coat the back of a metal spoon. The viscosity of a sauce will vary with the amount of thickening agent used. To determine the amount of roux required to achieve various levels of viscosity, use the following formula as a guide.

- Minimum viscosity: 10%
- Medium viscosity: 11.5%
- Maximum viscosity: 13%

To determine the amount of thickening agent required for a sauce, use the following formula:

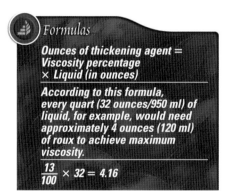

Formulas

Ounces of thickening agent = Viscosity percentage × Liquid (in ounces)

According to this formula, every quart (32 ounces/950 ml) of liquid, for example, would need approximately 4 ounces (120 ml) of roux to achieve maximum viscosity.

$$\frac{13}{100} \times 32 = 4.16$$

Leading Sauces

The *leading sauces,* also called the mother sauces, are the basic sauces from which many other sauces derive. The basic liquids used to create leading sauces are white stock, brown stock, tomato purée, milk, and clarified butter. Leading sauces can be categorized into brown sauces, white sauces, tomato sauces, warm butter sauces, and oil-based sauces.

Brown Sauces

Demi-glace is the classic brown sauce, but in recent times a lighter version of a brown sauce, called *jus lié,* has been made instead. This type of brown sauce is made by reducing and concentrating meat juices and then thickening them slightly with starches such as cornstarch or arrowroot. These sauces are made without roux and tend to lack the opacity of a fine demi-glace-based sauce, but they have a rich clean flavor and a more syrupy texture.

Making the classic demi-glace is a two-step process. A heavier brown sauce, espagnole, is made first and then is refined by adding an equal amount of brown stock. It is then simmered until the proper viscosity and flavor is achieved. Espagnole sauce is used only for this purpose.

As an alternative to the classic preparation of demi-glace, roast veal bones, mirepoix, and tomato paste. Add these to brown veal stock, and then simmer for several hours. The flavors become highly concentrated, and the mixture, after it is strained, can be blended with roux to thicken the sauce further, if desired.

As with all the leading sauces, a number of derivative sauces can be made by adding flavoring ingredients or garnishes to brown sauce.

White Sauces

The leading white sauces include béchamel and velouté. Béchamel is made by thickening milk with white roux. An onion piqué is added for additional flavor. Béchamel also serves as a base for some soufflés and a binder for fillings and stuffings, and it is used to hold croquettes and baked pasta dishes together.

Velouté is a blond sauce made from a light-colored stock thickened with blond roux. The various veloutés are named for the type of stock each contains. For example, sauce suprême is made with white chicken stock, sauce allemande is made with white veal stock, and sauce vin blanc is made from fish stock. Veloutés form the base for many sauces and thick soups.

Tomato Sauces

Tomato sauces are made by simmering a tomato product with flavorings; seasonings; and a liquid, such as stock or water. Tomato sauce can be vegetable based, but variations may include meat. Italian cuisine is famous for its many variations of tomato sauce.

Tomato sauce can be made with peeled, diced, ripe plum tomatoes, when in peak season, and shallots, onions, and garlic that have been sautéed in olive oil. Salt and pepper are added, and the sauce may be finished with chopped fresh basil. Plum tomatoes are used because of their high ratio of pulp to juice. For consistency, canned tomato products such as tomato purée, tomato paste, crushed tomatoes, or whole peeled tomatoes are often used.

Warm Butter Sauces

Warm butter sauces are semipermanent emulsions that are made by beating egg yolks with a reduction of an acidic liquid, clarified butter, and seasonings over a double boiler. Examples include hollandaise sauce, a versatile sauce that accompanies meat, fish, eggs, and vegetables; and béarnaise sauce, which is similar to hollandaise but with a much more intense flavor. Béarnaise sauce is often served with grilled meats and fish.

Oil-Based Sauces

Oil-based sauces are cold sauces that fall in one of two categories: mayonnaise-based and clear oil-based. Mayonnaise and vinaigrette are considered to be leading cold sauces.

Mayonnaise is a permanent emulsion of egg yolks and oil. Lemon juice or vinegar and mustard are often added. To make mayonnaise, whip the egg yolks, lemon juice or vinegar, and mustard if using, as the oil is slowly drizzled in. When one-third of the oil has been incorporated, the remaining oil can be drizzled in at a slightly faster pace. A mixer or food processor is ideal for making mayonnaise because it allows the oil to be added in a slow steady stream. Pasteurized eggs should be used to make mayonnaise because the egg yolks remain raw.

Clear oil sauces, such as vinaigrette, incorporate a mixture of oil, vinegar, herbs, and seasonings and are used primarily as a dressing for salads. However, vinaigrettes also can be used as marinades and toppings for seafood, meats, and vegetables. To make a vinaigrette, drizzle the oil slowly into the vinegar, and blend until the mixture is emulsified. Herbs and seasonings are usually added. Unlike mayonnaise, the emulsion is temporary; vinaigrettes must be whisked often to maintain even distribution of the liquids.

Oil-based sauces are primarily used in cold food applications, therefore both of these leading sauces and their methods of preparation are discussed in Chapter 25, Garde-Manger.

Preparing Espagnole Sauce

Preparation of this basic brown sauce is the first step in preparing espagnole. Either brown veal or beef stock can be used in this preparation.

To prepare espagnole sauce, follow these steps:

1 Gradually whisk hot brown stock into brown roux until it is completely dissolved.

2 Heat to a boil, reduce to a simmer, and skim as needed.

3 Render bacon in a saute pan, and then remove it from the pan. Drain off the excess fat, and sauté mirepoix until it browns.

4 Add tomato purée, and cook an additional 5 minutes.

5 Add the mirepoix mixture to the thickened stock.

6 Add the bouquet garni, continue to simmer, and skim as needed until proper consistency and flavor are achieved.

7 Strain through a chinois into a suitable container.

Preparing Brown Sauce

Brown sauce can be used as an alternative to the classic espagnole and demi-glace. Although it derives most of its thickening from the flour and reduction, brown sauce can be further thickened when used with butter or arrowroot.

Follow these steps to prepare a brown sauce:

 1 Brown bones and mirepoix in a preheated oven set at 425°F (218°C).

 **2** Remove pan from the oven, and place on a hot stove top. Add tomato paste or purée. Cook several minutes to reduce acidity in the tomatoes.

 **3** Dust bones with flour, stir, and cook until flour browns lightly.

 **4** Deglaze with brown stock or wine, and blend until syrupy.

 5 Remove bones and mirepoix from the pan, and place them in a stockpot.

 **6** Return pan to the stove top, and add additional stock. Bring to a boil.

 **7** Pour the liquid from the pan over the bones, scraping any browned bits and mirepoix into the stock pot. Blend well.

 8 Simmer approximately 2–3 hours, skimming as necessary.

 **9** Strain sauce through a chinois.

Preparing Béchamel Sauce

Béchamel is a white sauce made by thickening milk with white roux.

The procedure for making béchamel (and velouté) follows:

1

In a heavy saucepan, heat milk and an onion piqué, and simmer for 10 minutes.

2

Remove the onion piqué from the hot milk, and add the milk gradually to the blond roux, whisking constantly.

3

Heat to a boil, and reduce to a simmer. Simmer approximately 20 minutes or until proper flavor and consistency are achieved. Season with salt, white pepper, and nutmeg.

4

Strain the sauce through a chinois.

Preparing Tomato Sauce

A well-made tomato sauce is deep red, thick, and somewhat coarse in texture.

To make tomato sauce:

1

Heat olive oil in heavy stainless steel pot. Add diced onions and garlic, and cook over low heat until the onions are translucent. Take care not to burn the garlic.

2

Add chopped or crushed tomatoes or tomato purée to the pot. Bring to a boil, and reduce to a simmer. Cook between 20 minutes and one hour, depending on the tomato product used.

3

Remove from heat, and purée the sauce using a food mill, food processor, or immersion blender. For a more rustic look, the sauce may be left unpuréed.

4

If using fresh herbs such as basil or oregano, it is best to add them to the sauce when it is finished. Dry herbs should be added during the cooking process.

Preparing Hollandaise Sauce

A finished hollandaise sauce has a buttery acidic flavor and is light, smooth, and pale yellow in color. It should not show any separation.

To make hollandaise sauce:

1 Simmer white wine, vinegar, peppercorn, and bay leaf to make a reduction.

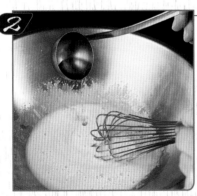

2 Blend cooled, strained reduction into egg yolks.

3 Whip egg yolk mixture over a double boiler, cooking until the eggs start to ribbon.

4 Remove egg yolk mixture from the heat. Gradually drizzle in clarified butter, whipping constantly to maintain an emulsion.

5 Blend a little hot water into the hollandaise sauce to achieve proper consistency. Season with salt and white pepper, and add a pinch of cayenne pepper.

Derivative or Compound Sauces

The leading sauces serve as a basis for numerous derivatives or **compound sauces.** See Figure 15-6. After sautéing, excess fat may be removed from the saucepan, and flavoring agents or garnishes can be added. The residue can be deglazed with wine, liqueur, stock, or demi-glace, and then the leading sauce is added.

Alternatively, flavoring agents can be strained from the sauce and garnishes added. When a roasted item is taken from the oven and set aside, the roasting pan is often put back on the range and deglazed with wine or stock. The mixture is then simmered and reduced. Strain the pan juices, and add them to the leading sauce along with the appropriate garnishes. Garnishes can also be prepared and added directly to the leading sauce without the addition of pan juices or additional flavoring agents.

Other Sauces

Not all sauces derive from the leading sauces; there are as many different sauce preparations as there are uses. Some sauces, such as curries, are inseparable from the other components of a dish. Others, like pasta sauces, add interest, flavor, or texture to a dish. Sauces based on butter can be as simple as browned butter or as varied as flavored butters. Pan drippings form the basis of sauces served with meat and poultry. Other sauces have a vegetable or fruit purée as their base. Among these other familiar sauces are compound butters, pan gravies, and various independent sauces.

Compound Butters

Compound butters are butters combined with one or more ingredients, such as herbs, spices, reduced stocks, or vegetable purées that change the color or flavor of the butter. To make compound butters, combine the ingredients in a food processor, and blend until smooth.

FIGURE 15-6

Leading Sauces and Their Derivatives

BÉCHAMEL
Cardinal, Crème, Mornay, Soubise

VELOUTÉ
Allemande
Albufera, Aurore, Curry, Hongroise
Suprême
Chivry, Curry, Poulette
Vin Blanc
Bercy, Diplomate, Normande, Anchois

DEMI-GLACE AND JUS LIÉ
Perigueux, Poivrade, Robert, Chasseur, Bigarade, Bordelaise, Porto

TOMATO
Provençale, Creole, Portuguese

WARM BUTTER SAUCES (HOLLANDAISE STYLE)
Hollandaise
Maltaise, Mousseline
Béarnaise
Choron, Foyot

OIL SAUCES
Mayonnaise
Rémoulade, Tartar
Vinaigrette
Ravigote, Tomato vinaigrette

FIGURE 15-7

Simple Compound Butters and Their Preparation

NAME	PREPARATION
Almond butter	*Pound almonds to a paste with a little water; blend with soft butter; pass through a sieve*
Anchovy butter	*Pound fish to a paste; blend with butter*
Bercy butter	*Reduce white wine; add finely chopped shallots, and combine with butter; add chopped parsley and lemon juice; season*
Caper butter	*Add finely chopped capers, anchovies, and lemon and orange juice to butter; top with three whole capers after piping into balls*
Chivry butter (**beurre ravigote**)	*Blanch parsley, chives, tarragon, chervil, and fresh burnet; pound with chopped, blanched shallots; add to butter; pass through fine sieve*
Colbert butter	*Combine melted meat glace with chopped tarragon (blanch first), and add to maître d'hôtel butter*
Curry butter	*Combine curry paste or powder and sugar with butter*
Garlic butter	*Grind garlic gloves and add to butter*
Green butter	*Combine spinach juice, celery salt, nutmeg, and white pepper; sprinkle or blend in chopped parsley; mix with butter*
Maître d'hôtel	*Mix lemon juice and chopped parsley with butter*
Mustard butter	*Combine mustard with butter*
Paprika butter	*Add paprika of choice to whipped butter*
Pepper butter	*Combine freshly ground black pepper, celery salt, and garlic salt; add to butter; use as a curl, if desired*
Salmon butter	*Blend smoked salmon with whipped butter, using the same method as anchovy butter*
Salmon and dill butter	*Mix cayenne, finely chopped onion, and chopped salmon with butter; spread on plastic wrap; chill; sprinkle with chopped dill; roll*
Sweet red pepper butter	*Grill or roast and peel sweet red peppers and add to butter; force the mixture through a sieve*
Tarragon butter	*Same process as chivry butter*
Tomato butter	*Add concentrated tomato purée to butter; can be used for soups and sauces*
Truffle butter	*Seal sticks of butter in jars of truffles overnight*

Compound butters are served as sauces on hot grilled foods, used to finish other sauces, or treated as a decorative finish. There are two types of compound butters: simple and complex.

Simple compound butters Simple compound butters are softened butter combined with puréed or finely chopped flavoring elements. See Figure 15-7 on page 260.

Complex compound butters Complex compound butters are made by combining clarified butter with flavoring ingredients. The flavoring ingredient may be edible or inedible. The shells of shrimp or lobster are an example of an inedible item used to create a complex compound butter. To extract the flavor of the shells, heat them with the clarified butter in a double boiler. Then strain and cool the butter. In the resulting shrimp or lobster butter, as in many other complex compound butters, only the flavor of the ingredient, not the ingredient itself, is present in the butter.

Other Butter Sauces

Butter may be prepared in several other ways for use as a sauce. These simple preparations include *beurre blanc, beurre noisette,* and *beurre noir.*

Beurre blanc *Beurre blanc,* or white butter, is an emulsified sauce with three main ingredients: whole butter, white wine, and shallots. Although an emulsion, *beurre blanc* does not include egg yolks, so it is lighter and thinner than the classic hollandaise or béarnaise sauces. Additional seasonings and flavorings complement this creamy butter sauce when served with steamed or grilled fish, chicken, or a variety of vegetables.

Beurre noisette *Beurre noisette,* or brown butter, is whole butter heated until light brown in color. Prepared *à la minute* and with care so that it does not burn or overbrown, this butter sauce has a distinctive nutty aroma that accents fish, white meats, eggs, and vegetables.

Beurre noir *Beurre noir,* or black butter, is whole butter heated until dark brown. Served with the same foods as *beurre noisette,* this butter sauce also often contains vinegar, capers, or chopped parsley.

Pan Gravies

Pan gravies are sauces that incorporate the pan drippings of roasted meat or poultry.

Prepare pan gravy by deglazing the roasting pan with water, stock, or demi-glace and then thickening the liquid with a roux. As an alternative, flour can be blended into the fat that remains in the roasting pan and cooked briefly. Stock is then added, and the mixture is simmered. The resulting sauce accompanies the roasted meat or poultry or can be served with side dishes such as noodles and potatoes.

Independent Sauces

Independent sauces do not use other sauces or a stock as a base. Often spicy, these sauces include both warm and cold preparations.

Independent sauces can be prepared in myriad ways with a variety of ingredients, typically infused in a cream, oil, vinegar, or vegetable purée. Applesauce, curry sauce, bread sauce, and raisin sauce are a few examples of warm independent sauces. Cold sauces include yogurt, chutney, cocktail sauce, cranberry sauce, Cumberland sauce, relish, salsa, and mint sauce.

Handling Sauces

Handle sauces carefully after cooking to preserve their consistency and to prevent the growth of bacteria. Follow the HACCP guidelines for hot holding, cooling, storing, and reheating sauces.

Hot Holding

Keep sauces hot for service in a bain marie or steam table. Hold at 140°F (60°C) or higher. If hollandaise sauce must be held for service, keep it at approximately 140°F (60°C) for no longer than 20 minutes. This temperature helps prevent the egg yolks in the sauce from curdling, and the acid in the sauce can keep bacterial growth down for a brief period. Hollandaise sauce may be kept hot in a bain marie, vacuum bottle, or ceramic container.

Some sauces develop a skin if held uncovered. There are several ways to avoid this: cover the sauce with the lid; spread melted butter over the surface of the sauce to seal it; or place oil, plastic wrap, or buttered parchment paper directly on top of the sauce.

Cooling and Storing

When cooling and storing sauces, transfer them to a clean container, and quickly cool them in a cold-water bath. Follow one of the cooling procedures described on page 250. Store cooled sauce under refrigeration in a plastic container with a tight-fitting lid. Label the container with the sauce's name and the date it was made.

Reheating

Before reheating the sauce, add a little stock or water to the saucepan beforehand to soften the cold sauce and keep it from burning.

As with stock, take care when reheating sauces. Move quickly through the temperature danger zone. Bring sauces up to at least 165°F (74°C) within 2 hours.

What's in a Name?

Interesting personalities and stories lie behind the names of some of the classical sauces. Béchamel, the standard white sauce, was developed for Louis XIV's majordomo, the Marquis de Béchamel. Soubise sauce, a compound that adds onions to basic béchamel, was created by chefs in the employ of the French prince of Soubise, Charles de Rohan. Made with cheese, Mornay sauce, another béchamel derivative, may have been created in the household of the Mornays, an important Huguenot family. Holland sauce—sauce hollandaise in French—was probably first prepared by French Huguenots in religious exile in neighboring Holland.

What Are Soups?

Simply defined, a soup is a liquid, savory food made with meat, fish, or vegetable stock as its base. Most soups are served warm, but sweetened fruit soups are often served chilled.

Soups can be served in a number of ways: as a combination of soup and sandwich or soup and salad; in a cup or a bowl before other courses; as an appetizer; or as the entrée. Soup should always complement the appetizer or entrée.

Types of Soups

There are four general categories of soup: clear, thin, thick, and specialty.

Clear Soups

These soups have clear, unthickened stock or broth as their base. Meat, poultry, or fish; vegetables; and aromatics are simmered together to produce clear soups. Clear soups include both broths and consommés and may be served plain or with a meat, vegetable, pasta, rice, or other garnish.

Broths A broth is a liquid that results from simmering meat, poultry, or fish with vegetables, herbs, and spices in water or stock. It contains no solid ingredients. Broth is more flavorful than stock because of the use of meat and poultry instead of bones.

Consommé A *consommé* is a clarified and fortified soup made from broth or stock and additional ingredients. Clarification removes impurities from the broth or stock, producing a full-bodied transparent soup without any fat and with a highly concentrated taste.

Thin Soups

Thin soups use water, stock, or milk as the liquid and include vegetables, meat, pasta, or grains for texture. Like clear soups, they are unthickened. Thin soups include vegetable soups and protein vegetable soups. Although most vegetable soups use a meat or poultry broth or stock, some have a vegetable broth as a base.

PROCESS

Preparing a Consommé

Consommé should have a rich flavor and be crystal clear.

Follow these steps to clarify a broth or stock into consommé:

1 **Combine lean ground meat, egg whites, mirepoix, tomato, and seasonings in a mixing bowl.**

2 **Add the ground meat mixture to cold stock and blend.**

3 **Place in a stockpot, and cook on the range over moderate heat, stirring often, until the stock comes to a simmer.**

4 **When a raft begins to form, stop stirring, and reduce the heat. Simmer gently.**

5 **Simmer for 1 1/2–2 hours, making sure that the raft does not break.**

6 **Slowly strain the consommé through a chinois lined with several layers of dampened cheesecloth. Adjust the seasonings as desired.**

Thick Soups

These soups are opaque instead of clear. Although they use stock or broth as a base, thick soups also contain a thickening agent such as cream, roux, or vegetable purée.

Vegetable purée soups Vegetable purée soups rely on starches in their main ingredients (usually vegetables, legumes, or rice) as thickeners. Many purée soups also incorporate cream or milk.

Cream soups Roux, liaison, or other thickeners produce the desired consistency in cream soups.

Velouté soups Preparation of velouté soups involves diluting and seasoning velouté sauce in which the main ingredient of the soup has cooked. The usual finish for a velouté soup is a liaison.

Specialty Soups

These soups require special ingredients or techniques that reflect the cuisine of a specific region. Specialty soups can be clear, thin, or thick. Bisques, chowders, international, and various cold soups are representative of specialty soups.

Bisques Bisques are thick soups usually made from shellfish. Traditionally thickened with rice, today bisques more commonly use roux as a thickener and contain cream.

Chowders Chowders have strong connections to the eastern United States, where their main ingredients—usually shellfish or fish—are readily available. Chowders may also feature vegetables as additional or main ingredients and typically contain diced potatoes and milk or cream.

International soups International soups are of foreign origin and include various preparations. International soups can be served hot or cold. Borscht, a beet soup, originates in Russia. Bouillabaisse is a fish-based soup flavored with saffron that comes from France. Gazpacho, a cold Spanish soup, is a thicker, puréed vegetable soup garnished with diced vegetables.

Cold soups Cold soups in the specialty category include both cooked cold soups and uncooked soups. Vichyssoise and consommé à la madrilène are examples of cooked cold soups. An example of an uncooked soup is fruit soup, made from various fruits and fruit and vegetable juices. These soups have gained recent popularity as a refreshing alternative during the hot summer months. Serve these soups cold in a chilled glass, soup plate, or cup.

Preparing Clear Soups

Stock or broth is the starting point for all clear soups. More flavorful than stock, broth can stand on its own as a dish. Broth is often clarified into a consommé.

Broth

Broths have more flavor than stocks because their preparation involves simmering meat as well as bones with other ingredients such as carrots, celery, leeks, and parsnips. Broths benefit from the substitution of stock for water as a cooking liquid and from the use of flavorful cuts of meat from the neck, shoulder, or shank.

To prepare a clear broth:

1. Cut the main ingredient. Brown meat or poultry, or sweat mirepoix or other vegetables in a stockpot.
2. Add water or stock to cover the ingredients, bring to a slow boil, and then reduce heat.
3. Simmer, skimming fats and impurities from the surface, until ingredients are tender.
4. To ensure a clear soup, strain the broth through a chinois.
5. Adjust seasonings, and serve.

Consommé

A well-prepared consommé has two distinctive features: rich flavor and perfect clarity. To achieve the concentrated flavor characteristic of consommé, reduce the broth or stock. To clarify the consommé, the following ingredients, known collectively as the *clearmeat,* or clarification, are necessary.

- A cold, flavorful broth or stock that is free of all visible fat. The liquid must be cold to prevent premature coagulation of albumin. The flavor of the broth or stock should be the same as that of the finished soup. When preparing a game consommé, for example, use a game broth or stock.
- Lean ground meat, poultry, or fish that adds flavor, color, and structure. The meat must be ground to allow even disbursement throughout the soup. It also should be very lean so that it does not add extra fat. The meat ingredient contains some albumin, which aids the clarification process.
- Egg whites, which contain large amounts of albumin. When albumin is heated, it coagulates, or solidifies, and combines with other particles in the broth or stock. The albumin carries these items to the surface of the broth or stock. There they form a *raft,* or floating mass. The coagulation of protein clarifies the broth or stock by attracting impurities to the raft and holding them there. Eight to ten egg whites per gallon of liquid are used for clarification.
- The mirepoix—celery, carrots, onions, and sometimes leeks—that contributes flavor, color to the consommé and structure to the raft. A rough chop of these vegetables is adequate.
- The acid ingredient—usually wine, lemon juice, or tomato products—to act as a catalyst, helping the albumin coagulate. The acid product also adds color and flavor to the consommé, so choose an ingredient that will complement the finished product. Use a tomato product for beef consommé, for instance, and white wine for fish consommé.
- Seasonings that add flavor. The bouquet garni is the most common seasoning for consommé. Salt has a tendency to make consommé cloudy. It may be added prior to clarification or immediately before service. Underseason slightly so that as reduction occurs, salt and other seasonings do not dominate the soup.

Consommé should be cooled and refrigerated if it is not used immediately. When the consommé is cold, remove any remaining fat from its surface. When reheating the consommé for service, blot the surface of the soup with a paper towel to remove traces of fat.

Preparing Thin Soups

When preparing thin soups, always use a clear, flavorful broth or stock. Choose vegetables and other ingredients that complement one another. Cut vegetables in uniform and visually attractive pieces. Add vegetables at junctures appropriate to their cooking times. Cook grains and pastas separately, and add them later.

Make thin soups as follows:

1. Sauté, sweat, or simmer the solid flavoring ingredients for the soup. Both vegetables and meats may be used to flavor and garnish the soup.
2. Add broth or stock to the flavoring ingredients, and heat to a simmer.
3. Add seasonings so that they will have sufficient time to release their flavor. Add other ingredients according to their cooking times.
4. Continue to simmer the soup until the ingredients are cooked and the desired flavor is achieved.
5. Use the process of *dépouillage* as the soup simmers.
6. Adjust the seasonings. Add separately prepared garnishes if serving immediately. Otherwise, hold for service, or cool and refrigerate.

Preparing Thick Soups

The preparation of thick soups involves the use of a thickening agent. Each kind of thick soup—purée, cream, and velouté—has a slightly different preparation process.

Purée

Purée soups are made by cooking legumes or starchy vegetables in broth, stock, or water and then puréeing the main ingredients. The main ingredients typically used give purée soups a coarser texture than that of cream or velouté soups. Legumes featured in purée soups include fresh or dried peas, navy beans, and lentils. Vegetables include broccoli, cauliflower, celery or celery root, potatoes, and turnips.

The procedure for preparing most purée soups involves these basic steps:

1. Sweat mirepoix or other vegetables in fat. Add flour if using, and cook several minutes, stirring to blend flour and fat.
2. Add the cooking liquid, main ingredients, and bouquet garni or other seasonings.
3. Cook at a simmer until the vegetables are tender enough for puréeing. Discard bouquet garni if using, and reserve some of the cooking liquid.
4. Use a food mill, food processor, immersion blender, or vertical cutter mixer (VCM) to purée the soup.
5. Add the reserved liquid or stock to achieve the required consistency. Add tempered cream if necessary.

6. Adjust the seasonings. Add separately prepared garnishes if serving immediately. Otherwise, hold for service, or cool and refrigerate.

The main ingredients for a purée soup and expectations for the final product will determine the techniques used, as the steps in the preparation of purée of carrot soup shown. Dried legumes are sometimes mashed instead of puréed.

Cream and Velouté

Cream soups and velouté soups have a smooth, velvety texture as a result of simmering the main ingredients with a roux or, more traditionally, with a béchamel or velouté sauce, and then straining and puréeing them and adding cream or liaison to finish. A variety of vegetables lend themselves to cream and velouté soups, including asparagus, broccoli, carrots, spinach, and squash.

> As the procedure for preparing purée of carrot soup demonstrates, some purée soups get their thick consistency from both the puréed vegetables and a starch that helps the purée remain suspended in the soup. **Singer** is the term for dusting sautéed or sweated ingredients with a starch such as flour, as in step 2. If the ingredients are not dusted with a starch, a thickening agent may be added later in the cooking process.

The procedure for making cream or velouté soups is essentially the same:

1. Sweat hard vegetables, such as carrots, in fat. Prepare soft or leafy vegetables, such as asparagus and spinach, by blanching.
2. Thicken by adding a roux and a liquid, a béchamel sauce, or a velouté sauce.
3. Bring to a boil, and then lower heat to a simmer. Add soft vegetables and a bouquet garni if desired.
4. Skim impurities and fat from the surface of the soup as it cooks. Simmer vegetables until tender. Remove bouquet garni.
5. Purée until smooth, and then strain.

6. Thin with hot white stock or milk.
7. Finish with tempered cream or a liaison. Adjust seasonings before serving.

> Heat and the acidity of certain ingredients can cause products in thick soups to curdle. Several precautions can be taken to avoid curdling. In general, dairy products with a higher fat content curdle less frequently than those with a lower fat content. Avoid adding cold cream or milk to hot soup; heat the cream or milk before adding, or temper it by adding a small amount of hot soup to it. Do not boil soup after adding milk or a liaison containing eggs. Thickening a soup with a starch prior to adding a dairy product helps to prevent curdling as well.

Preparing Specialty Soups

A variety of techniques are used to prepare specialty soups. Although some of these methods will be unique to a particular soup, in many cases other methods will be used to prepare clear, thin, and thick soups.

Bisque

Preparation of these shellfish-based cream soups is similar to that for any cream soup. Thicken a concentrated stock of shellfish, such as shrimp or lobster, with roux, and add cream to finish.

The basic procedure for these rich soups is as follows:

1. In a stockpot, sweat mirepoix and the main ingredient in fat over moderate heat.
2. Add a tomato product, and combine. Deglaze the pot with wine or cognac.
3. Add flour, and cook several minutes, stirring constantly to make a roux.
4. Add hot stock.
5. Simmer about one hour. Skim occasionally to remove impurities.

Preparing Purée of Carrot Soup

Purée soups are made with legumes or starchy vegetables.

To prepare pureé of carrot soup, follow these steps:

1 Sweat onions and carrots in clarified butter until onions are translucent.

2 Add flour, and cook 3–5 minutes, stirring constantly.

3 Add heated chicken or vegetable stock to the vegetables. Bring to a boil. Reduce heat to a simmer, and cook for about 30 minutes or until carrots are tender and soup has achieved the desired flavor.

4 Strain the soup and purée the vegetables, or purée using an immersion blender.

5 If not using an immersion blender, return the vegetable purée to the strained liquid in the soup pot.

6 Temper heavy cream, and add to soup. Heat to 165°F (74°C).

7 Adjust seasonings.

8 Add garnish appropriately.

6. Strain through a fine mesh china cap or cheesecloth.

7. Finish with tempered cream, and adjust seasonings before serving.

The usual garnish for a bisque is the sliced or diced flesh of the shellfish.

Chowder

The procedure for making chowders—clam, seafood, or corn—is also much the same as that for cream soups. Chowders, however, do not require puréeing or straining, which accounts for their chunky texture and frequent comparison to stews.

International Soups

Minestrone, hot-and-sour soup, bouillabaisse, Russian borscht, and Morrocan couscous are just a few international soups prepared in commercial kitchens. Preparation of these specialty soups and the ingredients required are specific to the cuisine from which the soups derive.

Cold Soups

The resulting product of a wide array of techniques and ingredients, cold soups, such as chilled consommé, vichyssoise, gazpacho, and avocado soup defy specific classification. It is possible, however, to group them in two general categories: cooked soups and uncooked soups.

Cooked cold soups Cooked cold soups require slightly different handling than hot soups do. Cold soups should be thinner than their hot versions. To achieve this, use less thickener or more liquid. Do not add the cream until the soup has chilled. This helps increase the shelf life of the soup. Finally, because cold blunts taste, cold soups often need more seasoning than hot soups. Taste cold soups just before serving, and adjust seasonings as needed. Examples of cooked cold soups include vichyssoise and consommé à la madrilène.

Uncooked cold soups Preparation of most uncooked cold soups is fairly simple. Much of the labor involves chopping or readying ingredients. Some recipes call for puréeing to thicken the soup and/or the addition of cream or yogurt to enrich the final product. Examples of uncooked cold soups include gazpacho and cold cucumber soup.

Handling Soups

Most soups can be prepared in advance of serving and reheated as needed. Stir soup occasionally during the cooking process to prevent ingredients from sticking to the bottom of the pot.

All soups, however, like other foods, require careful handling after preparation and cooking to prevent the growth of harmful microorganisms. Serve hot soups hot and cold soups cold. More specific guidelines for holding, storing, and reheating soups follow.

Holding

A soup's quality deteriorates if held on a steam table for an extended period. To maintain quality, keep the product fresh, and prevent cross-contamination, hold only small batches of soup at a time, replenishing the supply only when necessary.

Carefully monitor the temperature of soup to ensure safety. Keep hot soups 140°F (60°C) or higher when holding for service. Stir regularly to distribute heat throughout the soup and to prevent a skin from forming. Hold cold soups at 41°F (5°C) or lower until service.

Storage

Cool cooked soups from 140°F–70°F (60°C–21°C) within 2 hours and from 70°F–41°F (21°C–5°C) or lower in an additional 4 hours for a total of 6 hours. If these temperatures are not achieved within the allotted time, reheat the soup to 165°F (74°C) within two hours for 15 seconds. When making large batches of thick soup, do not add milk or cream before cooling and storing. Keep all soups under refrigeration at 41°F (5°C) or lower. Store soups in tightly sealed containers that have been labeled with the name of the soup and the date the soup was made. Use stored soup according to the FIFO method.

Reheating

Quickly reheat soup for service. Soup should reach an internal temperature of 165°F (74°C) for 15 seconds within 2 hours. Adjust the seasonings if needed.

Presenting Soups

Presentation is important, whether a soup is an appetizer or the entire meal. There are various facets to a soup's presentation, including garnishing, portion size, serving vessel, and temperature.

See Chapter 33: Principles of Dining Service for specific information on presentation and service.

Garnishing

A garnish enhances almost any soup's appearance. Garnishes run the gamut from a simple decoration such as fresh mint, seasoned croutons, or a rosette of sour cream to the actual ingredients of the soup to the carefully cut or shaped vegetables and other foods that adorn consommés and give them their names.

Except in the case of a consommé, which usually has a traditional garnish, a garnish is created that best accents a soup's color and flavor. When garnishing a soup, follow these guidelines:

- Cut meats or vegetables in uniform pieces so that they are similar in shape and size. Consommés in particular benefit from carefully cut garnishes because such additions are so clearly visible.
- Choose a garnish whose flavor and texture complements the soup.
- Cook garnishes only until just done. Vegetables should be tender but firm, meat or poultry should not fall apart, and pasta and rice should maintain their distinctive shapes. To avoid overcooking, hold these garnishes to the side until it is time to serve the soup.
- Cook starches or vegetables for garnishing separately. After the garnish is cooked, it is usually placed in a bouillon cup; then the hot or cold consommé is poured into the cup.
- Make sure that the garnish is attractive.

Typical garnishes The garnishes for many classic consommés are distinctive. See Figure 15-8 on page 268. Garnishes for soups include the actual vegetables in a clear vegetable soup, barley and lamb diced in Scotch broth, and a creatively cut vegetable in a cream or purée soup. Toppings on thick soups such as fresh herbs, grated cheese, chopped egg whites, sour cream, croutons, and crumbled bacon are other examples of garnishes. Soup often is served with both a garnish and a crisp accompaniment, such as breadsticks, melba toast, corn chips, or cheese straws.

Serving Soups

The type of soup, the meal at which it is served, and when during the meal it will be eaten determine portion size and thus the size and type of cup or bowl for service. An appetizer portion is usually 6–8 ounces (170–225 g), and a main course portion ranges from 10–12 ounces (285–340 g).

Temperature is also important to the presentation of soup. Hot soups should be held at 140°F (60°C) or higher and cold soups at 41°F (5°C) or lower. Hot soup will hold its temperature in a hot cup or bowl and cold soup in a chilled container.

FIGURE 15-8

Consommés and Their Garnishes

CONSOMMÉ À LA BOUQUETIÈRE
French beans, asparagus tips, green peas

CONSOMMÉ À LA BRUNOISE
small cubes of carrots, turnips, leeks, celery, peas, and chervil

CONSOMMÉ À LA CÉLESTINE
julienne of crêpes, with chopped truffles or fine herbs

CONSOMMÉ CHASSEUR
julienne of mushrooms and game quenelles

CONSOMMÉ JULIENNE
julienne of carrots, leeks, turnips, celery, cabbage, and green peas and chiffonade of chervil and sorrel

CONSOMMÉ MIKADO
diced tomato and chicken

CONSOMMÉ PRINTANIÈRE
carrots, peas and turnips, and chervil

CONSOMMÉ ROSSINI
profiteroles stuffed with foie gras purée and chopped truffles

CONSOMMÉ À LA ROYALE
cubes of royal custard

Vegetable Stock

INGREDIENTS	U.S. Standard	Metric
Vegetable oil	*as needed*	*as needed*
MIREPOIX		
Onions, *peeled*	*1 1/2 lbs.*	*680 g*
Leeks, *washed, trimmed*	*8 oz.*	*225 g*
Carrots, *washed, peeled, rewashed*	*8 oz.*	*225 g*
Celery, *washed, trimmed*	*8 oz.*	*225 g*
Garlic, *peeled and mashed*	*6 cloves*	*6 cloves*
White wine	*1 cup*	*240 ml*
Water, *cold*	*as needed*	*as needed*
BOUQUET GARNI		
White peppercorns, *whole*	*1 Tbsp.*	*15 ml*
Bay leaves	*3 each*	*3 each*
Parsley stems	*1 1/2 oz.*	*40 g*
Thyme leaves, *dried*	*1 tsp.*	*5 ml*

METHOD OF PREPARATION

1. Gather all the ingredients and equipment.

2. Heat the oil in a stockpot; add the mirepoix and garlic; cover and *sweat.*

3. Add the white wine. Reduce by half, and then add cold water to a height of 2–3 inches (5.08–7.63 cm) above the vegetables.

4. Add the bouquet garni, and simmer until the proper flavor is achieved.

5. Strain the stock through a *chinois,* and cool from 140°F (60°C) to 70°F (21°C) within 2 hours, and from 70°F (21°C) to 41°F (5°C) or lower in an additional 4 hours. Label, date, and refrigerate.

6. Reheat to 165°F (74°C) within 2 hours.

Chef's Notes

Add aromatic vegetables such as fennel, mushrooms, or tomato, as desired, for more flavor.

COOKING TECHNIQUES

Simmering:

1. Place the prepared product in an appropriately sized pot.
2. Bring the product to a boil, and then reduce the heat to allow the product to barely boil.
3. Cook until desired doneness is achieved.

GLOSSARY

Mirepoix: carrots, onion, celery, and sometimes leeks—rough-cut

Bouquet garni: bouquet of herbs and spices

Sweat: to extract moisture using low heat and a cover

Chinois: cone-shaped strainer

NUTRITION

Nutrition Facts

Yield: 1 gallon (3.8 liters)
Serving Size: 8 oz. (240 ml)

Amount Per Serving

Calories 70

Total Fat 3.5 g

Sodium 30 mg

Total Carbohydrate 8 g

Protein 1 g

Fish Stock

INGREDIENTS	U.S. Standard	Metric
White fish bones **and heads**	12 lbs.	5.4 kg
Vegetable oil	as needed	as needed
MIREPOIX		
Onions, peeled	1 1/2 lbs.	680 g
Celery, washed, trimmed	1 lb.	454 g
Leeks, washed, trimmed	1 lb.	454 g
White wine, dry	1 pt.	500 ml
Water, cold	3 gal.	11.2 l
BOUQUET GARNI		
Whole white **peppercorns,** crushed	1 Tbsp.	15 ml
Bay leaves	2 each	2 each
Parsley stems	1 1/2 oz.	40 g
Thyme leaves, dried	2 tsp.	10 ml

METHOD OF PREPARATION

1. Gather all the ingredients and equipment.

2. Remove the gills from the heads, and wash thoroughly in cold water to remove all traces of blood from the heads and the bones.

3. Place a thin layer of oil in a stockpot; add the mirepoix, cover, and *sweat* until onions are translucent. Add the fish bones and heads, re-cover, and allow to sweat until the fish bones turn opaque. Stir periodically, and do not allow mirepoix to brown.

4. Add the white wine, and reduce by half. Add the water and bouquet garni.

5. Bring to a boil, <u>immediately</u> turn to a simmer, and simmer gently until the proper quality (flavor, richness, body, color) is achieved, approximately 30 minutes. During the cooking process, occasionally crush the bones with a wooden spoon to release their gelatin. *Dépouille* often.

6. Strain the stock through a chinois into a suitable container, and place in a cooling sink or blast chiller. Cool from 140°F (60°C) to 70°F (21°C) within 2 hours, and from 70°F (21°C) to 41°F (5°C) or lower in an additional 4 hours. Label, date, and refrigerate.

7. Dépouille, then slowly and gently pour off the stock into another container until sediment begins to appear. Stop pouring at that point, and discard the sediment.

8. Label, date, and refrigerate the clean stock.

9. Reheat to 165°F (74°C) within 2 hours before using.

COOKING TECHNIQUES

Simmering:

1. Place the prepared product in an appropriately sized pot.
2. Bring the product to a boil, and then reduce the heat to allow the product to barely boil.
3. Cook until desired doneness is achieved.

GLOSSARY

Mirepoix: carrots, onion, celery, and sometimes leeks—rough-cut

Bouquet garni: bouquet of herbs and spices

Sweat: to extract moisture using low heat and a cover

Dépouille: skim off impurities or grease

NUTRITION

Nutrition Facts

Yield: 3 gallons (11.2 liters)
Serving Size: 8 oz. (240 ml)

Amount Per Serving

Calories 45

Total Fat 2 g

Sodium 350 mg

Total Carbohydrate 0 g

Protein 5 g

Court-Bouillon

INGREDIENTS	U.S. Standard	Metric
Water or appropriate stock	1 1/2 qts.	1.4 l
Dry white wine	3 oz.	90 ml
MIREPOIX		
Onions, peeled	4 oz.	115 g
Leeks, washed, trimmed	4 oz.	115 g
Celery, washed, trimmed	2 oz.	55 g
BOUQUET GARNI		
Whole peppercorns, white, black, or mix	1 tsp.	5 ml
Bay leaves	2 each	2 each
Parsley stems	1/2 oz.	15 g
Thyme leaves, dried	1 tsp.	5 ml

METHOD OF PREPARATION

1. Gather all the ingredients and equipment.

2. Place all the ingredients into an appropriate pan, heat to a boil, and *dépouille* as needed. Reduce to a simmer, and simmer gently until proper flavor is achieved. Strain into a *chinois,* if desired.

3. Hold at 140°F (60°C) or higher, or cool from 140°F (60°C) to 70°F (21°C) within 2 hours, and from 70°F (21°C) to 41°F (5°C) or lower in an additional 4 hours. Label, date, and refrigerate.

4. Reheat to 165°F (74°C) within 2 hours.

Chef's Notes

This is a basic outline for a court bouillon. Ingredients can change depending on the item to be poached and the desired flavors. Acid can be in the form of citrus juice, vinegar, wine, or a combination. Aromatics can change according to desired flavors. After poaching, some of the court bouillon can be strained and used in a sauce to accompany the poached item.

COOKING TECHNIQUES

Simmering:

1. Place the prepared product in an appropriately sized pot.
2. Bring the product to a boil, and then reduce the heat to allow the product to barely boil.
3. Cook until desired doneness is achieved.

GLOSSARY

Mirepoix: carrots, onion, celery, and sometimes leeks—rough-cut

Bouquet garni: bouquet of herbs and spices

Dépouille: skim off impurities or grease

Chinois: cone-shaped strainer

NUTRITION

271

Nutrition Facts

Yield: 1 quart (.95 liter)
Serving Size: 3 oz. (90 ml)

Amount Per Serving

Calories 20

Total Fat 0 g

Sodium 25 mg

Total Carbohydrate 4 g

Protein 0 g

Brown Stock—Beef, Veal, Lamb, Fowl, and Game

INGREDIENTS	U.S. Standard	Metric
Bones	50 lbs.	23 kg
Oil, vegetable	as needed	as needed
Tomato paste	as needed	as needed
Leeks, washed, trimmed, sliced	5 lbs.	2.3 kg
Cold liquid	15 gal.	56 l
MIREPOIX		
Carrots, washed, peeled	5 lbs.	2.3 kg
Celery, washed, trimmed	5 lbs.	2.3 kg
Onions, peeled	10 lbs.	4.5 kg
Red wine, dry	1 qt.	.95 l
BOUQUET GARNI		
Black peppercorns, whole	2 Tbsp.	30 ml
Bay leaves	4 each	4 each
Parsley stems	1 1/2 oz.	45 ml
Thyme leaves, dried	2 Tbsp.	30 ml

METHOD OF PREPARATION

1. Gather all the ingredients and equipment.

2. Preheat the oven to 425°F (218°C).

3. Place the bones in a roasting pan, and brush with oil. Roast in the oven until well browned.

4. Remove the pan from the oven, and spread the tomato paste lightly over the bones. This will result in additional color and flavor in the stock. Return the pan to the oven for a few minutes more. Be careful not to burn the tomato product.

5. Remove the bones from the oven, and drain and reserve the fat. Place the bones in a suitable stockpot or steam-jacketed kettle (with a spigot if available). Add the leeks. Add the cold liquid to a height of 6–8 inches (15.24–20.32 cm) above the bones.

6. Apply heat, bring to a boil, and immediately turn down to a simmer.

7. Using the same pan as for roasting the bones, add a small quantity of the reserved fat and the rest of the mirepoix, place on the stove top or back in the oven, and brown.

8. *Dépouille* the stock; then add the browned mirepoix.

9. Deglaze the roasting pan with the red wine, and add back to the stock.

10. Simmer until the proper quality (flavor, richness, body, color) is achieved, approximately 6–8 hours for beef or veal bones and 3–4 hours for chicken bones. Add bouquet garni during last 1–1 1/2 hours. Continue to dépouille as needed.

11. Strain the stock through a chinois into a suitable container, and place in a cooling sink or blast chiller. Cool from 140°F (60°C) to 70°F (21°C) within 2 hours, and from 70°F (21°C) to 41°F (5°C) or lower in an additional 4 hours. Label, date, and refrigerate.

12. Reheat to 165°F (74°C) within 2 hours.

Chef's Notes

▶ Leeks are added at the beginning of the stock-making process, with the bones and cold water, because the albumin that they contain is a protein that is soluble only in cold liquid. After it has been slowly released into the water, the albumin has the ability to naturally clarify the liquid by coagulating with the impurities. Gently simmering the stock, as opposed to boiling it, aids the albumin in the natural clarification process.

COOKING TECHNIQUES

Roasting:

1. Sear the food product, and brown evenly.
2. Elevate the food product in a roasting pan.
3. Determine doneness, and consider carryover cooking.
4. Let the food product rest before carving.

Simmering:

1. Place the prepared product in an appropriately sized pot.
2. Bring the product to a boil, and then reduce the heat to allow the product to barely boil.
3. Cook until desired doneness is achieved.

GLOSSARY

Mirepoix: carrots, onion, celery, and sometimes leeks—rough-cut

Bouquet garni: bouquet of herbs and spices

Dépouille: skim off impurities or grease

NUTRITION

Nutrition Facts

Yield: 12 gallons (45 liters)
Serving Size: 4 oz. (120 ml)

Amount Per Serving

Calories 20

Total Fat 0.5 g

Sodium 45 mg

Total Carbohydrate 2 g

Protein 2 g

White Stock (Chicken, Beef, Veal, Fowl and Game)

INGREDIENTS	U.S. Standard	Metric
Bones	50 lbs.	23 kg
Leeks, washed, trimmed, sliced	5 lbs.	2.3 kg
Cold liquid	as needed	as needed
MIREPOIX		
Carrots, washed, peeled	5 lbs.	2.3 kg
Celery, washed, trimmed	5 lbs.	2.3 kg
Onions, peeled	10 lbs.	4.5 kg
BOUQUET GARNI		
Black peppercorns, whole	2 Tbsp.	30 ml
Parsley stems	1 1/2 oz.	40 g
Thyme leaves, dried	2 Tbsp.	30 ml
Bay leaves	4 each	4 each

METHOD OF PREPARATION

1. Gather all the ingredients and equipment.

2. If necessary, split the bones and rinse thoroughly in cold water, removing all blood and fat, which causes discoloration.

3. Place the bones and leeks in a suitable stockpot or steam-jacketed kettle with a spigot.

4. Add the cold liquid to a height of 4–6 inches (10.16–15.24 cm) above the bones.

5. Apply heat, bring to a boil, and immediately turn down to a simmer; dépouille.

6. Add the rest of the mirepoix and the bouquet garni.

7. Simmer for approximately 2–3 hours or until proper quality (flavor, richness, body, color) is achieved, continuing to dépouille as needed.

8. Strain the stock through a *chinois,* and cool from 140°F (60°C) to 70°F (21°C) within 2 hours, and from 70°F (21°C) to 41°F (5°C) or lower in an additional 4 hours. Label, date, and refrigerate.

9. Reheat to 165°F (74°C) within 2 hours.

Chef's Notes

Leeks are added at the beginning of the stock-making process, with the bones and cold water, because the albumin that they contain is a protein that is soluble only in cold liquid. After it has been slowly released into the water, the albumin has the ability to naturally clarify the liquid by coagulating with the impurities. Gently simmering the stock, as opposed to boiling it, aids the albumin in the natural clarification process.

COOKING TECHNIQUES

Simmering:

1. Place the prepared product in an appropriately sized pot.
2. Bring the product to a boil, and then reduce the heat to allow the product to barely boil.
3. Cook until desired doneness is achieved.

GLOSSARY

Mirepoix: carrots, onion, celery, and sometimes leeks—rough-cut

Chinois: cone-shaped strainer

NUTRITION

Nutrition Facts

Yield: 12 gallon (45 liters)
Serving Size: 5 oz. (150 ml)

Amount Per Serving

Calories 50

Total Fat 2 g

Sodium 530 mg

Total Carbohydrate 6 g

Protein 2 g

Béchamel Sauce

INGREDIENTS

	U.S. Standard	Metric
Milk	4 qts.	3.8 l
Onion, piquet	1 each	1 each
Butter, clarified	6 oz.	170 g
Flour, all-purpose, sifted	6 oz.	170 g
Salt	TT	TT
White pepper, ground	TT	TT
Nutmeg	1/8 tsp.	.5 ml

METHOD OF PREPARATION

1. Gather all the ingredients and equipment.

2. In a saucepan, heat the milk with the onion piquet, and simmer for 10 minutes.

3. In another saucepan, heat the clarified butter over moderate heat.

4. Gradually add flour to the butter to make a roux. Using a wooden spoon, mix thoroughly, and cook it approximately 5–6 minutes to make a white roux. Remove from the heat, and cool slightly.

5. Remove the onion piquet from the milk.

6. Temper the milk into the roux by gradually adding the hot milk, whisking constantly. Heat to a boil; reduce to a simmer. Simmer until the proper quality factors of the sauce are achieved.

7. Season to taste with the salt, pepper, and nutmeg.

8. Strain through a fine *chinois* into a suitable container. Hold at 140°F (60°C) or higher, or cool from 140°F (60°C) to 70°F (21°C) within 2 hours, and from 70°F (21°C) to 41°F (5°C) or lower in an additional 4 hours. Label, date, and refrigerate.

9. Reheat to 165°F (74°C) within 2 hours.

NUTRITION

Nutrition Facts

Yield: 1 gallon (3.8 liters)
Serving Size: 2 oz. (60 ml)

Amount Per Serving

Calories 70

Total Fat 4 g

Sodium 65 mg

Total Carbohydrate 5 g

Protein 2 g

Espagnole Sauce

INGREDIENTS	U.S. Standard	Metric
Brown beef stock	1 gal.	3.8 l
Brown roux	11 1/2 oz.	325 g
Bacon	10 oz.	285 g
Tomato purée	8 oz.	240 ml
MIREPOIX		
Onions, peeled	1 lb.	454 g
Carrots, peeled, washed	8 oz.	225 g
Celery, washed, trimmed	8 oz.	225 g
BOUQUET GARNI		
Black peppercorns, whole	1 Tbsp.	15 ml
Bay leaves	3 each	3 each
Parsley stems	1 oz.	28 g
Thyme leaves, dried	2 tsp.	10 ml

METHOD OF PREPARATION

1. Gather all the ingredients and equipment.

2. In a saucepan, temper the hot brown stock into the brown roux.

3. Heat to a boil; reduce to a simmer, and *dépouille* as needed.

4. In a sauté pan, render the bacon. Remove the bacon, and drain any excess fat. Add the mirepoix, and sauté until browned.

5. Add the tomato purée, and simmer for 3–5 minutes to cook out the acidity. Add this mixture to the stock/roux mixture.

6. Add the bouquet garni, continuing to simmer and dépouille as needed, until the proper quality factors of the sauce are achieved.

7. Strain through a *chinois* into a suitable container. Hold at 140°F (60°C) or higher, or cool from 140°F (60°C) to 70°F (21°C) within 2 hours, and from 70°F (21°C) to 41°F (5°C) or lower in an additional 4 hours. Label, date, and refrigerate.

8. Reheat to 165°F (74°C) within 2 hours.

Chef's Notes

Espagnole sauce is often used as a base or an ingredient in compound sauces, braises, and stews. Therefore, espagnole should not be seasoned with salt and pepper at this stage because seasoning will be added as needed to the various dishes that may be made from this sauce.

COOKING TECHNIQUES

Boiling (At sea level):
1. Bring the cooking liquid to a rapid boil.
2. Stir the contents, and cook the food product throughout.
3. Serve hot.

Simmering:
1. Place the prepared product in an appropriately sized pot.
2. Bring the product to a boil, and then reduce the heat to allow the product to barely boil.
3. Cook until desired doneness is achieved.

GLOSSARY

Mirepoix: *carrots, onion, celery, and sometimes leeks—rough-cut*

Bouquet garni: *bouquet of herbs and spices*

Dépouille: *skim off impurities or grease*

Chinois: *cone-shaped strainer*

NUTRITION

Nutrition Facts
Yield: 1 gallon (3.8 liters)
Serving Size: 3 oz. (90 ml)

Amount Per Serving

Calories 50

Total Fat 3 g

Sodium 55 mg

Total Carbohydrate 4 g

Protein 2 g

Sauce Velouté (Chicken, Veal, Fish, or Vegetable)

Ingredients	U.S. Standard	Metric
Butter, clarified	8 oz.	240 ml
Flour, sifted	8 oz.	225 g
White stock, heated to a boil	5 qts.	4.75 l
Salt	TT	TT
White pepper, ground	TT	TT

Method of Preparation

1. Gather all the ingredients and equipment.

2. Heat the clarified butter in a saucepan over medium-low heat. Gradually stir in the sifted flour to make a roux.

3. Using a wooden spoon, mix the roux thoroughly, and cook 6–8 minutes to make a blonde roux. The roux will be light in color with a slightly nutty aroma.

4. Gradually temper the stock into the roux. Heat the sauce to a boil; reduce the heat, and simmer until the proper quality factors of the sauce are achieved. *Dépouille* as needed.

5. Season to taste with salt and pepper.

6. Strain through a *chinois mousseline* into a suitable container. Hold at 140°F (60°C) or higher, or cool from 140°F (60°C) to 70°F (21°C) within 2 hours, and from 70°F (21°C) to 41°F (5°C) or lower in an additional 4 hours. Label, date, and refrigerate.

7. Reheat to 165°F (74°C) within 2 hours.

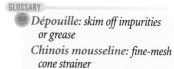

COOKING TECHNIQUES

Simmering:

1. Place the prepared product in an appropriately sized pot.
2. Bring the product to a boil, and then reduce the heat to allow the product to barely boil.
3. Cook until desired doneness is achieved.

GLOSSARY

Dépouille: skim off impurities or grease

Chinois mousseline: fine-mesh cone strainer

NUTRITION

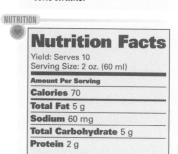

Nutrition Facts

Yield: Serves 10
Serving Size: 2 oz. (60 ml)

Amount Per Serving

Calories 70

Total Fat 5 g

Sodium 60 mg

Total Carbohydrate 5 g

Protein 2 g

Sauce Suprême

Nutrition Facts

Yield: 1 gallon (3.8 liters)
Serving Size: 2 oz. (60 ml)

Amount Per Serving	
Calories 50	
Total Fat 4 g	
Sodium 230 mg	
Total Carbohydrate 2 g	
Protein 2 g	

INGREDIENTS

INGREDIENTS	U.S. Standard	Metric
Chicken *velouté*	1 gal.	3.8 l
Heavy cream	8 oz.	240 ml
Salt	TT	TT
White pepper, ground	TT	TT

METHOD OF PREPARATION

1. Gather all the ingredients and equipment.
2. In a saucepan or stockpot, heat the chicken velouté. Reduce to a simmer.
3. *Temper* the heavy cream into the velouté.
4. Taste and season with salt and pepper as needed.

Sauce Allemande

INGREDIENTS

INGREDIENTS	U.S. Standard	Metric
Veal *velouté*	3 1/2 qts.	3.3 l
Egg yolks	4 oz.	120 ml
Heavy cream	8 oz.	240 ml
Lemon juice	2 oz.	60 ml
Salt	TT	TT
White pepper, ground	TT	TT

METHOD OF PREPARATION

1. Gather all the ingredients and equipment.
2. In a saucepan, heat the velouté to a boil.
3. Combine egg yolks and heavy cream in a mixing bowl, *temper,* and add to the velouté.
4. Whisk in the lemon juice; season with salt and pepper.
5. Hold at 140°F (60°C) or higher, or cool from 140°F (60°C) to 70°F (21°C) within 2 hours, and from 70°F (21°C) to 41°F (5°C) or lower in an additional 4 hours. Label, date, and refrigerate.

Nutrition Facts

Yield: 1 gallon (3.8 liters)
Serving Size: 2 oz. (60 ml)

Amount Per Serving	
Calories 60	
Total Fat 4.5 g	
Sodium 50 mg	
Total Carbohydrate 3 g	
Protein 1 g	

Tomato Sauce

Ingredients

Ingredients	U.S. Standard	Metric
Olive oil	as needed	as needed
Onions, peeled, diced *macédoine*	1 lb.	454 g
Garlic, peeled, mashed into a paste	8–10 cloves	8–10 cloves
Bay leaves, in a sachet	3 each	3 each
Basil, dried	2 Tbsp.	30 ml
Red pepper flakes, crushed	1/2 tsp.	2.5 g
Tomato paste	4 oz.	115 g
Tomatoes, crushed	6 lbs.	2.7 kg
Vegetable stock or water	1 1/2 qts.	1.4 l
Salt	TT	TT
Black pepper, ground	TT	TT

Method of Preparation

1. Gather all the ingredients and equipment.

2. Heat a thin layer of oil in a heavy pot, add the onions and garlic, and *sweat* until the onions are translucent.

3. Add the remaining ingredients; heat to a boil, and then reduce to a simmer.

4. Simmer until the proper quality factors of the sauce are achieved; stir and dépouille as needed.

5. Taste and adjust the seasoning with salt and pepper as needed. Remove bay leaf sachet.

6. Hold at 140°F (60°C) or higher, or cool from 140°F (60°C) to 70°F (21°C) within 2 hours, and from 70°F (21°C) to 41°F (5°C) or lower in an additional 4 hours. Label, date, and refrigerate.

7. Reheat to 165°F (74°C) within 2 hours.

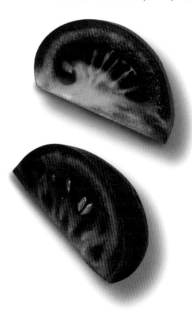

Hollandaise Sauce

INGREDIENTS

	U.S. Standard	Metric
REDUCTION		
Dry white wine	6 oz.	180 ml
White vinegar	1 1/2 oz.	45 ml
Whole black peppercorns, *crushed*	5 each	5 each
Bay leaf	1 each	1 each
Egg yolks, *pasteurized*	4 oz.	120 ml
Butter, *clarified and heated to 165°F (74°C)*	12 oz.	360 ml
Salt	TT	TT
White pepper, *ground*	TT	TT

METHOD OF PREPARATION

1. Gather all the ingredients and equipment.
2. Combine all of the ingredients for the reduction in a saucepan. Heat to a boil, turn to a simmer, and reduce the liquid slowly by half of the volume, strain, and cool.
3. In a bowl, whisk the cooled reduction into the pasteurized egg yolks.
4. Whisk the egg yolk mixture over a double boiler, cooking until the eggs start to ribbon and change color. Remove the eggs from the heat.
5. Slowly add the hot clarified butter to the eggs, whisking constantly.
6. Adjust the seasonings and serve immediately, or hold warm up to 20 minutes.

Béarnaise Sauce

INGREDIENTS

	U.S. Standard	Metric
REDUCTION		
Tarragon leaves, *dried*	3 Tbsp.	45 ml
Dry white wine	6 oz.	180 ml
White vinegar	1 1/2 oz.	45 ml
Black peppercorns, *crushed*	6 each	6 each
Bay leaves	2 each	2 each
Egg yolks, *pasteurized*	4 oz.	120 ml
Butter, *clarified and heated to 165°F (74°C)*	12 oz.	360 ml
Tarragon leaves, *washed, squeezed dry, and chopped*	1 Tbsp.	15 ml
Parsley, *washed, squeezed dry, and chopped*	1 Tbsp.	15 ml
Salt	TT	TT

METHOD OF PREPARATION

1. Gather all the ingredients and equipment.

2. Place all of the ingredients for the reduction in a saucepan, bring to a boil, turn down to a simmer, and reduce slowly to half of the volume. Strain and cool.

3. In a bowl, whisk the cooled reduction into the pasteurized egg yolks.

4. Over a double boiler, whip the egg yolk mixture until the eggs start to ribbon and change color. Then remove from the heat.

5. Slowly add the hot clarified butter to the egg mixture, whipping constantly.

6. Adjust the seasonings, and then fold in the fresh tarragon and parsley. Serve immediately, or hold warm for a maximum of 20 minutes.

COOKING TECHNIQUES

Simmering:

1. *Place the prepared product in an appropriately sized pot.*
2. *Bring the product to a boil, and then reduce the heat to allow the product to barely boil.*
3. *Cook until desired doneness is achieved.*

GLOSSARY

Reduction: evaporation of liquid by boiling

NUTRITION

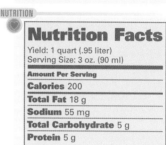

Nutrition Facts

Yield: 1 quart (.95 liter)
Serving Size: 3 oz. (90 ml)

Amount Per Serving

Calories 200

Total Fat 18 g

Sodium 55 mg

Total Carbohydrate 5 g

Protein 5 g

Demi-Glace

INGREDIENTS	U.S. Standard	Metric
Espagnole sauce	1 gal.	3.8 l
Brown stock	1 gal.	3.8 l
BOUQUET GARNI		
Black peppercorns, whole	1 Tbsp.	15 ml
Bay leaves	2 each	2 each
Parsley stems	1 oz.	28 g
Thyme leaves, dried	2 tsp.	10 ml
Tarragon, dried	1 Tbsp.	15 ml
Madeira wine	8 oz.	240 ml

METHOD OF PREPARATION

1. Gather all the ingredients and equipment.

2. In a saucepan, combine the espagnole sauce and brown stock, and heat to a boil. Reduce to a simmer.

3. *Dépouille* as needed. Add the bouquet garni.

4. Simmer until volume is reduced by half and the proper quality factors of the sauce are achieved.

5. Add the Madeira wine.

6. Strain through a *chinois* into a suitable container. Hold at 140°F (60°C) or higher, or cool from 140°F (60°C) to 70°F (21°C) within 2 hours, and from 70°F (21°C) to 41°F (5°C) or lower in an additional 4 hours. Label, date, and refrigerate.

7. Reheat to 165°F (74°C) within 2 hours.

Chef's Notes

Demi-glace is often used as a base or an ingredient in compound sauces, braises, and stews. Therefore, demi-glace should not be seasoned with salt and pepper at this stage because seasoning will be added as needed to the various dishes that may be made from this sauce.

COOKING TECHNIQUES

Simmering:

1. Place the prepared product in an appropriately sized pot.

2. Bring the product to a boil, and then reduce the heat to allow the product to barely boil.

3. Cook until desired doneness is achieved.

GLOSSARY

Bouquet garni: bouquet of herbs and spices

Dépouille: skim off impurities or grease

Chinois: cone-shaped strainer

NUTRITION

Nutrition Facts

Yield: 1 gallon (3.8 liters)
Serving Size: 2 oz. (60 ml)

Amount Per Serving

Calories 40

Total Fat 2 g

Sodium 230 mg

Total Carbohydrate 3 g

Protein 1 g

Sauce Bordelaise

COOKING TECHNIQUES

Simmering and Poaching:

1. Heat the cooking liquid to the proper temperature.
2. Submerge the food product completely.
3. Keep the cooked product moist and warm.

GLOSSARY

Reduction: *evaporation of liquid by boiling*

NUTRITION

Nutrition Facts

Yield: 1 quart (.95 liter)
Serving Size: 2 oz. (60 ml)

Amount Per Serving

Calories 90	
Total Fat 8 g	
Sodium 25 mg	
Total Carbohydrate 1 g	
Protein 1 g	

INGREDIENTS	U.S. Standard	Metric
REDUCTION		
Butter, clarified	as needed	as needed
Shallots, peeled and diced	1 oz.	28 g
Red Bordeaux wine	8 oz.	240 ml
Thyme leaves, dried	1/2 tsp.	2.5 ml
Bay leaves	2 each	2 each
Demi-glace	1 qt.	.95 l
Salt	TT	TT
White pepper, ground	TT	TT
Bone marrow, poached, shocked, drained, and diced	4 oz.	115 g

METHOD OF PREPARATION

1. Gather all the ingredients and equipment.
2. Melt a small amount of butter in a sauté pan, and add the shallots; sauté until shallots are softened.
3. Add the wine, thyme, and bay leaves, and then reduce by two-thirds.
4. Add the demi-glace, and bring to a boil immediately; turn down to a simmer, and simmer until proper quality factors of the sauce are achieved. Dépouille and strain.
5. Taste and season with salt and pepper as needed.
6. Hold at 140°F (60°C) or higher.
7. Just before serving, add the bone marrow.

Sauce Chasseur

INGREDIENTS

	U.S. Standard	Metric
REDUCTION		
Butter, clarified	as needed	as needed
Shallots, peeled, diced brunoise	2 oz.	55 g
Mushrooms, wiped clean, sliced 1/4" (6 mm)	4 oz.	115 g
Dry white wine	4 oz.	120 ml
Chervil leaves, dried	1/2 tsp.	2.5 ml
Tarragon leaves, dried	1 tsp.	5 ml
Demi-glace	1 1/2 pt.	720 ml
Tomato sauce	2 oz.	60 ml
Salt	TT	TT
White pepper, ground	TT	TT

METHOD OF PREPARATION

1. Gather all the ingredients and equipment.

2. In a sauté pan, heat a small amount of butter; add the shallots and mushrooms, and sauté until vegetables have softened.

3. Add the wine, and reduce the mixture by half.

4. Add the herbs to the reduction with the demi-glace and tomato sauce. Heat to a boil; reduce the heat, and simmer until the quality factors of the sauce are achieved. Dépouille.

5. Taste and season with salt and pepper as needed.

6. Hold at 140°F (60°C) or higher.

Beef Consommé

INGREDIENTS

INGREDIENTS	U.S. Standard	Metric
Ground beef, lean	1/2 lb.	225 g
MIREPOIX		
Onions, peeled and cut brunoise	4 oz.	115 g
Carrots, washed, peeled, cut brunoise	2 oz.	55 g
Celery, washed, trimmed, cut brunoise	2 oz.	55 g
Tomato paste	3 oz.	90 ml
Black peppercorns, crushed	5 each	5 each
White peppercorns, crushed	5 each	5 each
Bay leaves	1 each	1 each
Parsley stems	1/2 oz.	15 g
Thyme leaves	1/4 tsp.	1.5 ml
Salt, kosher	TT	TT
Egg whites, slightly beaten	9 each	9 each
White beef stock, cold (or beef broth, strong)	6 qts.	5.7 l
Madeira or sherry	1 Tbsp.	15 ml
White pepper, ground	TT	TT

METHOD OF PREPARATION

1. Gather all the ingredients and equipment.

2. In a mixing bowl, combine the lean ground beef, mirepoix, tomato paste, peppercorns, and herbs. Salt to taste. Mix the egg whites into the meat mixture until blended. Refrigerate.

3. In a *marmite*, blend the cold beef stock with the cold clarifying ingredients (meat/egg white mixture).

4. Place on moderate heat. Carefully watch the clarifying ingredients to make sure that they do not scorch. Stir occasionally until a raft forms (120°F/49°C), and then stop stirring.

5. Simmer the soup for 1 1/2 hours or to the desired strength, making sure that the raft does not break or sink. Remove the first cup of consommé through the spigot, and discard.

6. In a *chinois* lined with four to five layers of wet cheesecloth, slowly strain the liquid into a bain-marie insert to separate the clarifying ingredients from the liquid. Hold at 140°F (60°C) or higher.

7. Add the Madeira or sherry and adjust the seasonings to taste. (If consommé is strained through a spigot, there should be no fat on it; otherwise, dépouille all of the fat from the consommé.)

8. Serve hot with appropriate garnish, or cool from 140°F (60°C) to 70°F (21°C) within 2 hours, and from 70°F (21°C) to 41°F (5°C) or lower in an additional 4 hours. Label, date, and refrigerate.

COOKING TECHNIQUES

Simmering:
1. Place the prepared product in an appropriately sized pot.
2. Bring the product to a boil, and then reduce the heat to allow the product to barely boil.
3. Cook until desired doneness is achieved.

Boiling (At sea level):
1. Bring the cooking liquid to a rapid boil.
2. Stir the contents, and cook the food product throughout.
3. Serve hot.

GLOSSARY

Mirepoix: carrots, onion, celery, and sometimes leeks—rough-cut

Brunoise: 1/8" (3 mm) dice

Marmite: stockpot

Chinois: cone-shaped strainer

NUTRITION

Nutrition Facts
Yield: 1 gallon (3.8 liters)
Serving Size: 8 oz. (240 ml)

Amount Per Serving

Calories 70

Total Fat 2.5 g

Sodium 170 mg

Total Carbohydrate 4 g

Protein 6 g

Beef Bouillon

INGREDIENTS	U.S. Standard	Metric
White beef stock	1 gal.	3.8 l
Beef bones, split, washed	2 lbs.	910 g
Beef chuck, trimmed, cut into pieces	2 lbs.	910 g
BOUQUET GARNI		
Black peppercorns, crushed	6 each	6 each
Bay leaves	1 each	1 each
Parsley stems	1 oz.	28 g
Thyme leaves, dried	1 tsp.	5 ml
MIREPOIX		
Leeks, washed, trimmed	3 oz.	85 g
Onions, peeled	8 oz.	225 g
Carrots, washed, peeled	3 oz.	85 g
Celery, washed, trimmed	3 oz.	85 g
Salt	TT	TT
White pepper, ground	TT	TT
Parsley, fresh, washed, squeezed, and chopped	1/2 oz.	15 g

METHOD OF PREPARATION

1. Gather all the ingredients and equipment.

2. In a stockpot, combine the beef stock, bones, meat, bouquet garni, and leeks. Heat to a boil, and immediately reduce to a simmer.

3. Add the rest of the mirepoix, and simmer gently until the proper flavor is achieved. Dépouille as necessary.

4. Taste and adjust the seasonings with salt and pepper.

5. Strain the broth through a *chinois mousseline* lined with four or five layers of wet cheesecloth. Dépouille as needed.

6. Hold at 140°F (60°C) or higher. Serve in a preheated soup cup, garnished with parsley.

7. Cool from 140°F (60°C) to 70°F (21°C) within 2 hours, and from 70°F (21°C) to 41°F (5°C) or lower in an additional 4 hours. Label, date, and refrigerate.

8. Reheat to 165°F (74°C) within 2 hours.

Chef's Notes

• A bouillon is a fortified, partially clarified stock that is generally used for a soup.

• Leeks are added at the beginning of the process, with the bones, meat, and cold stock, because the albumin that they contain is a protein that is soluble only in cold liquid. After it has been slowly released into the water, the albumin has the ability to naturally clarify the liquid by coagulating with the impurities. Gently simmering the stock, as opposed to boiling it, aids the albumin with the natural clarification process.

COOKING TECHNIQUES

Boiling (At sea level):
1. Bring the cooking liquid to a rapid boil.
2. Stir the contents, and cook the food product throughout.
3. Serve hot.

Simmering:
1. Place the prepared product in an appropriately sized pot.
2. Bring the product to a boil, and then reduce the heat to allow the product to barely boil.
3. Cook until desired doneness is achieved.

GLOSSARY

Bouquet garni: bouquet of herbs and spices

Mirepoix: carrots, onion, celery, and sometimes leeks—rough-cut

Chinois mousseline: fine-mesh cone strainer

NUTRITION

Nutrition Facts

Yield: Serves 10
Serving Size: 8 oz. (240 ml)

Amount Per Serving

Calories 70

Total Fat 1.5 g

Sodium 140 mg

Total Carbohydrate 5 g

Protein 6 g

Purée of Celery Soup

INGREDIENTS	U.S. Standard	Metric
Butter	2 oz.	55 g
Celery, washed, trimmed, 1/2" (1.27 cm) rough-cut	1 lb.	454 g
Onion, peeled, 1/2" (1.27 cm) rough-cut	3 1/2 oz.	100 g
Garlic, peeled, mashed	1 clove	1 clove
Potatoes, peeled, washed, 1/2" (1.27 cm) rough-cut	12 oz.	340 g
Vegetable stock, heated to a boil	3 qts.	2.9 l
Salt	TT	TT
White pepper, ground	TT	TT
Ground nutmeg	pinch	pinch

METHOD OF PREPARATION

1. Gather all the ingredients and equipment.

2. In a stockpot, heat the butter, and sauté the celery and onions until translucent.

3. Add the garlic, potatoes, and stock. Heat to a boil. Reduce to a simmer, and simmer the soup for approximately 1 hour or until the celery and potatoes are very tender. Dépouille.

4. Purée the soup in a food processor or blender, strain, and bring to a simmer. Taste and season with the salt, pepper, and nutmeg as needed. Serve in a preheated soup cup, or hold at 140°F (60°C) or higher.

5. If necessary, cool from 140°F (60°C) to 70°F (21°C) within 2 hours, and from 70°F (21°C) to 41°F (5°C) or lower in an additional 4 hours.

6. Reheat to 165°F (74°C) within 2 hours before using.

Cream of Carrot Soup

INGREDIENTS

	U.S. Standard	Metric
Butter	3 oz.	85 g
Onions, peeled, diced brunoise	3 oz.	85 g
Carrots, peeled, washed, thinly sliced	16 oz.	454 g
Flour, all-purpose	2 oz.	55 g
Vegetable stock, heated to a boil	3 qts.	2.9 l
Rice	3 1/2 oz.	100 g
Egg yolks	2 each	2 each
Heavy cream	2 oz.	60 ml
Salt	TT	TT
White pepper, ground	TT	TT

METHOD OF PREPARATION

1. Gather all the ingredients and equipment.

2. Melt the butter in a stockpot. Add the onions, and sweat until translucent. Add the carrots and sweat for 5 minutes.

3. *Singe* the carrots and onions with the flour, and cook for 3 minutes. Add the boiling vegetable stock, and heat to a boil.

4. Add the rice, reduce the heat, and simmer the soup until the carrots and rice are very tender.

5. Purée the soup in a food processor, blender, or with an emersion blender; strain through a *chinois,* and return to the stove.

6. In a small bowl, whisk the egg yolk, and then add the cream to the egg. *Temper* this mixture into the soup, and heat to 165°F (74°C). Remove immediately from the stove or the soup will break. Taste and season with salt and pepper as needed.

6. Serve in a preheated cup, or hold at 140°F (60°C) or higher.

Chef's Notes

After egg yolks have been used as a final liaison in a dish, care must be taken to avoid breaking. When egg yolks, after being mixed with other liquids, are heated to a temperature exceeding 160°F (71°C), they begin to lose moisture. The proteins in them squeeze closely together, causing curdling or breaking. The soup will no longer be emulsified; clumps of yolk protein will be floating in the liquid of the soup.

COOKING TECHNIQUES

Sautéing:

1. Heat the sauté pan to the appropriate temperature.
2. Evenly brown the food product.
3. For a sauce, pour off any excess oil, reheat, and deglaze.

Simmering:

1. Place the prepared product in an appropriately sized pot.
2. Bring the product to a boil, and then reduce the heat to allow the product to barely boil.
3. Cook until desired doneness is achieved.

GLOSSARY

Brunoise: 1/8″ (3 mm) dice
Singe: to dust with flour
Chinois: cone-shaped strainer
Temper: to equalize products with two extreme temperatures or textures

NUTRITION

Nutrition Facts

Yield: Serves 10
Serving Size: 8 oz. (240 ml)

Amount Per Serving

Calories 210

Total Fat 12 g

Sodium 110 mg

Total Carbohydrate 20 g

Protein 6 g

Crème de Champignon avec Chanterelles

INGREDIENTS

	U.S. Standard	Metric
Butter	7 oz.	205 g
Mushrooms, cleaned and pulsed in a food processor (chop finely, but do not purée)	10 oz.	285 g
Flour, all-purpose	6 oz.	170 g
White chicken stock, heated to a boil	1 gal.	3.8 l
Chanterelle mushrooms, fresh, cleaned, and sliced	10 oz.	285 g
Heavy cream	8 oz.	240 ml
Salt	TT	TT
White pepper, ground	TT	TT

METHOD OF PREPARATION

1. Gather all the ingredients and equipment.

2. In a stock pot, heat 6 oz. (170 g) of butter, and cook the chopped mushrooms slowly over low heat.

3. Add the flour, and stir to make a roux. Cook for 4–6 minutes to make a blond roux. *Temper* in the stock, and then simmer soup gently for 30 minutes, stirring occasionally.

4. Heat the remaining 1 oz. (28 g) of butter in a sauté pan, and sauté the chanterelles for about 5 minutes until tender and cooked through.

5. Add the sautéed chanterelles to the soup, and simmer for 5 minutes more.

6. Temper the cream into the soup. Season with salt and pepper to taste.

COOKING TECHNIQUES

Simmering:
1. Place the prepared product in an appropriately sized pot.
2. Bring the product to a boil, and then reduce the heat to allow the product to barely boil.
3. Cook until desired doneness is achieved.

Sautéing:
1. Heat the sauté pan to the appropriate temperature.
2. Evenly brown the food product.
3. For a sauce, pour off any excess oil, reheat, and deglaze.

GLOSSARY

Temper: to equalize products with two extreme temperatures or textures

NUTRITION

Nutrition Facts
Yield: Serves 10
Serving Size: 8 oz. (240 ml)

Amount Per Serving

Calories 420

Total Fat 27 g

Sodium 180 mg

Total Carbohydrate 27 g

Protein 13 g

Shrimp Bisque

INGREDIENTS

INGREDIENTS	U.S. Standard	Metric
Shrimp, shell on	1 lb.	454 g
Butter	1 oz.	28 g
Shallots	2 oz.	55 g
Cognac	1 1/2 oz.	45 ml
Onions, peeled, rough-chopped	2 oz.	55 g
Carrots, peeled, washed, rough-chopped	2 oz.	55 g
Celery, washed, trimmed, rough-chopped	2 oz.	55 g
Bay leaf	1 each	1 each
Tomato purée	1 oz.	30 ml
Flour	1/2 c.	115 g
Shrimp or fish stock	1 1/2 qt.	1.4 l
Heavy cream	10 oz.	300 ml
Salt	TT	TT
White pepper, ground	TT	TT
Cayenne pepper	optional	optional

METHOD OF PREPARATION

1. Gather all the ingredients and equipment.

2. Peel and devein the shrimp; save shells.

3. Heat the butter in an appropriately sized stockpot over medium heat.

4. Add the shallots, and cook until translucent.

5. Add the peeled and deveined shrimp, and cook until shrimp are just beginning to turn opaque. Keep slightly undercooked to allow for carryover cooking. Add the cognac, and ignite. When the flame subsides, remove the shrimp, leaving other ingredients in the pot, and place in a hotel pan. Cool and then refrigerate.

6. Crush the shells in a food processor, and add them along with the onions, carrots, celery, and bay leaf to the stockpot with the shallots. Cook until the onions are translucent.

7. Add tomato purée, and cook for a few minutes.

8. Add flour, and blend well. Cook for about 5 minutes, stirring often.

9. Add shrimp stock slowly while stirring, and then bring to a boil. Reduce heat, and simmer about 30 minutes or until proper flavor and consistency is achieved.

10. Temper the heavy cream into the bisque.

11. Strain the bisque through a chinois. Taste and adjust seasoning with salt, pepper, and a pinch of cayenne if desired.

12. Dice the chilled shrimp and add to the bisque. Heat to 165°F (74°C), and serve or hold in a bain-marie at 140°F (60°C) or higher until service.

Simmering:

1. Place the prepared product in an appropriately sized pot.
2. Bring the product to a boil, and then reduce the heat to allow the product to barely boil.
3. Cook until desired doneness is achieved.

Sautéing:

1. Heat the sauté pan to the appropriate temperature.
2. Evenly brown the food product.
3. For a sauce, pour off any excess oil, reheat, and deglaze.

Nutrition Facts

Yield: Serves 10
Serving Size: 8 oz. (240 ml)

Amount Per Serving

Calories 270

Total Fat 21 g

Sodium 320 mg

Total Carbohydrate 9 g

Protein 11 g

Butternut Squash Bisque

INGREDIENTS

Ingredients	U.S. Standard	Metric
Butter, *clarified*	3 Tbsp.	45 g
Shallots, *chopped*	1/2 c.	115 g
Garlic, *chopped*	1 clove	1 clove
Pancetta, *chopped*	2 oz.	55 g
Butternut squash, *cubed*	2 1/2 lbs.	1.1 kg
Chicken stock	2 1/2 qts.	2.4 l
Parsley	1 sprig	1 sprig
Thyme	1 sprig	1 sprig
Sage	1 sprig	1 sprig
White truffle oil *(optional)*	2 Tbsp.	30 ml
Salt	TT	TT
White pepper	TT	TT
Pistachio nuts, *toasted and chopped*	3 Tbsp.	45 g

COOKING TECHNIQUES

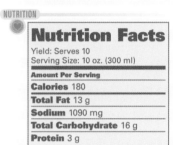

Simmering:
1. Place the prepared product in an appropriately sized pot.
2. Bring the product to a boil, and then reduce the heat to allow the product to barely boil.
3. Cook until desired doneness is achieved.

NUTRITION

Nutrition Facts

Yield: Serves 10
Serving Size: 10 oz. (300 ml)

Amount Per Serving

Calories 180

Total Fat 13 g

Sodium 1090 mg

Total Carbohydrate 16 g

Protein 3 g

METHOD OF PREPARATION

1. Gather all equipment and ingredients.

2. Heat butter in a stockpot, add shallots, garlic, and pancetta. Cook until shallots are soft.

3. Add squash, and cook about 10–15 minutes.

4. Add the chicken stock, bring to a boil, and reduce to a simmer.

5. Tie herbs together with kitchen string, and add them to the pot (tie the end of the string to the handle of the pot for easy retrieval). Simmer until squash is very tender, approximately 20 minutes.

6. Remove herbs and drain squash, reserving liquid.

7. Purée squash in blender or food processor, adding liquid as needed to make a smooth thick soup.

8. Return the soup to the stovetop, and simmer briefly. Add half the truffle oil, if using. Adjust seasoning with salt and pepper.

9. Garnish with toasted pistachio nuts and additional truffle oil if desired. Thinly sliced sautéed wild mushrooms or a dollop of whipped cream make attractive additional garnishes.

Fish Chowder

INGREDIENTS

INGREDIENTS	U.S. Standard	Metric
Salt pork, rind removed, diced brunoise	2 oz.	55 g
Vegetable oil	1 oz.	30 ml
Onions, peeled, diced macédoine	4 oz.	115 g
Bread flour	2 oz	55 g
Fish stock, heated	3 qts.	2.9 l
Potatoes, washed, peeled, and diced	5 1/2 oz.	155 g
Cod fillets, trimmed, bones removed, diced 1" (2.54 cm)	14 oz.	400 g
Heavy cream	4 1/2 oz.	135 ml
Salt	TT	TT
White pepper, ground	TT	TT
Parsley, washed, squeezed dry, chopped	1/2 oz.	15 g

METHOD OF PREPARATION

1. Gather all the ingredients and equipment.

2. In a large stockpot, combine the salt pork and oil, and *render* the salt pork over low heat until pork fat pieces are crispy and golden brown.

3. Add the onions, and sauté until translucent.

4. *Singe* the flour over the onions to create a roux. Cook over medium heat for 5–7 minutes.

5. Gradually whisk in the hot fish stock, blending until smooth. Heat to a boil. Reduce to a simmer.

6. Add the diced potatoes, and simmer gently.

7. When the potatoes are three-fourths cooked, add the diced cod, and finish cooking.

8. *Temper* the heavy cream into the soup. Taste and season with salt and pepper.

9. Serve in a preheated soup cup garnished with chopped parsley.

10. Hold at 140°F (60°C) or higher, or cool from 140°F (60°C) to 70°F (21°C) within 2 hours, and from 70°F (21°C) to 41°F (5°C) or lower in an additional 4 hours. Label, date, and refrigerate.

11. Reheat to 165°F (74°C) within 2 hours.

COOKING TECHNIQUES

Sautéing:
1. Heat the sauté pan to the appropriate temperature.
2. Evenly brown the food product.
3. For a sauce, pour off any excess oil, reheat, and deglaze.

Simmering:
1. Place the prepared product in an appropriately sized pot.
2. Bring the product to a boil, and then reduce the heat to allow the product to barely boil.
3. Cook until desired doneness is achieved.

GLOSSARY

Brunoise: 1/8" (3 mm) dice
Macédoine: 1/4" (6 mm) dice
Render: to melt fat
Singe: to dust with flour
Temper: to equalize products with two extreme temperatures or textures

NUTRITION

Nutrition Facts
Yield: Serves 10
Serving Size: 8 oz. (240 ml)

Amount Per Serving

Calories 230

Total Fat 11 g

Sodium 530 mg

Total Carbohydrate 14 g

Protein 17 g

Vegetable Soup, Asti Style

INGREDIENTS

	U.S. Standard	Metric
White beans, washed, soaked overnight in cold water	8 oz.	225 g
Pork, one piece, scored to the rind but not through	2 oz.	55 g
Oil	as needed	as needed
Onions, peeled, diced brunoise	3 oz.	85 g
Celery, washed, trimmed, diced brunoise	3 oz.	85 g
White cabbage, cored, cut chiffonade	7 oz.	205 g
Garlic, peeled and mashed	2 cloves	2 cloves
White chicken stock, heated to a boil	3 qts.	2.9 l
Potatoes, peeled, washed, diced macédoine	3 oz.	85 g
Basil, fresh, washed, dried, chopped	1/2 oz.	15 g
Salt	TT	TT
White pepper, ground	TT	TT
Pasta, ditalini style	4 oz.	115 g
Parmesan cheese, grated	2 oz.	55 g

METHOD OF PREPARATION

1. Gather all the ingredients and equipment.

2. Place the white beans into a saucepan; add twice their amount of cold water (either the soaking liquid or new water), bring to a boil, turn down to a simmer, and simmer gently until tender.

3. Meanwhile, in a large stockpot, *render* the piece of salt pork, fat side down, in a small amount of oil over low heat. When the salt pork has rendered enough fat to sauté the vegetables, remove the piece from the pot; save for later use, or discard.

4. Add the onions, celery, cabbage, and garlic to the rendered pork fat, and sauté until the onions are translucent.

5. Add the chicken stock; heat to a boil, and turn down to a simmer.

6. When white beans are tender, strain them, and add to the simmering soup.

7. In another saucepan, cover the potatoes with cold, salted water; cook until they are tender. Strain and add to the soup.

8. Simmer the soup for a total of 30–45 minutes, or until the proper flavor is achieved. Add the basil; taste and adjust seasonings with salt and pepper. Hold at 140°F (60°C) or higher.

9. In boiling, salted water, cook the pasta until it is al dente. Shock it under cold running water, drain, toss with a touch of oil, and set it aside.

10. For service, place some pasta in the bottom of a preheated soup cup. Ladle the hot soup over it. Top with 1/2 tsp. (5 g) of grated Parmesan cheese, and serve.

11. If necessary, cool from 140°F (60°C) to 70°F (21°C) within 2 hours, and from 70°F (21°C) to 41°F (5°C) or lower in an additional 4 hours. Label, date, and refrigerate.

12. Reheat to 165°F (74°C) within 2 hours.

Gazpacho

INGREDIENTS

	U.S. Standard	Metric
French bread, crust removed, sliced 1/2″ (1.27 cm) thick	12 slices	12 slices
Water	as needed	as needed
Olive oil	as needed	as needed
Tomato, concassé, 4 oz. (115 g) diced brunoise, rest rough-cut	2 1/4 lbs.	1 kg
Cucumber, peeled, seeded, 4 oz. (115 g) diced brunoise, rest rough-cut	3 each	3 each
Green bell peppers, seeded, 4 oz. (115 g) diced brunoise, rest rough-cut	1 1/4 lbs.	570 g
Onion, peeled, 1/2″ (1.27 cm) rough-cut	10 oz.	285 g
Garlic, chopped	6 cloves	6 cloves
Olive oil, extra virgin	5 oz.	150 ml
Sherry vinegar	2 oz.	60 ml
Salt	TT	TT
Black pepper, freshly ground	TT	TT

GLOSSARY

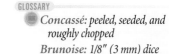

Concassé: peeled, seeded, and roughly chopped

Brunoise: 1/8″ (3 mm) dice

NUTRITION

Nutrition Facts

Yield: Serves 10
Serving Size: 10 oz. (300 ml)

Amount Per Serving

Calories 220

Total Fat 15 g

Sodium 105 mg

Total Carbohydrate 20 g

Protein 3 g

METHOD OF PREPARATION

1. Gather all the ingredients and equipment.

2. Crumble 8 slices of the French bread into a bowl. Add enough water to just moisten the bread, and let it sit for 15 minutes.

3. Cut the remaining bread into 1/2″ (1.27 cm) square croutons, toss lightly with olive oil, and bake in preheated 375°F (191°C) oven until crisp and golden.

4. Set the 4 oz. (115 g) each of brunoise tomato concassé, cucumber, and green pepper aside for garnish.

5. Place the rough-cut tomatoes, cucumber, and green peppers, along with the onion, garlic, and moistened bread in the food processor, and purée the mixture. With processor running, pour the olive oil into the purée in a slow, steady stream. If necessary, add a little water to achieve the proper consistency.

6. Add sherry vinegar, taste, and add salt and freshly ground pepper to taste. Chill until cold. After chilling, taste and adjust seasonings as needed.

7. Serve in cups or attractive glass bowls, garnished with croutons and the reserved brunoise of vegetables. Drizzle with extra virgin olive oil if desired.

16 Beef

People have been raising domesticated cattle for some 3,000 years. Christopher Columbus introduced domesticated cattle to the Americas in 1493, and soon after, cattle arrived in present-day Florida and Texas with the Spanish. Cattle have always had many uses: they carry heavy loads and pull carts and plows; supply milk, cheese, and butter; and provide a source for clothing, shelter, and food. Today, Americans prefer beef to all other meats.

A.D. 1493
Domesticated cattle first arrive in the Americas.

ca. 1500
European cookbooks begin to specify cuts of beef and other meats.

mid-1800s to 1900
Cattle ranching in the United States reaches its peak.

1906
Meat Inspection Act passed by Congress.

1950
Beef surpasses pork as the most popular meat.

shrinkage
fat cap
marbling
connective tissue
elastin
collagen
aging
dry aging
vacuum-packed aging
fast aging
carcass
forequarter
hindquarter
primal cut
subprimal cut
fabricated cut
variety meats
portion control

Cattle Terminology

Cattle is a general term for domesticated bovine animals raised on a farm or ranch for their meat, milk, or hides or for use as draft animals. Cattle are categorized by sex and age.

Calves Calves are young cattle of either sex. A male calf is known as a bull calf, and a female calf is called a heifer calf.

Bulls Bulls are mature, uncastrated male cattle used for breeding.

Steers Steers are male cattle that have been castrated before reaching sexual maturity, making them more docile and easier to maintain on a ranch or in a feedlot. Most beef that Americans eat comes from steers.

Stags Stags are male cattle that have undergone castration after they have matured.

Heifers Heifer calves grow into heifers and eventually become cows.

Cows Cows are mature female cattle, and are usually used as a source of milk.

Nutritional Makeup

Beef, like other meats, is animal muscle containing various nutrients that form part of a healthful diet.

Muscle Composition

The three main components of muscle are water, protein, and fat. These nutrients appear in the following proportions in most meats:

- 75% water
- 20% protein
- 5% fat

Muscle also contains vitamins, minerals, and trace amounts of carbohydrates.

Water Although most meats are about three-quarters water, the actual amount of water in meats varies depending on shrinkage. *Shrinkage,* or moisture loss, is the result of oxidation, which occurs during storage or aging or as a result of high temperatures and long cooking times. Oxidation causes meat to lose both water and weight.

Protein Protein is an essential nutrient that promotes growth, builds tissue, regulates body functions, and serves as an alternative to fats and carbohydrates as a source of energy. Most solid matter in meat is protein. When heat is applied to meat, the protein coagulates, or becomes firm. The degree of coagulation is one gauge for doneness. High heat can cause protein to lose moisture and become too firm, making the meat tough.

> *See Chapter 11: Cooking Techniques for more information on coagulation and doneness.*

Fat Fat surrounds the muscle tissue as a *fat cap* and lies within it (*marbling*). The fat cap may be left on a piece of meat during cooking to keep the meat moist, but barding or larding are acceptable alternative methods for retaining juice if there is no fat cap. Marbling also contributes to the juiciness of meat and makes it more tender and flavorful.

> See Chapter 11: Cooking Techniques for more information on barding and larding.

Vitamins and minerals Meat is an important source of Vitamins A and K as well as several B vitamins, including thiamin (B1), riboflavin (B2), niacin (B3), B6, and B12. Meat also adds minerals such as iron and phosphorus to the diet.

Carbohydrates Although present only in small amounts, carbohydrates contribute to the appearance and flavor of meat that is prepared with a dry technique such as roasting, sautéing, or broiling.

The Structure of Meat

Meat products consist of bones, muscle fibers, and connective tissue.

Bones Bone color is an indication of an animal's age. The redder the bone, the younger the animal. Older animals have white bones. Becoming familiar with the bone structure of an animal helps when learning the different cuts of meat and how to debone them. See Figure 16-5 on page 300

Muscle fibers Muscle fibers, or cells bundled together, make up the meat. The thickness of the fibers determines the texture or grain of the meat. Thick, tough fibers bound in large bundles make up coarsely textured meats, such as bottom round or brisket. Thinner, tender fibers in small bundles form finely grained meat, such as tenderloin.

Connective tissue *Connective tissue* is a web of proteins that performs several functions: it covers individual muscle fibers, bundles them together, and attaches them to bones. Connective tissue helps determine the texture of meat and is tough in general. Some meats are higher in connective tissue than others. Frequently used muscles such as those in the leg or shoulder have more connective tissue and thus

are tougher than those in the back (or loin). Meat from older animals is also tougher because as an animal ages, the connective tissue becomes more resistant to breaking down.

Elastin and collagen—the two kinds of connective tissue—differ in their ability to break down during the cooking process. *Elastin* is a hard, yellow connective tissue prevalent in older animals. Because it will not break down during cooking, elastin must be cut away from the meat or physically tenderized to reduce its effects. By contrast, *collagen,* the soft, white connective tissue, readily breaks down into water and gelatin with slow, moist cooking. Collagen also responds well to tenderizing.

Aging

Aging is the process by which naturally occurring enzymes (lactic acid) tenderize meat. After slaughter, chemical changes in the flesh of an animal cause rigor mortis, or a stiffening of the muscles. As rigor mortis disappears, the meat softens, or ripens, as a result of enzymatic action. This process takes up to several days for beef and must occur in a controlled, refrigerated environment so that the meat does not spoil. The result is flavorful, tender meat.

There are three methods of aging meat under refrigeration.

- *Dry aging*—This process involves hanging large, unpackaged cuts of meat in a controlled environment for six weeks. Temperature, humidity, and air flow must be carefully monitored to prevent spoilage. Although costly, dry aging produces extremely flavorful meat with a highly desirable texture. However, shrinkage is a major drawback of this method, with some cuts of meat losing as much as 20% of their weight through loss of moisture. Meat aged by this method also can develop mold, which requires trimming—a further reduction in weight.
- *Vacuum-packed aging*—Also known as Cryovac® aging, this process stores smaller cuts of meat for six weeks in air- and moisture-proof plastic vacuum packs that prevent the development of mold and bacteria. Instead, microorganisms and natural enzymes tenderize the

meat. This aging method does not result in weight loss, but the meats tend to lose more weight than do dry-aged meats during cooking.
- *Fast aging*—This method uses higher temperatures to reduce the time required for aging. Ultraviolet light is used to control bacteria.

Kobe Beef

Cattle raised in Kobe, Japan, are the source of a special grade of beef that is rich in flavor, has abundant marbling, and is extraordinarily tender. Kobe beef comes from the Wagyu breed of cattle and meets rigorous production standards. Wagyu cattle are famous for the extensive marbling of their meat, but this quality characteristic is not entirely the result of genetics. The daily routine and special diet of cattle raised for Kobe beef are quite unusual. The Wagyu cattle receive energizing massages with sake, the Japanese alcoholic rice beverage, and indulge in huge quantities of beer, making Kobe beef legendary and expensive. By USDA standards Kobe beef would receive the highest yield and quality grades. Its marbling and rareness in the marketplace actually put it well above the Prime grade. Once raised only in Kobe, Wagyu cattle now roam ranches in the United States and Australia, where land and feed are cheaper. Fabrication of the prized beef, however, takes place in Kobe, which earns it the name Kobe beef.

Inspection and Grading

Inspection and grading systems help producers, distributors, and consumers evaluate meat.

Inspection The Meat Inspection Act, passed in 1906, mandates the examination of all meats transported across state lines. This federal law guarantees that meat is wholesome and fit for consumption and that the animal from which it originated was not diseased; however, inspection is not a mark of quality.

USDA/FSIS The Food Safety and Inspection Service (FSIS), a public health agency within the United States Department of Agriculture (USDA), is responsible for conducting inspections. The FSIS checks meat to make sure that it is clean, safe, and properly packaged and labeled. Meat that satisfies inspection standards carries a USDA inspection stamp. All meat for foodservice operations must exhibit a USDA stamp.

Grading Unlike inspection, grading is completely voluntary. Grading measures meat quality and yield, allowing a comparison of meat. Quality grading indicates tenderness, juiciness, and flavor of the meat. Yield grades measure the amount of usable meat on beef.

Federal grading USDA graders evaluate the quality of meat. This evaluation is usually done 24 hours or more after slaughter and inspection. Graders base their assessment on the meat's color, texture, and firmness; the extent of marbling; and the animal's age.

The USDA also determines yield grades for meat. To measure yield, graders consider conformation (the shape and form of the animal and the proportion of meat to bone) and finish (the quality and distribution of fat around and within the meat).

The USDA issues stamps designating the quality or yield of meat products. See Figure 16-1 and Figure 16-2. Names describe the quality grade of meat.

Numbers indicate the yield grade. Yield grades range from 1 to 5, with Yield Grade 1 representing the leanest pieces of meat, and thus the greatest yield, and Yield Grade 5 indicating the pieces with the most fat, and thus the smallest yield.

Private grading Some meat producers, processors, and retailers use their own criteria to label meat with a quality assessment. This grading is not under the supervision of the USDA and is generally less consistent than the federal grading system.

Beef

297

FIGURE 16-1

The USDA uses the inspection stamp on the left to mark whole carcasses as wholesome and fit for consumption. The stamp on the right appears on fabricated or processed meat or its packaging. Both inspection stamps identify the slaughterhouse by number.

FIGURE 16-2

The USDA quality stamp carries a grade name, and the yield stamp provides a grade number.

Beef grading Because grading is voluntary, beef, like other meats, may receive a quality grade, a yield grade, both, or neither. All eight quality USDA grades apply to beef: Prime, Choice, Select, Standard, Commercial, Utility, Cutter, and Canner. See Figure 16-3. Beef at each grade level has unique quality characteristics. Produced only in limited quantities and served primarily in the finest foodservice establishments, USDA Prime beef displays abundant marbling and a thick layer of exterior fat. At the lower end, the USDA Utility, Cutter, and Canner grades of beef are appropriate only for processed meats, such as hamburger patties and hot dogs.

Beef yield grades describe the amount of boneless meat obtained from a side of beef. See Figure 16-4 for the proportion of edible meat to fat for each yield grade of beef.

Only the top three quality grades of beef usually receive yield grades. Most Prime and Choice beef is Yield Grade 3.

Kosher Considerations

Jewish dietary laws, known as *kashruth*, are also concerned with the fitness of food. These laws stipulate that Jews eat meat only from the forequarter (front portion) of animals that have split hooves and chew their cuds, such as cattle, deer, goats, oxen, and sheep. These animals may be slaughtered and examined only by a *shohet*, a person trained in these procedures who removes the veins and arteries from the animal and certifies it fit for consumption. Kosher meats also have to be federally inspected.

Jewish dietary laws also specify acceptable butchering practices. For meat to be kosher, or fit, butchers must prepare it in a certain way, which includes removing the blood. To extract the blood, they soak the meat in water and then cover it with salt.

Halal Considerations

Muslims follow special dietary laws as well and refer to foods fit for consumption as *halal*, or lawful. All fruits and vegetables are halal, and any of the following cooked meats: beef, lamb, and chicken. Fish and shellfish are also allowed to be consumed.

Pork, game, and birds of prey are not considered halal, and thus cannot be consumed. Meat-providing animals must be slaughtered and butchered following strict Muslim rituals and procedures.

FIGURE 16-3

Federal Grades of Meat

PRIME
Highest quality; most expensive; abundant marbling because of the young age of animals and the feed practices; extremely juicy and flavorful; limited supply

CHOICE
High quality; excellent value; very juicy and tender; abundant supply; widely available in the foodservice industry and retail markets

SELECT
Acceptable quality; good buy; generally lean with little marbling; less juicy and tender

STANDARD
Lower quality; economical; lacking marbling

COMMERCIAL
Low quality; economical; lacking tenderness; produced from older animals

UTILITY, CUTTER, CANNER
Lowest quality; used primarily by canners and processors; rarely used in foodservice operations

Purchasing Beef

In addition to inspection and grading, consider the following factors before purchasing meat of any kind:

- **Menu**—What meats do you need for dishes on the menu? Which meats lend themselves to the cooking techniques that will be used?
- **Price**—Are the most expensive cuts necessary in dishes you plan to prepare? What can customers afford? What are you willing to pay for top-quality meats?
- **Quality**—What are your general quality standards? What standards have you developed for specific dishes?

Always purchase beef and other meats only from USDA-approved processing plants. When placing an order, provide the product name, its IMPS/NAMP number (see Figure 16-7 on pages 305–307), the grade, the fat thickness, the weight range, and the form of delivery (chilled or frozen). To decide which cuts of meat to purchase, refer to the "The Meat Buyers Guide," published by the North American Meat Processors Association (NAMP). This guide provides the USDA's Institutional Meat Purchase Specifications (IMPS) for quality meats as well as photos of meat cuts

frequently used by foodservice operations. The purpose of the specifications is to ensure clarity and consistency in meat production and in purchasing.

FIGURE 16-4

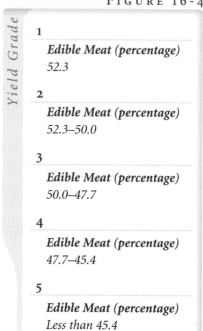

Yield Grade

1
Edible Meat (percentage)
52.3

2
Edible Meat (percentage)
52.3–50.0

3
Edible Meat (percentage)
50.0–47.7

4
Edible Meat (percentage)
47.7–45.4

5
Edible Meat (percentage)
Less than 45.4

Handling Beef Safely

Care in receiving and storing meat not only protects the health of customers but also reduces waste, thus conserving cost. The latter is an important consideration in recognizing how perishable and relatively costly meat is.

Receiving Beef

When receiving beef from a supplier, check it carefully to make sure that it is sanitary and matches the order placed. Look for inspection and grade stamps on the meat or its packaging. Closely examine the packaging for tears, leakage, and foreign objects. Beef in damaged or dirty packaging risks contamination. Also note the meat's temperature, color, odor, and texture. Beef, like other meats, should be delivered at 41°F (5°C) or lower. It should have a bright red color and no odor. Its texture should not be sticky or dry. Meat also should exhibit the fat thickness and degree of marbling requested. Do not accept beef that does not meet safety standards or specifications.

Storing Beef

Store beef immediately after delivery. Wrapping for cuts of fresh beef should be airtight. Exposure to air will cause the meat to turn brown. Use special care in handling and wrapping ground beef, as it is highly susceptible to contamination. Leave vacuum-packed beef in its packaging until ready for use.

To prevent cross-contamination, keep meat away from other foods. Always store meat on the lowest shelf of the refrigerator, below other foods. Place meat on trays so that juices do not contaminate other foods or drip onto the storage unit floor.

The ideal temperature for storage of fresh meats is 41°F (5°C) or lower. Use refrigerated fresh beef within two or three days of delivery for best results. Use ground beef within one to two days. Sealed vacuum-packed meat remains fresh under refrigeration for three to four weeks.

Choose airtight and moisture-proof wrap for frozen meat to guard against freezer burn. Keep frozen meat at 0°F to 10°F(−18°C to −12°C). Rotation of stock is important. Label packages with the date stored, and use the FIFO method. The recommended shelf life of frozen meat is four to six months.

Defrost frozen meat carefully. Allow time to defrost beef in the refrigerator. It is not recommended to defrost frozen meat in the microwave or under warm water, and frozen meat should never be defrosted at room temperature.

▌ *See Chapter 4: Food Safety for more information on storing food safely.*

Spoilage Indicators

The surface of beef will show the first signs of spoilage. Beef that has started to spoil may be dull red; green or brown meat is already spoiled and should be discarded. A sour odor and slimy texture are other signs that beef has deteriorated. Damaged packaging can indicate contamination.

Foodborne Illness Associated with Beef

Although the USDA inspects and guarantees the wholesomeness of beef for consumption, microorganisms remain on meat during processing. Among these microorganisms are bacteria, which are responsible for more foodborne illnesses than any other microbial contaminant. Illnesses caused by bacteria present in improperly handled or prepared beef include salmonellosis, listeriosis, staphylococcal food poisoning (enterotoxicosis), enteritis, gastroenteritis, botulism, and *E. coli* O157:H7 enterohemorrhagic (EHEC).

▌ *See Chapter 4: Food Safety and Chapter 11: Cooking Techniques for more information on handling and preparing beef.*

Radiation can kill dangerous microorganisms, such as *E. coli* and salmonella, that may be present in fresh and frozen beef and other meats. The radiation process does not change a meat's nutritional content or its flavor, texture, or appearance. However, irradiated beef has a longer shelf life than nonirradiated beef. Meats and other packaged foods that have undergone radiation must carry a label indicating this treatment as well as a radura symbol.

Primal, Subprimal, and Fabricated Cuts

Beef and other meats are available for purchase in various forms: carcasses; partial carcasses; and primal, subprimal, and fabricated cuts. Labor, equipment, facilities, and menu uses determine the form purchased.

The carcass is the whole animal after slaughter, without head, feet, hide, and entrails. It is typical to split a beef carcass into halves and then to cut each half into a front portion, or forequarter, and a rear portion, or hindquarter. A side or a quarter of beef represents a partial carcass.

Carcasses and partial carcasses are market forms whose use is not feasible in most foodservice operations. Only the largest operations are able to store and process these forms, reducing them to the preferred primal, subprimal, and fabricated cuts. See Figure 16-6.

A primal cut is a large, primary piece of meat, sometimes called a wholesale cut. A subprimal cut is a basic cut made from a primal cut. A fabricated cut is the smaller portion taken from a subprimal cut, such as a roast, steak, and ground meat. NAMP's "The Meat Buyers Guide" contains the names and numbers assigned to fabricated cuts of beef and other meats as well as photos of common cuts.

FIGURE 16-5
Skeletal structure

HOCK BONE

HIND SHANK (TIBIA)

PELVIC BONE

AITCH OR RUMP BONE — HIP BONE

KNEE CAP (PATELLA)

ROUND BONE (FEMUR)

TAIL BONES (CAUDAL VEREBRAE)

BALL OF FEMUR

SACRUM (SACRAL VERTEBRAE)

LOIN BONES (LUMBAR VERTEBRAE)

CHINE BONES

13TH RIB

RIB CARTILAGES (COSTAL CARTILAGES)

BACK BONES (THORACIC VERTEBRAE)

FEATHER BONES (SPINAL PROCESSES)

BREAST BONE (STERNUM)

BLADE BONE CARTILAGE

BLADE BONE (SCAPULA)

ELBOW (ULNA)

NECK BONES

1ST RIB

ATLAS BONE

ULNA RADIUS — FORE SHANK BONE

ARM BONE (HUMERUS)

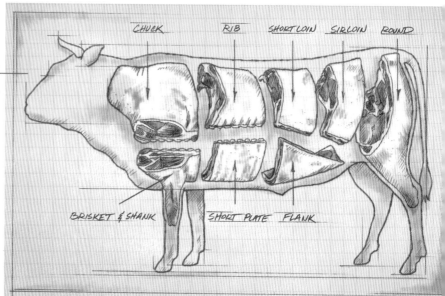

FIGURE 16-6
Location of primal cuts of beef

CHUCK · RIB · SHORT LOIN · SIRLOIN · ROUND

BRISKET & SHANK · SHORT PLATE · FLANK

Four primal cuts make up a forequarter of beef: chuck, primal rib, brisket, and short plate. A by-product of the forequarter is the foreshank, and it is listed below as such. For the location of the primal cuts, see Figure 16-6 on page 300.

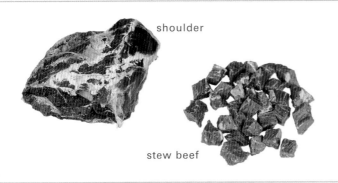

shoulder

stew beef

CHUCK *The chuck comes from the animal's shoulder. It includes part of the back bone and the first five rib bones as well as portions of arm bones and blade bones. The chuck makes up nearly 30% of the weight of the beef carcass. A fairly large proportion of the chuck is connective tissue, which accounts for the toughness of this meat. However, chuck has a great deal of flavor when prepared properly. A moist technique or a combination method such as stewing or braising is appropriate for this cut. Primal chuck yields various fabricated cuts: shoulder clod, chuck eye roll, chuck tender, triangle, chuck short ribs, cubed or tenderized steaks, stew meat, and ground chuck.*

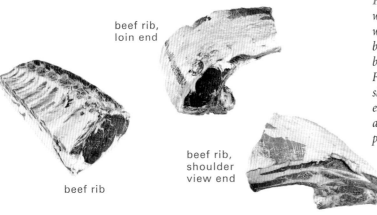

beef rib, loin end

beef rib, shoulder view end

beef rib

PRIMAL RIB *This primal cut comprises about 10% of the carcass weight. It includes ribs 6 through 12 and some of the back bone. As it is not well-exercised muscle, it is tender, owing its rich flavor to extensive marbling. Primal rib cuts benefit from dry cooking methods such as roasting, broiling, and grilling. Moist heat is the preferred method for short ribs. Fabricated cuts taken from the primal rib include rib roast, boneless rib eye, short ribs, and rib eye steaks. Rib roast, better known as prime rib, is an extremely popular meat dish. The word "prime," however, does not represent a USDA grade; rather, it indicates that the rib roast makes up most of the primal cut.*

brisket, split

brisket

BRISKET *Located below the chuck, the brisket constitutes a single primal cut. This cut consists of the breast (brisket) of the animal, including the rib bones and cartilage, and the breast bone. A combination technique such as braising is an excellent choice for beef brisket, which is very tough. Curing, another method of preparation for brisket, is the method used to produce corned beef. Fabricated cuts from this primal cut include boneless brisket and ground meat.*

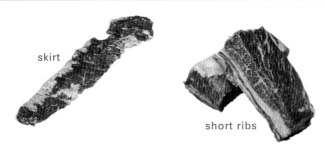

skirt

short ribs

SHORT PLATE *Short plate is the cut below primal rib on a side of beef. It contains rib bones and cartilage and the tip of the breast bone. Fabricated cuts from the short plate include ground beef, skirt steak, and short ribs. Moist cooking is appropriate for short ribs, which are quite meaty but also contain a large amount of connective tissue. Marination and grilling are excellent methods for skirt steak, which is sliced for fajitas.*

fore shank

FORESHANK *The foreshank is considered a by-product of the beef forequarter and may be attached to the chuck when purchased. The rich flavor of the foreshank and its abundant collagen, which turns to gelatin with moist heat, make it a choice ingredient in stocks and soups. Fabricated cuts include stew meat and ground beef.*

Beef

301

A beef hindquarter also yields four primal cuts: short loin, sirloin, round, and flank. For the location of these primal cuts, see Figure 16-6 on page 300.

SHORT LOIN The short loin is the first primal cut of the hindquarter, forming the front portion of the beef loin. It includes one rib and part of the back bone. The yield of this primal cut is substantial and represents the most palatable and popular, as well as the most expensive, cuts of beef. Among these is the tenderloin, the most tender piece of beef. Fabricated cuts from the short loin include club steaks, T-bone steaks, porterhouse steaks, strip loin, strip loin steaks, and short tenderloin. These cuts are best cooked using dry methods.

tenderloin, inside

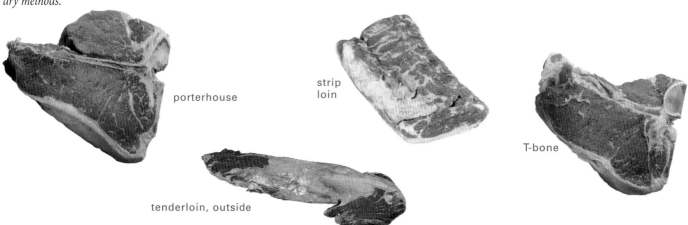

porterhouse

strip loin

T-bone

tenderloin, outside

SIRLOIN Located next to the short loin, the sirloin contains a portion of both the back bone and the hip bone. The subprimal and fabricated cuts taken from the sirloin have good flavor and are quite tender, though not as tender as the short loin cuts. Fabricated cuts from the sirloin include top sirloin roasts and steaks and top and bottom sirloin butt roasts and steaks. The dry techniques of broiling, roasting, and grilling are best for these cuts.

sirloin

ROUND The round is the hind leg of the animal, including the round, aitch, shank, and tail bones. It is an extremely large cut, constituting approximately 24% of the carcass weight. Very flavorful and fairly tender, the round yields various subprimal and fabricated cuts, including top round, bottom round (eye of round and outside round), knuckle, heel, and shank. Dry cooking such as roasting is appropriate for top round, which is relatively tender. The tougher bottom round benefits from combination cooking such as stewing or braising.

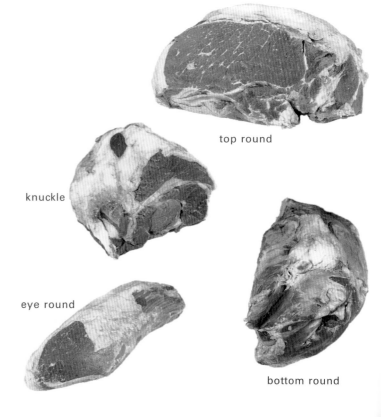

top round

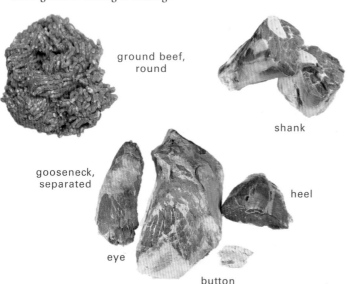

ground beef, round

shank

knuckle

gooseneck, separated

heel

eye round

eye

button

bottom round

FLANK Beneath the loin and behind the short plate is the flank. The flank contains a good amount of fat and connective tissue, which makes it tough. The flank yields flank steak. Moist cooking techniques are best for flank cuts except when flank steak is prepared as London broil and cut thinly across the grain.

flank

Variety Meats

Variety meats include internal organs, glands, and other meats that are removed during the processing of the carcass. Traditionally viewed as ethnic food items, variety meats have found their way onto American menus in limited quantities. High in protein, vitamins, and iron, variety meats are features of soups, stews, and other dishes.

All the beef variety meats except kidney are muscle tissue. These meats are tough in general and require long, moist cooking to become tender. Kidneys are the only glands from beef served with much frequency.

Heart
Tough but lean, the heart lends itself to braising or stewing. Ground heart can be added to meat loaves or to casseroles calling for chopped meat. Be sure to remove veins and fibers before cooking.

Liver
Beef liver is dark in color and has a strong flavor. It should be broiled, braised, or pan-fried. It is served with onions and is added to pies and puddings.

Tongue
The customary method for cooking tongue is simmering. After cooking, remove the skin and gristle. Cooked and chilled beef tongue is a favorite sliced meat for sandwiches. Smoking and curing are other methods of preparation before cooking.

Tripe
Tripe is the stomach lining of the animal. Although usually purchased partially cooked, tripe requires additional cooking to reach the desired tenderness. Simmering or stewing is an appropriate technique for tripe.

Oxtail
Before cooking, oxtails need to be cut into sections at the joints. Oxtails are rich in gelatin and also contain tasty meat, both of which augment the texture and flavor of soups and stews.

Kidney
Beef kidney is somewhat tough and has a relatively strong flavor. Braising helps tenderize this variety meat, which is a key ingredient in steak and kidney pie.

Fabricating Strip Steaks

Cutting a strip loin into steaks is an important fabrication skill that takes practice to achieve consistency in weight and size.

To fabricate strip steaks:

Square off the strip loin by trimming away 1–2 inches (3–5 cm) from the tail.

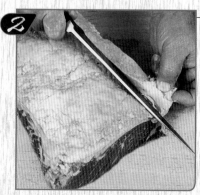

Turn the strip loin over, and remove excess fat.

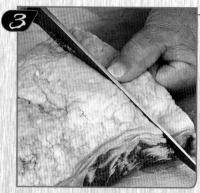

Cut the strip loin into steaks according to the weight and thickness desired.

Fabrication

Meats can be purchased in numerous ways. This decision depends on a variety of factors that require careful consideration and include butchering skills; available storage space; use of meat, bones, and trimmings on the menu; and cost per portion, including labor. Primal cuts can be fabricated into smaller cuts such as chops, roasts, steaks, stew beef, and ground beef.

In some cases, however, foodservice establishments use *portion control (PC) cuts,* fresh or individually quick frozen (IQF), cut to specification. A 12-ounce strip loin steak or an 8-ounce filet mignon are examples of a portion control cut. Portion control cuts should be used when there is little or no use of trimmings on the menu. These cuts ensure consistency and cost control and guarantee value for both the chef and the customer.

Whether working with the various available forms of meat or handling only prefabricated cuts, it is important to learn the primal cuts, their location on the carcass, and the smaller cuts made from them.

Butchering (Fabricating) Skills

Prefabricated portion control sirloin steak cuts are purchased most often because they offer a level of accuracy that cannot be guaranteed by cutting these in-house. However, because cuts of beef may need to be fabricated in-house, basic butchering skills are essential. Cutting a strip loin into steaks and peeling a tenderloin are common meat-cutting procedures.

Use a socle or croûton to enhance presentation of a portion of meat. When placed under a beef medallion, one of these rounds of toasted or fried bread, usually cut the same size as the steak, raises the meat on the plate, creating an optical illusion of a larger portion. This presentation technique can be used for classic preparations such as Tournedos Rossini and Tournedos a la Forestiere.

PROCESS

Peeling a Tenderloin

Exposing the meat of the tenderloin can be done two ways: pulling away the exterior fat, or as an alternative, purchasing the tenderloin peeled with the side muscle on (PSMO). The principal membrane will still remain and must be removed.

To peel a tenderloin by pulling away the exterior fat, follow these procedures:

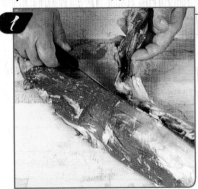

1 Remove the chain from the tenderloin.

2 Remove the silverskin without cutting into the meat by inserting the knife under the silverskin and cutting at a slight angle upward.

3 Cut the trimmed tenderloin into portions as needed, which may include filet steaks, tournedos, chateaubriand, and medallions.

4 Remove trim, and reserve for tips and kabobs.

Beef

FIGURE 16-7

305

Cuts of Beef

NAMP NUMBER	NAME	AVERAGE WEIGHT RANGE
103	Rib, primal	28–38 lbs./12.5–17.5 kg
104	Rib, oven-prepared, regular	22–30 lbs./10–13.5 kg
107	Rib, oven-prepared	19–26 lbs./8.5–12 kg
107A	Rib, oven-prepared, blade bone in	19–26 lbs./8.5–12 kg
109	Rib, roast-ready	16–22 lbs./7.5–10 kg
109A	Rib, roast-ready, special	16–22 lbs./7.5–10 kg
109B	Rib, blade meat	3 lbs. and up/1.5 kg and up
109C	Rib, roast-ready, cover off	15–21 lbs./7–9.5 kg
109D	Rib, roast-ready, cover off, short-cut	14–20 lbs./6.5–9 kg
109E	Rib, ribeye roll, lip-on, bone in	13–19 lbs./6–8.5 kg
110	Rib, roast-ready, boneless	13–19 lbs./6–8.5 kg
112	Rib, rib eye roll	6–10 lbs./2.5–4.5 kg
112A	Rib, rib eye roll, lip on	7–11 lbs./3–5 kg
113	Chuck, square-cut	79–106 lbs./36–48 kg
114	Chuck, shoulder clod	15–21 lbs./7–9.5 kg
114C	Beef chuck, shoulder clod, trimmed	12–18 lbs./5.5–8 kg
114D	Chuck, shoulder clod, top blade, roast	8–12 lbs./3.5–5.5 kg
114E	Chuck, shoulder clod, arm roast	8–12 lbs./3.5–5.5 kg
144A	Chuck, shoulder clod, roast	15–21 lbs./7–9.5 kg
144A	Chuck, shoulder clod, roast, tied	15–21 lbs./7–9.5 kg

NAMP NUMBER	NAME	AVERAGE WEIGHT RANGE
115	Chuck, square-cut, boneless	65–88 lbs./29.5–40 kg
115D	Chuck, pectoral	As requested
116A	Chuck, chuck roll	15–21 lbs./7–9.5 kg
116B	Chuck, chuck tender	15–21 lbs./7–9.5 kg
116D	Chuck, chuck roll eye	8–14 lbs./3.5–6.5 kg
116E	Chuck, under blade roast	8–14 lbs./3.5–6.5 kg
117	Foreshank	8–12 lbs./3.5–5.5 kg
118	Brisket	14–20 lbs./6.5–9 kg
120	Brisket, deckle off, boneless	8–12 lbs./3.5–5.5 kg
120A	Brisket, flat cut, boneless	6–10 lbs./2.5–4.5 kg
120B	Brisket, point cut, boneless	3–6 lbs./1.5–2.5 kg
120C	Brisket, 2-piece, boneless	8–12 lbs./3.5–5.5 kg
121	Plate, short plate	27–35 lbs./12.5–16 kg
121C	Plate, skirt steak (diaphragm), outer	2 lbs. and up/1 kg and up
121D	Plate, skirt steak, inner	3 lbs. and up/1.5 kg and up
121E	Plate, skirt steak, skinned, outer	2 lbs. and up/1 kg and up
123	Short ribs	3–5 lbs./1.5–2.5 kg
123A	Short plate, short ribs, trimmed	As requested
123B	Rib, short ribs, trimmed	As requested
123C	Rib, short ribs	As requested
123D	Short ribs, boneless	2–4 lbs./1–2 kg
124	Rib, back ribs	As requested
124A	Rib, rib fingers, boneless	As requested
125	Chuck, armbone	88–118 lbs./40–53.5 kg
126	Chuck, armbone, boneless (3-way)	70–90 lbs./32–41 kg
126A	Chuck, armbone, boneless, clod out	57–77 lbs./26–35 kg
158	Round, primal	71–95 lbs./32–43 kg
158A	Round, diamond-cut	76–102 lbs./34.5–46.5 kg
159	Round, primal, boneless	53–71 lbs./24–32 kg
160	Round, shank-off, partially boneless	57–76 lbs./26–34.5 kg
160B	Round, heel and shank out, semi-boneless	46–60 lbs./21–27 kg
161	Round, shank off, boneless	51–71 lbs./23–32 kg
161B	Round, heel and shank off, without knuckle, boneless	50–66 lbs./22.5–30 kg
163	Round, shank off, 3-way, boneless	50–66 lbs./22.5–30 kg
164	Round, rump and shank off	48–64 lbs./22–29 kg
165	Round, rump and shank off, boneless	43–57 lbs./19.5–26 kg
165A	Round, rump and shank off, boneless, special	46–60 lbs./21–27 kg
165B	Round, rump and shank off, boneless, special, tied	46–60 lbs./21–27 kg
166	Round, rump and shank off, boneless, tied	46–57 lbs./21–26 kg
166A	Round, rump partially removed, shank off, boneless, tied	52–70 lbs./23.5–32 kg
166B	Round, rump and shank partially removed, handle on	52–70 lbs./23.5–32 kg
167	Round, knuckle	9–13 lbs./4–6 kg
167A	Round, knuckle, peeled	8–12 lbs./3.5–5.5 kg
167B	Round, knuckle, full	12–16 lbs./5.5–7.5 kg
167D	Round, knuckle, peeled, 2-piece	7–12 lbs./3–5.5 kg
168	Round, top (inside), untrimmed	17–23 lbs./7.5–10.5 kg
169	Round, top (inside)	17–23 lbs./7.5–10.5 kg
170	Round, bottom (gooseneck)	23–31 lbs./10.5–14 kg
170A	Round, bottom (gooseneck), heel out	20–28 lbs./9–12.5 kg

NAMP NUMBER	NAME	AVERAGE WEIGHT RANGE
171	Round, bottom (gooseneck), untrimmed	21–29 lbs./9.5–13 kg
171A	Round, bottom (gooseneck), untrimmed, heel out	20–28 lbs./9–12.5 kg
171B	Round, outside round	10–16 lbs./4.5–7.5 kg
171C	Round, eye of round	3 lbs. and up/1.5 kg and up
172	Loin, full loin, trimmed	37–52 lbs./17–23.5 kg
172A	Loin, full loin, diamond-cut	42–57 lbs./19–26 kg
173	Loin, short loin	24–35 lbs./11–16 kg
174	Loin, short loin, short-cut	20–30 lbs./9–13.5 kg
175	Loin, strip loin	14–22 lbs./6.5–10 kg
176	Loin, strip loin, boneless	10–14 lbs./4.5–6.5 kg
179	Loin, strip loin, short-cut	10–14 lbs./4.5–6.5 kg
180	Loin, strip loin, short-cut, boneless	7–11 lbs./3–5 kg
181	Loin, sirloin	19–28 lbs./8.5–12.5 kg
181A	Loin, top sirloin, bone in	14–20 lbs./6.5–9 kg
182	Loin, sirloin butt, boneless	14–19 lbs./6.5–8.5 kg
183	Loin, sirloin butt, boneless, trimmed	10–15 lbs./4.5–7 kg
184	Loin, top sirloin butt	10–14 lbs./4.5–6.5 kg
184A	Loin, top sirloin butt, semi center-cut, boneless	9–13 lbs./4–6 kg
184B	Loin, top sirloin butt, center-cut, boneless, cap off	7–11 lbs./3–5 kg
184D	Loin, top sirloin, cap	2–4 lbs./1–2 kg
184E	Beef loin, top sirloin butt, boneless, 2-piece	9–13 lbs./4–6 kg
185	Loin, bottom sirloin butt	6–8 lbs./2.5–3.5 kg
185A	Loin, bottom sirloin butt, flap	3 lbs. and up/1.5 kg and up
185B	Loin, bottom sirloin butt, ball tip	3 lbs. and up/1.5 kg and up
185C	Loin, bottom sirloin butt, tri-tip	3 lbs. and up/1.5 kg and up
185D	Loin, bottom sirloin butt, tri-tip, defatted	3 lbs. and up/1.5 kg and up
186	Loin, bottom sirloin butt, trimmed	3–5 lbs./1.5–2.5 kg
189	Loin, full tenderloin	5–7 lbs./2.5–3 kg
189A	Loin, full tenderloin, side muscle on, defatted	4–6 lbs./2–2.5 kg
189B	Loin, full tenderloin, side muscle on, partially defatted	4–6 lbs./2–2.5 kg
190	Loin, full tenderloin, side muscle off, defatted	3 lbs. and up/1.5 kg and up
190A	Loin, full tenderloin, side muscle off, skinned	3 lbs. and up/1.5 kg and up
191	Loin, butt tenderloin	2–4 lbs./1–2 kg
191A	Loin, tenderloin, butt, defatted	2–4 lbs./1–2 kg
191B	Loin, tenderloin, butt, short	2 lbs. and up/1 kg and up
192	Loin, short tenderloin	3 lbs. and up/1.5 kg and up
192A	Loin, tenderloin, short	2–4 lbs./1–2 kg
193	Flank steak	1 lb. and up/.5 kg and up
130	Chuck, short ribs	3–5 lbs./1.5–2.5 kg
134	Beef bones	As requested
135	Diced beef	As requested
135A	Beef for stewing	As requested
135B	Beef for kabobs	As requested
136	Ground beef	As requested
136A	Ground beef and vegetable protein	As requested
136B	Beef patty mix	As requested
136C	Beef patty mix, lean	As requested
137	Ground beef, special	As requested
140	Hanging tender	As requested

Beef Tournedos Chasseur

INGREDIENTS

	U.S. Standard	Metric
Beef tenderloin, peeled	4 lbs.	1.8 kg
Butter, clarified	as needed	as needed
Salt	TT	TT
Black pepper, freshly ground	TT	TT
Mushroom caps, large, fluted	20 each	20 each
Croutons, round, brushed with butter, seasoned, toasted	20 each	20 each
Sauce chasseur, heated to a boil, held at 140°F (60°C) or higher	16 oz.	500 ml

METHOD OF PREPARATION

1. Gather all the ingredients and equipment.

2. Cut the beef tenderloin into 3-oz. (85-g) medallions, allowing 2 per portion.

3. Sauté the medallions to order in clarified butter, cooking until the desired internal temperature is reached. Season with salt and pepper to taste. Minimum internal temperature should be 145°F (63°C); however, remember to allow for carryover cooking.

4. Sauté the mushroom caps in clarified butter, and season to taste with salt and pepper.

5. Per portion: Place two medallions on two croutons on a preheated dinner plate, and *nappé* with sauce chasseur.

6. Garnish with two sautéed mushrooms caps. Serve immediately.

COOKING TECHNIQUES

Sautéing:
1. Heat the sauté pan to the appropriate temperature.
2. Evenly brown the food product.
3. For a sauce, pour off any excess oil, reheat, and deglaze.

GLOSSARY

Nappé: coated or to coat

NUTRITION

Nutrition Facts

Yield: Serves 10
Serving Size: 12 oz. (340 g)

Amount Per Serving

Calories 780

Total Fat 43 g

Sodium 960 mg

Total Carbohydrate 54 g

Protein 43 g

Braised Short Ribs of Beef

INGREDIENTS	U.S. Standard	Metric
Beef short ribs	5 lbs.	2.3 kg
Flour, seasoned	as needed	as needed
Oil	2 oz.	60 ml

MIREPOIX

Onions, peeled and diced	1/2 lb.	225 g
Carrots, washed, peeled, and chopped	1/2 lb.	225 g
Celery, washed, trimmed, and chopped	1/2 lb.	225 g
Garlic, peeled and crushed	1 head	1 head
Red wine	4 oz.	120 ml
Tomato purée	4 oz.	120 ml
Demi-glace, heated to a boil	1 qt.	960 ml
Marjoram, dried	1/2 Tbsp.	8 ml
Basil, dried	1/2 Tbsp.	8 ml
Salt	TT	TT
Black pepper, ground	TT	TT
Brown beef stock, heated to a boil	8 oz.	240 ml
Horseradish, prepared	1/2 tsp.	2.5 ml
Parsley, washed, squeezed dry, and chopped	2 oz.	55 g

METHOD OF PREPARATION

1. Gather all the ingredients and equipment.
2. Preheat the oven to 325°F–350°F (163°C–177°C).
3. Dredge the short ribs in the seasoned flour, and shake off any excess.
4. In a braising pan, heat the oil and sear the ribs until they are well browned. Remove the ribs from the pan and reserve.
5. In the same oil, sauté the mirepoix until lightly browned. Add the wine, tomato purée, and demi-glace with the herbs and seasonings, and bring to a boil. Return the ribs, and any juice that has accumulated, to the pan.
6. Cover with parchment paper and foil. Braise in the oven until the meat is fork-tender.
7. When the ribs are done, remove them from the braising pan and hold at 140°F (60°C) or higher. Depouille the braising liquid, add beef stock, simmer briefly or until desired consistency is achieved, and strain. Add the horseradish, and adjust the seasonings.
8. Serve the sauce over the short ribs on a preheated dinner plate. Garnish with chopped parsley.

Chicken-Fried Steak

INGREDIENTS

Ingredient	U.S. Standard	Metric
Beef steaks, cut top round	10 each (6 oz.)	10 each (170 g)
Salt	TT	TT
Eggs	4 each	4 each
Milk	4 oz.	120 ml
Black pepper	1 1/2 tsp.	7 ml
Flour, all-purpose	6 oz.	170 g
Oil, for frying	as needed	as needed

METHOD OF PREPARATION

1. Gather all the ingredients and equipment.
2. Pass the steaks through a meat tenderizer by cross-cut method, or pound well with a meat mallet to flatten and tenderize; season steaks with salt.
3. Blend eggs and milk.
4. Combine pepper with flour.
5. Dredge tenderized beef steaks in egg mixture; drain excess. Then dredge steaks in flour, shaking off the excess.
6. Shallow-fry steaks in small amount of oil until golden brown and crispy. Hold at 140°F (60°C) or higher.
7. Serve with traditional white gravy, chicken velouté, or forestière blanc.

Chef's Notes

Traditional white gravy is made by dusting the fat in the cooking pan with flour (*singe*) to make a roux. Milk is tempered in and cooked until thickened, seasoned, and served over the steak. Bacon fat may be used in place of cooking fat.

COOKING TECHNIQUES

Shallow-Frying:
1. Heat the cooking medium to the proper temperature.
2. Cook the food product throughout.
3. Season, and serve hot.

GLOSSARY

Singe: to dust with flour

NUTRITION

Nutrition Facts

Yield: Serves 10
Serving Size: 6 oz. (170 g) steak only, no sauce

Amount Per Serving

Calories 410

Total Fat 14 g

Sodium 390 mg

Total Carbohydrate 23 g

Protein 46 g

Poached Beef Tenderloin with Tapenade

INGREDIENTS	U.S. Standard	Metric
Beef tenderloin, peeled and trimmed	3 lbs.	1.4 kg
Beef stock	as needed	as needed
TAPENADE		
Anchovy fillets, minced	4 each	4 each
Garlic, minced	4 cloves	4 cloves
Niçoise or Kalamata olives, pitted and chopped	8 oz.	225 g
Capers, drained	2 oz.	55 g
Olive oil, extra virgin	4 Tbsp.	60 ml
Lemon juice	2 Tbsp.	30 ml
Parsley, fresh	1 Tbsp.	15 ml
Mizuna or mesclun greens	as needed	as needed
Vinaigrette dressing	as needed	as needed

METHOD OF PREPARATION

1. Gather all the ingredients and equipment.

2. Cut the tenderloin into 2 pieces. Truss to hold shape during cooking. Place the tenderloin pieces in a pot just large enough to hold them. They should not be pressed together, and the pot should not be so large that an excess amount of stock is needed to cook them.

3. Add cold stock to cover the tenderloin. Remove the tenderloin, and bring the stock to a boil. Reduce to a simmer.

4. Place tenderloin pieces back into the stock. Cook by maintaining a poaching temperature for about 15 minutes or until meat reaches 140°F (60°C) internal temperature.

5. Let meat rest, covered, in a 140°F (60°C) oven for about 5 minutes before slicing.

6. Place anchovies, garlic, olives, and capers in a food processor. Pulse several times until chopped fine.

7. Add olive oil, lemon juice, and chopped parsley; blend to combine.

8. Cut two slices of tenderloin per person and top with 2 Tbsp. (28 g) of tapenade per person. Garnish plate with mizuna or mesclun greens, tossed in vinaigrette if desired.

COOKING TECHNIQUES

Simmering and Poaching:

1. Heat the cooking liquid to the proper temperature.
2. Submerge the food product completely.
3. Keep the cooked product moist and warm.

NUTRITION

Nutrition Facts

Yield: Serves 10
Serving Size: 10 oz. (285 g)

Amount Per Serving

Calories 620

Total Fat 51 g

Sodium 1480 mg

Total Carbohydrate 15 g

Protein 26 g

Beef

Grilled Skewers of Asian Marinated Beef and Vegetables

INGREDIENTS

INGREDIENTS	U.S. Standard	Metric
Beef, top sirloin	2 lbs.	910 g
MARINADE		
Soy sauce	2 oz.	60 ml
Oil	2 oz.	60 ml
Honey	2 oz.	60 ml
Hoisin sauce	2 oz.	60 ml
Hot pepper sauce	1 tsp.	5 ml
Ginger, fresh, peeled, and grated	1 tsp.	5 ml
Black pepper, freshly ground	as needed	as needed
Red bell peppers, washed, seeded, and cut 1″ (2.54 cm)	2 each	2 each
Green bell peppers, washed, seeded, and cut 1″ (2.54 cm)	2 each	2 each
Onions, large, peeled, and cut 1″ (2.54 cm)	1 each	1 each
Mushroom caps, washed, stemmed	10 each	10 each

METHOD OF PREPARATION

1. Gather all the ingredients and equipment. Soak 10 wooden skewers in water to prevent burning on grill.

2. Trim and remove the excess fat from the top beef sirloin, and then slice it lengthwise, 1″ (2.54 cm) thick. Cut across the grain into cubes.

3. In a mixing bowl, mix together the marinade ingredients, and pour the marinade over the beef; marinate in a refrigerator for 2–4 hours.

4. Make skewers by alternating pieces of the beef and the various vegetables onto the skewers.

5. Grill the skewers to order. When serving, remove the wooden skewers.

Italian Meatballs in Marinara Sauce

INGREDIENTS

	U.S. Standard	Metric
Oil	1/2 oz.	15 ml
Onions, peeled and diced *brunoise*	5 oz.	140 g
Ground beef	2 1/2 lbs.	1.1 kg
Bread, white, cut into large cubes	10 oz.	285 g
Milk	as needed	as needed
Egg, whole	1 each	1 each
Parsley, washed, squeezed dry, chopped	1/2 oz.	15 g
Garlic, peeled and minced	2 cloves	2 cloves
Salt	TT	TT
Black pepper, ground	1/4 tsp.	1.25 ml
Marinara sauce, heated to a boil	1/2 gal.	1.9 l

METHOD OF PREPARATION

1. Gather all the ingredients and equipment.

2. Preheat the oven to 350°F (177°C).

3. Heat the oil in a sauté pan. Sauté the onions until translucent. Remove from the heat and cool.

4. Place the ground beef in a mixing bowl; add the cooled, sautéed onions.

5. Soak the white bread in the milk; squeeze out any excess milk, and then add to the meat.

6. Add the egg, parsley, garlic, salt, and pepper to the meat. Thoroughly mix all of the ingredients.

7. Shape into 2-oz. (55-g) round balls. Place each meatball on a sheet pan. Test for holding and taste by frying one meatball in a small pan.

8. Bake in the oven for 15 minutes or until the meatballs reach an internal temperature of 155°F (68°C). When done, transfer the meatballs to a hotel pan.

9. Pour the marinara sauce on the meatballs, and cover with parchment paper and foil. Bake for an additional 30 minutes. Hold at 140°F (60°C) or higher.

10. Serve the meatballs with any type of pasta.

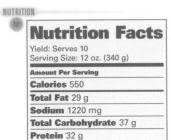

Nutrition Facts

Yield: Serves 10
Serving Size: 12 oz. (340 g)

Amount Per Serving

Calories 550	
Total Fat 29 g	
Sodium 1220 mg	
Total Carbohydrate 37 g	
Protein 32 g	

Beef

313

Roast Top Round of Beef

INGREDIENTS

Ingredient	U.S. Standard	Metric
Beef, top round	5 lbs.	2.3 kg
Salt	as needed	as needed
Black pepper	as needed	as needed
Garlic powder	as needed	as needed
Mustard powder	as needed	as needed
MIREPOIX		
Onions, peeled, diced	8 oz.	225 g
Celery, washed, peeled, and diced	8 oz.	225 g
Carrots, washed, peeled, and diced	8 oz.	225 g
Brown beef stock, heated to a boil	1 pint	500 ml

METHOD OF PREPARATION

1. Gather all the ingredients and equipment.

2. Preheat the oven to 350°F (177°C).

3. Trim the meat, and trim the thick fat to 1/4 inch (6 mm).

4. Rub the seasonings into the meat.

5. Place the mirepoix in the bottom of a roasting pan with the meat on top. Roast to an internal temperature of 140°F (60°C).

6. Remove the roast from the pan, and hold at 140°F (60°C) or higher. Allow to rest and carry over to 145°F (63°C) before serving.

7. Place the roasting pan on the stove, and remove excess fat. *Deglaze* the pan with beef stock, heat to a boil, and reduce to the proper consistency and flavor.

8. Strain the sauce, and adjust the seasonings.

9. Slice the meat against the grain. Serve on a preheated dinner plate with the seasoned sauce.

New England Boiled Dinner

Ingredients

Ingredients	U.S. Standard	Metric
Corned beef	6 lbs.	2.7 kg
Cold water	as needed	as needed
Pickling spices	2 oz.	55 g
Water or beef stock, (to boil vegetables)	4 1/4 qts.	4 l
White cabbage, washed, cored, cut into wedges	1 head	1 head
Carrots, washed, peeled, and **tournéed**	5 each	5 each
Turnips, washed, peeled, and **tournéed**	10 each	10 each
Potatoes, washed, peeled, and **tournéed**	10 each	10 each
Onions, small, peeled	10 each	10 each
Salt	TT	TT
White pepper, ground	TT	TT
Butter, heated to 165°F (73°C)	1 lb.	254 g
Parsley, fresh, washed, chopped	3 oz.	85 g
Horseradish, prepared	as needed	as needed
Caper sauce (recipe follows)	10 oz.	300 ml

Method of Preparation

1. Gather all the ingredients and equipment.

2. Place the beef in a large stockpot, and cover with water. Add pickling spices; heat the liquid to a boil. Skim the surface, reduce the heat, and simmer covered until the meat is fork-tender. This will require 2 1/2–3 hours cooking time. Remove the beef, and hold covered at 140°F (60°C) or higher. Strain the broth and dépouille. Reserve the broth for the caper sauce.

3. Place cabbage wedges in an appropriate pot, and pour in just enough hot broth to cover. Simmer gently until cabbage is tender. Drain, reserve broth, season to taste, and hold at 140°F (60°C) or higher.

4. In cold water or cold brown beef stock, boil the carrots, turnips, potatoes, and onions, using a separate pot for each item. Cook each vegetable until tender; drain and season to taste. Hold at 140°F (60°C) or higher.

5. Trim any excess fat from the beef, and slice thin against the grain on a bias. Arrange in a hotel pan, and cover with some of the hot broth. Hold at 140°F (60°C) or higher for service.

6. To serve, place the cabbage wedges on a preheated dinner plate. Lay the sliced beef over the cabbage, and arrange the remaining vegetables around the edge. Drizzle with hot butter, and garnish with parsley. Offer the horse-radish and caper sauce (recipe follows) separately.

COOKING TECHNIQUES

Simmering:
1. Place the prepared product in an appropriately sized pot.
2. Bring the product to a boil, and then reduce the heat to allow the product to barely boil.
3. Cook until desired doneness is achieved.

Boiling (At sea level):
1. Bring the cooking liquid to a rapid boil.
2. Stir the contents, and cook the food product throughout.
3. Serve hot.

GLOSSARY

Tournéed: trimmed to a large olive shape

NUTRITION

Nutrition Facts

Yield: Serves 10
Serving Size: 22 oz. (625 g)

Amount Per Serving	
Calories 710	
Total Fat 47 g	
Sodium 2150 mg	
Total Carbohydrate 50 g	
Protein 34 g	

Beef

315

Caper Sauce

INGREDIENTS	U.S. Standard	Metric
Reserved cooking broth, strained from corned beef	8 oz.	240 ml
White wine	4 oz.	120 ml
Heavy cream	8 oz.	240 ml
Capers, non-pareille, drained, rinsed, gently squeezed dry	3 oz.	85 g
White pepper	TT	TT

METHOD OF PREPARATION

1. Gather all the ingredients and equipment.

2. Combine the broth and wine in a small saucepan, simmer, and reduce to approximately 1 cup (240 ml).

3. Add the heavy cream, and continue to reduce until sauce thickens.

4. Stir in the capers and season with white pepper. Serve warm with corned beef.

COOKING TECHNIQUES

Simmering:

1. Place the prepared product in an appropriately sized pot.
2. Bring the product to a boil, and then reduce the heat to allow the product to barely boil.
3. Cook until desired doneness is achieved.

NUTRITION

Nutrition Facts

Yield: 11 oz.
Serving Size: 1 oz. (28 g)

Amount Per Serving

Calories 40

Total Fat 3.5 g

Sodium 115 mg

Total Carbohydrate 1 g

Protein 0 g

Japanese Beef and Vegetables

INGREDIENTS	U.S. Standard	Metric
Peanut oil	as needed	as needed
Top round of beef, trimmed, sliced 1/8" (3-mm) strips	2 1/2 lbs.	1.14 kg
Soy sauce	4 oz.	100 ml
Granulated sugar	3 Tbsp.	45 g
Scallions, washed, trimmed, cut 1" (2.54 cm) strips	10 each	10 each
Onions, peeled, sliced 1/2" (1.27 cm) thick	10 oz.	285 g
Mushrooms, washed, stemmed, sliced thin	10 oz.	285 g
Tofu	1 lb.	254 g
Spinach, fresh, washed, stemmed, cut chiffonade	1 lb.	254 g
Bamboo shoots, washed, cut julienne	1 lb.	254 g
Mirin, available in Asian markets	10 oz.	300 ml
Shirataki noodles, cooked, cooled, cut into thirds	1 1/2 lbs.	680 g

COOKING TECHNIQUES

Stir-Frying:
1. Heat the oil in a wok until hot but not smoking.
2. Keep the food in constant motion; use the entire cooking surface.

GLOSSARY

Chiffonade: ribbons of leafy greens

NUTRITION

Nutrition Facts

Yield: Serves 10
Serving Size: 14 oz. (400 g)

Amount Per Serving

Calories 490

Total Fat 15 g

Sodium 900 mg

Total Carbohydrate 38 g

Protein 5 g

METHOD OF PREPARATION

1. Gather all the ingredients and equipment.

2. In a wok or heavy sauté pan, heat a small amount of the peanut oil. Add the beef strips and stir-fry quickly to brown the meat. Season with soy sauce and sugar, and then remove and set aside.

3. Clean the wok or pan, and then heat some more peanut oil. Add the scallions, onions, mushrooms, tofu, spinach, and bamboo shoots. Stir-fry quickly for about 2 minutes. Add the mirin and noodles, and return the cooked meat to the mixture. Stir-fry an additional minute or just until hot and well incorporated.

4. Remove from wok or pan, and serve on a preheated dinner plate.

17 Veal

Although veal consumption has declined in the United States since the 1950s, veal's delicate flavor, consistent tenderness, and minimal fat content make it an appealing alternative to beef. Veal is the meat of calves. Because cows must give birth before they can produce milk and become dairy cows, veal is considered a by-product of the dairy industry.

Popular among inhabitants of the Italian peninsula since Roman times as well as among the French, the Germans, and the Spanish, veal came to the United States with immigrants from Europe, who appreciated its versatility, especially its easy pairing with sauces.

Veal Terminology

A calf is a bovine animal of either gender that has not yet reached maturity (nine months). Female calves mature and produce milk as dairy cows. Male calves become veal. Age at time of slaughter is the basis for the following categories of veal calves.

Bob veal (Baby veal) *Bob veal* are the youngest veal calves marketed. Calves in this category range from several days to 4 weeks old at time of slaughter. They make up about 15% of the veal market.

Vealer *Vealers* represent the largest segment of veal production. These calves range in age from 4 to 18 weeks. Calves between 8 and 16 weeks of age supply most of the veal on the market.

Calf The term *calf* refers to meat from veal calves 20 weeks or older. In contrast to meat from younger calves, calf is darker in color and exhibits some marbling and fat cover.

Types of Veal

Methods of veal production, in addition to the age of calves, have an impact on the characteristics of veal. Production methods define two types of veal: special-fed veal and grain-fed veal.

Special-fed veal (Formula veal) Most veal calves today are special-fed veal. Veal farmers feed these calves a milk- or soy-based formula that contains all the necessary nutrients, including vitamins, minerals, amino acids, fats, and carbohydrates. The calves live in individual pens just large enough to allow them to stand, stretch, and lie down. The liquid diet of the calves produces meat that is light pink in color, and the calves' restricted movement ensures that the meat is extremely tender.

Grain-fed veal (Market or average veal) These veal calves are free to roam and graze on grass and other plant foods. Their diet, which includes solid food, and their ability to exercise result in redder and somewhat less tender meat than that of special-fed veal. The flavor of grain-fed veal varies slightly from that of formula veal.

Quality Characteristics, Inspection, and Grading

Veal is tender and has a delicate flavor. Its lean meat should be pale pink, and its texture should be firm. Veal has no marbling and little external fat. Veal's lack of fat cover, which prevents drying and acts as a defense against bacteria, prohibits aging.

The USDA/FSIS mandates the inspection of veal. See Figure 17-1. Quality grades for veal are similar to those for beef. Prime and Choice are the top grades. Good is a medium grade suitable for institutions. Standard, Utility, and Cull grades are the lowest grades, appropriate for canning or other processing. The USDA does not issue yield grades for veal because it has very little fat in proportion to lean meat.

Purchasing Veal

When purchasing veal, consider the same factors that apply in the purchase of any meat: menu needs, cooking methods, price, and quality. Order specifications for veal should include the name of the cut with its IMPS/NAMP number (see Figure 17-4 on page 327), the portion weight and/or thickness as applicable, maximum surface fat thickness (for chops), and mode of delivery (chilled or frozen). Purchase only from plants inspected by the government, and refer to NAMP's "The Meat Buyers Guide" for information on purchasing veal.

Wiener Schnitzel: Its History and Preparation

German immigrants to the United States brought their cuisine with them, and many of these ethnic foods quickly became part of American cooking. Among these dishes was the breaded veal scallop known as Wiener schnitzel, or veal cutlet Viennese style. Prepared in German-American homes in the early 1800s, Wiener schnitzel was a popular menu offering of German restaurants in New York and other cities by the beginning of the twentieth century. Perfect Wiener schnitzel has a crisp crumb coating that does not stick to the meat.

The secret to making Wiener schnitzel is to bread the veal cutlet just before cooking and then cook it immediately and quickly. Otherwise, making Wiener schnitzel is a simple process. Pound the veal cutlet lightly to flatten it, and then season with salt and pepper. With flour, beaten eggs, and bread crumbs ready for breading, heat butter and oil in a sauté pan over moderate heat. Then bread the cutlet, place it in the hot butter, and pan-fry until golden brown—about 3 minutes on each side. Move the browned cutlet from the pan to a hot plate. Place a peeled lemon slice on top of the cutlet and an anchovy fillet rolled around a caper on top of the lemon slice.

Handling Veal Safely

Inspection ensures the wholesomeness of veal prior to delivery. Correct handling after receiving is essential to maintaining the safety and quality of veal.

Receiving Veal

Upon receipt, examine veal for signs of mishandling or contamination. Confirm that government inspection has taken place. Look at the packaging to make sure that it is not damaged. Tears, leakage, or indications of repacking may point to contamination. Check the meat's temperature, color, odor, and texture: veal should be received at 41°F (5°C) or lower; it should appear grayish pink; it should not have an off odor; and the texture should be firm and not sticky. Do not accept veal that does not meet these quality standards.

Storing Veal

For safe storage of veal, follow the same guidelines as for other meats. Upon delivery, store veal immediately at 41°F (5°C) or lower for fresh veal and between 0°F to 10°F (−18°C to −12°C) for frozen veal. Airtight wrapping is appropriate for both fresh and frozen products. Make sure that wrapping for frozen veal is moisture-proof to avoid freezer burn. To prevent cross-contamination, keep raw veal from other foods, in trays, and on the bottom shelves of storage units. Use fresh veal roasts and chops within three to five days and ground or stew meat within one to two days. Frozen roasts and chops keep well for four to six months; use frozen ground veal or stew meat within three to four months. To defrost, hold in the refrigerator at 41°F (5°C) or lower.

Spoilage Indicators

Spoiled veal may be sticky, slimy, or tacky and may smell sour. Damaged packaging may indicate spoilage. Always discard spoiled meat.

Foodborne Illness Associated with Veal

Enterohemorrhagic *E. coli* O175:H7 (EHEC) and salmonellosis are the main foodborne illnesses connected with improperly handled or prepared veal. *E. coli* bacteria form colonies in the digestive tract of cattle and can contaminate the muscle of animals at the time of slaughter. Cooking destroys the bacteria that cause this illness. Bacteria known as salmonellae cause salmonellosis. These bacteria also flourish in the digestive tracts of animals and may contaminate muscle at the time of slaughter. They cause illness when eaten. Thorough cooking and measures to prevent cross-contamination are effective methods for preventing salmonellosis.

See Chapter 4: Food Safety and Chapter 11: Cooking Techniques for more information about the safe handling and preparation of veal.

Primal, Subprimal, and Fabricated Cuts

Although a veal carcass is sometimes divided into sides, the more typical practice is to split the carcass between the ribs into a front portion (*foresaddle*) and a rear portion (*hindsaddle*). A veal foresaddle produces three primal cuts, and the hindsaddle produces two. See Figure 17-2 and Figure 17-3. As a result of the division into foresaddle and hindsaddle, each primal cut contains both halves, or sides, of the carcass. The primal rib, for instance, consists of a double rack with seven ribs from each side.

Scallops, escalopes, scaloppine, and schnitzel are all other names for cutlets. The term used depends on the cuisine. Other terms refer to a cutlet's preparation. A paillard, for instance, is a pounded and grilled cutlet.

FIGURE 17-2
Skeletal structure

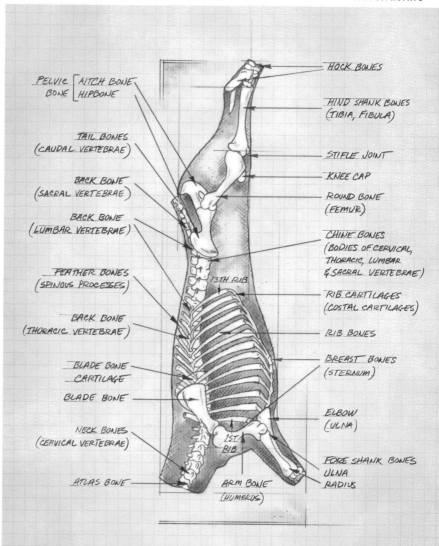

FIGURE 17-3
Location of primal cuts of veal

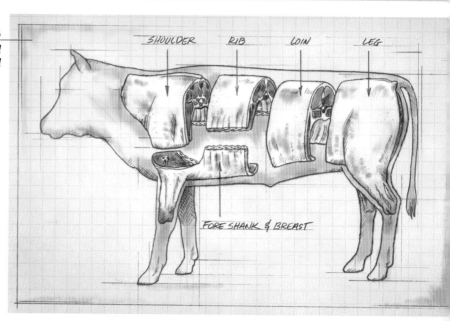

Primal, or wholesale, cuts from the foresaddle are the shoulder (chuck), breast, and rib. A by-product of the foresaddle is the foreshank. See Figure 17-3 on page 322 for the location of these primal cuts.

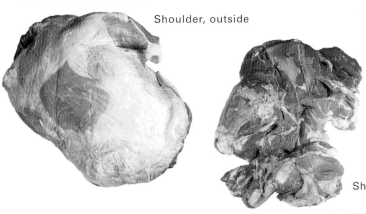

Shoulder, outside

Shoulder, inside

SHOULDER (CHUCK) The veal shoulder includes four rib bones, some of the backbone, and portions of the blade and arm bones. By weight, it makes up 21% of the carcass. Like beef chuck, this primal cut of veal contains a large amount of connective tissue, which makes it somewhat tough. Fabricated cuts from the shoulder include steaks and chops, which are suitable for broiling. These cuts, however, do not compare in tenderness with similar cuts from the loin or rib. Grinding or cubing veal chuck mitigates some of the toughness. Combination techniques such as braising and stewing also help tenderize veal shoulder meat.

BREAST Beneath the shoulder and the rib is the breast, which makes up a single primal cut. It includes rib bones, cartilage, and breastbones, and comprises about 16% of the carcass weight. Combination cooking such as braising and stewing offsets the presence of cartilage and a good deal of fat and connective tissue in the breast, which has quite a bit of flavor. Veal breast is often stuffed and rolled.

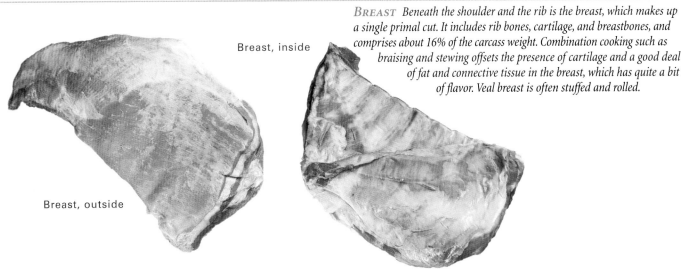

Breast, inside

Breast, outside

Veal

323

PRIMAL RIB (RACK) The comparatively small primal rib is very tender, popular, and expensive. It consists of a double rack of ribs and a portion of the backbone. The veal rack is suited to roasting whole, split, or boneless. When boned, it produces a short tenderloin and a rib eye. Medallions and steaks can be made from the rib eye. Chops fabricated from the veal rack may contain the bone or not. Grilling and sautéing are frequent cooking methods for veal chops.

Rib Chops

FORESHANK The foreshank is not considered a primal or even subprimal cut of veal, but instead is thought of as a by-product. It is commonly purchased attached to the chuck. Also full of flavor, but tough, the foreshank lends itself to braising whole or to slicing for osso bucco.

Foreshank

The hindsaddle consists of two primal cuts: the loin and the leg.
See Figure 17-3 on page 322 for the location of these primal cuts.

Loin (Saddle) *The loin is located directly behind the primal rib. It contains two ribs, with the loin eye on top and the tenderloin underneath. Both the loin eye and the tenderloin are extremely tender. The tenderloin is often cut into medallions, and boneless or bone-in chops are fabricated from the veal loin. Use dry cooking techniques such as broiling, grilling, roasting, and sautéing for these tender cuts, or a combination technique such as braising.*

Tenderloin

Loin

Leg *The leg is the largest primal cut of veal, accounting for 42% of the carcass weight. It includes both the leg and the sirloin and parts of the backbone, tailbone, hip bone, aitch bone, round bone, and hindshank. Cutlets are typical fabricated cuts. The leg, which is quite tender, also may be roasted whole. Moist, dry, and combination techniques are appropriate for leg cuts. When braised, cross cuts from the hindshank produce osso bucco.*

Leg, Stew Veal

Hindshank

Leg, Top Round

Leg

Variety Meats

Veal variety meats are perhaps the most popular and best-known variety meats. In addition to the more familiar calf's liver, tongue, and sweetbreads, foodservice establishments may offer calf's brains, heart, and kidney.

Liver

Calf's liver is milder in flavor, paler in color, and generally more tender than beef liver. Like beef liver, it is an excellent source of iron. To prepare, first trim and remove the outer skin and other tough membranes, and then slice. Cook calf's liver to order using a dry technique such as sautéing or broiling.

Tongue

Although not as tough as beef tongue, calf's tongue is still muscular and benefits from long simmering or braising in bouillon or broth. Pickling and smoking prepare it further for use as a cold sliced meat. Diced or julienned tongue serves as a garnish for soups and sauces.

Sweetbreads

Sweetbreads are a calf's thymus gland. Because the thymus gland shrinks with age, it is available only from young animals such as calves and lambs. Veal sweetbreads are a favorite because of their delicate taste and texture. Sautéing, shallow-frying, and poaching are appropriate cooking methods for sweetbreads.

Brains

A mild taste and delicate texture characterize calf's brains. Highly perishable and extremely fragile, brains require immediate use and careful handling. The usual procedure is to poach in court bouillon and then serve with butter or to cook further by battering and deep-frying.

Heart

Veal heart is relatively tender, which makes it suitable for sautéing or grilling. Cook only until medium rare if using a dry technique. Overcooking will make veal heart tough. Slow simmering and braising are also excellent cooking methods for veal heart.

Kidney

Sautéing and broiling enhance the rich taste and preserve the firm texture of calf's kidneys. Combination techniques are also appropriate cooking methods for kidneys, which enrich stews and are a feature of kidney pies.

Fabrication

The relatively small size of the veal carcass makes it easy to handle, and foodservice establishments sometimes purchase primal cuts or larger forms, such as a side, foresaddle, hindsaddle, or back, to make their own fabricated cuts. The decision to fabricate depends on many factors, including skill level, availability of equipment and storage facilities, and ability to use the variety of cuts larger forms produce. Some operations may also use portion control (PC) cuts, which are cut to specification. Portion control cuts are best used when there is little or no use of trimmings on the menu. Some portion control (PC) cuts may be purchased as individually quick frozen (IQF) cuts.

Butchering (Fabricating) Skills

If the foodservice establishment purchases primal cuts or larger forms of veal, various butchering procedures may be performed in-house, such as boning a veal loin and cutting it into boneless veal chops.

PROCESS

Cutting Veal Cutlets from a Top Round

Cutlets can be made from various large pieces of veal, such as top round.

To make veal cutlets, follow these steps:

1 **Slice against the grain from a fully trimmed top round.**

 To flatten, place each cutlet between two pieces of plastic wrap, and pound lightly.

Cutting Veal Breasts

Veal breasts can be stuffed prior to cooking.

To prepare a veal breast for stuffing or to make a boneless roast, follow these steps:

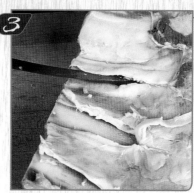

For a boneless roast, remove the bones using a boning knife to expose and cut them away from the meat.

Cut the veal breast into two sections.

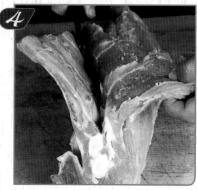

An alternative to step 3 would be to remove the meat from the bones by cutting directly between the meat and bones.

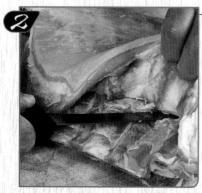

Using a boning knife, make a pocket between the bones and the meat, leaving about 2 inches (5 cm) attached to the end.

Trim the fat from the boned veal breast. Cut away the thick layer of fat from the breast.

Roll the veal breast inside out, tie it, and roast in a preheated oven.

FIGURE 17-4

NAMP NUMBER	NAME	AVERAGE WEIGHT RANGE
304	Foresaddle, 11 ribs	44–86 lbs./20–39 kg
304A	Forequarter, 11 ribs	17–43 lbs./7.5–19.5 kg
306	Hotel rack, 7 ribs	9–14 lbs./4–6.5 kg
306A	Hotel rack, 6 ribs	5–13 lbs./2.5–6 kg
306B	Hotel rack, chop-ready, 7 ribs	2–7 lbs./1–3 kg
306C	Hotel rack, chop-ready, 6 ribs	2–6 lbs./1–2.5 kg
306D	Hotel rack, chop-ready, 7 ribs, Frenched	2–7 lbs./1–3 kg
307	Rack, rib eye	3–5 lbs./1.5–2.5 kg
308	Chuck, 4 ribs	40–70 lbs./18–32 kg
309	Chuck, square-cut	20–36 lbs./9–16.5 kg
309B	Chuck, square-cut, boneless	19–33 lbs./8.5–15 kg
309D	Chuck, square-cut, neck off, boneless, tied	18–32 lbs./8–14.5 kg
309G	Chuck, square-cut, clod out, boneless, tied	15–30 lbs./7–13.5 kg
310	Chuck, shoulder clod	4–7 lbs./2–3 kg
310A	Chuck, shoulder clod, special	4–7 lbs./2–3 kg
310B	Chuck, shoulder clod, roast	4–7 lbs./2–3 kg
310C	Chuck, scotch tender	1/2–1 lb./up to .5 kg
311	Chuck, square-cut, clod out, boneless, tied	18–32 lbs./8–14.5 kg
312	Foreshank	2–4 lbs./1–2 kg
313	Breast	6–10 lbs./2.5–4.5 kg
314	Breast with pocket	6–10 lbs./2.5–4.5 kg
323	Short ribs	As requested
330	Hindsaddle, 2 ribs	50–88 lbs./22.5–40 kg
330A	Hindquarter, 2 ribs	18–63 lbs./8–28.5 kg
331	Loin	10–18 lbs./4.5–8 kg
332	Loin, trimmed	8–14 lbs./3.5–6.5 kg
334	Leg	40–70 lbs./18–32 kg
335	Leg, boneless, roast-ready, tied	15–26 lbs./7–12 kg
336	Leg, shank off, boneless, roast-ready, tied	11–19 lbs./5–8.5 kg
337	Hindshank	2–4 lbs./1–2 kg
338	Shank, osso bucco	1–3 lbs./.5–1.5 kg
341	Back, 9 ribs, trimmed	15–25 lbs./7–11.5 kg
344	Loin, strip loin, boneless	3–6 lbs./1.5–2.5 kg
344A	Loin, strip loin, boneless, special	2–5 lbs./1–2.5 kg
346	Loin, butt tenderloin	1–1 1/2 lbs./up to .5 kg
346A	Loin, butt tenderloin, skinned	1/2–1 lb./up to .5 kg
347	Loin, short tenderloin	1/2–1 lb./up to .5 kg
348	Leg, TBS, 4 parts	24–32 lbs./11–14.5 kg
348A	Leg, TBS, 3 parts	16–24 lbs./7.5–11 kg
349	Leg, top round, cap on	8–12 lbs./3.5–5.5 kg
349A	Leg, top round, cap off	6–8 lbs./2.5–3.5 kg
363	Leg, TBS, 4 parts	11–38 lbs./5–17.5 kg
363A	Leg, TBS, 3 parts	9–32 lbs./4–14.5 kg
363B	Leg, TBS, 3 parts	12–35 lbs./5.5–16 kg
388	Bones, mixed	As requested
389	Bones, marrow	As requested
395	Veal for stewing	As requested
395A	Veal for kabobs	As requested
396	Ground veal	As requested

Rolled Veal Scallops

INGREDIENTS

	U.S. Standard	Metric
FARCE		
Veal, ground	8 oz.	225 g
Pork, ground	8 oz.	225 g
Rice, cooked	8 oz.	225 g
Eggs	2 each	2 each
Oregano, dried	1/2 tsp.	2.5 ml
Basil, dried	1/2 tsp.	2.5 ml
Ginger, ground	1/4 tsp.	1.25 ml
Salt	TT	TT
White pepper, ground	TT	TT
Veal cutlets, pounded thin	10, 5 oz. each	10, 140 g each
Flour, all-purpose, seasoned	as needed	as needed
Vegetable oil	2 oz.	60 ml
Onions, peeled and diced brunoise	6 oz.	170 g
Carrots, washed, trimmed, and diced brunoise	8 oz.	225 g
Celery stalks, washed, trimmed, and diced brunoise	8 oz.	225 g
Garlic, peeled, sliced	3 cloves	3 cloves
Tomatoes, canned, crushed	1 lb.	454 g
White wine, dry	1 pt.	575 ml
Veal demi-glace, heated to a boil	1 pt.	500 ml
Salt	TT	TT
Black pepper, ground	TT	TT

METHOD OF PREPARATION

1. Gather all the ingredients and equipment.

2. Combine the *farce* ingredients, and mix well.

3. Lay out the pounded cutlets, and spread farce mixture on each.

4. Roll the cutlets, and secure with butcher's twine or toothpicks.

5. In a sauté pan, heat the oil.

6. Dredge the veal rolls in seasoned flour and *sear* on all sides, and then transfer the rolls to a hotel pan.

7. Sauté the vegetables in the same oil used to sear the veal. Add the wine and veal demi-glace, season with salt and pepper, and cook 10 minutes.

8. Pour the vegetable sauce over the veal, seal the pan with aluminum foil, and bake in a 325°F–350°F (163°C–177°C) oven until *fork-tender,* approximately 30–35 minutes. Hold at 140°F (60°C) or higher.

9. To serve, remove twine or toothpicks. Strain the sauce. Place one *roulade* on a preheated dinner plate, and *nappé* with the sauce.

COOKING TECHNIQUES

Sautéing:
1. Heat the sauté pan to the appropriate temperature.
2. Evenly brown the food product.
3. For a sauce, pour off any excess oil, reheat, and deglaze.

Simmering:
1. Place the prepared product in an appropriately sized pot.
2. Bring the product to a boil, and then reduce the heat to allow the product to barely boil.
3. Cook until desired doneness is achieved.

Baking:
1. Preheat the oven.
2. Place the food product on the appropriate rack.

GLOSSARY

Brunoise: 1/8″ (3 mm) dice
Farce: forcemeat stuffing
Sear: to brown quickly
Fork-tender: without resistance
Roulade: a rolled slice of meat or fish filled with a savory stuffing
Nappé: coated or to coat

NUTRITION

Nutrition Facts

Yield: Serves 10
Serving Size: 5 oz. (140 g)

Amount Per Serving

Calories 450

Total Fat 26 g

Sodium 160 mg

Total Carbohydrate 10 g

Protein 36 g

White Veal Stew with Asparagus

INGREDIENTS

	U.S. Standard	Metric
Stew veal, *trimmed, cut into 1" (2.54 cm) cubes*	4 lbs.	1.8 kg
White veal stock	2 qts.	1.9 l
White wine	1 c.	240 ml
Onion, *quartered*	1 each	1 each
Cloves	4 each	4 each
Bouquet garni	1 each	1 each
Clarified butter	2 1/2 oz.	75 ml
Flour	2 oz.	55 g
Green asparagus	2 lbs.	910 g
Egg yolks	3 each	3 each
Heavy cream	1 c.	240 ml
Lemon juice, *freshly squeezed*	1 Tbsp.	15 ml
White pepper	TT	TT
Salt	TT	TT

METHOD OF PREPARATION

1. Gather all the ingredients and equipment.
2. Put the veal into a braising pan, and add stock to cover. Add the wine, and bring to a boil.
3. Reduce to a simmer, dépouille, and discard the impurities that rises to the surface.
4. Stud the onion quarters with 1 clove each, and add to the pot along with the bouquet garni. Continue to simmer gently, and dépouille as needed until the veal is tender, about 1 1/2 hours.
5. Remove the veal, cover, and keep warm. Discard the bouquet garni and the *onion clouté.*
6. Make a white roux with 2 oz. (60 ml) of the clarified butter and the flour, and temper the cooking liquor into the roux. Bring to a simmer, and dépouille as needed.
7. Add the veal, and simmer gently 15 minutes longer. Hold if necessary at 140°F (60°C) or higher.
8. Meanwhile, remove the tips from the asparagus spears. Reserve the remaining asparagus for another use. Blanch the tips, shock, and set aside.
9. Just before service, reheat the stew to a boil, and reduce to a low simmer. Combine the egg yolks and the cream, and temper the mixture into the stew. Do not allow the stew to boil after adding the egg yolks.
10. Add the lemon juice. Taste, and season as needed with salt and pepper.
11. Heat the remaining 1/2 oz. (15 ml) of clarified butter in a sauté pan, and sauté the blanched asparagus tips to reheat.
12. Serve stew on preheated dinner plates (over buttered noodles or rice pilaf if desired), and garnish with asparagus tips.

COOKING TECHNIQUES

Stewing:
1. Sear, sauté, sweat, or blanch the main food product.
2. Deglaze the pan, if desired.
3. Cover the food product with simmering liquid.
4. Remove the bouquet garni.

GLOSSARY

Bouquet garni: bouquet of herbs and spices

Onion clouté: onion studded with cloves

Veal

NUTRITION

Nutrition Facts
Yield: Serves 10
Serving Size: 10 oz. (285 g)

Amount Per Serving

Calories 440

Total Fat 21 g

Sodium 170 mg

Total Carbohydrate 6 g

Protein 51 g

Osso Bucco

INGREDIENTS

	U.S. Standard	Metric
Veal shanks, 2" (5.08 cm) thick	10 each	10 each
Vegetable oil	as needed	as needed
Flour, seasoned	as needed	as needed
Onions, peeled, diced macédoine	8 oz.	225 g
Celery, trimmed, washed, diced macédoine	8 oz.	225 g
Carrots, peeled, washed, diced macédoine	8 oz.	225 g
Garlic, peeled, mashed into a purée	3 cloves	3 cloves
Sage leaves, dried, crushed	1 Tbsp.	15 ml
Tomatoes, canned whole, drained, seeded, diced	1 1/2 lbs.	680 g
Tomato purée	1 Tbsp.	15 g
Bay leaves	2 each	2 each
Marsala wine	4 oz.	120 ml
White veal stock	1 qt.	960 ml
Veal demi-glace	1 pt.	500 ml
Salt	TT	TT
Black Pepper, freshly ground	TT	TT

GREMOLADA GARNISH

	U.S. Standard	Metric
Lemons, washed, zested (zest finely minced)	2 each	2 each
Garlic, peeled, finely minced	6–8 cloves	6–8 cloves
Parsley, washed, squeezed dry, chopped	1 oz.	28 g

METHOD OF PREPARATION

1. Gather all the ingredients and equipment.

2. Preheat the oven to 325°F–350°F (163°C–177°C).

3. Heat a thin layer of oil in a braising pan to smoking point. Dredge the shanks in the seasoned flour, shaking off any excess, and sear the shanks well on all sides. Transfer the shanks to a sheet pan.

4. In the same braising pan, sauté the macédoine of vegetables until the onions are translucent.

5. Add the garlic, sage, tomatoes, tomato purée, bay leaves, Marsala, stock, and demi-glace; heat to a boil. Reduce the heat, simmer for 15 minutes, and then season to taste with salt and pepper.

6. Add the seared shanks to the pan, cover tightly, and place in the oven to braise until the meat is fork-tender, approximately 1 1/2–2 hours.

7. Remove the veal shanks and hold, covered tightly, with a bit of the braising liquid at 140°F (60°C) or higher.

8. Place the braising liquid on the stove top, bring to a boil, reduce the heat, and simmer until the proper flavor and consistency is achieved. Dépouille as needed. Remove the bay leaves, and adjust seasoning with salt and pepper to taste.

9. While the shanks are cooking, prepare the gremolada garnish by mixing the finely minced lemon zest, garlic, and parsley. Set aside for service.

10. To serve, place one shank on a preheated dinner plate, nappé with the sauce, and sprinkle generously with the gremolada.

Chef's Notes

If preferred, the sauce may be strained and reduced until proper flavor and consistency is achieved, in which case there is no need to macédoine the vegetables; a rough cut (mirepoix) will do.

COOKING TECHNIQUES

Braising:
1. Heat the braising pan to the proper temperature.
2. Sear and brown the food product to a golden color.
3. Degrease and deglaze.
4. Cook the food product in two-thirds liquid until fork-tender.

Sautéing:
1. Heat the sauté pan to the appropriate temperature.
2. Evenly brown the food product.
3. For a sauce, pour off any excess oil, reheat, and deglaze.

GLOSSARY

Macédoine: 1/4" (6 mm) dice

Mirepoix: carrots, onion, celery, and sometimes leeks—rough-cut

NUTRITION

Nutrition Facts

Yield: Serves 10
Serving Size: 12 oz. (340 g)

Amount Per Serving

Calories 340

Total Fat 12 g

Sodium 390 mg

Total Carbohydrate 17 g

Protein 37 g

Veal Paillard with Lemon

INGREDIENTS

	U.S. Standard	Metric
Veal top round or veal cutlets, 6 oz. (170 g) each	4 lbs.	1.8 kg
Lemons, washed	7 each	7 each
Butter, softened	6 oz.	170 g
Parsley, washed, squeezed dry, chopped	1 Tbsp.	15 ml
Salt	TT	TT
Black pepper, ground	TT	TT
Granulated garlic	TT	TT
Vegetable oil	as needed	as needed
Parsley, sprigs	10 each	10 each

METHOD OF PREPARATION

1. Gather all the ingredients and equipment.

2. Preheat the grill.

3. Cut the veal top round against the grain into 10 cutlets. Flatten between 2 pieces of plastic wrap. (Cutlets should be very thin but not torn.) Cover the veal, and store at 41°F (5°C) or lower while the sauce and garnish are prepared.

4. Juice 2 of the lemons, and then remove seeds. Prepare the rest of the lemons as desired for garnish.

5. Place the lemon juice in a nonreactive sauté pan over medium-high heat, and simmer until it reduces by one third. Add the butter, and swirl in until melted and *emulsified.* Add the chopped parsley. Taste, and season with salt and pepper, holding off the heat while the veal is cooked.

6. Season veal lightly with salt, pepper, and granulated garlic. Grill the *paillards* to order on a very hot grill, creating a diamond pattern on the most attractive side. Flip the veal over and finish the second side. Total cooking time will be about 1 1/2 minutes. *Baste* veal as needed with the vegetable oil to keep it moist.

7. Serve immediately on preheated dinner plates with lemon butter sauce, lemon garnish, and a sprig of parsley.

COOKING TECHNIQUES

Grilling/Broiling:
1. Clean and heat the grill or broiler.
2. To prevent sticking, brush the food product with oil.

Simmering:
1. Place the prepared product in an appropriately sized pot.
2. Bring the product to a boil, and then reduce the heat to allow the product to barely boil.
3. Cook until desired doneness is achieved.

GLOSSARY

Emulsify: to bind two ingredients together that do not normally mix

Paillard: a veal scallop or thin slice of beef that is quickly grilled or sautéed

Baste: to brush food as it cooks with melted butter or other fat, meat drippings, or liquid

NUTRITION

Nutrition Facts

Yield: Serves 10
Serving Size: 6 1/2 oz. (185 g)

Amount Per Serving

Calories 320

Total Fat 21 g

Sodium 120 mg

Total Carbohydrate 4 g

Protein 30 g

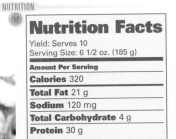

Grilled Veal Chops with Roasted Red Bell Pepper Butter

INGREDIENTS	U.S. Standard	Metric
Veal chops, bone in	10 each, 10 oz.	10 each, 285 g
Vegetable oil	2 oz.	60 ml
ROASTED RED PEPPER BUTTER		
Butter, soft	1 lb.	454 g
Red peppers, roasted, cleaned of skin and seeds	2 each	2 each
White pepper, ground	1 tsp.	5 ml
Salt	1/2 Tbsp.	8 ml
Parsley, washed, squeezed dry, and chopped	1 oz.	28 g
Salt	as needed	as needed
Black pepper, freshly ground	1 tsp.	5 ml

COOKING TECHNIQUES

Grilling/Broiling:
1. Clean and heat the grill or broiler.
2. To prevent sticking, brush the food product with oil.

NUTRITION

Nutrition Facts
Yield: Serves 10
Serving Size: 10 oz. (285 g)

Amount Per Serving

Calories 540

Total Fat 49 g

Sodium 810 mg

Total Carbohydrate 5 g

Protein 24 g

METHOD OF PREPARATION

1. Gather all the ingredients and equipment.

2. Trim chops of excess fat, and brush on both sides with oil; set aside.

3. Combine butter, roasted peppers, white pepper, and salt in a food processor or blender, and process until smooth. Add the parsley and process for one minute, just to incorporate; check and adjust seasoning as needed. Roll butter mixture in parchment paper into a 1″ (2.54 cm) thick cylinder shape, and freeze. When needed, slice into medallions and keep on ice.

4. Season chops with salt and pepper, grill to 140°F (60°C) internal temperature, and allow to rest and carry over to 145°F (63°C) before serving. Serve with roasted red pepper butter.

Veal Cutlets with Mushrooms

INGREDIENTS

	U.S. Standard	Metric
Veal cutlets, trimmed, silverskin removed	4 lbs.	1.8 kg
Vegetable oil	3 oz.	90 ml
Flour	as needed	as needed
Salt	TT	TT
White pepper, ground	TT	TT
Butter, clarified	3 oz.	90 ml
Shallots, peeled and diced brunoise	4 oz.	115 g
Mushrooms, cleaned	12 oz.	340 g
GLAÇAGE		
Hollandaise sauce	8 oz.	240 ml

METHOD OF PREPARATION

1. Gather all the ingredients and equipment.

2. Divide the veal into 2 1/2-oz. (75-g) cutlets, and pound each lightly with a meat mallet.

3. Heat the oil in a sauté pan.

4. Season the flour with salt and pepper. *Dredge* the cutlets in the seasoned flour, and shake off excess.

5. Place the veal into the hot oil, and sauté the veal until it is lightly browned and an internal temperature of 145°F (63°C) is achieved, turning once. Remove the veal, place in a hotel pan, and hold at 140°F (60°C) or higher.

6. Add the butter to the sauté pan, and sauté the shallots.

7. Purée the mushrooms in a robot coupe, then add them to the shallots. Simmer until almost dry, and then season with salt and pepper.

8. Lay out half of the sautéed cutlets on a half sheet pan. Spread the mushroom mixture evenly over the cutlets, and place the other half of the cutlets on top of the mushrooms.

9. Cover the layered cutlets with the hollandaise sauce, and glaze under a salamander or broiler.

10. Serve immediately on a preheated dinner plate.

COOKING TECHNIQUES

Sautéing:

1. Heat the sauté pan to the appropriate temperature.
2. Evenly brown the food product.
3. For a sauce, pour off any excess oil, reheat, and deglaze.

GLOSSARY

Brunoise: 1/8″ (3 mm) dice

Dredge: to coat with flour

NUTRITION

Nutrition Facts

Yield: Serves 10
Serving Size: 5 oz. (140 g)

Amount Per Serving

Calories 480	
Total Fat 39 g	
Sodium 370 mg	
Total Carbohydrate 8 g	
Protein 25 g	

Veal

333

18 Pork

621 B.C.
Eating of pork is prohibited
by Jewish dietary laws.

A.D. 700–1400
Salt pork is a staple food in Europe.

1800–1900
Pork becomes a mainstay of the American diet.

1994
A record 17.5 billion pounds of pork is produced by U.S. farmers.

Pork is meat from pigs, or domesticated swine, under one year old. Although Jewish and Islamic dietary laws have long prohibited the eating of meat from swine, pork was a regular feature on ancient Greek and Roman tables. By the Middle Ages it had became a food staple as salt pork. Columbus first brought pigs to the Americas in 1493. Later, pigs were brought to present-day Florida by Spanish explorers. The British supplied their colonies with pigs, and the colonists returned the favor by sending such products as bacon and ham to England. Today, pork is second only to beef in popularity.

KEY TERMS
trichinosis
processing
curing
brine
smoking

Types of Pork

Several hundred different breeds of pigs exist worldwide. Many of these are market pigs raised for pork. Others supply primarily bacon or lard.

Western Approximately 95% of pigs are raised in the midwestern states and North Carolina. Most pigs that are bred and sold are western breeds. They are typically three to six months old, are corn- and soy-fed, and have flesh that is white, firm, and dry.

Eastern Eastern pork varieties are of lower quality. The flesh is wet and yielding, and it is yellowish in color. Eastern pork is raised primarily for its fat content.

Quality Characteristics, Inspection, and Grading

Pork comes from young pigs between six months and one year of age. It is therefore naturally tender, making aging unnecessary. Quality pork should have firm flesh, tender texture, and an even covering of fat.

Inspection of pork by the USDA/FSIS is mandatory, as it is for other meats. The USDA does not issue a quality grade for pork because quality at the foodservice level is generally consistent. Pork yield grades, which range from 1 to 4, apply to carcasses only. A carcass with an appropriate proportion of fat to edible meat earns Yield Grade 1. Most pork is sold already cut and trimmed and does not carry a yield grade.

Purchasing Pork

As with other meats, specify what is needed when buying pork. Menu, price, and quality considerations will help determine the order. Order specifications should include the product name with its IMPS/NAMP number (see Figure 18-3 on page 344), its weight if a large cut or a roast is needed, the desired thickness of surface fat, and mode of delivery (chilled or frozen). Purchase pork only from USDA-inspected plants, and use NAMP's "The Meat Buyers Guide" as a reference when purchasing pork and other meats.

38
U.S.D
INSP'D & P'S'D

Handling Pork Safely

Many rules and regulations govern the production and slaughter of pigs, protecting both the animals and ultimately the public from disease, infection, and contamination. Proper handling of pork after purchase is essential to avoiding contamination and spoilage, thus safeguarding public health and saving foodservice operations money.

Receiving Pork

Check pork upon receiving to ensure that it is clean and meets specifications. Verify that inspection has taken place. Examine the packaging to make sure that it is intact. Torn or otherwise damaged packaging can be a sign of contamination. Leakage is another danger sign. Check the meat's temperature, color, odor, and texture. At delivery, the temperature of pork, like that of other meats, should be 41°F (5°C) or lower. The meat should have a light pink to reddish color, and the fat should appear white. There should be no perceptible odor. Meat texture should be firm, neither dry nor slick. Reject pork that fails to meet these quality and safety standards or specifications.

Storing Pork

Store pork immediately upon delivery, holding fresh meat at 41°F (5°C) or lower and frozen meat at a temperature that will keep it frozen, usually between 0°F–10°F (⁻18°C–⁻12°C). Use airtight wrapping for both fresh and frozen pork. Packaging for frozen pork should also be moisture-proof to prevent freezer burn. Store raw pork away from other foods, in trays and on the bottom shelves of the storage unit to avoid cross-contamination from drippings. Use fresh pork sausage within one to two days of receiving and fresh pork roasts and chops within two to five days. Frozen pork has a shelf life of three months. Thaw frozen pork in the refrigerator at 41°F (5°C) or lower.

Spoilage Indicators

Spoiled pork may have a dark color, appearing brown, green, or purple or displaying black, green, or white spots. The fat may be sticky or slimy, and the pork may have a sour odor. Damaged packaging may point to spoilage. Discard spoiled pork immediately.

Foodborne Illness Associated with Pork

Improperly handled or prepared pork can transmit various bacterial, viral, and parasitic illnesses. Bacteria in pork can cause salmonellosis, listeriosis, enteritis, and gastroenteritis. As a result of poor hygiene of workers or lack of refrigeration, ham can become the prime breeding ground for staphylococcal food poisoning (enterotoxicosis), another illness caused by bacteria. Pork is also frequently the source of the bacteria responsible for yersiniosis. Poor personal hygiene can contaminate cold cuts containing pork and cause the virus hepatitis A.

Undercooked pork, including pork sausage, can harbor the parasite roundworm, the ingestion of which causes an infection called *trichinosis*. Also linked with undercooked pork is toxoplasmosis, an illness caused by protozoan parasites.

To prevent trichinosis, freeze pork products fewer than 6 inches (15 cm) thick for 12 days at 30°F (–1°C) or for 30 days at 5°F (–15°C), cook pork to a minimum internal temperature of 145°F (63°C), and keep meat grinders and other equipment and utensils used to prepare raw pork clean and sanitary.

■ *See Chapter 4: Food Safety and Chapter 11: Cooking Techniques for more information on handling and preparing pork.*

Processing Pork

Although fresh pork is popular, it actually accounts for only a small amount of the pork consumed in the United States. Processed pork products are more common. About 70% of a pork carcass undergoes some kind of processing. Processing is the act of changing food by artificial means. Curing and smoking are common processing methods for pork, producing bacon, ham, and other food items.

Curing

Curing uses salt, sugar, spices, flavoring, and nitrites to preserve pork. Cured pork holds its flavor longer than fresh pork and resists spoilage better. The curing process also changes the color and flavor of pork. Cured ham, for instance, aquires an appealing pink color from nitrites.

There are several ways to cure pork, with dry curing being the oldest method. Dry curing involves rubbing seasonings such as salt on the pork, covering the meat's entire surface, and storing the meat under refrigeration until it absorbs the seasonings. Other methods of curing include the following:

Pickle curing Pickle curing involves submerging pork in *brine*—a mixture of water, salt, and other seasonings—until the mix completely penetrates the meat.

Injection curing In this method brine is injected directly into the pork to distribute it quickly and evenly.

Sugar curing Sugar curing involves covering pork with brine sweetened with brown sugar or molasses.

Smoking

Another processing method, *smoking* exposes pork to the smoke of fragrant hardwoods, such as hickory, to enhance its flavor and sometimes to cook it. It is common to smoke ham and bacon after curing them. The application of salt or brine helps the smoke enter and spread through the meat.

■ *See Chapter 25: Garde-Manger for more information on curing and smoking.*

Irradiation

Because microorganisms that cause illness often remain on meat during processing, changes have been made in the methods of processing meat. The FDA has approved the use of irradiation to eliminate potentially harmful microorganisms in pork. Irradiation exposes pork to moderate levels of radiation, destroying the cells that can cause spoilage. Radiation does not cook pork, nor does it have an adverse effect on its appearance, taste, or nutritional value. As effective as it is in enhancing food safety, irradiation is not, however, a substitute for proper handling and storage of meat.

Charcuterie

In the Middle Ages, merchants and craftspeople banded together in associations known as guilds to protect and promote their commercial interests. The guilds represented many trades, including those related to the preparation and sale of different foods. One group in the food trade was devoted to the business of charcuterie. Charcuterie was the "cooking of flesh," and more specifically the cooking of pig flesh, or pork. These medieval merchants, however, were more than just "cookers of flesh." Their expertise extended to all kinds of pork products and methods of preserving pork, such as curing. They made hams, bacon, sausages, and pâtés and dealt in pork by-products such as lard. Like other guild merchants, they maintained high standards for the quality of foods prepared and sold, buying only fresh, unspoiled pork from butchers who belonged to guilds. The activities of the guilds were well defined. The charcutiers could not slaughter pigs or cut up the carcasses—that was a butcher's job. Likewise, charcuterie did not include the preparation of meat pastries such as pâté en croûte, or pâté cooked in pastry—that was a baker's specialty. Certain charcutiers got around the latter restriction by foregoing the crust, but assembling the same ingredients, a creation that became known as a terrine. Today, terrines join a vast array of foods that are considered products of charcuterie. Only some use pork as the base.

Primal, Subprimal, and Fabricated Cuts

It is typical to split a pork carcass into halves and to take the primal cuts from each side. See Figure 18-1 and Figure 18-2.

See Figure 18-1 and Figure 18-2.

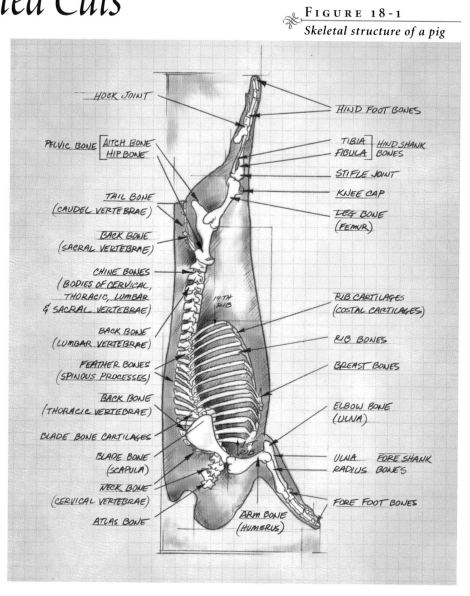

FIGURE 18-1
Skeletal structure of a pig

HOCK JOINT

HIND FOOT BONES

PELVIC BONE · AITCH BONE
HIP BONE

TIBIA · HIND SHANK
FIBULA · BONES

STIFLE JOINT

KNEE CAP

TAIL BONE
(CAUDEL VERTEBRAE)

LEG BONE
(FEMUR)

BACK BONE
(SACRAL VERTEBRAE)

CHINE BONES
(BODIES OF CERVICAL,
THORACIC, LUMBAR
& SACRAL VERTEBRAE)

RIB CARTILAGES
(COSTAL CARTILAGES)

14TH
RIB

BACK BONE
(LUMBAR VERTEBRAE)

RIB BONES

FEATHER BONES
(SPINOUS PROCESSES)

BREAST BONES

BACK BONE
(THORACIC VERTEBRAE)

ELBOW BONE
(ULNA)

BLADE BONE CARTILAGES

1ST
RIB

BLADE BONE
(SCAPULA)

ULNA · FORE SHANK
RADIUS · BONES

NECK BONE
(CERVICAL VERTEBRAE)

FORE FOOT BONES

ATLAS BONE

ARM BONE
(HUMERUS)

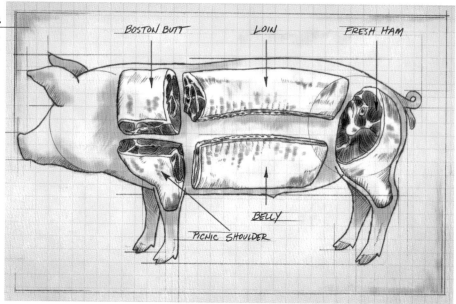

FIGURE 18-2
Location of the primal cuts of a pig

BOSTON BUTT   LOIN   FRESH HAM

PICNIC SHOULDER

BELLY

There are five primal cuts of pork: Boston butt, picnic shoulder, loin, belly, and ham. The loin is the largest cut. See Figure 18-2 on page 338 for the location of each of these primal cuts.

pork shoulder Boston butt

sausage

BOSTON BUTT Just above the shoulder is the square cut known as the Boston butt. This primal cut is high in fat and contains only a small piece of the blade bone. Boston butt is served smoked and boned as a cottage ham and used in sausages, ground pork, and cold cuts.

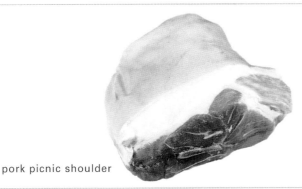

pork picnic shoulder

PICNIC SHOULDER The picnic shoulder, also known as the picnic ham, forms the lower part of the foreleg. It contains the arm and shank bones and makes up about 20% of the carcass weight. As a fairly frequently exercised muscle, the picnic shoulder is one of the toughest cuts of pork and is suited to various cooking methods. The high fat content of shoulder makes it excellent for roasting. Fabrication and further processing produce fresh and smoked picnic hams from this primal cut. Boned and cut into smaller pieces, shoulder meat also benefits from sautéing, braising, or stewing. The foreshank, or shoulder hock, adds rich flavor to soups and stews when simmered or braised.

LOIN The loin includes the entire rib section as well as the loin and part of the sirloin. Containing all the ribs, most of the backbone, and parts of the hipbone and blade bone, the loin makes up about 20% of the carcass weight. Many popular fabricated cuts come from the loin, including loin roasts, loin chops, backribs, and the most tender cut of all, pork tenderloin. Loin cuts lend themselves to a variety of cooking techniques. Dry cooking methods, such as roasting and sautéing, are ideal for pork loin. The whole tenderloin is often served grilled or roasted, or it is cut into medallions for sautéing. Loin chops are extremely popular, the best being the center-cut chops. Loin chops are also sometimes cured and smoked. Boneless pork loin is smoked to make Canadian bacon. Barbecuing is the preferred technique for pork backribs.

Pork

339

pork loin rib chop

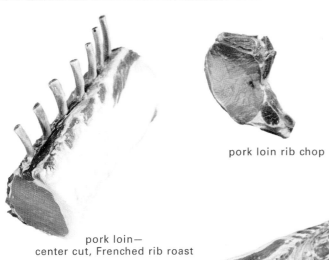

pork loin—
center cut, Frenched rib roast

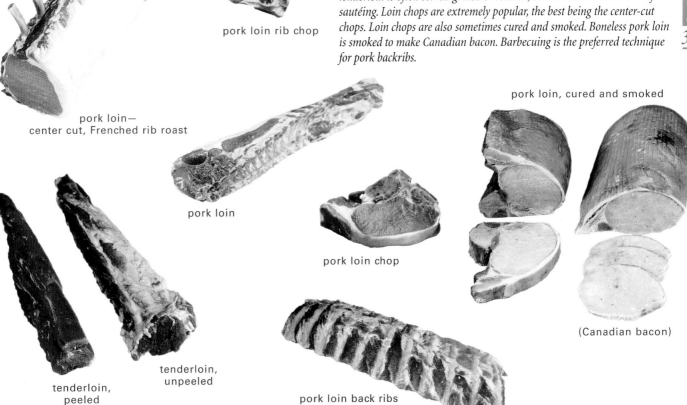

pork loin

pork loin, cured and smoked

pork loin chop

tenderloin,
peeled

tenderloin,
unpeeled

pork loin back ribs

(Canadian bacon)

BELLY *The belly is also a large primal cut, accounting for 16% of the carcass weight. It is very fatty and contains little lean meat. The belly and brisket spareribs are fabricated from the belly. The remaining meat is used for bacon, the market forms of which include slab, layout, shingle, and bulk. Spareribs are available fresh or smoked. The usual method of preparation is simmering followed by baking or grilling. Long, slow cooking in commercial smoking ovens or barbecue pits creates particularly succulent spareribs. Bacon generally undergoes curing and smoking. Pan-frying, griddling, and baking are the customary techniques for cooking bacon.*

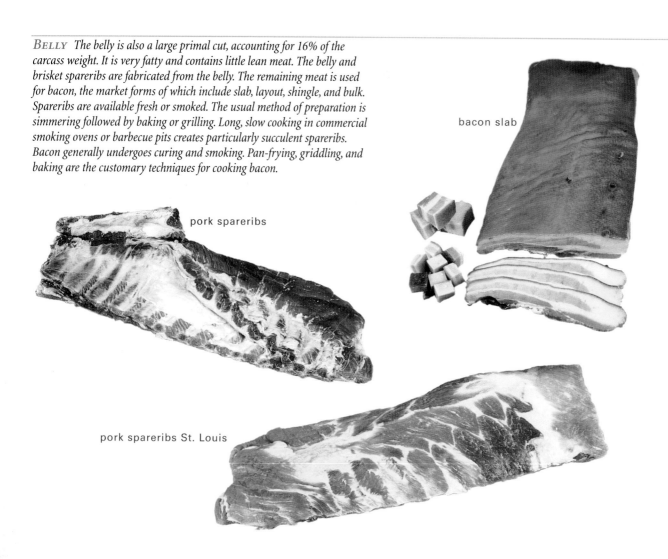

bacon slab

pork spareribs

pork spareribs St. Louis

HAM *The ham is a portion of the pig's hind leg. As part of the leg, it includes large muscles with scant connective tissue. Also containing the aitch, the leg, and the hind shank bones, the ham makes up approximately 24% of the carcass weight. Cured hams, such as prosciutto, and smoked hams, such as Westphalian and Smithfield hams, are popular varieties, and fresh ham makes an excellent roast. Fresh hams can be purchased with the bone in, boneless, or with the shank removed and prepared either by roasting or baking. Braising, stewing, or simmering is appropriate for the shank, or ham hock.*

pork fresh ham

ham, boneless, fully cooked

Variety Meats

Several pork variety meats are available for use in foodservice operations. Like variety meats from other animals, they are suited to many cooking techniques.

Heart
Smaller than veal or beef heart, pork heart adds flavor to stews, casseroles, and meat loaves. Simmering and braising are appropriate cooking techniques for the heart, which is quite tough.

Liver
Pork liver has a much stronger flavor than beef or calf liver. It is an important ingredient in various pâtés and sausages, including pâté de campagne (country-style terrine), liverwurst, and braunschweiger. Pork liver is usually added to pork butt and ground for these uses.

Kidney
Sautéing or broiling is an appropriate technique for cooking kidney. Fried pork kidney is a popular dish in Chinese and other Asian cuisines. Before cooking the kidney, cut it in half lengthwise, and remove the fat and connective tissue.

Fabrication

As with other meats, there are many factors to consider when deciding whether to purchase fabricated cuts of pork or cut them on site. Concerns as broad as quality control and available skills, labor, and facilities will affect the decision.

Portion Control

As with beef and veal, portion control (PC) cuts, either fresh or IQF, should be used when there will be no use for trimmings. Otherwise fabrication skills will be needed.

Butchering (Fabricating) Skills

Most foodservice establishments buy and use pork loin, a primal cut, requiring the use of butchering skills, including trimming and boning a pork loin, and tying a boneless pork roast.

Trimming and Boning a Pork Loin

Trimming and boning pork loin yields several fabricated cuts: the tenderloin, boneless loin, boneless chops, cutlets, and back ribs.

To perform this procedure, follow these steps:

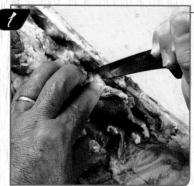

1 Using a boning knife, cut along the hip bone and backbone to loosen the tenderloin.

2 Cut downward along the backbone to free the tenderloin.

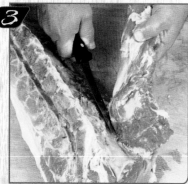

3 Remove the tenderloin.

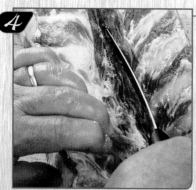

4 Starting at the chuck end of the tenderloin, separate the meat from the ribs, cutting as close to the bones as possible.

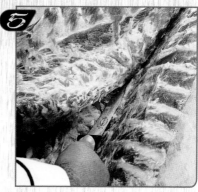

5 Cut under the muscle to release it from the feather bones.

6 Continue cutting along the loin, removing the meat from the backbone.

7 Cut along the hip bone to release the sirloin end.

8 A fully boned tenderloin should look like the one shown here.

Tying a Boneless Pork Roast

A boneless loin of pork is used to make this rolled and stuffed roast. The pork loin is butterflied, flattened, stuffed with spinach and seasonings, and then rolled and tied. This procedure can be used for tying most meats.

To perform this procedure, follow these steps:

1 **Leaving one end of twine attached to the roll, slide the twine under the rolled pork roast.**

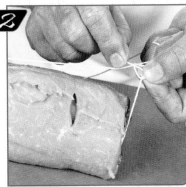

2 **Bring the twine up and over the roast, keeping the twine parallel to the bottom piece, and tie both pieces together. Remember, one section of twine is still attached to the roll.**

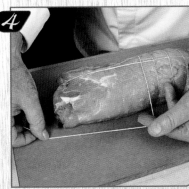

3 **Use your index finger to bring the attached section of twine down to the cutting board, and then wrap it under and around the roast.**

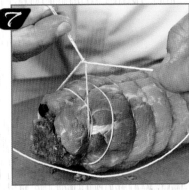

4 **Continue in a similar fashion, using your finger as a guide to measure the distance between the loops.**

5 **Wrap twine twice around the end of the roast.**

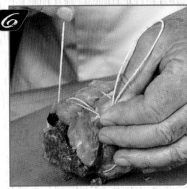

6 **Make a loop with the end attached to the roll to facilitate knotting.**

7 **Tie a knot to secure the roast, and cut the twine close to the knot.**

8 **Properly stuffed, rolled, and trussed pork roast should appear as shown.**

Pork

343

FIGURE 18-3

Cuts of Pork

NAMP NUMBER	NAME	AVERAGE WEIGHT RANGE
401	Leg, fresh ham	17–26 lbs./7.5–12 kg
401A	Leg, fresh ham, short shank	17–26 lbs./7.5–12 kg
401C	Leg, fresh ham, semi-boneless	16–20 lbs./7.5–9 kg
402	Leg, fresh ham, skinned	17–26 lbs./7.5–12 kg
402A	Leg, fresh ham, skinned, short shank	17–26 lbs./7.5–12 kg
402B	Leg, fresh ham, boneless, short shank	8–12 lbs./3.5–5.5 kg
402C	Leg, fresh ham, boneless, trimmed, tied	8–12 lbs./3.5–5.5 kg
402D	Leg, fresh ham, outside	6 lbs. and up/2.5 kg and up
402E	Leg, fresh ham, outside, trimmed, shank removed	6 lbs. and up/2.5 kg and up
402F	Leg, fresh ham, inside	3–5 lbs./1.5–2.5 kg
402G	Leg, fresh ham, TBS, 3-way, boneless	14–18 lbs./6.5–8 kg
403	Shoulder	12–20 lbs./5.5–9 kg
403B	Shoulder, outside	12–22 lbs./5.5–10 kg
403C	Shoulder, inside	4 lbs. and up/2 kg and up
404	Shoulder, skinned	12–20 lbs./5.5–9 kg
405	Shoulder, picnic	6–12 lbs./2.5–5.5 kg
405A	Shoulder, picnic, boneless	4–8 lbs./2–3.5 kg
405B	Shoulder, picnic, cushion, boneless	Amount as specified
406	Shoulder, Boston butt, bone in	4 lbs. and up/2 kg and up
406A	Shoulder, Boston butt, boneless	4 lbs. and up/2 kg and up
406B	Shoulder, Boston butt, boneless, special	4–8 lbs./2–3.5 kg
407	Shoulder, butt, cellar-trimmed, boneless	3–7 lbs/1.5–3 kg
408	Belly	12–18 lbs./5.5–8 kg
409	Belly, skinless	9–13 lbs./4–6 kg
409A	Belly, single, ribbed, skinless	12–18 lbs./5.5–8 kg
409B	Belly, center-cut, skinless	9–13 lbs./4–6 kg
410	Loin, bone in	14–22 lbs./6.5–10 kg
411	Loin, bone in, bladeless	14–22 lbs./6.5–10 kg
412	Loin, bone in, center-cut, 8 ribs	6–10 lbs./2.5–4.5 kg
412A	Loin, bone in, center-cut, 8 ribs, chine bone off	5–9 lbs./2.5–4 kg
412B	Loin, boneless, center-cut, 8 ribs, boneless	4–6 lbs./2–2.5 kg
412C	Loin, bone in, center-cut, 11 ribs	7–11 lbs./3–5 kg
412D	Loin, bone in, center-cut, 11 ribs, chine bone off	6–10 lbs./2.5–4.5 kg
412E	Loin, boneless, center-cut, 11 ribs, boneless	5–7 lbs./2.5–3 kg
413	Loin, boneless	8–12 lbs./3.5–5.5 kg
413A	Loin, boneless, roast	8–12 lbs./3.5–5.5 kg
413B	Loin, boneless, special	8–12 lbs./3.5–5.5 kg
414	Loin, Canadian back	4–6 lbs./2–2.5 kg
415	Tenderloin	1 lb. and up/.5 kg and up
415A	Tenderloin, side muscle off	1 lb. and up/.5 kg and up
416	Spareribs	2 1/2–5 1/2 lbs./1–2.5 kg
416A	Spareribs, St. Louis-style	2–3 lbs./1–1.5 kg
416B	Spareribs, breast bones	1/2–3/4 lb./.25–.5 kg
416C	Spareribs, breast-off	2–6 lbs./1–2.5 kg
416D	Breast bones	Over 1 lb./Over .5 kg
417	Shoulder hocks	3/4 lb. and up/.5 kg and up
417A	Leg, fresh ham, hocks	N/A
418	Trimmings	As requested
420	Pig's feet, front	1/2–3/4 lb./.25–.5 kg
421	Neck bones	Amount as specified
422	Loin, back ribs	1 1/2–2 1/4 lbs./.5–1 kg
423	Loin, country style ribs	3 lbs. and up/1.5 kg and up
435	Diced pork	As requested
435A	Pork for kabobs	As requested
496	Ground pork	As requested

Pork and Clams (Cataplana)

INGREDIENTS

	U.S. Standard	Metric
Pork loin, *boneless, trimmed, cut into 1–1 1/2" (2.54 cm–3.81 cm) cubes*	4 lbs.	1.8 kg
MARINADE		
Dry white wine	24 oz.	720 ml
Garlic, *peeled and minced*	6 cloves	6 cloves
Piri piri *(recipe follows)*	1 Tbsp.	15 ml
Spanish olive oil	as needed	as needed
Bay leaves	2 each	2 each
Spanish paprika	3 Tbsp.	45 ml
Cherrystone clams, *shells scrubbed well*	4 lbs.	1.8 kg
Onions, *peeled, thinly sliced*	1 lb.	454 g
Salt	TT	TT
Black pepper, *freshly ground*	TT	TT

METHOD OF PREPARATION

1. Gather all ingredients and equipment.

2. Place the pork cubes in a mixing bowl. Combine all of the ingredients for the marinade, and pour the mixture over the pork. Marinate in the refrigerator at 41°F (5°C) or lower for at least 2 hours. Strain the pork, reserve the marinade, and pat the meat dry.

3. Heat a thin layer of olive oil in a sauté pan to smoke point, and sear the pork cubes on all sides until well browned. Do not crowd the pan while searing—sear in batches or in 2 pans, if space allows.

4. Remove seared pork pieces to a small rondeau. Deglaze the sauté pan with some of the marinade, and add to the rondeau along with the rest of the marinade, bay leaves, and paprika; heat to a boil.

5. Reduce the heat, and simmer for approximately 45 minutes, until almost all of the liquid has evaporated. Do not allow to totally dry.

6. Add the scrubbed clams to the pot, cover tightly, and place on high heat to steam the clams open. Be careful not to scorch the bottom of the pot in the process. Add 1/2 c. (120 ml) of water or wine, if necessary, to moisten.

7. Meanwhile, heat olive oil in a sauté pan, and sauté the onions until they are translucent.

8. Remove the bay leaves from the pork and clam mixture, and then add the onions. Taste, and season with salt and pepper as needed.

9. Hold at 140°F (60°C) or higher.

10. Serve on a preheated dinner plate; the clams are traditionally served in their shells.

🌀 Searing:

1. Heat the sauté pan until it is very hot.
2. Place food product in the sauté pan.
3. Turn food product until entire surface of food product turns brown.

Sautéing:

1. Heat the sauté pan to the appropriate temperature.
2. Evenly brown the food product.
3. For a sauce, pour off any excess oil, reheat, and deglaze.

Simmering:

1. Place the prepared product in an appropriately sized pot.
2. Bring the product to a boil, and then reduce the heat to allow the product to barely boil.
3. Cook until desired doneness is achieved.

NUTRITION

Nutrition Facts

Yield: Serves 10
Serving Size: 15 oz. (430 g)

Amount Per Serving

Calories 690

Total Fat 39 g

Sodium 470 mg

Total Carbohydrate 11 g

Protein 60 g

Piri Piri

INGREDIENTS

	U.S. Standard	Metric
Piri Piri peppers *(or substitute Thai Peppers)*	3 oz.	85 g
Portuguese or Spanish olive oil	16 oz.	500 ml
Salt	1 tsp.	5 ml
Lemon zest *(wash lemon before zesting)*	1/2 tsp.	2.5 ml
Sherry vinegar	1 oz.	30 ml

METHOD OF PREPARATION

1. Gather all the ingredients and equipment.

2. Wearing gloves, remove tops of peppers. Cut lengthwise, and seed.

3. Place in a small bowl or glass jar along with all other ingredients, mix well, and store in the refrigerator for two weeks before using.

Chef's Notes

Piri Piri is a spicy condiment used in Portugal, as well as the name of the pepper used to make the condiment. It is best made at least two weeks in advance to allow flavors to meld and spiciness to develop.

NUTRITION

Nutrition Facts

Yield: 20 oz. (570 g)
Serving Size: 2 oz. (55 g)

Amount Per Serving

Calories 410

Total Fat 45 g

Sodium 230 mg

Total Carbohydrate 1 g

Protein 0 g

Pork Egg Rolls

INGREDIENTS

	U.S. Standard	Metric
Soy bean oil	1 oz.	30 ml
Ground pork	1 lb.	454 g
Mushrooms, *cleaned and thinly sliced*	4 oz.	115 g
Cabbage, *outer leaves removed, washed, cored, cut* **chiffonade**	1 lb.	454 g
Celery, *washed, trimmed and diced* **brunoise**	1 lb.	454 g
Soy sauce	8 oz.	240 ml
Sake	2 oz.	60 ml
Sugar	1 oz.	30 ml
Bean sprouts, *washed*	1 lb.	454 g
Egg roll wrappers	20 each	20 each
Eggs, *lightly beaten*	2 each	2 each
Frying oil	as needed	as needed
Mustard sauce *(Chinese mustard and water mixed)*	15 oz.	450 ml

METHOD OF PREPARATION

1. Gather all the ingredients and equipment.

2. Add the soy bean oil to a wok over high heat. Add the ground pork, and stir-fry for 2 minutes.

3. Add the mushrooms, cabbage, celery, soy sauce, sake, and sugar. Stir-fry for another minute. Drain the excess liquid, and then transfer the contents to a bowl.

4. Add the bean sprouts to the mixture, and cool in the refrigerator at 41°F (5°C) or lower.

5. To assemble each egg roll, shape approximately 2 oz. (55 g) of filling into a 4″ by 1″ (10 cm by 2.5 cm) cylinder. Place the filling diagonally across the center of a wrapper. Lift the lower triangular flap over the filling. Tuck the point under on the far side, leaving the upper point of the wrapper exposed. Bring each of the two small end flaps, one at a time, up to the top of the enclosed filling. Press the point down firmly. Brush the upper, exposed triangle of the dough with some of the lightly beaten egg. Roll the wrapper into a neat package—the beaten egg will seal the edges and keep the wrapper intact.

6. Place the filled egg rolls on a plate, and cover with a dry kitchen towel.

7. Preheat the fryolator to 350°F (177°C), or heat oil in the wok. Raise temperature to 375°F (191°C), and deep-fry the egg rolls for 3 to 4 minutes, or until golden brown and crisp. Place egg rolls on absorbent paper.

8. Serve two per order with mustard sauce on the side.

COOKING TECHNIQUES

Stir-Frying:
1. Heat the oil in a wok until hot but not smoking.
2. Keep the food in constant motion; use the entire cooking surface.

Deep-Frying:
1. Heat the frying liquid to the proper temperature.
2. Submerge the food product completely.
3. Fry the product until it is cooked throughout.

GLOSSARY

Chiffonade: *ribbons of leafy greens*

Brunoise: *1/8″ (3 mm) dice*

Sake: *rice wine*

NUTRITION

Nutrition Facts

Yield: Serves 10
Serving Size: 2 each (331 g)

Amount Per Serving

Calories 480

Total Fat 20 g

Sodium 1400 mg

Total Carbohydrate 54 g

Protein 19 g

Jerk-Spiced Barbecued Pork Skewers

INGREDIENTS

	U.S. Standard	Metric
Red chili peppers, *minced*	4 each	4 each
Garlic, *peeled, minced*	4 cloves	4 cloves
Scallions, *trimmed, finely chopped*	1 bunch	1 bunch
Salt	1 Tbsp.	15 ml
Cinnamon, *ground*	1 tsp.	5 ml
Nutmeg, *ground*	1 tsp.	5 ml
Allspice, *ground*	1 tsp.	5 ml
Clove, *ground*	1/4 tsp.	1.25 ml
Malt vinegar	1 c.	240 ml
Soy sauce	1 c.	240 ml
Dark rum	1 oz.	30 ml
Pork tenderloin	3 1/2 lbs.	1.6 kg

METHOD OF PREPARATION

1. Gather all the ingredients and equipment.

2. Preheat grill.

3. Soak 10 wooden skewers in water for a minimum of 1 hour.

4. Combine all ingredients except pork in a bowl and mix well.

5. Peel and trim pork tenderloin. Cut into 1-oz. (28-g) medallions, and flatten lightly to 1/2″ (1.27 cm).

6. Place medallions in a hotel pan, and cover with jerk marinade. Allow meat to marinate at least 1 hour.

7. Thread 4–5 medallions on each wooden skewer, patting them dry and being careful to secure pork well to skewer. Spray pork skewers lightly with vegetable oil spray, if desired, to minimize sticking when grilling.

8. Grill pork skewers on both sides until cooked to an internal temperature of 145°F (63°C). Grill to order, or hold at 140°F (60°C) or higher.

Pork Chops Normande Style

INGREDIENTS	U.S. Standard	Metric
Pork chops, trimmed of fat	10, 5 oz. each	10, 140 g each
Oil	2 oz.	55 g
Butter	2 oz.	60 ml
Salt	TT	TT
White pepper, ground	TT	TT
Red apples, washed, cored, and sliced	5 each	5 each
Yellow apples, washed, cored, and sliced	5 each	5 each
Apple cider	4 oz.	120 ml
Heavy cream	2 oz.	60 ml

METHOD OF PREPARATION

1. Gather all the ingredients and equipment.

2. Preheat the oven to 325°F (163°C).

3. In a sauté pan, heat the oil and butter. Season the pork chops with salt and pepper and *sear* until well browned, about 5 to 6 minutes. Remove the chops and reserve the fat.

4. Coat the bottom of a baking dish or roasting pan with some of the reserved fat. Place the apple slices on the bottom and arrange the pork chops on top. Fan the rest of the apple slices on each chop and add the apple cider.

5. Cover and bake in the oven for 20–25 minutes, or until 145°F (63°C) internal (pork) temperature is achieved.

6. Transfer the chops and the apples to a hotel pan, leaving the liquid in the pan. Hold chops covered at 140°F (60°C) or higher.

7. Heat the liquid in the roasting pan to a boil. Temper the cream and add to the pan juices. Simmer until the desired consistency and flavor is achieved. Season, and strain through a chinois into a suitable container, holding at 140°F (60°C) or higher.

8. To serve, arrange the chops on a preheated dinner plate. *Nappé* with sauce, and garnish with the apple slices.

COOKING TECHNIQUES

Searing:
1. Heat the sauté pan until it is very hot.
2. Place food product in the sauté pan.
3. Turn food product until entire surface of food product turns brown.

Baking:
1. Preheat the oven.
2. Place the food product on the appropriate rack.

GLOSSARY

Sear: to brown quickly
Nappé: coated or to coat

NUTRITION

Nutrition Facts

Yield: Serves 10
Serving Size: 5 oz. (140 g)

Amount Per Serving

Calories 700	
Total Fat 23 g	
Sodium 460 mg	
Total Carbohydrate 108 g	
Protein 26 g	

Pork Cutlets with Marsala

INGREDIENTS	U.S. Standard	Metric
Pork tenderloin	4 lbs.	1.8 kg
Olive oil	as needed	as needed
Flour	2 c.	225 g
Salt	TT	TT
Black pepper	TT	TT
Mushrooms, *cleaned and sliced*	1 lb.	454 g
Marsala	10 oz.	300 ml
Chicken stock	3 c.	720 ml
Butter	5 oz.	140 g
Parsley, *washed, squeezed dry, and chopped*	3 Tbsp.	45 g

METHOD OF PREPARATION

1. Gather all the ingredients and equipment.

2. Peel and trim pork tenderloin. To serve 3 slices per person, cut into 30 medallions, about 1 3/4 oz.–2 oz. (49 g–55 g) each.

3. Flatten medallions with a meat mallet to about 1/4″ (6 mm) thick.

4. Heat an appropriate amount of olive oil in a sauté pan.

5. Season the flour with salt and pepper. *Dredge* cutlets in seasoned flour, shaking off the excess.

6. Place cutlets into the hot olive oil. Do not overcrowd the pan. Brown cutlets on both sides. Remove the cutlets when brown, and hold at 140°F (60°C) or higher.

7. Add mushrooms to the sauté pan, and cook until soft.

8. Add the Marsala and reduce by half. Add chicken stock along with any juice that the sautéed cutlets may have dropped, and reduce by half.

9. Shut off the heat, and whisk in the butter; the sauce should thicken slightly. Season with salt, pepper, and parsley.

10. Serve 3 cutlets per serving, and *nappé* with sauce.

11. When cooking individual portions to order, choose an appropriately sized pan, and divide ingredients accordingly.

Roast Loin of Pork

INGREDIENTS

	U.S. Standard	Metric
Pork loin, *bone-in*	10 lbs.	4.5 kg
Salt	TT	TT
White pepper, *freshly ground*	TT	TT
Ginger, *ground*	1/2 tsp.	2.5 g
Garlic, *peeled and sliced into thin slivers*	3 cloves	3 cloves
Vegetable oil	as needed	as needed

MIREPOIX

	U.S. Standard	Metric
Onions, *peeled, diced 1/2" (1.27 cm)*	8 oz.	225 g
Carrots, *washed, peeled, diced 1/2" (1.27 cm)*	6 oz.	170 g
Celery, *washed, trimmed, diced 1/2" (1.27 cm)*	2 stalks	2 stalks
All-purpose flour	2 oz.	55 g
Brown veal stock, *heated to a boil*	1 1/2 pts.	720 ml
Veal demi-glace, *heated to a boil*	1 1/2 pts.	720 ml

METHOD OF PREPARATION

1. Gather all the ingredients and equipment.

2. Bone the meat, removing the loin in one piece (reserve bones); trim, *truss,* and season the meat with salt, pepper, and ginger. Using a paring knife, cut small slits all over the loin, and push the slivers of garlic into the slits.

3. In a roasting pan, heat a thin layer of oil until smoking, sear the loin on all sides, and then remove.

4. Place the mirepoix and reserved bones (cut between each of the bones to separate them) in the roasting pan, and place the seared pork on top. Roast in a preheated 325°F (163°C) oven until an internal temperature of 140°F (60°C) is reached.

5. Remove the pork, hold at 140°F (60°C) or higher, and allow to carry over to 145°F (63°C) before serving.

6. Place the roasting pan on the stove. Skim excess fat, leaving about 2 oz. (60 ml) in the pan. Add the flour to the pan to form a roux, and cook over low heat until golden brown.

7. Add the hot stock and hot demi-glace to the cooked roux in the roasting pan. Heat to a boil. Simmer the gravy, scraping the pan with a wooden spoon to loosen any particles, until proper flavor and consistency is achieved. *Dépouille,* and adjust the seasonings. Strain through a chinois, and hold for service.

COOKING TECHNIQUES

Roasting:
1. Sear the food product, and brown evenly.
2. Elevate the food product in a roasting pan.
3. Determine doneness, and consider carryover cooking.
4. Let the food product rest before carving.

GLOSSARY

Mirepoix: *carrots, onion, celery, and sometimes leeks—rough-cut*

Truss: *tie or secure*

Dépouille: *skim off impurities or grease*

NUTRITION

Nutrition Facts

Yield: Serves 10
Serving Size: 6 oz. (170 g)

Amount Per Serving
Calories 330
Total Fat 14 g
Sodium 850 mg
Total Carbohydrate 15 g
Protein 35 g

Barbecued Beer-Cured Pork Ribs

INGREDIENTS

	U.S. Standard	Metric
Pork spareribs, *portioned to 16 oz. (454 g)*	10 lbs.	4.5 kg
Beer	3 qts.	2.9 l
Water	to cover	to cover
Salt	TT	TT
Black peppercorns, *crushed*	2 Tbsp.	30 g
Garlic, *thinly sliced*	1 head	1 head
Rosemary leaves, *fresh, washed, and coarsely chopped*	1 oz.	28 g
Tarragon leaves, *fresh, washed, and chopped*	1 oz.	28 g
Oregano leaves, *dried*	1 Tbsp.	15 ml
Basil leaves, *dried*	1 Tbsp.	15 ml
Honey	10 oz.	300 ml
Barbecue sauce	2 qts.	1.9 l
Herb sprigs, *fresh*	to garnish	to garnish

METHOD OF PREPARATION

1. Gather all the ingredients and equipment.

2. Place the spareribs in a large pot, and then add all of the remaining ingredients except the honey and barbecue sauce.

3. Bring the liquid to a boil, reduce the heat, and simmer until the ribs are *fork-tender.* This will take approximately 1 1/2 hours.

4. When the ribs are tender, remove them from the liquid, and brush with honey on both sides while they are hot.

5. If possible, allow the ribs to cool to room temperature.

6. Grill or broil the ribs, brushing generously with barbecue sauce. Hold at 140°F (60°C) or higher.

7. Cut in portions, and serve on preheated dinner plates. Garnish with additional fresh herbs.

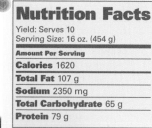

Nutrition Facts
Yield: Serves 10
Serving Size: 16 oz. (454 g)

Amount Per Serving

Calories 1620

Total Fat 107 g

Sodium 2350 mg

Total Carbohydrate 65 g

Protein 79 g

Baked Ham with Spiced Fennel-Pear Chutney

INGREDIENTS

	U.S. Standard	Metric
Ham, smoked, shankless, and trimmed	3–3.5 lbs.	1.5 kg
Cloves, whole	as needed	as needed
Mustard powder	1 oz.	28 g
Honey	7 oz.	210 ml
Brown sugar	4 oz.	115 g
Fennel seed, whole, lightly toasted, and then ground	2 tsp., whole	10 ml
White pepper, ground	1/2 tsp.	2.5 ml
Butter, clarified	2 oz.	60 ml
Onion, peeled, cut julienne	12 oz.	340 g
Fennel bulb, trimmed, cut julienne	1 1/2 lbs.	680 g
Bosc pears, ripe but firm, peeled, diced parmentier, rinsed with lemon juice to hold	1 1/2 lbs.	680 g
Raisins	4 oz.	115 g
White wine, dry	6 oz.	180 ml
Cider vinegar	4 oz.	120 ml
Brown sugar	4 oz.	115 g
Star anise	2 each	2 each
Cloves, ground	1/4 tsp.	1.25 ml
Salt	TT	TT
White pepper, ground	TT	TT

METHOD OF PREPARATION

1. Gather all the ingredients and equipment.
2. Score the fat on the surface of the ham into diamond shapes. Place a whole clove at the center of each diamond.
3. Mix the mustard, honey, brown sugar, 1 tsp. (5 ml) of the ground fennel seed (save the rest for the chutney), and pepper in a mixing bowl.
4. Place the ham on a rack in a roasting pan. Bake in a 350°F (177°C) oven. While baking, brush the honey glaze on the ham frequently. Bake until the ham is golden brown and has reached an internal temperature of 155°F (68°C), approximately 1 hour.
5. Remove the ham from the oven, hold, and let rest at 140°F (60°C) for 30 minutes before carving.
6. Meanwhile, prepare the chutney. Heat the butter in a large sauté pan. Add the onion, and sauté until translucent.
7. Add the fennel bulb, reduce the heat to low, and slowly cook until the onion and fennel are caramelized; stir often. This will take at least an hour. The vegetables need to caramelize, not merely brown; they will be very soft and golden when ready.
8. Add the pears, and continue to cook for about 15 more minutes, or until pears are starting to soften.
9. Add the raisins, white wine, vinegar, brown sugar, star anise, clove, and the rest of the ground fennel seed; bring to a boil, turn down to a simmer, and continue to simmer gently, stirring often, until all liquid has reduced to a thick, syrupy consistency and the pears are very tender and beginning to break down; this may take another hour. Remove the star anise.
10. Season to taste with salt and pepper. Hold at 140°F (60°C) or higher in a bain-marie for service.
11. Slice the ham, and serve 4-oz. (115-g) portions of ham on a preheated dinner plate with 3 oz. (85 g) of warm chutney.

COOKING TECHNIQUES

Baking:
1. Preheat the oven.
2. Place the food product on the appropriate rack.

Sautéing:
1. Heat the sauté pan to the appropriate temperature.
2. Evenly brown the food product.
3. For a sauce, pour off any excess oil, reheat, and deglaze.

Simmering:
1. Place the prepared product in an appropriately sized pot.
2. Bring the product to a boil, and then reduce the heat to allow the product to barely boil.
3. Cook until desired doneness is achieved.

GLOSSARY

Parmentier: 1/2" (1.27 cm) dice

NUTRITION

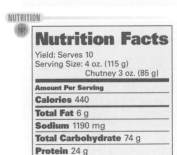

Nutrition Facts

Yield: Serves 10
Serving Size: 4 oz. (115 g)
Chutney 3 oz. (85 g)

Amount Per Serving

Calories 440

Total Fat 6 g

Sodium 1190 mg

Total Carbohydrate 74 g

Protein 24 g

19 Lamb

Although now infrequently prepared at home, lamb remains a popular choice of America dining out. In ancient societies lamb were important sacrificial animals. Later, people raised sheep primarily for their wool. Brought by Coronado in 1540, sheep grazed on Spanish lands in present-day Florida, Texas, New Mexico, California, and Arizona, as well as on farms in the American British colonies. Besides supplying early settler with wool, sheep provided food in the form of milk and mutton. More tender than mutton, lamb has a unique, mild flavor that welcomes sauces and other accompaniments.

A.D. 1279
Chinese incorporate lamb in their diet.

1540
Spanish explorer Coronado brings sheep to New Spain.

1600s
Sheep are raised for wool, milk, and mutton in America's British colonies.

1832
Cotswold sheep, raised since Roman times, are brought to the United States.

1993
Average per capita U.S. lamb consumption is 1.3 pounds a year.

KEY TERMS
mutton
yearling
baby lamb
genuine lamb
spring lamb
bracelet

Sheep Terminology

A lamb is a young animal belonging to the genus Ovis, which includes both domesticated and wild sheep.

There are several terms for the meat of ovine animals. Each indicates a specific level of muscle and bone development.

Lamb Lamb is meat from sheep under one year of age.

Mutton *Mutton* is meat from mature sheep. Sheep reach maturity at one year.

Yearling A *yearling* is a sheep between 12 and 20 months old. It produces yearling mutton.

Types of Lamb

Age at the time of slaughter and period of production determine various types of lamb.

Baby lamb The term *baby lamb* refers to meat from lamb sent to market before weaning, usually between 6 and 10 weeks old. Another term for baby lamb is hothouse lamb.

Genuine lamb *Genuine lamb* is meat from a sheep less than one year old.

Spring lamb *Spring lamb* is 3 to 5 months old and is produced between March and October. Spring lamb is milk-fed.

Although American demand for lamb is not great, domestic lamb production cannot meet U.S. consumer demands. Imported lamb, primarily from New Zealand, dominates the market. In general, lamb produced outside the country has a more pronounced flavor because lamb elsewhere are usually free-range, rather than grain-fed, as in the United States.

Lamb

Quality Characteristics, Inspection, and Grading

Lamb is tender but has a firm, fine texture. Its color ranges from light to darker red, and it should exhibit good marbling. Like beef, lamb can be aged for additional tenderizing. Aging also helps develop the flavor of lamb.

The USDA/FSIS requires inspection of lamb, as for other meats. USDA quality grades for lamb are Prime, Choice, Good, Utility, and Cull. With more marbling and external fat than the other grades, Prime lamb is more tender and flavorful. Ground or processed lamb usually carries a USDA Utility or Cull grade. Yield grades for lamb range from Yield Grade 1 to Yield Grade 5. Like beef, lamb may receive only a quality grade, only a yield grade, or both.

Purchasing Lamb

Various factors influence purchasing: the menu, cooking methods, price, and quality. When ordering lamb, specify the cut name with its IMPS/NAMP number (see Figure 19-3 on page 364), quality and/or yield grade, surface fat thickness, and state of refrigeration upon delivery (chilled or frozen). Purchase lamb only from government-inspected plants, and refer to NAMP's "The Meat Buyers Guide" for further information on purchasing lamb.

French Pré-Salé Lamb

In the opinion of many food connoisseurs, the best lamb in the world comes from the meadows of Brittany and Normandy in France. There, in the shadow of Mont St. Michel, lambs feed on the salty grass of the coastal marshes. Their diet gives the meat a distinctive delicate flavor and earns them the name pré-salé—"salty fields" in French. Pré-salé lamb is a rare and thus expensive variety. Some farmers in Canada have begun herding lambs on the salty marshland of Île Verte, an island in the St. Lawrence River. Locally produced pré-salé lamb now appears on the menus of the finest restaurants in Quebec City and Montreal, however both farmers and restauranteurs have an interest in limiting the production of pré-salé lambs. If these specialty lambs become too widely available, quality and authenticity may suffer.

Handling Lamb Safely

Although foodservice establishments rely on USDA inspection standards as a guarantee of lamb's fitness for consumption after slaughter, it is important to observe quality and safety standards for meat purchased and handled.

Receiving Lamb

On receiving, inspect lamb carefully to make sure it is safe and to the quality specified. Verify that the meat has passed government inspection. Packaging should be intact, without tears or other damage that could cause contamination. Check the meat's temperature, color, odor, and texture. Lamb, like other meats, should be 41°F (5°C) or lower at delivery. The meat should have a light red color, and the fat should be white. There should not be an unpleasant odor. The meat should not feel slimy or dry but should have a firm texture.

Storing Lamb

Follow the usual meat storage guidelines, but be aware that fresh lamb spoils quickly even when kept chilled. Immediately after delivery, store fresh lamb at 41°F (5°C) or lower. Freeze or keep lamb frozen between 0°F–10°F (⁻18°C–⁻12°C) or lower. Use airtight wrapping for fresh lamb and both airtight and moisture-proof packaging for frozen lamb to prevent freezer burn. Always store raw lamb apart from other foods, using trays and the bottom shelves of storage units to prevent cross-contamination. Use fresh lamb within three to five days, unless purchased in vacuum packaging, which allows lamb to be stored for longer periods of time. Keep frozen lamb no longer than six to nine months for best quality. Thaw frozen lamb in the refrigerator at 41°F (5°C) or lower.

Spoilage Indicators

Spoiled lamb may look brown instead of pink or light red. The surface of the lean meat may appear white. The fat may be soft and yellow in color, and the meat may be dry or slimy to the touch. The odor of the meat may seem off. Damaged packaging is often a sign of spoilage.

Foodborne Illness Associated with Lamb

Improperly handled or prepared lamb can carry a variety of bacteria and parasites that cause illnesses. Bacteria in lamb, as in other meats, can cause salmonellosis, listeriosis, and gastroenteritis.

See Chapter 4: Food Safety or Chapter 11: Cooking Techniques for more information on handling and preparing lamb safely.

Primal, Subprimal, and Fabricated Cuts

Like veal, a lamb carcass is divided between the ribs into the foresaddle and the hindsaddle. The foresaddle yields three primal cuts, and the hindsaddle produces two. Each primal cut contains both halves, or sides, of the carcass. See Figure 19-1 and Figure 19-2.

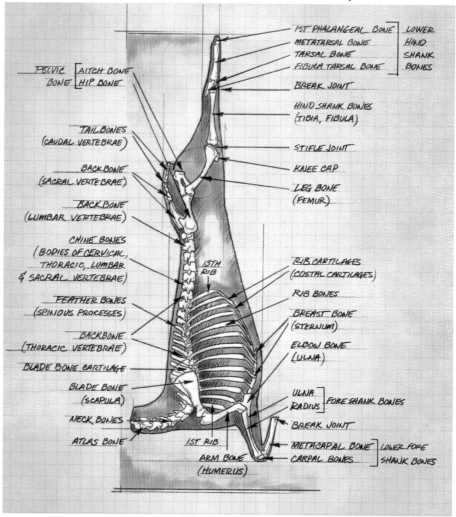

FIGURE 19-1
Skeletal structure of lamb

PELVIC BONE [AITCH BONE / HIP BONE]

TAIL BONES (CAUDAL VERTEBRAE)

BACKBONE (SACRAL VERTEBRAE)

BACKBONE (LUMBAR VERTEBRAE)

CHINE BONES (BODIES OF CERVICAL, THORACIC, LUMBAR & SACRAL VERTEBRAE)

FEATHER BONES (SPINOUS PROCESSES)

BACKBONE (THORACIC VERTEBRAE)

BLADE BONE CARTILAGE

BLADE BONE (SCAPULA)

NECK BONES

ATLAS BONE

13TH RIB

1ST RIB

ARM BONE (HUMERUS)

1ST PHALANGEAL BONE / METATARSAL BONE / TARSAL BONE / FIBULA TARSAL BONE [LOWER HIND SHANK BONES]

BREAK JOINT

HIND SHANK BONES (TIBIA, FIBULA)

STIFLE JOINT

KNEE CAP

LEG BONE (FEMUR)

RIB CARTILAGES (COSTAL CARTILAGES)

RIB BONES

BREAST BONE (STERNUM)

ELBOW BONE (ULNA)

ULNA / RADIUS [FORE SHANK BONES]

BREAK JOINT

METACAPAL BONE / CARPAL BONES [LOWER FORE SHANK BONES]

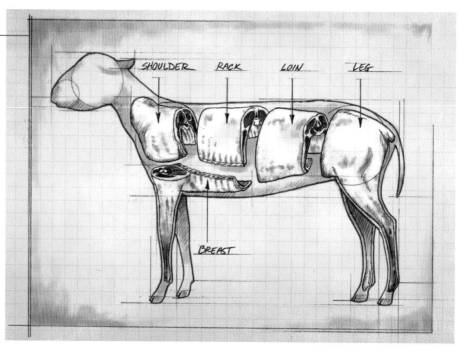

FIGURE 19-2
Location of primal cuts of lamb

SHOULDER   RACK   LOIN   LEG

BREAST

The three primal cuts from the foresaddle are the shoulder (chuck), the breast, and the primal rib, or rack. The foreshank is a by-product of the foresaddle, therefore it is not considered a primal cut. See Figure 19-2 on page 358.

SHOULDER (CHUCK) *The shoulder is the largest primal lamb cut, making up 36% of the carcass weight. In addition to four ribs, it contains the arm, blade, and neck bones and muscles that extend in cross directions. This primal cut's numerous bones and muscle groups make it difficult to divide the shoulder into fabricated cuts. Although roasts and chops are cut from the shoulder for roasting, grilling, or braising, most shoulder meat is ground for patties or cubed for stewing.*

lamb shoulder with arm
and blade chops

shoulder chuck arm

BREAST *The primal breast cut includes the breast and rib. The breast can be stuffed and roasted, with or without the bone. It is more common to separate the rib tips from the breast and serve them Denver style, an alternative to pork ribs.*

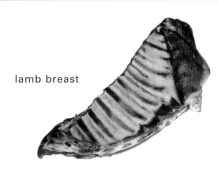

lamb breast

PRIMAL RIB (RACK) *Located between the shoulder and the loin, the primal rib, or rack, consists of eight ribs on each side and part of the backbone. The eye muscle of the rack is very tender. Split in half, the rack is suited to roasting, broiling, or grilling. A crown roast—two rib roasts sewn together in a circle that resembles a crown with the cleaned ribs upright—is a festive presentation for a roasted rack. It is also possible to cut a split rack into single or double rib chops.*

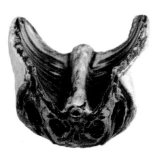

lamb hotel rack—view
from shoulder end

lamb rack—Frenched with rib chops

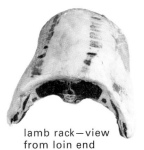

lamb rack—view
from loin end

FORESHANK *The foreshank is purchased as a by-product of the foresaddle. The shank is quite meaty and may be served as an entrée when braised. It also lends flavor to broths.*

foreshank attached to chuck

Lamb

359

The hindsaddle consists of two primal cuts: the loin and the leg. The hindshank is a by-product, rather than a primal cut, of the hindsaddle. See Figure 19-2 on page 358.

LOIN The loin is the primal cut between the rib and the leg. It accounts for about 13% of the carcass weight and includes one rib, a portion of the backbone, the loin-eye muscle, the tenderloin, and the flank. Dry methods such as roasting, grilling, or broiling are appropriate for loin cuts, which, with the exception of the flank, are very tender. Fabricated cuts include boneless or bone-in roasts and chops, medallions, and noisettes from the loin eye.

lamb loin— view from leg end

loin chops

lamb loin— view from rack end

LEG A large primal cut, the leg accounts for 34% of the carcass weight. It contains the tail, hip, aitch, and round, as well as part of the backbone. Although quite tender, the leg is not often cooked whole but split into two legs. With the bone in, a roasted leg of lamb may be the highlight of a buffet. When braised with a selection of vegetables, the bone-in leg is flavorful. Tender steaks come from the sirloin end of the bone-in leg. The boneless leg is suited to roasting, too, and also yields cutlets.

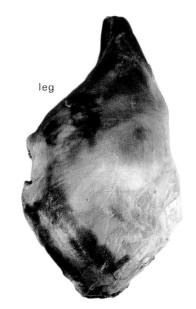

leg

lamb for stewing

HINDSHANK The hindshank is considered a by-product of the hindsaddle rather than a primal or subprimal cut. The shank portion of the leg is braised or commonly diced for use in stews or ground for patties.

hindshank

Variety Meats

Lamb variety meats are a common feature of dishes in Middle Eastern, Turkish, and Greek cuisine, which make heavy use of lamb. Different cooking methods may be used to prepare lamb variety meats.

Heart

Smaller than veal heart, lamb's heart is quite tender and lends itself to dry cooking. Sautéing or grilling is an appropriate cooking method. Avoid overcooking, which makes heart tough. Moist and combination methods are also good choices that further tenderize lamb's heart.

Liver

Although not as flavorful as calf's liver, lamb's liver has good taste and texture. It should be cooked to order, using a dry method such as sautéing or broiling. Lamb's liver becomes dry if overcooked. Basting or dredging keep lamb's liver tender and moist.

Kidney

The rich flavor and tenderness of lamb's kidneys make them a popular specialty item. Sautéing and broiling are the favored techniques for this variety meat.

Tongue

Lamb's tongue is tough muscle that requires moist or combination cooking to become palatable. Simmering makes lamb's tongue tender and increases its flavor. Braising is also appropriate. Lamb's tongue is a feature of various dishes in ethnic cuisines. It can be sliced and served hot or cold.

Fabrication

The small size of the lamb carcass facilitates handling, and foodservice establishments may choose to purchase the whole carcass or one of its large forms. The foresaddle, the hindsaddle, the back, and the bracelet are all available for purchase. The bracelet is the primal rack with the adjoining breast pieces. Uses for cuts and trimmings, as well as available skills, labor, and facilities, affect the decision to make fabricated cuts in-house from larger forms. Foodservice operations may elect to purchase portion control (PC) cuts for convenience.

Butchering (Fabricating) Skills

Fabrication skills are required when purchasing a whole lamb carcass or some of its larger forms or primal cuts. Basic lamb butchering procedures include Frenching a rack of lamb and trimming and boning a leg of lamb.

Frenching a Rack of Lamb

Frenching involves cutting away excess fat from the eye muscle and trimming meat and connective tissue from the ribs on a rack or chops.

To do this, follow these steps:

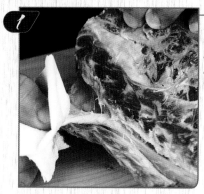

1 Loosen the fat cap slightly, and remove the back strap from the rack.

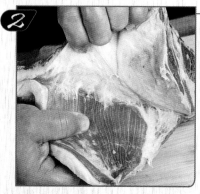

2 Pull away the fat cap.

3 Using a boning knife, remove the blade bone.

4 Lay the rack down with the bones facing up. Insert the boning knife through the meat in between the bones. Cut the membrane covering the rib bones to expose them.

5 Turn the rack over, fat cap side up, and cut across the rack perpendicular to the bones using the insert marks as a guide.

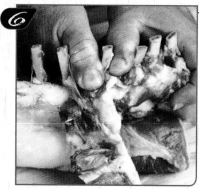

6 Push the cut meat and fat away from the ribs. Scrape any remaining meat from the bones using the back of the knife blade.

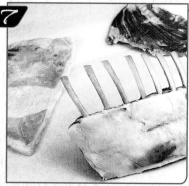

7 A fully Frenched lamb rack with rib chops should appear like the one shown here.

Boning a Leg of Lamb

After a leg of lamb has been trimmed and boned, it is ideal for roasting.

To remove the bone, follow these steps:

1 Loosen the tenderloin section from the leg. Using a boning knife, cut along the pelvic bone. Insert a steel into the hole of the pelvic bone to steady the leg and make cutting easier.

2 Continue gliding the blade of the knife along the pelvic bone to remove it.

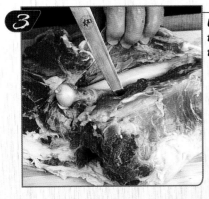

3 Using the tip of the knife, expose the leg bone.

4 Remove the hindshank at the joint.

5 Remove the leg bone.

6 A boned, rolled, and tied, or BRT, leg of lamb should look like the one shown here.

Lamb

363

FIGURE 19-3

Cuts of Lamb

NAMP NUMBER	NAME	AVERAGE WEIGHT RANGE
204	Rack	5–9 lbs./2.5–4 kg
204A	Rack, roast-ready, single	2–4 lbs./1–2 kg
204B	Rack, roast-ready	2–4 lbs./1–2 kg
204C	Rack, roast-ready, single, Frenched	1 1/2–3 1/2 lbs./.5–1.5 kg
204E	Rack, ribeye roll	1–3 lbs./.5–1.5 kg
206	Shoulder	19–27 lbs./8.5–12.5 kg
207	Shoulder, square-cut	13–19 lbs./6–8.5 kg
207A	Shoulder, outside	3–5 lbs./1.5–2.5 kg
208	Shoulder, square-cut, boneless	6–8 lbs./2.5–3.5 kg
208A	Shoulder, outside, boneless	2–5 lbs./1–2.5 kg
208B	Shoulder, arm out, boneless	3–6 lbs./1.5–2.5 kg
208C	Shoulder, inside roll, boneless	1–4 lbs./.5–2 kg
209	Breast	7–11 lbs./3–5 kg
209A	Ribs, Denver-style	5–9 lbs./2.5–4 kg
209B	Shoulder, ribs	1–4 lbs./.5–2 kg
210	Foreshank	2–3 lbs./1–1.5 kg
229A	Hindsaddle, long cut, trimmed	29–41 lbs./13–18.5 kg
230	Hindsaddle	27–38 lbs./12.5–17.5 kg
231	Loin	8–12 lbs./3.5–5.5 kg
232	Loin, trimmed	5–9 lbs./2.5–4 kg
232A	Loin, short-cut, trimmed	3–7 lbs./1.5–3 kg
232B	Loin, double, boneless, tied	2–5 lbs./1–2.5 kg
232D	Loin, short tenderloin	1/2–2 lbs./.25–1 kg
233	Leg	19–27 lbs./8.5–12.5 kg
233A	Leg, trotter off	9–14 lbs./4–6.5 kg
233B	Leg, boneless, tied	8–13 lbs./3.5–6 kg
233C	Leg, trotter off, partially boneless	4–7 lbs./2–3 kg
233E	Leg, steamship, 3/4, aitch bone removed	1 lb. and up/.5 kg and up
233F	Leg, hindshank	1 lb. and up/.5 kg and up
234	Leg, boneless	6–9 lbs./2.5–4 kg
234A	Leg, shank off, single, partially boneless	8–11 lbs./3.5–5 kg
234D	Leg, outside, boneless	8–11 lbs./3.5–5 kg
234E	Leg, inside, boneless	1–2 lbs./.5–1 kg
234F	Leg, sirloin tip, boneless	1/2–3 lbs./.25–1.5 kg
234G	Sirloin, boneless	2–4 lbs./1–2 kg
235	Back	12–16 lbs./5.5–7.5 kg
236	Back, trimmed	11–15 lbs./5–7 kg
238	Hindsaddle, long-cut trimmed	29–41 lbs./13–18.5 kg
240	Leg, three-quarters single	7–11 lbs./3–5 kg
241	Leg, steamship	6–10 lbs./2.5–4.5 kg
245	Sirloin, boneless	2–4 lbs./1–2 kg
246	Tenderloin	1/2–3 lbs./.25–1.5 kg
295	Lamb for stewing	As requested
295A	Lamb for kabobs	As requested
296	Ground lamb	As requested

Roast Rack of Lamb with Dijon Mustard Crust

INGREDIENTS	U.S. Standard	Metric
Oil	as needed	as needed
Rack of lamb, trimmed, frenched	5 lbs.	2.3 kg
Garlic, peeled, mashed to a purée	1 head	1 head
Parsley, washed, squeezed dry, chopped fine	1 oz.	28 g
Bread crumbs	10 oz.	285 g
Olive oil	1 1/2 oz.	45 ml
Dijon mustard	6 oz.	180 ml
Salt	TT	TT
Black pepper, ground	TT	TT

METHOD OF PREPARATION

1. Gather all the ingredients and equipment.

2. Preheat oven to 450°F (232°C).

3. Heat to smoking a thin layer of oil in a heavy-bottomed sauté pan, and then sear the racks until well browned on all sides. Do not crowd the pan; sear in batches if necessary. Place the lamb, meat side up, on a rack in a roasting pan.

4. Combine the garlic, parsley, bread crumbs, and olive oil in a small bowl. Mix well to combine.

5. Place the lamb in the preheated oven for 5 minutes. Remove from the oven and spread the mustard over the lamb. Season with salt and pepper, sprinkle the bread crumb mixture over the mustard, and press it down with a spoon or a spatula to make the crumbs adhere.

6. Return the lamb to the oven, and cook to an internal temperature of 140°F (60°C) for approximately 5–10 minutes more, depending on rack sizes. Hold at 140°F (60°C) or higher for at least 10 minutes to allow it to rest, and carry over to a final internal temperature of 145°F (63°C) before carving.

7. Serve 2 or 3 chops per portion (depending on the rack sizes) on a preheated dinner plate.

Chef's Notes

Fried parsley is recommended as a garnish.

COOKING TECHNIQUES

Roasting:

1. Sear the food product, and brown evenly.
2. Elevate the food product in a roasting pan.
3. Determine doneness, and consider carryover cooking.
4. Let the food product rest before carving.

NUTRITION

Nutrition Facts

Yield: Serves 10
Serving Size: 7 oz. (205 g)

Amount Per Serving

Calories 620

Total Fat 42 g

Sodium 820 mg

Total Carbohydrate 24 g

Protein 35 g

Lamb

Grilled Lamb Chops with Tomatoes and Olives

INGREDIENTS

	U.S. Standard	Metric
Lamb rib chops, one bone each	40 each	40 each
Olive oil	3 Tbsp.	45 ml
Salt	TT	TT
Black pepper, freshly ground	TT	TT
Tomatoes, ripe, concassé	2 lbs.	910 g
Garlic, peeled, finely chopped	4 cloves	4 cloves
Shallot, peeled, finely chopped	2 Tbsp.	30 g
Crushed red pepper	pinch	pinch
Olive oil, extra virgin	1 Tbsp.	15 ml
Oregano, fresh, washed, leaves stripped, chopped	1 Tbsp.	15 ml
Olives, Gaeta or Kalamata, pitted and chopped	15 each	15 each
Parsley, washed, squeezed dry, chopped	2 Tbsp.	30 ml

METHOD OF PREPARATION

1. Gather all the ingredients and equipment.

2. Preheat the grill.

3. Trim chops of excess fat, brush with the olive oil, and season with salt and pepper. Store at 41°F (5°C) or lower until needed for service.

4. Place the tomatoes concassé in a small bowl.

5. Sauté the chopped garlic, shallots, and crushed red pepper in the extra virgin olive oil until just soft. Do not allow garlic or shallots to brown. Add this mixture to the tomato concassé, and toss to combine.

6. Add the oregano and olives to the concassé mixture, and toss.

7. Taste, and season with salt as needed. Hold briefly at room temperature until service.

8. Grill the lamb chops on the preheated grill to an internal temperature of 140°F (60°C). Hold for 5 minutes at 140°F (60°C) to allow meat to rest and carry over to a final internal temperature of 145°F (63°C) before serving.

9. Serve 4 chops per portion on a preheated dinner plate along with 3–4 Tbsp. (45–60 g) of the tomato and olive sauce. Garnish with chopped parsley.

COOKING TECHNIQUES

Sautéing:
1. Heat the sauté pan to the appropriate temperature.
2. Evenly brown the food product.
3. For a sauce, pour off any excess oil, reheat, and deglaze.

Grilling/Broiling:
1. Clean and heat the grill or broiler.
2. To prevent sticking, brush the food product with oil.

GLOSSARY

Concassé: peeled, seeded, and roughly chopped

NUTRITION

Nutrition Facts

Yield: Serves 10
Serving Size: 10 oz. (285 g)

Amount Per Serving

Calories 900

Total Fat 75 g

Sodium 300 mg

Total Carbohydrate 5 g

Protein 51 g

Shepherd's Pie

INGREDIENTS

	U.S. Standard	Metric
DUCHESS POTATOES		
Potatoes, *peeled, washed, 1/2"* (1.27 cm) *rough cut*	2 1/2 lbs.	1.1 kg
Salt	TT	TT
Egg yolks	3 each	3 each
White pepper, *ground*	TT	TT
Nutmeg, *ground*	pinch	pinch
Oil	2 oz.	60 ml
Onions, *peeled, diced brunoise*	6 oz.	170 g
Ground lamb	2 1/2 lbs.	1.1 kg
Tomato purée	3 oz.	90 ml
Rosemary, *fresh, chopped*	1/2 tsp.	2.5 ml
Lamb demi-glace	8 oz.	240 ml
Black pepper, *ground*	TT	TT
Corn kernels	12 oz.	340 g
Eggs, *whole, lightly beaten*	1 each	1 each

METHOD OF PREPARATION

1. Gather all the ingredients and equipment.

2. Preheat the oven to 350°F (177°C).

3. Prepare the duchess potatoes. Place the potatoes in an appropriately sized pot; cover with cold, salted water; bring to a boil; and turn down to a simmer. Simmer until tender. Drain and dry on stove top.

4. Pass the potatoes through a food mill or ricer into a large bowl. Allow to cool slightly.

5. Temper the egg yolks into the potatoes, and season with salt, white pepper, and nutmeg. Spread a 1/3" (8 mm) thick layer of the duchess potatoes on the bottom of a hotel pan, and let sit for 15 minutes. Set the rest of the potatoes aside for the top of the pie.

6. Heat the oil in a sauté pan. Add onions, and sauté until translucent.

7. Add the ground lamb to the sauté pan, and cook until well browned. Drain off the excess fat. Add the tomato purée, rosemary, and demi-glace. Bring to a boil, turn down to a simmer, and simmer gently for 10–15 minutes until proper flavor is achieved. Taste, and season with salt and pepper as needed.

8. Place half of the sautéed meat mixture on top of the potatoes. Top with the corn kernels and then the rest of the meat.

9. Pipe the rest of the potatoes on top of the meat using a star tube with a pastry bag.

10. Brush the top of the potatoes with the beaten egg and bake to an internal temperature of 155°F (68°C) for about 30–45 minutes; top should be golden brown. Hold at 140°F (60°C) or higher.

11. Serve on preheated dinner plates.

Irish Lamb Stew

INGREDIENTS

	U.S. Standard	Metric
Lamb shanks, trimmed	10 each	10 each
Lamb stock, white	2 qts.	1.9 l
Leeks, split, washed, sliced 1/2" (1.27 cm)	1 lb.	254 g
Bouquet garni	1 each	1 each
Potatoes, cut tourné château	4 lbs.	1.8 kg
Carrots, cut tourné château	2 lbs.	910 g
Rutabaga, cut tourné château	2 lbs.	910 g
Salt	TT	TT
Black pepper, freshly ground	TT	TT
Parsley, washed, squeezed dry, and chopped	1 oz.	28 g
Irish soda bread (optional)	1 loaf	1 loaf

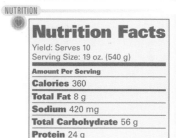
METHOD OF PREPARATION

1. Gather all the ingredients and equipment.

2. Place the lamb shanks, stock, leeks, and bouquet garni in a suitable rondeau, bring to a boil, turn to a simmer, cover, and allow to simmer gently until lamb is almost done. Or, bring ingredients to a boil, cover tightly, and place in a preheated 325°F–350°F (163°C–177°C) oven.

3. Cook the potatoes, carrots, and rutabaga separately until crisp/tender; shock, drain, and set aside.

4. When shanks are almost finished, remove them to a hotel pan, and hold briefly. Remove the bouquet garni from the stewing liquid and discard. Dépouille the liquid, and then purée in a blender or food processor until smooth. Strain if necessary. Taste, and season with salt and pepper as needed.

5. Place the lamb shanks and parcooked vegetables back into the rondeau, and add the sauce. Bring to a boil, turn down to a simmer, and simmer gently until all of the ingredients are tender, approximately 15 minutes.

6. Taste, and adjust seasonings as needed.

7. Serve on a preheated soup plate, sprinkled with chopped parsley. As an option, serve with a slice of warm Irish soda bread.

Braised Lamb Shank with Beans

INGREDIENTS	U.S. Standard	Metric
Pinto beans, rinsed and soaked overnight	30 oz.	855 g
Vegetable oil	as needed	as needed
Lamb shanks, trimmed	10 each	10 each
MIREPOIX		
Onions, sliced	10 oz.	285 g
Carrots, sliced	6 oz.	170 g
Celery, diced	10 oz.	285 g
Stewed tomatoes	2 15-oz. cans	900 ml
Lamb stock	2 qts.	1.9 l
Garlic, minced	1 head	1 head
Rosemary, fresh, washed, finely chopped	1 Tbsp.	15 ml
Black pepper, ground	1 tsp.	5 ml
Salt	TT	TT

METHOD OF PREPARATION

1. Gather all the ingredients and equipment.

2. Preheat oven to 325°F–350°F (163°C–177°C).

3. Place the soaked beans and their soaking liquid into a saucepan and heat to a boil. Immediately reduce heat to a simmer, and gently simmer the beans until they are al dente.

4. Heat a thin layer of oil in a rondeau to smoking. Add the shanks, and sear to brown well on all sides. Do not crowd the pan; sear in batches if necessary. Remove and hold.

5. Add the mirepoix to the rondeau, and sauté until the onions are translucent.

6. Add the stewed tomatoes, stock, garlic, rosemary, pepper, and a touch of salt (seasonings will be adjusted in final sauce). Bring to a boil.

7. Add the seared shanks back to the pan, cover tightly, and place in preheated oven until almost done.

8. Remove shanks from rondeau, and set aside. Strain the braising liquid through a chinois, dépouille, and taste; adjust salt and pepper as needed.

9. Return shanks to the rondeau. Drain the beans, and add to the rondeau with the shanks.

10. Add the strained sauce to the shanks with the beans, cover tightly, and finish cooking until shanks are fork-tender. Hold at 140°F (60°C) or higher until service.

11. Serve 1 shank per portion on preheated dinner plate with approximately 4 oz. (115 g) of beans; nappé with sauce.

NUTRITION

Nutrition Facts

Yield: Serves 10
Serving Size: 19 oz. (540 g)

Amount Per Serving

Calories 310

Total Fat 9 g

Sodium 500 mg

Total Carbohydrate 34 g

Protein 25 g

Lamb

Lamb Stew with Peas

INGREDIENTS

	U.S. Standard	Metric
Saffron	1/2 tsp.	3 g
Red wine, dry	6 oz.	180 ml
Olive oil	as needed	as needed
Lamb shoulder, trimmed, cut into 1" (2.54 cm) cubes	3 1/2 lbs.	1.6 kg
Onions, peeled, diced brunoise	8 oz.	225 g
Red peppers, washed, cored, diced brunoise	8 oz.	225 g
Tomato, concassé	8 oz.	225 g
Garlic, peeled, finely chopped	4 cloves	4 cloves
Chili peppers, washed, seeded, finely chopped	2 each	2 each
Spanish paprika	1 Tbsp.	15 ml
Demi-glace	1 pt.	500 ml
Green peas, fresh or frozen	10 oz.	300 ml
Salt	TT	TT
Black pepper, ground	TT	TT

METHOD OF PREPARATION

1. Gather all the ingredients and equipment.
2. Add the saffron to the red wine and allow to bloom until needed.
3. Heat to smoking a thin layer of oil in a rondeau.
4. Add the lamb, and sear until well browned on all sides. Do not crowd the pan; sear in batches if necessary. Remove and hold.
5. Add more oil if needed to the rondeau, add the onion, and sauté until lightly browned.
6. Add the red peppers, and sauté for 2 minutes. Add the tomato concassé, garlic, and chili peppers, and sauté for 5 minutes.
7. Add the red wine with the saffron, paprika, and demi-glace, and bring to a boil.
8. Return the meat to the rondeau, cover, and keep at a very low simmer on stove top. Or, place in a 325°F–350°F (163°C–177°C) oven until meat is fork-tender.
9. Add the peas and cook for another 5–10 minutes (depending on whether peas were frozen or fresh). Taste and season with salt and pepper as needed. Hold, covered, at 140°F (60°C) or higher until service.
10. Serve on preheated dinner plate.

Lamb Cutlets with Paprika

INGREDIENTS

INGREDIENTS	U.S. Standard	Metric
Lamb loin, boneless, trimmed	3 1/2 lbs.	1.6 kg
Flour, seasoned with salt and paprika	6 oz.	170 g
Vegetable oil	as needed	as needed
Garlic, finely chopped	6 cloves	6 cloves
Paprika, semi-hot	1 tsp.	5 ml
Red wine, dry	8 oz.	240 ml
Lamb demi-glace	1 qt.	960 ml
Heavy cream	6 oz.	180 ml
Salt	TT	TT
Black pepper, ground	TT	TT

METHOD OF PREPARATION

1. Gather all the ingredients and equipment.

2. Preheat oven to 325°F–350°F (163°C–177°C).

3. Slice loins into thirty 1 1/2-oz. (40-g) slices, and pound lightly with a wooden mallet.

4. Heat to smoking a thin layer of oil in a large sauté pan.

5. Dredge pounded cutlets in seasoned flour, shaking off the excess, and sear cutlets on both sides. Do not crowd pan; sear in batches or two pans. Place cutlets in a hotel pan, shingled, and hold at 140°F (60°C) or higher.

6. Add more oil to the sauté pan, turn heat to low, and add the garlic. Sauté for one minute. Add the paprika, and sauté a half minute more, being careful not to burn the paprika.

7. Add the red wine, bring to a boil, and reduce to half the volume.

8. Add the demi-glace, and bring to a boil.

9. Temper the heavy cream into the sauce, and let simmer for 10–15 minutes or until proper flavor and consistency is achieved. Taste, and season with salt and pepper as needed.

10. Pour the sauce on the lamb cutlets, cover tightly, and place in a preheated oven for 15 minutes.

11. Serve 3 cutlets per portion on preheated dinner plates.

COOKING TECHNIQUES

Sautéing:
1. Heat the sauté pan to the appropriate temperature.
2. Evenly brown the food product.
3. For a sauce, pour off any excess oil, reheat, and deglaze.

Braising:
1. Heat the braising pan to the proper temperature.
2. Sear and brown the food product to a golden color.
3. Degrease and deglaze.
4. Cook the food product in two-thirds liquid until fork-tender.

NUTRITION

Nutrition Facts

Yield: Serves 10
Serving Size: 8 oz. (225 g)

Amount Per Serving

Calories 330

Total Fat 15 g

Sodium 95 mg

Total Carbohydrate 15 g

Protein 28 g

A.D. 1387
Goose and various other birds are served at a large banquet held by England's King Richard II.

1523
Turkeys are brought to Spain from North America.

1873
Long Island duck industry starts up with Peking ducks from China.

1935
Americans pay more for chicken than for red meat.

1965
Cornish game hens are bred.

Poultry—large, domestic birds, such as chicken, turkey, duck, and goose—is popular around the world because it is relatively inexpensive, is generally low in fat, and lends itself to a variety of cooking methods. Poultry's mild taste makes it an ideal component of many dishes. Global preference for poultry is nothing new; the Chinese first domesticated ducks 4,000 years ago. Originally bred in Asia, chicken reached the Greeks at the height of their civilization. The Romans served all types of large birds, from swans to storks. Turkey, the great North American bird, is a traditional highlight of holiday tables.

Nutritional Makeup

Like other meats, poultry flesh is muscle, containing water, protein, and fat. In addition, poultry flesh contains carbohydrates, vitamin A and vitamin B complex, and minerals and is also a good source of calcium, iron, phosphorus, and potassium.

Muscle Composition

The proportions of the nutrients in poultry are generally the same as those in most meats: 75% water, 20% protein, and up to 5% fat.

Water Poultry flesh is about three-quarters water; the actual amount of water varies depending on shrinkage.

Protein When heat is applied to poultry flesh, the inherent protein coagulates, or becomes firm. The degree of coagulation is one gauge for doneness.

> *See Chapter 11: Cooking Techniques for more information on coagulation and testing for doneness.*

Fat Unlike beef and other red meats, poultry does not exhibit marbling of fat within the muscle tissue. The fat in birds occurs primarily in the skin, the abdomen, and the fat pad near the tail. Poultry fat is soft and has a relatively low melting point, making it easy to render during cooking. Breast meat in both chicken and turkey is especially low in fat.

Vitamins and minerals Poultry is also a good source of riboflavin (vitamin B2) and niacin (vitamin B3). Although present in a small amount, poultry does contain carbohydrates, as well.

The Structure of Poultry

Poultry consists of bones, connective tissue, and muscle fibers. Both the maturity of the bird and the quantity of connective tissue affect the tenderness of the flesh. The bird's skin color, however, does not have any effect on the flavor or quality of the poultry flesh.

Tenderness and Maturity

As with other meats, the tenderness of the product is linked to age. Thus the older the bird, the tougher the flesh. An increased amount of connective tissue also creates a tougher flesh. Most poultry is marketed young, so tender flesh is more likely to be purchased. There is a definite difference in the preparation of young versus old birds. A young bird can be cooked utilizing a dry technique such as sautéing, grilling, broiling, or roasting, but an older bird should be cooked slowly using the braising or stewing technique to override the inherent toughness.

Light Meat and Dark Meat

Poultry is not fabricated into different cuts as are beef and other meats, but the flesh of chicken and turkey is considered to be of two types: light meat and dark meat. The breast and wings have less connective tissue and fat and are light-colored. Dark meat, found on the drumsticks and thighs, consists of more connective tissue and fat. Because light meat is lower in fat than dark meat, it cooks more quickly. The difference in cooking time between light and dark meat needs to be considered when preparing a bird.

Inspection and Grading

Federal law requires inspection of poultry by the Food Safety Inspection Service (FSIS) of the United States Department of Agriculture (USDA). See Figure 20-1. USDA inspectors check poultry products to ensure that handling and processing have occurred in a sanitary environment and that the poultry is fit for consumption. Poultry that meets inspection standards receives a USDA inspection stamp. This round stamp appears on the packaging. All poultry intended for foodservice operations must exhibit a USDA stamp. Note that the inspection stamp guarantees wholesomeness, not quality or tenderness.

Poultry grading takes place after inspection. Unlike inspection, grading is voluntary. The USDA grading system is a means of indicating the overall quality of poultry. There are three levels of quality for poultry, indicated by the letter grades A, B, and C, with Grade A being the highest level. When grading poultry, the USDA considers lack of body deformity, amount of flesh, amount of fat, presence of pinfeathers, and condition of the bird (tears, cuts, broken bones, bruises, and blemishes). Grade A poultry must be free of deformities, have meaty flesh with ample fat, show no pinfeathers, and display no damage, imperfections, or discoloration. Grade A poultry is used almost exclusively in restaurants; Grades B and C poultry are best suited for processing.

The USDA grade is shown on a shield-shaped stamp. It must be noted that the stamp is a sign of general quality only. It makes no representations as to flavor or tenderness of the bird.

FIGURE 20-1

USDA inspection stamps

Kosher Considerations

According to *kashruth*—Jewish dietary laws—poultry is kosher, or fit for consumption. Chickens, turkeys, ducks, and geese are clean, or permitted, because these birds have a crop, a gizzard, and an extra talon. Birds of prey, such as eagles and hawks, do not share these attributes and thus are unclean, or forbidden for eating. As in the case of mammals, a *shohet* must carry out the slaughter of poultry following the procedure known as *shehitah*. In this process the shohet must kill the animal with a single knife stroke, bleed the carcass, and then remove all veins and arteries. The shohet also checks slaughtered birds for imperfections or disease, which would make them unfit. Salting and soaking flesh to extract blood is also required for poultry to be kosher.

Halal Considerations

As with beef, Muslims follow halal laws for consumption of cooked chicken. Birds of prey are not considered halal, and thus cannot be consumed. Chicken must be slaughtered and butchered following strict Muslim rituals and procedures.

Purchasing Poultry

Various factors influence the specifics of purchasing poultry including menu needs, price limitations, quality standards, storage facilities, preparation schedules, and skill levels. These and other considerations will determine the market form, class, and style of the poultry purchased.

Poultry *market forms,* or forms for purchase, include fresh, frozen, individually quick frozen (IQF), and fully cooked. Fresh poultry parts should be cooked within 48 hours, and fresh whole poultry should be prepared within 1–2 days. Frozen whole poultry keeps for up to 12 months. Frozen poultry parts will keep for 4–6 months. Fully cooked poultry, which is available frozen or canned, is a convenient choice for various preparations. Fresh poultry is usually less expensive than frozen.

In addition to market form, poultry is classified according to age and gender. The tenderness of the bird will vary with both of these factors.

Style is another consideration when making a purchase. *Style* refers to the amount of cleaning and processing of poultry prior to receiving it. Poultry is available live or *dressed*—killed, bled, and defeathered. Most establishments, however, purchase poultry ready to cook, or *RTC*—dressed, with head, feet, and organs removed. RTC poultry may be purchased whole, in parts, bone-in, boneless, or ground. To keep costs down, many operations opt to purchase poultry whole and then cut it into pieces in-house depending on their menu needs.

"The Poultry Buyers Guide," published by the North American Meat Processors Association (NAMP), is a useful reference for poultry purchasing. The guide uses a numbering system developed by NAMP and the USDA to indicate poultry species, classes, and parts and includes photos of poultry cuts frequently used. As in the case of red meat, the purpose of the system is to ensure clarity and consistency in purchasing.

Free-range poultry **refers to poultry that roams freely and eats outdoors. Most poultry today is raised indoors in a controlled environment and fed a prepared mixture of corn and soy bean meal, vitamins, minerals, animal proteins, and antibiotics. Some customers prefer free-range poultry because they believe that its more natural setting and diet make it safer and more flavorful than other poultry. Keep in mind, however, that because the free-range chicken is allowed to exercise more, its meat may be tougher. Also, the limited access to this type of poultry makes it more expensive. The USDA does not currently regulate the label "free-range" beyond requiring that such poultry have unlimited access to the outdoors.**

Handling Poultry Safely

After receiving poultry, handle it carefully to protect its quality, and store it immediately. Proper care will extend the shelf life of the product.

Receiving Poultry

Upon receiving poultry, check to make sure that it meets the required specifications and carries USDA inspection and grade stamps. Examine the packaging closely for tears or leakage. After looking at the packaging, check the temperature, color, odor, and texture of the poultry.

Modified atmosphere packaging (MAP) Poultry in modified atmosphere packaging (MAP) should also be delivered at 41°F (5°C) or lower. *Modified atmosphere packaging (MAP)* replaces air in food packaging with a gas such as carbon dioxide or nitrogen. This type of packaging helps extend the shelf life of fresh food items. The FDA has strict guidelines for the use of MAP. When receiving MAP poultry, reject packages that leak or have an expired code date and products that are discolored.

Ice pack Shipping in self-draining crushed ice is essential for fresh poultry that is not delivered in MAP. Temperature at delivery should be 41°F (5°C) or lower, and the poultry should be ivory or yellow in color with no discoloration. It should have a firm texture that is resilient to the touch.

Frozen and IQF Frozen and IQF poultry should arrive frozen. Reject poultry that shows any signs of thawing and refreezing, including drying and discoloration or ice crystals on the product. Liquid or chunks of ice in the packaging or staining on wrapping may also signal thawing and refreezing.

Storing Poultry

Both fresh and frozen poultry require careful storage. Fresh poultry is extremely perishable. Store immediately in a self-draining ice pack under refrigeration at 32°F–36°F (0°C–2°C), and use within 1–2 days. It should be noted, however, that poultry has a longer shelf life if shipped and stored at 28°F (–2°C). Hold fresh whole birds under refrigeration for 1–2 days. To prevent cross-contamination, keep raw poultry in the refrigerator away from cooked and ready-to-eat foods. Store on the lowest level, below all other foods, including raw meats.

Store already frozen poultry in its original packaging at 0°F–10°F (−18°C–−12°C). Whole frozen poultry has a shelf life of up to 12 months, and frozen poultry parts will keep for 4–6 months. Label all products with date of receipt, and use the FIFO method when pulling products for use.

To thaw, leave frozen poultry in its packaging, and hold under refrigeration. Allow 2–4 days for thawing whole birds. Never thaw poultry at room temperature, and do not refreeze. After poultry products have been cooked, they will keep for up to 4 days under refrigeration.

Spoilage Indicators

Spoilage in poultry is fairly easy to detect: the poultry may have a greenish or purplish color; the tips of wings may look dark; tackiness may be present under the wings and around the joints; and the poultry may have a bad odor. Spoiled poultry should be discarded.

Foodborne Illness Associated with Poultry

Improper handling and preparation of poultry can lead to outbreaks of dangerous foodborne illnesses caused by salmonella and campylobacter jejuni bacteria. These bacteria can create severe intestinal problems.

■ *See Chapter 4: Food Safety for more information.*

Proper preparation and cooking of poultry is crucial. To avoid cross-contamination from raw poultry and its juices, prepare poultry away from other raw and cooked foods on separate cutting boards and other work surfaces and with separate utensils. Carefully wash, rinse, and sanitize all surfaces and equipment that have come into contact with poultry. Practice good personal hygiene by washing hands thoroughly before and after handling raw or cooked poultry. Finally, always cook poultry thoroughly. Poultry should reach a minimum internal temperature of 165°F (74°C) for at least 15 seconds.

Poultry Classification

Poultry is a collective term for the various species, or kinds, of birds raised for human consumption.
The USDA identifies six kinds of poultry: chicken, turkey, duck, goose, guinea, and pigeon.
It further divides each kind of poultry into classifications based on age and gender as follows:

KIND	AGE	WEIGHT	GENDER	DESCRIPTION
Chicken				
Poussin	very young	1 lb. or less/ .5 kg or less	either	Weighs one pound or less, light flavor
Cornish hen	5–6 weeks	1.5 lbs. or less/ 1 kg or less	either	Young bird, very tender and flavorful, special breed
Broiler/fryer	9–12 weeks	3 lbs., 8 oz. or less/ 1.5 kg or less	either	Young bird, tender and fairly lean
Roaster	3–5 months	3 lbs., 8 oz.–5 lbs./ 1.5–2.5 kg	either	Young bird, tender
Capon	under 8 months	6–10 lbs./ 2.5–4.5 kg	castrated male	Slightly older bird, especially tender and flavorful, comparatively high in fat, expensive
Stewer	over 10 months	2 lbs., 8 oz.–8 lbs./ 1–3.5 kg	female	Mature hen, tough meat, coarse skin but good flavor
Turkey				
Fryer/roaster	under 16 weeks	4–9 lbs./2–4 kg	either (males are known as toms; females as hens)	Young bird, tender
Young turkey	5–7 months	8–22 lbs./ 3.5–10 kg	either	Young bird, tender
Yearling turkey	under 15 months	10–30 lbs./ 4.5–13.5 kg	either	Mature bird, still tender, skin somewhat coarse
Mature or old turkey	over 15 months	10–30 lbs./ 4.5–13.5 kg	either	Old bird; tough, coarse skin
Duck				
Broiler/fryer duckling	under 8 weeks	3 lbs., 8 oz.–4 lbs./ 1.5–2 kg	either	Young duck with soft windpipe, tender
Roaster duckling	under 16 weeks	4–6 lbs./2–2.5 kg	either	Young duck with hardening windpipe, tender, richly flavored
Mature duck	over 6 months	4–6 lbs./ 2–2.5 kg	either	Old duck with hard windpipe, tough
Goose				
Young goose	under 6 months	6–12 lbs./ 2.5–5.5 kg	either	Young bird, tender, rich flavor, considerable fat
Mature goose	over 6 months	10–16 lbs./ 4.5–7.5 kg	either	Old bird, tough
Guinea				
Young guinea	3 months	12 oz.–1 lb., 8 oz./ .5–1 kg	either	Tender meat, flexible breastbone
Mature guinea	over 3 months	1–2 lbs./1 kg	either	Tough flesh, hard breastbone
Pigeon				
Squab	4 weeks	12 oz.–1 lb., 8 oz./ .5–1 kg	either	Young bird, very tender, dark flesh, little fat
Pigeon	over 4 weeks	1–2 lbs./1 kg	either	Mature bird, coarse skin, tough flesh

Chicken

Chicken is the most common kind of poultry in the United States and around the world. Comparatively low in fat and containing both light and dark meat, chicken is suited to a range of dry and moist cooking techniques, depending on the type and age of bird.

Poussins A *poussin* is a very young, small chicken. At a pound (.5 k) or less in weight, poussins are smaller than Cornish hens but may be prepared in the same ways. Raised by special methods, poussins are costly.

Cornish hens The usual method of preparing a Cornish hen, sometimes called a Rock Cornish hen, is splitting and then grilling or broiling. Roasting is also appropriate for this special breed of chicken, which is plump for its small size and has a high proportion of light meat to dark.

Broilers/fryers Broilers/fryers are the most versatile class of chicken, ideal for sautéing and baking in addition to broiling and pan- and deep-frying.

Roasters Larger than broilers/fryers, roasters, as their name suggests, make excellent roasts, although they can be prepared by any cooking method such as broiling or frying.

Capons Similar in size to roasters, capons are castrated male chickens raised for their flavorful meat, which is largely light-colored. Capons also are best roasted.

Stewers Less tender than other birds, stewers should be cooked using a moist method such as simmering or a moist-dry combination technique such as braising or stewing, which brings out their full flavor. Simmering or braising is also the recommended cooking method for hens older than the average stewer and for roosters, mature male birds with tough and mostly dark meat.

Turkey

Second to chicken in popularity in the United States, turkey contains both light and dark meat and is fairly low in fat. Turkeys most often are roasted, although certain other cooking methods, such as deep-frying in the Cajun tradition, are also suitable for the whole bird. Roasting is an appropriate method not only for the fryer/roaster—an immature turkey with

the most tender meat—but also for young and yearling turkeys.

In addition, cooking turkey parts has become popular. Slicing turkey breast into cutlets for sautéing is a common method of preparation. Turkey legs lend themselves to inclusion in other dishes after braising or stewing. The flesh of older turkeys is tough and generally fit only for stewing, grinding, and other processing into such products as burgers, franks, sausage, and luncheon meats.

Duck

Roasting is the preferred method for preparing whole duck, whether a broiler/fryer or roaster duckling. Foodservice operations commonly use roaster duckling. This class of duck contains only dark meat and is quite fatty. Slashing the skin of a roaster duckling helps render the fat during roasting and keeps the skin crisp. Because duck is a water bird, it has a generous layer of fat under the skin. In addition to fat, it also has a high proportion of bone to meat, resulting in a lower yield than chicken or turkey.

Though not prepared as frequently as whole duck, duck parts such as breasts and legs are sometimes served. Duck breasts are best grilled, sautéed, or broiled. Braising or slow roasting is the best cooking method for duck legs. Simmering duck legs in rendered fat prepares them for curing as a confit.

▌ *See Chapter 25: Garde-Manger for more information on confits.*

Braising is a good method for tenderizing the tough flesh of a mature duck, although the meat of older ducks is appropriate for use only in processed products.

White Peking duck is the primary breed of duck raised in the United States. Long Island duckling is an example of this breed, first produced on Long Island, New York, after importation from its native China. Muscovy, moulard, and other imported breeds of duck are also available.

Goose

Roasting is the traditional European method of preparing goose, going back to the open-spit roasting of the Middle Ages and Renaissance. Like duck, goose is a water bird that has mostly dark meat and a layer of fat under the skin. Piercing the

The History of **Turkey**

The modern bird known as the turkey is a descendant of two species of turkey, both indigenous to the New World. In 1523 the first shipment of these birds was brought to Spain. The bird was quickly absorbed into European culinary culture. In fact, by the 1550s turkey was grouped with other large edible fowl and regulated by the London price market. In the New World, the settlers at Jamestown were saved from starvation by gifts of food from Native Americans, including turkey. It is disputed whether turkey was served at the first Thanksgiving celebration, but it was featured at the second celebration in 1621.

Because of its versatility, turkey was showcased in many recipes and preparations. There are sixteenth-century records of Italian and German turkey recipes. However, it was not until the seventeenth century that France followed suit. With today's efforts toward healthful eating, the lean quality of turkey meat makes this bird quite desirable. Now turkey is available in many processed forms, including those usually reserved for pork, such as bacon or ham.

 **PROCESS**

Trussing a Whole Chicken

Trussing a bird, such as a whole chicken, involves tying its wings and legs against its body to form a compact whole. A trussed bird cooks evenly, retains moisture, and is attractive when served.

There are various trussing methods. The following steps outline a simple method of trussing with butcher's twine:

1 **Remove the first joint from each of the wings.**

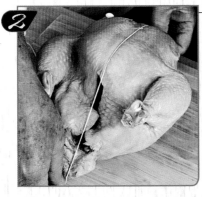

2 **After cutting a length of twine about two times the chicken's length, position the bird breast up with the neck closest to you.**

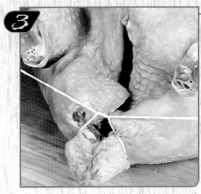

3 **Bring the twine around the tail, and tie a simple knot.**

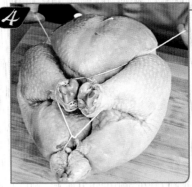

4 **Next, bring the twine up around the legs, and cross at the back of the breast.**

5 **Pull the twine under the chicken between the leg and breast, and tie under it to secure the remaining wing joint.**

6 **A properly trussed chicken should look like the one shown below.**

Poultry

379

Carving a Turkey

Always let a turkey or other large bird stand for at least 15 minutes before carving to allow juices to be redistributed.

To carve a turkey, follow these steps:

4 Cut the thigh meat parallel to the bone.

1 *Slice the skin between the leg and the breast to loosen the leg section from the carcass.*

5 **Remove the breast by cutting along the keel bone. Continue downward along the breastbone, and sever the joint at the wing.**

2 **Remove the legs by pulling them downward. Separate the thigh from the backbone by cutting at the joint.**

6 **Remove the wing.**

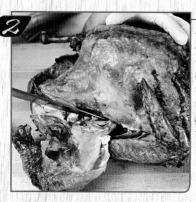

3 **Separate the drumstick from the thigh.**

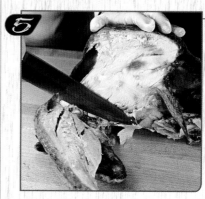

7 **Slice the breast at an angle across the grain. The bones and unservable trimmings can be used to make stock.**

skin with a fork and cooking at high temperatures help render goose fat. A fruit sauce provides an acidic accompaniment to cut the fat, highlighting the rich flavor and tender texture of young goose flesh. Mature goose is a great deal tougher and better for stewing or braising.

Smoked goose breast is a delicacy that involves salt curing before smoking. **Foie gras,** or fattened goose liver, is a specialty product served as a hot or cold appetizer and is used in garde-manger.

■ *See Chapter 25: Garde-Manger for more information on foie gras.*

Guinea Fowl

Indigenous to Africa, the guinea fowl was once a game bird. Today, it is a domesticated bird identified by the USDA as one of the six kinds of poultry. Like chicken and turkey, guinea has both light and dark meat. In flavor, it is similar to pheasant. Sautéing is appropriate for young guinea fowl, which are quite tender. Roasting is another choice, although barding is recommended to offset the bird's lean and somewhat dry meat. Combination methods (braising, stewing) are best for older and thus tougher birds.

Pigeon

Squab is a young pigeon that is not yet able to fly. Eaten since ancient times, squab originated in the Middle East and Asia. Squab has very tender, dark, lean meat with a delicate flavor. Grilling, roasting, broiling, and sautéing is suitable for young pigeons. Barding before roasting makes up for lack of fat. Older pigeons have tough flesh that can be used in stews, terrines, or pâtés.

Carving Skills

After whole poultry is roasted or baked and is allowed to rest, it needs to be carved. This can be done in the kitchen, at the table, or on a buffet, depending on service needs. When a larger bird is carved, the meat on the legs and breast is cut into slices rather than remaining whole.

Fabrication

Some of the same factors involved in deciding whether to fabricate meat on-site influence the decision to butcher poultry in-house: butchering skills; available storage space; use of flesh, bones, and cost per portion, including the time spent on the butchering process.

Portion Control

In some cases foodservice establishments use portion control (PC) cuts or individually quick frozen (IQF) cuts, which are cut to specification. These can provide excellent value to an operation when the menu does not allow for the utilization of the entire bird. Portion cuts can provide consistency and labor efficiency as well.

Fabricating Skills

It is important to know the basic butchering and preparation procedures for poultry. Portioning whole poultry and boning poultry breasts are essential skills.

Cutting a Chicken into Quarters

When one is familiar with a chicken's structure and the location of its joints, cutting it into pieces is an easy process.

To do so, follow these steps:

5 Use your thumb and index finger to remove the keel bone.

1 Remove the first two joints from the wings.

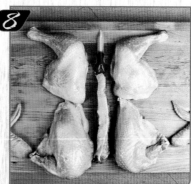

6 Cut the chicken completely in half.

2 Place the chicken neck down on the cutting board, and cut along the side of the backbone to split the chicken.

7 Place the chicken skin side up, and separate the leg and breast by cutting through the skin.

3 Repeat along the other side of the backbone, and remove the entire backbone.

8 A properly quartered chicken should look like the one shown here.

4 Place the split chicken skin side down, and make a small cut in the white cartilage at the front of the chicken.

Cutting a Chicken into Eighths

Cutting a chicken into eighths produces two drumsticks, two thighs, two breasts, and two wing pieces.

To cut a chicken into eighths, follow these steps:

1 Quarter the chicken as shown on page 382. Separate each drumstick portion of the leg from the thigh at the joint.

2 Cut each breast into two equal sections.

3 A chicken properly cut into eighths should look like the one shown here.

Boning a Chicken Leg

A boned chicken leg has many uses, including that of being stuffed with forcemeat to create a ballotine.

To remove the bone from a chicken leg, follow these steps:

1 Use the back of a French knife to break the lower part of the leg bone, keeping the end of the joint attached by the skin.

2 Use a boning knife to remove the backbone from the thigh if attached.

3 Use the tip of the boning knife to cut away the meat around the thighbone, and expose the bone as much as possible with your thumb and index finger.

4 Cut the meat around the joint, and pull up the thighbone. Cut to expose the remaining leg bone.

5 Scrape the meat away from the leg bone, using the back of the knife, and remove the bone.

Poultry

383

Boning a Chicken Breast

A boneless chicken breast can be prepared in a variety of ways, including poaching, sautéing, pan-frying, broiling, grilling, and baking.

To remove the bone from chicken breast, follow these steps:

1 **After the back-bone and leg sections have been cut from the chicken, place the chicken breast on the cutting board, and make a small cut into the white cartilage at the front of the breast.**

2 **Spread the breast open, and remove the keel bone and remaining cartilage.**

3 **Cut away the rib bones from the breast.**

4 **Extract the wishbone.**

5 **Remove the tenders from the breast, if desired.**

6 **Two fully boned chicken breasts should look like those shown here. One breast, skin side down, has the tenders attached, and the other, skin side up, has the tenders removed.**

Chicken Paprikash

INGREDIENTS

	U.S. Standard	Metric
Chickens, whole, 3–3 1/2 lbs. (1.4–1.6 kg)	3 each	3 each
Clarified butter	4 oz.	120 ml
Seasoned flour, for dredging	as needed	as needed
Onions, peeled, cut macédoine	l large	1 large
Green bell peppers, washed, seeded, cut macédoine	2 each	2 each
Tomato, concassé	1/2 c.	115 g
Hungarian sweet paprika	1 oz.	28 g
Hungarian hot paprika	TT	TT
Flour	2 oz.	55 g
White chicken stock, heated to a boil	2 qts.	1.9 l
Sour cream	8 oz.	225 g
Salt	TT	TT

METHOD OF PREPARATION

1. Gather all the ingredients and equipment.

2. Preheat over to 350°F (177°C).

3. Quarter chickens, removing wing tips and backs.

4. Heat the butter in a rondeau. *Dredge* the chicken pieces in flour, shaking off excess, and sear until well browned. Transfer the chicken to a hotel pan.

5. Add the onions to the rondeau, and sauté until translucent. Add the peppers and tomato, and sauté until peppers are tender.

6. Add the paprika and the 2 oz. (55 g) of flour to the vegetables, and continue to cook for 3 more minutes. Slowly add the stock while stirring to incorporate it into roux, and then season with salt to taste.

7. Add the seared chicken pieces back to the rondeau. The liquid should cover the chicken by two-thirds; add more stock if needed. Bring the liquid to a boil.

8. Cover tightly, and place in the oven at 325°F–350°F (163°C–177°C). Braise until the chicken is fork-tender and at least 165°F (74°C), approximately 35–40 minutes.

9. Transfer the chicken, along with a bit of the braising liquid, to a hotel pan, and hold, tightly covered, at 140°F (60°C) or higher.

10. Dépouille the braising liquid. Return to the heat, simmer, and reduce to proper flavor and consistency.

11. Temper the sour cream into the sauce, taste, and season as needed with salt. Heat to a minimum of 165°F (74°C), and hold at 140°F (60°C) or higher in a bain-marie.

12. To serve, place 1 piece of chicken on a preheated dinner plate, and nappé with sauce.

COOKING TECHNIQUES

Sautéing:
1. Heat the sauté pan to the appropriate temperature.
2. Evenly brown the food product.
3. For a sauce, pour off any excess oil, reheat, and deglaze.

Braising:
1. Heat the braising pan to the proper temperature.
2. Sear and brown the food product to a golden color.
3. Degrease and deglaze.
4. Cook the food product in two-thirds liquid until fork-tender.

GLOSSARY

Macédoine: 1/4″ (6 mm) dice
Dredge: to coat with flour

NUTRITION

Nutrition Facts

Yield: Serves 10
Serving Size: 8 oz. (225 g)

Amount Per Serving

Calories 310

Total Fat 20 g

Sodium 90 mg

Total Carbohydrate 15 g

Protein 23 g

Cider-Marinated Duck Breast with Spicy Mango Chutney

INGREDIENTS

	U.S. Standard	Metric
Duck breast, boneless, skin-on	5 each	5 each
Salt	TT	TT
Black pepper, freshly ground	TT	TT
Apple cider	1 pt.	500 ml
SPICY MANGO CHUTNEY		
Clarified butter	2 oz.	60 ml
Onions, peeled, cut macédoine	4 oz.	115 g
Granny Smith apples, washed, peeled, cored, cut macédoine	6 oz.	170 g
Mango, washed, peeled, cut macédoine	8 oz.	225 g
Garlic, peeled and mashed to a purée	1 clove	1 clove
Granulated sugar	2 oz.	55 g
Cider vinegar	1 oz.	30 ml
Chili peppers, dried, crushed, bruised	1/2 tsp.	2.5 ml
Thyme, dried	1/4 tsp.	1.25 ml

METHOD OF PREPARATION

1. Gather all the ingredients and equipment.

2. Preheat the grill.

3. Season the duck breasts with salt and pepper, and place them in a non-corrosive container. Add the cider, refrigerate at 41°F (5°C) or lower, and allow the duck to marinate for at least 1 hour.

4. In a small saucepan, heat the butter, add the onions, and sauté until translucent.

5. Add the remaining ingredients, and sauté until wilted. Reduce the heat and simmer, stirring frequently until the fruits are very soft and the mixture is thick. Taste, and adjust the seasoning as needed. Hold at 140°F (60°C) or higher.

6. Remove the duck breasts from the marinade and pat dry. Grill each duck breast, skin side down first, until skin is crisp and browned. Turn, and grill the flesh side for 2 minutes or to an internal temperature of 165°F (74°C). Remove, and place skin side up in hotel pan at 140°F (60°C) for 10 minutes before serving.

7. For service, thinly slice the duck breast on a diagonal, and fan out the meat on a preheated dinner plate. Place a 2 oz. (55 g) scoop of chutney in the center of the slices, and serve immediately.

Duck à l'Orange

INGREDIENTS

	U.S. Standard	Metric
Duck, whole	3 each	3 each
Salt	TT	TT
Black pepper, ground	TT	TT
Ginger, ground	1/2 tsp.	2.5 ml
Thyme, fresh, washed	3 sprigs	3 sprigs
Marjoram, fresh, washed	3 sprigs	3 sprigs
Rosemary, fresh, washed	3 sprigs	3 sprigs
Oranges, washed, segmented (zest 2 before segmenting; reserve zest and peels)	5 each	5 each
Grand Marnier®	2 oz.	60 ml
MIREPOIX		
Onions, peeled and diced	8 oz.	225 g
Carrots, washed, peeled, and diced	8 oz.	225 g
Celery, washed and sliced	8 oz.	225 g
SAUCE		
Orange juice	1 pt.	500 ml
Duck or chicken demi-glace	1 pt.	500 ml
Grand Marnier®	2 oz.	60 ml
Orange marmalade	2 oz.	55 g
Apricot jam	2 oz.	55 g
Orange zest	1 oz.	28 g

METHOD OF PREPARATION

1. Gather all the ingredients and equipment.

2. Preheat oven to 425°F (218°C).

3. Remove giblets from ducks and reserve. Season ducks inside with salt, pepper, and 1/4 tsp. (1.25 ml) of ginger. Place the herbs in the cavities along with some of the reserved orange peelings; *truss*.

4. Prick the skin all over the breast and fatty sides of the ducks, being careful to prick only into the fat but not into the meat. Rub Grand Marnier® on the skin of the ducks, and then season generously with salt, pepper, and the remaining ginger. Place mirepoix and the reserved giblets in a roasting pan, and set ducks on top.

5. Place to roast in preheated oven for 20 minutes. Baste with some of the rendered fat in the pan, and reduce temperature to 350°F (177°C). Roast the ducks to an internal temperature of 165°F (74°C).

6. When the ducks are done, set to cool slightly, and then disjoint and partially debone, reserving bones. Hold duck in a hotel pan, tightly covered, at 140°F (60°C) or higher until service. (Do not hold too long, or it will dry out.)

7. Pour excess fat from roasting pan. Place reserved bones into the roasting pan with the giblets and mirepoix; place the pan on the stove top, and brown for a few minutes. Add the orange juice, demi-glace, and remaining orange peel, bring to a boil, turn down to a simmer, and simmer for 15 minutes. Strain into a saucepan.

8. Add the remaining ingredients to the strained liquid, and heat to a boil. Turn to a simmer, and simmer until proper flavor and consistency is achieved. Dépouille. Taste, season as needed, and hold at 140°F (60°C) or higher in a bain-marie.

9. Place the orange segments in a sauté pan; add a little sauce, and heat.

10. To serve, place the duck on preheated dinner plates, nappé with the sauce, and ladle orange segments on top.

Roasting:
1. Sear the food product, and brown evenly.
2. Elevate the food product in a roasting pan.
3. Determine doneness, and consider carryover cooking.
4. Let the food product rest before carving.

Simmering:
1. Place the prepared product in an appropriately sized pot.
2. Bring the product to a boil, and then reduce the heat to allow the product to barely boil.
3. Cook until desired doneness is achieved.

GLOSSARY

Truss: tie or secure

NUTRITION

Nutrition Facts

Yield: Serves 10
Serving Size: 4 oz. (115 g)

Amount Per Serving

Calories 420

Total Fat 16 g

Sodium 190 mg

Total Carbohydrate 29 g

Protein 33 g

Chicken with Dumplings

INGREDIENTS

Ingredient	U.S. Standard	Metric
Chicken, whole, 3–3 1/2 lbs. (1.5–2 kg)	3 each	3 each
White chicken stock	1 gal.	3.8 l
MIREPOIX		
Carrots, washed and peeled	8 oz.	225 g
Onions, peeled	1 lb.	454 g
Celery, washed and trimmed	1 lb.	454 g
Leeks, washed and trimmed	8 oz.	225 g
Bay leaves	2 each	2 each
Salt	TT	TT
Black pepper, ground	TT	TT
DUMPLINGS		
Flour, all-purpose	3 c.	550 g
Salt	1 1/2 tsp.	7.5 g
Parsley, washed, squeezed dry, chopped	3 Tbsp.	45 g
Baking powder	4 1/2 tsp.	23 g
Butter	6 Tbsp.	90 g
Milk	10 oz.	285 g
Roux, blonde	4 oz.	115 g

METHOD OF PREPARATION

1. Gather all the ingredients and equipment.

2. Place the chicken in a stockpot, and add the stock (stock should cover chicken, add more if needed, or use a smaller stockpot). Heat to a boil, and after about 5 minutes, *dépouille.*

3. Add the mirepoix, bay leaves, and salt and pepper to taste. Turn down to a simmer, and cook until chickens reach an internal temperature of 165°F (74°C), approximately 1 hour. Carefully remove the chickens, and place in a hotel pan. Cover tightly, and hold at 140°F (60°C) or higher.

4. Strain the stock through a *chinois.* Place enough stock into a *rondeau* to reach a 2-inch (5.08 cm) depth. Place on the heat, bring to a boil, and then turn down to a simmer for cooking the dumplings. Place another 1 1/2 quarts (1.4 l) of stock in a saucepan for the sauce, and set aside.

5. To prepare the dumplings, combine the flour, salt, parsley, and baking powder. Cut the butter into the flour mixture with a fork (or fingertips), until mixture resembles coarse meal. Add the milk, and gently mix it by hand into the flour and butter mixture. Mix only until dough forms; overmixing will build up the gluten and result in tough dumplings.

6. Drop dough by spoonfuls into the simmering stock. Alternatively, dough can be rolled to a 1/2″ (1.27 cm) thickness, cut into desired shapes, and dropped into simmering stock. When dumplings are placed in the simmering stock, they will sink and then, after a few minutes, rise to the top. Allow them to cook for 5 minutes after they rise, and then cover and simmer for 10–15 minutes, or until they are cooked inside. Remove and hold at 140°F (60°C) or higher.

7. Heat the 1 1/2 quarts (1.4 l) of stock for the sauce to a boil, and then turn down to a simmer. Gently heat the roux. Temper the roux into the stock, and allow to simmer until proper flavor and texture are achieved. Taste and season as needed with salt and pepper. Strain the sauce through a chinois, and hold at 140°F (60°C) or higher in a *bain-marie* for service.

8. Cut the chickens into quarters, and partially debone. Place in a hotel pan; add a bit of stock and hold, covered, at 140°F (60°C) or higher until service.

9. To serve, place a portion of the chicken on a preheated dinner plate, arrange the dumplings around the chicken, and nappé with the sauce.

Cornish Game Hens with Honey-Dijon Glaze

INGREDIENTS

INGREDIENTS	U.S. Standard	Metric
Garlic, peeled, cloves separated	1 head	1 head
Honey	4 oz.	120 ml
Dijon mustard	2 1/2 oz.	75 ml
Butter	2 oz.	55 g
Thyme, fresh, washed, leaves stripped and chopped	1/2 oz.	15 ml
Cornish game hens	5 each	5 each
Salt	TT	TT
Black pepper, ground	TT	TT
Thyme, fresh, large sprigs, washed	1 1/2 oz.	45 ml
Parsley, flat leaf, sprigs, washed	4 oz. (5 each)	115 g (5 each)

METHOD OF PREPARATION

1. Gather all the ingredients and equipment.

2. Preheat oven to 350°F (177°C).

3. Divide the garlic cloves in half. Coarsely chop half of the garlic for the inside of the hens, and set aside. Finely mince the remaining cloves, and place in a small saucepan.

4. Add the honey, mustard, butter, and thyme to the minced garlic in the saucepan. Place over low heat and cook, stirring constantly until the mixture simmers and thickens slightly. Remove from heat, and set aside.

5. Rinse the inside cavities of the hens, and pat dry. Season the cavities well with salt, pepper, and the coarsely chopped garlic. Insert two sprigs each of thyme and parsley into the cavities.

6. Truss the hens, and season the outside of each with salt and pepper.

7. Line the bottom of a roasting pan with foil. Place the hens, breast side down, on a roasting rack. Do not crowd hens together; the heat of the oven must be allowed to totally circulate around each hen. Use a second pan if necessary.

8. Place hens in the preheated oven, and roast for 15 minutes. Remove hens from oven, and baste with the glaze. Return to the oven, and roast for 10 minutes more. Remove and rotate hens to breast side up, brush with glaze, and return to the oven. Continue basting the hens with the glaze every 10 minutes while roasting until they reach an internal temperature of 165°F (74°C) or higher, according to customer preference, at the thigh.

9. Allow hens to rest for at least 10 minutes before serving, or hold at 140°F (60°C) or higher until service.

10. Serve 1/2 of a hen per portion on a preheated dinner plate garnished with the remaining thyme sprigs.

NUTRITION

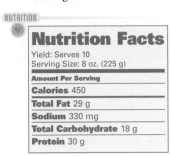

Nutrition Facts

Yield: Serves 10
Serving Size: 8 oz. (225 g)

Amount Per Serving

Calories 450

Total Fat 29 g

Sodium 330 mg

Total Carbohydrate 18 g

Protein 30 g

Roast Turkey with Giblet Gravy

Ingredients

	U.S. Standard	Metric
Whole turkey (10–12 lbs./4.5–5.5 kg), neck, giblets, wing tips removed and reserved	1 each	1 each
Chicken stock	3 qt.	2.9 l
Unsalted butter, softened	6 oz.	170 g
Salt	TT	TT
Black pepper, ground	TT	TT
Fresh sage leaves, washed, chopped	1 oz.	30 ml
Rosemary leaves, washed, chopped	1/2 oz.	15 ml
Garlic cloves, peeled, chopped	8 each	8 each
Onion, peeled, rough-chopped	1 1/2 lbs.	680 g
Celery, trimmed, washed, rough-chopped	1 lb.	454 g
Vegetable oil	3 oz.	90 ml
Carrots, peeled, washed, rough-chopped	1 lb.	454 g
Flour	2 oz.	55 g

Method of Preparation

1. Gather all the ingredients and equipment.

2. Preheat oven to 425°F (218°C).

3. In a medium saucepan, combine reserved neck, giblets, and wing tips with the chicken stock. Simmer gently until giblets are tender and liquid is reduced to 2 qt. (1.9 l). Strain and reserve both stock and giblets for gravy.

4. Meanwhile, blend the butter with 2 tsp. (10 ml) of salt, 2 tsp. (10 ml) of pepper, and half the chopped herbs.

5. Gently slide hand under the skin, starting at the neck, and loosen the skin from the breast and upper leg meat.

6. Spread the herb butter evenly under the skin. Season the cavity with the remaining herbs, salt, and pepper. Add the garlic, 1/2 the onions, and 1/2 the celery to the cavity, and then truss. Rub the surface of the bird with the oil.

7. Position the turkey on a roasting rack, breast side up, and roast at 425°F (218°C) for 25–30 minutes. Reduce the heat to 325°F (163°C), and continue cooking until thigh registers 155°F (68°C). Baste every 20 minutes with pan drippings.

8. Remove pan from oven, and place remaining onion, celery, and carrots beneath the rack and the meat. Continue roasting and basting until the meat is 165°F (74°C), or to customer preference, at the thigh, and the mirepoix is brown. Remove the vegetables from the cavity, and add to the mirepoix in the pan. Hold the turkey to rest, loosely covered, at 140°F (60°C) or higher while the sauce is produced.

9. Place the roasting pan over medium heat. *Singe* with flour, and stir to cook the roux.

10. Whisk the reserved giblet stock into the roux. Simmer 15–20 minutes to reduce, thicken, and fortify flavor.

11. Meanwhile, dice the reserved giblets macédoine. Strain sauce through a chinois mousseline, add the diced giblets, taste, and season with salt and pepper as needed. Hold covered at 140°F (60°C) or higher until service.

12. Slice the meat to order against the grain, and serve some light and dark meat in each portion. *Nappé* with gravy.

Provençal Herb-Baked Chicken

INGREDIENTS	U.S. Standard	Metric
Parsley, *washed, squeezed dry, chopped*	1 oz.	28 g
Rosemary, *fresh, washed leaves stripped and chopped*	1/2 oz.	15 ml
Thyme, *fresh, washed, leaves stripped and chopped*	1/2 oz.	15 ml
Sage, *fresh, washed, and chopped*	1/2 oz.	15 ml
Garlic, *fresh, peeled, mashed to a purée*	4 large cloves	4 large cloves
Olive oil	1/2 c.	120 ml
Chicken legs	10 each	10 each
Salt	TT	TT
Black pepper, *freshly ground*	TT	TT

METHOD OF PREPARATION

1. Gather all the ingredients and equipment.

2. Preheat the oven to 325°F–350°F (163°C–177°C).

3. Combine all herbs, garlic purée, and olive oil.

4. Trim chicken legs of excess fat, place in a bowl, and pour herb/oil mixture over them. Toss to coat.

5. Place chicken in a hotel pan, and season with salt and pepper to taste.

6. Bake in preheated oven to internal temperature of 165°F (74°C) for approximately 30–40 minutes.

7. Hold at 140°F (60°C) or higher.

COOKING TECHNIQUES

Baking:
1. Preheat the oven.
2. Place the food product on the appropriate rack.

NUTRITION

Nutrition Facts
Yield: Serves 10
Serving Size: 6 oz. (170 g)

Amount Per Serving
Calories 540
Total Fat 37 g
Sodium 480 mg
Total Carbohydrate 15 g
Protein 35 g

Roast Chicken with Fresh Herb Butter, Pearl Onions, and Garlic

INGREDIENTS

	U.S. Standard	Metric
Butter, softened	1/2 lb.	225 g
Parsley, flat-leaf	1 oz.	30 ml
Savory, fresh	1 oz.	30 ml
Salt	TT	TT
Black pepper, ground	TT	TT
Chicken, whole (3 1/2 lbs./1.5 kg)	3 each	3 each
Pearl onions, peeled, root intact	1 lb.	454 g
Garlic, cloves separated, peeled	3 heads	3 heads
Carrots, peeled, washed, 1/2" (1.27 cm) rough-chop	6 oz.	170 g
Celery, washed, 1/2" (1.27 cm) rough-chop	6 oz.	170 g
Flour	2 oz.	55 g
White wine	8 oz.	240 ml
Chicken stock	1 qt.	960 ml

METHOD OF PREPARATION

1. Gather all the ingredients and equipment.

2. Preheat the oven to 375°F (191°C).

3. Place butter into a medium-sized bowl. Chop 3 Tbsp. (45 ml) each of the parsley and savory, and add to the butter. Season with salt and pepper.

4. Wash the cavities of the chickens, and pat dry. Season well with salt and pepper. Place the remaining herb sprigs in the cavities.

5. Starting at the neck end, gently slide fingers under the skin and loosen the skin over the breast and thighs. Spread 4 Tbsp. (60 g) of herb butter under the skin, evenly coating the breast meat and the upper leg meat. Truss the chickens, and spread 2 Tbsp. (30 ml) of herb butter evenly over the surface of each.

6. Roast the chickens on a rack, breast side up, for 30 minutes.

7. Meanwhile, melt all but 2 Tbsp. (30 ml) of the remaining herb butter; set the butter aside at room temperature for the sauce, and keep the melted butter warm.

8. After 30 minutes, remove the chickens from oven, and position them breast side down. Scatter the pearl onions and garlic cloves around the chickens, and brush the vegetables and chickens with some of the melted butter. Return the pan to the oven.

9. Continue roasting the chicken to an internal temperature of 165°F (74°C) at the thigh (about 30 minutes longer). Remove the vegetables and chickens from the pan; drain any juice from the cavities into the roasting pan. Hold chicken and vegetables at 140°F (60°C) or higher until service.

10. Set the roasting pan on a medium-high heat. Add the carrots and celery; sauté until *caramelized.*

11. Pour off all but 2 oz. (60 ml) of fat from the roasting pan. Singe the carrots and celery with the flour, mixing it into the fat to create a roux. Whisk in the white wine and chicken stock, and simmer until proper flavor and consistency are achieved. Strain the sauce through a chinois. Whisk in the 2 Tbsp. (30 ml) of room temperature herb butter. Taste, and adjust seasoning with salt and pepper as needed. Hold at 140°F (60°C) or higher.

12. Serve a quarter of a chicken per portion on a preheated dinner plate, surrounded with roasted onions and garlic. Nappé with sauce.

COOKING TECHNIQUES

Roasting:
1. Sear the food product, and brown evenly.
2. Elevate the food product in a roasting pan.
3. Determine doneness, and consider carryover cooking.
4. Let the food product rest before carving.

Simmering:
1. Place the prepared product in an appropriately sized pot.
2. Bring the product to a boil, and then reduce the heat to allow the product to barely boil.
3. Cook until desired doneness is achieved.

GLOSSARY

Caramelize: to heat sugar in foods until it reduces to a clear syrup ranging in color from golden to dark brown

NUTRITION

Nutrition Facts

Yield: Serves 10
Serving Size: 14 oz. (400 g)

Amount Per Serving

Calories 920

Total Fat 65 g

Sodium 400 mg

Total Carbohydrate 18 g

Protein 61 g

Chicken Cacciatore

INGREDIENTS

INGREDIENTS	U.S. Standard	Metric
Chickens, 2 1/2–3 lbs. (1–1.5 kg) each	3 each	3 each
Olive oil	as needed	as needed
Flour, seasoned	2 cups	350 g
Onions, peeled, julienne	6 oz.	170 g
Mushrooms, wiped clean, sliced 1/4″ (6 mm)	10 oz.	285 g
Tomatoes, concassé	10 oz.	285 g
Garlic, peeled, chopped	3 cloves	3 cloves
Bay leaf	1 each	1 each
White wine, dry	8 oz.	240 ml
Brown chicken stock	1 pt.	500 ml
Salt	TT	TT
White pepper, ground	TT	TT
Oregano, washed, dried, chopped	1/2 oz.	15 ml

METHOD OF PREPARATION

1. Gather all the ingredients and equipment.

2. Cut off the wing tips; split the chicken into eighths.

3. Heat a thin layer of olive oil in a rondeau.

4. Dip chicken pieces in flour. Shake off excess, and sear in the hot oil. Do not crowd the pan; sear in batches if necessary. When browned, remove the chicken from the pan, and set aside.

5. Add onions and mushrooms to the rondeau, and sweat until onions are translucent.

6. Add tomatoes, garlic, bay leaf, wine, and chicken stock.

7. Bring to a boil; season with salt and pepper.

8. Return chicken pieces into the sauce, and braise in 325°F–350°F (163°C–177°C) oven, until meat is fork-tender or until an internal temperature of 165°F (74°C) is reached.

9. Remove chicken pieces from the braising liquid, and hold at 140°F (60°C) or higher, tightly covered. Add a small amount of the braising liquid to the chicken to keep it moist while holding.

10. Dépouille the braising liquid, and then simmer and reduce as needed to develop proper flavor and consistency. Taste, and season with salt and pepper. Hold at 140°F (60°C) or higher.

11. Serve chicken on preheated dinner plate, nappé with sauce, and garnish with fresh oregano.

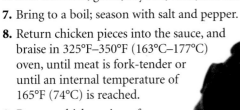

Sautéing:

1. Heat the sauté pan to the appropriate temperature.
2. Evenly brown the food product.
3. For a sauce, pour off any excess oil, reheat, and deglaze.

Braising:

1. Heat the braising pan to the proper temperature.
2. Sear and brown the food product to a golden color.
3. Degrease and deglaze.
4. Cook the food product in two-thirds liquid until fork-tender.

NUTRITION

Nutrition Facts

Yield: Serves 10
Serving Size: 10 oz. (285 g)

Amount Per Serving

Calories 510	
Total Fat 32 g	
Sodium 260 mg	
Total Carbohydrate 15 g	
Protein 34 g	

Buffalo Wings

INGREDIENTS

	U.S. Standard	Metric
Chicken wings, *second and third joints, tips removed*	*40 each*	*1.8 kg*
Hot sauce	*1/2 qt.*	*500 ml*
Butter, *melted*	*3 oz.*	*85 g*
Blue cheese dressing	*10 oz.*	*300 ml*
Celery, *washed, trimmed, cut baton, and held in ice water*	*2 lbs.*	*910 g*

METHOD OF PREPARATION

1. Gather all the ingredients and equipment.

2. Preheat the deep-fat fryer to 350°F (177°C).

3. Separate the two joints of the wings to end up with 80 pieces.

4. Close to service, fry the wings in batches until golden brown and thoroughly cooked until an internal temperature of 165°F (74°C) is reached. Remove, and drain on absorbent paper. Transfer the wings to a hotel pan lined with plenty of absorbent paper, and hold at 140°F (60°C) or higher until needed for service. Do not pile wings on top of one another, or they will get soggy.

5. For service, place the wings in a bowl, and coat them with the hot sauce and melted butter.

6. Place the coated wings on a preheated plate; serve 2 oz. (60 ml) of blue cheese dressing and celery sticks (well-drained) on the side for each portion.

COOKING TECHNIQUES

Deep-Frying:
1. Heat the frying liquid to the proper temperature.
2. Submerge the food product completely.
3. Fry the product until it is cooked throughout.

NUTRITION

Nutrition Facts

Yield: Serves 10
Serving Size: 7 oz. (205 g)

Amount Per Serving

Calories 590

Total Fat 49 g

Sodium 990 mg

Total Carbohydrate 6 g

Protein 30 g

Southern-Style Fried Chicken

INGREDIENTS

	U.S. Standard	Metric
MARINADE		
Buttermilk	1 pt.	500 ml
Cayenne pepper	1 tsp.	5 g
Garlic, *fresh, chopped*	1 Tbsp.	15 g
Worcestershire sauce	1 Tbsp.	15 ml
Onion, *peeled, minced*	1 Tbsp.	5 g
Chicken legs, *thighs and drumsticks separated*	10 each	10 each
Oil *(for frying)*	4 c.	960 ml
Flour, *seasoned*	2 c.	350 g
Salt	TT	TT

COOKING TECHNIQUES

Shallow-Frying:
1. Heat the cooking medium to the proper temperature.
2. Cook the food product throughout.
3. Season, and serve hot.

GLOSSARY
Dredge: to coat with flour

NUTRITION

Nutrition Facts

Yield: Serves 10
Serving Size: 8 oz. (225 g)

Amount Per Serving

Calories 550

Total Fat 39 g

Sodium 340 mg

Total Carbohydrate 13 g

Protein 36 g

METHOD OF PREPARATION

1. Gather all the ingredients and equipment.

2. Preheat oven to 350°F (177°C).

3. Combine ingredients for marinade, add chicken, and marinate for 1 hour. Drain and pat dry.

4. Heat the oil in an appropriate pan for shallow-frying to 350°F (177°C).

5. *Dredge* the chicken in flour, and shake off any excess.

6. Place the chicken into the hot oil, and fry evenly, turning once, until golden brown.

7. Remove chicken from oil, and place on a sheet pan lined with absorbent paper. Lightly season with salt. Transfer chicken to a wire rack set on a sheet pan.

8. Bake chicken in preheated oven until it reaches an internal temperature of 165°F (74°C).

21 Game

Game—wild species of animals and birds—has become an increasingly popular menu offering. Once the prize of the hunt, most game animals and birds consumed today are farm products raised to meet growing demand. Although prehistoric hunters first pursued animals that would be classified as game today, the ancient Egyptians pioneered raising wild species on farms for royalty to hunt. In the Middle Ages, game parks became common and continued in use for centuries. Game was essential to the survival of early European settlers in North America, who learned much from Native Americans about hunting game and gathering wild plants. In Europe kings and noblemen had their own hunting forests as well.

ca. 1150–1123 B.C.
Last Shang emperor of China has game park built for hunting.

621 B.C.
Jewish dietary law prohibits the eating of rabbit.

A.D. 650s to 1600
Game laws in Europe allow only royalty and nobles to hunt.

1621
First Thanksgiving at Plymouth, Massachusetts, includes venison.

1869
Passengers traveling across the United States on the Central Pacific Railroad dine on antelope, quail, and pheasant.

KEY TERMS
furred game
feathered game
wild game
domestic game
venison
jugging
entrails
ratite
fan
eviscerate

Types of Game

There are two general categories of game: furred game and feathered game. *Furred game* includes both large animals, such as deer, wild boar, elk, bear, and moose, and small animals, such as rabbit, squirrel, opossum, woodchuck, beaver, and muskrat. Pheasant, woodcock, ostrich, teal, and quail are examples of *feathered game*.

Game is further classified as wild or domestic. *Wild game* refers to animals and birds that grow and live in their native environment. Wild game is accessible only to hunters. It is for personal consumption only and cannot be sold. *Domestic game* refers to animals and birds that are bred and raised in a farmlike environment. Domestic game is commercially available, often throughout the year.

Nutrition and Quality

In general, both wild and domestic game are more active than other domesticated animals. Although some domestic game raised on farms live in restricted outdoor areas and feed on grains, other domestic game roam over acres of ranch or reserve land and forage for food. Greater movement and a freer lifestyle make game lower in fat, cholesterol, and calories than other meats. Game is also high in minerals and protein. One ounce of deer meat, for instance, has almost twice as much protein as one ounce of duck as well as considerably more protein than an ounce of chicken, pork, or lean beef.

Quality characteristics of game depend on a variety of factors, including the animal's age, diet, level of activity, and season of slaughter. Diet affects the flavor of game meat. Wild game has a very strong flavor. Farm- or ranch-bred game has a more subtle taste, though still stronger than meat from domesticated animals. Older animals have tougher flesh than do younger animals. Greater exercise makes wild game meat tougher and darker than that of domestic game. Game animals and birds harvested in the fall tend to be meatier because they have fed abundantly over the spring and summer.

Inspection of game for wholesomeness is voluntary. Because local health codes generally require that any meat intended for public consumption come from "an approved source," game inspection has become more widespread. Imported game is subject to random inspection by the Food and Drug Administration (FDA). Grading for quality is not available for game.

Handling Game Safely

Proper handling of game maintains its quality and ensures its fitness for consumption. Take the appropriate steps when purchasing, receiving, and storing game to check and preserve its freshness and quality.

Purchasing and Receiving Game

Both furred and feathered game are available fresh or frozen. Feathered game may be ordered cleaned and boned. It is advisable to purchase game only from suppliers that can certify their submission to federal or state inspectors.

As with other meats, examine game carefully upon receiving for signs of mishandling or contamination. Packaging should not show damage of any kind. Look for tears, leakage, or evidence of repacking. Check the temperature, color, odor, and texture of game meat at delivery. Fresh game, like other meats, should be 41°F (5°C) or lower. Frozen game should be frozen, without signs of thawing and refreezing such as ice crystals. Game meat should have good color and not give off a bad odor. It should be firm and not tacky. Do not accept game meat that does not meet these specifications.

Storing Game

Follow general meat storage guidelines for game. Refrigerate fresh game immediately at 41°F (5°C) or lower. Store frozen game at 0°F–10°F (⁻18°C–⁻12°C). Wrap both fresh and frozen products well. Keep raw game separate from other foods, in trays and on the bottom shelves of storage units, to prevent cross-contamination. Use fresh game birds and ground game within one to two days; cook fresh game animals within three to five days. Frozen game birds will keep for six months; frozen game animals will keep for six to nine months. Always thaw game gradually under refrigeration.

Foodborne Illness Associated with Game

Bacteria multiply quickly on raw or undercooked game that fall into the temperature danger zone between 41°F–140°F (5°C–60°C). Among these bacteria are Salmonella and E. coli, which may cause serious and sometimes fatal illnesses, especially in high-risk populations. Trichinella is a parasite often associated with wild game. Cooking game to the proper minimum temperatures is the only way to destroy the harmful bacteria and parasites that cause these and other illnesses.

Follow the minimum temperature guidelines for beef when cooking game animals such as bison, deer, and rabbit. Steak and chops should reach a minimum internal temperature of 145°F (63°C) for 15 seconds, roasts 145°F (63°C) for 3 minutes, stuffed meat 165°F (74°C), and ground meat 155°F (68°C).

Furred Game

Varieties of furred game available to foodservice operations vary by region and by season. Venison, rabbit, and wild boar are the most widely available game animals and appear most frequently on menus.

Venison

Venison is a general term for meat from various game animals, including antelope, caribou, deer, elk, moose, and pronghorn. The name of the animal is clearly displayed on the package label for all venison purchases. Farm-raised venison is available throughout the year. Very often it is meat from one of a variety of deer, including fallow deer (Mediterranean and generally European in origin), red deer (European with African and Asian relatives), roe deer (northern European), and white-tailed deer (North American).

Venison is dark, lean meat with little or no marbling. Although it has a generally mild aroma, it can have a gamy flavor that is lessened by soaking overnight. Loin, leg, and ribs (rack) are the most common venison cuts. Almost any cooking method suits the loin and rack, which are very tender. Dry techniques, such as grilling, roasting, and sautéing, cook these cuts best. Moist and combination methods should be used for the leg, which exercise has made less tender. Ground venison is often used as an ingredient for pâtés and sausages.

Rabbit

Rabbits are usually raised on ranches and are available all year. Often compared to chicken, rabbit meat is lean and quite tender and has a mild flavor. Roasting and sautéing are appropriate cooking methods for rabbit loin, which easily loses moisture. Rabbit legs, which are exercised more, are tougher and benefit from braising or stewing, which incorporates moist and dry cooking. Hares are typically larger than rabbits and are somewhat tougher. Hare is best cooked using a combination technique. **Jugging,** or preserving meat by cooking and storing it in fat, is another method used to prepare rabbit and hare. Casseroles and country-style pâtés sometimes feature rabbit.

Wild Boar

Wild boar is very popular in Europe. Known in Italy as *cinghiale*, wild boar is especially prominent in Tuscan cuisine. Related to domesticated hog, boar is raised today on farms and ranches and is available year-round. Boar meat is leaner than pork, has a more intense flavor, and tends to be very dark. Boar has many of the same culinary applications as pork; both are served as hams, sausages, and roasts. Cooking techniques for boar are also similar to those used for pork. They include both dry methods, such as grilling, and combination methods, such as braising and stewing.

Bison (Buffalo)

After having been hunted almost to extinction in the nineteenth century, North American bison, or buffalo, is making a comeback. Bison are raised on reserves or on ranches like beef cattle. Moist and full of flavor, bison meat bears similarities to lean beef and is suited to the same cooking techniques.

Secondary Varieties

Squirrel, opossum, woodchuck, and beaver are not used in foodservice. If farm-raised, bear may appear as a menu offering. The same cooking techniques used for large domestic game animals apply to cuts of bear.

Feathered Game

The game bird industry in the United States is huge, selling millions of birds each year to restaurants and consumers. Among the most popular varieties of feathered game are quail, pheasant, and partridge.

Quail

A favorite in Europe, North America, and Asia, quail are the smallest game birds. American quail go by various names—bobwhite, partridge, blue quail, California quail, mountain quail, and Montezuma quail—depending on the region. Quail meat is lean, dark, and mild-tasting. Grilling on skewers, roasting on a spit, broiling, sautéing, poaching, and braising are appropriate cooking techniques for quail. Usually served whole, quail are ideal for stuffing, often with rice or forcemeat. Stuffed whole quail may be presented in aspic. Hard-cooked quail eggs can be used in canapés and garnishes.

Pheasant

Originating in Asia, pheasant came to Europe during the Middle Ages and has become the most popular of all game birds. Farm-raised pheasant has a mild flavor and is generally meaty, with the female offering the juiciest and most tender flesh. Both female and young male pheasants are roasted, but the flesh of the larger and older male, which is drier, leaner, and tougher, is better suited to braising or stewing. Meat from an older bird can also be incorporated in a pâté. Pheasant stock makes an excellent base for consommé and sauces.

Partridge

Introduced to North America in the 1800s, partridges are native to Europe, Africa, and Asia. Farms and reserves provide a good supply of partridge in the United States today. Partridge meat has a gamier taste than that of quail or pheasant and is generally tougher. Often roasted whole, it can be cut into pieces and then sautéed, braised, or stewed.

Woodcock

Considered by some to be the best of all bird game, woodcock is extremely tender and has a distinct gamy taste. Woodcock hunting takes place in the spring and fall. Whole woodcock roasted with its **entrails,** or internal organs, intact offers the most flavor. Woodcock flesh is also used in pâtés, terrines, and mousses.

RHEA

EMU

FIGURE 21-1

Native to Africa, the ostrich is not only the largest member of the ratite family but the largest bird in the world, standing 7–8 feet tall. The emu is native to Australia and averages about 6 feet in height. The rhea, native to the Argentinian grasslands of South America, is the smallest ratite, at about 5 feet tall.

PHEASANT

OSTRICH

Ratites (Ostrich, Emu, Rhea)

Ostriches, emus, and rheas belong to the ratite family. See Figure 21-1 on page 400. *Ratites* are small-winged birds that do not fly. Considered red meat because of its dark cherry color, the flesh of these birds is extremely low in fat, cholesterol, and calories. After cooking, ratite meat looks and tastes much like beef although somewhat sweeter. It is available in a variety of retail cuts (medallions, steaks, fillets, and ground meat), mostly from the back, thigh (or *fan*), and leg. The more tender cuts are roasted, grilled, broiled, or sautéed and usually served medium rare to medium. The tougher cuts are cooked using combination methods.

> Inspection of ratites was once voluntary, as it is for other game. Since 2002, however, USDA inspection of ratites has been mandatory. HACCP systems and other sanitation operating procedures now apply to this special class of game bird.

Ratites are low in calories and fat and high in protein, comparing favorably with both red meat and poultry. The nutritional values for a 3.5-ounce (100-g) serving of ratite is shown in Figure 21-2.

FIGURE 21-2

Ratites

EMU
Calories 95
Protein 20 g
Fat 1.5 g

OSTRICH
Calories 100
Protein 25 g
Fat 2 g

RHEA
Calories 105
Protein 23 g
Fat 1.2 g

Preparation of Game

Game cookery involves certain preparatory procedures and techniques. Although domestic or commercially raised and wild game share many of the same preparatory techniques, differences do exist.

Domestic or commercially raised game is federally regulated and is prepared for market in much the same way as domestic livestock or poultry. Commercially raised game intended for sale or distribution must be slaughtered and processed in a USDA/FSIS-inspected facility before it is available for market. Game that has been trapped but not killed must also be slaughtered and processed at a USDA/FSIS site, whether intended for personal consumption or market sale.

Wild game is intended purely for personal use and enjoyment. Both large and small game must be bled, dressed, and cooled quickly to avoid damage to the meat and the spread of bacteria. Field dressing involves opening the body cavity and removing the internal organs. The carcass is then cleaned and dried inside and hung to quickly cool. When brought from the field to the kitchen, the carcass will benefit from 7–14 days' aging in 35°F–40°F (2°C–4°C) refrigeration. Meat should then cut easily away from the bone. Next, the bloodshot should be trimmed. Trim the fat away from the flesh to avoid the gamy taste often associated with wild meats. The meat is then ready to cut into steaks and chops or to be ground into sausage.

Both wild and commercially raised game benefit from marinating, barding, or larding the meat.

Aging

Hanging game before cooking helps the meat mature, or age. During the hanging process, carbohydrates in the tissue convert into lactic acid, tenderizing the meat and giving it a stronger flavor. Before hanging game, *eviscerate,* or remove the animal's entrails. Then hang the game in a cool, dark place with good air circulation. A refrigerator is ideal. Hang furred game by the hind legs and feathered game by the head. To help prevent contamination by bacteria, leave the coat or plumage intact until the hanging process is complete. Hanging times depend on the type and age of game. See Figure 21-3.

FIGURE 21-3

Hanging Times

HARE	WOODCOCK OR PHEASANT
2 days	*4 days*
THRUSH OR WILD DUCK	LARGE GAME
3 days	*6–8 days*

Barding a Game Bird

Game birds, such as a mature pheasant, are especially lean and are at risk of drying out during roasting. Barding, or covering a bird's surface with fat, provides moisture and adds flavor.

To bard a game bird, follow these steps:

1 — **Cover the bird with slices of bacon or pork fatback.**

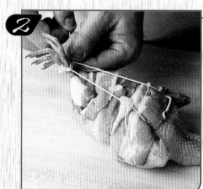

2 — **Secure the fat with butcher's twine.**

Marinating

Marinades have a traditional place in game cookery. Highly flavored and concentrated mixtures of wine, herbs, and spices are often prepared to tenderize game meat, especially that of furred animals, and to mitigate its robust flavor. Most commercially available game today is young, tender, and milder-tasting, therefore marinating is not a requirement. A marinade may be chosen to impart a particular taste to game or to keep it from drying out during cooking.

▍ *See Chapter 12: Seasoning and Flavoring Food for more information on marinades.*

Other Techniques

Because it is generally lean, game often benefits from barding and larding.

▍ *See Chapter 11: Cooking Techniques for more information on barding and larding.*

Fabrication

It is rarely necessary to fabricate large game animals. Commercially available furred game can be purchased already cut into subprimals or portions. Game birds are relatively small and are usually prepared whole, thus requiring little or no butchering.

Butchering (Fabricating) Skills

If smaller cuts of venison, boar, or bison are required, refer to the fabricating procedures for beef, pork, or lamb described in Chapters 16, 18, and 19. The procedure for fabricating a rabbit is explained on the following page.

Fabricating a Rabbit

Though it is rarely necessary to fabricate game, rabbit will need to be butchered in-house.

To fabricate a rabbit into eight sections, place the dressed rabbit on its back. Then follow these steps:

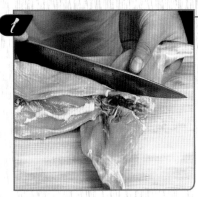

1 Remove kidneys and liver from belly cavity. Pull back the hind legs to expose the joint.

2 Cut through the joint to remove the leg. Repeat to remove the other hind leg.

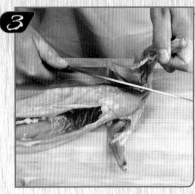

3 Pull the front leg away from the body to expose the joint.

4 Cut around and under the shoulder to separate. Repeat to remove the other front leg.

5 Cut the loin into four sections.

6 The rabbit cut into eight sections, along with liver, kidneys, and heart should look like the one shown here.

Venison Medallions

with Poivrade Sauce and Red Wine

INGREDIENTS	U.S. Standard	Metric
MARINADE		
Red wine	2 c.	500 ml
Water	2 c.	500 ml
Garlic, chopped	4 cloves	4 cloves
Juniper berries, crushed	6 each	6 each
Boneless venison loin, trimmed, cut into 20 medallions, about 2 oz. (55 g) each	3 1/2 lbs.	1.6 kg
POIVRADE SAUCE		
Butter	1 1/2 oz.	40 g
Onions, peeled, diced	4 oz.	115 g
White wine	10 oz.	300 ml
Red wine vinegar	4 oz.	120 ml
Black peppercorns	6 each	6 each
Parsley, washed	2 sprigs	2 sprigs
Thyme, washed	2 sprigs	2 sprigs
Bay leaf	2 each	2 each
Madeira wine	2 oz.	60 ml
Demi-glace	16 oz.	500 ml
Salt	TT	TT
Black pepper, freshly ground	TT	TT
Oil	as needed	as needed
Clarified butter	as needed	as needed
Cognac or brandy	5 oz.	150 ml
Whole butter, softened	2 oz.	55 g
Croutons, cut same size as the medallions, toasted	20 each	20 each

METHOD OF PREPARATION

1. Gather all the ingredients and equipment.

2. Combine the red wine, water, garlic, and juniper berries in a saucepan, and heat to a boil. Reduce heat, and simmer for about 5 minutes to meld the flavors. Chill to 41°F (5°C) or lower.

3. Add the venison medallions to the chilled marinade, and marinate, covered, at 41°F (5°C) or lower for 2 hours. Remove the meat, and pat dry. Discard the marinade.

4. While the venison is marinating, begin the sauce. Heat the butter, add the onions, and sauté until translucent. Add the wine, vinegar, peppercorns, parsley and thyme sprigs, bay leaves, Madeira, and demi-glace.

5. Simmer until reduced by one-third and good flavor and texture is achieved, about 35 minutes. Taste, and season with salt and pepper as needed. Strain through a chinois mousseline and reserve.

6. In a large sauté pan, add enough oil and butter to coat the bottom. Quickly sauté the medallions, turning once until browned and the internal temperature reaches 140°F (60°C). Season with salt and pepper, to taste. Hold at 140°F (60°C), and allow to carry over to a final internal temperature of 145°F (63°C).

7. Drain any fat from the sauté pan, add the cognac or brandy, and *flambé*. Add 16 oz. (454 g) of poivrade sauce. Simmer over low heat for 4 to 6 minutes. Whisk in the softened butter. Hold at 140°F (60°C) or higher.

8. To serve, place 2 croutons on a preheated dinner plate, place a medallion on each, and *nappé* with sauce.

Stewed Rabbit Ragù

with Pappardelle

INGREDIENTS

Ingredients	U.S. Standard	Metric
Flour	4 oz.	115 g
Paprika	1 Tbsp.	15 ml
Dried thyme leaves	1 tsp.	5 ml
Salt	as needed	as needed
Black pepper, ground	as needed	as needed
Olive oil	2–4 oz.	100 ml
Rabbit, cut into 6–8 pieces	3 each	3 each
Onion, peeled, cut macédoine	12 oz.	340 g
Celery, trimmed, washed, cut macédoine	4 oz.	115 g
Carrot, peeled, washed, cut macédoine	4 oz.	115 g
Garlic, peeled, chopped	8 cloves	8 cloves
Red pepper flakes	1 tsp.	5 ml
Dried oregano	1 Tbsp.	15 ml
Bay leaf	2 each	2 each
Canned whole tomatoes, drained, chopped	2 c.	500 ml
Dry white wine	2 c.	500 ml
Veal stock, white	3 c.	720 ml
Portabella mushrooms, gills removed, wiped clean, parmentier	1 lb.	454 g
Pappardelle, dried or fresh	2 lbs.	910 g
Flat leaf parsley, washed, squeezed dry, chopped	1/2 oz.	15 ml
Extra virgin olive oil	1 1/2 oz.	45 ml
Parmigiano regiano, shaved into long curls	3–4 oz.	100 g

METHOD OF PREPARATION

1. Gather all the ingredients and equipment.

2. In a medium-sized shallow container combine the flour, paprika, thyme, salt, and pepper.

3. Heat the olive oil in a large braising pan, and dredge the rabbit pieces in the seasoned flour, shaking to remove excess. Brown on both sides in the hot oil, and set aside.

4. Into the same pan add the onion, celery, and carrot. Sauté to brown. Add the garlic, dried herbs and spices, tomatoes, wine, and stock. Bring the mixture to a boil, and season lightly with salt and pepper.

5. Add the mushrooms, stir to incorporate, and then return the browned rabbit to the pan, nestling the pieces into the liquid. Simmer, covered, until the meat is very tender and falls from the bones.

6. Remove from heat. Place the rabbit on a cutting board to cool slightly. Remove and discard the bay leaves.

7. Pull the rabbit meat from the bones, breaking into small pieces. Discard the bones and any connective tissue.

8. Add the meat back to the sauce and incorporate gently. Adjust the seasoning to taste with salt and pepper. Simmer until hot and reduced to desired consistency and flavor.

9. Cook the pasta while the stew is being finished, and then gently toss the drained pasta with a bit of the braising liquid to moisten the pasta.

10. To serve, arrange a portion of pasta on a plate, top with the *ragù,* garnish with chopped parsley, drizzle with 1 tsp. (5 ml) of extra virgin olive oil, and top with 2–3 shavings of Parmigiano. Serve immediately.

Rabbit Fried in Herb Batter

COOKING TECHNIQUES

Deep-Frying:
1. Heat the frying liquid to the proper temperature.
2. Submerge the food product completely.
3. Fry the product until it is cooked throughout.

NUTRITION

Nutrition Facts

Yield: Serves 10
Serving Size: 10 oz. (285 g)

Amount Per Serving

Calories 380

Total Fat 7 g

Sodium 850 mg

Total Carbohydrate 24 g

Protein 51 g

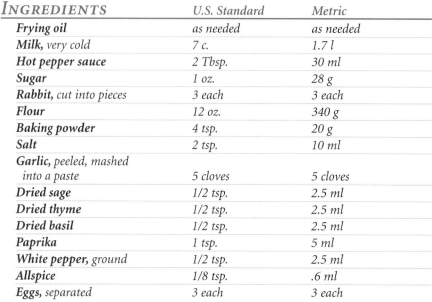

INGREDIENTS	U.S. Standard	Metric
Frying oil	as needed	as needed
Milk, very cold	7 c.	1.7 l
Hot pepper sauce	2 Tbsp.	30 ml
Sugar	1 oz.	28 g
Rabbit, cut into pieces	3 each	3 each
Flour	12 oz.	340 g
Baking powder	4 tsp.	20 g
Salt	2 tsp.	10 ml
Garlic, peeled, mashed into a paste	5 cloves	5 cloves
Dried sage	1/2 tsp.	2.5 ml
Dried thyme	1/2 tsp.	2.5 ml
Dried basil	1/2 tsp.	2.5 ml
Paprika	1 tsp.	5 ml
White pepper, ground	1/2 tsp.	2.5 ml
Allspice	1/8 tsp.	.6 ml
Eggs, separated	3 each	3 each

METHOD OF PREPARATION

1. Gather all the ingredients and equipment.
2. Heat the frying oil in a deep fryer to 350°F (177°C).
3. In a large container combine 5 cups (1.2 l) of the milk (keep the remaining 2 cups/500 ml cold), pepper sauce, and sugar, and whisk until the sugar dissolves. Add the rabbit, and marinate, covered, at 41°F (5°C) or lower for 2 hours.
4. Meanwhile, in a large bowl blend the flour with the baking powder, salt, garlic, herbs, and spices. Whisk the egg yolks and the remaining 2 cups (500 ml) of milk together, and add to the dry ingredients, blending to form a thick batter.
5. In another clean, dry bowl, whisk the egg whites to a medium peak, and fold into the batter. Hold the batter, covered on an ice bath.
6. Drain the rabbit pieces and pat dry; discard the marinade.
7. Working in batches, dip the rabbit pieces in the batter to coat completely.
8. Fry the battered pieces, a few at a time, to a rich brown color and an internal temperature of 145°F (63°C), about 10 minutes.
9. Remove from fryer, and drain on a wire rack. Sprinkle with salt, and hold uncovered in a dry oven at 140°F (60°C) or higher. Fry the remaining pieces in the same manner.
10. Serve the fried rabbit as soon as possible to maintain crispness.

Grilled Ostrich Medallions

with Mustard-Shallot Sauce and Wild Mushrooms

INGREDIENTS

	U.S. Standard	Metric
Shallots, *finely chopped**	3/4 c.	170 g
Garlic, *finely chopped**	10 cloves	10 cloves
Dry white wine, *divided**	3 1/2 c.	840 ml
Thyme leaves, *washed, leaves stripped, chopped**	6 Tbsp.	90 ml
Sugar	1 tsp.	5 g
Olive oil	4 oz.	120 ml
Salt	TT	TT
Black pepper, *freshly ground*	TT	TT
Ostrich, *top loin or tenderloin, trimmed, cut into 10 medallions*	3 1/2 lbs.	1.6 kg
Clarified butter*	4 oz.	115 g
Demi-glace	3 c.	720 ml
Dijon mustard	4 Tbsp.	60 ml
Thyme sprigs	3 each	3 each
Bay leaf	2 each	2 each
Heavy cream	8 oz.	240 ml
Assorted wild mushrooms, *whole (cut if large), cleaned*	1 1/2 lbs.	680 g

METHOD OF PREPARATION

1. Gather all the ingredients and equipment.
2. In a container large enough to hold the ostrich in one layer, combine 1/4 c. (44 g) of the shallots, half of the chopped garlic, 1 cup (240 ml) of the wine, 3 Tbsp. (45 ml) of the chopped thyme, sugar, and olive oil. Season with salt and pepper, whisking well. Lay the ostrich medallions into the marinade, cover, and hold at 41°F (5°C) or lower for 1 hour.
3. Preheat the grill to medium-high.
4. Meanwhile, make the sauce. In a medium-sized saucepan, sweat 1/4 c. (44 g) of the shallots in 2 oz. (60 ml) of the clarified butter. Add 1 1/2 cups (360 ml) of the wine, and reduce by half.
5. Add the demi-glace, mustard, thyme sprigs, and bay leaf, and reduce by one-third.
6. Add the heavy cream, return to a simmer, and simmer gently until good flavor and texture is achieved. Taste and season with salt and pepper as needed.
7. Strain through a fine chinois, and hold covered at 140°F (60°C) or higher.
8. While the sauce is reducing, sauté the mushrooms in the remaining clarified butter in a large sauté pan along with the remaining 1/4 c. (44 g) of chopped shallots and chopped garlic until lightly browned. Season with salt and pepper.
9. Add the remaining 1 c. (240 ml) wine and 3 Tbsp. (45 ml) of chopped thyme, and reduce until nearly dry. Hold covered at 140°F (60°C) or higher.
10. Remove the ostrich from the marinade, and pat dry. Grill the ostrich to 145°F (63°C).
11. To serve, arrange a portion of mushrooms with a grilled medallion on a preheated dinner plate. *Nappé* with the sauce, and serve immediately.

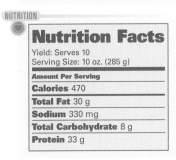

Nutrition Facts

Yield: Serves 10
Serving Size: 10 oz. (285 g)

Amount Per Serving

Calories 470	
Total Fat 30 g	
Sodium 330 mg	
Total Carbohydrate 8 g	
Protein 33 g	

Note: Milligrams are higher in analysis than label because of adding the sauce.

Venison Stew

with Pearl Onions, Artichokes, and Sun-Dried Tomatoes

INGREDIENTS

	U.S. Standard	Metric
GREMOLADA		
Lemon zest, washed, finely grated	4 tsp.	20 ml
Parsley, washed, squeezed dry, chopped	4 tsp.	20 ml
Garlic, peeled, finely chopped	2 cloves	2 cloves
Olive oil	2 oz.	60 ml
Venison stew meat, trimmed, cut into 1 1/2" (3.8 cm) cubes	4 lbs.	1.8 kg
Pearl onions, trimmed, peeled	1 pt.	454 g
Carrots, tourné 1" (2.54 cm)	30 each	30 each
Red wine	1 pt.	500 ml
Brown veal stock	1 qt.	960 ml
Parsley stems	6 each	6 each
Thyme sprigs	2 each	2 each
Bay leaves	2 each	2 each
Celery stalks, 4" (10.1 cm) long	2 each	2 each
Sun-dried tomatoes, sliced 1/2" (1.27 cm)	3 oz.	85 g
Frozen artichoke hearts, thawed	1 1/2 lbs.	680 g
Salt	TT	TT
Black pepper, freshly ground	TT	TT
Brown roux	3 oz.	85 g

METHOD OF PREPARATION

1. Gather all the ingredients and equipment.

2. Combine the lemon zest, parsley, and garlic for the gremolada, and set aside.

3. For the stew, heat half of the olive oil in a braising pan, and brown half of the meat well. Hold browned meat, and repeat with remaining oil and meat.

4. Sauté the onions and carrots in the same pan until lightly browned. Return the seared meat to the pan.

5. Add the wine and stock, and bring to a boil.

6. Meanwhile tie the parsley stems, thyme, and bay leaves with the celery to create a bouquet garni.

7. Add the bouquet garni, sun-dried tomatoes, and artichokes to the pan. Bring to a boil, and season lightly with salt and pepper. Reduce to a simmer.

8. Cut a piece of parchment paper to the diameter of the pot, and lay it directly onto the surface of the stew.

9. Cover with a lid, and simmer gently for 20–30 minutes, or until the meat is fork-tender.

10. Carefully drain the cooking liquids into a saucepan. Hold the stew, covered tightly, at 140°F (60°C) or higher.

11. Thicken the cooking liquid by tempering in the brown roux, and then simmer until desired consistency is achieved.

12. Add the sauce back to the meat. Sprinkle with the gremolada, and mix gently but thoroughly. Taste, and adjust the seasoning with salt and pepper as needed. Serve immediately, or hold at 140°F (60°C) or higher.

COOKING TECHNIQUES

Stewing:
1. Sear, sauté, sweat, or blanch the main food product.
2. Deglaze the pan, if desired.
3. Cover the food product with simmering liquid.
4. Remove the bouquet garni.

NUTRITION

Nutrition Facts
Yield: Serves 10
Serving Size: 12 oz. (340 g)

Amount Per Serving
Calories 380

Total Fat 11 g
Sodium 170 mg
Total Carbohydrate 23 g
Protein 42 g

Buffalo Chili

INGREDIENTS

INGREDIENTS	U.S. Standard	Metric
Salad oil	2 oz.	60 ml
Onion, cut macédoine	12 oz.	340 g
Garlic, peeled, chopped	15 cloves	15 cloves
Ground buffalo	2 lbs.	910 g
Chili powder	1/2 c.	120 ml
Ground coriander	1 tsp.	5 ml
Ground cumin	1 Tbsp.	15 ml
Dried oregano	2 Tbsp.	30 ml
Salt	1 Tbsp.	15 ml
Cayenne	1/2 tsp.	2.5 ml
Brown sugar	1 Tbsp.	15 g
Vinegar	1 Tbsp.	15 ml
Tomatoes, concassé	1 1/2 lbs.	680 g
Beef stock	1 pt.	500 ml
Red kidney beans, canned, drained	1 1/2 lbs.	680 g

METHOD OF PREPARATION

1. Gather all the ingredients and equipment.

2. In a large, heavy rondeau heat the salad oil, and sweat the onion and garlic until softened.

3. Increase the heat. Add the ground buffalo, and brown well, mixing and breaking up large clumps.

4. Add the chili powder, coriander, cumin, and oregano. Blend well, and cook, stirring to warm the spices, about 1–2 minutes.

5. Add the salt, cayenne, sugar, vinegar, tomatoes, and stock, and simmer, stirring occasionally for 1–1 1/2 hours until thickened. Add the drained beans, and simmer 20 minutes longer. Taste, and adjust the seasoning as needed. Hold covered at 140°F (60°C) or higher, or serve immediately.

Squab with Sweet Sausages and Porcini

INGREDIENTS

Ingredients	U.S. Standard	Metric
Porcini, dried	1 oz.	28 g
Italian sweet sausages (mild)	1 lb.	454 g
Squab	10 each	10 each
Salt	TT	TT
Black pepper, ground	TT	TT
Butter, whole	2 oz.	55 g
Garlic, minced	6 cloves	6 cloves
Onion, peeled, chopped	12 oz.	340 g
Red bell peppers, cored, seeded, thinly sliced	2 each	2 each
Canned plum tomatoes (save juice)	3 c.	720 ml
Red pepper flakes	1 tsp.	5 ml
Tomato paste	3 Tbsp.	45 ml
Dry white wine	1/2 c.	120 ml
Basil, washed, dried, chopped	2 Tbsp.	30 ml
Juice of orange	1 each	1 each
Zest of orange (wash before zesting)	2 each	2 each
Cooked rice, cooked with porcini soaking liquid (optional)	2 1/2 c.	550 g

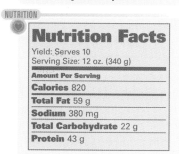

COOKING TECHNIQUES

Braising:
1. Heat the braising pan to the proper temperature.
2. Sear and brown the food product to a golden color.
3. Degrease and deglaze.
4. Cook the food product in two-thirds liquid until fork-tender.

NUTRITION

Nutrition Facts
Yield: Serves 10
Serving Size: 12 oz. (340 g)

Amount Per Serving

Calories 820

Total Fat 59 g

Sodium 380 mg

Total Carbohydrate 22 g

Protein 43 g

METHOD OF PREPARATION

1. Gather all the ingredients and equipment.

2. Soak the porcini in 3 cups (720 ml) of warm water for 30 minutes. Drain, and reserve the water to cook the rice. Hold the mushrooms for the braising liquid.

3. Pierce the sausages to release fat. Cook them for 10 minutes in a covered, dry braising pan over moderate heat. Remove the lid, and allow sausages to brown on all sides. Remove sausages to cool, slice in 1″ (2.54 cm) pieces, and set aside.

4. Meanwhile, rinse and dry the cavities of the squab, season well with salt and pepper, and truss. Sear the squab in the fat from the sausages. Remove, and set aside. Pour off all but 1 tablespoon (15 ml) of the fat in the pan. Add the butter to the pan, and melt. Add the garlic, onions, and peppers, and sauté over a moderately low flame until the vegetables are tender.

5. Return the sausage slices to the pan, and add the porcini, tomatoes, red pepper flakes, tomato paste, wine, basil, orange juice, zest, and salt to taste. Simmer for 10 minutes to blend the flavors.

6. Return the squab to the sauce and simmer, covered, for 20 minutes or until the temperature at the thigh is 165°F (74°C). Taste the braising liquid, and adjust with salt if needed. Dépouille.

7. Hold covered at 140°F (60°C) or higher, or serve immediately on preheated dinner plates with rice cooked with the porcini soaking water.

Pheasant Braised

with Red Cabbage and Apple Cider

INGREDIENTS	U.S. Standard	Metric
Bay leaf	2 each	2 each
Black peppercorns	1 Tbsp.	15 ml
Juniper berries	5 each	5 each
Thyme sprigs	3 each	3 each
Celery seed	1 tsp.	5 ml
Bacon	1/2 lb.	225 g
Butter, whole	4 oz.	115 g
Onions, diced macédoine	12 oz.	340 g
Brown sugar	2 oz.	55 g
Red cabbage, core removed, cut chiffonade	3 lbs.	1.4 kg
Tart apples, cored, peeled, grated	4 each	4 each
Potatoes, peeled, grated	8 oz.	225 g
Apple cider	1 pt.	500 ml
Dry white wine	1 c.	240 ml
Cider vinegar	2 oz.	60 ml
Salt	TT	TT
Ground black pepper	TT	TT
Clarified butter	1 1/2 oz.	45 ml
Vegetable oil	1 1/2 oz.	45 ml
Pheasant, cut into 8 pieces	3 each	3 each

METHOD OF PREPARATION

1. Gather all the ingredients and equipment.

2. Preheat the oven to 350°F (177°C).

3. Make a sachet of the bay leaf, peppercorns, juniper berries, thyme sprig, and celery seed; set aside.

4. In a braising pan, render the bacon until crisp. Remove bacon, rough chop, and hold at 41°F (5°C) or lower.

5. Add the whole butter to the pan with the bacon fat, and melt.

6. Add the onion to the pan, and sweat until softened. Stir in the brown sugar.

7. Add the cabbage, apples, potatoes, cider, wine, vinegar, and sachet. Season with salt and pepper. Mix well, cover, and simmer together for about 10 minutes, stirring periodically.

8. Meanwhile, heat the clarified butter and vegetable oil together in a large sauté pan. Season the pheasant pieces with salt and pepper, and sear them carefully in the hot fortified butter until well browned (the skin tends to stick if the pan is too cold or they are moved too soon).

9. Lay the seared pheasant pieces on top of the cabbage. Cover tightly, and braise in the preheated oven until fork-tender, about 45 minutes to 1 hour.

10. Remove the pheasant pieces to a hotel pan, cover, and hold at 140°F (60°C) or higher.

11. Adjust the liquid in the cooked cabbage if it seems too dry or too soupy, and remove sachet.

12. Add the reserved bacon bits, cover, and hold at 140°F (60°C) or higher.

13. Serve two pieces (one piece each, leg and breast) of pheasant per portion on top of a bed of cabbage on a preheated dinner plate.

Chef's Notes

If a crispy skin is desired, the cooked pheasant can be brushed with some butter and run briefly under a broiler.

COOKING TECHNIQUES

Braising:

1. Heat the braising pan to the proper temperature.
2. Sear and brown the food product to a golden color.
3. Degrease and deglaze.
4. Cook the food product in two-thirds liquid until fork-tender.

NUTRITION

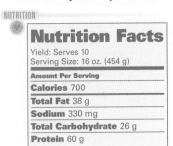

Nutrition Facts

Yield: Serves 10
Serving Size: 16 oz. (454 g)

Amount Per Serving

Calories 700

Total Fat 38 g

Sodium 330 mg

Total Carbohydrate 26 g

Protein 60 g

Prosciutto-Stuffed Quail

INGREDIENTS	U.S. Standard	Metric
STUFFING		
Prosciutto ham, diced brunoise	5 oz.	140 g
Apple, washed, peeled, cored, and diced brunoise	5 oz.	140 g
Pistachio nuts, shelled and peeled	2 oz.	55 g
Dried dates, pitted and chopped	2 oz.	55 g
Bread crumbs	1 oz.	28 g
Butter, melted	1 oz.	30 ml
Ginger, ground	1/4 tsp.	1.25 ml
Thyme, ground	1/4 tsp.	1.25 ml
White pepper, ground	1/4 tsp.	1.25 ml
Salt	TT	TT
Quail, partially deboned	10 each	10 each
Olive oil	2 oz.	60 ml
Marsala wine	4 oz.	120 ml
Demi-glace, heated to a boil and seasoned	1 pt.	500 ml

METHOD OF PREPARATION

1. Gather all the ingredients and equipment.

2. Preheat the oven to 325°F (163°C).

3. Combine ingredients for stuffing, and mix well.

4. Rinse the quails, and pat dry. Fill the quails with the stuffing mixture. Fold the wings under the birds.

5. In a sauté pan, heat the olive oil until it is almost smoking. Sear the birds on all sides. Transfer the birds to a hotel pan.

6. Discard the fat from the pan, and deglaze with Marsala wine. Cook to reduce by half. Add the demi-glace; return to a boil, and then pour over the quails.

7. Bake in the oven for 10 minutes or until tender, or until the internal temperature reaches 165°F (74°C).

8. To serve, place the quail on preheated dinner plates, and nappé with sauce.

COOKING TECHNIQUES

Sautéing:
1. Heat the sauté pan to the appropriate temperature.
2. Evenly brown the food product.
3. For a sauce, pour off any excess oil, reheat, and deglaze.

Baking:
1. Preheat the oven.
2. Place the food product on the appropriate rack.

NUTRITION

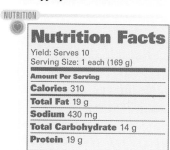

Nutrition Facts
Yield: Serves 10
Serving Size: 1 each (169 g)

Amount Per Serving

Calories 310

Total Fat 19 g

Sodium 430 mg

Total Carbohydrate 14 g

Protein 19 g

Roast Partridge Dijon Style

INGREDIENTS	U.S. Standard	Metric
Whole partridge	5 each	5 each
Dijon mustard (reserve 3 Tbsp./45 g)	12 oz.	360 ml
Bacon	20 slices	20 slices
Game fumet	6 oz.	180 ml
Cognac	4 oz.	120 ml
Heavy cream	1 pint	500 ml
Salt	TT	TT
Black pepper, ground	TT	TT
White bread, toasted, cut in diagonals	10 slices	10 slices

METHOD OF PREPARATION

1. Gather all the ingredients and equipment.

2. Trim the partridges, and spread the mustard over each bird. Bard each with three or four slices of bacon, and truss.

3. Place the birds in a roasting pan. Roast in an oven at 425°F (218°C) for 20–25 minutes.

4. Remove the birds from the roasting pan, and hold warm at 140°F (60°C) or higher. Take 2 oz. (60 ml) of the fat from the roasting pan, and place in a skillet. Add the fumet, stir, and heat to a boil. Add the cognac, and cook for 3 minutes.

5. Add the cream and 3 Tbsp. (45 g) of Dijon mustard. Stir, simmer, and reduce the sauce slowly. Season with salt and pepper. Remove the string and barding from the birds.

6. Cut the partridges in half. Set each half on top of two toast diagonals, and spoon the sauce on top.

COOKING TECHNIQUES

Roasting:

1. Sear the food product, and brown evenly.
2. Elevate the food product in a roasting pan.
3. Determine doneness, and consider carryover cooking.
4. Let the food product rest before carving.

NUTRITION

Nutrition Facts

Yield: Serves 10
Serving Size: 1/2 each (199 g)

Amount Per Serving

Calories 390

Total Fat 18 g

Sodium 700 mg

Total Carbohydrate 3 g

Protein 38 g

22 *Fish and Shellfish*

Rock paintings made thousands of years ago show pictures of fish and the tools people used to catch them. Waste heaps, called kitchen middens, filled with fish bones and mollusk shells provide even older evidence of the kinds and quantities of fish and shellfish people ate in prehistoric times. Clearly, fish and shellfish have provided an important source of protein from the earliest times. Early fishers probably caught fish by grabbing them from shallow rivers or by picking up those washed in by the ocean's tide. Later, people used traps and nets to capture fish and shellfish. Development of sailing vessels brought humans to the seemingly inexhaustible food supplies of the sea.

A.D. 1903
A cannery in San Pedro, California, launches the canned tuna industry.

1914
Brooklyn-born Bob Birdseye pioneers frozen fish.

1965
Arkansas farmers open catfish farms to supplement farm income.

1976
U.S. extends its fishing rights to 200 miles offshore and limits catch of certain species.

Fish and Shellfish Consumption

With more than 30,000 species in the oceans and lakes, fish and shellfish supply the bulk of the animal protein people consume in most parts of the world. The average American still relies most on red meat and poultry for protein, but Americans now eat 3.5 pounds more fish and shellfish per year than they did just twenty years ago. Americans annually consume more than 4 billion pounds—nearly 15 pounds per person—of domestic and imported fish and shellfish. The newest star in the American fish world is salmon. Since 1989, salmon consumption in the United States has nearly quadrupled. Increased awareness of the health benefits that come from eating fish, the availability of high-quality fish and shellfish in all parts of the country, the growing cultural diversity of the country, and the demand for foods from a variety of traditions all have boosted Americans' consumption of fish and shellfish.

Nearly 75% of all the fish and shellfish consumed in the United States is eaten in restaurants. Fish and shellfish, prepared using a variety of cooking methods, appear in nearly every course on the menu in a seemingly endless range of dishes. The diversity that fish and shellfish offer, as well as consumers' increased demand, makes fish cookery an important focus for today's chefs.

Nutritional Benefits

Fish and shellfish are composed of protein, fat, water, vitamins, and minerals. Fish and shellfish are high in iron, potassium, phosphorus, and vitamins A, B, and D. Canned fish with edible bones are also an especially good source of calcium. Compared with other forms of animal protein, fish and shellfish are relatively low in calories. Commonly used cooking methods such as grilling, broiling, poaching, and steaming contribute little or no fat, which also increases the nutritional standing.

The fat content of fish and shellfish ranges from 0.5% to 20%. Cod, sole, flounder, halibut, and snapper are some popular lean fish varieties. Nutritionists consider even high-fat fish a dietary plus. Salmon, tuna, mackerel, sardines, and anchovies are high-fat fish, rich in omega-3 fatty acids. Research indicates that omega-3 fatty acids are helpful in preventing heart disease and in boosting the functioning of the body's immune system.

Inspection and Grading of Fish and Shellfish

The U.S. Food and Drug Administration (FDA) requires fish and shellfish processors, repackers, and warehouses to follow the HACCP food safety system. Inspection of fish and shellfish, however, is voluntary. The National Oceanic and Atmospheric Administration (NOAA), under the control of the U.S. Department of Commerce, runs the government's fee-for-service inspection program. Owners of fishing vessels, fish processors, distributors, brokers, retailers, chefs, exporters, and importers are among the groups who can pay for inspection services.

Specific inspection marks designate the type of inspection the federal inspector performs. Recognize these marks and understand their significance to make informed decisions about fish and shellfish. See Figure 22-1.

The "U.S. Grade A" mark indicates that the fish or shellfish has been processed under federal inspection in an approved facility. It also indicates that the product meets the highest standards for quality. U.S. Grade A fish is practically free from defects, with a good flavor and odor. Most fish consumed in restaurants is U.S. Grade A.

Grading criteria vary according to the type of fish and shellfish, and specific federal criteria exist only for the most popular kinds of fish. Inspectors grade the highest quality as U.S. Grade A, fish and shellfish of good quality are classified as U.S. Grade B, and fish and shellfish of fairly good quality are labeled U.S. Grade C. Some products, such as frozen salmon and fresh scallops, have only Grade A and Grade B designations. In these cases, fish below Grade B are classified as substandard.

The "Processed Under Federal Inspection" (PUFI) mark indicates that the product has been inspected in an approved facility and is certified to be safe, wholesome, and properly labeled. The PUFI mark also indicates that the fish or shellfish conforms to standards established in a purchasers' approved specification sheet.

The "Lot Inspection" mark identifies fish or shellfish that was officially sampled and inspected and that meets all approved criteria or purchase specifications.

The "Retail" mark identifies retail or foodservice establishments that use the U.S. Department of Commerce HACCP-based service or other approved sanitation and product evaluation service. The mark assures consumers that the facility follows proper procedures for sanitation and handling of fishery products.

The USDC "HACCP" mark can be used in conjunction with other inspection marks to signify that the fish or shellfish was produced under the HACCP-based program.

FIGURE 22-1

Federal Inspection Marks

Structure of Fish

Fish and shellfish are two different types of seafood. Fish are cold-blooded animals that live in either salt water or freshwater. They have fins for swimming, gills for breathing, backbones, and internal skeletons of bones and cartilage. Fish flesh is composed of short muscle fibers with little connective tissue, so fish are naturally tender. Experts classify fish into three categories, according to their shape and skeletal structure.

Round Fish

Round fish swim upright—that is, in a vertical position. A round fish has one eye on each side of its head and a body that may be round, oval, or compressed. The backbone lies along the upper edge of the fish's body. See Figure 22-2. Trout and cod are two popular types of round fish.

Flat Fish

Flat fish are so named because they swim flat, or horizontally, through the water. Flat fish spend much of their time resting flat on the ocean floor. A flat fish has a backbone that runs horizontally through the center of its body and two eyes on top of its head. See Figure 22-3. As protection from predators, the skin on the top of most flat fish is dark, and the underside is white. Three common types of flat fish are flounder, sole, and halibut. Flat fish have small scales and dorsal and anal fins that run the length of the body.

Boneless Fish

Boneless fish, such as sharks and rays, have cartilage instead of bones. Many boneless fish have smooth skin instead of scales. They are sometimes grouped with round fish.

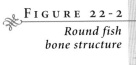

FIGURE 22-2
Round fish bone structure

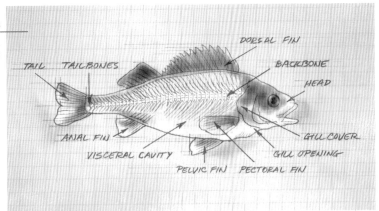

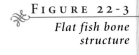

FIGURE 22-3
Flat fish bone structure

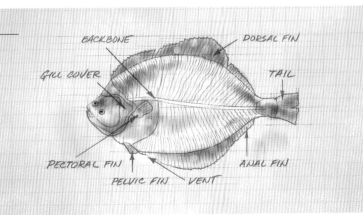

Handling and Storing Fish Safely

Proper temperature is key to maintaining the quality and safety of fish, from the time the fish is caught to the time it is cooked and served. Handle and store fish carefully, and use it quickly.

Receiving Fish

Foodservice establishments must thoroughly inspect incoming fish for freshness and quality before accepting it. The quality of fish can deteriorate quickly; the U.S. Grade A stamp is no guarantee that the fish is still at peak quality and wholesomeness by the time it is received. Arrange for the frequent delivery of fresh fish, and accept only what will be used within a day or two.

Fresh Fish

Evaluate fresh fish on the basis of its smell, feel, and appearance.

- **Smell**—Fresh fish should have the odor of the ocean or of fresh seaweed. It should not smell "fishy." As the fish ages, off odors intensify. Fish with an ammonia-like smell is unfit for consumption.

To check whole, gutted fish, bend the head backward, and sniff the gut cavity. If there is an off-odor, the fish is not at peak freshness. Check fillets and steaks by sniffing the surface of the cut fish.

- **Feel**—Top-quality fish feels firm to the touch. Check by pressing your finger onto the fish surface. The flesh should spring back, leaving no indentation. Whole fish should feel moist and slick, with scales that are firmly attached. Cut fish should not feel slimy.

- **Appearance**—Examine the eyes, gills, skin, and flesh. On most types of fish, the eyes should be clear and rounded. The gills should look bright red. As the fish ages, the gills turn from red to pink and then eventually to gray or brown. Cut fish should have a sheen of moisture and be free from bruises or blood spots. When bent, the flesh should not separate. If it does, the connective tissue between the muscles has begun to deteriorate.

Frozen Fish

Frozen fish should be solidly frozen when received. Look for well-wrapped fish with no off-odor. Examine frozen fish for white or dark spots and fading or discoloration of red or pink flesh. These characteristics could indicate freezer burn. Check whole fish for ice crystals inside the fish. These could indicate that the fish was partially thawed and then refrozen. Some frozen fish are coated with a thin layer of ice to minimize moisture loss. Such fish should have a shiny, glazed surface.

Canned and Vacuum-Sealed Pouches

Check canned fish for signs of container damage. Do not accept swollen or dented cans. **Vacuum-packed** fish can include fresh, frozen, or cooked fish, packed in sealed, airtight pouches from which most oxygen is removed. Cooked tuna is also available vacuum-packed and requires no refrigeration. Vacuum packaging extends the shelf life of fresh and frozen fish, but fresh and frozen vacuum-sealed products must follow the same temperature receiving and handling requirements as conventionally packaged fish. Check frozen vacuum-packed fish for signs that the product has thawed and been refrozen. Check all vacuum packaging carefully for tears, holes, or leakage.

Storing Fish

All animal products spoil because of bacterial action. Following proper procedures for storing fresh, frozen, canned, and vacuum-packed fish ensures wholesome, good-tasting fish.

Fresh Fish

The best way to preserve the freshness of fish is to keep it well chilled and serve it as soon as possible. Store fresh fish at 41°F (5°C) or lower. To store fresh whole fish at the correct temperature, keep the fish on crushed ice in the refrigerator, in a drip pan to allow for drainage. Cut fish, such as fillets or steaks, should be stored in watertight containers or wrapped in plastic bags and covered on all sides with crushed ice. Drain and change the ice daily on both whole and cut fish. Use fresh fish within one or two days, checking for freshness again just before use. Wrap and freeze fresh fish if there is more than can be used immediately.

Frozen Fish

Store frozen fish between 0°F–10°F (-18°C–-12°C), and wrap fish well to prevent freezer burn. Frozen fatty fish maintains its quality for up to two months, and frozen lean fish keeps well for six months. Prior to use, thaw frozen fish in the refrigerator. Allow 18–36 hours for thawing to take place. Never thaw frozen fish at room temperature. If necessary, thaw well-wrapped frozen fish under cold running water.

Small pieces of fish can be cooked from a frozen state. Doing so minimizes *drip loss,* the loss of moisture that occurs as fish thaws. Fish also can be partially thawed and then prepped and cooked. Partially thawed fish handles more easily than fish that has thawed completely. Follow the manufacturer's directions for cooking frozen prepared or breaded fish products, as many should not thaw before cooking. Never refreeze fish. Remember to check for quality before preparing all frozen or thawed fish.

Canned and Vacuum-Sealed Pouches

Store canned fish and vacuum-sealed pouches of cooked tuna in a cool, dry place. Once opened, the product should be used immediately, or unused portions should be refrigerated in labeled, covered containers. Use the opened product within a day or two. Store vacuum-sealed fresh or frozen fish just as any other fresh or frozen fish.

Foodborne Illness

The very qualities that make fish desirable—its high protein and moisture content—make it susceptible to rapid bacterial decay. Fish that is improperly handled, stored, or cooked carries a high risk of transmitting illness to humans. Some fish also can be afflicted with parasites. Anisakiasis is an illness caused by parasitic roundworms that live in the organs of some fish. Following proper cooking methods can destroy these parasites. Obtaining fish from reputable sources; checking quality upon receipt and prior to preparation; and storing, cooking, and serving fish at appropriate temperatures will minimize the risk of foodborne illness.

Varieties of Fish

There are hundreds of different fish from which to choose when deciding what to prepare and serve. The following varieties represent the kinds of fish most commonly served in the United States.

Saltwater Fish

Saltwater fish spend all or most of their lives in salt water. Saltwater fish can include fish caught in the wild and those raised through aquaculture fish farms.

Mercury Poisoning in Fish

The U.S. Food and Drug Administration (FDA) warns women who are pregnant, nursing, or of childbearing age and at risk of getting pregnant to limit their consumption of certain kinds of fish. The FDA also suggests that young children should limit the amounts and kinds of fish they eat.

The risk comes from mercury. Mercury that is naturally present in the air and released through industrial pollution enters lakes, rivers, and oceans. Once there, bacteria in the water change the mercury to methylmercury. Fish absorb methylmercury in the water when they feed on smaller fish and other aquatic organisms. Methylmercury is a toxin that can seriously damage the brain and nervous system of the developing human fetus. Learning deficiencies and delayed mental development are two potential results of methylmercury exposure.

Levels of methylmercury are particularly high in some large fish that live for many years, such as shark, swordfish, king mackerel, and tilefish. Mercury levels in these fish build up over time, creating dangerously high levels. The FDA recommends that pregnant women exclude these fish from their diets and limit the consumption of other types of fish to no more than 12 ounces of cooked fish per week.

Groups such as the National Academy of Sciences and the U.S. Public Interest Research Group believe the risks of exposure to methylmercury in the womb are far greater than the FDA admits. The U.S. Public Interest Research Group claims that fresh tuna, sea bass, halibut, and several other types of fish are equally risky for pregnant women. On the other hand, the group says that farm-raised trout, shrimp, wild Pacific salmon, and haddock are safe.

Round Fish

Round fish have a backbone along the upper edge of the body. Anchovies, various types of bass, and cod are among the popular types of round fish.

Anchovy

An anchovy is a tiny, round saltwater fish, with a pronounced flavor and a firm texture when fresh. Most anchovies are salted and canned in oil. Anchovies also form the basis for commercially packaged anchovy paste. Use canned anchovies and anchovy paste in Caesar salad, in canapés, and as a flavoring in sauces or other prepared dishes. Cook fresh anchovies with herbs and oil on the grill, or serve lightly sautéed.

Black Sea Bass

Black sea bass are round saltwater fish from the Atlantic coastline. This black-scaled fish has firm, moderately fatty white flesh and a delicate flavor from its diet of crabs and shrimp. The fish typically weighs 1–2 pounds (450–900 g), although some may reach 5 pounds (2.2 kg). Black sea bass lends itself to any cooking technique and may be cooked whole or in fillets.

Striped Bass

Wild striped bass, sometimes incorrectly called rockfish, are no longer available for commercial sale because of overfishing and pollution on the East Coast. A true striped bass is anadromous, meaning that it migrates from salt water to spawn in freshwater. Foodservice operations purchase a hybrid striped bass that has been aquafarmed. Farm-raised striped bass range in size from 1 to 5 pounds (450 g to 2.2 kg) and have six to eight stripes on their greenish silver bodies. The mild, sweet flavor and firm texture of this fish make it suitable for steaming, baking, poaching, or broiling.

Cod

Cod is a family of round fish from the Atlantic and Pacific Oceans. Cod has lean, firm flesh and a mild flavor. The best-known cod species is the Atlantic cod, which has a distinctive single whisker sticking out of its chin. Atlantic cod generally weigh around 10 pounds (4.4 kg). Cod weighing less than 2.5 pounds (1.1 kg) are labeled as scrod. Cod most often sells in fillets, which can be poached, deep-fried, sautéed, braised, or used in soups and stews. Cod that has been salted and dried is often called *baccalà*.

Haddock

Haddock is a round saltwater fish with a firm texture and a mild flavor. Haddock is closely related to cod, but the fish are generally smaller, weighing 2–5 pounds (900 g–2.3 kg). A variety of cooking techniques are used to prepare whole haddock, haddock fillets, and steaks. Finnan haddie, traditionally eaten at breakfast in the British Isles, is haddock that has been boned, salted, and smoked.

Mackerel

Spanish and king mackerel are two common members of the mackerel family. Tuna, another mackerel, is discussed separately. Mackerel is a saltwater fish whose oily and full-flavored taste is best when broiled, baked, grilled, or smoked. King mackerel weigh 5–15 pounds (2.2–6.6 kg) and grow to be about 3 feet (1 m) long. King mackerel is often cut into steaks. Spanish mackerel are typically 2 feet long (60 cm) and weigh about 3 pounds (1.3 kg). They are sold whole and as skin-on fillets.

Bluefish

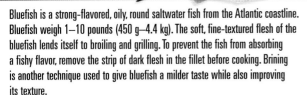

Bluefish is a strong-flavored, oily, round saltwater fish from the Atlantic coastline. Bluefish weigh 1–10 pounds (450 g–4.4 kg). The soft, fine-textured flesh of the bluefish lends itself to broiling and grilling. To prevent the fish from absorbing a fishy flavor, remove the strip of dark flesh in the fillet before cooking. Brining is another technique used to give bluefish a milder taste while also improving its texture.

Grouper

Grouper is a family of approximately four hundred varieties of round saltwater sea bass. Yellowfin grouper, black grouper, and red grouper are three of the most common types. Some grouper weigh nearly 1,000 pounds (440 kg), although most weigh less than 20 pounds (8.8 kg). Grouper are very lean with a moderately firm texture when cooked and a flavor that can range from delicate to mildly pronounced. Remove the tough, strong-flavored skin before baking, broiling, grilling, or deep-frying the fish.

Pompano

Pompano is a round saltwater fish from the East Coast and the Gulf of Mexico. Pompano, which are members of the jack family, usually weigh less than 2 pounds (900 g) and are quite expensive. Cook this firm-textured, rich fish using most any cooking methods, but baking pompano in parchment paper *(en papillote)* is one well-known technique. For more on cooking fish in parchment, see page 425.

Mahi-Mahi

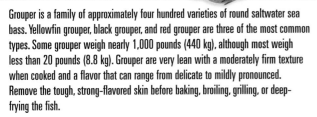

Mahi-mahi is a round saltwater fish commonly found off Florida and in other warm waters. It has firm, flavorful flesh that lends itself to grilling or broiling. Also called dolphinfish, mahi-mahi is unrelated to the dolphin that is a mammal. Although mahi-mahi can grow to be 50 pounds (22 kg), most are caught at around 15 pounds (6.6 kg). Mahi-mahi sells whole or in fillets.

Snapper

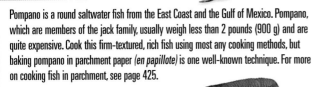

Snapper are a group of several hundred varieties of round saltwater fish found in tropical and semitropical waters. Red snapper is one species. Red snapper is really pink, and it turns white when cooked. Snapper is lean with a rather soft texture and a delicate flavor. Most snapper are sold whole or in fillets with the skin attached to make identification easier. Snapper can be prepared using a variety of cooking methods, often reserving the heads and bones for stock.

Tuna

Tuna is a round saltwater fish and a member of the mackerel family. Yellowfin, bluefin, blackfin, bonito, bigeye, and albacore are some common varieties of tuna. Tuna are large fish that can weigh up to several hundred pounds each. Raw tuna ranges in color from deep pink to dark red, and it has a mild flavor and firm meatlike texture when cooked. Only the freshest and best tuna is served raw in sashimi or sushi. Thick tuna steaks are also grilled or broiled until the steaks are rare or medium rare. Canned white tuna comes from albacore. Yellowfin or skipjack may be used in canned light tuna. Use canned tuna, packed in water or oil, in salads, sandwiches, and some sauces.

Swordfish

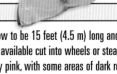

Swordfish is a saltwater fish that can grow to be 15 feet (4.5 m) long and 1,000 pounds (440 kg). Swordfish are typically available cut into wheels or steaks. The flesh varies in color from white to slightly pink, with some areas of dark red. The firm-textured swordfish lends itself to grilling and broiling and has a mild, flavorful taste.

Monkfish

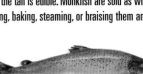

Monkfish are lean, round saltwater fish with a delicate flavor. Cooked monkfish has a flake-free texture somewhat like that of lobster, earning monkfish the nickname "poor man's lobster." Monkfish have a grotesque appearance and black, scaleless skin that must be removed prior to cooking. Only the tail is edible. Monkfish are sold as whole tails or fillets. Prepare monkfish by frying, baking, steaming, or braising them and by using them in soups and stews.

Salmon

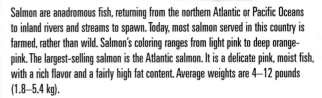

Salmon are anadromous fish, returning from the northern Atlantic or Pacific Oceans to inland rivers and streams to spawn. Today, most salmon served in this country is farmed, rather than wild. Salmon's coloring ranges from light pink to deep orange-pink. The largest-selling salmon is the Atlantic salmon. It is a delicate pink, moist fish, with a rich flavor and a fairly high fat content. Average weights are 4–12 pounds (1.8–5.4 kg).

Coho is a Pacific salmon that is available wild or farmed. Farmed coho is available year-round. Coho contains less fat than Atlantic salmon, so it is flakier but somewhat less flavorful when cooked. Wild coho weigh 3–12 pounds (1.3–5.4 kg). Farmed baby coho weigh less than 1 pound (450 g). Chinook, also called king salmon, is another Pacific variety. It is the largest and fattest of all salmon. Chinook has a very rich flavor, black gums, and larger scales than other salmon varieties.

Top quality, reasonably priced salmon are available year-round and the fish are popular with the public, so salmon holds a starring place on many menus. Salmon lends itself to most cooking techniques, with the possible exception of frying. Salmon is available whole and as steaks and fillets. Salmon is also sold cured, smoked, or canned.

Shark

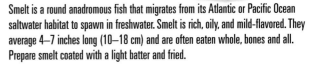

Shark is a lean, boneless saltwater fish with a moderately firm texture and sweet flavor. Mako and blacktip are two of the shark species commonly marketed in this country. Mako is usually sold as steaks and is pale pink with red blotches when raw. Blacktip is pale pink except for a ruby-colored ring just beneath the skin. This ring of flesh should be removed with the skin before cooking. Use any cooking technique to prepare shark; grilled shark steaks are especially popular.

Smelt

Smelt is a round anadromous fish that migrates from its Atlantic or Pacific Ocean saltwater habitat to spawn in freshwater. Smelt is rich, oily, and mild-flavored. They average 4–7 inches long (10–18 cm) and are often eaten whole, bones and all. Prepare smelt coated with a light batter and fried.

Flat Fish

Flat fish swim horizontally through the water. This type of fish has a backbone that runs horizontally through the center of the body. Sole, flounder, and halibut are the most common flat fish.

Dover Sole

Dover sole is a lean, white, firm-fleshed flat fish with a delicate flavor. Pacific flounder is sometimes sold as Dover sole, but it is not the same product. True Dover sole comes from the coastal regions of the Atlantic Ocean and Mediterranean Sea off England, Europe, and Africa. Dover sole is small and expensive. Use the fundamentals of classical cuisine when preparing Dover sole.

Flounder

Flounder is a lean, fine-textured, flat saltwater fish with a delicate flavor. In the United States flounder is sometimes called sole. English sole, dab, and lemon sole are some common varieties of flounder. Flounder is available whole and as fillets. To keep the fragile fish from falling apart during cooking, poach, steam, bake, sauté, or deep-fry flounder.

Halibut

Halibut is a flat saltwater fish with a firm flesh and mild flavor. Both Atlantic and Pacific halibut are available. Some members of the halibut family grow to be 300 pounds (135 kg). California halibut is much smaller than Atlantic or Pacific halibut and is actually a flounder. Halibut is often sold as steaks. This fish easily dries out during cooking; broil, bake, grill, or poach halibut with a sauce.

Farmed Freshwater Fish

Some popular fish are farm raised in freshwater.

Catfish

Virtually all commercially available catfish is farm raised. Aquafarming provides a year-round supply and eliminates undesirable flavors once associated with wild catfish. Channel catfish is the most common variety in this country. Catfish has a firm texture and a mild flavor. Serve catfish fried in a light batter.

Trout

Farm-raised trout ranges in color from pure white to salmon-colored, and it has a soft, flaky texture when cooked and a moderate fat content. The most commonly available species is rainbow trout. There is also a trout species on the West Coast that spends part of its life at sea and part in freshwater. These trout are called salmon trout or steelhead. Trout's delicate flavor is easily overwhelmed by strong sauces or spices; choose simple presentations involving poaching, steaming, baking, or pan-frying.

Tilapia

Tilapia is raised on freshwater aquafarms throughout the world. The fish grow to be up to 3 pounds (1.3 kg) and are available whole and as fillets. Tilapia has a very mild flavor somewhat like that of catfish and a slightly firm texture when cooked. Braise skinless fillets, or pan-fry tilapia whole or as fillets.

Whitefish

Whitefish includes several varieties of freshwater fish, most of which is harvested in Canada. Whitefish are moderately fatty and are a primary ingredient in prepared gefilte fish. Whitefish are frequently smoked and also can be baked, broiled, or grilled.

Market Forms of Fish

Foodservice operations can purchase fish whole or in a variety of other market forms, including dressed, as fillets, cubed, or as individually quick frozen fillets or steaks.

Fresh Fish

Foodservice operations should purchase fresh fish in a form that makes sense for their establishment. Fish fabrication requires foodservice personnel with the prerequisite skills for cutting fish and the space in which to store whole and cut fish. Another consideration is whether the operation can make use of the bones and trim that result when whole fish are cut. Operations that regularly serve whole fish, those with high volumes, or those that are upscale or specialty operations may find it advantageous to do their own fish fabrication. Many establishments, however, save money when they buy fish already cut and processed. See Figure 22-4.

Whole

Whole fish refers to the whole fish as it comes from the water. The internal organs remain intact. This form of fish has the shortest shelf life.

Drawn

Drawn fish are whole fish whose internal organs are removed. Drawn fish have the longest shelf life. Foodservice operations that purchase whole fish frequently choose drawn fish.

Dressed

Dressed fish are those with internal organs, gills, fins, and scales removed. Sometimes heads are removed in dressed fish.

Fillets

Fish *fillets* are the most popular market form used in foodservice operations. Both boned and boneless fillets may be available. Depending on the fish, fillets can be with or without skin. Round fish provide two fillets, one from each side. Flat fish produce four fillets, two from the top and two from the bottom of the fish. Smaller flat fish may be cut into two fillets.

Butterflied

Butterflied fish are dressed and then cut open so the two sides lie open and attached at the skin, like an open book.

Steaks

Fish steaks are cross-sectional cuts of dressed fish. The skin usually remains on steaks. Steaks often contain a small section of the backbone, although steaks cut from large fish, such as swordfish, are boneless.

Cubes

Cubes are cut from leftover pieces of large fish. Use cubes in kabobs, stews, soups, or stir-fries.

Frozen Fish

Modern processing methods deliver high-quality, fresh-tasting frozen fish, usually for less than what would be paid for fresh fish. Foodservice operations use more frozen fish than fresh fish. Frozen fish is packaged in a variety of forms.

IQF *IQF* stands for individually quick frozen. Fish fillets or steaks are coated with a thin glaze of water and then quickly frozen piece by piece. Fish in this form remains separated, not frozen together in a mass, making it easy to remove from the freezer an exact number of pieces. The quality of IQF fish remains high because quick freezing inhibits the formation of ice crystals.

Block Block-frozen fish are fillets or fillet pieces frozen into a mass. All fish in the block are from a single species of fish. Block-frozen fish cannot be made of minced or reformed fish. The entire block of fish must be thawed at one time.

Shatter pack Frozen fish are glazed and then packaged together in shatter packs. Poly sheets are placed between layers of fish, which are then block-frozen in a blast freezer. When lightly tapped, the layers of fish fillets separate easily.

Canned and Vacuum-Sealed Pouches

Tuna, salmon, and anchovies are among the most common forms of canned fish. Vacuum-sealed pouches of cooked tuna combine fresh taste with the convenience of a product that requires no refrigeration and has a long shelf life.

FIGURE 22-4
Market forms of fish

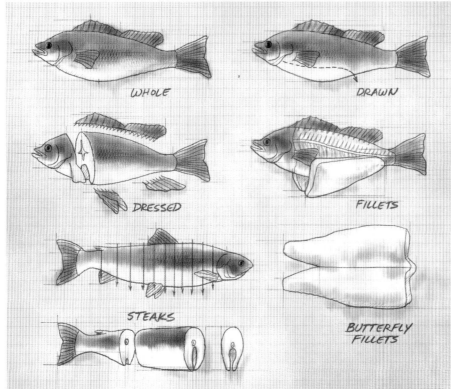

WHOLE

DRAWN

DRESSED

FILLETS

STEAKS

BUTTERFLY FILLETS

Fish Cooking Basics

Fish lends itself to a variety of cooking techniques. Dishes can be elaborate or simple, rich and full-flavored, or lean and mild. Fish has little connective tissue and is naturally tender, so long cooking times are unnecessary with fish. In fact, careful attention must be given to time and temperature, and the cooking process must be monitored to keep fish from overcooking.

■ *See Chapter 11: Cooking Techniques for more information.*

Baking

Whole fish, steaks, and fillets can be baked. Sometimes a fish is baked in a sauce, such as tomato or curry, to create a more elaborate dish and to keep the fish from becoming dry. Cooking methods can be combined, first browning the fish in a small amount of oil in a sauté pan to give it color and flavor and then baking it to finish the cooking. Lean fish requires frequent basting with oil or butter to keep it from drying out during baking.

Fatty fish, such as pompano and salmon, are less likely to dry out than some other types of fish and are therefore the best candidates for dry baking. Generally, bake fish at 350°F–400°F (177°C–204°C), presentation side up, in a well-oiled or buttered pan. Use the lower temperature for large fish to ensure even baking. Sprinkle the fish with seasonings such as salt, spices, and lemon juice, and generously brush it with melted butter or oil before the fish goes into the oven. Cook the fish until the internal temperature, taken in the thickest part of the fish, is 145°F (63°C) or higher for 15 seconds.

Moist cooking also can be used to bake fish. Add vegetables and liquid to a large piece of fish or a whole fish as it bakes, and then use the liquids from moist cooking as the basis of an accompanying sauce.

Another option is to bake fish *en papillote.* This technique involves wrapping fish in parchment paper, often with vegetables, herbs, and flavored butter, and then baking it in the oven. Cooking fish *en papillote* produces a steaming effect and keeps the meat moist while preserving nutrients and natural flavors. Limit the amount of fat in the dish by eliminating the use of flavored butters or other oil.

Broiling and Grilling

Broiling and grilling take advantage of high heat to quickly prepare fish dishes. Guests sometimes prefer broiled or grilled dishes because these limit the need for added fat. A lemon wedge or grilled vegetables are fine accompaniments to broiled or grilled fish. Grilled or broiled fish is sometimes topped with a lemon- or herb-flavored butter or served with a sauce.

Broiling or grilling imparts a smoky flavor to fish and gives the fish good color and a lightly charred surface. Fatty fish is the best choice for grilling and broiling, although any variety can be broiled. To keep the meat from sticking and to help moisten lean fish, brush butter or oil on the fish before broiling. Turning thicker cuts of fish during the grilling or broiling process will help these cuts cook evenly. Avoid very thick cuts because the high heat will finish cooking the outside before the interior is done. Take care to avoid overcooking. The high temperatures associated with broiling and grilling can quickly turn a perfect dish into a dry, tasteless one, because residual heat will continue to cook the fish after it is removed from the broiler or grill.

Sautéing and Pan-Frying

Sautéing and pan-frying are similar but not identical techniques for cooking fish. Both are dry cooking methods performed in a sauté pan. Sautéing adds flavor and lightly browns the surface of the fish in a small amount of oil or clarified butter. Coat the fish with flour before sautéing, if desired. Pan-frying requires more fat; always coat the fish in seasoned batter, flour, or breading before cooking.

Both fatty and lean fish lend themselves to sautéing and pan-frying. Use steaks or fillets that are uniform in size and thickness for best results. Thin pieces of fish work well. When dredging or breading large quantities of fish, do so in small batches.

Always heat the pan and the fat before adding the fish. Sauté fish using just a thin coating of oil or clarified butter in the bottom of the pan. For pan-frying, add oil or clarified butter to reach about one-third up the side of the pan. Place the fish in the hot oil, presentation side down. Sauté thin slices of fish over high heat to quickly brown the surface. Cook thicker pieces over lower heat so that they do not get too brown before the fish cooks through. Avoid adding too much fish to the pan at one time, or the fat will cool and the fish will simmer in its own juices. Turn pieces once halfway through the cook time.

Deep-Frying

In the United States, deep-frying is the most popular way to fry fish. Foodservice operations deep-fry frozen, prebreaded fish fillets as well as fresh, breaded, or batter-dipped fish. The breading or batter forms a crispy, attractive coating that protects the fish during cooking. If using frozen, prebreaded fish fillets, cook them from the frozen state to prevent them from getting soggy or breaking up while cooking. Drain deep-fried fish well, and serve immediately. Lemon wedges, tartar sauce, or cocktail sauce are appropriate accompaniments.

Poaching

Poaching is a moist-heat technique in which fish cooks in liquid at very low heat. Fish requires gentle handling, therefore it is rarely simmered or boiled. Poached fish can be served hot or cold. Hollandaise sauce or a sauce made from the poaching liquid often accompanies poached fish served hot. When the fish is served cold, a mayonnaise-type sauce may be offered with the dish. Steaks, fillets, and whole fish are appropriate for poaching. Poach lean white fish, such as sole, halibut, or cod, as well as fatty fish, such as salmon or trout.

Cooking Fish En Papillote

Cooking fish en papillote *involves wrapping the fish in parchment paper with vegetables and flavorings and then baking it in the oven.*

To cook fish en papillote, *follow these steps:*

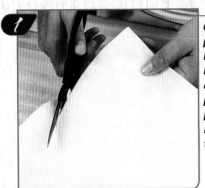

1 Cut parchment paper into a heart-sized shape large enough to contain the fish portion. Fold the parchment paper in half, and crease the folded edge.

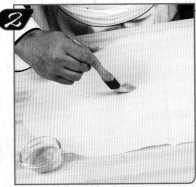

2 Brush the parchment paper with clarified butter. Place the buttered side face down on the baking dish.

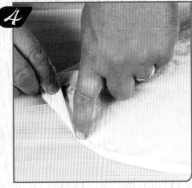

3 Place the fish, vegetables, and flavored butter on one half of the parchment paper.

4 Fold the parchment paper over the fish, and crimp the edges to seal the package, forming an envelope.

5 Bake the sealed envelope in a preheated oven.

6 Slit open the package, pull back the parchment, and serve with the juices that accumulated during the cooking process.

Fish and Shellfish

425

Two different poaching techniques may be used. In *submersion poaching,* completely cover the fish with a liquid such as fish stock or court bouillon. Fish gain flavor and seasoning as they poach because the poaching liquid may include herbs, spices, wine, and vegetables. Starting whole fish in a cold liquid will help preserve their appearance. Start fillets or steaks in liquid that has been raised to a simmer.

Shallow poaching combines poaching with steaming. The fish cooks on a base of vegetables in a liquid, called a cuisson. Heat the cuisson on the stove top, and then pour it over the fish and vegetables, covering the fish halfway. Place buttered parchment paper or a lid over the pan, and then cook the fish in the oven or on the range.

Steaming

Steaming is a moist-heat technique in which fish cooks on the range over, not in, boiling water. Steaming in a covered pan allows the fish to cook without added fat while preserving natural flavors and valuable nutrients. Either lean or fatty fish can be steamed. To flavor the fish, season the raw fish with salt, pepper, herbs, and spices; add flavor by steaming the fish over court bouillon.

Determining Doneness

Fish cooks quickly and is easily overcooked. On the other hand, undercooking fish can be a health hazard. Follow the guidelines below to determine when fish is done.

- Fish starts flaking. Fish that flakes readily is probably overdone. Properly cooked fish should just begin to flake.
- Bones separate from the fish easily.
- Flesh springs back when pressed. Undercooked fish can be soft or mushy.
- Fish becomes opaque. Raw fish is translucent. As the proteins coagulate and the fish cooks, the flesh changes color.
- Cooked fish should have an internal temperature of 145°F (63°C) or higher for 15 seconds.
- Broiled or grilled fish should have a browned, crispy surface and a juicy, tender interior.
- Sautéed and pan-fried fish should have a slightly brown or crispy surface with a juicy, tender interior.
- Deep-fried fish should have a rich, golden brown color.

Types of Shellfish

Shellfish have shells that protect their bodies but no internal skeletons or backbones. Shellfish are found in both freshwater and saltwater habitats. Mollusks and crustaceans are two forms of shellfish.

Foodborne Organisms and Shellfish

Like other forms of seafood, shellfish spoil rapidly because of bacterial action. Shellfish also can carry parasites, and those taken from contaminated water can transmit disease to humans. Oysters, clams, and mussels feed by taking in nutrients and oxygen as they pump water across their gills. During this process the animal may ingest bacteria, viruses, and other impurities present in the water. Shellfish can carry the virus that causes hepatitis A, the bacteria that causes cholera, the Norwalk virus, and various toxins. Although thorough cooking destroys some of these hazards, many people eat raw or lightly cooked shellfish. To minimize the risk, the FDA has established standards for shellfish. When serving raw or undercooked shellfish, the FDA Food Code mandates that a disclosure and a reminder be publicly available warning the public of the potential risk of consuming these food items: Consuming raw or undercooked meats, poultry, seafood, shellfish, or eggs may increase the risk of contracting foodborne illness. The reminder may be related to specific foods, such as shellfish, or in general pertaining to any raw or undercooked animal products. Shellfish must be taken from approved waters, each container of shellfish must have a tag tracing its origins, and foodservice operations must keep shellfish tags on file for 90 days after receiving the shellfish.

Mollusks

Mollusks live in salt water and have shells that protect their soft bodies. Although all mollusks have shells, the shells are not all alike. Mollusks are grouped according to their type of shell. There are three major groups.

Univalves *Univalves* have a single, one-piece shell that covers the body. Univalves are marine snails that use a single foot to attach themselves to rocks. Abalone, whelks, periwinkles, and conch are univalves.

Bivalves *Bivalves* have two shells hinged together. Mussels, oysters, clams, and scallops are bivalves.

Cephalopods *Cephalopods* have thin internal shells but no outer protection. Cephalopods have tentacles that attach at the head near the mouth. They also have well-developed eyes. Octopus, squid, and cuttlefish are cephalopods.

Oysters

Oysters are bivalves with rough, asymmetrical shells. The bottom shell is round and deep, and the top shell is rather flat. Oysters have a soft, gray flesh with a high percentage of water and are available year-round. Restaurants frequently offer raw oysters as an appetizer or a first course. Oyster stews or soups may be listed on the soup menu, and cooked oyster dishes may appear as entrées or on the lunch menu, such as the popular po'boy sandwich made with fried oysters.

There are four main varieties of oysters in the United States: Atlantic, or American, oysters; Olympias, tiny oysters from the coast of the Pacific Ocean; Japanese, or Pacific, oysters, which are large oysters from the Pacific Coast; and European flat oysters, sometimes called Belon oysters, that are farm raised and have flatter shells than their Atlantic counterparts. Oysters also are named for the region from which they are harvested. Bluepoint oysters, Long Island oysters, Florida Gulf oysters, and Chesapeake Bay oysters are all Atlantic oysters. Where an oyster is harvested is significant because an oyster picks up the flavors from the water in which it grows. The water's temperature also affects the oyster's flavor. Oysters from warmer waters tend to be milder than those from northern, cooler parts.

Market Forms

Oysters are available live in the shell and **shucked,** or removed from the shell, in fresh or frozen form. Shucked oysters are graded by size, ranging from Very Small to Extra Large. See Figure 22-5. Although canned oysters are available, they are rarely used.

Handling and Storing Oysters

To determine whether oysters in the shell are alive, look for tightly closed shells. Avoid oysters with a gap between the shells because this leak may have allowed the oyster to dry out. Live and shucked oysters should have a sweet, mild smell. Shucked oysters should be plump and clear.

Store live oysters flat in cardboard containers in the refrigerator. Drape the oysters with seaweed or damp towels. Check them daily, and remove any dead oysters. Live oysters should keep a week in the refrigerator. Treat shucked oysters the same way you would treat fish fillets, keeping them refrigerated in containers surrounded by ice. Keep frozen shucked oysters in the freezer until needed. Thaw frozen oysters in the refrigerator.

Culinary Applications and Determining Doneness

Raw oysters may be served as a first course or an appetizer, garnished with lemon wedges, hot sauce, or another sauce. Cooked oysters can be poached, deep-fried, prepared in a soup or stew, or baked in their own liquid or with a sauce. To keep oysters juicy and plump, cook them just until they are heated through. Overcooking toughens oysters and causes them to shrivel.

FIGURE 22-5

Oyster Grades per Gallon	
VERY SMALL	*Over 500*
SMALL OR STANDARDS	*301–500*
MEDIUM OR SELECT	*211–300*
LARGE OR EXTRA SELECTS	*161–210*
EXTRA LARGE OR COUNTS	*160 or fewer*

Clams

Clams are bivalves that are harvested from the ocean along the East and West Coasts. Atlantic clams are divided into two major groups: soft-shell and hard-shell. Within the major groups are dozens of varieties of

Shucking Oysters

Commercial kitchens may purchase oysters in a variety of market forms, including in the shell.

To shuck an oyster, follow these steps:

1 Scrub the oyster shell under cold, running water.

2 Insert the oyster knife into the hinge at the back of the oyster, between the top and bottom shells.

3  Twist the knife to separate the shells and break the hinge.

4  Slide the knife under the top shell to break the abductor muscle, which holds the shell shut. Remove the top shell.

5  Slide the knife under the oyster to cut the abductor muscle, and loosen the meat. Be careful to remove any shell fragments before cooking or serving.

Shucking a Hard-Shell Clam

Clams purchased in the shell should be live, with tightly closed shells. Before use, shuck the hard shell.

To do so, follow these steps:

1 Scrub the clam shell under cold running water.

2  Hold the clam firmly between your thumb and fingers. Position the clam knife between the shells, and squeeze the knife with your fingers to separate the shells.

3 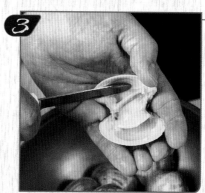 Run the tip of the knife against the top shell to loosen the clam meat.

4 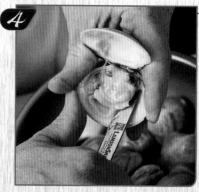 Keeping the clam as intact as possible, slide the knife under the clam meat to loosen it from the bottom shell. Be careful to remove any shell fragments before cooking or serving.

clams. Clams are available year-round, although specific varieties may not be. One variety can almost always be successfully substituted for another in recipes. Steamed clams may be part of the appetizer menu, and clam chowder and soups can serve as a first course or a light lunch. Fried clams, served on a bun or with side dishes, can be offered as a supper or a luncheon entrée. The traditional clambake makes steamed clams, along with other shellfish, the focus of a substantial dinner.

Soft-Shell Clams

Soft-shell clams are tender and sweet. Their shells are not really soft but are thinner and more fragile than those of hard-shell clams.

Steamers or longnecks Soft-shell clams are sometimes called longnecks because of the long, tubelike siphon that extends from the side of the shell. The clam's neck prevents the clam from closing completely. Longnecks also are called steamers because most people prepare soft-shell clams by steaming them and serving them with melted butter. See Figure 22-6.

FIGURE 22-8

Types of Hard-Shell Clams

SURF

LARGE QUAHOG

CHERRYSTONE

LITTLENECK

PACIFIC LITTLENECK

MANILA

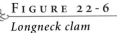
FIGURE 22-6
Longneck clam

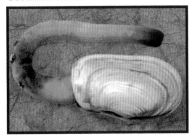
FIGURE 22-7
Geoduck clam

Geoducks Geoducks come from the coast of the Pacific Ocean. Each of these huge soft-shell clams has a large siphon, up to 3 feet (1 m) long, that protrudes from the clam's shell. Geoducks are tender and rich with a briny flavor. See Figure 22-7.

Hard-Shell Clams

Hard-shell clams, also called quahogs, are classified by size. See Figure 22-8.

Surf clams Surf clams are large white clams that grow to be about 8 inches (20 cm) across. Surf clams are too large to be cooked and served whole, so they are often cut or minced and packed as frozen or canned clams for fritters or for chowders. Foodservice operations sometimes serve fried clams made from strips of surf clams.

Large quahogs Large quahogs, also called chowder clams, are about 3 inches (8 cm) across and come two to four per pound (450 g). Chowder clams do not have the same delicate flavor as some smaller clams, but they are practical for soups.

Cherrystones Cherrystones are medium-sized clams about 2.5–3 inches (6–8 cm) across. They come five to seven clams per pound (450 g). Cherrystones can be served raw, but more often they are cooked.

Littlenecks At 1.5–2.25 inches (4–6 cm) across, littlenecks are the smallest quahogs. These clams weigh about 2 ounces (30 g)

each and are considered the sweetest and tenderest of the clams. Littlenecks are served raw on the half shell or steamed.

Pacific littlenecks The Pacific littleneck is a small Pacific coast clam that is generally considered slightly tougher than the Atlantic littleneck.

Manila clams Manila clams are Pacific coast clams that can grow to be quite large. The 1-inch (2.5-cm) Manila clams are especially prized and suitable for serving raw or steamed.

Market Forms

Whole clams are available live in the shell. Shucked clams are available frozen or fresh. Canned clams come chopped, minced, or whole.

Handling and Storing Clams

Clams in the shell should be alive. A tightly closed shell indicates that the clam inside is alive. Whole clams and shucked clams should smell fresh. Handle whole clams carefully to avoid damaging their shells. Store whole clams for up to one week in their original packaging with the shellfish tag attached. Store shucked fresh clams in the refrigerator, packed in containers on ice. Keep frozen shucked clams solidly frozen until needed. Thaw them in the refrigerator. Inspect canned clams before use.

Fish and Shellfish

429

Cleaning and Debearding Mussels

When preparing mussels, remove the beard just prior to cooking. Pulling the beard from the mussel shortens its shelf life.

To clean and debeard live mussels, follow these steps:

1 Scrub the mussel shell under cold running water to remove sand and barnacles.

2 Rinse under cold running water.

3 Grasp the beard (byssus)—the fine hairs sticking out between the two shells—and pull it away toward the hinged end of the shell.

4 As shown, wild mussels have a distinctive large beard that needs to be removed; cultivated mussels are usually sold with their beards trimmed off.

Culinary Applications and Determining Doneness

In addition to being served raw on the half shell, clams can be served steamed, in chowder, deep-fried, baked on the half shell with toppings, in sauces, and poached. Clams become rubbery when overcooked, so cook shucked clams just until heated throughout. Steam clams in the shell just until the shells pop open.

Mussels

Mussels are bivalves that are harvested in the wild and farmed around the world. They are available year-round. Mussels resemble clams, but they are smaller, with thin, dark shells and tan-colored meat. Mussels appear on both appetizer and entrée menus.

Common Varieties, Appearance, and Characteristics

The most common mussels are blue mussels, which are 2–3 inches (5–8 cm) long and have blue-black shells. See Figure 22-9. Blue mussels are harvested in the wild along the Atlantic Coast and aquafarmed along both the Atlantic and Pacific Oceans. The meat of the blue mussel is sweet and plump with a firm, somewhat chewy texture. Cultivated, or farmed, mussels have yellow- or orange-colored meat and a more delicate flavor than wild mussels. They are generally larger than wild mussels and command a higher market price. One pound (450 g) includes 10–20 mussels.

FIGURE 22-9
Blue mussels

FIGURE 22-10
New Zealand green mussels

Fully cultivated mussels Fully cultivated mussels are farmed from rafts floating in the open ocean. Ropes are suspended from the rafts, providing places for mussel larvae to attach. From the ropes, mussels feed by taking in plankton and other nutrients as they filter water through their bodies. Mussels grown on ropes mature more quickly than mussels on the bottom of the ocean floor because rope-grown mussels have greater access to the food supply.

Partially cultivated mussels Another technique for cultivating mussels involves collecting mussel larvae and small mussels from the wild and transporting them to the ocean bottom in sheltered cultivation beds. Deep water in the cultivation areas allows mussels to remain submerged with a continuous supply of nutrients. The harvesting of mussels involves scraping or pumping the mussels up from the ocean floor. Some bottom-cultivated mussels are allowed a year more of growth than rope-cultivated mussels. This results in a larger mussel with a more well-developed flavor.

Wild mussels Wild mussels grow along the coasts of the Atlantic and Pacific Oceans and the Mediterranean Sea. This supply does not meet demand, so Europeans began cultivating mussels hundreds of years ago. One problem with wild mussels is their susceptibility to contamination from polluted waters. Wild mussels also are generally smaller and more leathery in texture than cultivated mussels.

New Zealand green mussels At 3–4 inches (8–10 cm) wide, New Zealand green mussels are much larger than blue mussels. See Figure 22-10 on page 430. These mussels, with their green-tipped shells, come from both New Zealand and parts of Southeast Asia. In general, green mussels are more expensive than blue mussels.

Market Forms

Whole mussels are sold live in the shell, cooked and frozen in the shell, and as shucked, cooked products packed "fresh" or frozen in vacuum packages. Cooked, shucked mussels are often packed in brine or their natural juices. A variety of smoked or marinated mussel meat products is also available.

Handling and Storing Mussels

Except for commercially frozen mussels in the shell, mussels in the shell should be alive. The shell should be firmly closed or should close tightly when tapped. Discard mussels with cracked or open shells. Mussel shells that feel light are probably empty and should be

thrown out. Very heavy mussels probably contain a great deal of sand and also should be discarded.

Refrigerate live mussels in a paper bag or in their original container. Storing mussels on self-draining ice can extend shelf life. Though mussels can last between 7–10 days, it is best to use them within 2–3 days because harvesting and processing conditions, such as trimming the beard—the fine hairs that stick out between the shells—can affect quality and shelf life. Removing the beard kills the mussel and should not be done until mussels are ready to be prepared for service.

Culinary Applications and Determining Doneness

Mussels are almost never served raw. Typically they are steamed, accompanied by the broth in which they cooked. Herbs, aromatic vegetables, and wine may be added to the pot in which mussels steam. Mussels can also be broiled on the half shell, baked in sauce, or served fried, in soups, or in traditional dishes such as *paella*.

To avoid the toughness that comes from overcooking, cook mussels just until shells open and the mussels are heated through. Discard unopened mussels.

> **When serving steamed mussels as a first course, allow about 1/2–3/4 pound (225–335 g) per person. An entrée should contain about 1 1/2 pounds (675 g) of steamed mussels. The number of mussels per serving will depend on the size of the mussels.**

Scallops

Scallops are bivalves that are taken year-round from both shallow and deep seawater around the world. Europeans generally eat the entire scallop, including the roe, or eggs. What Americans think of as a scallop is actually only the abductor muscle, the part that closes the scallop's two shells. Scallops appear on the menu as appetizers and entrées. Scallop *seviche* is a popular first course in which raw scallops are marinated in lime juice and tossed with chilies and other seasonings. The acid in the limes tenderizes the fish and turns it opaque, just as if it had been cooked.

FIGURE 22-11
Sea scallop

FIGURE 22-12
Bay scallop

FIGURE 22-13
Calico scallop

Common Varieties, Appearance, and Characteristics

Most scallops are marketed already shucked, so the scallop's beautiful fan-shaped shells may be unfamiliar. Depending on the species, scallop shells can be smooth or ridged and range in size from only a few inches wide to up to 12 inches (5–30 cm).

Scallops have a sweet flavor and plump yet tender texture. Raw scallops range in color from ivory to creamy pink. The size depends on the species. There are hundreds of different species, but only three that are common in the United States.

Sea scallops Sea scallops are the largest of the scallops. See Figure 22-11 on page 431. One pound (450 g) may contain 20–30 medium sea scallops or 10–15 large ones. Although sea scallops are moist and have a delicate sweet flavor, their texture is firmer than that of the smaller scallops.

Bay scallops True bay scallops come from waters along the Atlantic Coast. They are harvested from October through March. Bay scallops are very tiny, about 1/2 inch (1.5 cm) wide and 3/4 inch (2 cm) thick. See Figure 22-12 on page 431. A pound (450 g) of bay scallops can include 70–90 smaller bay scallops or 40–50 larger ones. Bay scallops have the sweetest and most desirable flavor of all common American varieties.

Calico scallops Calico scallops, with a shape and size like that of miniature marshmallows, are even smaller than bay scallops. See Figure 22-13 on page 431. Although these scallops are often sold as bay scallops, most people do not consider the flavor to be as fine. A pound (450 g) may contain 70–110 calico scallops. To remove calico scallops from the shell, processors lightly steam them. Although these scallops are marketed as raw, the steaming process partially cooks the meat, resulting in scallops that look pale white and opaque around the edges. This process destroys some of the scallop's flavor.

Market Forms

The most common market form is fresh shucked scallops. Scallops may be sold by either the pound or gallon and may be labeled "wet" or "dry." Wet pack scallops, which have a pure white, shiny appearance, have been soaked to increase their keeping qualities and to add bulk. Wet pack scallops

are generally less expensive. Dry pack scallops have more color, ranging from ivory to pinkish, and they tend to remain separated rather than clumped together in a mass. One problem with wet pack scallops is their tendency to release a great deal of water when heated. This can prevent the scallops from browning properly.

Scallops are also available in 5-pound frozen blocks (2.3 kg) and in IQF form.

Handling and Storing Scallops

Store fresh scallops in covered containers in the refrigerator, and use them within a day or two. Thaw frozen scallops in the refrigerator before use. Remove the tough tendon from the side of the scallop before using scallops. If sautéing scallops, dry them well before placing them in the prepared sauté pan.

Culinary Applications and Determining Doneness

Scallops lend themselves to a variety of cooking techniques, including sautéing, grilling, braising, deep-frying, and poaching. Scallops served on the shell and broiled *au gratin* are a classic first course.

For more even cooking, large sea scallops can be sliced into thin discs before cooking. Even whole scallops cook in a matter of minutes, and overcooked scallops become dry and firm. Remove scallops from the heat when they change from translucent to opaque.

Squid

Squid is a cephalopod with eight short tentacles and two long ones. See Figure 22-14. Squid, often listed on menus by its Italian name, *calamari*, is most common in this country as an appetizer, often served fried. As squid's popularity has grown, restaurants increasingly offer squid baked or stuffed or in a variety of entrées, such as stews and stir-fries.

Common Varieties, Appearance, and Characteristics

Squid range in size from 1 inch (2.5 cm) up to 70 feet (21 m), but most foodservice operations serve small squid. See Figure 22-14. On average 1 pound (450 g) contains about eight to ten squid. The most widely available varieties of squid are the Atlantic longfin, the Atlantic shortfin, and the California or Pacific squid. Some people

FIGURE 22-14
Squid

consider the California squid to be the most desirable.

Squid has a firm, somewhat chewy texture and a mild, sweet flavor. Both the tentacles and hollow body tube, called the *mantle,* are edible.

Market Forms

Squid is marketed cleaned or uncleaned and whole or cut into steaks or rings. Cleaned squid tubes or cleaned tubes and tentacles also are sold separately. Squid is sold either fresh or frozen.

Handling and Storing Squid

Store fresh squid refrigerated for no more than a day or two. Thaw frozen squid in the refrigerator. Unless whole cleaned squid or squid parts are purchased, squid must be cleaned before use. To do this:

1. Pull off the squid's head, removing the internal organs.
2. Peel the skin from the mantle. Discard the skin.
3. Pull the clear quill from the mantle. Discard the quill, and rinse the mantle under cold, running water.
4. Cut the tentacles from the head, just above the eyes. Discard the head and organs.
5. Pull out the hard beak from the center of the tentacles.

Culinary Applications and Determining Doneness

Squid rings and tentacles are often coated with batter and deep-fried, garnished with lemon wedges or a dipping sauce. Squid also can be sautéed with herbs or simmered slowly to make a stew. Stuffed squid tubes can be grilled or braised. Raw squid is used in sushi.

Squid is notorious for being tough, but correctly prepared squid should not be chewy or rubbery. To avoid this problem, cook squid quickly (about 2 minutes) over moderately high heat, or simmer it slowly for 30 minutes or more. Cooked squid should be pale and almost white. Remove deep-fried squid before the coating turns brown to avoid overcooking the meat. When stuffing squid, remove the pointy tip from the end of the mantle. This will prevent the mantle from bursting when cooking.

Octopus

Octopus is a cephalopod with eight equal-sized tentacles. See Figure 22-15. It can range in size from 1 ounce to 50 pounds (from 30 g to 23 kg), but the most common weight is 2–3 pounds (1–1.5 kg). See Figure 22-15. Before cooking, an octopus looks reddish gray; cooking turns the skin purple. Both the body and the tentacles are edible, and the meat is flavorful and chewy. Octopus can appear on the menu as either an appetizer or entrée, pickled, or as the base of a hearty salad. Raw octopus is used in sushi.

Market Forms

Octopus most often is sold whole and already cleaned. It comes in fresh, frozen, and cooked forms, as well as smoked and canned. Tiny baby octopus also is available, although at a higher price than more mature specimens.

Handling and Storing Octopus

If the octopus is uncleaned, cut off the head just above the eyes, and turn it inside out to remove the internal organs. Discard the eyes, and remove the beak from the main body of the octopus. Skin the body and tentacles, and then cut the octopus into appropriate sizes, or leave baby ones whole.

✤ FIGURE 22-15
Octopus

Store fresh octopus in a container on ice in the refrigerator, and use it within a day or two. Store frozen octopus in the freezer, and then thaw in the refrigerator.

Culinary Applications and Determining Doneness

Octopus is prepared in cold salads, fried, and simmered in stews. Baby octopus can be cooked whole, but cut larger octopus into strips or meaty chunks. Octopus meat is chewy, so it needs to be tenderized with a mallet or through long, moist-heat cooking. The Japanese rub octopus with daikon and then cook it quickly in highly salted water before using thin slices in marinated salads and sauced dishes. Octopus meat turns white when cooked. Slow-simmered octopus should be firm and meaty but not chewy.

Crustaceans

Crustaceans have hard, outer segmented shells and jointed legs.
They breathe through gills. Some crustaceans grow in salt water and
some in freshwater.

Lobster

Once so plentiful that they were used for fish bait, lobster now is rare enough that eating it is considered by many to be a luxury. Lobster appears on the menu as a cold or warm appetizer, in salads and soups, as an extravagant filling for sandwiches, and as an elegant entrée.

Although lobsters can grow as large as 20 pounds (9 kg), the most common market forms are less than 2 pounds (900 g). See Figure 22-16. Lobster shells are brown or blue-black and turn red when heated. Lobster meat is white with a rich, sweet flavor and firm texture. The claw, legs, and tail meat are especially prized. Lobster shells also are used to add flavor to stock and soups; the **tomalley,** or liver, is added to stuffing; and the **coral,** or eggs, is used in composed butters or sauces.

Common Varieties, Appearance, and Characteristics

American lobster, also called Maine lobster, is the most popular variety in the United States and is also considered to be the highest quality. Found off the Atlantic coast of Canada and the United States, Maine lobsters have large heavy claws with abundant meat and four additional pairs of legs. A similar lobster, called the European lobster, lives in the Mediterranean and in waters off the coastlines of South Africa and Europe. European lobsters have slightly darker shells than American lobsters. Spiny lobsters, also called rock lobsters, have no heavy front claws; all five pairs of legs are about the same size. Generally only the tails of spiny lobsters, called "rock lobster tails," appear in markets. Spiny lobsters taken from waters off Florida, Brazil, and the Caribbean are known as warm-water tails. The flavor of cold-water tails, taken from the waters surrounding South Africa, Australia, and New Zealand, is considered superior to that of warm-water tails. Rock lobster tails are not as sweet as Maine lobster, and the texture is firmer and stringier.

Market Forms

Whole lobsters are available live, frozen, or as fresh-cooked meat. IQF uncooked lobster tails also are available. Live lobsters are classified by weight. See Figure 22-17.

Handling and Storing Lobsters

Live lobsters can be stored in special saltwater tanks or kept refrigerated, wrapped in seaweed or wet paper. If lobsters are kept in a live tank, avoid rapid changes in water temperature. Live lobsters should be approximately the same temperature as the water in the tank before they are submerged. Extreme temperature change can quickly kill the lobsters. A live lobster will wiggle and curl its tail when picked up. Lobsters that are dying show little movement. Such lobsters are called "sleepers" and must be cooked immediately. Lobsters must be cooked live or killed immediately before cooking. Dead lobsters are unsafe to eat and must be thrown out.

When cooking a whole lobster, plunge it headfirst into boiling water to quickly kill it. Before splitting a live lobster or cutting it into pieces, pierce the lobster's head with the point of a French knife to quickly kill the lobster. Refrigerate cooked lobster meat, and use it within two days.

Lobster Classifications

CHICKEN
1 pound (450 g)

QUARTERS
1 1/4 pounds (575 g)

SELECTS
1 1/2 to 2 1/4 pounds (675 to 1,025 g)

JUMBOS
over 2 1/2 pounds (1,130 g)

Culinary Applications and Determining Doneness

The simplest and most popular way to cook a lobster is by dropping it in boiling water, bringing the water back to a boil, and then reducing the heat and simmering the lobster for a few minutes. It should take no longer than 8 minutes to cook a 1 1/2-pound (675-g) lobster. For every additional pound, cook about 2 minutes. Lobster can also be steamed or broiled. Simmering, steaming, and broiling are appropriate techniques when serving whole lobster or when the meat is needed for another dish, such as a cold salad, an appetizer, or an aspic. Lobster is also baked in sauce or *au gratin*. Rock lobster tails are prepared by steaming, simmering, or broiling. For the customer's convenience, split the whole lobster or tail, and crack the claws before service.

Remove the lobster from the heat just as the meat turns opaque. The texture should be firm but not tough. Avoid boiling or other high-temperature techniques, and keep cooking times to a minimum.

Shrimp

Americans eat more shrimp than any other shellfish. Shrimp are found worldwide, but most shrimp eaten in this country are caught in warm waters off the Atlantic, Pacific, and Gulf Coasts. American restaurants typically serve only the shrimp's tails. Shrimp most often appear on the menu as appetizers and as entrées, but shrimp also are used in soups, sandwiches, and salads.

Common Varieties, Appearance, and Characteristics

Thousands of varieties of shrimp swim the world's seas, but only about a dozen species are commonly marketed in the United States. Shrimp come in a range of colors, including white, pink, brown, and blue. See Figure 22-18. However, the shells' color changes when the shrimp are cooked. Most consumers consider the variety of shrimp less important than their size.

Tropical shrimp Most of the shrimp Americans eat are tropical shrimp, which come from warm, shallow waters. Gulf of Mexico white shrimp grow along the coastline from North and South Carolina to Florida and in the Gulf of Mexico. They are known for their firm texture and nutlike flavor. Gulf of Mexico pink shrimp are pink or pale orange when raw and have a taste that some rank highest among domestic shrimp. Gulf of Mexico browns come from Texas and have brown or grayish shells. They are somewhat less flavorful than either Gulf of Mexico white or Gulf of

✼ FIGURE 22-18

Black tiger shrimp have distinctive dark shells with yellow markings; tropical or gulf shrimp have lighter shells.

Deveining Shrimp

Whether served hot or cold, shrimp need to be deveined before preparation.

To devein a shrimp, follow these steps:

1 **Remove the shell.**

2

Make a shallow cut along the backside of the shrimp.

3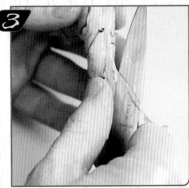

Remove the intestinal tract or "vein."

Mexico pink shrimp. Black tiger shrimp have very dark shells with yellow markings. Those sold in this country have been farm raised in Thailand, Indonesia, Taiwan, or China. Black tiger shrimp are sometimes less expensive than other common varieties because they lack the flavor of whites and pinks.

Less common varieties Foodservice operations sometimes offer other, less common, varieties of shrimp. Rock shrimp are small shrimp with a flavor somewhat like that of lobster. They grow in cold, deep waters. Sand shrimp, uncommon in most parts of the United States except for California, are quite popular in Europe, where they are sometimes eaten shell and all. Freshwater shrimp grow in brackish water rather than in saltwater habitats. Freshwater shrimp are also called *prawns,* a term often applied to all large shrimp, regardless of origin.

Market Forms

Shrimp purchased headless and raw in the shell, either fresh or frozen, are called *green shrimp.* Frozen green shrimp may come packed in 5-pound (2.3-kg) blocks. Peeled and deveined shrimp, called P/D shrimp, and PDC shrimp—peeled, deveined, and cooked shrimp—are two common forms. (Ice-glazed P/D and PDC shrimp sell IQF.) Shrimp are categorized by size and sold as counts per pound. Marketers inconsistently apply names such as "jumbo," "large," and "medium." On the other hand, shrimp counts tell the purveyor approximately how many shrimp a pound (450 g) contains. A pound of the largest available shrimp may contain 10 or fewer shrimp. A pound of smaller shrimp might contain 36–45 shrimp. Common sizes used in food service include U/10 (fewer than 10 per pound), U/15 (fewer than 15 per pound), 21/25 (21–25 per pound), and 41/50 (41–50 per pound). Regardless of size range, the shrimp within the package should be uniform in size. In general, the larger the shrimp, the greater the price per pound. A pound of green shrimp will yield about 3/4 pound (340 g) of peeled shrimp.

Handling and Storing

Store well-wrapped frozen shrimp between 0°F–10°F (-18°C–-12°C). Thaw frozen shrimp in their original wrapping in the refrigerator. Store fresh or thawed shrimp wrapped and on ice in the refrigerator or covered and refrigerated. Use thawed or fresh shrimp within a day or two.

For cold service, peel and devein the shrimp after cooking. If the shrimp will be served hot, peel and devein them before cooking. To improve the appearance of large shrimp, reduce cooking time, or to enlarge the surface area for breading, butterfly the shrimp by deepening the cut down the back of the shrimp (where the intestinal vein is removed). Then spread the shrimp open.

Culinary Applications and Determining Doneness

Shrimp are prepared in the shell by simmering, grilling, or broiling. Peel-and-eat shrimp may be served hot or cold. Shrimp can also be sautéed, baked in sauce, added to a soup or stew, or deep-fried in batter. Shrimp cook in a matter of minutes, turning pink when done. The shell turns pink to orange-red when done, and the flesh changes from translucent to white in appearance. To avoid tough, chewy shrimp, avoid cooking shrimp on high heat or for any longer than necessary.

Crab

There are thousands of crab species worldwide, each with a slightly different taste and characteristics. The appetizer menu may spotlight crab legs or claws or include a warm crabmeat dip or a first course with crabmeat as the key ingredient. Crab-enriched soups and salads are another way to offer crab. Whole crab or crabmeat-based dishes are often among a restaurant's most impressive entrées.

Common Varieties, Appearance, and Characteristics

The types of crab harvested in different parts of the country vary greatly in taste and appearance. Foodservice operations along the Atlantic and Pacific Coasts often specialize in crab native to a particular region. See Figure 22-19.

Alaskan crab King crab and snow crab are two varieties of Alaskan crab. The king crab is a very large crab, weighing 6–20 pounds (2.7–9 kg) apiece. Foodservice operations serve meaty king crab legs and claws in the shell. This sweet, snow-white meat is easy to remove because of the crab's large size. Snow crab is more abundant than king crab and sometimes substitutes

FIGURE 22-19

KING CRAB

DUNGENESS CRAB

BLUE CRAB

SOFT-SHELL CRAB

STONE CRAB CLAWS

for it. However, the snow crab's legs are thinner, and the meat is more difficult to remove from the shell. The meat is white with a touch of pink and has a mild, salty flavor.

Pacific crab Dungeness crab comes from the coastline of the Pacific Ocean from Mexico to Alaska, with Oregon and Washington supplying the most. Known for their delicate, sweet, pink-tinged meat, Dungeness crabs weigh 1 1/2–4 pounds (680 g–1.8 kg) apiece.

Atlantic crab Blue crab, with its distinctive bluish green shell, comes from the Atlantic coast. Blue crab makes up about half of all crab marketed in the United States. Blue crabs are small, with an average weight of 5 ounces (142 g). Picking the meat from the whole crab can provide a challenge, although one with a succulent reward. Most blue crabs are harvested as hard-shell crabs. However, the blue crab periodically molts, or sheds its shell. For six hours after molting, the crab's new shell is soft. Blue crabs harvested during this brief period are called soft-shell crabs. Soft-shell crabs can be eaten whole, shell and all.

Caribbean and Gulf crab Stone crabs come from waters of the Caribbean and the Gulf of Mexico. Only crab claws are harvested from the stone crab. One of the crab's claws is broken and removed from the crab, and the live crab is thrown back into the water. Within the next year or so, a new claw will grow. Each claw weighs 2 1/2–5 1/2 ounces (75–155 g). Stone crab claws are mild and sweet, somewhat reminiscent of lobster.

Market Forms

Most crab is marketed cooked and frozen—some as claws, as in king crab and stone crab—and some as whole crab or picked meat. Soft-shell crab is sold fresh or frozen. Fresh, whole crabs are regional specialties that may be difficult to obtain outside the catch area. Cooked crabmeat is available frozen or canned, and some is pasteurized to improve the shelf life. Cooked blue crabmeat is sold in three grades. The top grade, called lump, jumbo, or backfin, contains large chunks of body meat. The second grade, called flake, contains smaller pieces from the body. The lowest-quality meat is brownish claw meat. Picked crabmeat from Dungeness crabs is different. The top grade comes from the legs and is

PROCESS

Preparing a Soft-Shell Crab

Soft-shell crab is available both fresh or frozen and can be used in a variety of dishes.

To prepare a soft-shell crab, follow these steps:

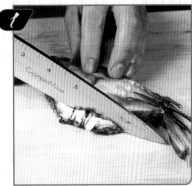

1 Cut off the front part of the crab, just behind the eyes.

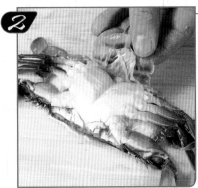

2 Turn the crab on its back, and remove the flap or "apron." A twisting motion works best.

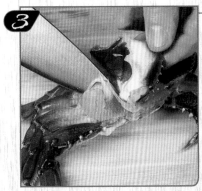

3 Turn the crab over, and pull back the soft shell on each side. Scrape away any of the gills.

sometimes called fry-legs. Broken leg meat is second, and body meat is third.

Handling and Storing Crabs

Keep live crabs alive, packed in damp seaweed in the refrigerator, until you are ready to cook them. Kill crabs quickly by plunging them into boiling water or piercing a sharp knife or metal skewer into the underside behind the eyes. Thaw frozen crabmeat in the refrigerator, and use it quickly once thawed. Thawed crabmeat can be watery, so drain it well before use. The liquid also can be added to sauce or other cooked dishes.

Culinary Applications and Determining Doneness

Whole live crabs are cooked by simmering them in broth or seasoned water. When cooking soft-shell crab, sauté the crabs to maintain the crispiness of their edible shells. Prepare frozen Dungeness crab legs, which come to the kitchen already cooked, by broiling, baking, or warming in the microwave. Lump or flake crabmeat tastes delicious when mixed with other ingredients and fried into crab cakes, added to stews and soups, or added to enrich a stuffing or sauce.

Like other shellfish, crab becomes tough when overcooked. Whole hard-shell crabs turn red when cooked, and the meat becomes slightly opaque. Precooked crabmeat needs only gentle warming.

Crayfish

Crayfish, also called crawfish, are freshwater crustaceans. Crayfish look much like miniature lobsters and are about 3–6 inches (8–15 cm) long. Crayfish plays a prominent role in Creole and Cajun cuisine and is a much-sought-after delicacy in France. Crayfish appear on the menu as a hot or cold appetizer or an entrée and in soups, stews, and sauces. Crayfish is sometimes

used to garnish plated seafood dishes or the seafood buffet because it is so colorful and attractive.

Common Varieties, Appearance, and Characteristics

About 250 different crayfish species grow in North America. Three species dominate the commercial market.

Red swamp Red swamp crayfish come from the Louisiana delta. The red swamp crayfish, which is the largest of the three popular species, turns a brilliant red when cooked.

White river White river crayfish grow in northern Louisiana.

Pacific Pacific crayfish come from California and Oregon.

Market Forms

Crayfish sell in live and frozen forms. Frozen tail meat is also available.

Handling and Storing

Unless frozen crayfish are bought, crayfish should be alive when received. The crayfish should squirm when lifted, not hang limp. Store live crayfish in the refrigerator, in a bowl covered with a damp towel. Use the crayfish within 24 hours. Thaw frozen crayfish in the refrigerator, and use it promptly.

Cooking Applications and Determining Doneness

Live crayfish are cooked by dropping them in boiling water and simmering them for a few minutes. Creole spices, herbs, or vegetables are added to the boiling liquid, and then the crayfish is served like lobster, to be eaten with the hands. Whole crayfish or tails are used to make bisques, soups, and sauces, or just the shells are used to add flavor. Crayfish is a key ingredient in Cajun specialties such as étouffé, gumbo, and jambalaya. Crayfish cook quickly, and their shells turn red when cooked.

Other Seafood

Foodservice operations sometimes serve other less well-known types of seafood, such as eel, conch, and sea urchin. Some items, such as frogs and snails, are typically listed as seafood on the menu, even though these are really primarily land animals. See Figure 22-20 on page 439.

Surimi

Surimi is a Japanese word meaning "formed fish." In this country most surimi is made from either of two cod family members: pollock or whiting. To make surimi, the whole fish is skinned, boned, rinsed, and ground into a paste. Flavoring ingredients, sometimes made from real shellfish, are added to the fish paste. Finally the product is shaped, colored, and cooked. Sometimes labeled "imitation crabmeat" or "imitation lobster," surimi provides an inexpensive, if imperfect, alternative for shellfish in salads, casseroles, and soups. Culinary historians credit the invention of surimi to the Japanese, who have been making it since A.D. 1100.

FIGURE 22-20

Other Seafood

FROG LEGS

Market Forms
Frozen or fresh legs, sold in pairs

Menu Application and Cooking Techniques
Appetizer or entrée; fried or sautéed

SURIMI

Market Forms
Fresh, frozen, or cooked

Menu Application and Cooking Techniques
Appetizer, salad, or entrée; cold with cocktail sauce or in sushi; warmed, as a substitute for crab or lobster

EEL

Market Forms
Fresh, smoked, or pickled

Menu Application and Cooking Techniques
Appetizer, soup, or entrée; baked, stewed, or grilled

CONCH

Market Forms
Fresh, canned, or frozen

Menu Application and Cooking Techniques
Appetizer, soup, salad, or entrée; simmered for soup or chowder, seviche, steamed, or sautéed

ABALONE

Market Forms
Frozen or canned

Menu Application and Cooking Techniques
Appetizer or entrée; seviche, grilled, sautéed, or simmered

LANGOUSTINES

Market Forms
Frozen

Menu Application and Cooking Techniques
Appetizer, salad, or entrée; simmered or sautéed

SEA URCHIN

Market Forms
Fresh

Menu Application and Cooking Techniques
Appetizer or in sauces; only the roe is eaten

SNAILS (ESCARGOT)

Market Forms
Fresh in shell or canned

Menu Application and Cooking Techniques
Appetizer; boiled then baked or broiled in seasoned butter

Fish and Shellfish

439

Fish and Shellfish Fabrication

Some foodservice establishments carry out all their own fabrication of fish and shellfish. Even restaurants that purchase most fish and shellfish already cut may find it necessary to carry out some fabrication procedures themselves, such as shucking oysters and deveining shrimp.

Portion Control

If its employees are experienced, one advantage the foodservice operation has when it carries out its own fabrication is that it has greater control over portion size and cut. When a restaurant purchases fish and shellfish already fabricated, the chef must choose from among the vendors' offerings and may lose the ability to present customers with a greater variety of sizes and cuts. On the other hand, the restaurant must compare per-pound prices of gilled and gutted fish with per-pound prices for specific cuts of fish. An employee who is inexperienced at fabricating fish can create excessive waste or fewer usable portions.

In choosing what cuts to make, the person fabricating the fish considers the fish and cooking technique preferred by the restaurant.

Fillet A fillet is a boneless piece of fish, cut from either side of a round fish or from the top and bottom of a flat fish. In most instances, fabrication includes removing the skin from the fillet.

Tranche A *tranche* is a slice of fish made by cutting through a fish fillet while holding the knife at an angle. The object of the cut is to increase the surface area of the fish. The greater the angle of the cut, the greater the surface area of the *tranche*. See Figure 22-22.

Goujonette A *goujonette* is a finger-sized strip of fish, cut from the fillet. See Figure 22-23 on page 441.

Darne A *darne* is a thick cross-sectional slice made from a large fish. It usually refers to a horseshoe-shaped cut of salmon that has the bone intact and is often grilled or poached. See Figure 22-24 on page 441.

Paupiette A *paupiette* is a thin fillet of white flesh fish that is rolled into a spiral, often around a filling of vegetables or ground fish. See Figure 22-25 on page 441.

Fabricating Skills

With practice and experience, fabrication can be carried out on a variety of fish.

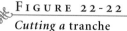

FIGURE 22-22
Cutting a **tranche**

✄ **FIGURE 22-23**
Cutting goujonettes

✄ **FIGURE 22-24**
Cutting a darne

✄ **FIGURE 22-25**
Rolling paupiettes

 PROCESS

Gutting a Round Fish

To maintain quality and extend shelf life, remove the viscera from whole fish as soon as possible.

To gut a round fish, follow these steps:

1 Using either a boning or fillet knife, make a horizontal cut along the belly to uncover the viscera.

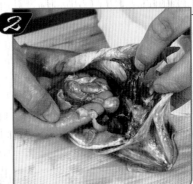

2 Remove the viscera.

3 Rinse the belly cavity of the fish under cold water.

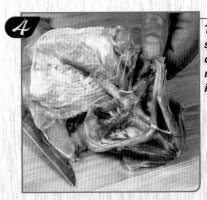

4 The cavity should be free of blood and remnants of the internal organs.

Filleting a Round Fish

The ability to fillet a round fish is a fabrication skill that results in better portion control and decreased waste.

To fillet a round fish, follow these steps:

1  Make a diagonal cut under the gills at the back of the head.

2  Starting from the tail, slide the knife along the backbone of the fish. Continue cutting along the backbone until reaching the belly cavity, and then gently lift the fillet and sever the rib bones without cutting through the fillet.

3  Turn the fish over, and repeat the process to separate the other fillet from the backbone.

4 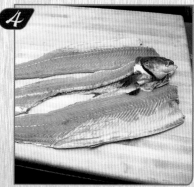 Lay each half of the round fish on the cutting board, skin side down.

5  Slide the knife under the rib bones to remove them from each fillet.

6  Trim the belly fat from each fillet.

7 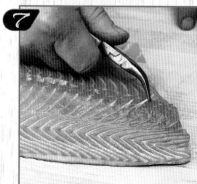 Run your fingers over the fillets to feel the pin bones. Remove the pin bones with tweezers or needle-nose pliers.

8  Position the fillet on the cutting board, and, working from the tail end, remove the skin by sliding the knife between the skin and the fillet, pulling the skin firmly toward you.

Filleting a Flat Fish

There are several ways to fillet flat fish, producing either half or quarter fillets. Some chefs pull the skin from the head toward the tail. Fillets can be cut with the skin on, without removing the head. This is one method that works particularly well.

To fillet a flat fish, follow these steps:

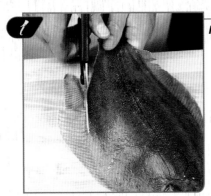

1 Remove the fins.

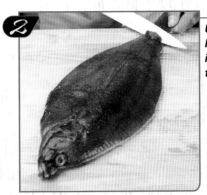

2 Using a fillet knife, make a cut in the skin near the tail.

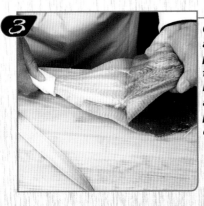

3 Grip the skin at the tail, and pull the skin toward the head. Remove the skin, and repeat the process on the other side.

4 Remove the head.

5 Cut quarter fillets by sliding the knife down the backbone and along the rib bones.

6 Turn the fillet over, and repeat the process on the other side.

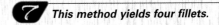

7 This method yields four fillets.

443

Salmon Fillet en Papillote

INGREDIENTS

	U.S. Standard	Metric
Parchment paper, cut into heart shape	10 each	10 each
Butter, melted	2 oz.	55 g
Salmon fillets, 6 oz. (170 g) each	10 fillets	10 fillets
Leeks, white section, sliced and blanched	5 oz.	140 g
Carrots, cut julienne, blanched	8 oz.	225 g
Celeriac, cut julienne, blanched	8 oz.	225 g
Butter, cut into 1/2-oz. (15-g) patties	5 oz.	140 g
Lemon juice (from fresh lemons)	2 each	2 each
White wine	2 oz.	60 ml
Salt	1/2 tsp.	2.5 ml
White pepper, ground	1/2 tsp.	2.5 ml

METHOD OF PREPARATION

1. Gather all the ingredients and equipment.
2. Fold the parchment in half, and crease the folded edge.
3. Brush paper hearts with the melted butter, and place buttered side down on baking dish.
4. Place a fillet on half of the paper.
5. Mix blanched vegetables, and divide on all fillets.
6. Place a butter patty on each fillet. Drizzle each fillet with lemon juice and white wine.
7. Season the fillets with salt and pepper to taste. Fold over the upper half of paper, and crimp the edges. Place *papillons* on a sheet pan, and refrigerate for one hour to let marinate.
8. Bake at 350°F (177°C) to order for 8–10 minutes, depending on thickness of fillets.
9. Serve the papillons closed to the guest. It is the waiter's duty to cut the papillon open at the table.

Shrimp Créole

Ingredients

Ingredients	U.S. Standard	Metric
Lime juice	4 oz.	120 ml
Salt	1 Tbsp.	15 g
Shrimp (16/20)	4 lbs.	1.8 kg
Cold water	as needed	as needed
Shallots, peeled and diced brunoise	6 oz.	170 g
Scallions, peeled and thinly sliced	6 oz.	170 g
Garlic, peeled and finely minced	12 cloves	12 cloves
Chili peppers, washed, seeded, and diced brunoise	3 each	3 each
Tomato, concassé	1 lb.	454 g
Fresh parsley, washed, squeezed dry, and chopped	3 oz.	90 ml
Thyme, ground	1/2 tsp.	3 g
Bay leaves	3 each	3 each
Salt	TT	TT
Olive oil	6 oz.	180 ml

Method of Preparation

1. Gather all the ingredients and equipment.

2. Preheat the oven to 375°F (191°C).

3. Combine the lime juice and salt, add the shrimp, and cover with water. Marinate and refrigerate at 41°F (5°C) or lower for 1 hour.

4. Mix all of the remaining ingredients, and allow mixture to stand for 1 hour. Drain the shrimp, and place in a baking pan. Pour the vegetable mixture over the shrimp.

5. Cover the pan tightly with aluminum foil, and braise in the oven, approximately 8–10 minutes, or until the shrimp are firm.

6. Serve immediately on a preheated plate, and *nappé* with the vegetable mixture. Remove bay leaves before serving.

COOKING TECHNIQUES

Braising:

1. Heat the braising pan to the proper temperature.
2. Sear and brown the food product to a golden color.
3. Degrease and deglaze.
4. Cook the food product in two-thirds liquid until fork-tender.

GLOSSARY

Brunoise: 1/8" (3 mm) dice

Concassé: peeled, seeded, and roughly chopped

Nappé: coated or to coat

NUTRITION

Nutrition Facts

Yield: Serves 10
Serving Size: 11 oz. (310 g)

Amount Per Serving

Calories 390

Total Fat 20 g

Sodium 1000 mg

Total Carbohydrate 12 g

Protein 39 g

Pan Seared Snapper with Floridian Fruit Vinaigrette

INGREDIENTS

	U.S. Standard	Metric
Red snapper, cut into 5-oz. (140-g) fillets; skin on	4 lbs.	1.8 kg
Salt	TT	TT
White pepper, ground	TT	TT
Lemon juice, freshly squeezed	3 oz.	90 ml
Vegetable oil or butter, clarified	3 oz.	90 ml
Floridian fruit vinaigrette	as needed	as needed

METHOD OF PREPARATION

1. Gather all the ingredients and equipment.

2. Place the snapper fillets in a hotel pan. Sprinkle the fillets on both sides with salt and pepper. Drizzle lemon juice over each fillet. Place in a cooler at 41°F (5°C) or lower, and let marinate for 30 minutes or until service.

3. Heat clarified butter or vegetable oil in a sauté pan. Add fillets, presentation side down first, and sauté until lightly browned on each side. Cook to an internal temperature of 145°F (63°C).

4. Place pan-seared fillet on a preheated dinner plate, and nappé with Floridian Fruit Vinaigrette.

NUTRITION

Nutrition Facts

Yield: Serves 10
Serving Size: 7 oz. (205 g)

Amount Per Serving

Calories 200

Total Fat 10 g

Sodium 130 mg

Total Carbohydrate 1 g

Protein 27 g

Floridian Fruit Vinaigrette

NUTRITION

Nutrition Facts

Yield: Serves 1 1/2 qts. (1.4 l)
Serving Size: 1 oz. (30 ml)

Amount Per Serving

Calories 40

Total Fat 0 g

Sodium 0 g

Total Carbohydrate 9 g

Protein 0 g

INGREDIENTS

	U.S. Standard	Metric
Oranges, peeled and sectioned	5 each	5 each
Apples, peeled, cored and thinly sliced	2 each	2 each
Strawberries, washed, stemmed and cut lengthwise	8 oz.	225 g
Lemons, peeled and sectioned	2 each	2 each
Grapes, red seedless, washed and stemmed	8 oz.	225 g
Sugar, granulated	8 oz.	225 g
Cointreau	2 oz.	60 ml

METHOD OF PREPARATION

1. Gather all the ingredients and equipment.

2. Place all of the ingredients, except the liqueur, into the bowl of a food processor, and purée.

3. Transfer the purée into a glass or crock container. Add the Cointreau, and mix well. Refrigerate at 41°F (5°C) or lower for at least 12 hours or overnight.

Mussels Steamed with Cider and Fresh Thyme

INGREDIENTS

INGREDIENTS	U.S. Standard	Metric
Mussels	8 lbs.	3.6 kg
Butter	2 oz.	55 g
Shallots, peeled, diced brunoise	3/4 c.	180 ml
Thyme leaves, washed, chopped	2 Tbsp.	30 ml
Black pepper, freshly ground	1/2 tsp.	2.5 ml
Apple cider	2 1/2 c.	600 ml
Cider vinegar	1 oz.	30 ml

METHOD OF PREPARATION

1. Gather all the ingredients and equipment.

2. Scrub and debeard the mussels. Wash shells well under cold water.

3. Melt the butter in a stockpot large enough to accommodate the mussels with room to spare. Add the shallots to the hot butter, and sauté until softened.

4. Add the rest of the ingredients, along with the cleaned mussels, cover pot with a tight-fitting lid, and raise heat to high. Allow mussels to steam, shaking the pot periodically, until they are all opened, about 8–10 minutes (for all 8 lbs. at once). Discard any that do not open.

5. Serve immediately in warm bowls with some of the broth on the side.

COOKING TECHNIQUES

Steaming (Traditional):
1. Place a rack over a pot of water.
2. Prevent steam vapors from escaping.
3. Shock or cook the food product throughout.

Sautéing:
1. Heat the sauté pan to the appropriate temperature.
2. Evenly brown the food product.
3. For a sauce, pour off any excess oil, reheat, and deglaze.

GLOSSARY

Brunoise: 1/8″ (3 mm) dice

NUTRITION

Nutrition Facts

Yield: Serves 10
Serving Size: 14 oz. (400 g) with shells, 7 oz. meat (205 g)

Amount Per Serving	
Calories 410	
Total Fat 14 g	
Sodium 740 mg	
Total Carbohydrate 20 g	
Protein 48 g	

Baked Stuffed Lobster Fisherman Style

INGREDIENTS

	U.S. Standard	Metric
Lobsters, 1 1/4 lbs. (570 g) each	10 each	10 each
Butter, clarified	10 ounces	300 ml
Scallops (30 ct.)	1 lb.	454 g
Shrimp (16/20), peeled, deveined, halved lengthwise	10 each	10 each
Ritz® cracker crumbs	5 cups	450 g
Dry sherry	2 Tbsp.	30 ml
Parsley, chopped	1/4 cup	60 g
Butter or pan spray	as needed	as needed
Lemon wedges	10 each	10 each

METHOD OF PREPARATION

1. Gather all equipment and ingredients.

2. Heat oven to 400°F (204°C).

3. Lay the live lobster on its back, using one hand to hold the tail down with a towel.

4. Insert a French knife into the head, and cut down to the shell. Continue cutting down the length of the lobster without cutting through the shell. Carefully spread the lobster open, gently cracking the shell as necessary.

5. Remove the head sac and the liver (tomalley). Discard both.

6. Remove the roe from the female lobsters, and set aside.

7. Cut off the claws at the joint closest to the carapace.

8. Plunge the claws into boiling salted water, and simmer about 3 minutes. Plunge into ice water to cool quickly.

9. Remove the meat from the claws, keeping the claws intact. Remove any cartilage from the claws. Remove the meat from the knuckles.

10. Heat the clarified butter, and sauté the scallops and shrimp until just barely cooked. Remove the scallops and shrimp and set aside.

11. Add the roe to the butter, and cook until it turns bright red. Crush the cooked roe.

12. Put the Ritz® cracker crumbs into a large bowl. Add the butter, parsley, cooked roe, and sherry. Blend to combine.

13. Place two shrimp halves in the cavity of the lobster. Add a couple of scallops and the lobster meat from the knuckles. Slice one scallop in half, and place the two halves in the tail section. Sprinkle with cracker crumb mixture.

14. Lay the two claws on top of the crumb mixture in the carapace. Top with more crumbs, and sprinkle some into the tail section.

15. Place lobsters on a sheet pan with a little salted water. Top with a little extra butter or spray with pan spray. Cover with foil, and bake 15 minutes. Remove foil, and bake an additional 3–5 minutes or until crumbs just begin to brown. Serve with extra melted butter and lemon wedges if desired.

NUTRITION

Nutrition Facts

Yield: Serves 10
Serving Size: 1 9-oz. (255-g) lobster

Amount Per Serving

Calories 460

Total Fat 27 g

Sodium 650 mg

Total Carbohydrate 14 g

Protein 39 g

Bouillabaisse Marseillaise

INGREDIENTS

	U.S. Standard	Metric
Cod, *skinned and boneless, cut into 10 cubes*	20 oz.	570 g
Catfish, *cut into 10 cubes*	20 oz.	570 g
Scallops	20 each	20 each
Mussels	20 each	20 each
Littleneck clams	20 each	20 each
Lobster tail, *cut into 3 pieces (and claws)*	1 1/4 lbs.	570 g
Olive oil	4 oz.	120 ml
Saffron	1/2 tsp.	2.5 ml
Salt	1 tsp.	5 ml
Black pepper, *ground*	1/2 tsp.	2.5 ml
Fish stock, *concentrated*	3 qts.	2.9 l
Croutons, *garlic-flavored*	20 each	20 each

METHOD OF PREPARATION

1. Gather all the ingredients and equipment.
2. Place all of the seafood in the pot, and add the oil and spices. Place in the refrigerator, and marinate for 1 hour.
3. Pour the cold, flavored, seasoned fish stock to cover the seafood, and poach until the shells open.
4. Taste, and adjust the seasonings.
5. Serve in a bowl with garlic croutons. Place a small plate on the side (to place shells).

Simmering:

1. Place the prepared product in an appropriately sized pot.
2. Bring the product to a boil, and then reduce the heat to allow the product to barely boil.
3. Cook until desired doneness is achieved.

NUTRITION

Nutrition Facts

Yield: Serves 10
Serving Size: 20 oz. (570 g)

Amount Per Serving

Calories 410

Total Fat 18 g

Sodium 1,160 mg

Total Carbohydrate 6 g

Protein 51 g

Fish and Shellfish

449

Linguine with Littlenecks and White Wine (Linguine alla Vongole)

INGREDIENTS

	U.S. Standard	Metric
Littleneck clams	50 each	50 each
Olive oil	4 oz.	120 ml
Shallots, peeled, thinly sliced	5 each	5 each
Garlic, peeled, thinly sliced	8 cloves	8 cloves
Crushed red pepper flakes	2 tsp.	10 g
Bay leaves	2 each	2 each
Dry white wine	16 oz.	500 ml
Clam juice	24 oz.	720 ml
Butter, in pieces, room temperature	3 oz.	85 g
Linguine	2 lbs.	910 g
Flat-leaf parsley, washed, squeezed dry, chopped	1/2 c.	120 ml
Extra virgin olive oil	10 Tbsp.	150 ml

METHOD OF PREPARATION

1. Gather all the ingredients and equipment.

2. Wash clams thoroughly, scrubbing the shells well.

3. Fill a large pot with salted water, and set on the stove to boil for linguine.

4. In a large, wide pot, heat the olive oil until hot but not smoking.

5. Add the shallots, garlic, and pepper flakes. Cook while stirring until barely golden, about 30 seconds.

6. Add the bay leaves, wine, clam juice, and clams. Simmer, covered, until clamshells open, about 4–5 minutes (discard any unopened shells). Remove clams and place in a bowl with a bit of the broth. Cover loosely, and hold at 140°F (60°C) or higher.

7. Strain liquid through 4–5 layers of wet cheesecloth. Return to a boil, and reduce until flavorful. Swirl in the butter.

8. Cook the linguine in the boiling salted water until al dente, and then drain, but do not rinse.

9. Add the pasta to the sauce along with the chopped parsley. Toss to combine.

10. Serve immediately on preheated dinner plates garnished with 5 clams each and a drizzle of extra virgin olive oil.

Maryland Crab Cakes

INGREDIENTS	U.S. Standard	Metric
Crabmeat, lump or jumbo	1 1/2 lbs.	680 g
Mayonnaise	1/2 c.	115 g
Egg, lightly beaten	1 each	1 each
Parsley, washed, squeezed dry, finely chopped	2 Tbsp.	30 ml
Lemon juice, freshly squeezed	1 Tbsp.	15 ml
Tabasco® sauce	1 1/2 tsp.	8 ml
Worcestershire sauce	1 tsp.	5 ml
Dijon mustard	1 tsp.	5 ml
Old Bay® seasoning	1 1/2 tsp.	8 ml
Bread crumbs, lightly toasted	1/3 c.	30 g
Fresh bread crumbs	1 1/2 c.	135 g
Clarified butter	4 oz.	120 ml
Vegetable oil	4 oz.	120 ml
Lemon wedges	10 each	10 each

METHOD OF PREPARATION

1. Gather all the ingredients and equipment.

2. Pick over crabmeat to remove any shell fragments.

3. Place cleaned crab in a bowl, and add all ingredients up to and including the toasted bread crumbs.

4. Form the mixture into 10 equal portions; shape each portion into round cakes about 1/2″–3/4″ (1.27 cm–1.9 cm) thick.

5. Dip each cake into the fresh bread crumbs to lightly coat.

6. Chill cakes well to firm.

7. Combine the clarified butter and vegetable oil to make a fortified butter.

8. Just before serving, shallow-fry the cakes to a golden brown crust, using the fortified butter as needed. Remove onto absorbent paper or a rack to drain.

9. Serve immediately with a lemon wedge.

COOKING TECHNIQUES

Shallow-Frying:
1. Heat the cooking medium to the proper temperature.
2. Cook the food product throughout.
3. Season, and serve hot.

NUTRITION

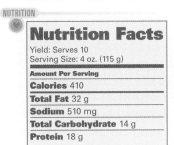

Nutrition Facts
Yield: Serves 10
Serving Size: 4 oz. (115 g)

Amount Per Serving

Calories 410

Total Fat 32 g

Sodium 510 mg

Total Carbohydrate 14 g

Protein 18 g

Fried Fisherman's Platter

with Beer Batter and Tartar Sauce

INGREDIENTS

	U.S. Standard	Metric
Cod fillets	1 1/2 lbs.	680 g
Shrimp (21/25 or 16/20)	1 lb.	454 g
Seasoned flour	as needed	as needed
Beer batter (recipe follows)	1 batch	1 batch
Sea scallops	1 lb.	454 g
Oysters, shucked	20 each	20 each
Frying clams, shucked	1 lb.	454 g
Eggs	4 each	4 each
Milk	1 c.	240 ml
Bread crumbs or dry breading mix	1 lb.	454 g
French fries, preblanched in fryer, drained, and held on absorbent paper	2 1/2 lbs.	1.1 kg
Salt	TT	TT
Lemons, cut in wedges	3 each	3 each
Tartar sauce (recipe follows)	1 qt.	960 ml

METHOD OF PREPARATION

1. Gather all the ingredients and equipment.

2. Preheat fryer to 350°F (177°C).

3. Trim cod, and cut into pieces about 2–2 1/2 oz. (70 g) each.

4. Peel the shrimp, leaving the tail section attached. Remove the vein from the back of the shrimp.

5. If cooking individual orders, divide seafood into 10 portions, and cook each portion separately as needed.

6. Dredge fish pieces in seasoned flour, and shake off excess. Then dip fish into the beer batter, and deep-fry until crisp, golden brown, and cooked to an internal temperature of 145°F (63°C). Drain and remove, spread on a sheet pan lined with absorbent paper, and hold briefly at 140°F (60°C) or higher.

7. Repeat the process using seasoned flour and beer batter to cook the shrimp; leave the tail section unbattered.

8. Remove the side "muscle" from the scallops.

9. Whisk the eggs to break up, and then whisk in the milk. Using the standard breading procedure, coat the scallops, oysters, and clams, and fry until golden brown and cooked to an internal temperature of 145°F (63°C); or use dry breading mix. Drain, spread on a sheet pan lined with plenty of absorbent paper, season lightly with salt, and hold briefly at 140°F (60°C) or higher.

10. While the seafood is cooking, refry the blanched fries to crisp, golden brown, drain, and season with salt; hold briefly at 140°F (60°C) or higher on absorbent paper.

11. Serve one portion of each seafood along with 4 oz. (115 g) of French fries on a preheated dinner plate with lemon wedges and tartar sauce.

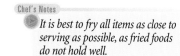

Chef's Notes

It is best to fry all items as close to serving as possible, as fried foods do not hold well.

COOKING TECHNIQUES

Deep-Frying:
1. *Heat the frying liquid to the proper temperature.*
2. *Submerge the food product completely.*
3. *Fry the product until it is cooked throughout.*

NUTRITION

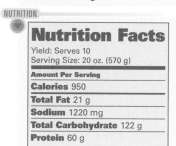

Nutrition Facts
Yield: Serves 10
Serving Size: 20 oz. (570 g)

Amount Per Serving

Calories 950

Total Fat 21 g

Sodium 1220 mg

Total Carbohydrate 122 g

Protein 60 g

Beer Batter

INGREDIENTS

	U.S. Standard	Metric
Flour, all-purpose	1 1/2 lbs.	680 g
Salt	1 tsp.	5 ml
White pepper	1/2 tsp.	2.5 ml
Eggs, whole, separated	6 each	6 each
Beer	18 oz.	540 ml

Chef's Notes
 This batter can be used with fish or vegetables.

METHOD OF PREPARATION

1. Gather all the ingredients and equipment.

2. In a large bowl, combine the flour, salt, and pepper; mix well.

3. In another bowl, lightly beat the yolks, and whisk in the beer.

4. Add the liquid ingredients to the dry ingredients, and mix to a smooth batter.

5. Whip the egg whites to a soft peak, and then gently fold whites into the batter.

Tartar Sauce

Chef's Notes

• Serve this sauce cold. It can be served with fish, seafood, grilled entrées, or vegetables.

• For Southern-type preparations, add Cajun spice to taste, and mix well.

• Onions can be replaced with chopped chives.

GLOSSARY

Brunoise: 1/8" (3 mm) dice

NUTRITION

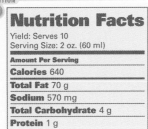

Nutrition Facts

Yield: Serves 10
Serving Size: 2 oz. (60 ml)

Amount Per Serving

Calories 640

Total Fat 70 g

Sodium 570 mg

Total Carbohydrate 4 g

Protein 1 g

INGREDIENTS

	U.S. Standard	Metric
Mayonnaise	1 3/4 pts.	785 g
Dill pickles, diced brunoise	2 oz.	55 g
Onions, peeled, diced brunoise	2 oz.	55 g
Capers, drained, rinsed, rough-chopped	1/4 oz.	8 g
Chervil leaves, washed, dried, chopped	1/4 oz.	8 g
Tarragon leaves, washed, dried, chopped	1/4 oz.	8 g
Parsley, washed, squeezed dry, chopped	1/4 oz.	8 g
Lemon juice, freshly squeezed, seeds removed	1/4 oz.	8 g

METHOD OF PREPARATION

1. Gather all the ingredients and equipment.

2. Mix all of the ingredients together in a bowl, and refrigerate at 41°F (5°C) or lower for at least one hour.

Oriental Shrimp Curry

INGREDIENTS

	U.S. Standard	Metric
Shrimp (10/20)	40 each	40 each
Salt	TT	TT
White vinegar	2 Tbsp.	30 ml
Coconut, grated	8 oz.	225 g
Coconut milk	10 oz.	300 ml
Coriander seeds, ground	4 oz.	115 g
Vegetable oil	3 oz.	90 ml
Ginger root, peeled and finely chopped	2 Tbsp.	30 g
Onions, peeled and cut julienne	4 oz.	115 g
Garlic, peeled and finely chopped	2 Tbsp.	30 g
Turmeric	1 tsp.	5 ml
Cumin	1/2 tsp.	2.5 ml
Cayenne pepper	TT	TT
Black pepper, ground	TT	TT

METHOD OF PREPARATION

1. Gather all the ingredients and equipment.

2. Peel the shrimp, leaving the tail section on. Devein and wash the shrimp.

3. Combine the salt and white vinegar, add the shrimp, and marinate for 1 hour. Strain the shrimp, and reserve the marinade.

4. In a food processor, purée the coconut, coconut milk, and coriander seeds. Strain through a cheesecloth, and reserve.

5. In a wok, over high heat, add the oil. Sauté the ginger root and onions. Then add the garlic and stir-fry for about 2 minutes. Add the turmeric, cumin, cayenne pepper, and black pepper.

6. Add the shrimp, marinade, and coconut mixture, and simmer until the shrimp are thoroughly cooked.

7. To serve, ladle the soup into a preheated cup. Serve immediately, or hold the soup at 140°F (60°C) or higher.

Nutrition Facts

Yield: Serves 10
Serving Size: 4 oz. (115 g)

Amount Per Serving

Calories 230

Total Fat 16 g

Sodium 115 mg

Total Carbohydrate 18 g

Protein 8 g

Baked Cod Pizziaoli (Marzanese Style)

INGREDIENTS

Ingredients	U.S. Standard	Metric
Cod fillets	3.5 lbs.	1.6 kg
French or Italian bread, *crusts removed*	10 oz.	285 g
Water	about 4 oz.	120 ml
Garlic cloves, *peeled and chopped*	2 each	2 each
Olive oil	2 Tbsp.	30 ml
Crushed tomato, *canned*	2 cups	500 ml
Salt	TT	TT
Pepper	TT	TT
Oregano, *dry*	1 1/2–2 tsp.	10 ml

METHOD OF PREPARATION

1. Gather all the ingredients and equipment. Preheat oven to 400°F (204°C).

2. Cut cod into 10 pieces, about 5 1/2 oz. (155 g) each. Arrange pieces in a hotel pan.

3. Make a *panada* out of the bread and water by breaking up bread into small pieces and moistening with water. Squeeze out any excess water.

4. Pat moistened bread panada over each piece of fish. The panada should be about 1/4″ (6 mm) thick.

5. Heat the garlic in the olive oil until softened but not browned. Add the garlic and oil to the crushed tomatoes.

6. Neatly spoon the tomato mixture over the fish fillets, keeping the tomato on top of the fish.

7. Season each piece with salt and pepper, and sprinkle with the oregano.

8. Add a small amount of water to the pan, and cover with foil.

9. Bake about 8–10 minutes, or until the fish is almost cooked. Remove the foil, and bake a few minutes longer. The internal temperature of the fish should be 145°F (63°C).

Baking:
1. Preheat the oven.
2. Place the food product on the appropriate rack.

Panada: a thick paste made by mixing bread crumbs, flour, rice, etc., with a liquid such as water, stock, or milk

Nutrition Facts

Yield: Serves 10
Serving Size: 8 oz. (225 g)

Amount Per Serving

Calories 250

Total Fat 5 g

Sodium 320 mg

Total Carbohydrate 17 g

Protein 31 g

23 Protein Alternatives

11,000 B.C.
Wild grains grow in the Near East.

7000 B.C.
The Greeks cultivate lentils and other legumes.

22 B.C.
The Japanese ferment soy beans to make soy sauce and miso paste.

A.D. 1904
Peanut butter is introduced as a health food for the elderly.

1999
The U.S. Food and Drug Administration recommends that Americans eat soy protein to reduce the risk of coronary heart disease.

About 1.5 million years ago, early humans obtained almost all their dietary needs from meat. Climate patterns marked the disappearance of the mastodon and the mammoth, the main sources of meat, forcing humans to find food that provided protein and fat. It was n[ot] long before humans began to use legumes and grains for a significant source of prote[in] and a viable alternative to meat. Tens of thousands of years ago, people gathered beans in Central Asia, southeastern Afghanistan, and the Himalayan foothills. People in ancient India, Egypt, the Middle East, and Central Asia sowed lenti[ls]. According to Chinese legend, cultivation of soy beans began in the fifteen[th] century B.C. The Chinese have grown rice since 4000 B.C., and peop[le] in present-day Mexico ate maize (corn) prior to that. Today muc[h] of the world still relies on legumes and grains as a major source of protein. In the United States, consumers increasingly choose plant-based foods to meet some or all of the body's protein needs.

KEY TERMS
protein alternatives
satiety
isoflavones
tempeh
seitan
textured soy protein
tofu
silken tofu
soy-based analogs
mutual supplementation
legumes
grains
mycoprotein

Why People Choose Alternative Sources of Protein

The human body needs protein to carry out basic functions and sustain life. Animal products such as meat, milk, cheese, and eggs are major sources of protein. Plants such as legumes and grains contain high levels of protein, too. Some people choose to replace some or all of the animal proteins in their diet with these plant-based protein alternatives. The decision to choose protein alternatives can be related to health, the environment, or religious traditions and ethics.

Health In the United States, most people have adequate access to protein. In fact, a major problem in developed countries is the overconsumption of protein.

- Many high-protein foods, such as meat, eggs, and dairy products, contain high levels of saturated fat, a known contributor to heart disease and cancer. Researchers now believe that regardless of fat content, animal protein may raise blood cholesterol. Diets high in animal protein may also contribute to bone loss as well as to kidney and liver problems.
- Plant proteins pose few health risks when consumed in moderation. Most alternative sources of protein are naturally low in saturated fats. Some high-protein plants, such as soy beans, may even lower blood cholesterol. Protein alternatives offer foods that are rich in fiber and lower in calories than comparable meals based on animal protein. Soy, rice, and nut milks and soy and rice cheese provide options for people who are lactose intolerant.

Environment Some people choose protein alternatives because raising plant proteins takes less of a toll on the environment than raising livestock does.

- Livestock are high on the food chain. It takes ten pounds of grain to produce a pound of beef, but only one pound of grain to produce a loaf of bread. Growing food crops such as legumes and grains requires less land, energy, and water than producing meat and milk products.
- Large feedlots and factory-style animal farms create huge quantities of waste, which can pollute the surrounding soil and water. Fishing also has environmental impacts. Overfishing threatens certain fish species. Nonfood fish and other aquatic animals can be injured or killed during the harvest of some food fish.

Religious traditions and ethics Religious traditions and ethics influence some people's decision to use other sources of protein. Some religious faiths forbid the consumption of particular animal products, such as pork or shellfish, and others ban all meats or animal products.

- Buddhist philosophy requires followers to abstain from eating animal products, including those from cattle, horses, dogs, monkeys, and chickens.
- Jewish and Muslim dietary laws define pork and other animal products as being unclean and thus unfit for consumption.
- Some people choose to eat other sources of protein because of the manner in which animals are slaughtered for food. Some believe that it is wrong to consume any products, even those such as milk, cheese, eggs, or honey, taken from live animals.

Nutritional Considerations

Researchers evaluate the quality of a food's protein by looking at its digestibility and its balance of amino acids. Proteins are classified as either complete or incomplete. A complete protein contains all the essential amino acids needed by the human body. An incomplete protein contains some essential amino acids, but not all. Combining two or more incomplete but complementary proteins allows the body to obtain complete protein. Soy beans provide complete protein. The other legumes and grains that make up protein alternatives provide incomplete protein.

Alternative sources of protein offer the body more than just protein. They contribute vitamins, minerals, fat, carbohydrates, and fiber to the diet. Because of their high dietary fiber, some protein alternatives, most notably legumes, cause a feeling of fullness, or *satiety,* sooner than animal protein sources do. Legumes also satisfy hunger longer than some other food sources. Both of these characteristics can be powerful aids in controlling weight.

The health benefits of eating foods with soy protein are impressive. The U.S. Food and Drug Administration recommends that Americans include soy foods in the diet in order to reduce the risk of coronary heart disease. Soy has been shown to reduce blood levels of bad (LDL) cholesterol and reduce plaque buildup in the arteries. Soy is also a rich source of isoflavones. *Isoflavones* are phytochemicals, a group of plant compounds that may help reduce the risk of certain diseases, particularly cancer.

Tempeh

Tempeh is a chunky, tender cake made from whole soy beans that have been fermented. In addition to soy beans, tempeh sometimes contains other grains, such as rice or millet. Tempeh has a flavor described as smoky, yeasty, or nutty.

Nutritional Information

Tempeh is an excellent source of cholesterol-free protein that is naturally low in saturated fat. Tempeh is also rich in dietary fiber. One 3-ounce serving contributes more than one-fourth of the adult daily requirement for dietary fiber. Soy beans, the principal ingredient in tempeh, are rich in isoflavones. In addition, the fermentation process used in making tempeh helps reduce the compounds that make legumes hard for some people to digest.

Tempeh is a traditional food of Indonesia, where people eat an average of 860 grams (nearly two pounds) of tempeh per month. Traditional Indonesian tempeh is fermented in bright green banana leaves. The finished tempeh cakes are sold still wrapped in banana leaves. A 225-gram piece of tempeh (slightly less than half a pound) sells for under a quarter in Indonesia.

Purchasing, Handling, and Storing Tempeh

Tempeh is available fresh or frozen. Frozen tempeh can be stored for months without loss of quality. After it has thawed, keep tempeh in the refrigerator, where it will stay fresh for about ten days. Tempeh should have a fragrant, musty odor. The only visible mold should be that from the white tempeh culture. Tempeh cakes should not feel slimy.

Production Methods

To make tempeh, soy beans are cooked and dehulled. Then the beans are inoculated with the mycelium of *Rhizopus* mold. The beans ferment for 18 to 24 hours and form a compact cake.

Culinary Applications

Tempeh has a chewy consistency. It can be grilled or used in soups, casseroles, or chili. Sliced, fried tempeh has a texture and flavor similar to that of southern-fried chicken. Form tempeh into burgers, or steam and purée it for use in dressings and spreads.

Seitan

Seitan is a protein alternative made from wheat gluten. Sometimes called wheat meat, seitan has a firm, chewy, and meatlike texture. Russian and Southeast Asian farmers, vegetarian monks of China, and Mormons are some of the groups of people who have traditionally relied upon seitan as a significant source of protein. Seitan has a mild, almost neutral taste and absorbs other flavors well.

Nutritional Information

Seitan is naturally low in sodium and fat and high in protein. One ounce (30 grams) of raw gluten contains 7.5 grams of protein. The starch and bran from the wheat are washed out during the production of seitan. Its exact nutritional content varies depending on the ingredients added during processing. Flavoring ingredients added to commercially prepared seitan can contain a great deal of sodium. One 3-1/2-ounce serving (100 grams) contains 118 calories, 18% protein, and less than 1% fat.

❧ FIGURE 23-1
Seitan may be used as a meat replacement in sautés and stir-fries.

Purchasing, Handling, and Storing Seitan

Commercially prepared seitan is packed in marinades or broth in refrigerated tubs or vacuum packs. It is also sold as foil- or plastic-wrapped cakes. Seitan cutlets, slices, burgers, and strips are available fresh or frozen. Fresh seitan in broth, when refrigerated, retains its freshness for about one week. Frozen, individually wrapped slices or cutlets retain their quality for about one month. Thaw frozen seitan in the refrigerator before using.

Production Methods

The traditional method for making seitan is to combine water and flour or wheat gluten to form thick dough. Knead the dough, and if using flour, rinse the dough repeatedly in water to remove the wheat starch and bran. After the dough reaches the desired consistency, slowly simmer it in broth. Packaged wheat gluten eliminates the need for rinsing.

Culinary Applications

Because seitan is fully cooked, add it to cooked dishes at the last minute so that it retains its texture and flavor. Seitan easily absorbs flavors, making it a welcome addition to stews or soups. Seitan can replace meat in stir-fried or sautéed foods. See Figure 23-1. Baking, braising, or deep-frying are other methods for cooking seitan.

Textured Soy Protein

Textured soy protein is a bland-tasting, processed, dehydrated soy bean protein made from soy bean flour or soy protein concentrate. Rehydrated textured soy protein has a texture similar to that of ground beef and functions as a meat extender or as a replacement for ground meat, poultry, or fish. Textured soy protein is sometimes called TVP®, textured vegetable protein, or TSP®, textured soy protein. Both TVP® and TSP® are proprietary names for products created by Archer Daniels Midland and PMS Foods, respectively.

Nutritional Information

Textured soy protein made from soy flour contains about 50% protein as well as dietary fiber and carbohydrates. One ounce (30 grams) contains approximately 80 calories, 12 grams of protein, and no fat. Textured soy protein made from soy protein concentrate contains about 70% protein.

Purchasing, Handling, and Storing Textured Soy Protein

The forms of dehydrated textured soy protein include flakes, granules, and chunks, either plain or flavored. Flavored varieties may contain salt, flavorings, and other additives. Dehydrated textured soy protein is sold in bags or in bulk and can be stored in airtight containers for several months. After it is rehydrated, textured soy protein must be kept refrigerated and used within a few days.

Production Methods

Textured soy protein production involves refining and defatting soy bean flour and then running the flour through an extrusion machine that shapes the textured soy protein into many different forms and sizes. Rehydrate textured soy protein in boiling water before use. One pound (450 g) of dry product yields approximately three pounds (1,360 g) of rehydrated textured soy protein. It is not necessary to rehydrate textured soy protein before adding it to soups or sauces, provided that the recipe contains enough liquid.

Culinary Applications

Hydrated textured soy protein has a chewy, fibrous, meatlike texture suitable for stews, soups, and sauces. Because it is naturally bland, textured soy protein absorbs the flavor of the marinade or sauce in which it cooks. Textured soy protein frequently replaces some or all of the meat in chili, spaghetti sauce, or tacos. It can also be formed into loaves or patties and then baked or fried. Many commercial meat analogs contain textured soy protein.

Tofu

Tofu, also called soy bean curd, is a soft, cheeselike food made from soy milk that has been heated and curdled with a coagulant. Tofu has a bland taste and easily absorbs the flavors of other ingredients with which it cooks.

Nutritional Information

Tofu is a source of high-quality protein and B vitamins. It is low in sodium and relatively low in calories. Tofu made with calcium salts can be a good source of calcium. Nutritional counts depend on the variety of tofu, but in general, the firmer the tofu, the higher the protein, fat, and calorie count. A 1/2-cup serving of firm, water-packed tofu has 97 calories, 10 grams of protein, and 5.6 grams of fat.

Purchasing, Handling, and Storing Tofu

There are two main types of tofu sold in the United States: water-packed and silken. Water-packed tofu has a solid, dense texture that holds its shape well in cooked dishes. Water-packed tofu comes in firm and extra-firm consistencies. Although Chinese- and Japanese-style tofus differ, both are classified as water-packed. Chinese tofu is denser and coarser than Japanese tofu. Japanese tofu has a softer consistency, less protein, and fewer calories than does Chinese tofu.

Silken tofu is made using a different process from that for water-packed tofu and has a consistency that is much softer, like flan or custard. Silken tofu is sold fresh in tubs or packed in aseptic bricks. It can be purchased in extra-firm, firm, soft, and reduced-fat varieties.

Except for tofu packed in aseptic bricks, tofu must be received and stored cold. Refrigerate aseptic bricks after opening them. Water-packed tofu should be rinsed, covered with fresh water, and refrigerated. Change the water daily, and use the tofu within one week. Silken tofu need not be covered with water, but it should be refrigerated and used within three days of opening. It is possible to freeze tofu for up to five months to extend its shelf life. Freezing tofu changes its texture—a plus if a product should have a chewy, meatlike texture. Tofu is also available in smoked, fermented, marinated, and pickled varieties. Pressed tofu, a Chinese specialty, is tofu with even more of the water removed, which results in a meaty, chewy texture. Spices or other flavors and coloring are sometimes added to pressed tofu.

Production Methods

Tofu is made from whole soy beans that have been soaked and ground and then boiled and filtered to produce soy milk. The warm soy milk is then curdled with the addition of calcium sulphate or with *nigari*, lye that remains after the production of sea salt. Curds are separated from the whey and then pressed to squeeze out most of the remaining liquid.

Culinary Applications

Tofu can form the basis of a main course, or it can enrich other dishes. Tofu can be reshaped and formed into cakes or loaves, deep-fried or grilled as an appetizer, tossed with vegetables in a stir-fry, or cubed and added to soups and casseroles. Puréed silken tofu can be used in dips, cream sauces, and desserts.

Soy-based Analogs

Soy-based analogs are soy products formulated to simulate the taste, texture, and cooking characteristics of animal products. The two main categories of analogs are dairy items and meat and fish products.

Dairy Items

Soy milk serves as the replacement for milk, cheese, and yogurt.

Milk Soy milk is made from soy beans that have been soaked, ground fine, boiled, and strained. It contains no lactose or casein, so it is suitable for those who cannot tolerate cow's milk. Soy milk offers more protein than cow's milk and is a good source of B vitamins. It is cholesterol-free and low in fat and sodium. Forms of soy milk include powder that must be reconstituted in water, ready-to-use liquid in quart and half-gallon containers, and liquid in aseptic packaging. Soy milk can be fortified with calcium, vitamin D, and vitamin B-12 and flavored with vanilla, chocolate, or strawberry. It is also available in whole, low-fat, and nonfat forms. Unopened aseptic packages of soy milk remain usable when stored at room temperature for several months. Keep soy milk powder in closed containers in the refrigerator or freezer. Refrigerate opened containers of soy milk, and use them within five days.

Soy milk can substitute for cow's milk in most recipes. Soy milk's thick, rich texture makes it especially suitable for sauces and soups. However, high heat and acidic ingredients such as wine or lemon juice can cause soy milk to curdle.

Cheese Soy cheese is made from soy milk with the possible addition of casein, a milk protein. Soy cheese comes in full-fat, low-fat, and nonfat versions of cheeses such as cheddar, mozzarella, Parmesan, and cream cheese. Serve soy cheese chilled or at room temperature. Most soy cheese melts well when heated.

Yogurt Soy yogurt is made from soy milk to which live bacteria are added. Its flavor and consistency are similar to those of cow's milk yogurt, and it can be used in the same way. Both plain and fruit-flavored soy yogurts are available. Use soy yogurt within approximately one week of purchase.

Meat and Fish Products

Meat and fish analogs simulate various kinds of meat and fish products. Soy beans or soy bean-based products, such as textured soy bean protein or tofu, form the basis of analogs, with the addition of other ingredients. Wheat or other grains are common ingredients in meat analogs. Some meat analogs also contain eggs, flavorings, and additives. Fat and sodium counts vary widely among products and manufacturers; some meat analogs are available in fat-free forms.

Meat analogs are available fresh, frozen, canned, or dried. It is usually possible to prepare and serve meat and fish analogs in the same manner as the meat or fish they replace.

Chicken Analog chicken products include nuggets and patties.

Burgers Analog burgers, preformed into patties, look and taste like beef hamburgers.

Sausage Analog sausage is produced as preformed links or patties. Sausage crumbles also are available.

Bacon Analog breakfast strips have the shape and coloring of bacon.

Deli meats Analog cold cuts resemble sliced, deli-style cold cut meats.

Fish Analog fish products are formed into nuggets, strips, and breaded fillets.

Legumes and Grains

With the exception of soy beans, most legumes and grains lack one or more essential amino acids. *Mutual supplementation* is the strategy of eating two protein-rich foods that, when combined, contain all of the essential amino acids. For example, many legumes supply adequate amounts of the amino acids isoleucine and lysine but lack methionine and tryptophan. Grains have the opposite strengths and weaknesses. Eating legumes and grains together provides the body with all the essential amino acids it needs. Recent studies show that it is beneficial to eat complementary proteins in the same dish or at the same meal for the body to get the energy and protein needed.

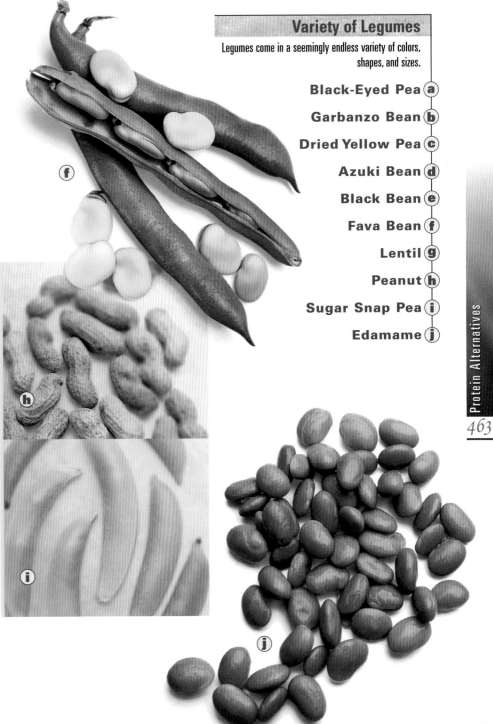

Variety of Legumes

Legumes come in a seemingly endless variety of colors, shapes, and sizes.

Black-Eyed Pea **a**
Garbanzo Bean **b**
Dried Yellow Pea **c**
Azuki Bean **d**
Black Bean **e**
Fava Bean **f**
Lentil **g**
Peanut **h**
Sugar Snap Pea **i**
Edamame **j**

Protein Alternatives

463

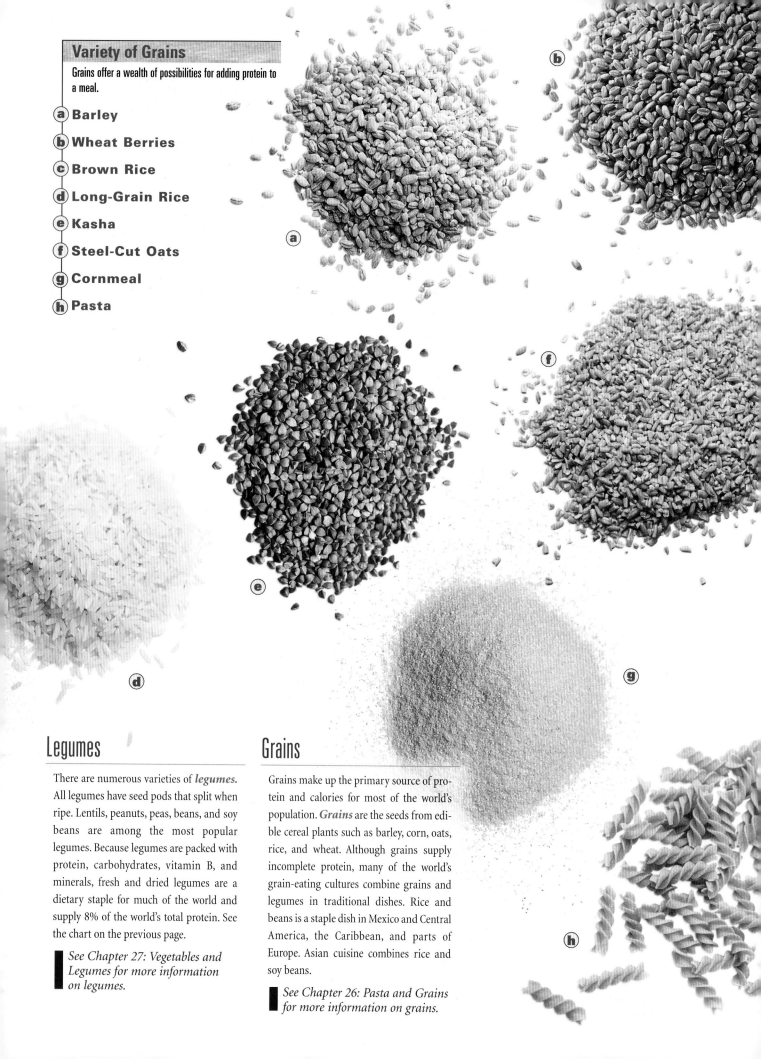

Variety of Grains

Grains offer a wealth of possibilities for adding protein to a meal.

ⓐ **Barley**

ⓑ **Wheat Berries**

ⓒ **Brown Rice**

ⓓ **Long-Grain Rice**

ⓔ **Kasha**

ⓕ **Steel-Cut Oats**

ⓖ **Cornmeal**

ⓗ **Pasta**

Legumes

There are numerous varieties of *legumes.* All legumes have seed pods that split when ripe. Lentils, peanuts, peas, beans, and soy beans are among the most popular legumes. Because legumes are packed with protein, carbohydrates, vitamin B, and minerals, fresh and dried legumes are a dietary staple for much of the world and supply 8% of the world's total protein. See the chart on the previous page.

▌ *See Chapter 27: Vegetables and Legumes for more information on legumes.*

Grains

Grains make up the primary source of protein and calories for most of the world's population. *Grains* are the seeds from edible cereal plants such as barley, corn, oats, rice, and wheat. Although grains supply incomplete protein, many of the world's grain-eating cultures combine grains and legumes in traditional dishes. Rice and beans is a staple dish in Mexico and Central America, the Caribbean, and parts of Europe. Asian cuisine combines rice and soy beans.

▌ *See Chapter 26: Pasta and Grains for more information on grains.*

Using Vegetables and Grains as Meat Alternatives

Because people enjoy the texture, appearance, and culinary applications of meat so much, the food industry has developed vegetable and grain products that mimic meat's characteristics.

Meat Alternatives and Texture

The taste and mouth feel of meat influence some people to choose protein alternatives with meatlike properties. For instance, the large, dark brown portobello mushroom not only looks like a hamburger but also has a similarly dense, chewy texture. A grilled portobello sandwich is a common vegetarian dish. Portobello mushrooms are also grilled or sautéed and served as an entrée. In February 2002, Quorn Foods, Inc. introduced to the United States new products made from *mycoprotein,* fermented fungi. It contains all nine essential amino acids, is cholesterol free, and is low in fat, especially saturated fat. Its texture is similar to that of chicken breast, and it can be transformed into products resembling ground beef, chicken nuggets, patties, cutlets, and chicken tenders.

Formed Vegetable Items

Some vegetables are ground and formed into patties or other shapes for use as meat alternatives. Veggie burgers, meant to imitate the appearance and texture of hamburgers, can be made from a variety of ingredients, including grains; legumes, such as soy beans; and fresh vegetables, such as shredded carrots, green beans, peppers, and zucchini. Vegetable pâté recipes that resemble meat loaf products contain nuts, vegetables, and a grain binder. However, not all veggie burgers are free from animal products. Eggs may form the binding ingredient in veggie burgers. Cheese or meat-based natural flavors may be added for flavor or enrichment.

Seitan Piccata

INGREDIENTS

	U.S. Standard	Metric
HERB CRUST		
Flour, unbleached, all-purpose	2 c.	350 g
Polenta or cornmeal	1/2 c.	175 g
Thyme, dried	2 1/2 tsp.	13 ml
Basil, dried	2 1/2 tsp.	13 ml
Oregano, dried	2 1/2 tsp.	13 ml
Paprika	2 tsp.	10 ml
White pepper, freshly ground	1 1/4 tsp.	6 ml
SOY MILK MIXTURE		
Soy milk	1 1/2 c.	360 ml
Dijon mustard	3 1/2 tsp.	17.5 ml
Seitan, ten 4-oz. (115-g) portions	2 1/2 lbs.	1.14 kg
PICCATA SAUCE		
Lemons, washed	9 each	9 each
Garlic, minced	1 Tbsp.	15 g
Fresh lemon juice	10 oz.	300 ml
Nonalcoholic wine or dry white wine	10 oz.	300 ml
Orange juice	10 oz.	300 ml
Honey	4 oz.	120 ml
Nutritional yeast	1 1/2 Tbsp.	22 ml
White pepper, freshly ground	3/4 tsp.	4 ml
Sea salt	3/4 tsp.	4 ml
Arrowroot	1 1/2 Tbsp.	22 ml
Water, cold	2 1/2 oz.	75 ml
Capers, drained	1 1/2 Tbsp.	22 g
Salt	TT	TT
Canola oil	as needed	as needed
Lemon slices, thinly sliced	10 slices	10 slices
Basil, fresh, washed, dried, finely chopped	1/2 oz.	15 ml
Chives, fresh, washed	20 each	20 each

METHOD OF PREPARATION

1. Gather all the ingredients and equipment.

2. In a shallow bowl, combine all the dry ingredients for the herb crust.

3. In another bowl, combine the soy milk and mustard.

4. Dip seitan slices into the soy milk mixture, then dredge with the crust mixture, dip again in the soymilk mixture, and dredge once again in the crust mixture. Place on a sheet pan lined with parchment paper.

5. Peel 3 of the lemons for the sauce. Using a paring knife, clean off all the white pith, leaving just the yellow rind. Cut the skin (pith and rind) off the remaining lemons, and section them. Remove the seeds as you go, and discard the skins.

6. Combine the cleaned lemon peels, lemon sections, and the listed sauce ingredients from garlic to sea salt in a saucepot. Heat to a simmer.

7. Dissolve the arrowroot in the cold water, and thicken the sauce with this mixture. Simmer for 5 more minutes. Strain, add capers to strained sauce, and reheat to a simmer; taste and adjust salt and pepper as needed. Hold in a bain-marie at 140°F (60°C) or higher until service.

8. In a large nonstick sauté pan or skillet, sauté the breaded seitan, in batches, in the canola oil over medium-high heat until lightly browned, about 2 to 3 minutes per side. Hold warm at 140°F (60°C) or higher on a platter.

9. Serve 4 oz. (115 g) of seitan with 3 oz. (90 ml) of sauce on preheated plates garnished with lemon, chopped basil, and two chives each.

Vegetable Walnut and Pine Nut Pâté

INGREDIENTS

	U.S. Standard	Metric
Onions, peeled, cut macédoine	1 c.	225 g
Carrots, peeled, cut macédoine	1 c.	225 g
Celery, washed, cut macédoine	1 c.	225 g
Olive oil	1 Tbsp.	15 ml
Black pepper	pinch	pinch
Garlic, peeled and minced	1 tsp.	5 g
Scallions, cut brunoise	1/2 cup	115 g
Red wine vinegar	2 tsp.	10 ml
Soy sauce	1 Tbsp.	15 g
Dijon mustard	1 Tbsp.	15 ml
Sea salt	1/4 tsp.	1.25 ml
Liquid smoke	3 drops	3 drops
Vegetable stock	1/4 c.	60 ml
Walnuts, toasted, chopped (see Chef's Notes)	2/3 c.	170 g
Pine nuts, toasted, chopped (see Chef's Notes)	1/3 c.	85 g

METHOD OF PREPARATION

1. Gather all the ingredients and equipment.

2. Sauté the onions, carrots, and celery in olive oil over medium heat for 5 minutes.

3. Add the pepper, garlic, and scallions, and sauté for 5 minutes more. Turn the heat to low, and add all remaining ingredients, except for the stock and nuts. Continue sautéing for 5 additional minutes.

4. Turn the ingredients into a food processor. Deglaze the pan with the vegetable stock, and pour into the food processor. Process the mixture to a smooth pâté. Chill the pâté before serving.

5. Garnish the pâté with the nuts, and serve with crackers, flat breads, chutney, or crudités.

Chef's Notes

To toast the nuts: Place on a sheet pan in a 350°F (177°C) oven for 4–5 minutes. Stir and check after 3 minutes. Keep the nuts at the edge of the pan from burning.

COOKING TECHNIQUES

Sautéing:

1. Heat the sauté pan to the appropriate temperature.
2. Evenly brown the food product.
3. For a sauce, pour off any excess oil, reheat, and deglaze.

GLOSSARY

Macédoine: 1/4" (6 mm) dice

NUTRITION

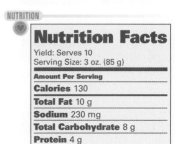

Nutrition Facts		
Yield: Serves 10		
Serving Size: 3 oz. (85 g)		
Amount Per Serving		
Calories 130		
Total Fat 10 g		
Sodium 230 mg		
Total Carbohydrate 8 g		
Protein 4 g		

Smoked Tempeh and Potato Sausages

INGREDIENTS

	U.S. Standard	Metric
Smoked tempeh, marinated, finely crumbled	8 oz.	225 g
Russet potato	1 each	1 each
Scallions, finely chopped	3 each	3 each
Flour, unbleached	1/4 c.	55 g
Sage, dried	1 tsp.	5 ml
Thyme, dried	1/2 tsp.	2.5 ml
Nutmeg, ground	1/4 tsp.	1.25 ml
Black pepper, ground	1/2 tsp.	2.5 ml
Chipotle pepper	1 tsp.	5 ml
Tamari soy sauce	2 tsp.	10 ml
Sea salt	TT	TT
Canola oil (optional)	2 Tbsp.	30 ml

METHOD OF PREPARATION

1. Gather all the ingredients and equipment.

2. In a large bowl, combine all the ingredients except the oil, and mix well.

3. Form the mixture into ten 1/2″ (1.27 cm) thick patties. In a large sauté pan or skillet, cook in oil over medium heat on both sides until browned. Or, cook in a dry nonstick pan and use cooking spray.

4. Serve warm.

Quick Sloppy Joes

INGREDIENTS

Ingredient	U.S. Standard	Metric
Onion, small, chopped	1 each	1 each
Oil, vegetable	2 tsp.	10 ml
Tempeh, grated	16 oz.	454 g
Paprika	2 tsp.	10 ml
Chili powder	2 tsp.	10 ml
Garlic powder	1/2 tsp.	2.5 ml
Honey	1 tsp.	5 ml
Molasses	1 tsp.	5 ml
Salt	1/4 tsp.	1.25 ml
Tomato paste	6 oz.	180 ml
Vegetable stock or water	2 c.	500 ml

METHOD OF PREPARATION

1. Gather all the ingredients and equipment.

2. Sauté onion in oil in a large sauté pan over medium heat for 2 minutes. Add tempeh, and sauté 5 minutes longer.

3. Reduce heat, add remaining ingredients, and simmer 5 minutes. Serve warm.

COOKING TECHNIQUES

Sautéing:
1. Heat the sauté pan to the appropriate temperature.
2. Evenly brown the food product.
3. For a sauce, pour off any excess oil, reheat, and deglaze.

NUTRITION

Nutrition Facts

Yield: Serves 10
Serving Size: 4 oz. (115 g)

Amount Per Serving

Calories 120

Total Fat 6 g

Sodium 85 mg

Total Carbohydrate 10 g

Protein 9 g

Open-Faced "Burgers"

INGREDIENTS

	U.S. Standard	Metric
Millet, uncooked	1 c.	240 ml
Quinoa, uncooked	1/2 c.	120 ml
Water or vegetable stock	3 c.	720 ml
Salt	1 tsp.	5 g
Olive oil	2 Tbsp.	30 ml
Onion, diced brunoise	1 1/2 c.	350 g
Carrots, shredded	1 c.	250 g
Celery, diced brunoise	1/2 c.	115 g
Garlic, medium size, minced	1 clove	1 clove
Oregano, dried	1/2 tsp.	2.5 ml
Thyme, dried	1/2 tsp.	2.5 ml
Sunflower seeds, toasted and ground	1 1/2 c.	360 ml
Whole wheat flour	1/4 c.	50 g
Rice vinegar	2 Tbsp.	30 ml
Tamari or reduced-sodium soy sauce	2 Tbsp.	30 ml
Green pepper, diced brunoise	1/4 c.	50 g
Portabella mushrooms, stemmed, wiped clean	10 each	10 each
Onions, large, sliced	2 each	2 each
Red pepper purée	1 c.	240 ml
Tomatoes, large, sliced	3 each	3 each
Arugula, washed	10 oz.	285 g

COOKING TECHNIQUES

Mixing:
1. Follow the proper mixing procedure: creaming, blending, whipping, or combination.

Baking:
1. Preheat the oven.
2. Place the food product on the appropriate rack.

NUTRITION

Nutrition Facts
Yield: Serves 10
Serving Size: 15 oz. (430 g)

Amount Per Serving

Calories 420

Total Fat 15 g

Sodium 390 mg

Total Carbohydrate 61 g

Protein 14 g

METHOD OF PREPARATION

1. Gather all the ingredients and equipment.

2. In a fine-meshed sieve, rinse millet and quinoa under cold running water until water runs clear. In medium saucepan, combine millet, quinoa, water (or vegetable stock), and salt. Bring to a boil over medium-high heat. Stir, cover, and return to a rapid boil. Reduce heat to low, and simmer covered until liquid has been absorbed and steam holes appear, about 20 minutes.

3. Meanwhile, in large nonstick skillet, heat 1 tablespoon (15 ml) of oil over medium-low heat. Add onions and cook about 5 minutes until translucent. Stir in carrots, celery, garlic, oregano, and thyme. Continue cooking for 10 minutes, stirring occasionally.

4. Preheat oven to 350°F (177°C). With the remaining oil, lightly oil a large sheet pan. In a large bowl, combine millet mixture, sautéed vegetables, ground sunflower seeds, flour, vinegar, tamari, and green pepper. Mix well. Use 1/2 cup (112 g) of the mixture, firmly packed, for each patty, and form into ten round or oval patties. Place on prepared sheet pan, and bake until lightly browned, about 30 minutes.

5. Broil or grill the portabella mushroom caps and the onion slices.

6. To serve, spoon 2 Tbsp. (30 ml) of red pepper purée onto a preheated plate. Top each with a broiled mushroom, a burger, a broiled onion, and tomato slice. Ring plates with 1 oz. (28 g) of arugula, and serve hot.

Lentil Loaf

INGREDIENTS

	U.S. Standard	Metric
Lentils, *cooked*	1 c.	225 g
Tomato, *concassé*	1/2 c.	115 g
Zucchini or yellow squash, *washed, diced brunoise*	1/2 c.	115 g
Green onions and tops, *trimmed, diced brunoise*	1/4 c.	60 ml
Carrots, *peeled, washed, and diced brunoise*	1/4 c.	115 g
Garlic, *peeled, and finely chopped*	3 cloves	3 cloves
Bread crumbs, *unseasoned*	1/4 c.	115 g
Cumin, *ground*	1/2–3/4 tsp.	4 ml
Ketchup	1/8 c.	30 ml
Salt	TT	TT
Black pepper, *ground*	TT	TT
Egg white	1 each	1 each
Olive oil, *cooking spray*	as needed	as needed

TOMATO TOPPING

	U.S. Standard	Metric
Tomato paste	1/4 c.	60 ml
Ketchup	1/4 c.	60 ml

COOKING TECHNIQUES

Baking:
1. Preheat the oven.
2. Place the food product on the appropriate rack.

NUTRITION

Nutrition Facts

Yield: Serves 10
Serving Size: 3 oz. (85 g)

Amount Per Serving

Calories 80

Total Fat 1 g

Sodium 340 mg

Total Carbohydrate 15 g

Protein 4 g

METHOD OF PREPARATION

1. Gather all the ingredients and equipment.

2. Process the lentils in the food processor, or mash with a fork until finely chopped, but not smooth. (Some whole lentils should still be visible). Mix in tomato, zucchini, green onions, carrots, garlic, bread crumbs, cumin, and ketchup. Season to taste with salt and pepper. Mix in egg white.

3. Spray loaf pan with cooking spray. Spread lentil mixture evenly in pan.

4. Combine ingredients for tomato topping, and spread mixture evenly over top.

5. Bake at 350°F (177°C) until center is firm, approximately 35 minutes. Tomato topping should be well caramelized.

6. Loosen the loaf around the edge with a knife. Invert onto a platter, and slice into 3-oz. (85-g) portions.

Broccoli with "Cheese" Sauce

INGREDIENTS

	U.S. Standard	Metric
Potato, *peeled and roughly chopped*	3/4 c.	170 g
Water	2 c.	500 ml
Vegetable stock	2 c.	500 ml
Cornstarch	1/3 c.	75 g
Lemon juice, *fresh*	1/4 c.	60 ml
Pimiento, *canned, roughly chopped*	7 oz.	205 g
Nutritional yeast	1/2 c.	115 g
Onion powder	1 tsp.	5 ml
Salt *(optional)*	1 tsp.	5 ml
Broccoli, *florets*	3 lbs.	1.4 kg

METHOD OF PREPARATION

1. Gather all the ingredients and equipment.

2. Place the potato in a saucepan with 1 cup (240 ml) of the water and 1 cup (240 ml) of the stock. Bring to a boil, and cook until tender, approximately 15 minutes. Place potato along with its cooking liquid into blender or food processor, and process until smooth; add more water and vegetable stock if purée is too thick.

3. Dissolve the cornstarch in the lemon juice.

4. Place potato purée along with the cornstarch and lemon juice, pimiento, yeast, onion powder, and salt into saucepan, and cook mixture over medium heat, stirring constantly until thickened, about 5–6 minutes. Correct consistency with leftover water and vegetable stock as needed; boil both first.

5. Meanwhile, steam the broccoli until tender, about 8 minutes. Drain well.

6. Place the drained broccoli in a bowl, and pour the sauce over it, mixing gently.

COOKING TECHNIQUES

Boiling (At sea level):
1. Bring the cooking liquid to a rapid boil.
2. Stir the contents, and cook the food product throughout.
3. Serve hot.

Simmering:
1. Place the prepared product in an appropriately sized pot.
2. Bring the product to a boil, and then reduce the heat to allow the product to barely boil.
3. Cook until desired doneness is achieved.

NUTRITION

Nutrition Facts

Yield: Serves 10
Serving Size: 7 oz. (205 g)

Amount Per Serving

Calories 90

Total Fat 0.5 g

Sodium 55 mg

Total Carbohydrate 17 g

Protein 7 g

Scrambled Tofu

INGREDIENTS	U.S. Standard	Metric
Onion, *peeled, diced macédoine*	8 oz.	225 g
Sweet bell peppers, *washed, seeded, diced macédoine*	8 oz.	225 g
Garlic, *peeled, minced*	2 cloves	2 cloves
Olive oil	1 Tbsp.	15 ml
Tofu, *extra firm, diced macédoine*	8 oz.	225 g
Tofu, *soft, mashed*	8 oz.	225 g
Nutritional yeast	4 Tbsp.	60 g
Tumeric	1/4 tsp.	2 g
Soy sauce	2 Tbsp.	30 ml
Tomato, *washed, chopped*	8 oz.	225 g

METHOD OF PREPARATION

1. Gather all the ingredients and equipment.

2. Sauté the onion, bell pepper, and garlic in the oil until soft.

3. Add the tofu, nutritional yeast, turmeric, and soy sauce. Simmer until heated.

4. Add chopped tomato, and serve.

Sautéing:
1. Heat the sauté pan to the appropriate temperature.
2. Evenly brown the food product.
3. For a sauce, pour off any excess oil, reheat, and deglaze.

Nutrition Facts

Yield: Serves 10
Serving Size: 4 oz. (115 g)

Amount Per Serving

Calories 70

Total Fat 3 g

Sodium 130 mg

Total Carbohydrate 7 g

Protein 6 g

Protein Alternatives

473

A.D.1762
The word "sandwich" is coined after
John Montagu, England's Fourth Earl of Sandwich.

1889
Raffaele Esposito of Naples, Italy, makes what is reported
to be the first pizza to celebrate a visit from Italian King Umberto I
and Queen Margherita.

1905
Gennaro Lombardi opens the first pizzeria in the United States, in New York City.

1955
McDonald's founder Ray Kroc opens the first company-operated McDonald's in Des Plaines, Illinois.

Sandwiches and pizzas are among the most popular foods in the United States. Whether simple or sophisticated, the basic components of sandwiches and pizza are similar—a bread component and a filling. The origins, however, are as diverse as the immigrants who brought them to the Americas. The submarine sandwich and the traditional pizza both have Italian roots. The "all-American" hot dog, first introduced in 1904 at the St. Louis World's Fair, traces its lineage to German sausages, and the hamburger is named for Hamburg, Germany. Ultimately, the hamburger inspired the American Big Mac, arguably the world's most famous triple-decker sandwich.

Sandwiches

It is believed that sandwiches were invented in 1762 when John Montagu, England's Fourth Earl of Sandwich, could not tear himself away from the gaming table. Instead, he asked his servant to bring him cold meat between two pieces of bread. From those noble beginnings, many bread, spread, and filling combinations came to be called sandwiches.

Sandwich Types

Two kinds of sandwiches are prepared in commercial kitchens: those served hot and those served cold. Within those categories are a variety of combinations, but the fundamentals are the same: become familiar with classic sandwich ingredients; choose appropriate breads, fillings, spreads, condiments, and garnishes; use preparation methods that are efficient and cost-effective; and plate the sandwich attractively.

Hot Sandwich Varieties

Hot sandwiches come in a variety of forms, including the hamburger; the sloppy joe; the open-faced hot roast beef; the French dip; the Reuben; several varieties of grilled cheese; hot wraps, such as the bean or beef burrito; and the taco, comprised of fillings that may include beef, pork, and chicken.

Hot closed sandwich A *hot closed sandwich* contains a hot filling such as pulled pork, Italian meatballs, grilled or fried chicken breast, or fish filet between two slices of bread or a split roll or bun. A variety of condiments usually accompanies these sandwiches and might include bottled sauces, such as ketchup or steak sauce; mustards; a variety of pickle types, either sliced or whole; relishes; or chutneys. Hamburgers, cheeseburgers, and other hot closed sandwiches may be presented as open sandwiches in order to display attractive garnishes such as sliced tomato, lettuce leaves, or sliced raw onion on the top half of a sliced bun, but such sandwiches are generally eaten as closed sandwiches.

Hot open-faced sandwich A *hot open-faced sandwich* is made with buttered or unbuttered bread and a hot filling, such as a stack of thinly sliced roast beef, pork, or turkey breast. A hot open-faced sandwich is not covered with an additional slice of bread, but many are served with a sauce, melted cheese, or gravy ladled over the foundation bread and filling. Mashed potatoes often accompany hot roast beef or hot turkey sandwiches, but hot open-faced sandwiches also can have more complex flavors and presentation techniques. Sliced prime rib, served *au jus* on firm French bread, makes an interesting open-faced sandwich. A Kentucky Hot Brown sandwich combines bread triangles stacked with thinly sliced turkey breast in a gratin dish, covered with velouté sauce, augmented with heavy cream, Romano cheese, and sherry; and baked.

> *See Chapter 15: Stocks, Sauces, and Soups for information on making sauces.*

Grilled sandwich A *grilled sandwich* is hot from the inside out and includes the grilled cheese, the Reuben, and the tuna melt. Fillings are placed between two slices of bread, the outsides of the bread are spread with soft butter or margarine, and both sides of the sandwich are grilled on a hot griddle. The filling of a grilled sandwich is warmed, not cooked, during grilling, so filling ingredients that require cooking, such as bacon, need to be completely cooked before assembling the sandwich.

❧ F I G U R E   2 4 - 3
A pita sandwich is an example of a cold closed sandwich.

❧ F I G U R E   2 4 - 1

A hot triple-decker sandwich may include meat, seafood, cheeses, and condiments layered between bread.

Hot triple-decker Called a *triple-decker sandwich* because it is made with three pieces of bread or a bun sliced into three layers, a hot triple-decker sandwich has fillings between each layer of bread. See Figure 24-1. It may include a meat item, cheese, and condiments or garnishes layered between bread slices.

Wraps *Wraps* are made with soft flat breads wrapped around a filling. See Figure 24-2. Soft tacos, burritos, fajitas, and enchiladas are examples of wraps. Soft tacos and burritos may contain meats such as beef or chicken or a protein alternative such as refried beans. The fillings are generally

enclosed in soft flour tortillas, which are heated briefly on a grill to soften them before they are wrapped around the hot filling. The lower part of the tortilla is folded up so that the filling is overlapped by 2 or 3 inches (5–8 cm). Then the tortilla is rolled from right to left or left to right, forming a cylindrical wrap with a closed bottom to prevent the filling from falling out of the bottom as the wrap is eaten.

Fajita fillings are served at the table in a sizzling skillet or on a platter and are accompanied by a covered basket of warm flour tortillas. Fillings often include seasoned chicken or beef pieces, sliced or cubed green peppers, and sliced onions.

Similar in style to a fajita, a *mooshi sandwich* is made by wrapping thinly sliced stir-fried vegetables and meats or seafood in thin pancakes.

Enchiladas, consisting of rolled flour tortillas filled with a mixture containing meats or cheeses, are usually served covered with a hot sauce spiced with chili. A variety of condiments and garnishes accompany enchiladas, including diced, seeded tomatoes; grated cheese; salsas, sour cream, guacamole, and *pico de gallo* (a sauce made from a variety of fresh ingredients that may include chopped seeded tomatoes or tomatillos, cilantro, lime or lemon juice, and chopped green chilies); and various bottled hot sauces.

Cold Sandwiches

Cold sandwiches, often called deli-style sandwiches, are made with sliced deli meats, such as salami and bologna, or cold roast beef, pork, or turkey; and cheeses, such as Swiss, cheddar, mozzarella, and provolone. Bound salads such as tuna salad, chicken salad, or egg salad are also popular cold-sandwich fillings.

Cold closed sandwiches A *cold closed sandwich* usually is made with either a split roll or two pieces of bread encasing a cold filling and includes vegetable-stuffed pita pockets and the hero sandwich. *Pita* is flat bread that is easily split into two layers to form a pocket. See Figure 24-3. It is stuffed with cold cuts and vegetables, such as lettuce, tomato, sliced green peppers, olives, or raw onions.

The hero assumes different identities and variations depending on the location where it is served. Called a submarine in New Jersey; a blimp, torpedo, or grinder in New England; a hoagie in Pennsylvania; and a po' boy in New Orleans, this sandwich may have originated in Atlantic City, New York, or San Francisco—all of which claim to be the hero's birthplace.

❧ F I G U R E   2 4 - 2
Wraps, such as the ones shown here, include soft tacos, burritos, fajitas, enchiladas, and mooshi.

Making a Triple-Decker Sandwich

The process for making a triple-decker sandwich, either hot or cold, is relatively easy to make: select a bread, a spread, fillings, and garnish.

To make a cold triple-decker sandwich, follow these steps:

1 Complete mise en place.

2

Spread each slice of bread with mayonnaise or other appropriate spread.

3

Top the first slice of bread with lettuce, and arrange the filling on top of it. Place the second piece of bread on top of the filling.

4

Top the second piece of bread with lettuce, tomato slices, and bacon.

5

Place the third slice of bread on top of the bacon, mayonnaise side down. Insert frill picks. Slice into triangles using a serrated knife.

6 Plate with accompaniments, such as potato chips or French fries, and serve.

Cold open-faced sandwich A *cold open-faced sandwich* includes *canapés,* bite-sized sandwiches usually served as hors d'oeuvre, and chicken salad, tuna salad, and egg salad sandwiches.

Cold triple-decker Like the hot variety, a cold triple-decker sandwich, also called a *club sandwich,* is made with three slices of bread layered with fillings such as sliced turkey breast, bacon, tomato, and lettuce. Some vary the traditional club sandwich by adding sliced avocado or cucumber to the layers.

Finger sandwich A *finger sandwich* often uses thinly sliced breads with the crusts removed. Finger sandwiches may be cut into triangles or other decorative shapes and are usually small enough to be eaten in one or two bites.

Selecting Sandwich Breads

Choosing a bread variety that is fresh, flavorful, attractive, and appropriate for the filling gives a sandwich a solid foundation. White bread sliced from a Pullman loaf or other sliced breads, such as rye, whole wheat, multigrain, oat, or pumpernickel, are popular choices. Croissants, *focaccia* (an Italian flat bread), pita, kaiser rolls, and tortillas also make flavorful sandwich breads.

Many commercial bakeries and food-service providers can supply fresh breads and rolls daily, including those baked with a variety of cheeses, such as Asiago or cheddar; breads flavored with herbs, such as dill, onion, rosemary, or garlic; and breads flavored with fruits, nuts, and seeds. See Figure 24-4.

See Chapter 30: Yeast Breads and Rolls for information on baking breads used for sandwiches.

Based on the Filling

When choosing bread, select one that will complement the filling. Fillings with delicate flavors will not stand up to highly flavored, robust breads. More flavorful breads, on the other hand, enhance or complement highly flavored fillings.

For finger sandwiches, choose a bread with texture because the bread must stand up to being sliced thinly and must still hold a circle, diamond, or triangle shape after the filling is applied and the sandwich is cut.

Hot fillings tend to soften breads. For that reason, choose a firmer bread or bun for hamburgers, roast beef, barbecued pork, or other hot fillings.

> To use a fragile bread like banana nut bread for a finger sandwich, minimize crumbling or breakage by freezing the bread before spreading it with a softened and flavored cream cheese.

Based on Cultural Traditions

Many sandwiches have their origins in regional or ethnic cuisines. In New Orleans, the *muffaletta* is served on a round loaf of Italian bread cut lengthwise and brushed with olive oil before adding cheese, meats, and pickled olive salad and cutting the loaf into quarters. A Philly cheese steak sandwich is served on a traditional crusty roll.

Ethnic considerations also help determine bread choices. Mexican and Spanish tacos are traditionally made with a corn tortilla, a Native American taco with fried bread, and the typical Americanized version with a crisp corn taco shell or a soft flour tortilla.

Based on Customer Preference

Many customers have developed their own ideas about how their sandwiches should be made. It is not unusual for people to request specialty breads for sandwiches such as croissants, herbed sourdough, pita, or focaccia.

Based on Signature Styles

Some restaurants base their image on signature-style sandwich breads, billing themselves as bakeries that also prepare sandwiches on fresh, fragrant, site-baked breads. An Italian sandwich made with sliced focaccia, fresh ripe tomatoes, handmade smoked mozzarella, extra-virgin olive oil, and fresh basil leaves might be a typical sandwich in such an establishment.

Sandwich Spreads

Sandwich spreads help keep sandwich breads firm by creating a barrier between the moisture from the filling and the bread. Spreads also add flavor and body to a sandwich.

FIGURE 24-4
Sandwich bread varieties may include white, pumpernickel, rye, pita, rolls, and tortillas.

Butter

Butter provides an effective moisture barrier, good flavor, and satisfying richness to a sandwich. To use butter, first soften it to keep it from tearing the bread. Plain butter is common, but flavored whipped butters, such as red chili butter or garlic butter, may be used to add additional flavors to robust sandwiches.

Mayonnaise

Mayonnaise, a combination of oil and egg yolks, can be used plain or flavored to add another interesting flavor dimension to a sandwich. Some common flavored mayonnaise varieties include garlic, tomato and sweet red pepper, mustard-flavored, caper and herb, apple-horseradish, cilantro and hot pepper, and curry yogurt.

See Chapter 15: Stocks, Sauces, and Soups or Chapter 25: Garde-Manger for additional information on mayonnaise.

Cheese Spreads

Cheese spreads also provide a moisture barrier between the filling and the bread and add a more varied flavor component than do other spreads. For example, cream cheese can be blended with a number of flavor components, including herbs, onions, garlic, fruits, nuts, and a variety of spices. Other cheese speads include combinations of different cheeses, mayonnaise, and herbs or minced vegetables.

Vegetable Spreads

Vegetable spreads have become popular sandwich spreads. See Figure 24-5. Cheeseburgers with guacamole and bacon are now a staple at many establishments. Grilled tuna becomes a gourmet sandwich with the addition of *tapenade,* a spread made with anchovies, capers, black olives, olive oil, and lemon juice.

Sandwich Fillings

The variety of sandwich fillings continues to expand as new combinations of flavors are developed. Hot and cold meats, poultry, fish, cheeses, vegetables, and combinations of these fillings are all available on today's sandwich menu.

Beef

Several classic sandwiches contain beef fillings, such as salami, pastrami, crumbled ground beef in tacos and burritos, sloppy

FIGURE 24-5

Spreads, such as salsa, pesto, and tapenade have become quite popular.

joes, and many others. The hamburger and roast beef are two of the most popular beef fillings.

Pork

Ham and bacon are two very popular sandwich filling choices, as are pork sausages of various shapes, sizes, and flavors. Pulled pork sandwiches, made from bits of whole pork shoulders that have been slowly smoked in pits, are a Southern staple. They are typically served on a white bun with a side of barbecue sauce.

Poultry

Poultry, such as sliced turkey breast and boneless chicken breast, is used as a sandwich filling. Turkey also is used as an alternative meat for hot dogs, ham, and pastrami. Chicken breasts can be fried or grilled and seasoned in a variety of ways and are complemented by a variety of sauces, including ranch or blue cheese dressings or hot sauces that create a spicy Buffalo chicken sandwich.

Seafood

Fresh, smoked, and canned tuna, salmon, shrimp, lobster, and crab salads are popular choices for seafood sandwiches. Particular varieties of fish tend to be regional favorites. In Florida, for example, the grouper sandwich is a staple, and along the Northwest coast, fresh salmon is a popular choice. Seafood sandwiches can be as simple as fried fish or tuna salad or as exotic as deep-fried soft-shelled crabs and New Orleans's famous shrimp and oyster po' boys.

Cold Cuts

Sandwiches made with cold cuts include the classic bologna and cheese as well as combinations of prosciutto and soppressata (a spicy Italian pressed sausage) on rosemary-scented foccacia. Italian prosciutto di Parma, Spanish Serrano ham, and German Westphalian ham are increasingly popular sandwich choices.

Eggs

Eggs are popular sandwich fare, served in a number of ways. A classic Denver sandwich mounds sautéed onions, diced ham, and green peppers on a grill and covers the mixture with a beaten egg, which binds the ingredients together. Denver sandwiches most often are served on sliced and toasted white bread. Some varieties of egg sandwiches have become staples for people on the go. McDonalds has made the Egg McMuffin one of America's favorite breakfast sandwiches. Eggs Benedict, the classic hot open-faced sandwich made with an English muffin, Canadian bacon, a poached egg, and hollandaise sauce was probably the inspiration for the Egg McMuffin. *Huevos rancheros,* the classic Mexican egg sandwich, wraps a warm tortilla around a fried egg, salsa, and cheese.

Protein Alternatives

Sandwiches made from protein alternatives, including veggie burgers, meat substitutes made from soy protein, and falafel are becoming common menu items.

 See Chapter 23: Protein Alternatives for more information.

Vegetables

Vegetables often are used as sandwich fillings. Pita bread sandwiches stuffed with the ingredients found in a Greek salad make for a healthy, nutritious, and simple-to-eat meal. Roasted red peppers with fresh mozzarella on bruschetta, an Italian bread slathered with fresh olive oil, salt, and herbs, is a flavorful open-faced sandwich that also doubles as an appetizer. Diced tomatoes, white beans, and prosciutto also are common toppings for bruschetta. See Figure 24-6. Various wraps and burritos may include corn, tomatoes, onions, peppers, and avocados.

Cheese

A wide variety of cheeses is used in sandwiches, but the most common is processed American cheese, served on hamburgers or in grilled cheese sandwiches. However, other cheeses are becoming increasingly popular. Fresh cream cheese, white and yellow cheddar, gouda, Swiss, mozzarella, provolone, and blue cheese are just a few cheeses that accompany sandwiches made from cold cuts, cooked meats, and vegetables. Hot open-faced sandwiches frequently are covered with melted cheese.

Preparation Techniques

Sandwich preparation begins with mise en place, with all the ingredients needed for the sandwich within easy reach so that the motion required for assembly is minimal.

Utensils and Equipment

Sandwiches are made at the sandwich workstation. Utensils for the workstation include
- a sandwich unit—a refrigerated unit that holds meats, cheeses, vegetables, and condiments and serves as a work space.

- sharp knives, including a French knife and a bread knife.
- assorted cutters for shaping breads.
- serving spoons or scoops for controlling portions of spreads and fillings.
- spatulas for spreading or lifting fillings and spreads.
- a toaster for toasting bread.
- tongs for moving food items.
- cutting boards.

Guarding Against Bacteria

Sandwiches often combine hot and cold items, the perfect environment for the growth of bacteria. To guard against bacteria and avoid cross-contamination, use gloves or utensils when handling ready-to-eat foods. Wash your hands well and often, and minimize the cross-use of utensils. Wash, rinse, and sanitize all work surfaces and utensils frequently. Keep hot foods hot and cold foods cold.

Cutting Sandwiches

The way a sandwich is cut adds to its visual appeal. Use a serrated knife to cut sandwiches, using only slight pressure to avoid compressing the filling. Cut sandwiches into neat, uniform shapes, and arrange them on a plate in a manner that displays the filling attractively. When using frill picks to anchor the bread and filling, insert them before cutting the sandwich.

FIGURE 24-6

Bruschetta is often topped with chopped tomato, olive oil, fresh herbs, and shaved or grated pecorino romano cheese.

Pizza

Pizza is thought to have evolved from focaccia, which has been a popular bread in Italy for more than 1,000 years. Today it is one of the most common foods consumed, with about 3 billion pizzas, worth more than $30 billion, served each year in the United States.

Pizza Techniques

At the most basic level, pizza includes the following ingredients: a crust made from a raised yeast dough, rolled into a circle, square, or rectangle; a sauce, generally with a tomato base; and toppings ranging from cheese to various meats and vegetables. The pizza is baked at a high temperature in a pizza oven and served.

Making Pizza Dough

Pizza dough is made like any other standard dough, as the basic steps for making a pizza show.

▌ *See Chapter 30: Yeast Breads and Rolls for more information on making yeast doughs.*

Dividing the dough Divide the dough into even portions, depending on the size of the pizzas being made. A single serving pizza requires 4–6 ounces (113–170 g) of dough. After dividing the dough, spray or smooth oil onto the surface to keep the dough from sticking to the bowl or pan sides as it rises.

Retarding the dough Cover the bowl or pan with food-grade plastic wrap, and let the dough rest for several hours or overnight in the refrigerator.

Preliminary shaping of dough Remove the dough from the refrigerator, and allow it to warm to room temperature for 30 minutes before rolling it out. Roll or press the dough into disks.

Final shaping of dough Shape the dough by hand-tossing, rolling, or pressing it into the desired shape and size. Place the shaped dough on a pizza peel dusted with cornmeal or semolina flour so that the dough can be easily slid into the oven. The final diameter of the pizza will be about 6–9 inches (15–29 cm) for a six-ounce (170-g) crust. To shape pizza dough in a pizza pan, drizzle a small amount of olive oil on the pizza pan or sheet pan. Spread it around so that the entire surface is covered with a very thin coating. Sprinkle cornmeal on the pan to prevent the pizza from sticking and to aid in crisping the crust. Gently stretch or roll out the dough to the desired shape, place it into the pizza pan, and push the dough into the shape of the pan. Drizzle the dough lightly with olive oil if desired, and add toppings.

Building the pizza Place the desired toppings on the pizza dough. For a typical tomato sauce-cheese-meat pizza, start with seasoned tomato sauce, spreading a thin layer over the dough. Then add the cheese—most pizzas are made with mozzarella cheese. Finally, add a layer of toppings, such as sliced pepperoni, ham, prosciutto, or sausage; seafood; and vegetables, such as artichoke hearts, peppers (red, green, or banana), onions, or mushrooms. Most restaurants offer a choice of toppings; restaurants that make specialty pizzas may offer only a choice of pizzas with specific ingredient combinations such as feta cheese, spinach, black olives, and mushrooms.

> **Avoid adding too many heavy toppings to the pizza; their weight can cause the crust to develop improperly.**

Baking the pizza Pizza is baked at a very high temperature on the floor of the pizza oven. Carry the pizza to the oven on the pizza peel, and slide it gently off the peel into the preheated oven. If the peel was prepared carefully with cornmeal or flour, the pizza should slide easily into the oven. If it does not, a gentle shake should dislodge it. Bake 5–8 minutes, depending on the temperature of the oven and the size and thickness of the pizza. Remove the pizza from the oven when the cheese has melted and has begun to bubble and brown. Do not overbake it.

Resting the pizza Let the pizza rest for 3–4 minutes before cutting it into wedges or squares. The waiting time allows the cheese to set and prevents tearing. Use a large French knife or a rotary pizza cutter to cut the pizza for serving.

Serving the pizza Pizzas can be served as an appetizer or as the main course. Some pizza restaurants serve pizza on cardboard disks; some serve it on a wooden cutting board. Upscale establishments generally plate the pizza before serving it.

Beef Fajita

INGREDIENTS

	U.S. Standard	Metric
Beef, top round	2 1/2 lbs.	1.14 kg
MARINADE		
Lime juice, fresh	3 oz.	90 ml
Tomato juice	6 oz.	180 ml
Hot sauce	1/2 tsp.	2.5 ml
Garlic, peeled and minced	1 clove	1 clove
Vegetable oil	2 oz.	60 ml
Red onion, large, peeled, and thinly sliced	1 each	1 each
Jalapeño pepper, washed, seeded, and finely minced	1 each	1 each
Green pepper, large, washed, seeded, and thinly sliced	1 each	1 each
Cumin, ground	1/2 tsp.	2.5 ml
Chili powder	1/2 Tbsp.	8 ml
Salt	TT	TT
Cilantro, fresh, washed, squeezed dry, and chopped	1 oz.	28 g
Flour tortillas	10 each	10 each
Tomatoes, large, concassé	20 oz.	600 ml
Cheddar cheese, shredded	10 oz.	285 g
Sour cream	20 oz.	600 ml
Scallions, cleaned, thinly sliced on bias	10 oz.	300 ml

METHOD OF PREPARATION

1. Gather all the ingredients and equipment.

2. Trim and remove the excess fat and silverskin from the beef. Cut the meat into thin strips against the grain.

3. Combine the marinade ingredients; pour over the meat. Marinate for 1–2 hours in the refrigerator.

4. Remove the meat from the marinade, and sear in a hot sauté pan in oil; add the red onion, jalapeño, and green pepper and sauté until the beef and vegetables are tender. Drain any excess fat. Add the ground cumin, chili powder, salt, and cilantro. Taste and adjust seasonings as needed. Place mixture in a hotel pan, cover, and hold at 140°F (60°C) or higher until needed.

5. To prepare individual portions, warm the tortillas on a sheet pan, either in a 350°F (177°C) oven or lightly under the broiler; do not dry them out. Place approximately 4 oz. (115 g) of the meat mixture on a tortilla, and top with 2 oz. (55 g) tomato, 1 oz. (28 g) cheese, 2 oz. (55 g) sour cream, and 1 oz. (28 g) scallion.

6. Roll the tortilla around the filling, tucking in the ends. Place the rolled tortillas seam-side down in hotel pans and hold, covered, at 140°F (60°C) or higher or serve.

French Dip Sandwich

INGREDIENTS	U.S. Standard	Metric
Top round of beef	2 1/2 lbs.	1.14 kg
Salt	TT	TT
Black pepper, ground	TT	TT
Meat glaze	2 cups	500 ml
Brown beef stock	2 cups	500 ml
French bread, cut in 6" (15 cm) lengths	10 each	10 each

METHOD OF PREPARATION

1. Gather all the ingredients and equipment.

2. Preheat oven to 425°F (218°C).

3. Trim the beef, season with salt and pepper, and place in preheated oven. Immediately reduce oven temperature to 350°F (177°C), and roast beef to an internal temperature of 140°F (60°C). Hold at 140°F (60°C) or higher. Allow to rest and carry over for about 20 minutes to an internal temperature of 145°F (63°C) before slicing.

4. Meanwhile, make a dipping *jus* by combining the meat glaze and the beef stock; bring to a boil. Season to taste with the salt and pepper. Keep hot in a *bain-marie* until service.

5. Heat the French bread sections in the oven until a crispy crust forms. Cut each in half and top with 4 oz. (115 g) of thinly sliced beef. Cover with the top of the French bread, and serve with a 3-oz. (90-ml) side portion of hot jus for dipping.

COOKING TECHNIQUES

Roasting:
1. Sear the food product, and brown evenly.
2. Elevate the food product in a roasting pan.
3. Determine doneness, and consider carryover cooking.
4. Let the food product rest before carving.

GLOSSARY

Jus: a flavorful sauce of unthickened natural meat juices

Bain-marie: hot water bath

NUTRITION

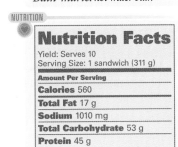

Nutrition Facts

Yield: Serves 10
Serving Size: 1 sandwich (311 g)

Amount Per Serving

Calories 560

Total Fat 17 g

Sodium 1010 mg

Total Carbohydrate 53 g

Protein 45 g

Pizza with Eggplant and Tomato

INGREDIENTS

	U.S. Standard	Metric
Pizza dough	2 1/2 lbs.	1.14 kg
Flour, bread	as needed	as needed
Olive oil	6 oz.	180 ml
Eggplant, peeled, diced parmentier	2 lbs.	910 ml
Garlic, chopped	4 cloves	4 cloves
Oregano, fresh, washed, dried, and chopped	3 Tbsp.	45 ml
Plum tomatoes, sliced 1/4″ (6 mm) thick	1 lb.	454 g
Mozzarella cheese, fresh, diced macédoine	1 lb.	454 g
Salt	TT	TT
Black pepper, ground	TT	TT
Parsley, washed, squeezed dry, chopped	3 Tbsp.	45 g

METHOD OF PREPARATION

1. Gather all the ingredients and equipment

2. Preheat the oven to 450°F (232°C).

3. Divide dough into ten 4-oz. (115 g) portions, and roll or shape each portion into a circle about 1/4″ (6 mm) thick, using flour as needed. Place the rolled dough on sheet pans lined with parchment paper.

4. Heat 4 oz. (120 ml) of the olive oil in a large sauté pan. Add the eggplant, and sauté until lightly browned and tender, stirring often. Add garlic and cook 2 minutes longer. Remove pan from heat, and stir in the chopped oregano; set aside.

5. Divide the tomato slices over each pizza, and brush with the remaining 2 oz. (60 ml) of olive oil.

6. Divide eggplant and mozzarella over pizzas. Season each pizza with salt and pepper.

7. Bake about 10 minutes or until the crust is cooked. Cut the pizza into quarters, and place on a preheated plate to serve, garnished with chopped parsley.

Chef's Notes

As an alternative to parchment paper, pizzas can be baked on lightly oiled sheet pans sprinkled with a little cornmeal.

COOKING TECHNIQUES

Baking:
1. Preheat the oven.
2. Place the food product on the appropriate rack.

Sautéing:
1. Heat the sauté pan to the appropriate temperature.
2. Evenly brown the food product.
3. For a sauce, pour off any excess oil, reheat, and deglaze.

GLOSSARY

Parmentier: 1/2″ (1.27 cm) dice
Macédoine: 1/4″ (6 mm) dice

NUTRITION

Nutrition Facts

Yield: Serves 10
Serving Size: 12 oz. (340 g)

Amount Per Serving

Calories 630	
Total Fat 29 g	
Sodium 1050 mg	
Total Carbohydrate 67 g	
Protein 24 g	

Monte Cristo Sandwich

INGREDIENTS

	U.S. Standard	Metric
White bread	30 slices	30 slices
Turkey breast, cooked, sliced thin	10 oz.	285 g
Virginia ham, sliced	10 oz.	285 g
Swiss cheese, sliced	10 oz.	285 g
Eggs, slightly beaten and seasoned with salt and pepper	5 each	5 each
Butter	as needed	as needed

METHOD OF PREPARATION

1. Gather all the ingredients and equipment.
2. Place a slice of bread on a sheet pan. Place 1 oz. (28 g) of turkey on the bread, and top with another slice of bread.
3. Place 1 oz. (28 g) each of ham and Swiss cheese on top of the second slice of bread; cover with a third slice of bread.
4. Dip the sandwich in the egg to coat. Cook on both sides to a golden brown on a well-buttered griddle.
5. To serve, cut in half on the diagonal.

Chef's Notes

French fries or warm potato chips are recommended accompaniments.

COOKING TECHNIQUES

Griddling:

1. Clean and heat the griddle.
2. To prevent sticking, coat the griddle with a thin layer of oil.
3. Place food product onto the griddle.
4. Cook the product, turning over when necessary, until desire doneness.

NUTRITION

Nutrition Facts

Yield: Serves 10
Serving Size: 1 sandwich (144 g)

Amount Per Serving

Calories 350	
Total Fat 22 g	
Sodium 1090 mg	
Total Carbohydrate 15 g	
Protein 25 g	

Hot Italian Grinder

INGREDIENTS

Ingredients	U.S. Standard	Metric
Olive oil	1 cup	240 ml
Red wine vinegar	3 Tbsp.	45 ml
Oregano, dried	1 1/2 tsp.	8 ml
Basil, dried	1 1/2 tsp.	8 ml
Salt	TT	TT
Black pepper, freshly ground	TT	TT
Tomatoes, washed, cored, and sliced thin	5 each	5 each
Red onions, peeled, sliced into thin rings	2 each	2 each
Rolls, submarine style, split but not cut in half	10 each	10 each
Capicola, sliced thin	10 oz.	285 g
Salami, sliced thin	10 oz.	285 g
Mortadella, sliced thin	10 oz.	285 g
Provolone cheese, sliced thin	10 oz.	285 g
Lettuce, washed, cut chiffonade	1 head	1 head
Pepperoncini, marinated rings, drained	6 oz.	170 g

METHOD OF PREPARATION

1. Gather all the ingredients and equipment.
2. Preheat oven to 375°F (191°C).
3. Combine the olive oil, vinegar, oregano, and basil; whisk well and season to taste with salt and pepper.
4. Add the tomatoes and onions to the vinaigrette, and allow vegetables to marinate for at least an hour.
5. Brush the inside of each roll with some of the vinaigrette. Lay 1 oz. (28 g) each of the meats and then the cheese inside the rolls.
6. Place on sheet pans, and bake for 5–10 minutes, or until meats are warm and bread is lightly toasted.
7. Remove from the oven and top with the lettuce chiffonade, marinated tomato and onion slices, and pepperoncini rings.
8. Serve immediately.

COOKING TECHNIQUES

Baking:
1. Preheat the oven.
2. Place the food product on the appropriate rack.

NUTRITION

Nutrition Facts

Yield: Serves 10
Serving Size: 1 sandwich
13 oz. (370 g)

Amount Per Serving

Calories 970

Total Fat 58 g

Sodium 2420 mg

Total Carbohydrate 77 g

Protein 32 g

Tuna Melt

INGREDIENTS

INGREDIENTS	U.S. Standard	Metric
English muffin, *large, halved*	5 each	5 each
Mayonnaise	5 oz.	140 g
Iceberg lettuce, *washed and separated*	1/2 head	1/2 head
Tomatoes, *washed, cored, and sliced*	3 each	3 each
Tuna salad	2 1/2 lbs.	1.14 kg
Provolone cheese, *thinly sliced*	10 slices	10 slices

METHOD OF PREPARATION

1. Gather all the ingredients and equipment.

2. Toast the English muffin halves, and spread with mayonnaise.

3. Top each with lettuce, tomato, and tuna salad.

4. Put a slice of provolone cheese on top of the tuna salad, and place the sandwich in a salamander until the cheese melts.

5. Serve with seasoned French fries and coleslaw.

COOKING TECHNIQUES

Baking:
1. Preheat the oven.
2. Place the food product on the appropriate rack.

NUTRITION

Nutrition Facts

Yield: Serves 10
Serving Size: 1 sandwich (half an English muffin) (477 g)

Amount Per Serving

Calories 540	
Total Fat 25 g	
Sodium 970 mg	
Total Carbohydrate 52 g	
Protein 30 g	

Sandwiches and Pizza

487

Philadelphia Steak Sandwich

INGREDIENTS

	U.S. Standard	Metric
Vegetable oil	as needed	as needed
Onions, medium size, peeled, cut julienne	3 each	3 each
Green bell peppers, washed, seeded, cut julienne	3 each.	3 each
Beef top round, sliced or shredded paper-thin	3 lbs.	1.4 kg
Salt	TT	TT
Black pepper	TT	TT
Rolls, French style, split lengthwise	10 each	10 each
Provolone cheese, sliced thin	10 each	10 each

METHOD OF PREPARATION

1. Gather all the ingredients and equipment.

2. Heat an appropriate amount of oil in a large sauté pan over medium-high heat.

3. Add the onions and green peppers, and stir-fry for 4 minutes; remove from pan, and hold at 140°F (60°C) or higher.

4. Add more oil to the pan if necessary, and sauté the sliced top round of beef to an internal temperature of 145°F (63°C); season to taste. Mix with the vegetables.

5. Place the beef and vegetable mixture on the bottom half of each roll. Top with cheese, and melt under a salamander or in an oven. Cover with the top of the roll and serve.

COOKING TECHNIQUES

Sautéing:
1. Heat the sauté pan to the appropriate temperature.
2. Evenly brown the food product.
3. For a sauce, pour off any excess oil, reheat, and deglaze.

Stir-Frying:
1. Heat the oil in a wok until hot but not smoking.
2. Keep the food in constant motion; use the entire cooking surface.

GLOSSARY

Julienne: 1/8″ × 1/8″ × 1″–2″ strips (3 mm × 3 mm × 2.5–5 cm strips)

NUTRITION

Nutrition Facts
Yield: Serves 10
Serving Size: 1 sandwich (248 g)

Amount Per Serving

Calories 440

Total Fat 21 g

Sodium 500 mg

Total Carbohydrate 23 g

Protein 37 g

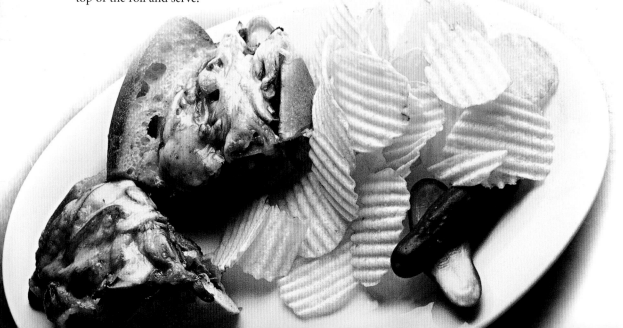

Clam Roll

INGREDIENTS

INGREDIENTS	U.S. Standard	Metric
Frying oil	as needed	as needed
Clams, whole, frying, drained	2 1/2 lbs.	1.14 kg
Eggs, whole, lightly beaten	3 each	3 each
Milk	4 oz.	120 ml
Flour, seasoned	as needed	as needed
Bread crumbs	as needed	as needed
Parker rolls, split, but not cut in half	10 each	10 each
Butter, clarified	as needed	as needed
Tartar sauce	as needed	as needed
Romaine lettuce, washed, chiffonade	1 head	1 head
Lemon wedges	as needed	as needed

METHOD OF PREPARATION

1. Gather all the ingredients and equipment.
2. Preheat deep-fat fryer to 375°F (191°C).
3. Combine the eggs and the milk to make an egg wash.
4. *Dredge* the clams in seasoned flour; shake off the excess.
5. Dip in the egg wash, and transfer into the bread crumbs.
6. Roll the clams in the bread crumbs to coat.
7. Fry the clams *à la minute* in the hot fryer until golden brown. Lay out on absorbent paper.
8. Transfer to a hotel pan lined with absorbent paper, and keep the pan uncovered and hot at 140°F (60°C) to hold. Do not pile clams on top of one another, or they will get soggy.
9. Brush the inside of the rolls with clarified butter, and toast under the salamander or broiler until golden.
10. To serve, spread both halves of the rolls with tartar sauce, place a small amount of lettuce chiffonade in the bottom of the roll, and top with fried clams.
11. Serve with extra tartar sauce and a lemon wedge on the side.

COOKING TECHNIQUES

Deep-Frying:
1. Heat the frying liquid to the proper temperature.
2. Submerge the food product completely.
3. Fry the product until it is cooked throughout.

GLOSSARY

Chiffonade: ribbons of leafy greens

Dredge: to coat with flour

À la minute: cooked to order

NUTRITION

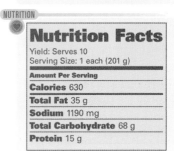

Nutrition Facts

Yield: Serves 10
Serving Size: 1 each (201 g)

Amount Per Serving

Calories 630

Total Fat 35 g

Sodium 1190 mg

Total Carbohydrate 68 g

Protein 15 g

3000 B.C.
Sumerians use salt to preserve meat.

A.D. 1100s
Garde-manger provides cold food storage and preparation.

late 1500s
Charcuterie guild oversees preservation and sales of pork products.

1790
Guild members and garde-manger household staffs turn to restaurants and hotels for work.

1889
Escoffier includes garde-manger in brigade system at Savoy in London.

Before the invention of refrigeration, the garde-manger —literally, "keeper of food to be eaten"—was a place for storing cold food until it was needed in the kitchen. This storage room or pantry eventually became a convenient work space for the preparation of an array of cold foods. Today, the garde-manger may be an entire department in a large hotel, fine restaurant, or catering company. Garde-manger staff members focus on the preparation and creative presentation of cold food items, including appetizers, salads, terrines, pâtés, galantines, smoked meats, and cheeses. Today's garde-manger chefs earn their place in this long tradition through meticulous work and artistic expression.

History and Traditions

The garde-manger's original purpose—to preserve food—has been a concern since prehistory. Hunters and gatherers first faced the challenge of keeping food for later use. They likely stumbled on ways to do so, finding brine-coated fish drying in the sun by the sea or hanging meat by the fire to keep it away from animals, and later noticing its dry texture and enjoying its smoky flavor. The Sumerians appear to have been the first to salt meat in order to preserve it. Later the Chinese, Greeks, and Romans salted fish and other foods. Cured pork such as bacon and ham, prepared in the Roman province of Gaul (now France), was served to connoisseurs in Rome, the capital of the Roman Empire.

By the Middle Ages, peasant farmers had developed many ways to preserve meat after the autumn slaughter of livestock. Salted, pickled, dried, and smoked meats filled the storerooms of the nobility. The special chambers for keeping food became known as the garde-manger. A variety of food items common in the garde-manger of noble households eventually found their way into medieval markets, where individual guilds, or merchant groups, began to oversee their preparation and trade. The guild known as charcuterie, for instance, prepared and sold pork products, including pâté, bacon, ham, and sausage.

The guilds exercised enormous power over commerce in food and other goods until the late eighteenth century, when they were finally abolished. By then, many noble households had also dissolved. Former guild members and garde-manger staff found work in the hotels and restaurants that had begun to develop from traditional inns and taverns. Gradually a kitchen hierarchy emerged, in which different workers had distinct responsibilities or areas of specialization. In the late nineteenth century, Escoffier organized kitchen procedures and staff into what is now known as the brigade system. The garde-manger, or cold-foods chef, was among the primary figures in the classic brigade.

The Garde-Manger Brigade

Once limited to the preparation of preserved and cold foods, the garde-manger station today has a broader scope. In addition to such traditional items as sausages, pâtés, and cheeses, it is often responsible for the preparation of salads, cold sauces or dressings, sandwiches, and both hot and cold hors d'oeuvre and appetizers. Foods prepared by the garde-manger appear at banquets, buffets, and other formal and informal parties. The presentation of these foods often includes elaborate centerpieces and artistically designed platters.

To perform these varied duties, the classic garde-manger station has its own brigade. The chef garde-manger supervises operations and oversees the positions in the garde-manger. See Figure 25-1.

The modern garde-manger is generally less structured than the classic brigade. Like the scope of the contemporary station, the skills and duties are broader than in the past, embracing many areas of food preparation.

FIGURE 25-1

The Brigade

BOUCHER
Butchers all meats and poultry except those that are preserved

POISSONNIER
Responsible for cleaning, preparing, and storing fish and shellfish and creating fish sauces

BUFFETIER
Maintains the buffet

HORS D'OEUVRIER
Creates and prepares all hors d'oeuvre

CHARCUTIER
Makes all sausage and smoked items

COMMIS
Works as an apprentice learning the duties of garde-manger

The Garde-Manger Work Station

A carefully planned and well-equipped work station is essential to the work of the garde-manger, which incorporates both basic cooking techniques and specialized skills. Although much of the equipment, smallwares, and tools found in the garde-manger forms part of all kitchen stations, the garde-manger contains certain items especially suited to its work.

Equipment

The properly outfitted garde-manger commonly features equipment such as:
- Cold (refrigerated) surfaces for food preparation
- Walk-in refrigerators and freezers
- Reach-in refrigerators
- Ice-carving tools
- Stoves and ranges
- Food slicers
- Mandolines
- Food processors
- Meat grinders
- Sausage presses
- Smokers

See Figure 25-2.

UPRIGHT SMOKER

FIGURE 25-2

Food processors, meat grinders, sausage presses, smokers, and aspic cutters are essential equipment in the garde-manger work station.

MEAT GRINDER

SAUSAGE PRESS

ASPIC CUTTERS

FOOD PROCESSOR

Smallwares and Tools

In addition to many smallwares and tools used at other work stations, the garde-manger requires specialized pieces. See Figure 25-3.

FIGURE 25-3
Garde-manger small-wares and tools

TERRINE MOLD

MELON BALLER

PÂTÉ MOLDS

BUTTER CUTTER

PASTRY BAGS

EGG SLICER

PASTRY TIPS

SMALL MOLDS

TOURNÉ KNIFE

EGG WEDGER

ICE-CARVING TOOLS

SPATULAS

LARDING NEEDLE

LARGE CUTTERS

Salads

The salad course originally consisted of leafy greens dressed with a vinaigrette, served after the main course to cleanse the palate. The practice of eating fresh greens with oil and vinegar originated with the Romans, who often gathered salad ingredients—lettuces and herbs—from home gardens. Related to the Latin word for salt, which the Romans sprinkled on their greens, salad refers to a mixture of one or more ingredients, including not only leafy greens but also vegetables, meat, fish, fruits, nuts, and grains.

Salad Components

A salad may contain ingredients from four components: the foundation, the body, the garnish, and the dressing. Some or all of these components may appear in a salad.

Foundation The foundation is the base ingredient of a salad. Leafy greens such as romaine, bibb, Boston, or iceberg lettuce often serve as a salad's foundation. Used whole or cut into a chiffonade, the lettuce leaves provide a base for other salad ingredients. Specially prepared vegetables or fruits, such as a julienne of red pepper or a poached and sliced pear, sometimes function as a salad's foundation.

Body The main ingredients of a salad make up its body. The body creates the salad's identity and often gives the salad its name. Garden-fresh vegetables, for example, form the body of a garden salad. The body of a protein salad might be meat, poultry, fish, or legumes.

Garnish The garnish contributes to a salad's visual appeal and very often to its flavor. A garnish should be colorful, edible, and the same temperature as the salad itself. Most important, the garnish should be simple so that it does not overpower the presentation of the salad. Common salad garnishes include herbs, hard-cooked eggs, olives, fruits, cheese, and nuts. Some salads, such as fruit salads, do not require a garnish or dressing.

Dressing The dressing is a sauce that complements a salad's flavor and sometimes binds the salad ingredients together. Salad dressings fall into three groups: vinaigrettes (raspberry, balsamic), cream-style or fatty (Roquefort, blue cheese), and simple (oil and vinegar, flavored oils).

Nutritional Aspects of Salads

Salads can be extremely healthful foods. Greens, which form the foundation or the body of many salads, are low in fat and calories and a good source of vitamins A and C and minerals such as calcium and iron. Darker greens contain even greater amounts of vitamins, as well as minerals such as potassium and folic acid. Meat, poultry, fish, cheese, and legumes add protein to salads.

Salad Greens

A variety of greens are available for use in salads. See Figure 25-4. Although all are leafy vegetables, not all are green. More tender greens such as arugula and butterhead are preferred over greens such as collards and chard that require cooking to make them more palatable. Baby varieties of sturdier greens not usually used in salads, such as beet greens and mustard greens, also make excellent additions. Salad greens can be classified into two general categories: mild greens and flavor-adding greens. Flavor-adding greens can be either spicy or bitter.

FIGURE 25-4

ARUGULA

Description	Category
Spicy or peppery flavor; resembles dandelion leaves; 2–4 inches (5–10 centimeters)	Flavor-adding greens

BABY LETTUCES (LOLLO ROSSO, RED SAILS, BABY GREEN BIBB, BABY RED ROMAINE, BABY RED OAK LEAF, BABY RED BIBB, PIRATE)

Description	Category
Delicately flavored and textured; wrinkled or wavy leaves; deep greens tinted blue, red, or purple	Mild greens

BUTTERHEAD LETTUCE

Description	Category
Delicate in texture; rosettes loosely formed by thick, soft leaves; also known as Boston or bibb lettuce; buttery flavor; forms cups when peeled from the head	Mild greens

CURLY ENDIVE

Description	Category
Bitter tasting; creamy white or a pale yellow-green; crisp, pointy, spearlike leaves; can be pale; heads compact and tight; 4–6 inches long (10–15 centimeters)	Flavor-adding greens

CRESS

Description
Pungent; peppery tasting; stem extends into a leaf that is higher in the middle and shorter on the sides; medium green

Category
Flavor-adding greens

DANDELION

Description
Bitter tasting; dark green in color; leaves are long, narrow, and spike-shaped; ribs are white or red

Category
Flavor-adding greens

BELGIAN ENDIVE

Description
Bitter tasting; creamy white or a pale yellow-green; crisp, pointy, spear-like leaves; can be pale; heads compact and tight; 4–6 inches long (10–15 centimeters)

Category
Flavor-adding greens

ESCAROLE

Description
Bitter tasting; leaves possess a lightly nutty flavor; leaves are green; heads are a greenish yellow

Category
Flavor-adding greens

FRISÉE

Description
Tightly compacted green leaves surrounding butter-colored inner leaves; delicate in flavor, slightly bitter

Category
Flavor-adding greens

ICEBERG LETTUCE

Description
Leaves are tightly packed (dense); pale green; crisp leaves and firm heads

Category
Mild greens

LOOSE-LEAF LETTUCE

Description
Red, green, and oak leaf lettuce; loosely packed with deep indents; leaves curl along crisp edges

Category
Mild greens

MÂCHE

Description
Delicate leaves; dark green; also called lamb's tongue because of its shape and appearance; tender; slightly nutty flavor

Category
Mild greens

MIZUNA

Description
Tender, elongated, spiky leaves; light to dark green; slightly peppery flavor

Category
Flavor-adding greens

TAT-SOI

Description
Dark-green, delicate, spoon-shaped leaves with tender white nibs and white to pale green stems; spicy-sweet flavor

Category
Flavor-adding greens

TREVISO RADICCHIO

Description

Elongated leaves well suited for grilling; less bitter than the round varieties; greenish to purple-red elongated leaves; also can be grilled or braised

Category

Flavor-adding greens

RADICCHIO

Description

Bitter tasting; purple-red leaves are tightly packed to form a compact head; crisp

Category

Flavor-adding greens

ROMAINE OR COS

Description

Cylindrical, not rounded heads; leaves are crinkled or ribbed and appear ruffled; leaves become sweeter and are not as dark, coarse, or crisp as you get closer to the center of the head; loosely packed

Category

Mild greens

SORREL

Description

Leaves are small and green; resembles spinach; sour, almost lemon tasting

Category

Flavor-adding greens

SPINACH

Description

Deep green to black leaves; oval; crisp; flat leaf varieties work best in salads; curly-leaf varieties work well if young and tender; the more mature curly-leaf greens hold up well to warm salad dressings

Category

Flavor-adding greens

Salad Mixes

Mixing different greens produces a salad with unique tastes and interesting textures. It is possible to create proprietary salad mixes or to purchase prepared mixes.

Making Proprietary Mixes

Proprietary mixes of salad greens allow a foodservice establishment to create salads unique to that establishment. Blends of green, white, and red lettuces add interesting flavors and textures as well as improve appearance. However, many establishments do not produce enough volume to purchase, store, and keep fresh large cases of various greens. Many rely on prepared mixes of greens that can be purchased from suppliers.

Prepared Mixes

A variety of fresh, prewashed salad mixes can be purchased with either whole leaf or ripped greens. See Figure 25-5. They are virtually ready to use, and offer consistency and value in economizing on space, labor, and waste. Despite being sold as prewashed, prepared mixes should still be washed before using. Salad mix packages range from 1 pound to 10 pounds (.5 kg to 5 kg). Most baby and exotic greens come in 3-pound (1.5-kg) boxes.

Mesclun This salad mix is a blend of small leaves of lettuces and other greens. Mesclun may also feature herbs and flowers. The varied colors, subtle flavors, and tender texture of mesclun make it a popular mix.

Oriental mix This mix takes its name from the various oriental greens it contains. Oriental mix includes such greens as tat-soi, pak-choi, shungi ku, mizuna, and red shiso, combined with the leaves of red oak, arugula, beet greens, Swiss chard, amaranth, sorrel, and purslane.

Baby mix The young and extremely tender leaves in this mix give it its name. Baby romaine, red oak, green oak, lollo rosso, and other greens create a colorful, generally mild mix of delicate leaves.

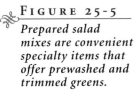

FIGURE 25-5
Prepared salad mixes are convenient specialty items that offer prewashed and trimmed greens.

PROCESS

Cleaning Greens

A water bath is ideal for washing greens because it is gentle and allows dirt and debris to settle at the bottom of the bowl. This procedure works well for whole leaves, baby greens, or cut lettuce.

To clean greens, follow these steps:

1 **Soak the greens for several minutes using a cold-water bath in a bowl, or use a sanitized sink if cleaning a large amount of greens.**

2 **Lift the greens out of the water with care, and drain them in a colander.**

3 **Gently pat dry with paper towels.**

4 **As an alternative, use a salad spinner to spin-dry wet greens.**

Using Herbs

When used in moderation, herbs are a welcome addition to salad mixes, providing an accent of distinctive flavors and interesting fragrances. Choose herbs with tender leaves and relatively flat surfaces. Basil, chervil, chives, cilantro, dill, mint varieties, and parsley are appropriate. Before adding large leaf herbs to a mix, tear, chop, or cut them chiffonade.

> *See Chapter 12: Seasoning and Flavoring Food for more information about these and other possible herb choices.*

Using Flowers

Edible flowers add flavor, aroma, color, and texture to salad mixes. Garden flowers such as nasturtiums, pansies, primroses, calendulas, marigolds, and roses have become popular salad accents, as are flowers from various herbs, including chives, thyme, oregano, and sage. Add whole flowers or individual petals to salad mixes.

Make sure that the flowers you incorporate in salad mixes are edible and pesticide-free. Always clean flowers and petals carefully. Insects, eggs or egg casings, and dirt can easily escape notice in the folds and crevices of petals and other flower parts. Soak flowers in 10% salted ice water to remove insects.

Handling Salad Greens

Careful handling and preparation will help salad greens maintain their freshness and quality from time of purchase to service.

Receiving

If possible, purchase salad greens daily, and select those that are fresh and crisp. Greens should show no signs of spoilage (discoloration, wilting), mishandling (blemishes, tears, bruising), or insect infestation (eggs, egg cases).

Storing

Salad greens, like other fresh produce, are highly perishable. Upon receipt, quickly refrigerate them at several degrees above freezing (34°F–38°F/1°C–3°C). Keep salad greens in their original packaging, away from tomatoes, apples, and other ripening fruits, which cause greens to wilt. Use soft-leaved greens such as bibb and Boston lettuce as soon as possible. Under optimum conditions, crisper varieties, such as romaine and iceberg lettuce, may keep up to a week or more.

> **If greens have wilted slightly, submerge them in ice water for 30 to 60 minutes and then refrigerate them. As a general rule, do not wash salad greens until ready to use. Excess water can cause a loss of quality, flavor, and nutrients.**

Preparing

Preparation of salad greens involves washing, drying, crisping, and cutting or tearing. Cleaning removes insects and any dirt, sand, dust, or grit that may have collected in the leaves.

Refrigerate salad greens not being used immediately in a colander or other perforated container that will allow air to circulate and any remaining water to drain off. Do not pack or seal. Cover lightly with clean, damp toweling. Be sure to use washed greens within 24–48 hours.

When it is time to mix salad greens, cut or tear them into bite-sized pieces. Although many advocate tearing instead of cutting to avoid bruising or discoloring, others insist that tearing can damage greens in the same way. Cutting is faster than tearing, and it is a more expedient method in a large foodservice operation. To guarantee speed and to prevent "rusting" of cut greens, use a sharp, stainless steel blade.

PROCESS

Dressing Greens

A dressing is both a sauce and a seasoning and can be served warm or chilled.

Follow these steps to apply dressing to greens:

1 Pour dressing into a bowl, and add greens that have been properly cleaned.

2 Gently toss to lightly coat the greens.

3 Add additional ingredients, and toss briefly.

4 Plate and garnish. For the salad presented in this process, a little extra dressing and a cracker leaf were used to add flavor, interest, and texture.

Foodborne Illness Associated with Salads

Correct handling of salad ingredients helps prevent foodborne illness. Thorough cleaning, sanitary preparation, and proper cooling and storage are essential.

Poorly washed lettuce can harbor bacteria that cause the shigellosis and *E. coli* O157:H7 enterohemorrhagic (EHEC) infections. Contaminated or improperly refrigerated salad dressings may foster the growth of bacteria that cause staphylococcal food poisoning (enterotoxicosis). The risk of botulism exists when oil and garlic mixtures do not contain an acid ingredient and are not refrigerated. Improperly chilled or inadequately cooked meat, poultry, fish, and dairy products included in a salad may cause gastroenteritis and other bacterial infections.

Salads may also transmit the hepatitis A virus as well as viral forms of gastroenteritis (Norwalk virus and rotavirus) when sanitary practices are ignored and cross-contamination occurs. Giardiasis, an infection caused by protozoan parasites, can result from poor personal hygiene among staff and inadequate washing of food items.

Salad Dressings

A dressing is both a sauce and a seasoning. As such, it should complement the flavors and textures of the salad ingredients, not dominate them.

Guidelines for Dressing Salads

Apply dressing immediately before serving because greens wilt quickly after they have been coated.

Customer preference Some customers prefer to apply dressing to their salads themselves. On request, serve dressing on the side in a saucier to accommodate customers' preferences.

Bound salads Certain heavy dressings, such as mayonnaise, are an exception to the practice of applying dressing immediately before serving. Mayonnaise and certain other dressings mixed into some salads ahead of time serve to bind the salad ingredients together. Known as *bound salads,* they include tuna salad, egg salad, and potato salad.

Types of Dressings

Salad dressings vary widely. Most, however, fall into one of three broad categories: vinaigrette, cream-style or fatty, and simple.

Vinaigrette Dressings (Temporary Emulsions)

A *vinaigrette* is a temporary emulsion of oil and vinegar. The mixture is temporary because oil and vinegar have a natural tendency to separate.

Emulsions Adding pasteurized eggs to a vinaigrette creates a more permanent emulsion. Egg yolk will stick to the drops of oil and keep them separated and scattered, allowing them to combine uniformly with the vinegar and stay combined. An emulsified vinaigrette is heavier than the basic vinaigrette and adheres to greens especially well. Mustard can be used as an emulsifier, too.

Variations Various oils and vinegars are available for use in vinaigrettes. Mild oils such as canola and safflower oil go well with flavored vinegars. Olive oil has more flavor and is a good match with red wine vinegar. Balsamic and sherry vinegars complement nut oils and more robust olive oils. Citrus juice can be substituted for all or part of the vinegar; adjust the oil proportion accordingly. The ratio of oil to vinegar is a matter of taste in general. Salt and pepper are the basic seasonings for a simple vinaigrette. Other ingredients may be added, including herbs, spices, mustard, garlic, and shallots, to enhance the flavor of a vinaigrette.

Cream-Style or Fatty Dressings (Permanent Emulsions)

Cream-style or fatty dressings are permanent emulsions, or mixtures whose ingredients stay combined after they have been blended together. These dressings use mayonnaise or dairy products as a base. Mayonnaise itself is a permanent emulsion created by whipping together oil, lemon juice, pasteurized egg yolk, and various flavorings. Buttermilk and sour cream are dairy products commonly featured in cream-style dressings.

Variations Cream-style dressings usually contain other ingredients, such as herbs, spices, onions, capers, garlic, tomato paste, and hard-boiled eggs. These additional ingredients add color, texture, and flavor to salads. Common cream-style dressings include creamy French, Thousand Island, Russian, ranch, blue cheese, and creamy Italian.

Simple Dressings

The simplest salad dressings are not emulsions or blended mixtures. They are simple liquids that contribute moisture and flavor to salads.

Lemon juice On its own, freshly squeezed lemon juice is an acidic dressing that gives a tang to salad.

Olive oil More flavorful than vegetable oils, olive oil is a fruity, aromatic dressing when used alone on a salad.

Flavored vinegars Vinegars flavored with fruit, herbs, or garlic are popular dressings because they add vivid flavor to salads but no fat.

Making a Vinaigrette

Vinaigrette is a basic salad dressing. The usual proportion is three parts oil to one part vinegar. Whole-grain mustard is included in this procedure to help emulsify the dressing and provide flavor and body.

Follow these steps to make a vinaigrette:

Combine mustard and seasonings in a bowl. A pinch of sugar can be added, if desired. Blend well.

Slowly drizzle oil into mustard, whipping vigorously to maintain an emulsion.

Gradually add vinegar, whipping constantly. Adjust seasonings.

Types of Salads

In addition to being a separate course, a salad may be an appetizer, an accompaniment, the main course, or a dessert. The point at which a salad is served during a meal helps determine the salad's ingredients, dressing, and presentation.

Appetizer Salads

Served before the main course, an appetizer salad should whet the appetite. It may be as simple as a tossed green salad dressed with a vinaigrette and finished with a garnish, or it may be a more elaborate offering that features fish, shellfish, poultry, meat, or legumes. The appetizer salad often makes the first impression on the customer, so it should be visually appealing and should stimulate the palate with bright flavor and crisp texture.

Accompaniment Salads

Served with the main course and acting as a complement to it, an accompaniment salad is essentially a side dish. It should be relatively light and add flavor but should not overwhelm the main course. An accompaniment salad typically does not include food items featured in the main course. Vegetable salads frequently accompany the main course. If the main course is light, a protein or pasta salad is an appropriate accompaniment.

Main-Course Salads

A salad served as the main course constitutes a full meal, and its size and ingredients should reflect this. A main-course salad should be substantial and nutritionally balanced, supplying protein along with greens, vegetables, fruits, or a combination of these. It should also offer an attractively presented mix of flavors, textures, and colors. Chicken salad; egg salad; or meat, chicken, or seafood salads can be satisfying as a main course.

Separate Salads

Depending on the type of service, the separate salad course may come before or after the main course. In American service the salad course precedes the entrée as an appetizer salad; in Europe it follows the entrée. A salad served after the main course cleanses the palate and renews the appetite. Lightly dressed greens or a citrus salad, for example, provides the ideal break between the main course and dessert.

Dessert Salads

Salads served as dessert are often sweet and usually contain fruits, nuts, and/or gelatin. Dressings for dessert salads may incorporate cream or liqueur.

Hors d'Oeuvre (Appetizers)

The garde-manger is responsible for the production of all hors d'oeuvre, *or appetizers. The literal meaning of the French term hors d'oeuvre is "outside the work." In a culinary context, the term refers generally to food items served "outside the meal or the main part of the meal." Such foods are features of the cuisines of many cultures. Spanish tapas, Mediterranean meze, the dishes included in a Scandinavian smörgasbord, and the offerings of the Russian zakuski table are rooted in the hors d'oeuvre tradition.*

Hors d'oeuvre come in various forms. Method and time of service help define three general categories of hors d'oeuvre: single foods, hors d'oeuvre variés, and finger foods.

Single Food

An hors d'oeuvre may consist of a single garnished food item. Served hot or cold as the first course of a meal, this type of hors d'oeuvre is commonly called an appetizer. The food is plated or presented in a coupe or other appropriate dish to a seated customer. Seafood cocktail, pâté, frog legs, mussels marinière, and salade composée are examples of popular single-food hors d'oeuvre.

Hors d'Oeuvre Variés

Hors d'oeuvre variés are an assortment of light, tasty items presented plated, on a platter, or on a cart *(voiture)*. These special service carts come equipped with heating elements to keep food warm. They also can be refrigerated. Plated hors d'oeuvre variés, which frequently feature seafood or charcuterie, provide a selection of food items for each guest. For presentation of hors d'oeuvre variés on a platter, ravier dishes are especially appropriate. Each of these small, often oval-shaped glass or crystal dishes holds eight small portions of a food item. To serve hors d'oeuvre on a cart, or voiture, you may use larger raviers, platters, or bowls. The customer selects directly from the cart, which is prepared in the kitchen before service and then left in the dining room.

Finger Foods

Served prior to a meal or as the only foods at receptions and other events, this type of hors d'oeuvre is true to its name. Finger foods do not require a knife or fork and can usually be eaten in one or two bites. Presentation is buffet-style on separate platters arranged on a table or passed on trays butler-style by serving staff.

Finger foods may be hot or cold. Chicken teriyaki, spanakopita, clams casino, and stuffed mushrooms are popular hot finger hors d'oeuvre. Examples of cold finger hors d'oeuvre are deviled eggs, crudités, shrimp, canapés, barquettes, and tartlets.

Composed Hors d'Oeuvre

Hors d'oeuvre range from very simple to elaborate. At the more intricate end of the spectrum are *composed hors d'oeuvre,* which contain two or more food elements. Examples of composed hors d'oeuvre include special items such as canapés, barquettes, tartlets, bouchées, and vol-au-vents.

Making Canapés

The base for this canapé was made by cutting circles out of white bread with a fluted cutter.

To make this canapé, follow these steps:

1 Brush base with clarified butter. Bake in a 375°F (189°C) oven until golden brown and crisp.

2 A slice of lobster, carefully placed on the base, is used as a nourishing element.

3 A lobster and sour cream spread is piped in a decorative fashion.

4 A small broccoli floret is used as a colorful garnish.

Canapés

Canapés are small, open-face sandwiches. Light and flavorful, they help stimulate the appetite at cocktail parties and other predinner gatherings. Canapés are usually served cold. The average allowance for a function is 8–10 canapés per hour per person.

The word *canapé* means "sofa" in French, and the image is an apt one. Like a sofa's platform and cushion, the main components of a canapé are a base and a topping. A canapé frequently has other layers, including a spread, a liner, and a garnish.

Base Various items can serve as the *base* of a canapé. A crouton—a crustless piece of toasted or fried bread—is a common base. A thin slice of fresh bread, a cracker, sliced vegetables, and small pastry shells are other possible bases. Shapes for the base are usually geometric: rounds, rectangles, right triangles, squares, ovals, and isosceles triangles.

Spread The *spread* is a seasoned, easily applied mixture that adheres well to the base. Spreads include flavored butter, softened cream cheese, mayonnaise, and sour cream. Besides enhancing the flavor of the canapé, the spread keeps the base from becoming soggy and helps secure other food items to the base.

Liner Usually a green, such as a baby lettuce leaf, the *liner* is an optional ingredient that contributes to the texture and visual appeal of a canapé. It also acts as a moisture barrier between the base and topping.

Topping Also called the nourishing element, the *topping* is the main part of the canapé, contributing flavor, texture, color, and nutrients. Fish, meat, cheese, vegetables, or fruits are examples of nourishing elements that top canapés.

Garnish The garnish is a decorative, edible final addition to the canapé that adds color, flavor, and texture. Simple garnishes include chopped parsley, lemon or orange zest, a sprig of watercress, black olive rings, pimiento strips or dice, capers, sliced red onion, peas, and compound butter piped through a pastry tube.

FIGURE 25-6

The different shapes, textures, and colors of canapés create a visually pleasing display.

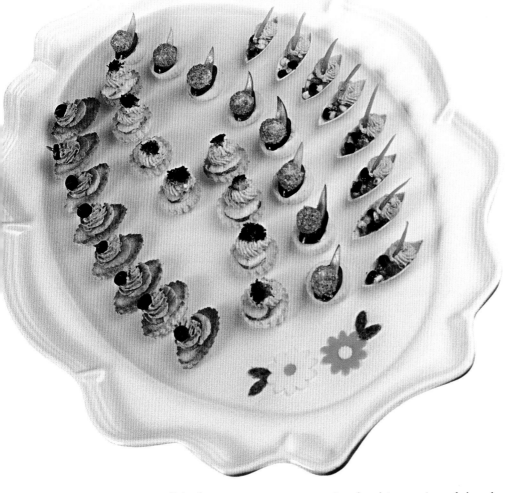

Barquettes and Tartlets

Barquettes and *tartlets* are small edible containers made from a savory pie crust or short dough baked in a tiny mold. They can be served as hot or cold hors d'oeuvre using savory ingredients. A barquette looks like a little boat; a tartlet is round like a small pie. Each holds a flavored spread or other filling and is topped with a garnish. Barquettes and tartlets are also considered sweet desserts when filled with cream or assorted fruits. Fillings for these baked shells can be moist, and they should be assembled just before serving.

Bouchées and Vol-au-Vents

Bouchées and *vol-au-vents* are edible containers made from puff pastry. The main difference between a bouchée (which means "mouthful") and a vol-au-vent (meaning "flying in the wind") is size. Bouchées are 1 1/2–2 inches (4–5 cm) in diameter; vol-au-vents are a minimum of 4 inches (10 cm). Usually served as an appetizer, bouchées require a fork and knife. Vol-au-vents are served as plated appetizers or entrées. A smaller version of the bouchée, known as a bouchette ("little mouthful"), is a familiar finger food.

Baked ahead of time and then cooled, these pastry shells hold a variety of fillings, which are always served hot. To keep the crust crisp, fill bouchées and vol-au-vents as close to service as possible. Bouchées and vol-au-vents can accommodate ragoûts, fricassées, fondues, and salpicons. Pâtés, flavored cream cheeses, and mousses are more appropriate fillings for bouchettes. See Figure 25-6.

Caviar

Caviar is a luxury food item that many consider the premier hors d'oeuvre. The term *caviar* refers to the salted roe (eggs) of sturgeon from the Caspian Sea. Roe from other fish, such as salmon and American sturgeon, can carry the label caviar only with identification of their source.

Techniques of Production

A sturgeon may weigh as much as 2,000 pounds (907 kg), and 10%–12% of its body weight can consist of eggs. Some sturgeon carry as many as 4 million eggs. The eggs are contained in sacs, which are harvested from the live fish and then gently rubbed over a sieve until their membrane breaks, releasing the eggs. After the eggs are rinsed and drained, they receive a grade based on grain, size, flavor, firmness, color, shine, and fragrance. Then the roe is salted. The salt helps preserve the roe and extract flavor from it. High quality roe is only lightly salted and receives the label *malassol*, meaning "little salt"; roe of lesser quality receives more salt.

Beluga, osetra, and sevruga are the main species of sturgeon used for producing caviar. The size and color of caviar vary from species to species.

Beluga Beluga is the largest species of sturgeon, with the female weighing an average of 800–2,000 pounds (363–907 kg) and measuring 6 1/2 to 26 feet (2–8 m) long. It takes nearly 20 years for the female to mature and reproduce, making beluga caviar the scarcest and most expensive. Beluga eggs are dark gray, large, heavy, firm, and well separated.

Osetra Osetra is a medium-sized sturgeon species. Its female weighs 400–700 pounds (181–318 kg) on average and is 4–7 feet (1–2 m) long. The maturation period for an osetra female is about 13 years. Osetra eggs are golden yellow to brown, even-grained, and oily. They have a nutty or fruity flavor. Many consider osetra the best caviar of all.

Sevruga Sevruga is a small species of sturgeon with a long, pointed muzzle. The female weighs an average of 80–120 pounds (36–54 kg) and is 3–5 feet (.9–1.5 m) long. It is mature and ready to reproduce at about seven years of age. Sevruga eggs are small and range in color from light to dark gray. Caviar from the sevruga sturgeon has a strong flavor.

Pressed caviar Made from the ripest sevruga and osetra eggs, *pressed caviar* is a processed product with an intense flavor. The sturgeon eggs are packed and hung in linen bags. As they drain, they lose their shape and press together, producing an extremely salty and oily black paste with the consistency of

FIGURE 25-7

Beluga, osetra, and sevruga eggs vary in size, with beluga at one end of the scale, sevruga at the other, and osetra in between. It is more difficult to distinguish individual eggs in pressed caviar.

jam. Pressed caviar is served on bread and often accompanied by a Russian vodka or brut Champagne. See Figure 25-7.

Other Fish

A variety of other fish, including salmon, whitefish, lumpfish, mullet, cod, carp, and even tuna, are the source of other types of caviar. Caviar from fish other than sturgeon is relatively inexpensive and of lesser quality.

Purchasing and Storing Caviar

Fresh caviar is available for purchase in jars or tins weighing from 1 ounce (28 g) to 4 pounds (2 kg). Frozen caviar is also available but is appropriate for use only as a garnish. Eggs should be whole, plump, shiny, and moist with natural oils. Excessive oiliness indicates broken eggs and is undesirable. Eggs should smell fresh and should have a subtle flavor that is both nutty and salty.

Store caviar at 32°F (0°C). Under refrigeration and unopened, caviar will keep for up to a month. After it has been opened, it has a life of 2–3 days. Avoid cross-contamination after opening. Always use a clean utensil to take caviar from its container.

Serving Caviar

Caviar may be served in its own jar on a bed of crushed ice. The lid from the jar may be included in the presentation as proof of the product's authenticity. Provide non-metal flatware, such as tortoise-shell or mother of pearl, for caviar service because metal reacts with caviar and affects its flavor. A gold serving spoon is always appropriate. Accompaniments such as chopped egg, herbs, onion, and lemon are often served with caviar but they tend to detract

from the natural flavor. Caviar goes well, however, with lightly buttered toast, which helps reveal its flavor. Blinis served hot with crème fraîche or sour cream also complement fresh caviar.

Sushi

Sushi preparation falls under the duty of the garde-manger. *Sushi* is cooked or raw fish or shellfish commonly served with rice. There are several varieties of sushi served in food service. See Figure 25-8. The most common ones follow:

- **Nigiri-sushi**—Strips of raw fish or cooked fish or shellfish served on top of a mound of seasoned rice.
- **Maki-sushi**—Sliced raw fish and seasoned rice rolled in nori seaweed sheets.

- **Chirashi-sushi**—Strips or cubes of raw or cooked fish or shellfish mixed with seasoned rice and vegetables.

Typical fish or shellfish varieties used in sushi are tuna, mackerel, yellowtail, clams, eel, and octopus. Roe may also be used. Make sure that the fish or shellfish used is of the highest quality and is very fresh. Before using fresh fish, it is advisable to freeze the product 7 days at –4°F (–20°C) or lower to kill parasites.

Sushi is served with sauces, condiments, and garnishes such as soy sauce, wasabi, and julienned daikon or carrots and is presented in small Japanese-style bowls or on a tray. Japanese chopsticks are used with sushi.

FIGURE 25-8
Examples of sushi

Making California Rolls

The method for making California rolls is similar to that of other forms of maki-sushi. Raw or cooked fish, rolled omelets, and various vegetables can be used.

To make California rolls, follow this procedure:

1 Blend rice wine and sugar mixture into the warm rice with a wooden spoon or paddle, using a cut-and-fold technique. A fan helps cool the rice.

2 Lay a bamboo mat on a cutting board, and place a nori sheet shiny side down on the mat.

3 Moisten hands, and spread about 3/4 cup of rice over the nori sheet, leaving about 1 inch of the sheet uncovered at the far side. A small amount of wasabi may be spread on the rice if desired.

4 Lay avocado strips, surimi or crab legs, cucumber, and cooked egg if desired along the center of the rice.

5 Lift the bamboo mat, and begin rolling the nori sheet.

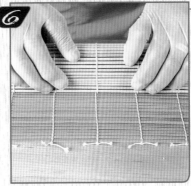

6 Pull the mat back as you roll to avoid rolling the mat into the rice. A small amount of water brushed on the edge of the nori sheet helps seal the roll.

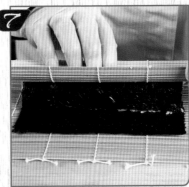

7 Press the mat to make an even shape. Rolls may be shaped round, oval, or square.

8 Remove the roll from the mat, and slice in half with a very sharp knife. Cut each half into 3 or 4 portions. A slightly wet knife prevents sticking.

9 Serve California rolls with tamari, pickled ginger, and wasabi.

Forcemeats

Forcemeats are also an important product of the garde-manger. Forcemeats are uncooked ground meats, poultry, fish, shellfish, and sometimes vegetables or fruits that are seasoned and then emulsified with fat. The term forcemeat comes from the early French word farce, meaning "stuffing." The French terms farce, farci ("stuffed"), and farcír ("to stuff") refer to the use of forcemeats as stuffing for various food items.

Types of Forcemeats

Forcemeats have a rich taste and a satisfying consistency. The texture varies according to the processing of ingredients and the planned use of the forcemeat. The four basic types are straight, country-style, gratin, and mousseline.

- To make *straight forcemeat,* combine meat and fat cut into small pieces, and process them further by curing or seasoning and then grinding, sieving, and binding.
- To make *country-style forcemeat,* mix coarsely ground pork with pork fat, and add varying amounts of liver and garnishings.
- For *gratin forcemeat,* sauté and chill the main ingredient (often liver) before grinding it. The gratin, or "browned" element, usually makes up no more than a quarter of the total weight.
- For the light forcemeat called a *mousseline,* add cream to ground white meat, such as chicken, veal, or fish.

To make a mousseline, use a food processor with a chilled bowl, and follow these steps.

1. Dice the main ingredient, and chill.
2. Place the ingredients into a chilled bowl, and grind in a food processor until smooth. Add eggs or egg whites, and process lightly until blended.
3. Keep the food processor running, and slowly pour in the cream. Stop the machine as needed to scrape down the sides of the processor bowl.
4. Stop processing when all the cream has been incorporated and the mixture is smooth.
5. Pass the mixture through a fine sieve to remove pieces of bone or sinew and to achieve greater smoothness.

Forcemeat Derivatives

The four types of forcemeats are the basis for various food items: terrines, galantines, ballotines, roulades, pâtés, quenelles, mousses, and sausages.

- A *terrine* is a smooth or coarsely ground forcemeat mixture baked, covered, in an earthenware or ceramic mold. Terrines are served cold.
- Also served cold, a *galantine* is boned poultry or game stuffed and rolled in its own skin and poached.
- A *ballotine* is essentially the same as a galantine, although it can be served hot or cold.
- A *roulade* is similar to a galantine, but it may contain meat or fish and is rolled in cheesecloth or plastic wrap instead of skin.
- A *pâté* is a rich, smooth or coarsely ground forcemeat enclosed in a thin layer of fat and baked in a mold.
- A *pâté en croûte* incorporates the same forcemeat mixture as a simple pâté, but it is baked in pastry dough with or without a mold.
- *Pâté en terrine* contains either a smooth or coarse mixture of forcemeat, and it is baked in a mold lined with a thin layer of fat or plastic wrap.
- A *quenelle* is a fine forcemeat mixture with an ovoid shape formed by using two spoons and poaching in seasoned liquid.
- A *mousse* is a very fine savory or sweet mixture of poultry, fish, vegetables, or fruit and whipped cream or beaten egg whites. Raw mousses are wrapped in plastic or poured into a container before cooking. Cooked mousses incorporate already-cooked foods with a binder such as gelatin or aspic. For more information on aspic, see page 517.
- Sausage is a forcemeat of ground meat, poultry, game, fish, and even vegetables or fruit enclosed in a natural or synthetic casing. Sausages may be smoke-cured, dried, or cooked.

Making Country-Style Pâté

Pork butt and pork liver are the main ingredients in a country-style pâté, or *pâté de campagne.* To make a country-style pâté:

1. Combine ground pork, liver, and seasonings with a panada of cream, eggs, flour, and brandy. (See page 511 for more information on panadas.) Mix until sticky to the touch.
2. Line a terrine with plastic wrap and slices of fatback, allowing some to hang over the sides. Fill the mold with the forcemeat, and fold the liners inward.
3. Cover the terrine, and poach in a 170°F (77°C) water bath or in a 300°F (149°C) oven for 1 to 1 1/4 hours. Remove and allow to cool to an internal temperature of 90°F–100°F (32°C–38°C).
4. Drain the juices from the terrine, peel back the plastic liner, and coat the pâté with aspic. Cover, and refrigerate for 48 hours.

Making Pâté en Croûte

When making pâté en croûte, a rectangular mold promotes even baking and facilitates slicing. The traditional method, however, does not use a mold and results in an oval-shaped pâté.

1. Roll out the dough, and cut it into the correct shape to fit a rectangular mold.
2. Line a buttered mold with the lightly floured dough, pressing it into the corners with a dough ball.
3. Layer with thinly sliced ham or fatback.
4. Fill with forcemeat, layering in garnish, to 1/2 inch (1 cm) from the top of the mold. Fold the fatback over the forcemeat.
5. Top with the remaining piece of dough, and brush with egg wash.
6. Cut holes in the top dough to allow steam to escape during baking. Surround each hole with a ring of dough. Egg wash will allow the ring of dough to adhere to the top crust. Line the whole with aluminum foil to create a chimney.
7. Bake at 400°F (204°C) for 15 minutes. Reduce heat to 350°F (177°C), and bake until the pâté reaches the appropriate

internal temperature. For large pâté en croûte, cover partially with foil after initially browning the crust, and then remove the foil to crisp the crust toward the final 15 minutes of baking.

8. Cool 1–2 hours. Then pour warm aspic through a funnel into the holes in the surface. Refrigerate for 1–3 days before slicing.

Making a Galantine

Dating from the time of the French Revolution, galantines usually feature poultry as the main ingredient, formed into a large roll and glazed with chaud-froid sauce. They are typically made as follows:

1. Remove the poultry skin in one piece, and trim it into a rectangle shape.
2. Make a forcemeat from the meat of the bird, and refrigerate it.
3. Lay out the skin on a piece of plastic wrap or cheesecloth.
4. Spread the forcemeat evenly over the skin, and then place seared breast meat or tenderloins in the middle of the forcemeat.
5. Roll the galantine in the plastic wrap or cheesecloth, and secure it with foil. If using cheesecloth, ensure that the ends are tight.
6. Poach the galantine in stock until the forcemeat reaches the appropriate internal temperature.
7. Cool the galantine in the cooking liquid until handling is possible, and then remove the foil. Wrap the galantine in fresh material. Refrigerate overnight before slicing.

Panadas

To make a *panada,* add liquid (water, stock, or milk) to a starch such as flour, potato, rice, or bread. In addition to binding other ingredients, a panada tenderizes and adds smoothness and moisture to forcemeats. It also produces a higher yield.

There are five basic kinds of panadas: bread, flour, potato, rice, and frangipane. Bread cooked in boiling milk is the type of panada used in meat loaf, fish, forcemeats, and hamburger. Flour cooked with boiling water or stock and butter is featured in quenelles. White meat quenelles contain cooked mashed potatoes with milk. Various forcemeats feature rice puréed in white stock. Frangipane, a flour panada with added egg yolks, is used in chicken or fish forcemeats.

Basic Elements

Forcemeats have four basic elements: the main ingredient or nourishing element, fats, binders, and seasonings. Careful portioning of fat to other ingredients is key to a forcemeat's emulsification. Tasting is essential to its correct seasoning.

Main Ingredient

The main ingredient occurs in the largest proportion of all ingredients in a forcemeat. Also known as the nourishing element, it contributes flavor, texture, color, and nutrients. Meat, poultry, fish, vegetables, and fruit are common nourishing elements in forcemeats.

Fat

Fats improve moisture and enrich a forcemeat's flavor. Butter, cream, and natural animal fats such as pork fat, egg yolk, and jowl fat are commonly used in forcemeats.

Binder

The proteins in meat, poultry, and fish bind with the fat and liquids in forcemeat mixtures, acting as a stabilizer. For greater shape and smoothness, other *binders* may be added. Panadas and egg whites are the most common binders. It is also possible to use gelatin or velouté.

Seasoning

Seasoning for forcemeats varies according to the recipe used. Salt, herbs and spices, and marinades help heighten the flavor of forcemeats.

Working with Forcemeats

Taking sanitary precautions will ensure that forcemeats are safe for consumption. Following basic steps in assembling forcemeats will help guarantee consistent quality.

Safety Guidelines

Keeping ingredients and equipment cold is essential. To avoid the risk of foodborne illness and to achieve maximum quality with forcemeats, take the following precautions:

- Work in a cold room over an ice bath.
- Maintain a temperature below 41°F (5°C) for food products and equipment.
- Avoid overworking the food.
- Wash hands frequently.

Assembling Forcemeats

Knowing the basic steps in assembling forcemeats is helpful, no matter what formula is followed.

Progressive grinding, or grinding with successively smaller plates, is the standard method for making forcemeats. To do so:

1. Pass chunks of meat through a grinder, using a large grinder plate. The texture will be coarse.
2. Grind the meat a second time, using a medium plate to produce a medium-coarse grind. Add fat during the second grind.
3. If a finer forcemeat is needed, pass the meat and fat through a small die, or transfer the ground mixture to a food processor or VCM and process to the desired consistency.

After grinding the forcemeat, mix it by hand, adding seasonings, random garnish, and the binder. The *random garnish* is an ingredient such as nuts, truffles, olives, or mushrooms that is folded into the forcemeat. Add cream, if required, as a last step.

Working with Foie Gras

Foie gras, the fattened liver of a duck or goose, has been a delicacy since ancient times. It is available in three grades. A-grade foie gras, which is the largest and firmest, is blemish-free and suitable for grilling, roasting, or sautéing. B- and C-grade liver is lighter and usually displays some imperfections, making it appropriate for various forcemeat applications, including terrines, pâtés, roulades, and mousses.

Foie gras is expensive and deserves special care from purchase through use. Always inspect foie gras for quality and freshness. Weigh the product to ensure the accuracy of the filled order. Pack ice around foie gras, and store it in the refrigerator.

Before using foie gras, temper it in salt water for several hours to make handling easier. Then separate and devein the lobes. Marination is often the next step after cleaning. Recipes for terrines, pâtés, and roulades typically require a marinade of Armagnac, cognac, port, or a Sauternes wine with additional seasonings. Marination time is usually 12–24 hours.

Foie gras is the highlight of many classic preparations. Presentation is varied. Foie gras terrines and pâtés may be sliced and plated or served in their molds or crocks. Toasted croutons may be provided as an accompaniment to foie gras mousse, or a foie gras roulade may be baked in brioche for an appetizer. Truffles are a traditional accompaniment to foie gras. Carefully chosen wines and other beverages also complement this special food item.

The Foie Gras Process

Foie gras has evolved as a delicacy that graced the tables of ancient Egyptians, became the food of kings under Louis XVI, and is most recently appreciated as a rare treat by fine diners. As early as 2500 B.C., Egyptians took advantage of the oversized liver produced by migrating geese who would gorge themselves before their migratory flight. Later, Greeks and Romans experimented by overfeeding geese with figs in the hope that the flavor of the fig would be absorbed into the liver. As an alternative to the fat from pork, Jewish peoples used this goose fat.

The process of producing the perfect foie gras involves months of painstaking effort. Geese or ducks are raised outdoors in pens or in fenced fields. To promote rapid growth, the fowl are fed special poultry feed made from corn or other grains, soy bean meal, meat by-products, vitamins, and minerals. The geese or ducks are ready for market by four months of age. Two to three weeks prior to their market day slaughter, the geese or ducks are force-fed a special feed to enhance liver growth. Tubes are positioned in their mouths and the feed is funneled in. The birds are fed this special formula four or more times a day, with the total amount of feed increasing each day. At the time of slaughter, the liver has grown to almost seven times its original size.

Foie gras is available in four forms: raw, fresh, semi-cooked pasteurized, and preserved. Raw foie gras is a popular holiday treat. Typically sold at the end of the calendar year, it comes well-lobed, smooth, and not yellowed. Fresh foie gras is cooked and sold by delicatessens. Fresh foie gras is perishable, lasting, at most, a week covered and refrigerated. Semi-cooked pasteurized foie gras comes canned, and the label should state how the foie gras was canned. For example, duck foie gras prepared with truffles would be labeled foie gras de canard entire truffé. Preserved foie gras, like fine wine, improves with age. This type of foie gras is found in jars and is preserved by its own fat.

Making a Pâté

This pâté is made with pork forcemeat wrapped in prosciutto. A broccoli inlay provides flavor and enhances the appearance.

Follow these steps to make pâté:

1 Prepare mise en place for pâté.

2 Keeping the ingredients and equipment as cold as possible, grind the pork. This is referred to as the first grind.

3 Bacon is added, and the meat is prepared for the second grind.

4 The bacon and pork are ground together for the second grind. Notice the color change of the forcemeat as the fat is combined with the already ground pork.

5 Forcemeat is added to the food processor.

6 Process forcemeat with egg whites.

7 Add seasonings and cream to the forcemeat.

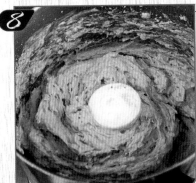

8 Continue processing until the forcemeat is smooth.

9 Remove forcemeat to a chilled bowl surrounded with ice. Add accessory ingredients, and blend.

10 Lightly spray mold with vegetable oil pan spray, and lay the prosciutto into the mold. Keeping the prosciutto on the plastic wrap makes it easy to remove the cooked pâté from the mold.

11 Pipe forcemeat into mold.

12 Make a channel down the center of the forcemeat using a small spatula.

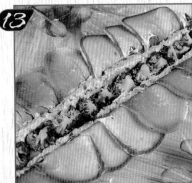

13 Add small broccoli florets, cover with more forcemeat, and fold prosciutto over to seal. Close with plastic wrap.

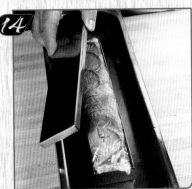

14 Cover, and bake in a water bath.

Curing, Smoking, and Food Preservation

Food preservation has been central to the garde-manger from its beginnings. Preservation techniques used in the garde-manger today surpass their original purpose of keeping food safe for later consumption. They create new flavors and textures for meats and other foods. The main preserving methods of the garde-manger are curing, smoking, drying, and preserving in fat.

Curing

To cure a food product, either dry it in granular salt (*dry cure*) or immerse it in a salt solution (*wet cure*, or brine). *Salaison* is the term used for a meat preserved with a dry or wet cure.

Dry cures Salt is the simplest dry cure. Used alone, however, it produces a rather harsh flavor. In addition to salt, dry cures frequently contain sweetener and flavorings. The mixture may also incorporate a prepared curing blend such as TCM (Tinted Cure Mix) or Prague Powder I or II to enhance color and flavor as well as assist in the curing process.

To use a dry cure, rub the mixture over the surface of the food. Then put the food in a container or wrap it in cheesecloth or paper, packing it with any additional mixture, and refrigerate it for the required length of time, which varies. During refrigeration, turn the food regularly to keep it evenly coated. Large items often require additional rubbing during curing. After curing, wash the food product to remove the curing mixture, and either cook the food item or allow it to mature by drying, aging, or smoking. Prosciutto is an example of a meat preserved with a dry cure. The usual procedure is to cure the ham for approximately four weeks and then hang it to air-dry.

Wet cures (brines) A wet cure, or brine, is a dry cure dissolved in water. Brines usually contain sea salt, a sweetener, spices, and herbs. To make a brine, combine the mix with water, and bring it to a boil. After the solution has cooled, immerse the food product in it, refrigerate, and soak for the required time. The brine should completely cover small food items. A weight may be needed to keep the item submerged. If the food product is large, perforate it with a sharp knife or inject it with brine to ensure that the salt solution reaches the center and to shorten curing time. Brining times will vary. After brining, rinse the food product, and either cook by boiling, poaching, or baking or allow it to mature by drying or smoking. Common examples of brined meats include bacon, tongue, brisket, corned beef, and pastrami.

Smoking

Originally a means of preserving food, smoking is popular today for the unique flavors it imparts to a variety of foods. The main chemical components of smoke—tar, creosote, alcohol, and formaldehyde—supply both flavor and small quantities of preserving agents. The best woods for smoking are low in resin, which makes food bitter. Commonly used woods include hickory, cherry, apple, maple, oak, mesquite, and alder.

Smoking alone is not enough to preserve food. Pretreat products to be smoked with a dry cure or brine. Curing will ensure a longer shelf life. (Curing is not necessary for certain food products, including processed items such as cheese.) After curing, air-dry the food product, and rub it with oil to prevent a crust from forming during the smoking process.

The process for smoking depends on the method used. The four methods of smoking are cold, hot, pan, and liquid.

Cold smoking *Cold smoking*, also known as slow smoking, is the best and only true method, according to the definition of smoking. The cold process imparts flavor but does not cook the food product, and it must be cured before cold smoking or cooked afterward. Temperatures for cold smoking generally range from 50°F–95°F (10°C– 35°C). Smoking times vary with the size of the food item and the equipment used. Shrimp or scallops, for example, may require only one hour of smoking, but smoking a ham may take as long as four days.

Hot smoking *Hot smoking,* or fast smoking, cooks and smokes the food product at the same time. Commonly used in commercial settings, this method requires temperatures above 140°F (60°C). Smoking time depends on the size of the food product. Chicken may take 20 minutes to 2 hours to smoke, but a pork butt will take much longer. Hot smoked foods do not require further cooking, although many undergo reheating or are ingredients in recipes that involve additional cooking.

Pan smoking Generally considered a hot-smoking method, *pan smoking* also occurs at temperatures above 140°F (60°C). Sometimes called roast smoking, this method smokes food in a covered pan. Line the bottom of a hotel pan with wood chips, and place on a burner or flat top on high heat. When the wood begins to smoke, put the food in the pan on a roasting rack and cover, sealing the edges of the pan well. Adjust heat as needed. Then smoke the food product to the desired doneness, generally 7–15 minutes.

Liquid smoking This method gives food a smoky flavor without subjecting it to an actual smoking process. *Liquid smoking* involves the use of a liquid with a smoke flavor made by rubbing resin, which builds up on the walls of a smokehouse or chimney, with a liquid. Liquid smoke can be purchased ready to use or prepared in-house. Rub the smoke-flavored liquid into the scored skin or flesh of the food product, and allow it to marinate for a few hours. After the smoke flavor has penetrated the food product, slow roast at 325°F (163°C) until done.

PROCESS

Making Gravlax

Gravlax is cured, unsmoked salmon. The dry cure used for this dish contains dill, cracked peppercorns, salt, and sugar. Brandy, aquavit, or lemon juice is often added.

To make gravlax, follow these steps:

1   **Lay salmon fillet, skin side down, on cheesecloth or plastic wrap. Brush lightly with lemon juice, aquavit, or brandy, if desired.**

2   **Combine kosher salt, granulated sugar, and cracked white peppercorns. Spread the mixture evenly on the fillet.**

3   **Top with fresh dill.**

4   **Wrap the fillet in the cheesecloth or plastic wrap, and place it in a hotel pan.**

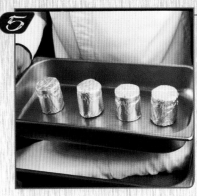

5   **Top with another hotel pan, and add weights. Refrigerate for three days.**

6   **Unwrap the salmon fillet, and remove any excess spices and herbs. Slice the gravlax very thinly on the bias, and serve with mustard dill sauce.**

Drying

Air-drying may be an important step before and after smoking. It may also replace smoking as a stage in preserving food items. Certain foods take weeks or months to air-dry. Careful monitoring of temperature and humidity is essential to successful and safe air-drying. Mechanical drying, an alternative to natural air drying, offers more precise temperature and humidity control.

A lengthy air-drying period is the final step in the preparation of various cured and cold-smoked hams. Among these are the Italian prosciutto di Parma, Spain's Serrano ham, Smithfield ham from the United States, and Westphalian ham from Germany. The process for beef jerky and the Italian beef product bresaola also includes air-drying.

Preserving in Fat

Confits and rillettes, two classic methods of food preservation, use fat as a preservative.

Confits A *confit* is meat cooked and preserved in its own fat. The meat is usually poultry, especially duck or goose, or small game, such as rabbit. To make a confit, simmer cured bird or animal parts in rendered fat, preferably the fat of the same bird or animal. After cooking the pieces, pack them in a crock, and cover them with the fat. The fat seals out the air, keeping the meat from spoiling. A confit may be stored in the refrigerator for several weeks. In general, however, confits are served hot. Traditionally, duck or goose confit was an important element of dishes such as cassoulet. Today a variety of other ingredients are used for confits, including fish and vegetables, which stew in butter or oil until they develop the consistency of jam.

Rillettes A *rillette* is also preserved meat. To prepare a rillette, slowly cook meat such as pork or poultry, particularly duck or goose, in broth or fat with vegetables and seasonings. After cooking the meat, mash it, and mix it with some of the cooking fat. Then pack it into a mold, sealing it with rendered fat. Like confits, rillettes will keep for several weeks under refrigeration. Rillettes are usually served cold as a spread for bread or toast. A rillette may be used to top a canapé or to fill a puff pastry such as a profiterole.

Making Fresh Cheese

The garde-manger also prepares fresh cheeses. These include mascarpone, mozzarella, queso blanco, fromage blanc, and ricotta and are relatively easy to make because they do not require cooking or ripening. These mild and creamy cheeses are often the highlight of an appetizer, a salad, a sandwich, or another menu item.

Basic Techniques

All cheeses are pressed milk curd, and the preparation steps are the same, regardless of the kind of cheese. The basic steps are acidifying the milk, salting the curds, coagulating the milk, draining the whey, shaping the cheese, and ripening it.

Acidifying the milk Begin by souring milk with an acid such as vinegar, lemon juice, citric acid, or tartaric acid or with an enzyme such as rennet that produces lactic acid. The acid or enzyme promotes the formation of curds and inhibits the growth of dangerous microorganisms.

Salting the curds As the acid or enzyme starter is added, or soon thereafter, stir salt into the milk. The salt prevents spoilage and contributes to both the flavor and the texture of the cheese.

Coagulating the milk At this stage the acid or enzyme starter does its work. The acid causes the proteins in the milk to coagulate, or tighten, forming curds.

Draining the whey Break up the curds to let the whey drain off. The *whey* is the part of the milk that does not coagulate.

Shaping the cheese Place the curds in a cheesecloth bag or in the basket or mold that tradition indicates for the type of cheese. Then hang the cheese, or set it on a rack to drain and dry further. For fresh cheeses, draining and shaping is usually a single step.

Ripening the cheese Allow the cheese to ripen, or age. Ripening procedures, locations, and materials vary widely, according to the type of cheese. As already noted, fresh cheeses do not undergo ripening.

Making Mozzarella

A mild, soft Italian cheese frequently eaten alone dressed with olive oil and herbs, mozzarella is an example of a *pasta filata*, or "spun paste." To create mozzarella and other *pasta filata* cheeses, such as Provolone, stretch and spin the curds to the desired consistency after immersing them in hot water.

Aspic

Aspic is a clear, savory jelly with many applications in the garde-manger. Aspic can be made from a variety of foods, including meat, fish, and vegetables.

Meat The classical method of making aspic involves cooking bones, cartilage, and tendons for several hours. These high-gelatin ingredients produce a thick stock, which turns into a gelatinous mass when the liquid cools. Contemporary preparations of aspic shorten the cooking process by adding gelatin directly to bouillon or consommé. Today, gelatin is conveniently available in the form of leaves or powders.

Fish Isinglass, gelatin obtained from fish, can also serve as the basis for aspic.

Vegetable Agar-agar is a vegetable or seaweed alternative to gelatin that may be used in preparing meat-free aspic.

Uses of Aspic

Aspic is a versatile product. It functions as a binder to lend structure to other foods, as a decorative element that adds color to dishes and food displays, or as a lining for metal platters to protect food from contamination, drying, and discoloration. Aspic also frequently serves as a food coating. As such, it may complement another food's flavor, prevent oxidation and drying, or improve the appearance of food, especially for buffet display, by adding shine.

Applying Aspic

Aspic intended as a food coating should be completely clear and contain no bubbles, food particles, streaks, or fingerprints. See Figure 25-9. Be sure to clean and sanitize all utensils. Always wear gloves to handle foods coated with aspic.

Lining a Platter with Aspic

Aspic has many uses within the garde-manger repertoire, including that of adding a decorative touch and clean look to platters and plates.

To line a platter with aspic, follow this procedure:

Arrange the decorations on the platter in the desired pattern.

Level the platter with shims, and pour the aspic in an even layer.

Use a blowtorch to smooth out any imperfections.

Applying Aspic

Lay foods to be coated neatly on a coating rack, and chill them while preparing aspic.

Follow these steps to apply aspic:

1 Melt aspic in a double boiler, heating only as much as can be used in 15 to 20 minutes.

2 Temper aspic over an ice bath, bringing it to a temperature below 85°F (29°C) and stirring it gently to prevent air bubbles from forming.

3 To coat the food product, start at one side of the rack, and move to the opposite side. Then refrigerate the coated food.

4 Prepare aspic for a second coating by bringing it to the appropriate temperature.

Repeat the aspic application process as needed to create a clear, even coating on all food. One even coating of aspic is usually adequate for a buffet of short duration, but two to three coatings are necessary for a buffet whose presentation will last several hours. Use a minimum of three layers of aspic for foods presented for culinary competition.

Methods of Application

Aspic can be applied to chilled foods by spraying, ladling, brushing, or dipping.

Spray Pour tempered aspic into a spray bottle, and mist it over chilled food products. Keep the spray bottle in a hot water bath to prevent the aspic from cooling and solidifying within the spraying mechanism.

Ladle Ladle tempered aspic over food products laid out on a coating rack. Use this method for coating large pieces.

Brush Use a natural bristle brush to paint tempered aspic onto food products. Although not often used because of the likelihood of streaking, brushing is a good method if the food requires only a thin coating and the time before service is limited.

Dip Dip the food products into a container of tempered aspic, and then place them on a clean surface and refrigerate. Dipping ensures a clean, smooth coating.

FIGURE 25-9

Food coated with aspic

Chaud-Froid

Chaud-froid, a term literally translated as "hot-cold," refers to the preparation of foods that are cooked, cooled, and then coated with a sauce, usually brown or white, that sets up or gels to form an attractive and lasting presentation. These pieces are then decorated or garnished and finished with a coating or clear aspic. Chaud-froid sauces are prepared hot and served cold. Chaud-froid sauces add shine, color, and a savory flavor to foods. Typically applied to meat, fish, game, or poultry, the type of food to be coated determines both the color and flavor of the sauce to be used. Chaud-froid sauces can also be used to coat platters. In recent times, chaud-froid has fallen out of favor as a leading preparation for cold buffets.

Varieties of Chaud-Froid

Chaud-froid sauces comes in two basic forms: brown chaud-froid and white chaud-froid. A third type of chaud-froid, tomato, made from tomato pulp and aspic, is seldom used today.

Brown chaud-froid A brown chaud-froid is used for brown or red meats and is made from brown stock and aspic. An orange variation can be made with demi-glace, orange juice and zest, Madeira, and aspic.

White chaud-froid White meats such as pork or poultry, poached items, or fish benefit from a white chaud-froid. Traditionally, white chaud-froid was made primarily by adding aspic to béchamel or velouté sauce. Chaud-froid made with mayonnaise and aspic is called mayonnaise collée. Most modern white chaud-froid sauces are made by adding gelatin to milk.

Planning a Buffet

Paramount to the success of planning a buffet is the presentation, appearance, and flavor of the foods to be served. As with any menu planning, gastronomics, economics, and practicalities must be taken into consideration, too.

Buffet planning begins with a theme, or central concept or motif, and the menu, but other aspects of planning include the design: table placement; available space; number of zones, or buffet areas; and décor.

Theme

A buffet is a carefully planned presentation of a multitude of food items from which diners make their selections. Before determining which food items will be served and presented on the menu, the theme must be determined. The theme sets the mood of the event or affair, and spans the spectrum from black-and-white formal to casual dining. The theme may be event-focused, such as that of a wedding, charity luncheon, or holiday party, or may be based on ethnic food items—Greek, Italian, Mexican, and so on.

The theme in turn drives the selection of the food items, menu design, décor, music, lighting, linens, and dinnerware. In deciding the theme and all that accompanies the buffet, cost must be considered.

FIGURE 25-10

The size and shape of the dining room, along with the theme, food selection, and number of guests, influence the shape of the buffet table.

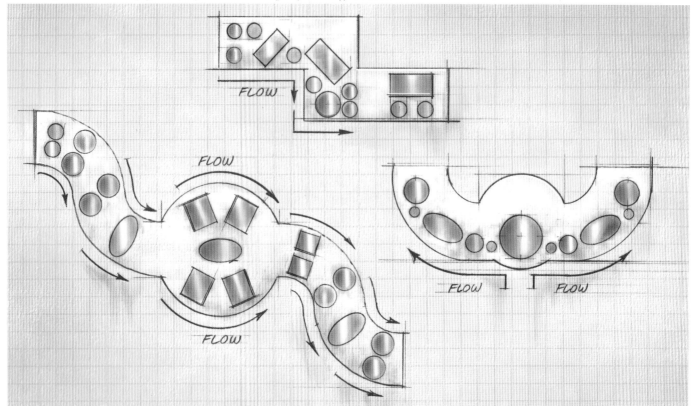

The Menu

The buffet menu is generally à la carte with food choices representative of first-course items, such as soups and salads; entrées; accompaniments, such as vegetables and potatoes; desserts; and beverages. All food selections should coincide with the theme of the buffet and offer variety in presentation.

Menu planning has three main aspects: gastronomic, economic, and pragmatic.

Gastronomic Plan the menu as a whole meal rather than as a succession of independent, unrelated courses. Integrating different ingredients, colors, and textures in the menu as well as a range of cooking techniques will help achieve this effect.

- A variety of ingredients enhances the menu presentation. Give guests choices among main ingredients. Instead of two meat entrées, for example, provide a meat entrée and a fish entrée. Do not repeat ingredients. If you offer shrimp cocktail as the appetizer, do not use shrimp as the entrée.
- Color and texture contrasts are also important. Aim for a variety of colors and food textures on the buffet table.

Guests should have a choice between vegetable and protein salads or clear and cream or hot and cold soups, for example.

- Use the buffet as an opportunity to showcase different cooking methods. Balance a cold poached fish as an entrée selection with freshly grilled chicken breasts.

Economic Pay close attention to cost when planning the menu. Creating and presenting a visually appealing and satisfying meal within budget is a challenge that requires a careful balance of expensive or elaborate dishes and items that are less costly in terms of expense and time.

Pragmatic When planning the menu, think about available equipment, the staff's skill level, and the type of service needed. Also take into consideration the religious or ethnic dietary needs of guests.

See Chapter 6: Menu Development for information on menu design and Chapter 10: Sensory Perception for information on presentation.

Buffet Design

Buffet design involves determining the arrangement of a buffet; the number of zones; table placement, size, and shape;

space for service; and centerpieces and other decoration.

Zones A zone is a buffet area designed for the smooth and speedy flow of patron traffic. A single buffet zone may serve 75 to 125 people. For larger groups, additional zones may be needed to ensure rapid service and shorter lines. Each zone should contain the same menu items.

A zone may consist of a single table that patrons approach along one side only. A single table may also serve as two zones, with identical foods on both sides of the table and patrons forming a line on each side. The two-sided approach is practical for large groups. Another arrangement that accommodates large groups is several zones on a single table that guests approach on one side. See Figure 25-10 for various traffic flow and zone options for one-sided and two-sided buffet service.

Table placement, size, and shape The configuration of the dining room and seating arrangements often dictate the size and shape of the buffet table or tables. Tables of various shapes strategically placed in the dining room can influence the buffet's initial visual impact on the guest, contributing to an impression of abundance and beauty.

Space for service The table arrangement should also accommodate servers and staff. Servers or runners need to replenish the buffet and keep it neat. They should have enough space to do so without disturbing food displays or guests. Convenient access to the kitchen is essential for quick replacement of food items. Space may also be needed at a buffet where servers may carve or prepare food at the table. Staff on site can also explain to guests what is being served.

Presentation

Presentation of the food items is key to the success of a buffet. Food selections should be plentiful and visually appealing in an effort to please the eye and stimulate the appetite. Sometimes this means presenting food simply, letting the natural colors and textures take center stage. In other cases presentations can be more elaborate or intricate.

Before beginning to cook, plan the way the food will be presented—how the food will look on the buffet; what the focus of the presentation will be; and how the guest's visual, textural, and flavor interest will be engaged throughout the meal. Present contrasts in food color and appearance, shapes, height, texture, flavor, and temperatures.

> See Chapter 10: Sensory Perception for more information on presentation.

Hot food items When serving hot food items, such as soups, meats, and vegetables, follow the proper holding and serving procedures as outlined by HACCP. Serve hot foods hot, and typically from chafing dishes placed near the end of the buffet table. Foods should be portioned in the kitchen prior to replenishing the buffet.

Cold food items As with hot foods, cold foods should be held and served following HACCP guidelines. Serve cold foods cold, and present them in an artistic manner.

Centerpieces

A centerpiece (pièce montée) enhances the appearance of the buffet table. It provides a focal point when guests first enter the dining room and reinforces the theme of the buffet. A buffet centerpiece often incorporates an illuminated tray, baskets of fruit, vases of flowers, ice carvings, sculptures, or a candelabra.

Color contrast, shape, size, medium, and cost are all factors to consider when planning a centerpiece. Common media for centerpiece production include ice, vegetables, salt dough, sugar pastillage, chocolate, and marzipan. The availability of the product, the ease with which it can be stored and transported, and the risk of breakage all affect cost.

Ice Carving

Ice carvings are one of the most impressive and sought-after centerpieces for the buffet table. The cost of producing ice sculptures can vary greatly, depending on the availability of ice, skilled artisans, and a proper storage facility. When not produced in-house, ice sculptures can be expensive.

Safety
Goggles, gloves, and heavyweight boots with nonslip soles are essential safety equipment for ice carving. Plastic goggles protect the eyes from flying pieces of ice, and gloves made of carbon mesh protect the hands from cuts. Heavy-duty, water-resistant boots, preferably with steel toes, guard against injury from pieces of ice and keep feet dry while sculpting.

Making a Template
Usually one solid block of ice is used to create an ice carving. Before carving, a *template,* or pattern for the design of the sculpture, must be created. Draw the template on a sheet of paper the same size as the block of ice. Transfer the design by using the grid method of copying. When duplicating the design, draw the template slightly larger than needed to allow for the melting that occurs while finishing the centerpiece. Every design should include a substantial base to ensure stability.

Tempering the Ice
Before carving, temper the ice by removing it from the freezer; otherwise it will be very brittle and break easily. Ice tempers in about half an hour, or when the block begins to clear. Tempering should occur in a relatively cool environment of 40°F–68°F (4°C–20°C).

Display
Present the completed ice carving on a raised socle that can also act as a drip pan. The drip pan should have a drain, a rubber hose that drains the water from the drip pan to a bucket underneath the buffet table, and a light. The drain carries away the melted ice, and the light illuminates the carving. Additional colored lights can be placed at the back or under the ice carving. Make sure that the electric wiring is well insulated so that melting water does not cause a short circuit. Use greenery and in-season floral decorations to call attention to the centerpiece.

Vegetable Carving

Vegetable carvings can also be used as a centerpiece. Production costs depend on the availability of produce, the variety of vegetables used, and the skill of the carver. Unlike ice carvings, vegetable carvings are limited in size. They are useful for decorating small areas on a buffet, a dining table, or a platter.

Vegetable carvings vary in size, shape, and color. Intricate vegetable carvings can be created with simple tools, such as a vegetable peeler, paring knife or tourné knife, French knife, or channel knife. Specialty carving tools are also available. Numerous books detail procedures for vegetable and fruit carvings. Those that include step-by-step sequences illustrated with color photographs are the most useful.

The following basic rules apply to vegetable carving:

- Wash the vegetables well.
- Hold the vegetables at room temperature before carving.
- After carving, immerse the vegetables in ice water to facilitate crispness.
- To reuse vegetable centerpieces and thus save on costs, soak them in ice water.

Food Display

A centerpiece can also consist of foods other than vegetables. Such a centerpiece, which displays a large, uncut portion of the main food, is called a *grosse pièce* ("large piece"). A cold roast with garnishes or a whole terrine surrounded by individual slices offers a focal point for a buffet table or platter. An accompaniment such as a sauce or condiment can also serve as a centerpiece if presented in an eye-catching dish or bowl.

Platter Design

Platters are the primary means for displaying foods on a buffet. Platter shapes and sizes and the materials from which platters are made vary greatly. The selection of platters and the arrangement of food on them are a critical part of the aesthetics of the buffet table.

Blueprints

After choosing appropriate platters on the basis of the buffet menu, develop platter *blueprints,* or drawings of what the platters will look like with food displayed on them. Each platter should have its own blueprint, which should detail the following: foods that will be presented, lining and decoration for the platter, space requirements based on platter size, and size and shape of garnishes. A platter blueprint will provide a visual key to the finished foods and their locations on the platter. It will also help ensure that each platter offers color and texture contrasts, as well as diverse shapes and heights of food.

Selecting Food Elements

A balanced platter has five basic food elements: the main piece, the utilization piece, the enhancing salad, the garnish, and the starch. The main piece represents the main food item on the platter. It is often a solid or semisolid cut of meat or a food item such as

a pâté, terrine, or galantine. The utilization piece usually consists of the trimmings and extra pieces from the main piece. The enhancing salad is specially designed to add flavor, balance, texture, and color to the platter. The various garnishes on the platter should be flavorful, functional, and colorful. The starch is often a cracker, crouton, or socle added to an element of the platter for nutritional balance and texture.

Guidelines for Presentation

Careful planning of the layout of food elements is vital to the success of the presentation. For eye appeal and ease of service, follow these guidelines:

- Maintain a natural frame on the platter.
- On bordered platters, position the foods at least 1 inch (2.5 cm) from the inner edge. On borderless platters, position the foods at least 2 inches (5 cm) from the edge.
- Use the one-quarter concept. Visualize an imaginary grid over the platter blueprint and later over the finished presentation. Are the five basic food elements equally distributed in each quarter of the grid? If not, rearrange the presentation.
- Confirm the alignment and order of sliced foods. Shingle the slices of food neatly in a row toward the guest. Display the pieces in the exact order in which they were sliced.
- Do not crowd the platter or leave it looking empty. The amount of food presented on the platter should look appetizing.
- Place taller food items toward the rear of the platter.
- Make portions consistent. For example, if there are eight portions of the main item, there should also be eight portions of every other element.
- Confirm that the portion size is correct. Slices should be no more than one-quarter of an inch thick.

Criteria for Evaluation

When you have determined the basic food elements of a platter and their arrangement, evaluate the presentation to make sure that it is balanced. Ask these questions:

- *Do the foods represent a variety of cooking methods?* Determine whether adding or removing a particular cooking method would improve the platter.

- *Are the foods presented a pleasing mix of colors?* Some colors should contrast with others.
- *Which foods offer a variety of textures?* For example, are all of the elements containing meat finely ground, or does at least one piece exhibit the natural texture or grain of the meat? Do foods with a crispy texture balance foods with a soft texture?
- *Are the flavors of the foods complementary?* Rich foods should counterbalance leaner preparations. Hot and spicy foods should offset foods seasoned with milder aromatics. Cured, smoked foods should have sweet or acidic accompaniments.
- *Is the height of the foods proportional to their importance?* Are the main items the highest? Does the centerpiece dominate the platter?
- *Do the foods offer a variety of shapes?* Foods should be displayed in proper proportions.
- *Does the platter provide nutritional balance?* Are proteins, carbohydrates, and vegetables well represented in the five food elements?

The overall effect of a buffet platter should be one of variety and harmony.

Making an Ice Carving

Make a template for the sculpture by copying an image from a book onto a transparency. A paper cut the size of the block of ice is hung on a wall, and the image is projected onto the paper using an overhead projector. Trace the image with a marker onto the paper.

Follow these steps to make an ice carving:

1 Place the prepared template over the block of ice, and smooth it to make it stay in place.

2 Use a chipper to score the ice, transferring the design onto the ice block.

3 Remove the template, and score the ice to highlight the design.

4 Rough out the design with a chain saw. For safety reasons, remove large pieces of ice from the work area.

5 Sanding helps smooth out the design.

6 A variety of tools can be used to provide detail.

7 A finished ice sculpture

Classic Italian Balsamic Dressing

INGREDIENTS

	U.S. Standard	Metric
Balsamic vinegar	8 oz.	240 ml
Granulated sugar	1 oz.	28 g
Garlic, *peeled and mashed into a paste*	1 clove	1 clove
Shallots, *peeled and minced*	1 oz.	28 g
Olive oil	12 oz.	360 ml
Oregano, *fresh, washed, and roughly chopped*	2 Tbsp.	30 g
Marjoram	1/2 tsp.	2.5 ml
Basil, *fresh, washed, and roughly chopped*	2 Tbsp.	30 g
Salt	TT	TT
Black pepper	TT	TT

Chef's Notes

Using an emersion blender will make a stronger emulsion, which may not separate for several hours.

NUTRITION

Nutrition Facts

Yield: Serves 10
Serving Size: 2 oz. (55 g)

Amount Per Serving

Calories 330

Total Fat 34 g

Sodium 20 mg

Total Carbohydrate 7 g

Protein 0 g

METHOD OF PREPARATION

1. Gather all the ingredients and equipment.

2. In a medium mixing bowl, whisk together the balsamic vinegar, sugar, garlic, and shallots until the sugar dissolves.

3. Drizzle in the oil slowly, while whisking.

4. Blend in the fresh herbs, taste, and season with salt and pepper.

5. Hold covered at 41°F (5°C) or lower. Mix to blend if necessary before service.

Salmon Pâté

INGREDIENTS

	U.S. Standard	Metric
Salmon inlay	1 each	1 each
Fillets of salmon, lean, cut into cubes	1 1/2 lbs.	680 g
Salt	1 to 1 1/2 tsp.	5 to 8 ml
Nutmeg	1/2 tsp.	2.5 ml
Cayenne	1 pinch	1 pinch
Dill	1 Tbsp.	15 ml
Egg whites	3 each	3 each
Heavy cream	1/2 c.	120 ml
Zucchini, washed, skin left on, diced brunoise	1 each	1 each

Nutrition Facts

Yield: Serves 10
Serving Size: 2 oz. (55 g)

Amount Per Serving

Calories 80

Total Fat 5 g

Sodium 180 mg

Total Carbohydrate 1 g

Protein 7 g

METHOD OF PREPARATION

1. Gather all the ingredients and equipment.

2. Combine the fish and seasoning in the bowl of a food processor fitted with the metal blade. Process by frequently turning the machine on and off and scraping the mixture from the sides of the bowl until a smooth consistency is achieved.

3. With the food processor running, add the egg whites, and slowly add the heavy cream through the feed tube. Process until the mixture is well blended and fluffy. Fold in zucchini, test the seasoning, and correct, if necessary. Place the salmon inlay in the middle.

4. Mousseline (forcemeat) keeps refrigerated for about 1 day or for up to 3 months if frozen. Mold, and cook in a water bath to an internal temperature of 145°F (63°C).

Pork Pâté

with Broccoli Inlay

INGREDIENTS

	U.S. Standard	Metric
Bacon slices	12 each	12 each
Pork, cubed, chilled	1 1/2 lbs.	680 g
Pork fat	6 oz.	170 g
Olive oil	1 Tbsp.	15 ml
Spanish onions, diced	1/2 each	1/2 each
Orange pepper, diced	1/2 each	1/2 each
Yellow sun-dried tomatoes, diced	12 each	12 each
Chef's spice	3 full tsp.	15 ml
Egg whites	6 each	6 each
Heavy cream	3/4 c.	180 ml
Prosciutto, diced	2 oz.	55 g
Broccoli, blanched	1/2 bunch	1/2 bunch

NUTRITION

Nutrition Facts

Yield: Serves 10
Serving Size: 2 oz. (55 g)

Amount Per Serving

Calories 380

Total Fat 30 g

Sodium 360 mg

Total Carbohydrate 5 g

Protein 22 g

METHOD OF PREPARATION

1. Gather all the ingredients and equipment.

2. Lay bacon slices on plastic wrap (bacon slices should touch) along the length of the pâté or terrine mold.

3. Fold plastic wrap over the bacon, and roll with a rolling pin.

4. Place the bacon slices in the mold.

5. Grind the pork cubes through a large grinding plate. Repeat the process (use a smaller plate if possible), adding the fat on the second grind. Keep ground meat chilled when task is complete.

6. Heat olive oil in a sauté pan. Sauté onions, pepper, and sun-dried tomatoes until wilted. Place vegetables on a shallow tray. Cool to 41°F (5°C) or lower.

7. Place ground meat in a food processor. Blend the meat; add seasoning and egg whites slowly, and finally add the cream.

8. Remove forcemeat from food processor. Fold in the sautéed vegetables and diced prosciutto in a stainless steel bowl over ice.

9. Test the forcemeat, and adjust the seasoning.

10. Place forcemeat in a pastry bag. Pipe the forcemeat into the pâté mold until it is half full.

11. Cut the broccoli into small florets. Place in the center of the pâté.

12. Fill the pâté with the remaining forcemeat. Fold the bacon over the top. Cover with plastic wrap and foil. Place in a water bath in a 350°F (177°C) oven, and bake until the internal temperature is 150°F (66°C).

13. Cool immediately, and chill overnight. Slice and serve.

Veal and Ham Pie

INGREDIENTS	U.S. Standard	Metric
PÂTÉ DOUGH		
Bread flour	18 oz.	510 g
Salt	1/2 oz.	15 g
Granulated sugar	1 Tbsp.	15 ml
Primex	2 1/2 oz.	75 g
Butter	3 1/2 oz.	100 g
Egg	1 each	1 each
Egg white	1 each	1 each
Cold water	3 oz.	90 ml
Lemon juice	2 oz.	60 ml
FORCEMEAT		
Clarified butter	2 oz.	60 ml
Onion, *peeled and diced*	1/2 each	1/2 each
Carrots, *diced*	1 each	1 each
Shallots, *peeled and diced*	8 each	8 each
Port wine	4 oz.	120 ml
Veal, *ground*	1 lb.	454 g
Bacon, *cut julienne*	4 oz.	115 g
Egg whites	4 each	4 each
Chef's spice	1 tsp.	5 ml
Parsley, *washed, chopped, squeezed dry*	2 Tbsp.	30 g
Heavy cream	6 oz.	175 ml
Ham, *diced*	8 oz.	225 g
Pistachios, *whole, blanched, peeled*	2 oz.	55 g
Shiitake mushroom caps, *blanched*	12 each	12 each

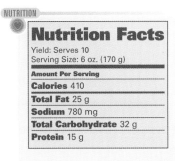

Nutrition Facts

Yield: Serves 10
Serving Size: 6 oz. (170 g)

Amount Per Serving

Calories 410

Total Fat 25 g

Sodium 780 mg

Total Carbohydrate 32 g

Protein 15 g

METHOD OF PREPARATION

Pâté dough:

1. Gather all the ingredients and equipment. Blend flour, salt, sugar, primex, and butter until mixture is crumbly.

2. Add egg, egg white, water, and lemon juice. Blend mixture until smooth dough is formed.

3. Place in a plastic bag, and rest for 1 hour in the refrigerator.

Forcemeat:

4. Heat butter in a sauté pan, and sauté onions, carrots, and shallots until wilted. Add wine, and reduce until almost dry. Place in a shallow pan, and chill.

5. Place ground veal in a food processor. Blend well; add bacon, and chop until one mixture is formed.

6. Slowly add egg whites. Add seasoning and parsley, and slowly add cream.

7. Test the forcemeat. Adjust seasoning, if necessary.

8. Place veal mixture in a stainless steel bowl over ice. Fold in ham, pistachios, and mushrooms.

Assembly:

9. Roll dough on a floured surface to 1/8" (3 mm) thick. Place dough in an oiled mold as demonstrated.

10. Pipe forcemeat into the mold with a pastry bag. Place blanched mushroom caps on top of forcemeat.

11. Fold dough over the top, as demonstrated. Wash all seams, and top with egg wash (1 egg, 2 Tbsp. milk).

12. Place 2 chimneys on top of the pâté as demonstrated.

13. Bake in a 400°F (204°C) oven 15 minutes, reduce temperature to 350°F (177°C), and bake until the internal temperature is 150°F (66°C). Then fill with aspic. Cool overnight.

Stuffed Breast Of Turkey

with Sun-Dried Tomato Pâté

INGREDIENTS

	U.S. Standard	Metric
SUN-DRIED TOMATO FORCEMEAT		
Lean turkey meat, diced	1 1/2 lbs.	680 g
Egg whites	3 each	3 each
Bacon	4 strips	4 strips
Fresh chives, chopped	1 Tbsp.	15 ml
Poultry seasoning	1 Tbsp.	15 ml
Heavy cream	1 c.	240 ml
Red sun-dried tomatoes, diced	3 oz.	85 g
Yellow sun-dried tomatoes, diced	3 oz.	85 g
Shallots, peeled and minced	2 each	2 each
Dried apricots, diced	2 oz.	55 g
Turkey breast	1/2 each	1/2 each
Leek greens, blanched	4 each	4 each
Ham bars	4 oz.	115 g

METHOD OF PREPARATION

1. Gather all the ingredients and equipment.

2. Chill diced turkey well. Grind in a food processor; add egg whites, bacon, herbs, seasoning, and cream.

3. Add sun-dried tomatoes, shallots, and apricots. Run food processor just to combine the ingredients.

4. Flatten the turkey breast with a mallet.

5. Place a small amount of forcemeat on top.

6. Wrap ham bars with leeks. Place on top of forcemeat as an inlay. Cover with additional forcemeat.

7. Rope and cover with plastic wrap and then foil. Bake in a 350°F (177°C) oven to 165°F (74°C) internal temperature.

8. Cool, unwrap, and slice.

Ham Mousse Tartlets

INGREDIENTS	U.S. Standard	Metric
CRACKER DOUGH		
Flour	3/4 c.	115 g
Cornmeal	1 1/2 oz.	40 g
Sugar	1 tsp.	5 ml
Butter	2 1/2 tsp.	12.5 g
Ice water	1/3 c.	83.3 ml
HAM MOUSSE		
Baked ham, *diced*	10 oz.	285 g
Cream cheese	6 oz.	170 g
Sour cream	3 Tbsp.	45 g
Instant gel powder	1 tsp.	5 g
Green pepper, *cut julienne*	for garnish	for garnish

METHOD OF PREPARATION

For cracker dough:

1. Gather all the ingredients and equipment. Mix flour, cornmeal, sugar, and butter until the mixture is crumbly.

2. Add water, and form into a smooth dough. Chill for 1 hour.

3. Roll the cracker dough out in the pasta machine until similar to pasta dough. Dusting with flour may be necessary.

4. Place the dough on parchment paper and freeze the dough. Cut into circles a little larger than a tartlet mold. Place the dough in mold. Place an empty mold on top. Spray all contact areas with spray shortening.

5. Refreeze the shells with any excess dough hanging over the edge.

6. When frozen, remove the excess dough with a sharp knife.

7. Bake in a 300°F (149°C) oven for 5–6 minutes.

For ham mousse:

8. Place ham in a food processor, and grind until smooth.

9. Soften cream cheese with your hands, and add to food processor.

10. Blend until one mixture is formed.

11. Add sour cream and instant gel powder, and blend well.

Assembly:

12. Place ham mousse in a pastry bag with a star tube. Pipe a rosette of ham mousse in each shell, and garnish with a julienne cut of green pepper.

Chef's Notes

You may also garnish the tartlets with marinated vegetables from the Turkey Platter (platter 7).

NUTRITION

Nutrition Facts

Yield: Serves 10
Serving Size: 2 oz. (55 g)

Amount Per Serving

Calories 190

Total Fat 11 g

Sodium 85 mg

Total Carbohydrate 11 g

Protein 11 g

Garde-Manger

529

Crusted Lemon Crackers

with Pistachio Boursin Cheese Rolls

INGREDIENTS

	U.S. Standard	Metric
Flour	3/4 c.	170 g
Cornmeal	1 1/2 oz.	40 g
Sugar	1 tsp.	5 ml
Salt	1 tsp.	5 ml
Butter	2 1/2 tsp.	12.5 g
Ice water	1/3 c.	75 ml
Lemon, *zest only, finely chopped*	1 each	1 each
Boursin cheese	1 package	1 package
Cream cheese	1 Tbsp.	15 g
Pistachios, *ground and sieved*	as needed	as needed
Chives or diamond-cut red pepper	for garnish	for garnish

METHOD OF PREPARATION

1. Gather all the ingredients and equipment.

2. Place the flour, cornmeal, sugar, salt, and butter in a stainless steel bowl. Blend until the mixture is crumbly.

3. Add the water and lemon zest. Blend until a smooth dough is formed.

4. Place in a plastic bag, and chill.

5. Take a small piece of dough, dredge in flour, and roll in a pasta machine to a thickness similar to that of pasta.

6. Place the dough on a parchment papered tray. Freeze the dough.

7. Cut the dough with a small, round crinkle cutter while frozen.

8. Spray a round-bottomed mold with shortening. Place the crackers in the mold so that the edge will stand up. Bake in a 300°F (149°C) oven 6–8 minutes until the dough is set.

9. Combine the Boursin and cream cheeses, and form into small balls. Coat with ground pistachios.

10. Garnish with a chive or diamond-cut red pepper.

11. Place on crackers as demonstrated.

Roasted Venison Loin

with Red Pepper Mousse, Garnished with Apricots and Currants

INGREDIENTS

	U.S. Standard	Metric
Venison loin, chilled	1 each	1 each
Venison trimmings, cut into cubes, chilled	1/4 lb.	115 g
Lean pork cubes	1/4 lb.	115 g
Bacon, cut julienne	2 oz.	55 g
Red pepper, roasted	1 each	1 each
Paprika	1 tsp.	5 ml
Chef's spice*	1 tsp.	5 ml
Egg whites	2 each	2 each
Heavy cream	1 oz.	30 ml
Apricots, diced	12 each	12 each
Currants	1/2 c.	115 g
Caul fat	8 oz.	225 g

Chef's Notes

*Chef's spice is your choice; a prepared blend or your own mixture or rub.

NUTRITION

Nutrition Facts

Yield: Serves 10
Serving Size: 4 oz. (115 g)

Amount Per Serving

Calories 360

Total Fat 20 g

Sodium 130 mg

Total Carbohydrate 6 g

Protein 37 g

METHOD OF PREPARATION

1. Gather all the ingredients and equipment.

2. Remove venison loin from the bone. Trim off all fat and silverskin. Set aside.

3. Place the chopped venison and pork cubes in a robot coupe. Add bacon, and blend until one mixture is formed.

4. Peel the skin from the roasted red pepper. Remove the seeds and stem, and dice the pepper. Add the pepper to the meat mixture. Blend well. Add seasonings, and slowly add egg whites and cream.

5. Test the forcemeat, and adjust the seasonings. Place the forcemeat in a stainless steel bowl over ice.

6. Fold in apricots and currants.

7. Stretch a large piece of caul fat on a cutting board that is the length of the venison loin.

8. Spread the mousse over the top of the venison loin. Place the loin forcemeat side down on the caul fat.

9. Wrap the fat around the loin so that a seam is formed.

10. Place the venison loin on a wire rack, seam side down.

11. Spray the loin with shortening. Sprinkle your favorite seasoning over the roast.

12. Place in a 350°F (177°C) oven until a temperature of 145°F (63°C) is achieved.

13. Chill overnight. Slice and serve.

Smoked Beef Tenderloin of Beef

with a Whole-Grain Mustard Crust

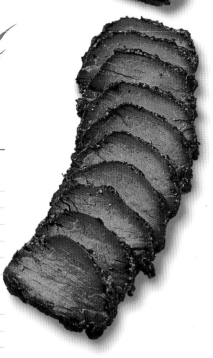

INGREDIENTS	U.S. Standard	Metric
HONEY BRINE		
Water	1 gal.	3.8 l
Kosher salt	6 1/2 oz.	185 g
Sugar	8 oz.	225 g
Pepper, black	2 tsp.	10 ml
Cloves	2 tsp.	10 ml
Honey	6 oz.	180 ml
TENDERLOIN		
Beef tenderloin	1 each	1 each
Whole-grain mustard	2/3 c.	170 g
Instant gel	3 tsp.	15 g
Egg whites	1 each	1 each
Montreal steak seasoning	as needed	as needed

METHOD OF PREPARATION

For honey brine:

1. Gather all the ingredients and equipment.

2. Combine all ingredients in a saucepan. Bring to a boil; reduce to a simmer for 20 minutes.

3. Place in a shallow hotel pan, and cool to 41°F (5°C) or lower.

For tenderloin:

4. Gather all ingredients and equipment.

5. Trim the tenderloin, removing all fat, silverskin, and connective tissue.

6. Truss the trimmed tenderloin with butcher's string, and place in the cooled honey brine for 2–3 hours.

7. When curing is complete, remove the tenderloin from the brine. Pat dry with paper towels.

8. Blend the mustard, instant gel, and egg whites in a mixing bowl.

9. Put the tenderloin on a wire rack, and place in a 200°F (93°C) smoker for 30 minutes.

10. When smoking is complete, coat the tenderloin with the mustard mixture and Montreal steak seasoning. Place the tenderloin in a 350°F (177°C) oven until the internal temperature reaches 140°F (60°C) for 12 minutes.

11. Remove the tenderloin from the oven, and cool immediately to 41°F (5°C) or lower. Chill overnight.

NUTRITION

Nutrition Facts

Yield: Serves 10
Serving Size: 3 oz. (85 g)

Amount Per Serving

Calories 200

Total Fat 9 g

Sodium 520 mg

Total Carbohydrate 6 g

Protein 25 g

Bow Tie Pasta Salad

with Lump Crabmeat

Chef's Notes

Chopped lobster may also be added for garnish.

INGREDIENTS

Ingredients	U.S. Standard	Metric
Bow tie pasta	3 c.	675 g
Sour cream	1/2 c.	115 g
Whole-grain mustard	2 Tbsp.	30 g
Mayonnaise	1/2 c.	115 g
Chef's spice	1 Tbsp.	15 ml
Fresh chives, chopped	1/4 c.	60 ml
Fresh basil, chopped	2 Tbsp.	30 ml
Sugar	1 tsp.	5 ml
Yellow pepper, seeds removed, diced	1/2 each	1/2 each
Red pepper, seeds removed, diced	1/2 each	1/2 each
Onion, diced	1/2 each	1/2 each
Carrot, peeled, diced	1/2 each	1/2 each
Crabmeat, drained	1/2 pound	225 g
Kalamata olives, cut in half, pits removed	12 each	12 each
Heavy cream	as needed	as needed

NUTRITION

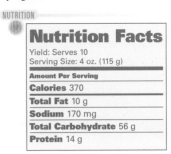

Nutrition Facts

Yield: Serves 10
Serving Size: 4 oz. (115 g)

Amount Per Serving

Calories 370

Total Fat 10 g

Sodium 170 mg

Total Carbohydrate 56 g

Protein 14 g

METHOD OF PREPARATION

1. Gather all the ingredients and equipment.

2. Blanch pasta in boiling salted water until al dente. Drain, cool, and drain again. Place pasta in a stainless steel bowl.

3. Blend sour cream, mustard, mayonnaise, seasonings, herbs, and sugar in a stainless steel bowl. Blend well.

4. Combine peppers, onion, carrot, crabmeat, and olives with the pasta. Add dressing, and combine until well mixed. Adjust seasoning, and keep chilled. Add heavy cream as needed to adjust consistency.

Mango Salsa

INGREDIENTS

	U.S. Standard	Metric
Mango, *peeled and finely diced*	1 each	1 each
Chile peppers, *finely diced*	2 each	2 each
Garlic, *peeled and* *finely chopped*	1 clove	1 clove
Scallions, *finely chopped*	4 each	4 each
Olive oil	1 Tbsp.	15 g
Sugar	1 tsp.	5 ml
Plum tomatoes, *seeds removed,* *diced*	2 each	2 each
Amaretto liquor	1 oz.	30 ml
Orange, *juice and zest*	1 each	1 each

METHOD OF PREPARATION

1. Gather all the ingredients and equipment.

2. Mix all ingredients in a stainless steel bowl. Adjust seasoning, and serve in a sauceboat.

Roasted Red Bliss Potato Salad

INGREDIENTS

	U.S. Standard	Metric
Red bliss potatoes, B size	8 each	8 each
Oil	as needed	as needed
Chef's spice	1 Tbsp.	15 ml
Bacon, finely chopped	10 slices	10 slices
Mayonnaise	1/2 c.	115 g
Sugar	1 Tbsp.	15 ml
Red onion, diced	1/2 each	1/2 each
Cucumber, peeled, deseeded, diced	1 each	1 each
Broccoli florets, blanched	1/2 bunch	1/2 bunch
Heavy cream or buttermilk	1/4 c.	60 ml

METHOD OF PREPARATION

1. Gather all the ingredients and equipment.

2. Wash potatoes, and pat dry with paper towels.

3. Rub the potatoes with oil, and sprinkle with chef's spice. Place on a half baking sheet.

4. Roast in a 350°F (177°C) oven until fork-tender. Chill in refrigerator overnight.

5. Leaving skins on, dice the potatoes, and place in a stainless steel bowl.

6. Place the bacon in a sauté pan. Brown the bacon, place the browned bits on absorbent paper towels, discard the fat, and sprinkle the cooled bacon over the potatoes.

7. In a separate mixing bowl, combine mayonnaise, sugar, red onion, cucumbers, and broccoli. Blend well with cream or buttermilk.

8. Add the dressing to the potatoes, and gently incorporate.

9. Chill and serve. Drain excess dressing, if necessary.

Garbanzo Bean Salad

INGREDIENTS

	U.S. Standard	Metric
Olive oil	1/4 c.	60 ml
White vinegar	2 Tbsp.	30 ml
Fresh chives, *chopped*	2 Tbsp.	30 ml
Salt and pepper	TT	TT
Roasted red pepper/garlic seasoning	1 tsp.	5 ml
Garbanzo beans, *drained and washed*	1 can (28 oz.)	840 g
Snow peas, *blanched, cut julienne*	1 c.	225 g
Red peppers, *seeds removed and diced*	1/4 c.	50 g
Yellow peppers, *seeds removed and diced*	1/4 c.	50 g
Orange peppers, *seeds removed and diced*	1/4 c.	50 g
Red onions, *peeled and diced*	1/4 c.	50 g
Plum tomatoes, *seeds removed and diced*	3 each	3 each

METHOD OF PREPARATION

1. Gather all the ingredients and equipment.
2. Combine oil, vinegar, and seasonings in a stainless steel bowl.
3. Add vegetables, and blend well.
4. Adjust seasoning, and serve.

Mayonnaise

INGREDIENTS

	U.S. Standard	Metric
Egg yolks, *pasteurized*	12 oz.	360 ml
Dijon mustard	4 oz.	120 ml
Salt	TT	TT
Sugar	4 oz.	115 g
White vinegar	3 oz.	90 ml
Vegetable oil	3 qt.	2.9 l
Lemon juice	4 oz.	120 ml

METHOD OF PREPARATION

1. Gather all the ingredients and equipment.

2. In a mixing bowl, combine the egg yolks, mustard, salt, sugar, and vinegar.

3. Whip the mixture to combine, then slowly add the oil in a thin, steady stream. Continue to whip, allowing air to be incorporated, and add the lemon juice.

4. Adjust the seasoning as needed.

5. Label, date, and refrigerate.

NUTRITION

Nutrition Facts

Yield: 1 gallon (3.8 l)
Serving Size: 1 Tbsp. (15 ml)

Amount Per Serving

Calories 100

Total Fat 11 g

Sodium 40 mg

Total Carbohydrate 1 g

Protein 0 g

Horseradish Sour Cream Sauce

INGREDIENTS

	U.S. Standard	Metric
Mayonnaise	1 c.	225 g
Sour cream	1 c.	225 g
Horseradish	1/2 c.	115 g
Onion powder	1 Tbsp.	15 ml
Parsley, *washed, finely chopped, squeezed dry*	2 Tbsp.	30 ml
Tabasco® sauce	1 tsp.	5 ml
Salt and pepper	as needed	as needed
Heavy cream	2 Tbsp.	30 ml

METHOD OF PREPARATION

1. Gather all the ingredients and equipment.

2. Blend all ingredients in a stainless steel bowl.

3. Check seasoning.

4. Serve in a sauceboat.

NUTRITION

Nutrition Facts

Yield: Serves 10
Serving Size: 1 oz. (60 ml)

Amount Per Serving

Calories 120

Total Fat 11 g

Sodium 170 mg

Total Carbohydrate 7 g

Protein 1 g

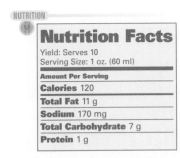

Garde-Manger

Pasta and Grains

The history of grains is really the story of human civilization. Hunters supplemented their meat-based diets with wild grains. Soon, they learned to cultivate these plants. By about 10,000 B.C., people near the Mediterranean Sea were farming barley and wheat. Other civilizations rose with the cultivation of other grains—millet and rice in India and China, and maize (corn) in the Americas. Today, grains are used in a variety of ways, as entrées, or in side dishes.

Pasta came much later. The Chinese noodle dates back to the first century A.D. The origination of Italian pasta is less certain. In fact, the term pasta was not commonly used until after World War II. It was referred to as dough or noodles. Some insist that pasta-making tools depicted on a fourth-century B.C. Etruscan artwork prove that pasta was consumed on the Italian peninsula prior to contact with China. Others claim that Marco Polo introduced pasta to Italy after he returned from China in 1298, telling stories of Chinese noodles.

10,000 B.C.
People in Jericho plant barley and wheat.

7500 B.C.
The Japanese grow buckwheat and barley.

3000 B.C.
People in China and India grow millet and rice.

A.D. 100
Europeans cultivate oats.

1520
Rice reaches the Americas.

1943
Converted rice is developed.

Pasta in the Italian Tradition

Pasta was a staple food in Italy for centuries before its popularity spread to other parts of Europe. In 1533 Catherine de' Medici left Italy to marry the future king of France. She took her cooks with her and, at her wedding banquet, introduced pasta to the rest of Europe.

Thomas Jefferson is credited with introducing pasta in the United States after he developed a taste for it while living in Paris in the late 1700s. However, not until thousands of Italians moved to the United States in the late nineteenth century did pasta become popular here. Now establishments from family-style eateries to those specializing in elaborate continental cuisine offer pasta in one form or another.

Pasta

Italian-style pasta is made from an unleavened dough composed of wheat flour and liquid. The liquid is primarily water, egg, or a mixture of the two. Pasta is made in one of two basic methods. Cut pasta is made from dough that has been rolled, flattened, and then cut. A second type of pasta is *extruded,* a process whereby the dough is forced through a pierced disk or plate, like that of a meat grinder. The shape of the hole through which the dough passes determines whether the pasta will be curved, straight, ribbed, and so on.

Pasta comes in either fresh or dried forms and can be made in a commercial kitchen. Both fresh and dried pastas are available in a variety of flavors. Green pasta is a basic wheat pasta to which spinach has been added for flavor and color. Red pasta may contain tomato or red pepper. Black pasta may have squid or cuttlefish ink added to it. Other pasta flavors include herb and spice mixtures as well as beet and pumpkin.

Pasta Flours

The best-quality dried pastas are made from high-protein *semolina flour* that is coarsely ground from hard durum wheat. Semolina has a high gluten content, which produces a smooth dough with a creamy yellow color. Lesser-quality pastas may be made from softer flours.

A dough made entirely from semolina produces a pasta that is quite firm when cooked. The dough also requires a great deal of kneading. When making fresh pasta, substitute unbleached all-purpose flour, bread flour, or a mixture of all-purpose flour and hard durum wheat for semolina. Each of these choices will create a dough that is easier to work with than that made with only

FIGURE 26-1

Italian-Style Pastas

ACINI DE PEPE

Description
Means "peppercorns" in Italian; tiny, pellet-shaped pasta

Uses
In light soups, broths, and cold salads

CAPELLI D'ANGELO

Description
Also called angel hair; the finest strand pasta

Uses
In sauces; with seafood, tomatoes, or garlic; or broken in soups

CHITARRA

Description
Named after the guitar strings traditionally used to cut the pasta; rods, similar to spaghetti but square instead of round

Uses
In tomato-based sauces or with other medium-bodied sauces

CONCHIGLIE

Description
Means "conch shell" in Italian; shaped like shells; the smallest pasta shells are called conchigliette; the largest, which can be stuffed, are called conchiglioni

Uses
In salads or with meat or seafood sauces; filled with cheese, seafood, or meat and then baked; in soups

DITALINI

Description
Means "thimble" in Italian; tiny tubes; a slightly larger version is called ditali

Uses
In vegetable soups, broth or hearty soups, such as minestrone

FARFALLE

Description

Means "butterfly" in Italian; made from flat, wide noodles squeezed in the center to resemble bow-ties or butterflies; also called bow-tie pasta or butterfly pasta

Uses

In pasta salad, with chunky meat or vegetable sauces or baked with artichokes or seafood

FETTUCCINI

Description

Means "little ribbons" in Italian; a ribbon pasta made with or without eggs; flat and long

Uses

With rich cream sauces, such as Alfredo, or other smooth sauces

LINGUINE

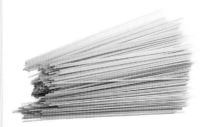

Description

Means "little tongues" in Italian; a ribbon pasta; similar to fettuccini, but narrower

Uses

With clam or marinara sauce and with seafood

ORZO

Description

Means "barley" in Italian; small rice-shaped pasta

Uses

In pilaf, salads, and soups

PAPPARDELLE

Description

Means "gulp down" in Italian; wide, flat ribbons, about 1 inch in width (3 cm by 6 cm)

Uses

With meats, ragùs, or fish; baked with hearty sauces

PENNE

Description	Uses
Means "pens" in Italian; hollow tubes, cut on the diagonal like a pen nib	*With hearty sauces; baked in a casserole with meat, cheese, and sauce*

RIGATONI

Description	Uses
Medium-width tube with ridges	*Baked with chunky tomato or meat sauces*

SPAGHETTI

Description	Uses
Means "little strings" in Italian; long thin strands; a thinner version is called spaghettini	*Served with thin meat or tomato sauce, oil, butter, or other thin sauces*

TAGLIATELLE

Description	Uses
Ribbon pasta similar to fettuccini, but slightly wider and thinner	*Added to meat sauce, or served with clams or shrimp*

---

semolina. Most doughs made without semolina are softer and result in a pasta that remains tender when cooked. Pastas intended to be stuffed are nearly always made without semolina because the pasta needs to be moist enough to shape and seal easily when stuffing. It is imperative that the pasta not be too dry.

Pasta Shapes and Sizes

Pastas come in long, thin rods, strips, or ribbons of various widths; hollow tubes; and fanciful shapes. See Figure 26-1 on pages 540–542. Some pastas stand up to thick, chunky ragùs, but others are best with lighter sauces. Traditionally, spaghetti can hold a smooth tomato sauce, but a heavier or chunky sauce needs a sturdier pasta, such as thick-walled pasta tubes called macaroni. Thicker pastas also hold up well in salads and baked dishes. Large tubes and shells can be filled easily. Shaped pastas and pasta with ridges trap sauce more effectively than smooth-surface pastas and pasta rods. Fresh pasta and egg pastas pair well with cream or butter sauces.

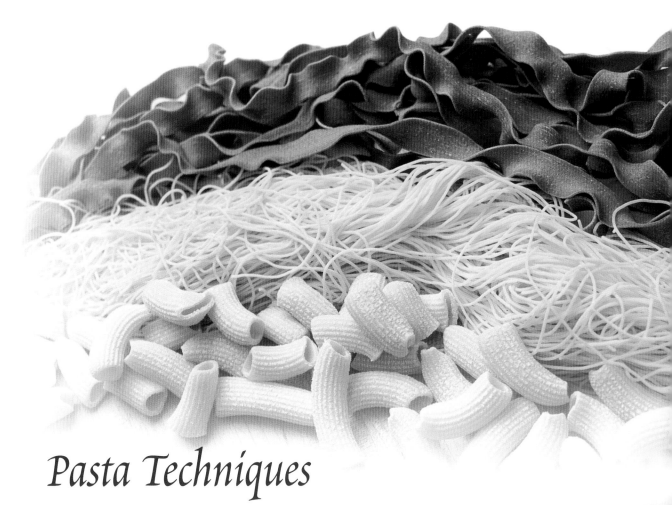

Pasta Techniques

Making pasta is a relatively simple procedure that begins with dough. Pasta can be made either by hand—kneading the dough, stretching it, rolling it with a rolling pin, and cutting it with a French knife—or with the aid of a pasta machine. Pasta machines make the work less time-consuming and are available in electric or manual models.

Commercial kitchens that use electric pasta machines often opt for an extrusion machine that kneads the dough and then extrudes it through a disk that shapes the dough. Foodservice operations that use this type of pasta machine most likely produce large volumes of pasta. Many establishments use a manual, hand-cranked model instead. This type of pasta machine has one set of rollers that kneads the dough and presses it into a thin sheet and another set that cuts the dough into varying pasta shapes.

Drying Pasta

Fresh pasta can be laid flat or curled into nests on parchment-lined trays, covered, and stored in the refrigerator for a day or two. For longer storage, place the trays in a dry place, and allow the pasta to harden and dry thoroughly. Then wrap and store the pasta in a cool, dry place.

Egg pasta, when dried at room temperature, is considered safe because the water is diminished to the point that bacteria cannot reproduce. It can be left out after drying. Fresh egg pasta does not have to be dried prior to use, but it cannot be left out as dried egg pasta can.

Making Fresh Pasta

When making fresh pasta, you can mix pasta dough in a food processor, with an electric mixer, or by hand. When mixing dough by hand, traditionalists prefer to work on a flat surface, such as a wooden board.

To mix the dough the traditional way:

1 Measure the flour. If using more than one type of flour, mix them together.

2 Mound the flour on a flat work surface. Using your hand, scoop out a "well" in the center of the flour.

3 Break the eggs into a cup. Slide the eggs from the cup into the well. Add salt or olive oil if desired.

4 Use a fork to lightly mix the eggs, and then begin incorporating flour from the sides of the well into the egg mixture. Use your hand to support the outside wall of the mound so that the eggs do not spill down the side while mixing.

5 Continue pulling flour into the egg until the mixture becomes too thick to work with a fork.

6 Use your hands to incorporate the remaining flour.

7 When most of the liquid is absorbed and the dough forms a homogenous mass, begin the kneading process. If the dough is too moist, work in small amounts of flour.

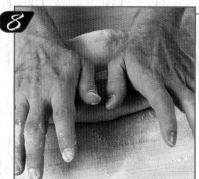

8 Use the palms of your hands to knead the dough until it becomes satiny.

9 When done, cover or wrap the dough, and allow it to rest for at least thirty minutes.

Rolling and Cutting Fresh Pasta

Fresh pasta can be rolled and cut by hand or with a machine. When working by hand, it is important to roll the dough from the center outward to stretch the dough. Roll the dough to the desired thickness, let it dry for a short period, and then cut the dough to the desired width. Using a machine to roll and cut the dough is more practical in the commercial kitchen.

To roll and cut pasta with a hand-cranked pasta roller, follow these steps:

1 Cut the prepared dough into pieces that are sized appropriately for the pasta roller. To prevent dough from drying out, cover the pieces not being rolled.

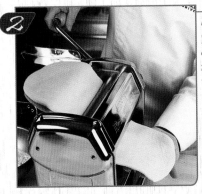

2 Use the heel of your hand, fingers, or a rolling pin to flatten a piece of the dough. Set the rollers to the highest setting, and then use one hand to feed the dough between the rollers while cranking the pasta roller with the other hand.

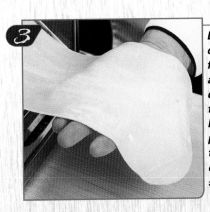

3 Lightly dust the dough with flour, fold it in thirds, and feed the dough through the rollers again. Repeat the process several times until the dough feels very smooth.

4 Tighten the rollers a notch to create a thinner dough. Feed the dough through the rollers, and repeat, this time without folding the dough.

5 Adjust the rollers to achieve another level of thinness each time the dough passes through until the desired thickness is achieved.

6 Select the cutting blade attachment appropriate to the type of pasta being made, and pass the dough through the blades.

7 Hang the pasta to dry, or place on parchment-lined sheet pans dusted lightly with semolina or flour.

Making Ravioli

Ravioli is a classic Italian dish, typically stuffed with either cheese or meat, but it may also include vegetables, seafood, and herbs.

To make ravioli, follow these steps:

1
Place a thin sheet of pasta on a flat work surface. Using a spoon, pastry bag, or small scoop, drop small portions of filling spaced evenly apart on the pasta sheet. Use only half the pasta sheet if you plan to fold the other half over to form the top section.

2
Brush lightly with egg wash or water between the fillings. As an alternative, the entire sheet of pasta can be brushed prior to depositing the filling.

3 If the filling was deposited on half the sheet, fold the other half of the pasta sheet over the half with the filling. If using two sheets of pasta, cover the filling with another sheet of pasta.

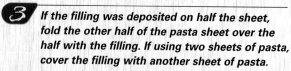

4
Using your fingertips, a dowel, or a wooden kitchen spoon, press around each mound of filling to seal the layers and remove air bubbles.

5
Use a ravioli cutter, a pastry wheel, or a French knife to cut the ravioli.

Other Dishes Made from Fresh Dough

A variety of dishes can be prepared using fresh dough. Ravioli, gnocchi, and spätzle are three classic preparations. Gnocchi and spätzle are not, strictly speaking, pasta. However, they are prepared and served in much the same way as some Italian-style pastas.

Ravioli *Ravioli* is a stuffed pasta made from small square or circular envelopes of egg and flour dough. Cheese and meat are traditional fillings, but ravioli can be stuffed with a variety of ingredients, including lobster, mushrooms, herbs, and vegetables.

Gnocchi *Gnocchi* are little Italian dumplings often made from a mixture of potatoes and wheat flour. The potato must have sufficient starch to bind the flour and keep the gnocchi light in texture. A little ricotta cheese is sometimes added. The addition of eggs makes the dough a little easier to handle, but too much egg makes the gnocchi tough and heavy. A different style of gnocchi can be made using a base of semolina or cornmeal instead of potatoes.

Spätzle *Spätzle* are tiny dumplings from the Alsace region of France and southern Germany. Spätzle are made from a thick batter of wheat flour, eggs, and a liquid, such as milk, cream, or water. They can be served as a side dish, boiled and then finished in a sauté pan with butter.

PROCESS

Making Gnocchi

Gnocchi are little Italian dumplings that are usually served with butter or a tomato-based sauce.

To make gnocchi, follow these steps:

1 Cook peeled potatoes in lightly salted water until soft. When done, drain the potatoes, and place them in a moderately hot oven until the potatoes dry.

2 Force the potatoes through a ricer or food mill.

3

Add flour, and begin to mix thoroughly.

4

Eggs may be added if desired.

5

Continue to mix until completely blended.

6

Remove the dough from the bowl to a flat work surface, and knead very gently until a smooth ball of dough forms. Do not overwork the dough.

7

Cut off a few small pieces of dough, and roll each piece into a long, finger-thick rope. Cut the ropes of dough into pieces, each about 1 inch (25 mm) wide. The back of a fork can be used to make grooves in each piece.

8

Simmer the gnocchi in salted water until they rise to the surface, about two to three minutes. Remove them with a slotted spoon.

Making Spätzle

Spätzle are made with wheat flour, eggs, and a liquid—either milk, cream, or water.

To prepare spätzle, follow these steps:

1 Follow the recipe for the batter as presented on page 563.

2 Let the batter rest for at least ten minutes.

3  Over a pot of boiling salted water, force the batter through a spätzle maker or colander with large holes, dropping the batter carefully into the pot.

4  Cook the spätzle until they float to the top of the water; this should happen in a matter of minutes. Simmer them for another one to two minutes before removing them with a skimmer.

5 For later service, rinse the spätzle in cold water, and drain well. Cover, and refrigerate until ready to use.

6  Just before serving, lightly sauté the spätzle in butter until hot.

Handling and Storing Pasta

Requirements for handling and storing pasta vary, depending on whether the pasta is dry or fresh. Most commercially prepared pasta is dried; however, some types are available fresh or frozen.

Purchasing Pasta

Pasta is purchased by weight in 1-, 5-, 10-, and 20-pound (454-, 2,268-, 4,536-, 9,072-gram) units. Dried pasta is packed in bags or boxes in flat, tube, or shaped forms. Fresh tubes and shapes do not hold their shape well. For this reason, most commercially available fresh pasta is flat. Linguine, fettuccine, and angel hair pasta are widely available fresh, frozen, or dried. Some stuffed pastas, such as ravioli and tortellini, are also available fresh, frozen, or dried. Flavored pastas come fresh, frozen, or dried.

Receiving Pasta

Dry pasta should be received dry and in good condition. Check packaging for leaks, tears, or signs of water damage or insect infestation. Fresh pasta should be at proper temperatures for refrigerated or frozen products. Make sure that frozen pasta is free from ice crystals.

Storing Pasta

Dry pasta should be stored in a cool, dry place. Dry pasta can be safely held for several months at temperatures from 50°F–70°F (10°C–21°C). Keep fresh pasta tightly wrapped and refrigerated. Use fresh pasta within a few days of the time it is made or received. Well-wrapped frozen pasta will keep for a few weeks in the freezer.

Quality Characteristics of Pasta

The best-quality dried pasta is made entirely from semolina flour. It is yellow, not white or gray. Dry pasta should be brittle, and when snapped, the break should be clean and sharp. Cooked pasta should hold its shape and retain some of its firmness. Inferior pasta is gummy or soft when cooked. To be labeled egg pasta, the pasta must contain at least 5.5% egg solids. Egg pastas are usually sold as flat noodles.

Foodborne illness associated with pastas can come from fresh pasta, stuffed pasta, and baked pasta dishes that have not been properly handled or refrigerated. Cook fresh pasta promptly, or hold it in the refrigerator or freezer. Quickly cool, drain, and then refrigerate unused cooked pasta and baked pasta.

Cooking Pasta

Part of pasta's appeal is its rapid cooking time and the simplicity of the actual cooking process. For these reasons, become familiar with the recipe, and complete mise en place prior to cooking. Pasta can be cooked in boiling salted water or broth. Sometimes pasta will be boiled for a short period and then finished in the oven with other ingredients.

Cooking Fresh and Dry Pasta

Fresh and dry pasta require different cooking times. Fresh pasta cooks more quickly than dry pasta does because of its higher moisture content. Fresh pasta cooks in only one to two minutes after the water returns to a boil.

Boiling

Pasta is usually cooked to order, using a tall-sided pot. Cooked fresh pasta is tender and fragile, so serve it as soon as it is done cooking. Cook, cool, and then reheat dry pasta by placing it in boiling salted water just long enough to heat it through. However, it is best to serve dry pasta immediately after it is cooked.

To boil pasta:

1. Use at least 1 gallon (3.75 liters) of water for every pound of pasta (4 liters per 450 grams). Add 1 ounce (30 grams) of salt to the water.
2. Bring the water to a rolling boil. Drop the pasta into the water.
3. Push the pasta down into the water, and stir at once. Bring the water back to a full boil.
4. Stir occasionally as the pasta continues to cook. The combination of rapid convection, the high ratio of water to pasta, and the stirring motion will keep the pasta from sticking together.
5. As soon as the pasta is firm, drain it into a colander. For immediate service, remove the pasta from the colander, and finish the dish. For later service, rinse the pasta in the colander with cold, running water until it is cool. Toss it with a small amount of oil to keep the cooled pasta from sticking, and store it, covered, in the refrigerator.

Baking

Probably the best-known baked pasta dish is lasagna, in which wide flat noodles are boiled and then layered in a casserole with other ingredients, such as cheese, meat, spinach or other vegetables, and sauce. Manicotti and cannelloni are other popular stuffed pasta dishes. Most of the time, pasta is partially cooked before it is layered or stuffed. When the dish is assembled, it is finished by baking it in the oven.

Determining Doneness

Italian-style pastas are cooked ***al dente,*** which means "to the bite." The pasta should be slightly firm when bitten. Pasta cooked beyond *al dente* quickly becomes sticky and unappetizing.

Cooking times vary depending on the shape and thickness of the pasta, the type of flour used, altitude, and whether the pasta is fresh or dry. The best way to determine doneness is to taste the pasta. Properly cooked pasta should be tender but firm, with a uniform color on the exterior surface. It should not taste raw or doughy. Alternately, a fork can be used to cut through a piece of pasta to test for doneness. When the pasta cuts easily, it is done. Begin testing well before you think it is fully cooked. Remove it from the heat, and drain immediately when the pasta is just a little too firm. Residual heat will continue to cook the pasta.

Serving Pasta

Plate and immediately serve pasta that is cooked to order. Do not rinse pasta unless chilling it for later service. Have the sauce or other garnish ready to add as soon as the pasta is done. Pasta loses heat rapidly; heating the serving bowls or plates will help maintain proper temperature.

When pasta is served as part of a buffet, choose a sturdy pasta that will retain its shape and texture. Baked pasta dishes work well for both buffet and banquet service.

Sauces for Pasta

There are many ways to finish pasta; sauce is one of the most common. Pasta sauces can be categorized into six basic types: ragù, cream, vegetable, olive oil-based, seafood, and uncooked.

Ragù

Originally, *ragù* referred to a cubed meat sauce without tomatoes that was developed in Bologna for lasagna and other pasta dishes. Today ragù refers to any meat- or poultry-based sauce prepared by stewing or braising. Common ingredients include minced beef, poultry, bacon, or other meat; mushrooms, leeks, or onions; and a liquid, such as stock or wine, water, milk, or cream. Tomatoes now are frequently added to ragùs; the meat stays in the sauce.

Cream Sauces

Cream sauces for pasta are rich white sauces based on cream or thickened milk. Cream sauces stick to smooth pasta, such as fettuccini, better than other types of pasta sauces do. To add another layer of flavor and richness to a cream sauce, add cheese or another flavoring ingredient.

Vegetable Sauces

The most common vegetable sauce for pasta is based on the tomato. However, other vegetables can be used as the base, including finely chopped mirepoix and garlic. Flavorings and olive oil can also be added. The sauce is cooked, tossed with pasta, and served.

Olive Oil-Based Sauces

Olive oil-based sauces are the simplest of pasta sauces to make—flavoring ingredients, such as garlic and herbs, are added to olive oil. Unlike other pasta sauces, many olive oil-based sauces are appropriate for either warm or cold pasta. The sauce itself may be cooked or uncooked.

Seafood Sauces

Seafood sauces are made from either shellfish or fish and are categorized as either red or white. Red seafood sauces contain tomatoes. White seafood sauces are based on stock, wine, or sometimes cream.

When using shellfish such as mussels as the base, steam them with water or white wine, and then combine the cooking liquid with olive oil or cream. Toss with pasta, and serve. To make a seafood sauce using crustaceans, sauté the food item, season, and toss with pasta. Serve immediately. Other seafood choices for this type of sauce include squid, octopus, and clams.

Uncooked Pasta Sauces

Many uncooked pasta sauces overlap with olive oil-based sauces. Vegetables, herbs, capers, olives, and cheese are common ingredients in uncooked pasta sauces. One way to use uncooked sauces is by tossing pasta with olive oil, basil, and fresh diced tomatoes.

Fettucine Alfredo

One of the most famous and luxurious of all the cream sauce pasta preparations is fettuccine Alfredo, which combines fettuccine with butter, cream, and fresh Parmesan. In 1914 Roman chef Alfredo Di Lelio created the dish for his pregnant wife. The dish proved so successful that Di Lelio soon began preparing it tableside for service in his restaurant. Then in 1927 two of Hollywood's biggest stars, Douglas Fairbanks and Mary Pickford, discovered the dish while on their honeymoon in Rome. Legend has it that the two stars ate the dish every night for a week and then presented Alfredo with a golden fork and spoon, which he used to toss the pasta on their final night at his restaurant. Fairbanks and Pickford took tales of the dish back to California with them, where it became a popular restaurant specialty.

Asian Noodles

Like Italian-style pastas, Asian pastas are quite varied in taste, texture, and uses. However, Asian pastas do not have the range of shapes and sizes of Italian-style pastas. Their taste and textural differences come from the various flours or starches used in the dough. The most well-known Asian pastas are made from wheat, rice, and buckwheat flours. However, other important varieties are made from vegetable starches derived from sweet potatoes, mung beans, potatoes, and corn.

The choice of flour and style of noodle varies from country to country. Chinese noodles are made from wheat, rice, or mung beans. The Japanese use almost no rice noodles, preferring wheat or buckwheat noodles instead. Thai and Vietnamese cuisines rely most heavily on rice noodles, and Korean cuisine uses buckwheat, sweet potato, rice, and wheat noodles. See Figure 26-2.

Cooking Asian Noodles

Cooking methods for Asian noodles vary depending on the type of noodle being prepared. Many require a brief soak in hot water prior to boiling or stir-frying. This removes excess starch and prevents sticking. Other noodles are soaked in cold water before being used in stir-fries or other dishes. Do not presoak noodles that are deep-fried, such as mung bean threads, thin rice noodles, or rice vermicelli.

FIGURE 26-2

Asian Noodles

HOKKIEN

Description
Egg and wheat noodle popular in Malaysia and Singapore; resembles thick yellow spaghetti; available fresh or dried

Uses
Soups, stir-fried with meat and vegetables, or with a sauce

MIAN

Description
Also spelled mein; Chinese wheat noodles, cut in ribbons of various widths, including vermicelli; can be made with or without eggs; available fresh or dried

Uses
Soups, stir-fried with meat and vegetables, or with a sauce; deep-fried

MUNG BEAN THREADS

Description
Also called cellophane noodles or bean threads; very thin, gelatinous noodles popular in Chinese and Southeast Asian cuisine; made from mung beans; have little flavor of their own

Uses
Soups, stir-fries, salads, and fried as a garnish or as a base for sauce

RAMEN

Description
Deep-fried noodles sold dried in packages with seasonings and dehydrated vegetables; also available in fresh and frozen varieties

Uses
A thick soup or in salad

RICE NOODLES, FLAT

Description
Also known as rice sticks; known by various names, depending on the country; especially popular in Southeast Asia; made with rice flour, cut into various widths

Uses
Soups, stir-fries, or in the Thai noodle specialty, Phad Thai

RICE NOODLES, THIN

Description
Also called thin rice sticks; known by various names, depending on the country; made with rice flour, cut very thin

Uses
Soups, deep-fried as a garnish, or as a bed for sauces

SOBA

Description
Chewy Japanese buckwheat or buckwheat and wheat noodles; light brown strands of various widths; available fresh or dried

Uses
Cold salad, soups, or with sauce

SOMEN

Description
A thin, white Japanese wheat noodle, lightly coated with oil before being cut into strands; varieties flavored with green tea are green; those with egg are yellowish

Uses
Served cold, in soups, and in stir-fries

UDON

Description
Thick Japanese wheat flour noodles with a soft but chewy texture; available fresh or dried

Uses
Stir-fries, soups, or stews

Grains

Grains are the seeds of edible grasses: a nutritional staple that, for much of the world, provides the largest share of calories and nutrients people eat each day. Grains supply carbohydrates, protein, vitamins, and minerals. They are a source of antioxidants, a class of nutrients that helps protect the body from substances that attack healthy cells. In addition, grains supply dietary fiber, which is thought to reduce the risk of some forms of cancer. Wheat, corn, and rice are three of the most commonly eaten grains. Others include oats, barley, rye, and buckwheat.

Whole grains are seed kernels that have not been *milled*, or ground. They contain an outer *hull*, or husk that protects the kernel and contains the *bran*, the outer covering; the *endosperm*, the main part of the seed from which flour or meal is made; and the *germ*, which is actually the embryo that produces the new plant. The germ is the only part of the seed that contains fat. During milling, the germ, endosperm, and bran can be separated.

Milling breaks down grain into finer and finer particles. Most milling is performed by crushing the seeds between a series of metal rollers. Stone grinding, in which the kernels are ground with a stone mill rather than a metal one, is a more precise and expensive method of milling grain. Either grinding technique can produce cracked grains, such as cracked wheat, which has been broken or cracked open; meals, such as cornmeal, grits, and cream of rice; and flour, the most finely milled product.

■ See Chapter 29: Fundamentals of Baking and Pastry for more information on types of flour.

Receiving and Storing Grains

Grains are sold by weight. Storage requirements vary by type of grain. Most grains are stored at room temperature in tightly sealed containers. Some grains, such as rice, store best when protected from light.

In general, the less processed the grain, the higher the oil content and the shorter the shelf life. Off odors indicate that the natural oils in whole and lightly processed grains have become rancid. Discard any grains that do not smell fresh. After grains are cooked, serve them promptly, or keep them under refrigeration. The greatest risk of foodborne illness comes from *bacillus cereus*, a bacterium that can develop in cooked rice that has been held for too long without refrigeration.

Rice

Today rice grows in a variety of habitats, from the mountain climate of the Himalayas in Nepal to the deserts of Egypt. About 11% of the world's tillable land is devoted to rice cultivation. Rice is a staple in the diet of more than half the world's population. Within the United States, rice consumption has more than doubled since 1972 because of the growing ethnic diversity of the country and because of interest in incorporating more grains into the diet.

Types and Characteristics of Rice

Grains of rice are actually the seeds of a grassy aquatic plant. Most of the rice that people eat is in the form of the whole grain. Rice is also ground into flour, starch, flakes, and meal. Rice noodles, for instance, are made from rice flour. Rice is categorized into three basic grain types: short-grain, medium-grain, and long-grain.

Short-grain *Short-grain rice* has small, roundish grains. It has the highest starch level of the three major types, causing it to become sticky and tender when cooked. The Japanese traditionally prefer short-grain rice for sushi and for eating plain. Short-grain rice such as arborio, vialone nano, carnaroli, valencia, and kokuko are used in risotto, sushi, and the Spanish rice dish *paella*.

Medium-grain *Medium-grain rice* has slightly longer grains than short-grain rice. As it cools, it becomes sticky. Medium-grain rice should be eaten as is as soon as it is prepared or used in rice puddings or rice molds.

Long-grain *Long-grain rice* is the most universally popular rice. Long-grain rice is firm and fluffy when cooked, and the grains separate easily. It is versatile and can be used in most rice preparations. Carolina and basmati are examples of long-grained rice.

Processed Rice

All three types of rice grain can be processed to remove the hull, polish the rice, or otherwise change its characteristics.

Brown rice *Brown rice* owes its color to the bran layer left on the kernels. Bran is an important source of fiber and vitamin B, making brown rice nutritionally superior to white rice. However, use of brown rice is limited because it has a nuttier taste and a firmer "bite" than white rice; it also takes about twice as long to cook.

White rice *White rice,* sometimes called polished rice, has had the husk, bran, and germ removed, creating a softer, lighter rice that cooks more quickly and with less water. *Enriched rice* is white rice that has vitamins and minerals added to make up for some of those lost with the removal of the bran.

Converted rice *Converted rice* has been soaked, pressure-steamed, dried, and then milled to remove the bran. This process removes some of the surface starch, creating rice grains that stay fluffy and

FIGURE 26-3

Specialty Rices

ARBORIO

Characteristics

Short-grained white rice that is creamy when cooked; white color and mild flavor

Uses

An excellent rice for risotto-style preparation

BASMATI

Characteristics

From India; slender, very long grains with a creamy color and a slightly sweet flavor and aroma

Uses

Indian cuisine; with curry or in side dishes, including pilaf

VALENCIA

Characteristics

Short-grained rice with a high starch content and exceptional ability to absorb liquids

Uses

Classic rice for paella

JASMINE

Characteristics

From Thailand and Vietnam; an aromatic long-grained rice, similar to Basmati; some-times called perfumed rice or fragrant rice

Uses

Thai and Vietnamese cuisines; as a side dish

RED RICE

Characteristics

Any of a variety of rices with red hulls; the best red rice is a long-grained aromatic rice with an earthy flavor

Uses

With meat and bean dishes known as Wehani

SUSHI RICE

Characteristics

Any of a variety of short-grained, sticky rices suitable for use in sushi; sushi rice can also refer to the vinegared-cooked rice that is shaped into sushi

Uses

For sushi and Japanese-style boiled rice

WILD RICE

Characteristics

Not a "true" rice, as it comes from an unrelated aquatic grass; very slender, long grains with brown to black hulls; nutty and chewy

Uses

Combined with white rice and served as a side dish; with game or as stuffing for poultry

Pasta and Grains

555

separated, even when served from a steam table. Converted rice has a beige cast, not the pure white of regular white rice. The hull is retained during the initial processing, therefore more nutrients remain in the kernel. This rice is sometimes referred to as parboiled, but it actually requires a longer cook time and a higher ratio of liquid to rice than regular white rice.

Instant rice Instant rice has been partially or fully cooked and then dehydrated and packaged. Although it saves time, the product offers inferior texture and flavor, becoming soft soon after cooking.

Specialty Rices

In addition to white and brown rice, a variety of other rices are used in commercial kitchens, depending on the dish. See Figure 26-3 on page 555 for information about some of the most widely used specialty rices.

Corn

Corn is eaten both fresh as a vegetable and dried as a grain. As a dried grain, it comes in two main forms: cornmeal and hominy.

Cornmeal

Cornmeal can be white, yellow, or blue, depending on the type of corn from which the meal is ground, and can be used to make baked goods and polenta.

Polenta *Polenta* is a kind of porridge that becomes solid when cold. Polenta is sometimes served just after cooking while still soft, but it is more often allowed to cool and harden. It can then be fried, grilled, or baked and served as a side dish, an appetizer, or a main course. It is often topped with cheese, tomato, or other sauces.

Hominy

Hominy is the dried corn kernel with the hull and germ removed. Hominy is made by soaking dried corn in lye until the kernel swells and the outer layers loosen for easily removal. It can be served as a side dish or added to soups. Grits and masa harina are made from hominy.

Grits *Grits,* also called hominy grits, are made from hominy that has been coarsely ground into meal. Cook grits in water, and serve them as a cereal or side dish.

Masa harina *Masa harina* is flour made from finely ground hominy. It is used to make corn tortillas and some breads.

Wheat

Wheat is best known as a flour for use in bread, pasta, and other baked goods. Wheat also comes in a variety of other forms.

Semolina Ground more coarsely than other wheat flours, semolina resembles meal. It is ground from durum wheat from which the bran and germ have been removed. Semolina can be used to make Italian-style pastas or cooked and served as a hot cereal or side dish.

Couscous *Couscous* is not a whole grain flour but a granular semolina flour, resembling small, creamy, yellow pellets or kernels. It is served topped with butter or cheese or mixed with other ingredients and served as a side dish. *Israeli couscous* is made from the same dough as regular couscous, but it is extruded like pasta and then toasted. When cooked, Israeli couscous expands to the size of small pearls.

Wheat berries *Wheat berries* are whole, unprocessed kernels of wheat. Wheat berries can be served as a hot cereal, used in pilaf, or added to bread.

Cracked wheat *Cracked wheat* is the wheat kernel that has been cracked open and broken into fragments. Use it in the same way as wheat berries in cereal and pilaf and as a crunchy, nutritious addition to bread.

Bulgur *Bulgur* is similar to cracked wheat in that it is made from crushed wheat kernels. However, bulgur is steamed and dried during processing. Bulgur has a chewy texture that is delicious in pilaf or in meat and vegetable dishes. Bulgur is the primary ingredient in the Middle Eastern salad tabbouleh.

SEMOLINA

COUSCOUS

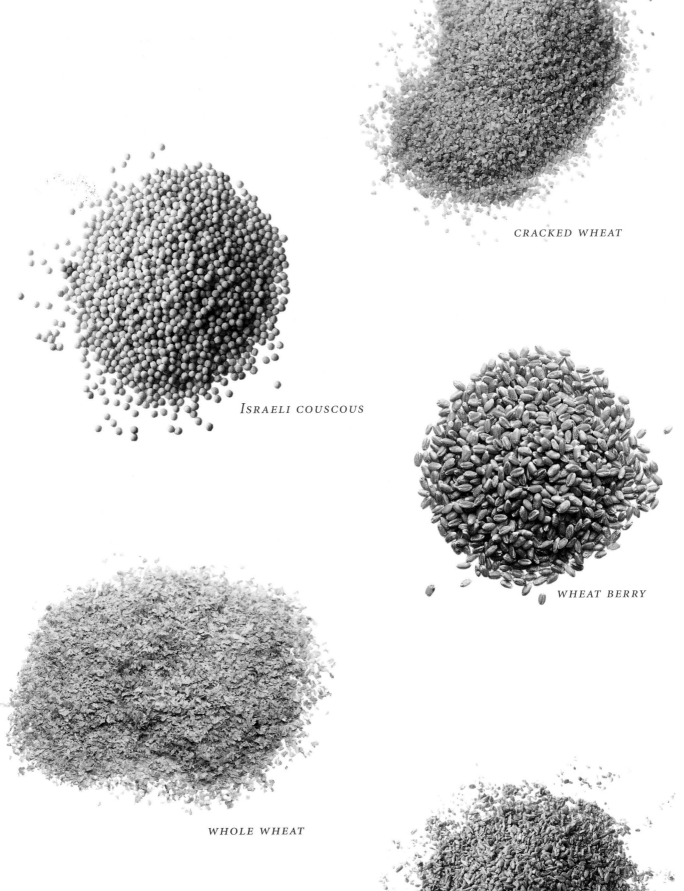

CRACKED WHEAT

ISRAELI COUSCOUS

WHEAT BERRY

WHOLE WHEAT

BULGUR

Other Grains

A variety of other grains add interest and texture to meals, including spelt, oats, kasha, and rye.

Spelt *Spelt* is an ancient variety of wheat whose small brown grains can be cooked like rice or ground into flour for use in baking. It has a mild, somewhat nutty flavor.

Oats Oats are the berries of oat grass, available as oatmeal, also called rolled oats; as a whole grain, called oat berries or oat groats; and as a toasted and cracked grain form known as steel-cut oats. All forms of oats can be used as cereal and in baked goods. Food items made from oats include muesli and porridge.

Kasha *Kasha* is hulled, roasted, and crushed buckwheat, also called buckwheat groats. Kasha has a strong, nutty flavor and is used in cold salads and as a side dish.

Rye Rye is a grain used primarily in the United States as rye flour. It is heavy and dark and is used in breads and to make rye whiskey.

Amaranth *Amaranth,* sometimes called Inca wheat, was the staple grain of the ancient Incas and Aztecs. Amaranth is available as a whole grain which can be used as a cereal or as flour for baking.

Millet *Millet* is another ancient grain eaten as a cooked cereal, in bread, or in place of rice. It is mostly used in countries such as China, Africa, India, and Nigeria. Millet is used in curries, stews, and stuffings.

Quinoa *Quinoa* is a small, bead-shaped grain with white or pink kernels. High in protein and commonly eaten in Columbia, Argentina, and Chile, quinoa is used in stews, soups, salads, bread, and tortillas. It can also be ground into flour for baked goods. Quinoa leaves can be enjoyed as a green vegetable.

Barley Barley is available as a whole grain with only the outer hull removed; as Scotch barley that has been husked and slightly ground; and as pearl barley, a polished form with the hull and bran removed. Barley has a chewy texture and a slightly sweet flavor. For a hearty consistency, add barley to soups and stews, or use it in stuffing and in pilaf side dishes.

SPELT

ROLLED OATS

KASHA

STEEL-CUT OATS

RYE

AMARANTH

MILLET

QUINOA

BARLEY

Cooking Rice and Other Grains

Cook grains with water to moisten them and make them tender. Depending on the grain, grains may be rinsed in cold water to remove debris and excess starch before the cooking process begins. Most grains are cooked until they become tender, but firmness or chewiness may be a desirable characteristic in some cooked grains. There are three basic methods to cook grains: boiling, steaming, and braising.

Boiling

Grains can be boiled, using much the same procedure as for cooking pasta. Add the grain to boiling salted water, simmer until the grain reaches the desired degree of tenderness, and then drain off the water. Serve boiled grains plain or with seasonings, or combine them with other ingredients for salads or casseroles.

Steaming

The most common approach to cooking grains is that of steaming. Combine the grain with boiling water or stock, stir, cover, and simmer until the grain absorbs the liquid. Because the ratio of liquid to grain varies by grain (see Figure 26-4), consult a recipe or package directions.

Grains can steam in a saucepan on the range, in the oven, or in a convection steamer. For steaming rice, a rice cooker is often used. The rice cooker controls the cooking time and prevents burning by automatically shutting off when the rice is done.

Braising

Braising involves sautéing the grain kernels in fat before adding a liquid. The initial sauté develops the flavor of the grain and helps keep the grains of long grain rice separated. There are two basic ways to cook grains through braising: the *pilaf method* and the *risotto method*.

The pilaf method In the *pilaf method,* sauté the grain in hot oil or butter with onions, shallots, or other aromatic vegetables and then add a hot liquid, such as stock or water. The pilaf method is most often used when cooking rice, but it works equally well with other grains such as barley and bulgur.

The risotto method The *risotto method* begins the same way as the pilaf method. However, instead of adding all the liquid at once, add it a little at a time, waiting for the grain to absorb it before adding more. Never allow the risotto to dry out completely. The risotto method requires constant stirring to create a firm but creamy dish. The cooking liquid can include wine, stock, or broth. Many different grains can be cooked with this method, but true risotto is made from Italian short-grain rice. It is best to let risotto rest a few minutes before serving, but the time it takes to deliver the dish to the customer is usually time enough to develop the proper texture and flavor of a good risotto.

Pressure Cooking

Some whole grains have tough outer hulls and require longer cook times to soften the grain and bring out its flavor. A pressure cooker can be used to cook these grains rapidly and evenly. In addition to saving time, pressure cookers minimize loss of nutrients and flavor.

Preparing Other Grains

Special techniques are used to make polenta. Polenta, also called cornmeal, can be served moist with butter and topped with grated cheese.

FIGURE 26-4

Liquid to Rice Ratios

COOKING RICE

Type of Rice	Liquid (by volume)	Rice
Arborio	3 to 3.5	1
Basmati	1.75	1
Brown, long grain	2.5	1
Converted	2	1
White, long grain	2	1
White, short grain	1 to 1.25	1
Wild	3	1

The ratio of liquid to rice varies by type of rice. The age and moisture content of the rice and the degree of moisture lost during cooking also affect the amount of liquid needed.

Using the Pilaf Method

Grains may be cooked using the pilaf method in hot oil or butter with the addition of onions, shallots, and aromatic vegetables.

To cook grains with the pilaf method:

1 Heat a small amount of oil or butter in a heavy pan. Sauté the aromatic vegetables until they are translucent.

2 Add the dry grain, stirring to coat each piece with oil. Sauté briefly without browning.

3 Add the hot stock or other liquid, and bring to a boil.

4 Lower the heat, and then cover and cook until the liquid is absorbed. The pot can also be transferred to an oven to finish cooking.

5 Remove the pilaf from the heat, and allow it to rest for five minutes to absorb any remaining liquid.

6 Use a braising fork to fluff and separate the grains.

Using the Risotto Method

When preparing grains using the risotto method, constant stirring is required to create a firm, creamy dish.

To use the risotto method:

1 Heat the oil or butter in a heavy pan. Add the onion or other aromatics, and sauté until translucent.

2 Add the dry grains, and stir to coat the grains in the fat. Sauté, but do not allow the grains to brown. Add wine if desired, and stir constantly until the liquid is almost absorbed. It is best not to use cold wine for this process.

3 Add a portion of hot stock, usually about 1/4 to 1/5 the total amount of liquid called for in the recipe.

4 Add additional ingredients according to the recipe, and repeat step 3, continuously adding stock in portions, waiting for the liquid to be absorbed before adding more.

5 When the rice is tender but still al dente, remove the rice from the heat.

6 Add butter, grated cheese, and other finishing ingredients according to the recipe.

Making Polenta

As an alternative to the method used below, cornmeal may be blended into cold liquid and heated to a simmer. Instant polenta cooks in about 5 minutes. A whisk helps blend the cornmeal with the water, but use a wooden spoon to stir the polenta once it starts to cook and thicken.

To make polenta, follow these steps:

1 Bring water to a boil in a heavy saucepan.

2 **Sprinkle the cornmeal over the water, stirring constantly to prevent lumps.**

3 Reduce the heat, and simmer for about forty-five minutes, stirring periodically, until the polenta pulls away easily from the sides of the pot.

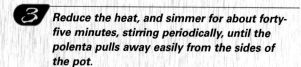

4 **Reduce heat, and add butter, grated cheese, and seasonings, along with other flavoring ingredients. Serve soft, or prepare the polenta to harden as follows.**

5 **Pour the polenta into a lightly greased sheet pan. Use a spatula to spread the polenta evenly.**

6 Refrigerate until chilled and firm.

7 **Using a mold or French knife, cut the polenta into shapes.**

8 **Finish the preparation by grilling, sautéing, deep-frying, or baking.**

Egg Spätzle

INGREDIENTS

Ingredients	U.S. Standard	Metric
Flour, all-purpose	1 lb.	454 g
Nutmeg, ground	small pinch	small pinch
Salt	1 tsp.	5 ml
Eggs	5 each	5 each
Milk	4 oz.	120 ml
Butter	3 oz.	85 g

METHOD OF PREPARATION

1. Gather all the ingredients and equipment.

2. In a 5-qt. mixer, combine the flour, nutmeg, and salt.

3. Beat the eggs in a small bowl, add the milk, and whisk to blend.

4. Using a paddle, with the machine running, add the egg mixture in a steady stream, and beat to make a smooth elastic batter. Mixture can be beaten with a wooden spoon or by hand if desired. Let the batter rest, covered, for about 15 minutes (to relax the gluten).

5. In the meantime, set a large pot of salted water on the stove top, and bring to a boil.

6. Press the batter through a large-holed colander or spätzle cutter, or cut off of a board into the boiling water. Cook uncovered, until spätzles rise to the top.

7. Use a *skimmer* or slotted spoon to transfer spätzle to a bowl of very cold water to stop the cooking process. Cook spätzle in batches, repeating process until all batter is used. Drain well, cover, and set aside until service.

8. Just before service, melt the butter in a large sauté pan, and sauté spätzle until heated through.

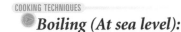

COOKING TECHNIQUES

Boiling (At sea level):
1. Bring the cooking liquid to a rapid boil.
2. Stir the contents, and cook the food product throughout.
3. Serve hot.

Sautéing:
1. Heat the sauté pan to the appropriate temperature.
2. Evenly brown the food product.
3. For a sauce, pour off any excess oil, reheat, and deglaze.

GLOSSARY
Skimmer: long-handled, round, perforated tool

NUTRITION

Nutrition Facts
Yield: Serves 10
Serving Size: 3 oz. (85 g)

Amount Per Serving

Calories 280

Total Fat 11 g

Sodium 260 mg

Total Carbohydrate 36 g

Protein 7 g

Spaghetti Putanesca

INGREDIENTS

	U.S. Standard	Metric
Olive oil	4 oz.	120 ml
Garlic, peeled and coarsely chopped	12 cloves	12 cloves
Anchovy fillets, oil drained, chopped	2 oz.	55 g
Tomato, concassé	2 lbs.	910 g
Olives, black pitted (Calamata or Gaeta), cut 1/3 slices	5 oz.	140 g
Black pepper, freshly ground	1/2 Tbsp.	7.5 ml
Salt	TT	TT
Spaghetti	1 1/2 lbs.	680 g

METHOD OF PREPARATION

1. Gather all the ingredients and equipment.

2. In a sauté pan, heat the oil, and sauté garlic for 2–3 minutes. Add the anchovies and sauté for 1 minute more.

3. Add the remaining ingredients, except the spaghetti, and simmer until the tomatoes are reduced to a sauce, approximately 20 minutes.

4. Meanwhile, cook the spaghetti in a large pot of boiling, salted water until *al dente;* drain well. (If sauce is not finished, rinse the spaghetti in cold water, drain well, and toss lightly with olive oil to hold.)

5. When the sauce is ready, add the spaghetti to the sauce, and toss together. Taste, and adjust the seasoning as needed.

6. Serve immediately, or hold briefly at 140°F (60°C) or higher.

COOKING TECHNIQUES

Sautéing:
1. Heat the sauté pan to the appropriate temperature.
2. Evenly brown the food product.
3. For a sauce, pour off any excess oil, reheat, and deglaze.

Boiling (At sea level):
1. Bring the cooking liquid to a rapid boil.
2. Stir the contents, and cook the food product throughout.
3. Serve hot.

Simmering:
1. Place the prepared product in an appropriately sized pot.
2. Bring the product to a boil, and then reduce the heat to allow the product to barely boil.
3. Cook until desired doneness is achieved.

GLOSSARY

Concassé: peeled, seeded, and roughly chopped

Al dente: to the bite

NUTRITION

Nutrition Facts	
Yield: Serves 10	
Serving Size: 7 oz. (205 g)	
Amount Per Serving	
Calories 430	
Total Fat 16 g	
Sodium 980 mg	
Total Carbohydrate 59 g	
Protein 11 g	

Fettuccine Alfredo

INGREDIENTS

	U.S. Standard	Metric
Cream, heavy	2 c.	500 ml
Butter	1 oz.	28 g
Water, boiling, salted	1 1/2 gal.	5.7 l
Fettuccine, fresh	1 1/2 lbs.	680 g
Parmesan cheese, freshly grated	5 oz.	140 g
Salt	TT	TT
Pepper	TT	TT

METHOD OF PREPARATION

1. Gather all the ingredients and equipment.

2. Combine 1 cup of cream and the butter in a sauté pan. Bring to a simmer, reduce by one-fourth, and remove from heat; keep warm.

3. Drop the noodles into boiling salted water, return to a full boil, cook until al dente, and drain. The noodles must be slightly undercooked because they will cook further in the cream.

4. Put the drained noodles in the pan with the hot cream and butter. Over low heat, toss the noodles with two forks until they are well coated with the cream.

5. Add the remainder of the cream and the cheese, and toss to mix well. (If noodles seem dry at this point, add a little more cream.)

6. Add salt and pepper to taste.

7. Plate and serve immediately. Offer additional grated cheese at the table.

Boiling (At sea level):
1. Bring the cooking liquid to a rapid boil.
2. Stir the contents, and cook the food product throughout.
3. Serve hot.

Nutrition Facts

Yield: Serves 10
Serving Size: 6 oz. (170 g)

Amount Per Serving

Calories 430

Total Fat 26 g

Sodium 550 mg

Total Carbohydrate 40 g

Protein 14 g

Risotto with Porcini Mushrooms

INGREDIENTS

Ingredient	U.S. Standard	Metric
Olive oil	4 Tbsp.	60 ml
Onion, *finely chopped*	1/4 c.	55 g
Garlic, *chopped*	1 clove	1 clove
Porcini mushrooms, *fresh-sliced (see Chef's Notes)*	4 oz.	115 g
Arborio or Carnaroli rice	1 lb.	454 g
White wine, *dry*	1/2 c.	120 ml
Vegetable stock, *heated to a boil*	2 qts.	1.9 l
Butter	2 Tbsp.	30 g
Parmigiano-reggiano cheese, *grated*	3 Tbsp.	45 g
Salt	TT	TT
Pepper	TT	TT

METHOD OF PREPARATION

1. Gather all the ingredients and equipment.

2. Heat olive oil in appropriately sized saucepan.

3. Add onions, and cook over medium heat until translucent.

4. Add the garlic, and sauté for another couple of minutes.

5. Add mushrooms, and sauté briefly.

6. Add rice to sauté pan, and toss with onions, garlic, and mushrooms. Heat, stirring constantly for a few minutes.

7. Add white wine to pan, and simmer until wine reduces and blends into rice.

8. Add stock in stages, 1–2 cups at a time, stirring constantly. Each addition of stock must absorb into the rice before adding more.

9. Continue process until the rice is al dente, and the dish has a creamy consistency; this should take about 20 minutes. Do not let the last addition dry completely—allow some moisture to stay so that the overall texture of the dish is creamy and not gummy. Moisten with more stock if needed but make sure that the rice remains a bit firm (al dente).

10. Blend in butter and Parmigiano-reggiano cheese; add more or less as desired. Taste, and season as needed.

11. Garnish with additional Parmigiano-reggiano and assorted mushrooms, if desired. Serve immediately.

NUTRITION

Nutrition Facts

Yield: Serves 10
Serving Size: 8 oz. (225 g)

Amount Per Serving

Calories 180

Total Fat 9 g

Sodium 110 mg

Total Carbohydrate 15 g

Protein 6 g

Polenta with Tomato and Fontina Cheese

INGREDIENTS

	U.S. Standard	Metric
White chicken stock, heated to a boil	1 1/2 qts.	1.4 l
Salt	TT	TT
White pepper, ground	TT	TT
Butter	4 oz.	115 g
Cornmeal, yellow	12 oz.	340 g
Tomato, concassé	2 c.	500 ml
Olive oil	1 1/2 oz.	45 ml
Parsley, washed, squeezed dry, chopped	1/2 oz.	15 ml
Fontina cheese, shredded	4 oz.	115 g

METHOD OF PREPARATION

1. Gather all the ingredients and equipment.

2. In a saucepan, combine the stock, salt, pepper, and butter. Heat to a boil.

3. Slowly pour the cornmeal into the boiling stock, stirring constantly. Reduce the heat, and simmer for about 30 minutes or until polenta is very thick. Stir constantly to prevent the bottom from sticking.

4. Taste, and adjust seasoning as needed. Spread the cooked polenta onto a plastic- or parchment-lined sheet pan, 1/2″ –3/4″ (1.27–1.9 cm) thick. Cool to 41°F (5°C) or lower. When totally cooled, cut into desired shape for service.

5. Combine the tomato concassé, olive oil, and parsley; season to taste with salt and pepper.

6. Preheat the oven to 350°F (177°C).

7. For service, arrange the polenta pieces on parchment-lined trays, and sprinkle with Fontina. Top each with a bit of the seasoned concassé, and place in the oven. Bake until the polenta is hot throughout. Hold briefly at 140°F (60°C) or higher, or serve immediately.

Asian Barley and Mushroom Salad

COOKING TECHNIQUES

Simmering:

1. Place the prepared product in an appropriately sized pot.
2. Bring the product to a boil, and then reduce the heat to allow the product to barely boil.
3. Cook until desired doneness is achieved.

Sautéing:

1. Heat the sauté pan to the appropriate temperature.
2. Evenly brown the food product.
3. For a sauce, pour off any excess oil, reheat, and deglaze.

GLOSSARY

Macédoine: 1/4" (3 mm) dice
Julienne: 1/8" × 1/8" × 1 1/2"–2" (3 mm × 3 mm × 2.5–5 cm) strips

NUTRITION

Nutrition Facts

Yield: Serves 10
Serving Size: 8 oz. (225 g)

Amount Per Serving

Calories 410

Total Fat 29 g

Sodium 510 mg

Total Carbohydrate 3 g

Protein 6 g

INGREDIENTS

	U.S. Standard	Metric
Chicken stock	6 c.	1.4 l
Salt	as needed	as needed
Barley, rinsed	1 lb.	454 g
Shiitake mushroom caps, diced macédoine	12 oz.	340 g
Salad oil	8 oz.	240 ml
Soy sauce	2 oz.	60 ml
Rice vinegar	3 oz.	90 ml
Sesame oil	2 Tbsp.	30 ml
Garlic, minced	2 Tbsp.	30 g
Ground cumin	1/2 tsp.	2 g
Ground coriander	1/2 tsp.	2 g
Red pepper flakes	1/2 tsp.	2 g
Salt	TT	TT
Celery, washed, trimmed, julienne	4 oz.	115 g
Carrots, peeled, washed, julienne	4 oz.	115 g
Snow peas, stringed, 1/4" (6 mm) bias cut, blanched, shocked	6 oz.	170 g
Green onions, 1/4" (6 mm) bias cut	5 each	5 each
Peanuts, toasted, coarsely chopped	1 1/2 c.	360 ml
Sesame seeds, toasted	1/4 c.	60 ml

METHOD OF PREPARATION

1. Gather all the ingredients and equipment.

2. In a medium stockpot, bring the chicken stock and 2 tsp. (10 g) of salt to a boil. Stir in the barley; reduce heat, and simmer, covered, until the barley is tender (about 45 minutes). Add small amounts of liquid if pot gets too dry. Strain any liquid, and turn out cooked barley onto a sheet pan to cool slightly.

3. As the barley cooks, sauté the chopped mushrooms in 2 oz. (60 ml) of oil; set aside.

4. For the dressing, place the soy sauce, rice vinegar, sesame oil, garlic, and spices into a large bowl, and whisk to blend. Drizzle in 6 oz. (180 ml) salad oil while whisking. Taste, and season with salt, if needed.

5. Add the warm barley and cooked mushrooms to the dressing. Combine well, and then mix in the celery, carrots, snow peas, green onions, and chopped peanuts. Taste, and season with salt, if needed. Chill at 41°F (5°C) or lower.

6. Top the barley salad with the toasted sesame seeds at service.

Rice Pilaf

INGREDIENTS	U.S. Standard	Metric
Butter, clarified	1 oz.	28 g
Onions, peeled and diced brunoise	8 oz.	225 g
Rice, long grain, converted	1 lb.	454 g
White chicken stock, heated to a boil	1 qt.	950 ml
Salt	TT	TT
White pepper, ground	TT	TT

METHOD OF PREPARATION

1. Gather all the ingredients and equipment.
2. Preheat the oven to 350°F (177°C).
3. Place the butter in a braising pan, and heat.
4. Add the onions, and sauté until translucent.
5. Add the rice, and stir to coat all of the grains with butter.
6. Add the chicken stock and seasonings, and heat the liquid to a boil.
7. Cover the pot with a lid, and place in the oven. Steam for 17–20 minutes, or until all of the stock is absorbed and the rice is tender.
8. When done, mix with a fork, and adjust the seasoning, if necessary. Serve immediately, or hold at 140°F (60°C) or higher.

COOKING TECHNIQUES

Sautéing:
1. Heat the sauté pan to the appropriate temperature.
2. Evenly brown the food product.
3. For a sauce, pour off any excess oil, reheat, and deglaze.

Simmering:
1. Place the prepared product in an appropriately sized pot.
2. Bring the product to a boil, and then reduce the heat to allow the product to barely boil.
3. Cook until desired doneness is achieved.

Steaming (Traditional):
1. Place a rack over a pot of water.
2. Prevent steam vapors from escaping.
3. Shock or cook the food product throughout.

GLOSSARY

Brunoise: 1/8″ (3 mm) dice

NUTRITION

Nutrition Facts
Yield: Serves 10
Serving Size: 3 oz. (85 g)

Amount Per Serving

Calories 220

Total Fat 3 g

Sodium 960 mg

Total Carbohydrate 42 g

Protein 4 g

Potato Gnocchi with Butter and Sage

INGREDIENTS

	U.S. Standard	Metric
Baking potatoes	5 lbs.	2.3 kg
Salt	TT	TT
Egg, whole	1 each	1 each
Flour, all-purpose	1 1/4 lbs.	570 g
Butter, melted	as needed	as needed
Black pepper, freshly ground	TT	TT
Fresh sage leaves, cut chiffonade	4 Tbsp.	60 ml
Parmigiano reggiano, grated	TT	TT

METHOD OF PREPARATION

1. Gather all the ingredients and equipment.

2. Wash and peel potatoes, place them in a pot, and cover with cold water. Potatoes may be cooked with skins on, if desired, and then peeled. Bring water to a boil, add salt, and reduce to a simmer. Cook potatoes until tender. Drain the potatoes, and let them dry at room temperature until cool enough to handle.

3. Press potatoes through a *ricer* into a large mixing bowl.

4. Beat the egg lightly, and blend into the cooled potatoes. Add the flour in batches. Mix gently to combine. The amount of flour used depends on the potatoes. Test before adding all the flour. (See Chef's Notes.) Add more flour if necessary.

5. Gently knead the mixture until it forms a smooth dough. Do not overknead, or too much gluten will be built, which will in turn toughen the gnocchi. Divide the dough into small balls, and roll them on a lightly floured board into long ropes about 3/4″ (1.9 cm) thick.

6. Cut the ropes into 1/2″–1″ (1.27–2.54 cm) pieces, depending on the size gnocchi desired. They will puff up a bit when cooked.

7. Place a large pot of salted water on the stove top, and allow to come to a boil while the gnocchi is formed.

8. Form the gnocchi by rolling each piece off the tines of a fork to leave a shallow depression. If the dough sticks, dip hands and fork in flour before forming. Hold on a parchment-lined sheet pan.

9. Drop the gnocchi in batches into the boiling, salted water. When the gnocchi rise to the surface, allow them to simmer gently for a few minutes to cook through, and then remove them with a slotted spoon or skimmer, and shock to stop the cooking. Drain well, and set aside until service.

10. For service, sauté the gnocchi in melted butter in batches, seasoning with salt and pepper to taste. Lastly, toss in the chiffonade of sage.

11. Serve hot with grated Parmigiano sprinkled lightly on top.

Chef's Notes

Test a few gnocchi by dropping them into a small pot of boiling, salted water before finishing the entire batch. Too little flour will cause gnocchi to begin to disintegrate in the water. Too much flour will make gnocchi tough and heavy. Properly made gnocchi should be light in texture, but they should hold their shape without becoming sticky or watery.

COOKING TECHNIQUES

Boiling (At sea level):
1. Bring the cooking liquid to a rapid boil.
2. Stir the contents, and cook the food product throughout.
3. Serve hot.

Sautéing:
1. Heat the sauté pan to the appropriate temperature.
2. Evenly brown the food product.
3. For a sauce, pour off any excess oil, reheat, and deglaze.

GLOSSARY

Chiffonade: ribbons of leafy greens

Ricer: kitchen utensil used to mash or rice cooked foods

NUTRITION

Nutrition Facts

Yield: Serves 10
Serving Size: 8 oz. (225 g)

Amount Per Serving

Calories 500

Total Fat 11 g

Sodium 95 mg

Total Carbohydrate 89 g

Protein 11 g

Spinach and Ricotta Ravioli

with Tomato Basil Sauce

INGREDIENTS	U.S. Standard	Metric
RAVIOLI		
Fresh spinach, *washed, stemmed, blanched*	2 lbs.	910 g
Ricotta cheese	1 lb.	454 g
Eggs	2 each	2 each
Parmesan cheese, *freshly grated*	4 oz.	115 g
Nutmeg	1/4 tsp.	1.25 ml
Salt	TT	TT
Black pepper, *ground*	TT	TT
Fresh pasta dough	2 lbs.	910 g
Flour	as needed	as needed
SAUCE		
Olive oil	3 oz.	90 ml
Garlic, *crushed*	4 cloves	4 cloves
Tomatoes, *concassé, with juice*	3 lbs.	1.4 kg
Salt	TT	TT
Red pepper flakes	1/4 tsp.	1.25 ml
Parsley sprigs, *washed*	4 each	4 each
Basil sprigs, *washed*	4 each	4 each
Basil leaves, *chiffonade*	1/3 c.	75 ml
Parmesan cheese, *shavings*	3 oz.	85 g

METHOD OF PREPARATION

To make ravioli:

1. Gather all the ingredients and equipment.

2. Finely chop the cooked spinach, and squeeze out as much moisture as possible. Place in a medium mixing bowl. Blend in the ricotta, eggs, parmesan, nutmeg, salt, and pepper. Set aside, covered, at 41°F (5°C) or lower.

3. Either by hand or using a machine, roll out the dough, 1/4 at a time, until very thin. Fill and form the ravioli as each sheet is stretched, or hold, covered (it dries out quickly), until all the dough is rolled out.

4. Lay out a sheet of pasta. Moisten very lightly with water. Place filling in rows about 2″ (5.08 cm) apart. Lay a second sheet of pasta over the filling, and press down gently but firmly, pushing out as much air as possible from between mounds.

5. Cut the ravioli between the mounds to form squares. Check each to ensure that the edges are sealed. Lay out on a lightly floured pan to dry 30 minutes. Turn them over at least once to dry evenly. Cook the ravioli in rapidly boiling salted water until just tender, about 3–4 minutes. Serve immediately with sauce.

To make sauce:

1. Gather all the ingredients and equipment.

2. In a large sautoir, heat the olive oil until fragrant. Add the crushed garlic, and cook gently until the color turns to a light brown. Remove and discard the garlic.

3. Add the chopped tomatoes to the garlic oil along with any juice. Bring to a boil, season with salt and red pepper flakes, and add the sprigs of basil and parsley.

4. Simmer the sauce for 20–30 minutes, adding a few ounces of water if it thickens too much. Remove and discard the whole sprigs of herbs, and blend in the basil chiffonade. Adjust the seasoning, and serve with the ravioli. Top each portion with some of the Parmesan shavings.

27 / Vegetables and Legumes

Humans have been cultivating food plants since before the rise of civilization. Ancient Egyptians and Sumerians (circa 3000 B.C.) enjoyed a diet of vegetables that has remained essentially the same to this day. European explorations of the Renaissance era were driven by the search for new routes to the spice-laden Indies. As a result of this exploration, spices and produce from these native lands were introduced to European cuisine.

Christopher Columbus's New World held a wealth of new vegetables, including beans, corn, squash, tomatoes, potatoes, and sweet potatoes. This harvest eventually transformed the European diet and the world-wide distribution of flora. European colonists brought vegetables from the Americas back to Europe and they introduced their native plants to the New World.

3000 B.C.
Egyptians and Sumerians use vegetables in their diets.

A.D. 1492
Christopher Columbus discovers the New World and its array of vegetables.

1730
Europeans bring from the Americas to Europe a bounty of new vegetables and incorporate them into their diets.

2002
Chefs use vegetables creatively to enhance the flavor, color, and nutritional value of meals.

A Variety of Healthful Choices

Vegetables, plants or parts of plants, form part of the human diet. The nutritional value of vegetables is generally very high. They consist of 65%–95% water and contain a variety of minerals, vitamins, volatile oils, and enzymes, all of which are important to regulating body functions. Vegetables usually contain few fats, carbohydrates, or protein, but are very high in fiber.

Vegetables provide a broad and vivid palette of colors, shapes, textures, and flavors from which to choose. They can complement a main course or serve as a complete entrée.

Vegetables are at their best at the peak of their season, when they are fully ripe, readily available, and reasonably priced. To ensure the availability of high quality, local, seasonal produce, it is important to support local producers and growers whenever possible. Modern transportation and the awareness of certain suppliers that have relationships with farmers around the world create value, consistency, and quality, making year-round access possible.

However, most produce is available year-round in the United States, thanks to an efficient distribution chain. Avocados harvested in California in February, for example, can be found in supermarkets in Boston within a day or two of being picked. Mandarin oranges from the People's Republic of China are widely available from early fall through spring in most U.S. markets. Because vegetables are highly perishable, they must be moved to market as quickly as possible.

Genetically Engineered Tomatoes

Genetically engineered foods are a topic of controversy among consumers, food producers, and scientists. Although advocates promote the benefits of genetically altering vegetables to enhance characteristics such as sweetness, appearance, and rate of growth or to solve storage and shipping problems, others argue that so-called "Frankenfoods" are potential time bombs, laden with little-understood problems.

· The availability of seasonal produce provides an argument in support of genetically engineered foods. Consumers in the northern regions of the United States must rely on tomatoes shipped out of season from the South if they want fresh tomatoes.

To withstand the rigors of shipping, tomatoes must be picked at a stage the growers call "mature-green," which occurs when the plant has absorbed all the vitamins and nutrients it can but has not started to produce the natural ethylene gas that triggers ripening.

The next step, called "de-greening" or "ripening initiation," involves putting the green tomatoes in ripening rooms where ethylene gas is released. The green tomatoes spend 3 to 4 days in the ripening room before they are shipped at temperatures not lower than 50°F (10°C). Cooler temperatures destroy tomato flavor.

Unfortunately, many consumers think that tomatoes shipped in winter lack the taste and texture of vine-ripened tomatoes. Therefore, Calgene, Inc., a biotechnology company with headquarters in Davis, California, has developed a tomato with a gene that slows the natural softening process that accompanies ripening. The company says that their Flavr Savr™ tomato spends more days on the vine than other tomatoes, resulting in more flavor, yet it remains firm enough to be shipped.

Types of Fresh Vegetables

Vegetables can be divided into several categories on the basis of either their botanical relationship or their edible parts: leafy vegetables, brassicas, shoots, fruit-vegetables, squashes and gourds, bulbs, roots and tubers, pods and seeds, mushrooms and truffles, and legumes.

Leafy Vegetables

Leafy vegetables are tender green vegetables that may be served raw, as in a salad, or cooked. Most greens, including mustard, sorrel, spinach, Swiss chard, dandelion greens, and turnip greens have strong, spicy flavors. Composed largely of water, these greens are drastically reduced by cooking. Lettuces and other milder greens are usually eaten raw. Leafy vegetables should be crisp and fresh with brightly colored leaves and should be free of any brown spots.

CHICORY/ENDIVE

SORREL

CHICORY/ENDIVE

Nutritional Advantage—Fat-free; source of folate, beta-carotene, vitamins A and B

Purchasing Specifications—Fresh and crisp with a dark green color on outer leaves

Packaging and Weight—25 lbs.; 24 per carton (California); 18 lbs.; 12–18 per carton (Florida)

Storage Requirements—Refrigerate at 38°F (3°C); 90% relative humidity

Market Form—Fresh

Flavor—Slightly bitter taste; prickly texture

Uses—Salads; sauté; braise

ESCAROLE

SORREL

Nutritional Advantage—Low in fat and calories; sodium-free; high in vitamins A and C, iron, fiber; contains some magnesium, calcium, phosphorus, potassium

Purchasing Specifications—Light green leaves resembling spinach; crisp, not limp

Packaging and Weight—35-lb. half-crates; 32-lb. 4/5 bushel crates

Storage Requirements—Refrigerate at 40°F (4°C)

Market Form—Bunched in leaves

Flavor—Tart, lemony taste

Uses—Soups, sauces; serve with spinach, fish, chicken

ESCAROLE

Nutritional Advantage—Source of folate, vitamins A and C, calcium, potassium

Purchasing Specifications—Pale green leaves, firm stalk

Packaging and Weight—Bundled by the pound; California: 25 lbs. (24 count); Florida: 18 lbs. (12–18 count)

Storage Requirements—Refrigerate at 38°F (3°C); 90% relative humidity

Market Form—Fresh

Flavor—Slightly bitter

Uses—Salads; soups; grill; sauté; braise

LETTUCE

ICEBERG, ROMAINE, BUTTER, LEAF

Nutritional Advantage—Fat-free; source of folate, vitamin C, potassium, iron

Purchasing Specifications—Good medium to light green color, red in some varieties; generally crisp leaves; soft-leafed lettuces should not be wilted

Packaging and Weight—By the case, 24 count

Storage Requirements—Refrigerate at 38°F–45°F (3°C–7°C) with 90% relative humidity

Market Form—Fresh

Flavor—Usually sweet; may have bitter edges; crisp texture

Uses—Salads, bedding

SPINACH

SPINACH

Nutritional Advantage—Contains antioxidants such as lutein and other cholesterol-lowering nutrients; fat-free, high in vitamins A and C, a source of iron, fiber, beta-carotene, calcium, folic acid

Purchasing Specifications—Crisp, bright green leaves

Packaging and Weight—10-lb. cartons of 8 film bags, each 10 oz.

Storage Requirements—Refrigerate at 37°F (3°C); 95%–98% relative humidity

Market Form—Fresh, canned, or frozen

Flavor—Slightly acidic taste

Uses—Salads, stews, pasta, stuffings; cream, boil, purée

SWISS CHARD

SWISS CHARD

Nutritional Advantage—Low in calories; source of vitamins A and C, potassium, iron, calcium, fiber

Purchasing Specifications—Crinkled, glossy, red, white, green or multicolored leaves with tender, light-colored stems

Packaging and Weight—35-lb. half-crates; 32 lb. 4/5 bushel crates; or 10- and 20-ounce bunches

Storage Requirements—Refrigerate at 34°F (1°C)

Market Form—Bunched in leaves

Flavor—Somewhat beetlike in taste; a cross between celery and asparagus

Uses—Soups, salads, pasta; serve with vegetables

WATERCRESS

WATERCRESS

Nutritional Advantage—Low calories, low sodium, fat-free; high in vitamins A and C; a source of potassium, iodine, iron, sulphur, oxalic acid. *Oxalic acid can cause reactions in individuals with kidney or bladder sensitivity

Purchasing Specifications—Fresh, crisp, rich green color

Packaging and Weight—12- or 24-count case

Storage Requirements—Refrigerate at 38°F (3°C); 90% relative humidity

Market Form—Fresh

Flavor—Mild, spicy flavor

Uses—Soups, salads, Chinese-style dishes

Brassicas

Brassicas include broccoli, cauliflower, kohlrabi, and red and green cabbages, and all are used for their heads, flowers, or leaves. These quick-growing, cool-weather vegetables are inexpensive, readily available, and easily prepared. Brassicas can be consumed either raw or cooked; they should be firm and heavy with good color. Many brassicas have been a dietary staple since ancient times.

BOK CHOY

BOK CHOY

Nutritional Advantage—Low calories; fat-free; high in potassium, calcium, fiber, vitamins A and C

Purchasing Specifications—Thick, firm white stalks with crisp, large dark green leaves

Packaging and Weight—50-lb. crate, 70-lb. bushel

Storage Requirements—Refrigerate at 35°F–45°F (2°C–7°C); 90% relative humidity

Market Form—Fresh

Uses—Soups, steamed dishes, salads, edible garnish, in dumplings; boil, steam, stir-fry, braise

BRUSSELS SPROUTS

Nutritional Advantage—Low in fat and sodium; a source of fiber, protein, folate, iron, carbohydrates, vitamin C

Purchasing Specifications—Firm texture; fresh, appealing light green color; compact leaves

Packaging and Weight—25-lb. loose-pack cartons or 9-lb. trays

Storage Requirements—Refrigerate at 35°F–45°F (2°C–7°C); 95% relative humidity

Market Form—Fresh and frozen

Uses—Side dish; can also accompany sharply seasoned dishes; braise, steam, or boil

BROCCOLI

Nutritional Advantage—Source of protein, fiber, potassium, calcium, iron, magnesium, vitamins A and C, folic acid, lutein, beta-carotene

Purchasing Specifications—Light green stalks with consistently thick, dark green bud clusters that may have a tinge of purple; stalks are tender and firm

Packaging and Weight—Wax-treated containers: 18 bunches (23-lb.)

Storage Requirements—Refrigerate at 35°F–45°F (2°C–7°C); 95% relative humidity

Market Form—Fresh or frozen

Uses—Hot or chilled in salads, quiches, soufflés, pasta dishes, stir-fries; sauté or steam

BROCCOLI

CABBAGE

SAVOY, GREEN, RED

Nutritional Advantage—Low in sodium and calories; fat-free; high in vitamin C, protein, fiber, carbohydrates, folate, calcium, iron

Purchasing Specifications—Hard head, heavy for its size; green and red cabbage should be smooth with compacted leaves; Savoy cabbage leaves should be looser and more crinkly

Packaging and Weight—Bushel: 30 lbs.

Storage Requirements—Refrigerate at 35°F–45°F (2°C–7°C); 90% relative humidity

Market Form—Fresh

Uses—Casseroles, sauerkraut, sides, salads, coleslaw, soups, stews, cabbage rolls, stir-fries; pickle, braise, bake, steam, or boil

GREEN CABBAGE

RED CABBAGE

CAULIFLOWER

Nutritional Advantage—Fat-free; rich in vitamins C, E, and vitamin B-complex; a source of calcium, dietary fiber; contains some protein, phosphorus, magnesium, iron, potassium

Purchasing Specifications—A firm and compact head of white to cream-white curds surrounded by a crown of well-trimmed, turgid green leaves

Packaging and Weight—42-lb. crate (12–15 heads); 1/2 bushel: 20 lbs. (12 count)

Storage Requirements—Store at 35°F–45°F (2°C–7°C); 90% relative humidity

Market Form—Fresh or frozen

Uses—Crudité trays, salads, stir-fries; side or garnish; steam or purée

CAULIFLOWER

KALE

KALE

Nutritional Advantage—Low in calories and sodium; fat-free; high in vitamins A and C; source of iron, calcium, magnesium, potassium, protein, dietary fiber

Purchasing Specifications—Fresh, crisp, green leaves

Packaging and Weight—Bushel carton: 18–25 lbs.

Storage Requirements—Store in a moist environment at 40°F (4°C); 90% relative humidity

Market Form—Fresh

Uses—Salad accent, steamed side, soups or garnish; steam, braise, blanch, layer with pasta

KOHLRABI

Nutritional Advantage—Low in calories and sodium; fat-free; high in vitamin C; a source of potassium and vitamin B6

Purchasing Specifications—Small to medium-sized light green bulbs; smooth, not cracked; attached leaves should be firm and green

Packaging and Weight—25-lb. film bags; 50-lb. film and mesh bags; 24-lb. cartons that hold 24 1-lb. film bags

Storage Requirements—Refrigerate at 32°F (0°C); 98%–100% relative humidity

Market Form—Fresh

Uses—Dips, chicken broths, spring fricassées, cream soups; as a food enhancer; braise, sauté, steam, boil, purée, pickle

Shoot Vegetables

Shoot, or *stalk,* vegetables such as celery, asparagus, artichokes, and fennel are plant stems with a high percentage of cellulose fiber. Shoot vegetables should be harvested while they are young and tender. They should be firm and without any browning. Older shoot vegetables with tough fibers should be trimmed before cooking.

ARTICHOKES

ASPARAGUS

ARTICHOKES

Nutritional Advantage—*High in sodium and calories; fat-free; a source of fiber, magnesium, folacin, potassium, iron, calcium, vitamin C*

Purchasing Specifications—*Firm, heavy, and compact; light green in color*

Packaging and Weight—*Packaged in wax-treated cartons by count and loose pack, 20–25 lbs. (18, 24 and 36, 48, 60)*

Storage Requirements—*Refrigerate at 38°F (3°C); 90%–95% relative humidity*

Market Form—*Fresh, canned (hearts and bottoms), or frozen*

Uses—*Salads, stews, soups, stir-fries; serve with cream and cheese sauces; batter and pan-fry, bake, boil, steam*

ASPARAGUS

Nutritional Advantage—*Fat- and sodium-free; a source of vitamins A and C, fiber, protein, iron, calcium, folic acid, potassium, glutathione*

Purchasing Specifications—*Straight, thin, round spears; should snap easily; crisp, compacted tips*

Packaging and Weight—*1/2 carton: 15 lbs.; Pyramid crates; loose 30 lbs.*

Storage Requirements—*Refrigerate at 35°F–40°F (2°C–4°C); 90% relative humidity*

Market Form—*Fresh, canned, or frozen*

Uses—*Drizzle with butter, light seasonings, delicate sauces; serve as a side or edible garnish; add to pasta or vegetable medleys; use in cream soups*

BAMBOO SHOOTS

Nutritional Advantage—*Low in fat; source of vitamin B6, carbohydrates, protein, zinc, fiber*

Purchasing Specifications—*Canned shoots are peeled and cut into strips; whole fresh shoots are cone-shaped, about 4″ long*

Packaging and Weight—*8 oz. vacuum packed, 8-oz. cans*

Storage Requirements—*Store canned shoots in a cool, dry place at 50°F–70°F (10°C–21°C), 50%–60% relative humidity, 6″ off the floor*

Market Form—*Usually canned, though fresh, whole shoots may be available*

Uses—*Chilled in salads; vegetable medleys, stir-fries, or soups; sauté, braise, boil, stew, or simmer*

BAMBOO SHOOTS

BELGIAN ENDIVE

Nutritional Advantage—*Sodium- and fat-free; source of folate and trace amounts of beta-carotene, vitamins A and B*

Purchasing Specifications—*Firm, cigar-shaped heads with compacted white leaves; should be unblemished*

Packaging and Weight—*10-lb. box or 25-lb. bushel*

Storage Requirements—*Keeps briefly at 35°F–45°F (2°C–7°C); 90% relative humidity*

Market Form—*Fresh*

Uses—*A salad or sandwich accent, side, in soups, unusual appetizer; bake, braise, blanch, steam*

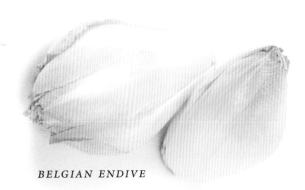

BELGIAN ENDIVE

FENNEL

FENNEL

Nutritional Advantage—*A source of vitamins A and C, niacin, potassium, calcium, iron, carbohydrates, fiber*

Purchasing Specifications—*Large, bright, compact bulb with fresh edges, if cut, and no browning or dryness; feathery and divided leaves*

Packaging and Weight—*24 bulbs per case*

Storage Requirements—*Refrigerate at 32°F–34°F (0°C–1°C)*

Market Form—*Fresh*

Uses—*Fresh salads; as a garnish; serve sliced with olive oil and black pepper; braise or grill*

CELERY

CELERY

Nutritional Advantage—*A source of vitamins C, A, E, and B-complex, potassium, folic acid, protein, dietary fiber, iron, magnesium, phosphorus, calcium*

Purchasing Specifications—*Straight, firm, light green stalks with fresh leaves*

Packaging and Weight—*Whole heads: carton: 50–56 lbs. (18, 24, 36, 48 count); Hearts: carton: 25–28 lbs. (12, 18, 24 count)*

Storage Requirements—*Refrigerate at 35°F–45°F (2°C–7°C); 90%–95% relative humidity*

Market Form—*Fresh*

Uses—*Add to stir-fries, stocks, soups or poultry stuffing; excellent stir stick for iced tomato drinks; adds crunch to salads (tuna, shrimp, chicken, or potato salad)*

FIDDLEHEAD FERN

Nutritional Advantage—*Source of fiber, antioxidants, bioflavonoids (chemicals produced in plants that can protect against disease)*

Purchasing Specifications—*Small, firm, tightly coiled with a deep green color; resemble the heads of violins*

Packaging and Weight—*10-lb. box*

Storage Requirements—*Keep tightly wrapped and cooled; refrigerate at 35°F (2°C) for no more than two days*

Market Form—*Fresh, frozen, canned*

Uses—*Edible garnish; accompaniment; serve with melted butter or lemon, boil; prepare and serve like artichoke hearts or asparagus*

PALM HEARTS

Nutritional Advantage—*Source of fiber*

Purchasing Specifications—*Ivory color, cylinder shape; firm and smooth texture; 4″ long*

Packaging and Weight—*#303 cans, 8 oz. vacuum packed*

Storage Requirements—*Wrap in plastic; refrigerate*

Market Form—*Fresh, precooked, canned*

Uses—*Add to salads, pasta, main dishes; appetizer (hearts of palm ceviche)*

PALM HEARTS

Fruit-Vegetables

Fruit-vegetables are botanically fruit because they develop from the ovary of flowering plants and contain one or more seeds. However, they are prepared and served as savory vegetables. Fruit-vegetables include eggplants, tomatoes, sweet peppers, chilies, and avocados, and they should have smooth, unblemished skin.

AVOCADO

AVOCADO

Nutritional Advantage—Sodium-free; a source of fiber, vitamins B6, C, and E, potassium, folate; fat content varies through the harvest season—at the season's start, the fat content could be 2 g and at the end 6 g

Purchasing Specifications—Firm; oblong; dark green to black skin

Packaging and Weight—1/2 carton: 15 lbs.; carton: 24-5 lb. case: 48 each; pyramid: 30-lbs. holding 12 bunches

Storage Requirements—Refrigerate at 36°F–40°F (2°C–4°C)

Market Form—Fresh, purée in cans

Uses—Excellent in Mexican dishes (burritos, tostadas, rice, guacamole, salsa, relishes); add to salads, sandwiches, soups or dips; eat out-of-hand as a snack

CHILI PEPPERS

Nutritional Advantage—Fat-free; high in fiber; source of vitamins A, B, and C, iron, thiamine, niacin, magnesium, riboflavin

Purchasing Specifications—Firm, smooth and shiny; though dried peppers will be somewhat wrinkled

Packaging and Weight—10-lb. half-crate, 25-lb. bushel/crate

Storage Requirements—Store at 40°F–50°F (4°C–10°C); 85% relative humidity

Market Form—Fresh, dried

Uses—Salads, sauces, pickled (en escabeche); to flavor soups, ceviches, sauces, meats, poultry, chutneys, dips, and salsa

EGGPLANT

Nutritional Advantage—Sodium- and fat-free; source of potassium, vitamins A, B-complex, C

Purchasing Specifications—Firm, plump, unblemished, even-colored dark purple skin

Packaging and Weight—33-lb. bushel; crates: 12–18, 24, or 30 count in each

Storage Requirements—Refrigerate at 45°F–50°F (2°C–7°C), 85% relative humidity

Market Form—Fresh

Uses—Pizza topping, combine with other vegetables, appetizer, dip, main entrée; fry, grill, stuff, braise, steam

EGGPLANT

TOMATOES

Nutritional Advantage—*Sodium- and fat-free; a source of vitamins A and C, calcium, iron, potassium, lycopene (antioxidant)*

Purchasing Specifications—*Shiny skin, firm flesh, good shape; should be unblemished*

Packaging and Weight—*Flat: 10 lbs. (40 count); lug: 28–30 lbs. (108, 126, or 147 count); carton: 25 lbs. (12 count, or 1-pint trays)*

Storage Requirements—*Store unripened at 65°F–70°F (18°C–21°C); 85%–88% relative humidity; until fully ripe, tomatoes should not be refrigerated*

Market Form—*Fresh, canned, or dried*

Uses—*Slice for sandwiches, stuff, add to salads, stir-fries, sauces, soups*

TOMATOES

BELL PEPPERS

PEPPERS (BELL)

Nutritional Advantage—*Sodium- and fat-free; source of vitamins A and C, potassium, calcium, carbohydrates, dietary fiber, protein, iron*

Purchasing Specifications—*Bright, strong, thick, glossy skin; well-formed and without bruises*

Packaging and Weight—*Bushel: 24 lbs.; box: 11 lbs.*

Storage Requirements—*Store at 40°F (4°C); 85% relative humidity*

Market Form—*Fresh*

Uses—*Add to stuffings; as a snack; salad enhancer; stir-fries, salsas, sauces, pasta; roast, grill, bake, stuff, sauté*

Vegetables and Legumes

581

Squashes and Gourds

Squashes and gourds include a large family of almost 750 species. Squashes are fleshy fruits in the gourd family. They range in size, shape, color, and peak season. They may be classified as either winter squash (October through March) or summer squash (April through September). All squashes have a center cavity filled with seeds, and squash blossoms are edible.

Gourds are identified by their large, complex root systems, trailing vines, and large leaves. They generally grow in warm regions worldwide.

Squashes and gourds should be firm and free of blemishes and mold.

SUMMER SQUASH

WINTER SQUASH

SUMMER SQUASHES

CHAYOTE, CROOKNECK, PATTY PAN, YELLOW, ZUCCHINI

Nutritional Advantage—*A source of vitamins A and C, iron, calcium, niacin, riboflavin, thiamine*

Purchasing Specifications—*Firm, soft shell; shiny, tender rinds; should show no soft spots or blemishes*

Packaging and Weight—*Carton: 20 lbs.; bushel/carton: 50 lbs.*

Storage Requirements—*Refrigerate at 35°F–40°F (2°C–4°C); 85%–90% relative humidity*

Market Form—*Fresh and frozen*

Uses—*Soups, stews, casseroles, stir-fries, braises; with dip; in breads; braise, deep-fry, purée, stuff, steam, boil, sauté, fry*

WINTER SQUASHES

ACORN, BUTTERNUT, HUBBARD, PUMPKIN, SPAGHETTI

Nutritional Advantage—*Fat-free and sodium-free; a source of vitamins A and C, beta carotene, potassium, magnesium, folate, vitamin B6, thiamine*

Purchasing Specifications—*Heavy; dull color; hard rind; no blemishes, soft spots, or cracks in the shell*

Packaging and Weight—*Each carton: 50 lb.*

Storage Requirements—*Store at 50°F (10°C); low relative humidity*

Market Form—*Fresh*

Uses—*Blend with butter, brown sugar, and apples to stuff; soups; purée, bake, sauté with vegetables; flavor desserts, pies, breads, cookies, muffins, puddings*

OTHER SQUASHES

CUCUMBERS

Nutritional Advantage—*Sodium- and fat-free; a source of vitamins A and C, iron, calcium, protein, dietary fiber*

Purchasing Specifications—*Firm, well-shaped; crisp; medium size; dark green skin*

Packaging and Weight—*25–28-lb. carton (24 count), 30–32-lb. carton (35–40 count), 50–55-lb. Los Angeles lugs (60, 70, 80 or 90 count)*

Storage Requirements—*Store at 45°F–50°F (7°C–10°C); 85% relative humidity*

Market Form—*Fresh*

Uses—*An edible garnish; serve as a side; add to salads*

CUCUMBERS

Bulb Vegetables

Bulb vegetables are mostly used for seasoning and flavoring other food. Onions are among the most commonly used bulb vegetables in the world. Virtually every culture's cuisine uses these strongly flavored members of the lily family. The bulb family includes onions (Bermuda, Spanish, white, red, and so on), garlic, leeks, scallions, and shallots. Bulb vegetables should be firm and fresh, and should have good color.

LEEKS

ONIONS

SCALLIONS

SHALLOTS

GARLIC

Nutritional Advantage—Sodium- and fat-free; a source of iron, vitamins; contains mild antibiotic properties

Purchasing Specifications—Plump bulbs, tightly compressed cloves, tight and unbroken sheath, mold-free

Packaging and Weight—25- or 30-lb. crate; purchased by the pound

Storage Requirements—Store fresh garlic in a cool, dark place at 65°F (18°C) or lower; 65% relative humidity. Do not refrigerate fresh garlic; refrigerate peeled garlic in a tightly sealed jar at 41°F (5°C) or lower

Uses—Flavoring for meat, poultry, vegetables, soups, stew, salads, sauces, or casseroles; chop, mince, press

LEEKS

Nutritional Advantage—Vitamin C, folate, iron

Purchasing Specifications—Fresh green tops, clean white bases

Packaging and Weight—Bunch: 12–15; bushel baskets or hampers: 24–30 lbs.; carton: 12 count

Storage Requirements—Refrigerate at 40°F–50°F (4°C–10°C); 90% relative humidity

Market Form—Fresh

Uses—Popular bistro appetizer; onion substitute in tomato sauces and risottos; julienne for cream sauces; braise

ONIONS (GLOBE)

Nutritional Advantage—Cholesterol-, sodium-, and fat-free; source of vitamins A, B-complex, and C, calcium, potassium, magnesium, fiber

Purchasing Specifications—Hard; crinkly, thin papery, dry skin; tight at the neck; no stem, decay, or wetness

Packaging and Weight—10-, 25- and 50-lb. mesh sacks

Storage Requirements—50°F–60°F (10°C–16°C); 65%–70% relative humidity; dark place

Market Form—Fresh

Uses—Flavor soups, stews, casseroles, meat dishes; add to salads; sandwich topper; stir-fry

SCALLIONS

Nutritional Advantage—Cholesterol-, sodium-, and fat-free

Purchasing Specifications—Blanched ends, fresh green tops

Packaging and Weight—7–12-lb. half carton (24-bunch count); 15–25-lb. carton (48 count)

Storage Requirements—Refrigerate at 40°F–50°F (4°C–10°C); 90% relative humidity

Market Form—Fresh

Uses—Flavor stir-fries and Oriental dishes, vegetable ragoûts, salsas, soups, and garnishes; chop, slice, mince, or blanch

SHALLOTS

Nutritional Advantage—Contains mineral salts, protein, and sulphur

Purchasing Specifications—Plump, well-shaped; should not be dry or have any sprouts; skin is papery and purple; interior is bronze

Packaging and Weight—Bag: 5- or 10-lb., by the quart

Storage Requirements—Store in a cool, dark, dry place at 40°F–60°F (4°C–16°C); 60%–70% relative humidity; or refrigerate at 35°F (2°C) at 60%–70% relative humidity

Market Form—Fresh

Uses—Use like garlic; add to appetizers, dressings, marinades, soups, stews, casseroles, salads, sauces, poultry, fish, and meat dishes

Roots and Tubers

Roots are the deep taproots of plants, and *tubers* are the fat, underground stems. This group of vegetables includes beets, carrots, celeriac (celery root), parsnips, turnips, and radishes. Potatoes are the most popular tuber. Quality roots and tubers should be firm, without blemishes, and unwrinkled and should have good color.

CARROTS

CARROTS

Nutritional Advantage—90 mg sodium; cholesterol- and fat-free; source of vitamin A, potassium, calcium

Purchasing Specifications—Tops trimmed, smooth; well-shaped; deep vibrant orange

Packaging and Weight—By the bunch (if not topped); topped: 25-, 50-, or 100-lb. bags; bushels: 50 lbs.; crates: 50 lbs.

Storage Requirements—35°F–45°F (2°C–7°C); 90% relative humidity

Market Form—Fresh, frozen, canned

Uses—Casseroles, soups, stews; out-of-hand as a snack; edible garnish; with dressing or dip; salad, stir-fry; in desserts (cakes, muffins, puddings); bake, boil, steam, purée

BEETS

Nutritional Advantage—A source of protein, fiber, folic acid, vitamin A, potassium; beet greens are high in beta-carotene, folic acid

Purchasing Specifications—Dark purple-red color, small to medium size, smooth, globular form, firm flesh

Packaging and Weight—Bushel: 50 lbs.; bunch: 1-1/2 lbs.; bag: 1 crate (20–25 lbs.)

Storage Requirements—35°F–45°F (1°C–7°C); 95% relative humidity

Market Form—Fresh, canned

Uses—Decorative garnish; pickle, steam, boil, add to soups and salads

CELERIAC

CELERIAC (CELERY ROOT)

Nutritional Advantage—Cholesterol- and fat-free; source of vitamin C, some potassium, phosphorus, iron, magnesium, calcium

Purchasing Specifications—Not wilted, firm; tan exterior, creamy white center

Packaging and Weight—1/2 bushel: 20 lbs.

Storage Requirements—35°F–45°F (2°C–7°C); 98%–100% relative humidity

Market Form—Fresh

Uses—Salads, soups, stuffings, fritters, purées; grate, braise, bake, eat raw

JICAMA

Nutritional Advantage—Sodium-, cholesterol-, and fat-free; high in vitamin C, potassium

Purchasing Specifications—Ball-shaped; thin brown skin, crunchy white flesh

Packaging and Weight—50-lb. box

Storage Requirements—55°F–65°F (13°C–18°C); 65%–70% relative humidity

Market Form—Fresh

Uses—Adds crunch; add to fruit cups, stir-fries, fruit and vegetable salads; appetizer (chilled with a chili dip)

JICAMA

PARSNIPS

PARSNIPS

Nutritional Advantage—Source of vitamins C, E, fiber, folacin, magnesium, manganese, potassium, trace amounts of protein

Purchasing Specifications—Firm, smooth, well-shaped; small to medium in size

Packaging and Weight—Bag: 12–20 oz.; bag: 25 lbs.; cello wrap: 12 (1-lb.) bags; 28–30-lb. bushel

Storage Requirements—38°F (3°C); 90% relative humidity

Market Form—Fresh

Uses—Add to soups, stews; stir-fry in peanut oil for a snack; as a fritter (appetizer); carrot substitute; sauté, glaze, roast, boil, steam

POTATOES

POTATOES

Nutritional Advantage—Source of fiber, potassium, vitamin C, protein, thiamine, niacin, folacin, magnesium, iron

Purchasing Specifications—Oblong and irregular in size; fairly clean, smooth, firm; no wet spots

Packaging and Weight—50-lb. carton; sack: 50 or 100 lbs.

Storage Requirements—45°F–50°F (7°C–10°C); dark ventilated space

Market Form—Fresh, canned, frozen

Uses—Salad, side, French-fried, baked, au gratin, casseroles, soups, stews; mash, roast, steam, boil, scallop, purée, cream, sauté

RUTABAGA

Nutritional Advantage—Cholesterol- and fat-free; source of vitamin C

Purchasing Specifications—Long and yellow, smooth, firm; not cracked or shriveled; dense flesh free of blemishes

Packaging and Weight—Carton/bag: 50 lbs.

Storage Requirements—35°F (2°C)

Market Form—Fresh

Uses—Serve as a side; boil, steam, bake, mash, purée, or sauté

RUTABAGA

TURNIPS

TURNIPS

Nutritional Advantage—Cholesterol- and fat-free; source of vitamin C, complex carbohydrates, protein, fiber, calcium, potassium, folic acid

Purchasing Specifications—Purple top with a white tip; small to medium size, somewhat rounded, firm, not blemished or cracked

Packaging and Weight—1/2 bushel: 25 lbs.; bag: 25 or 50 lbs.; carton: 43–47 lbs. (24 bushel count)

Storage Requirements—35°F (2°C); 90%–95% relative humidity

Market Form—Fresh, canned

Uses—Serve as a side; boil, steam, bake, mash; add to soups, casseroles; use the leaves like spinach

Pods and Seeds

Pods and seeds include peas, green beans, haricorts verts (string beans), corn, legumes, and okra. In all cases the parts consumed are the seeds, although sometimes the pod is eaten as well. Seed vegetables generally contain more carbohydrates and protein than do other vegetables. Pod and seed vegetables should be firm, well shaped, and unblemished.

BEAN SPROUTS

BEAN SPROUTS

MUNG, ALFALFA

Nutritional Advantage—*Source of vitamin A, niacin, thiamine, riboflavin, protein, mineral enzymes; high in potassium*

Purchasing Specifications—*Straight, crisp, fresh, brightly colored, snap easily; the younger the sprout, the more tender*

Packaging and Weight—*Containers holding twelve 8-oz. cellophane bags; 10-lb. lugs and crates; loose pack, 10-lb. bags, 10-lb. flats*

Storage Requirements—*Clean and refrigerate; 90% relative humidity*

Market Form—*Fresh*

Uses—*Salads, sandwiches, stir-fries*

CORN

Nutritional Advantage—*Source of fiber, vitamin A, C, iron, potassium, dietary fiber*

Purchasing Specifications—*Plump, consistently sized kernels, fresh green husk, silky brown ends*

Packaging and Weight—*50-lb. bags holding 5 dozen ears; crate: 48 count*

Storage Requirements—*Highly perishable; refrigerate briefly at 35°F–40°F (2°C–4°C); 40% relative humidity*

Market Form—*Fresh, frozen, canned*

Uses—*On the cob, side, stir-fries, casseroles, vegetable medleys, salads; pickled; creamed; fritters, bread; boil, grill, steam*

CORN

The Many Uses of Corn

Corn is available in a variety of forms: fresh, on the cob; popcorn; cornflakes; cornbread; and cornstarch as a thickener for sauces or lemon meringue pie.

But corn has many other uses. According to food historian Margaret Visser, author of Much Depends on Dinner, there is nothing in a modern kitchen that does not have some relationship with corn.

Nonculinary uses of corn include:

- *Ethanol*—Corn growers and environmentalists hope to increase the production of ethanol as an environmentally friendly alternative to our growing dependence on foreign oil.

- *Biodegradable corn plastic*—Scientists have developed an earth-friendly polymer from the lactic acid produced during the corn fermentation process.

- *BioTred™*—Goodyear Tire has developed the world's first tire compound made from corn. These tires offer environmental and economic advantages.

- *HarvestForm™*—The John Deere Company uses this new polymer composite made from soy bean and corn resins in its combine panels, replacing metal materials.

GREEN BEANS

SHELLING PEAS

OKRA

GREEN BEANS

SNAP, STRING

Nutritional Advantage—Source of fiber, vitamins A and C, calcium, protein, iron

Purchasing Specifications—Long, bright green or yellow, straight pods, snap easily

Packaging and Weight—Bushel; Florida: 22 lbs.; Texas and Georgia: 20 lbs.

Storage Requirements—45°F–50°F (7°C–10°C); 85% relative humidity

Market Form—Fresh, frozen, canned

Uses—Side dish, add to casseroles, soups, stews, stir-fries

SHELLING PEAS

Nutritional Advantage—Source of fiber, vitamins A and C, iron, calcium, potassium, protein, folic acid

Purchasing Specifications—Bright green pods that snap easily and are well filled

Packaging and Weight—Carton/tub: 25 lbs.; lug: 10 lbs.

Storage Requirements—38°F (3°C); 90% relative humidity

Market Form—Fresh, canned, frozen

Uses—Add to soups, salads, stews; as a side

OKRA

Nutritional Advantage—Low-sodium; cholesterol- and fat-free; source of vitamins A, B, and C, folacin, magnesium, potassium, calcium

Purchasing Specifications—Tender, fresh, unblemished pointed pods, not shriveled; 3–4″ long

Packaging and Weight—Bushel: 25 lbs.

Storage Requirements—Refrigerate at 35°F–40°F (2°C–4°C); 85%–90% relative humidity

Market Form—Fresh, frozen

Uses—Steam, braise, sauté, deep-fry; add to stir-fries, soups; cook with meats

Mushrooms and Truffles

Mushrooms are members of the fungi family, which have no seeds, stems, or flowers. Although they are not technically a vegetable, mushrooms are usually prepared and served as such. Mushroom varieties include white, button, portabella, shiitake, crimini or Italian brown, and cloud ear. Wild mushrooms are also used in commercial kitchens and are sold by specialty purveyors. Wild mushrooms have a stronger earthy or nutty flavor than do cultivated mushrooms.

Mushrooms should be clean and free of soft spots and blemishes. If the mushrooms are dirty, gently rinse them under running water just prior to serving them, but do not allow them to soak up water as this will deteriorate them. Allow the mushrooms to dry on towels before preparing them.

Truffles grow near the roots of oak or beech trees. The two principal varieties are Périgord (black) and Piedmont (white). Truffles, especially the Piedmont variety, are strongly scented and flavored, and are usually added sparingly to soups, sauces, pasta, and other items. Black truffles are often used as a garnish or to flavor pâtés, terrines, and egg dishes. Fresh truffles are extremely expensive and perishable, so they are usually purchased canned, dried, or processed.

MUSHROOMS

Nutritional Advantage—Protein, potassium, niacin, B vitamins, calcium, magnesium, phosphorus

Purchasing Specifications—Firm, fresh, well shaped; cap and stem intact

Packaging and Weight—1-, 3-, and 10-lb. cartons or baskets; button cups; flats

Storage Requirements—Refrigerate fresh mushrooms at 35°F (2°C); 85%–90% relative humidity; dried mushrooms can be stored in a cool, dry place for several months

Market Form—Fresh, canned, dried

Uses—Edible garnish, pizza topping, stuffed, stir-fried, cooked with meat, poultry, seafood, soups, sauces, salads, soups, stews, pasta, rice; deep-fry, sauté, braise

TRUFFLES
PÉRIGORD, PIEDMONT

Nutritional Advantage—Sugar-free; source of vitamin B, protein, copper

Purchasing Specifications—Scaly skin; irregular shape; violet to black or white; a sweet, earthy aroma

Packaging and Weight—Carton: 3, 5, 10 lbs.

Storage Requirements—Store in alcohol or uncooked rice; refrigerate at 41°F (5°C); 90%–95% relative humidity

Market Form—Fresh, canned, dried, processed

Uses—Shave over salads, accompany smoked meats, top with cream sauces, pasta, stuffing; sauté

Legumes

Legumes are plants that have double-seamed pods containing a single row of seeds. Beans, peas, lentils, soy beans, and peanuts are among the most common legumes. Unlike other vegetables, legumes are not picked fresh. They are left on the vine until the bean or pea is plump and beginning to dry. These dried seeds, such as dried peas and lentils, are called *pulses*.

Legumes come in many different forms, colors, sizes, and textures. They are versatile, nutritious, and economical and have a long shelf life. Legumes are an excellent source of protein, complex carbohydrates, and dietary fiber and are often used as a meat substitute. They are a staple of many cuisines worldwide and an essential part of a vegetarian diet. Legumes should be bright in color and uniform in size; they should not be marked, damaged, or shriveled.

BEANS

BEANS

(FAVA, BLACK TURTLE, GREAT NORTHERN, KIDNEY, LIMA, NAVY, PINTO, SOY)

Nutritional Advantage—High in fiber, iron, protein, vitamins A and C, potassium

Purchasing Specifications—Shiny green pods; well-shaped, lightly colored beans

Packaging and Weight—Bushel: 26–30 lbs.

Storage Requirements—Refrigerate briefly at 45°F–50°F (7°C–10°C); 85% relative humidity

Market Form—Fresh, dried, frozen, canned

Uses—With rice, pasta; in soups, stews, casseroles, stir-fries, vegetable salads; mash, bake, simmer

PEAS

PEAS

Nutritional Advantage—Sodium-, cholesterol-, and fat-free; source of vitamins A, B, and C, dietary fiber, iron, zinc, potassium, and calcium

Purchasing Specifications—Bright green to yellow; whole or split

Packaging and Weight—Carton/tub: 25 lbs.; lug: 10 lbs.

Storage Requirements—38°F (3°C); 90% relative humidity

Market Form—Dried

Uses—Soups, casseroles; simmer, sauté

Purchasing and Storing Fresh Vegetables

Fresh vegetables are packed and shipped in cartons and can be purchased by weight or count. The specification will depend on the vegetable's weight and size.

Some vegetables, such as onions and lettuce, can be purchased cleaned, trimmed, and cut as needed, although the cost is higher.

Grading

For sellers and buyers of vegetables, the U.S. Department of Agriculture (USDA) grading service ensures that vegetable products meet certain standards of quality and condition. This provides the food industry with a common language with which to describe quality, determine the best use of a particular shipment, and gauge storage life.

The USDA has established 159 official grade standards for 85 fresh vegetables, fruits, tree nuts, peanuts, and related commodities. This grading service is voluntary and is paid for by user fees. Grading is performed either as the produce is packed for shipment or upon its arrival at the delivery site. An official certificate, accepted as evidence in all federal courts, shows which USDA grade standards a product meets.

Most fresh vegetables are graded as Extra Fancy, Fancy, Extra No. 1, or No. 1. U.S. Extra Fancy is the premium classification. Others, such as onions, potatoes, and carrots, are graded by an alphabetical system in which Grade A is the premium quality.

Receiving

When vegetables arrive in a commercial kitchen, they should be examined for quality; spoilage; debris, such as bits of metal or glass; vermin; and insect infestation. Match the purchase order against the invoice to ensure that all products ordered have been delivered with the correct form, size, quality, quantity, and price.

Ripening

Most vegetables are purchased when they are at their peak ripeness, but they may continue to ripen when exposed to oxygen. The rate of ripening depends on the type of vegetable and how it is stored.

Some vegetables—most notably fruit-vegetables such as tomatoes and avocados—are often purchased unripened to minimize damage during shipping. Once received, the ripening process can be hastened by exposing these vegetables to ethylene gas produced by bananas and other fruits.

Storing

Different vegetables require different storage conditions. Starchy vegetables, such as potatoes, winter squash, and onions, should be stored in a dry location at a temperature between 40°F–60°F (4°C–16°C), depending on the vegetable. If these vegetables are refrigerated, they will lose texture and flavor. Most other vegetables should be refrigerated at temperatures between 34°F–40°F (2°C–4°C) with high humidity.

Refer to the charts throughout the chapter for storage requirements for specific vegetables.

Purchasing and Storing Potatoes

Potatoes are typically purchased in 50-lb. bags or cartons. The number of potatoes received depends on their size. Selection of potatoes depends on their intended use.

FIGURE 27-1

Market Forms of Potatoes

MARKET FORM	SPECIFICATIONS
Fresh, unprocessed	Store in a cool, dark, dry place
Peeled, treated to prevent browning	Keep refrigerated (below 40°F or 4°C) for 5–7 days
Canned, whole, cooked	Store at 50°F (10°C) at 60%–70% relative humidity
French fries, blanched in deep fat and frozen	Available in several sizes and cuts; cook from the frozen state; refrigerated French fries are also available
Frozen, prepared products	Available as hash browns, puffs, stuffed, baked, and croquettes
Dehydrated	Granules or flakes; can be reconstituted as mashed potatoes with hot water or milk; with butter or other flavorings

NEW POTATOES

WAXY OR NEW POTATOES

Characteristics—High moisture content, high sugar content, low starch

Appearance—Usually small and round, though some varieties are large, and may be elongated; flesh is white, yellow, or blue; skin is white, red, yellow, or blue

Uses—Boil whole for salads, soups, hash browns, and any other preparation where the potato must hold its shape; not suitable for deep-frying

MATURE POTATOES

MATURE OR STARCHY POTATOES

Characteristics—High starch content, low moisture and sugar

Appearance—Russets or Idahos are long, regularly shaped, and have slightly rough skin; all-purpose (or chef's) potatoes are not always as dry and starchy as russets; they may be irregularly shaped and therefore less expensive than russets

Uses—Light, dry, mealy when cooked; ideal for baking and deep-frying; may be used for mashing; well suited for any preparation where shape does not matter

Types of Potatoes

Possibly the most popular vegetable in the world and one of the most important staples in a commercial kitchen, potatoes are versatile, economical, and highly nutritious. Because potatoes function as both a starch and a vegetable, most foodservice operations use them in some form in every meal. Potatoes are classified according to their starch content, which determines their best use, and include russet, Yukon gold, red, and sweet.

Quality Characteristics

High-quality potatoes are firm and smooth, not soft or shriveled. Their skins are dry and free of eyes. If eyes are present, they should be few and shallow. High-quality potatoes show no signs of sprouts.

One of the most important indicators of a high-quality potato is the absence of green areas on the outside of the potato. Green areas develop on potatoes that have been stored in light. These areas contain solanine, which is bitter tasting, and in large quantities, poisonous. Any green areas should be cut off before cooking.

When receiving potatoes, check to ensure that they meet these quality characteristics.

Storing Potatoes

Potatoes should be kept in a cool, dry place at a temperature between 55°F–60°F (13°C–16°C). They can be stored briefly at room temperature if they are to be used immediately.

Do not refrigerate potatoes. At temperatures below 45°F (7°C), the starch in the potatoes converts to sugar. If potatoes have been refrigerated, they should be stored at 50°F (10°C) for a period of two weeks so that the sugar can revert to starch.

New potatoes do not store well. Purchase only a week's supply at a time.

Market Forms

Potatoes are available in a variety of market forms. See Figure 27-1. Fresh, unprocessed potatoes that have been well prepared offer the best possible quality and economy. However, there are a number of processed potato products that also offer good value and convenience, particularly if time is at a premium.

Purchasing and Storing Preserved Vegetables

Because fresh produce is highly perishable and subject to inconsistency in climate and weather changes throughout the growing season, many foodservice operations turn to processed vegetables—canned or frozen—to meet their demand for a consistent product year-round. Although processed vegetables cannot duplicate the flavor or quality of fresh produce, they can offer some valuable advantages.

- *Convenience—Vegetables are washed, peeled, and ready to use and are packaged with other vegetables.*

- *Long shelf life—Because canned or frozen vegetables are preserved, they keep longer.*

- *Little to no preparation—Most are ready to serve; they provide substantial labor and cost savings.*

Canned Vegetables

Nearly all vegetables are available in a variety of can sizes. See Figure 27-2. When receiving canned vegetables, check for dents, bulges, and evidence of swelling, rust, or leaks, which may indicate spoilage. Small dents are harmless, but larger dents may indicate that the can's inner lining has been damaged. Bulging cans also may be a sign of botulism. Discard immediately.

■ *See Chapter 4: Food Safety for more information.*

Most canned vegetables are packed in a packing medium that protects the food and will be drained from the product. Different grades and different varieties of vegetables will vary in drained weight. Typically, drained weights are 60%–65% of the total contents. Some canned products, such as tomato paste or cream-style corn, have no drained weight because the entire contents are used.

The U.S. Department of Agriculture has established U.S. grade standards of quality and provides an inspection service to certify the quality of processed vegetables. The grades are:

- U.S. Grade A, also labeled as Fancy— These vegetables are selected for color, tenderness, and freedom from blemishes. They are the highest-quality vegetables produced for processing.

- U.S. Grade B, also referred to as Extra Standard—These vegetables are of excellent quality but may be more mature than Grade A or have other imperfections.

- U.S. Grade C, also labeled as Standard— These vegetables are not as uniform in color and flavor as are the higher grades of vegetables. They are a thrifty buy if used in casseroles, soups, or other foods in which appearance is not a consideration.

FIGURE 27-2

Commercial Can Sizes

Container Common Name	Typical Net Weight/oz.	Maximum Volume Capacity (fl. oz./ Approx. Cups)	Typical Number of Cans per Case	Cans Needed to Equal 1 #10 Can	Typical Contents
#10	109.43	105.10/13 1/8	6	1.00	Vegetables, fruits, entrées
#3 cylinder (#3 tall)	51.60	49.57/6 1/8	12	2.12	Condensed soups
#3 vacuum	23.90	22.90/2 3/4	24	4.59	Sweet potatoes
#300 cylinder	19.40	18.70/2 1/3	24	5.61	Asparagus
#303	16.88	16.20/2	24/12	6.49	Many fruits and vegetables
#300	15.22	14.60/1 3/4	48/24	7.19	Diced sweet red peppers, tomato products
#1 Juice (12A or #211 cylinder)	13.56	13.05/1 5/8	48	8.05	Vegetable juices, nectars
8 oz. (8 oz. tall)	8.68	8.32/1	48	12.66	Individual entrées
8 oz. (8 oz. short)	7.93	7.60/7/8	48	13.82	Vegetables
6 oz. (6 oz.)	6.08	5.80/3/4	48	18.18	Tomato paste, individual juices

Frozen Vegetables

Although more expensive than canned vegetables, frozen vegetables are generally more nutritious and flavorful because nutrients in canned vegetables leak into the packing medium.

Frozen vegetables are graded according to USDA standards:

- U.S. Grade A—carefully selected for color, texture, tenderness, and freedom from blemishes
- U.S. Grade B—more mature and less tender than Grade A vegetables
- U.S. Grade C—less uniform in color and flavor, usually more mature

Frozen vegetables are packed in cases containing 1- to 2-lbs. (450-gram to 1.8-kilogram) boxes or bags, or in bulk form, and need to be stored in a freezer until they are used. Packages should be sealed and moisture-proof.

When receiving frozen vegetables, ensure that the temperature is between 0°F–10°F (‾18°C–‾12°F). Look for ice crystals; a large buildup of ice indicates poor handling. Check for signs of leakage from the carton when received; this is an indication that the carton has been thawing.

Dried Vegetables

Before modern canning methods and freezing technology were available, drying was an important way of preserving many vegetables. Freeze-dried and other dehydrated vegetables, such as potatoes, onions, carrots, celery, beans, tomatoes, peppers, and mushrooms, are gaining popularity in the commercial kitchen.

To reconstitute dried vegetables, follow the manufacturer's instructions. Many of these products must be soaked in water for a specified length of time and temperature. Dried mushrooms, for example, should be soaked in tepid water until soft and then gently squeezed dry before cooking. In many cases the soaking liquid can be strained and used as a flavoring in soups or sauces.

Store dried vegetables at 50°F–70°F (10°C–21°C) in a dry, well-ventilated place, at 15% relative humidity or less. Keep them well sealed and 6″ off the floor.

Cooking Vegetables

Cooking affects the color, texture, flavor, and nutrients of vegetables. These changes can produce attractive, succulent results when vegetables are properly cooked. However, improperly cooked vegetables are unappetizing and result in waste.

Controlling Texture Changes

The fiber structure of vegetables includes cellulose and pectins, which give the vegetables shape and firmness. The amount of fiber varies from vegetable to vegetable and from age to age. For example, mature carrots have more fiber than do young carrots. Tomatoes are lower in fiber than turnips are. The tips of asparagus have less fiber than the stalks.

Cooking breaks down some components, causing some vegetables to lose shape and firmness. Longer cooking times mean softer vegetables. Additives, such as alkalis, in the cooking liquid also destroy fiber as well as valuable vitamins.

Fiber can be made firmer by adding acids such as lemon juice, vinegar, or tomato products to the cooking liquid, which extends the cooking time. However, care is needed when using acids as they can affect the color and flavor of the food. Using sugar strengthens the cell structure, a technique that is also useful when cooking fruit.

Controlling Nutrient Loss

Vegetables are a primary source of vitamins A and C and are rich in other essential nutrients. Overcooking, high temperatures, oxygen, leaching (dissolving into water or other liquid), and alkalis (hard water, baking soda) cause nutrient loss. Plant enzymes, which are active at warm temperatures but killed by high heat, destroy vitamins.

Some loss of nutrients is inevitable, no matter which cooking method is used. However, nutrient loss can be minimized by washing vegetables only briefly and keeping them whole, if possible. Cutting vegetables before washing them increases potential nutrient loss. Soaking cut vegetables in water for 15 minutes or more can result in as much as a 30% loss of nutrients. If boiling or simmering vegetables, certain rules apply.

Below-ground or root vegetables These vegetables are often dense, fibrous, and starchy. A gradual cooking process ensures even cooking. Start cooking the vegetables in cold, seasoned liquid, and gradually bring to a boil, reduce to a simmer, and cook to desired doneness.

Above-ground vegetables Often less dense, fibrous, and starchy than root vegetables, these vegetables therefore may be cooked more quickly. Start cooking above-ground vegetables in a boiling, seasoned liquid. The heat may be reduced to a simmer for more delicate vegetables.

The size and the cut of the vegetable The size and cut of the vegetable may cause the first two rules to vary. For example, if a root vegetable is small, such as a new potato versus an all-purpose potato, then it may be cooked by starting it in a boiling seasoned liquid. Because of its large size, the all-purpose potato should be cooked in a cold seasoned liquid and gradually brought to a boil before reducing it to a simmer. However, if the all-purpose potato is washed and diced in a macédoine style, it will cook much more quickly and therefore may be cooked by starting it in a boiling seasoned liquid.

Heat and Pigmentation

Preserving as much natural color as possible when cooking vegetables is as important as preserving flavor and nutrients.

Pigments, the compounds that give vegetables their color, react in different ways to heat, acid, and other elements.

Foods that have a distinctive green color, such as peas, broccoli, and spinach, contain chlorophyll. Overcooking, covering during cooking, and acidic ingredients added during cooking or holding change the color from dark green to olive. Additives that reduce acidity, such as baking soda (alkalis), tend to brighten the color but leave the vegetables soft and devoid of key nutrients. Salt and sugar added to cooking liquid tend to brighten the green color as well.

Red betalains dominate beets and give them their distinctive color. Acids, such as lemon juice or vinegar, turn the beets bright red. Betalains are water soluble, so beets are usually cooked with the skin on to retain as much color as possible. When beets are cooked in very alkaline water, they tend to turn yellowish brown or black.

Carotenoids are orange-red pigments, characteristic of produce such as carrots, winter squash, peaches, citrus fruits, red peppers, and tomatoes. Carotenoids are very stable and respond little to heat variance, acids, or alkalis.

Anthoxanthins, part of the flavonoid family, give produce such as apples, onions, potatoes, cauliflower, and parsnips their pale yellow to white color. When a base (or alkali) is added to the cooking liquid, the produce turns more yellow, whereas acids tend to make the produce whiter.

Anthocyanins, also in the flavonoid family, provide the purple, blue, and red colors in grapes, berries, cherries, and eggplant. Many of these products become a more vibrant red in the presence of acid. In alkaline water they tend to turn grayish blue. Because of this, anthocyanins are sometimes referred to as "nature's pH meter."

A good example of how the variety of pigments interact and change the color of a vegetable during cooking can be demonstrated by cooking red cabbage in alkaline-rich water. Anthocyanins in the red cabbage turn bluish. The small amount of anthoxanthins, the white pigment present in the cabbage, turns yellow. The red cabbage turns a greenish color, the result of blending yellow with blue.

Maintaining the proper texture and the vibrant, natural colors of produce adds color, interest, and appeal.

Preparing Vegetables for Cooking

Before cooking or serving raw vegetables, prepare them by washing, trimming, peeling, slicing, dicing, mincing, shredding, fluting, or fanning. Much of this work can be performed with a French knife; some tasks require special equipment. Some recipes require vegetables to be shaped. Most vegetables that will be cooked need to be cut into uniform pieces.

See Chapter 7: Equipment and Chapter 8: Knives, Hand Tools, and Smallwares for more information.

Washing Vegetables

Wash leafy green vegetables in several changes of cold water. Lift the greens from the water so that any sand or debris can sink to the bottom. Drain in a colander, and refrigerate until ready to cook. Cover loosely with wet cheesecloth or a damp paper towel to prevent drying without cutting off air circulation.

Peeling, Cutting, and Shaping Vegetables

Peeling, cutting, and shaping vegetables can determine how they taste after they have been cooked. Inedible skins, stems, and stalks are usually removed before cooking. An exception to this is when the shape and color of the skin is part of the vegetable's appeal, as it is with certain winter squashes. Vegetables may be cut into uniform pieces with a food processor, a mandolin, or a French knife.

Cooking Vegetables With Dry Heat

Cooking vegetables with dry heat, such as broiling, grilling, baking, and roasting, preserves flavors and nutrients because the nutrients do not leach into water or other liquid. This method also adds flavor and textural interest to the vegetables. For more intense flavoring, brush butter, seasonings, flavorings, or flavored oil on the vegetables before cooking.

Broiling and grilling Both of these cooking methods cook vegetables quickly over high heat, which browns the vegetables, adding flavor. Tender vegetables with high moisture can be grilled raw. Dense

PROCESS

Preparing Roasted Red Peppers

Roasting peppers over an open flame gives them a rich, smoky flavor that makes them ideal for use in appetizers, salads, sauces, side dishes, and entrée preparations. Do not handle with bare hands if using them in preparations that require no further cooking.

To roast and trim peppers:

Wash peppers, and then place them on a pre-heated grill. Char the peppers, turning them occasionally, until they are blackened on all sides.

Place warm peppers in a bowl or hotel pan, and cover with plastic wrap. Let sit about 15 minutes or until cool enough to handle.

Use a paring knife to peel away the charred skin.

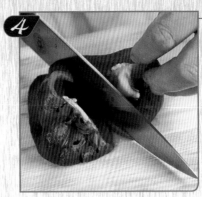

Cut the peppers in half to expose the core and seeds.

Remove the core.

Use a paring knife to scrape away the seeds.

Vegetables and Legumes

595

vegetables contain more starch and must be parboiled before grilling. To ensure even cooking, cut vegetables into uniform or equal shapes and slices. Grill vegetables long enough to create well-browned cross-hatch marks on both sides. Potatoes, tomatoes, eggplant, peppers, squash, and corn are just a few of the vegetables that benefit from broiling or grilling. See Figure 27-3.

Small vegetables, such as mushrooms or tomatoes, can be threaded onto skewers for grilling. For larger vegetables, such as squash or eggplant, slice and place them directly on the grill.

The size of the vegetable can affect the broiling process. To broil, arrange the sliced vegetables on a sheet pan. Vegetables that are already cooked can be broiled to reheat them.

Baking Baked vegetables are cooked at a lower temperature for a longer time than grilled or broiled vegetables. Squash, onions, potatoes, and other root vegetables are excellent choices for this method. See Figure 27-4. Before baking, thoroughly clean the vegetable, and peel if necessary. Some vegetables are baked with the skin on. They can be either left whole or cut into uniform pieces.

Roasting Roast vegetables to add to their flavor. Roasted vegetables, such as squash or

eggplant, should be washed, trimmed, and cut, if needed. The skins can be left on to protect the interior from drying out. Add water or another liquid to the roasting pan to provide steam and prevent scorching. Cooking time controls oven temperatures. For vegetables that require longer cooking times, the oven temperature should be on a lower setting; vegetables that cook fast use higher temperature settings. Rotate the pan to ensure even cooking. Vegetables are done when they can be easily pierced by a chef's fork.

Sautéing Sautéing cooks vegetables quickly in a small amount of butter or oil over moderately high heat. Because this method is quick, have all vegetables prepared and cut before starting. Blanch any firm vegetables, such as broccoli, Brussels sprouts, carrots, and potatoes, before sautéing them. Choose a complementary cooking fat, and introduce additional seasonings to optimize the vegetable's flavor. Sautéed vegetables should be brightly colored and slightly crisp.

To begin, heat the oil or cooking fat. Keep in mind that vegetables will use less heat than meat, fish, or poultry. Adjust the heat accordingly. Vegetables should be added individually, by order of cooking time. Start with vegetables that require a

longer cooking time, and end with those needing less time to cook.

Deep-frying Deep-fried vegetables are often coated with a batter or breading before they are submerged in hot oil. Potatoes, deep-fried as either French fries or chips, are an exception. Other vegetables that can be deep-fried include onions, mushrooms, cauliflower, eggplant, and zucchini; blanch cauliflower and broccoli before deep-frying. See Figure 27-5 on page 597. Vegetables should be cut into uniform pieces and thoroughly dried before deep-frying. The thinner the cut of the vegetable, the crispier the end product will be.

Vegetable oils such as corn, canola, and safflower work well for deep-frying. These oils are able to reach high temperatures without breaking down or smoking, and they hold a neutral flavor. Olive oil or duck or goose fat may be used to give vegetables a distinct flavor.

To season deep-fried vegetables, wait until vegetables are in a pan lined with absorbent paper. Seasoning over a fryer can speed up the breakdown of the frying oil. Use a fry basket, tongs, a spider, or a skimmer to remove vegetables from the fryer.

Cooking Vegetables with Moist Heat

Moist cooking methods for vegetables include blanching, steaming, simmering, poaching, and braising. Before cooking the vegetables, clean and cut them into uniform pieces. Preserve water-soluble vitamins by cooking vegetables for the minimum amount of time.

Green vegetables should be cooked uncovered so that the acid can escape. Red vegetables should be cooked covered to retain the acid. They may also need an acid such as vinegar added to the cooking liquid to replace lost acid.

Blanching Blanching involves a two-step process. Vegetables are plunged into boiling water until they are lightly cooked but still firm. Vegetables are then shocked, or submerged in an ice bath, to stop the cooking process. Vegetables are often blanched to loosen their skins before peeling or to

FIGURE 27-3
Many vegetables benefit from being grilled or broiled. These methods preserve nutrients while adding flavor, texture, and visual appeal.

FIGURE 27-4
Vegetables can be baked with their skin on or removed, and they can be left whole or cut into uniform pieces.

FIGURE 27-5
Deep-fried vegetables often are coated with a batter or breading before frying.

FIGURE 27-6
Steaming vegetables results in more color and flavor.

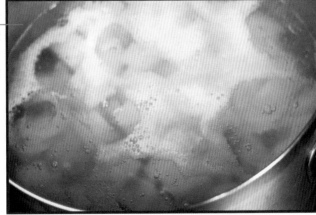

FIGURE 27-7
Simmering results in soft, colorful, flavorful vegetables.

FIGURE 27-8
Braised vegetables are cooked in their own juices, either whole or in large pieces.

increase their color and flavor before being frozen. Blanched vegetables become fully cooked by using a second cooking method, such as grilling or broiling.

Steaming Steaming captures a vegetable's pure, undiluted flavor. Water is the most common liquid used to steam vegetables. The cooking time required determines the amount of liquid needed. The longer the cooking time, the more liquid is needed. When steaming small quantities of vegetables, place a perforated container above boiling water. Larger quantities should be steamed in tiered steamers or pressure or convection cookers to properly circulate the steam. Steaming results in colorful, flavorful vegetables. See Figure 27-6.

Simmering Simmering, like steaming, can produce colorful, flavorful vegetables. See Figure 27-7. Simmering, as opposed to boiling, reduces the break-up of fragile vegetables during cooking. When simmering green vegetables, allow for the liquid to reach a slightly higher temperature, and more convection, to avoid extending cooking time. This helps minimize the loss of color and nutrients.

Poaching Poached vegetables cook in just enough liquid to cover them. The liquid absorbs much of the flavor of the vegetables and seasoning used during the poaching process. This liquid can be used in the final stages of poaching to create a flavorful finishing sauce.

Braising Braised vegetables either cook in their own juices or cook with added stock, fumets, meat glace, or demi-glace. See Figure 27-8. Vegetables are cooked whole or cut into pieces. If desired, vegetables may be lightly sautéed or blanched as part of the process. Cover and finish cooking on the range or in an oven with moderate heat. Save the braising liquid, reduce it, and serve it as a sauce for the vegetables or blend it into a prepared sauce such as demi-glace. Popular braising vegetables include cabbages, celery, leeks, onions, endive, and some lettuces.

Purchasing and Storing Legumes

Legumes may be purchased as whole beans, bean flours, bean sprouts, whole peas, split peas, pea flours, and lentils, and dried, precooked, frozen, canned, and presoaked. Like vegetables, they are graded on quality characteristics and should be stored properly.

Grading

Legumes receive a grade based on the quality characteristics of color, uniformity, and damage. The USDA grades legumes as
- U.S. No. 1—the highest quality mark given to legumes;
- U.S. No. 2—above average quality;
- U.S. No. 3—medium or average quality.

Market Forms

Legumes are widely available dried, precooked, frozen, canned, or presoaked. They are almost interchangeable, although some traditional recipes specify a particular type of bean or other legume. Canned legumes such as chickpeas or kidney beans are precooked and packed in a broth or oil or with a sauce. They may be used straight from the can in almost any recipe.

Storing Legumes

Store dried legumes in a cool, dark place.

Cleaning and Soaking Legumes

Most dried legumes, generally the most economical and versatile choice, must be rehydrated before cooking. Lentils and split peas are the exception. They can be cooked without soaking and will cook more quickly than dried beans.

Handling and Storing Cooked Legumes

When preparing legumes, use one of the following methods to cool them quickly:
- Divide the hot legumes into smaller quantities, and put them into shallow, precooled pans. Refrigerate, and stir occasionally.
- Use an ice bath to bring down the temperature of the food. Divide the cooked legumes into several small, shallow pans, and place in ice water in the sink.
- Use cold paddles filled with water, and freeze. Sanitize the paddles after each use.

Store extra legumes in a container, labeled by name and date, in the refrigerator. Cooked, refrigerated legumes can be stored for about three days. Cooked, cooled legumes can be packaged in an airtight, moisture-proof container and frozen.

Soaking Legumes

Legumes often are soaked before cooking.

To soak legumes:

1 Pick through the beans carefully, removing any grit, small pebbles, or other debris.

2 Place the beans in a bowl, and cover with water, removing any skins or beans that float to the surface.

3 Drain the beans in a colander, and rinse under cold, running water.

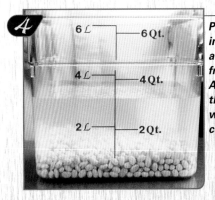

4 Place the beans in a container, and cover with fresh cold water. Allow about three cups of water for each cup of beans.

5 Soak the beans for several hours, overnight, or as directed in the recipe.

6 Drain beans, and cook according to the recipe. The soaking water may be discarded or preserved for use in the recipe.

Quick-Soaking Legumes

When preparing legumes, you can accelerate the soaking time by using the quick-soaking technique.

To do this:

1 Rinse and pick through the beans.

2 Place the beans in a saucepan, and add cool water to cover by about two inches.

3 Bring to a boil, and simmer for two minutes.

4 Remove from the heat, cover, and let soak for one hour.

5 Drain beans, and proceed with the recipe.

Braised Red Cabbage

INGREDIENTS

	U.S. Standard	Metric
Duck fat	4 oz.	115 g
Onions, *peeled and diced brunoise*	4 oz.	115 g
Red wine vinegar	1 oz.	30 ml
Sugar	3 oz.	85 g
Red cabbage, *core removed, cut chiffonade*	4 lbs.	1.8 kg
Sour apples, *washed, peeled, and grated*	10 oz.	285 g
Salt	TT	TT
White pepper	TT	TT

METHOD OF PREPARATION

1. Gather all the equipment and ingredients.
2. Heat the duck fat in a braising pan.
3. Add the onions to the hot fat, and sauté.
4. Add the red wine vinegar and sugar, and simmer briefly to melt sugar.
5. Add the red cabbage and the apples; toss well to coat with the fat.
6. Cover, and braise over medium heat until tender.
7. Season with salt and pepper.

COOKING TECHNIQUES

Sautéing:
1. Heat the sauté pan to the appropriate temperature.
2. Evenly brown the food product.
3. For a sauce, pour off any excess oil, reheat, and deglaze.

Braising:
1. Heat the braising pan to the proper temperature.
2. Sear and brown the food product to a golden color.
3. Degrease and deglaze.
4. Cook the food product in two-thirds liquid until fork-tender.

GLOSSARY

Brunoise: *1/8" (3 mm) dice*

Chiffonade: *ribbons of leafy greens*

NUTRITION

Nutrition Facts

Yield: Serves 10
Serving Size: 8 oz. (225 g)

Amount Per Serving

Calories 200	
Total Fat 12 g	
Sodium 60 mg	
Total Carbohydrate 23 g	
Protein 3 g	

Roasted Beets

INGREDIENTS

	U.S. Standard	Metric
Beets, *fresh, washed, trimmed, leaving 1" (2.54 cm) of stem and root intact*	4 lbs.	1.8 kg
Butter, *clarified*	4 oz.	115 g
Salt	TT	TT
Black pepper, *freshly ground*	TT	TT

METHOD OF PREPARATION

1. Gather all the equipment and ingredients.

2. Preheat the oven to 350°F (177°C).

3. Place beets on a sheet pan, and roast in the oven until fork-tender. Should take approximately 1–1 1/2 hours, depending on size of beets.

4. Remove from the oven. Allow the beets to cool enough to handle. Trim the ends, and peel. Cut or slice beets as desired.

5. For service, heat a saucepan, and melt the butter. Add the beets, and sauté until heated thoroughly. Season to taste and serve, or hold at 140°F (60°C) or higher.

COOKING TECHNIQUES

Roasting:

1. Sear the food product, and brown evenly.
2. Elevate the food product in a roasting pan.
3. Determine doneness, and consider carryover cooking.
4. Let the food product rest before carving.

Sautéing:

1. Heat the sauté pan to the appropriate temperature.
2. Evenly brown the food product.
3. For a sauce, pour off any excess oil, reheat, and deglaze.

NUTRITION

Nutrition Facts

Yield: Serves 10
Serving Size: 5 oz. (140 g)

Amount Per Serving

Calories 170

Total Fat 9 g

Sodium 160 mg

Total Carbohydrate 17 g

Protein 3 g

Grilled Fresh Vegetables

Grilling/Broiling:

1. Clean and heat the grill or broiler.
2. To prevent sticking, brush the food product with oil.

Steaming (Traditional):

1. Place a rack over a pot of water.
2. Prevent steam vapors from escaping.
3. Shock or cook the food product throughout.

Blanch: to parcook

Al dente: to the bite

Nutrition Facts

Yield: Serves 10
Serving Size: 5.5 oz. (155 g)

Amount Per Serving

Calories 80	
Total Fat 4.5 g	
Sodium 95 mg	
Total Carbohydrate 8 g	
Protein 3 g	

INGREDIENTS

	U.S. Standard	Metric
Carrots, washed, peeled, and cut on the bias, 1" (2.54 cm) thick	6 oz.	170 g
Onions, peeled and cut into 1" (2.54 cm) dice	6 oz.	170 g
Zucchini, washed, trimmed, cut on the bias, 1" (2.54 cm) thick	6 oz.	170 g
Yellow squash, washed, trimmed, cut on the bias, 1" (2.54 cm) thick	6 oz.	170 g
Mushrooms, cleaned and stemmed	1 lb.	454 g
Cherry tomatoes, washed and stemmed	1 lb.	454 g
Olive oil	as needed	as needed
Salt	TT	TT
Black pepper, ground	TT	TT

METHOD OF PREPARATION

1. Gather all the equipment and ingredients.
2. Preheat the grill or broiler.
3. *Blanch* or steam the carrots and onions until *al dente,* shock, and strain.
4. Arrange the vegetables on skewers, alternating colors for eye appeal.
5. Brush the vegetables with olive oil and grill, turning frequently until they are crisp/tender. Season and serve immediately, or hold minimally at 140°F (60°C) or higher.

Ratatouille

Ingredients

Ingredients	U.S. Standard	Metric
Olive oil	4 oz.	120 ml
Onions, peeled and diced brunoise	4 oz.	115 g
Garlic, peeled, mashed into a purée	1/4 head	1/4 head
Green bell peppers, washed, seeded, sliced	1 lb.	454 g
Tomatoes, washed, cored, and cut into wedges	1 lb.	454 g
Eggplant, washed and diced parmentier	1 lb.	454 g
Zucchini, washed and diced parmentier	1 lb.	454 g
Green beans, washed, blanched and shocked	1 lb.	454 g
Tomato purée	4 oz.	120 ml
Salt	TT	TT
Black pepper, ground	TT	TT

Method of Preparation

1. Gather all the equipment and ingredients.

2. Heat olive oil in a rondeau. Add onions, and sauté until translucent.

3. Add all other vegetables, and sauté for 5 minutes.

4. Stir in tomato purée. Season, cover, and bake in a 350°F (177°C) oven until the vegetables are tender.

COOKING TECHNIQUES

Sautéing:
1. Heat the sauté pan to the appropriate temperature.
2. Evenly brown the food product.
3. For a sauce, pour off any excess oil, reheat, and deglaze.

Steaming (Traditional):
1. Place a rack over a pot of water.
2. Prevent steam vapors from escaping.
3. Shock or cook the food product throughout.

GLOSSARY

Brunoise: 1/8″ (3 mm) dice
Parmentier: 1/2″ (1.27 cm) dice
Blanch: to parcook

NUTRITION

Nutrition Facts
Yield: Serves 10
Serving Size: 9 oz. (255 g)

Amount Per Serving	
Calories 170	
Total Fat 12 g	
Sodium 70 mg	
Total Carbohydrate 17 g	
Protein 4 g	

Stir-fried Vegetables

INGREDIENTS

Ingredients	U.S. Standard	Metric
Carrots, washed, peeled, and cut julienne	1 lb.	454 g
Turnips, washed, peeled, and cut julienne	10 oz.	285 g
Green beans, trimmed and French cut	10 oz.	285 g
Butter	4 oz.	115 g
Vidalia onions, peeled and cut julienne	6 oz.	170 g
Red peppers, washed, cored, and cut julienne	10 oz.	285 g
Cubanelle peppers, washed, cored, and cut julienne	10 oz.	285 g
Salt	TT	TT
White pepper, ground	TT	TT
Parsley, washed, squeezed dry, and chopped	2 oz.	55 g

METHOD OF PREPARATION

1. Gather all the equipment and ingredients.
2. Separately blanch the carrots, turnips, and green beans; drain and shock. When cold, strain to remove all moisture.
3. Heat butter in a wok or skillet; add the onions and peppers, and stir-fry for three minutes.
4. Add the blanched vegetables; add seasonings, and stir-fry until vegetables are al dente and heated through. Sprinkle with chopped parsley.

COOKING TECHNIQUES

Blanching:
1. Plunge food briefly into boiling water.
2. Quickly plunge food into cold water to stop the cooking process.

Stir-Frying:
1. Heat the oil in a wok until hot but not smoking.
2. Keep the food in constant motion; use the entire cooking surface.

GLOSSARY

Julienne: 1/8″ × 1/8″ × 1″–2″ (3 mm × 3 mm × 2.5–5 cm) strips

NUTRITION

Nutrition Facts
Yield: Serves 10
Serving Size: 7 oz. (205 g)

Amount Per Serving

Calories 190

Total Fat 14 g

Sodium 270 mg

Total Carbohydrate 14 g

Protein 2 g

Red and Black Lentils with Prosciutto

INGREDIENTS

	U.S. Standard	Metric
Dried red lentils, washed, drained	12 oz.	340 g
Dried black lentils, washed, drained	12 oz.	340 g
Water	as needed	as needed
Olive oil	3 oz.	90 ml
Leeks, trimmed, split lengthwise, thinly sliced, washed	5 oz.	140 g
Prosciutto, diced brunoise	5 oz.	140 g
Rosemary, fresh, washed, leaves stripped, chopped	1 1/2 tsp.	8 ml
Salt	TT	TT
Black pepper, ground	TT	TT

METHOD OF PREPARATION

1. Gather all the ingredients and equipment.

2. Place both varieties of lentils in a saucepan. Add water to cover, heat to a boil, and immediately turn down to a simmer. Continue to simmer gently until the lentils are tender, and then drain. Dépouille as needed.

3. In the meantime, heat the oil in a sauté pan, add the leeks, and sauté until translucent. Add the prosciutto and rosemary, and sauté for 1 minute more.

4. Add the drained lentils. Mix well and heat throughout. Taste and season with salt and pepper as needed.

5. Serve immediately, or hold at 140°F (60°C) or higher.

This is a perfect accompaniment to lamb.

COOKING TECHNIQUES

Simmering:
1. Place the prepared product in an appropriately sized pot.
2. Bring the product to a boil, and then reduce the heat to allow the product to barely boil.
3. Cook until desired doneness is achieved.

Sautéing:
1. Heat the sauté pan to the appropriate temperature.
2. Evenly brown the food product.
3. For a sauce, pour off any excess oil, reheat, and deglaze.

GLOSSARY

Brunoise: 1/8" (3 mm) dice

NUTRITION

Nutrition Facts

Yield: Serves 10
Serving Size: 4 oz. (115 g)

Amount Per Serving

Calories 380	
Total Fat 11 g	
Sodium 320 mg	
Total Carbohydrate 49 g	
Protein 25 g	

Roasted New Potatoes with Garlic and Rosemary

INGREDIENTS

	U.S. Standard	Metric
Red Bliss potatoes, washed	30 small	30 small
Olive oil	3 oz.	90 ml
Garlic, peeled and minced	4 cloves	4 cloves
Rosemary, fresh, washed and chopped	1 oz.	30 ml
Salt	TT	TT
White pepper, ground	TT	TT

METHOD OF PREPARATION

1. Gather all the ingredients and equipment.

2. Preheat the oven to 350°F (177°C).

3. Shape the potatoes as desired, and hold them in cold water.

4. In a mixing bowl, combine all of the remaining ingredients. Drain the potatoes well, and then toss in the oil mixture until they are well coated.

5. Place the potatoes in a shallow roasting pan, and place in the oven. Roast about 45 minutes or until the potatoes are fork-tender.

COOKING TECHNIQUES

Roasting:

1. Sear the food product, and brown evenly.
2. Elevate the food product in a roasting pan.
3. Determine doneness, and consider carryover cooking.
4. Let the food product rest before carving.

NUTRITION

Nutrition Facts

Yield: Serves 10
Serving Size: 3 each; 6 oz. (170 g)

Amount Per Serving

Calories 120

Total Fat 6 g

Sodium 460 mg

Total Carbohydrate 14 g

Protein 1 g

Potato Croquettes

INGREDIENTS	U.S. Standard	Metric
Potatoes, *Russet*	3 lbs.	1.4 kg
Salt	1 1/2 tsp.	8 ml
Egg yolks	3 each	3 each
Salt	TT	TT
White pepper	TT	TT
Nutmeg	TT	TT
Flour, *all-purpose*	1 3/4 oz.	49 g
Eggs	3 each	3 each
Bread crumbs, *fine*	4 oz.	115 g
Vegetable oil	as needed	as needed

METHOD OF PREPARATION

1. Gather all the ingredients and equipment.
2. Wash and peel potatoes, and cut into even-sized chunks.
3. Steam potatoes, or cook in lightly salted water (enough to cover), and drain well.
4. When cooked, dry potatoes briefly in the oven.
5. Pass potatoes through a wire sieve or ricer.
6. Add egg yolks to potatoes, and season to taste with salt, pepper, and nutmeg.
7. Dust the work area generously with flour.
8. Using a pastry bag with a straight tube, press the tubular rolls about 1/2″ (1.27 cm) thick, directly onto floured table.
9. Cut tubes into 1 1/2″ (3.81 cm) long sections.
10. Roll croquettes in flour.
11. Beat eggs, and mix with a small amount of water.
12. Dredge floured croquettes, first in egg mixture, and then in bread crumbs. Roll to shape evenly and to press crumbs to croquettes.
13. Fill pan 1″ (2.54 cm) deep with oil. Deep-fry until golden brown.
14. Drain on absorbent paper or a sheet pan and wire rack.

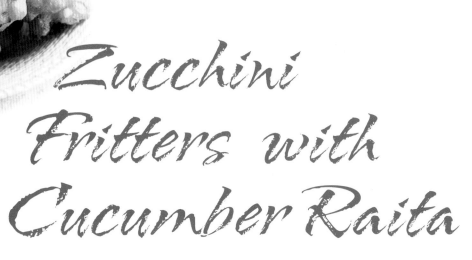

Zucchini Fritters with Cucumber Raita

INGREDIENTS

	U.S. Standard	Metric
Oil	for frying	for frying
Zucchini	3 lbs.	1.4 kg
Salt	1/2 Tbsp.	8 ml
Flour	1 cup	240 ml
Baking powder	1/4 tsp.	1.25 ml
Eggs, beaten	2 each	2 each
Milk	3 oz.	90 ml
Onion, peeled and diced brunoise	2 oz.	55 g
Salt	TT	TT
White pepper, ground	TT	TT

METHOD OF PREPARATION

1. Gather all the ingredients and equipment.
2. Preheat fryolator to 350°F (177°C).
3. Wash, trim, and grate the zucchini. Do not peel. Sprinkle with salt.
4. Drain in a colander for 30 minutes.
5. Squeeze the zucchini, a handful at a time, to remove as much moisture as possible.
6. In a separate bowl, mix the flour and baking powder.
7. In another bowl, combine the eggs, milk, and onion.
8. Add the flour mixture to the egg mixture, and whip until smooth.
9. Add the grated zucchini. Stir until incorporated. Season with salt and pepper.
10. Drop by spoonfuls into hot oil, and fry until golden brown on all sides. Test one fritter first to check seasoning, and reseason as needed before cooking the rest.
11. Drain on absorbent towels, and then transfer to a hotel pan lined with absorbent towels. Hold briefly at 140°F (60°C) or higher if necessary. To retain crispness, do not stack fritters on top of each other.
12. Serve hot with Cucumber Raita (recipe follows).

COOKING TECHNIQUES

Frying:
1. Heat the frying liquid to the appropriate temperature.
2. Place the food product into the hot liquid.
3. Cook the product, turning frequently, until golden brown and tender.

NUTRITION

Nutrition Facts
Yield: Serves 10
Serving Size: 6 oz. (170 g)

Amount Per Serving

Calories 280

Total Fat 25 g

Sodium 240 mg

Total Carbohydrate 12 g

Protein 4 g

Cucumber Raita

INGREDIENTS

	U.S. Standard	Metric
Cucumber, medium, peeled and seeded	1 each	1 each
Yogurt, plain	1 cup	240 ml
Salt	3/4 tsp.	4 ml
Cumin, ground	1 tsp.	5 ml
Garlic, fresh, peeled, mashed	1 clove	1 clove
Cilantro, fresh, washed, squeezed dry, chopped	1/2 oz.	15 ml

METHOD OF PREPARATION

1. Gather all the ingredients and equipment.
2. Finely grate the cucumber.
3. In a bowl, combine the cucumber with all other ingredients, and mix well.
4. Serve with Zucchini Fritters.

Honey Lime Carrots

INGREDIENTS

	U.S. Standard	Metric
Carrots, washed, peeled, cut batonnette	3 lbs.	1.4 kg
Butter	2 oz.	55 g
Sugar, brown	2 oz.	55 g
Honey	2 oz.	55 g
Salt	1 tsp.	5 g
Lime juice	2 each	2 each
Parsley, washed, squeezed dry, and chopped	2 oz.	60 ml

METHOD OF PREPARATION

1. Gather all the equipment and ingredients.
2. Preheat steamer.
3. Place carrots in a hotel pan, steam al dente, and shock. Drain well to remove all moisture.
4. For service, melt butter in a sauté pan, add the sugar and honey, and swirl to melt.
5. Add the carrots, salt, and lime juice, and sauté until carrots are heated through.
6. Toss in the parsley and serve.

French-Fried Potatoes

INGREDIENTS

	U.S. Standard	Metric
Potatoes, washed, peeled, cut into strips 2" × 1/4" (5.08 cm × 6 mm)	5 lbs.	2.3 kg
Oil	as needed	as needed
Salt	TT	TT

METHOD OF PREPARATION

1. Gather all the ingredients and equipment.

2. Keep the potatoes in cold water for 1 hour to remove some of the starch. Drain, and pat dry with absorbent paper.

3. Half-fill the frying basket with potatoes. Dip the potatoes in the oil in a deep-fat fryer at 325°F (163°C), and blanch until almost done. Drain, remove, and spread on a sheet pan lined with absorbent paper. Hold until needed.

4. Cook only the quantity of potatoes needed, half-filling the basket each time.

5. Dip the basket in the oil in a deep-fat fryer set at 375°F (191°C).

6. Fry to a golden brown. The potatoes should be crisp outside but soft inside.

7. Drain on absorbent paper.

8. Lightly salt the potatoes.

COOKING TECHNIQUES

Deep-Frying:

1. Heat the frying liquid to the proper temperature.
2. Submerge the food product completely.
3. Fry the product until it is cooked throughout.

NUTRITION

Nutrition Facts

Yield: Serves 10
Serving Size: 4 oz. (115 g)

Amount Per Serving

Calories 230

Total Fat 9 g

Sodium 35 mg

Total Carbohydrate 35 g

Protein 4 g

Bouquet of Vegetables

COOKING TECHNIQUES

Boiling (At sea level):
1. Bring the cooking liquid to a rapid boil.
2. Stir the contents, and cook the food product throughout.
3. Serve hot.

Sautéing:
1. Heat the sauté pan to the appropriate temperature.
2. Evenly brown the food product.
3. For a sauce, pour off any excess oil, reheat, and deglaze.

GLOSSARY
Al dente: to the bite
Nappé: coated or to coat

NUTRITION

Nutrition Facts
Yield: Serves 10
Serving Size: 10 oz. (285 g)

Amount Per Serving	
Calories 380	
Total Fat 34 g	
Sodium 210 mg	
Total Carbohydrate 15 g	
Protein 5 g	

INGREDIENTS

INGREDIENTS	U.S. Standard	Metric
Carrots, washed, peeled, and chopped	1 lb.	454 g
Green beans, washed and trimmed	1 lb.	454 g
Cauliflower, core removed, washed, florets cut (reserve stems)	1 head	1 head
Asparagus, washed, trimmed, stalks peeled	1 lb.	454 g
Butter	8 oz.	225 g
Salt	TT	TT
White pepper, ground	TT	TT
Cherry tomatoes, washed	30 each	30 each
Hollandaise sauce, heated to 140°F (60°C)	5 oz.	150 ml
Mimosa butter	5 oz.	150 ml

METHOD OF PREPARATION

1. Gather all the equipment and ingredients.

2. In separate saucepans, cook the carrots, green beans, cauliflower, and asparagus in boiling, salted water until *al dente.* Shock in ice water, and drain.

3. At the time of service, heat the butter in a sauté pan, and separately reheat or sauté all of the vegetables, including the cherry tomatoes. Add seasoning to taste.

4. To serve, arrange the vegetables on preheated dinner plates. *Nappé* the asparagus with hollandaise sauce and the cauliflower with mimosa butter.

Evidence shows that people have enjoyed fruit since prehistoric times. Scientists have carbon-dated apple seeds from as far back as 6500 B.C., and the ancient Romans first cultivated the wild apple to produce sweeter, juicier fruit. Ancient Phoenician, Mesopotamian, and Egyptian civilizations used grapes extensively, and as long as 4,000 years ago China cultivated drupes. Apricot trees were likely first cultivated in England in the 1300s, from where settlers then brought them to North America and planted them throughout the English colonies. Colonists first planted pear trees in America in 1620.

2000 B.C.
Chinese cultivate drupes.

A.D. 1300
English grow apricot trees.

1620
Colonists plant pear trees in America.

KEY TERMS

phytonutrients
supremes
achenes
fraise des bois
drupe
tapenade
bloom
papain
ethylene gas
acidulate

Fruit

Fruits play an important role in a balanced diet. Although they consist mainly of water and supply little protein, fruits do provide essential vitamins and minerals. Oranges and strawberries are excellent sources of vitamin C. The natural sugars in fruit provide quick energy, and fruit acids aid digestion. Fruit is also an important source of fiber. Fruits are rich in antioxidants called phytonutrients, which appear to be active agents in fighting heart disease, cancers, and other age-related illnesses. The U.S. Department of Agriculture's Food Guide Pyramid recommends two to four servings of fruit daily for optimum health.

Fruit-Supplying States and Nations

California, Florida, and Washington are the top three fruit-producing states in the United States. California is the leading producer of grapes, strawberries, peaches, nectarines, and kiwi fruit and a major producer of citrus fruit, apples, pears, plums, and sweet cherries. Florida, second in fruit production, is the leading provider of citrus fruit in the United States, accounting for 79.9% of all citrus fruit grown domestically. Washington ranks third in overall fruit production, but it ranks first in domestic production of apples, pears, and sweet cherries. It supplies 52% of apples, 45% of sweet cherries, and 38% of pears.

Among international fruit sources, Mexico and Chile are the leading suppliers of fresh and frozen fruit, excluding bananas, imported by the United States. The main sources of bananas, which constitute 70% of all fresh fruit imports, are Costa Rica, Ecuador, Guatemala, Colombia, and Honduras. Countries in South America and Southeast Asia provide much of the fruit juice consumed in the United States. Brazil is a major supplier of orange juice. Argentina and Chile provide apple juice and grape juice. The main international sources of pineapple juice are the Philippines and Thailand.

Types of Fresh Fruit

Fresh fruits are those that have not been canned, frozen, or dried. They may be ripe or unripe, depending on the type of fruit, how it was harvested, and the storage conditions used.

Fruits can be divided into eight categories: citrus fruits, melons, berries, drupes, pomes, grapes, tropical fruits, and exotic fruits.

> See Chapter 27: Vegetables and Legumes for information on fruit-vegetables such as tomatoes, eggplant, capsicum peppers, and avocados.

Citrus Fruits

Citrus fruits grow in tropical and subtropical climates. Their origin has been traced to Southeast Asia, particularly Malaysia, more than 6,000 years ago. The classification includes lemons, limes, grapefruit, tangerines, kumquats, oranges, and several hybrids.

Citrus fruits are identified by their thick rind, composed of the bitter white pith covered by a thin layer of brightly colored skin, or zest. Citrus fruits are acidic and have a strong aroma. The flesh is segmented and juicy, and it varies in flavor from bitter to tart to sweet.

Citrus fruits are a source of vitamin C, folic acid, dietary fiber, and potassium. The pulp, skin, and juice of citrus fruits are all edible.

Lemons Lemons are the most commonly used citrus fruits. Their strongly acidic flavor makes them nearly unpalatable raw, but they are well suited for flavoring desserts and confections. Lemon juice is often used in sauces, particularly with fish, seafood, and poultry. The zest adds flavor to pastries and savory dishes.

Limes Small, thin-skinned limes can often be used interchangeably with lemons. Limes are too tart to eat raw, but curries and desserts often include their juice. The zest adds color and flavor to a variety of dishes.

Grapefruits The grapefruit is a large, round hybrid of the orange and the pomelo. Grapefruits have yellow skin, thick rind, and tart flesh. They are available in white-fleshed and the sweeter pink- or ruby-fleshed varieties. They are best eaten raw or lightly broiled with a topping of brown sugar. Grapefruit segments are available canned in syrup.

Kumquats Kumquats are very small, oval-shaped, orange fruits with a soft, sweet skin and slightly bitter flesh. They can be eaten whole, either raw or preserved in syrup, and used in jams and preserves.

Mandarins Mandarins, a hybrid of the orange and the tangerine, have loose, smooth, deep orange skin that can be easily peeled to reveal sweet flesh. Mandarins can be eaten raw alone or in salads, or they can be juiced.

Tangelos Tangelos are a hybrid of the mandarin and the pomelo, with a smooth, deep orange skin that is easily peeled. Tangelos are large, though smaller than the pomelo, and slightly elongated on one end, resulting in a bell shape. Their juicy, seedless flesh can be an ingredient in salads or main dishes.

Tangerines Tangerines are small, dark oranges with loose, easily removed rinds. They are most often eaten fresh, but they are also available canned like mandarin oranges.

Oranges Oranges are round fruits with a juicy orange flesh and a thin orange skin. They may be either sweet or bitter. Oranges can be juiced for beverages or sauces, eaten raw, added to salads, cooked in desserts, or used as a garnish.

PROCESS

Segmenting an Orange

Citrus segments are known as *supremes*. Orange segments may be added to salads, cooked in desserts, or used as a garnish.

To segment an orange:

1 Cut off both ends of the orange to create a flat surface and expose the flesh.

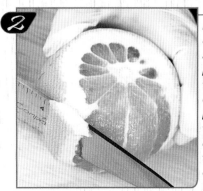

2 Lay the cut side flat on a cutting board, and remove the peel. Take caution to waste as little of the orange as possible while trimming away the entire pith. Follow the rounded shape of the orange.

3 Cut alongside each membrane, cutting down to the center of the orange.

4 Remove the orange segment from the membrane.

LEMONS

LEMONS

EUREKA, LISBON, BEARSS, AVON, HARNEY, VILLAFRANCO, MEYER

Description and Purchasing Specifications— Oval shape with a thin yellow to orange skin. Firm, heavy, fine-textured skin.

Packaging and Receiving—75, 95, 115, 140, 165, 200, and 235 count cartons

Grade and Size—U.S. No. 1, Combination, No. 2

Storage and Usage—45°F–48°F (7°C–9°C), 89%–91% relative humidity. Garnish, juice, beverage enhancer, desserts.

Flavor—Very tart, bitter. Meyer lemons are sweet in comparison with other lemons.

Yield—49%

LIMES

LIMES

KEY, MEXICAN, PERSIAN, TAHITI

Description and Purchasing Specifications— Round or oval shape with a bright green skin. Fully ripe, heavy, smooth skin.

Packaging and Receiving—10-lb. (4.4-k), 20-lb. (8.8-k), and 38-lb. (16.8-k) cartons (27, 48, 54, and 63 count)

Grade and Size—U.S. No. 1, Combination, No. 2

Storage and Usage—58°F–60°F (14°C–16°C), 90% relative humidity. Used like lemons; can also be used in salad dressings.

Flavor—Tart, slightly sweeter than lemons.

Yield—N/A

Fruit

615

Zesting a Lemon

The thin strips of the rind, or zest, of a lemon add intense flavor to foods. When zesting, it is important to avoid the pith because it is very bitter.

To zest a lemon:

1 Wash the lemon very well before cutting.

2 Draw a five-hole zester across the skin to remove the zest, being careful to avoid cutting into the pith.

3 Use a French knife to chop the zest into tiny pieces.

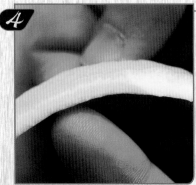

4 The peel includes the bitter white pith. The zest is only the outer yellow skin.

GRAPEFRUITS

DUNCAN, MARSH, WHITE, PINK, RUBY RED

Description and Purchasing Specifications—Large, round, yellow to pink skin, acidic flesh. Firm, plump, heavy, well-shaped, smooth outer peel.

Packaging and Receiving—18, 24, 32, 40, 48, and 56 count boxes; 5-lb. (2-k 225-g) and 8-lb. (4-k) bags

Grade and Size—Fresh: U.S. Fancy, No. 1, No. 2, Combination, No. 3. Canned: Grade B

Storage and Usage—40°F–45°F (4°C–7°C), 85% relative humidity. Eaten raw, juiced, or in marmalade.

Flavor—Juicy, acidic; sweetness varies.

Yield—47%

KUMQUATS

Description and Purchasing Specifications— *Small oval fruit whose flesh contains tiny, edible white seeds. Firm, unblemished skin, not shriveled.*

Packaging and Receiving—*1-lb. (450-g) and 2-lb. (900-g) baskets*

Grade and Size—*None*

Storage and Usage—*40°F (4°C), 90%–95% relative humidity. Garnish, salad ingredient, raw or cooked, jams and preserves.*

Flavor—*Sweet peel, sour pulp, tart flavor.*

Yield—*94%*

MANDARINS, TANGERINES, CLEMENTINES, TANGELOS, AND UGLI FRUITS

Description and Purchasing Specifications— *Small, very sweet oranges. Soft, heavy for size, loose skin with deep orange color. Ugli fruit has deeply pock-marked green to orange skin.*

Packaging and Receiving—*54, 66, 80, 100, 120, and 156 count bushels or boxes*

Grade and Size—*U.S. Fancy, No. 1, No. 2, No. 3*

Storage and Usage—*38°F–40°F (3°C–4°C), 90%–95% relative humidity. Raw, juice, salad, garnish.*

Flavor—*Juicy and sweet.*

Yield—*72%*

BLOOD ORANGES

ORANGES

NAVEL, RUBY RED, TEMPLE, VALENCIA, BLOOD

Description and Purchasing Specifications— *Round, thick-skinned fruit. Firm, heavy, good color from pale orange-yellow to deep orange-red, unblemished skin.*

Packaging and Receiving—*40-lb. (17.7-k) case; California and Arizona: 48, 56, 72, 88, 113, 138, and 168 count. Florida: 100, 125, 163, 200, 252, and 324 count*

Grade and Size—*U.S. Fancy, No. 1, Combination, No. 2, No. 3*

Storage and Usage—*45°F–48°F (7°C–9°C), 90% relative humidity. Eaten raw, juiced, or as a garnish.*

Flavor—*Sweet, juicy, with an acidic bite.*

Yield—*70%*

Fruit

617

Melons

Melons are divided into two categories: sweet (or dessert) melons and watermelons. They vary in shape, size, color, and taste. Melons can be oval, oblong, or long and slender. They may have smooth, grooved, or netted surfaces. The color of a melon's flesh can be white, pink, green, orange, or yellow, and its flavor ranges from sweet to spicy.

Because melons are almost 90% water, cooking gives the flesh a mushy consistency. Most melons are served chilled and sliced, sometimes with a bit of lime or lemon juice. Melons blend well in fruit salad and complement cured meats such as prosciutto.

Melons should always be vine-ripened, yield slightly to pressure at the blossom end, and give off a pleasant aroma.

Cantaloupes Cantaloupes, or muskmelons, have sweet, moist, orange flesh and a strong aroma. They can be eaten alone or served with ham or other rich meats. Peak season for cantaloupes is summer, but Mexican imports provide a year-round supply.

Casaba melons These teardrop-shaped melons have coarse yellow skin and a thick, ridged rind. The sweet flesh is creamy white to yellow with no aroma. Casaba melons are used like cantaloupes. Purchase melons with a deep skin color and no dark spots or moist patches. Peak season is September and October.

Cranshaw (or Crenshaw) melons Cranshaws are large, pear-shaped sweet melons with a strong aroma. The orange-pink flesh is very flavorful with a strong, spicy accent. The skin is mottled green and yellow with a ridged rind. Cranshaws are available from July through October, with peak season occurring in August and September.

Honeydews Honeydews are large, oval, sweet melons with a smooth rind that ranges from white to pale green. The flesh is usually pale green, but it can also be pink or gold. Honeydews have a mild, sweet flavor. They are available almost year-round, with peak season from June through October.

Juan Canary melons These rather large melons have a bright yellow skin that has a waxy feel when ripe. The flesh has a unique, sweet flavor that makes it suitable as a side dish or as an ingredient in fruit salad.

Muskmelons Unlike other sweet or dessert melons, muskmelons are further divided into the net-skinned varieties, including cantaloupes and Persian melons, and the smooth-skinned varieties, including casabas and honeydews.

Persian melons Persian melons are larger than cantaloupes, with dark green skin covered with yellow netting.

Santa Claus melons Santa Claus melons, or Christmas melons, are large, elongated sweet melons with a smooth, green-and-yellow-striped rind. The flesh is creamy white or yellow, with a taste similar to that of casaba melons. Santa Claus melon is a winter variety, with peak availability during December.

Watermelons Watermelons belong to a different genus than sweet melons. Native to tropical Africa, they are grown commercially in Texas and other Southern states. Watermelons are large, weighing up to 30 pounds (13.5 kilograms). They are round or oval-shaped with a thick rind. The skin may be green, green-and-white striped, or mottled with white. The crisp, juicy flesh may be pale pink to deep red. Most watermelons are flecked with small, hard, dark seeds, though more expensive seedless hybrids are available.

CANTALOUPE

CANTALOUPES (MUSKMELONS)

Description and Purchasing Specifications—*Round-to-oval shaped melon with a netted skin. Pleasant aroma, heavy, firm, good skin, sweet salmon-colored flesh.*

Packaging and Receiving—*12-lb. (5.3-k) to 15-lb. (6.6-k) crate; 18, 23, 27, 36, and 46 count. 38-lb. to 41-lb. half-cartons; 9, 12, 18, and 23 count. 53-lb. to 55-lb. two-thirds cartons; 12, 14, 18, 24, and 30 count. 80-lb. to 85-lb. jumbo crates; 18 to 45 count*

Grade and Size—*Frozen: Grade A. Fresh: U.S. Fancy, No. 1*

Storage and Usage—*38°F–40°F (3°C–4°C), 90% relative humidity. Store in a warm, dark space if melon is hard. Eaten raw or in salads, as a dessert, or side dish.*

Flavor—*Moist, mildly sweet.*

Yield—*58%*

CASABA MELONS

Description and Purchasing Specifications—*Large, round melon, yellow rind. Creamy white flesh.*

Packaging and Receiving—*4 to 8 count cartons*

Grade and Size—*U.S. No. 1*

Storage and Usage—*40°F (4°C), 95% relative humidity. Eaten raw, as a side dish or in salads, beverages, and desserts.*

Flavor—*Sweet, juicy.*

Yield—*59%*

CRANSHAW OR CRENSHAW MELONS

CRANSHAW

Description and Purchasing Specifications—*Light yellow-red skin, soft pink flesh.*

Packaging and Receiving—*4 to 8 count carton*

Grade and Size—*U.S. No. 1*

Storage and Usage—*40°F (4°C), 95% relative humidity. Eaten raw as a dessert, as a side dish, or in fruit salad.*

Flavor—*Sweet, spicy flavor.*

Yield—*66%*

HONEYDEWS

HONEYDEWS

Description and Purchasing Specifications—*Large, heavy melon with a waxy, creamy white to yellow skin and thick green flesh.*

Packaging and Receiving—*4, 5, 6, 8, 9, and 12 count crates*

Grade and Size—*Fresh: U.S. No. 1. Frozen: Grade A*

Storage and Usage—*45°F (7°C), 90%–95% relative humidity. Store in a warm, dark space if melon is hard. Eaten raw as a side dish or dessert or in a salad.*

Flavor—*Firm, moist, slightly sweet flavor.*

Yield—*58%*

JUAN CANARY MELONS

JUAN CANARY

Description and Purchasing Specifications—*Oval melon, pale green to white flesh. Uniform canary yellow skin, fairly large and firm.*

Packaging and Receiving—*4 to 8 count carton*

Grade and Size—*U.S. No. 1, Commercial, No. 2*

Storage and Usage—*50°F (10°C), 90%–95% relative humidity. Eaten raw, as a side dish, or in fruit salad.*

Flavor—*Distinctive sweet flavor.*

Yield—*N/A*

PERSIAN MELONS

Description and Purchasing Specifications—*Finely netted, dark green rind with slight tan cracks. Firm orange/pink flesh.*

Packaging and Receiving—*4 to 8 count carton*

Grade and Size—*U.S. No. 1, Commercial, No. 2*

Storage and Usage—*40°F (4°C), 95% relative humidity. Eaten raw as a side dish, dessert, or in fruit salad.*

Flavor—*Very sweet and buttery.*

Yield—*N/A*

SANTA CLAUS MELONS

Description and Purchasing Specifications—*Oblong with a mottled green and yellow rind and light netting.*

Packaging and Receiving—*8 to 10 count carton*

Grade and Size—*U.S. No. 1, Commercial, No. 2*

Storage and Usage—*Ripen: 65°F–72°F (18°C–22°C), 95% relative humidity. Store: 50°F (10°C), 90%–95% relative humidity. Eaten raw as a side dish, dessert, or in fruit salad.*

Flavor—*Sweet, light green flesh.*

Yield—*N/A*

WATERMELONS
CHARLESTON GRAY, CARMON BALL, SEEDLESS, PICNIC, ICEBOX

Description and Purchasing Specifications—*Symmetrical shape, heavy for its size.*

Packaging and Receiving—*8 to 15 count cartons. Carmon Ball: 20 to 25 lb. is best*

Grade and Size—*U.S. Fancy, No. 1, No. 2*

Storage and Usage—*50°F–60°F (10°C–16°C), 90% relative humidity. Eaten raw in salads, as a side dish, or dessert.*

Flavor—*Sweet, moist flesh, usually pale pink to dark red.*

Yield—*49%*

WATERMELON

Berries

A good source of potassium, fiber, and vitamin C, berries grow on bushes and vines in many parts of the world. Berries are juicy with thin skins and numerous tiny seeds. Berries can be added to many kinds of dishes or used to make jams, jellies, and preserves. Berries are eaten raw, featured in desserts, and baked.

When purchasing fresh berries, avoid fruit that is soft or moldy. Berries do not ripen further after picking, so choose plump, fully colored ones. Highly perishable, berries can be loosely packed and refrigerated for two to four days or frozen to store them for longer periods.

Blackberries Blackberries resemble raspberries, but their color ranges from deep purple to black. They are larger and heavier with shiny skin. Wild blackberries are rather common, but there is only limited commercial production. Mid-June through August is their peak season.

Blueberries These small, firm berries with deep blue skin and lighter blue flesh originated in North America. Blueberries are cultivated from Maine to Oregon, with fresh blueberries in peak season mid-June to mid-August. Frozen blueberries are available year-round.

Boysenberries Boysenberries are large, juicy, and very sweet. They are often used for preserves and syrups as well as in baked goods, desserts, and salads.

Cranberries Cranberries are firm berries with blotchy red skin and a tart flavor. They grow in bogs in Massachusetts, Wisconsin, and New Jersey. Fresh cranberries are widely available from September through October, but they are seldom served raw. They are usually frozen, canned, dried, or made into jelly, and their unique flavor is added to sauces, relishes, pies, pastries, and breads.

Currants Currants are tart berries that are extremely small and grow in clusters on bushes. Most currants are a bright, jewel-like red, but varieties with a black or golden color are also grown. Sauces, jams, and jellies use all types of currants. Black currants, however, are the basis of *crème de cassis*, a liqueur. Peak season is late summer.

Raspberries Raspberries are extremely delicate berries available year-round. They are usually marketed frozen. A cool climate crop, raspberries are cultivated from Washington state to western New York, but they are also imported from New Zealand and South America. Domestically, peak season is May through November.

Gooseberries Fresh gooseberries, in both sweet and tart varieties, are available only for a short time in the summer. Sweet gooseberries can be eaten raw, and tart varieties are used in preserves and baked desserts.

Strawberries Strawberries are botanically classified as a perennial herb, though they are commonly considered berries. The skin is a vivid red color and is covered with minute, black seeds called *achenes*. Look for berries with good color that still have the green leafy hulls. Avoid soft or brown-spotted berries. The most flavorful and aromatic strawberries are the small alpine berries called *fraise des bois*. These are seldom available domestically.

CRANBERRIES

BLACKBERRIES

BLUEBERRIES

BOYSENBERRIES

CURRANTS

RASPBERRIES

GOLDEN RASPBERRIES

ELDERBERRIES

GOOSEBERRIES

MULBERRIES

BLACKBERRIES, BLUEBERRIES, BOYSENBERRIES, CRANBERRIES, CURRANTS, RASPBERRIES, GOLDEN RASPBERRIES, ELDERBERRIES, GOOSEBERRIES, MULBERRIES

Description and Purchasing Specifications—No mold or insect damage. Firm, plump, well-colored.

Packaging and Receiving—12 pints per flat tray

Grade and Size—Fresh: U.S. No. 1. Canned: Grade B. Frozen: Grade A

Storage and Usage—40°F (4°C), 90%–95% relative humidity. Eaten raw, in salads, jams, jellies, syrups, and baked desserts.

Flavor—Berries vary in flavor, from rather tart (cranberries) to very sweet and juicy (blackberries).

Yield—92%–97%

STRAWBERRIES

Description and Purchasing Specifications—Fresh strawberries should have an intact green hull.

Packaging and Receiving—5-lb. (2.2-k) to 10-lb. (4.4-k) boxes, or 24-quart (22.8-l) crates

Grade and Size—U.S. No. 1, Combination, No. 2

Storage and Usage—40°F (4°C), 90%–95% relative humidity. Eaten raw, in jams, preserves, and baked desserts.

Flavor—Quite sweet, succulent.

Yield—87%

Drupes

A *drupe,* or stone fruit, is a type of fruit with one large, hard stone, or pit, often containing toxic acids. This category includes apricots, cherries, peaches, nectarines, plums, and olives. With their soft flesh and thin skin, drupes are delicate and bruise easily. Care must be taken when packing and transporting drupes because they are also highly perishable. They should not be washed until just before use. Drupes are delicious fresh or dried, and are used as flavoring for many brandies and liqueurs.

In North America, stone fruits are in season during the summer, but they need varying periods of cold temperatures in the winter in order to flower in the spring.

Peaches grow best in Georgia, where winters are mild. Cherries grow better in the upper Midwest and the Pacific Northwest, where winters are cold. Apricots thrive in hot, dry regions such as Central California.

Apricots Apricots are small, round fruits with succulent flesh. Their color ranges from yellow to bright orange. They can be eaten raw, or they can be poached, baked, stewed, candied, dried, or processed into jams and preserves. Apricot juice, or nectar, is widely available.

Apricots are often used in sweet and savory sauces, compotes, quick breads, pastries, custards, and mousses. Early summer is their peak season. Select firm apricots that are well shaped and plump. Avoid mushy or greenish-yellow ones.

Cherries Cherries are available in sweet and sour varieties. Northern states, especially Washington, Oregon, Michigan, and New York, are the largest suppliers. Sweet cherries are round or heart-shaped, and their color varies from yellow to deep red to almost black. The flesh is sweet and juicy. Deep red Bing cherries are the most popular variety, though yellow-red Royal Ann and Rainier cherries are grown in some regions. Select plump, firm cherries with the green stems still attached. Refrigerate fresh cherries, and avoid washing them until ready for use.

APRICOTS

MOORPACK, ROYAL, TILTON, BLENHEIM

Description and Purchasing Specifications—
Plump, firm, no worms or insect damage, bright golden yellow to orange color.

Packaging and Receiving—*Fresh: 24-lb. (10.6-k) to 28-lb. (12.4-k) lugs, 12-lb. (5.3-k) flats. Dried: 5-lb. (2.2-k) boxes*

Grade and Size—*Fresh: U.S. No. 1, No. 2. Canned: Grade B. Dried: Grade A*

Storage and Usage—
Refrigerate at 40°F–45°F (4°C–7°C), 80%–90% relative humidity. Eaten raw or cooked in sauces, jams, or desserts.

Flavor—*Very sweet, chewy fruit.*

Yield—*94%*

CHERRIES

BING, LAMBERT, RAINIER, BURLAT, BROOKS, TULARE, LAPINS, CHELAN, SWEETHEART

Description and Purchasing Specifications—*Bright skin, firm, smooth, green stem still attached, matured, no mold.*

Packaging and Receiving—*Fresh: 18-lb. (8-k) to 20-lb. (8.8-k) lugs and baskets. Frozen: 30-lb. (13.3-k) crates*

Grade and Size—*Canned or frozen: Grade A. Fresh: U.S. No. 1, Commercial*

Storage and Usage—*40°F–50°F (4°C–10°C), 80%–90% relative humidity. Eaten raw or prepared as garnish or pastry filling.*

Flavor—*Sweet, juicy, crisp.*

Yield—*88%*

Sour cherries are seldom eaten raw. The most common varieties are Montmorency and Morello. They are usually available canned, frozen, or as prepared pie and pastry filling that has been cooked with sugar and starch. All varieties of cherries are available dried.

Peaches and nectarines Peaches and nectarines are closely related, and although their flavors are slightly different, they can be used interchangeably. Peaches have a thin, fuzzy skin; the skin of nectarines is smooth. Flesh color varies from white to pale orange.

Fresh peaches and nectarines can be eaten raw, used in pies and pastries, and prepared as jams, preserves, chutneys, and relishes. They are available as freestones, with a stone that separates easily from the flesh, or clingstones, with a stone that is firmly attached to the flesh. Freestones are best eaten raw, but clingstones hold their shape better when cooked or canned. Choose fruit that has an appealing aroma and a color ranging from creamy yellow to yellow to yellow-orange. Avoid those with green skin, which indicates that the peaches were harvested too soon, because they will not ripen further.

Plums Plums have a round to oval shape with skin color that may be yellow, green, red, or deep purple. The flesh is sweet and juicy and varies from pale yellow to dark red. There are dozens of varieties of plums, but only a few are commonly available.

Plums are used in tarts, pies, cobblers, jams, and preserves. Fresh plums are available from June to October. Select plump fruit with smooth, unblemished skin. Plums will ripen at room temperature, and then they should be refrigerated. Dried plums, called prunes, are produced from special plum varieties.

Olives Olives are fruit, but they are not usually categorized with other fruit. Native to the Mediterranean region and also grown in California, olives come in a variety of sizes and flavors. Raw olives are inedible and must be soaked and pickled before they can be eaten. Green olives are harvested when unripe, and black olives are harvested when fully ripe. Olives may be served as appetizers, used as garnishes, baked in breads, added to salads or pasta, or used in stews, sauces, and soups. *Tapenade*, a dip or condiment made from minced ripe olives, is a Mediterranean specialty.

> See Chapter 12: Seasoning and Flavoring Food for more information on olives.

PEACHES

ALBERTA, HALE, BLAKE, RED TOP, O'HENRY, JUNE LADY, FLAVOR CREST

Description and Purchasing Specifications— *Creamy yellow with varying degrees of red blush or fuzz, fresh looking, not too hard.*

Packaging and Receiving— *40-lb. (16-k) bushels, 48 to 80 count. 22-lb. (9.7-k) lugs*

Grade and Size— *Dried: Grade A. Canned or Frozen: Grade B. Fresh: U.S. Fancy, Extra Fancy No. 1, No. 1, No. 2*

Storage and Usage— *Ripen: 65°F–72°F (18°C –22°C), 95% relative humidity. Store: 32°F (0°C), 90% relative humidity. Eaten raw or in desserts, pastries, jams, or relishes.*

Flavor— *Very sweet and juicy with a hint of dryness about the skin.*

Yield— *76%*

NECTARINES

Description and Purchasing Specifications— *Red with orange-yellow shading, no green, firm and plump.*

Packaging and Receiving— *19-lb. to 23-lb. lugs, (50 to 84 count)*

Grade and Size— *U.S. Fancy, Extra Fancy No. 1, No. 1, No. 2*

Storage and Usage— *Ripen: 65°F–72°F (18°C–22°C), 95% relative humidity. Store: 40°F (4°C), 95% relative humidity. Eaten raw or in desserts, pastries, jams, or relishes.*

Flavor— *Crisp, juicy, sweet with a slight tang.*

Yield— *86%*

PLUMS

PURPLE, RED, YELLOW, GREEN, ANGELENO, KELSEY, FRENCH, STANLEY, FELLENBURG (EUROPEAN), BURBANK (JAPANESE)

Description and Purchasing Specifications— *Full, deep color, no bruises or blemishes, flesh just beginning to soften. Thin red to purple skin, meaty green to yellow flesh.*

Packaging and Receiving— *25-lb. (11.1-k) lugs*

Grade and Size— *Fresh: U.S. Fancy, No. 1, Combination, No. 2. Canned: Grade B. Frozen: Grade A*

Storage and Usage— *Ripen: 65°F–72°F (18°C–22°C), 95% relative humidity. Store: 32°F (0°C), 90% relative humidity. Eaten raw or in jams and jellies.*

Flavor— *Very sweet, meaty and juicy flavor.*

Yield— *90%*

GOLDEN DELICIOUS

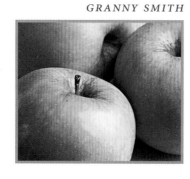

GRANNY SMITH

McIntosh

Pomes

Pomes are tree fruits with a central core that contains many small seeds. The skin is thin, and the flesh is firm. The most familiar pomes are apples, pears, and quinces.

Apples

There are hundreds of varieties of apples. They vary in shape, color, texture, taste, and nutritional value. Their variety, convenience, flavor, and availability are keys to the enduring popularity of apples. Apples grow in temperate zones throughout the world, though they grow best in cool climate countries such as China, Russia, Germany, France, England, and the northern United States (Washington, Michigan, and New York).

Apples are a source of vitamin C, folic acid, and potassium. The high fiber content of apples aids in the digestive process. Apples also contain antioxidants that can improve the immune system and help prevent heart disease.

Apples can be baked, stewed, cooked in pies and sauces, and prepared as a condiment for meats and other savory dishes. Apples are pressed to make juice and cider.

Commercial growers harvest apples before they are fully ripe and store them until they are sold. Though the peak season is autumn, fresh apples are plentiful year-round.

APPLES

GOLDEN DELICIOUS, GRANNY SMITH, JONATHAN, MCINTOSH, NEWTOWN, RED DELICIOUS, YELLOW DELICIOUS, WINESAP, YORK, GALA, FUJI, ROME

Description and Purchasing Specifications—*Fragrant, well-colored. Color varies from pale greenish-yellow (Golden Delicious) to deep green (Granny Smith) to deep red (Winesap). Firm, no bruises or spots.*

Packaging and Receiving—*40-lb. (17.7-k) boxes; 88, 100, 113, 125, 138, 150, and 163 count. 40-lb. (17.7-k) bushels. 46-oz. (1.175-k) or 10-lb. (4.4-k) canned*

Grade and Size—*Fresh: U.S. Extra Fancy, Fancy, No. 1. Canned: Grade A*

Storage and Usage—*31°F–32°F (–1°C–0°C), 85%–90% relative humidity. Eaten raw, cooked in pies, sauces; used for a garnish or as juices.*

Flavor—*Crispy, mildly sweet to tart.*

Yield—*76%*

COURTLAND

RED DELICIOUS

RED BARTLETT

BARTLETT

BOSC

PEARS

BARTLETT, RED BARTLETT, BOSC, COMICE, FORELLE, SECKEL, ANJOU

Description and Purchasing Specifications—*Bright color depending on variety, firm, no bruises or damage to the skin.*

Packaging and Receiving—*Boxes packed 20 to 245 count; 110 to 135 count is recommended.*

Grade and Size—*Washington Extra Fancy, U.S. No. 1, No. 2, Combination*

Storage and Usage—*Ripen: 60°F–65°F (16°C–18°C), 95% relative humidity. Store: 40°F (4°C), 95% relative humidity. Eaten raw or cooked in salads, compotes, or preserves.*

Flavor—*Tart, sweet, juicy.*

Yield—*78%*

COMICE

ASIAN

ANJOU

Pears Washington, Oregon, and California produce more than 90% of the pears sold in the United States. Pears are also grown in New York, Michigan, and Pennsylvania. The main international producers are Chile, Canada, New Zealand, Australia, and Argentina. Pears are a source of fiber and vitamin C and are available year-round.

Pears ripen at room temperature after harvesting. Choose pears with smooth, unbroken skin and intact stems. When fully ripe, pears have a good aroma and yield slightly to pressure near the stem. Pears can be eaten raw, alone or as a complement to cheese. They are added to fruit salads, preserves, and pastries; made into cider; baked; and used as a garnish for meat.

Quinces Quinces are large, fragrant, yellow fruits that resemble pears but have an uneven shape. See Figure 28-1. Quinces are too astringent to eat raw, but they develop a sweet flavor and delicate rosy pink tone when cooked. The hard flesh is very high in pectin, encouraging gelling when added to other fruit jams and preserves.

South America and Europe are the main producers of fresh quinces, which are available from October through January. Look for firm, yellow fruits. Cut away any small blemishes, taking care to avoid damaging the fruit. Quinces can be stored up to a month under refrigeration.

FIGURE 28-1

Quinces are large, fragrant fruits, uneven in shape and high in pectin.

BLACK

RED FLAME

THOMPSON SEEDLESS

Grapes

Fresh table grapes are plump, sweet, and juicy. They are classified by color, with green grapes referred to as white and red grapes referred to as black. White grapes have thinner skins, firmer flesh, and less intense flavor than black grapes.

California supplies nearly all the grapes sold in the United States. Table grapes are used as an ingredient in fruit salads or as an accompaniment to fish, cheese, or desserts. They are available year-round. Select those that are unblemished and still attached to the stem. A dusty white coating, or **bloom,** indicates that the grapes have been recently harvested. Grapes are always picked ripe and do not ripen further once off the vine. All grapes should be rinsed before use.

Champagne grapes Champagne grapes, with their reddish-purple color, are classified as the Black Corinth variety and were originally used to make raisins and wine.

These sweet, juicy grapes are so tiny that they are most often eaten by the bunch rather than one by one.

Concord grapes The Concord grape is an American original, first cultivated in 1849 in Concord, Massachusetts. Deep purple in color, Concords are intensely sweet and juicy with a nice aroma. Concords are commonly used for jelly and juice.

Emperor grapes Emperor grapes are eaten fresh in salads, as a snack, or as a dessert. Select large, plump, firm grapes. Red varieties are best when the red color dominates most or all of the grapes.

Red Flame grapes Red Flame grapes are a seedless hybrid with a variegated red color. They are large, round, and slightly tart in flavor.

Thompson seedless grapes Pale green Thompson seedless grapes are sweet with a crisp texture. They are the predominant commercial table variety.

GRAPES

CHAMPAGNE, CONCORD, BLACK, RED EMPEROR, RED FLAME, THOMPSON SEEDLESS

Description and Purchasing Specifications—*Plump, well colored, pliable green stem.*

Packaging and Receiving—*18-lb. (8-k) to 22-lb. (9.7-k) lugs*

Grade and Size—*U.S. Fancy, No. 1*

Storage and Usage—*36°F–40°F (2°C–4°C), 90% relative humidity. Eaten raw alone, in salads, or as garnish; prepared as juices, jellies.*

Flavor—*Ranges from very sweet and juicy (Concords) to firm and slightly tart (Red Flame).*

Yield—*94%*

Tropical Fruits

Modern transportation and refrigeration methods make tropical fruits available year-round. Tropical fruits are native to the tropical and subtropical regions of the world. The flavors of different tropical fruits usually complement one another, and they make excellent accents for fish, poultry, and rich or spicy meats.

Bananas The most popular tropical fruit in the United States is the banana. Ranging from seven to nine inches in length, bananas are actually the berries of a large tropical herb. They have soft, sweet flesh and a thick, yellow skin that peels easily. Bananas are harvested before ripening and ripen at room temperature. Brown flecks in the yellow skin signal that they are fully ripe. They are available year-round.

Plantains Plantains are also called "cooking bananas" because they are used as a vegetable in tropical or ethnic dishes. Plantains are larger than bananas, but they are not as sweet.

Coconuts Coconuts are the seeds of the tropical coconut palm tree. The shell is a thick, hard, dark brown oval covered with coarse fibers. Inside the shell is a layer of sweet, moist, white flesh. The flesh surrounds clear liquid called coconut water. This liquid is different from coconut milk or cream, which is processed from the flesh.

Shredded or flaked coconut flesh, either sweetened or unsweetened, is readily available. Coconut is often featured in desserts, candies, and Indian and Caribbean cuisines. Look for fresh coconuts that are heavy and without cracks, moisture, or mold.

Dates Dates grow on the date palm tree to a length of one to two inches (2.5–5 cm). Their coloring when ripe is golden to dark brown, and they have papery skin and a single grooved seed inside the flesh. They have a sticky texture and sweet taste and can be served with other fruits, stuffed with cheese as an appetizer, or baked in breads, muffins, and pastries.

Kiwis Originally called Chinese gooseberries, kiwis are small, oval fruits with fuzzy brown skin and bright green flesh surrounding a white core that is bordered with numerous tiny black seeds. Sweet but bland, kiwis are often served raw, alone or sliced for fruit salads or garnishes. Puréed kiwis add flavor to sorbets or mousses. Like fresh pineapples and papayas, kiwis have an enzyme that tenderizes meat and prevents gelling.

Mangoes These oval- or kidney-shaped fruits have thin, smooth skin, with color that ranges from yellow to red to green. The bright orange, juicy flesh is firmly attached to a large pit. Mangoes usually weigh between six ounces and one pound. As they ripen, they lose their green coloring.

The flavor of mangoes is a slightly acidic blend of sweet and spicy. Puréed mangoes are added to drinks and sauces, and the sliced or cubed flesh can be used in desserts, salads, pickles, or chutneys. Mexico provides most of the mangoes consumed in the United States. Peak season is from May through August. When purchasing mangoes, look for firm fruit that yields to gentle pressure and which has no blemishes or wrinkles. When ripe, mangoes have a good fragrance. They will ripen at room temperature, and then they can be refrigerated for as long as one week.

Papayas Papayas are greenish yellow with a golden to pinkish flesh and a center cavity full of edible, silver-black seeds. Ripe papayas can be served raw sprinkled with lemon or lime juice. Puréed papayas add flavor to sweet or spicy sauces, chilled soups, or sorbets. Papayas contain an enzyme called *papain.* It is an excellent meat tenderizer because of its action in breaking down proteins.

Papayas are available year-round, but peak season is April through June. As papayas ripen, their skin color changes from green to yellow; the ripest fruit has the greatest proportion of yellow to green. Papayas will ripen at room temperature, and they can be refrigerated for up to one week.

Pitting and Cutting Mangoes

The pit of the mango is quite large with a relatively flat oval shape, about 3/4 inch (2 cm) thick. It is located in the center, and conforms to the basic shape of the mango.

To pit and cut a mango, follow these steps:

Hold the mango in a vertical position. Slice downward gliding the knife along the pit. Turn the mango and repeat to separate the other half from the pit.

Take one section of the mango, and make lengthwise and then crosswise cuts, without cutting through the skin.

Fold the skin back, and cut away the cubes of mango.

Passion fruit A passion fruit is about the size of a large egg with firm, tough, purple skin. The orange-yellow pulp surrounds large, edible, black seeds. Passion fruit has a rich, sweet flavor reminiscent of citrus. The fruit should be heavy with dark, shriveled skin and a strong fragrance. Bottles or frozen packs of flavorful passion fruit purée are commonly available. Fresh passion fruit will ripen at room temperature; it then can be refrigerated. Peak season is February and March.

Pineapples Pineapples resemble oversized pinecones, with their rough, brown skin and prickly eyes. The sweet, juicy, pale yellow flesh surrounds an edible but tough core that is usually removed. Raw pineapple can be served alone or in salads. Baked or grilled pineapple slices often accompany pork or ham. In Southeast Asian cuisine, pineapple is used in curries, soups, and stews. Pineapple juice can also be mixed into punch or cocktails.

Pineapples do not ripen after harvesting, so they must be picked when completely ripe, which makes them very perishable. They are available year-round but are most plentiful March through June. Look for heavy pineapples with a strong, sweet aroma, avoiding any with soft spots or dried leaves. The skin should have an even greenish brown or golden color. Use fresh pineapples immediately. Canned pineapple is available as slices, as cubes, or crushed, dried, or candied.

BANANAS

CAVENDISH, BURRO, MANZANO, RED, PETITES, GROS MICHEL

Description and Purchasing Specifications— *Firm, uniform shape and color, strong peel, bright.*

Packaging and Receiving— *In bunches, 25-lb. (11.1-k) boxes, 40-lb. cases*

Grade and Size— *U.S. No. 1, No. 2*

Storage and Usage— *50°F–60°F (10°C–16°C). Eaten raw, in salads, or baked in breads and muffins.*

Flavor— *Sweet and sticky.*

Yield— *68%*

PLANTAINS

BANANAS

PLANTAINS

Description and Purchasing Specifications— *No bruises, gouges, black spots, or mold on the skin.*

Packaging and Receiving— *25-lb. (11.1-k), 40-lb. (17.7-k), and 50-lb. (22.2-k) cartons*

Grade and Size— *U.S. No. 1, No. 2*

Storage and Usage— *50°F–60°F (10°C–16°C). Cooked as side dish when green; in desserts when ripe.*

Flavor— *Less sweet than bananas.*

Yield— *72%*

COCONUTS

Description and Purchasing Specifications— *Heavy for their size, no cracks, no wetness around the eyes.*

Packaging and Receiving— *40-lb. (17.7 k) or 50-lb. (22.2-k) sacks and cartons*

Grade and Size— *N/A*

Storage and Usage— *Room temperature. Refrigeration will dry the liquid. Used in fruit salad, pastries, candies.*

Flavor— *Sweet, nutty flavor.*

Yield— *53%*

COCONUTS

Peeling, Coring, and Trimming a Pineapple

Pineapples have a rough, brown skin and prickly eyes, so to eat the fruit, one must peel, core, and trim it first.

To perform this technique, follow these steps:

5 Remove the core from the quarters.

1 Cut off both ends of the pineapple to create a flat surface and expose the flesh.

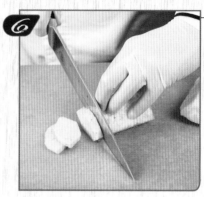

6 Slice the pineapple quarters to the desired thickness.

2 Using a French knife, cut downward to remove the peel.

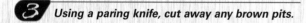

3 Using a paring knife, cut away any brown pits.

4 Cut the pineapple in half lengthwise, and then cut it into quarters.

DATES

DEGLET NOOR, ZAHIDI,
KHADRAWY, HALAWY,
MEDJOOL

**Description and Purchasing
Specifications**—*No sugar
crystallization or insect damage.
Plump with smooth, golden
brown skin.*

Packaging and Receiving—*Bulk: 15 lbs. (6.6 k) Chopped:
30 lbs. (13.3 k)*

Grade and Size—*Fresh: None. Dried: Grade A*

Storage and Usage—*50°F–60°F (10°C–16°C), 30%–40%
relative humidity. Fresh or dried, stuffed as appetizer, in
baked goods and pastries.*

Flavor—*Rich, sticky-sweet flavor.*

Yield—*90%*

MANGOES

TOMMY ATKINS, KEITT,
ATAULFO, HADEN, KENT,
VAN DYKE

**Description and Purchasing
Specifications**—*Strong fruity
fragrance, tight skin, full and
firm shape.*

Packaging and Receiving—*10-lb. (4.4-k) to 12-lb. (5.3-k)
flats. 24-lb. (10.6-k) lugs (16 count)*

Grade and Size—*None*

Storage and Usage—*50°F–55°F (10°C–13°C), 85%
relative humidity. Eaten raw in salads, chutneys, or
desserts; puréed in sauces or drinks.*

Flavor—*Smooth texture, sweet taste.*

Yield—*69%*

PASSION FRUIT

EDGEHILL, BLACK KNIGHT,
KAHUNA, PURPLE GIANT

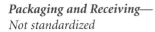

**Description and Purchasing
Specifications**—*Heavy, large,
wrinkled dark purple to black
indicates ripeness.*

Packaging and Receiving—
Not standardized

Grade and Size—*U.S. No. 1*

Storage and Usage—*Refrigerate 41°F–45°F (5°C–7°C),
90%–95% relative humidity. Used in sauces, custard, ice cream.*

Flavor—*Very aromatic, distinctive sweet flavor. Seeds and
pulp are edible.*

Yield—*64%*

KIWIS

HAYWARD, GOLDEN

**Description and Purchasing
Specifications**—*Ripe kiwis
have soft, furry, and unwrinkled
skin that gives under gentle
pressure; 2 to 3 inches long.*

Packaging and Receiving—
*Single-layer flat cartons. New Zealand: 5 lbs. (2.2 k) to 6 lbs. (2.6 k)
California: 11 lbs. (4.8 k) to 12 lbs. (5.3 k) 25 to 46 count*

Grade and Size—*U.S. No. 1, No. 2, Fancy*

Storage and Usage—*40°F (4°C), 90%–95% relative humidity.
Eaten raw in salad or as garnish, puréed for sorbet and mousse.*

Flavor—*Sweet, slightly bland.*

Yield—*84%*

PAPAYAS (HAWAII)

WAIMANALO, KAPOHO,
SUNRISE

**Description and Purchasing
Specifications**—*Good yellow-
green to full yellow-orange
color, firm and unblemished,
no dark spots on the peel.*

Packaging and Receiving—*10-lb. (4.4-k) cartons.
6 to 14 count*

Grade and Size—*Hawaii: Fancy, No. 1, No. 2. No U.S. grade*

Storage and Usage—*90%–95% relative humidity. Mature
green to yellow papaya: 55°F (13°C); partially ripe yellow
papaya: 50°F (10°C); ripe to full yellow papaya: 45°F (7°C).
Eaten raw or puréed in soups, sauces, and drinks.*

Flavor—*Sweet and juicy. Seeds and pulp are edible.*

Yield—*67%*

PINEAPPLES

SMOOTH CAYENNE, GOLD,
QUEEN, RED SPANISH,
SUGARLOAF, CABAIANI

**Description and Purchasing
Specifications**—*Heavy for
their size, well shaped, fresh-
looking, dark green crown
leaves. Dry, crisp shell.
Greenish yellow to golden color.*

Packaging and Receiving—*35-lb. (15.5-k) crates, 9 to 21 count*

Grade and Size—*U.S. No. 1*

Storage and Usage—*45°F–50°F (7°C–10°C), 85%–90% relative humidity. Eaten raw in salads or alone; cooked, served
with pork; used for curries, stews, soups; juice.*

Flavor—*Sweet, crisp, meaty flesh, white to yellow in color.*

Yield—*52%*

Exotic Fruits

Improved transportation and storage methods have brought such exotic fruits as figs, persimmons, cherimoyas, and star fruits to North American menus.

a Cherimoyas

Cherimoya, also known as custard apple, is native to Central America. The conical cherimoya measures from four to eight inches (10–20 cm) long, and its average weight ranges from five to eighteen ounces (140–510 g). There are two types of skin: smooth and marked with fingerprint-like swirls or covered with conical protuberances. Ripe cherimoya has sweet, juicy flesh and an appealing aroma. The glossy, dark seeds that stud the flesh are highly toxic and must be discarded.

b Figs

Figs have an extremely sweet flavor, and their tiny seeds add crunchiness to the soft flesh. Figs are pear shaped with various skin colors, including dark, yellow, and white. Sliced figs may be added to salads, but the fruit may also be baked, poached, or made into jams and preserves. A popular appetizer features figs served with prosciutto or other cured meats.

Mission figs are a dark-skinned variety whose name stems from their cultivation in early mission settlements along the Pacific coast. Their thin skin surrounds sweet flesh and small seeds. They can be purchased fresh, dried, or canned. The more common Calimyrna fig is large and yellow with large seeds. These are also available dried.

Figs should be harvested when fully ripe, but ripened figs are delicate and hard to transport. Peak season for most figs is June through October, but June is the only month when fresh Calimyrna figs are available.

c Guavas

Guava is a small fruit with an oval or pear shape, an aroma that is strong, and flesh that is mild with some graininess. Guava juice is served plain or blended with the juices of other tropical fruits. Guavas are well suited for use in jams and preserves. The fruit is best when it is fully ripened and slightly soft. It will ripen at room temperature.

d Feijoa

Feijoa, or pineapple guava, is a distant relative of the guava. It has a flavor reminiscent of pineapple and guava, sometimes with a suggestion of mint. The fruit's size varies from just under an inch to about three inches long. Skin color is blue-green to blue or grayish green, occasionally with areas of orange or red. The waxy skin can be smooth or rough and pebbly. Feijoa has an intense and long-lasting aroma with grainy, white, and thick flesh and numerous edible seeds.

e Loquats

Loquats are about the size of an apricot, globular to pear shaped, with yellow-orange skin. The tender, juicy flesh is creamy to orange, with a flavor that ranges from sweet to tart, depending on the variety. The flavor is similar to that of apricots, cherries, and plums.

Because fresh loquats bruise easily when transported, they are usually only available in areas where they are grown. California and Florida have some commercial production, but limited imports come from Chile and Spain. Loquats ripen at room temperature. To prepare them, peel, remove the seeds, and slice into fruit salads.

f Lychee

The lychee, a native of southern China, may be round, oval, or heart shaped and one to one-and-a-half inches long. This sweet, tender fruit is encased in a leathery rind that varies in color from pink to red. The white flesh is firm and juicy.

g Persimmons

Persimmons have shiny orange skin and the shape of an acorn. The jellylike flesh is bright orange with a mild taste similar to that of honey and plums. Ripe persimmons can be refrigerated. The fruit should be peeled and the seeds discarded before use.

Underripe persimmons are almost inedible; they have a strong tannic taste and chalky texture. When completely ripe, they are very soft, and the skin is almost translucent. Persimmons may be eaten raw, topped with cream cheese, or included in fruit salads. Fresh persimmons are available from October through January.

h Pomegranates

Pomegranates are native to Iran. Round, bright red, and about the size of an orange, pomegranates have a hard shell encasing hundreds of small, brilliant red seeds surrounded by a juicy red pulp. An inedible yellow membrane surrounds groups of seeds and divides the fruit into segments. Pulp and seeds are tangy and sweet, and the seeds are crunchy. Seeds can be used as an attractive garnish, while the juice is popular in Mediterranean cuisines. Grenadine syrup is produced from concentrated pomegranate juice.

Select pomegranates that are heavy but not rock hard, cracked, or heavily bruised. Whole pomegranates can be refrigerated for several weeks. The fruit's peak season is in October, but pomegranates are available from September to December.

i Prickly pears

Prickly pears, also called cactus pears or barbary figs, are the berries of several kinds of cactus. They grow to the size of a large egg and have a barrel or pear shape. Their skin is green or purple, thick, and covered with small thorns and stinging fibers. Prickly pears have spongy, pink-red flesh with scattered, tiny black seeds. Ripe prickly pear has a sweet flavor. It can be peeled and diced and eaten raw or puréed for jams, sauces, custards, or sorbets.

Look for heavy fruits that have deep color. Avoid soft fruits or those with bruises. Ripe prickly pears can be refrigerated for about a week. Peak season is September through December.

j Pomelo

Pomelo is native to Southeast Asia and is the largest of all the citrus fruits. An ancestor of the grapefruit, it ranges from nearly round to pear shaped and grows up to 12 inches (30.5 cm) wide. The thick skin may be greenish-yellow or pale yellow, the flesh color varies from greenish-yellow or pale yellow to pink or red, and the taste is sweeter and less acidic than that of grapefruit.

When purchasing pomelo, look for firm, unbruised fruit that has a sweet aroma and is heavy for its size. Ripe pomelos can be refrigerated for up to one week. Skinned segments can be broken apart and used in salads and desserts or made into preserves. Extracted juice makes an excellent beverage. The peel can be candied.

k Rhubarb

Botanically, rhubarb is a vegetable, though it is usually prepared as a fruit. Rhubarb grows abundantly in temperate and cold climates. The pinkish-red stalks are edible and do not need to be peeled. The leaves contain high amounts of toxic oxalic acid.

Rhubarb is extremely acidic and very bitter when raw. It requires large amounts of sugar to develop the characteristic sweet-sour taste. Rhubarb can be used for pies, stewing, or preserves, and it is sometimes combined with other fruits, such as strawberries. Choose crisp stalks without blemishes. Cooked rhubarb has an appealing pink color. Peak season for fresh rhubarb is February to May, but frozen rhubarb is readily available year-round.

l Star fruits

Star fruits are also known as carambola. They have an oval shape with five raised ribs running the length of the fruit. When sliced into cross sections, the resulting shape is like a star. An edible, orange-yellow skin encases the light yellow flesh. Sweet but bland, star fruit's taste is similar to that of plums. Sliced star fruit is often added to fruit salads or used as a garnish.

Look for fruit that is deep golden yellow, with brown along the edges of the ribs. There should be a strong floral aroma. Unripe fruit will ripen at room temperature and can be refrigerated for up to two weeks. Fresh star fruit is available from August to February.

Purchasing and Storing Fresh Fruit

Fresh fruit may be ripe or unripe at the time of purchase, depending on how it ripens, the storage methods used, and the duration of its peak ripeness. To get the maximum benefit from fresh fruit, it is important to consider several factors: size, the grade or quality, the stage of ripeness, and the nutritional content. All of these factors affect how the fruit can be used for cost-effectiveness, flavor, and presentation.

Grading Fresh Fruit

The USDA's voluntary fruit grading program bases grades on size, uniformity of shape, color, texture, and the absence of flaws. Most fruits purchased are U.S. Fancy, the highest grade. Lower grades are U.S. No. 1, U.S. No. 2, and U.S. No. 3. Fruits with grades lower than U.S. Fancy may have some cosmetic or other minor defects that do not affect the nutritional quality. They are adequate for use in sauces, jams, jellies, or preserves.

Receiving

Fresh fruits are sold by count or by weight and are packed in flats, lugs, or cartons. Lugs are shallow wooden containers that hold various amounts of produce weighing up to 40 pounds. Flats are shallow boxes used to ship pints and quarts of produce such as berries.

Some fruits, such as melons, berries, and pineapples, may have been cleaned, peeled, or cut before shipping. These prepared fruits are purchased in bulk, often with sugar and preservatives added. Prepared fruit is a labor-saving convenience, but it can be more costly than unprocessed fruit. There may also be changes to its texture, visual appeal, and nutrients.

Ripening and Storing Fresh Fruit

For sensory appeal, flavor, and nutrition, fresh fruits should be used at the height of ripeness. Some fruits, such as pineapples, must be harvested when fully ripe and transported quickly to market because they only ripen when on the plant. Others, such as bananas, are harvested when unripe and continue to ripen afterward.

Because the quality of fruits begins to deteriorate after they reach peak ripeness, it is important to know how long and under what conditions various fruits can be stored before spoilage sets in. As fruits ripen, they give off colorless, odorless *ethylene gas.* To speed up the ripening process, place unripened fruits near other fruits that emit high levels of ethylene gas, such as bananas or apples. To slow the ripening process, keep fruits chilled and separated from other fruits.

Purchasing Fresh Fruit

As fruits ripen, they change from hard and inedible to succulent and flavorful, often with an appealing aroma. Ripening fruit may change in size, color, weight, or texture. Most fruit is harvested long before it ripens in order to avoid damage during shipping and spoilage at the destination. The following chart shows how various fruits ripen after harvesting.

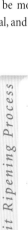

Fruit Ripening Process

BANANAS
After harvest, changes in color, texture, moisture content, and sweetness

APPLES, PEARS, CHERIMOYAS, MANGOES, KIWI, PAPAYAS
After harvest, becomes sweeter

APRICOTS, NECTARINES, PEACHES, MELONS (EXCEPT WATERMELON), BLUEBERRIES, FIGS, PASSION FRUIT, PERSIMMONS
After harvest, changes in color, texture, and moisture content; no change in sweetness

CITRUS FRUITS, CHERRIES, GRAPES, SOFT BERRIES, PINEAPPLES, WATERMELONS, OLIVES
No changes after harvest

Purchasing and Storing Preserved Fruit

In addition to fresh fruit, foodservice operations often use preserved fruit that has been canned, frozen, or dried.

Canned Fruit

Most fruits can be canned successfully. Pineapple, peaches, and pears may be preserved in water; fruit juice; or heavy, medium, or light syrup. They may also be preserved in a solid pack can that contains little or no added water.

The heat used in the canning process destroys microorganisms, and the sealed, airtight can eliminates oxidation. Canned fruit is softer than fresh fruit, but the process has little or no effect on nutritional value.

Canned fruits are available in standard-sized cans. See Figure 28-2. When receiving canned fruits, inspect the cans for any signs of damage such as dents or bulges. Return cans with bulges immediately without opening them because bulges can indicate the presence of the botulism toxin. Damaged cans in storage or prep areas should be discarded.

■ *See Chapter 4: Food Safety for more information.*

FIGURE 28-2

Standard Sizes of Canned Goods

NO. 1/2

Average Weight	Cups per Can	Cans per Case
8 oz. (225 g)	1	8

NO. 1 TALL (OR 303)

Average Weight	Cups per Can	Cans per Case
16 oz. (450 g)	2	2 or 4 doz.

NO. 2

Average Weight	Cups per Can	Cans per Case
20 oz. (565 g)	2-1/2	2 doz.

NO. 2-1/2

Average Weight	Cups per Can	Cans per Case
28 oz. (785 g)	3-1/2	2 doz.

NO. 3

Average Weight	Cups per Can	Cans per Case
33 oz. (930 g)	4	2 doz.

NO. 3 CYLINDER

Average Weight	Cups per Can	Cans per Case
46 oz. (1 k 165 g)	5-2/3	1 doz.

NO. 5

Average Weight	Cups per Can	Cans per Case
3 lb. 8 oz. (1.258 k)	5-1/2	1 doz.

NO. 10

Average Weight	Cups per Can	Cans per Case
6 lb. 10 oz. (2.6 k)	13	6

A Food Revolution

The ability to preserve food in impermeable cans has had a dramatic effect on human history. The French emperor Napoleon offered a 12,000 franc reward to anyone who could prevent military food supplies from spoiling before they reached the soldiers. In 1795, chef Nicholas Appert won the competition by canning meats and vegetables in jars sealed with pitch. By 1804, Appert opened a factory to vacuum pack foods. In 1810, Englishman Peter Durand patented the use of metal containers for canning. By the time of the Battle of Waterloo, fought between the English and Napolean's French forces in 1815, both sides were well supplied with nonperishable foodstuffs.

Although there is a popular perception that canned foods are less nutritious than either frozen or fresh foods, an analysis of 84 fresh, frozen, and canned foods conducted at the University of Illinois demonstrated that once foods are prepared for the table, canned foods are equal, and often superior, in nutrients.

Today canned fruits are frequently processed with relatively little sugar. Canning companies are also producing more low-sodium and sodium-free canned goods. Experiments with thinner metals may produce cans that would require less processing time while maintaining flavor and texture.

Fruit

635

Store cans in a cool, dry area. Once opened, any remaining fruit should be transferred to a clean storage container and refrigerated.

Frozen Fruit

Freezing is an effective method of preserving fruits. It inhibits the growth of the microorganisms responsible for spoilage, but it does not destroy nutrients. Freezing does alter the appearance and texture of fruits, however. This happens because ice crystals form in the water contained in the cells, causing the cell walls to burst.

Today many fruits are individually quick frozen (IQF), especially berries and pear and apple slices. This method speeds the freezing process, reducing the formation of ice crystals.

The grades for frozen fruits are U.S. Grade A (Fancy), U.S. Grade B (Choice or Extra Standard), or U.S. Grade C (Standard). When a government inspector has graded the fruit, the initials U.S. can be used. However, if the quality of the fruit meets the standards of the grade, packers may use the grade names, but not the initials, without outside inspection.

Processors often trim and slice fruits before freezing. Most frozen stone fruits have been peeled, pitted, and sliced. Other fruits, such as berries, are frozen whole. Packing fruit in sugar syrup before freezing not only adds flavor but also prevents browning. Frozen purées of some fruits are also available. Moisture-proof packaging is essential for frozen fruit, as is a constant temperature of 0°F–10°F (⁻18°C–⁻12°C). Freezer burn can result from changes in temperature.

Dried Fruit

The earliest method for preserving food is drying. When ripe fruits are dried, the moisture loss results in concentrated flavor and sweetness. Drying substantially prolongs the shelf life of fruit.

Almost any fruit can be dried, but the most common dried fruits are plums (prunes), grapes (raisins, sultanas, and currants), apricots, and figs. Fruit may be sun-dried or passed through a commercial dryer that quickly extracts moisture. The commercial procedure is more cost effective for producing large quantities of dried fruits.

Dried fruits remain moist and soft because they retain between 16% and 25% of their moisture. They are often treated with sulfur dioxide to retard oxidation which causes browning, and to extend their shelf life.

Dried fruits are very versatile. They are often used in baked goods such as breads, muffins, and pastries, added to salads or cereals, stewed for chutneys and compotes, used in stuffing for poultry or roasted meats, or eaten raw.

Before using dried fruits, reconstitute them by soaking them in hot water or another liquid such as wine, brandy, or rum. Some dried fruits benefit from being simmered for a short time before use.

When purchasing dried fruits, check the list of ingredients for sulfites, a preservative. People who are allergic to sulfites can suffer a life-threatening reaction to them. Store dried fruits in airtight containers, away from moisture and sunlight.

Cooking Fruit

Although fruits are usually served raw, some fruits can be cooked for use in either sweet or savory dishes. Puréed fruit can be added to sauces and mousses and used as jam. Cooking fresh fruits requires careful attention; even brief cooking changes the texture and can reduce fruits too much. Adding sugar can counteract this process. The fruit's cells will absorb sugar slowly, thus firming the fruit. Acids such as lemon juice also help fruits maintain firmness during cooking. Alkalis such as baking soda, however, break down cells.

Preparing Fruit for Cooking

Wash fruit in cold water, and drain well. Remove any stems, and peel any fruit that requires it. Some fruits, such as apples or pears, may need to be cored. Remove any seeds or pits, and cut away any bruises. Cut fruit in halves, quarters, slices, or chunks.

Fruits such as apples and peaches will start to brown when the flesh is exposed to air. To prevent this, *acidulate* the fruit by dipping it in citrus juice, vinegar, or water that has been treated with ascorbic acid (vitamin C). This step is not necessary for all fruit.

Cooking with Dry Heat

The methods for cooking fruit with dry heat are broiling, grilling, baking, sautéing, and deep-frying.

Broiling and Grilling
Fruits are usually broiled or grilled quickly, just to the point where the sugar browns but before the fruit's structure begins to break down. Apples, bananas, pineapples, grapefruit, peaches, and persimmons are all suitable for broiling or grilling. Cut or slice the fruit into the desired form. The flavor of broiled or grilled fruit can be enhanced by adding a glaze made of sugar, honey, a liqueur, or lemon juice, sometimes in combination with a spice such as cinnamon, nutmeg, or ginger.

Place fruit on an oiled sheet pan or platter for broiling. Put fruit pieces on skewers or on a clean grill grate for grilling. Thick slices of fruit may need to be turned to brown on all sides and heat through. Broiled or grilled fruits can complement meat, fish, or poultry dishes. Fruits cooked in this manner also serve as dessert or enhance other desserts as a topping.

Baking
Fruits suitable for baking include pomes, drupes, and tropical fruits, which make excellent hot desserts. Fruits with strong skins can be baked unpeeled. The skins of apples and pears hold in moisture and flavor while baking. After coring, fill the center cavity with sweet or savory fillings. Other fruits may need to be peeled, cored, or pitted before baking.

Different fruits can be combined to blend sweet and tart flavors. Strawberries and rhubarb are a classic combination, as are apples with blackberries or plums.

Baked fruit desserts can take several different forms: fruits topped with a crust (cobbler), a strudel, or a batter (buckle). Wrap poached fruit in puff pastry or phyllo dough, and then bake and serve as a hot dessert.

Fruits to be baked should be ripe but firm and then peeled, pitted, cored, or sliced as required. Add sweeteners or other flavorings if necessary. Prepare the fruits as directed by the recipe. Bake the fruit uncovered in a moderate oven until tender.

Sautéing
Sautéing fruits briefly in butter and sugar gives them a rich flavor and syrupy texture. Added spices or liqueur can enhance the fruits' flavor. Fruits that may be sautéed include pineapples, cherries, bananas, pears, and apples. Flambéing fruits (as for bananas Foster) gives a dramatic effect. Sautéing fruits with sugar creates a syrup or glaze, and this sweet mixture often serves as a topping for ice cream or cake or as a filling for crêpes. For savory fruit mixtures, sauté fruit with onions, shallots, or garlic.

For sautéing, fruits should be washed and trimmed as necessary and then cut into uniform pieces. The fat, usually butter, should be heated in a sauté pan before adding the fruit pieces. Do not overcrowd the fruit; this will result in the fruit stewing in its own juices. Cook quickly over high heat.

Deep-frying
Few fruits deep-fry satisfactorily. However, apples, pears, pineapples, bananas, and firm peaches can be coated in batter and deep-fried. Make sure that fruit pieces are clean, trimmed as necessary, and cut into uniform pieces. Use paper towels to dry them thoroughly so that the batter or other coating adheres properly. Then immerse the fruit pieces a few at a time in hot oil, and fry them until golden brown and cooked through. Drain and roll in sugar, and serve with an appropriate sauce or dusted with confectioner's sugar.

Cooking with Moist Heat

Poaching and simmering are the moist cooking methods used to cook fruits.

Poaching
Poaching infuses fruit with the flavors of spices or wine while gently softening its flesh. Serve poached fruit hot or cold. It can accompany meat or poultry dishes, though it is often used in pastries.

In poaching, fruits cook gradually because of the low temperature of the liquid (160°F–185°F/71°C–85°C). In this way, the fruit retains its shape. Water, sugar syrup, wine, liquor, or a liqueur can serve as the poaching liquid. Allow the fruit to remain in the liquid while cooling. It is possible to use the liquid several times, or it can be thickened into a glaze or sauce.

Wash, peel, core, and slice the fruit as needed. In a deep saucepan, combine the poaching liquid with ingredients such as sugar or spices. Place the fruit so that the liquid covers it, and put the saucepan over a medium-high flame. Bring the liquid to a boil, and then reduce the temperature. Continue to poach until the fruit can be easily pierced by a small knife.

Simmering

Simmering softens fruit and is used to stew fruit or to make compotes. Use fresh, frozen, canned, or dried fruits for simmering. Simmering liquids include water, liquor, wine, a liqueur, or fruit juice. Add sugar, honey, spices, or other flavorings as desired. Hot or cold simmered fruit functions as a first course, an accompaniment to meat or poultry, or a dessert.

Wash and prepare fruit as needed. Bring the cooking liquid to a simmer, and cook the fruit to the desired tenderness. Add sweeteners if preferred.

COMPECHE

Main Ingredients	*Complements*
Sour orange juice, chile, garlic	Seafood

PINEAPPLE

Main Ingredients	*Complements*
Pineapple, chile, onion	Grilled pork, whitefish

MANGO

Main Ingredients	*Complements*
Mango, chile, tamarind, shrimp, onion, garlic, fresh cilantro, red pepper	Grilled pork, chicken, crabmeat, tuna

PAPAYA

Main Ingredients	*Complements*
Papaya, black beans, red bell peppers, red onions, pineapple juice, lime juice, cilantro, cumin, chile	Grilled fish

APRICOT-FIG

Main Ingredients	*Complements*
Apricots, figs, raisins, onions, vinegar, almonds, ginger, red chile, lemon	Lamb

WATERMELON

Main Ingredients	*Complements*
Watermelon, cucumbers, red onion, carrot, vinegar, sugar, fresh mint, cilantro	Grilled shellfish

PEACH

Main Ingredients	*Complements*
Ripe or semi-ripe peaches, peppers, red onion, orange juice, lime juice, molasses, chile pepper, parsley, garlic	Grilled fish

Fruit Salsas

More than just a dip, salsa is a healthful, low-calorie accent to many foods, from steaks and chops to seafood and salads. Thanks to the growing popularity of ethnic foods, especially Mexican and Tex-Mex, salsa has become such a staple that it has replaced catsup as the most popular condiment in the world.

Although less familiar than tomato-based salsas, fruit salsas have become increasingly popular. Diced and julienned fruits combined with herbs, spices, and other flavorings make an excellent accompaniment to a variety of dishes. Many people enjoy the flavor combination of hot and sweet or hot and tart, which adds zest to low-fat and low-calorie dishes.

The chart on the left outlines some of the most popular examples of fruit-based salsas.

Freshly prepared fruit salsas are highly perishable.

- *Use very fresh fruit (you may substitute dried fruit, if necessary).*
- *Avoid frozen fruit because freezing destroys fruit's texture.*
- *Serve fruit salsas warm or cold to accompany fish or poultry, or use them as dessert toppings or pastry fillings.*

Brown Rice with Peaches and Almonds

INGREDIENTS

INGREDIENTS	U.S. Standard	Metric
Salad oil	2 oz.	60 ml
Onion, peeled, cut macédoine	1 1/2 c.	285 g
Bay leaves	2 each	2 each
Cardamom, ground	1/2 tsp.	2.5 g
Brown Basmati rice, rinsed	2 c.	450 g
Water	4 c.	960 ml
Currants	1 c.	225 g
Salt	2 tsp.	10 ml
White pepper, ground	1/2 tsp.	2.5 ml
Sliced almonds, toasted	1 c.	150 g
Ripe peaches, large, peeled, pitted, cut macédoine	6 each	6 each
Mint, washed, dried, chopped fine	1/4 c.	55 g

METHOD OF PREPARATION

1. Gather all the ingredients and equipment.

2. In a rondeau, heat the oil over medium heat. Sweat the onions in the oil until translucent.

3. Add the bay leaves, cardamom, and rice, and stir with the onions until fragrant.

4. Add the water, currants, salt, and pepper, and bring to a boil. Cover tightly, lower the heat, and simmer for about 40 minutes, or until the rice is tender and liquid is absorbed.

5. Fold in the almonds, peaches, and mint. Allow mixture to stand covered for 5 minutes.

6. Serve immediately, or hold covered at 140°F (60°C) or higher for a short while.

Chef's Notes

Other fruits, such as nectarines or apricots, can replace peaches.

COOKING TECHNIQUES

Simmering:

1. Place the prepared product in an appropriately sized pot.

2. Bring the product to a boil, and then reduce the heat to allow the product to barely boil.

3. Cook until desired doneness is achieved.

NUTRITION

Nutrition Facts

Yield: Serves 10
Serving Size: 6 oz. (170 g)

Amount Per Serving	
Calories 300	
Total Fat 12 g	
Sodium 470 mg	
Total Carbohydrate 45 g	
Protein 6 g	

Fruit

639

Cold Fruit Soup

INGREDIENTS

	U.S. Standard	Metric
Cantaloupe melon, peeled, seeded, cubed	7 c.	900 g
Orange juice, freshly squeezed	3/4 c.	180 ml
Vanilla yogurt	1 1/2 c.	350 g
Sour cream	1/2 c.	115 g
Brown sugar	4 Tbsp.	60 g
Melon-flavored liqueur	2 oz.	60 ml
Strawberries, fresh, cut macédoine	2 c.	170 g
Blueberries, fresh	2 c.	170 g
Peaches, fresh, peeled, cut macédoine	2 c.	170 g

METHOD OF PREPARATION

1. Gather all the ingredients and equipment.

2. Combine the melon, orange juice, yogurt, sour cream, brown sugar, and liqueur in a bowl.

3. Purée the mixture in batches until smooth. Transfer the purée to a stainless steel insert when it is finished.

4. Stir in one cup each of the strawberries, blueberries, and peaches. Reserve the remaining fruit, individually, for garnish.

5. Cover the soup, and chill in an ice bath at 41°F (5°C) or lower.

6. To serve, ladle a portion of soup into a cold bowl, and garnish with some of each of the reserved fruits.

Chef's Notes

- The fruits added to the purée can be varied according to availability. Different berries can replace the strawberries and blueberries. Apricots or nectarines would be a nice replacement for the peaches.
- This could also be finished with an additional dollop of yogurt or sour cream for presentation.

NUTRITION

Nutrition Facts

Yield: Serves 10
Serving Size: 8 oz. (225 g)

Amount Per Serving

Calories 180

Total Fat 4 g

Sodium 45 mg

Total Carbohydrate 36 g

Protein 4 g

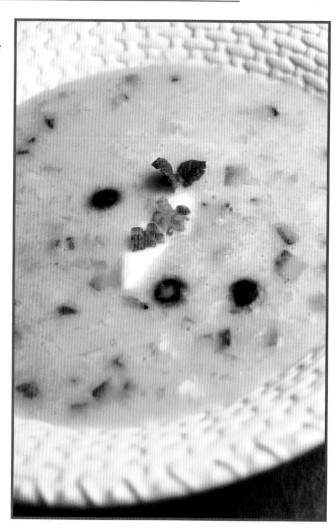

Mango and Roasted Corn Salsa

INGREDIENTS

	U.S. Standard	Metric
Corn kernels, fresh	2 c.	454 g
Vegetable oil	2 tsp.	10 g
Mango, peeled, diced macédoine	2 c.	454 g
Pineapple, fresh, peeled, diced macédoine	3/4 c.	170 g
Sweet red pepper, diced macédoine	1/4 c.	50 g
Red onion, peeled, diced macédoine	3 Tbsp.	45 g
Sugar	2 Tbsp.	30 g
Lime juice, fresh	1/4 c.	60 ml
Orange juice, fresh	1/4 c.	60 ml
Mint, fresh, minced	3 Tbsp.	45 g
Cilantro, fresh, minced	2 Tbsp.	30 g
Ginger, fresh, peeled, grated	1 tsp.	5 g
Salt	1/2 tsp.	2.5 ml

METHOD OF PREPARATION

1. Gather all the ingredients and equipment.

2. Preheat the oven to 375°F (191°C). Toss the corn with the oil, and spread on a parchment-lined half sheet pan. Bake for 10–15 minutes, or until it turns a pale brown. Cool.

3. Combine the corn with all the remaining ingredients, and mix well.

4. Cover and hold at 41°F (5°C) or lower. Be sure to mix again, gently, just before service.

Grilled Coconut-Dipped Pineapple with Spiced Rum Syrup

INGREDIENTS

Ingredient	U.S. Standard	Metric
Sugar	5 c.	1.2 kg
Water	2 c.	500 ml
Lime zest, *wash lime, grate fine*	2 tsp.	10 g
Orange zest, *wash orange, grate fine*	2 Tbsp.	60 g
Lime juice, *freshly squeezed*	1 oz.	30 ml
Black pepper, *freshly ground*	1/4 tsp.	2 g
Ginger, *fresh, peeled, finely minced*	4 tsp.	20 g
Star anise	3 each	3 each
Dark rum	1/2 c.	120 ml
Vanilla extract	1 tsp.	5 ml
Golden pineapple	2 each	2 each
Coconut milk, *unsweetened*	28 oz.	840 ml
Mace, *ground*	1 tsp.	5 ml
Vegetable oil	as needed	as needed
Mint springs, *washed (to garnish)*	as needed	as needed

METHOD OF PREPARATION

1. Gather all the ingredients and equipment.

2. Preheat the grill to medium heat.

3. Combine 1 1/2 cups (350 g) of sugar, the water, zests, lime juice, spices, and rum in a nonreactive saucepan. Bring the mixture to a boil, reduce the heat, and simmer for 20 minutes to reduce and concentrate flavors. Add the vanilla, strain, and set aside, covered, to cool to room temperature.

4. Cut the top and the bottom off the pineapple, and peel it by standing it upright and slicing off the skin in long strips. Remove any remaining "eyes" with the tip of a vegetable peeler. Slice the pineapple into 1/2″ (1.27 cm) thick slices, and then use a round cutter to remove the core from each slice.

5. Shake the coconut milk well, and pour into a shallow container. Mix the remaining 3 1/2 cups (790 g) of sugar and the mace together in another shallow container.

6. When ready to cook, brush the grates of the grill with vegetable oil. Dip each pineapple ring into the coconut milk to coat completely. Let excess drip off, and then dip into the sugar-mace mixture, coating both sides.

7. Grill the pineapple slices until well marked on both sides, about 3–5 minutes per side. Remove, and hold at 140°F (60°C) or higher. Serve 3 slices each with a pool of the rum syrup and a mint garnish.

NUTRITION

Nutrition Facts

Yield: Serves 10
Serving Size: 6 oz. (170 g)

Amount Per Serving

Calories 390	
Total Fat 1 g	
Sodium 30 mg	
Total Carbohydrate 92 g	
Protein 1 g	

Madris Chutney

INGREDIENTS

	U.S. Standard	Metric
Oranges, scrubbed	3 each	3 each
Sugar	1 c.	225 g
Brown sugar	1/2 c.	115 g
Salt	1 tsp.	5 g
Red pepper flakes	1/8 tsp.	1 g
Malt vinegar	2 c.	500 ml
Onion, peeled, diced 1/4" (6 mm)	6 oz.	170 g
Dates, pitted, chopped	8 oz.	225 g
Dried apricots, chopped	8 oz.	225 g
Garlic cloves, minced	1 each	1 each
Ginger, fresh, finely minced	5 Tbsp.	75 g
Mustard seed	1 Tbsp.	15 g

METHOD OF PREPARATION

1. Gather all the ingredients and equipment.

2. Remove the zest from the oranges. Reserve. Remove the white pith and seeds, and discard. Chop the orange flesh and set aside.

3. In a large saucepan, combine the sugars, salt, pepper flakes, and vinegar, and bring to a boil to dissolve the sugar.

4. Add half of the reserved zest and all the remaining ingredients, including the orange flesh. Stir well.

5. Simmer over a medium-low heat, stirring frequently until the mixture is reduced and thick, about 1 hour. Stir in the rest of the zest.

6. Cover, and cool in the refrigerator at 41°F (5°C) or lower.

Chef's Notes

- This mixture will stay good in the refrigerator for several months in tightly closed containers.
- The hot mixture can be sealed in hot sterilized jars and kept in a cool, dark place.

NUTRITION

Nutrition Facts

Yield: 1 quart (560 g)
Serving Size: 2 oz. (55 g)

Amount Per Serving

Calories 180

Total Fat 0 g

Sodium 160 mg

Total Carbohydrate 45 g

Protein 1 g

Fruit

643

Fundamentals of Baking and Pastry

The earliest foods for humans were fruits, nuts, berries, and grains. With the ability to harness fire, humans discovered that toasting grains enhanced their flavor and that gruel was more palatable when cooked on a stone near the fire.

Production of coarse flatbread began around 10,000 B.C., and the Egyptians began baking leavened bread around 3,000 B.C. By the time of the ancient Greeks, around 600 B.C., enclosed ovens, heated by wood fires, were in use. Ancient Rome was the site of the first mass production of breads, and the first bakers' guilds were introduced there around 170 B.C.

During the Middle Ages, baking guilds were established in England. Strict guidelines were set, and standard weights and measures were established. Severe penalties were enforced if these standards were not followed.

After the French Revolution freed many of the servants of the nobility, chefs and bakers were able to set up independent businesses. Giving the general public access to high-quality artisan products, these businesses became the forerunners of the bakeries and pastry shops of today.

10,000 B.C.
Production of coarse flatbread is begun.

3,000 B.C.
Egyptians bake leavened bread.

600 B.C.
Enclosed ovens are used for baked breads.

A.D. 1493
Christopher Columbus brings sugarcane cuttings to the Caribbean.

1600
Bakers and pastry chefs begin to become two distinct groups.

Bakeshop Formulas

A baker or pastry chef uses a formula, and each ingredient is measured in precise amounts. This measurement, often called a baker's percentage, includes the percentage of each ingredient in relation to the weight of flour in the final baked product.

Precision is essential in baking because most baked products are made from the same seven basic ingredients—flour, water, sugar, salt, egg, fat, and a leavening agent. The distinction between two baked products often lies in the ratio of each ingredient to another, as well as in the use of different varieties of each product. Bear in mind that adjustments are no longer possible after an item goes into the oven.

Bakeshop Measurements

In the bakeshop, ingredients are generally calculated by weight or volume. Weight—a measure of the force of gravitational attraction between two objects—is defined in many baking books as the mass or the heaviness of an ingredient. Mass is sometimes defined as the amount of matter, or for our purposes, the weight of an object.

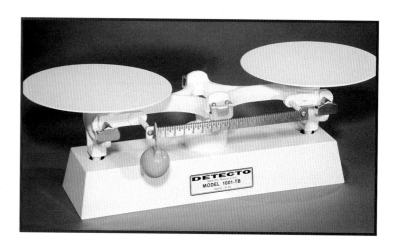

Scaling and Volume Measurement

Volume is the amount of space that an ingredient takes up. In other words, weight measures the mass or heaviness of something, and volume measures the space it occupies. The problem is that the two methods of measurement often produce very different results. In professional baking, volume measures are generally liquids, such as water, milk, oils, egg whites, etc. See Figure 29-1. Syrups such as honey, corn syrup, and molasses must be weighed on a baker's scale because they are much heavier than water.

Exact and constant quantity is significant, so bakers tend to weigh most ingredients on a digital electronic scale or on a *balance scale,* which has two platforms. The left platform holds the item being weighed; the right platform holds weights. Bakers refer to weighing as *scaling.* Most of the dry ingredients used in baking, such as flour and sugar, are easily and accurately weighed. Liquid ingredients, such as water and milk, also can be scaled but often are measured by their volume.

Formula vs. Recipe

In professional baking, exact measures and procedures are essential for consistent products. Most professional bakers rely on formulas and formula procedures for consistent finished products. A *formula* is a list of ingredients based on the ratio of ingredients to one another. If one ingredient in a formula is changed, all the other ingredients must be changed according to the percentage change in the ingredient. A *recipe* is a list of ingredients and set of instructions on how to produce a certain product. A recipe is often adjusted by adding ingredients, seasonings, or flavoring without further adjustments to the other ingredients in the recipe. Recipes typically are not used in baking.

Baker's Percentage

Bakers frequently convert entire formulas to baker's percentages to make the desired number of servings. A baker's percentage means that each ingredient is a certain percentage, by weight, of the sum of flour in the formula. The weight of flour is important because it is the central ingredient in baked goods. Flour in professional baking formulas is always considered to be 100%. This means that all the ingredients in a formula are based on the amount of flour in the formula. In the United States, flour is measured in pounds; in countries that use the metric system, it is measured in grams.

Baking with Formulas

The key to baking with formulas rather than recipes is to understand that all ingredients are in ratio, or in relationship, to the total flour weight. Once the total amount of flour needed to produce the desired quantity of baked goods has been established, the weight of all the other ingredients can be calculated, assuming that the ratio of those ingredients to the total flour weight is known. The ratio of every ingredient is expressed as a percentage of the total flour weight. The following examples demonstrate how to use basic math equations to determine either the weight or the percentage of every ingredient in a formula.

FIGURE 29-1

Volume Measures

HALF PINT		
Cups	*Ounces*	*Pounds*
1	8	1/2
PINT		
Cups	*Ounces*	*Pounds*
2	16	1
QUART		
Cups	*Ounces*	*Pounds*
4	32	2
HALF GALLON		
Cups	*Ounces*	*Pounds*
8	64	4
GALLON		
Cups	*Ounces*	*Pounds*
16	128	8

To convert the weight of an ingredient into a percentage using the *Baker's Math System*, use the following equation:

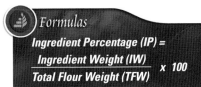

Formulas

Ingredient Percentage (IP) =

$$\frac{\text{Ingredient Weight (IW)}}{\text{Total Flour Weight (TFW)}} \times 100$$

For example, if yeast is 8 ounces and the total flour weight is 25 pounds, first calculate the yeast percentage by converting both figures to pounds or both figures to ounces.

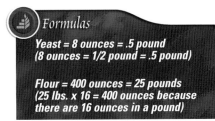

Formulas

Yeast = 8 ounces = .5 pound
(8 ounces = 1/2 pound = .5 pound)

Flour = 400 ounces = 25 pounds
(25 lbs. x 16 = 400 ounces because there are 16 ounces in a pound)

Then, to calculate the yeast percentage:

Formulas

$$\frac{8 \text{ ounces}}{400 \text{ ounces}} \times 100 = 2(\%)$$

OR

Formulas

$$\frac{.5 \text{ lb.}}{25 \text{ lbs.}} \times 100 = 2(\%)$$

In either instance, the answer is 2%.

For the sake of clarity, conversion examples are in U.S. Standard measurements. These examples also apply to metric measurements. See Appendix for metric conversions.

If a formula is expressed in percentages, the weight of every ingredient can be found regardless of batch size, by using the following two equations:

First, find the total flour weight (TFW) by using this equation—

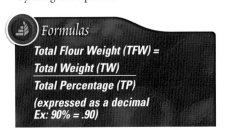

Formulas

Total Flour Weight (TFW) =

Total Weight (TW)
─────────────────
Total Percentage (TP)

(expressed as a decimal
Ex: 90% = .90)

PROCESS

Using a Balance Scale

Professional bakers and pastry chefs use a twin platform/single-beam balance scale or a digital electronic scale for measuring.

To use a balance scale, follow these procedures:

1 Set the weight on the horizontal bar to zero and make sure the scale is in balance. Position the scoop on the left side of the scale. Add a counterweight, or *tare weight*, to adjust for the weight of the scoop.

2 To obtain the exact amount of an ingredient, add weights to the right side of the scale that equal the desired weight of the ingredient. Move the weight on the horizontal bar to make adjustments for ounces.

3 Add the ingredient to the scoop on the left side of the scale until the scale is balanced.

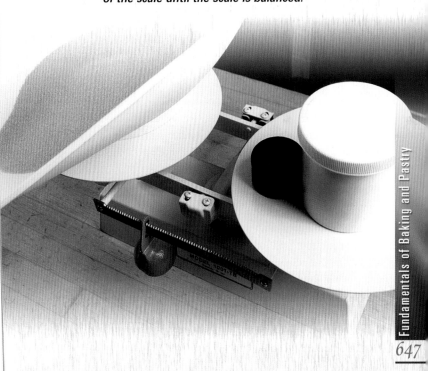

For example: In the following formula for Lean Bread Dough, the total percentage (TP) of the formula is 168% and the total weight (TW) is 42 pounds. Therefore:

Formulas

$$\frac{42\ lbs.}{1.68\ (168\%)} = 25$$

Formulas

Formula for Lean Bread Dough

16 pounds	Water	64%
8 ounces or .5 pound	Comp. yeast	2%
25 pounds	Bread flour	100%
8 ounces or .5 pound	Salt	2%
42 pounds total weight		168%

Thus the total flour weight for this batch will be 25 pounds. Then, to calculate the weight of all the other ingredients, use the following equation:

Formulas

**Ingredient (individual) Weight (IW) =
Total Flour Weight (TFW) x Ingredient Percentage (IP)
(expressed as a decimal)**

For example: In the above formula for Lean Bread Dough water is listed as 64% (.64). To find the water weight multiply the total flour weight times the water percentage—25 lbs. × .64 (64%) = 16 lbs. Thus, the water weight is 16 pounds.

To find the total flour weight from any other ingredient in the formula, use the following equation:

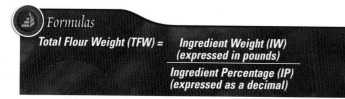

Formulas

**Total Flour Weight (TFW) =   Ingredient Weight (IW)
(expressed in pounds)**

**Ingredient Percentage (IP)
(expressed as a decimal)**

For example, all the percentages for the lean bread formula remain the same, but a batch that calls for only 4 ounces of yeast has been requested:

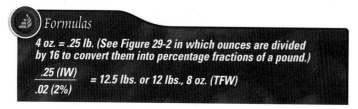

Formulas

4 oz. = .25 lb. (See Figure 29-2 in which ounces are divided by 16 to convert them into percentage fractions of a pound.)

$$\frac{.25\ (IW)}{.02\ (2\%)} = 12.5\ lbs.\ or\ 12\ lbs.,\ 8\ oz.\ (TFW)$$

FIGURE 29-2

Conversion Chart

OUNCE WEIGHT	DECIMAL POUND WEIGHT
1	.0625
2	.1250
3	.1875
4	.25
5	.3125
6	.375
7	.4375
8	.5
9	.5625
10	.625
11	.6875
12	.75
13	.8125
14	.875
15	.9375
16	1.00

Using the above equations and chart (see Figure 29-2), a baker has the tools:

1. To convert pounds to ounces: Pound Weight × 16

2. To convert ounces to pounds: $\dfrac{Ounce\ Weight}{16}$

3. To find the ingredient percentage (IP) of any ingredient:
$$\frac{Ingredient\ Weight\ (IW)}{Total\ Flour\ Weight\ (TFW)} \times 100$$

4. To find the total flour weight (TFW) of any formula:
$$\frac{Total\ Weight\ (TW)}{Total\ Percentage\ (TP)}$$

5. To find the ingredient weight (IW) of any ingredient:
Total Flour Weight (TFW) × Ingredient Percentage (IP)

6. To find the total flour weight (TFW) from any ingredient:
$$\frac{Ingredient\ Weight\ (IW)}{Ingredient\ Percentage\ (IP)}$$

Using these equations enables the conversion of recipes into formulas or formulas into recipes. The specific ingredient weights for any batch size can be calculated, or a general formula from a specific recipe can be created.

Large Bakeshop Equipment

Bakeshop equipment is constantly exposed to wet, sticky ingredients and extreme changes in temperature, so it is important that it be durable and of good quality. It also must be able to withstand the demanding workload of commercial bakeshops.

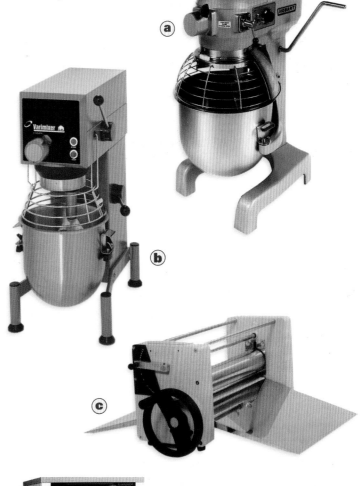

Large Bakeshop Equipment

Large bakeshop equipment is just some of the basic equipment found in a specialized foodservice operation. These items are used in a variety of ways, as described below, to prepare baked goods.

ⓐ Mixers
Mixers are pieces of bakery equipment used to beat, knead, blend, or whip.

ⓑ Stationary mixer
Stationary mixers can be equipped with a variety of optional attachments, which may include the standard flat paddle, spiral dough hooks, and wire whisks. These machines are extremely versatile and are essential to the baker and pastry chef. Stationary mixer sizes are based on the bowl size in quart measure. The standard sizes of most professional mixers are 12, 20, 30, 60, and 80 quarts, and some can be as large as 140 quarts. It should be noted that 80-quart mixers can be converted to use 40- and 60-quart bowls and attachments by the addition of adaptors to the 80-quart mixer. A 12-quart bowl and attachments can be adapted to be used on the 20-quart machine.

ⓒ Sheeter
A sheeter is used primarily to roll out smooth dough with little effort. The baker controls the amounts of force and pressure applied to the dough. Many sheeters are designed for laminated doughs like puff pastry, croissant, and Danish doughs. Sheeters also can mold bread and cut and evenly divide doughs using special cutters that can be attached to the sheeter.

ⓓ Proofing cabinet
The proofing cabinet has been designed to control the ideal conditions of proofing, the final stage of the fermentation process before the product is baked. Both the temperature and the humidity in the proofing cabinet can be adjusted.

ⓔ Retarder/Proofer
A retarder/proofer is designed as a refrigerating unit to help slow down, or retard, the fermentation process when needed. It can then be converted to a proofer for the proper temperature and humidity for the final proofing of yeast items. This unit is very important in the production of artisan-style breads and in high-production bakeshops.

Bakery Ovens

Commercial ovens, used to produce a vast array of baked goods, are invaluable pieces of bakeshop equipment. There are gas and electric models, some of which are equipped with convection fans that circulate the oven's heated air. Some commercial ovens have steam injection systems that produce proper oven spring and crust development for baking breads. There are even old-world type ovens lined with bricks and fueled by wood for baking specialty breads.

(a) Deck oven

A deck oven is also known as a stack oven because two or three separate ovens can be "piggybacked" on top of one another to save space. Each has separate baking controls. Deck ovens are used for many production tasks in the bakeshop and pastry shop, including pizza production, artisan bread work, and fine pastry baking. These ovens are either gas or electric and can be equipped with steam injection.

(b) Roll-in rack oven

The roll-in rack oven, also called a rotary rack oven, is a high-volume production unit. It comes either as a single-rack (18–20 shelves) or double-rack (36–40 shelves) oven. These racks are rolled into the oven with the product already on them. The racks are either hooked to the top of the oven or they ride on a carousel to rotate for even baking. These ovens usually are made of stainless steel inside and out and come with a steam injection system for crusty breads. Most roll-in rack ovens use convection heat.

(c) Convection oven

A gas or electric convection oven is equipped with a fan that provides continuous circulation of hot air around the food. Baking occurs not only more evenly, but also up to 25% faster and at temperatures approximately 50°F (10°C) lower than in a conventional oven.

(d) Reel oven

A reel oven contains shelves that rotate like a Ferris wheel. The standard time for the reel to make a complete revolution is about two minutes. A reel oven can bake a large quantity of products evenly, exposing them to the same temperature and humidity. These ovens are not seen often in today's industry because they take up a large amount of valuable bakery space and time, since each pan must be handled separately.

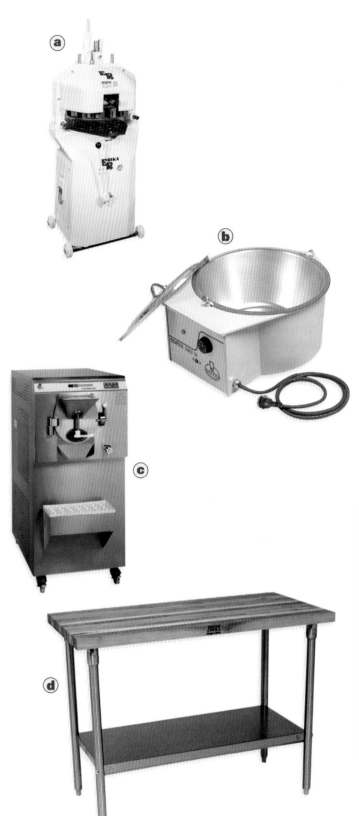

Miscellaneous Items

In addition to large bakeshop equipment and bakery ovens, these items may be used in a bakeshop.

ⓐ Dough divider

Dough dividers relieve the baker of tedious work by evenly flattening and dividing dough into standard 18–36 equal pieces. Some units also are equipped with a rounding plate that rounds the items with the simple move of a lever.

ⓑ Chocolate tempering machine

Pastry chefs use a chocolate tempering machine to keep chocolate stable. This tempering process aligns all the fats in a pattern and gives the finished product the glossy shine that denotes fine chocolate. These machines help the pastry chef quickly and accurately accomplish this task with consistent results.

ⓒ Ice cream machine

An ice cream machine freezes (usually employing compressors) and incorporates air (overrun), providing a base product with which to work. These machines reduce time and effort in the production of ice cream.

ⓓ Wood-top work table

Wood-top tables serve the baker/pastry chef in the kitchen. Wood is the surface of choice for most bakers when working with doughs and processing bakery products. For durability, most high-quality wood-top tables are made from a hardwood, like maple.

Bakeshop Smallwares

Commercial bakeshops require a range of hand tools for dividing, molding, portioning, and finishing products. Numerous utensils are used to shape, score, finish, and decorate various pastries and bakery goods.

Bakeshop Equipment

Bakeshop equipment includes all the smallwares and hand tools to get the product made.

(a) Sheet pans

Sheet pans come in standard full size (18 x 26 in./45 x 65 cm) or half size (18 x 13 in./45 x 33 cm). Perforated baking sheet pans are the same size and are used for baking breads. They allow air to flow completely around the product, thereby producing crispier crusts than regular sheet pans.

(b) Loaf pan

Loaf pans are used primarily for pan or loaf bread, but they also may be used for some quick breads.

(c) Tube pans

Tube pans are used for angel food cakes as well as for many specialty cakes.

(d) Springform pans

These pans contain a clamp that can be used to release the pan's bottom from its circular wall. They are commonly used to bake cheesecakes.

(e) Tart pan

Tart pans are round, shallow pans with removable bottoms for the production of various large fruit tarts. Individual tart pans are one piece.

(f) Brioche tins

Brioche tins are small individual fluted cups with sloped sides. They are also made in larger sizes and different shapes.

(g) Muffin and cupcake tins

These are pans with 6–24 cups arranged for even baking. The cups vary in ounce capacities.

(h) Molds

Molds are pans with distinctive shapes. They range in size and shape from small, round ceramic pans to long, narrow bread molds.

(i) Rings

Rings are containers with no bottom. They come in assorted heights and are usually round, but they also can be square. Rings are used to produce round and square dessert items.

(j) Parchment paper

Parchment is a silicon-based sheet of paper used to prevent baked goods from sticking to sheet pans and other baking surfaces. The use of parchment paper eliminates the need for pan grease on sheet pans and can be used to make piping bags for pastry decorating.

(k) Pastry bags and tips

Pastry bags come in various sizes and materials, including plastic, nylon, plastic-lined cotton, and polyester. The premade bags are generally cone-shaped with one wide open end and the other end tapering to a narrow opening that can be fitted with decorator tips of various sizes. Fill the larger end with batter, icing, fillings, or whipped cream.

(l) Pastry brushes

These flat-edged brushes come in a variety of shapes and sizes. Some are used to brush on liquids and oils; others are used to dust off excess flour. Brushes are used before, during, or after baking.

(m) Pastry cutters

Pastry cutters have straight or fluted edges and are used to cut dough into specific shapes.

(n) Pastry wheels

Pastry wheels are small sharp wheels on handles used for cutting pastry into strips or for decorating the tops of pies and tarts. Some are fluted for decorating pastry dough strips.

(o) Bench scrapers

This rectangular utensil, also called a dough cutter, has a stainless steel blade and a handle made of slip-resistant plastic or wood. The bench scraper can be used to clean and scrape surfaces and to cut and portion dough.

(p) Rolling pins

These long, cylindrical tools are made from hardwood and have handles on each side. The French rolling pin also is made from hardwood, but it does not have handles and is tapered at the ends. Rolling pins are used for rolling laminated doughs, pie dough, pastry doughs, and shortbread cookie dough.

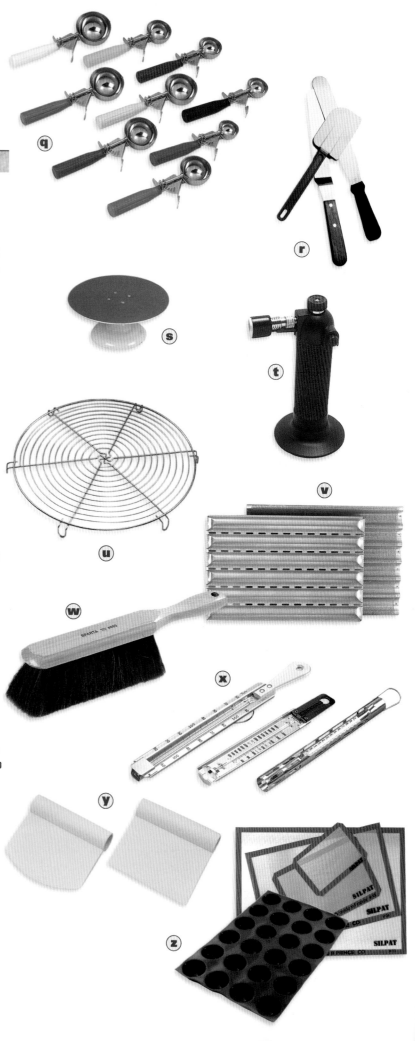

Bakeshop Equipment *continued*

(q) Scoops

Scoops are rounded tools used to dip out foods.

(r) Spatulas (offset and regular)

Spatulas are used for spreading products such as fillings, toppings, and icing on cake. They come in a variety of sizes depending on the intended purpose. An offset spatula, or turner, has a bent stainless steel blade.

(s) Turntable

A turntable helps the cake decorator quickly turn and adjust cakes, facilitating the process of icing a cake.

(t) Blowtorch

A kitchen blowtorch is used to brown items quickly, such as lemon meringue pie, baked Alaska, or crème brûlée.

(u) Cooling rack

Cooling racks are slotted shelves that allow air to pass through them to rapidly cool products that have come out of the oven.

(v) Baguette screens

Baguette screens are metal perforated pans that are curved to create a cylindrical finished product similar to the French baguette.

(w) Bench brush

Bench brushes are longer than pastry brushes and are used to brush the flour from the bench or dough or flour from a piece of equipment.

(x) Candy thermometers

A candy thermometer is a high-temperature instrument used to measure the temperature of a sugar solution as it moves through its various stages of hardness. It is usually a glass tube housed in a protective wire cage. Today's digital thermometers are very accurate and easy to read, but be careful that the plastic housing probe does not get too close to the heat source.

(y) Bowl scrapers

A bowl scraper is a plastic card-shaped item that is curved and beveled on one side. The baker uses it to scrape or clean out products from bowls. This tool can be used to spread icing on cakes or to hand-mix batters that contain an egg mixture that should not be deflated. Bowl scrapers also can be used to "cut" fat into dry ingredients to make pie dough and biscuit items.

(z) Nonstick bake sheets

Nonstick bake sheets are flexible, silicon-coated, nonstick molds, trays, and mats. They are the size of a full sheet pan and extremely versatile. Both are rubberlike and can withstand temperatures of -10°F–450°F (-23°C–232°C).

Bakeshop Ingredients

Most baked goods are made from the same basic ingredients: flour, fats, sweeteners, leaveners, thickeners, a liquid, and various flavorings.

Wheat Flour

Wheat and wheat flour are the most essential ingredients used in baking. Wheat flour gives structure and strength to most baked goods. It is classified two ways, by the season it is sown—spring or winter, and by the kernel—hard or soft.

Hard wheat is higher in protein content and is used mostly in the production of bread items. Soft wheat is lower in protein content and is used in the production of pastry items such as cakes, cookies, and pie dough.

The protein found in wheat flour is called *gluten.* Gluten is found in ample amounts only in wheat flour and forms a tough, rubbery, and elastic substance when mixed or kneaded with water or other liquids. Gluten affects the texture of baked goods. Yeast dough items need an extensive amount of gluten to help hold the gases during the fermentation and baking processes. Pastry items such as pie dough, biscuits, cakes, and cookies need a lesser amount of gluten because these items have a more tender finished quality.

Gluten is made up of two other proteins: glutenin and gliadin. *Glutenin* gives a baked good strength and structure and helps retain the gases during leavening and baking. *Gliadin* gives a dough its elastic or stretching ability, allowing it to expand during the leavening and baking processes.

Wheat flour is the only grain and flour that has an abundant amount of these vital proteins. Rye, corn, rice, and oats lack the proper amount of glutenin and gliadin.

The Wheat Kernel

The wheat kernel contains three sections: bran, germ, and endosperm. See Figure 29-3.

Bran The *bran* is the outer protective coating for the kernel. It is high in fiber and mineral content and is generally removed during the milling process.

Germ The *germ* contains high levels of fat and oils (vitamin E) and gives wheat its nutty taste. This section is where the embryo is formed and is removed during the milling process. Wheat flour with a high amount of wheat germ has a tendency to turn rancid if not stored properly.

Endosperm The *endosperm* is the innermost portion of the kernel. It contains mostly carbohydrates, starches, and proteins. When the bran and germ are removed during the milling process, what is left is the starchy endosperm. When just the endosperm is milled, 100% "straight flour" is produced. Straight flour is the most commonly used flour in today's bakeshop.

Milling Process

After the wheat has been harvested, it is sent to the mill for processing into flour. While at the mill, its beard and shaft are removed by threshing the wheat. This process leaves only the edible wheat kernel. The kernel goes through a washing and tempering process before it can be ground and sifted into flour.

FIGURE 29-3
Wheat kernel

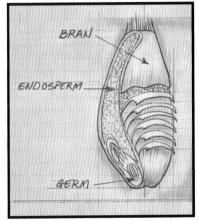

When 100% of the whole kernel is ground and sifted, it is called whole-wheat flour. Whole-wheat flour is an excellent food source. It contains substantial amounts of proteins, vitamins, minerals, fats, and carbohydrates for human consumption.

Whole-wheat flour contains the bran and germ, so it has a detrimental effect on the gluten production in baked goods. Baked goods that have a high amount of whole-wheat flour tend to be flat and less leavened.

For baked goods to have a lighter and less dense texture, the bran and germ are removed to expose only the creamy, starchy endosperm. Millers have been removing the outer bran and germ for thousands of years.

In ancient times, aristocrats desired white flour because the finished baked goods were lighter in texture and easier to digest. The whole-grain flour was left for the peasants.

Straight Flour

Straight flour is 100% milled endosperm. All the bran and germ have been removed during the milling process. Straight flour contains about 70% starch. The first grinding and sifting of straight flour is called first clear or clear flour.

Ash content is an indicator of the quality of the milled flour. High ash content—0.75%–1.0%—indicates a lower-quality milled wheat flour; low ash content—0.7% to less than 0.5%—indicates a higher-quality milled wheat flour. The ash content is determined by flash burning a small amount of milled straight flour and finding out how much mineral or ash content remains. The percentage of the remaining minerals or ash determines the quality of the milled wheat flour.

First clear or clear flour This type of flour is milled from the outer portion of the endosperm. It is high in mineral or ash content because it contains some residue of bran, giving clear flour its gray to tan color. Baked goods that use clear flour leave the crumb darker and less creamy or white in color. First clear is generally used in multigrain and rye breads.

Patent flour Patent flour is milled from the center of the endosperm. It is considered pure flour because of the low mineral or ash content. Patent flour has a more consistent amount of protein, and is used in high-end production. Most flours used today are said to be of patent quality.

Wheat Flour Treatments and Additives

When wheat flour is milled into straight flour by removing the bran and germ, some of the vital minerals and vitamins are removed during the milling process. Most millers are required by law to enrich their flour with the vital minerals and vitamins that were removed before the flour can be sold to the general public.

Flour that will be used for bread production sometimes has other added ingredients, such as malted barley and ascorbic acid. The miller also may add enzymes if the wheat is found to be lacking in a group of enzymes known as *diastase,* which convert starches into sugars and are essential in yeast breads.

Aging and Bleaching

Bakers throughout the centuries have been trying to improve bread. When wheat is first milled, it does not make very good bread. The gluten is rather inelastic and the flour has a yellow color. Over time the oxygen in the air matures the proteins. The high cost of storage and the great demand for high-quality baked goods has required flour to be bleached with chemicals, such as chlorine, benzyl peroxide, and bromates, in an effort to whiten it and mature the proteins. These products affect the bonding properties of flour and increase the flour's strength and elasticity. Bromates increase the oxygen levels in wheat, which are essential in the aging process. Chemical aging in flour takes a very short time, about three to four days.

Not all flour is chemically aged or bleached. Many millers in the United States have stopped using this process and have gone back to a more natural aging process.

When wheat is milled, oxygen is mixed into the flour slowly, so the aging process takes a longer time. This natural aging process generally takes up to seven days. Naturally aged flour is usually not bleached. Unbleached flour gives bread a more creamy color to the finished crumb. This natural aging process is a growing trend in the milling industry today. Some states, including California, have banned the use of chemically treated and bleached flour.

Common Additives

The USDA requires all millers to state what has been added at the mill and what type of aging or bleaching process has been performed on the flour.

The following are common additives in flour:

- malted barley or wheat, which helps in the fermentation process
- ascorbic acid, a dough conditioner that aids in the mixing process; this additive helps strengthen the flour so it can perform better with modern mixers
- bleaching agents, which help keep the flour white in color; chlorine gas is used in cake flour processing
- chemical aging agents, such as potassium bromates or benzyl peroxide
- enrichments, including vitamins, minerals, folic acid, and iron

FIGURE 29-4
Hard-wheat flour

Hard-Wheat Flour

Hard wheat makes up about 75% of U.S. wheat production. The difference between hard and soft wheat is the amount of protein in the kernel. The protein in the kernel runs from about 7%–14%. Hard wheat kernels have a higher percentage of protein. When these wheats are milled, they break into larger fragments because there are fewer free starch granules. Hard wheats also form strong bonds in the baking process. They are known as hard red, white spring wheat, or hard red winter wheat, with red being the most common. See Figure 29-4 and Figure 29-5 on page 657.

High-gluten flour High-gluten flour is wheat flour that has a protein content of 13% or greater. Generally, the gluten protein is added at the mill. High-gluten flour is used for making hard, crusty products such as pizza dough, bagels, and multigrain breads.

FIGURE 29-5

FIGURE 29-6
Soft-wheat flour

FIGURE 29-7

Characteristics of Hard Wheat

Hard-Wheat Flour

- *coarse to the feel*
- *absorbs large amounts of water (50%–75% of its weight in water)*
- *flows evenly when used for dusting the work bench*
- *will not pack when squeezed*
- *excellent for yeast dough items*

Characteristics of Soft Wheat

Soft-Wheat Flour

- *soft and silky to the feel*
- *absorbs less water than does hard wheat (25%–50% of its weight)*
- *will not flow evenly if used to dust the work bench*
- *will pack if squeezed*
- *excellent for cakes, cookies, and fine pastries*

Patent or bread flour Patent or bread flour is the most commonly used flour in the bakery because of its high quality. This type of flour has a protein content of 11%–12% and an ash content of 0.5%– 0.7%. It is excellent for French and Italian styles of breads, laminated doughs, and most high-quality bread items.

Clear flour Clear flour has a dark color that makes it unsuitable for white bread. This color makes the flour appropriate for mixing with other grains that have their own color and do not require the purity of patent or bread flour.

Whole-wheat flour As its name implies, whole-wheat flour consists of the entire wheat kernel, including the bran, endosperm, and germ.

Soft-Wheat Flour

Soft-wheat flour has a lower protein content—6%–11%—than hard-wheat flour. Soft winter wheat is the most common soft-wheat flour in the United States. See Figure 29-6 and Figure 29-7.

Pastry flour Pastry flour, like clear flour, has more color, a creamy texture, and a slightly higher gluten content than other soft flours. Pastry flour is considered to be of medium strength, silky smooth, with the ability to be squeezed into a ball. Its application in the bakeshop is for items such as pie crusts, cookies, brownies, cake doughnuts, and muffins, where low gluten is desired but the color and extraction rate are not as important.

Cake flour Cake flour is much finer than the coarser hard flours, which allows it to carry maximum quantities of sugar and liquids. Cake flour is very high in starch content. Finely ground cake flour also provides excellent volume and crumb color to products such as high-ratio cakes, layer cakes, foam cakes, sheet cakes, cupcakes, and loaf cakes. Cake flour is generally bleached to keep it snowy white during and after the baking process.

Flour Blends

Flour blends include flours of varying strengths blended together to produce flours that are better suited to meet the specific needs of the baker.

All-purpose flour All-purpose flour is a blend of hard and soft wheats that produces a final product with a moderate gluten content. This flour is the most popular in homes, supermarkets, and common cookbooks but is not used extensively in professional bakeshops. Professional bakers generally blend their own flours to suit their needs.

Sylvester Graham

Sylvester Graham was one of the first supporters of whole-wheat flour. In the 1820s, he advocated the important benefits of eating whole grains.

Graham supported his position on the whole grain being used by quoting scripture in his work: "not putting asunder what God has joined together." He went on to claim that coarse wheat was the cure and preventive measure for many intestinal diseases as well as other disorders. His influence was felt well into the twentieth century, causing John Harvey Kellogg to advocate for roughage in the diet to prevent "intestinal toxemia." To this day Graham's name is associated with whole wheat and the whole-wheat cracker that was named after him.

Fats

Fats have been used over time by bakers to add moisture and tenderness to baked goods. They also add shelf life to products because they help retain moisture. The flakiness of many products, such as Danish, puff pastries, croissants, and pies, would not be possible without fats. Some fats, including butter and lard, add flavor to baked goods. See Figure 29-8.

Fats and oils are components of the same class of chemicals, triglycerides. *Triglycerides* are made up of glycerol and fatty acids, which we call fats, oils, and shortenings. The difference between fats and oils is generally their melting point. Oils are liquid at room temperature, and fats are solid or waxy and plastic in consistency.

Fats used in baking are called *shortenings* because of their function in the product, which is to shorten the gluten strands and help lubricate the gluten during the mixing and kneading processes. The high melting point of most shortenings gives a mouth feel of tenderness.

Fats in solid form are also creamed. Mixing fats with sugar increases the amount of fat-coated air cells and aids in the leavening process. The fats most commonly used by the baker/pastry chef are shortening, butter, margarine, and sometimes lard. The oils most commonly used in the bakeshop are made from vegetable or nut oils, such as soy bean, canola, peanut, and corn. Olive oils are rarely used in the bakeshop because of their strong taste and aroma.

To gain optimal use when working with fats, it is important to keep them cool—approximately 60°F (16°C). Fats are less effective in warm environments because they shorten the gluten too much and capture air for leavening.

Shortening

Usually produced from vegetable oils, shortening is made by injecting hydrogen gas into heated oils. The amount of gas dictates the firmness of the shortening. Shortening is 100% fat, compared with butter and margarine, which are about 80% fat.

All shortenings are white in color and tasteless and must have a waxy to plastic consistency at room temperature. Shortenings have a wide variety of uses in the bakeshop.

FIGURE 29-8

Baking fats and oils add moisture to baked goods.

There are two basic kinds of shortenings: all-purpose and high-ratio.

All-purpose shortening This type of shortening is made from 100% vegetable oils. All-purpose shortening is used in a variety of baked goods that require a fat. It generally is used in creaming and is the fat used in pie dough and biscuits. All-purpose shortening also can be used for frying doughnuts. See Figure 29-9.

High-ratio shortening *High-ratio shortening* is made from 100% vegetable oils that are hydrogenated like all-purpose shortening but with the addition of mono- and diglycerides. These are emulsifing agents that increase moisture absorption and retention, giving high-ratio cakes the ability to contain greater amounts of liquids and sugars. High-ratio shortening can be used in the production of sweet dough items and icings.

It should be noted that even though all-purpose and high-ratio shortenings are made from 100% vegetable oils, these shortenings are not interchangeable. Do not substitute one shortening for the other because they do not perform the same way in different applications.

High-ratio liquid shortening Liquid shortenings are oils, primarily from plants, that have been combined with emulsifiers and solid fats but are still liquid at room temperature. They are used in place of solid shortenings because they have the ability to blend faster and more easily with other ingredients.

Puff-pastry shortening Puff-pastry shortening is 80%–100% fat and has a mild to salty flavor. This shortening is designed to have a texture that is soft enough to roll out evenly between the layers of a laminated dough and spread thin. Regular shortenings have no flavor and are harder, breaking up in colder dough and giving finished products uneven lift. Puff-pastry shortening has an extremely high melting point for better steam leavening. One of the disadvantages of using this type of fat is that it leaves a waxy feel to the palate.

Butter

Butter is a dairy product made from churning milk fat after it has ripened. Its unique flavor is the reason why butter is used when flavor is most important. It also adds a creamy mouth feel to baked products because of its low melting point. The United States produces primarily sweet cream butter, which includes lightly salted, unsalted, and whipped butter. The USDA requires butter to have a fat content of 80%. Cultured butter, a rich butter made from cultured cream, is found mainly in Europe. This butter has a fat content of 82% or higher.

All butters are hard and brittle when cold. They work best in baked goods when they are close to room temperature, which makes the butter smoother and creamier. Butter

FIGURE 29-9

All-purpose shortening is used to make biscuits.

creams better when it is soft and waxy. It is the recommended fat to use in laminated dough items like croissants, Danish, and puff pastry. Butter gives baked products an excellent taste and aroma. Products made with butter have a richer crust and crumb color. Although butter is preferred by most bakers and pastry chefs, it is very expensive to use and has a low melting point. It must be handled with extreme care.

Margarine

Margarine was invented in France in the 1800s and was used as a butter substitute. Margarine was made from either animal fats or vegetable oils, but it has always been considered inferior to butter. Today many improvements have been made in the production of margarine.

Margarine's main purpose in the bakeshop is to reduce the cost. Most bakers blend margarine with butter to cut the cost of baked goods, making margarine/butter blends common in today's bakeshops.

The federal guidelines for margarine are that it be 80% oil, have at least 15,000 added IUs of vitamin A, and be an aqueous solution such as one made of milk products and water. Ingredients such as salt, vitamins, and those that enhance the taste, texture, or stability may also be added. As it is made from vegetable oils, margarine also contains vitamin E. Margarine products that have less than 80% oil are frequently called "spreads" or lowfat, reduced-fat, or fat-free margarine. These products are rarely used in a production bakeshop.

Lard

The quality of lard, which is rendered and clarified pork fat, depends on two variables:
- from which section or interior organ the fat comes
- the method of rendering

Lard rendered from the outer parts of the carcass has a lower melting point than those fats from the body cavity (leaf lard). Lard can be processed in many ways, including prime steam, dry render, open kettle, or continuous. It is then normally filtered and bleached. Typically, processed lard is roughly the consistency of vegetable shortening and has a nutlike flavor. Lard is richer than many other fats because it is harder and has a higher melting point. Consequently, it makes extremely tender products like biscuits and pie dough. Lard is used mostly in regional and ethnic baking.

FIGURE 29-10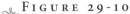

Sweeteners have many purposes in baking.

Oils Oils come primarily from plants that have been purified of fibrous materials and most colors. Oils have been deodorized, and their color ranges from clear to slightly yellow. They are used primarily in the production of muffins and quick-bread batters.

Considerations when selecting fats
When selecting fats, consider the following:
- the cost of the fat
- its purpose and function in the product
- storage and temperature conditions to which the fat and final product will be subjected
- the look of the final product
- the desired flavor and texture

Each fat has a variety of characteristics that distinguish it from other products. If flavor is an important factor, choose butter.

Storing fats and oils When choosing fats or oils, storage facilities, the time and temperature they will be subjected to, and the holding time must be considered.

Sweeteners

Sugars or sweeteners have many purposes in baking, including the following:
- adding flavor and sweetness
- adding color through the browning of the crust
- serving as food for yeast
- aiding in the retention of moisture
- breaking up the gluten and tenderizing products
- serving as a base for icings
- helping stabilize egg foams

The word *sugar* usually refers to table sugars derived from sugarcane or sugar beets. Although the chemical classification for regular sugars is sucrose, other sugars of numerous chemical structures also are used. See Figure 29-10.

Types of Sugars

Sugars belong to a group of chemical components called carbohydrates, a group that also includes starches. The following is a list of the types of sugars:
- sucrose, made from sugarcane or sugar beets
- carbohydrates, contained in wheat and other grains
- maltose, or malt sugar
- fructose, contained in fruits and vegetables
- lactose, contained in milk products
- glucose, contained in fruits and vegetables

Brown sugar Brown sugar was originally an unrefined or partially refined sugar that retained some molasses. Molasses, a cane sugar derivative, is the brownish liquid residue present after heating up raw cane sugar/sucrose and using a centrifuge to refine, or drain off the liquid. Molasses contains primarily the uncrystallizable sugars as well as some residual sucrose and other nutrients.

Today brown sugar generally is a product consisting of white or refined sugar to which molasses has been added. Brown sugar comes in different stages of refinement from dark brown to light brown. The less molasses added, the lighter the color. Brown sugar helps retain moisture in baked goods. It also gives cookies a soft, chewy texture.

Granulated sugar Standard granulated sugar, also called table sugar, is derived from either refined sugarcane or sugar beets and is the most commonly used type of sugar. Granulated sugar is white in color because all the molasses and impurities have been removed.

Coarse sugar Coarse, or sanding, sugars are larger particles used primarily for decoration on cookies, cakes, and other bakery items.

Fine and superfine sugar Very fine and ultrafine sugars (also known as caster sugar to the British) contain smaller crystals than granulated sugar but not as fine as powdered sugar. These types of sugar are used when you want the sugar to dissolve rapidly in a mix, giving the baker a more uniform batter.

Confectioners' or powdered sugar These are granulated sugars that are produced by grinding the crystals finer and mixing the sugar with a small amount of starch (about 3%) to prevent caking. They are grouped by the finished crystal size, which is indicated by X's. The most commonly sold form is 6X, but 10X is the finest. These sugars are referred to as icing sugars because they are used primarily for cold work, such as icings and whipped cream.

Inverts and Syrups

Inverts and syrups are liquid forms of sugar. They are hygroscopic, which means they have the ability to hold and retain moisture. When used in baked goods, inverts and syrups help retain moisture and keep the product softer and less crispy. They also increase the shelf life of the product.

Invert sugars Invert sugars are liquids produced from ordinary sugar. The sugar is boiled with a solution of hydrochloric acid and water, which changes the disaccharide sucrose to monosaccharides. Invert sugar is somewhat sweeter than table sugar and can aid in moisture retention and are sometimes used as fat substitutes in fat-reduced products.

Corn syrup Corn syrup is a natural product made from converting cornstarch to a liquid through the use of enzymes. It is very economical and is the most common syrup used in the foodservice industry. Corn syrup is added to products to prevent recrystallization of sugars in candy making or sugar work. Corn syrup also helps retain moisture in baked goods.

Maple syrup Maple syrup is natural sugar harvested from the sugar maple tree. Depending on how sweet the sap is, it can take 25–75 gallons of raw sap to make a gallon of maple syrup. Sugar maple sap is about 2% sugar, making it a very expensive sweetener that is not used often in commercial bakeries except as a flavoring.

Honey Honey was most likely the first sugar used by humans. It is produced by bees from the nectar of flowers. Honeybees are essential in the pollination of fruit, flowers, and nut trees. The most common honeys are clover honey and orange blossom honey. Clover honey is used for its robust flavor and is amber to light tan in color. Orange blossom honey is also amber to very light tan in color and has a mellower taste than clover honey. Other types of honey come from a number of flowers or blossoms, including apple blossom, rose hips, and sage.

Flower nectar is about 80% water and 20% sugar. In the hive it is converted into an invert sugar and dried to about 70% sugar. The remaining product consists of oils, gums, and water. The oils give each honey its unique characteristics. Honey's high acid content can be counteracted by the use of baking soda, which helps reduce the acid's bitter taste in baked goods.

Glucose Glucose is similar to corn syrup. It is prized by bakers and pastry chefs because of its purity. Glucose is produced from corn, rice, or potatoes. It is used in the same way as corn syrup because it, too, prevents the recrystallization of sugar in candy making and sugar work.

Malt syrup Malt syrup or malt extract is a concentrated water extract from barley grain or corn that has been allowed to sprout. The sprouting permits changes to take place in the grain, making it relatively high in vitamins and a valuable nutritional additive to bakery goods. Malt syrup contains diastatic enzymes that help break down starches into sugars. These enzymes are excellent for yeast fermentation. Malt syrups are used in the production of beer and other alcoholic beverages. Sometimes bakers use as a flavoring agent a nondiastatic malt that has the enzymes removed.

Leaveners

A *leavening agent* is a substance that causes a baked good to rise by adding carbon dioxide (CO_2), steam (water vapor), or air into the mix. These gases increase in molecular size because of the heat of the oven, stretching the gluten or protein cell walls in the manufactured goods. The end result is a baked good that is light, fine textured, and increased in volume. Leavening agents can be produced in a baked good either physically (air and steam), chemically (by using baking soda or baking powder), or biologically (through the fermentation process). See Figure 29-11.

Physical

Air and steam are important physical leavening agents.

Air Air is classified as a physical leavening agent because it occurs as a result of a physical action, such as sifting, creaming, and whipping. In the making of Genoese sponge, for example, the flour is double sifted to increase the air, and the egg mixture is whipped to produce foam. In other cookie- and cake-making methods, fats and sugars are creamed, which incorporates air and aids in the leavening process.

Steam Steam is created at the stage in the baking process when water is heated to

FIGURE 29-11
Leaveners cause baked goods to rise.

212°F (100°C) and converts into steam. This action swells the cell structure, causing the product to rise. Liquids containing water in some form are part of all baked products, and steam is a chief leavening agent. In the production of pie dough, puff pastry, and pâte á choux (cream puffs or éclairs), steam is the primary leavening agent.

Chemical

Baking powder and baking soda are the main chemical leaveners.

Baking powder Baking powder is composed of an alkaline such as baking soda, an acid/salt such as cream of tartar or aluminum sulfate, and a moisture absorber such as cornstarch. When mixed with a liquid, baking powder releases carbon dioxide gas (CO_2). Baking powders are used as leaveners in cakes, muffins, cookies, and quick breads. They come in three basic types:

- Slow-acting baking powders react to the heat of the oven.
- Fast-acting baking powders react to the liquid in the formula.
- Double-acting baking powder is a mixture of both fast- and slow-acting baking powders. Two-thirds of its power reacts in the presence of a liquid. One-third of its power reacts when it comes in contact with heat from the oven. These are known as its action rates: 2/3 moisture and 1/3 heat. Though slow- and fast-acting baking powder can be purchased for the baking industry, double-acting baking powder is the ingredient used by most bakers today.

Baking soda Baking soda, or sodium bicarbonate, is a chemical leavener that requires the presence of moisture and an acid to release CO_2 gas into the baked good. Baking soda neutralizes or changes the pH levels in the product that help release CO_2. Buttermilk, chocolate or cocoa powder, yogurt, fruits, honey, molasses, and sour cream are common sources of acid used in baking. Baking soda has the ability to weaken gluten strands, which helps tenderize the baked good during baking. Baking soda also has the ability to darken the color of the baked good. Products such as devil's food cake have a richer color if the proper amount of baking soda is used. If baking soda is not mixed completely or is out of ratio with the acid, it may leave a soapy aftertaste and can weaken the gluten strands so much that the product has an undesirable texture and grain. Too much baking soda can cause the product to rise and fall before it can set in the oven, making the product inedible.

Biological

Yeast is a living organism, a single-celled fungus that multiplies quickly in a warm, moist environment. The cell division that occurs in yeast is called "budding." During the process of *fermentation,* yeast metabolizes carbohydrates into carbon dioxide gas and alcohol, which causes the gluten in the dough to swell. Yeast products get their characteristic aroma and taste from this fermentation process. For proper fermentation to occur, yeast needs food (sugars and carbohydrates), warmth (proper water temperature, room environment, and mixer speed), and moisture. The ideal temperature for yeast to thrive is 78°F–82°F (26°C–28°C). Yeast cell reproduction ceases if the temperature of the dough reaches 138°F (59°C). This is called thermal death point, or TDP.

Commercial baker's yeast was first discovered in the 1800s by the French chemist Louis Pasteur, who is responsible for discovering how yeast cells reproduce. He was able to collect and grow yeast cells in the lab and then introduce them into bread. This was an important discovery because it gave bakers a fast and reliable way to produce bread. The yeast cells that Pasteur discovered are called *Saccaramyces Cerevisiae,* or baker's yeast. The three types of baker's yeast most frequently used in bakeshops are compressed, dry active, and instant dry yeast.

Compressed yeast Compressed yeast, sometimes called fresh or wet compressed yeast, is partially dried to about a 70% moisture level. Compressed yeast is the standard in most formulas unless otherwise stated. It should be tan in color, have a crumbly texture, and smell like freshly baked bread. Compressed yeast quickly deteriorates at room temperature, so it must be refrigerated when not in use. To use compressed fresh yeast, crumble it into water to create a slurry, or crumble it directly into the dough as it is being mixed. Compressed yeast has a shelf life of about 24–30 days if properly stored.

Dry active yeast Dry active yeast is the same as compressed yeast but with all but 8% of the moisture removed, leaving granules of yeast dormant. Dry active yeast must be rehydrated in a portion of the formula's liquid that is approximately 110°F (43°C) before being added to other ingredients. This type of yeast is normally sold in vacuum-sealed bags of 1- or 2-pound quantities. Unopened packages can be stored in a cool, dry place for several months. Once opened, containers of dry active yeast should be kept frozen. When substituting active dry yeast for compressed yeast, cut the amount of yeast in half. That is, if a formula calls for 2 ounces of compressed yeast, use just 1 ounce of dry active yeast.

Instant dry yeast Instant dry yeast is similar in appearance to dry active yeast but is a different strain of yeast cells. Its leavening action is much more rapid, so use one-third the amount of compressed yeast in the formula. If a formula calls for 3 ounces of compressed yeast, use only 1 ounce of instant dry yeast. Carbon dioxide is created earlier and in greater quantities than in compressed or dry active yeast, speeding up the fermentation of the dough. To use instant dry yeast, blend it with the dry ingredients. Then add it to the water or liquid ingredients. Instant dry yeast lasts at least 24 months in unopened packages or when stored frozen. Once opened, it lasts about 6 months. This is a very popular yeast in today's bakeshops because of the amount used in a formula and the longer shelf life. This yeast is also very reliable and gives bakers a consistent finished product.

Liquid yeast Liquid yeast is primarily used in large commercial bakeshops and in brewing. Various grains are wetted and inoculated with yeast spores, which begins the process of cultivation. The end product is a yeast slurry that can be added to the mix in a continuous stream by commercial producers without slowing down production. This type of yeast is rarely used in small commercial bakeries.

Sourdough starters Sourdough starters, the forerunners of modern yeast baking, were accidentally introduced into grain mashes by wild yeast from the air. Today starters are used for the unique flavor they bring to the final product, such as San Francisco sourdough bread. Sourdough starters often are fortified with yeast for reliability and consistency.

Storing Leavening Agents

Dry yeast products as well as baking soda and baking powder must always be kept securely closed when not being used. If not sealed properly, they can attract moisture from their surrounding environment and lose some of their leavening ability. They must be kept in a cool storage area because heat also brings about deterioration of the product. Yeast should be kept in the refrigerator and purchased just before use.

Thickeners

Most thickening agents are forms of starch derived from the roots or seeds of certain plants. When used in conjunction with proteins, starches perform many valuable functions in the bakeshop, including:

- quickly thickening fillings and sauces
- producing glossy fillings and glazes
- offsetting the action of certain acids
- maintaining a filler's thickness and consistency upon cooling
- maintaining the flavor and color of fruit fillings and glazes

See Figure 29-12.

Arrowroot

Arrowroot is a root starch like tapioca. It is similar to cornstarch but more expensive. A sauce made from arrowroot has a very clear appearance. Arrowroot is often used in frozen foods because the sauce will not break down when frozen.

Cornstarch

Cornstarch is a grain starch like flour. A powdery dense flour with almost twice the thickening power of flour, cornstarch creates sauces and fillings that are glossy and almost clear.

Flour

When flour is used in baking, the starch interacts with the proteins and forms a dough. Flour also absorbs water and gelatinizes during baking, giving firm structure to the end product. When used as a thickener, flour leaves a pasty aftertaste, which is why it is usually cooked with fat to make a roux.

Potato Starch

Potato starch has a clear finish and the texture of salve. It is used in some baked goods because it produces a moist crumb, which can be seen in products such as citrus sponge cake and macaroon cookies.

Tapioca

A starchy substance extracted from the root of the cassava plant, tapioca, like cornstarch, is used as a thickening agent for fruit fillings and glazes. It is sold in various forms, the most common being pearled tapioca.

Eggs

Eggs are used for thickening when flavor and leavening are also important. The protein structure of the egg captures air. As heat is applied, the egg begins to dehydrate and coagulate, creating a soft gel.

Modified Food Starch

Modified food starch helps in the reduction of "set-back"—the process in which the starch weeps and begins to thin, generally in the presence of an acid. Modified food starches do not have some of the difficulties that unmodified starches have, such as rupturing and losing viscosity.

Pregelatinized Starches

Pregelatinized starches are precooked and dried and need no further cooking to absorb water. They are used in products such as instant puddings. When using pregelatinized starches, mix them with sugar (about one part starch to four parts sugar) before adding the liquid. Use pregelatinized starches to thicken sauces quickly and to thicken coulis-type sauces.

Gelling Agents

Gelling agents come from both plants and animals. These agents are fluid at high temperatures and set as they cool. Three commonly used gelling agents are gelatin, agar-agar, and pectin.

Gelatin Gelatin is the generic term used to identify a group of protein-related material that is found in the collagen of animals, particularly bones and pork skins. It has fairly strong gelling power, allowing molds to hold their shape after they have been unmolded.

Agar-agar Agar-agar is a water-soluble plant gum derived from seaweed. It sets up a gel that is stiff, clear, and reversible. Agar-agar is used in some pies, jellies, and icings.

Pectin Pectin is a fiber that occurs naturally in many fruits and becomes soft in water. It is used to thicken many types of fruit-based items, such as jams, jellies, and glazes. Pectin can be purchased in liquid or powdered form.

Liquids

Liquid is necessary in baking to combine all the ingredients into a homogeneous mass. Liquids also dissolve and readily disperse all the ingredients, allowing them to bind together. Water, milk, and cream are the most common liquids used in baking.

Water

Water is a solvent used for the redistribution of salt, sugar, and other water-soluble ingredients. It also is used to hydrate the flour to form gluten. Water is added during the mixing stage of all bakery products through one of two methods, either directly to the mix or through the use of eggs, milk, juices, or other liquid products.

Milk and Cream Products

Milk and cream products not only add moisture but also bring sweetness, flavor, and fat to products such as custards and ice creams. Milk also contains important minerals and proteins, improves the flavor and texture of certain baked goods, and extends product shelf life.

Other dairy products used in the bakeshop include buttermilk, sour cream, yogurt, heavy cream, and dried milk solids such as nonfat dry milk.

Pasteurization Milk and dairy products are a favorable medium for harmful bacteria growth. If milk and dairy products are not stored properly, serious illness can occur.

In the early 1860s a French chemist named Louis Pasteur developed a way to use heat to prevent spoilage of beer and wine without damaging the quality of the product. This process, called pasteurization, applies to milk as well.

Today all milk products and some dairy products are required by law to be pasteurized. There are two methods of pasteurization. The holding process requires the product to be heated to more than 144°F (62°C) for 30 minutes and then rapidly cooled to 45°F (7°C). The second method is called the high temperature method in which the product is heated to 161°F (72°C), held for 15 minutes, and then cooled rapidly to 45°F (7°C).

Homogenization Homogenization is the process that helps prevent the separation of dairy fats from liquids. This process makes the dairy product more desirable to the public. Though homogenization is not required by law, as pasteurization is, this process is done as a convenience to the general public.

Non-Dairy Toppings

Rich's® Whip Topping, nondairy topping, and Cool Whip® nondairy whipped topping are examples of nondairy products available on the market. These products have become increasingly popular as the industry has realized that more and more people are lactose-intolerant. Imitation toppings are made with soy and gums, which mimic milk and cream, respectively.

Flavorings

Although flavorings do not usually impact the baking method, they do add to the unique and identifying flavor, aroma, and color of the final baked good. There are many items available to enhance the final product, from extracts and spices to fruits and nuts. See Figure 29-13.

Extracts and Essences

Extracts and essences are concentrated flavorings derived from various foods or plants. Extracts are liquid flavorings that

contain alcohol and usually are derived through evaporation or distillation. Essences are concentrates, usually oily substances extracted from food. Vanilla extract, the most commonly used in the bakeshop, is the exception. It is made by soaking the vanilla bean in alcohol, with no high temperatures involved, to extract flavor.

Fruit

Fruits add not only color and flavor to baked goods but also small amounts of moisture and nutritional value. Fruits also may add texture and visual appeal to the finished product and can improve moisture retention and sweetness. Juices, purées, skins, zests, and pulps all may be used.

Compounds

Compounds are mixtures of flavors bound to sugars or other dry ingredients to enhance the taste of products. They also may be blends of flavors in a dry form such as butter, lemon, orange, and vanilla.

Seasonings and Herbs

Seasonings and herbs are the fragrant leaves and seeds of plants. Seasonings are sometimes referred to as spices. They can be made from the bark, roots, flower buds, or seeds of a plant. Herbs are the tender leaves with no woody stems or branches.

Spices come in ground or whole form. Ground spices release their flavor quickly and keep for about three months. The flavor of whole spices comes out during the baking process.

Nuts

Nuts provide flavor, color, and texture to baked goods. They are used in a variety of forms, including whole, halved, broken, chopped, chipped, or ground. Store nuts in a cool, dry place to prevent them from turning rancid. Nuts can be used as a topping as well as an ingredient.

Salt

Although many salts are known, the one most significant to the baker is sodium chloride, or table salt. Salt is naturally present in many foods and is necessary for human life. It is obtained from several different sources, but the two most important are salt deposits from the ground and from oceans and lakes.

Salt that is mined from the ground consists of large, irregular pieces with many impurities. It is generally referred to as rock salt and used mostly for home freezing. Rock salt is sometimes purified and used for koshering, or meat curing.

Table salt is mined by pumping water into underground salt deposits. The brine, or salt-laden water, leaves behind crystals as it evaporates. To keep the salt from absorbing moisture and clumping together, chemicals are often added. Iodine is an important nutrient added to salt in the United States.

Evaporation is another processing method. Water from lakes, ponds, or seas is evaporated and the impurities removed until the salt has dried and crystallized. Then it is further purified and ground and graded for use.

One additional method is the vacuum process, in which the brine is placed in vacuum pans and boiled off, leaving lump salt that is then handled in the same way as described earlier, in evaporation.

> The Romans who mined salt in Cheshire were paid in salt, and it is from the Latin word *salarium* that the word *salary* is derived. It is even thought that the word *soldier* comes from *sal dare,* which means "to give salt."

Functions of Salt

Salt has many functions in the bakeshop. Listed below are some of salt's most important functions.

Flavor Salt enhances the flavors of products by adding its own unique flavor and bringing out the flavor of other ingredients.

Controlling yeast activity By lowering the yeast's ability to produce gas (CO_2), salt slows down the fermentation process.

Strength and structure Salt interacts with gluten in flour-based products, toughening the gluten and giving the item more strength and structure.

Stretch and texture As salt interacts with gluten, it also gives the item more stretching ability. The final product in turn has a finer texture.

Preventing bacterial growth Salt changes the pH level of doughs and helps in reducing water activity, thereby aiding in the prevention of bacterial growth in doughs.

Bleaching Salt is such a good bleaching agent that it helps keep the crumb in bread less creamy in color if desired.

Aiding in digestion Salt helps make food more digestible.

Aerating properly Salt's ability to control fermentation also helps in aerating doughs properly.

Effects of Too Much or Too Little Salt

Although salt has many benefits in the bakeshop, it must be measured accurately. Too much salt causes the dough to ferment slowly and have a strong salty flavor. If the product contains too little salt, it will become tasteless and rise uncontrollably, with poor structure and texture.

Chocolate

Chocolate, a popular bakeshop ingredient, adds body, bulk, flavor, and color to cookies, cakes, candies, and pastries. It comes from the bean pods of the tropical cacao tree and was first discovered by the Europeans through the Spanish explorations of Juan Carlos Cortez, who found it in his dealings with the Aztecs. Chocolate is grown in Mexico, Ecuador, Brazil, and in some parts of Africa. See Figure 29-14.

The cacao is a delicate tree that requires six years to grow to maturity. When the fruit ripens, it is collected and grouped together. The berry is divided from the pod, which contains 30–40 cacao berries. They are removed, washed, fermented, and allowed to dry naturally in the sun or they are blown dry through mechanical means. Once it is dry, cacao is transferred to a processing center, where it is roasted, cracked, and then separated into the nibs. The nibs are then shipped to manufacturers, where they are roasted twice and processed into a variety of chocolate or cocoa products, including:

- Cocoa butter, a natural vegetable fat
- Chocolate liquor, a thick, dark brown semifluid

If other ingredients are added (milk powder, sugar, etc.), the chocolate is then refined another time. The final step for most chocolate is *conching,* a process by which huge granite rollers slowly combine the heated chocolate liquor, eliminating some remaining water and unstable acids. The conching continues for 12–72 hours. During this process, other ingredients may be added, such as small amounts of cocoa butter and lecithin. Lecithin reduces the fat requirement, reduces viscosity, and emulsifies the sugar and fat. Soy lecithin, a mixture of fatty substances that are derived from the processing of soy beans, also may be added. These ingredients give chocolate its silky texture. See Figure 29-15 on page 665.

FIGURE 29-14

Chocolate comes from the bean pods of the cacao tree.

Couverture Chocolate

Couverture, the French word for "coating," is a term used not for coating chocolate but for high-quality dark, milk, and white chocolates. Couverture is made from chocolate mass (chocolate and cocoa butter) and extra cocoa butter. Other ingredients can be added to produce any of the aforementioned forms. If couverture chocolate is used to coat candies or other products, it must be *tempered,* carefully melted and cooled off to just the right temperature.

Compound Chocolate

Compound, or coating, chocolate is not made of cocoa butter but of hydrogenated fat and lecithin. It is therefore more stable and does not have to be tempered like other chocolates for dipping, coating, or molding. Despite its convenience, it does not have the mouth feel of couverture chocolate.

Dark Chocolate

Pure chocolate or dark chocolate is marketed as unsweetened chocolate and also called baking or bitter chocolate. U.S. standards require that unsweetened chocolate contain 50%–58% cocoa butter. It has no added sugar or milk solids, giving it a bitter taste. Dark chocolate is not meant to be eaten plain but is used as a flavoring for products such as fillings, mousses, and marzipan. Since it contains all the cocoa butter from the bean, it gives products a very rich flavor.

The addition of sugar, lecithin, and vanilla creates, depending on the amount of sugar added, bittersweet, semisweet, or sweet chocolate. Bittersweet chocolate must contain at least 35% chocolate liquor; semisweet and sweet chocolate contain 15%–35% chocolate liquor.

Milk Chocolate

Milk chocolate is made from cocoa paste that has been finely ground and conched. Extra cocoa butter, sugar, and vanilla also have been added. Milk chocolate must contain at least 12% milk solids and 10% chocolate liquor. Milk chocolate is rarely melted and added to batters because of its somewhat low chocolate liquor content. Instead it is added to a variety of confections or used as a coating chocolate.

White Chocolate

White chocolate is not really chocolate at all but a mixture of sugar, cocoa butter, lecithin, vanilla, and dried or condensed milk. This product cannot be officially classified as chocolate because it contains no chocolate liquor. It is used as a confectionery or may be eaten alone.

Cocoa Powder

Cocoa powder is the dry, brown powder that is left after cocoa butter has been removed from the chocolate liquor. Cocoa powder can be either alkalized cocoa (known as Dutch-process cocoa powder) or nonalkalized (regular).

Dutch-process cocoa has been treated with an alkali solution of potassium carbonate to make it milder, less acidic, and darker. It also is less likely to lump than regular cocoa. Dutch-process cocoa can be substituted for unsweetened chocolate by adjusting the amounts of cocoa and shortening.

Regular cocoa has no added sweeteners or flavorings. Commonly used in baking, it absorbs moisture and provides structure.

FIGURE 29-15
Chocolate is a popular bakeshop ingredient.

The Mixing Process and Gluten Development

As mentioned earlier, gluten is the part of the wheat protein that, when hydrated, mixed, and kneaded properly, develops into a tough, rubbery, and elastic substance. Wheat flour is the only grain to have the proteins gliadin and glutenin together naturally. Gliadin gives dough its stretching ability and allows the dough to expand during leavening and baking; glutenin gives dough its strength and structure and helps the dough retain gases during leavening and baking. Together they create a cell structure that gives bread products their form and structure and enables them to swell with gas during fermentation and baking.

Controlling Gluten

The presence of certain ingredients affects gluten formation.

Flour

Different types of flour have varying degrees of gluten-forming proteins. Bread flour, for example, has a high gluten content. Pastry flour and cake flour have lower gluten contents.

Liquid

Liquids such as water must be mixed or kneaded for the gluten structure in flour to form.

Shortenings and Fats

Shortenings and fats lubricate the gluten and shorten the gluten strand, which tenderizes baked goods. Shortening also prevents water from hydrating too quickly, giving the dough a longer mixing time. In the production of pie dough and biscuits, the gluten-developed flour envelops the fat, allowing the fat to melt and create steam so that the product will have a flaky and tender texture.

Salt

Salt strengthens the gluten, conditioning it and giving it more rigidity and stability. Too much salt in a dough will prevent gluten development.

Sugar

Sugar slows gluten development because of its hygroscopic tendencies, which compete with the gluten for water. If a dough has a high percentage of sugar, it is best to add the sugar in stages to help in the development of the gluten strands.

Mixing Method

Mixing, or mechanical manipulation, is very important to the distribution of ingredients. It also aids in the full and proper hydration of the gluten. Yeast dough items need an ample amount of gluten development for consistent finished products. Pastry items like cookies, cakes, pie dough, and biscuits require less gluten because they require a more tender finished quality. If a yeast dough is underdeveloped, the bread will be flat and less aerated. Pastry items with too much gluten development will give a product a tough and less desirable finished texture.

The Baking Process

All doughs and batters go through the same changes during the baking process. The following are the stages of baking.

Gas Formation and Expansion

The first stage of baking, gas formation and expansion, produces a boost in volume known as oven spring. Carbon dioxide (CO_2), air, and steam are the main gases that cause the leavening of baked goods.

Carbon dioxide is released by the activity of yeast and by baking soda and baking powder. Air is added to batters and doughs during the mixing process. Steam forms during baking, as the dough's moisture is heated.

The rise continues until the internal product's temperature reaches 140°F (60°C).

Gases Trapped in Air Cells

Proteins in dough, such as gluten and egg, trap the gases that are formed during baking. If these proteins were not present, the gases would escape, causing little leavening in the baked good.

Gelatinization of Starches

After the heat has permeated the dough and the product has reached a temperature of 140°F (60°C), the next stage, gelatinization of starches, begins. During this stage, the starches gain structure as they absorb moisture, expand, and become firm.

Coagulation of Proteins

As the baking process continues, the proteins begin to coagulate until the structure becomes set at a temperature of 165°F (74°C). The interior temperature of the dough will not exceed 212°F (100°C) because of the water and alcohol evaporation taking place.

The baking temperature is crucial because of the way it affects the coagulation. Temperatures that are too high cause the coagulation process to begin too early, which causes the baked good to have a split crust or a low volume. Low temperatures do not allow the proteins to coagulate soon enough, causing the product to collapse.

Water Evaporation

Water evaporation occurs throughout the baking process. Bakers must consider this moisture loss when they scale the dough. Although factors such as baking time and proportion of surface area to volume affect the percentage of weight loss, all dough loses about 10% of its original mass as a result of evaporation.

Melting of Shortenings and Fats

The next stage of baking, melting of shortenings and fats, occurs at varying temperatures, depending on the type of shortening or fat being used. This melting process aids in the production of a tender item, as shortening and fat break gluten and emulsify the product.

Crust Formation and Browning

As water evaporates and leaves the surface dry, crust is formed. Sugar and starch on the surface of the product begin to brown, or caramelize, at 266°F (130°C) as they react to chemical changes from the heat. The baker generally washes the product with water, milk, or egg wash to increase browning and to add moisture to the bakery item. This moisture helps give the final product good form and shape.

Carryover Baking

Baked products continue to bake for a short time after they have been removed from a hot oven because of a process called carryover baking. This process occurs because the chemical and physical reactions that take place during baking do not stop immediately. The heat contained in the product causes it to continue to bake. Therefore bakers must keep this in mind, or they will end up with overbaked products.

Breads and yeast-leavened baked goods have always been one of the principal foods for humans. The oldest forms of bread were known as flat breads because they contained no leavening agent. They were no more than toasted grains or a porridge mixture baked on a hot rock.

How and when the first yeast-leavened bread was discovered no one knows. On the basis of information found in the writings and drawings from excavated crypts (from 6,500 to 7,000 years ago), we can be quite certain that ancient Egyptians put aside a bit of fermented dough from one day's baking to add to the next. This was the first sourdough starter.

The Greeks and Romans mixed a wheat porridge with wine, which triggered fermentation in the dough. The Gauls and Iberians added the foamy head from ale to their dough to bring about fermentation. From these humble beginnings came the various types of yeast breads and flat breads available today.

1680 B.C.
Leavened bread is invented in Egypt.

A.D. 1654
Nicolas de Bonnefons' Les Délices de la campagne, the first real collection of bread recipes, is published.

1850
Sourdough bakers proliferate in San Francisco.

1857
Louis Pasteur's analysis of fermentation sheds light on the leavening process during baking.

1868
Compressed yeast is produced commercially for the first time in the United States in Cincinnati, Ohio.

KEY TERMS

straight-dough method
cleanup
modified straight-dough method
sponge method
pre-fermented dough
pâte fermenté
poolish
biga
pickup
punching down
stippling
oven spring
staling
lean/hard dough
enriched soft/medium dough
sweet/rich dough
laminated dough/rolled-in fat dough
autolysis

Yeast Doughs

All breads generally contain four basic ingredients: wheat, water, salt, and yeast.

Wheat Wheat is the backbone ingredient in breads. It gives yeast dough structure and bulk and provides some of its nutrients. The quality of the wheat is revealed by its ability to produce a consistent and superior finished product.

Water Water is the solvent that disperses the various ingredients in the dough and provides hydration of the proteins to develop gluten. Water is vital in helping control the temperature of the dough.

Salt Salt aids in flavor enhancement and retention of moisture, strengthens gluten, and aids in controlling fermentation. Salt also helps develop the bread's texture and crumb. However, it can have a negative impact on products if too much is added. Tuscan bread is one of the few breads that does not contain salt.

Yeast This microorganism rapidly reproduces when suitable food, warmth, and moisture are present. Yeast converts sugars found in the dough into carbon dioxide and alcohol. The carbon dioxide makes bread rise and gives it a light texture. The alcohol gives bread its unique taste and aroma but generally evaporates from the dough during baking. Today most yeast is produced commercially and sold in many forms, including wet or compressed yeast, dry active yeast, and instant yeast. See Figure 30-1.

FIGURE 30-1
Yeast is sold in many forms.

Other Ingredients

Yeast bread, with few exceptions, must contain the four basic ingredients of wheat, water, salt, and yeast. Other ingredients, such as sugars, fats, and dairy products, are added to change the texture or characteristics of the bread.

Sugar Up to a point, sugar nourishes the yeast and increases fermentation. Sugar acts as a tenderizer and also adds color to the crust, helps products retain moisture, and enhances the flavor.

Shortening Shortening also has a tenderizing effect on the dough. Its other benefits include:

- aids in retaining moisture
- helps lubricate the gluten strands, thus causing an increase in volume
- gives the bread a softer crust and crumb

Dry milk solids (DMS) Dry milk solids, or DMS, which contain no more than 5% moisture, are the most concentrated form of milk. DMS adds flavor, increases water absorption, aids in even crust color, and improves the texture and grain of the bread. Because of its concentration, DMS is high in nutrients and protein.

Regular Yeast Dough Products

Many yeast dough products are commonly produced in the bakery. Some of the most common include lean/hard dough, enriched soft/medium dough, sweet/rich dough, and laminated dough/rolled-in fat dough. See types of dough on page 677.

Mixing Methods

There are three methods used to mix yeast dough into a unified, malleable mass: the straight-dough method, the modified straight-dough method, and the sponge method. Each of these methods affects yeast activity and gluten formation and gives finished products specific characteristics.

Three objectives must be achieved in any of the mixing methods:

1. a uniform and complete mixture of all the ingredients

2. proper gluten development

3. initiation of fermentation through yeast nourishment

Straight-Dough Method

The *straight-dough method,* also known as the bulk fermentation method, is a simple mixing method in which all the ingredients are mixed together in one operation. To prepare dough using this method, simply combine and mix the ingredients together until the dough is smooth and elastic.

There are three basic methods of mixing a straight dough: short, improved, and intensive. Each method gives a bread its own unique texture and grain. See Figure 30-2 on page 671.

Short mix The short-mix method creates a light gluten development and soft dough consistency. A short mix is a specialty mixing method that duplicates the hand mixing and kneading procedure. It is used extensively in the production of artisan-style breads, for which hand kneading is desired over machine mixing and kneading. To prepare dough using this method, add all the ingredients to the mixing bowl with a dough hook attachment, and mix on first speed for 6–8 minutes until well incorporated. Knead the dough on second speed for only 2–4 more minutes to develop some gluten strands. Then place the dough on a floured worktable, and stretch and fold it to develop the gluten slightly. The result of this method is a dough with an open crumb structure and creamy color. Because this method has a slight gluten development, the fermentation process is much longer—up to three hours or more with a series of stretching and folding of the dough during the fermentation process. Classic Italian bread like ciabatta requires this method of mixing to achieve its open texture and grain.

Improved mix This method is the most common method of mixing and kneading yeast dough items, such as French baguettes and soft dinner rolls. The improved method gives the finished bread a good crust and crumb structure. To prepare dough using this method, place all the ingredients in the mixing bowl with a dough hook attachment, and mix on first speed until properly incorporated or until the dough achieves what is called cleanup. *Cleanup* is when the ingredients have been properly hydrated and the dough has a cohesive consistency. When this is achieved, the mixer's speed is increased to second speed to develop the gluten properly. This method, which requires a one- to two-hour fermentation period, gives dough sufficient strength and structure.

Intensive mix As the name implies, this method calls for the dough to be mixed for an extended amount of time. Doughs that have a high sugar or fat content, such as most sweet/rich dough items, require this method. This method gives dough a well-organized gluten structure and a closed grain. Some doughs must be kneaded for up to 15–20 minutes on second speed to achieve the proper gluten development. Because of the high sugar and fat content, these items have a shorter fermentation period of one hour or less. Most intensive mixed dough items are placed in the walk-in to assist in slowing down the fermentation process and to help keep the high fat content at a plastic or waxy consistency that is greater than normal. Sweet rolls and French brioches are two of the many items that require this method of mixing.

Modified Straight-Dough Method

The *modified straight-dough method* employs the straight-dough method and the creaming method of mixing. (See page 692 in Chapter 31.) This method helps ensure an even distribution of fats and sugars and can be used to prepare sweet/rich dough items. To use this method:

1. Rehydrate dry yeast or soften fresh yeast in part of the water.
2. Combine the fat, sugar, salt, milk solids, and flavorings in the bottom of the mixing bowl, and mix on second speed with the paddle attachment until the mixture is smooth and creamy. Scrape the bowl and paddle attachment.
3. With the mixer still on second speed, add the eggs gradually until they are absorbed into the mixture. Scrape the bowl and paddle attachment as often as possible.
4. Add about half the flour, and mix until incorporated.
5. Add the other liquids and yeast mixture to the dough. Add the remaining flour, and mix until a smooth, developed dough is formed.

Sponge Method

The *sponge method,* which allows the dough to ferment and develop gases and flavor before it is mixed with the other ingredients, is used to develop a heightened flavor and a lighter, airy texture appropriate for crusty hearth breads and sweet doughs. It involves a three-step process:

1. Combine the liquid, the yeast, and part of the flour (and sometimes a small amount of sugar). Mix and allow to ferment until the dough has doubled in size or until it starts to fall in the center of the fermented mixture.
2. Punch down, and add the remaining flour and ingredients, mixing until a smooth, uniform dough is formed.
3. Mix and knead the dough to the desired consistency.

Pre-Fermented Dough Method

The sponge method has a number of variations, including the addition of a *pre-fermented dough* (old dough). These methods are used to develop a bread with a unique taste, flavor, and texture. Because

FIGURE 30-2

Each mixing method gives bread its own unique texture.

yeast at one time was very hard to obtain and store, these methods were employed to help in the fermentation process.

A pre-fermented, or "old," dough is introduced to a "new" dough to develop a bread item with added flavor, increased fermentation, and a richer crust and crumb color. The amount of pre-fermented dough added to a bread dough is generally 50%–100% of the total flour weight. Breads that use a pre-fermented dough have a unique acidic taste and a superior crumb structure.

There are three types of pre-fermented doughs: pâte fermenté, poolish, and biga.

Pâte fermenté *Pâte fermenté* is a piece of overfermented, or old, dough that contains the same ingredients as a new dough. This method is one of the oldest forms of bread making. The pâte fermenté must be at least 3–24 hours old before it is added to the final dough. Adding this old dough to the new dough helps increase the fermentation process because less yeast is required in the final dough, giving the bread a unique taste, texture, and aroma. To increase the flavor and texture of a bread, add a predetermined amount of pâte fermenté to the final dough, and remove and reserve that same amount after the dough has been developed for use in the next day's production. If this procedure continues to be nurtured over a long period of time, the bread will take on a more acidic flavor and the crust will have a rich golden color. This procedure is used mostly in European-style breads and yeast pastries.

Poolish A *poolish* is a mixture of equal parts of flour and water with a small amount of added yeast. This method allows the water to break down some of the starches in the flour, converting them to sugar. The yeast has a better environment for fermentation, and the final dough acquires a tangy, nutty taste. A poolish must be at least 3 hours old, or it can be retarded

for up to 48 hours before being added to the final dough. The final dough contains the poolish, water, yeast, flour, and salt. Unlike a pâte fermenté that can be reserved and used in the next day's production, poolishes are used as part of the final dough. Some items that use a poolish in their production are French baguettes and Italian ciabatta.

Biga A *biga* is a firm mixture of water, flour, and yeast. It is used in the same way as a poolish, except that the mixture is firmer in consistency. This procedure gives a bread a more closed crumb structure with the same results in taste, texture, and aroma. The amount of biga added to the final dough can range from 20%–100% of the flour weight. Bigas are used in classic European-style breads.

Using Sourdough Starters

Before the development of commercially available yeasts during the nineteenth century, sourdough yeast starters were the leaveners used in most bread production. At first, flour and liquid were mixed together and left outside, where wild airborne yeasts would settle in the mixture and ferment. Part of this mixture was used to leaven bread. Another part was saved, mixed with more flour and liquid, and set aside for later use.

Today, these sours are a simple mixture of flour, water, sugar, and sometimes yeast, which is added for consistency and reliability. A portion of the starter is used as the base leavener for some bread formulas, which are popular because of their sour flavor. After fermentation, sour starters can be kept going in the right environment for years simply by adding equal parts of flour and water. Because sourdough starters are difficult to control and maintain, they are generally used and produced only by trained artisan bakers.

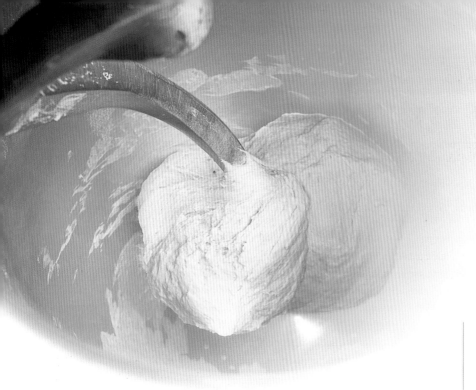

The Desired Dough Temperature (DDT) or 240 Factor

The dough temperature is of great importance when working with yeast-raised dough because proper temperature and humidity are needed for fermentation. A warm, moist environment (78°F–82°F/26°C–28°C) with a humidity of approximately 85% creates the ideal conditions for yeast to thrive. Each type of dough has its own particular desired dough temperature (DDT). The average final dough temperature is approximately 80°F (27°C). The three varieties of dough most frequently used and their DDTs are:

Lean/hard dough 75°F–78°F (24°C–26°C)

Soft/medium dough 80°F–81°F (about 27°C)

Sweet/rich dough 75°F–82°F (24°C–28°C)

Calculating the DDT

When it is said that the DDT is 80°F (27°C), the temperature of the dough should be 80°F (27°C) after the dough has been mixed. Dough is affected by several factors in the bakeshop: flour temperature, room temperature, friction temperature caused by the mixer speed, and water temperature. Dough temperatures can rise by 10°F–20°F ($^{-}$12°C–$^{-}$6°C) if kneaded on first speed; by 20°F–30°F ($^{-}$6°C–$^{-}$1°C) if kneaded on second speed, which is the recommended speed for mixing most yeast dough items; and by 30°F–40°F ($^{-}$1°C–4°C) if kneaded on third speed.

Because most bakeshops are not operating under perfect conditions and the temperature of the friction from the mixing process must be taken into consideration, the water temperature is the only variable that can be controlled by the baker. Therefore, its temperature must be calculated. Commercial bakers have developed a formula for calculating the correct water temperature so that the DDT can be achieved no matter what the other temperatures may be.

1. Check the DDT in the formula.
2. Multiply DDT × 3 = total temperature factor (TTF).
   Example: DDT = 80°F (27°C) × 3 (flour, room, and water temperatures) = 240°F (116°C)
3. Calculate the temperature of the flour and room and the desired friction factor.
4. Subtract the result of Step 3 from 240°F (116°C) in Step 2.
5. The result of Step 4 is the correct water temperature needed to achieve the DDT.

In some instances, as with sponge dough, high amounts of scraps in the dough, sour starters, or soaking stages (rustic wheats), the multiplication factor in Step 2 must be increased. Flour temperature is usually 66°F–68°F (19°C–20°C). The friction temperature depends on the mixer used.

1. DDT = 80°F (27°C)
   Flour temperature = 66°F (19°C)
   Room temperature = 70°F (21°C)
   Friction temperature = 30°F ($^{-}$1°C)
2. 80°F (27°C) × 3 = 240°F (116°C)
3. 66°F + 70°F + 30°F = 166°F (74°C)
4. 240°F − 166°F = 74°F (23°C)
5. The ideal water temperature is 74°F (23°C).

It is necessary to calculate water temperature because different doughs succeed best at different temperatures. The temperature of the water can be adjusted by using ice to cool the water.

Making Bread

Many steps are involved in bread making.

Scaling Ingredients and Measuring Liquids

Unlike a chef who uses recipes, a baker working with a formula must scale all ingredients to ensure the precision of the operation.

Baker's Scale

A two-platform baker's scale is used to weigh, or scale, the exact quantities required in baking. Most dry ingredients are scaled easily and accurately. Flour, however, may need some slight adjustments because of the milling process. The baker's formula will help to achieve the desired result.

Volume Measurement

Some wet ingredients can be measured by volume in a graduated container marked in ounces, cups, quarts, gallons, and the metric equivalents. Items such as water, milk, and some thin juices are measured this way.

Mixing

Using the dough hook attachment on a vertical mixer, mix for the amount of time stated in the formula. The first phase can be divided into two operations: the pickup and the cleanup.

Pickup The *pickup* is when the ingredients are first incorporated and the dough starts to form.

Cleanup The cleanup occurs when the dough is properly hydrated, forms a ball, and begins to clear the bottom of the bowl.

Development After the ingredients have been mixed together and the yeast has been distributed, the gluten must be developed to its proper consistency.

Overmixing or undermixing dough causes the bread to have poor volume and texture. Through trial and error and experience, a baker learns to tell by sight and feel when a dough is at its optimum development. Properly developed dough should feel smooth and elastic. A lean dough should be tacky but not too sticky to the touch. Sometimes a little more flour or water can be added if the dough has not achieved the correct consistency. Rich doughs are normally developed fully because of the high fat and sugar content. Mixing times given in most bread formulas are only guidelines. Small mixers might need to be run at a lower speed to avoid damage to the machine. Large, high-performance mixers may take less time but can damage the dough by overmixing.

> To test whether the gluten has been properly developed, remove a small piece of the dough (2–3 ounces/55–85 grams), and test how elastic and pliable it is by gently stretching the dough until it can form a thin membrane, or "window." If the dough is rough and difficult to stretch, knead it longer. If the dough is smooth, stretches easily, and a window has been achieved, it has been kneaded enough.

Floor Fermentation Period

Fermentation is the development and growth of the yeast cells, which convert the dough's sugars and starches into food and produce the by-products of carbon dioxide gas and alcohol.

To allow the fermentation process to take place, transfer the dough from the mixing bowl to a lightly flour-dusted or oiled container. Then cover it to prevent a crust from forming. Let the dough rest in a warm, draft-free place at a temperature of about 80°F (27°C).

During the floor fermentation period, the gluten becomes smoother and more elastic. An underfermented, or young, dough does not develop to its proper size and quality. It lacks volume and flavor and is dry and tough. An overfermented, or old, dough becomes sticky and soft because the yeast has depleted the food supply, and the dough will not rise during the final proof or baking stage.

Punching down is done at the end of the floor fermentation period. It is a method of collapsing the dough's cell structure so that carbon dioxide is expelled. Punching down also redistributes the yeast and its food supplies for promoting continued growth, tightens the gluten, and equalizes the temperature throughout the dough. This is accomplished by pressing down in the center of the dough with both fists and then pulling the sides up, folding them to the middle. After this is completed, turn the dough upside down in the bowl. The dough must rest for a few minutes on the bench before dividing begins.

Dividing

Using a twin-platform balance scale, cut or divide the dough with a bench scraper or dough divider into equally weighted portions in relation to the product being made. Never pull or tear the dough because this will allow the gases to escape too fast and will hinder the gluten development. During scaling, an additional amount of dough is added to each piece to compensate for the loss of water during the baking step. This weight loss is approximately 10%–13% of the weight of the dough. For example, to achieve a 1-pound (.5 kg) loaf of bread, the baker would normally divide the dough into 1-pound 2-ounce (.5 kg) pieces, an adjustment of approximately 12%. Dividing should be done as fast and accurately as possible to prevent the dough from becoming old.

Round Rest or Preshaping

After scaling, the portions of dough are fashioned into smooth, round balls or preshaped into the desired form. This practice forms a kind of covering by stretching the gluten on the outside of the dough into a smooth layer. Rounding aids in the later shaping of the dough and also helps preserve gases formed by the yeast.

Benching or Intermediate Proofing

Rounded and preshaped portions of dough are allowed to rest on the bench or bench box, covered, for 10–15 minutes. This helps relax the gluten to make the shaping of the dough simpler. Fermentation is also continuing during this time.

Shaping

After the dough has been properly rested, it is shaped into a variety of large or small loaves or into one of the many roll forms. A slight punching down of the dough is required before shaping the dough. All seams must be sealed straight and tight. These seams must be placed on the bottom of any molded item. Shaping gives the dough its final look.

Panning

Panning the bread or rolls is important because heat must be able to move evenly around all sides of the product during the baking process. When baking items in pans, be sure to match the pan size with the weight of the dough. If too much or too little dough is used, the item will not form properly. Rolls should be placed evenly on parchment-lined sheet pans. If a hard roll dough is being baked on parchment-lined sheet pans, a small amount of cornmeal is sprinkled on the paper to give a more rustic appearance to the finished product. Generally the washing of the dough with water or egg wash to develop a shiny crust during baking is done when the dough is panned. It is imperative to wash the dough evenly so that the finished product will have an attractive crust.

Final Proof

During the final proof stage, the final rise of the dough occurs. This is the last process of yeast fermentation before baking. A proof box, a special cabinet that controls both the temperature and the humidity, is used for final proofing.

Proofing temperatures The temperature for final proof should be 78°F–100°F (26°C–38°C) with an increased humidity of 70%–90%. This helps keep the crust moist and allows the dough to double in size. The

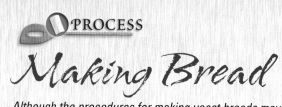

PROCESS

Making Bread

Although the procedures for making yeast breads may vary, the general steps are the same.

To make yeast bread, follow these basic steps:

1 Scale the ingredients, and measure all liquids.

2 Mix the liquid and dry ingredients together.

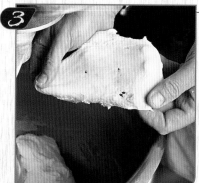

3 Continue mixing until proper gluten development is achieved.

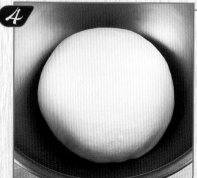

4 Transfer the dough from the mixing bowl to a flour-dusted or oiled container to allow the floor fermentation period to take place.

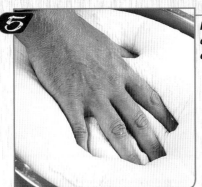

5 Punch down the dough to release carbon dioxide.

6 Cut or divide the dough with a bench scraper or dough divider into equal portions.

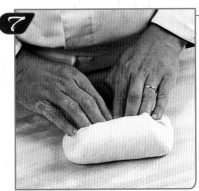

7 Round or pre-shape the portioned dough.

8 Bench rest, or proof, the dough for about 30 minutes.

9 Begin shaping the dough into the appropriate form.

10 Use the heel of your hand to seal the seam.

11 For baguettes, roll into a smooth, even cylinder.

12 Pan according to the style of bread being made.

13 Place the dough in the proofing cabinet for final proof. Stipple proofed loaves as required.

14 Bake the dough according to the formula.

dough should be light and airy to the touch and should close around a finger indentation slowly without collapsing.

Proofing time The proofing time is dependent on the type of dough and its size and shape.

Stippling Some items, particularly lean/hard doughs, are stippled before, during, or after final proof. See Figure 30-3. *Stippling* is making decorative cuts on the top of various types of breads and rolls. Stippling not only gives items a decorative look but also lightens the product by allowing the crumb to move upward and expand during baking. For most bread, stippling is done during the last 20% of the final proof, or when the loaf has reached three-quarters of its maximum volume. Use a razor rather than a serrated knife for stippling because the knife tends to pull across the dough. The stippling should produce a clear, sharp look. To stipple bread dough:

1. Holding the blade almost parallel to the length of the dough, cut just under the surface of the dough, not too deep, and make a straight cut.
2. Overlap the cuts by one-third the length of each cut, making all cuts of equal length. The cuts should cover the full length of the dough.

Baking

Baking transforms the raw dough into an appetizing, pleasing product. Baking times and temperatures are determined by three primary factors: the type of dough (lean or rich), the size of each piece, and the desired crust. Two universal rules apply to the type of dough:

1. The leaner the dough, the higher the oven temperature and the shorter the baking time.
2. The richer the dough, the lower the oven temperature and the longer the baking time.

Baking with Steam

Steam is of benefit to some types of bread products, such as French and Italian breads, which require a thin, hard, crispy crust. In most professional bakeries this is accomplished through the injection of steam into the oven during baking. Steam provides a moist environment that prevents a crust from forming too rapidly. When the steam

FIGURE 30-3

Stippling gives bread a decorative look.

is released by the opening of the oven's damper, a crisp crust is formed. Ovens have different steam systems. Some are turned on after the product is placed in the oven; others are turned on before. Steam has three major effects on a product:

1. The moisture aids in achieving good expansion of the dough.
2. It helps in the formation of a thin and crispy crust.
3. Steam aids in the development of excellent crust color.

As the product is baked, the internal temperature rises, and four major changes take place: oven spring, structure formation, crust development, and alcohol burn-off.

Oven Spring

Oven spring is a rapid blooming or expansion of the dough caused by yeast's reaction to the heat of the oven. This final leavening effort occurs during the first 5 minutes of baking, before a crust has been formed and the internal temperatures become hot enough to kill the yeast cells (138°F–140°F/59°C–60°C). This is called the thermal death point, or TDP.

Structure Formation

When the internal temperature reaches 130°F (54°C), the starch granules begin to enlarge from the transfer of moisture; as they swell, they become set in the gluten structure. At 150°F (66°C), the starches gelatinize and become the chief structure of the dough, rather than the gluten, which begins to dry out and coagulate at 165°F (74°C). The crumb is also formed during this stage.

Crust Development

The crust forms at 165°F (74°C) as the exposed starches and sugar at the surface of the dough brown and thicken. This finalizes the composition of the product.

At this point, the product looks done, but additional baking time is needed.

Alcohol Burn-Off

The alcohol given off by the yeast occurs as a by-product during fermentation and burns off at 176°F (80°C). The finished bread has an approximate internal temperature of 220°F (104°C).

Cooling

Bread that has just been taken out of the oven still continues to bake a few minutes after it has been removed because of carry-over baking. Fresh baked bread should be allowed to cool in a well-ventilated area before it is consumed. This allows the bread to finish baking and helps in the establishment of a good crust and crumb. Pan breads should be kept in the baking pans for a few minutes before removing the bread. Do not let bread sit in the pans after it has cooled. Condensation will form on the crust and make the bread soggy.

Young and old doughs have undesirable end results. Young doughs, which have been underfermented and underproofed, lack volume and flavor and are dry and tough. They have not been able to expand to the appropriate volume, and the ingredients have not had enough time to blend and mature in flavor. Moisture has not been able to move about the dough to moisten the ingredients properly.

Old dough is overfermented, giving it so much volume that the structure can no longer support it properly. Old dough lacks color because the yeast has consumed too much of the sugars that form the crust. It also has an alcohol odor that comes from overproduction of gases during the long fermentation.

Staling and Storage

Staling and storage are two very important aspects of dough production. Staling, the change in texture and aroma of baked goods as moisture is lost, begins as soon as the product is taken out of the oven. The product loses freshness as starches firm from dehydration and free water molecules are absorbed by the drier ingredients of the baked item. There are two ways to slow this process: with proper packaging and by adding ingredients.

Postponing Staling with Packaging

Bread products should never be wrapped when they are still warm. Many foodservice operations keep bread for only one day. For longer storage periods, wrap bread tightly in moisture-proof bags or store it in a freezer to prevent staling. Items with thin, crisp crusts, such as French bread, should be wrapped in paper. If wrapped in plastic, they lose crispness and become soggy. Soft dough products can be packaged in either plastic or paper. Sweet dough items should be wrapped in plastic or packaged in a pastry box.

Postponing Staling by Adding Ingredients

Staling can be slowed by adding certain ingredients to the dough.

Syrups Syrups aid in moisture retention. The most commonly used syrups are malt, honey, and corn syrup.

Fat Fat postpones staling by helping retain the product's tenderness.

High-gluten flour High-gluten flour has a higher hydration rate than bread flour, so a bread formulated with high-gluten flour can retain more water.

FIGURE 30-4
Lean/hard dough breads have a thin, crispy, and chewy crust.

Types of Dough

There are four basic types of dough: lean/hard dough, enriched soft/medium dough, sweet/rich dough, and laminated dough/rolled-in fat dough.

Lean/Hard Dough

Lean/hard dough is made with the four basic ingredients and contains little or no sugar or fat. Breads made with lean dough have a thin, crispy crust and chewy crumb. These breads are usually baked directly on the hearth, or oven surface, because they generally hold their own shape during baking. Classic French baguettes and some crusty Italian breads are lean/hard doughs. Steam is generally injected in the oven chamber to achieve a thin, crisp crust, which is desirable in most lean/hard dough items. See Figure 30-4.

Makeup of Items Made with Lean/Hard Dough

As their name implies, lean/hard dough items are low in fat (0%–1%) and sugar. They have a relatively hard, chewy crumb and a hard crust.

French and Italian breads These breads are light, crusty, yeast-raised breads made with lean/hard dough. The dark brown, intensely crisp crust is created by steaming during the baking process. French and Italian breads sometimes may contain small amounts of sugar or malt and high-gluten flour, which allows the bread to withstand long fermentation. French and Italian breads come in many shapes.

FIGURE 30-5
Sweet/rich dough products are popular in the United States.

Baguettes and batards Baguettes are a long, chewy, and crispy French bread. The weight and size are controlled by French law. A French baguette is generally scaled between 8 and 16 ounces (225 and 454 grams), according to the style of baguette. Baguette dough can be shaped and formed many ways. The French batard is the same weight as a baguette but has a shorter and fatter shape.

Hearth breads Hearth breads are lean/hard doughs with thick, hard crusts that are placed directly on the oven surface. This was accomplished in the past by using a wooden board known as a peel. Today a tool known as an oven loader is used. An over loader is a tablelike device with a cotton belt that deposits the bread onto the hearth. Baking these breads directly on the hearth gives them their dark bottom crust and rich flavor. Breads not baked on the oven surface generally lose some of the chewiness and rich flavor. Many multigrain and sourdough breads are baked in this fashion.

Bagels and bialys Bagels and bialys are very chewy lean/hard dough rings. They usually are boiled and then baked. The boiling process reduces the starch on the crust and gives the product a chewy texture.

Kaiser rolls (or Vienna rolls) These large, round rolls are made of a lean/hard dough and have a traditional fanlike stipple marked on the top. Named for the kaisers who ruled Austria in the 19th century, these breads are used mostly for sandwiches.

Enriched Soft/Medium Dough

Enriched soft/medium dough produces a soft crumb and crust. It is one of the most popular types of yeast-raised products in the United States. Variations of enriched soft/medium dough products include single knots, onion rolls, double knots, cloverleaf rolls, figure-8 knots, Parker House rolls, butter flake rolls, hamburger buns, and hot dog buns.

Key Ingredients

Enriched soft/medium dough contains the four basic ingredients as well as sugar, shortening, dry milk powder, and sometimes eggs. The sugar and shortening may run 2%–8% of the flour weight.

Sweet/Rich Dough

Sweet/rich doughs, used in many breakfast pastries and breads, contain as much as 8%–25% or more sugars and fats. Most sweet dough items contain egg products. Sweet doughs are generally high in both fats and sugars, whereas rich doughs have less sugar but a higher percentage of fats.

Sweet/rich dough items are generally glazed with a glossy egg wash or finished off with a coating of icing. Some items, such as yeast-raised coffee cakes and sweet rolls, are filled with fruit. See Figure 30-5.

Sweet rolls Sweet rolls come in a variety of shapes and sizes. Some items that can be made using a sweet roll dough are cinnamon rolls, pecan sticky buns, and filled yeast coffee cakes.

Brioches Brioches are the richest of these products, containing approximately 70% butter and 50% eggs. They are extremely smooth and rich. Although brioches may be baked as pan loaves or in a number of shapes and sizes, the classical French way to prepare them, called brioche parisienne, is in a fluted cup with a ball on top. If at all possible, brioches should be made a day in advance.

Kugelhopfs These Alsatian yeast cakes originated in Austria. From the German *Kugel,* which means "ball," the kugekhopf is baked in a deep, crownlike mold. It is flavored with raisins or currants and is best served the day after it is prepared.

Panettones These large, round Italian cakes are made from raised doughs that have been enriched with egg yolks and flavored with raisins, lemon peel, and candied orange. Panettones have an extremely light texture.

Laminated Dough/Rolled-in Fat Dough

Laminated dough/rolled-in fat dough has many layers of dough and fat, which add to the flavor, tenderness, and flakiness of the baked good. This layering is known as a physical leavener. The fat that has been folded into the layers melts, and steam is created in the baking process. This steam is strong enough to push the dough up, creating height and flakiness. Croissants and Danish dough are two laminated doughs that are aided in the leavening by the use of yeast fermentation.

Yeast-raised laminated doughs Croissants and Danish dough are very similar in makeup and development. Croissants are made from a lean/hard dough, whereas Danish doughs are made with a sweet/rich dough. Both contain large amounts of fat in the roll-in procedure.

According to legend, the croissant was created in Budapest, Hungary, in 1686 to celebrate the defeat of the Turkish Army. Hungarian bakers created this flaky treat to represent the crescent moon on the Turkish flag. The croissant traveled from the pastry shops of Hungary to the cafés of Paris, where today it is considered a French creation.

PROCESS

Making Laminated Dough

Laminated doughs are used to make items such as croissants, Danish, and puff pastries.

The following is a general procedure for laminated dough, though formulas and techniques vary according to the product being made.

1   Mix dough according to the straight-dough mixing method. Let dough rest in the refrigerator for about 30 minutes.

2  While the dough is resting, soften the roll-in fat, and spot it on two-thirds of a piece of parchment paper, leaving about a one-inch border around the outside edge.

3 Smooth and level the roll-in fat with a bench scraper, maintaining the one-inch border.

4  Roll out the dough 1/2"–3/4" (1.27 cm–1.9 cm) thick in a rectangular shape about the size of a full sheet pan. Place the roll-in fat over two-thirds of the dough.

5  Fold the third of the dough without the roll-in fat over the center third. Fold the remaining third of the dough on top.

6 Rest the dough 20–30 minutes in the refrigerator.

7 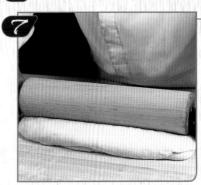 Place the dough on a bench and turn 90 degrees; roll out the dough again as previously done.

8 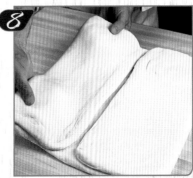 Make a book fold by folding one quarter of the dough to the center. Fold the other quarter to the center as well. Leave a 1" (2.54-cm) gap down the middle to facilitate future folds.

9  Fold the ends over to make a rectangular package. Mark the dough in the top corner with your thumb to indicate the number of turns.

10 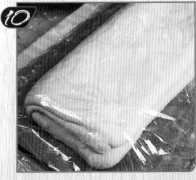 Lightly dust with flour a bread board or sheet pan covered with parchment paper, and place dough on top. Cover with plastic wrap, and chill. Repeat the process until you have made three book-like folds.

FIGURE 30-6

1. DO NOT OVERMIX.

Laminated doughs need an ample amount of gluten development for proper leavening during makeup and baking. Too much gluten in the dough will make it difficult to laminate the rolled-in fat, and the finished product will be tough and less palatable. If there is too little gluten, the dough will not be able to hold the leavening agents properly and the finished product will not rise and will have a greasy texture. The straight-dough method, using the short mixing method, is recommended in the production of laminated doughs. Unlike most bread doughs, laminated doughs have a slight to medium amount of gluten development during the mixing and kneading process. It is important to mix and knead the dough until a smooth mass is achieved. Laminated doughs can be made by hand or mixed on first speed until the dough is developed. However, the dough must be underdeveloped because the gluten development will occur during the lamination of the rolled-in fat into the dough.

2. KEEP THE DOUGH COLD.

There are three reasons for the dough to be kept cold or retarded.

   a. Low yeast activity: *Steam leavening, which is a physical leavener, is the primary leavening agent in laminated dough products. Yeast is only a secondary leavening agent and should work to its potential at the final proofing stage and in the oven.*

   b. Relaxed gluten strands: *Cold temperatures keep the gluten development to a minimum. Because laminated doughs need an ample but not excessive amount of gluten, colder dough temperatures have a retarding effect on the gluten strands.*

   c. Rolled-in fat consistency: *The rolled-in fats used in laminated dough production must maintain a waxy and plastic consistency for the leavening action to perform to its potential. If the fat gets too warm, it will not leaven correctly and the product will be flat and greasy.*

3. KEEP THE DOUGH AND FAT AT THE SAME CONSISTENCY AND TEMPERATURE.

The consistency and temperature of the dough and the rolled-in fat should remain the same. Before the rolled-in fat can be incorporated in the dough, it is very important that the dough and the fat be at the same consistency. The dough should be cold and firm but relaxed, and the rolled-in fat should be cold, waxy, and plastic in consistency. The dough and rolled-in fat temperature should be at about 70°F–75°F (21°C–24°C) before the dough can be laminated. If the fat is too cold, it will break the gluten strands during lamination. Fat that is too warm will make the finished product flat and greasy. Dough that is too cold will be difficult to roll out. In dough that is too warm, the yeast activity will increase, and the fat will have a tendency to melt.

Danish dough Danish dough is made from a richer dough than that of croissants and is used like a yeast-raised puff pastry. There are countless uses for Danish dough, but in the United States, Danish pastries are generally consumed as a breakfast food or served with coffee or tea. Danish pastries are usually filled with fruit or cheese and topped with a syrupy glaze or icing.

Rules for Laminated Dough

There are a number of rules that must be followed to produce a consistent, superior laminated dough. See Figure 30-6.

Types of Fats Used for Lamination

The type of fat used in lamination plays an important role in the flavor and leavening ability and ultimately the quality of the product. Choosing the correct type of fat will affect the cost, flavor, and leavening ability.

Unsalted butter Unsalted butter is the best choice for the production of most laminated dough products. Unsalted butter gives products a rich flavor, melt-in-the-mouth finish, and excellent crust color and aroma. Because unsalted butter is only 80% butterfat and the rest solids and moisture, a small amount of bread flour should be blended with the fat before it is used in the lamination process to keep the moisture in the fat.

Unsalted butter has several disadvantages. Butter has a low melting point, which makes it difficult to control its temperature in warm environments. This low melting point also lessens its leavening ability. Furthermore, unsalted butter is very expensive in today's market. Despite these disadvantages, however, unsalted butter is still the recommended rolled-in fat to use in the production of croissants and Danish pastries.

Baker's margarine Baker's margarine, which has a melting point below 90°F (32°C), can be used as a substitute for unsalted butter in most laminated doughs when the quality of unsalted butter is not needed. The primary advantage of using baker's margarine is to cut costs. Professionals will sometimes blend unsalted butter and baker's margarine to lower production costs while still achieving the buttery taste and aroma of the final product.

Shortening or puff pastry shortening Shortening has a very high melting point over 100°F (38°C), which has an excellent effect on the leavening ability of a laminated dough. Because shortening is 100% fat, it creates a much higher leavening and flakiness in a laminated product than unsalted butter and baker's margarine. Shortening is very inexpensive to use, but it leaves a waxy aftertaste that is not desirable in croissants and Danish pastries.

PROCESS

Shaping Croissants

Remove the dough from the refrigerator, and punch down to release any buildup of carbon dioxide. Divide dough according to batch size. Roll out the dough, dusting lightly with flour as needed. Stacking two sheets on top of each other (Step 3) improves speed but is not necessary.

Follow this procedure for shaping croissants:

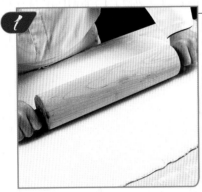

1 Roll dough into a rectangle between 16"–20" (40.64 cm–50.8 cm) wide and about 1/8" (3 mm) thick. The size of the rectangle is actually dependent on the amount of dough you are working with.

2 Use a pastry wheel to cut dough in half, forming two long rectangles.

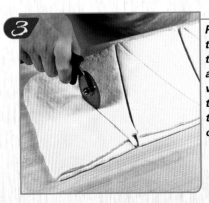

3 Place one half of the dough on top of the other, and use a pastry wheel to cut triangles. Stack triangles on top of one another.

4 Take one triangle in hand, point facing you, and gently stretch it out.

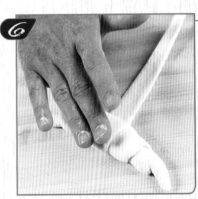

5 Begin rolling from the back toward you (toward the point).

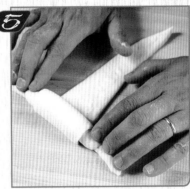

6 Stretch the point a bit before completing the roll.

7 Shape into a crescent with the point tucked under, facing the inside of the crescent. Place the croissants on a parchment-lined sheet pan; egg wash and proof before baking.

Shaping and Finishing Danish

Remove the dough from the refrigerator, and punch down to release any buildup of carbon dioxide. Divide dough according to batch size. Roll out the dough, dusting lightly with flour as needed. Fold the dough in half, making sure that the edges are square. Brush lightly with egg wash, and sprinkle with sugar and spices before folding to improve flavor. Begin to shape and finish.

To shape and finish Danish, follow these steps:

1 Lay the strip in front of you to facilitate twisting.

2 Twist the dough into a spiral strip.

3 Roll into pin-wheels or other desired shape.

4 Place shaped Danish on sheet pan lined with parchment paper, and proof. When half proofed, add filling.

5 Bake until finished and desired color is achieved. Apply glaze when the Danish are still warm. Drizzle with fondant icing when cool.

Croissant & Danish Production

To make croissants and Danish, follow these production steps:

1. Scale all ingredients accurately.
2. Mix ingredients using the straight-dough method. Mix on first speed for 4 minutes and on second speed for 5 minutes. Do not overmix or develop too much gluten.
3. Place dough on a dusted sheet pan, cover, and place in the walk-in for 20–30 minutes.
4. Blend the butter and the extra flour until smooth, plastic, and waxy in consistency. The butter should not be lumpy. Spread or spot the butter evenly over 2/3 of a parchment-lined sheet pan. Smooth and level with a bench scraper. Place in the walk-in until ready for lamination.
5. When the dough is ready for lamina-tion, take out the dough and butter from the walk-in. Dust a worktable with bread flour. Roll out the dough to about the size of a sheet pan.
6. Put the butter on 2/3 of the dough. Remove the parchment paper. Make sure that the butter is plastic and waxy in consistency. The butter cannot be too cold or too soft.
7. Start the lamination by doing a tri-fold. Place 1/3 of the unbuttered dough on top of the buttered dough. Make sure that the dough is even at the edges.
8. Place the remaining 1/3 of buttered dough over the top of the rest of the dough. Make sure that the edges are even.
9. Wrap the dough in plastic wrap, and place in the walk-in to rest for 20–30 minutes.
10. After the dough has been relaxed in the walk-in for the required time, dust a worktable with flour. Take out the dough, and sheet it out to the size of a sheet pan. Perform another quarter-fold. Cover and place in the walk-in for another 20–30 minutes so that the dough can relax.
11. When the dough has had its proper rest period, roll out the dough for the final quarter-fold. Wrap the dough in plastic wrap, and place in the walk-in for 8–24 hours before rolling out the final product.

Whole Grain Breads

Before the age of modern milling, wheat and other grains were crushed between rocks. This produced a very coarse flour that left breads flat and chewy. As the milling process evolved, the whole grains were crushed and sifted to a finer powder that helped slightly improve the leavening ability and gave bread a less chewy texture. These breads were made with the prominent grains of the region: rye in central Europe, barley in the Middle East, and rice in Asia. The breads were very rustic in appearance and in texture. With the onset of artisan breads in today's market, this style of bread is becoming more popular. It is important to understand the correct usage and application of these grains in baking.

Using Whole-Wheat Flour in Formulas

Several types of whole-wheat flour are available. A coarse ground wheat, such as cracked wheat, and stone ground, which is a finer product, are both good choices. When using a coarsely ground product, the wheat is often hydrated with the liquid from the formula ahead of time to improve hydration. Salt is also added at this time to strengthen the gluten. As the wheat kernels soften, there is a reduced chance of tearing apart the gluten fibers and damaging the dough during the mixing process. This process, called *autolysis,* helps extract the sucrose (sugar) in the wheat and gives the bread a sweeter and nuttier taste. When using stone-ground wheat, it is not necessary to soak the wheat because the proteins and starches are visible and gluten development is almost immediate.

When producing whole-wheat bread, most bakers add a portion of clear flour to the dough to produce a lighter bread and a dough that is easier to handle. When producing a 100% whole-wheat bread, 5%–10% vital wheat gluten is often added to strengthen the dough.

Using Rye Flour

Gluten is not formed in rye flour, so a 100% rye bread will produce a dense and chewy flat bread. For this reason, most rye breads contain a percentage of wheat flour to produce the needed gluten.

Because of rye bread's high starch content, it has a long shelf life. Its gliadin content gives it some elasticity, but the wheat flour is still required to achieve the finished light product that most people prefer.

Rye flour is higher in ash content (minerals) than wheat flour is. The greater amount of ash found in rye gives the yeast cells in the fermentation process a better environment in which to thrive and multiply. Breads with a high rye content will ferment faster. The amount of yeast is also reduced in a rye formula because the ash content helps accelerate the fermentation process.

Rye has a higher acid content than other grains, so breads with a higher rye content will have a more acidic taste.

Grades and Types of Rye

Grades and types of rye include coarse rye or pumpernickel, dark rye, medium rye, and light rye.

Coarse rye or pumpernickel This is a very coarse milled grain. It contains all parts of the rye kernel: bran, endosperm, and germ. This is a specialty rye that is used mostly in ethnic or regional breads.

Dark rye This flour is a finely ground whole rye. It is very dark in color and high in bran and germ content.

Medium rye Most of the bran and germ have been removed from this flour. It is very similar to clear flour.

Light rye The bran and germ have been completely removed from this flour, and only the endosperm is milled. This flour is gray to ash white in color. It is very high in starch but low in protein content. This flour is commonly used in rye bread production.

Considerations When Working with Rye Bread Dough

Some considerations when working with rye bread dough include the following:

- Mixing times should be reduced by 25% because of the higher starch content and lower gluten.
- Fermentation time decreases by 25%.
- The amount of yeast is reduced by 25%.
- The dough requires a lighter shaping and handling because of its weaker gluten structure.
- The dough requires docking (making small holes in the surface of the dough) or stippling before baking to prevent premature crust formation.
- Steam is added during baking to help assist in a greater oven spring. Steam injection will also give a shinier and glossier crust color.

Most American rye breads are 5%–10% rye with color and other ingredients added to give them rye's characteristic dark color and taste. European rye breads must contain 60% rye by law, or they cannot be called rye bread.

Using Other Grains

These grains include any plant from the grass family that produces an edible grain (seed), such as barley, corn, millet, oats, and wild rice. Because grains are both inexpensive and a widely available source of protein and carbohydrates, they are a staple throughout the world. These grains are generally combined with wheat in bread products because they do not produce gluten and therefore cannot retain the gases for leavening.

Soft Dinner Roll Dough

Yield: 28 lbs., 3 oz.

INGREDIENTS	U.S. Standard	Baker's Percentage
Water	8 lbs.	53.00
Sugar, granulated	1 lb., 1 oz.	7.00
Dry milk solids (DMS)	1 lb., 1 oz.	7.00
Salt	5 oz.	2.00
Eggs, whole	1 lb., 1 oz.	7.00
Yeast, compressed	10 oz.	4.00
Flour, bread	15 lbs.	100.00
Shortening, all-purpose	1 lb., 1 oz.	7.00
Egg wash	as needed	

METHOD OF PREPARATION

1. Gather all the ingredients and equipment.
2. Calculate final dough temperature for 80°F (27°C).
3. Place water in mixing bowl.
4. Combine the sugar, DMS, and salt, and dissolve in water.
5. Add the whole eggs, and mix well.
6. Add the yeast, and dissolve well.
7. Add the bread flour, and mix just until dough begins to form.
8. Add the shortening, and continue mixing on second speed until final clear, about 15 minutes.
9. Place the dough onto a lightly floured surface, and cover with plastic sheet. Proof for 60–90 minutes.
10. Divide dough into 4-lb. pieces, and round. Place rounded pieces into a floured proofing box, and allow to proof for an additional 30–45 minutes.
11. Using a dough divider, cut dough units into 36 parts. Allow pieces to bench rest for 15 minutes, and then shape as desired.
12. Place finished shapes, 5 × 7, onto parchment-lined sheet pans, and egg wash.
13. Final proof at 95°F (35°C) with 75% humidity, until double in size.
14. Bake at 400°F (204°C) for 12–15 minutes.

Sweet Dough

Yield: *19 lbs., 6 1/2 oz.*

INGREDIENTS	U.S. Standard	Baker's Percentage
Sugar, *granulated*	1 lb., 10 oz.	18.00
Dry milk solids (DMS)	9 oz.	6.25
Salt	2 oz.	1.40
Shortening, *all-purpose*	1 lb., 10 oz.	18.00
Eggs, *whole*	1 lb., 10 oz.	18.00
Water	3 lbs., 12 oz.	42.00
Vanilla extract	1 1/2 oz.	1.00
Lemon extract	1 1/2 oz.	1.00
Yeast, *compressed*	14 1/2 oz.	10.00
Flour, *bread*	9 lbs.	100.00

METHOD OF PREPARATION

1. Gather all the ingredients and equipment.

2. Preheat oven to 360°F (182°C).

3. Using a paddle, cream sugar, DMS, salt, and shortening.

4. Add eggs slowly, scraping the bowl between additions.

5. Change the paddle to the dough hook.

6. Add the water, vanilla, lemon extract, and yeast to the cream mixture. Mix until blended, and scrape bowl.

7. Sift flour, and add to cream mixture. Mix on speed two until a smooth, cohesive dough is obtained, approximately 15–18 minutes.

8. Remove dough from bowl, and place on a floured, parchment-lined sheet pan. Cover dough, and refrigerate until chilled.

9. Remove dough from the refrigerator, and place on a floured surface. Punch, and give the dough a 3-fold. Cover with plastic, and allow to proof for one hour.

10. Prepare desired products—cinnamon rolls, sticky buns, or coffee rolls.

11. Proof final products at 95°F (35°C) with 75% humidity, until almost double in size. Bake 15–30 minutes, depending on product size and type.

30% Medium Wheat Dough

Yield: *18 lbs., 9 1/4 oz.*

INGREDIENTS	U.S. Standard	Baker's Percentage
Water	6 lbs.	60.00
Sugar, granulated	10 oz.	6.25
Dry milk solids (DMS)	10 oz.	6.25
Salt	3 1/4 oz.	2.00
Yeast, compressed	8 oz.	5.00
Flour, bread	7 lbs.	70.00
Flour, whole-wheat	3 lbs.	30.00
Shortening, all-purpose	10 oz.	6.25
Egg wash	as needed	

METHOD OF PREPARATION

1. Gather all the ingredients and equipment.
2. Calculate final dough temperature for 78°F (26°C).
3. Place water into mixing bowl.
4. Scale together the sugar, DMS, and salt. Dissolve in the water.
5. Add the yeast, and dissolve well.
6. Add the bread flour and whole-wheat flour, and mix on low speed until dough is formed, about 3 minutes.
7. Add the shortening, change mixing speed to medium, and continue to mix until final clear is achieved, about 10–12 minutes.
8. Turn dough out onto a floured surface, cover with a plastic sheet, and allow to ferment for 60–90 minutes.
9. Divide dough into 4-lb. units. Round, and place into proof box until double in size, about 30 minutes.
10. Divide dough units using the dough divider, and allow the individual pieces to bench rest for 20–30 minutes.
11. Shape pieces into appropriate shapes, as demonstrated by instructor.
12. Place pieces 5 × 7 onto parchment-lined sheet pans.
13. Egg wash, and sprinkle with an assortment of seeds, if desired.
14. Proof at 95°F (35°C) with 75% humidity for 40–60 minutes, or until rolls have almost doubled in size.
15. Bake at 375°F (191°C) for 12–15 minutes, or until a high degree of color has been achieved.

Croissant Dough

Yield: 12 lbs., 1 1/2 oz.

INGREDIENTS	U.S. Standard	Baker's Percentage
Water, cold	2 lbs., 12 oz.	55.00
Sugar, granulated	5 oz.	6.25
Salt	2.5 oz.	3.125
Dry milk solids (DMS)	5 oz.	6.25
Yeast, compressed	5 oz.	6.25
Flour, bread	5 lbs.	100.00
Shortening, all-purpose	5 oz.	6.25
Butter, unsalted (60°F/16°C)	3 lbs.	60.00
Flour, bread	2 1/2 oz.	
Egg wash	as needed	

Chef's Notes

Variations for filled croissants:
Cream cheese and fruit
Ham and cheese
Almond
Chocolate

PASTRY TECHNIQUES

Laminating:
1. Allow a proper time to rest dough.
2. Roll the dough out to a 1/2-inch to 3/4-inch thickness.
3. Evenly spread the fat.
4. Allow a proper time for the dough to rest.
5. Refrigerate for several hours.

METHOD OF PREPARATION

1. Gather all the ingredients and equipment.
2. Place the cold water into a mixing bowl.
3. Combine sugar, salt, and DMS, add to the cold water, and dissolve well. Place the dough hook onto the mixer.
4. Add the yeast to the water mixture to dissolve.
5. Add the bread flour, and mix until all the flour has been absorbed and dough has formed.
6. Add the shortening to the dough, and mix on low speed for 3 minutes.
7. Change the mixing speed to medium, and continue mixing for 8 additional minutes.
8. Remove dough from the mixing bowl, place onto a floured surface, and cover with plastic. Ferment for 45–60 minutes.
9. Punch the dough, and place it on a floured, parchment-lined sheet pan. Cover with plastic wrap, and refrigerate for one hour.
10. Remove dough from refrigerator, and place on a floured surface.
11. Combine butter with 2 1/2 oz. bread flour to make roll-in.
12. Shape the dough into a 16″ × 24″ rectangle, and cover two-thirds of surface area with the roll-in butter. Do a 3-fold.
13. Place dough back on floured, parchment-lined sheet pan. Cover with plastic wrap, and refrigerate for 30 minutes.
14. Remove dough from the refrigerator, and place onto a floured surface. Using a rolling pin, shape the dough into a rectangle 2 ft. × 5 ft.
15. Shrink the dough, and give it a 3-fold.
16. Return the dough to refrigerator for 30 more minutes.
17. Repeat steps 13, 14, and 15 two more times.
18. Cover dough with plastic wrap, and return to refrigerator for 12 to 24 hours.
19. Remove the dough from the refrigerator and divide into 3 equal sections.
20. Place one section of dough onto a floured surface and roll it out into a rectangle, 12″ wide by 1/8″ thick by approximately 5 ft. long.
21. Using a pastry wheel, cut the dough into triangles having a 5″ wide base.
22. Egg wash the surface of the dough lightly, and roll each piece up and place into a crescent shape.
23. Place rolls 3 × 6 on parchment-lined sheet trays.
24. Proof at 85°F (29°C) with 70% humidity, until almost double in size (about 40 to 60 minutes).
25. Remove from the proof box, egg wash carefully, and place into the oven.
26. Bake at 375°F (191°C) for 15 to 20 minutes.

Challah Bread

Yield: *15 lbs., 1/4 oz.*

INGREDIENTS

Ingredients	U.S. Standard	Baker's Percentage
Water	*3 lbs., 4 oz.*	*40.00*
Egg yolks	*1 lb., 10 oz.*	*20.00*
Oil, *vegetable*	*13 oz.*	*10.25*
Yeast, *compressed*	*4 3/4 oz.*	*3.75*
Malt syrup	*3/4 oz.*	*.60*
Egg-yellow food coloring	*5 drops*	
Sugar, *granulated*	*12 oz.*	*9.375*
Flour, *high-gluten bread*	*8 lbs.*	*100.00*
Salt	*2 1/2 oz.*	*2.00*
Dough conditioner *(optional)*	*1 1/4 oz.*	*1.00*
Egg wash	*as needed*	

METHOD OF PREPARATION

1. Gather all the ingredients and equipment.
2. Calculate final dough temperature for 78°F (26°C).
3. Place the water, egg yolks, oil, yeast, malt, and egg-yellow food coloring into a mixing bowl, and mix together well.
4. Add the sugar to the mix, and blend in.
5. Place the dough hook on the mixer.
6. Add the flour, salt, and dough conditioner (optional).
7. Mix on low speed for 3 minutes.
8. Change mixing speed to medium, and continue mixing for 8–10 minutes.
9. Remove the dough from the bowl, and place onto a floured surface. Cover with a plastic sheet.
10. Allow the dough to ferment for 1 hour.
11. Divide the dough into 2 equal portions. Round, cover, and place in a proof box for 30 minutes.
12. Using the dough divider, divide the dough into 36 pieces.
13. Round the individual pieces, and allow to bench rest for 30 minutes.
14. Shape as demonstrated by the instructor.
15. Place finished loaves, 3 per pan, onto parchment-lined sheet pans that have been dusted with cornmeal.
16. Final proof at 95°F (35°C) with 75% humidity for 40–60 minutes, or until loaves have reached 3/4 proof. Egg wash.
17. Bake at 360°F (182°C) for approximately 30 minutes.

Lean Bread Dough

Yield: 24 lbs., 12 1/2 oz.

INGREDIENTS	U.S. Standard	Baker's Percentage
Water	9 lbs.	60.00
Yeast, *compressed*	5 oz.	2.00
Salt	5 oz.	2.00
Flour, *high-gluten bread*	15 lbs.	100.00
Malt diastase	2 1/2 oz.	1.00
Dough conditioner *(optional)*	2 1/2 oz.	1.00

METHOD OF PREPARATION

1. Gather all the ingredients and equipment.
2. Calculate the final dough temperature for 78°F (26°C).
3. Place water into mixing bowl.
4. Dissolve the yeast into the water.
5. Dissolve the salt into the water.
6. Add the flour, malt, and dough conditioner. Mix for 3 minutes on low speed, and 8–10 minutes on second speed, until a final clear is achieved.
7. Remove the dough from the bowl, and place onto a floured surface.
8. Cover the dough with a plastic sheet, and ferment for 1–1 1/2 hours.
9. Punch and fold dough, cover with plastic, and ferment for an additional 30 minutes.
10. Divide dough into the appropriate weights, round into smooth balls, and bench rest in proof box for about 30 minutes.
11. Shape, pan, and proof at 95°F (35°C) with 75% humidity, until almost double in size, about 40–60 minutes.
12. Bake at 425°F (218°C) with steam for the first 5 minutes. Release the steam, lower oven temperature to 400°F (204°C), and continue baking for an additional 25–30 minutes.

Chef's Notes

This dough may be used to produce: baguettes (long and cylindrical loaves), batards (short and cylindrical loaves), boules (round loaves), crusty rolls, soft crust rolls, pizza, and calzones.

GLOSSARY

Malt diastase: a group of enzymes, found in wheat flour, which break down some of the starch and sugars

Quick breads such as muffins, biscuits, and scones are a less time-consuming alternative to yeast-leavened products. They are relatively easy to produce, and they do not need the special equipment required for yeast dough items.

Cakes have a long history, going back to the cheese and honey cakes of the ancient Greeks and Romans. The Italians and French took cake to a new level during the Renaissance by using sponge cake to make layer cakes and tortes. Many classic cakes enjoyed today are the fruits of their efforts.

Cookies—literally "small cakes"—are among the most ubiquitous sweets in the world. Almost every culture has enjoyed the different types and styles of these unique baked goods. Among the many varieties include Italy's biscotti, France's madeleines and petits fours secs, Eastern Europe's rugelach, Germany's Lebkuchen, Scotland's shortbread, Scandinavia's spritz rings, Sweden's raspberry turnovers, China's sesame seed cookies, and America's peanut butter and chocolate chip cookies.

A.D. 1220
French monks eat cake made with eggs on feast days.

1270
Paris cookie makers are recognized as a guild.

1830s
Cornbread is a staple among rural Americans.

1856
Commercial baking powder becomes available in the United States.

1897
A recipe for brownies is published in the Sears, Roebuck catalog.

1930
The chocolate chip cookie is invented at the Toll House Inn in Massachusetts.

1948
Prepared cake mixes are introduced in the United States.

Cakes, and Cookies

Menu Alternatives

Quick breads, cakes, and cookies have many menu applications. In their different forms, quick breads—biscuits, muffins, scones, and loaf breads—can be served at breakfast, lunch, or dinner, or anytime with a cup of coffee or tea. Quick breads are also a rich addition to a breadbasket served at dinner. Cakes provide a sweet conclusion to any meal and are also often the confectionery highlight of a special occasion, such as a wedding or afternoon tea. Cookies have a variety of uses on any menu. Often served on holidays, they also make an excellent accompaniment to an elegant dessert.

Mixing Methods

Many excellent formulas have had poor results because the ingredients were improperly scaled or mixed or the formula improperly carried out. A formula represents only the raw materials; knowing how to implement the formula properly, as well as using the best ingredients possible, can mean the difference between the product's success or failure.

Mixing should accomplish the following objectives:

- Achieve a uniform and complete mixture of all ingredients specified in the formula

- Form and incorporate air cells, the amount depending on the method of mixing suited to the formula

- Contribute to the development of a desirable grain and texture in the baked product

To produce quick breads, cakes, and cookies, use one or more of the following basic mixing methods. For quick breads, such as muffins and loaf breads that have a breadlike texture, apply the blending method. Biscuits, scones, and soda breads use the biscuit or rubbing method, and quick breads that have a cakelike texture require the creaming method. Cakes may use the whipping or sponge method, depending on the desired finished product. The creaming method of mixing generally is used in cookie production, but it also is used in the production of both quick breads and cakes.

Blending Method

Quick bread formulas calling for oil involve the *blending method.* See Figure 31-1. When using this method, the dry ingredients—with the exception of sugar—are sifted together and set aside. The oil and eggs are blended together with the sugar. The dry ingredients are then added to the egg mixture and mixed on low speed until just incorporated. Water or other liquids are added according to the recipe and blended together. If fruit is added, it is gently folded into the mixture. Be careful not to overmix, which will produce a tough, undesirable final product. Overmixing may also cause *tunneling,* or the formation of holes within the baked good.

Biscuit or Rubbing Method

The *biscuit method,* also known as the rubbing method, involves rubbing or cutting fats into flour to create a mixture with the consistency of cornmeal or rice. It produces light and flaky quick breads. The fat should be solid and cold to ensure that it does not blend into the flour. Although cutting the fat into the flour with your fingers or a pastry blender is best, a mixer on low speed with a paddle or pastry knife attachment also may be used. After combining the fat and flour, whisk the eggs and liquid ingredients together, and add them to the mixture, mixing just until combined. The eggs and liquid also should be cold. The resulting dough will be soft, loose, and quite wet. Kneading the dough lightly (20–30 seconds) on a well-floured workbench helps make it somewhat more manageable and adds volume and flakiness. Overkneading will make the final product tough and difficult to roll out and cut.

Creaming Method

Formulas for quick breads that have a cake-like texture and some cakes and cookies requiring butter or solid fats use the *creaming method.* To cream properly, the fat must be in a soft and waxy state. For best results, blend the fat and sugar on medium speed with a paddle attachment until the mixture lightens in color and texture, and increases in volume. Small air cells form during the creaming process and are incorporated into the mixture. This helps increase

⚓ **FIGURE 31-1**
Blending quickbread

the product's volume and makes it softer. Overcreaming or undercreaming will have a dramatic effect on the finished product, resulting in less volume and poor texture.

Various controlling factors contribute to proper creaming, including the temperature of the fat, eggs, and bakeshop and the speed of the mixer. To incorporate air cells in a mixture properly, the fats should be 70°F (21°C). Cold fats require a longer mixing time for maximum creaming; warm fats (above 75°F/24°C) are too soft and cannot hold the proper amount of air cells in the mix, resulting in poor volume.

The addition of eggs must always be gradual so that they can emulsify properly into the fat and sugar mixture. The egg yolks contain lecithin, a natural emulsifier that coats the surface of the air cells formed during creaming and holds the liquid without curdling. Curdling occurs when there is more liquid than the fat-coated cells have the capacity to retain. It is important to scrape the bowl frequently at this stage to ensure proper incorporation of the ingredients.

Bakeshop temperature also affects creaming. Creaming takes place faster in cooler weather than in extreme heat. Mixing at higher speeds creates friction and reduces or destroys the proper amount of air cells. Adjustments of temperatures, the correct

speed of the mixer, and allowances for mixing times are necessary for proper control.

In the final stage, add all the sifted dry ingredients, and mix on low speed. If more liquids are added to the mixture, alternate dry ingredients with liquid ingredients, beginning and ending with dry, until all the ingredients are in the bowl. Flour and other dry ingredients absorb excess liquid and also help prevent curdling.

Whipping, Sponge, or Foaming Method

The *whipping method,* also known as the sponge or foaming method, involves whipping whole eggs, egg yolks, or egg whites with sugar into a foam. As the eggs are beaten, they trap air. The trapped air provides leavening for the baked good. The basic whipping method, using whole eggs, produces a *génoise* sponge cake. Variations on the basic method produce angel food cake and chiffon cake.

For the basic *génoise* method, warm both eggs and sugar to about 110°F (43°C) before whipping. Do this by heating the mixture in a double boiler. Warming softens the egg yolks, allows quicker whipping, and helps increase air volume in the mixture.

The Blending Method

Use the blending method to make muffins and loaf breads such as banana bread and cranberry bread, as well as pancakes and waffles. Muffins made by this method have a breadlike texture similar to that of loaf breads.

To apply the blending method, follow these steps:

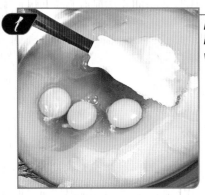

1 Blend liquid ingredients with sugar.

2 Add remaining dry ingredients to the liquid mixture.

3 Add water, and blend together.

4 Add additional ingredients such as berries or nuts.

5 With a portion scoop, lift some batter from the mixing bowl, taking care not to mix the batter when scooping it out.

6 **Finish by adding coarse sugar, nuts, or appropriate garnish if desired.**

The Biscuit or Rubbing Method

The biscuit method produces not only biscuits but also scones, shortcakes, and soda breads. It is very similar to the method used to make pie dough.

To use this method, follow these steps:

4 Turn the dough onto a well-floured work-bench, and knead for development.

1 Sift all dry ingredients into the mixing bowl.

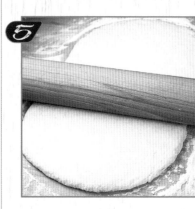

5 Allow the dough to rest about 15 minutes. Use a rolling pin to roll the dough about 1 inch (2.54 cm) thick.

2 Rub or cut the fat into the sifted dry ingredients.

6 Cut out biscuits close together to avoid excess scraps. Place about 1 inch (2.54 cm) apart on parchment-lined sheet pans.

3 Add liquid ingredients (often milk and eggs blended together), and mix lightly, until just slightly developed and incorporated.

The Creaming Method

The creaming method is a procedure that is common for producing both cakes and cookies. The following procedure demonstrates the use of the creaming method in the production of chocolate chip cookies.

To apply the creaming method, follow these steps:

1  Combine butter and/or shortening and sugar in a mixing bowl. Spices may be added at this time if desired.

2 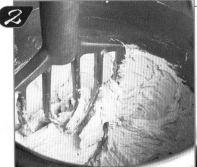 Mix at moderate speed using a paddle until the mixture is smooth. For cakes and less dense cookies, mix longer until creamy and light.

3  Add eggs gradually, mixing on low speed until combined.

4 Scrape down the bowl and paddle attachment as necessary.

5  Add the sifted dry ingredients, and mix only until ingredients are just combined. If more liquids are needed, alternate the dry and the liquid ingredients.

6 Add additional ingredients such as nuts and chocolate chips to finish.

The Whipping Method

The whipping method is used for génoise, angel food, and chiffon sponge cakes. Each has its own formula that involves the use of whole egg, egg white, or a combination of egg yolks with egg white folded in. This procedure is for a chiffon sponge used to make a jelly roll.

To make a jelly roll (chiffon sponge) using the whipping method, follow these steps:

1 Place egg yolks, honey, oil, and flavorings in a bowl, and whip to full volume. Finish by slowly adding simple syrup on low speed in a slow, steady stream. Pour batter into a large mixing bowl.

2 Whip egg whites to medium peaks, slowly adding granulated sugar to make a meringue.

3 Blend a small portion of egg white into the egg yolk mixture to lighten it.

4 Add the remaining egg whites, and fold until just incorporated. Do not overmix.

5 Fold in the dry ingredients by hand.

6 Spread batter evenly into a parchment-lined sheet pan. Bake at 420°F (216°C) for about 10–15 minutes. Test for doneness.

Angel Food Cake Variation

Angel food cakes use egg whites only and a large amount of sugar. They contain no fat. To whip the egg whites properly, add the sugar gradually. A high-volume foam develops as the egg whites and sugar are whipped together.

Follow these steps for angel food cake:

1. Whip the egg whites with cream of tartar, gradually adding part of the sugar, until the mixture forms medium stiff, but not dry, peaks.

2. Sift the remaining sugar with the dry ingredients. Fold this mixture gently into the egg-white foam until just blended.

Chiffon Variation

Chiffon cakes are similar to angel food cakes in that they rely on whipped egg whites for volume, but they also incorporate egg yolks and vegetable oil.

The procedure for making chiffon cake is similar to that for angel food cake, except that it involves whipping yolks and whites separately. Follow these steps for chiffon cake:

1. Sift the dry ingredients, including part of the sugar, together.

2. Whip together the egg yolks, oil, and other liquid ingredients until a stable foam has formed and the mixture forms ribbons when the whip is lifted.

3. Whip the egg whites with the remaining sugar until the mixture forms medium peaks. Set aside.

4. Blend a small portion of the whipped egg whites into the egg yolk mixture to lighten it. Fold the remaining egg whites into the batter.

5. Fold in the dry ingredients. Alternately, some recipes may require that the dry ingredients be folded into the yolk mixture prior to adding the whipped egg whites.

Quick Breads

Quick breads are "quick" because their preparation, unlike that of yeast breads, does not involve time-consuming processes such as proofing and rising. Quick breads have the texture of bread or cake but contain no yeast. Instead, they use chemical ingredients such as baking soda or double-acting baking powder for leavening. Often flavored with nuts, fruits, or spices, most quick breads have relatively heavy batters that require muffin tins or loaf pans for baking. Quick breads include biscuits, scones, soda breads, muffins, loaf breads, pancakes, and waffles. Quick breads are best served warm and may be garnished lightly with sanding sugar, streusel, or other toppings for better eye appeal.

▍ *See Chapter 14: Breakfast Cookery for more information on pancakes and waffles.*

Quick Bread Doughs and Batters

Various mixing methods—blending, biscuit or rubbing method, and creaming—produce quick breads. The consistency of the quick bread's dough or batter determines the mixing method used.

Quick breads can be made from soft doughs or batters. Although somewhat sticky, *soft doughs* have a thick, pliable consistency that makes them ideal for rolling and cutting into various shapes before baking. The biscuit mixing method produces soft doughs. Soft dough products include buttermilk biscuits and scones.

Quick breads such as muffins and loaf breads are batter products. Batters can be thin and pourable like pancake and waffle batters, or they can be thicker ones like muffins and loaf breads, which are deposited with a spoon or portion scoop.

Quick Breads, Gluten, and Leavening

Quick breads differ from yeast breads in that they require very little development of gluten. Too much gluten makes quick bread doughs and batters overly heavy and does not allow them to achieve their proper leavening, texture, and grain. A light and tender quality is desirable in most quick bread items. Care must be taken not to overmix quick breads, as this overworks the gluten, making the baked product tough and rubbery with low volume and tunneling throughout the dense crumb.

Quick breads rely on chemical ingredients instead of yeast fermentation for leavening or aeration. These chemical ingredients allow quick bread doughs and batters to rise quickly without the time-consuming process of proofing.

Types of Chemical Leaveners

Baking soda and double-acting baking powder are the two most commonly used chemical leavening ingredients in the bakeshop today. Both create the leavening agent carbon dioxide gas, which causes the rising or aeration of the baked good. Besides creating the essential leavening gases, chemical leaveners also help tenderize gluten, which makes for a more tender finished product. Baking soda and double-acting baking powder create a strong chemical reaction. The proper scaling and use of these leavening ingredients are vital in the success of the finished product.

Baking Soda

Baking soda, also known as sodium bicarbonate, is one of the oldest known chemical ingredients used in baking. Baking soda produces a chemical reaction in a baked good when it comes in contact with an acid ingredient, such as buttermilk, molasses, cocoa powder, or fruit juice. With the addition of moisture, baking soda helps neutralize the acid ingredient, making the dough or batter less acidic. This chemical reaction produces carbon dioxide gases. These gases are trapped in the dough and help the product rise during baking. Baking soda also darkens the color of baked goods and is utilized to give chocolate cake and brownies their rich deep color.

Double-Acting Baking Powder

Double-acting baking powder is the most common chemical ingredient used in baking. As the name implies, double-acting baking powder has two action rates, fast-acting and slow-acting. The fast-acting portion reacts when baking powder comes in contact with moisture. The slow-acting portion reacts when the product is heated in the oven. Double-acting baking powder contains three basic ingredients: baking soda, cornstarch, and some type of dry acidic ingredient, like cream of tartar. When double-acting baking powder is sifted with the dry ingredients and moisture is added to make a batter or dough, the baking soda and the acidic ingredients combine and create a very fast chemical reaction. This reaction produces carbon dioxide gas that gets trapped in the batter or dough. When the product is baked, a slower chemical reaction takes place, producing more gases. The remaining gases expand during the baking process, causing the product to leaven. Cornstarch acts as a drying agent that helps absorb excess moisture in the air and prevents the baking soda and other acidic ingredients from reacting during storage.

Effects of Improper Use of Chemical Leaveners

Improperly scaling and using chemical leavening ingredients will have a negative effect on the finished product. These chemical leaveners will give a baked good an undesirable soapy taste and aroma. The crumb structure will be loose and crumbly, and the product will rise and then fall before it sets during baking.

Chemical leaveners are effective only if they are fresh, and they deteriorate quickly if improperly stored. To maintain quality, keep chemical leaveners in airtight containers in a cool, dry place. To prevent contamination and absorption of moisture, keep the lids on the containers even if using the leaveners often during the day.

Quick Bread Ingredients

In addition to chemical leaveners, quick breads typically include flour, eggs, fat, sugar, salt, and a liquid.

Flour The use of hard- and soft-wheat flours produces the best quick breads. Hard wheat is used for structure building and soft wheat for its tenderizing quality. Grains such as oats and cornmeal add extra flavor and texture to quick breads. Toasted wheat germ and bran give a healthful nutty taste and texture.

Eggs Eggs provide structure, volume, moisture content, and nutritional value to quick bread products.

Fat Fats have a tenderizing effect on baked goods. They also help quick breads stay moist by retaining moisture content. Fats are essential to the creaming process by creating fat-coated air cells that aid in the leavening process during baking.

Sugar Sugar and other sweeteners, such as molasses and brown sugar, have a tenderizing effect on baked goods. They play an important part in creaming, too, because the sugar acts as an abrasive and helps incorporate air into the fat. Sweeteners also impart color and add flavor to quick breads.

Salt The principal use of salt is to accent flavor. Salt also aids in gluten development.

Liquid Liquid provides moisture, helps incorporate the dry ingredients into a dough or batter, and aids in producing gluten. Water, milk, and buttermilk are typical liquids for quick breads.

Preparing Quick Breads

Muffins and loaf breads are two of the most common types of quick breads. These two products are similar in consistency and differ only in the portioning and style of baking. Most muffin and loaf bread items can be interchangeable. For example, a loaf bread, such as banana nut bread, may be baked as a banana nut muffin, and vice versa.

Making Muffins

The blending method or the creaming method may be used to make muffins. The product will show the difference. The creaming method produces muffins with a fine, cakelike texture; the blending method results in more breadlike muffins.

Muffins should meet the same quality standards as other quick breads. They should

PROCESS

Baking Loaf Breads

Baking loaf breads is a relatively easy process to follow.
After mixing the batter, follow these guidelines:

1 Heat the oven to 375°F (191°C), and properly grease the bottoms and sides of the loaf pans.

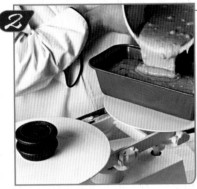

2 Scale an appropriate amount of batter into the prepared pans. Let the batter rest for several minutes.

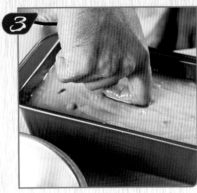

3 To prevent uneven splitting of the crust, make a shallow trough of oil down the center of the top of the batter. Garnish the top. Then place the pans in the oven.

4 Bake the loaves for the time specified in the formula. A wooden pick or skewer inserted into the center of the loaf should come out clean but moist.

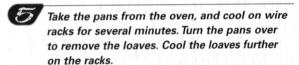

5 Take the pans from the oven, and cool on wire racks for several minutes. Turn the pans over to remove the loaves. Cool the loaves further on the racks.

Quick Breads, Cakes, and Cookies

699

have a golden-brown surface. Muffins should be moist and tender on the inside and break apart without crumbling. Their grain should be even and show no tunneling, a sign of overmixing. Finally, muffins should have a sweet flavor. A bitter aftertaste indicates an excess of leavening ingredients.

Making Loaf Breads

Similar in preparation to muffins, loaf breads are products of either the blending method or the creaming method and differ only according to the finished product desired.

Loaf breads share quality characteristics with other quick breads. The texture should be uniform, with no tunneling. They should have a moist and tender crumb. Their crusts should be light brown and not too thick. The top of loaf breads should be rounded with a split down the center. The flavor of a quick bread loaf will depend on the ingredients used. Fruits, nuts, and even vegetables such as zucchini give loaf breads their unique flavors.

Cooling and Storing Quick Breads

Cooling procedures depend on the baked product. Let muffins and loaf breads cool briefly in their pans before turning them onto a wire rack. Set biscuits and scones directly on cooling racks after baking. Most quick breads are best served while still warm. Make them daily or throughout the day as needed, and serve them immediately. If storage is necessary, make sure that quick breads have cooled completely before wrapping them tightly in plastic wrap. Moisture will collect inside the wrap if baked items are still warm at the time of storage. Store at room temperature, and serve within a few days. Quick breads also may be frozen in plastic wrap for a maximum of three months.

Since the advent of quick bread mixes in the 1930s, many commercial mixes have become available. Such mixes are convenient for large foodservice operations because they are less labor intensive and are consistent in uniformity and flavor.

Cakes

Ever popular as desserts, cakes run the gamut from a simple pound cake dusted lightly with confectioner's sugar to the rich chocolate layers of a Black Forest torte to wedding cake with its elaborate structure and special decorations. Although flavorings and added ingredients differentiate the seemingly limitless variety of cakes, the mixing method used to make a cake determines its texture and general characteristics. Mixing methods, together with ingredients, distinguish two general categories of cakes: layer cakes and sponge cakes.

Layer cakes, or shortened cakes, use the blending or creaming method to mix fat (butter or shortening) with sugar. Although these cakes usually include baking powder for leavening, air cells created during mixing also act as a leavening agent and contribute to their generally light and fine texture.

Sponge or foam cakes, on the other hand, use the whipping method or one of its variations and depend on the air whipped into eggs or egg whites for leavening. Sponge cakes have a springy texture and are more pliable than layer cakes.

Types of Cakes

Ingredients, texture, and taste determine the five types of cakes within the categories of layer cakes and sponge cakes. Pound cakes and high-ratio cakes are examples of layer cakes. Sponge cakes include *génoise* cakes, angel food cakes, and chiffon cakes.

Pound Cakes

The forerunner of the modern layer cake, *pound cake,* or English cake, originated in seventeenth-century England. Traditional pound cake contained a pound each of butter, sugar, flour, and eggs, as well as fruits, nuts, and spices for flavoring. Variations on the basic formula have been popular for hundreds of years. Pound cakes today often feature vanilla, almond, or lemon flavoring, poppyseeds, or chocolate. Because of pound cake's low ratio of liquid and sugar to the flour weight, the creaming method is used.

High-Ratio Cakes

High-ratio cakes contain a high ratio of liquid and sugar to flour, which produces a more moist and tender cake than a pound cake. High-ratio cake formulas also call for **emulsified shortening,** a type of fat that absorbs the large amounts of liquids, sugars, and other fats. Because of the large amounts of liquids, sugars, and other fats that must be absorbed into the emulsified shortening, the blending method is used. The blending method used for cakes is different from the method used for quick breads.

1. Place the sifted dry ingredients in the mixing bowl.
2. Add the shortening and half the liquid ingredients.
3. Mix on low speed until blended, and then mix on medium speed until lightened (approximately 4–5 minutes).
4. Gradually add the remaining liquid ingredients, and blend until smooth.

Use of the paddle attachment limits the amount of air mixed into the batter, resulting in a tight grain, which is particularly desirable for the assembly of wedding cakes.

Sponge or Foam Cakes

Sponge cakes, or foam cakes, have a base of whole eggs whipped into a foam. Large amounts of air whipped into the eggs create the cake's light, airy texture. Perhaps the most common example of this type of cake is the European-style sponge cake known as *génoise,* which contains a higher ratio of eggs to other ingredients and usually incorporates a small amount of melted butter for increased tenderness and richness. *Génoise* forms the basis for many classic tortes.

Angel Food Cakes

Made with whipped egg whites but no yolks, **angel food cakes** are extremely light and usually quite tall. Their height depends on three important variables: the proper whipping technique, the gentle folding of the dry ingredients, and the speed with which the mixture is put into the oven to avoid air cell depletion. These cakes are baked in ungreased tube pans. The absence of grease prevents the delicate foam from losing volume and allows the batter to attach to the sides of the pan as it rises. Angel food cakes contain no fat but have a large proportion of sugar, which provides tenderness and moisture to the finished product. The classic version of angel food cake is white, but variations may include cocoa or nuts. Angel food cake may be served plain or glazed with chocolate, fruit glaze, or flat icing.

Chiffon Cakes

Like angel food cakes, *chiffon cakes* include whipped egg whites, or a **meringue,** and thus have a very light texture. The addition of egg yolks and vegetable oil, however, makes chiffon cakes very moist and decidedly richer than angel food cakes. Lemon, orange, chocolate, and walnut are all popular variations of this classic sponge cake. Like *génoise,* chiffon sponge cakes are used in many classic tortes. They usually are selected because of their lightness.

Preparing Cakes

Proper mixing and the ingredients used greatly contribute to the outcome of a cake formula; however, other procedures also affect the end result. Batter scaling, pan preparation, panning, baking, cooling, and storing contribute to the quality of the finished product.

FIGURE 31-2
Balance scale

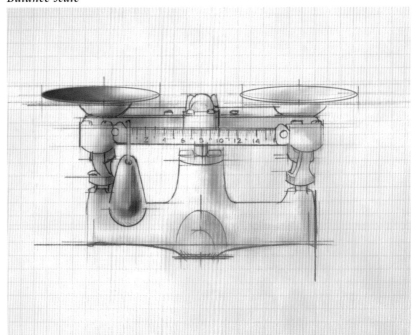

Batter Scaling

To ensure that the size of cakes is consistent, always scale batter before panning it. See Figure 31-2 on page 701. To scale batters by weight, follow these steps:

1. Place a prepared baking pan on the left side of the scale, and balance the scale to tare.
2. Set the scale for the weight desired.
3. Place batter in the pan until the scale balances.

Pan Preparation

Always prepare baking pans before mixing cake batter so that they are ready for filling when the batter is ready and there is no loss of aeration. Depending on the type of cake, the pans are prepared differently.

- Layer cake pans are greased, and often a parchment liner is used.
- Pound cake pans either are greased or a pan liner is used.
- *Génoise* sponge cake pans are lightly greased and lined with parchment paper.
- Angel food cake pans are never greased.
- Chiffon cake pans are lightly greased and lined with parchment paper.

Panning

To prevent batter from spilling over the sides of the pan as the cake rises during baking, make sure that the pans are one-half to two-thirds full. After placing the batter in the pans, use an offset spatula to distribute it evenly. Take care to spread the batter lightly; overworking it will cause air cells to collapse, and the cake will not rise as it should. As a final step for all but foam cakes, tap the pan firmly on a flat surface to disperse large air bubbles before baking.

Baking Cakes

Because baking is the final step in the chemical process that begins with the mixing of the batter, conditions for baking are as important to a cake's success as the ingredients and mixing method used. To achieve the desired results, follow these guidelines for baking:

- Before preparing the batter, preheat the oven. Batter that has to wait for the oven to heat loses leavening and will not rise as it should.
- Set the oven to the correct temperature. Temperatures that are too high or too low can affect how quickly and evenly the cake sets and rises, with negative results.
- Check that the oven and shelves are level to ensure even baking.
- Make sure that pans do not touch each other. Air needs to flow freely around the pans for the cakes to bake evenly.
- Keep the oven door closed, and do not disturb the cakes during baking. Cakes may fall if disturbed before they have fully risen and set. A cake is done when it meets the following criteria:
  - The cake has pulled away slightly from the sides of the pan.
  - The center of the top of the cake springs back when lightly pressed.
  - A cake tester or pick inserted into the center of the cake comes out clean.

Cooling and Storing Cakes

As a general rule, allow cakes to rest 10–15 minutes on a wire rack before attempting to remove them from their pans. Then turn the cakes out of their pans and onto the racks to cool further. A sheet cake requires special handling to remove from the pan. Lightly sprinkle the top of the sheet cake with granulated sugar, and place an empty sheet pan with bottom down on top of the cake. Turn the pans upside down, and remove the top pan. Then carefully peel away from the cake the parchment paper used to line the pan.

Angel food cakes need to cool upside down. After cooling, use a spatula or knife to loosen the cake. Invert onto a parchment-lined sheet pan or place a cardboard cake circle on top of the cake pan, invert, and carefully remove the pan from the cake. See Figure 31-3. Use the same procedures to cool and remove a chiffon cake from the pan.

To stay moist, cakes need to be wrapped as soon as they are cool. Store

 ## FIGURE 31-3

Gravity keeps an angel food cake from collapsing when inverted in its pan.

High-Altitude Baking

Baking at high altitudes requires fine-tuning of cake formulas. Atmospheric, or air, pressure is lower at high altitudes than at sea level, causing liquid to boil at a lower temperature and evaporate more readily. If a cake loses liquid while baking, it will be tough and have little flavor. To compensate for the evaporation of liquid and other effects of high altitudes, cake ingredients, oven temperature, and pan preparation must be adjusted. Follow these general guidelines:

- Decrease the amount of baking soda or baking powder. The gases released during leavening expand more at high altitudes, so less leavener is needed.

- Cream or whip cake batters for a shorter period of time. Less aeration is needed in batters prepared at high altitudes.

- Increase amounts of eggs and flour. Both supply proteins that contribute to a cake's structure, and cakes need more structure at high altitudes.

- Decrease amounts of sugar and shortening. These ingredients have a tenderizing effect that is less desirable at high altitudes, where a cake needs a firm structure.

- Increase liquids to counteract evaporation and prevent drying. Batters also need more liquid because the amount of flour, which absorbs moisture, will increase, and the amount of sugar and fat, which adds moisture, will decrease.

- Above 3,500 feet, increase baking temperatures about 25°F (14°C) to help prevent evaporation of liquid.

- Give pans a heavier coating of grease. Layer cakes are more likely to stick to pans at high altitudes. Remove cakes from pans promptly.

Consult Figure 31-4 for approximate adjustment percentages for layer cake ingredients at different altitudes.

FIGURE 31-4

High-Fat Cake Formula Adjustments at High Altitudes

	APPROXIMATE ADJUSTMENT
INGREDIENT	2,500 feet (762 m)
Baking powder	−20%
Eggs	+2 1/2%
Flour	—
Fat	—
Sugar	−3%
Liquid	+9%
INGREDIENT	5,000 feet (1,524 m)
Baking powder	−40%
Eggs	+9%
Flour	+4%
Fat	—
Sugar	−6%
Liquid	+15%
INGREDIENT	7,500 feet (2,286 m)
Baking powder	−60%
Eggs	+15%
Flour	+9%
Fat	−9%
Sugar	−9%
Liquid	+22%

baked cakes wrapped in plastic in the refrigerator until needed. Properly wrapped undecorated cakes will keep in the freezer for up to a month.

Icings

Icing is a decorative, sweet coating for cake and other baked goods. Icings are distinguished by their use of syrups and confectioner's sugar. With the exception of fudge icing, icings do not contain fat.

There are five basic types of icings: fudge icing, boiled icing, fondant, flat or water icing, and royal icing.

Fudge Icing

Rich and thick, *fudge icing* is appropriate for cakes, cupcakes, and brownies. To prepare fudge icing:

1. Place chocolate fudge icing base in bowl, and mix until smooth.
2. Prepare a hot syrup of sugar, water, corn syrup, and shortening, and boil the mixture until it reaches 240°F (116°C).
3. Add the syrup to the chocolate fudge icing base, and mix until smooth.
4. Add sifted confectioner's sugar, and mix until smooth.

Flavors added to fudge icing may include vanilla, coffee, and almond. Fudge icing is smooth and heavy and stays moist for long periods. To store, cover the icing tightly to prevent drying. Because fudge icing is often too thick for easy spreading, heat it in a water bath to provide the proper consistency for spreading.

Boiled Icing

Boiled icing is known variously as foam icing, seven-minute icing, and white mountain icing. To prepare boiled icing:

1. Cook sugar, water, and corn syrup or glucose to 250°F (121°C).
2. Prepare a common meringue by whipping egg whites and sugar to medium peaks.
3. Slowly add the syrup to the meringue, and continue to whip until cool.

Because boiled icing breaks down easily, use it the same day. Boiled icing is often applied with a homestyle appearance. Cover the cake with generous amounts of the icing, and create swirls and peaks.

■ *See Chapter 32: Desserts for more on meringues.*

Fondant

Probably best known as the coating for Napoleons and petits fours, *fondant* is a heavy, white icing made of glucose, sugar, and water. It is cooked to 240°F (116°C), cooled to about 108°F (42°C), and then agitated quickly on oiled marble or in a mixing bowl to crystallize the sugar and create a smooth, ivory-colored icing. Because it is difficult to make, many bakers purchase fondant ready-made. To use it as a coating or glaze, heat over a water bath to 98°F–100°F (37°C–38°C), stirring constantly. If heated to over 100°F (38°C), fondant will lose its shine and have a dull, grainy finish. Simple syrup is often added to thin the icing and enable it to flow freely. Flavorings and light, pastel colorings may be added to fondant as desired.

Flat or Water Icing

Used primarily on coffee cakes, breakfast pastries, and angel food cakes, *flat or water icing* is a mixture of warm water and confectioner's sugar that also sometimes includes flavoring. Corn syrup or honey is often added to prevent the icing from drying and flaking after application. To make flat icing, mix the ingredients together until smooth, and put the mixture into a double boiler. Warm to 100°F (38°C).

Royal Icing

Royal icing, or decorator's icing, has many decorating applications, including fine piping, gingerbread house assembly, and pastillage showpieces. It also may be used to decorate dummy cakes for display purposes. To make royal icing, blend confectioner's sugar, egg whites, and cream of tartar or lemon juice until the mixture has a smooth consistency. Light, pastel coloring may be added as desired. To prevent drying and hardening during storage, keep it covered with a damp cloth and wrapped airtight with plastic wrap. After it has been applied, royal icing will harden.

Buttercreams

By combining different ingredients with fat (butter or shortening), various types of the rich coating known as *buttercream* are created. Each buttercream has its own unique characteristics of flavor, sweetness, and texture. Buttercreams are sometimes referred to as icings; however, it is important to distinguish them from icings that are based on syrups and sugars.

Types of Buttercreams

There are five types of buttercreams: American, German, Swiss, Italian, and French.

American buttercream American buttercream is sweet and slightly grainy and leaves a fatty coating in the mouth.

1. Cream butter and emulsified shortening.
2. Add and combine confectioner's sugar.
3. Add pasteurized egg whites or milk, and then whip until light.

German buttercream German buttercream is sweet and leaves a slight fatty coating in the mouth. It is slightly smoother than American buttercream.

1. Cream butter and emulsified shortening.
2. Add fondant, and mix until smooth. Then whip until light.

Swiss buttercream Swiss buttercream is smooth with a buttery flavor. It has an excellent mouth feel.

1. Heat egg whites and sugar in a double boiler. Whip until the mixture is slightly warm and stiff peaks form.
2. Add softened butter, and whip until smooth.

Italian buttercream Italian buttercream is smooth with a buttery flavor. It has an excellent mouth feel. Swiss and Italian buttercreams produce virtually identical results, but the Swiss method is easier to prepare.

1. Cook sugar and water to 240°F (116°C).
2. Slowly add sugar syrup to common meringue. Whip until the mixture is slightly warm and stiff peaks form.
3. Add softened butter, and whip until smooth.

French buttercream French buttercream uses the same method as Italian buttercream, replacing the egg whites with egg yolks and butter and then whipping until ribbons form.

Buttercream Tips

For better results when preparing buttercreams, follow these guidelines.

- Shortenings or margarines with a high melting point may be substituted for part of the butter to stabilize the mixture, especially if icing and serving the cake in a hot climate.
- Warm butter or margarine to 75°F (24°C).
- Whip the buttercream at medium speed on a three-speed mixer for 10–20 minutes to produce high volume and a smooth consistency.

Assembling a Cake

Careful assemblage and meticulous attention to detail allow a baker to create a beautiful finished product.

When assembling a cake:

1 Use a serrated knife to level and trim the top of the cake.

Slice the cake into three layers, keeping as level as possible.

Transfer each layer to a cardboard cake circle.

Brush the bottom layer with simple syrup. Spread filling over the bottom layer, and top with the middle layer.

Brush the middle layer with simple syrup, and then spread the filling on top of the second layer. Top with the third layer. Refrigerate several minutes to set the icing.

Ice the top of the cake, and then apply icing to the sides. Sometimes a pre-coat or skim coat is applied first to prevent the appearance of crumbs in the icing. If using a skim coat, refrigerate the cake before applying the final coat of icing.

Smooth icing on top of cake by working from sides inward, holding the spatula at a 45-degree angle. Finish icing and smoothing the entire surface.

Pipe rosettes, spacing evenly to mark individual portions.

Use an appropriate garnish for each cake. Candy mocha beans are being used for this cake.

Quick Breads, Cakes, and Cookies

Making a Jelly Roll

Prepare and bake chiffon sponge using the whipping method described on page 692. Remove from the oven, cool at room temperature, and then follow the steps described below.

To make a jelly roll:

Flip the jelly roll sponge onto a sheet of parchment paper dusted lightly with granulated sugar. Peel back and remove the parchment paper that was used during baking. Spread with a thin layer of seedless fruit preserves.

Spread with a 1/16-inch (1.5-mm) layer of buttercream.

Roll up jelly roll, using the parchment paper to help shape. Place on a cakeboard, and refrigerate for about 30 minutes to firm up the jelly roll.

Ice jelly roll with buttercream. Smooth using a strip of parchment paper.

Refrigerate and chill iced jelly roll for about 20 minutes or until buttercream is firm.

Place the jelly roll on a glazing screen. Using a ladle, glaze jelly roll with chocolate glaze.

Trim both ends of glazed jelly roll. Score and decorate as desired.

- Use only natural products such as coffee, melted chocolate, and pure liquors as flavoring. To prevent curdling, flavorings should be either concentrated or fat-based, rather than water-based.
- Use colors only to enhance the visual perception of flavors.

Glazes

Glazes also may be used on cakes. *Glazes* are thin coatings that add color, shine, and flavor; preserve moisture; and enhance the overall appearance of a product. The types of glazes are fruit or mirror, commercial, preserve, and chocolate glazes.

Fruit or mirror glazes Fruit or mirror glazes use fruit purées or juices and gelatin to help them set properly. These opaque glazes are poured on cakes that are assembled in rings.

Commercial glazes Commercial glazes are either neutral or fruit flavored. Neutral glazes may be flavored and colored as desired. The methods to prepare them vary according to the manufacturer. Some require just heating or melting; others require that water be added before heating and melting. These glazes are either brushed or sprayed on pound cakes or fruit arrangements on cheesecakes, tortes, and tarts.

Preserve glazes These glazes are made with fruit preserves and simple syrup that are heated and then strained. Preserve glazes are used in the same way as commercial glazes.

Chocolate glazes Chocolate glazes are made with equal parts of chocolate and shortening or clarified butter. Chocolate glazes are poured over tortes, jelly rolls, cheesecakes, and angel food cakes.

Syrups

Simple syrup is brushed on layers of cake to add moisture and flavor. To make simple syrup, use equal parts of sugar and water, bring to a boil, and cool. The methods used to flavor the syrup vary. Vanilla or liquor can be added to the syrup after it has been cooled. Sometimes, lemon or orange rind is added when the syrup is coming to a boil.

PROCESS

Making a Paper Cone for Piping

A paper cone is ideal for piping decorations on petite fours, making chocolate garnishes, and adding names to celebration cakes.

To make a paper cone, follow these steps:

1 Cut a triangle with equal sides in length from a piece of parchment paper.

2 Form a cone by bringing one end of the triangle toward the point facing you, tucking under to form a closed, pointed tip.

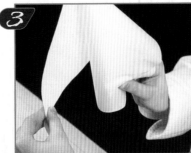

3 Grasp the unfolded corner in one hand and lift the cone, pinching the edge so it does not unravel.

4 Holding the tip in one hand, fold one of the points into the cone.

5 Crease to form the completed cone.

707

Quick Breads, Cakes, and Cookies

Using a Pastry Bag to Decorate

Pastry bags are used in both sweet and savory preparations to make attractive presentations, garnishes, and decorations. Filling a bag properly is an important skill to master.

Follow these guidelines to use a pastry bag:

1 Insert the desired tip into the bag. Using your finger and thumb as a guide, snip the tip of the bag to expose the tip.

2 Fold down the bag over your hand and fill it approximately halfway.

3 Grip the top of the bag in your palm to close the open end, and twist to secure.

4 Squeeze the bag from the top to push the filling through the tip. Use your other hand to guide the bag.

Assembling and Decorating Cakes

Careful assembly and tasteful decoration contribute not only to a cake's visual appeal but also to its overall flavor. These final stages of cake production require a knowledge of various techniques, a sense of design, and close attention to detail.

Mise en Place

Before beginning to assemble a cake, prepare all cake components, and gather the necessary equipment and tools. Cakes should be thoroughly cooled. Icings and fillings should be ready and held as required. Have fresh fruit and other decorations at hand if desired. Use a serrated knife to cut layers, spatulas for spreading filling and icing, and paper cones or pastry bags and tips for decorating. A turntable makes decorating easier. Circles and other pieces of cardboard may be needed to assemble and display the cake.

Cake Assembly

The process of assembly will vary according to cake type, shape, and size.

Decorating Techniques

Cake decorations range from simple garnishes such as chopped nuts, fresh fruit, and shaved chocolate to elaborate designs that include bead or shell borders, basketweave patterns, and flowers and leaves. Cakes often carry messages matched to the occasion. Many of these more elaborate decorations can be created by using a pastry bag and special tips. To write messages on cakes, use a paper cone filled with icing.

Cookies

The word cookie derives from the Dutch word koekje, meaning "small cake." The description is fitting in its generality, for the term cookie encompasses a vast array of offerings. In fact, there are more varieties of cookies than any other type of baked good.

Texture of Cookies

A cookie's texture is perhaps its main identifying characteristic. Biscotti are hard and crisp, for example, but macaroons are soft and chewy. Certain other cookies, such as chocolate chip cookies, can be either crisp or chewy depending on the formula used. Generally speaking, however, cookies can be classified by texture as crisp, chewy, or soft. Various factors influence cookie texture, including proportions of ingredients and baking conditions.

Crisp-Textured Cookies
Crisp cookies have a relatively low moisture content. They are usually high in fat and sugar or contain more flour than do other cookies. Because they generally have a greater amount of sugar than other cookies, crisp cookies tend to *spread,* or expand, more during baking. As they spread, they become thin and dry.

Chewy-Textured Cookies
Chewy cookies are high in moisture. They have a high ratio of eggs or other liquids to dry ingredients and usually contain less fat than do crispy cookies. The development of gluten during the mixing stage also contributes to the chewy texture of these cookies. Gluten provides elasticity, giving the cookie its chewiness. Certain flours have more gluten than others. Although pastry flour is appropriate for making cookies, combine cake flour and bread flour to create a chewier texture.

Soft or Cake-Textured Cookies
Soft cookies, like chewy cookies, are relatively low in fat but high in moisture. Batter for these cookies contains a high ratio of liquid, such as eggs, to fat and sugar. Formulas for soft cookies often call for corn syrup, molasses, or honey in addition to granulated sugar. These liquid sweeteners help the cookies retain moisture after baking and thus contribute to their cakelike texture.

Cookie Ingredients and Spread

Most cookies contain the same basic ingredients: sugar, fat, flour, liquid, and leavening agents. In addition to contributing to a cookie's texture, different proportions of these ingredients help determine a cookie's spread.

Sugar

If sugar is too coarse or is overworked during mixing, the cookie will spread too much during baking. Likewise, the finer the grain of sugar, the less spread during baking. (Finer grains absorb more moisture from the batter and ultimately cause the cookie to spread less.) For this reason, fine-granulated sugar is ideal to produce the proper spread. An equal combination of granulated sugar and confectioner's sugar can be used if fine-granulated sugar is not available.

Fat

Compared with other baked goods, most cookies have high levels of fat. American-style cookies such as chocolate chip and oatmeal raisin, prepared by the creaming method, are especially high in fat. These and other cookies often use only butter, which creates more spread. A combination of shortening and butter creates less spread.

Flour

Flour provides much of the structure in a cookie. A strong flour helps maintain structure and offsets the high fat content of most cookies. On their own, however, strong flours can develop too much gluten for cookie production. Pastry flour works well in many cookie formulas, as do blends of hard and soft flours. It is worth experimenting with blends to see which help achieve the desired spread.

Liquid

Eggs are the chief source of liquid, and therefore moisture, in a cookie. Eggs also offer structure to the batter and thus contribute to the shape of the cookie. In addition, they provide flavor. Cookie batter with a great amount of liquid spreads more than batter with less liquid.

Leavening Ingredients

Most cookies use chemical leavening ingredients such as baking soda or baking powder. Baking soda helps relax gluten and thus contributes to spread. Baking powder, though not often used in cookies, also helps create spread and aeration in a finished product.

Mixing Cookies

The mixing methods used for cookies are similar to those used for cakes. The major difference between them is the ratio of liquid to dry ingredients. In general, cookies have a lower ratio of liquid to dry ingredients. For more information on the various mixing methods for cookies, see page 692.

It is important to note that properly employing the creaming method creates the appropriate spread during baking. Fat and sugars that are overcreamed during the first stage of mixing will create excessive air cells, resulting in a cookie with too much spread during baking. Flour that is overmixed during the last stage will overdevelop the gluten, resulting in a cookie with less spread during baking.

Cookie Varieties

Cookies also can be classified according to their makeup:

1. Bagged or pressed
2. Bar
3. Dropped or deposit
4. Icebox or refrigerator
5. Molded
6. Rolled
7. Sheet
8. Wafer

Bagged or pressed cookies *Bagged or pressed cookies,* which include macaroons and spritz rings, should be shaped as soon as the dough has been made. The dough for these cookies must be firm enough to hold its shape yet soft enough to pass through a pastry bag.

1. Fit a tip of the appropriate size and shape on a pastry bag.
2. Press out cookies onto properly prepared baking sheets.

Bar cookies As their name implies, *bar cookies* are shaped into long bars before being baked and cut. Some bar cookies—Italian biscotti, French biscotte, German

FIGURE 31-5

To ensure even spread, always leave space between cookies.

zwieback, and Jewish mandelbrot—are called *twice-baked cookies* because they are baked until done, cut into strips, and then baked again. To make bar cookies:

1. Scale the dough according to the formula, and shape dough pieces into sheet-pan-length cylinders. Space cylinders well apart on properly greased sheet pans.
2. Use the fingers to flatten the dough into strips 3–4 inches wide and 1/4 inch thick (8–10 cm wide, 6 mm thick).
3. Brush with egg, if called for in the formula, and bake as directed.
4. While they are still warm, cut baked cookies into bars 1 3/4 inches wide (4 1/2 cm).

Dropped or deposit cookies *Dropped or deposit cookies* are made from a soft dough or batter, usually produced using the creaming method. Examples of dropped cookies include chocolate chip, macadamia chunk, and oatmeal raisin cookies.

1. Using the proper-sized scoop or spoon to portion the dough, drop uniform cookies onto parchment-lined baking sheets. Allowing ample room for spreading, place cookies in even rows. See Figure 31-5 on page 710.
2. If necessary, lightly flatten batter mounds with a weight dipped in sugar.
3. Bake as directed in the formula, until cookies are moist but done and golden brown on the bottoms.

Icebox or refrigerator cookies *Icebox or refrigerator cookies* are especially convenient for high-production kitchens because a large batch of dough can be made in advance and used as needed. Icebox cookies include chocolate chip, peanut butter, and macadamia nut cookies, as well as almond shortbread.

1. Scale the dough into uniform sized pieces, and form into cylinders of the desired diameter.
2. Using wax or parchment paper, wrap the cylinders on sheet pans, and refrigerate overnight or for several days.
3. After unwrapping the dough, cut it into uniform slices of the desired thickness.
4. Place cookies on parchment-lined sheet pans, allowing ample space between them, and bake as directed.

Molded cookies As their name implies, *molded cookies* have been formed into their desired shape. These cookies may be hand-shaped into fingers or crescents or flattened and stamped with a design. Crescent cookies are an example of a molded cookie.

1. Roll out the dough into cylinders of the desired thickness, and use a bench scraper or knife to cut the dough into pieces of the desired size.
2. Put the pieces on properly prepared baking sheets, leaving enough space between them.
3. After pressing the cookies, flatten them with a weight that has been dipped in sugar. Note: As an alternative, the dough can be hand-shaped as desired after Step 1.

Rolled cookies Made from a stiff, chilled dough, *rolled cookies* are uncommon in large foodservice operations because of the time-consuming work that they require. Examples of rolled cookies include sugar cookies, shortbread, and gingerbread cookies.

1. Thoroughly chill the dough.
2. Place the dough on a lightly floured workbench or canvas, and roll it out into 1/8-inch thickness.
3. Use cookie cutters to cut out the dough in desired shapes, and place on properly prepared baking sheets. Because rerolled scraps make tough cookies, cut cookies as close together as possible.

Sheet cookies *Sheet cookies* range from rich, dense squares similar to sheet cake to double- or triple-layer cookies that are baked in stages. Examples include brownies, Swiss leckerli, and nut squares.

1. Spread the mixture evenly into properly prepared sheet pans.
2. Brush with egg wash or add topping, if required.
3. Bake and cool as directed.
4. Apply topping or icing, if required, and cut into rectangles or squares.

Wafers Light, crisp cookies with marks similar to waffles made by cooking plates, *wafers* can be served plain, filled with praline cream or with jam, rolled up, or shaped like fans. They are made with pourable batters that spread by using templates to give desired shapes. The wafers are first baked and then molded while still warm. The batter has a buttery, sweet flavor that is often enhanced with ground nuts or citrus zest.

Baking Cookies

Whatever method is used to portion cookies onto sheet pans, it is imperative that they be of equal size and shape and placed in uniform rows, either staggered or straight. This will allow even baking throughout the product. Because they contain so much sugar and are relatively small, cookies brown quickly and sometimes burn on the bottom. To prevent this, *double-pan* the cookies, placing the sheet pan inside another pan of the same size before baking.

Baking temperatures for most cookies are moderate (between 350°F–375°F/ 177°C–191°C). If the temperature is too low, cookies may spread too much and become hard and dry. Too high a temperature risks burning cookies and reduces spreading. Cookies usually are done when their bottoms and edges are a light golden brown. Cookies may be removed when slightly underbaked, as they will continue to bake and brown on the pan, even after they have been removed from the oven—a phenomenon known as *carryover baking.*

Decorating Cookies

There are many ways to decorate cookies. For example, they may be sprinkled with sugar before baking, dipped in chocolate, or sprinkled with confectioner's sugar after baking. Each type of cookie usually has a particular form of decoration. A cookie formula often specifies appropriate or traditional decoration.

Cooling and Storing Cookies

When cookies are cool and firm enough to handle, remove them from the pan. Exposing cookies to high humidity for any length of time can affect their unique texture and cause them to become soggy. Cookies should be tightly wrapped in plastic or kept in airtight containers, unrefrigerated.

Making Almond Lace (Florentines)

Almond lace is often used as a cup, holder, or garnish for desserts.

Follow these steps to make almond lace:

1 Gather equipment and ingredients. Preheat oven to 350°F (177°C).

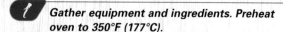

2

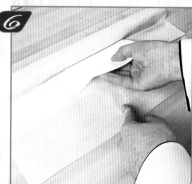

Place flour, sugar, and slightly softened butter in a bowl, and place on a mixer. Use a paddle to blend together.

3

Add corn syrup, and mix until creamy.

4

Add crushed almonds, and mix until the nuts are evenly dispersed.

5

Remove from the mixer. Place 1 pound (454 g) of dough on parchment paper lengthwise, and roll into a thin log shape.

6

Use a bench or bowl scraper to tighten the log. Refrigerate or freeze until firm.

7

When the dough is firm, slice the log into 1/2-ounce (14-g) portions. Roll into smooth balls, and place on a sheet pan topped with a nonstick silicone baking mat.

8

Bake approximately 5–7 minutes or until golden brown, and quickly remove them from the pan with an offset spatula.

9

Shape as desired while warm.

Working with Tulip Paste

Tulip paste is used to make shaped cookies.

Follow these steps to work with tulip paste:

1 Use an offset spatula to spread paste onto a silicone baking mat. Use a template to make the desired shape.

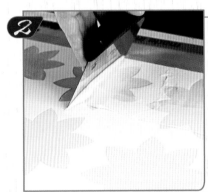

2 Smooth and level paste with a bench scraper.

3 Place silicone baking mat on an upside-down sheet pan, and bake in a 350°F (177°C) oven about 5 minutes or until lightly browned.

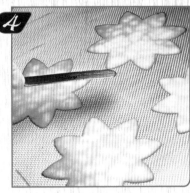

4 Remove the cookies using an offset spatula.

5 Shape as desired while still warm.

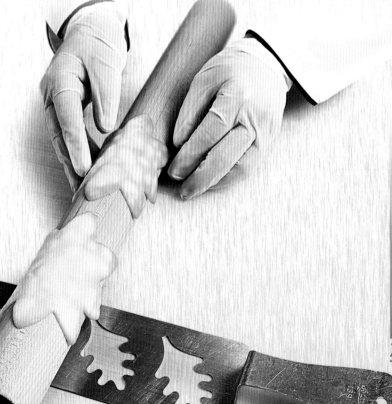

Yellow Pound Cake

Yield: 11 lbs., 6 oz. (5187 g)

INGREDIENTS

	U.S. Standard	Metric
Flour, *cake*	2 lbs., 8 oz.	1135 g
Sugar, *granulated*	3 lbs., 4 oz.	1480 g
Salt	1 1/2 oz.	40 g
Baking powder	1/2 oz.	15 g
Dry milk solids (DMS)	3 oz.	85 g
Shortening, *high-ratio*	1 lb., 12 oz.	795 g
Water	20 oz.	600 ml
Vanilla extract	1/2 oz.	15 ml
Lemon compound	1/2 oz.	15 g
Eggs, *whole*	2 lbs.	910 g
Water	4 oz.	120 ml

METHOD OF PREPARATION

1. Gather all the ingredients and equipment.

2. Preheat oven to 360°F (182°C).

3. Sift the dry ingredients together, and place in mixing bowl.

4. Add the high-ratio shortening.

5. Combine the 20 oz. (600 ml) of water with vanilla and lemon compound. Add to the dry ingredients.

6. Using a paddle, mix on low speed for 4 minutes.

7. Combine the eggs and 4 oz. (120 ml) of water.

8. Add the egg mixture into the batter in 3 stages, scraping the bowl between additions. Allow each addition to completely emulsify.

9. Continue mixing the batter for an additional 4 minutes, until mixture is smooth.

10. Scale 20 oz. (600 ml) batter into a 3″ × 7″ (7.5 cm × 17.5 cm) loaf pan.

11. Bake at 360°F (182°C) for approximately 60–75 minutes.

PASTRY TECHNIQUES

Blending:

1. Combine the dry ingredients on low speed.
2. Add the softened fat(s) and liquid(s).
3. Mix the ingredients on low speed.
4. Increase the speed gradually.

Cranberry Orange Bread

Yield: *8 lbs., 14 1/2 oz. (4040 g)*

INGREDIENTS	U.S. Standard	Metric
Sugar, *granulated*	*1 lb., 8 oz.*	*680 g*
Shortening, *all-purpose*	*8 oz.*	*225 g*
Baking soda	*1/2 oz.*	*15 g*
Salt	*1/2 oz.*	*15 g*
Cinnamon, *ground*	*1/2 oz.*	*15 g*
Eggs, *whole*	*8 oz.*	*225 g*
Flour, *bread*	*2 lbs.*	*910 g*
Flour, *cake*	*8 oz.*	*225 g*
Baking powder	*1 oz.*	*28 g*
Water	*28 oz.*	*840 ml*
Oranges, *3 each, juice and zest*	*2 oz.*	*55 g*
Orange compound	*2 oz.*	*55 g*
Cranberries, *coarsely chopped*	*1 lb.*	*454 g*
Pecans, *coarsely chopped*	*8 oz.*	*225 g*

METHOD OF PREPARATION

1. Gather all the ingredients and equipment.
2. Preheat oven to 375°F (191°C).
3. Grease or line with paper, seven 3″ × 7″ (7.5 cm × 17.5 cm) loaf pans.
4. Using a paddle, cream sugar, shortening, baking soda, salt, and cinnamon. Mix on medium speed for 3 minutes.
5. Add the eggs in stages. Scrape down. Blend until smooth.
6. Sift together bread flour, cake flour, and baking powder. Divide flour mixture into thirds.
7. Combine water, juice, zest, and compound.
8. Add 1/3 of the flour mixture to the batter, and then add 1/3 of the water and juice mixture. Scrape bowl.
9. Repeat Step 7 two more times. Mix until smooth.
10. Fold the cranberries and pecans into mixture.
11. Scale 22 oz. (660 ml) batter into seven 3″ × 7″ (7.5 cm × 17.5 cm) loaf pans.
12. Bake at 375°F (191°C) for approximately 35–40 minutes.

PASTRY TECHNIQUES

Creaming:
1. Soften the fats on low speed.
2. Add the sugar(s) and cream; increase the speed slowly.
3. Add the eggs one at a time; scrape the bowl frequently.
4. Add the dry ingredients in stages.

Combining:
1. Prepare the components to be combined.
2. Add one to the other, using the appropriate mixing method (if needed).

Quick Breads, Cakes, and Cookies

715

Corn Bread

Yield: *1 sheet pan*
9 lbs., 6 oz. (4256 g)

INGREDIENTS

	U.S. Standard	Metric
Water	30 oz.	900 ml
Eggs, whole	1 lb.	454 g
Oil, vegetable	12 oz.	360 ml
Vanilla extract	1 oz.	30 ml
Flour, bread	1 lb., 12 oz.	795 g
Flour, pastry	12 oz.	340 g
Sugar, granulated	1 lb., 10 oz.	740 g
Dry milk solids (DMS)	6 oz.	170 g
Baking powder	2 oz.	55 g
Salt	1 oz.	28 g
Cornmeal	1 lb.	454 g

METHOD OF PREPARATION

1. Gather all the ingredients and equipment.

2. Preheat oven to 375°F (191°C).

3. Grease a sheet pan, and line it with parchment paper.

4. Using a paddle, blend well the water, eggs, oil, and vanilla extract.

5. Sift the bread flour, pastry flour, sugar, DMS, baking powder, and salt twice.

6. Add the cornmeal to sifted dry ingredients.

7. Add all dry ingredients to the liquid ingredients, and mix just until blended.

8. Scrape the bowl well, and mix until smooth.

9. Deposit the mixture onto the prepared sheet pan, and spread.

10. Bake at 375°F (191°C) for approximately 22–25 minutes.

Chef's Notes

This formula may be used for corn muffins or corn sticks.

Cheese, jalapeño, and spices may be added.

PASTRY TECHNIQUES

Blending:

1. Combine the dry ingredients on low speed.
2. Add the softened fat(s) and liquid(s).
3. Mix the ingredients on low speed.
4. Increase the speed gradually.

Buttermilk Scones

Yield: 12 lbs., 3 oz. (5528 g)

Combining:

1. Prepare the components to be combined.
2. Add one to the other, using the appropriate mixing method (if needed).

Rolling:

1. Prepare the rolling surface by dusting with the appropriate medium (flour, cornstarch, or other).
2. Use the appropriate style of pin (stick pin or ball-bearing pin) to roll the dough to desired thickness; rotate the dough during rolling to prevent sticking.

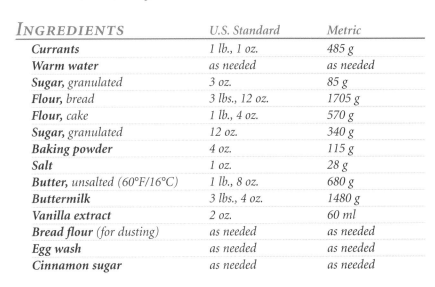

INGREDIENTS	U.S. Standard	Metric
Currants	1 lb., 1 oz.	485 g
Warm water	as needed	as needed
Sugar, granulated	3 oz.	85 g
Flour, bread	3 lbs., 12 oz.	1705 g
Flour, cake	1 lb., 4 oz.	570 g
Sugar, granulated	12 oz.	340 g
Baking powder	4 oz.	115 g
Salt	1 oz.	28 g
Butter, unsalted (60°F/16°C)	1 lb., 8 oz.	680 g
Buttermilk	3 lbs., 4 oz.	1480 g
Vanilla extract	2 oz.	60 ml
Bread flour (for dusting)	as needed	as needed
Egg wash	as needed	as needed
Cinnamon sugar	as needed	as needed

METHOD OF PREPARATION

1. Gather all the ingredients and equipment.
2. Preheat oven to 450°F (232°C).
3. Place currants in small bowl, add enough warm water to cover, and 3 oz. (85 g) of sugar. Let sit for 15 minutes.
4. Line two sheet pans with parchment paper.
5. Sift together the bread flour, cake flour, sugar, baking powder, and salt twice.
6. Add the butter to the dry mixture, and rub together until fat pieces are the size of small peas.
7. Combine buttermilk and vanilla extract.
8. Add the liquids to the dry mixture, and mix only until ingredients are moistened.
9. Drain the currants well, and add the currants to the dough. Mix just until blended into dough.
10. Scale into 1-lb. (454-g) pieces.
11. Round the dough pieces, and let rest on a floured surface for 15 minutes. Cover with plastic.
12. Flatten dough to a 5″ (12.7 cm) round disk. Divide the disk into quarters. Place 4 × 6 on sheet pans.
13. Egg wash, and sprinkle with cinnamon sugar. Rest for 20 minutes.
14. Bake in a 450°F (232°C) for 15–20 minutes.

Chocolate Chip Cookies

Yield: *27 lbs., 4 oz. (12,361 g)*

INGREDIENTS

INGREDIENTS	U.S. Standard	Metric
Butter, unsalted, 75°F (24°C)	2 lbs.	910 g
Shortening, all-purpose	2 lbs.	910 g
Sugar, granulated	3 lbs.	1365 g
Sugar, light brown	2 lbs.	910 g
Salt	1 1/2 oz.	40 g
Eggs, whole	2 lbs.	910 g
Vanilla extract	2 oz.	60 ml
Flour, cake	3 lbs.	1365 g
Flour, pastry	3 lbs.	1365 g
Baking soda	1/2 oz.	15 g
Chocolate chips	9 lbs.	4082 g

METHOD OF PREPARATION

1. Gather all the ingredients and equipment.

2. Preheat oven to 375°F (191°C).

3. Using a paddle, cream the butter, shortening, granulated sugar, brown sugar, and salt.

4. Combine eggs and vanilla extract. Add in stages to the cream mixture. Scrape bowl. Blend until smooth.

5. Sift together the cake flour, pastry flour, and baking soda twice.

6. Add flour mixture to creamed mixture; mix only until blended.

7. Scrape bowl, and blend until smooth.

8. Add chocolate chips to batter, and mix until combined.

9. Using a 1 3/4-oz. (52.5-ml) scoop, deposit cookies 4 × 5 onto a parchment-lined sheet pan.

10. Bake at 375°F (191°C) for approximately 12–15 minutes.

PASTRY TECHNIQUES

Creaming:

1. Soften the fats on low speed.
2. Add the sugar(s) and cream; increase the speed slowly.
3. Add the eggs one at a time; scrape the bowl frequently.
4. Add the dry ingredients in stages.

Blending:

1. Combine the dry ingredients on low speed.
2. Add the softened fat(s) and liquid(s).
3. Mix the ingredients on low speed.
4. Increase the speed gradually.

Oatmeal Cookies

Yield: *6 lbs., 15 oz. (3147 g)*

INGREDIENTS	U.S. Standard	Metric
Butter, unsalted, 75°F (24°C)	9 oz.	255 g
Shortening, high-ratio	9 oz.	255 g
Sugar, brown	1 lb., 7 oz.	655 g
Sugar, granulated	1 lb., 7 oz.	655 g
Salt	1/2 oz.	15 g
Molasses	2 oz.	55 g
Eggs, whole	7 oz.	205 g
Vanilla extract	1 oz.	30 ml
Flour, pastry	1 lb., 4 oz.	570 g
Ground cinnamon	1/2 oz.	2.5 ml
Baking soda	1/4 oz.	8 g
Oatmeal	1 lb.	454 g

METHOD OF PREPARATION

1. Gather all the ingredients and equipment.

2. Preheat oven to 375°F (191°C).

3. Using a paddle, cream the butter, shortening, brown sugar, granulated sugar, and salt.

4. Combine molasses, eggs, and vanilla extract. Add in stages to the cream mixture, scraping bowl. Blend until smooth.

5. Sift together pastry flour, cinnamon, and baking soda twice.

6. Add flour mixture and oatmeal to creamed mixture. Mix until blended.

7. Scrape bowl and blend until smooth.

8. Using a 1 3/4-oz. (52.5-ml) scoop, deposit cookies 4 × 5 onto a parchment-lined sheet pan.

9. Bake at 375°F (191°C) for approximately 12 to 15 minutes.

PASTRY TECHNIQUES

Creaming:

1. Soften the fats on low speed.
2. Add the sugar(s) and cream; increase the speed slowly.
3. Add the eggs one at a time; scrape the bowl frequently.
4. Add the dry ingredients in stages.

Blending:

1. Combine the dry ingredients on low speed.
2. Add the softened fat(s) and liquid(s).
3. Mix the ingredients on low speed.
4. Increase the speed gradually.

Chocolate Fudge Brownies

Yield: 1 sheet pan
9 lbs., 4 1/2 oz. (4210 g)

INGREDIENTS

Ingredients	U.S. Standard	Metric
Sugar, granulated	3 lbs.	1365 g
Shortening, all-purpose	1 lb., 8 oz.	680 g
Corn syrup	8 oz.	240 ml
Cocoa powder (sifted)	8 oz.	225 g
Vanilla extract	1/2 oz.	15 ml
Eggs, whole	12 oz.	340 g
Flour, pastry	2 lbs.	910 g
Walnuts, pieces (toasted)	1 lb.	454 g

METHOD OF PREPARATION

1. Gather all the ingredients and equipment.
2. Preheat oven to 375°F (191°C).
3. Using a paddle, cream the sugar, shortening, corn syrup, and cocoa powder.
4. Combine the vanilla extract with the eggs. Add in stages to the creamed mixture. Scrape bowl. Blend until smooth.
5. Add the pastry flour to creamed mixture, and mix only until blended.
6. Scrape the bowl, and blend until smooth.
7. Add the walnuts to batter, and mix until combined.
8. Scale the batter onto a greased, paper-lined sheet pan.
9. Spread the batter evenly with a spatula. Clean the edge of the pan.
10. Bake at 375°F (191°C) for 25–30 minutes or until firm, but not dry. Do not overbake.
11. Remove from oven, and cool completely.
12. Cover with fudge icing. Recipe follows.
13. Cut with sharp knife into desired shapes.

PASTRY TECHNIQUES

Creaming:
1. Soften the fats on low speed.
2. Add the sugar(s) and cream; increase the speed slowly.
3. Add the eggs one at a time; scrape the bowl frequently.
4. Add the dry ingredients in stages.

Combining:
1. Prepare the components to be combined.
2. Add one to the other, using the appropriate mixing method (if needed).

Spreading:
1. Using an icing spatula or off-set spatula, smooth the icing or other spreading medium over the surface area.

Chocolate Fudge Icing

Yield: *2 lbs., 5 1/4 oz. (1056 g)*

INGREDIENTS	U.S. Standard	Metric
Corn syrup	*1 oz.*	*30 ml*
Shortening, *all-purpose*	*3/4 oz.*	*22 g*
Water	*4 1/2 oz.*	*135 ml*
Fudge base	*8 oz.*	*225 g*
Sugar, *confectioner's (sifted)*	*1 lb., 6 oz.*	*625 g*

METHOD OF PREPARATION

1. Gather all the ingredients and equipment.

2. Place the corn syrup, shortening, and water in a pot, and bring to a boil. Remove from heat.

3. Place the fudge base and sugar in a mixing bowl with paddle. Mix until well blended.

4. Gradually add the boiling water mixture into the fudge base while mixer is on low.

5. Combine until well blended.

Combining:

1. Prepare the components to be combined.

2. Add one to the other, using the appropriate mixing method (if needed).

Peanut Butter Cookies

Yield: 17 lbs., 10 1/2 oz. (8009 g)

INGREDIENTS	U.S. Standard	Metric
Butter, *unsalted (75°F/24°C)*	3 lbs.	1365 g
Sugar, *granulated*	2 lbs.	910 g
Sugar, *light brown*	2 lbs.	910 g
Salt	1 oz.	28 g
Peanut butter	3 lbs.	1365 g
Vanilla extract	1 oz.	30 ml
Eggs, *whole*	1 lb.	454 g
Flour, *pastry*	4 lbs.	1820 g
Baking soda	1/2 oz.	15 g
Peanuts, *roasted and chopped*	2 lbs., 8 oz.	1135 g

METHOD OF PREPARATION

1. Gather all the ingredients and equipment.

2. Preheat oven to 375°F (191°C).

3. Using a paddle, cream the butter, granulated sugar, brown sugar, salt, and peanut butter.

4. Combine the vanilla extract with the eggs. Add in stages to the creamed mixture. Scrape bowl. Blend until smooth.

5. Sift together the pastry flour and baking soda twice.

6. Add flour mixture to creamed mixture, and mix only until blended.

7. Scrape the bowl, and blend until smooth.

8. Add the peanuts to batter, and mix until combined.

9. Using a 1 3/4-oz. (52.5-ml) scoop, deposit cookies 4 × 5 onto parchment-lined sheet pans.

10. Using a fork, flatten the cookie slightly, making a crosshatch design.

11. Bake at 375°F (191°C) for approximately 12–15 minutes.

PASTRY TECHNIQUES

Creaming:
1. Soften the fats on low speed.
2. Add the sugar(s) and cream; increase the speed slowly.
3. Add the eggs one at a time; scrape the bowl frequently.
4. Add the dry ingredients in stages.

Combining:
1. Prepare the components to be combined.
2. Add one to the other, using the appropriate mixing method (if needed).

Jelly Roll Sponge Cake

Yield: 3 full sheet pans
6 lbs., 5 1/4 oz. (2870 g)

INGREDIENTS

INGREDIENTS	U.S. Standard	Metric
Flour, bread	12 oz.	340 g
Flour, cake	4 oz.	115 g
Baking powder	1/2 oz.	15 g
Salt	1/4 oz.	8 g
Egg yolks (room temperature)	1 lb., 5 oz.	595 g
Honey	5 oz.	150 ml
Oil, vegetable	5 oz.	150 ml
Vanilla extract	1 oz.	30 ml
Lemon compound	1/2 oz.	15 g
Simple syrup, 100°F (38°C)	8 oz.	240 ml
Egg whites, 100°F (38°C)	1 lb., 14 oz.	855 g
Sugar, granulated	14 oz.	400 g

METHOD OF PREPARATION

1. Gather all the ingredients and equipment.
2. Preheat oven to 420°F (216°C).
3. Sift together the bread flour, cake flour, baking powder, and salt.
4. Place the egg yolks, honey, oil, vanilla, and lemon compound in a mixing bowl, and whip to full volume.
5. When the mixture is just about full volume, reduce the mixing speed to medium, and slowly add the warm simple syrup in a slow, steady stream.
6. In another mixing bowl, whip the egg whites to medium peak, slowly adding the sugar to make a meringue.
7. When both mixtures are completed, remove from machine. Gently fold the meringue into the yolk mixture.
8. Fold in the dry ingredients.
9. Scale 2 lbs., 2 oz. (970 g) of batter into parchment-lined sheet pans.
10. Using an offset spatula, evenly spread the mixture on the pan.
11. Bake at 420°F (216°C) for approximately 12–15 minutes.
12. Allow to cool to just warm.

• Check crust color—golden brown is desired.
• Check cake for firmness—it should spring back when lightly touched.

PASTRY TECHNIQUES

Whipping:
1. Hold the whip at a 55° angle.
2. Stir vigorously, using a circular motion perpendicular to the bowl.

Folding:
Perform steps 1, 2, and 3 in one continuous motion.
1. Run a bowl scraper under the mixture, across the bottom of the bowl.
2. Turn the bowl counterclockwise.
3. Bring the bottom mixture to the top.

Spreading:
1. Using an icing spatula or off-set spatula, smooth the icing or other spreading medium over the surface area.

Basic Muffin

Yield: 30 lbs., 12 oz. (13,948 g)

INGREDIENTS

	U.S. Standard	Metric
Sugar, granulated	5 lbs.	2275 g
Salt	1 1/2 oz.	40 g
Dry milk solids (DMS)	1 lb.	454 g
Eggs, whole	2 lbs.	910 g
Oil, vegetable	48 oz.	1.4 l
Water	80 oz.	2.4 l
Vanilla extract	2 oz.	60 ml
Lemon compound	2 oz.	55 g
Flour, high-gluten bread	9 lbs., 8 oz.	4309 g
Baking powder	6 1/2 oz.	185 g
Fruit, fresh or frozen	4 lbs., 8 oz.	2045 g

METHOD OF PREPARATION

1. Gather all the ingredients and equipment.
2. Preheat oven to 400°F (204°C).
3. Grease muffin pans or line with paper liners.
4. Place the sugar, salt, and DMS into a mixing bowl.
5. Using the paddle, add the eggs slowly to the sugar mixture.
6. Slowly add the vegetable oil.
7. Add the water and flavorings. Scrape bowl. Blend until smooth.
8. Sift together the flour and baking powder.
9. Rinse the fruit, and pat dry. Dredge the fruit with a small amount of flour. Set aside.
10. Add remaining flour mixture to batter, and blend on low speed.
11. Remove from the mixer. Fold fruit into batter.
12. Using a 3 3/4-oz. (112.5-ml) scoop, deposit the batter into muffin tins.
13. Bake at 400°F (204°C) approximately 20–30 minutes.

PASTRY TECHNIQUES

Blending:
1. Combine the dry ingredients on low speed.
2. Add the softened fat(s) and liquid(s).
3. Mix the ingredients on low speed.
4. Increase the speed gradually.

Buttermilk Biscuits

Yield: *13 lbs., 13 3/4 oz. (6287 g)*

INGREDIENTS	U.S. Standard	Metric
Flour, *bread*	*3 lbs., 5 oz.*	*1505 g*
Flour, *pastry*	*3 lbs., 5 oz.*	*1505 g*
Sugar, *granulated*	*1 lb.*	*454 g*
Dry milk solids (DMS)	*8 oz.*	*225 g*
Salt	*1 1/4 oz.*	*38 g*
Baking powder	*6 oz.*	*170 g*
Butter, *unsalted 60°F (16°C)*	*1 lb., 8 oz.*	*680 g*
Buttermilk	*32 oz.*	*960 ml*
Water	*16 oz.*	*500 ml*
Eggs, *whole*	*11 oz.*	*310 g*
Vanilla extract	*1 oz.*	*30 ml*
Bread flour *(for dusting)*	*as needed*	*as needed*
Egg wash	*as needed*	*as needed*

METHOD OF PREPARATION

1. Gather all the ingredients and equipment.

2. Preheat oven to 425°F (218°C).

3. Line two sheet pans with parchment paper.

4. Sift together the bread flour, pastry flour, sugar, DMS, salt, and baking powder twice.

5. Add the butter to the dry mixture, and rub together until fat pieces are the size of small peas.

6. Blend together buttermilk, water, eggs, and vanilla.

7. Add the liquids to the dry mixture, and combine only until ingredients are moistened.

8. Place the dough onto a floured canvas. Press dough out to a rectangle of 18″ × 16″ (45 cm × 40 cm).

9. Give the dough a three-fold.

10. Cover the dough with a plastic cover, and allow dough to rest for 15–20 minutes.

11. Roll the dough out to 3/4″ (1.9 cm) thick.

12. Cut biscuits using a biscuit cutter (2 1/2″/6.4 cm), and place 5 × 8 on parchment-lined pans.

13. Egg wash, and allow to rest for 20 minutes.

14. Bake 15–20 minutes.

Combining:

1. Prepare the components to be combined.

2. Add one to the other, using the appropriate mixing method (if needed).

Rolling:

1. Prepare the rolling surface by dusting with the appropriate medium (flour, cornstarch, or other).

2. Use the appropriate style of pin (stick pin or ball-bearing pin) to roll the dough to desired thickness; rotate the dough during rolling to prevent sticking.

32 Desserts

A.D. 1191
Snow from the mountains of Lebanon, flavored with fruit, is served to Crusaders by Saracen leader Saladin.

1440s on
A Paris pastry guild begins to make sweet items from milk, eggs, and cream.

1795
Pumpkin pie is among the native specialties in the first cookbook published in America.

1846
The hand-cranked ice cream freezer is invented.

The word dessert comes from the French word desservir, which means "to remove all dishes from the table." Desserts have come a long way from the simple fruit that finished a French meal during the Renaissance. It was probably the French bourgeoisie who rejected the upper-class restriction of fruit alone for the last course of dinner. By the late sixteenth century, dishes sweetened with sugar were all the rage across Europe. (Before this time sugar was commonly used only as a medicine or as a spice.) Today, dessert may be pastry, pudding, custard, mousse, or a frozen specialty such as ice cream or sorbet.

Dessert Presentation

Restaurant patrons often order dessert as the culmination of a satisfying dining experience. Delicious and elegant dessert offerings give restaurants a final chance to impress customers.

While the preparation of desserts is very much a science, the presentation of desserts can be a sophisticated art. Desserts need to be visually pleasing as well as delicious. In recent years, more time has been devoted to the creative arrangement of desserts on the plate.

Modern desserts focus on taste and presentation. Chocolate is a favorite dessert item that can be plated in a creative manner. Nuts add crunch as well as texture to a dish. As customers become more health conscious, fruit in almost any form is a delicious and attractive dessert offering. Sorbets and ice cream are popular as single dessert items and as accompaniments to other desserts, such as pies and tarts.

Plated Desserts

Good plate presentation is the result of careful attention to the texture, temperature, shape, flavor, and color of the food. The extra effort involved in plating enhances a dessert's visual appeal and thus increases its perceived value.

Components of a Plated Dessert

A plated dessert has four basic components: the main item, the sauce, the garnish, and the crunch. See Figure 32-1 on page 728.

Main item The main item, or entrée item, is the focal point of the dish. Plated, the main item is usually 3–5 ounces (85–140 g) in weight.

Sauce Sauces complement or contrast with the flavor of the main item. More than one sauce may be used, but sauces should never be added to the plate merely for color. The flavors of the individual sauces must always be considered as well.

Garnish The garnish adds interest. It varies widely, from a dusting of powdered sugar on the plate to an intricately stenciled and shaped tuile cookie. Garnishes add to the perceived value of a plated dessert. All garnishes used on a plated dessert must be edible.

Crunch Used when the main item does not contain flour, the *crunch* is often a decorative cookie that offers textural contrast to the main item. Usually a crunch and a garnish are the same item— a tuile or almond lace garnish, for example. The crunch and/or garnish should not overwhelm or detract from the main item on the plate.

Plating Contrasts

Contrasts are an integral part of plate design and provide interest for the customer. Most plates feature contrasts in at least one or two of the following areas:

Texture Texture contrasts are very effective. Smooth, velvety-textured components, crunchy components, and chewy-textured items, when placed together, make a dessert more interesting to eat.

Desserts

727

Temperature Temperature contrasts are another important component. The combination of hot and cold items on the same plate adds interest to the overall dessert. Always serve hot items hot and cold items cold.

Shape Visual contrasts also add to the interest of a plate. Use components of different shapes and sizes to increase customer interest in the plate. Careful use of shape and size can easily draw attention to the plate's main item.

Flavor The fact that desserts are sweet does not mean that everything on the plate must be sweet. Try contrasting sweet and sour flavors or dark, heavy flavors and light ones to make the dessert more appealing. Sometimes savory components can be included to balance the predominate sweet flavors. Keep in mind that the driving force of the plate comes from the flavor(s) of the entrée item. Make sure that all of the other flavors on the plate complement that of the main item.

Color Color is one of the easiest and most visually exciting ways to add contrast to a plate. Each addition of new color to the plate means that flavors are being added as well. Avoid adding color just for the sake of color.

Tips for Plating

Dessert plating requires a great deal of mise en place as well as time management and organizational skills. The following general guidelines may be useful. They are intended as suggestions, not steadfast rules.

- Consider the kind of plate to be used before designing the dessert. Its size, color, and shape will greatly influence the final plate design.
- Make designs and contrasts interesting but simple. Complex plate design confuses the eye and the palate.
- Balance the different aspects of the plate—textures, shapes, flavors, and colors. Asymmetric or symmetric balance may be used, as long as the main item is the focal point of the plate.
- Do not allow stronger, contrasting flavors to overpower subtle flavors.
- Make sure that the components of the plate work together as a single offering. They should come together harmoniously, not just fill space.
- Use the placement and shape of the components to create a flow or movement that leads the eye toward the main item.
- Take care that all the items on the plate are edible.
- Avoid unnatural colors such as blue.

FIGURE 32-1

The various components of a plated dessert offer contrasts in texture, temperature, shape, flavor, and color.

Pies and Fruit Tarts

Brought to America by European settlers, sweet and savory pies offered food that traveled well, was fairly easy to prepare, and did not require high-quality ingredients. Initially pies offered a way of preserving fruit, not only because of the high sugar content of their fillings but also because they could contain fruit that was past its prime.

Tarts are the European version of the American pie. The two products have much in common, such as bottom crusts and a variety of fillings. There are, however, some distinctions between these two items.

Pies are usually deeper than tarts and thus can accommodate more filling. They are generally made with an unsweetened crust and can be either open-faced or covered with a top crust. Slices of pie often do not hold up without the support of the pie pan and are cut directly before service.

Tarts are made primarily with a sweet, or short, dough and require less filling than pies do because the traditional tart form is only about 1 inch deep. Tarts are never made with a top crust, and their sides are usually fluted. Tart forms have a removable bottom, and unlike a pie, a tart can be removed from this form and displayed in its entirety.

Types of Pie Dough

The dough is arguably the most important element in a pie. The baked dough's flakiness and tenderness are crucial to a pie's success, whatever its filling may be. Flour, fat, cold liquid, and salt are the basic dough ingredients, with sugar or dry milk solids (DMS) as optional additions used either to sweeten or to enrich the dough. How well the fat is distributed into the flour determines the flakiness of the crust. To achieve a tender crust, great care must be taken when preparing the dough.

There are two types of pie dough: flaky and mealy. In both doughs, the cold fat is cut into the flour with ice-cold water used to bind the mixture. A flaky pie dough can consist of either a long or a short flake. To produce *long-flake pie dough,* cut the fat into nickel-sized pieces; long-flake pie dough is used only as a top crust. *Short-flake pie dough* requires hazelnut-sized pieces of fat and can be used as either a top crust or a bottom crust. To make *mealy pie dough,* cut the fat into small, pea-sized bits and incorporate it completely into the flour, leaving no lumps; mealy pie dough is used only for bottom crusts. Mealy pie dough does not flake, and therefore is not tender. Its denser nature makes it an ideal watertight lining for moist fillings, such as custards, that are not cooked prior to putting them into the pie shell.

Dough Ingredients

Also known as 3-2-1 dough, pie dough usually contains 3 parts flour to 2 parts fat to 1 part liquid by weight. Salt and sugar also can be added to the pie dough. It is important to understand what each of these ingredients contributes to the quality of the dough.

Flour Pie dough calls for pastry flour. Pastry flour contains a relatively small amount of gluten but enough to hold the dough together and give it elasticity for rolling. Bread flour has too much gluten; it will produce an overly tough dough. Cake flour has too little gluten; because of the small amount of gluten, the dough will crack and crumble when rolled out.

Fat Butter, lard, and all-purpose shortening are the fats most commonly used for pie dough. Each has its pros and cons. Butter has excellent flavor, but its low melting point and high water content make the dough extremely hard to work with and will cause it to lose its shape during baking. Pie dough that uses butter alone as a fat will result in a crust that is mealy and crumbly. Lard's higher melting point results in a lighter, flakier crust than butter alone; however, because the quality of lard is not consistent, it can give crust an undesirable flavor. Lard is also unacceptable for use in kosher, halal, and vegetarian diets. All-purpose shortening is the best choice for pie dough. Its high melting point, close to that of lard, produces a light, flaky crust. Shortening also has a consistently good quality and imparts no flavor to pie dough. The combination of both shortening and butter produces optimum flakiness and flavor in a pie dough.

> Be sure to use all-purpose, not high-ratio, shortening for pie dough. The latter contains emulsifiers in the form of mono- and diglycerides, which enable it to absorb moisture. If used in a pie dough, high-ratio shortening will cause the crust to absorb too much moisture. The result is a heavy, soggy crust.

Cold liquid Cold liquid helps the gluten in the flour develop properly. Water is the most frequently used liquid because it provides needed moisture without adding extra components that will affect the quality and tenderness of the dough. Milk is an alternative liquid that enriches dough and adds to crust color. The additional sugar and fat in milk, however, may produce a heavy, soggy crust that is more tender than flaky. Whether water or milk, the liquid should be ice-cold to preserve the solid state of the fat. It is the melting of the fat and the release of steam that give the dough structure and contribute to the flakiness of the baked crust.

Salt Salt's main purpose is to enhance the flavor of the dough. It also acts as a gluten conditioner, slowing its development and tenderizing the crust. For even distribution, sift the salt with the flour or dissolve it in the liquid.

Sugar When added to pie dough, sugar provides flavor. However, it also absorbs moisture, often producing a mushy crust. It is preferable to sprinkle sugar on top of the dough before baking. This technique not

PROCESS

Rolling and Panning Pie Dough

Roll out the dough on a clean, flat surface lightly dusted with flour. Also dust the rolling pin and the dough with just enough flour to prevent the dough from sticking. The addition of too much flour will result in a tough product.

To roll and pan the dough, follow these steps:

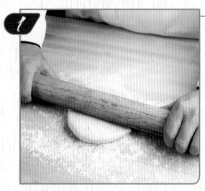

1 Lightly flatten the dough with the rolling pin.

2 Place the rolling pin at a diagonal, and roll the dough from the center to the outer edge.

3 Roll the dough to the outer edge in the opposite direction, also at a diagonal, to form a round about 1/8-inch (3-mm) thick and 1–2 inches (2.54 cm–5.08 cm) larger in diameter than the pan.

4 Roll the dough onto the rolling pin. Then place the pin over the pan, and unroll the dough. Gently place the dough in the pan, making sure that it fully contours to the sloping sides of the pan with no air pockets.

only adds sweetness but also creates caramelization.

Preparing Pies and Tarts

The manner in which the pie dough is handled is just as important as using the right ingredients and the correct proportions. The proper techniques for making, shaping, filling, and baking the pie are necessary to achieve the best results.

Making Pie Dough

Although large amounts of dough may require machine mixing, hand mixing is best for pie dough. Mixing by hand gives greater control over gluten development, fat distribution, the size of fat pieces, and ultimately the

FIGURE 32-2

To create a flaky dough, cut or rub the fat in coarsely.

A flaky dough should have nickel-to hazelnut-size pieces of fat.

To make a mealy dough, continue cutting or rubbing in the fat until it is the size of small peas.

flakiness of the crust. Avoid overmixing or overworking the dough, which will result in a tough crust. See Figure 32-2 on page 730.

To mix pie dough, use the biscuit, or rub-in, method and follow these steps:

1. To prevent clumping, sift the flour and salt together, and place in a bowl.

2. Using your hands or a pastry cutter, cut the fat into the flour. (If mixing by machine, use the dough hook attachment.) The fat should be well distributed and still in large pieces, about the size of hazelnuts.

3. Sprinkle the cold liquid over the mixture a little at a time, and mix until the dough holds together in a ball.

Wrap mixed dough tightly in plastic wrap, and refrigerate. Before using the dough, let it rest for at least 1–2 hours so that the gluten can relax. Chilling firms the flour and fat, making the dough easier to handle and roll and resulting in a flakier crust. Do not refrigerate dough longer than a week, however; it will begin to oxidize, and the flour and water will start to ferment, turning the dough gray. For storage longer than a week, freeze the dough in 8- to 10-ounce (225- to 285-g) portions. Then thaw overnight in the refrigerator before use.

Shaping Pie Dough

After pie dough is made and chilled, it is ready to be shaped. To shape dough, roll it out and fit it into a pie pan or tart shell, or place it on top of pie filling.

Single-crust pies For a single-crust pie, fluting is the next step after panning the dough. *Fluting* is a decorative method of finishing a pie crust by making folds or pleats in the dough at regular intervals around the edge of the pie. See Figure 32-3. After filling, certain single-crust pies are topped with a *streusel topping* (a crumbled mixture of flour, fat, sugar, and often spices and nuts) before baking. Other single-crust pies are finished with a meringue or a whipped cream topping.

Some single-crust pies do not use pie dough at all. Instead, they feature *crumb crusts,* usually made from finely ground cookies or graham crackers. Sweeten the crumbs with sugar as needed, and add spices and nuts as desired. Then moisten the crumb mixture with melted butter, and press it into a pie pan. The crust is chilled and then baked before filling. Crumb crusts are used primarily for ice cream pies or pies with a cream cheese filling.

FIGURE 32-3

To flute a single-crust pie, fold under the dough that extends beyond the pan's rim so that it is even with the pan's edge. Then make a fluted ridge of dough around the pie by pressing the dough between your fingers.

Two-crust pies Two-crust pies feature both a bottom crust and either a full top crust or a lattice crust. To create a full top crust, roll out the dough as for a bottom crust, but make the round large enough to hang over the edge of the pan by 1–2 inches (25–50 mm). Roll the crust onto a rolling pin, or fold it in half. After lifting and placing the crust on top of the filled pie, use fluting to seal the top crust to the bottom crust. Vents should then be cut into the top crust to allow steam to be released from the fruit as it cooks. If vents are not provided, the steam will release at the seams of the top and bottom crusts, usually resulting in the top crust's sliding off the pie. A *lattice crust* is a crust of interwoven strips of dough evenly placed across the top of a pie. The top crust, or lattice, can then be brushed with an egg wash and sprinkled with sugar before baking, giving the final product a wonderful sheen. See Figure 32-4.

Pie Fillings

Pies contain a variety of fillings. Some of these fillings are baked with the crust, and others are added after the crust has been baked.

Fruit fillings Fruit fillings consist of fresh, canned, frozen, or dried fruit mixed with sweeteners, spices, and starches (flour, cornstarch, tapioca, modified food starch, or pregelatinized starch). Depending on the fruit used, a prebaked crust may be filled with an already cooked fruit filling or with fruit juice filling, or the fruit filling may be baked with the crust.

Cream fillings Cream fillings are essentially flavored pastry cream—a smooth, thick custard made from eggs. These fillings are precooked and thickened with cornstarch and/or flour. After the cream filling is cooked, place it in a prebaked crust, and top it with a meringue or with whipped cream. If a meringue is used as a topping, bake it in a 400°F (204°C) oven until lightly browned, or caramelize the meringue beneath a salamander or by using a propane blowtorch.

Custard fillings Custards are dairy based, containing milk, cream, or a combination of both. Eggs are then added to the dairy base. As the custard bakes, the egg proteins in it coagulate, thickening the filling.

FIGURE 32-4

A lattice crust features an over-under pattern of dough strips that is particularly attractive for fruit pies.

FIGURE 32-4

Chiffon fillings Chiffon filling is made by adding gelatin to a warm, cooked custard or to a warm fruit purée. After this mixture has cooled, a meringue is folded into it to make the filling light and fluffy. The mixture is then placed in a prebaked crust and chilled.

Fruit Tarts

Although tarts may have many different kinds of fillings, (See Figure 32-5) their base is made of a short dough shell. *Short dough* is a mixture of butter, sugar, pastry flour, and eggs. The term *short* refers to the action of the butter, which shortens and tenderizes the gluten strands in the flour. Classic examples of tarts include fruit tart with pastry cream, Linzertorte, and Swiss apple flan.

Short dough is prepared quite differently from pie dough. Another name for short dough is 1-2-3 dough, which refers to its ingredients by weight: 1 part sugar to 2 parts butter to 3 parts flour (3 eggs are also added). Instead of cutting in the fat by hand, as for pie dough, short dough is made by the creaming method.

1. Mix sugar, eggs, and butter at low speed with a dough hook.
2. When the ingredients are just combined, add the flour, and continue to mix until the dough is smooth.
3. Let the dough rest in the refrigerator, preferably overnight, to relax the gluten and firm the butter.
4. Avoid overmixing because the incorporation of too much air will make the dough extremely difficult to work

with, resulting in an undesirable end product.

Fruit tart with pastry cream There are many variations on this classic fruit tart. Its basic components are a prebaked short dough shell, a pastry cream filling, fruit arranged decoratively on top of the filling, glaze, and nuts (usually toasted almonds) on the sides of the tart as a finish. (For more on pastry cream, see page 740.)

Linzertorte Actually a tart rather than a torte or cake, this pastry originated in the town of Linz, Austria. The traditional Linzertorte has a hazelnut crust and contains a filling of sweet raspberry jam. It is finished with a lattice-style top crust.

Swiss apple flan This tart contains a mixture of custard and tart apples. The apples are arranged in a spiral on a semi-baked crust over which the custard filling is then poured. After baking, the top is brushed with a light glaze.

Baking Pies and Tarts

Baking procedures and times vary with the type of pie or tart. Follow these general guidelines:

1. When *blind baking,* or baking an unfilled pie crust, it is necessary to dock, or pierce, the unbaked dough. This will allow steam to escape and will prevent blisters from forming during baking. Placing an empty pie pan on top of the dough and then turning the pan upside down to bake, or lining the shell with parchment paper and then filling it with dried

beans or pastry weights, will prevent both blistering and shrinkage.

2. Set fruit pies on a preheated sheet pan to catch drippings.

3. Bake fruit pies at high heat (400°F–425°F/204°C–218°C) to set the bottom crust so that it does not absorb moisture from the filling. For custard pies, reduce the oven temperature to 325°F–350°F (163°C–177°C) after ten minutes to cook the pie slowly.

4. Test custard pies for doneness by shaking the pan to check for firmness or by inserting a knife near the center of the pie; the knife will come out clean when the pie is done. Fruit pies will begin to bubble toward the end of the baking process. Crusts should be golden brown. Fruit should be tender but not mushy when a knife is inserted into the pie.

Cooling and Storing Pies and Tarts

Unbaked pie crusts and unbaked fruit pies may be stored, tightly wrapped, in the freezer for up to two months. Always cool a blind-baked crust before filling. Prebaked crusts will stay fresh for two to three days at room temperature. Wrapped in plastic, these crusts will keep in the freezer for up to three months. Refrigerate cream, custard, and chiffon pies to prevent the growth of bacteria. Freezing is not appropriate for baked fruit pies or cream, custard, or chiffon pies.

FIGURE 32-5

Fruit tarts can have many different fillings.

Custards

Custard is made of eggs, sugar, and milk or cream that thickens as the egg proteins coagulate during baking. Ostensibly, custard is one of the simplest desserts to prepare; however, the delicacy of its ingredients makes it one of the most difficult to bake. Overbaking curdles custard and fills it with air pockets; underbaking produces a runny product with little texture. The egg-to-dairy ratio and the type of dairy used are determining factors in custard's final texture. A greater proportion of eggs and egg yolks and the use of cream instead of milk make custard especially creamy and rich.

To bake custard, a process known as wet slow baking is used. *Wet slow baking* involves insulating the food item in a water bath during baking. The water bath protects the delicate ingredients of the product, promotes even baking, keeps the product from drying out, and prevents cracking on its surface. The water bath also prevents the eggs from leavening, resulting in a silky end product. To use wet slow baking for custard, place the custard in ramekins in hot water, and bake them slowly in a low-temperature oven (300°F–325°F/149°C–163°C). For the water bath to be effective, monitor and replenish it if needed.

Types of Custard

There are many types of custard. Classic examples include crème caramel, flan, crème brûlée, pots de crème, and bread pudding. See Figure 32-6 on page 735.

Crème caramel Crème caramel is a custard baked over caramelized sugar. To make crème caramel, cover the bottom of the ramekin with caramelized sugar before pouring in the custard base. After baking it in a water bath, allow the custard to cool slightly. Then invert it to display its golden brown surface and to allow the caramel sauce created by the melted sugar to pour down the sides.

FIGURE 32-6

Custard is simple to prepare yet difficult to bake.

Flan Perhaps the forerunner of crème caramel, flan was the invention of Spanish nuns. Its use spread quickly to Central and South America, where it became a popular dessert. Although made in much the same way as crème caramel, flan has a higher proportion of cream to milk and sometimes even contains cream cheese. In addition, in making flan, the caramelized sugar is mixed with a sugar syrup before being poured into the ramekin. This creates a stickier syrup that melts more readily than the caramel of crème caramel.

Crème brûlée Crème brûlée, or burnt cream, has been a popular English dessert since the 1600s, but the French popularized the custard in the nineteenth century. A richer custard than flan or crème caramel, crème brûlée contains heavy cream, eggs, and additional egg yolks rather than just milk and whole eggs. The small amount of egg whites (and their albumen protein) means that the crème brûlée lacks the structure needed to be neatly unmolded from its ramekin. Therefore, it is served in the same ramekin in which it is baked. Before service the dessert is sprinkled with sugar and then caramelized either with a blowtorch or by placing it briefly under a salamander.

Pots de crème A rich custard made with eggs and egg yolks, milk, and heavy cream, pots de crème bake in special molds that cover the top of the custard, except for a tiny hole for steam. If the special molds are not available, bake this custard in a ramekin covered with foil with a steam hole. Pots de crème differ from the custards already described in that they do not contain any form of caramelized sugar.

Bread pudding The procedure for making this dessert is simple: a custard base is poured over stale bread. After the bread has absorbed the liquid, the mixture is baked in a water bath. The drier the bread, the more custard it will absorb and the more tender the pudding. Although originally developed to use day-old French bread, many variations are used today, including croissants, Danishes, cornbread, and cake layers. Some bread puddings incorporate dried and fresh fruits and various nuts as well.

Cheesecakes

Cheesecake is a baked custard that contains a soft cheese. The type of cheese used typically depends on the region or locale. Fresh, soft cheeses form the basis of German, Austrian, and Scandinavian cheesecakes; Italian and other Mediterranean cheesecakes usually have ricotta as a base. In the United States, most cheesecakes feature cream cheese as the main ingredient, although Neufchâtel cheese or a combination of baker's cheese and cream cheese also produce quality cheesecakes. Neufchâtel, a soft, white French cheese, is a flavorful lowfat alternative to cream cheese, which is high in butterfat. Baker's cheese, which is somewhat bland and about 75% water, helps cut the fat of cream cheese without adding flavor.

To make cheesecake, use a variation on the creaming method of mixing.

▌ See Chapter 31: Quick Breads, Cakes, and Cookies for more information on the creaming method.

After being mixed, the batter should contain no large lumps. Softening the cheese(s) with the butter (if used) before mixing, adding the eggs very slowly, and scraping the bowl constantly during mixing help ensure a lump-free batter. Avoid overmixing or mixing the batter on high speed because the batter will incorporate too much air, resulting in holes or cracks on the surface of the cake during baking. If lumps occur, the batter can be pushed through a large sieve to separate the lumps from the mixture.

Types of Cheesecake

The variations of cheesecakes are seemingly endless. The flavor possibilities are limitless, as are the various doughs, crumbs, and cakes used as the base for such cakes. There are two basic types of cheesecake: New York, or deli-style, cheesecake and French-style cheesecake.

New York (Deli-style) Extremely rich and quite dense, New York, or deli-style, cheesecake usually has a graham-cracker or cookie crust. Fruit is a popular topping for this type of cheesecake. The creamy nature of the New York-style cheesecake comes from its being baked in a water bath. The water bath contributes to the cheesecake's texture and also prevents the cake from rising and cracking.

French-style French-style cheesecake is lighter than New York style cheesecake. Some or all of the eggs used are separated; the whites are beaten and folded into the custard mixture before baking. A vanilla layer cake or cake crumbs traditionally serve as a base for this type of cheesecake.

Soufflés

Soufflés are a versatile food that can be savory or sweet and served as an entrée or a dessert. The term soufflé comes from the French verb souffler, which means "to blow up." A soufflé has two main components: a base and egg whites. The base contains all the flavor elements of the soufflé. The egg whites help "blow up" the soufflé, giving it its height and fluffy texture. To make a soufflé, fold whipped egg whites into the base. The air incorporated in the egg whites during whipping expands during baking, and the soufflé rises dramatically.

Soufflé Bases

The two most common types of soufflé bases are pâte à choux and custard. ***Pâte à choux*** is a paste composed of bread flour, water or milk, fat, eggs, and salt. Piped into rounds, fingers, or other shapes and then baked, the paste expands into a light pastry with a hollow, slightly moist center.

For a pâte à choux base, bring the milk to a boil, add the softened butter and flour, and while the mixture is still on the burner, continue to beat it. Remove from the heat, and add the eggs. Fold in the whipped egg whites while the batter is still warm, but not hot. Most soufflés with a pâte à choux base require a water bath during baking. A pâte à choux base is excellent for fruit soufflés because it is heavy enough to support the weight of the fruit.

The procedure for making a custard base is similar to that for a crème anglaise or pastry cream. Fold the whipped egg whites into the base while the cream is warm, but not hot. A custard base can easily be flavored with various liquors, chocolate, or fruit purées. Most custard-based soufflés do not need the added insulation of a water bath; they should be baked in a hot oven (400°F–410°F/204°C–210°C).

Making Soufflés

Follow these guidelines for success in making soufflés:

1. Both the base and the egg whites should be at room temperature. Egg whites at room temperature achieve greater volume when whipped, and the base and eggs combine more readily if they are at the same temperature.
2. Whip the egg whites to stiff peaks. Make sure that the egg whites are completely clean (no yolks or pieces of yolks present). The whisk and bowl must also be completely clean and grease free.
3. If the soufflé batter is prepared in advance, do not fold in the egg whites until just before baking.
4. Use a round ramekin with striated sides for baking. The striations, or grooves, on the outside of the baking dish will encourage proper distribution of heat throughout the batter.
5. Use a properly sized dish for the amount of batter. In an appropriately sized dish, the soufflé will rise to a beautiful crown. If the dish is too small, the batter will rise out of the dish and spill down the sides.
6. Use a collar of parchment paper if there is more batter than the dish will accommodate. Make the collar twice as high and 1 1/3 times the diameter of the dish, butter it, and then wrap it around the outside of the dish.
7. Fill the soufflé dish three-quarters of the way to the top.

Serving Soufflés

Baking *à la minute* is essential, and timing with the dining room is crucial for the proper service of a soufflé. Soufflés must be served immediately because they can collapse in as little as three minutes after removal from the oven. Thus communication with the servers is essential for successful service of a soufflé.

Meringues

Meringues consist of whipped egg whites and sugar. The use of a meringue depends on its ratio of sugar to egg. Soft meringues, which are relatively low in sugar, are important components of soufflés and various cakes. Harder meringues, with an equal or slightly greater proportion of sugar to egg whites, form part of icings or top pies and other desserts. Meringues with twice as much sugar as egg whites in weight are pastry items, piped into decorative shapes and dried slowly at a low oven temperature. During this process, known as dry slow baking, the moisture in the eggs evaporates, and the meringue becomes a crisp shell. This sugary structure is perfect for filling with fruit, ice cream, or mousse.

The Science of Meringues

Albumen and ovalbumen proteins in egg whites help increase the foam that forms meringues. When egg whites are whipped, they incorporate air bubbles, which the albumen proteins stabilize. At the same time, these proteins form a network around the air bubbles and hold the water in the foam in place. Egg whites consist of almost 85% water. This redistribution of protein is called denaturization. When the foam is heated, the air expands, but the ovalbumen protein coagulates, preventing the collapse of the structure of the meringue as the water in the whites evaporates.

The sugar in the meringue not only flavors and sweetens it but also plays an important role in stabilizing the foam, particularly during baking. Sugar bonds with the meringue's protein structure and creates a smooth, stable foam. However, because sugar can also hinder the development of the foam and decrease its volume, add it only after the meringue has begun to increase in volume. Sugar also should be added gradually, in a slow, steady stream. Adding the sugar too early or too quickly can keep the foam from whipping properly.

Acid in the form of lemon juice or cream of tartar may be added to the foam during whipping to change its pH level and stabilize it. Too much acid, however, will prevent the coagulation of the proteins during baking and alter the taste of the meringue. Copper bowls, long considered the best utensil for whipping egg whites, were thought to have the same stabilizing effect as acid. Today, though, this theory is the subject of some debate. The current general consensus is that a stainless steel bowl is best. Aluminum bowls give meringues a grayish tint, and plastic bowls retain fats from previous use that hinder whipping. Fats will interfere with coagulation of the proteins and reduce volume drastically.

Types of Meringue

There are three basic types of meringue: common meringue (French), Swiss meringue, and Italian meringue. All have a 2 to 1 ratio of sugar to egg whites; they differ only in procedure and final product.

Common meringue Also known as a cold or French meringue, a *common meringue* is the quickest and easiest of the three types to make. Beat egg whites at high speed until frothy, and then add granulated sugar in a slow, steady stream until the foam reaches the desired volume. The structure of this meringue is weaker than that of the others because no heat is used. Its texture is also grainier. A common meringue is used primarily for cookies and must be formed and baked immediately after whipping.

Swiss meringue To make a *Swiss meringue,* heat both the sugar and the egg whites to 120°F (49°C) over a water bath while lightly whisking. At this temperature, the mixture will feel warm to the touch, and the sugar granules will have mostly dissolved. Take the mixture off the heat, and whip at high speed until it is completely cooled. This meringue is used in fillings and buttercreams.

Italian meringue For an *Italian meringue,* heat the sugar in a sugar syrup to 245°F–250°F (118°C–121°C), reserving a small handful of sugar to help leaven the egg whites during whipping. When the sugar syrup reaches 238°F (114°C), beat the egg whites to full volume while adding the reserved sugar. Then pour the syrup into the whipped egg whites in a thin, steady stream, and mix at medium speed until cool. When adding the hot syrup, be careful to avoid pouring it into the whip attachment, or the resulting splatters will cause lumps of sugar to form in the meringue.

The heat used for Swiss and Italian meringues helps their ingredients form a strong bond and structure, making the texture of both stronger than that of a common meringue.

Items Made from Meringue

Meringues have many dessert applications. Items made from meringues include the following:

Vacherin *Vacherin* is the French term for a meringue that is piped into a basket shape to hold mousses, creams, fruits, and so on.

Filigrees Filigrees are delicate ornaments into which meringue can be piped. These are then baked and used to decorate cakes, pastries, and desserts.

Swans Meringues in the form of swans can be filled with mousse or whipped cream for an elegant dessert.

Pavlovas Created in Sydney to celebrate a perfomance of prima ballerina Anna Pavlova, this classic Australian dessert is a meringue cup usually filled with a whipped cream and topped with fresh fruit.

Baking and Storing Meringues

Use one of the following methods to bake, or dry, meringues:

- Place meringues in a 200°F–250°F (93°C–121°C) oven until they are set. This method is fast but tends to color the meringues slightly.
- Leave the meringues overnight in a gas oven with just the pilot light for heat. This method takes longer, but the meringues will retain their white color.

Meringues should not be bone dry or spongy. Ideally meringues are crisp shells with a light, almost chewy center.

The high sugar content of meringues makes them very susceptible to moisture. Use meringues immediately after baking, or store in airtight containers until needed. Do not freeze or refrigerate meringues because they will absorb too much moisture and dissolve.

Dessert Creams

Dessert creams, in all of their various guises, form the backbone of a restaurant's dessert repertoire. Dessert creams include mousse, Bavarian cream, and pastry cream.

Mousse

A *mousse* is basically a mixture of whipped cream, whipped egg whites or egg yolks, and flavorings. It is often stabilized with gelatin. The term *mousse* means "foam" in French, and if made correctly, a mousse will seem like a light foam to the palate.

Mousses are fairly straightforward to make. First, prepare the base, which can be as simple as melted chocolate, crème anglaise, or puréed fruit. If egg yolks are used, the usual procedure is to make a pâte à bombe with part of the sugar and then add any flavorings to this mixture. A *pâte à bombe* consists of whipped egg yolks and hot sugar syrup. For mousses that are not chocolate based, gelatin is then added in order to help the mixture set. After the base is made (and cooled, if necessary), fold in the whipped cream. If a meringue is used, it is folded in last because of its delicate nature. Pasteurized whites are needed if a common (uncooked) meringue is being used. To thicken properly, some mousses need to set for a few hours or overnight. If the mousse is to be served individually, be sure to pipe it into serving glasses before refrigerating to prevent the mousse from setting in a mass.

Mousses are extremely versatile. They are used as the main item in a plated dessert and as a component of such items as mousse tortes and mousse-filled pastries.

Bavarian Cream

A *Bavarian cream* is crème anglaise with the addition of gelatin for thickening and whipped cream for lightness. This dessert cream is firm enough to mold and even slice. It can be served by itself or as a filling for a cake.

There are two primary bases used in making a Bavarian cream. One method uses a base made of crème anglaise, and the other uses a base made from a pâte à bombe.

- A crème anglaise uses a base of milk, heavy cream, sugar, and eggs or egg yolks cooked over a water bath. The gelatin is bloomed in either cold water or some cold milk from the recipe. After it has bloomed, the gelatin is added to the hot crème anglaise. The mixture is cooled over an ice bath. After the mixture has been chilled and the gelatin just begins to set, the whipped cream is folded in. (For more on crème anglaise, see pages 751 and 753.)
- The pâte à bombe base is a mixture of whipped egg yolks and hot sugar syrup. For this base, allow the gelatin to bloom and dissolve separately, add it to the bombe, and fold in the whipped cream while the mixture is still warm.

Timing is a critical element in making a Bavarian cream. If the mixture becomes too cold and the gelatin begins to set too much before the whipped cream is added, the mixture will lump badly. Likewise, if the mixture is too warm when the whipped cream is added, it will lose both its volume and texture, ultimately disintegrating in the mixture. The amount of gelatin used also plays a role in the success of a Bavarian cream. Too much gelatin will make the cream tough and rubbery; too little will not allow the dessert to hold its shape when unmolded.

Chocolate mousse is perhaps the most difficult mousse to prepare because its consistency depends on the tempering of ingredients of various temperatures and consistencies. If great care is not taken, the melted chocolate will seize and create lumps. It is therefore important to have all of the ingredients ready to be incorporated at the same time. If the chocolate is allowed to sit for too long, the whipped cream and meringue cannot be fully incorporated.

The base can be flavored in a number of ways. Chocolate, fruits, nuts, spices, and liquors can all be successfully used. Certain fruits contain enzymes that will inhibit the setting of the gelatin. For this reason, either cook the fruits or substitute a vegetable-based thickener such as agar-agar for the gelatin.

The cream should set for at least 2–3 hours before service. To unmold, dip the inverted mold in hot water for a few seconds, or heat it with a blowtorch. To avoid a mess, unmold Bavarian cream onto parchment paper, and then transfer it to plates or serving dishes. Alternatively, silicone fleximolds offer an easier solution. Simply place the fleximold on a sheet pan, fill with the Bavarian cream mixture, and freeze. Once frozen, the Bavarian cream will simply pop out. Place on a parchment-lined sheet pan, and keep in the refrigerator until service.

Bavarian cream also can be used as a cake filling. It is the classic filling for both charlotte russe and charlotte royale. Charlotte russe is a Bavarian cream surrounded by ladyfingers, usually molded in a charlotte mold. Charlotte royale is a cake made with jelly rolls and Bavarian cream. Line a large bowl with plastic wrap and slices of jelly roll. Fill with Bavarian cream, top with a layer of sponge cake, and chill. To serve, invert the bowl on a serving plate, remove the bowl and the plastic wrap, and brush on some apricot glaze.

Pastry Cream

Pastry cream is essentially an egg custard thickened with cornstarch and/or flour. It has many applications in the bakeshop. Pastry cream serves as a filling for a variety of pastries, including cream puffs, éclairs, napoleons, cakes, and cream pies.

To make pastry cream, follow the steps to the right, and follow these guidelines when preparing this versatile cream:

1. Always mix the cornstarch and/or flour with a small portion of the sugar, and then whisk with a small amount of the liquid (usually milk) to make a slurry. This will help prevent lumps from forming in the finished cream.

2. The milk or cream must boil for 3 minutes to activate the thickening powers of the starch, to get rid of the starchy flavor, and to allow the cream to regain its translucency and shine.

PROCESS

Making Pastry Cream

The procedure for making a vanilla pastry cream follows. To make a lower fat version of pastry cream, eliminate the butter and use only egg whites in place of the egg yolks and whole eggs.

Follow these steps to make pastry cream:

Gather ingredients for pastry cream.

Combine the starch, half the sugar, and salt, if using, in a bowl. Add a small portion of milk, and blend.

Add eggs to milk mixture.

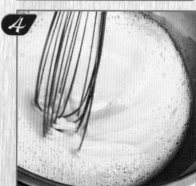

Beat eggs and milk until combined.

Put remaining milk into a saucepan with the remaining sugar, and scald over moderate heat.

Add vanilla.

Temper hot milk into egg mixture.

Add butter, and blend until combined.

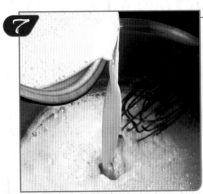

Combine tempered egg mixture and hot milk in the saucepan.

Pour into a stainless steel hotel pan or sheet pan lined with parchment paper.

Heat until mixture thickens.

Cover with parchment paper or plastic wrap, and refrigerate.

3. Whisk the eggs with a portion of the milk, and then add them to the slurry so that the cornstarch can absorb them more readily. The cornstarch stabilizes the eggs in the mixture so that they do not curdle when the cream is boiling. Tempering the egg mixture first by whisking a small amount of the hot liquid into it in a steady stream also helps prevent curdling.

4. Whisk the pastry cream constantly while it is thickening.

History of Ice Cream

It is a testament to ice cream's worldwide popularity that so many countries in so many different corners of the world insist on claiming responsibility for its origin. Some claim that the Roman Emperor Nero enjoyed a form of ice cream in the first century A.D. Others say that the Chinese were responsible for the first ice cream, a concoction of milk and seasoned rice, eaten over 4,000 years ago.

The first mention of ices goes back thousands of years to the Chinese. The Chinese method of making ices involved no churning and created a hard product that required chipping and scraping, a technique the Italians used later to make granita.

The sweetened ices traveled with explorers along the spice trade route. Thus ices moved from China to the Middle East. In the Middle East, Arabs flavored the crushed ices with fruit and honey—a concoction they called sharbat, *the forerunner of sherbet and sorbet. As spices traveled to Europe, so too did ices. They eventually made their way to Italy, where Italian chefs developed and refined the churning process to produce* sorbetti. *These ices arrived in France with great pomp and circumstance in 1533, when Catherine de Medici married the duke of Orleans, later to become King Henry II. Guests enjoyed a different flavor of ice for every day of the wedding celebration.*

The French can take credit for adding cream to these ices. In the 1600s, Paris cafés began to offer crèmes glacées *and fancy sherbets. At about the same time, English royals tasted ice cream for the first time at Windsor Castle. A taste for* sorbet *quickly spread from the nobility to the working classes in France and eventually became a common offering of French coffeehouses, where it is still served today.*

By the 1700s, middle-class English cookbooks included ice creams, and the idea soon crossed the ocean to the American colonies. In 1846 a dairymaid from Philadelphia named Nancy Johnson made an important advance in the production of ice cream when she invented a portable hand-cranked ice cream freezer. This single accomplishment greatly improved the quality of ice cream. With the steady addition of air and the constant movement of the mixture, ice cream was smoother than ever before and contained less grit. A favorite American treat was born. With the exception of the Italians, who pride themselves on their sorbetto, granita, and, of course, their gelato, Americans eat more ice cream per capita than anyone else in the world.

Frozen Desserts

Frozen desserts are enjoyed year-round and have many uses. They work well as single dessert items, or as side items for desserts such as apple pie or brownies.

Ice Cream

Ice cream can range from the rich, French crème anglaise or premium ice cream to the light and airy American ice cream. The differences depend on both the ingredients used and the manner in which the ice cream is made. See Figure 32-7 on page 744.

Milk and cream The butterfat in milk and cream is the chief contributor to ice cream's texture, body, and richness. Ice creams usually contain 14%–16% butterfat but no more than 22%–25%. An excess of butterfat will adversely affect the mix's whipping ability and impair the ice cream's overrun. *Overrun* is an increase in volume as a result of the incorporation of air. Too much fat will also freeze separately during *churning,* or mixing, giving the ice cream a grainy texture. Serum solids, or solids in milk and cream other than butterfat, should total at least 20%. These solids contribute to whipping capabilities. Excessive serum solids, however, can cause the lactose in the milk to crystallize, giving the ice cream a sandy texture.

Sugar Total sugar content in ice creams should be 14%–16% and never more than 18%. Sugar enhances not only the flavor but also the smoothness of ice cream. Sugar inhibits freezing, however, so too much sugar interferes with ice cream's firmness.

Flavoring Flavorings for ice cream include fruits, nuts, extracts, and liqueurs. Ice cream needs more flavoring than many other products because taste buds are less sensitive when cold.

Eggs Eggs contribute to the flavor, color, and fat content of ice cream and, because they contain the emulsifier lecithin, eggs also add to the body of ice cream. When using eggs in an ice-cream base, heat the mixture to at least 145°F (63°C).

Ice creams fall into two categories according to their ingredients and methods of preparation: French-style ice cream and American-style ice cream. French-style ice cream is thick and custardlike. It contains eggs and has a crème anglaise or pâte à bombe base. The French ice cream base is always cooked. American-style ice cream is usually not cooked. It is simply a basic mixture of milk, cream, sugar, and flavorings.

Freezing and Overrun

After the base is prepared, the ice-cream mix must be frozen. Churning is necessary during the freezing process to prevent large ice crystals from forming. Churning also incorporates air into the mix, which increases its volume. This increase in volume is expressed as a percentage of the total volume of the mix. The USDA requires that the overrun for products called ice cream not exceed 50%. Overrun is one of the differentiating characteristics between premium and less expensive brands of ice cream. There is a great deal more overrun in American ice cream than in French ice cream.

The ice-cream mix can absorb air only when it still contains sufficient liquid components. Therefore, if the base is frozen too quickly, the end product will be undesirable. During the freezing process, one-third of the water changes to ice. Insufficient air makes ice cream heavy and gritty. Too much air gives the ice cream a foamy, snowy texture.

Several factors determine the overrun of ice cream:

- The type of freezing equipment used
- How long the ice cream base is frozen or churned
- The amount of mix in relation to freezer capacity (for maximum overrun, the freezer should be filled only halfway)
- The amount of solids in the mix (total solids—fat, sugar, nonfat milk solids, and egg solids—should be approximately 40%)

Hardening

Ice cream should come out of the ice cream machine at a temperature of 22°F–26°F (⁻6°C–⁻3°C). The product is then ready for service. Ice cream also may be stored for up to one week in a hardening cabinet. A hardening cabinet has a constant temperature of 6°F–10°F (⁻14°C–⁻12°C). Under these conditions, another one-third of the water in the ice cream changes to ice crystals. After the hardening period, the ice cream can be placed in serving cabinets.

Before it hardens, pack the ice cream in an airtight container to prevent ice crystals from forming on its surface and to guard against absorption of odors from the freezer. Carefully monitor temperature during storage because fluctuations in temperature can coarsen the texture of the ice cream and shorten its shelf life.

Ice Cream Desserts

Ice cream is used extensively in many types of desserts. The following is a short list of the most popular ice cream desserts.

- **Baked Alaska**—This dessert features ice cream on a sponge cake base, enclosed in meringue, which is then caramelized.
- **Bombe**—A bombe is several layers of ice cream molded in a spherical or dome shape and decorated with an Italian meringue, which is then browned.
- **Coupe**—A coupe consists of ice cream served in a dessert glass with fruit or sauce and whipped cream.
- **Ice-cream pie**—Various flavors of ice cream are used as a pie filling. The crust is usually made of cookie or graham-cracker crumbs.
- **Neapolitan**—This three-layer ice-cream "cake" usually features vanilla, chocolate, and strawberry ice creams.
- **Parfait**—This attractive dessert presents ice cream alternating with topping or sauce in a tall glass.
- **Sundae**—A sundae is an elaborate concoction of one or more types of ice cream, sauce (hot fudge, butterscotch, and so on), and toppings such as fruit, nuts, and candies, typically garnished with Chantilly cream and a maraschino cherry.

Following strict sanitation standards is absolutely necessary when making and storing ice cream. Do not touch ice cream mixtures with bare hands. Clean ice cream freezers and machines carefully after each use. Keep storage units sanitary, and maintain proper temperatures for storage (6°F–10°F/¯14°C–¯12°C for ice cream and frozen yogurt). To avoid growth and transfer of bacteria, use running water to rinse portioning implements, and then sanitize. Many machines have automatic sanitizing systems.

Qualities of Ice Cream

Smoothness of texture, richness, flavor, and mouth feel are the main criteria for grading ice cream. The butterfat in the milk products used is the chief contributor to these qualities. Butterfat provides body and richness and is largely responsible for the velvety-smooth texture of ice cream. Size of ice crystals also affects texture, and overrun and solids other than butterfat help create its body. Ingredients such as eggs add to an ice cream's richness and flavor.

Manufacturers of ice cream often use gums, gelatins, and chemicals to create texture and body without costly ingredients such as cream and eggs. These additives act as stabilizers, altering the texture and body of ice cream.

Gelato

Gelato is an Italian-style ice cream characterized by a relatively dense texture. The mix for this ice cream incorporates less air during the churning process.

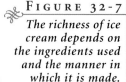 **FIGURE 32-7**
The richness of ice cream depends on the ingredients used and the manner in which it is made.

Sherbet and Sorbet

Sherbet and sorbet are sweetened water-based products infused with various flavors. Sherbet also may contain a dairy product and/or egg whites. Sherbet's additional ingredients make it smoother and slightly richer than sorbet. Sorbet often includes alcohol as flavoring. Sorbet was initially used as an intermezzo, something served between courses to cleanse the palate. As America has become increasingly interested in fat-free dessert options, sorbet has gained in popularity.

Stabilization is even more important for sherbet and sorbet than for ice cream because of the danger of sugar separation and a resulting crumbly texture.

Sherbet and sorbet use most of the same stabilizers as ice cream. The approximate amount of these basic additives for sherbets and sorbets is as follows:

Gelatin (200 bloom)	0.45%
Agar-agar	0.20%
Pectin	0.18%

In general, the sugar content of these products is about double that of ice cream, ranging from 25% to 35%. Sources of sugar include cane or beet sugar, corn syrup solids, honey, and other invert sugars. The sugar content of any fruit used must also be taken into account. Sugar density is measured by the Baumé scale, with a workable sorbet base between 18 and 21 degrees.

To make good sherbets and sorbets, it is necessary to control both the sugar content and the overrun. Overrun affects the firmness of these products.

Sherbet and sorbet differ from ice cream in several other significant ways. Although cooking the sugar base of sherbet or sorbet to a certain density ensures that the product freezes well and has sufficient body, the lack of total solids, particularly butterfat, gives these frozen products a coarser texture than ice cream. Sherbet and sorbet also have a higher sugar content than ice cream, which gives them a lower melting point. Their coarser texture and lower melting point cause a greater cooling characteristic while being consumed. Sherbet and sorbet also have a much lower overrun.

Sherbets and sorbets can be difficult to produce. Common problems in their production and recommended solutions follow.

Separation of sugar syrup Various factors cause separation of the concentrated sugar syrup for sherbet and sorbet: too much sugar in the base mixture, excess overrun, and a lack of total solids to bind the mixture. To prevent separation, reduce the amount of sugar in the formula, and add stabilizers in the form of gelatin, agar-agar, pectin, or egg whites to the base mixture. The usual amount of gelatin necessary is 2 teaspoons per quart of the base mixture. Fruits high in pectin, such as citrus fruits, blueberries, cranberries, and apples, should not require the support of a stabilizer.

Crystallization of sugar and ice Exposure to air in the freezer, fluctuation of storage temperatures, and use of granulated sugar to make the sugar syrup promote sugar and ice crystallization. To avoid crystallization, store the product in airtight containers. Monitor the cabinet temperature, and substitute an invert sugar such as glucose or honey for at least part of the granulated sugar. Granulated sugar can cause the extraction of water onto the surface of the mixture as soon as it has frozen, causing ice and sugar crystals to form; the use of an invert will help prevent this.

Coarse or crumbly texture Low sugar content in the base mixture, inefficient freezing methods, and too much overrun can result in a coarse or crumbly texture in the final product. To attain the desired texture, adjust the sugar content and add an invert to the total percentage of sugar, use more efficient freezing techniques, and freeze the base mixture with less overrun.

Granita

Granita (French *granité*) is an Italian ice that is also made with a sweetened, flavored water base. Its name derives from the Italian word *grana*, which means "grainy." The texture of a granita is similar to that of a snow cone or crushed ice. Although the basic mixture for a granita is similar to that for a sorbet, the two products differ in several ways. Granitas contain less sugar than sorbets, and the sugar syrup for granitas is thinner. The freezing process also differs. Although sorbets are churned during freezing, granitas are still-frozen (that is, frozen without any movement) in a shallow pan and scraped after they become solid. The result is a coarsely textured, refreshing dessert.

Frozen Yogurt

Although it is often promoted as a healthful alternative to ice cream, frozen yogurt actually has much in common with ice cream. It has yogurt as a base, but it also may contain milk or cream as well as various stabilizers to improve its smoothness, body, and richness. Different fruits, liqueurs, and other flavorings create frozen yogurt flavors.

Plating Frozen Desserts

Many of the general guidelines for plating desserts apply to frozen desserts. Some procedures are specific to frozen desserts, however. Always temper ice cream and other frozen desserts for 24 hours before service so that they will soften somewhat. Holding these items at 8°F–15°F (⁻13°C–⁻9°C) will accomplish this.

Standard scoops help in the proper portioning of frozen desserts such as ice cream. Pull the scoop across the surface of the product to avoid packing it. This method will roll the product into a ball for serving. Use of a cold plate is vital to effective service of an ice-cream dessert. It is also important to place something on the plate to anchor the scoop of ice cream. Examples are a cup made of tuile, almond lace, or tempered chocolate. Toasted, ground nuts or cake crumbs also can be sprinkled on the plate with the ice-cream scoop placed neatly on top. This prevents the ice cream from rolling around the plate as it is taken from the kitchen to the guest.

Pâte à Choux

Pâte à choux is the basis for various savory items and sweet pastries such as éclairs, cream puffs, and profiteroles. In fact, a literal translation of pâte à choux is "cabbage paste"—a reference to the cabbagelike shape of cream puffs. This pastry dough is also known as éclair paste.

Uses for Pâte à Choux

A variety of products use pâte à choux shells. These include the following:

Beignets To make these deliciously sweet pastries, deep-fry pâte à choux squares or strips, and then dredge them in cinnamon and sugar.

Churros Similar to beignets, these Spanish and Mexican pastries are deep-fried sticks of pâte à choux rolled in cinnamon sugar.

Cream puffs These pastries are baked pâte à choux rounds filled with pastry cream or Chantilly cream.

Éclairs Filled with pastry cream, whipped cream, or sometimes ice cream, these pâte à choux pastries are oblong versions of cream puffs. It is common to glaze the tops of éclairs with fondant or chocolate. See Figure 32-8.

Paris-Brest This pastry is made by piping the pâte à choux into a large ring, topping it with slivered almonds, and then baking it. The filling is praline-flavored pastry cream or whipped cream.

Profiteroles Basically small cream puffs, these pastries often have ice cream as a filling and are served with a topping of chocolate sauce.

Croquembouche This pyramid-shaped structure of filled pâte à choux puffs is traditional at Christmas and at wedding celebrations in France. The puffs are filled with pastry cream. Caramelized sugar holds the layers of puffs together. The entire structure is finished with spun sugar.

Saint-Honoré Named for the patron saint of pastry chefs (and the Paris street that is home to so many patisseries, or pastry shops), this classic pâte à choux dessert cake has a round puff-pastry base with a ring of pâte à choux piped along its edge. After it is baked, it is filled with a mixture of pastry cream and whipped cream. Chantilly cream is then piped out in a woven pattern over the entire puff pastry base. Profiteroles filled with cream and dipped in light caramel decorate the top of the cake.

Swans These pâte à choux pastries are made by cutting a shell-shaped puff in half horizontally and filling one half with Chantilly cream. The remaining piece is cut in half vertically and inserted in the sides of the filling to resemble wings. A neck (piped and baked separately) is placed at the front of the filled shell.

FIGURE 32-8
Éclairs are oblong versions of cream puffs.

Making Pâte à Choux

Baked pâte à choux shells may be stored for several days at room temperature or several weeks in the freezer. After the shells are filled, the pastries should be served within several hours, before they become soggy.

To make pâte à choux, follow these steps:

1 *Bring butter, salt, sugar, and water or milk to a boil. Add sifted flour all at once.*

2 *Stir constantly with a wooden spoon for about 5 minutes or until the mixture forms a ball that does not stick to the sides of the pot.*

3 Transfer the mixture to a mixer, and blend on low speed until slightly cooled.

4 *Add eggs gradually, mixing on low speed.*

5 *Pâte à choux mixture should be somewhat sticky and elastic.*

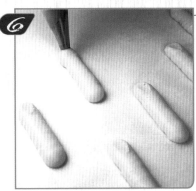

6 *Pipe into desired shapes on sheet pans lined with parchment paper.*

7 Bake immediately at 425°F–475°F (218°C–246°C). After 15 minutes, reduce the oven temperature to 375°F–425°F (191°C–218°C) for the final baking time to ensure that the product becomes firm and dry but not too brown. A perfectly baked pâte à choux puff should have a crisp, golden brown outer shell and a dry center when broken open.

Puff Pastry

Puff pastry is one of the basic doughs used widely in the bakeshop and kitchen. Although its ingredients are basic, its preparation involves considerable expertise. Puff pastry is a nonyeast laminated dough composed of many of layers of butter and dough. When baked, these layers of fat and dough create a light, buttery-flavored pastry.

Ingredients of Puff Pastry

Water, salt, butter, and flour form the basic mixture for puff pastry. The term for the flour and water mixture that makes up the dough is *détrempe.*

Flour The flour for puff pastry is often a combination of hard and soft flours. The flour must be strong enough to support the high percentage of rolled-in, or layered-in, fat and to withstand the repeated rolling and folding necessary to create the flaky layers of dough.

Fat The fat used in puff pastry is of great importance. Butter is the most widely accepted fat for this pastry dough, largely because of its incomparable taste and wonderful mouth feel. In addition, butter contains a great deal of moisture, which creates steam during baking. To save on food cost, a combination of puff-pastry shortening and butter instead of butter alone is used.

Other ingredients Salt, in addition to providing flavor, strengthens the strands of gluten in the flour. A very small amount of acid, such as lemon juice, is sometimes added to relax the gliadin in the gluten; this makes rolling the dough easier and quicker and results in less shrinkage when the pastry is baked.

Making Puff Pastry

Correct techniques and procedures are absolutely necessary when making puff pastry. If too much flour is added to the *détrempe,* for example, or if the dough is worked too much, the mixture will be rubbery, difficult to manipulate, and likely to shrink when baked. It is also important to let the dough rest for at least 30 minutes before making the first fold and after each successive fold.

Preparing the rolled-in fat also requires great care. To ensure a structure of even layers, the fat and flour must be close to the same consistency and temperature. This is acheived by adding a small amount of flour to the rolled-in fat, making the fat easier to handle. If rolled out properly, puff-pastry dough will have alternating layers of fat and dough. Depending on the number of folds, these layers can number between 500 and 1,500.

There are many methods of rolling the fat into the dough. The most common is the *block, or French, method.* In this technique the first fold is made after spreading the block of rolled-in fat over two-thirds of the dough. In another version of the block method, the dough is rolled into a square slightly larger than the block of fat, the fat is placed diagonally on the dough, and the flaps of dough are folded toward the center and sealed; then the first fold is made. After the initial fold, fold the dough, using either a single turn (*threefold*) or a double turn (*fourfold*). The dough should be refrigerated for at least 30 minutes after each fold. A combination of these types of folds is also possible. Generally, for puff pastry, either two fourfolds or a threefold/fourfold/threefold/fourfold alternation is customary. Too many folds will result in a compact product, and not enough folds will result in too few layers to produce the desired flaky texture.

The *blitz* ("lightning"), *or Scottish, method* is easier and faster than either version of the block method. Instead of using a block of fat, add the fat to the dough, and mix only enough to incorporate; large pieces of fat will be visible throughout the dough. Then fold the dough using the same procedures as in the block method.

The blitz method is popular in high-volume bakeshops because it reduces procedure time and produces dough quickly. It produces a slightly more compact product than the block

method does. The block method allows a more even distribution of fat with a reduced amount of dusting flour (if the dough absorbs too much flour during rolling and turning, it will be tough).

The blitz method is used primarily when the dough does not need to puff too much in the end product. Examples of this would be when lining tart pans or making fleurons or napoleons.

> **Rolling puff-pastry dough too thin or too hard can damage the structure of the layers. Be careful not to roll over the edges of the dough because this will prevent the sides of the dough from rising. Use equal pressure when rolling out the dough so that the butter is evenly dispersed. If the dough is too thick, the butter tends to melt during baking, reducing the flakiness of the final product.**

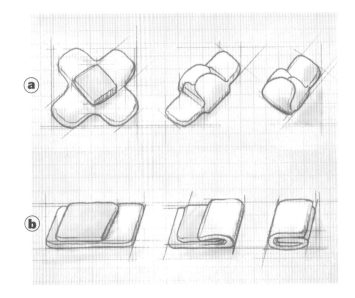

Block Method of Roll-in, Threefold, and Fourfold

(a) Block Method
In this version of the block method, place the block of fat on a square of dough, and fold the flaps toward the center.

(b) Threefold and Fourfold
After rolling the dough in a rectangle and placing the fat on it, fold using either a single turn (threefold) or a double turn (fourfold).

Baking Puff Pastry

Puff pastry requires a uniform oven temperature. If properly made, the dough should rise to approximately four times its initial height. Bake small puff-pastry items at 415°F–425°F (213°C–218°C), and use slightly lower temperatures for larger items. Do not set the oven temperature below 400°F (204°C). Low oven temperatures will cause butter to melt before it can create the steam needed to produce flakiness, resulting in puff pastry that does not puff up. To avoid fluctuations in temperature, do not open the oven door frequently during baking.

Storing Puff Pastry

Puff-pastry dough can be kept for up to a week. If kept too long, the flour and water in puff-pastry dough, as in pie dough, will begin to ferment and oxidize, turning the dough gray and giving it an off taste. Keep dough covered at all times. Puff-pastry dough freezes well. For best results, cut all the pieces at one time, wrap them well, and freeze. Then simply take them out of the freezer, and bake as needed.

Items Made from Puff Pastry

Puff pastry can be used to create a variety of items, both savory and sweet. Vol-au-vents and bouchées are puff-pastry containers with savory applications. See Figure 32-9.

See Chapter 25: Garde-Manger for more on vol-au-vents and bouchées.

Dessert items made from puff pastry include the following:

Napoleons Also known as *mille feuilles à la crème* ("thousand leaves with cream"), napoleons are among the best-known puff items. Docking—making small holes in the surface of a dough—before baking prevents the puff pastry for napoleons from rising as much as it otherwise would. Napoleons are rectangular with a pastry cream filling. They are finished with white fondant icing and chocolate feathering.

Palmiers These puff pastries, known in the United States as elephant ears, may be large or the size of petits fours. Gently rolled out with granulated sugar and cinnamon, they are folded in a fourfold to look like a palm leaf.

Turnovers These fruit-filled pastries resemble slippers and are also known as *chaussons* ("slippers" in French).

Sacristans These twisted puff creations are coated with almond or cinnamon sugar and look like corkscrews. Their ecclesiastical name derives from the use of a corkscrew to open wine for use in the celebration of church sacraments.

Pithiviers Named for the town of Pithiviers, about 50 miles south of Paris, this large, dome-shaped gateau is a puff-pastry structure filled with *frangipane* (almond cream). The top of the dome is scored with curved lines before baking. The finished product is meant to resemble the sun.

FIGURE 32-9

Puff pastry can be used to create a variety of dessert items.

Stretch Doughs

Three basic doughs make up this category of fine pastry: phyllo, strudel, and cannoli. All three are unleavened and stretched to a thinness that makes them crispy, light, and delicate. Phyllo and strudel doughs are paper-thin; cannoli dough is slightly thicker.

Phyllo Dough

Phyllo dough is a paper-thin pastry dough that, when layered and baked, produces a crisp, golden-brown crust of extraordinary flakiness. Although *phyllo* is a Greek word meaning "leaf," these leaflike sheets of pastry are thought to have originated in Turkey and then gained popularity throughout the Near East and eastern Mediterranean, particularly in Greece. Phyllo dough is the basis for both sweet pastries such as baklava (phyllo layered with nuts and coated with honey) and savory dishes such as spanakopita (phyllo triangles filled with feta cheese and spinach).

> **Phyllo dough will dry out in less than 3 minutes if left exposed to the air. When working with phyllo, keep it covered with a lightly moistened cloth. Wrap unused dough airtight, and refrigerate.**

Although puff-pastry dough may contain as much as 50% fat, phyllo dough contains only a small amount of vegetable oil to bind the dough and thus is virtually fat-free. It has gained in popularity as consumers look for lowfat alternatives to puff pastry. Products that use phyllo dough as a replacement for puff-pastry dough are lighter and flakier in texture and have little or no greasy aftertaste.

Baklava, perhaps the best-known pastry made from phyllo dough, features butter-coated layers of phyllo alternating with layers of nuts, usually walnuts and pistachios. The butter adds to the dough's flakiness, evaporating during baking and creating steam, which pushes the layers apart. After the pastry is baked, a hot rose-or citrus-scented honey syrup traditional in Middle Eastern and eastern Mediterranean cooking is poured over it. The pastry is left to rest overnight to allow the layers of phyllo and nuts to absorb the syrup. Shredded phyllo dough, known as *kataifi,* has many uses. It appears not only as the main ingredient of various

pastries but in the form of decorative cups and holders for plated dessert presentations.

Strudel

Strudel dough, which is stretched until it is paper-thin, is a version of the Turkish phyllo dough. It was brought to Austria by the Hungarians, who had learned to make it from the Turks. Pastry made from the paper-thin dough quickly became a popular menu item in Vienna's many coffeehouses. Today strudel, particularly apple strudel, is one of the most famous of all Austrian pastries.

Proper development is the key to making strudel dough. A strong flour, such as bread flour, is necessary. Vinegar included in the dough helps relax the gliadin, the component of gluten that provides elasticity. Allowing the dough to rest before stretching is also important. If properly made and rested, the dough will stretch over an entire pastry bench. Being able to read a newspaper through the stretched dough is the traditional test of thinness for strudel dough.

For added flavor and flakiness, phyllo and strudel dough are brushed with butter between layers to make baklava and strudel. After it has been filled, commonly with fruits, nuts, or cheese, it is rolled into a log, placed on a sheet pan, and brushed with butter. Vents are cut along its length to allow steam to escape as it bakes. A very hot oven (400°F–425°F/204°C–218°C) is necessary to ensure a crisp, golden brown crust and to prevent the filling from overcooking. Strudel is best served hot, sprinkled with confectioner's sugar.

Cannoli

The word *cannoli* means "pipes," which is an accurate description of the shape of this pastry. A favorite dessert originating in Sicily, *cannoli* are cylinders of sweet, crispy pastry with fillings that range from sweet ricotta cheese, sometimes laced with chocolate chips, to pastry cream with fruit and nuts. The pastry is stretched or rolled and wrapped around metal tubes and then deep-fried until crisp and golden brown. The pastry shells can be fried ahead of time. They should be stored tightly covered at room temperature and filled just before service.

Crêpes

The thin, delicate pancake known by the French term *crêpe* can be part of an elegant dessert. Preparing batter for crêpes several hours before it is needed allows the flour to absorb the liquid ingredients. Crêpes also may be cooked in advance and then frozen until needed. Make sure that the crêpes are tightly wrapped and that there is paper separating each individual layer to prevent them from sticking together. A crêpe pan, which is the size of an individual crêpe, is extremely useful.

There are many varieties of both savory and sweet crêpes. The following sweet crêpes are classic desserts:

Crêpes Suzette Flavored with oranges, sugar, and spices, these crêpes are flambéed with orange liqueur and cognac.

Crêpes Jacques These crêpes are filled with sautéed bananas and seasoned with butter and spices.

Crêpes Empire This dessert features crêpes filled with pineapple macerated in kirsch or cherry brandy.

Dessert Sauces

Sauces are an integral part of plated desserts. They add flavor and provide contrasts in texture, flavor, and color. Dessert sauces can range from the traditional crème anglaise, caramel sauce, chocolate sauce, and fruit coulis to reductions of liquors, juices, and poaching liquids.

Types of Sauces

The following basic sauces are often used for plating a dessert:

Coulis Fresh, canned, or frozen fruits may be used to make a *coulis.* The procedure is simple: purée fruit, and adjust the sauce's flavor with simple syrup. An acid in the form of lemon, orange, or lime juice can help increase the fruit's natural flavor. A coulis requires no cooking.

Cooked fruit sauce This sauce is a coulis that is reduced to thicken or alter its color or flavor. For the reduction, use a wide, shallow pan over low heat.

Thickened sauce The addition of a thickening agent such as cornstarch, arrowroot, or an instant starch creates this sauce's consistency. When a slurry is used, it should be cooked for 3 minutes to activate the cornstarch, decrease the starchy flavor, and regain the sauce's original vibrant color.

Crème anglaise *Crème anglaise* is a classic custard sauce made from egg yolks, milk, cream, and sugar. Flavor crème anglaise as desired with chocolate, liqueurs, extracts, nuts, or fruit compounds. Served hot or cold, crème anglaise is an accompaniment to pastries, cakes, soufflés, and fruit dishes. It also can be used to decorate dessert plates.

Sabayon This classic sauce of egg yolks, sugar, and Marsala wine is also known by its Italian name, *zabaglione.* Vigorously whisk the mixture over a water bath until it turns a

Caramelizing Sugar

Sugar that has been cooked to a caramel state can be used to line ramekins for crème caramel, as a base for caramel sauce, or to make an attractive garnish.

To caramelize sugar, follow these steps:

1 Combine sugar and water in a copper pan. Heat over medium to high heat and bring to a boil.

2
As the sugar cooks, crystals may form on the sides of the pan. Dissolve the crystals with a brush dipped in clean water.

3
Dip a spoon into the sugar to test the color.

4
Caramelized sugar should be a light amber color, at a temperature of approximately 320°F–325°F (160°C–163°C).

5
Once the sugar has cooled and the proper consistency is achieved, an attractive garnish can be made by dipping a hazelnut into the sugar and pulling it out. The excess will solidify, then be snipped with scissors to finish.

light lemon color and thickens. The sauce should be cooked to at least 145°F (63°C) to form a thick, fluffy mixture. Sabayon serves as an accompaniment to fresh fruits. Classically, the sauce is spooned over a flat dish of fruit, which is then placed under a salamander until it is lightly caramelized.

Egg-yolk-based (curd) sauces Made with egg yolks, sugar, and butter and usually flavored with citrus, these sauces are referred to as curds. They are tart yet sweet and generally thicker than other sauces.

Caramel sauce To make caramel sauce, combine caramelized sugar with heavy cream and butter. Citrus juice, liqueur, or fruit juices may be used to enhance flavor.

Chocolate sauce There are several types of chocolate sauce. Custard-based sauce uses a crème anglaise flavored with chocolate. Syrup- or ganache-based sauce follows the procedure for ganache, though often uses a sugar syrup instead of heavy cream. Cocoa-based sauce can be made by combining a paste of cocoa and water and cooking it with sugar over low heat until it boils.

Preserve-based sauces These sauces combine sugar syrup and a preserve. The best-known preserve-based sauce is Melba sauce. Melba sauce is made from raspberries and was invented to accompany the classic ice-cream dessert, peach Melba.

Reductions Almost any sauce can be reduced to thicken it. This sauce category, however, generally encompasses reductions of juices or sweet wines.

Guidelines for Sauce Presentation

A sauce's consistency and appearance are often critical to the success of the design of a plated dessert. Most sauces should be smooth in texture and thick enough to coat the back of a spoon. When used on plated desserts, sauces should be thick enough to hold a line when dispensed through a sauce bottle. Multiple sauces that are "married" for feathering into a design should be of the same consistency; a heavy sauce will sink into a thin sauce and ruin the design. Similar consistencies will also prevent one sauce from bleeding into another.

There are many techniques for using sauces to create visual appeal. Painting a plate with sauces introduces color and creates flow.

Making Crème Anglaise

Take care not to boil the final mixture, or it will curdle. The final product should be smooth and thick.

To make crème anglaise, follow these steps:

1 Put milk, heavy cream, half the granulated sugar, vanilla beans, and salt in a pot, and bring to a boil.

2 Whip egg yolks slightly with the remaining granulated sugar.

3 Temper the egg yolks with boiling milk.

4 Add the tempered mixture to the hot milk.

5 Cook the mixture to 185°F (85°C), stirring constantly. Never let the temperature go above 190°F (88°C). The mixture should coat the back of a spoon.

6 Strain the mixture into a container set in an ice bath. Cool, stirring constantly.

Pâte à Choux

INGREDIENTS

Ingredient	U.S. Standard	Metric
Flour, bread	1 lb.	454 g
Salt	1/4 oz.	8 g
Water	24 oz.	720 ml
Oil, vegetable	12 oz.	360 ml
Eggs, whole	1 lb., 8 oz.	680 g
Egg whites	6 oz.	170 g

METHOD OF PREPARATION

1. Gather all the ingredients and equipment.
2. Preheat oven to 425°F (218°C).
3. Sift the bread flour and salt, and set aside.
4. Place water and oil in a heavy-bottomed pan, and bring to a boil.
5. Add the flour mixture all at once.
6. Stirring with a wooden spoon, cook the roux 3–5 minutes. Stir constantly, until the mixture forms a ball that does not stick to the inside of the pot.
7. Remove from heat, and place mixture into a mixing bowl with paddle attachment. Cool mixture on low speed 2–3 minutes.
8. Combine whole eggs and whites.
9. Add eggs gradually, making sure that each egg is fully incorporated before the next addition.
10. Pipe into the desired shapes on a parchment-lined sheet pan.
11. Bake for 15 minutes at 425°F (218°C). Then reduce heat to 400°F (204°C) until golden brown and dry in appearance.

Chef's Notes

Product variations include éclairs, profiteroles, swans, Paris-Brest, gateau Saint Honoré, and beignets soufflé.

NUTRITION

Nutrition Facts

Yield: 5 lbs., 2 1/4 oz. (2332 g)
Serving Size: 6 oz. (170 g)

Amount Per Serving

Calories 290

Total Fat 21 g

Sodium 200 mg

Total Carbohydrate 17 g

Protein 8 g

Crème Brûlée

INGREDIENTS

	U.S. Standard	Metric
Egg yolks	6 oz.	170 g
Sugar, granulated	2 oz.	55 g
Vanilla extract		
(or vanilla bean, 1 each)	TT	TT
Cream, heavy	16 oz.	500 ml
Sugar, granulated	as needed	as needed

METHOD OF PREPARATION

1. Gather all the ingredients and equipment.
2. Scale ingredients.
3. Whisk the egg yolks and sugar together.
4. Add the vanilla extract or vanilla bean.
5. Add the heavy cream.
6. Stir until everything is completely incorporated.
7. Strain the mixture through a *chinoise mousseline,* and remove any foam on top.
8. Place custard molds or ramekins on a sheet pan or in a hotel pan.
9. Fill custard molds or ramekins with mixture to the top.
10. Fill the pan with water.
11. Bake at 325°F (163°C) until firm to the touch.
12. Refrigerate until thoroughly chilled.
13. When the custard is ready to be served, sprinkle the top with some granulated sugar.
14. Using a salamander, broiler, or a propane torch, caramelize the sugar until light golden brown.
15. Serve immediately.

Nutrition Facts

Yield: 1 1/2 lbs. (680 g)
Serving Size: 1 oz. (28 g)

Amount Per Serving
Calories 100
Total Fat 9 g
Sodium 10 mg
Total Carbohydrate 4 g
Protein 2 g

Strudel

INGREDIENTS

INGREDIENTS	U.S. Standard	Metric
Dough		
Flour, bread	2 lbs., 8 oz.	1135 g
Oil	8 oz.	240 ml
Salt	1 1/2 oz.	40 g
Eggs, whole	8 oz.	225 g
Vinegar, white	1 tsp.	5 ml
Water, lukewarm	14 oz.	420 ml
For rolling out dough/filling		
Flour, bread	as needed	as needed
Butter, melted	as needed	as needed
Cake crumbs	4 oz.	115 g
Confectionary sugar	as needed	as needed

METHOD OF PREPARATION

1. Gather all the ingredients and equipment.
2. Scale ingredients.

Preparation of dough:

3. Place the bread flour, oil, salt, eggs, vinegar, and water in a bowl with a dough hook.
4. Mix on medium speed for 8–10 minutes, or until gluten is fully developed.
5. Remove dough from the mixer, and brush the top with oil.
6. Place in a bowl, and cover with plastic wrap.
7. Place bowl in a warm place at 70°F (21°C) for approximately 1 hour.

Preparation of rolling strudel:

8. Cover the bench with a *pastry cloth,* and dust lightly with flour.
9. Have the melted butter, cake crumbs, and rested dough ready.
10. Roll the dough into a rectangle about 2 ft. (60 cm) long.
11. Lightly dust the back of your hands with flour, and pull out the edges.
12. Pull out the dough uniformly by stretching the opposite corners. Avoid thin areas to prevent tearing the dough.
13. Continue to pull the dough until it covers the bench.
14. Trim off any excess dough with a pastry wheel, and discard scraps.
15. Lightly brush the dough with melted butter.
16. Sprinkle the cake crumbs along the length of one side of the dough.
17. Place the strudel filling on top of the crumbs.
18. Roll up the dough away from you, using the pastry cloth to support and guide the dough.
19. Transfer the strudel to a sheet pan by using the cloth as a guide.
20. With a pastry brush, brush the top of the strudel with melted butter.
21. Cut vents along the top of the strudel to allow steam to escape.
22. Bake at 400°F (204°C) for 20 minutes, or until the strudel is golden brown and its sides are dry and firm to the touch.
23. Serve fresh and warm, dusted with confectionary sugar.

GLOSSARY

Pastry cloth: a large, lightweight canvas cloth on which pastry dough can be rolled out

NUTRITION

Nutrition Facts

Yield: 4 lbs., 8 oz. (2045 g)
Serving Size: 1 oz. (28 g)

Amount Per Serving

Calories 90

Total Fat 3.5 g

Sodium 230 mg

Total Carbohydrate 12 g

Protein 2 g

Tarte Tatin

INGREDIENTS

	U.S. Standard	Metric
Apples, Granny Smith	2–3 each	2–3 each
Butter, unsalted, softened	1 oz.	28 g
Sugar, granulated	2 oz.	55 g
Puff pastry, 8″ (20 cm) circle, 1/4″ (6 mm) thick	1 each	1 each

METHOD OF PREPARATION

1. Gather all the ingredients and equipment.

2. Scale ingredients.

3. Preheat the oven to 425°F (218°C).

4. Peel, core, and cut the apples into quarters.

5. In an 8″ (20 cm) Teflon®-coated sauté pan, spread the softened butter on the bottom.

6. Sprinkle the granulated sugar over the softened butter.

7. Place each apple quarter on its side in the pan, the thinner portion of the apple being placed towards the center of pan.

8. Place the pan over medium heat, and cook the sugar, butter, and apples until the sugar begins to caramelize and the apples begin to soften.

9. When the sugar has caramelized, remove the pan from the heat, and lay the puff pastry circle over the top of the apples.

10. Turn the oven temperature to 400°F (204°C). Immediately place the pan into the oven, and bake for approximately 15–20 minutes; remove from the oven when the puff pastry is baked completely.

11. After removing the tart from the oven, invert it immediately onto a preheated serving plate.

Chef's Notes

Pears and mangos are great substitutes for the apples.

NUTRITION

Nutrition Facts

Yield: one 8″ (20 cm) tart
Serving Size: 1 8″ (20 cm) tart (510 g)

Amount Per Serving

Calories 850

Total Fat 38 g

Sodium 105 mg

Total Carbohydrate 130 g

Protein 3 g

Pastry Cream

INGREDIENTS

Ingredients	U.S. Standard	Metric
Milk, whole	16 oz.	500 ml
Sugar, granulated	4 oz.	115 g
Salt	pinch	pinch
Cornstarch	1 1/2 oz.	40 g
Flour, cake	1/4 oz.	8 g
Egg yolks	2 oz.	55 g
Eggs, whole	1 oz.	28 g
Vanilla extract	TT	TT
Butter, unsalted	1 oz.	28 g

METHOD OF PREPARATION

1. Gather all the ingredients and equipment.
2. Scale ingredients.
3. Place three quarters of the milk, half of the granulated sugar, and the salt in a pot; bring to a boil.
4. Place the cornstarch, the remaining granulated sugar, and flour in a bowl; slowly add the remaining milk, and whisk together well.
5. Add the egg yolks and whole eggs to the cornstarch mixture; combine well.
6. *Temper* the cornstarch mixture, and add to the boiling milk.
7. Bring the mixture back to a second boil, stirring constantly; cook for 3 minutes.
8. Remove from the heat; stir in the vanilla extract and butter.
9. Whisk well.
10. Cool properly, and refrigerate.

Chef's Notes
- Place buttered parchment paper on top of cream to avoid forming a hard skin on top.
- Store at 41°F (5°C) or lower.
- Keep for a maximum of two days only.

PASTRY TECHNIQUES

Tempering:
1. Whisk the eggs vigorously while ladling hot liquid into them.

GLOSSARY

Temper: to equalize products with two extreme temperatures or textures

NUTRITION

Nutrition Facts
Yield: 1 lb., 9 3/4 oz. (732 g)
Serving Size: 1 oz. (28 g)

Amount Per Serving

Calories 50

Total Fat 2.5 g

Sodium 15 mg

Total Carbohydrate 7 g

Protein 1 g

Bavarian Cream

INGREDIENTS

INGREDIENTS	U.S. Standard	Metric
Gelatin sheets	5 sheets	5 sheets
(or powdered gelatin)	1/2 oz.	15 g
Cream, heavy	16 oz.	500 ml
Milk, whole	16 oz.	500 ml
Sugar, granulated	4 oz.	115 g
Egg yolks	5 oz.	140 g
Vanilla extract	TT	TT
Flavorings	TT	TT

METHOD OF PREPARATION

1. Gather all the ingredients and equipment.
2. Scale ingredients.
3. Bloom the gelatin in cold water, and set aside.
4. Whip the cream to a medium peak, and place in refrigerator.
5. Scald the milk and sugar in a pot.
6. Temper the egg yolks with the hot milk mixture, stirring constantly.
7. Return to stove, and heat until the mixture reaches nappé.
8. Strain the hot mixture through a chinoise mousseline on top of the bloomed gelatin.
9. Stir until the gelatin is completely dissolved.
10. Cool immediately over an ice bath; stir frequently to prevent the gelatin from setting up.
11. When the mixture is cool and begins to thicken, fold in the whipped cream and vanilla extract and flavorings if desired.
12. Immediately pour into desired forms or molds.
13. Refrigerate or freeze the molds immediately.

Chef's Notes

Numerous different flavorings can be added such as liqueurs, extracts, compounds, and purées.

PASTRY TECHNIQUES

Blooming:
Gelatin sheets or leaves:
1. Fan the sheets out.
2. Cover the sheets in liquid.
3. Sheets are bloomed when softened.

Granular gelatin:
1. Sprinkle the gelatin.
2. Gelatin is ready when it has the consistency of cream of wheat.

Whipping:
1. Hold the whip at a 55° angle.
2. Stir vigorously, using a circular motion perpendicular to the bowl.

Folding:
Perform steps 1, 2, and 3 in one continuous motion.
1. Run a bowl scraper under the mixture, across the bottom of the bowl.
2. Turn the bowl counterclockwise.
3. Bring the bottom mixture to the top.

Scalding:
1. Heat the liquid on high heat.
2. Do not boil the liquid.

Tempering:
1. Whisk the eggs vigorously while ladling hot liquid into them.

NUTRITION

Nutrition Facts
Yield: 2 lbs., 9 oz. (1165 g)
Serving Size: 1 oz. (28 g)

Amount Per Serving

Calories 70

Total Fat 6 g

Sodium 10 mg

Total Carbohydrate 4 g

Protein 1 g

Desserts

Chocolate Mousse

Ingredients

Ingredients	U.S. Standard	Metric
Cream, heavy	8 oz.	240 ml
Semi-sweet couverture or bittersweet	6 oz.	170 g
Egg yolks, pasteurized	2 oz.	55 g
Egg whites, pasteurized	2 1/2 oz.	75 g
Liqueur (optional)	1 oz.	28 g

Method of Preparation

1. Gather all the ingredients and equipment.
2. Scale ingredients.
3. Whip the heavy cream to a medium peak, and hold in the refrigerator.
4. Finely chop the chocolate, and melt over double boiler.
5. Fold the egg yolks into the chocolate.
6. Fold in the liqueur.
7. In a clean dry bowl whip the egg whites to a wet-medium peak.
8. Fold the whipped cream into the chocolate mixture in two stages; do not overfold.
9. Fold the whipped egg whites into the chocolate mixture; be careful not to overfold.
10. Pipe into the desired forms or glasses, and either let set in the refrigerator or freeze until set.

Chef's Notes

If using fresh egg yolks, the egg yolks must be heated over a double boiler with 4 oz. (115 g) of sugar, whipping constantly to prevent overheating. The egg yolks must reach 145°F (63°C).

PASTRY TECHNIQUES

Whipping:
1. Hold the whip at a 55° angle.
2. Stir vigorously, using a circular motion perpendicular to the bowl.

Melting:
1. Prepare the food product to be melted.
2. Place the food product in an appropriately sized pot over direct heat or over a double boiler.
3. Stir frequently or occasionally, depending on the delicacy of the product, until melted.

OR

1. Place the product on a sheet pan or in a bowl, and place in a low-temperature oven until melted.

Folding:
Perform steps 1, 2, and 3 in one continuous motion.
1. Run a bowl scraper under the mixture, across the bottom of the bowl.
2. Turn the bowl counterclockwise.
3. Bring the bottom mixture to the top.

NUTRITION

Nutrition Facts
Yield: 1 lb., 3 1/2 oz. (554 g)
Serving Size: 1 oz. (28 g)

Amount Per Serving	
Calories 100	
Total Fat 9 g	
Sodium 15 mg	
Total Carbohydrate 5 g	
Protein 2 g	

Fruit Mousse

INGREDIENTS

	U.S. Standard	Metric
Gelatin sheets	2 1/2 each	2 1/2 each
(or powdered gelatin)	1/4 oz.	8 g
Cream, heavy	16 oz.	500 ml
Sugar, powdered	2 oz.	55 g
Fruit purée	10 oz.	285 g

METHOD OF PREPARATION

1. Gather all the ingredients and equipment.
2. Scale ingredients.
3. Bloom the gelatin sheets or powdered gelatin.
4. Whip the heavy cream and powdered sugar to soft peaks, and refrigerate.
5. Dissolve the bloomed gelatin over a double boiler.
6. Add the fruit purée to the gelatin.
7. Let the mixture cool, but do not let it become firm.
8. Fold the whipped cream into the purée mixture.
9. Allow the mixture to set slightly and then pipe into a *ramekin,* glasses, or *flexipan.*

PASTRY TECHNIQUES

Blooming:
Gelatin sheets or leaves:
1. Fan the sheets out.
2. Cover the sheets in liquid.
3. Sheets are bloomed when softened.

Granular gelatin:
1. Sprinkle the gelatin.
2. Gelatin is ready when it has the consistency of cream of wheat.

Whipping:
1. Hold the whip at a 55° angle.
2. Stir vigorously, using a circular motion perpendicular to the bowl.

Folding:
Perform steps 1, 2, and 3 in one continuous motion.
1. Run a bowl scraper under the mixture, across the bottom of the bowl.
2. Turn the bowl counterclockwise.
3. Bring the bottom mixture to the top.

GLOSSARY

Ramekin: a single serving dish

Flexipan: silicone sheet that can be molded to hold mousse

NUTRITION

Nutrition Facts
Yield: 1 lb., 12 oz. (795 g)
Serving Size: 1 oz. (28 g)

Amount Per Serving

Calories 70

Total Fat 6 g

Sodium 10 mg

Total Carbohydrate 4 g

Protein 1 g

Crème Anglaise (Vanilla Sauce)

INGREDIENTS

	U.S. Standard	Metric
Milk, whole	8 oz.	240 ml
Cream, heavy	8 oz.	240 ml
Sugar, granulated	4 oz.	115 g
Salt	pinch	pinch
Egg yolks	4 1/2 oz.	130 g
Vanilla extract (or vanilla bean)	TT	TT

METHOD OF PREPARATION

1. Gather all the ingredients and equipment.
2. Scale ingredients.
3. Place the milk, heavy cream, sugar, salt, and vanilla bean (if using) in a saucepan.
4. Scald the milk mixture.
5. Place the egg yolks in a bowl, and whip slightly.
6. Temper the hot milk mixture into the yolks, stirring constantly with a wooden spoon.
7. Return to the stove on moderate heat, and cook to 175°F (80°C) until the mixture coats the back of a wooden spoon (nappé).
8. When the mixture reaches nappé, remove it from the heat, strain, and put over an ice bath immediately.
9. Add vanilla extract, if using.
10. Refrigerate in a covered container.

Chef's Notes
- Vanilla sauce can be stored for only 2–3 days.
- To produce a thicker sauce, replace milk with heavy cream.

PASTRY TECHNIQUES

Scalding:
1. Heat the liquid on high heat.
2. Do not boil the liquid.

Tempering:
1. Whisk the eggs vigorously while ladling hot liquid into them.

GLOSSARY
Nappé: coated or to coat

NUTRITION

Nutrition Facts
Yield: 1 lb., 8 1/2 oz. (696 g)
Serving Size: 1 oz. (28 g)

Amount Per Serving

Calories 80

Total Fat 5 g

Sodium 15 mg

Total Carbohydrate 6 g

Protein 1 g

Fruit Coulis

INGREDIENTS

	U.S. Standard	Metric
Fruit, fresh or frozen	12 oz.	340 g
Simple syrup	3 oz.	85 g
Lemon juice	1/2 lemon	1/2 lemon
Sugar, granulated	as needed	as needed
Cornstarch or instant starch	as needed	as needed

METHOD OF PREPARATION

1. Gather all the ingredients and equipment.
2. Scale ingredients.
3. Prepare the fruit: clean and slice, or thaw as needed.
4. Simmer the fruit with simple syrup for approximately 5 minutes.
5. Add the lemon juice, and taste; adjust the acidity level as needed.
6. Add more granulated sugar if needed.
7. Purée the mixture, and strain, if necessary, to remove any seeds and skins.
8. Thicken with a cornstarch slurry or instant starch, if desired.
9. Store in refrigerator in a covered container.

GLOSSARY
Instant starch: starch that is pre-cooked and therefore requires no heating to enable it to absorb water and gelatinize

Cornstarch slurry: the act of adding water to cornstarch, before it is used, whipping it to eliminate any lumps

NUTRITION

Nutrition Facts
Yield: 15 oz. (430 g)
Serving Size: 1 oz. (28 g)

Amount Per Serving

Calories 40

Total Fat 0 g

Sodium 0 mg

Total Carbohydrate 10 g

Protein 0 g

Chocolate Sauce (Chocolate Base)

INGREDIENTS

	U.S. Standard	Metric
Semi-sweet couverture or bittersweet	8 oz.	225 g
Cream, heavy	8 oz.	240 ml

METHOD OF PREPARATION

1. Gather all the ingredients and equipment.
2. Scale ingredients.
3. Finely chop the chocolate, and set aside in a bowl.
4. Scald the cream.
5. Add the chopped chocolate all at once to the scalded cream in the pot.
6. Whisk until smooth.
7. Transfer to a covered container, and refrigerate.

Chef's Notes
- The sauce will need to be reheated before use. This can be done in a microwave or on a double boiler.
- The hot pot helps melt the chocolate.

PASTRY TECHNIQUES
Scalding:
1. Heat the liquid on high heat.
2. Do not boil the liquid.

NUTRITION

Nutrition Facts

Yield: 1 lb. (454 g)
Serving Size: 1 oz. (28 g)

Amount Per Serving

Calories 120

Total Fat 10 g

Sodium 5 mg

Total Carbohydrate 8 g

Protein 1 g

Chocolate Sauce (Cocoa Powder Base)

INGREDIENTS

	U.S. Standard	Metric
Cocoa powder	4 oz.	115 g
Water	8 oz.	240 ml
Sugar, granulated	8 oz.	225 g
Semi-sweet couverture or bittersweet, finely chopped	2 oz.	55 g

METHOD OF PREPARATION

1. Gather all the ingredients and equipment.
2. Scale ingredients.
3. Whisk together cocoa powder, water, and granulated sugar in a saucepan.
4. Bring to a boil.
5. Add chopped chocolate, and continue to whisk until the chocolate is melted.
6. Strain through a *chinoise mousseline*.
7. Refrigerate in a covered container.

Chef's Notes
- Sauce will thicken slightly as it cools.
- Sauce will need to be reheated slightly before used.

GLOSSARY
Couverture: term describing professional quality coating, creating chocolate that is extremely glossy

Chinoise mousseline: fine-mesh cone strainer

NUTRITION

Nutrition Facts

Yield: 1 lb., 6 oz. (625 g)
Serving Size: 1 oz. (28 g)

Amount Per Serving

Calories 60

Total Fat 1.5 g

Sodium 0 mg

Total Carbohydrate 15 g

Protein 1 g

Caramel Sauce

INGREDIENTS

	U.S. Standard	Metric
Sugar, granulated	12 oz.	340 g
Water	as needed	as needed
Butter, unsalted	2 oz.	55 g
Cream, heavy	7 oz.	210 ml

METHOD OF PREPARATION

1. Gather all the ingredients and equipment.

2. Scale ingredients.

3. Place sugar in a saucepan, and add just enough water to make the mixture look gritty.

4. Wipe down the sides of the saucepan with a wet paper towel or brush.

5. Place on high heat until the water evaporates and the sugar starts to caramelize.

6. Keep the sides of the saucepan clean by wiping down with a wet paper towel or brush. Do not stir.

7. When the desired color is reached, take the saucepan off the heat, and stir in the butter and heavy cream.

8. Store in the refrigerator in a covered container.

Chef's Notes

- Be careful when cooking sugar because there will be a tremendous amount of carryover heat.
- To clean the saucepan, simply fill with water and bring to a boil.
- The sauce will thicken in the refrigerator. It will need to be reheated before use.

NUTRITION

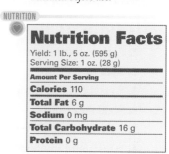

Nutrition Facts

Yield: 1 lb., 5 oz. (595 g)
Serving Size: 1 oz. (28 g)

Amount Per Serving

Calories 110

Total Fat 6 g

Sodium 0 mg

Total Carbohydrate 16 g

Protein 0 g

American Ice Cream

INGREDIENTS

	U.S. Standard	Metric
Cream, heavy	10 1/2 oz.	315 ml
Milk, whole	21 oz.	630 ml
Sugar, granulated	10 1/2 oz.	300 g
Vanilla extract	TT	TT
Salt	pinch	pinch

METHOD OF PREPARATION

1. Gather all the ingredients and equipment.

2. Scale ingredients.

3. Place heavy cream, milk, sugar, vanilla extract, and salt in a sauce pot, and heat to 180°F (82°C).

4. Strain through a *chinoise mousseline.*

5. Cool immediately over an ice bath, stirring occasionally.

6. Freeze in an ice cream machine according to the machine's directions.

7. Serve immediately, or store in a covered container in the freezer.

GLOSSARY

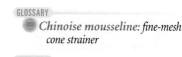

Chinoise mousseline: fine-mesh cone strainer

NUTRITION

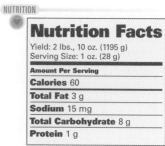

Nutrition Facts

Yield: 2 lbs., 10 oz. (1195 g)
Serving Size: 1 oz. (28 g)

Amount Per Serving

Calories 60

Total Fat 3 g

Sodium 15 mg

Total Carbohydrate 8 g

Protein 1 g

French Vanilla Ice Cream

INGREDIENTS	U.S. Standard	Metric
Milk, whole	16 oz.	500 ml
Cream, heavy	16 oz.	500 ml
Salt	pinch	pinch
Sugar, granulated	9 oz.	255 g
Vanilla extract	1/2 oz.	15 g
(or vanilla bean)	1/2 each	1/2 each
Egg yolks, pasteurized	8 oz.	225 g

METHOD OF PREPARATION

1. Gather all the ingredients and equipment.
2. Scale ingredients.
3. Place the milk, heavy cream, salt, granulated sugar, and vanilla extract or bean (if desired), in a saucepan, and bring to a scald.
4. Temper the hot milk mixture into the egg yolks.
5. Return to the stove, and bring to a nappé, stirring constantly.
6. Strain through *chinoise mousseline.*
7. Cool immediately over an ice bath, stirring occasionally.
8. Freeze in an ice cream machine according to the machine's directions.
9. Serve immediately, or store in a covered container in the freezer.

PASTRY TECHNIQUES

Scalding:
1. Heat the liquid on high heat.
2. Do not boil the liquid.

Tempering:
1. Whisk the eggs vigorously while ladling hot liquid into them.

GLOSSARY
Chinoise mousseline: fine-mesh cone strainer

NUTRITION

Nutrition Facts
Yield: 3 lbs., 1 1/2 oz. (1405 g)
Serving Size: 1 oz. (28 g)

Amount Per Serving

Calories 70

Total Fat 5 g

Sodium 15 mg

Total Carbohydrate 6 g

Protein 1 g

Fruit Sorbet

INGREDIENTS	U.S. Standard	Metric
Simple syrup	16 oz.	500 ml
Lemon zest	1/4 each	1/4 each
Lemon juice	1/2 oz.	15 g
Fruit purée	1 lb.	454 g

METHOD OF PREPARATION

1. Gather all the ingredients and equipment.
2. Scale ingredients.
3. Place simple syrup in a pot, and simmer. When it measures between 20–28 on the *Baumé* unit of a hydrometer, remove from heat and cool.
4. Add lemon zest, juice, and fruit purée to the simple syrup mixture.
5. Strain.
6. Freeze in an ice cream machine according to the machine's directions.
7. Serve immediately, or store in a covered container in freezer.
8. Refreeze leftover sorbet daily.

PASTRY TECHNIQUES

Freezing
1. Prepare the product.
2. Place the product in the freezing cabinet for the appropriate length of time.

GLOSSARY
Baumé scale: a scale used to measure the specific gravity of liquids

NUTRITION

Nutrition Facts
Yield: 2 lbs. (910 g)
Serving Size: 1 oz. (28 g)

Amount Per Serving

Calories 50

Total Fat 0 g

Sodium 15 mg

Total Carbohydrate 14 g

Protein 0 g

Lemon Sorbet

INGREDIENTS	U.S. Standard	Metric
Sugar, granulated	1 lb.	454 g
Water	26 1/2 oz.	795 ml
Lemon juice, fresh	5 oz.	140 g
Salt	pinch	pinch
Lemon, zest	1 1/2 each	1 1/2 each
Egg whites, pasteurized	2 oz.	55 g

METHOD OF PREPARATION

1. Gather all the ingredients and equipment.
2. Scale ingredients.
3. Place granulated sugar, water, lemon juice, salt, and lemon zest in a bowl, and whisk together.
4. Add the egg whites.
5. Whisk until well combined.
6. Freeze in an ice cream machine according to the manufacturer's directions.
7. Store in a covered container in the freezer.

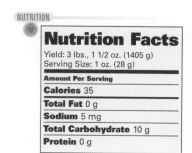
Tulip, Tuile, or Cigarette Paste

INGREDIENTS	U.S. Standard	Metric
Sugar, powdered	12 oz.	340 g
Butter, unsalted	7 oz.	205 g
Flour, bread	10 oz.	285 g
Egg whites	7 oz.	205 g

METHOD OF PREPARATION

1. Gather all the ingredients and equipment.
2. Scale ingredients.
3. Sift the powdered sugar.
4. With a paddle, cream together butter, powdered sugar, and bread flour on low speed until mixture resembles cornmeal.
5. Add the egg whites slowly in two stages on second speed, mixing well after each addition.
6. Scrape the bowl.
7. Mix for an additional minute, or until blended.
8. Store in the refrigerator in a covered container.

Baking:

9. Butter a sheet pan and freeze until butter is firm, or use a *silpat*.
10. Place stencil on sheet pan or silpat, and spread the batter evenly over the stencil.
11. Bake at 350°F (177°C) for 5 minutes, or until very light brown around the edges.
12. Remove from the pan immediately; mold into desired shape while hot.

Chef's Notes

- *Batter could be piped onto a sheet pan or silpat and then baked.*
- *For best results, allow the batter to return to room temperature before using.*
- *Batter can be flavored with extract, cocoa powder, and spices.*
- *Batter can also be colored with food colorings.*
- *After cookies are made, store in an airtight container.*
- *It is best to serve cookies the same day that they are made.*

GLOSSARY

Silpat: a silicone baking sheet that will not stick to the sheet pan

Short Dough/1-2-3 Cookie Dough

INGREDIENTS

INGREDIENTS	U.S. Standard	Metric
Sugar, granulated	1 lb.	454 g
Butter, unsalted, room temperature	2 lbs.	910 g
Eggs, whole	6 oz.	170 g
Flour, cake or pastry	3 lbs.	1365 g

METHOD OF PREPARATION

1. Gather all the ingredients and equipment.

2. Scale ingredients.

3. Place the sugar and butter in a bowl; cream well on second speed.

4. Scrape the bowl, and continue to cream.

5. Add the eggs in three stages, and blend well after each addition.

6. Add the flour in 2 or 3 stages, and mix on lowest speed until well blended.

7. Chill the dough before using.

Chef's Notes
- For best results, have the butter at room temperature.
- Chill dough thoroughly to relax the gluten and for ease of handling
- Uses for short dough: tart/tartlette shells; sugar cookies; petit four sec.
- Nuts or spiced or dried fruit, can be added.
- For cookies, bake at 350°F (177°C).
- For blind baking, set at 400°F (204°C).

GLOSSARY
Blind baking: to bake a pastry shell before it is filled

NUTRITION

Nutrition Facts

Yield: 6 lbs., 6 oz. (2892 g)
Serving Size: 1 oz. (28 g)

Amount Per Serving

Calories 130

Total Fat 7 g

Sodium 0 mg

Total Carbohydrate 15 g

Protein 1 g

Apple Strudel Filling

INGREDIENTS

INGREDIENTS	U.S. Standard	Metric
Apples, Granny Smith	1 lb., 8 oz.	680 g
Cinnamon, ground	1/4 oz.	8 g
Sugar, granulated	4 oz.	115 g
Raisins, seedless (dark or golden)	3 oz.	85 g
Walnuts, chopped, toasted	3 oz.	85 g

METHOD OF PREPARATION

1. Gather all the ingredients and equipment.

2. Scale ingredients.

3. Peel, core, and slice the apples approximately 1/4″ (6 mm) thick.

4. In a bowl, combine the apples, cinnamon, sugar, raisins, and walnuts.

Chef's Notes
- Pears can be substituted for apples.
- Other nuts can be used in place of walnuts.
- Other dried fruits can be used in place of raisins.

NUTRITION

Nutrition Facts

Yield: 2 lbs., 2 oz. (970 g)
Serving Size: 1 oz. (28 g)

Amount Per Serving

Calories 50

Total Fat 1.5 g

Sodium 0 mg

Total Carbohydrate 9 g

Protein 1 g

Walnut Strudel Filling

INGREDIENTS

Ingredients	U.S. Standard	Metric
Walnuts, rough-chopped, toasted	1 lb.	454 g
Butter, unsalted	4 oz.	115 g
Sugar, granulated	6 oz.	170 g
Raisins, golden or dark	4 oz.	115 g
Lemon zest	1/4 each	1/4 each
Milk, whole	12 oz.	360 ml
Cake crumbs, dry	4 oz.	115 g
Brandy	1 1/2 oz.	45 ml

METHOD OF PREPARATION

1. Gather all the ingredients and equipment.

2. Scale ingredients.

3. Place the walnuts, butter, granulated sugar, raisins, lemon zest, and milk in a pot.

4. Bring to a boil.

5. Reduce the heat, and simmer until two-thirds of the liquid is evaporated.

6. Remove from the heat, and then add the cake crumbs and brandy. Stir to incorporate well.

7. Cool and store in the refrigerator until ready to use.

Chef's Notes

• Any nut or combination of nuts can be substituted for the walnuts.

• For best flavor, nuts should be lightly toasted.

• Other dried fruit can replace the raisins.

NUTRITION

Nutrition Facts

Yield: 2 lbs., 15 1/2 oz. (1347 g)
Serving Size: 1 oz. (28 g)

Amount Per Serving

Calories 110

Total Fat 9 g

Sodium 0 mg

Total Carbohydrate 8 g

Protein 2 g

Chocolate Molten Cake

INGREDIENTS

INGREDIENTS	U.S. Standard	Metric
Butter, *unsalted*	as needed	as needed
Sugar, *granulated*	as needed	as needed
Semi-sweet couverture	12 oz.	340 g
Butter, *unsalted*	12 oz.	340 g
Eggs, *whole, slightly beaten*	12 oz.	340 g
Sugar, *granulated*	3 oz.	85 g
Flour, *bread*	3 oz.	85 g
Truffles	as needed	as needed

METHOD OF PREPARATION

1. Gather all the ingredients and equipment.
2. Scale ingredients.
3. Butter the ramekins, and sprinkle with granulated sugar, knocking out any excess sugar.
4. Chop the chocolate into fine pieces.
5. Cut butter into chunks, and place in pot.
6. Melt butter, add chopped chocolate, and then whisk until melted.
7. Take off the heat as soon as both the chocolate and butter are completely melted.
8. Lightly whisk eggs and sugar together.
9. Add the egg-sugar mixture to the chocolate-butter mixture, and stir until well incorporated.
10. Using a piano wire whisk, add the bread flour to the chocolate mixture.
11. Pour into buttered ramekins until they are about three-quarters filled, or pour into 4-oz. (115-g) aluminum tins.
12. Place in 350°F–400°F (177°C–204°C) oven.
13. After the sides of the cakes have set (approximately 10–12 minutes), take the cakes out of the oven, and add a truffle. Make sure that the truffle is completely submerged in the cake mixture at the center of the ramekin.
14. Return ramekins to the oven.
15. Bake for an additional 5 minutes, or until the center of the cake has begun to set up.
16. Remove from oven, invert onto plate, and serve immediately.

PASTRY TECHNIQUES

Melting:

1. Prepare the food product to be melted.
2. Place the food product in an appropriately sized pot over direct heat or over a double boiler.
3. Stir frequently or occasionally, depending on the delicacy of the product, until melted.

OR

1. Place the product on a sheet pan or in a bowl, and place in a low-temperature oven until melted.

NUTRITION

Nutrition Facts

Yield: 2 lbs., 10 oz. (1195 g)
Serving Size: 1 oz. (28 g)

Amount Per Serving

Calories 130

Total Fat 11 g

Sodium 10 mg

Total Carbohydrate 9 g

Protein 2 g

Gingerbread Cake with Lemon Glaze

INGREDIENTS	U.S. Standard	Metric
CAKE		
Pastry flour	7 oz.	205 g
Baking soda	1/8 oz. (1 1/4 tsp.)	6 ml
Ginger, ground	1/8 oz. (1 1/2 tsp.)	7 ml
Cinnamon, ground	1/16 oz. (3/4 tsp.)	3.75 ml
Salt	1/8 oz. (1 1/4 tsp.)	6 ml
Eggs, whole	2 oz.	55 g
Sugar, granulated	4 oz.	115 g
Molasses, dark	6 oz.	170 g
Oil, vegetable	4 oz.	115 g
Water, boiling	4 oz.	120 ml
LEMON GLAZE		
Sugar, powdered	3 oz.	85 g
Lemon juice	1 1/2 oz.	40 g

METHOD OF PREPARATION

1. Gather all the ingredients and equipment.
2. Scale ingredients.
3. Preheat oven to 350°F (177°C).
4. Grease and flour ramekins or muffin tins or cake pans.

Cake:

5. Sift together the pastry flour, baking soda, ginger, cinnamon, and salt in a large bowl.
6. Whisk the egg, granulated sugar, molasses, and oil together.
7. Whisk wet ingredients into dry ingredients, and mix thoroughly.
8. Pour the hot water over the mixture, and whisk thoroughly.
9. Half-fill each of the *ramekins* or muffin tins with batter.
10. Bake until the batter sets up and is firm to the touch.

Lemon glaze:

11. Whisk the powdered sugar and lemon juice together until completely smooth.
12. Using a pastry brush, brush the tops of the cake with the glaze while the cakes are still hot.

PASTRY TECHNIQUES

Baking:
1. Preheat the oven.
2. Position the item appropriately in the oven.
3. Check for appropriate firmness and/or color.

GLOSSARY

Ramekin: single-serving dish

NUTRITION

Nutrition Facts
Yield: 1 lb., 9 7/16 oz. (725 g)
Serving Size: 1 oz. (28 g)

Amount Per Serving

Calories 110

Total Fat 4.5 g

Sodium 190 mg

Total Carbohydrate 18 g

Protein 1 g

Milk Chocolate Truffles

INGREDIENTS	U.S. Standard	Metric
Milk chocolate couverture	2 lbs., 8 oz.	1135 g
Cream, heavy	16 oz.	500 ml
Flavorings (compounds	2 tsp.	10 ml
or liquor)	4 oz.	120 ml

METHOD OF PREPARATION

1. Gather all the ingredients and equipment.
2. Scale ingredients.
3. Chop the couverture into fine pieces, and place in a bowl.
4. Scald the heavy cream.
5. Pour the scalded cream over the chopped couverture.
6. Whisk until mixture is smooth and all lumps have been removed.
7. Add flavoring or liquor.
8. Pour mixture into a clean container, and place in refrigerator.
9. Allow mixture to cool until the consistency is like that of soft fudge.
10. Take out of the refrigerator, and scoop out of the containers with a melon baller or a small sorbet scoop.
11. Place on a tray.
12. After the mixture has been portioned, begin to roll into balls.
13. Garnish if desired.
14. Store in covered containers in a cool area.

Nutrition Facts

Yield: 3 lbs., 8 oz. (1590 g)
Serving Size: 1 oz. (28 g)

Amount Per Serving

Calories 130

Total Fat 9 g

Sodium 0 mg

Total Carbohydrate 14 g

Protein 2 g

White Chocolate Truffles

INGREDIENTS	U.S. Standard	Metric
White chocolate	3 lbs.	1365 g
Cream, heavy	16 oz.	500 ml
Flavorings (compounds	2 tsp.	10 ml
or liquor)	4 oz.	120 ml

METHOD OF PREPARATION

1. Gather all the ingredients and equipment.
2. Scale ingredients.
3. Chop the chocolate into fine pieces, and place in a bowl.
4. Scald the heavy cream.
5. Pour the scalded cream over the chopped chocolate.
6. Whisk until mixture is smooth and all lumps have been removed.
7. Add flavoring or liquor.
8. Pour mixture into a clean container, and place in refrigerator.
9. Allow to cool until the consistency is like that of soft fudge.
10. Take out of the refrigerator, and scoop out of the containers with a melon baller or a small sorbet scoop.
11. Place on a tray.
12. After the mixture has been portioned, begin to roll into balls.
13. Garnish if desired.
14. Store in covered containers in a cool area.

Dark Chocolate Truffles

INGREDIENTS	U.S. Standard	Metric
Dark couverture	2 lbs.	910 g
Cream, heavy	1 lb.	454 g
Flavorings (compounds	2 tsp.	10 ml
or liquor)	4 oz.	120 ml

METHOD OF PREPARATION

1. Gather all the ingredients and equipment.
2. Scale ingredients.
3. Chop the couverture into fine pieces, and place in a bowl.
4. Scald the heavy cream.
5. Pour the scalded cream over the chopped couverture.
6. Whisk until mixture is smooth and all lumps have been removed.
7. Add flavoring or liquor.
8. Pour mixture into a clean container, and place in refrigerator.
9. Allow to cool until the consistency is like that of soft fudge.
10. Take out of the refrigerator, and scoop out of the containers with a melon baller or a small sorbet scoop.
11. Place on a tray.
12. After the mixture has been portioned, begin to roll into balls.
13. Garnish if desired.
14. Store in a covered container in a cool area.

Poaching Liquid for Fruits

INGREDIENTS

INGREDIENTS	U.S. Standard	Metric
Wine, red or white	16 oz.	500 ml
Water	16 oz.	500 ml
Sugar, granulated	8 oz.	225 g
Spices, whole	TT	TT
Fruit, peeled and cored	as desired	as desired

METHOD OF PREPARATION

1. Gather all the ingredients and equipment.
2. Scale ingredients.
3. Place all ingredients in a pot, except the fruit.
4. Bring to a simmer at 180°F–185°F (82°C–85°C).
5. Place fruit in the liquid, and place a piece of parchment paper directly over the top of the liquid.
6. Fruit should be removed when a paring knife inserted into the fruit comes out easily.

NUTRITION

Nutrition Facts

Yield: 2 lbs., 8 oz. (1135 g)
Serving Size: 1 oz. (28 g)

Amount Per Serving

Calories 30

Total Fat 0 g

Sodium 0 mg

Total Carbohydrate 6 g

Protein 0 g

Simple Syrup

INGREDIENTS

INGREDIENTS	U.S. Standard	Metric
Sugar, granulated	1 lb.	454 g
Water	16 oz.	500 ml
Lemon, sliced	1/2 each	1/2 each

METHOD OF PREPARATION

1. Gather all the ingredients and equipment.
2. Scale ingredients.
3. Place the sugar and water in a saucepot, and bring to a boil.
4. Remove from the heat, and add the lemon slices.
5. Cool.
6. Store in the refrigerator in a covered container until needed.

NUTRITION

Nutrition Facts

Yield: 2 lbs. (910 g)
Serving Size: 1 oz. (28 g)

Amount Per Serving

Calories 60

Total Fat 0 g

Sodium 0 mg

Total Carbohydrate 14 g

Protein 0 g

Desserts

Basic Pie Dough

INGREDIENTS	U.S. Standard	Metric
Shortening, all-purpose	1 lb.	454 g
Flour, pastry	1 lb., 8 oz.	680 g
Water (ice cold)	8 oz.	240 ml
Sugar, granulated	2 oz.	55 g
Dry milk solids (DMS)	1 oz.	28 g
Salt	1/2 oz.	15 g

METHOD OF PREPARATION

1. Gather all the ingredients and equipment.

2. Chill shortening to 60°F (16°C).

3. Sift the pastry flour.

4. Add chilled shortening to flour. Cut or rub the shortening until the fat pieces are the size of a pea.

5. In cold water dissolve the sugar, DMS, and salt.

6. Add the water mixture to the flour and fat. Incorporate until all the flour is moistened. Do not overmix the dough.

7. Place dough on parchment-lined sheet pan dusted with flour.

8. Cover with plastic wrap, and refrigerate for 3 hours, preferably overnight.

Chef's Notes
- *Work as quickly as possible to keep dough chilled.*
- *To minimize dough scrap, scale first piece of dough at 8 oz. (225 g) for a 9" (23 cm) bottom and the second piece at 6 oz. (170 g) for the top.*

PASTRY TECHNIQUES

Mixing:
1. *Follow the proper mixing procedure: creaming, blending, whipping, or combination.*

NUTRITION

Nutrition Facts
Yield: 3 lbs., 3 1/2 oz. (1467 g)
(4 pie crusts)
Serving Size: 14 oz. (1 pie crust)
(400 g)

Amount Per Serving

Calories 1630

Total Fat 116 g

Sodium 1380 mg

Total Carbohydrate 139 g

Protein 23 g

Dutch Apple Pie

INGREDIENTS	U.S. Standard	Metric
Basic pie dough	*for one pie*	*for one pie*
FILLING		
Hard baking apples	*1 lb., 8 oz.*	*680 g*
Sugar, *granulated*	*4 oz.*	*115 g*
Cinnamon, *ground*	*1/4 oz.*	*8 g*
Salt	*1/4 oz.*	*8 g*
Flour, *cake*	*2 oz.*	*55 g*
Raisins	*4 oz.*	*115 g*
STREUSEL TOPPING		
Flour, *pastry*	*1 lb.*	*454 g*
Sugar, *granulated*	*5 oz.*	*140 g*
Butter, *unsalted, 60°F (16°C)*	*8 oz.*	*225 g*

METHOD OF PREPARATION

1. Gather all the ingredients and equipment.
2. Preheat oven to 375°F (191°C).
3. Prepare one 9″ (23 cm) unbaked pie shell.

Filling:

4. Peel and core the apples, and cut into 8 wedges each. Set aside.
5. Combine the sugar, cinnamon, salt, and cake flour.
6. Add the apples to the flour mixture, and dredge well.
7. Add the raisins.
8. Place the mixture into the pie shell.

Streusel topping:

9. Place all the dry ingredients into a stainless bowl.
10. Rub the cold butter into the flour mixture until fat pieces are about the size of peas.
11. Generously sprinkle the streusel topping over the pie.
12. Bake at 375°F (191°C) for 40–60 minutes.

Chef's Notes

4 oz. (115 g) of nuts or oatmeal may be added to streusel.

PASTRY TECHNIQUES

Baking:
1. Preheat the oven.
2. Position the item appropriately in the oven.
3. Check for appropriate firmness and/or color.

NUTRITION

Nutrition Facts

Yield: one 9″ (23 cm) pie,
3 lbs., 1/2 oz. (1809 g)
Serving Size: 8 oz. (225 g)

Amount Per Serving

Calories 500

Total Fat 21 g

Sodium 300 mg

Total Carbohydrate 77 g

Protein 7 g

Chocolate Cream Pie Filling

INGREDIENTS	U.S. Standard	Metric
Milk, whole	112 oz.	3.3 l
Cream, heavy	16 oz.	500 ml
Sugar, granulated	1 lb., 4 oz.	570 g
Salt	1/4 oz.	8 g
Cocoa powder	8 oz.	225 g
Cornstarch	10 oz.	285 g
Sugar, granulated	1 lb.	454 g
Milk, whole	32 oz.	960 ml
Eggs, whole	12 oz.	340 g
Vanilla extract	2 oz.	60 ml
Butter, unsalted	8 oz.	225 g

METHOD OF PREPARATION

1. Gather all the ingredients and equipment.

2. Place milk, cream, sugar, and salt into a heavy-bottomed saucepan. Bring to a boil.

3. In a bowl combine cocoa powder, cornstarch, and granulated sugar; whisk in cold milk.

4. Add the eggs to the slurry, and whisk well.

5. Temper hot milk and cream mixture with slurry and egg mixture.

6. Whisking constantly, continue cooking for 2–3 minutes.

7. Remove from the stove, and whisk in vanilla extract and butter.

To finish:

8. Place mixture into baked pie shell. Cover with plastic wrap directly on filling, and chill.

9. When chilled, cover with chantilly cream, and garnish with chocolate shavings.

PASTRY TECHNIQUES

Tempering:
1. Whisk the eggs vigorously while ladling hot liquid into them.

NUTRITION

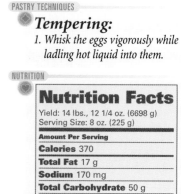

Nutrition Facts
Yield: 14 lbs., 12 1/4 oz. (6698 g)
Serving Size: 8 oz. (225 g)

Amount Per Serving
Calories 370
Total Fat 17 g
Sodium 170 mg
Total Carbohydrate 50 g
Protein 7 g

Chocolate Soufflé

INGREDIENTS	U.S. Standard	Metric
Butter, unsalted	as needed	as needed
Sugar, granulated	as needed	as needed
Semi-sweet couverture	8 oz.	225 g
Unsweetened chocolate	2 oz.	55 g
Egg yolks	5 oz.	140 g
Sugar, granulated	5 oz.	140 g
Salt	pinch	pinch
Cream, heavy	2 oz.	60 ml
Espresso, instant	1/4 oz.	8 g
Rum or brandy	1 1/2 oz.	45 ml
Egg whites	10 oz.	285 g

METHOD OF PREPARATION

1. Gather all the ingredients and equipment.

2. Scale ingredients.

3. Butter the soufflé dishes, and sprinkle with granulated sugar, knocking out any excess.

4. Set the dishes on a sheet pan and set aside.

5. Chop the chocolates very fine, and place in a bowl.

6. With a whisk, ribbon the egg yolks, sugar, and salt.

7. Melt both of the chocolates together, stirring occasionally over a double boiler.

8. Gently stir the melted chocolates into the egg yolk-sugar mixture.

9. Stir in the heavy cream, instant espresso, and liquor into the yolk-chocolate mixture.

10. Whip the egg whites to a medium peak by hand.

11. Carefully fold the egg whites into the chocolate mixture.

12. Immediately pour the batter into the prepared *soufflé dishes* until they are approximately three-fourths filled.

13. Bake in a deck oven at 400°F (204°C) for 30 minutes or until done.

14. Serve immediately.

Chef's Notes

- Be careful when opening and closing the doors during baking.
- Dust with powdered sugar or cocoa prior to serving.

PASTRY TECHNIQUES

Whipping:
1. Hold the whip at a 55° angle.
2. Stir vigorously, using a circular motion perpendicular to the bowl.

Melting:
1. Prepare the food product to be melted.
2. Place the food product in an appropriately sized pot over direct heat or over a double boiler.
3. Stir frequently or occasionally, depending on the delicacy of the product, until melted.

OR

1. Place the product on a sheet pan or in a bowl, and place in a low-temperature oven until melted.

Folding:
Perform steps 1, 2, and 3 in one continuous motion.
1. Run a bowl scraper under the mixture, across the bottom of the bowl.
2. Turn the bowl counterclockwise.
3. Bring the bottom mixture to the top.

Ribboning:
1. Use a high speed on the mixer.
2. Do not overwhip the egg yolks.

GLOSSARY

Couverture: professional quality coating, creating chocolate that is extremely glossy

Soufflé dish: round baking dish with straight sides

NUTRITION

Nutrition Facts
Yield: 2 lbs., 1 3/4 oz. (959 g)
Serving Size: 1 oz. (28 g)

Amount Per Serving

Calories 100

Total Fat 6 g

Sodium 20 mg

Total Carbohydrate 10 g

Protein 2 g

Service is a critical ingredient in a restaurant's recipe for success. Guests often have different expectations for service, depending on the kind of establishment they visit. Cleanliness, consistency, and friendly, competent service may bring customers back to fastfood restaurants, but guests' expectations for service are much higher for fine dining establishments. In addition to delicious food and elegant décor, guests expect the service to enhance a fine dining experience. It is the "added value" that guests expect from fine restaurants.

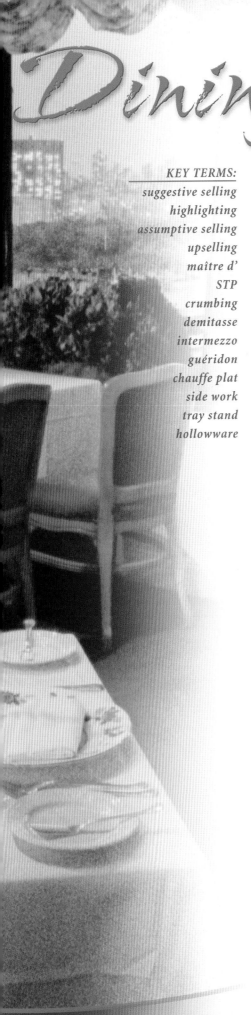

Dining Service

Quality Service

Although the components of service may seem intangible, poor service can drive away customers, even if the rest of the dining experience is excellent. For that reason, the entire staff needs to be aware of these service components:

Smiling

Eye contact with the guest

Reaching out with hospitality to every guest

Viewing every guest as special

Inviting guests to return

Creating a warm environment

Exceeding guests' expectations

Origin and History of Service

Restaurants are a relatively new development in the course of human history, but people have always had complex rules and forms of etiquette that govern how they eat.

Great civilizations of the past enjoyed elaborate banquets, and travelers have always had wayside stations where they could buy food and drink. An actual restaurant where anybody could go to enjoy a complete meal prepared and served by someone else, however, dates back only to 1765.

That was the year that A. Boulanger, a soup vendor, opened his business in Paris, offering only a "restorative," or "restaurant," of sheep's feet simmered in white wine. From this humble beginning grew the tradition of luxurious restaurants for which Paris is famous.

In the United States, Giovanni and Pietro Delmonico opened a café in New York City in 1827. Three years later, they opened the Restaurant Français in an adjacent building, becoming the first U.S. restaurateurs.

The Server

Quality service cannot be left to chance. It requires training that is refined through practice and experience. With this combination, a professional server becomes the restaurant's representative and salesperson as well as a skilled server.

Server as Representative

Because the server has more contact with the guest than any other restaurant employee, the server is the restaurant's ambassador. He or she sets the mood in the dining room, making guests feel welcome, relaxed, and secure in the knowledge that their needs will be met. Courtesy, friendliness, and superior interpersonal skills are the hallmark of server-ambassadors.

Server as Salesperson

A successful ambassador for the restaurant is a skilled salesperson. A skilled server helps guests have a satisfying dining experience by explaining menu options, describing any specials in detail, suggesting wines or other beverages to complement the food, and helping tailor choices to diners' needs.

Successful selling involves not only making guests feel pampered but also increasing revenues both for the restaurant and the server. Effective servers encourage guests to add to their original orders by guiding them to new, unusual, or premium items. This process, called *suggestive selling,* incorporates three sales techniques: highlighting, assumptive selling, and upselling.

Highlighting Drawing a guest's attention to particular menu items as an order is placed is called *highlighting*. Using vivid and enthusiastic descriptions may encourage guests to try specials or to order other items that the chef is eager to sell. If the kitchen staff is backed up, a good server may suggest items that require little preparation to help the kitchen run smoothly and speed up service for guests.

Assumptive selling The sales technique of *assumptive selling* guides the guest's choices by asking open-ended questions. The server might ask the guest for a wine preference, implying that wine would complement the menu selections. Not only does this technique increase sales, it also makes the guest feel that his or her needs are being attended to.

Upselling Sales can be increased by *upselling,* a technique for suggesting that guests order items of better quality or a larger size than what was originally contemplated. Taking an order for scotch, for example, might involve suggesting Dewar's® or Chivas Regal®, higher-priced alternatives to bar scotch. Although the technique is not always successful, upselling consistently increases the establishment's sales and the server's own income.

Server as Skilled Professional

Each member of a restaurant's service team—busser/runner, server, captain, wine steward, bartender, host, and *maitre d',* or manager—should strive for a positive attitude, good appearance, excellent communication skills, thorough job knowledge, and timeliness.

Positive attitude A positive attitude is essential when dealing with the public. Personal problems should not interfere with the guests' dining pleasure. A positive attitude reflects a sincere desire to please the customer and is a server's most important attribute.

Appearance In order to create a positive first impression for both the establishment and the service personnel, good personal hygiene; clean, neat attire; and professional body language are essential. See Figure 33-1.

Body language Attitude is often apparent through body language. Slouching suggests carelessness, whereas standing tall creates an aura of pride and professionalism. See Figure 33-1. Similarly, eating, drinking, smoking, or chewing gum while on duty is unprofessional. Guests wish to be confident that their food is being handled hygienically. Servers should be continually aware of what is touched.

Communication skills Servers communicate with patrons orally, in writing, and more subtly through their gestures and actions. Strong communication skills are essential to interact with guests and other front-of-the-house and kitchen staff members. Take care to write orders clearly if the establishment does not use a computerized ordering system. Guest checks should be clear and accurate. Address guests and fellow staff members professionally. Addressing guests as "you guys," for

FIGURE 33-1

Key Elements of Professional Appearance

PERSONAL HYGIENE

Restrain hair that is longer than collar length; shampoo frequently.

Keep hands clean; always wash hands after using the restroom, as required by law.

Trim and clean fingernails.

Keep teeth clean and breath fresh.

Use deodorant as necessary to avoid body odor.

Avoid cologne or perfume; scents may detract from aromas of the food and wine; some patrons are allergic to or offended by perfumes.

PERSONAL ATTIRE

Keep jewelry to a minimum.

Keep shoes clean and shined.

Keep uniforms clean and well pressed.

BODY LANGUAGE

Maintain good posture.

Move quickly, but do not appear rushed.

Avoid touching your nose, mouth, hair, or face.

Avoid searching for pencils or pads, and keep your hands out of your pockets.

Avoid squatting down or bending over the table to use it as a writing surface.

example, undermines the guest's perception of the server as a professional. Keep communications with customers friendly, but not familiar. Similarly, keep communication with co-workers professional, not personal, while on duty.

Job knowledge Job knowledge includes a thorough understanding of the workplace. Familiarity with the food, wine, and beverage menus is essential in making recommendations or answering customers' questions. Be prepared to answer questions about local events or landmarks or to deal with customer complaints or problems.

Complete understanding of the server's responsibility in serving alcohol is also a key element, which is discussed further in Chapter 35, Mixology.

Thorough knowledge of the many other elements of the job includes the manual skills of serving and clearing tables and using a computerized point-of-sale system.

Timeliness Timeliness refers to the ability to work safely, efficiently, and quickly. Servers are generally responsible for a station or a section of the dining room, typically three or four tables. Professional service depends on working quickly, but safely and accurately among tables. Being well organized and prioritizing tasks effectively is essential to good service.

The Sequence of Service

The service sequence varies from one restaurant to another, but the following is a general guideline for service in most establishments.

Reservation Systems

The guest's first contact with an establishment may be through the reservation system. Many destination restaurants and usually the most upscale ones continue to accept reservations, but most other restaurants accept reservations only on special occasion days, such as Mother's Day, and for larger parties.

Although online services are available, manual reservation systems depend on the host or hostess to answer the phone, record the details, and, if it is the management's policy, record credit card numbers as a guarantee. He or she may also answer questions, give accurate directions to the restaurant, and provide clear information about parking.

Greeting the Guest

Because first impressions are lasting, it is critical that the initial greeting be warm, relaxed, and hospitable.

Greeting guests is usually the responsibility of the dining room host or hostess, or maître d', but all front-of-the-house employees should be trained to greet guests properly. Good management requires that someone is always at the door to greet guests. If the restaurant uses a reservation system, ask the guest for the name under which the reservation was made. If a guest must wait for a table, be honest about the length of the wait; nothing irritates a guest more than to be misled about how long the wait will be.

Seating the Guest and Presenting the Menu

It is usually the responsibility of the maître d' to lead guests to their table and ensure that they are seated comfortably. All menus should be presentable and up-to-date. They may also contain inserts such as the day's specials. Chairs should be pulled out for the guests. Present menus and wine lists, if used, first to women in the party, then to men, and finally to the party's host. The maître d' should convey any special requests or important information, such as a guest's allergies, to the server.

Greeting by the Server

Allow the guests to relax and settle into their seats for a few moments before approaching the table. Then, making good eye contact and standing erect, welcome the guests to the restaurant or, depending on the establishment's policy, introduce yourself by name: "Hello. I'm Bob, and I'll be your server. Please let me know if there is anything I can do to make your meal more enjoyable." Reading the guests' comfort level and perhaps the occasion helps personalize and adjust service to the specific needs of the party.

Greeting Guests

Following a set sequence for interacting with guests ensures consistently good service.

When greeting guests, follow this five-step model.

Make sure that guests are seated comfortably.

Keep greetings friendly and professional.

Present menus to guests as soon as they are seated.

Helping guests find appropriate areas to hang their coats creates a welcoming atmosphere.

Escorting guests to their tables is part of good service.

The Beverage Order

Because the beverage order is the first point of service, it is especially important that it be smooth and error-free. Be knowledgeable about popular drinks, brands of liquor, and wines and beers available by the glass.

Take the beverage order from children and women first, men second, and the host last. See Figure 33-2. Clarify any preferences for alcoholic beverages such as "straight up" or "with a twist." If possible, serve beverages from the right side. Check back for a second round when the first round is about three-quarters consumed, and remove any empty glasses before serving fresh drinks. If one customer orders another "round" of drinks, make sure that it is the intention of each guest to have another drink at that time.

Selling the Menu and Specials

There are three basic systems of menu presentation: à la carte, prix fixe, and table d'hôte.

À la carte The à la carte menu is one in which each item on the menu is priced individually.

Prix fixe One fixed price applies to any multiple-course meal, regardless of the entrée chosen.

Table d'hôte With table d'hôte service, the price of a multiple-course meal is determined by the choice of entrée. For instance, a meal that includes steak au poivre as the entrée is typically more expensive than a meal that includes chicken.

> See Chapter 6: Menu Development for more information on types of menus.

Describing the Menu

Providing clear, accurate, and appealing descriptions of menu items not only helps guests decide on their food orders but also provides an opportunity for additional selling. Begin by offering a confident explanation of any daily specials or other particularly outstanding or appealing selections. Using descriptive adjectives, appropriate hand gestures, and good eye contact with guests increases their comfort level and helps steer their selections. Food descriptions should include how the item is prepared, the sauce with which it is served, the accompaniments, and an endorsement.

Each kind of food may include different descriptive details. For example, soup descriptions generally include the major ingredients, the stock, the texture, and if appropriate, the temperature (such as for chilled gazpacho). Salad descriptions might identify whether the salad is tossed or arranged, whether cooked ingredients are served warm or cold, and the kind or kinds of dressings available. Entrées, on the other hand, include descriptions of the ingredients, such as a cut of meat; the type of preparation, such as sautéed or braised; and the way the entrée is served, such as with a specific kind of sauce. If any menu items have been sold out, be sure to give that information to the guest before you ask whether he or she is ready to order.

After the guest chooses the items in the food order, suggest a range of wines to complement the food or describe the dessert menu.

Describe the selections as appealingly as possible, but take care to avoid misrepresentation. The National Restaurant Association (NRA) has established these guidelines for representation:

- **Quantity**—Be specific and accurate; a "four-egg omelet" must contain four eggs.
- **Quality**—"Angus beef" must be certified as Angus.
- **Price**—A cover charge, service charge, or gratuity must be stipulated.
- **Brand names**—The advertised product must be the one served; for example, another brand of hot sauce cannot be substituted for Tabasco® sauce.

✦ FIGURE 33-2
Taking the beverage order

- **Product identification**—Blue cheese must not be substituted for Roquefort cheese, for example.
- **Point of origin**—Salmon advertised as Atlantic salmon cannot come from elsewhere.
- **Merchandising terms**—Fish advertised as "fresh" must not have been previously frozen.
- **Food preparation**—A steak advertised as "charcoal-grilled" must be grilled over charcoal, not merely broiled.
- **Verbal and visual presentation**—If a server represents bread as "baked on the premises," the bread cannot be delivered already baked to the restaurant.
- **Nutritional and dietary claims**—Descriptions must be accurate; a food sold as "fat-free," for example, must be totally free of fat, not merely low in fat.

Taking the Order

In most restaurants, tables are numbered to make taking the order and organizing the workflow easier. Each server is responsible for a specific group of tables, called a station.

Seat Numbering

In addition to numbering tables, each seat, and thus, each guest, also has a number, which usually flows clockwise around the table from a fixed point, such as the entrance to the restaurant. Using this system, the seat closest to the entrance at each freestanding table is numbered position 1. At a booth or banquette table, the numbering begins depends on the position at which a server

stands to take an order. Using this system helps improve communication among staff members to provide better service. A busy server can easily ask another server to check on the coffee at table 5, for instance, and to make sure that positions 3 and 4 have fresh hot water for their tea.

Position of Server

Carefully gauge when a party is ready to order—not always an easy task, but one that is vital to maintain the flow of service. Similarly, evaluate whether the guest has made, or needs assistance in making, a selection.

When taking the order at a table, stand to the right of each guest when possible. If there is a guest of honor, take that person's order first, and then take the children's and women's orders, followed by the men's, and finally the host's orders. Ask for all the details for an order from each guest and remove the menu before moving on to the next person. When appropriate, ask about the cooking temperatures, such as the degree of doneness for a steak or eggs. Repeating the order to the guest helps avoid mistakes. If a guest has special requests, be sure to check with the chef before the order is taken to see whether the request can be honored.

Timing is equally important in determining exactly when to take the order and transmit it to the kitchen so as not to overburden the kitchen staff.

Writing the Order

In traditional classical service, a cold item is served before a hot one, and a liquid item precedes a solid one. In the United States, courses are generally served in the following sequence: **1.** Appetizer, **2.** Soup, **3.** Salad, **4.** Intermezzo, **5.** Entrée, **6.** Cheese, **7.** Dessert, **8.** Coffee.

The exact sequencing depends somewhat on each guest's order. Assume, for example, that the first guest at a table orders an appetizer, a soup, and a salad. The second guest orders only soup, and the third orders only a salad. Using the system described above, bring the first guest an appetizer. After clearing the appetizer, bring soup for the first and second guests. After clearing the soup, bring salad for the first and third guests.

Orders should be written in the correct sequence on a small order pad or a guest check or entered into a point-of-sale (POS) computer system. See Figure 33-3. Beverage orders are normally placed on the back of the check. Each guest's seat position should be written next to the order, and the women's seat numbers circled for quicker identification.

Servers generally use a kind of "shorthand" to note information and communicate with the kitchen staff and among themselves. See Figure 33-4 and Figure 33-5.

FIGURE 33-3
Orders should be written in correct sequence.

FIGURE 33-4

Kitchen "Shorthand"		
Blkn- or B&B	Black and blue
R	Rare
M/R	Medium rare
M	Medium
M/W	Medium well
86	Sold out of item
68	Item is again available
SOS	Sauce on the side
LOS	Light on sauce
Hold	Chef waits to prepare until server discusses the item

FIGURE 33-5

Service Slang		
deuce	a party of 2
4 top	a party of 4
fire	to request an item from the kitchen
split	divide item in two

Transmitting the Order to the Kitchen

Orders are transmitted to the kitchen either verbally, with a written order form, or by a computerized point-of-sale (POS) system. See Figure 33-6. Be familiar with handwritten checks, and understand check-writing principles in case a computerized system crashes.

Begin preparing a guest check by filling out the information at the top of each check in the boxes provided for date, server number or initials, table number, and number of guests. In the far left column, list the quantity of each item ordered, and in the center column, write the item ordered and next to it, the number of each guest's position.

Prepare the check by transferring the order from the order pad to a guest check. First, determine whether there are more items in a particular course, such as the appetizers, than there are guests. Two people might, for example, order three appetizers. Also check to see whether the same guest number appears twice for one course as when, for example, one guest ordered two appetizers and another ordered none.

Copy the order pad onto the guest check the way it is written, leaving a space between the separate courses. For example, if a guest has an appetizer as an entrée, list the appetizer with the other guests' entrées.

FIGURE 33-6

Customer orders can be placed with kitchen staff either verbally, in written form, or via a POS system.

Service Guidelines

Although styles of table service can range from those used in elegant, formal dining to those appropriate to relaxed, casual meals, customers are always entitled to courteous, knowledgeable service from servers who take pride in their work.

Protocol

The following are the standard protocol or precedence of service:

1. The guest of honor, if there is one, is served first, and the host last.
2. Serve children, women, and men in that order.
3. Serve and clear beverages and food from the guest's right side.
4. Clear soiled dishes from the guest's right side.
5. Carry flatware on a serviette or a *STP,* or standard transport plate.
6. Carry glassware on a beverage tray.
7. Do not reuse flatware for a subsequent course.
8. Wait until everyone at the table has finished a course before clearing.
9. Do not reach across a guest if you can approach from the other side.
10. Do not touch a guest, and do not allow a guest to touch you.
11. Try not to interrupt guests who are engaged in conversation.
12. Serve and clear with the hand farthest from the guest.

Etiquette

Most guests are less concerned with the techniques of service than with the manner in which they were served. Intrusive service is annoying, regardless of how skilled the server is. Considerate service is both efficient and pleasant, and it is likely to persuade a guest to return. See Figure 33-7.

1. Carry plates and drinks so that your fingers are well away from the food or rim of a glass.
2. Never rush the guest by bringing the courses to the table too quickly.
3. Position the plate of food in front of the guest as the chef intended.
4. Try to anticipate your guest's requests rather than simply responding to them.
5. Take the time to groom the table before serving each course.
6. Serve each guest in a timely manner so that he or she does not have to make repeated requests for service.

7. Take note of any physical limitations or characteristics preferences such as left-handedness, and make the necessary adjustments.

Adjusting Flatware

Another aspect of service involves adjusting the flatware to suit the service order before each course arrives and then clearing it after each course. Readjust flatware after each course is cleared, and replace any that is missing or has been used. Clean flatware should be carried on a serviette or STP. See Figure 33-8.

If the server notices a utensil from a preceding course on the table while placing new flatware, he or she should pick it up, place it in the fingers holding the STP, and treat it as a used utensil.

FIGURE 33-7

The guests' convenience and comfort dictate the actions of the professional server.

FIGURE 33-8

Attention to detail confirms the guest's impression that the establishment is one to which he or she wishes to return.

FIGURE 33-9

When clearing a table, the professional server works with a seemingly effortless artistry that guests hardly notice.

FIGURE 33-10

Frequent crumbing keeps the table free of food particles.

Clearing

When clearing a table, first make sure that all guests have finished a course. Clear from the right side, but avoid reaching across the table. Walk around the table clockwise, keeping the cleared plates in the left hand, away from the guests, and avoid overstacking them on your arm. Clearing plates with flatware requires crossing the fork over the knife to prevent utensils from sliding off onto the floor, or worse, the customer. When using food service trays, separate flatware from serviceware according to type, and ensure that the tray is properly balanced by placing heavier items at the center of the tray. Glassware should be cleared separately onto beverage trays to avoid excessive breakage. Clearing the table should be conducted as quietly and unobtrusively as possible. See Figure 33-9.

Crumbing the Table

As the name implies, *crumbing* is the procedure for clearing the table of crumbs and other food particles. It should be done between the entrée and dessert courses, and as needed, as quickly, quietly, and unobtrusively as possible. See Figure 33-10.

To clear the table of crumbs and other food particles between courses, follow these steps.

1. Move glasses or utensils, if necessary, to ensure that the table is clean.
2. Crumb from the center of the table outward, away from the guest, and at a diagonal to an open corner.
3. Use a crumbing utensil such as a special brush, if available, or a folded service towel to sweep the crumbs onto a plate or small pan.

Changing Ashtrays

Another duty of the server is changing ashtrays in the establishment's smoking section. Do not allow more than a couple of cigarette butts to accumulate before changing an ashtray. To make sure that ashes do not fly into guests' food or beverages, invert a clean ashtray and hold it over the soiled one. Dispose of the contents of the dirty ashtray safely, and then place the clean ashtray on the table.

Checking Back with Guests

Though it is imperative to check on guests' satisfaction, checking too often is annoying and intrusive. Instead, check visually, from a distance. If a guest's body language suggests displeasure with a course, return to the table, and ask whether the dish is prepared to his or her liking. Avoid such phrases as, "Is everything okay?" If body language suggests that all is well, check back only after the entrée has been served and the guest has had time to taste the food. Avoid asking guests about the food when their mouths are full.

Presentation of the Check

Present the check as soon as there are direct or indirect signs that the guest has finished the meal or the server deems it appropriate. The check should be accurate, legible, and unspoiled as it is presented to the host or placed in the center of the table. See Figure 33-11.

Avoid hovering over the guest waiting for payment, but keep a close eye on the check folder for either a credit card or cash payment and pick it up as soon as possible. Always be discreet, tactful, and gracious.

Handling Money

Checks are commonly paid either by credit card or cash, though sometimes the guest may have a gift certificate or other voucher for the meal. If the guest is paying by credit card, check the card for the cardholder's signature and the expiration date. Process the card appropriately and according to restaurant policy. Return the card with the check and voucher to the guest, along with a pen for signing the voucher.

After the transaction is completed, remove the check to ensure that the credit card voucher has been signed and that the voucher has been left in the check folder. Occasionally, an authorization issue occurs with the credit card. If there is difficulty, draw the cardholder aside and explain that there is a problem processing the card. Avoid embarrassing the cardholder in front of guests.

If the guest is paying with cash, ensure that you receive the correct amount, and return any change with a selection of bills to ensure flexibility in leaving a tip. It is inappropriate to ask the guest whether change is needed.

Farewell

When guests are ready to leave, assist them with their chairs and their coats. Check the table to ensure that guests have not left any belongings behind, and thank them for their patronage. See Figure 33-12.

After the guests have departed, clear the table, and place any accessories such as flowers or candles on a tray, not on a chair. Change the table linens, neatly folding the soiled linens and taking care not to spill crumbs on the floor. Avoid allowing the surface of the table to be revealed during service.

In resetting a tablecloth, use the following guidelines.

- The hem of the cloth should be face down.
- The corners of the cloth should line up with the corners of the table.
- If a base cloth is used, the corners of the decorative cloth should line up with the base cloth's corners.
- The center crease of the cloth should be centered on the table and point upward.
- Use the backs of the hands to smooth the cloth.
- Replace the accessories, place folded napkins at each place setting, and reset flatware, glassware, and any other serviceware according to the establishment's specifications.

FIGURE 33-11
When presenting the check, make sure that it is presentable and legible.

FIGURE 33-12
Gracious service from beginning to end is the key to return business.

Service Techniques

Individual foodservice operations may incorporate specific service techniques, but many procedures are universal.

Beverage Service Techniques

Although hot and cold beverage service varies among establishments, most follow common procedures in serving all beverages. Place the drinks sequentially on the beverage tray so that the first drink served is closest to the server and the last drink is farthest away. Carry beverages on a well-balanced beverage tray with the left hand, and serve with the right hand from the guest's right side. Never place your fingers near the rim of the cup or glass. The server should hold a stemmed glass by the stem and a base glass by the bottom third of the glass. Make sure that glassware, cups, saucers, and utensils are clean, and present a new glass or cup and saucer with each new beverage. Never overfill the glass or cup. Use a cold glass for cold beverages and a warm cup for hot beverages. Place a cocktail/beverage napkin under the glass when serving on a hard uncovered surface. If a beverage is spilled, remove the glass or cup and saucer, and replace it with a new beverage.

Cold Beverage Service

Cold beverage service includes presenting water, soft drinks, milk, liquor, and wine. Glasses should be carried on a beverage or cocktail tray. Clean stemmed glasses may be carried by hand safely and expeditiously to save time. The technique is very specific to avoid any contact with the bowl of the glass. Glasses are placed upside down, with the stem between the fingers and the bowls of the glasses touching one another.

Water Service

Most, but not all, restaurants in the United States serve water to guests automatically. Generally, restaurants that do not serve water automatically prefer to sell bottled water or other beverages.

For water service, the protocol is as follows:

1. Preset water glasses to the right of the guest's cover, or place setting, usually above and in line with the entrée knife.
2. Bring a pitcher filled with ice water and plenty of ice to the table.
3. Using a neatly folded service towel or STP to catch any drips, pour water into the water glass, being careful not to overfill. The glass should be about three-fourths full.
4. Refill the glass as needed, never allowing the glass to be less than one-fourth full. Water service in the United States requires constant attention.
5. If the water pitcher has an insufficiently wide spout, it may be necessary to remove the glass from the table and pour water behind the guest to avoid spills on the table.

Mineral Water

Mineral water should be served cold and poured into a glass that is shaped differently from the water goblet for easier identification. Avoid adding ice unless the guest requests it. Guests often order mineral water because they dislike tap water's taste. Melting ice will add tap water flavors to the mineral water.

Other Cold Beverages

When serving beverages such as soft drinks, milk, and iced tea, use the appropriate glasses. If using garnishes, ensure that they are appropriate and fresh. Place the beverage to the right of the guest's cover.

When serving bottled beverages, place the appropriate glass before the guest, and proceed to fill it no more than two-thirds of the way to the top. Leave the bottle to the guest's right with the label facing the guest.

Wine Service

Familiarity with an establishment's wine list and the basic principles of pairing wine with food is critical to a server's success. Before suggesting a wine to guests, however, first ask what kinds of wines they like to avoid making pointless suggestions.

Be aware of any wines that may not be available or that have a different vintage year from that stated on the wine list. Use the following tips to help guests select wines:

1. Take the wine order from the host, either by name or bin number.
2. Check the wine label and vintage for accuracy before presenting the bottle to the guest.
3. Preset the appropriate wine glasses by handling the stems only, and bring the bucket to the table if serving a white wine. In formal settings, an additional tasting glass may be brought for the host to taste the wine.
4. Determine who will be having wine, and ensure that all guests are of legal drinking age.
5. Present the wine to the host for verification, and repeat the wine's brand, variety or classification, appellation, and vintage.
6. Determine when the guests want their wine poured.
7. Pour 1 ounce (30 ml) of wine for the host for tasting purposes. If the wine is refused, determine the reason and find the manager. A faulty cork occasionally compromises the flavor of the wine. In that event, the manager may replace the wine with another bottle.
8. Avoid reaching in front of the guest to pour. Delicately pour wine in a continuous flow for each person from the right side and with the right hand, twisting the bottle at the end of each pour to avoid drips.
9. Return the wine to the wine bucket or to the chiller on the table with the label facing the host.
10. Avoid overpouring wine.
11. Discreetly allow the host to know when the bottle is empty and determine whether another bottle is desired. If the host orders another bottle of wine, bring a clean glass for tasting, even if it is the same wine.

12. If guests switch to a different wine, bring clean and appropriate wine glasses.

13. When guests have finished the bottle and do not require another, remove it from the table before removing the wine glasses.

Opening Procedures for White, Rosé, and Dessert Wines

To open white, rosé, and dessert wines:

1. If using a wine bucket or chiller, put equal amounts of ice and water into it until it is three-quarters full. Place it in either a wine bucket stand or on the table to the right of the host.

2. Present the wine, label facing the host, from the right side. Read the wine's primary identification: the brand, variety or classification; the appellation; and the vintage.

3. Then place the wine bottle in the bucket, draping a service napkin in the form of a collar around the neck of the bottle. When opening it, for additional support, rest the bottle on the side of the bucket.

4. Remove the top of the seal by cutting it above or below the lip of the wine bottle. If the seal is torn, remove it from the bottle entirely and put it in your pocket. If the bottle has an exaggerated lip at its top with a small seal affixed to the surface of the cork, perforate the seal with the worm of the corkscrew before proceeding with cork removal.

5. Insert the worm of the corkscrew into the center of the cork, and twist until four turns of the worm are in the cork. Place the corkscrew lever onto the lip of the bottle, break the seal, and pull the cork straight out, using the lever. If necessary, use a delicate wriggling motion to remove the cork completely. Unscrew the cork from the corkscrew.

6. Use a clean napkin to wipe any particles from the mouth of the bottle.

7. Present the cork to the host's right side by placing it on a doily on a plate. (The host will examine the condition of the cork to determine the storage conditions of the wine.) Remove the plate and cork from the table after the guest has been served the wine.

8. Remove the bottle from the chiller or bucket, holding the bottle over the long folded portion of the service towel collar, leaving the label exposed to the guests' view.

9. Pour about 1 ounce (30 ml) of the wine into a tasting glass for the host's approval.

10. After the wine has been approved, pour wine for the other guests, serving the host last.

11. After pouring the wine in 3- or 4-ounce (89- or 118-ml) servings, place the bottle back into the ice bucket or chiller, and fold a service towel over the top of the bucket.

12. Avoid pouring more than 3 or 4 ounces (89 or 118 ml) of wine at a time to prevent warming that may impair the flavor. Pouring smaller servings is especially important with dessert wines, which often are consumed more slowly so that guests can savor their flavors.

Opening Procedures for Red Wine

Red wine is not generally chilled in an ice bucket or chiller, so the procedures for opening red wine differ from those for chilled wines.

1. Bring a wine coaster or doilied bread-and-butter plate to the table along with the bottle of wine.

2. Present the wine bottle from the right side, with the label facing the host.

3. Place the bottle on the coaster or the doilied bread-and-butter plate, and remove the top portion of the seal as previously described.

4. Use the same opening procedures described above, and use the doilied plate to present the cork to the host.

5. After approval, pour 4–6 ounces (118–177 ml) of the wine, depending on the style of glass used, or use standard rules of protocol.

6. Place the bottle on the coaster or doilied bread-and-butter plate toward the center of the table, label facing the host.

7. Remove and pocket the cork.

Decanting Red Wine

Red wines are decanted for three reasons:

• Decanting allows some wines to "breathe" so that the full aromatic bouquet can be revealed.

• Careful decanting removes the wine and leaves any accumulated sediment in the bottle.

• Decanting allows wines from a cellar to reach their proper serving temperatures more speedily, a process called *chambréing*.

Do not begin decanting red wine more than a half-hour before it is to be served. Pour the wine from the bottle carefully into a glass or crystal decanter (33-ounce, or 1-liter, minimum), in a slow but steady stream.

If decanting an old wine, pour slowly and continuously so as not to loosen the sediment. Stop pouring as soon as you see sediment approaching the neck of the bottle.

Young red wines—a young claret from Bordeaux, for example—may be high in tannins. Aerating such a wine by decanting it allows the hard tannins to seem less astringent and makes the wine easier to drink. Avoid decanting more delicate red wines such as Pinot Noir. The server should use the opening procedures described earlier for red wine.

Older red wines (10 years or more) ideally need to stand upright for from 24 to 48 hours prior to serving. If the bottle has just been brought from the cellar, however, place it in a cradle or wine basket and open it there, taking care not to disturb any sediment.

When serving from a wine cradle, a lighted candle on a plate or a flashlight should be placed to the right of the decanter so that the server can clearly observe the flow of wine down the neck of the bottle. Stop pouring as soon as the sediment approaches the neck, and do not interrupt the flow because that will loosen the sediment and allow it to spread through the wine.

For very expensive older red wines, the guest might choose to be served the remaining wine, regardless of the sediment. In that case, use a special silver funnel with a strainer to pour this wine into a separate glass.

Chambréing Wine

Chambré is a French word meaning "brought to room temperature." Although all wines should be stored in a cool cellar at 50°F (10°C), red wines should be served at warmer temperatures, up to 65°F (18°C). Using a warm decanter is the most effective way of bringing wines to their optimum serving temperature.

Opening Procedures for Sparkling Wines

Sparkling wines should be chilled to 40°F–45°F (4°C–7°C) before opening. The most efficient way to chill sparkling wines is with a sparkling wine bucket, which is taller than conventional wine buckets. Chilling the wine from storage temperature to serving temperature should take about 20 minutes. Insufficient chilling may cause the cork to exit the bottle explosively; some of the wine may overflow, and carbonation may be lost.

1. At the table, remove the sparkling wine from the ice bucket, and wipe it dry with a service towel.
2. Holding the bottle at chest height at a 45° angle, find the perforation or wire loop, and pull it out from under the foil.
3. Remove the top part of the foil, and then twist the wire loop counterclockwise about 5 1/2 times until the wire cage can be lifted from the lip of the bottle. Put the cage in your pocket.
4. Still holding the bottle at a 45° angle, grasp the cork in your left hand, and twist the bottle counterclockwise with your right. Do not twist the cork, which may break.
5. As the cork is being expelled from the bottle, carefully counterbalance the pressure by gently holding it in and tilting it toward yourself. Allow the slightest amount of gas to escape to help preserve the bubbly character of the wine. The guests should hear a soft hiss rather than a loud pop.
6. Continue to hold the bottle at a 45° angle for several seconds to equalize the pressure.
7. Present the cork on a doilied plate to the guest.
8. Wrap a service towel around the neck of the bottle. Pour a 1-ounce (30-ml) taste for the host's approval.
9. After the wine is approved, pour it for each of the guests. Pour the wine down the center of an appropriate fluted or tulip glass, waiting for foam to subside. Continue to pour until the glass is three-fourths full.
10. After pouring, put the bottle back into the bucket with a service towel draped over it.

Service Temperatures of Wine

Serving wine at its appropriate temperature is important. Neglecting this aspect will, at the least, diminish the guest's appreciation of the wine, and at worst, destroy the wine's character and taste.

The senses of taste and smell are important to the appreciation of wine. The volatile compounds of red wine are released at higher temperatures than those of white wine, so red wine's aromas are easier to detect at 60°F–65°F (16°C–18°C). White wines should be chilled so that their acidity is less pronounced on the palate. As a general guideline, the higher the acidity in wine, the lower the serving temperature should be to preserve the balance of the wine on the palate.

See Figure 33-13 for general serving temperatures of various wines.

Hot Beverage Service

The quality of hot beverage service is critical because it is often a guest's final impression of a dining experience. Coffee or tea may be served as a one-step or two-step procedure, depending on the number of guests at the table.

One-step service means that the warmed cups and saucers, spoons, and condiments are brought to the table on a beverage tray at the same time as the coffee or teapot. The serviceware and condiments are placed appropriately on the table first, and then the server pours coffee into the cup.

A two-step service requires the preset being brought and placed on the table first and then the server returning with the coffee or teapot to pour it into the cups.

1. Coffee or teapots and cups should be warmed prior to service.
2. When using a beverage tray, the lip of the cup and spoons should not come into direct contact with the tray's surface.
3. The cup and saucer should be placed to the right of the cover, with the handle at a 4 o'clock position. The spoon may be placed to the right or above the cup on the saucer or directly on the table to the right of the cup and saucer.
4. Cream, half-and-half, or milk should be kept refrigerated and poured into a creamer immediately prior to service. (In upscale restaurants, the cream or milk might be heated.)
5. If unwrapped sugar cubes are used, tongs should be provided. The creamer and sugar bowl should be placed in front of the guest of honor or women at the table.

Coffee Service

Depending on the style of meal, coffee cups may be either preset on the table or brought to the table when the guest orders coffee. Breakfast service often requires presetting coffee cups, saucers, spoons, and sugar and sweeteners. Here are the fundamentals of coffee service:

1. While pouring, catch drips with a service towel or STP.
2. Pour the coffee into each cup at the table, until it is only three-fourths full, unless the guest has specified "black" coffee.
3. When using individual pots, place the pot to the right of the guest.

FIGURE 33-13

Serving Temperatures for Wine

DESSERT AND SPARKLING WINES
40°F–45°F (4°C–7°C)

WHITE WINES, ROSÉS, SHERRIES, BEST CHAMPAGNES
45°F–50°F (7°C–10°C)

BEST QUALITY DRY WHITES, LIGHT REDS (BEAUJOLAIS NOUVEAU, FOR EXAMPLE)
50°F–55°F (10°C–13°C)

LIGHT REDS, ORDINARY BORDEAUX, CHIANTI
55°F–60°F (13°C–16°C)

FULL-BODIED REDS
60°F–65°F (16°C–18°C)

4. If a guest orders more coffee after a considerable time has passed, replace the cup with a new one.

5. If a French press is offered, ask the guests whether they prefer to press the plunger and serve themselves.

There are five fundamentals for brewing the perfect cup of coffee.

Proportion The proportion of coffee to water must be measured accurately. The recommended formula is 1 ounce (30 ml) of coffee to 20 ounces (591 ml) of fresh, cold water. Prepackaged coffee packs are designed for specific brewing capacity.

Grind Coffee beans can be ground from coarse to fine, which will determine, along with the roast level and blend, the intensity and balance of taste and flavors. The brew cycle of the coffee machine determines the grind. Fine grind will require 1–4 minutes; drip/medium grind requires 4–6 minutes; and regular/coarse grind will require 6–8 minutes.

Water The quality and temperature of the water helps determine the flavor and quality of coffee, but unless the water is hard, purification is usually not necessary.

Freshness Coffee beans lose essential oils and aroma when exposed to air, light, heat, and moisture. To preserve freshness, keep coffee sealed and refrigerated. Grinding coffee beans immediately before brewing ensures that they are at their best.

Equipment The cleaner the equipment, the better the coffee will taste. Clean the grinder, dispenser, coffeemaker, filter devices, spray heads, and brewing containers thoroughly at the end of each shift.

Coffee is brewed at temperatures between 195°F–205°F (90°C–96°C). Establishments may use different kinds of equipment depending on the volume of fresh brewed coffee they typically serve. For amounts of less than 3 gallons (11.36 l) of coffee per hour, a French press or a single pot brewer is appropriate. For 3–6 gallons (11.36 l–22.71 l) per hour, an air pot brewing system gives the best results. Any amount of more than 6 gallons (22.71 l) requires either a modular system or an automatic urn system.

Although French presses are more costly to maintain and more labor intensive, many upscale establishments use them to ensure the freshest and most flavorful coffee. French presses come in 10- to 20-ounce (296- to 591-ml) sizes and use medium grind coffee at a rate of 1–1 1/2 ounces (30 ml–44 ml) per 20 ounces (591 ml) of boiling water.

Pour the coffee into the French press pot, and add boiling water. The grounds will float to the top. Then stir the grounds rapidly 2 or 3 times and cover the pot. Wait for 3 minutes before slowly pressing the plunger.

Single pot brewers yield 60 ounces (1.77 l), or 12 5-ounce (148-ml) servings, and may be pour-through or plumbed systems. Each pot requires 3 ounces (89 ml) of ground coffee.

Air pot brewers dispense brewed coffee into an insulated serving decanter that holds it at 185°F (85°C) for an hour. Because additional heat is not applied, the flavor of the coffee does not deteriorate as it does in single pot brewers. Most air pots hold 75 ounces, (2.22 l) or 15 5-ounce (148-ml) servings, and use 3 1/2 ounces (104 ml) of coffee.

High volume foodservice operations generally use an automatic urn that yields 60 5-ounce (148-ml) servings of coffee, brewed with 2 1/2 gallons (9.46 l) of water to one pound (.45 kg) of coarse-ground coffee. Unless the urn is equipped with an automatic mixing device, draw the stronger coffee from the bottom of the urn, and pour it back into the brew (but not through the grounds) to ensure uniform strength.

Modular brewers combine a fixed-location brewing module (the heating and volume control) with mobile brewed coffee containers of various capacities (5, 10, and 20 l). Heating systems keep coffee at 185°F (85°C).

Most brewers, except the French press, use paper filters that eliminate soluble solids to keep coffee clear. Because paper filters are thrown away after each use, sanitation is easier with these brewers; however, filters can pick up odors that affect the coffee's flavor if stored near aromatic foods.

Espresso Brewed by passing steam and boiling water quickly through finely ground coffee, *espresso* is so named because an espresso machine takes only 17–23 seconds to make 1 ounce (30 ml) of espresso. Although the process is swift, the flavor captures the essence of the coffee bean. Traditionally served in a warm *demitasse,* or half cup, espresso is accompanied by a demitasse spoon and sugar.

The following steps are used to brew espresso:

1. Make sure that the demitasse is warm.

2. Grind the coffee, and hold it for no longer than an hour before brewing.

3. Place the portafilter under the doser, and pull the lever to release the grounds into the portafilter; then, with the portafilter on the countertop, tamp the grounds firmly, and wipe any excess grounds from the rim.

4. Insert the portafilter into the machine, and press the button to pour the shot. (Be sure to use the shot within 30 seconds, or the espresso will no longer be hot.)

5. After the espresso is made, remove the portafilter, knock out the grounds, and rinse the portafilter under hot water.

Espresso uses a specific blend of freshly ground Italian roasted beans to yield a concentrated beverage consisting of the heart, body, and crema. Crema is the emulsified coffee oils that float on the surface of freshly brewed espresso. Espresso machines usually brew only one or two demitasses at a time, but a shot of espresso is critical in drink recipes for caffé latte, café mocha, and cappuccino.

Espresso-based drinks Espresso-based drinks include cappuccino, café latte, and caffé mocha.

> See Chapter 34: Principles of Beverage Service for more information on espresso-based drinks.

Tea Service

Tea generally refers to a beverage that is made from an infusion of the leaves of *Camellia sinensis* prepared in boiling water. See Figure 33-14 on page 793. There are, however, a number of herbal blends that also fall into this category. The following fundamentals are essential to steeping the perfect cup of tea:

Proportion The proportion of tea to the volume of water will determine the final taste. Depending on the type and quality of tea leaves, 1 rounded teaspoon of tea is required for 6 ounces (177 ml) of water.

Water Trace chemicals and minerals in tap water may alter the flavors in tea. For that reason, many restaurants may use bottled spring water, distilled water, or filtered water for steeping tea.

Freshness Light, temperature, humidity, and oxygen all affect tea leaves, so it is essential to store tea in a sealed container.

Infusion Two factors are important to consider when infusing tea in fresh water.

- **Temperature**—Tea must be infused in water ranging from 160°F (71°C) to boiling point temperatures in order to release all its aromas and flavors. Generally, the greater the fermentation of the tea, the higher the temperature of the water.
- **Steeping time**—The time needed to steep tea leaves is also based on their level of fermentation or oxidation. Greater levels of oxidation require more steeping time. Teas can be steeped more than once, but later infusion will require more time. Avoid using color as a determining factor for the infusing time because color does not necessarily correspond to better flavor.

Equipment A wide variety of equipment is appropriate for steeping tea—teapots, teacups, kettles, and many others. Regardless of the kind of equipment, it must be spotless. Constant use leads to buildup of mineral deposits from water and tea that may create off-flavors.

Most establishments use commercial-grade bagged tea because it is convenient, but higher-quality loose teas are often used in fine dining establishments.

Use the following procedures when serving tea:

1. When a guest requests tea, bring a selection of the available teas for the guest's perusal.
2. After the guest selects a tea, place the packet on a doilied bread-and-butter plate, or put the loose tea in a tea strainer.
3. Preset a warm cup on a saucer, a spoon on the table to the right of the guest, sugar and sweeteners, and lemon

wedges or a creamer with milk, depending on the guest's request.

4. If using a teabag, the guest may determine how strong or weak the tea should be. Place the teapot with the teabag propped against it on a doilied bread-and-butter plate to the right of the cup.
5. For service using loose-leaf tea, place the tea in a warmed teapot, and fill the pot with boiling water. After the tea has steeped for the required time, strain the tea into the cup through a tea strainer.

High Tea Service

Afternoon, or "high" tea—a light, midday meal that bridges the gap between early-morning breakfasts and late-evening dinners—is a Victorian tradition.

The tradition has gained renewed popularity in recent years, and many cosmopolitan hotels and restaurants offer an afternoon tea service. It provides an opportunity to sell light foods and beverages when demand for full-service meals is low.

High tea includes a loose tea selection with more detailed service and food accompaniments such as finger sandwiches, tartlets, scones, cookies, or cakes.

Iced Tea

More than 80% of the tea consumed in the United States is iced tea. Iced tea can be prepared from powdered tea concentrate, a commercial liquid tea concentrate, or a concentrate made on the premises.

To make iced tea from a liquid concentrate, steep the tea for about ten minutes in a quarter of the quantity of boiling water needed for fresh hot tea. Remove the tea bags, or strain loose-leaf tea. Dissolve sugar or other sweetener in the hot concentrate. To serve, blend one part concentrate and two parts fresh water, served in a highball glass or tall goblet filled with ice.

Bread-and-Butter Service

The sequence of bread service varies from restaurant to restaurant, but typically bread is served as a welcoming gesture after water has been poured or after the food order has been taken. See Figure 33-15. Bread and butter may be served in a number of ways, from the informal breaking off of sections from a loaf to formal Russian or English service.

FIGURE 33-15

Bread service often creates a first impression of food quality.

Classic Bread Service

1. Line a small breadbasket with a clean, folded napkin.
2. Use tongs to place the bread in the center of the fold. Never handle bread or rolls with bare hands.
3. Allow 1 1/2 rolls of bread per guest for the initial serving.
4. Place the breadbasket in the center of the table and the fresh butter where it is most convenient for the women at the table.
5. When replenishing bread, replenish the butter as well.

Butter service Butter may be served in the form of wrapped patties, chips, curls, balls, florets, or whipped or compounded in a ramekin, dish, or specialty butter cup. The butter should be served near room temperature so that it is easy to spread.

Olive oil As Italian-style cuisine dominates much of the restaurant industry,

FIGURE 33-14

Types of Tea

GREEN TEA
Steeped at 160°F–180°F (71°C–82°C) for 2–3 minutes

OOLONG TEA
Steeped at 195°F–212°F (91°C–100°C) for 3–4 minutes

BLACK TEA
Steeped at 200°F–212°F (93°C–100°C) for 4–5 minutes

olive oil has become a much more visible alternative accompaniment to bread. It should be served directly from the bottle if the container is elegant and 600 ml or less. Otherwise, it should be served from a cruet or handled dispenser that is integrated into the décor of the room. A teaspoon and doilied underliner should also accompany the dispenser or bottle.

Appetizer Service

Appetizers are usually a smaller food presentation, often a substitute for soup or salad, and present an opportunity for the chef to display some creativity. They may be hot or cold. The general guidelines for serving appetizers follow:

1. When a guest orders both hot and cold appetizers, serve the cold appetizer first, unless the guest requests otherwise.
2. If an appetizer is being shared, divide it skillfully, if possible, at the table.
3. Adjust any specialized flatware before serving the appetizer, and remove after clearing the appetizer.
4. Provide fingerbowls if necessary either before or immediately after clearing the appetizer.

Soup Service

Soups fall into two distinct categories: clear soups, such as consommé, and thick or cream soups, including chowder. Clear soups are served in a soup cup with a bouillon spoon. Thick soups are best served in a bowl or soup plate with a soup or potage spoon. In either case, an underliner or doilied plate under the cup/bowl helps prevent accidents.

If soups are carried on a food tray into the dining room, assemble the cups and bowls onto the liners in the dining room, not in the kitchen, to avoid soup spills onto the liners. Also, the rim of a soup plate should be wiped clean, if necessary, before being placed in front of the guest.

Salad Service

Salads can be served before or after an entrée. In the United States, the convention is to serve the salad before the entrée, but in Europe it usually follows the entrée.

Cold salads should be served on chilled plates with a salad knife and fork. If requested, salad oil and vinegar should be presented in clean, filled cruets. If freshly ground pepper is available, it should be offered to the guest when serving the salad. The salad course is a good opportunity to service the table in ways such as replenishing bread and pouring wine.

Intermezzo Service

An *intermezzo* is a pause or intermission between two courses. Usually a sorbet, sherbet, or granita is served to cleanse the palate between two courses of very different flavors.

Serve the intermezzo as quickly as possible. This is a very short course, usually lasting no longer than five minutes.

Entrée Service

Entrée service will depend on the establishment's style of service (see pages 795–803). There are, however, some general guidelines that apply:

- Hot entrées should be served on a hot plate. Use a clean, folded service towel for handling hot plates, and inform the guest that the plate is hot.
- Be aware of the intended presentation, and serve the plate so that the guest can appreciate the full effect of the chef's efforts.

- Whether using a tray or carrying plates by hand, hold them as level as possible to prevent spoiling the presentation.
- Allow about an inch between the plate's edge and the table edge to lessen the risk of spilling onto the guest's clothing.
- If the guest leaves the table after the entrée has been served, keep the food warm by either taking the plate back to the kitchen or covering it with a plate cover until the guest returns.
- When clearing the entrée course, remove empty wine glasses, salt and pepper shakers, and bread-and-butter plates and knives, unless guests are opting for a salad or cheese course after the entrée.

Cheese Service

Cheeses are best when served at room temperature. Semi-firm and firm cheeses will take an hour to warm to room temperature, and soft and semi-soft cheeses will usually need a half hour. Very large pieces of cheese will need more time.

When serving cheeses, arrange them on marble or wooden cheese boards, trays, or a cheese cart so that they are easily cut. The cheese should be cut according to its shape so that the rind is evenly distributed. See Figure

FIGURE 33-16

Cheese should be served at room temperature and cut according to its shape.

33-16 on page 794. Each cheese should be provided with a separate knife. Bread or crackers should accompany the cheese course, and if fruit is served, ensure that it is washed, dried, and cut into bite-sized portions.

Dessert Service

The dessert course can be both the guests' most anticipated course and the kitchen's last chance to impress the guests. See Figure 33-17. Some restaurants use rolling pastry carts or display desserts at their entrance to tempt guests. Other upscale, white-tablecloth restaurants offer made-to-order desserts that require customers to select a dessert at the same time as placing their original meal order.

Dessert service procedures may vary with service styles and the types of dessert. However, the fork should be placed to the left of the cover and the spoon to the right. If the dessert fork and spoon are part of the place setting, the spoon is placed above the fork with their respective handles pointed toward the appropriate side.

FIGURE 33-17
Often the most anticipated part of the meal, dessert may be the last chance to make a good impression.

Styles of Service

Western styles of service evolved and became formalized over the last three centuries. They generally reflect social and gastronomic developments in Europe and the United States.

The terms used to describe the major styles of service can be confusing, however. The United States and Europe interpret them differently. French, Russian, and English services have very different meanings in Europe than they do in the United States. The descriptions that follow use United States interpretations.

Traditional Service Styles

In traditional Russian service, the food was carried from the kitchen, presented, and then finished in front of the guest. This formal protocol was exported to France in the mid-1800s by Prince Alexander Kourakine, where it was incorporated into French service.

Historically, French service had been an elaborate ritual of presenting platters of food from which guests helped themselves, usually with assistance from servants. In the nineteenth century, however, French service began to incorporate elements of Russian service, in which the server completed the preparation of a dish at the table. Steak au poivre flambéed at table is one example.

Today, American, or plated, service (known as "*à l'assiette*" service in France), is the most popular service around the world. Simple and quick, because all food is plated in the kitchen, this service has several advantages. It enables a chef to demonstrate and highlight creativity and artistry in the presentation of a dish. It also keeps most food at the best possible serving temperature. This style has evolved to accommodate many types of dining establishments, from upscale fine dining to bistros.

Although most restaurants rely on American service, most will also incorporate elements from other techniques to the advantage of a particular presentation for the guest.

Major service styles include:
- American or plated
  - Booth service
  - Banquette service
  - Banquet
- Family-style
- French
- Russian/English
- Butler
- Buffet

American or Plated Service

American service can take several forms, depending on the establishment's environment.

À la Carte Environment

In an à la carte environment, food is completely prepared, plated, sauced, and garnished in the kitchen. The organization of the dining room most often consists of a server for a station of 3–5 tables; however, backwaiter, busser, and other positions may also be incorporated into the staffing.

In the most upscale restaurants, a more formalized brigade system is common. In most establishments, one server is responsible for serving a table, including bringing out each course from the kitchen on a tray or by hand and serving it to the guest. This approach is efficient and streamlined, requiring less equipment and fewer and less extensively trained service staff than other service styles. It is also highly adaptable and easily tailored to any dining environment.

Generally, food and beverages are served from the right if possible. The server proceeds around a free-standing table in a clockwise manner.

Booth service In establishments with booths—tables that rest against a wall with high-backed and benchlike seats—guests are numbered clockwise around the booth for the purpose of organizing the kitchen order and food service. Service begins with the guest seated farthest away from the server. When clearing the tableware, service staff starts with the guests seated closest to the server.

Banquette service In a banquette, guests are seated facing the server, with their backs to the wall. As with booth service, the server should number the guests clockwise from the focal point as they take food and beverage orders. Serving should be done as unobtrusively as possible, serving with the hand farthest from the guest.

The Banquet Environment

In the United States, a banquet—a predetermined meal for a set number of guests—usually uses the American service style.

Servers at a banquet work as a team, under the direction of a maître d' or captain, to ensure that all guests are served each

Serving Children and People with Disabilities

According to the National Restaurant Association (NRA), families are dining out on average 3.5 times a week. Clearly, these numbers show that servers must address the needs of children.

The following guidelines apply to children up to age eight.

• Ask whether a booster seat or high chair is needed.

• Ensure that the seats are clean and that the trays on high chairs are clean and sanitized.

• Remove any sharp objects from the table.

• Remove glassware from the covers of small children. If lidded plastic containers are available for children's beverages, parents generally appreciate their use.

• Talk to the children as you serve them.

• If your establishment offers children's activities such as paper placemats and crayons, bring these to the table.

• If parents approve, help children select an appropriate menu item.

• Serve children as quickly as possible, and serve them first.

• After the guests depart, make sure that the area beneath the table is thoroughly swept.

Under the Americans with Disabilities Act (ADA), restaurants are required to provide accommodations for wheelchair users and other disabled guests.

Servers should address disabled guests directly, without assuming that they want or need help.

course at the same time. The table with the guest of honor is always served first. Depending on the number of courses and allotted meal time, servers are assigned a station of 20–30 guests.

Menu selections are usually limited to two or three choices (a split menu) and are generally preordered by the party's host. Communication between the service staff and chef is critical to ensuring that service proceeds smoothly.

Advantages American service has several advantages. Service is generally faster. The service staff needs less training because the service is easier to master. Equipment costs are limited and less space is required between tables, so more guests can be seated and more turns included. Chefs also have greater cost and presentation controls under this system.

Disadvantages American service lacks the elegance of French or English/Russian service, and a sense of theater that makes the dining experience memorable is sometimes lost. Also, guests cannot choose their own portion sizes.

Family-Style Service

In family-style restaurants, the chef prepares the dishes in the kitchen, and then servers place platters, casseroles, or tureens in the center of the guests' table with appropriate serving utensils. Guests serve themselves using plates that servers place in front of them. Table clearing follows the protocol for American service. This service style may also be used for select courses in a banquet setting.

Advantages Family-style service minimizes the costs of dining room labor and helps create a warm, familial atmosphere. Guests can decide what size portions they want, and the meal is perceived as a good value for customers.

Disadvantages The lack of portion control can result in considerable food waste, and there is no control over plate presentation. Some guests may miss the personalized service of other serving styles.

French Service

French service is usually associated with elegant settings when expense is not a determining factor and when food prepa-

rations are enhanced by it. Because a key element of French service is tableside preparation and plating, servers prepare and plate special dishes tableside in full view of the guest.

In order to deliver such elaborate and labor-intensive service, a restaurant generally requires a team of highly skilled and knowledgeable servers—called a brigade—who need to work together closely.

General Rules of French Service

As with American service, food and beverages are served from the right with the right hand. With the exception of bread-and-butter plates and knives, all dishes are cleared from the right with the right hand, and servers move clockwise around the table whenever possible.

Food is prepared tableside or plated on a *guéridon,* or side stand. Today, as restaurants blend service techniques, some plates are prepared and plated in the kitchen. The serving of these dishes must be coordinated with the tableside items as they are completed so that all plates can be presented to the guests at the same time.

Because French service is perceived as synonymous with elegant restaurants, specifically designed flatware for specific courses, such as a fish knife and fish fork, is more commonly found in restaurants using this service.

Show plates for decorative purposes are preset on the cover, and if removed, may be replaced by service plates after the guest has ordered. If one guest decides not to join others at the table in selecting a course, that guest has a service or show plate placed in front of him or her. Plates that are prepared in the kitchen may be served *sous cloche,* or "under a bell." These large, domed plate covers are removed by servers simultaneously in front of the guests to add to the theater of dining.

Advantages French service is elegant, stylish, and highly personalized. It is ideal for presenting certain dishes such as Dover sole.

Disadvantages French service takes much longer than American service, reducing the ability to turn tables. Equipment such as guéridons and specialty carts require floor space, limiting the number of tables in a restaurant. For these reasons, as well as the cost of the equipment used and

the larger, highly skilled servers required, menu prices need to be higher.

The Brigade

In a dining room using French service, the brigade, or service team, may consist of as many as six positions:

Dining room manager The dining room manager, known as the *chef de service* or *chef de salle* in France, must be in close contact with every department of the restaurant and know all aspects of the business. The manager holds ultimate responsibility and is accountable for the success of the dining room.

Sommelier The *sommelier* is the wine steward, who must have extensive knowledge of wines, spirits, and beverages and may be in charge of the purchasing, service, sales training, and control of these beverages, especially wine.

Captain The captain, known as the *chef de rang,* supervises and organizes all aspects of service for his or her station or room, including taking orders and synchronizing service for the station.

Waiter or front waiter Known as the *commis de rang,* the front waiter assists the captain and should be able to perform all duties of the captain in his or her absence. The front waiter's primary duties are the actual service of food and beverages to guests.

Back waiter The back waiter, or *commis de suite,* is the bridge between the brigade and the kitchen, with primary responsibilities including placing and picking up orders from the kitchen.

Busser The busser, or *commis debarrasseur,* is usually an entry-level position, primarily responsible for clearing and grooming the table.

Tableside Service

Tableside preparation is generally associated with fine dining, but other dining environments have also adapted tableside preparation as an enhancement of the dining experience. Four general types of tableside service include assembling, saucing and garnishing, sautéing and flambéing, and carving and deboning.

Assembling Salads and other dishes that involve a quick and simple assembly of ingredients may be completed tableside. Examples include Caesar salad and steak tartare.

Preparing Caesar Salad

The best Caesar Salads are prepared tableside not only for presentation but because the lettuce remains crisp.

To prepare Caesar Salad tableside, follow these steps:

1 Attractively arrange mise en place on a guéridon.

2 Use the tines of two forks to mash garlic and season the bowl. A little kosher salt can also be added, if desired.

3 Add anchovy, and continue to mash, using a spoon.

4 Add pasteurized raw egg yolk, and blend with garlic and anchovy. Add Dijon mustard.

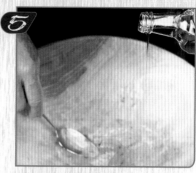

5 Drizzle olive oil into egg mixture, stirring constantly to maintain an emulsion.

6 Blend in lemon juice, freshly ground black pepper, and wine vinegar, if using.

7 Add romaine lettuce, using a napkin to break it into appropriately sized pieces.

8 Toss salad with serving set, adding croutons and grated Parmigiano Reggiano cheese.

9 Plate salad attractively, using the serving set.

10 Add additional freshly grated cheese and freshly ground black pepper to the customer's desire.

PROCESS

Preparing Bananas Foster

Bananas Foster is a dessert that can be prepared tableside with flair and a touch of "theatre" to dining.

To prepare bananas Foster, follow these steps:

1 Arrange mise en place attractively on a guéridon.

2 Slice the ends off a banana, and cut the banana in half lengthwise, using a fork to keep the banana steady.

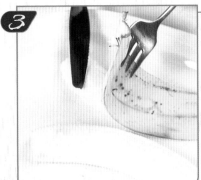

3 Remove the skin, using the service set. Cut the banana into quarters.

4 Melt butter and brown sugar in a preheated pan.

5 Use a lemon to stir the mixture. The lemon prevents the caramelized sugar from sticking to the utensil, and the juice prevents the sugar caramel from hardening.

6 Place banana quarters in the pan with the sliced side down. Lightly brown the bananas, and turn them over.

7 Remove pan from the heat, and add liqueur.

8 Place pan back over the heat, and flambé, tilting the pan and drawing it toward you as the sauce gently simmers.

9 Plate the bananas over ice cream in a decorative fashion, and nappé with the caramel sauce.

Principles of Dining Service

Carving a Duck Tableside

Carving ducks, poultry, and other meat requires dexterity and skill especially in a dining room to impress guests positively.

To carve a duck tableside, follow these steps:

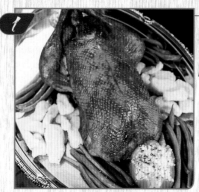

1 Present the duck to the guests on a decorated platter.

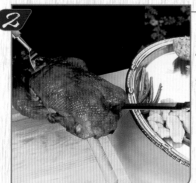

2 Transfer the whole duck to a carving board without piercing the skin.

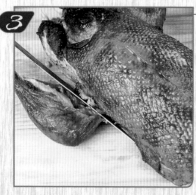

3 Remove the leg section by separating the thigh from the backbone.

4 Separate the drumstick from the thigh.

5 Remove the breast by cutting lengthwise down the keel bone and sliding the knife along the breastbone. Slice the breast into even slices. Repeat the process to remove the other breast.

6 Place the duck on a warm plate along with accompaniments.

Boning and Serving Whole Trout

Boning fish tableside requires dexterity and speed so that the guests may enjoy the food without bones while it is still warm.

For an elegant tableside presentation for trout, follow these steps:

1

Present the trout to the guests on a decorated platter.

2

Use a fork and fish knife to remove the fins.

3

Slide the fish knife under the skin, and peel the skin toward the tail.

4

Gently remove the fillets by pushing them away from the bones.

5

Insert the tines of the fork into the backbone, and lift the head while separating the bottom fillets.

6

Delicately plate the fillets with the service set.

Saucing and garnishing Servers may put the finishing touches of saucing and garnishing on dishes that have been prepared in the kitchen.

Sautéing and flambéing Both sautéing and flambéing are used for items that can be cooked quickly at the tableside or hot beverages or desserts that are flamed as part of the preparation.

Carving and deboning Fish, poultry, game, and meats may be carved or deboned at the table. Carving also includes peeling and slicing fruits and cheese to make them more manageable for guests.

Food safety In the dining room, as in every part of an operation, it is critical to follow food safety guidelines and HACCP procedures.

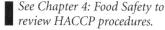 *See Chapter 4: Food Safety to review HACCP procedures.*

Tableside Equipment

Tableside service requires a number of indispensable pieces of equipment, including a service set, guéridon, réchaud, and blazer pans.

Service set The service set consists of a large fork and spoon that the service staff uses in a "pincer" or "pliers" technique to avoid touching food items with their hands.

Guéridon The *guéridon* is a portable workstation used for all tableside preparations.

Réchaud The réchaud is a portable stove used for cooking and flambéing food and also for keeping food warm.

Blazer pans Oval, rectangular, or round blazer pans are made from copper or stainless steel and are shaped to suit particular items, such as crêpes Suzette, that are prepared tableside.

Chauffe plats *Chauffe plats* are heat-retaining panels that keep food warm during tableside plating or when direct flame is not needed.

Flaming swords Flaming swords are used in flambé service. Food items flambéed on the sword are presented, flaming, to the guests before being removed from the sword and plated.

Wagon or slicing cart The slicing cart, called the *voiture-à-trancher* in French, is used for carving larger cuts of meats tableside, such as roast beef or leg of lamb.

Russian, English, or Silver Service

In Europe, English service refers to a service in which the server spoons or plates portions directly onto a dish that is in front of the guest. In the United States, this kind of service is often called Russian service, and sometimes silver service. Regardless of its name, however, the service does have some general principles.

General Rules of Russian/English-Silver Service

When using silver service, all food is prepared, portioned, and garnished before being placed on platters, tureens, or service plates. Unlike French service, silver service can involve a single server or a team of servers. All servers, however, have a clean service towel, usually draped over their left forearm.

Beverages, plates, and bowls on underliners are set in front of the guest from the right side, and food items are served with the right hand from the left side of the guest. Service proceeds counterclockwise around the table. Use service sets to transfer food from the platter to the guest's plate.

Tureen Service

When soup is ordered, tureen service is a part of this service. Preset warmed soup plates or bowls on underliners in front of the guests. Before it leaves the kitchen, the soup tureen should be placed on a STP/serviette underliner with a ladle in or beside it. Remove the cover before approaching the table. With the tureen in the left hand, approach and serve guests from the left, drawing the handle of the soup ladle toward yourself, using the right hand to avoid spillage. Return the ladle to the tureen before serving the next guest. Service proceeds counterclockwise around the table.

Platter Service

Another aspect of this service is platter service. The chef prepares and places food on a platter in the kitchen. Warmed plates are preset in front of the guests before the food is presented.

With platters held on the left forearm and hand, hold the platter parallel to the table to the left of the guest, without touching the table. Using the pincer technique, place the portion onto the guest's plate. Each platter requires a clean service set. Sauces are generally served separately, or there is a separate serving spoon for the sauce. The server proceeds counterclockwise.

Casserole Service

In casserole service, the dinner plate and any accompaniments are preset on the table from the guest's right side. Hold the casserole dish in the left hand and a service set in the right. The contents of the casserole are served from the left of the guest and as close to the plate as possible. Clearing is done from the guest's right, with the server using the right hand.

Advantages Russian (English, silver) service is faster than French service and requires less extensively trained staff. It also allows guests to determine their own portion size and gives the chef greater quality control than French service.

Disadvantages Initial equipment costs in Russian service are high, and servers need to be skilled in using service sets. More space is needed between guests for server access. Additionally, there can be considerable temperature loss in foods served on a platter. Finally, the last guests served may receive the food from a platter whose appearance is unappetizing.

Butler Service

Butler service is similar to Russian service but allows for the guest to select the food portion from the platter or tureen. This type of service is used most often at receptions, with servers carrying trays of hors d'oeuvres from which guests make a selection. It is important that cocktail napkins be offered to the guest in a convenient manner. There should be trays placed conveniently about the room for guests to dispose of frill picks, used napkins, and any other associated item.

At a full service meal, the handles of the utensils for the platters must be directed toward the guest for their convenience. Should the course be presented a second time, new service utensils should be used.

The advantages of this service are that guests may choose their own portion size, items can be creatively displayed on trays, and serving guests in stand-up receptions is cost-efficient.

Butler service has several disadvantages. Portion control is difficult. If guests choose not to serve themselves, the host might be embarrassed. If guests are not dexterous, the presentation of food on their plates might not be as appealing. Finally, more space is needed between chairs to allow server access.

Buffet Service

Buffet service can be conducted in an à la carte or banquet environment and is becoming a popular dining option because it is relatively efficient and economical to set up. Although the menu may be limited, guests can select from a variety of options and choose the quantity and combinations they prefer.

Except for the kitchen staff, buffets often require very little service staffing. A buffet table is used to display both hot and cold prepared foods. Cold food platters are kept chilled, and hot dishes are kept warm in chafing pans. Hot and cold foods are held at their appropriate temperatures to ensure food safety and appetizing flavors.

Today, three types of buffet service—simple, modified deluxe, and deluxe—are common.

Simple Buffet Service

The simple buffet is basically unstaffed. Customers serve themselves, and the server is responsible only for setting tables, replenishing food items, clearing tables, presenting checks, and breaking down the buffet table. The simple buffet is commonly used in conference centers and hotels, where the buffet table can be wheeled into a meeting room so that guests can serve themselves without disrupting the meeting.

Modified Deluxe Buffet Service

Although customers select soups, appetizers, salads, entrées, and possibly desserts from a buffet table using the modified deluxe buffet service, staff members serve beverages and assist at the buffet to various levels, depending on the establishment. In more elaborate environments, the buffet may be plated partially or entirely by *buffetiers*; in casual restaurants, the guests serve themselves. Often a chef assists at the carving station. Large parties, such as an office Christmas party or an anniversary celebration, often use this service.

Deluxe Buffet

The deluxe buffet provides the most service. With the exception of the entrée, all courses are plated and served. In a buffet service, the server invites guests to the buffet table, or, in an à la carte environment, informs guests of the choices available, and makes recommendations. The server is responsible for serving and clearing beverages and serving any plated course using American service. As needed, the server clears and replaces soiled plates and flatware.

In addition to the servers, buffets require a *buffetier*, whose responsibilities include being familiar with and able to describe all the ingredients and methods of preparation for each food item. The *buffetiers* supervise the correct positioning of the buffet tables and the organization of the display. Cold items are displayed first, and hot items are last. The *buffetier* also estimates the number of guests that a buffet table can accommodate and oversees all the details for the comfort and safety of the guests.

Buffetiers are responsible for the smooth operation of the buffet and the safe handling of the food. They ensure that food is at the correct temperature. Hot foods are placed in a chafing pan. The insert pan should be at least one-third full of hot water, using at least two heat sources, unless an electric heating element is used.

The buffet surface and plates are checked for cleanliness (including both sides of the plates). Chilled plates are available for appetizers and salads. Dinner plates are heated so that they are warm, but not hot, to the touch.

Service utensils have clean handles; those with soiled ones are replaced. Chafing pans are kept covered when guests are not using them. Hinged chafers have the hinged side away from the guests.

Any pan with shingled food items has the first piece on top of, not under, the piece behind it. For two-sided buffets, food is shingled in two opposite lines.

Food is reordered when a pan is one-third full and replaced before the pan is empty or when the appearance of the food has diminished because it has been in the pan too long. Food is never transferred from one pan to another in the dining room.

Accompaniments and condiments are placed near the appropriate item with appropriate service ware; salad dressing choices, for example, are near the salads with appropriate utensils for serving.

Plates and bowls are replaced before they are all used but are never stacked more than 30 plates high.

Hot pans are removed safely by using two servers, one to remove the used pan, the other to replace it with a full one; used pans are not removed until a replacement is ready because the steaming pans pose a risk to guests.

Guests are cautioned before the staff approaches the buffet with a hot pan, and chafing pans are changed using service towels.

The buffet is broken down safely by discarding leftover food, wiping the table clean, covering chafing pans and extinguishing all canned fuel containers before moving them, and safely discarding hot water.

Advantages Buffet service minimizes dining room labor costs, and customers have a wider selection of food from which to choose. They also can determine their own portions. Buffets can present an impressive display of food, and, if properly managed, reduce service time.

Disadvantages Buffets produce a considerable amount of food waste and leftovers. Because of the time lag between the first table of guests to be invited to the buffet table and the last, the buffet table may look less attractive for later guests unless it is well maintained. Guests may have to wait in long lines, and guests with physical disabilities may also be at a disadvantage at a buffet. There is also a potential for food contamination and cross-contamination by guests, unless carefully managed and supervised.

The Dining Room Environment

The dining room sets the stage for a guest's expectations. The décor, background music, lighting levels, and furnishings all suggest the style of service and hint at the menu.

Just as significant as the overall environment are the smaller details. Tableware and flatware should reflect the type of service and food being served. Every detail of the menu should give the impression that it has received the same care and attention as the dining room ambience.

The quality of service begins with behind-the-scenes work, or side work. Typically, side work includes setting tables for service; cleaning and refilling salt and pepper shakers, sugar bowls, and vinegar and oil cruets; folding napkins for service; polishing glasses and flatware; and stocking side stations.

Dining Room Equipment and Serviceware

Dining room equipment and serviceware make the server's job easier, complement the décor, and are appropriate to the style of service.

The Table

The size of the tables and the amount of space needed for each guest are primary concerns in laying out the dining room. The table should be firmly footed and not wobble when a customer leans on it. The menu and service style determine the type of table cover, which, in turn, influences the amount of space needed for the cover.

The cover can be as simple as a napkin and bread-and-butter plate, or it can be an elaborate arrangement of show plates, cutlery for each course, water glass, and three wine glasses at each setting. Table linens add to a sense of elegance and formality and also help reduce noise.

How the tables are spaced and the kind of seating offered are significant because they affect the flow of traffic and the comfort level of the guests. In a fine-dining restaurant, for instance, chairs will be comfortable enough to encourage leisurely dining. In a restaurant where fast turnover is critical, chairs will be less inviting.

Table Settings

Table settings are determined by menu type and include à la carte, both the traditional and modern or basic; prix fixe; and a banquet preset.

À la carte There are two possibilities for presetting the cover for à la carte dining: the traditional and the modern. In a true à la carte situation, the establishment does not know what or how many courses a guest will choose. The preset cover, therefore, does not include silverware or flatware. If the establishment offers a complimentary *amuse-bouche*, a small, bite-sized sampler, then a cocktail fork might be included.

The traditional setup would include little but the show plate, napkin, and a bread-and-butter plate and knife. The modern or basic place setting is dictated by aesthetics and the assumption that the guest will order at least an entrée. This less barren place setting includes a show plate, napkin, dinner knife, dinner fork, bread-and-butter plate, butter knife, and water glass. See Figure 33-18.

Prix fixe The difference between a prix fixe setting and a modern à la carte is quite often blurred, but because a prix fixe menu includes a soup/appetizer and salad course, the flatware for those courses is included in the preset. A wine glass might also be included in the cover either as a suggestive marketing tool or because many restaurants choose to include specific glasses of wine for specific courses as part of a prix fixe menu. See Figure 33-19 on page 805.

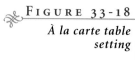

FIGURE 33-18

À la carte table setting

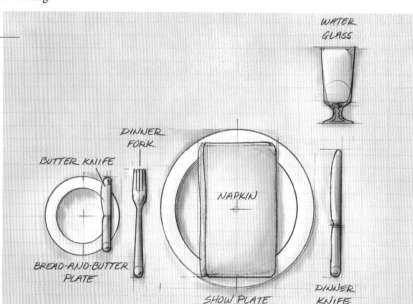

Banquet or preset A preset menu is one that has been determined ahead of time. The table setting will depend on what is being served, and includes all utensils and glassware for each course, including a bread-and-butter plate, butter knife, salad fork, dinner fork, dinner knife, spoon, coffee cup, wine glass, water glass, dessert spoon, dessert fork, napkin, and show plate. See Figure 33-20.

The Service Tray

The service tray allows a server to carry several items to a table at one time. The trays are often lined with cork or rubber to prevent slippage. If the trays are not lined, a service napkin serves this purpose.

Carry service trays in the left hand and just above the shoulder to ease maneuvering through a doorway without the door swinging back and hitting the tray. Balance items as evenly as possible on the tray, with taller or heavier items placed toward the center; avoid carrying glassware intermingled with other service ware. Be alert both for guests who may stop suddenly and for other servers. Signal servers by saying "Behind you" to avoid collisions.

When clearing a table, remove all flatware from the plates, and place it to the side of the tray. Never stack plates on top of food. Cover the tray with a service towel before carrying the tray through the dining room to the kitchen. Remove the tray as soon as the table is cleared.

The Beverage Tray

The beverage tray is a round, handheld tray on which to carry beverages. When using a beverage tray, make sure that it is clean and dry before use.

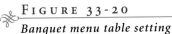

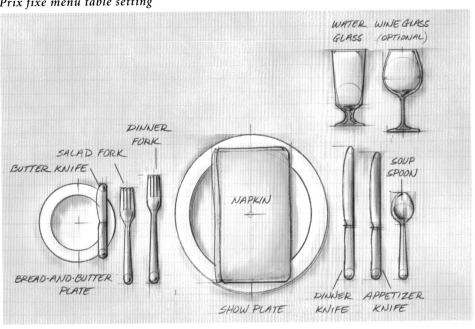

FIGURE 33-19
Prix fixe menu table setting

FIGURE 33-20
Banquet menu table setting

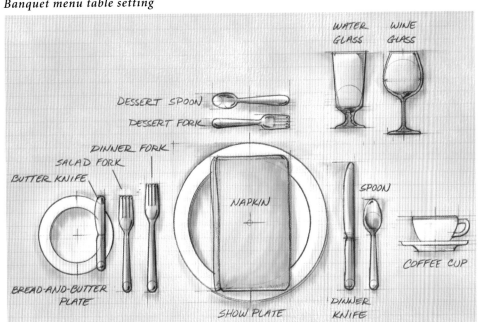

Carry the tray at waist level and in the left hand, holding it under the center of the tray, not by the edge. Avoid tilting the beverage tray when placing beverages on the table by tucking the left elbow close to your body. Never allow guests to remove beverages from the tray.

Cleaning, sanitizing, and storing service trays The food or beverage tray must always be clean. After clearing a table and unloading the tray, brush off any food particles, and wipe with a clean service towel. A service towel used to prevent slippage should be clean and folded neatly. The trays should be washed, rinsed, and sanitized at the end of the day as part of the final cleanup. They may be left to air-dry.

Tray Stands/Jacks

Tray stands, or jacks, are collapsible frames on which to rest trays. The frames may be plastic, wood, or metal. When not in use, tray stands should be collapsed and stored away from busy traffic areas. When using a tray stand, carry it collapsed on the right side when walking through the dining room. When picking up or putting down a full tray, make sure that the legs of the stand are parallel to the server and that the tray is lifted by bending the knees, keeping the back straight.

Glassware

Glassware available for foodservice operations includes common glass, fully tempered, and lead crystal.

- **Fully tempered glassware**—Commercial operations commonly use this type of glassware because it is stronger than other types, although it has the disadvantage of shattering if broken.
- **Lead crystal glassware**—Also called 24% lead crystal, this glassware is known for its brilliance and clarity, but it is expensive. For that reason, it is best suited to fine-dining establishments.

Handling glassware Regardless of type, glassware should be stored upside down in an appropriate rack. Check glassware frequently to ensure that it is free from cracks or chips and that it is thoroughly cleaned. Use a beverage tray to carry glasses in the dining room. It is more efficient to carry clean stemmed glassware by hand, inverting the glasses and placing their bases between the fingers and (the weight of the base of the next glass.) Depending on dexterity, hand size, and experience, the server may carry as many as 16 glasses this way.

When presetting a set number of glasses onto a cover, use generally accepted industry standards. Wine or beverage glasses are placed to the right of the water goblet in a sequence from right to left, the one furthest to the right being used first.

Standard sizes and shapes Glassware is available in a variety of sizes and shapes. Standard sizes and shapes are shown in Figure 33-21.

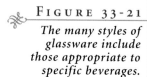
FIGURE 33-21
The many styles of glassware include those appropriate to specific beverages.

BORDEAUX   BORDEAUX WHITE   BURGUNDY RED   BURGUNDY WHITE   RHEINGAU   HOCK WINE   VINTAGE CHAMPAGNE

MOSCATO   CHAMPAGNE FLUTE   PORT   BRANDY SNIFTER   SHERRY   FOOTED PILSNER   MUG

PILSNER   ROCKS   FOOTED ROCKS   HIGHBALL   FOOTED HIGHBALL   ZOMBIE SLING   OLD-FASHIONED   WHISKEY SOUR

PONY   COCKTAIL   MARTINI   CORDIAL   LINED SHOT   MIXING GLASS

Corkscrews

Corkscrews are essential serviceware for conducting wine service. Types and shapes of corkscrews vary, but a good corkscrew has a sharp yet supple worm—the spiral driver that bites into the cork. The worm should cut into the cork, rather than tear it.

The most common corkscrew in the foodservice industry is the "waiter's friend," a simple T-shaped tool, that, when open, includes a small knife for cutting away the foil that covers the cork.

Tableware/Plateware

Tableware is available in a variety of different materials. The choice of tableware generally depends on the kind of establishment. Most use restaurant china, a blend of china and porcelain characterized by strength, durability, and low absorption, that was developed specifically for commercial operations. Some upscale restaurants and hotels use specially developed commercial porcelain tableware. Porcelain is hard, light, nonabsorbent, and strong, and its white, translucent appearance lends an aura of elegance to table settings.

Handling tableware/plateware When handling tableware/plateware, routinely check for cleanliness, and ensure that it is free from stains, cracks, chips, or crazing—hairline cracks in the glaze.

Hold plates with fingers under the plate and the rim of the plate resting against the thumb. The thumb should not be resting on the rim.

Depending on the restaurant environment and dexterity of the server, between three and four plates can generally be carried by hand or on a service tray. In a banquet, stackable plate covers allow a server to carry up to 12 entrées on a tray so that an entire table can be served at the same time.

Store all china according to type on appropriate shelving or racks. Do not overstack cups, and do not stack cups with handles. Bleach coffee cups once every two weeks, or according to your establishment's schedule, to remove stains.

Flatware and Cutlery

Flatware is the generic term for all dining utensils; cutlery refers specifically to knives. See Figure 33-22. Many styles and compositions of metals, ranging from stainless steel to sterling silver, are used for flatware. The choice of flatware is dictated

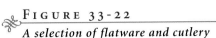

FIGURE 33-22
A selection of flatware and cutlery

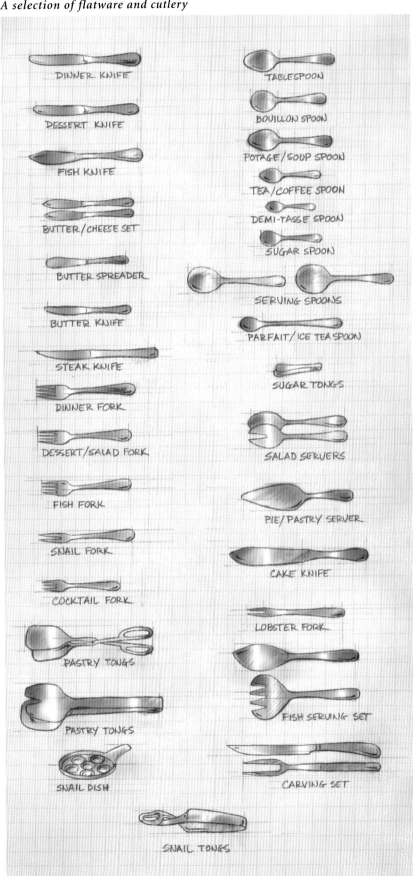

by the décor, style, menu, and pricing structure of the establishment.

Handling flatware Wipe all flatware with a clean service towel before placing it on a table. Handle flatware by its midsection so that fingers never come in contact with the blade, prongs, or bowl. Carry flatware on a STP or serviette, and place it on a table by group or category, depending on the size of the party.

Flatware is not placed in a napkin pocket fold when using an STP but merely laid on top of a square napkin fold. Flatware pieces should be parallel to one another and perpendicular to the table, except for the dessert service, which is placed horizontally above the plate, with the spoon placed above the fork.

Cleaning, sanitizing, and storing flatware and cutlery Flatware and cutlery should be washed and rinsed at high temperatures in the dishwasher and allowed to dry before being put away.

Hollowware

Hollowware includes service pieces such as water pitchers, teapots, sauceboats, and cake plates among other items. Properly cleaned and maintained, hollowware enhances presentation. See Figure 33-23.

Hollowware can generally be cleaned using normal dishwashing procedures, but to look its best, it may need occasional polishing, particularly if the pieces are silver plate or sterling silver. Use a clean service towel to wipe stainless steel free of watermarks or smudges.

FIGURE 33-23

Attractive hollowware enhances a table's appearance.

Centerpieces

Centerpieces are decorative attention-getters that many establishments use to enhance their table presentations. They can be small and discreet, such as a bud vase with a single flower, or large and flamboyant, such as an ice sculpture on a buffet table. The choice and style of centerpieces will depend on the establishment's concept and overall mood.

Of the five types of centerpieces—floral and foliage, edible, sculpted, ceramic, and lighting—floral and foliage pieces are the most common.

Floral and Foliage

Floral and foliage centerpieces can be made from fresh flowers and greenery, dried flowers, or silk or synthetic flowers and foliage. When choosing a floral centerpiece, several factors affect the final selection:

- **Expense**—Fresh arrangements are expensive and need to be replaced frequently. Good-quality dried and artificial arrangements are initially expensive but can last almost indefinitely with good care and storage.
- **Proportion**—The centerpiece should enhance, not dominate, the table setting. Avoid large arrangements that obstruct conversation or create a visual barrier.
- **Scent**—Strong scents and perfumes may irritate or trigger allergies in some guests. In addition, strong scents may overpower the aromas of food and beverages.
- **Color coordination and seasonality**—Fresh and dried flowers and artificial arrangements should coordinate with the décor and reflect the season.
- **Caution**—Dried and artificial arrangements may pose a danger if placed too close to candles. Be aware of local fire ordinances that may restrict their use.

Table Accessories

Table accessories include a variety of items that make serving convenient and dining more enjoyable for guests, such as ashtrays and matches, salt and pepper shakers, and condiments such as vinegar or ketchup, sugar, and creamers. In a fine-dining environment, table accessories are kept to a minimum, but in a high-volume restaurant in which servers are under severe time constraints, several accessories may be on the table.

Linens

Along with china, flatware, and glassware, linens are one of the "big four" in the food-service industry. Linens are high-maintenance items. They are expensive to purchase and must be changed after every guest. Frequent laundering is labor intensive and expensive. For those reasons, many establishments prefer to use paper placemats or vinyl or glass tabletops. Other establishments rent linens from a restaurant supplier or other specialist.

Table fabrics can vary from bright and cheerful cottons or chintz to elegant white linen. The style and colors will reflect the environment and atmosphere of the dining room.

Linens may be 100% natural fiber, a 50-50 blend of cotton and polyester, or 100% polyester. Polyester is easily maintained and colorfast, but cotton or other natural fiber linens are generally more attractive and hold folds better. Creasing is particularly important for folded napkins and formally pleated table skirting and draping.

Standard size and shapes for linens follow:

FIGURE 33-24

Open and closed pleats give tables a uniform appearance.

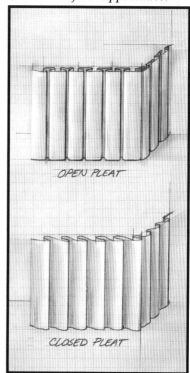

OPEN PLEAT

CLOSED PLEAT

Table Linen Sizes	SQUARE AND RECTANGULAR TABLE COVERS	ROUND TABLE COVERS	NAPKINS
	36" × 36"	51" round	17" × 17"
	45" × 45"	60" round	20" × 20"
	54" × 54"	69"/72" round	22" × 22"
	63" × 63"	81" round	
	72" × 72"	87" round	
	83" × 83"	90" round	
	54" × 72"	120" round	
	54" × 96"	132" round	
	54" × 108"/110"		
	54" × 120"		

Skirting

Skirting refers to the specialized linen used for draping tables. Skirting provides a uniform appearance, is more economical than tablecloths, and requires less labor to maintain. Clips, pins, or tapes attach skirting to a table.

Skirting is available in three types of pleating: sheer, accordion, and box. Sheer pleating is used for lace and other sheer fabrics in overlays. The accordion pleat is a closed pleat; the box pleat is an open pleat often used with more substantial fabrics. See Figure 33-24.

Folding Napkins

Decoratively folded napkins add distinction to a table setting. The folds can be whimsical, elegant, or a combination of both. The choice of folds depends on the personal taste of the owner/operator or manager, but most establishments refrain from using elaborate folds because of the labor involved and sensitivity to sanitation. It is imperative to ensure that servers have washed their hands prior to handling linen.

Handling Linens

When handling linen, servers select only the amount needed for a shift plus a 5% overage for emergencies. Treat linens with care, placing them only on clean surfaces.

When storing linen, place newly received linen under the existing inventory. Ensure that the folds of the linen are facing out, and that it is stored by type, size, and color.

Place tablecloths on tables with the seams facing down and centerfold facing up. Remove any debris from the tablecloth before folding and bagging it for laundering.

To guests, providing good service may seem simple; for servers, good service is a product of knowledge, training, and diligent observation of food service principles.

Pommes Normande

INGREDIENTS

	U.S. Standard	Metric
Sugar, granulated	1 Tbsp.	15 ml
Butter	1 oz.	28 g
Apples, sweet, peeled, cored, and cut in 1/4" (6 mm) slices	2 each	2 each
Calvados or Applejack	2 oz.	60 ml
Cinnamon-sugar mixture	1/2 tsp.	2.5 ml
Heavy cream	2 oz.	60 ml

METHOD OF PREPARATION

1. Gather all the ingredients and equipment.
2. Heat a crêpe pan; add sugar and butter, and allow to lightly caramelize.
3. Add apples, and sauté.
4. Remove pan from heat, add Calvados or Applejack, return to heat, and flame.
5. Sprinkle cinnamon-sugar over flame.
6. When flame subsides, remove apples to preheated dessert dishes. Add cream to pan, bring to a boil, and blend well.
7. Spoon sauce over apples.

Chef's Notes

- Substitute brown sugar for granulated sugar, if desired.
- Substitute nutmeg for cinnamon, if desired.

COOKING TECHNIQUES

Sautéing:

1. Heat the sauté pan to the appropriate temperature.
2. Evenly brown the food product.
3. For a sauce, pour off any excess oil, reheat, and deglaze.

NUTRITION

Nutrition Facts	
Yield: Serves 2 Serving Size: 5 oz. (140 g)	
Amount Per Serving	
Calories 300	
Total Fat 19 g	
Sodium 100 mg	
Total Carbohydrate 23 g	
Protein 1 g	

Shrimp Sauté with Garlic

INGREDIENTS

	U.S. Standard	Metric
Butter, clarified	2 oz.	60 ml
Shrimp, peeled, deveined, and butterflied	8 each	8 each
Sherry	1 oz.	30 ml
Garlic, crushed	1 tsp.	5 g
Lemon juice, freshly squeezed	2 oz.	60 ml
Salt	TT	TT
Cayenne pepper	TT	TT
Parsley, freshly chopped	1 Tbsp.	15 ml

METHOD OF PREPARATION

1. Gather all the ingredients and equipment.

2. Heat pan, add butter, and melt.

3. Add shrimp, and sauté on both sides.

4. Remove pan from heat, and pour in sherry; return to heat.

5. Add garlic and lemon juice, and season to taste. Mix well, and simmer 2 minutes.

6. Place 4 shrimp per portion on preheated dinner plate. Spoon sauce over the shrimp, and garnish with parsley. Serve immediately.

COOKING TECHNIQUES

Sautéing:
1. Heat the sauté pan to the appropriate temperature.
2. Evenly brown the food product.
3. For a sauce, pour off any excess oil, reheat, and deglaze.

NUTRITION

Nutrition Facts
Yield: Serves 2
Serving Size: 4 shrimp (84 g)

Amount Per Serving

Calories 200

Total Fat 15 g

Sodium 115 mg

Total Carbohydrate 3 g

Protein 5 g

Zabaglione

INGREDIENTS	U.S. Standard	Metric
Egg yolks, pasteurized	2 oz.	55 g
Sugar, granulated	2 tsp.	10 g
Marsala	3 oz.	90 ml

METHOD OF PREPARATION

1. Gather all the ingredients and equipment.

2. Beat egg yolks and sugar in a cold zabaglione pan.

3. When some volume is reached, add Marsala, and beat a little more.

4. Apply low heat, and whisk, keeping sides of the pan clean so as not to cook yolk on sides. (This could become mixed with the final product.)

5. When mixture has reached a ribbonlike texture (determined by testing on the back of a spoon), pour into champagne glasses.

NUTRITION

Nutrition Facts

Yield: Serves 2
Serving Size: 2 oz. (55 g)

Amount Per Serving

Calories 180

Total Fat 9 g

Sodium 15 mg

Total Carbohydrate 10 g

Protein 5 g

Veal Piccata

INGREDIENTS

	U.S. Standard	Metric
Olive oil	1 oz.	30 ml
Butter	1 oz.	28 g
Veal, *scaloppine*	6, 2 oz. each	6, 55 g each
Flour, *seasoned*	as needed	as needed
Salt	TT	TT
Black pepper, *ground*	TT	TT
Lemon juice, *freshly squeezed*	2 Tbsp.	30 ml
Dry white wine	3 oz.	90 ml
Lemon pinwheels, *without rind*	4 slices	4 slices

METHOD OF PREPARATION

1. Gather all the ingredients and equipment.

2. In a heated sauté pan, add olive oil and butter.

3. Lightly coat the scaloppine with flour, shaking off excess.

4. Sauté the scaloppine on both sides, and season to taste.

5. After turning scaloppini, add the lemon juice.

6. Add wine, and simmer. Cook veal to an internal temperature of 145°F (63°C).

7. Remove the scaloppine to a preheated dinner plate, overlapping slices, and nappé with sauce.

8. Garnish with lemon pinwheels on side of plate.

COOKING TECHNIQUES

Sautéing:

1. Heat the sauté pan to the appropriate temperature.
2. Evenly brown the food product.
3. For a sauce, pour off any excess oil, reheat, and deglaze.

NUTRITION

Nutrition Facts

Yield: Serves 2
Serving Size: 6 oz. (170 g)

Amount Per Serving

Calories 440

Total Fat 29 g

Sodium 135 mg

Total Carbohydrate 8 g

Protein 29 g

Flaming Steak with Peppercorns

INGREDIENTS

INGREDIENTS	U.S. Standard	Metric
Butter	1 oz.	28 g
Olive oil	1 tsp.	5 ml
Sirloin steaks, coated with crushed black peppercorns	2, 5 oz. each	2, 140 g each
Cognac	2 oz.	60 ml
Demi-glace	4 oz.	120 ml
Salt	TT	TT

METHOD OF PREPARATION

1. Gather all the ingredients and equipment.

2. Heat a Suzette pan until very hot; add butter and oil.

3. When butter is melted, add the steaks.

4. Remove pan from heat, and add Cognac; return to heat, and flame.

5. When flame subsides, remove steaks, and place on preheated dinner plates.

6. Add demi-glace to pan, and mix with Cognac. Season with salt.

7. Spoon sauce alongside steak.

Chef's Notes

- Dijon mustard may be lightly brushed on steak before coating with peppercorns, or added to mustard sauce in pan.
- Medallions of tenderloin may be substituted for sirloin.
- Green peppercorns also may be used.
- Supplement with light cream.

COOKING TECHNIQUES

Sautéing:

1. Heat the sauté pan to the appropriate temperature.
2. Evenly brown the food product.
3. For a sauce, pour off any excess oil, reheat, and deglaze.

NUTRITION

Nutrition Facts

Yield: Serves 2
Serving Size: 5 oz. (140 g)

Amount Per Serving

Calories 490	
Total Fat 37 g	
Sodium 200 mg	
Total Carbohydrate 0 g	
Protein 28 g	

Caesar Salad

INGREDIENTS

	U.S. Standard	Metric
Garlic, peeled and cut in half	l large clove	1 large clove
Salt	1 tsp.	5 ml
Anchovy fillet	1 large	1 large
Dijon mustard	1 tsp.	5 g
Olive oil	1 oz.	30 ml
White wine vinegar	1/2 tsp.	2.5 ml
Lemon juice, freshly squeezed	1 oz.	30 ml
Egg yolk, pasteurized	1 each	1 each
Black pepper, ground	1 tsp.	5 g
Romaine lettuce, washed, dried, torn into pieces	4 oz.	115 g
Croutons	4 oz.	115 g
Parmesan cheese, grated	1 Tbsp.	15 g

METHOD OF PREPARATION

1. Gather all the ingredients and equipment.

2. Season the bowl with garlic, using salt as an abrasive, and then discard the garlic pieces.

3. Add anchovy, and mash with a fork. Move the anchovy to one side of the bowl, and add the mustard.

4. Blend oil into the mustard, slowly and steadily.

5. Add the wine vinegar, lemon juice, egg yolk, and pepper. Mix well.

6. Add romaine, and toss lettuce. Toss all the above by rotating service spoon and fork from back to front of bowl until lettuce is fully coated.

7. Add croutons, and toss.

8. Add cheese, and toss. Serve immediately.

Chef's Notes

- Supplement with 2 dashes Worcestershire sauce and 1 dash of Tabasco® sauce when adding lemon juice.
- Supplement with 2 dashes of soy sauce when adding lemon juice.
- Blend oil and lemon juice and emulsify; then add dry mustard instead of Dijon.
- Pasteurized egg yolk is recommended.

NUTRITION

Nutrition Facts

Yield: Serves 2
Serving Size: 2 oz. (133 g)

Amount Per Serving

Calories 300

Total Fat 20 g

Sodium 620 mg

Total Carbohydrate 24 g

Protein 8 g

Banana Flambé

INGREDIENTS

INGREDIENTS	U.S. Standard	Metric
Sugar, granulated	2 Tbsp.	30 ml
Butter	1 oz.	28 g
Bananas, split in half lengthwise and crosswise	2 each	2 each
Dark rum (preferably Myers®)	1 1/2 oz.	45 ml
Cinnamon-sugar mixture	1/2 tsp.	2.5 ml
Banana liqueur	1 1/2 oz.	45 ml
Vanilla ice cream, 4 oz. (115 g) in coupe	2 scoops	2 scoops

METHOD OF PREPARATION

1. Gather all the ingredients and equipment.
2. Heat Suzette pan, and add sugar and butter.
3. Lightly caramelize; then add bananas, and coat with caramel.
4. Remove pan from réchaud, and add rum; return pan to réchaud, and flame.
5. While still flaming, sprinkle cinnamon-sugar over pan.
6. Lower flame and remove pan from heat. Add banana liqueur, and return pan to réchaud. Allow sauce to reduce.
7. Arrange four quarters of banana around ice cream, and nappé with sauce, covering ice cream.

Chef's Notes

- *Replace granulated sugar with brown sugar or honey, if desired.*
- *Supplement with lime or lemon juice.*
- *Serve with lemon wedges.*

NUTRITION

Nutrition Facts

Yield: Serves 2
Serving Size: 1 each (272 g)

Amount Per Serving

Calories 530

Total Fat 25 g

Sodium 210 mg

Total Carbohydrate 67 g

Protein 5 g

Crêpes Suzette

INGREDIENTS	U.S. Standard	Metric
Sugar, granulated	2 Tbsp.	30 ml
Butter	1 oz.	28 g
Oranges, zest	2 each	2 each
Lemon, zest	1 each	1 each
Grand Marnier®	2 oz.	60 ml
Orange juice	4 oz.	120 ml
Crêpes	4 each	4 each
Cognac	1 oz.	30 ml

METHOD OF PREPARATION

1. Gather all the ingredients and equipment.

2. Heat Suzette pan, and add sugar. Add butter, and mix until all sugar is dissolved.

3. While sugar is dissolving, add the zest of one orange and the lemon.

4. Remove pan from heat and add Grand Marnier®.

5. Add orange juice. (If sugar caramelizes too quickly, add juice to the pan while zesting.)

6. Return pan to the heat, but do not flambé. Dip crêpes in the sauce, one at a time; then fold into quarters. Move crêpes to the side of the pan.

7. When all crêpes are folded, remove the pan from the heat, and add Cognac; return pan to the heat, and flame.

8. Heat sauce to a boil. Serve two crêpes on a preheated plate, and nappé with sauce.

9. Garnish with additional orange zest.

NUTRITION

Nutrition Facts

Yield: Serves 2
Serving Size: 2 each (216 g)

Amount Per Serving

Calories 390

Total Fat 23 g

Sodium 260 mg

Total Carbohydrate 20 g

Protein 15 g

Café Diable

INGREDIENTS

INGREDIENTS	U.S. Standard	Metric
Sugar	1 tsp.	5 ml
Cinnamon stick	1 each	1 each
Orange, *for horse's neck* (see note at the right)	1 each	1 each
Cognac	1 oz.	30 ml
Grand Marnier®	1 oz.	30 ml
Espresso	5 oz.	150 ml

METHOD OF PREPARATION

1. Gather all the ingredients and equipment.

2. In a diable réchaud, add sugar, cinnamon stick, horse's neck, Cognac, and Grand Marnier®.

3. When liqueurs start to steam, pierce one end of horse's neck with a long-handled fork. With the other hand, use a ladle to remove a small amount of liqueur from the bottom of the réchaud, and expose it to the flame until it ignites.

4. Raise the horse's neck about 12 inches above the pan, and pour liqueur down rind. Continue until cloves glow bright red. Extinguish the flame in the réchaud by pouring in espresso.

Chef's Notes

"Horse's neck" is the skin of an orange that has been removed by carefully peeling from top to bottom while rotating orange in hand. Stud with cloves approximately 1" (2.54 cm) apart.

NUTRITION

Nutrition Facts

Yield: Serves 2
Serving Size: 1 each (105 ml)

Amount Per Serving

Calories 60

Total Fat 0 g

Sodium 10 mg

Total Carbohydrate 3 g

Protein 0 g

Irish Coffee

INGREDIENTS

INGREDIENTS	U.S. Standard	Metric
Lemon wedges	2 each	2 each
Sugar, *granulated*	2 Tbsp.	30 ml
Irish whiskey	2 oz.	60 ml
Coffee	10 oz.	300 ml
Heavy cream, *whipped*	2 oz.	60 ml

METHOD OF PREPARATION

1. Gather all the ingredients and equipment.

2. Rim footed glass with lemon, and dip it in sugar.

3. Heat glass over flame slightly, rotating glass.

4. Remove glass from heat, add whiskey, return to heat, and flame. Swirl glass so that flame rises. Flame for approximately 1 minute.

5. Add coffee, and fill to about 1/2" (1.27 cm) below the rim.

6. Add whipped cream.

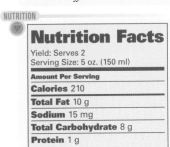

Chef's Notes

Use liqueurs from any country to create different international coffees.

- Jamaica: Jamaican Rum and Tia Maria
- Mexico: Kahlua
- Lover's Coffee: Amaretto

NUTRITION

Nutrition Facts

Yield: Serves 2
Serving Size: 5 oz. (150 ml)

Amount Per Serving

Calories 210

Total Fat 10 g

Sodium 15 mg

Total Carbohydrate 8 g

Protein 1 g

Beverage development began in ancient civilizations. Sumerians and Babylonians brewed and stored beer in clay pots as early as 6000 B.C. Winemaking may have migrated to Europe from ancient Egypt. With distillation came "visebaugh," an ancestor of whiskey, which the early Celts called "the water of life." European monks, meanwhile, developed liqueurs, or cordials, from spirits, sweeteners, and flavorings such as herbs and berries.

In Asia, early civilizations learned to make tea, and in the Americas, Mayan and Aztec rulers sipped drinks made from chocolate. Coffee growing developed in Ethiopia and was brought to Arabia, Turkey, Central and South America, and the Pacific Islands. Although many have been revered and condemned in turn because they had psychotropic or stimulant properties, beverages today are an important part of restaurant service and an important profit center.

A.D. 1191
Tea first arrives in Japan from China; in 1350, Japan's shogun prohibits tea drinking.

1450
Moka, in southwest Arabia, becomes a leading port for the export of coffee.

1510
Benedictine, the world's oldest cordial, is developed at the Benedictine Abbey in Normandy, France.

1668
In New York City, coffee replaces beer as the favorite breakfast drink.

1720
Arabica coffee plants are introduced into the New World.

1776
When the Revolutionary War causes a shortage of rum, Scots-Irish immigrants begin distilling whiskey.

Beverage Service

Coffee

Fifty-two percent of Americans start the day with a cup of coffee, and 29% drink specialty coffees such as latte, espresso, or cappuccino. In fact, coffee is the third most popular beverage in the world after water and tea. For a quick history of coffee, see Figure 34-1 on page 822.

Economic Significance of Coffee

Worldwide, more than 25 million acres are devoted to coffee growing. About 20 million people work in the industry, and coffee is, after oil, the world's second most traded commodity.

The Coffee Plant

Coffee trees produce berries that resemble cherries. The berries, bright red when ripe, normally contain two seeds, or beans, that are processed, roasted, ground, and brewed into liquid coffee. Although more than 25 wild species of coffee trees have been identified, only two, *C. arabica* and *C. robusta* (now reclassified as *C. canephora*), are cultivated for commercial use.

Initially planted from nursery-grown seedlings, the coffee tree begins producing fruit in four to six years and continues to do so for about 40 years. A self-pollinating evergreen, the coffee tree blooms with fragrant white flowers and produces about 2,000 berries—enough to produce a pound and a half of roasted coffee beans. Most growing regions have a single yearly harvest, but regions with two distinct rainy seasons have two harvests.

Coffea arabica About 75% of the world's coffee production comes from *C. arabica* plants. *Arabica,* the highest-quality coffee, grows best in a narrow band on either side of the equator at altitudes ranging from 2,000 to 6,000 feet (610 to 1,829 m). In Central and South America and East Africa, where the majority of coffee grows, year-round temperatures of about 70°F (21°C) and abundant rainfall provide the plants with ideal conditions. Most *arabica* fruits ripen at different times on the same plant and grow in rugged terrain, so harvesting is labor-intensive. Only ripe berries yield superior coffee, and they generally must be picked by hand. *Arabica* is also lower-yielding and more susceptible to disease than *robusta*. Still, consumers willingly pay a higher price for *arabica's* sweet aroma and winy, fresh, and slightly acid taste.

Coffea robusta *Coffea canephora,* or **robusta,** is hardier than *arabica,* and grows well at lower altitudes in wet valleys and tropical forest climates. Like *arabica,* a *robusta* plant begins to mature four to six years after being transplanted. It is also easier to cultivate, and growers can often use machines to harvest it. Large coffee roasters often use these less expensive *robusta* beans as a supplement in their blends and for making instant coffees. *Robusta's* heavy, earthy aroma and flavor also make it ideal for making espresso with its characteristic thicker viscosity.

Varietal and specialty coffees About 10% of the world's coffee bean crop is classified as gourmet or specialty quality coffee. A varietal coffee is a coffee from a single growing region. Antigua Guatemalan, Jamaican Blue Mountain, Hawaiian Kona, Costa Rican Tarrazu, Kenyan AA, Ethiopian Yergachev, or Sumatran Gayo Mountain are all examples of varietal coffees. Specialty coffees are often blended by the roaster from two or more varieties of beans that complement one another. Roasters who blend coffees generally do so using their own judgment, and their blends often define the roaster's image for the public.

Certified organic coffee The market for organically grown and processed products has expanded considerably in the last few years. There is a difference between products that claim to be "organic" and those that are "certified organic," however.

Certified organic coffees have been endorsed by an accredited, independent, third-party inspection. Detailed record keeping must demonstrate that the coffee has at least 95% certified organic ingredients, which are grown without the use of synthetic fertilizers or pesticides. The grower must also practice shade-tree canopy preservation to provide habitats for migratory birds in order for the coffee to be designated as "bird friendly." Finally, certified organic coffee must be kept separate from all other coffee throughout its production and processing.

Coffee Production

A number of conditions determine which of three methods growers use to harvest coffee. Where the terrain is too rugged for mechanical harvesting, growers use the most expensive *selective method,* picking only ripe berries from the tree by hand. For varieties that ripen their berries at the same time, one swift movement sweeps the branches clean of berries using the *strip method.* The *mechanical method* of harvesting is most common on coffee plantations, where the trees are planted on relatively flat terrain in even rows. In this method, the harvester straddles the row and agitates the trees, causing the beans to fall onto a conveyor belt.

Processing

As with growing and harvesting techniques, processing methods depend on the kinds of beans and the conditions where the trees grew. Where sufficient water is available, a wet method of processing is used, mostly for *arabica* coffees. Both the kind of bean and the method of processing give the *arabica* variety its characteristic high quality. In areas where water is not plentiful, processors use the dry method.

Wet method Using the *wet method,* coffee processors first depulp the berries

FIGURE 34-1

CIRCA A.D. 1000
A decoction is first made from the dried hulls and beans of the coffee plant.

CIRCA LATE 1200S
The practice of roasting coffee beans begins in Yemen.

CIRCA LATE 1400S
Dervishes and Muslim pilgrims spread the practice of drinking coffee throughout the Near East, Middle East, and North Africa.

CIRCA 1599
Although the Roman Catholic Church initially calls it "Satan's latest trap to catch Christian souls," coffee gains widespread popularity throughout Europe.

1616
The Dutch begin cultivating coffee in Ceylon and Java.

1720
Gabriel Mathieu de Clieu, a French naval officer, smuggles a coffee seedling into Martinique. The plant is the ancestor of most of the arabica *beans cultivated around the world.*

1740
London has more than 2,000 coffeehouses.

1773
Coffee becomes America's patriotic beverage following the Boston Tea Party.

1971
Starbucks® opens its first store in Seattle's Pike Place Market, and freshly roasted whole beans, gourmet blends, and specialty coffees become trendy.

PRESENT
Today, coffee is brewed and served in more ways, to more people, than at any other time in history.

mechanically. Depulping exposes the parchment-covered beans, which then soak in tanks of water until fermentation softens the mucilage layer for easy removal. Timing is critical because fermentation must not affect the bean itself. The beans are then washed to remove the fermented layer and spread in the sun on drying patios for 7 to 21 days. More modern drying methods include drum dryers that tumble the beans for two to three days at temperatures from 122°F–140°F (50°C–60°C). Through the drying process, the moisture content of the beans drops from about 70% to about 11%. After a rest period of 20 to 30 days, the parchment and silver skin are peeled off by a hulling machine before the coffee is roasted to fill orders.

High-quality beans that are processed by the wet method generally have cleaner flavors, few if any undesirable characteristics, and a more acid taste.

Dry method In areas where water is scarce, processors use the *dry method* of processing to produce sweet, smooth, complex coffee tastes. The method is used primarily in areas such as Yemen or Ethiopia where *robusta* is the dominant coffee crop, but it can also be used for *arabicas* if water supplies are insufficient.

Processors using this method allow the coffee cherries to dry partially on the tree and then spread them to dry in the sun for 14 to 21 days. Mechanical huskers then remove the dry pulp and parchment. Beans that have been prepared by the dry method have a heavier body but may sometimes develop off flavors.

Levels of Roasting

Five common but imprecise levels of roasting give different "roasts" their distinctive flavors and aromas.

ⓐ Green beans
Unroasted coffee beans range in color from blue-green to yellow.

ⓑ Cinnamon roast
Cinnamon roast is the lightest commercially available roast. These beans have no visible oils on their surface, and the flavor and body are light.

ⓒ Full City roast
Full City roast is a medium roast.

ⓓ Vienna roast
Vienna roast describes both a medium roast that is chocolate brown with dark speckles and a particular blend of different roasts. (Photo not shown.)

ⓔ French roast
Sometimes called New Orleans roast, this coffee has been heavily roasted to bring out a strong, characteristically bitter flavor and aroma.

ⓕ Italian roast
Italian roast is the darkest stage of roasting. The beans become carbonized and coated with a film of oil. These beans are usually reserved for espresso.

Sorting and Grading

Dried beans are graded by size, density, and color. Size grading uses screens to separate beans according to their diameter. A number 10 bean, for example, has a diameter of 10/64 inch (4 mm). The beans are sized by passing them through the appropriate screens. Density is determined by subjecting the beans to an air jet calibrated to separate heavier beans from lighter ones. Color sorting is usually accomplished by hand, but some processors color-sort electronically. Finally, the beans are packed in burlap or plastic bags and shipped to roasters across the world.

The sorting and grading process varies from country to country. In general, though, coffee beans come in six export grades, with the top grade being SHB, or strictly hard beans, grown at a high altitude of at least 4,000 feet (1.2 km) above sea level.

Coffee Classifications

The dried, but still green, coffee beans are classified according to botanical variety, processing method, and altitude of growth. The International Coffee Organization has classified green coffee beans, for example, as Colombian milds, other mild *arabicas*, Brazilian and other *arabicas*, and *robustas*. In recent decades the organization has lost its standing, and the above classifications are no longer so readily accepted.

They do, however, provide useful descriptions of the wide variability in coffees.

Colombian milds Grown primarily in Colombia, Kenya, and Tanzania, these coffees constitute 16% of the world's production and are graded principally on bean size. These beans produce sweet, highly aromatic brewed coffee with thick body.

Other mild *arabicas* This classification encompasses most of the *arabicas* grown in Central and South America. Accounting for about 26% of the world's production, these beans are graded according to growing altitude, density, color, and number of defects. See Figure 34-2 on page 824. Their taste is typical of medium-altitude coffee, grown at 2,000–4,000 feet (610–1,220 m)— winy to sour, with moderate aromatics and a smooth body.

Brazilian and other *arabicas* Grown in Brazil and Ethiopia, these beans make up about 37% of the world's coffee production. They are graded by the growing area, which determines the taste characteristics and the number of imperfections. The brewed coffee made from these beans has a winy-to-sour taste, moderate aromatics, and smooth body.

Robustas Accounting for 21% of global coffee production, *robustas* are graded on density, size, and the number of defects.

These beans produce a brew with neutral-to-sharp taste, pungent aromatics, and heavy body. Because *robustas* are 10% to 40% less expensive than *arabicas*, they are often used as filler in blended coffees.

The Roasting Process

Roasting coffee beans brings out their full flavor and aroma, and their flavors depend on the degree to which the beans are caramelized during the roasting process. Many complex chemical changes take place during roasting, which generally takes from 8 to 16 minutes at temperatures of approximately 500°F (260°C). As they reach a temperature of about 400°F (204°C), the beans begin to turn brown, and the oils, called coffee essence, start to emerge. This process, called *pyrolosis,* produces the distinctive flavor and aroma of the coffee.

Espresso and Espresso Beverages

Properly made, *espresso* is thick, dark, and intensely fragrant, with a bittersweet taste. It is topped with creamy golden foam called the *crema.* A single *demitasse,* or half-size cup, serving contains only 1–1 1/4 ounces (30–37 ml) and is served immediately after

Figure 34-2

SCAA Green Arabica Coffee Classification System

Effective Spring 2000

Full Black Bean: Predominately opaque black.

Full Sour Bean: Predominately reddish or yellowish brown.

Dried Cherry/Pod: Bean partially or fully enclosed in dark outer fruit husk.

Fungus Damaged Bean: Exhibiting yellowish or brownish fungal attack.

Severe Insect Damage Bean: With three or more insect perforations.

Foreign Matter: *Any* non-coffee item, such as sticks or stones.

Specialty Grade
No Category 1 Defects Allowed.
No more than 5 Full Defects.

Premium Grade
Category 1 and 2 Defects Allowed.
No more than 8 Full Defects.

Standard Method of Classification

Sample Weights:
Green Coffee - 350 grams
Roasted Coffee - 100 grams

Green Coffee Moisture Content:
Washed Coffees should be between 10 - 12% upon import.

Scent of the Green Coffee:
Coffee must be free of foreign odor.

Bean Size:
No more than 5% variance from purchase contract specification, measured referencing retention on standard grading screens.

Table of Defect Equivalents:

Category 1 Defects	Full Defect Equivalents	Category 2 Defects	Full Defect Equivalents
Full Black	1	Partial Black	3
Full Sour	1	Partial Sour	3
Dried Cherry/Pod	1	Parchment/Pergamino	5
Fungus Damaged	1	Floater	5
Severe Insect Damage	5	Immature/Unripe	5
Foreign Matter	1	Withered	5
		Shell	5
		Broken/Chipped/Cut	5
		Hull/Husk	5
		Slight Insect Damage	10

Roast Uniformity:
Specialty Grade – No quakers allowed
Premium Grade – Maximum 3 quakers allowed

Cupping Methodology:
Cupping is the professional technique for evaluating coffee's fragrance, aroma, taste, body and aftertaste. 150 milliliters of hot water are poured directly onto 7.25 to 9 grams of roast and ground coffee and allowed to steep. Using a large spoon, the coffee is stirred then vigorously sipped at various temperatures to reveal its full flavor characteristics.

Flavor Characteristics:
Upon cupping, sample must exhibit distinctive attributes in the areas of taste, acidity, body and aroma as determined between buyer and seller. Must be free from faults and taints.

Quaker: An unripe bean that does not fully develop during roasting.

Partial Black Bean: Less than one-half opaque black.

Partial Sour Bean: Less than one-half reddish or yellowish-brown.

Parchment/Pergamino Bean: Partially or fully enclosed in dried parchment.

Floater Bean: Light in color and low in density.

Broken/Chipped/Cut: A cut bean or fragment.

Immature/Unripe Bean: Underdeveloped and greenish with silverskin attached.

Hull/Husk: Fragment of a dried cherry/pod.

Withered Bean: Lightish green bean with a wrinkled surface.

Slight Insect Damage Bean: With less than three insect perforations.

Shell: Part of a malformed bean consisting of a cavity.

Green Coffee Color Gradient
Unroasted coffee's color ranges from a blue-green to a pale yellow depending upon origin, processing or age.

| Blue-Green | Bluish-Green | Green | Greenish | Yellow-Green | Yellowish | Pale Yellow |

Specialty Coffee Association Of America

1 World Trade Center, Suite #1200
Long Beach, California 90831
tel: 562.624.4100 • fax: 562.624.4101
www.scaa.org

Courtesy of SCAA

The Origins of Espresso

In 1903 Luigi Bezzera, an Italian manufacturer, was unhappy about the amount of time his workers spent on their coffee breaks. He thought that by shortening the brewing process, which took as long as 20 minutes, he could shorten the breaks.

Bezzera decided to brew the coffee under pressure. He invented a machine he called the "Fast Coffee Machine." Not only did Bezzera's machine reduce the brew time to a mere 20 seconds, but it also made a better cup of coffee than traditional methods made. The quick brewing time extracted the coffee's best qualities while leaving the unfavorable qualities, such as bitterness, behind.

Later Achilles Gaggia, a barkeeper, decided to improve on the basic espresso machine, adding a lever and piston that produced more pressure in the brew chamber. Today, Gaggia espresso machines and related equipment are familiar sights behind the counters of the world's coffee bars.

brewing. Espresso may be combined with ice, cold milk, steamed milk, whipped cream, mocha, and other flavorings to create a wide range of recipes.

There are several popular espresso-based drinks served in foodservice operations:

Americano—*Americano* is a single shot of espresso with 6 to 8 ounces (177 to 237 ml) of hot water added.

Caffe latte—*Caffe latte* is a single shot of espresso topped with steamed skim milk and a layer of frothed skim milk.

Cappuccino—*Cappuccino* is a single shot of espresso, topped with 4 1/2 ounces (133 ml) of thick foam of steamed milk served in a 6- to 8-ounce (177- to 237-ml) cup or glass with sugar on the side.

Caffe breve (brief)—a single shot of espresso and 4 ounces (118 ml) of steamed half-and-half, served in a 6-ounce (177-ml) cup with sugar on the side.

Corretto (corrected)—a single shot of espresso with a 1-ounce (30 ml) shot of liqueur served in a demitasse.

Doppio (double)—a double shot of espresso served with sugar on the side.

Espresso *macchiato* (marked)—a single or double shot of espresso topped with a heaping teaspoon of steamed milk.

Lungo (long)—a single shot of espresso served in a demitasse with sugar on the side.

Ristretto (restricted)—a shot of espresso, served in a demitasse with sugar to the side and a "water-back."

Decaffeinated Coffee

Caffeine, a nitrogen compound found in plants, is a mild stimulant that may increase the heart rate and cause sleeplessness in sensitive people. As little as 10 milligrams can cause discomfort.

The Food and Drug Administration (FDA) guidelines state that coffee labeled *decaffeinated* must have 97% of the caffeine removed from the green coffee bean prior to roasting, so decaffeinated coffee has about two to five milligrams of caffeine per serving. Three main processes decaffeinate coffee beans. Because caffeine is water-soluble, each process begins with moistened green coffee beans.

Conventional water method In this process, the green beans are treated with steam and water to open their cellular structure and then flushed with a decaffeinating agent such as methylene chloride or ethyl acetate. The beans are then treated with steam and water to evaporate all remaining traces of the decaffeinating agent. No traceable amount of the agent is left in the beans.

Swiss water processing Swiss water processing is similar to the water method but uses charcoal filtration rather than chemicals.

Supercritical carbon dioxide decaffeination This method uses carbon dioxide as the solvent agent. The carbon dioxide is passed through the coffee beans under tremendous pressure (250–300 times atmospheric pressure), typically extracting 96%–98% of the caffeine. This method, while expensive, is popular because carbon dioxide is abundant and reusable.

Degassing and Packaging Coffee

Preserving the maximum flavor, freshness, and aroma of coffee while packaging it for distribution is a complex problem.

After coffee beans are roasted, they produce carbon dioxide gas equal to about three times their volume. If the carbon dioxide is not released prior to most commercial packaging, the pressure of the escaping gas will burst the package. Unfortunately, when the carbon dioxide dissipates, the beans can absorb oxygen and become somewhat stale.

Packers have developed ingenious packaging solutions for the gas problem. Greaseproof, moisture-proof, resealable bags are nitrogen-flushed to displace oxygen. A one-way valve allows carbon dioxide to pass out of the bag while preventing air from entering it. After packages have been opened, however, storage conditions have an important effect on the coffee's flavor and quality.

Storing Coffee

To keep coffee's taste and aroma from dissipating, store it away from air, moisture, and heat. Buy smaller quantities of whole beans, and store the coffee in tightly sealed containers. It is preferable to keep previously opened coffee containers in a freezer. Freezing coffee for up to ten days will not seriously compromise the coffee's flavor. Unopened preportioned nitrogen-flushed coffee packs generally have a "use by" date and can be stored in a cool room.

Tasting Terms

Humans perceive taste through receptors on taste buds located primarily on the tongue. But taste is also affected by texture and mouth feel. Although taste is a somewhat subjective sensation, people have generally agreed on the meaning of several taste descriptors: sweet, sour, bitter, mellow, bland, fresh, and sharp, for example. Coffee tastes, too, have an agreed-on vocabulary.

Acidity This desirable characteristic refers to the lively, palate-cleansing tartness of the coffee. It is a characteristic of *arabica* from high-altitude growing regions. Acidity should not be confused with bitterness.

Body Body refers to the sense of heaviness or thickness of a coffee. Descriptors for this sensation would range from thin, light, and watery to buttery, heavy, and thick. Sumatran can be the heaviest coffee, and Mexican and Ethiopian coffees tend to be the lightest. Several factors, such as the type of grind, amount of water used, and brewing method, can also affect the coffee's body.

Flavor Flavor is the most important tasting term, referring to the overall impression of aromas, flavors, and body. Coffee can often be described as mellow or harsh, grassy or earthy. There are also special descriptors such as "chocolaty" or "winy" (winelike) that can be used to describe coffee's flavor.

Crema Crema is the amber foam that floats on top of a well-made espresso. The foam is composed of oils and colloids—suspended coffee particles. This mixture gives espresso a rich, full mouth feel.

Mocha Named for the Yemeni port of Moka on the Red Sea, from which coffee was first traded, mocha was a term used to describe coffee in Europe during the sixteenth century. When chocolate was brought from the Americas to Europe, Europeans believed it to have a flavor similar to coffee. *Mocha* is a term now used to describe a blend of coffee and chocolate.

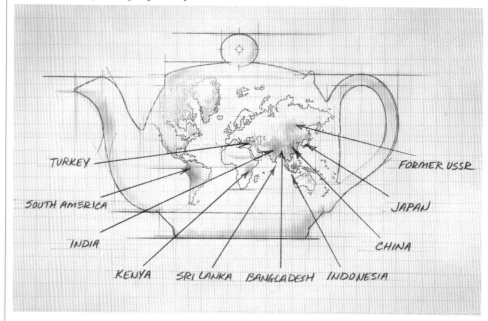

Tea

Legend has it that a Chinese emperor discovered tea in 2737 B.C. when a fragrant leaf or two from a nearby camellia tree blew into some water he was boiling. Tasting the brew, he declared it delectable, and thus was born tea cultivation. However, it was not until the Ming dynasty (A.D. 1368–1644) that tea consumption became a part of everyday life in China.

By the 1600s, explorers and traders were importing tea to Europe and then further abroad to America. Tea drinking soon became fashionable among British aristocrats.

In the late 1700s, afternoon tea became an everyday ritual among members of English society. Tea among the upper classes included not only the hot beverage but also delicate, crustless sandwiches and pastries. These offerings soon expanded to include toasted bread with jam, as well as scones and crumpets. The working classes soon developed their own ritual, with "high tea" consisting of meats, cheese, and breads taken as their principal evening meal.

FIGURE 34-4

Tea, the world's most popular beverage after water, begins with these first-flush leaves of the Camellia sinensis tree.

FIGURE 34-5

Even today, hand-harvesting of tea remains a painstaking task.

Tea Production

Today, tea is the most popular beverage in the world after water. It is available in a wide variety of forms, ranging from the modest, inexpensive tea bag to extremely rare, and proportionately expensive, herbs gathered by hand in remote regions of the world. See Figure 34-3 on page 826.

Tea is processed from the leaves of *Camellia sinensis*, a tree or shrub that grows best at higher altitudes under damp, tropical conditions.

The leaves are hand-harvested or plucked from the plants' youngest shoots, called the first and second flush. See Figure 34-4 and 34-5. About 4,200 pounds (1,905 kg) of fresh tea leaves produce 1,000 pounds (454 kg) of finished tea.

Although tea grows in many other regions, India, China, Sri Lanka, Indonesia, and Kenya account for most of the world's commercial production and exports. Teas often take their names from the regions in which they are grown.

Tea Classification

Although all tea comes from basically the same plant species, there are approximately 1,500 grades and 2,000 different blends of teas. Three general classifications of tea define the level of enzymatic oxidation that leaves undergo during processing. See Figure 34-6 on page 828.

Green Tea

Green tea is unfermented and yellowish-green with a slightly bitter flavor. Steaming or heating the leaves immediately after picking prevents enzymatic oxidation that turns tea leaves into black tea. After heating, the leaves are rolled and dried. Green teas need to be stored properly and served fresh. Green teas are produced primarily in China, Taiwan, and Japan.

Examples of green tea include:

Gyokuro—the finest grade of exported Japanese tea.

Tencha—the powdered tea used in Japanese tea ceremonies.

Sencha—the most common Japanese tea, popular in restaurants and sushi bars.

Gunpowder—the highest Chinese grade; it is rolled into tiny balls.

Imperial—a grade from Sri Lanka, China, or India.

Shou Mei—Chinese green tea known as "old man's eyebrows."

Oolong Tea

Oolong tea combines the characteristics of black and green teas. The leaves are partially oxidized; then the process is interrupted, and the leaves are rolled and dried.

Oolong is often flavored with scented agents such as jasmine flowers. It is also graded by leaf size and age.

Examples of oolong tea include:

Formosa Oolong—a delicate, large-leafed oolong tea with a taste reminiscent of ripe peaches. Unique and expensive, it is suited to breakfast or afternoon tea.

Black Dragon—a kind of tea from Taiwan.

Pouchong—grown both in China and Taiwan.

Black Tea

When steeped, *black tea* is strongly flavored and amber or coppery brown. The color and flavor result from plucked leaves being dried, or *withered,* and then rolled in special machines to release the enzymes that give the tea its color, specific taste, and aroma. See Figure 34-7. The leaves are then "fired," or heated and compressed, to their final shape.

Teas are also sorted by leaf size and according to their brewing time. Larger leaves take longer to brew than smaller leaves. Size classifications include souchong, or large-leaf tea; pekoe, or medium-leaf tea; and orange pekoe, or the smallest whole-leaf tea.

Broken tea leaves are categorized as either fannings and dust—used for tea bags—and broken orange pekoe—of high-quality, and generally results in a darker brew of the kind most commonly steeped from tea bags. Black teas are the best known and most popular in the West, but most teas sold in the United States are blends. Even the same tea blend or type of tea will taste different from blender to blender, however. Some of the most popular types of teas are:

Assam—a rich, black tea from Northern India, valued as a breakfast tea by connoisseurs.

Ceylon—a full-flavored black tea with a delicate fragrance; ideal for iced tea because it does not turn cloudy when cold.

Darjeeling—a full-bodied, black tea with a Muscat flavor, grown in the foothills of the Himalayas.

Earl Grey—a popular choice for afternoon tea, Earl Grey is flavored with oil of bergamot.

English Breakfast—a full-bodied, robust blend of Indian and Sri Lankan teas.

Lapsang Souchong—a tarry, smoky flavor and aroma, best suited to afternoon tea or as a dinner beverage.

FIGURE 34-6

Three general classifications of tea: green, oolong, and black (shown left to right in the teapots).

FIGURE 34-7

Withering, or drying, tea leaves produces black tea.

Iced Tea and Tea Bags

Iced tea and the tea bag have "happy accidents" in common. Iced tea was invented at the 1904 World's Fair in St. Louis, Missouri, when, with the temperature soaring and fairgoers ignoring the hot brew, tea merchant Richard Blechynden dumped a load of ice into the tea and served it cold.

In 1908 New York tea merchant Thomas Sullivan carefully wrapped samples of his product in muslin bags for restaurant managers to test. When he realized that the restaurants were brewing his samples in the bag to avoid the mess of tea leaves, the tea bag was born.

At about the same time, Thomas Lipton, a British merchant and owner of several tea plantations, began marketing his high-quality tea blend in convenient, inexpensive boxes that were affordable by middle- and working-class people.

By the mid-1990s, according to the Tea Council, only a little more than 1% of the tea brewed in the United States was prepared from loose tea. Approximately 60% was prepared from tea bags, with iced tea mixes accounting for another 25%. The remaining tea was made from instant tea.

Infusions

Many other "teas" are produced by infusing roots, stems, seeds, berries, flowers, leaves, herbs, and spices in water. *Infusion* involves steeping flavoring agents in water. The following are the different types of infusions:

Scented teas Scented teas are made by blending aromatic petals from flowers such as jasmine, lavender, gardenias, or magnolias with tea leaves.

Flavored teas Flavored teas gain their distinct character by the addition of the essence of citrus fruits, berries, vanilla, or other flavoring components to tea leaves.

Spiced teas Blending flavoring agents such as cinnamon, nutmeg, coriander, and cloves with tea leaves produces spiced teas.

Herbal teas Herbal teas, or *tisanes,* are infusions made from such herbs as chamomile, spearmint, ginseng, and lemon balm. These beverages do not contain any real tea at all; however, they are prepared in the same way as tea infusions.

Beer

The making of the first beer, like the brewing of coffee and the steeping of tea, was also a happy accident. More than 8,000 years ago, early peoples discovered that wild barley, when soaked in water, produced a liquid that fermented on contact with natural yeasts. The resulting beverage was probably cloudy, muddy brown, and very different from today's beer, but drinking it evoked feelings of happiness and relaxation. According to clay tablets found in Mesopotamia dating to about 6000 B.C., the earliest known recipe of any kind is for making beer. The brewing of beer was also well established and already regulated.

Brewing Develops

Regulation did not slow beer's development, however. By about 4000 B.C., the Babylonians were brewing about 16 varieties of beer—and giving it a better flavor by adding such ingredients as dates and honey. Egyptians added their own touches to the brew. Around 3000 B.C., Egyptians brewed beer from barley bread soaked in water and added their own flavorings, such as herbs and fruits. The Egyptians passed their brewing knowledge on to the Greeks and Romans, and beer became increasingly popular throughout Europe, partly because the alcohol eliminated disease-causing bacteria that often contaminated water in early times.

In the tenth century A.D., beer brewing, which was universally done in homes, began to develop along two divergent paths. The Celtic and Anglo-Saxon peoples of Britain continued to brew ales without hops, but Belgians and Germans began using hops as a natural preservative and flavor enhancer. The nineteenth century marked the beginning of lager (German for "storage") beers. The use of ice-packed caves in the Bavarian Alps to store and preserve beers allowed for slow-acting yeast strains to adapt, and new beer styles were developed.

From the earliest Puritan settlements in the United States, the dominant beer styles were ales, porters, and stouts until an influx of German immigrants in the mid-1800s introduced lagers. The advent of commercial refrigeration in 1860, pasteurization in 1876, and railroad distribution all ushered in the modern era of beer brewing. By 1880 about 2,300 breweries were scattered across the United States. The beer industry was destroyed by Prohibition, but after it was repealed in 1933, four breweries, Anheuser-Busch®, Miller®, Coors®, and Stroh's®, came to dominate the market, with a combined 97% share of total sales.

Craft and Microbreweries

The proliferation of local craft and microbreweries in the 1980s and 1990s was a reaction to the rather uniformly bland taste of the big four breweries' beer, the growth of the home-brew industry, and the passage of legislation that granted tax advantages to microbreweries. These developments have given Americans an unparalleled choice of beer styles. See Figure 34-8 on page 830. During the same period, however, major brewers also expanded their portfolios of products.

Primary Brewing Ingredients

Although the brewing industry offers consumers an expanded list of choices, all beers generally have four essential ingredients: water, malted grain (usually barley, but sometimes wheat), hops, and yeast. Most have a fifth ingredient, called an adjunct, such as rice or corn, for lightness and economy.

Water

Water makes up 90%–96% of beer, and its quality greatly affects the beverage's quality. In the 1960s, one brewery acknowledged water's importance with its "From the land of sky blue waters" slogan. Brewers are well advised to pay attention to a good water source. The lack of certain minerals may prevent yeasts from fermenting, and water's mineral content (hardness or softness) impacts the brewing process and the beer's ultimate flavor. "Burton" ale, for example, has a distinct taste profile that comes from a particularly high mineral concentration in the water source.

Malted Barley

Barley, the most significant solid ingredient in brewing, provides nutrients for yeast and contributes body, flavor, and color to beer. Although other cereal grains such as wheat, oats, and rye can also be brewed into beer, barley is by far the most popular and practical for malting. See Figure 34-9.

Malting, the essential process at the beginning of brewing, has three essential steps—steeping, germinating, and kilning. In the malting process, the grains are *steeped,* or soaked, by being sprayed with water, aerated, and held at 50°F (10°C) and 100% humidity over a period of five days. During that time the barley *germinates,* or grows, and the sprouting barley forms enzymes that convert starches to sugars essential to fermentation. After germination, the malt is *kilned,* or dried. Time, temperature, and moisture level in the kilning process determines the flavor and color characteristics of the malt. Most beers use a *pale malt,* but small amounts of specially kilned malts impart other specific flavors and colors to beer.

Specialty malts include:

- **Black malt**—Roasted at high temperatures, this malt is black and has a burned flavor often perceived as bitterness.
- **Chocolate malt**—This dark brown malt is roasted for a shorter time than black malt, is sweeter (with a less burned or bitter flavor), and gives beer some chocolate flavor notes.
- **Crystal or caramel malt**—Golden to reddish hues and a caramel or toffee flavor result from barely roasting the malt.

Hops

The cone-shaped flowers of the *hop* vine *(humulus lupulus)* help preserve beer and impart aromas and bitterness to it. The bitterness of hops balance the sweetness of malt. Hops, like spices, come in several varieties, and the kind of hops, the amount used, and the contact time all determine the level of bitterness and aroma hops impart to beer. Hop aromas vary from herbal, piney, and tobacco-like to citrusy. In addition to their antiseptic quality, hops also help beer retain the foam that forms the head when beer is poured.

Yeast

Yeast, a single-celled fungus, is essential to fermentation. Yeast cells produce alcohol and natural carbonation in beer. Although the results of yeast growth have long been appreciated in bread making and brewing, it wasn't until 1876 that Louis Pasteur first described yeast's role in fermentation. To a great degree, the strain of yeast in brewing determines the type and style of beer. Smooth, light lagers, for example, are made with the strain *Saccharomyces carlsbergensis.* Hearty, robust ales are made with *Saccharomyces cerevisiae,* or, as it is now known, *S. uvarum.* See Figure 34-10 on page 831.

Adjuncts

Adjuncts include sugars or starches made from unmalted grains other than barley, used to produce a lighter, smoother beer with a clean finish. Most American beers have cornmeal or ground rice added to their recipes. Adjuncts can also refer to fruits and fruit purées, such as apricots, that are added to make Belgian-style lambic beers.

The Brewing Process

Milling, mashing, lautering, boiling, fermenting, and lagering (or aging) are the essential steps in brewing beer. Although the equipment used has been refined over the ages and the processes better understood, the basic method remains the same as that practiced in ancient Sumaria or Egypt. See Figure 34-11 on page 832.

Milling

After kilning, the malted barley needs to be *milled,* or ground into a coarse meal called *grist,* to expose the interior starches to the brewing water. Milling is best done immediately prior to making the beer to preserve freshness and flavor.

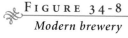
FIGURE 34-8
Modern brewery

FIGURE 34-9
Malted barley is the heart and soul of beer. It determines its color, flavor, and aroma.

Mashing

The grist then goes to a large container called a *mash tun,* where it is mashed together with hot water. At a critical temperature range, the starches from the grist are converted by malt enzymes into fermentable sugars, in a process called *saccharification.* By adjusting the temperature and length of saccharification, the brewer can influence a beer's body and alcohol content.

Lautering

The sweet brown liquid or extract, called the *wort,* is separated from the mash bed and transferred carefully to a brew in a process called *lautering.* Hot water, called liquor, is sprayed over the mash bed to prevent it from collapsing and creating a cloudy wort. Lautering also enables better sugar extraction from the malt.

Boiling

The bacteria-vulnerable wort is boiled for 1–2 hours in the kettle to sterilize it and to incorporate the needed compounds of the hops, which determine the level of bitterness. To extract the aromatic qualities of hops, they are added for a short period to the boiling wort.

Fermenting

The boiling wort is cooled and transferred to the fermenting tank, carefully using a whirlpool action so that it is separated from the unwanted proteins, called a *trub,* which then collect at the bottom of the

kettle. Oxygen is generally injected into the wort to promote initial yeast growth. The appropriate yeast is added.

Ales, porters, and stouts are made with yeast that rises to the surface and works at a higher temperature for a shorter duration than it does in bottom-fermented beers.

Lager, Pilsner, and Bock beers are produced by yeasts that work at a colder temperature, from the bottom of the fermentation container. Ales take only a few days to ferment, but lagers take up to six weeks.

Lagering, Storing, and Conditioning

After fermentation is complete, the brewer transfers the beer to storage vats for *conditioning*—a process that may last from three days to three months. Here the beer may also be lagered. During *lagering,* stubborn sugars continue to ferment. Some brewers *kräusen* their beers, a process in which unfermented wort is added to the aging beer to cause a secondary fermentation. Adding hops at this stage, called dry hopping, may also be done to increase hop aromas. Following this stage, the beer is put into casks, kegs, bottles, or cans for storage.

Beer Types and Styles

The two broad categories of beer, top-fermented and bottom-fermented, also have several varieties. See Figure 34-12 on page 833.

Ales

Ales were the original beers until the advent of hops and refrigeration. Ales are top-fermented beers that exhibit a variety of characteristics. Often described in literature as "nut brown ale," the beer has flavors described as sweet, fruity, pale, mild, or bitter. Ale styles include:

- **Brown ale**—This is a sweet, lightly hopped full-bodied beer with a reddish to brown color.
- **India pale ale**—This is a distinctively dry and bitter beer with some fruity and floral notes and a color that ranges from light to copper.
- **Scottish ale**—Rich and mouth-filling, this beer is amber to dark brown with a sweet, malty flavor and higher alcohol content than some other ales.
- **Stout**—Stout is a dark, heavy, top-fermented beer made with a high proportion of roasted malt or barley. Stout is often quite sweet and strong, but it also includes different styles such as dry, imperial, oatmeal, and milk stout.
- **Porter**—This is a dark chocolate-colored ale somewhat between an ale and a stout; it is generally drier than a stout with varying levels of bitterness.
- **Sake**—Sake is a Japanese rice beer/wine which is high in alcohol (16%) and varies in style. The best-crafted sake is served chilled like a white wine; commercial-grade sake is served warm.

Lagers

Lagers are bottom-fermented beers; they ferment for a longer time and at cooler temperatures than ales, and as a result, have crisp, clean, more heavily carbonated characters. Most lagers have lighter coloration than other beers and are less "hoppy" and lighter-bodied.

Lagers include:

- **American pilsner**—This is a pale gold, crisp, carbonated pilsner that is weaker and lighter in body than its German counterparts. American pilsner is the prevalent beer style in the United States.
- **European pilsner**—This beer is the model of a clean, dry beer that is light-bodied with a floral finish.
- **American dry lager**—This beer is pale gold and light-bodied with high carbonation and low bitterness.
- **Bock**—Bock is a dark brown beer with strong malt and hops flavors.

FIGURE 34-10

Yeast + sugar = alcohol + CO₂—Note the froth from fermentation's CO₂.

FIGURE 34-11
The brewing process

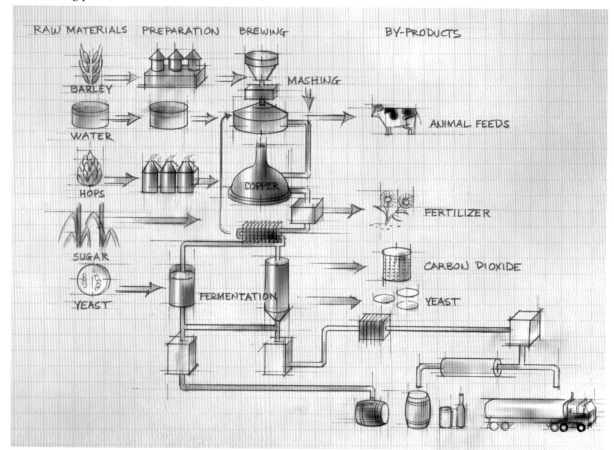

Courtesy of British Beer and Pub Association

- **Malt liquor**—This variety is pale, light-flavored, and sweet with high alcohol content (up to 6%).

Specialty Beers

A specialty beer has an adjunct such as fruits, spices, or smoke.

- **Abbey or Trappist**—This rich, dark beer is produced by five Trappist monasteries in Belgium.
- **Lambic**—Lambic is a somewhat sour wheat beer with fruit adjuncts such as cherry (*kriek*), peach (*pêche*), or raspberries (*framboise*). It is fermented by a wild yeast colony that lives in the cellar of monasteries and generally has low carbonation.
- **Faro**—Faro is a lambic beer with rock candy added to re-ferment it and add sweetness to balance the sourness.
- **Gueuze**—This beer is a blend of aged lambics with new lambics.
- **Rauchbier**—The malt of this beer is wood-smoked, giving the beer a very smoky flavor.

Combination Styles

This category of beers includes those that are made from a combination of top- and bottom-fermented brewing styles.

- **Altbier**—Altbier is an amber-colored beer that is aromatic and malty, but bitter. It is basically an ale that is cold lagered.
- **Bière de garde**—This complex, highly aromatic, and alcoholic beer needs bottle aging.
- **Kölsch**—Kölsch is a pale, cold beer that is drier, less bitter, and more delicate than an Altbier.
- **Steam beer**—This unique amber-colored American invention is ale made with lager yeast. It has good body and hops aroma.
- **Wheat/Weisse/Weizen/Weiss-bier**—This wheat beer should be very carbonated and sour with citric and spicy notes. Bottle-conditioned wheat beers are cloudy and known as *Hefe Weizen*.

Storing Beer

Although it is best consumed as soon as it is packaged, pasteurized beer has a shelf life of about three months. Beer bottles are colored brown to filter out light because beers exposed to fluorescent light or sunlight will smell "skunky." Beers that are exposed to heat will smell "cardboardy." Beer is at its best when stored in a cool, dark room with a temperature between 50°F–55°F (10°C–13°C). Unpasteurized and draft beers keep only two or three weeks and must be kept refrigerated at all times.

Serving Beer

Ideally, the different beer types require different service temperatures to maximize the taster's appreciation. Ales should be served between 55°F–60°F (13°C–16°C). Lagers, on the other hand, should be served at 45°F–50°F (7°C–10°C).

FIGURE 34-12

Major Styles of Beer

PILSNER

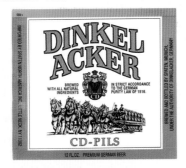

INDIAN PALE ALE

HEFE-WEIZEN/WEISSE

BOCK

LAGER

AMBER ALE

AMERICAN PILSNER

PORTER

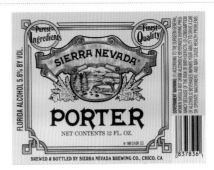

PALE ALE

STOUT

Different beer types also benefit from different glass shapes. Beer glasses range from tulip-shaped, stemmed ale glasses and thick tall stout tumblers to lager mugs with handles and V-shaped pilsner glasses. See Figure 34-13. The most significant factor for a glass, however, is that it is clean, properly rinsed, and air-dried. It should not be frosted. Lack of cleanliness or detergent residue will prevent the beer foam, or head, from forming. See Figure 34-14.

The head preserves the beer's aromas and helps retain the carbonation. A quality beer will have a thin lace-patterned film of small bubbles and foam that is referred to as Belgian or Brussels lace.

To serve a beer from a bottle, allow the glass to remain on a flat surface. Pour the beer over the edge of the glass so that the stream flows vertically into the center of the glass. Reduce the flow after the head is formed, and stop when the head reaches the top of the glass. If guests prefer less foam, pour the beer along the side of the glass.

Draft Beer

Guests often prefer draft beer because it is generally fresher and has a more pleasing carbonation than bottled or canned beers. When drawing draft beer from a keg, hold the glass 1 inch below the tap at a 45° angle, and open the tap. As the glass becomes half full, pour the beer vertically. Close the tap after the head has risen slightly above the rim. See Figures 34-14 and 34-15.

Quality Characteristics of Beer

Quality beers are marked by a number of characteristics. For the most part, the beer's color should be clear and uniform, and the head should have tightly knitted, small bubbles that do not quickly dissipate. The head of the beer should be no less than half its original height after a minute. Aromas should be clean and refreshing, and the flavors and body should be balanced with either the sweetness of malt or the bitterness of the hops predominating, depending on the beer style. The first sip should invite the taster for another, and the finish should be pleasant but not lingering.

Poorly made beer, on the other hand, is characterized as having tastes and smells of butter, cabbage, cheese, green apples, bandages, mold, musk, rotten eggs, or turpentine.

FIGURE 34-15
Many customers prefer draft beer for its fresh taste and pleasant carbonation.

Pairing Beer and Food

Beer can be an ideal companion to many different foods. Just as different wines complement different dishes, some beers pair well with certain foods. The right combination can make for an unforgettable dining experience.

Although there are no hard-and-fast rules for which beer is best served with which food, here are some general guidelines:

- The flavor of the beer should either complement or contrast nicely with the food with which it is paired. Pale ale, for example, contrasts well with the robust, smoky flavors of barbecue. The same ale would also complement fish or shellfish.
- If preparing ethnic foods, beer from the same region usually pairs very well with the flavors. A rich, dark lager from Germany is an excellent match for bratwurst and grilled onions, for example.
- If the beer style has a dominant taste, then the food should contrast with it— a bitter ale with food that is salty or a little sweet, for example.

Spirits and Liqueurs

A *spirit* is a highly alcoholic beverage produced by both fermentation and distillation. Alcoholic *distillation* is the process by which alcohol from a fermented liquid is evaporated, captured, and cooled to liquid form. Spirits are made from fermented products such as grapes, sugarcane, apples, potatoes, and grains. The fermented liquids are then distilled to create such spirits as whiskey, brandy, tequila, vodka, and rum.

Liqueurs, also known as cordials, are highly refined, sweet spirits to which flavorings such as fruits, nuts, herbs, or spices have been added. They are often enjoyed before dining as *apéritifs* or after dinner as *digestifs*. They are also essential parts of many cocktails. Most liqueurs contain between 17% and 30% alcohol by volume, and some may contain as much as 50%. See Figure 34-16 on page 836.

Liquor and Liqueurs in History

As is the case with many early processes, no one knows for sure who discovered the method of distillation or exactly when it happened. Because alcohol and water boil at different temperatures, a distiller can heat a fermented beverage to the boiling point for ethyl alcohol (173°F/78°C), capture the vapor, and then cool it to condense it into liquid alcohol. Water, with its higher boiling point of 212°F (100°C), is left behind.

Many experts speculate that the Chinese used this process with rice wines around 800 B.C., as did the Greeks and the Egyptians with other wines. Aristotle described distilling seawater to capture freshwater in about 400 B.C., but the first recorded distillation of alcoholic beverages in Europe did not occur until circa A.D. 900.

Culinary Relevance

From cocktails and apéritifs with canapés before dinner to brandy or a liqueur with coffee after dinner, spirits and liqueurs are indispensable parts of dining for many people.

Unlike wine and beer, spirits are not usually prominent features in the preparation of savory foods, though they are sometimes used as an ingredient in a marinade or a basting sauce. For dessert tableside preparations and for pastry chefs, however, liquors and liqueurs are invaluable flavoring agents.

FIGURE 34-16

Types and Origins of Alcoholic Beverages

FERMENTED

Grape	*Other Fruits*	*Grain*	*Miscellaneous*
Wines:	Cider	Beer:	Palm Pulque
Aromatized/Apéritif	Citrus	Ale Pilsner	
Sparkling	Cherry	Stout Lager	
Table	Others	Porter Bock	
Dessert		Sake	
Fortified		Others	

DISTILLED

Grain	*Sugarcane*	*Plants and Roots*	*Fruit*
Whiskeys Vodka	Rum	Arak	Brandy Spirits:
		Okolehao	
American Imported	Light Dark	Tequila	Grape: Cognac
Bourbon Canadian	Puerto Rican Barbados	Neutral	Armagnac
Light Irish	Virgin Islands Jamaica	spirit	Marc
Corn Scotch	Others		Grappa
Sour mash			Others
Tennessee			Apple: Applejack
Blended			Calvados
Straight			Cherry: Kirsch
Rye			Pear: Poire
Bottled in			Plum: Mirabelle
bond			Quetsch
			Slivovitz
			Raspberry: Framboise

COMPOUNDED

Gin	*Liqueurs*	*Bitters:*	*Miscellaneous:*
	Flowers	Aromatic	Aquavit
London Dry	Fruits	Fruits	Anise
Holland	Plants		Prepared cocktails
Flavored	Spices		
	Others		

The Distillation Process

Monks and alchemists improved on the process of distillation over the centuries. In 1205, Arnaud de Villeneuve became the first person to distill wine in France. In Great Britain, with the dissolution of the monasteries in the sixteenth century, monks began to share their knowledge with distillers. Over the years, the distillation process has been refined, but the essential process remains basically the same.

As noted, distilling spirits is possible because water and ethyl alcohol, the two primary components of a fermented beverage, have different boiling points. The alcohol is vaporized and then recondensed in an apparatus called a *still.*

All alcoholic beverages fall into one of three categories:

- Fermented beverages made from products such as grains and fruits with alcoholic strengths ranging from 3.2%–14%
- Distilled spirits resulting from a distillation of fermented beverages
- Compounded beverages made from combining either a fermented beverage or spirit with a flavoring agent

Production Processes

There are five necessary steps in the production of distilled spirits: mashing, fermenting, distilling, aging or filtering, and blending. For a flavored spirit or liqueur, there is an additional step of compounding.

Mashing

Corn, barley, and rye are the principal grains used in making beverage-quality alcohol. The process begins with milling the grains to break down the hull and free the starch that will eventually convert to alcohol.

The next step is to turn the grain starch into grain sugar by mixing the grain meal with water to form a *mash.* Then, barley malt is added, and the end result is *maltose,* or grain sugar. See Figure 34-17.

Fermenting

Fermentation begins when yeast is added to the mash. As the yeast grows, it digests the sugar and releases alcohol and carbon dioxide. As the yeast multiplies, creating grain alcohol, the alcohol mixes with *congeners,* or flavoring agents.

Distilling

When the fermented liquid is heated to vaporize the alcohol, some water and some congeners are left behind. When the alcohol vapor is cooled, it condenses into clear ethyl alcohol. Spirits such as whiskey are distilled to the 140–160 proof (70%–80% alcohol) range. At higher proof levels, fewer congeners stay behind, the spirit loses flavor characteristics of the grain, and a rather harsh neutral spirit results. See Figure 34-18.

Aging or Filtering

To dispel the harshness of this clear spirit, the liquid is either aged or *filtered.* See Figure 34-19. Aging takes place in charred oak barrels that give color to the spirit, absorb impurities, and mellow the flavor. The character of the spirit depends on aging time—sometimes as long as 18–24 years. Clear spirits, such as vodka, are filtered in activated charcoal systems to mellow them, with the higher-quality clear spirits being filtered as many as four times.

Blending

After the aging or filtering is completed, the spirits are reduced in *proof,* or percentage of alcohol by volume, to the desired concentration by the addition of demineralized water. In the blending process, spirits of different ages and sometimes from different grains are blended into the final product, which is then bottled and packaged for sale. Once bottled, aging and changes to the product cease.

Compounding

Compounding blends spirits with other flavorings, including sweeteners. Infusion involves steeping flavoring agents using heat; maceration steeps them by cold method. Percolation allows the spirit to trickle through a flavoring agent, rather like water trickles through ground coffee, except that the process takes place repeatedly.

FIGURE 34-17
The process of turning grain into mead whiskey begins with germination.

FIGURE 34-18
The principles of distilling have not changed since early Celts first produced their fiery "water of life."

FIGURE 34-19
Virtually all straight whiskies are aged at least four years.

Redistillation involves distilling a spirit with a flavoring agent; gin, for example, is redistilled with juniper berries.

American Whiskies

The United States government requires that all whiskies be made from a grain mash, distilled at 90% alcohol by volume (ABV) or less and reduced to no more than 62.5% ABV (125 proof) before aging in oak barrels. (The exception is corn whiskey, which does not have to be aged in oak.) Whiskies must have the aroma, taste, and characteristics that are generally attributed to whiskey and must be bottled at no less than 40% ABV (80 proof).

The following eight designations are rigidly defined by law and regulated accordingly:

Straight

Straight whiskey is unblended and contains no neutral spirits. It must be aged at least two years but generally is aged four years in new charred oak. Old Charter® (10 years old) is an example.

Bourbon

Bourbon whiskey must contain a minimum of 51% corn, be produced in Kentucky, be distilled at less than 80% ABV (160 proof), and be aged for a minimum of two years in new charred barrels, although most are aged longer. This straight whiskey has seen a renaissance with the introduction of single batch and single barrel high-end bourbons. Examples include Maker's Mark, Jim Beam® 80 proof, Early Times®, and Old Grand-Dad® 86 proof.

Corn

Corn whiskey must contain at least 80% corn, be distilled at less than 80% ABV (160 proof), and be aged for a minimum of two years in new or used uncharred barrels.

Sour Mash

Sour mash is a result of the fermentation process, in which the mash is soured with a lactic culture like sourdough bread. Examples include Jim Beam® Black Label 90 proof and Chester Graves® 90 proof.

Tennessee

Tennessee whiskey differs from bourbon only in that the distillate is leached or filtered through sugar maple charcoal in mellowing vats before being diluted with demineralized water and aged in charred oak barrels. One of the more popular examples is Jack Daniel's® Black Label 90 proof.

Blended

Blended whiskeys are lightbodied with at least 20% straight whiskey, the balance being made up of unaged neutral spirits. Seagram's 7 Crown® 80 proof and Corby's Reserve® 80 proof are examples.

Bottled in Bond

Bottled in bond is a straight whiskey produced by one distiller. It is required to be aged at least four years, bottled at 100 proof, and stored in bonded warehouses under government supervision. Examples include Old Forrester® 100 proof, Beam's® 100 proof, and Old Grand-Dad® B/B 100 proof.

Rye

By definition, rye whiskey must be produced from a grain mash containing at least 51% rye grain. It may not be distilled at higher than 160 proof and must be aged in new charred oak barrels. One example is Jim Beam Rye®, which is 86 proof.

For a list of proprietary brand names of American whiskies, see Figure 34-25 on page 842.

Imported Whiskies

A variety of imported whiskies are available in the United States for consumption, including Canadian, Irish, and Scotch whiskies.

Canadian

Virtually all Canadian whiskey is six years old or older. Anything aged for less time must be labeled as such. All Canadian whiskey

FIGURE 34-21

Every Scotch whiskey has a distinctive flavor that is a result of climate, peat or fuel, and water used in the process.

is aged in oak casks for at least three years, but most typically from six to eight years.

By U.S. law, imported Canadian whiskey must be produced in Canada and must contain no distilled spirits fewer than three years old. It is often referred to simply as rye whiskey or rye, even though it contains more corn and other grains. This lighter-tasting whiskey is the third most popularly demanded spirit category after vodka and liqueurs. Examples include Seagram's VO®, Canadian Club®, and Seagram's Crown Royal®.

FIGURE 34-20

Distillation and production process for Scotch

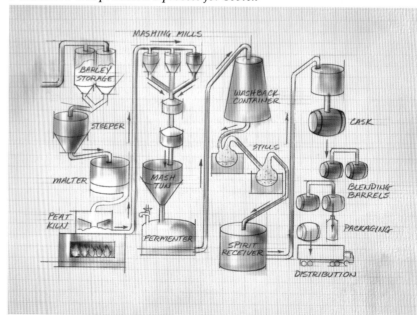

Irish Whiskies

Irish whiskey must be produced in Ireland, triple-distilled, usually in pot stills, from Irish grain, aged in wooden casks for three years, and bottled at not less than 40% ABV. Its base is barley, with oats and other grains added for additional flavor. The soft mineral content of the water and triple distillation gives Irish whiskey a heavier and smoother character than its Scottish counterpart. Examples include Jameson® 80-proof, Murphy Irish® 86 proof, and Dunphy's Irish®.

Scotch Whiskies

Scotch whiskies include blended Scotch whiskey, vatted malt scotches, and single malts. Blended Scotch whiskey contains a mixture of grain whiskey and malt whiskey and can contain as many as 40 different malt whiskies.

Vatted malt scotches or pure malt scotches are blends from more than one distillery. Single malt is a whiskey brewed from a single batch of wort from one particular distillery. Scotland has more than 100 distilleries, each of which produces a distinctive single malt whiskey, but the different malts may be grouped as follows.

- **Highland malts**—These malts are sweeter and have more body and character than Lowland malts.
- **Lowland malts**—These malts are drier than Highland malts. They are usually lighter, and there are fewer differences among them than among malts from other regions.
- **Islay malts**—Islay malts are the most pungent and heavily peaty of all the malts. They take their characteristics from the peat that is used to dry the barley and from their closeness to the sea.
- **Campbeltown single malts**—These malts have a distinctive, briny taste. With two distilleries, this region produces three single malts, each with its own character.

See Figure 34-20 and Figure 34-21 on page 838 to learn how Scotch is distilled and produced and Figure 34-22 to view some popular Scotch brands. For a list of proprietary brand imported whiskies, see Figure 34-25 on page 842.

Gin

An unaged liquor, gin is made from grains such as barley, corn, or rye and is flavored with juniper berries, coriander, and other herbs and spices. Gin is valued for its ability to blend harmoniously with other substances. Examples of classic gin pairings include the martini (with dry vermouth) and gin and tonic water.

English gin is similar to American gin, but it is generally distilled at a lower proof than Dutch or Genever gin. Those gins are much more highly flavored and fuller-bodied than English gin and are not, therefore, as well suited to mixing with other ingredients. See Figure 34-25 on page 842 for a list of gins by brand name.

Vodka

Vodka is produced primarily from grain, potatoes, molasses, or beets. Russian vodkas are made from wheat and Polish vodkas from rye.

FIGURE 34-22

Popular Brands of Scotch

BLENDED AND SINGLE-MALT SCOTCHES

Highlands

Lowland

Islay

Speyside

Courtesy Schieffelin & Somerset Co.

In the United States, domestic vodka is defined as a "neutral spirit," refined to be without distinctive taste, aroma, color, or other characteristics. As a neutral spirit, vodka lends itself well to mixing with other beverages or fortifying other spirits and is preeminent in the U.S. market.

The super premium vodkas are triple or quadruple distilled and demand higher prices because they are less harsh and have a lower congener content. For a list of brand-name vodkas, see Figure 34-25 on page 842.

Rum

Most rum is made from fermented sugar juice, sugarcane syrup, sugarcane molasses, and other sugarcane by-products. Rum is produced wherever sugarcane grows—primarily in the Caribbean in Puerto Rico, the Virgin Islands, Jamaica, Barbados, Trinidad, Martinique, and Haiti. See Figure 34-25 on page 842. Rums are classified as white, golden, or dark.

White rum White rums are generally highest in alcohol, light-bodied and clear, with a subtle flavor. If they are aged in oak casks, they are usually filtered to remove any color. Primarily used as a mixer, white rum blends particularly well with fruit flavors.

Golden rum Golden, or amber, rum is medium bodied, and usually aged for at least three years in oak casks. Its taste is smooth and mellow.

Dark rum Dark rum is the traditional, full-bodied, rich rum, dominated by overtones of caramel. The best are produced in pot stills and are usually aged for a minimum of six years in oak barrels. The best of these rums are consumed straight up.

Brandy

The word brandy has its roots in the Dutch word *brandewijn*, which means "distilled wine." Dutch traders distilled the highly acidic white wines of the Cognac region to limit taxes. (Ten barrels of wine produce only one barrel of cognac.) People soon discovered that the longer the distilled beverage aged, the better it tasted. Other brandies are distilled from fruit wines and pulp. Although many countries produce brandies, the best known are distilled from grape wine, especially Cognac and Armagnac. See Figure 34-25 on page 842.

Cognac

Cognacs are the world's elite brandies. Their high quality stems from the kinds of grapes from which they are distilled, the soil and climate of the Cognac region, and the skill of the distillers.

Cognac is distilled twice in pure copper alembic stills soon after the base wine (made from Ugni Blanc, Colombard, and Folle Blanche grapes) has finished fermenting. The first distillation produces a 30% alcoholic liquid called the *broullis* which is redistilled to make the *bonne chauffe*. Then the brandy is aged in Limousin and Tronçais oak barrels, in which a slow oxidative reduction gives cognac its distinctive flavor. The resulting evaporation is called "the angels' share."

The soil's impact is codified into the appellation laws. The more chalk, the better the appellation. The best area, in the heart of Cognac, is Grande Champagne followed by Petite Champagne. The other subdivisions include: Borderie, Fins Bois, Bon Bois, and Bois Ordinaire. Labels with "Fine Champagne" are a blend of 50% Grande and 50% Petite Champagne cognac.

Like all spirits and brandies, cognac ages only as long as it remains in wood, but after 60 years, there are diminished returns.

- **VS**—Very Special or Superior is aged no less than 3 years.
- **VSOP**—Very Special (Superior) Old Pale cannot be aged less than 5 years.
- **XO**—Extra Old or Extra Ordinary are house blends that must be aged at least 6 years, but usually are aged 12 or more years.

- **Vintage**—Vintage Cognacs are allowed as of 1988 under special control procedures.

The most notable houses for cognac include Martell®, Hennessy®, Rémy Martin®, Courvoisier®, Otard-Dupuy®, Camus®, Hine®, Delamain®, Salignac®, and Castillon®. See Figure 34-23.

Armagnac

Armagnac brandy is the oldest in France; documented references to the spirit go back to the fifteenth century. Armagnac is mostly produced in the unique alembic armagnaçais, a type of column still that dates back to the earliest days of brandy production. Although Armagnac shares Cognac's high standard, the two brandies are very different. Armagnac is an Appellation Contrôlée French grape brandy from Gascony, produced under strict controls and inspection procedures.

Three growing zones—Bas-Armagnac, Ténarèze, and Haut-Armagnac—may use the appellation on their label. Like Cognac, Armagnac's unique character comes from a combination of climate, soils, and grape varieties. Also like Cognac, most Armagnacs are blends, although some single vintages or single vineyard varieties are available. Blended Armagnacs generally have a higher proportion of older vintages than Cognac and thus may be a better value.

Most Armagnacs shipped to the United States are classified as V.O., V.S.O.P., or Réserve, which indicates that the youngest brandy in the blend is a Comte 4, or was aged in oak four years. Armagnacs have a prune, violet, or spice aroma and tend to be drier and more rustic than cognacs.

FIGURE 34-23
Popular Cognac labels

American Brandies

Most brandies produced in the United States may not enjoy the reputation of their French counterparts, but brandies made by artisans such as RMS®, Germain Robain®, and Jepson® stand up to the very best France has to offer.

Pomace Brandies

Pomace brandies are made from the pressed skin, pulp, seeds, and stems of grapes that remain after wine pressing. They are seldom aged, and are usually harsh and raw, although they may have a fruity aroma that is generally missing from more refined brandies. Many regard pomace brandy as an acquired taste.

Marc Marc is the pomace brandy that is produced in all wine-producing regions of France. It is generally consumed locally and is not exported.

Grappa Grappa, produced primarily in Italy, has been called the "firewater style" of pomace. In recent years, however, some single variety grappas have been produced with smoother, more elegant results.

Serving Brandies

Traditionally, brandy is served in a short, squat, tulip-shaped glass called a *snifter*. The shape of the glass concentrates and emphasizes the brandy's aroma. The brandy should be at room temperature when it is poured. The glass does not need to be heated—the heat of the hand should be enough to release the aromatic qualities of a good brandy. See Figure 34-24.

Tasting Brandies

The brandy should be swirled and the glass brought up gently to the nose to appreciate its many complex aromas—dried fruits, nuts, spices, and flowers. Small, slow sips should be taken, with the brandy sitting on the tongue for a moment before rolling it in the mouth. The contrast between the "velvet flame" and the smoothness should be noted. Some very well-aged (20- to 25-year-old) brandies take on a nutty, fatty richness that is often referred to as *rancio*. Even after the glass has been emptied, the aromas from the *fond du verre* can still be enjoyed. It is said that a glass that has held a fine brandy will still retain the bouquet the next day.

Evaluating Brandies

Brandies are evaluated solely on their unique tastes. Taste is, of course, highly subjective, but the skilled taster analyzes and identifies the sensations the brandy arouses and classifies them according to a brandy's character.

Tequila

Tequila is a distillate made from the fermented and distilled juice of the agave plant. This cactus-shaped plant that is related to the lily takes nine years to develop a large bulbous core, weighing up to 170 pounds (77 kg), called a *piña*. The pressure-cooked and shredded *piña* is made into mash, fermented, and then distilled into tequila. Tequila is produced only in the Mexican state of Jalisco. There are three type of tequila: white tequila, *reposado*, and *añejo*.

- **White tequila**—Labeled *blanco* or plata (silver), this unaged spirit can include up to 49% other neutral spirits.
- ***Reposado* tequila**—Aged 2 to 11 months, *reposado* must be made from 100% blue agave.
- ***Añejo* tequila**—Aged a minimum of one year, *añejo* is more frequently held for three years in small barrels.

Tequila has become extremely popular in the United States, with 75% of it poured for margaritas. Mescal, being a closely related spirit, is also made from the agave (sometimes called the maguey) but cannot be called tequila if it is not made in Jalisco. For brand names, see Figure 35-25 on page 842.

Aquavit

Aquavit is a distilled liquor from Scandinavia. It ranges from about 42% to 45% ABV. Distilled from a fermented potato or grain mash, it is usually flavored with caraway or cumin seeds but may also be flavored with citrus peel, cardamom, aniseed, or fennel. Aquavit is usually served chilled, often straight out of the freezer, in small glasses that are emptied in one shot. It is not typically mixed with any other beverage.

Bitters

As the name suggests, bitters are a very bitter, or bittersweet, liquid distilled from various herbs and roots. Bitters are used sparingly in cocktails and cooking to add a dry zest. Because they are both a digestive aid and an appetite stimulant, bitters are used in both before- and after-dinner mixed drinks. Bitters are highly alcoholic and should never be used in nonalcoholic drinks.

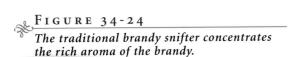

FIGURE 34-24
The traditional brandy snifter concentrates the rich aroma of the brandy.

FIGURE 34-25

AMERICAN WHISKEY

Seagram's 7®

Bourbon

Jim Beam® (blended)

Old Grand-Dad®
(straight, bonded)

Early Times®
(straight)

Wild Turkey®
(straight)

Tennessee Whiskey

Jack Daniel's®
(sour mash)

IMPORTED WHISKEY

Canadian

Canadian Club®

Seagram's VO®

Seagram's Crown Royal®

Irish Whiskey

Jameson®

Bushmills®

Scotch Whiskey

Cutty Sark®

J&B®

Dewar's®
(White Label)

Johnnie Walker®
(Red)

Johnnie Walker®
(Black) 12 years old

Chivas Regal®
12 years old

Haig & Haig Pinch®
12 years old

Glenfiddich®
(straight malt)
10 years old

Glenmorangie®
(straight malt)
12 years old

GIN

Beefeater®

Boodles®

Tanqueray®

Bols Genever®

Bombay®

Bombay Sapphire®

VODKA

Smirnoff®

Belvedere®

Absolut®

Stolichnaya®

Skye®

Wyborowa® (Vee-ba-rova)

Grey Goose®

FLAVORED VODKAS

Absolut Citron®

Absolut Pepper®

Stolichnaya Pertsovstra®

Stolichnaya Limonnaya®

RUM

Haiti

Barbancourt®

Jamaican Rum

Appleton®—White

Appleton®—Gold

Appleton®—Dark

Myers'®—Platinum

Myers'®—Gold

Myers'®—Dark

Puerto Rican Rum

Bacardi®—Silver

Bacardi®—Gold

Bacardi®—Amber

Bacardi®—151

Bacardi®—Black

Captain Morgan®—Spiced

Barbados

Gosling Barbados®

Mount Gay Eclipse®

BRANDY (AMERICAN)

Christian Brothers®

Germain-Robin Fine®

Cognac

Courvoisier®, VSOP, XO

Courvoisier®, Napoléon

Hennessy®, VS, VSOP, XO

Martell®, VS, VSOP, XO

Rémy Martin®, VS, VSOP, XO

Rémy Martin®, Louis XIII

Armagnac

Clés des Ducs®

St. Vivant®

Marquis de Caussade®

Armagnac de Montal®

TEQUILA

Jose Cuervo®—Silver

Jose Cuervo®—Gold

Sauza®

Two Fingers®

Liqueur Production Process

Liqueurs still retain the mystique of secret elixirs and potions concocted by monks and alchemists—most often in secret. Benedictine and Chartreuse, for example, are herbal blends developed by ancient religious orders. The Benedictine order first made its famous liqueur in 1510, mixing herbs, plant parts, and spices into a Cognac base. The recipe for Chartreuse predates the American Revolution and is so secret that only five monks at a time are permitted to know the 130-ingredient recipe.

A Variety of Processes

Production methods of liqueurs vary widely from one liqueur to another. In some cases, the exact manner of production is also a carefully guarded secret. But in general, there are four basic methods.

Infusion
Infusions steep flavoring agents in a hot liquid, usually water or fruit juice, much like steeping tea. Because the resulting "tea" must be strong enough to impart flavor to the entire blended liqueur, however, the infusion is generally much stronger than tea.

Maceration
When an aromatic or flavoring agent is immersed in the base spirit until the spirit absorbs the flavoring or aroma, the process is called maceration. The maker might, for example, macerate fresh strawberries in a spirit to avoid losing the aroma, flavor, and color of the berries. Because heating can cause evaporation of both the alcohol and esters, maceration is a cool process that may take as much as a year. The final result is called a *tincture* and is the basis of the liqueur.

Percolation
In percolation, the flavoring agents are placed in a container above the base liquor, which is then bubbled up through it—a process that can take weeks—to absorb the flavors and form a product called an *extract.*

Redistillation
Redistillation, used mostly for flavoring agents like seeds, citrus peel, or mint, employs an extraction method. The flavoring agent is steeped in spirits for several days and then placed in a still with other spirits and distilled. Using a vacuum enables the distillation to take place at lower temperatures so that more of the flavors are retained.

Proprietary Brands

There are two general types of liqueur: *generics* are liqueurs such as crème de menthe or crème de cacao that are not proprietary—any producer of alcoholic beverages can produce them; *proprietaries* are trademarked liqueurs made according to specific, usually highly secret recipes. Examples include Grand Marnier®, Southern Comfort®, or Benedictine®. See Figure 34-27 on pages 844–845 for popular brands of liqueurs and cordials.

Flavor Classifications
Although liqueurs come in a great variety of flavors, they generally fall into these classifications:

- **Fruit-flavored**—These liqueurs are popular and bear a label that identifies the fruit that flavors the liqueur, such as Midori®, made with melon.
- **Seed-based**—Although one seed predominates in the liqueur, the beverage usually is made from several kinds of seeds.
- **Herbs**—Among the most complex, herbal liqueurs may contain a dozen or a hundred herbs; except for mint or anise seed, however, the herbal flavor does not predominate.
- **Crème**—Called crème liqueurs for their creamy texture and sweet taste, crèmes take their name from the dominant flavoring ingredient, such as a fruit (crème de banana).
- **Peels**—The most frequently used peels are those in the citrus family, such as orange or lemon.
- **Fruit brandies**—These fall into three general groups: brandies flavored with apples and pears; those using stone fruits like plums, peaches, or apricots; and those flavored with berries, such as blackberries or elderberries.
- **Nut liqueurs**—Among these are such favorites as Amaretto (almonds) and Frangelico (hazelnuts).

Serving Liqueurs

Liqueurs or cordials may contain essential oils in addition to their sweet flavors and alcohol. A dash of liqueur gives a cocktail added smoothness, texture, and palatability.

In France, certain liqueurs were used in the form of highballs. Crème de cassis, for example, was mixed frappés with wine to make Kir. Frappés, a popular way of serving liqueurs, are made by filling a small stem glass with shaved ice and pouring liqueur over it. See Figure 34-26.

FIGURE 34-26

A variety of liqueurs is a traditional and elegant end to an evening of fine dining.

FIGURE 34-27

ALIZE®

From France; blend of passion fruit and cognac

AMARETTO

Aromatic liqueur made from apricots and almonds steeped in aquavit (fusion of alcohol)

AMARETTO DI SARONNO®

Brand name of Amaretto

ANISETTE

Sweet, mild, liqueur with licorice-like flavor

B&B LIQUEUR D.O.M.®

Delicate finesse of Benedictine D.O.M., with drier cognac; amber

BENEDICTINE D.O.M.®

Classic French herbal liqueur; amber

BOGGS CRANBERRY LIQUEUR®

Tart, tangy taste of juice of cranberries; red color

CAMPARI®

Italian bittersweet spirit apéritif; infusion of aromatic and bitter herbs; light ruby red color

CHAMBORD LIQUEUR ROYALE DE FRANCE®

From France; rich aroma and taste of framboises (small black raspberries) and other fruits and herbs combined with honey; dark purple color

CHARTREUSE®

Classic herb liqueur with subtle flavor and aroma drawn from 130 wild mountain herbs distilled and blended in brandy

CHERRY MARNIER®

French cherry-flavored liqueur

COCORIBE®

Coconut flavor with light rum

COINTREAU®

Classic French specialty orange liqueur; fragrant, mellow bouquet, with subtle hint of orange; blends sweet and bitter Mediterranean and tropical orange peels; clear color

CREAM LIQUEURS

Bailey's® (dominant brand), Carolans®, Emmets®, Leroux®, Myers®, O'Darby®
Fresh cream blended with spirits and natural flavorings; Irish whiskey is the most widely used spirit; brandy, cordials, rum, and vodka are also used

CRÈME DE BANANA®

Flavor of fresh, ripe bananas; yellow color

CRÈME DE CACAO (BROWN)

Rich, creamy, deep chocolate flavor drawn from cocoa and vanilla beans, with hint of spices

CRÈME DE CACAO (WHITE)

Less intense chocolate flavor; clear color

CRÈME DE CASSIS

Full, rich, flavor of black currants; very dark purple

CRÈME DE FRAMBOISE

Raspberry-flavored liqueur

CRÈME DE MENTHE (GREEN)

Refreshing, tangy, natural mint flavor; cool, clean

CRÈME DE MENTHE (WHITE)

Virtually identical to green crème de menthe; lack of color makes it useful in more drink recipes

CURAÇAO

From the the island of Curaçao in the Netherlands Antilles; clear amber color; similar to Triple Sec but sweeter and more subtle; lower proof; clear, orange, or blue color

DRAMBUIE®

Old Scotch whiskey, delicately honeyed and spiced

FRANGELICO®

Wild hazelnuts (filberts) blended with spirits, berries, and herbs; amber

FRUIT-FLAVORED BRANDIES

Flavor and aroma of fresh, ripe fruit defined by product name (apricot, blackberry, and so on); higher proof and drier than fruit liqueurs

FRUIT-FLAVORED LIQUEURS

Flavor and aroma of fresh, ripe fruit, defined by product name (apricot, blackberry, and so on); lower proof and sweeter than fruit brandies

GOLDWASSER

Flavor blend of herbs, seeds, roots, and citrus peels; tiny flakes of gold imperceptible to the tongue that shimmer in this clear liqueur

GRAND MARNIER®

From France; classic cognac-based orange liqueur; flavor and bouquet from peels of wild bitter oranges

HONEY BLONDE®

From Denmark; honey-based liqueur

IRISH MIST®

From Ireland; flavor blend of four whiskeys, honeys from heather, clover; essence of a dozen herbs

JÄGERMEISTER®

Distinctive flavor blend of 56 roots, herbs, and fruits

KAHLÚA®

Flavor aroma of choicest coffees; dark brown color

KAHLÚA ROYALE®

Blends Kahlúa, fine brandy, a hint of chocolate, and oranges

KÜMMEL

One of the oldest liqueurs; fairly dry and usually 70 proof or more; essential flavor is caraway with a hint of cumin seed and anise; clear color

LA GRANDE PASSION®

From France; blends Armagnac with passion fruit

LEMONIER®

From France; lemon peel liqueur

LIQUORE GALLIANO®

From Italy; natural golden liqueur; distinctive flavor of anise and vanilla; rich, sweet, palatable; natural flavorings of seeds, herbs, and spices

LIQUORE STREGA®

From Italy; rich, fragrant, golden liqueur with flavors of more than 70 herbs

LOCHAN ORA®

From Scotland; distinctive scotch-based liqueur with subtle flavors drawn from Curaçao and Ceylon; gold color

MALIBU®

From Canada; flavor blend of white rum and coconut

MANDARINE NAPOLÉON®

From Belgium; a tangerine liqueur; flavor and bouquet of ripe Andalusian tangerines and cognac; orange color

METAXA®

From Greece; brandylike liqueur from grape base, slightly sweet, with distinctive flavor

MIDORI®

From Japan; light, refreshing taste of fresh honeydew melon; green color

MONTE TECA®

From Mexico; tequila-based liqueur; rich, golden taste

OPAL NERA®

From Italy; anise and elder-flower flavor with hint of lemon; color of black opal

OUZO®

From Greece; sweet, white liqueur; licorice-like anise flavor, slightly drier and stronger proof than anisette; when water or ice is added, it turns milky white

PEAR WILLIAM

From Loire Vally in France; delicate flavor of Anjou pears; clear color

PERNOD®

From France; blends select anise seed, special flavorings, and natural herbs with spirits

PETER HEERING®

From Denmark; famous cherry-flavored liqueur produced since 1818; formerly known as Cherry Heering®; dark red color

PIMM'S CUP®

From England; tall "sling" drinks (Pimm's Cup No. one is the gin sling)

PRALINE LIQUEUR®

Rich, mellow vanilla- and pecan-based flavor of the original New Orleans praline confection

RICARD®

From France; anise and herb liqueur

ROCK AND RYE

Whiskey-based liqueur containing crystals of rock candy, flavored with fruits (sometimes has pieces)

SABRA®

From Israel; flavors of orange and chocolate

SAMBUCA ROMANO®

Liqueur flavored with elderberry and anise

SCHNAPPS

Apple Barrel®, Aspen Glacial® (peppermint), Cool Mint®, Cristal® (anise), DeKuyper Peachtree® (peach), Dr. McGillicuddy®, (menthomint), Rumple Minze® (peppermint), Silver Schnapps® (100-proof, peppermint), Steel® (85-proof peppermint)

Predominantly for after-dinner sipping; often too sweet and syrupy for straight drinking; good with many mixers

SLOE GIN

Bouquet and tangy fruity flavor resembling wild cherries; made from fresh fruit of the sloe berry; red color

SOUTHERN COMFORT®

From America; high-proof, peach-flavored liqueur with a bourbon whiskey base

TIA MARIA®

From Jamaica; coffee-flavored liqueur; dark brown color

TRIPLE SEC®

Crystal-clear orange flavor; like curaçao but drier and higher proof; flavor blends peels of tangy, bittersweet green curaçao and sweet oranges

TRUFFLES®

Combination of spirits and imported chocolate

TUACA®

From Italy; brandy base with hint of herbs, vanilla, and fruit peels; golden color

VANDERMINT®

From Holland; Dutch chocolate with a hint of mint

YUKON JACK®

100-proof blend of sweetened Canadian whiskies

WILD TURKEY LIQUEUR®

Bourbon base; herbs, spices, and other natural flavorings; amber color

35 Mixology

A.D. 1637
Boston establishes the first malt house.

1783
Evan Williams starts the first distillery in Kentucky.

1874
The first Manhattan is said to have been mixed at the Manhattan Club in New York.

1933
Jay Sindler obtains a patent for the swizzle stick.

1943
Chef Joe Sheridan concocts Irish coffee.

"In Nevada, for a time," Mark Twain wrote in Roughing It, *" . . . the lawyer, the editor, the banker, the chief desperado, the chief gambler, and the saloon-keeper occupied the same level in society, and it was the highest."* Perhaps the bartender in early Nevada society earned his accolades for skills other than mixing drinks, for the beverage choices were meager in early saloons.

Today, however, bartenders are highly skilled professionals who must understand complex local, state, and federal laws; possess a working knowledge of psychology and current events; and master hundreds of beverage recipes and techniques.

Mixology

Mixology is the study of cocktails, mixed drinks, and their ingredients. Those who study mixology—mixologists or bartenders—generally work in restaurants, bars, hotels, private clubs and resorts, and on cruise lines. Each environment has its own challenges, but all share some basic principles for setting up and managing an efficient and profitable operation.

The Bartender

Good bartenders share a common set of traits and follow certain guidelines that spell success or failure for the bar operation. See Figure 35-1 on page 848. They must have expertise in mixology and thorough knowledge of and adherence to sanitary laws regarding alcohol service. They should possess good organizational skills and practice good cost control. The ability to recognize behavioral cues indicating levels of intoxication is critical to an establishment's survival in today's society.

Bar Opening Procedures

Follow appropriate procedures for opening the bar to ensure efficiency. Develop and use checklists to make sure that each task is completed every time the bar is opened. To open a bar:

1. Begin by checking the cash register. First, ensure that the previous shift has been closed out properly. Then count the bank, or cash that has been issued in the presence of a manager, and ensure that it is correct. Make sure that there are ample quantities of guest checks or paper for the POS printer.

2. Place clean ashtrays and books of matches on the bar if appropriate.

3. Fill the three-compartment sink: (1) wash, (2) rinse, (3) sanitize. Wash any soiled glasses, and leave them on the drain board. See Figure 35-2 on page 849.

4. Check bottled drinks; rotate and restock them according to established bar stocks. Restock liquor issued for the day, and turn in empty bottles for inventory control.

5. Clean the soda gun. Check soda levels and carbon dioxide pressure.

6. Check fruit garnishes, fruit juices, cream, and other bar mixes. Wash containers, refill, and refrigerate.

7. Prepare garnishes sufficient for one shift.

8. Check all sundry supplies and bar implements.

9. Wash and polish the bar counter, drain and wash sinks and ice bins, and wipe the neck of each bottle on the back bar. Line up the bottles with labels and pourers facing the same direction.

10. Visit the rest room to check your appearance.

11. Keep the register key with you at all times.

12. Open the bar on time. All mise en place should be complete and the bar fully stocked and ready.

Hand-Washing Glasses

It is especially important to keep the glasses clean and sanitized. Here is the proper method for hand-washing glasses:

1. Wash glasses in the first compartment of the sink. Use warm water—at least 110°F–120°F (43°C–49°C)—a washing compound, and a brush.
2. Use the second compartment to immerse the glasses in clean, warm water of at least 110°F (43°C). Change this rinse water often. Never rinse glasses in dirty water.
3. Sanitize the glasses in the third sink compartment using water containing a chemical sanitizer. The water temperature and immersion time vary depending on the chemical compound used. Drain and air-dry glasses. Store them inverted on shelving lined with air mats.

Chemical Usage

Several different chemical solutions are available for sanitizing hand-washed glasses, including the following:

- A solution of water and at least 50 parts per million (ppm) of available chlorine.
  Temperature: not less than 55°F (13°C)
  Time: at least 7 seconds
- A solution of water and at least 220 ppm of a quaternary ammonium compound (quats).
  Temperature: not less than 75°F (24°C)
  Time: at least 30 seconds
- A solution of water and at least 12.5 ppm of available iodine in a solution with a pH not less than 5.0.
  Temperature: not less than 75°F (24°C)
  Time: at least 30 seconds

A field test kit should be used to measure the chemical concentration at any time.

Bar Closing Procedures

Closing the bar properly helps ensure efficient operation. To close the bar:

1. Wipe and thoroughly clean speed rack; wipe bottles and replace.
2. Sanitize empty shelves for clean glasses.
3. Collect all used glassware, and place it on the counter above the sink area. Wash hands.
4. Wash glassware, one type at a time, washing cream-drink glasses last. Replace on shelf covered with air mats.
5. Rinse and wash sinks, and dry them to prevent rust or scale.
6. Wash and polish drain board and other parts of the sink.
7. Clean out ice bin, and wipe dry.
8. Sweep floor, and remove trash container.

FIGURE 35-1

The Good Bartender's Guidelines

- *Recognize the faces of regular customers, know the drinks they prefer, and offer a friendly greeting when they arrive.*
- *Handle complaints courteously. Remedy the problem or mix another drink, recording the latter for cost-control purposes.*
- *Step back or move away from customers to avoid giving the impression of eavesdropping on a conversation. Do not join a conversation unless invited to do so.*
- *Never hurry the customers or appear impatient if they are slow drinkers, but be attentive to the need for refills.*
- *Cooperate with and be helpful to other employees. Customers can sense when there is tension among staff members.*
- *Answer the telephone quietly. Ask who is calling and tell the caller you will check to see whether the party is present. Then the customer can decide whether to take the call.*

- *Use a fresh cocktail napkin with each drink.*
- *Unless a customer specifically requests otherwise, use a fresh glass for every drink.*
- *Use the appropriate glass and garnish for each drink.*
- *Pick up glasses by the stem or base only; never pick up a glass by the rim or put your fingers in the glass.*
- *Avoid overfilling a glass; one-quarter of an inch (6 mm) from the rim is a good rule of thumb.*
- *Use a measure for drinks; measuring ensures consistent quality and contains costs.*
- *Keep the bar dry and clean, emptying ashtrays frequently and taking care not to let ashes spill.*
- *Follow standardized recipes or house recipes, but keep customers' preferences in mind. Some may ask for a "light" drink; others prefer a stronger one. Being too rigid may cause unhappy customers; being too generous drives up costs.*

- *Place the glass on the bar or rail so that the customer can see what you are doing. Then use the shaker or mixer.*
- *Return bottles to their proper places immediately. This practice saves time and preserves the ambience.*
- *When pouring two identical drinks, prepare a double recipe, and half-fill each glass. Then pour additional liquid until the glasses are evenly filled.*
- *In preparing a shaken drink, shake rapidly. Shaking too long dilutes the drink. A ten-second shake adds one-half to three-quarters of an ounce (15 to 22 ml) of additional liquid to the drink.*
- *Ring drinks on the guest check, and place it face down in front of the customer. If need be, itemize by writing the order on the check.*
- *Never sit, eat, or smoke at the bar, even when off duty. To do so is unprofessional and contrary to sanitation codes.*

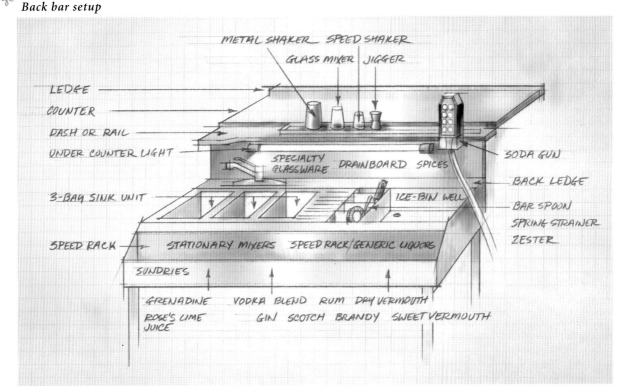

9. Wrap or store fruit garnishes appropriately, and refrigerate them for the next day.

10. Top up all fruit juice containers and refrigerate; wash and store empties.

11. Fill in the day's requisition for liquor, wine, and beer.

12. Stock coolers for the next shift.

13. Run appropriate closing procedures on POS system and, if using a manual system, count guest checks and correlate with issue register. Note any unused checks. Close out cash register according to house policy.

14. Check security, and lock up.

Back Bar Setup

The back bar should be set up to display bottles in an attractive manner that will promote sales, but the arrangement should also be functional for the bartender. See Figure 35-2. Standardize and arrange the setup for greatest efficiency as follows:

First Row Sequence
Proprietary-brand distilled spirits in sequence of products: Scotches, Canadians, imported whites, and Americans

Brands—arranged in order:
- Chivas Regal®
- Dewars®
- Canadian Club®
- Seagram's VO®
- Seagram's 7®
- Smirnoff®
- Stolichnaya® or Absolut®
- Beefeater®
- Tanqueray®
- Tequila
- Old Grand-Dad®
- Jack Daniel's®

Second Row Sequence
Generic liqueurs and flavored brandies

Brands—arranged alphabetically:
- Apricot-flavored brandy
- Crème de banana
- Crème de cacao (dark)
- Crème de cacao (light)
- Crème de menthe (green)
- Crème de menthe (white)
- Curaçao® (blue)
- Curaçao® (orange)
- Peach schnapps
- Peppermint schnapps
- Triple sec

Third Row Sequence
Rums and proprietary-brand liqueurs, arranged alphabetically, followed by seldom-used brands

Brands—arranged in order:
- Bacardi® light rum
- Mount Gay® gold rum
- Myers'® dark rum
- Amaretto di Saronno®
- Campari®
- Cognac
- Cointreau®
- Drambuie®
- Frangelico®
- Galliano®
- Kahlua®
- Midori®
- Peter Heering®
- Southern Comfort®

Cocktails and Mixed Drinks

The terms cocktail and mixed drink are often used as though they were synonymous. There are, however, several important differences. See Figure 35-3. A *cocktail* is a fairly short drink, made by mixing liquor or wine with fruit juices, eggs, and/or bitters. Cocktails are created by mixing together two or more ingredients to make a new flavor that is both pleasing and palatable. Unless the drink is made to the specifications of a particular customer, no single ingredient should overshadow the others. Although cocktails are stirred or shaken with ice in bar glasses or cocktail shakers, they are served *up*, or without ice, in stemmed glasses. If the guest prefers, the cocktail may be served *on the rocks*, or with ice.

Mixed drinks, on the other hand, are tall drinks, served over ice. Mixed drinks combine liquor with a mixer—one as simple as club soda or as complex as several kinds of fruit juices, various carbonated beverages, and even puréed fruits. Generally served in a base glass, mixed drinks are served with ice.

To summarize, cocktails can be differentiated from mixed drinks by the following characteristics:

1. Presentation: Cocktails are short and served up unless called for on the rocks. Mixed drinks are tall, served with ice.

2. Procedure: Cocktails are stirred or shaken. Mixed drinks are served ice down-pour or speed-shaken.

3. Glassware: Cocktails are served in a stemmed glass, and mixed drinks are served in a tall base glass.

A Long History

Experts differ on the origins of the word *cocktail*. Everyone does agree, however, that the cocktail, like jazz, was born in America. And like jazz, New York Times restaurant critic William Grimes writes, other countries can copy the cocktail, but seldom improve it. By 1889, the Century Dictionary had formalized the term, defining the cocktail as "an American drink, strong, stimulating, and cold."

Most researchers agree that the origin of the cocktail dates back to the time of the American Revolution, when Americans were unable to import rum and other spirits from Great Britain.

Americans began distilling whiskey, some of it of dubious quality. Mixing this whiskey with sugar and bitters improved the taste, and the cocktail was born. As the distillers' skills improved, however, distinctive and high-quality whiskies, such as Kentucky bourbon, began to develop. Eventually whiskey found its way into one of America's earliest classic cocktails, the mint julep.

The first recorded reference to the julep occurs in 1787, when the drink was described as a combination of rum, water, and sugar. By the 1830s, however, the julep recipe had acquired mint and ice. Juleps were served ice cold but were created differently depending on social class. The wealthy made them with expensive brandy, and common folk used whiskey.

Making Cocktails and Mixed Drinks

Four basic procedures are used in making cocktails and mixed drinks. All use *stir, shake, ice down-pour,* or *speed-shake* methods.

For cocktails served up:

- **Stir procedure**—Gently agitate with ice to chill and blend the cocktail ingredients.
- **Shake procedure**—Agitate energetically with ice to disperse or incorporate heavy ingredients.

For mixed drinks or cocktails requested on the rocks:

- **Ice down-pour procedure**—Place ice in a service glass, and then add liquor and mixer; serve as is.
- **Speed-shake procedure**—In a service glass, agitate with ice to disperse or incorporate heavier ingredients.

✣ FIGURE 35-3
Cocktails and mixed drinks differ with regard to presentation, procedure, and glassware.

Performing the Stir Procedure

Drinks prepared using the stir procedure are served cold, but the ice is strained out to prevent diluting the liquor and mixer. Drinks prepared this way are usually served with a garnish.

To perform the stir procedure, follow these steps:

Add the liquor.

1 Chill a stemmed glass by filling it with ice, and place it on the rail.

5 Hold the mixing glass with fingers closed at the base, and stir. Holding the bar spoon by its helix, roll it back and forth between thumb and index finger for 3–4 seconds. Gently remove the bar spoon.

2 Put ice into a mixing glass until it is one-fourth full.

6 Remove the ice from the chilled serving glass.

7 Using a spring strainer over the mouth of the glass, strain ingredients into the serving glass.

3 Pour the base into the mixing glass.

8 Garnish and serve.

Performing the Ice Down-Pour Procedure

For mixed drinks and cocktails requested on the rocks, the ice down-pour procedure is used. These drinks are served cold over ice.

To perform the ice down-pour procedure, follow these steps:

1 Fill base glass with ice.

2 Add measured liquor(s) and/or liqueur(s).

3 Garnish.

4 Add the stirrer or sip stix, and serve.

Bar Terminology

The *jigger,* a legal measure of 1.5 ounces (45 ml), and a *shot,* a measure of liquid (quantity determined by house) served straight up, are bartending tools of the trade. Other terms include:

- **Back**—A chaser on the side.
- **Float**—The final ingredient added to the drink after the usual procedure is performed; a float finds its own space and should not be incorporated into the drink.
- **Free-pour**—Pouring spirits or liqueurs without using a measuring device, such as a jigger.
- **Hold/no garbage**—Served without garnishes.
- **Light**—A drink containing a reduced amount of liquor but the normal amount of mixer.
- **On the rocks**—Served on ice, usually in a rocks glass.
- **Straight up or neat**—Served without ice; the drink never comes into contact with ice.
- **Tall/Long**—A drink served in an 8- to 16-ounce (240- to 500-ml) highball or zombie glass; the amount of the mixer is increased, not the amount of liquor.
- **Up**—Prepared with ice to chill, but served strained from the ice in a stemmed glass.

FIGURE 35-4

Bases for Alcoholic Beverages

VERMOUTH
Cocktails

SOURS
Short sours–cocktails
Long sours–mixed drinks

CREAMS
Short creams–cocktails
Long creams–mixed drinks

POLYNESIAN OR TROPICAL
Mixed drinks

CARBONATED AND JUICE-BASED HIGHBALLS
Mixed drinks

CORDIALS (LIQUEURS)
Two-liquor drinks

WINES AND PUNCHES

SPECIALTIES
Cream- and ice cream-based drinks; coffees mixed with spirits

FIGURE 35-5

VERMOUTH BASE (SERVED UP)

Name of Drink	Procedure	Glass
Martini	Stir	Cocktail
Manhattan	Stir	Cocktail
Rob Roy	Stir	Cocktail
Gibson	Stir	Cocktail
Negroni	Stir	Cocktail

VERMOUTH BASE (SERVED ON THE ROCKS)

Name of Drink	Procedure	Glass
Martini	Ice down-pour	Rocks
Manhattan	Ice down-pour	Rocks
Rob Roy	Ice down-pour	Rocks
Gibson	Ice down-pour	Rocks
Negroni	Ice down-pour	Rocks

SHORT SOURS (SERVED UP)

Name of Drink	Procedure	Glass
All sours (i.e. whiskey)	Shake	Sour
Bacardi® Cocktail	Shake	Cocktail
Ward 8	Shake	Cocktail
Between the Sheets	Shake	Cocktail
Side Car	Shake	Cocktail
Daiquiri	Shake	Cocktail
Margarita	Shake	Champagne coupe
Jack Rose Cocktail	Shake	Cocktail
Kamikaze	Shake	Cocktail
Gimlet	Shake	Cocktail

SHORT SOURS (SERVED ON THE ROCKS)

Name of Drink	Procedure	Glass
All sours (whiskey)	Speed-shake	Rocks
Bacardi® Cocktail	Speed-shake	Rocks
Ward 8	Speed-shake	Rocks
Between the Sheets	Speed-shake	Rocks
Side Car	Speed-shake	Rocks
Daiquiri	Speed-shake	Rocks
Margarita	Speed-shake	Rocks
Jack Rose Cocktail	Speed-shake	Rocks
Kamikaze	Speed-shake	Rocks
Gimlet	Speed-shake	Rocks

SHORT CREAM BASE (SERVED UP)

Name of Drink	Procedure	Glass
Brandy Alexander	Shake	Champagne coupe
Grasshopper	Shake	Champagne coupe
Golden Dream	Shake	Champagne coupe
Pink Squirrel	Shake	Champagne coupe

SHORT CREAM BASE (SERVED ON THE ROCKS)

Name of Drink	Procedure	Glass
Brandy Alexander	Speed-shake	Rocks
Grasshopper	Speed-shake	Rocks
Golden Dream	Speed-shake	Rocks
Pink Squirrel	Speed-shake	Rocks

FIGURE 35-6

LONG CREAM BASE

Name of Drink	Procedure	Glass
Orgasm	Speed-shake	Highball
Toasted Almond Bar	Speed-shake	Highball
Girl Scout Cookie	Speed-shake	Highball
White Russian	Speed-shake	Highball

TROPICAL-POLYNESIAN

Name of Drink	Procedure	Glass
Mai Tai	Speed-shake	Collins
Planter's Punch	Speed-shake	Collins
Zombie	Speed-shake	Sling/zombie
Piña Colada	Speed-shake	Sling/zombie

LONG SOURS

Name of Drink	Procedure	Glass
(Tom) Collins	Speed-shake	Collins
Ward 8	Speed shake	Collins
Sloe Gin Fizz	Speed-shake	Collins
Singapore Sling	Speed-shake	Sling/zombie
Long Island Iced Tea	Speed-shake	Sling/zombie

HIGHBALL

Name of Drink	Procedure	Glass
Soda Highball	Ice down-pour	Highball
Juice Highball*	Ice down-pour	Highball

CORDIALS

Name of Drink	Procedure	Glass
All Cordials	Ice down-pour	Rocks

Exception to the rule for juice-based drinks: speed-shake juice-based highballs that have a liqueur with a juice mixer.

Eight Bases for Alcoholic Beverages

It is important to become familiar with the types of alcohol that are used as the bases for many cocktails and mixed drinks. See Figure 35-4 on page 852. Note that the base ingredient or mixer for both mixed drinks and cocktails does not change but the liquor changes according to the name of the drink. See Figure 35-5 and Figure 35-6.

Vermouth-Based Drinks

The martini remains a universally popular cocktail. It is a dry, sharp, appetite-whetting drink that has become progressively drier over the years. There is no martini recipe on which all bartenders agree. By the time it came to be called a martini, the drink had become a mixture of equal parts gin and dry vermouth.

The Manhattan was named for Manhattan, New York, where bartenders in speakeasies cut the harshness of bootlegged liquor with syrups and aromatic flavorings. In addition to whiskey or bourbon, the original Manhattan contained bitters,

Performing the Shake Procedure

Mixologists use the shake procedure to incorporate spirits and mixer ingredients more fully. The ice is strained from the drink before serving it.

To perform the shake procedure, follow these steps:

1  Put ice into a mixing glass until it is one-third full.

2  Add spirit(s) and/or liqueur(s).

3  Add mixer and/or base ingredient(s).

4  Place a metal cup or base over the top of the mixing glass, making sure that the metal cup is sitting evenly, not at an angle.

5  Give the top (bottom of the metal shaker) a light tap to create a vacuum.

6  Pick up the whole unit from the bar, and flip it over so that the metal is facing down and the glass is near your shoulder.

7 In a quick, even movement, move the unit back and forth several times in a rapid succession.

8  With the metal shaker still on the bottom, hold the unit in the left hand for balance. Press the index finger against the metal shaker. Make a fist with the right hand.

9 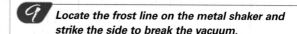 Locate the frost line on the metal shaker and strike the side to break the vacuum.

10  Twist off the mixing glass, and strain the liquid through the spring strainer into a glass.

Performing the Speed-Shake Procedure

The speed-shake procedure is appropriate for mixing spirits and heavier mixers. Drinks that are speed shaken are generally served tall with ice.

To perform the speed-shake procedure, follow these steps:

Place a base glass filled to the rim with ice on the bar or rail.

Pour liquor(s) and/or liqueur(s).

Add the mixer and/or the base ingredient(s).

Place the metal speed shaker over the glass.

Pick up the unit; flip it, ensuring that the metal speed shaker is on the bottom; and shake the container back and forth in quick, even movements for three or four seconds.

Pour the drink from the speed shaker into the chilled glass, and garnish, including a sip stix.

sugar, and much more vermouth than today's recipe. Although the recipe for a basic Manhattan is sweet vermouth and whiskey, using dry vermouth creates a Dry Manhattan. Using both sweet and dry vermouth makes the drink a Perfect Manhattan.

In Rob Roys, Scotch replaces the whiskey or bourbon used in the Manhattan recipe. Like regular Manhattans, Dry Rob Roys and Perfect Rob Roys vary according to the type of vermouth used in their preparation.

Vermouth-based cocktails are served up in cocktail glasses, and unless a customer requests the cocktail on the rocks, they are stirred. For an on-the-rocks version, use the ice down-pour method, and serve the drink in a rocks glass.

Garnishes Vermouth-based drinks may be garnished in a variety of ways.

- A martini may contain either a cocktail olive or lemon zest.
- A Manhattan or a Rob Roy contains a maraschino cherry. When making a Rob Roy with dry vermouth rather than sweet vermouth, use lemon zest. When the drink contains both sweet and dry vermouth, the garnish is optional. Use either a cherry or lemon zest.
- A Negroni, which contains Campari® (a slightly bitter Italian apéritif), is garnished with an orange slice or lemon zest.
- Garnish a Gibson with a cocktail onion.

Sours

Sours are drinks that use a sour base, such as lemon or lime juice. They can be classified as short sours and long sours. Traditionally, bartenders have used simple syrup, lemon or lime juice, and egg whites as a sour mix. Today, commercially made sour mixes are generally used. Short sours are composed of liquor(s) and/or liqueur(s) with commercially prepared lemon sour mix or lime juice. Long sours contain the same ingredients, with the addition of carbonated soda to cut the sour taste. Serve a long sour, garnished with a cherry and an orange slice, in a tall glass.

Use cocktail or sour glasses for short sours. The only short sours served with garnishes are sour-type cocktails, such as whiskey sours or apricot sours, and the garnish is a cherry. If a customer requests the cocktail on the rocks, however, use the

speed-shake procedure, and serve the cocktail in a rocks glass.

Cream- and Ice Cream-Based Drinks

Cream drinks are usually very sweet, smooth, and pleasing to the palate. They are perfect after-dinner drinks, and many customers order them instead of dessert.

All cream-based drinks may use ice cream instead of cream. Usually, vanilla ice cream is the flavor of choice, but any flavor that blends well with the liqueur's flavor will work, including coffee, strawberry, peach, or chocolate. Sherbets also may be used to make *freezes,* or frozen drinks.

Prepare cream drinks by using either a shake or a blend procedure. The *blend procedure* uses a blender, mixing the ingredients more thoroughly and giving the drink a creamier, frothier texture.

The blend procedure is appropriate for any drink that is shaken, but it should always be used when incorporating ice or solids, such as strawberries, into a Strawberry Daiquiri. To use the blend procedure:

1. Place the ice in the blender; add the remaining ingredients.
2. The blender container should be one-fourth full; the ice should be covered with the other ingredients.
3. When using a two-speed blender, blend for 3 seconds on low and then 7–10 seconds on high.
4. Using a cocktail spoon to maintain an even flow, pour the blended ingredients into an appropriate glass.

Short cream drinks Serve short cream drinks up in a Champagne coupe. The only cream-based drink that has a garnish is the Alexander, which requires a sprinkle of nutmeg.

Long cream drinks Long cream drinks are generally prepared using the speed-shake procedure and are served in a highball glass; they receive no garnish.

Cordials or Two-Liquor Drinks

Cordials are a sweet alcoholic beverage in which two-liquor drinks are combined with a distilled spirit or brandy. The spirit helps cut the pronounced sweetness of the cordial. Except for drinks like the Mud Slide, which requires the speed-shake procedure, two-liquor drinks are served on the rocks in a rocks glass, using the ice down-pour procedure with the spirits poured in first.

Some cordials are considered layered drinks, poured carefully into the glass so that the ingredients do not mix, but remain in layers because the cordials and spirits each have different specific gravities.

The cordial *pousse-café,* French for "coffee-pusher," requires a very steady hand to layer the different colored liqueurs, one on top of the other, in a pony glass. Each layer is created by pouring individual liqueurs into the glass over the back of the a cocktail spoon. Generally, the last ingredient is flamed to add to the drama. As many as 56 different ingredients can be used to make *pousse-café.* Knowing the specific gravity of each ingredient allows bartenders to pour the most dense liqueur first and the least dense last.

Highballs

Highballs consist of carbonated mixers, water or juices, and the appropriate liquor, served tall in highball glasses on ice. See Figure 35-7. Highballs with carbonated mixers or water require only the ice down-pour procedure to have their ingredients fully incorporated. Highballs made with liqueurs are speed-shaken to incorporate their ingredients. The basic recipe, however, is the same: 1 1/2 ounces (45 ml) of liquor (or customer preference); 4 ounces

FIGURE 35-7

Examples of Popular Highballs

Highball
Whiskey and ginger ale

Spritzer
White wine and club soda

Wine cooler
Red wine and ginger ale

Vodka and Tonic
Vodka and tonic water

Scotch and Soda
Scotch and club soda

7 and 7
Seagram's 7 Crown® and 7 Up®

Presbyterian
Whiskey, ginger ale, and club soda

*Some drinks also may be ordered on the rocks with a splash of mix according to customer preference, such as the classic Old Fashioned.

(120 ml) of soda or other mixer; pour the liquor over ice cubes in a highball glass; top with any flavored soda; and serve.

Highball history Mixed drinks and highballs have origins as fabled as those of the cocktail and the cordial. Many grew out of the habits of different occupations in different locations.

One of the first mixed drinks was called Gin and Tonic by British troops in the late 1800s. Like many of the original cordials, the drink grew out of the desire to add "a spoon full of sugar" to help the "medicine go down." Required to take daily doses of bitter quinine, a medicine used to ward off malaria, British soldiers in India began adding sugar and water to the dose. Before long, they discovered that adding gin, their favorite liquor, made the medicine go down even better, and Gin and Tonic was born.

Highballs were named by a different group of workers. In the 1800s, railroaders typically used a ball placed on a high pole as a signal to fast, oncoming trains that they could maintain speed; the track was clear. When the men had time enough to stop for a fast drink of whiskey and ginger ale, they coined the term "highball" as a name for their drink.

The popular Screwdriver, too, was named by American workers, this time in Iran's oil fields, where alcohol is forbidden. Their habit of using screwdrivers to mix drinks secretly made from vodka and orange juice ultimately gave the Screwdriver its name.

Polynesian-Tropicals

These drinks, such as Mai Tai, Piña Colada, Zombie, and Planter's Punch, are usually rum-based with tropical fruit flavors—pineapple, orange, or coconut—to bring sweetness to the mix. Polynesian-tropicals are generally prepared using a blender or the speed-shake procedure and are garnished with a combination of a cherry and a slice of orange or pineapple chunk.

VERMOUTH-BASE
stir and/or ice down-pour

MARTINI (CLASSIC)

Gin	1 1/2 ounces (45 ml)
Dry vermouth	3/4 ounce (22 ml)
Olive or zest	garnish

DRY MARTINI

Gin	2 ounces (60 ml)
Dry vermouth	1/2 ounce (15 ml)
Olive or zest	garnish

VODKA MARTINI

Vodka	1 1/2 ounces (45 ml)
Dry vermouth	3/4 ounce (22 ml)
Olive or zest	garnish

EXTRA-DRY MARTINI

Gin	2 1/4 ounces (67 ml)
Dry vermouth	1/4 ounce (8 ml)
Olive or zest	garnish

SMOKY MARTINI OR SILVER BULLET

Gin	1 1/2 ounces (45 ml)
Dry vermouth	1/4 ounce (8 ml)
Scotch *(float)*	1/2 ounce (15 ml)
Olive or zest	garnish

GIBSON

Gin or vodka	1 1/2 ounces (45 ml)
Dry vermouth	3/4 ounce (22 ml)
Cocktail onions	garnish

MANHATTAN

Bourbon or blended	1 1/2 ounces (45 ml)
Sweet vermouth	3/4 ounce (22 ml)
Cherry	garnish

Classic recipe includes a dash of bitters.

SOUTHERN COMFORT/DELUXE MANHATTAN

Southern Comfort®	1 1/2 ounces (45 ml)
Dry vermouth	3/4 ounce (22 ml)
Cherry or zest	garnish

PERFECT MANHATTAN

Bourbon or blended	1 1/2 ounces (45 ml)
Dry vermouth and sweet vermouth, combined	3/4 ounce (22 ml)
Cherry or zest	garnish

DRY MANHATTAN

Bourbon or blended	1 1/2 ounces (45 ml)
Dry vermouth	3/4 ounce (22 ml)
Zest	garnish

ROB ROY

Scotch	1 1/2 ounces (45 ml)
Sweet vermouth	3/4 ounce (22 ml)
Cherry	garnish

Classic recipe includes a dash of bitters.

DRY ROB ROY

Scotch	1 1/2 ounces (45 ml)
Dry vermouth	3/4 ounce (22 ml)
Zest	garnish

PERFECT ROB ROY

Scotch	1 1/2 ounces (45 ml)
Dry vermouth and sweet vermouth, combined	3/4 ounce (22 ml)
Cherry or zest	garnish

NEGRONI

Gin	1 ounce (30 ml)
Sweet vermouth	1 ounce (30 ml)
Campari®	1 ounce (30 ml)
One-half slice of orange	garnish

Build over ice in an old-fashioned glass.

SHORT SOURS
shake or speed-shake

WHISKEY SOUR

Whiskey	1 1/2 ounces (45 ml)
Lemon mix	2 ounces (60 ml)
Cherry	garnish

Serve in a sour glass.

DAIQUIRI

Light rum	1 1/2 ounces (45 ml)
Lemon mix	1 ounce (30 ml)

BACARDI® COCKTAIL

Bacardi® light rum	1 1/2 ounces (45 ml)
Lemon mix	1 ounce (30 ml)
Grenadine	1/2 ounce (15 ml)

WARD 8

Whiskey	1 1/2 ounces (45 ml)
Lemon mix	1 ounce (30 ml)
Grenadine	1/2 ounce (15 ml)
Cherry or orange slice	garnish

Serve on the rocks.

JACK ROSE COCKTAIL

Applejack	1 1/2 ounces (45 ml)
Grenadine	1/2 ounce (15 ml)
Lemon mix	1 ounce (30 ml)

MARGARITA

Tequila	1 1/2 ounces (45 ml)
Lemon mix	1 ounce (30 ml)
Triple sec	3/4 ounce (22 ml)

Rim champagne coupe with salt. To rim or frost a glass, moisten the rim of the glass with a wedge of citrus fruit, and then dip the glass into a small container of salt or sugar. Set the glass aside. Blend or shake.

BETWEEN THE SHEETS

B—brandy	1/2 ounce (15 ml)
L—lemon mix	1/2 ounce (15 ml)
T—triple sec	1/2 ounce (15 ml)
Rye—rum	1/2 ounce (15 ml)

Using the "BLT on Rye" mnemonic is a handy way to remember the ingredients of this drink. The drink does not contain rye whiskey.

SIDECAR

Brandy	1 1/2 ounces (45 ml)
Triple sec	3/4 ounce (22 ml)
Lemon mix	1/2 ounce (15 ml)

KAMIKAZE

Gin or vodka	1 1/2 ounces (45 ml)
Rose's Lime Juice®	1/2 ounce (15 ml)
Triple sec	3/4 ounce (22 ml)
Lime wedge (optional)	garnish

STONE SOUR

Apricot brandy	1 1/2 ounces (45 ml)
Orange juice	1 ounce (30 ml)
Lemon mix	1 ounce (30 ml)
Cherry	garnish

GIMLET

Gin or vodka	1 1/2 ounces (45 ml)
Rose's Lime Juice®	3/4 ounce (22 ml)
Lime wedge (optional)	garnish

LONG SOURS
shake or speed-shake

TOM COLLINS

Gin	1 1/2 ounces (45 ml)
Lemon mix	2 ounces (60 ml)
Club soda and 7-Up®	to fill
Cherry and one-half orange slice	garnish

Also known as a John Collins

Speed-shake—Collins

Variations

Mike Collins—whiskey

Joe or Ivan Collins—vodka

Pedro Collins—rum

Sandy Collins—scotch

SINGAPORE SLING

Gin	1 1/2 ounces (45 ml)
Lemon mix	2 ounces (60 ml)
Club soda and 7-Up®	equal parts to fill
Cherry flavored brandy or liqueur (float)	1/2 ounce (15 ml)

Classic recipe includes 1 dash of Angostura bitters

Speed-shake—Sling/Zombie

SLOE GIN FIZZ

Sloe gin	1 1/2 ounces (45 ml)
Lemon mix	2 ounces (60 ml)
Club soda	to fill
Cherry and one-half orange slice	garnish

Speed-shake—Collins

LONG ISLAND ICED TEA

Vodka	1/2 ounce (15 ml)
Gin	1/2 ounce (15 ml)
Rum	1/2 ounce (15 ml)
Tequila	1/2 ounce (15 ml)
Triple sec	1/2 ounce (15 ml)
Lemon mix	1 ounce (30 ml)
Coke® (float)	1 ounce (30 ml)
Lemon wheel	garnish

Speed-shake—Sling/Zombie

FROZEN CREAM-BASED DRINKS *blend or shake*

SUMMER RUM FREEZE

Bacardi® rum	1 1/2 ounces (45 ml)
Lime sherbet	2 scoops
Pineapple juice	3 ounces (90 ml)
Cream or milk	3/4 ounce (22 ml)
Pineapple spear or lime wheel	garnish

Place ingredients in the blender. Blend until creamy. Pour into a tall goblet.

SHORT-CREAMS *blend or shake*

BRANDY ALEXANDER

Brandy	1 ounce (30 ml)
Dark crème de cacao	1 ounce (30 ml)
Cream or milk	1 ounce (30 ml)
Nutmeg	garnish

GRASSHOPPER

Light crème de cacao	1 ounce (30 ml)
Green crème de menthe	1 ounce (30 ml)
Cream or milk	1 ounce (30 ml)

GOLDEN DREAM

Galliano®	1 1/2 ounces (45 ml)
Cointreau®	1 ounce (30 ml)
Orange juice	1 ounce (30 ml)
Cream or milk	1 ounce (30 ml)

PINK SQUIRREL

Light crème de cacao	1 ounce (30 ml)
Crème de Noyaux® or crème de almond	1 ounce (30 ml)
Cream or milk	1 ounce (30 ml)

LONG-CREAMS *speed-shake*

ORGASM

Amaretto	1 ounce (30 ml)
Vodka	1/2 ounce (15 ml)
Kahlua®	1/2 ounce (15 ml)
Cream or milk	4 ounces (120 ml)

Classic recipe: short cream with Bailey's Irish Cream® instead of milk.

WHITE RUSSIAN

Vodka	1 1/2 ounces (45 ml)
Kahlua®	1/2 ounce (15 ml)
Cream or milk	4 ounces (120 ml)

Traditionally a layered drink with half-and-half cream set on top of a Black Russian. Today, prepare using speed-shake, serve tall.

GIRL SCOUT COOKIE

Peppermint schnapps	1/2 ounce (15 ml)
Dark crème de cacao	1/2 ounce (15 ml)
Milk	4 ounces (120 ml)

TOASTED ALMOND BAR

Amaretto	3/4 ounce (22 ml)
Dark crème de cacao	3/4 ounce (22 ml)
Milk	4 ounces (120 ml)

CORDIALS *ice down-pour*

BLACK RUSSIAN

Vodka	1 1/2 ounces (45 ml)
Kahlua®	3/4 ounce (22 ml)

GODFATHER

Scotch	1 1/2 ounces (45 ml)
Amaretto	3/4 ounce (22 ml)

SICILIAN KISS

Southern Comfort®	1 1/2 ounces (45 ml)
Amaretto	3/4 ounce (22 ml)

MUD SLIDE

Vodka	3/4 ounce (22 ml)
Kahlua®	3/4 ounce (22 ml)
Bailey's Irish Cream®	3/4 ounce (22 ml)
Speed-shake	

AFTER 5

Kahlua®	1/3 ounce (10 ml)
Bailey's Irish Cream®	1/3 ounce (10 ml)
Peppermint schnapps	1/3 ounce (10 ml)
Layered in order	

STINGER

Brandy	1 1/2 ounces (45 ml)
White crème de menthe	3/4 ounce (22 ml)

GODMOTHER

Vodka	1 1/2 ounces (45 ml)
Amaretto	3/4 ounce (22 ml)

RUSTY NAIL OR QUEEN ANNE

Scotch	1 1/2 ounces (45 ml)
Drambuie®	3/4 ounce (22 ml)

B-52

Kahlua®	1/3 ounce (10 ml)
Bailey's Irish Cream®	1/3 ounce (10 ml)
Grand Marnier®	1/3 ounce (10 ml)

CLASSIC MIXED DRINK

OLD FASHIONED

Sugar	1 package
Bitters	2 or 3 dashes
Club soda	splash
Stemless cherry or orange slice	garnish

Muddle (crush using a muddler) the ingredients
to release the oils and juice of the fruit. Then add
2 ounces (60 ml) blended whiskey or bourbon and
a splash of club soda. Serve on the rocks. Garnish with
orange slice and cherry.

JUICE-BASED HIGHBALLS

COMFORTABLE SCREW

Southern Comfort®	1 1/2 ounces (45 ml)
Orange juice	4 ounces (120 ml)
Orange slice	garnish
Speed-shake	

BOCCE BALL

Amaretto di Saronno®	1 1/2 ounces (45 ml)
Orange juice	4 ounces (120 ml)
Club soda (float)	
Speed-shake	

CAPE CODDER

Vodka	1 1/2 ounces (45 ml)
Cranberry juice	4 ounces (120 ml)

HARVEY WALLBANGER

Vodka	1 1/2 ounces (45 ml)
Orange juice	4 ounces (120 ml)
Galliano® (float)	1/2 ounce (15 ml)
Orange slice and cherry garnish	

TEQUILA SUNRISE

Vodka	1 1/2 ounces (45 ml)
Orange juice	4 ounces (120 ml)
Grenadine (float)	1/2 ounce (15 ml)
Orange slice and cherry garnish	

MADRAS

Vodka	1 1/2 ounces (45 ml)
Cranberry juice	2 ounces (60 ml)
Orange juice	2 ounces (60 ml)

SALTY DOG

Vodka	1 1/2 ounces (45 ml)
Grapefruit juice	4 ounces (120 ml)
Rim glass with salt.	

PEARL HARBOR

Midori®	1 ounce (30 ml)
Vodka	1/2 ounce (15 ml)
Pineapple juice	4 ounces (120 ml)
Speed-shake	

WOO-WOO

Peachtree® Schnapps	1 ounce (45 ml)
Vodka	1/2 ounce (15 ml)
Cranberry juice	to within 1/4 inch of rim
Speed-shake	

BASIC BLOODY MARY MIX

Liquor	1 1/2 ounces (45 ml)
Tomato juice	4 ounces (120 ml)
Salt and pepper	dash
Lea & Perrins® Worcestershire sauce	dash
Tabasco® sauce	dash
Lemon mix	dash
Horseradish (optional)	1 teaspoon (5 ml)
Celery salt (optional)	dash
Celery stalk or lime wedge	garnish

Speed-shake; serve in a goblet.

Variations

Bloody Mary—vodka

Bloody Maria—tequila

Virgin Mary—nonalcoholic Bloody Mary

Bloody Jane or Red Snapper—Bloody Mary mix and gin

ALABAMA SLAMMER

Sloe gin	1/2 ounce (15 ml)
Banana liqueur	1/2 ounce (15 ml)

Orange juice	to within 1/4 inch (6 mm) of rim
Southern Comfort® (float)	1/2 ounce (15 ml)
Speed-shake	

SEX ON THE BEACH

Peachtree® schnapps	1 ounce (30 ml)
Vodka	1 ounce (30 ml)
Orange juice	2 ounces (60 ml)
Cranberry juice	2 ounces (60 ml)
Speed-shake	

SEA BREEZE

Vodka	1 1/2 ounces (44 ml)
Grapefruit juice	2 ounces (60 ml)
Cranberry juice	2 ounces (60 ml)

TOOTSIE ROLL

Dark crème de cacao	1 1/2 ounces (45 ml)
Orange juice	4 ounces (120 ml)
Speed-shake	

SCARLET O'HARA

Southern Comfort®	1 1/2 ounces (45 ml)
Cranberry juice	4 ounces (120 ml)
Speed-shake	

BLOODY CAESAR

| Vodka | 1 1/2 ounces (45 ml) |
| Clamato® juice | 4 ounces (120 ml) |

Speed-shake; serve in a salt- and pepper-rimmed goblet.

FUZZY NAVEL

Peachtree® schnapps	1 1/2 ounces (45 ml)
Orange juice	to within 1/4 inch (6 mm) of the rim
Speed-shake	

WATERMELON

Southern Comfort®	1 ounce (30 ml)
Crème de Noyaux® or crème de almond	1 ounce (30 ml)
Pineapple juice	4 ounces (120 ml)

POLYNESIAN-TROPICALS

The mnemonics to the left of the ingredients list are an aid for remembering specific ingredients; blend or speed-shake.

MAI TAI

S—Sugar or simple syrup	1/2 ounce (15 ml)
C—Orange curaçao	1/2 ounce (15 ml)
R—Myers'® rum (dark)	1 ounce (30 ml)
R—Mt. Gay® rum (gold)	1 ounce (30 ml)
O—Amaretto	1/2 ounce (15 ml)
L—Lemon mix	3 ounces (90 ml)

PIÑA COLADA

C—Coco Lopez®	1/2 ounce (15 ml)
P—Pineapple juice	3 ounces (90 ml)
R—Mt. Gay® rum (gold)	2 ounces (60 ml)

PLANTER'S PUNCH

G—Grenadine	1/2 ounce (15 ml)
L—Lemon mix	1 ounce (30 ml)
O—Orange juice	3 ounces (90 ml)
M—White rum	1 ounce (30 ml)
M—Myers'® rum (dark)	1 ounce (30 ml)
P—Pineapple juice	1 ounce (30 ml)
S—Sugar or simple syrup	1/2 ounce (15 ml)

ZOMBIE

G—Grenadine	1/2 ounce (15 ml)
R—Light rum (bar)	1 ounce (30 ml)
R—Myers'® rum (dark)	1 ounce (30 ml)
L—Lemon mix	2 ounces (60 ml)
O—Orange juice	1 1/2 ounces (45 ml)
C—Orange curaçao	1 ounce (30 ml)

NONALCOHOLIC COCKTAILS AND MIXED DRINKS

SHIRLEY TEMPLE

Ginger ale	6 ounces (180 ml)
Grenadine	1 ounce (30 ml)
Cherries	garnish

FLORIDA COCKTAIL

Grape juice	2 ounces (60 ml)
Orange juice	1 ounce (30 ml)
Lemon mix	2 ounces (60 ml)
Club soda	fill to 1/4 inch (6 mm) from the rim
Fresh mint leaves	garnish
Speed-shake	

PUSSYFOOT

Lemon mix	2 ounces (60 ml)
Orange juice	2 ounces (60 ml)
Rose's Lime Juice	1 ounce (30 ml)
Grenadine	1/2 ounce (15 ml)
Pasteurized egg yolk	1 ounce (30 ml)
Orange slice and cherry	garnish
Shake	

Nonalcoholic cocktails and mixed drinks are an important aspect of mixology. Designated drivers, abstainers from alcoholic beverages, and young people may want to take part in social occasions where others are enjoying alcoholic beverages. Nonalcoholic options must be available to them. Bartenders should use their imaginations and creativity to cater to this market.

Alcohol and the Law

The first liquor-control laws in America's English colonies became effective in 1733, when Georgia's governor prohibited the importation of hard liquor into that colony. Since that time, governments have passed a variety of liquor laws—some to control and deter the consumption of alcohol and others to raise money. Popularly known as "sin taxes," laws taxing such items as alcohol and tobacco are popular with legislators because they do not tax necessities.

609-984-2830
609/635-6028

Early Alcohol Laws

Shortly after the United States became an independent country, a tax on alcohol prompted the first confrontation between citizens and federal troops. The 1794 Whiskey Rebellion sent Pennsylvania farmers, who found it cheaper to transport alcohol than the grain used to make it, into the streets to protest a tax on spirits. Twenty years later, Indiana prohibited the sale of liquor on Sunday, and by 1833 more than 5,000 temperance groups with more than a million members lobbied for an outright ban on the sale of alcohol. A string of controls across the country, including Maine's 1846 prohibition law, made complete prohibition of the sale of alcoholic beverages an idea whose popularity would continue to grow.

Prohibition

On January 16, 1920, the Eighteenth Amendment, which banned the sale of liquor in the United States, became law.

Prohibition was a failure—many ordinary citizens turned into lawbreakers, paving the way for the development of organized crime, and costing the United States government approximately $1 billion each year in lost revenues and enforcement expenses. Experts estimate that about $36 billion spent for bootlegged and smuggled liquor traveled from the wallets of ordinary citizens into the pockets of criminals.

In the end, Americans opted for regulation over the expensive and largely ineffective Eighteenth Amendment. In 1933, the Twenty-first Amendment repealed Prohibition, setting up a climate for new regulations.

ATF

Federal laws governed trade practices and required permits, and in 1972, the new *Bureau of Alcohol, Tobacco, and Firearms (ATF)* received its charter. The ATF has jurisdiction over the making and distribution of distilled spirits. For example, government regulations require that distilled spirits be bottled in similar containers with affixed Internal Revenue tax stamps. The stamp must span the crevice where the bottle cap ends and the bottle begins so that upon opening the bottle the stamp will tear, but a portion of the stamp must remain affixed to each opened bottle. Failure to comply may result in a fine of up to $10,000, imprisonment of not more than five years, or both. Note that it violates federal law to use empty liquor bottles for any reason or to marry the contents of two or more bottles of the same liquor.

The ATF has control over three areas:

· **Consumer protection**—Alcoholic beverages must conform to the Standards of Identity.
· **Trade practices**—The sale of illegal spirits is prohibited.
· **Revenue collection**—The bureau collects revenues from distillers on the basis of production of proof gallons.

Retail dealers who sell alcoholic beverages must pay a special federal tax. When the tax is paid in full, the dealer will be issued a special tax stamp for the class of business for which the tax is paid.

Legal Definitions

The ATF uses specific definitions to levy taxes on alcoholic beverages:

Alcohol—A volatile, colorless liquid obtained through the fermentation of a liquid containing sugar.

Alcoholic beverage—Any potable liquid containing from 0.5% to 75.5% ethyl alcohol by volume.

Spirit—A potable alcoholic beverage obtained from the distillation of a liquid containing alcohol.

Proof (American method)—The strength of a liquor, once called "gunpowder proof."

To test the strength of the liquor, distillers used to pour it on gunpowder and throw a struck match on it. If the liquor blazed, it was too strong. Liquor at the proper strength, mixed with the powder, would burn slowly with a blue flame. The addition of 50% water produced a slow, steady flame. That strength was called "100 proof." Today, regulations apply the same scale on the following basis: Pure 100% alcohol is 200 proof, and 1 degree of proof is equal to 0.5% alcohol. Dividing the proof number by 2 yields the percentage of alcohol by volume. Proof, therefore, indicates the strength.

Conversely, the proof number is always twice the percentage of alcohol in the beverage. The remainder of the content in the beverage includes distilled water, coloring, and flavoring components.

Proof Gallon Taxes

All alcoholic beverages, whether they are produced in the United States or imported, are subject to Internal Revenue taxes; imported alcoholic beverages are also subject to customs duties. The alcoholic content of the beverage determines the tax rate. The standard one-gallon proof contains 100 proof, or 50%, alcohol. If a gallon contains 150 proof alcohol, it is taxed as 1.5 proof gallons. The trade term for a spirit of more than 100 proof is an overproof spirit.

A tax gallon, then, is the measure used to determine how much tax is paid, according to the rate of taxation and/or duties times the number of tax gallons of spirits. For beverages containing less than 100 proof alcohol, the tax is paid on actual gallons.

The federal government taxes wines at different rates, ranging from $1.07 to $3.30 per gallon and depending on alcohol content and degree and type of carbonation. The beer tax is $18 per 31 gallons (117 L) and 5 cents on each 12-ounce (355 ml) can. The tax on distilled spirits is $13.50 per proof gallon. These taxes are paid by on-premise and off-premise retailers, who must track the sale of each category and maintain written records that are subject to both ATF or local government audit.

Duties

Import duties are imposed in addition to the federal, state, and local excise taxes charged for alcoholic beverages, so imported spirits are often more expensive than domestic varieties. Negotiated trade agreements can change the amount of duties charged on imported alcoholic beverages. Wines, in particular, are commonly available from countries all over the world, especially Mexico, Canada, the Caribbean nations, European countries, and Australia.

Fifty percent of the average retail price of a bottle of spirits consists of federal, state, and local taxes.

State Controls

With the repeal of Prohibition, the federal government turned over most alcoholic beverage control to the individual states. This has resulted in the enormous differences in controls between states and even within states. State control of the sale of alcoholic beverages falls into two categories: open-license states and control states.

Open-License States

Open-license states grant licenses to private enterprises to operate as wholesalers of alcoholic beverages to both on- and off-premise retailers and to the retailers themselves. Strict rules may govern the manner in which both tiers of the distribution system operate. For example, no *tied house* relationships, whereby the distributor operates or owns part interest in a retailer, may exist. Most states also have *local option laws* that leave the decision to allow the sale of alcoholic beverages up to local communities.

In addition to these state controls, some states have "dry" communities, and it is illegal to transport alcoholic beverages into them from neighboring "wet" communities. Each state and municipality also may enforce different hours for opening and closing establishments that sell liquor and have different provisions with respect to the number of licenses permitted in a given area or in proximity to places of worship, schools, or hospitals.

Control States

Eighteen control states operate to varying degrees as the sole distributors of alcoholic beverages to on- and off-premise retailers. In some of these states, the state acts as the only off-premise outlet for liquor sold to consumers. In such cases, beer and certain wines may be sold through private enterprises, such as grocery stores. To prevent consumers or operators of bars and restaurants from purchasing alcoholic beverages across state lines, some control states require a special stamp or mark on each bottle to prove that the item was purchased legally within the state.

State Laws

Those who work in establishments that serve alcohol need to make sure that they are familiar with all the state laws governing the sale of alcoholic beverages. Failure to know the law can have serious consequences for the employer and the employee. Some consequences are legal; others are a matter of conscience, escpecially if innocent people are injured by someone who should not have been served alcohol.

Dram Shop Laws

For bars and restaurants and their personnel, dram shop laws are the most critical issue affecting the sale of alcoholic beverages. Dram shop laws originated in the nineteenth century in England and were first enacted in the United States in 1873. In states with *dram shop laws,* restaurants, bars, and their employees are held liable for illegal acts committed by patrons under the influence of alcohol served to them in the establishment. These laws are also known as third-party liability laws. Lawyers began using these laws in the mid-1980s to litigate civil actions. Many such suits resulted in unprecedented multimillion dollar awards.

Negligence Laws

Even in states that do not have dram shop laws, courts generally apply common law to alcohol-related cases. Basing their decisions on precedents, courts normally favor the victim over the persons who served or sold the liquor.

Generally, in non-dram shop states, courts base their decisions on Alcohol Beverage Control (ABC) regulations, either because state laws were violated or because sellers or servers were negligent in serving alcohol to an obviously inebriated person or to a minor.

In addition to facing third-party liability and negligence laws, the operator of a restaurant, tavern, or bar; the employees of such an establishment; or the host of a private party may be subject to criminal liability. If convicted, these persons could receive prison sentences.

Finally, the establishment and its employees can face administrative liability, whereby the state or Alcohol Control Board can levy a fine or suspend or revoke a liquor license.

Drunken Driving Laws

The hope of preventing thousands of deaths caused by drunk drivers has encouraged many states to strengthen drunken driving laws. In these states, offenses that are commonly referred to as DWI, driving while intoxicated, or DUI, driving under the influence, are no longer treated lightly. These offenses are punishable under *per se* laws, dictating that a single piece of evidence, such as the results of a Breathalyzer™ test or the refusal to take such a test, is sufficient evidence to presume guilt.

Impact of Laws on Industry

As we have seen, criminal, administrative, and civil sanctions exist for servers, managers, or owners of establishments who fail to make reasonable efforts to ensure that alcohol consumption occurs in a responsible and moderate fashion.

An establishment and its servers must be acquainted with all pertinent laws and regulations and must undergo alcohol intervention training such as TiPS (Training for Intervention ProcedureS) to demonstrate

that negligence has not occurred. Each server should know which persons cannot legally be served. These include anyone:

- who is legally intoxicated or who would become intoxicated if served an alcoholic beverage
- who is a known alcoholic
- with a propensity toward alcoholism
- who is legally under age

All states mandate than only those persons who are 21 years of age or older may purchase or be served alcoholic beverages. Because forging identification has become easier with today's technology, establishments need to stay abreast of publications on identification issues, which are updated yearly.

As a precaution, a server should check identification for anyone who looks younger than 25 years old. Some national chains have made it a policy to check identification of all who purchase alcoholic beverages, regardless of age.

Legally acceptable forms of identification include:

- a state-issued driver's license with photograph
- a state-issued identification card with photograph
- a military identification card with photograph
- a United States passport

An establishment's employees are not required to accept any identification issued outside the state in which the establishment is located. Some states, such as Rhode Island, require that employees have a "Minors Book" located at the bar. Anyone who presents proper identification but who appears underage or "illegal" for some other reason must sign the book before being served. A good guide to follow is that if there is sufficient reason to question the legal age of a patron, politely refuse to serve that person any alcoholic beverage.

The Effects of Alcohol

Alcohol is a food product, but it is classified as an intoxicating drug that depresses the brain and other parts of the central nervous system. Although alcohol is fairly high in calories, it has little nutritional value. An ounce of pure alcohol has 210 calories; one ounce of whiskey (43% alcohol, or 86 proof) has 75 calories. A 12-ounce (355-ml) container of beer has between 120 and 210 calories. Although moderate consumption of alcohol, especially wine, may have some health benefits, long-term abuse will result in permanent damage to the liver, kidneys, and brain, as well as to the central nervous, digestive, and circulatory systems.

Absorption Rate Factors

Because alcohol requires no digestion, it is absorbed and transported by the bloodstream throughout the body in a very short time. A small amount enters the capillaries in the mouth even before the beverage is swallowed. About 20% of the remaining alcohol is absorbed quickly through the stomach lining. However, the presence of food in the stomach slows the absorption of alcohol because alcohol mixes with the stomach's contents and is digested along with the food.

During the initial stage of the digestive process, the "door" between the stomach and the small intestine, called the *pylorus valve*, generally remains closed, trapping food and alcohol in the stomach. Too much alcohol may cause a *pylorospasm*, in which the alcohol-sensitive pylorus valve prevents the food and alcohol from moving through the system.

Pylorospasms trap sufficient alcohol in the stomach to cause irritation and distress. The drinker may elect to stop drinking at this point because he or she feels ill when the stomach lining secretes excess amounts of hydrochloric acid. This process is a self-protective mechanism

that can prevent the overconsumption of alcohol, but not all people recognize the symptoms.

When alcohol reaches the small intestine, the remaining 80% is absorbed into the bloodstream. The faster the alcohol is absorbed, the more likely the consumer is to become intoxicated. The higher the alcohol content of the beverage, the more quickly it is absorbed into the bloodstream. Alcohol mixed with carbonated beverages is absorbed faster than alcohol of the same proof mixed with fruit juice. Several other factors also influence the rate of absorption of alcohol, including the following:

- the rate of consumption
- the gender of the consumer
- the height, weight, and physical condition of the consumer
- the mood of the consumer
- the amount of food in the consumer's stomach
- the presence of medications, some of which can speed up the effects of alcohol

Levels of Intoxication

Learning to recognize and understand the effects of alcohol will help servers determine whether to serve or continue to serve alcoholic beverages to a guest. The brain and other parts of the central nervous system are affected more quickly than are other organs of the body. When blood alcohol content is sufficient to cause *intoxication,* or drunkenness, it also impairs memory, motor control, and judgment. These behavioral clues can help determine when a patron has become intoxicated:

- **Loss of inhibitions**—An intoxicated person becomes talkative, relaxed, and overfriendly and exhibits mood swings. Depending on how extreme his or her actions are, the person may fit into a happy category or one of pronounced excitement.
- **Loss of judgment**—An intoxicated person often exhibits erratic behavior. He or she may use foul language, become angry, or act impulsively. The person may be excited to the point of confusion.
- **Loss of reaction**—An intoxicated person may lose his or her train of thought easily. He or she may exhibit unfocused eyes, slurred speech, and unsteady hands.

- **Loss of coordination**—An intoxicated person may suffer loss of balance, drowsiness, and lack of dexterity. When a drinker reaches this stage, he or she is approaching the fourth stage of intoxication.

Figure 35-8 is based on the effects of alcohol consumption on a man weighing 150–160 pounds (68–73 kg). One drink represents 1 ounce (30 ml) of 100 proof distilled spirits, 3 ounces (90 ml) of sherry, 5 ounces (150 ml) of wine, or 12 ounces (355 ml) of beer. Note that a woman who weighs 120–130 pounds (54–60 kg) becomes intoxicated faster than a man of similar weight. This more rapid intoxication takes place because women generally have less water and more body fat than men. The higher rate of water in a man's body dilutes the alcohol, lowering the blood-alcohol level.

Industry Responsibilities

Although the food and beverage industry cannot be responsible for all the problems associated with excess alcohol consumption,

servers and establishment operators can ensure that the behavior of staff members promotes responsible consumption of alcoholic beverages by:

- Checking identification as a routine in every case in which there is doubt about a patron's age.
- Recognizing the signs of intoxication and refraining from serving anyone who has consumed too many drinks or who exhibits signs of intoxication.
- Declining to serve any customer who appears to have consumed excess alcohol elsewhere.
- Encouraging impaired customers to call for a cab or contact a friend to get a ride home, or offering to make the call yourself. Persuading the customer to surrender the car keys when warranted.
- Observing responsible and reasonable standards in serving and consuming alcohol to set a good example for fellow employees and friends.

FIGURE 35-8

Stage	Drinks per Hour	Blood Alcohol	Rate to Metabolize
Happy	1	0.02	Less than 1 hour **Loss of inhibitions:** *talkative, relaxed*
Excited	2	0.05	Two hours **Loss of judgment:** *loud, boisterous, inappropriate remarks and behavior*
Confused	4	0.10	Four hours **Loss of reactions:** *slurred speech, staggering, mood swings, double vision, some loss of coordination*
Stupor	8	0.20	Eight hours **Loss of coordination:** *after 6 hours, still legally drunk; emotional, erratic behavior; inability to stand; loss of memory; barely conscious, approaching paralysis*
Coma	1 pint	0.40–0.50	**Unable to metabolize:** *comatose, and dangerously close to death; brain centers are anesthetized*
Death		0.60–0.70	

Stages of Intoxication

36 Enology

ca. 6000 B.C.
Winemaking developed in Asia Minor and spread to the Fertile Crescent.

ca. 4000 B.C. to A.D. 350
Egyptians begin labeling wine with place of origin, variety of grape, winemaker, and vintage.

A.D. 350–1200
Monasteries preserve winemaking and viticultural knowledge to satisfy need for sacramental wines.

1400–1700
Fortifying, sulfuring, and bottling wines in glass revolutionizes winemaking.

1863–1890
Phylloxera devastates Europe's vineyards; grafting vines to American rootstock saves viticulture.

1950–present
Modern technology and science help the U.S. earn deserved reputation for fine wines.

It is little wonder that the ancient Greek god Dionysus was known as the god of wine and ecstasy. Few beverages excite as many senses as wine does. Brilliant colors, inviting aromas, complex bouquets, subtle tastes and textures— the products of the winemaker's art —have made wine an integral part of ceremonies and social and religious rituals, enhancing well-prepared meals and cementing friendships. Today, science has also revealed the long-term health benefits of moderate wine consumption.

Introduction to Wine

The simple definition of wine—the fermented juice of grapes—does little to explain why academics in such diverse fields as biology, chemistry, microbiology, geography, horticulture, sociology, economics, and medicine have all been fascinated with the study of wine. Perhaps the interest stems from the simple fact that from the vineyard to the table, wine is the perfect blend of art and science, a study of infinite variety and nearly endless permutations.

There are many species of grapes and thousands of varieties within each species. It is the Vitis vinifera species, however, that produces most wines. Of the 5,000 varieties of Vitis vinifera (the name means "wine bearing"), the wine market is concerned with no more than 50. Because winemaking is so complex, however, the history of winemaking has been characterized by continual challenges for winemakers and growers alike.

The History of Wine

Winemaking is a natural phenomenon: grapes have sugars that wild yeasts convert to ethyl alcohol. Today, winemakers choose varieties of grapes and the yeasts that ferment them into wines with infinite care, but the first winemakers took the gift that nature provided and slowly learned to modify and improve the process.

Until the nineteenth century, the history of wine making may be viewed as the struggle against spoilage. Wood inadvertently became an added flavor component after the Romans adopted it from the ancient Gauls of France as a standard medium for transportation and storage. Modern winemakers, however, have little excuse for making a bad wine. The art and the science of grape growing and winemaking are based on centuries of experimentation and learning about conditions that make for good wines—and sometimes great ones.

Wine and religion Over the centuries, wine has been inextricably linked to religion. From the ancient Greeks and Romans to Jewish and Christian traditions, wine has been associated with mystical and religious experiences because of the symbolism of annual rebirth of the vine, not to mention its psychological impact.

The earliest years The earliest traces of winemaking may date to 6000 B.C. in the Caucasus region. By 4000 B.C. winemaking had spread to Mesopotamia, Babylon, and Egypt. In fact, the Egyptians had already begun the practice of labeling wines to indicate the place of origin, the grape, the name of the winemaker, and the vintage.

Written references to grapes appear in the Bible, which notes that Noah planted a vineyard after the great flood, said to have occurred about 5600 B.C. When the Phoenicians or Minoans introduced winemaking to Greece in about 2000 B.C., its sale led to the wealth on which the great Greek civilization was built.

Winemaking technology continued to develop under the Roman Empire. Winemakers began understanding wine production and the relationships between varieties and soil, climate, aging, and storing temperatures. Later, Romans introduced winemaking to the Gauls (modern-day French). Between A.D. 350 and 1200, some monastic orders, particularly the Benedictines, Carthusians, and Cistercians, preserved and improved winemaking knowledge in Europe. See Figure 36-1 on page 869. In the process, they cultivated vineyards dedicated to producing wine for sacramental, medicinal, and income purposes.

Trade expands winemaking As world exploration and trade expanded in the 1400s, Europeans looked for ways to preserve wine during long trade voyages. Dutch and English traders learned to fortify French wines by adding brandy to stabilize them. The process of adding sulfur to prevent spoilage became more widespread and continues to this day, although more judiciously. Exploration and trade also introduced winemaking to the Americas, Australia, and South Africa as Europeans begin to settle in the New World.

Technology advances winemaking In the mid-1600s, glass bottles strong enough for commercial use were developed, though they were not widely used until late in the century. By the end of the century, the use of corks became commonplace. These developments were important to better quality control and marketing of brands.

During the 1700s, Dom Pérignon, cellar master at the monastery in Hautvillers at Épernay, made significant advances in the science of winemaking. He began to understand the different characteristics of varieties; the role of terroir; the cuvée, or blending of different varieties; and the role of temperature in fermentation and cellaring.

In the years following the French Revolution (1789–1815), monastic orders lost their landholdings. Their vineyards were distributed to supporters of the Revolution; the Napoleonic Code of Law then granted equal inheritance rights to heirs, resulting in ever-smaller landholdings. *Négociants,* or merchants, took on an increasingly important role of not only distributing, but also "raising " the wines purchased from the owners of these small vineyards.

In 1851, *oidium,* a powdery mildew fungus, devastated many of France's vineyards, particularly in Bordeaux. Growers learned to use sulfur and lime to combat the problem—a solution that is still used today.

By 1855, wine brokers played a pivotal role in creating a list of the best wine producers for the *Paris Exposition Universelle.* The list ultimately became the foundation for the Classification of 1855 of Bordeaux wines, rating the best 61 wines, primarily of the Médoc region. The list, nearly unchanged, survives to this day.

The problem of wine spoilage, however, continued to plague winemakers. A solution was desperately needed. In 1862, Napoleon III invited Louis Pasteur, France's premier scientist, to tackle the problem. Pasteur soon discovered that bacteria present in wine, especially acetobacter, the organism that turns wine to vinegar, could be controlled if the bacteria were deprived of light and oxygen. He suggested several solutions: Fill wine bottles as full as possible. Use colored glass to deprive bacteria of light. Store wine bottles on their sides so that corks remain moist and swell, keeping oxygen from seeping into the bottles. Store wine in a cool environment to retard bacterial growth. Pasteur also developed a pasteurization process for wine, which would later be used primarily to treat milk.

Biological challenges In 1863 the European wine industry faced its biggest challenge when *Phylloxera vastatrix,* a microscopic pest, was accidentally introduced to vineyards in France through the importation of American vines. By 1880, *Phylloxera* infestations had become so widespread that the pest was known as the "Blight of Europe." It took nearly 40 years for France and the rest of Europe to understand the life cycle of the pest and find a solution to the havoc it caused. Through the efforts of Jules-Emile Planchon and C. V. Riley of Missouri, grafting the *Vitis vinifera* vines to native American *vitis* species, particularly *riparia* and *rupestris* rootstock, gave the vines resistance to the pest. *Phylloxera* still remains a problem, devastating California vineyards not only in the 1880s but once again in the 1990s. Of major wine producing regions, only Chile remains free of the pest.

Hybridizing *vitis* species to combat *Phylloxera* proved relatively disappointing because the quality of most hybrids was inferior. Only a few hybrid varieties, notably Seyval Blanc and Vidal Blanc for whites and Chambourcin and Maréchal Foche for reds, are still grown for wines, especially in New England.

Interaction between Europe and North America resulted in another imported blight that attacked Europe's vines. When grafting began to enjoy success, huge quantities of American rootstock were imported to Europe. With them came downy mildew, a plague that weakened the vines, reduced the crops, and killed outright 30% of France's vines. It took four years for growers to learn that spraying the vines with copper sulfate could prevent this mold. The spray is still used today.

Then, in 1920, another "blight" plagued the wine industry, this time in the United States. The Volstead Act made the production and sale of alcoholic beverages illegal. Prohibition devastated most wineries; others could produce only sacramental or medicinal wines. However, a legal loophole allowed citizens to make up to 200 gallons of wine per year for home consumption. The planting of high-yielding table grape varieties doubled grape production. When Prohibition was repealed in December of 1933, it left a legacy of second-rate wines—a legacy that would last for over 30 years.

Improved quality control During this same period, France was focusing on improving quality in wines. The country developed the *Appellation Contrôlée* system. First adopted for the production of Roquefort cheese, the system delimited the name of a wine to a particular region, but it also determined which varieties were best suited to the particular environment of that region in order to achieve authenticity. Thus, the concept of terroir was born. The system recognized that not only soil, but also the complete ecosystem of an area, including climate, wind, temperature, rainfall, sunlight, and topographical features, affected a wine's quality.

American wines improve Ernest and Julio Gallo preserved American wine consumption during the 1930s to the 1960s by producing well-made "table wine" that was readily accessible to the American table. In the 1950s fine winemaking was again recognized as feasible in California as a result of the action of a few creative vintners.

James Zellerback, who replicated a Burgundian cellar down to the kind of oak used for aging, developed an impressive Chardonnay. Inspired by his success, J. Heitz and Robert Mondavi visited Europe and came away impressed with the importance of varietals. American winemakers began to plant top-quality vines. The University of California-Davis School of Oenology became a world leader in the study of viticulture and winemaking.

A blind wine tasting held in 1976 in Paris, France, resulted in French judges' rating some American wines as superior to the best that France had to offer. Consequently, a "grape rush" occurred, especially in Napa Valley. Tax advantages inspired heavy investments in vineyards, and more than 210 wineries are now operating in the Napa Valley alone. Europeans have made major investments in such American wineries.

Beginning in 1981, certain geographic areas became identified as *American Viticultural Areas (AVA)* as a result of the concept and centrality of place or terroir. The Napa Wine Growers Association was able to make its appellation a critical marketing decision in the U.S. consumer's

mind. As other regions have copied Napa, there are currently approximately 140 AVAs.

In California, *Phylloxera* reasserted itself in vines grafted on AxR1 rootstock that offered insufficient resistance to the pest. Most California vines had to be replanted in the 1990s. This disaster allowed producers to apply recently acquired knowledge to plant more appropriate clones and realign vineyards to optimize sunlight by spacing more efficiently and more densely—all contributing to improved quality.

Despite the problems that periodically surface in viticulture, areas around the world have thrown their resources into viticulture in the recognition that great wines are made in the vineyard. New World wines have made inroads in fine wine markets, offering consumers throughout the world ever improving quality. Concurrently, there has been a major shift from consuming "table" wines to premium and super-premium wines in both the New World and the Old World. Although consumption in the United States remains low at 2 gallons per adult versus 15 gallons per adult in France, excitement is palpable among U.S. consumers, who are discovering wines from around the world.

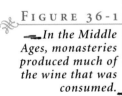

FIGURE 36-1

In the Middle Ages, monasteries produced much of the wine that was consumed.

Winemaking

The critical elements in producing good wine are the grape; the climate; viticulture, or growing conditions; and vinification, or the process of winemaking.

The Grape

The essence of wine is the grape used to produce it. A thorough knowledge of the categories, composition, and varieties of grapes is essential to the wine maker's art.

Grape categories Grapes are generally divided into four categories, Native American *Vitis* species such as Labrusca, two subdivisions of *Vitis vinifera,* and a hybrid, or cross between native American species and *vinifera.*

- **Native American *Vitis*** North American wild grapes of these species do not have the acid and sugar balance of *vinifera* and typically have a "foxy" flavor that many associate with Concord grape juice. For that reason, wine made from such species does not generally pair well with food.
- ***Vitis vinifera*** grapes, typified by varieties like Thompson Seedless, are primarily used as table grapes because their undistinguished quality makes them unsuitable for fine wines. In Europe and the United States, winemakers blend these grapes into table or jug wines, although this category is declining in importance.
- ***Vitis vinifera*** grapes that produce fine wines, on the other hand, have a distinct character that makes them the focus of the winemaker's art. These varieties are also the focus of this chapter.
- **French-American hybrid** grapes generally produce less satisfactory wines than *vinifera* varieties, though some, such as Seyval Blanc and Vidal Blanc, can be made into palatable, if not distinctive, wines.

Grape composition The well-known adage "fine wine is created in the vineyard" recognizes the pivotal role of grape varieties in creating a fine wine. The grape captures the sun's energy, stores it as sugar, and retains the water and minerals absorbed by the vine's root system. In exceptional growing years, wines are made in which the alcohol, sweetness, acidity, and *tannins,* a chemical component found in grape skins, stems, and *pips* (seeds), are perfectly balanced and flavors are fully developed. The key to fine wine is always balance—and balance begins with perfectly balanced grapes. See Figure 36-2.

Grapes consist of 70%–85% water, 15%–30% sugar and extracts, 0.3%–1.8% acids, and 0%–0.2% tannins, but by the time grapes are fermented, the resulting wine has developed more than 300 organic compounds; 200 of them have distinct odors.

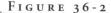

FIGURE 36-2

Each part of the grape contributes to the flavor and aroma of the wine.

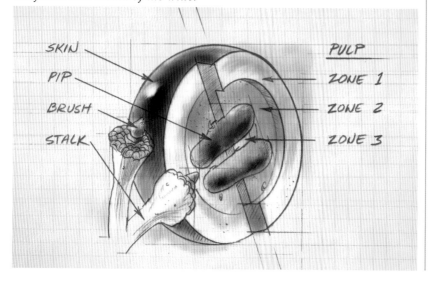

Aromas, fragrances derived from the grape itself, include compounds found in all fruits. *Bouquets,* those fragrances that result from fermentation and aging, sometimes take years to develop as the wine slowly evolves and changes chemical composition.

When grapes ferment into wine, the fermentation process creates alcohol from sugar stored in the grape. If the sugars are fermented completely, the wine is dry. If the sugars are not completely fermented, the wine retains varying degrees of sweetness. In addition, ethanol, the main form of alcohol produced by fermentation, is perceived as sweetness.

In red wines, tannins and phenolics found in the grape's skins, stems, and pips are important to the wine's balance and mouth feel.

Tannins vary in astringency, from a chalky "dried-out" feeling in the mouth to a great deal of spice and harshness. They provide significant textural components and act as a preservative in red wine. In white wines, tannins are generally negligible because the skins, stems, and seeds from which tannins are derived are removed very early in the winemaking process, although wood or oak tannins can be a factor, especially with Chardonnays.

The acid component in wine not only provides balance but also allows wine to age well. Several acids—tartaric, malic, lactic, and citric—are found in wine, each with unique characteristics. Tartaric acid, with its very acidic taste, is uncommon in most other fruits and vegetables, but it is important in grapes, and therefore in wines. Because tartaric acid's salt, potassium bitartrate, is only partially soluble in alcohol, it may precipitate out in the wine. Sometimes, therefore, crystals of potassium bitartrate may be present on the cork or floating in the wine. The crystals look like glass, but they are not harmful; in fact, as a by-product of winemaking, they are sold for culinary use as cream of tartar.

Malic acid is also found in green apples, such as Granny Smiths, and may be perceived as tart or acidic in wine. Malic acids are partially converted to lactic acid in wines that undergo malolactic fermentation. Almost all red wines and, with the exception of Chardonnay, almost no white wines undergo this secondary fermentation. This conversion reduces the overall perception of the wine's acidity, making it seem "softer." Citric acids generally disappear during fermentation, so wines usually contain only trace amounts of citric acid. Acids are, however, important to wine because they give it liveliness and balance the alcohol and/or sugars.

Grape Varieties

The world of wine owes much of its variety to the genetic instability of *vitis vinifera*, the "wine vine." More than 5,000 identified varieties, and hundreds of different clones of certain of these varieties, have resulted from this instability. Most wine connoisseurs, however, are primarily interested in only 50 or so of these, divided into white and black grape varieties. Most wines produced in the New World are sold using varietal names—those that identify the wine by the variety from which the wine is made. In the Old World, wines may be made from essentially the same grape variety, but their names are most often based on a geographic region or appellation rather than on grape variety. That is because the characteristics of soil, moisture, temperature, and orientation have profound effects on the grapes of each region. A wine labeled *Domaine Leflaive Puligny-Montrachet*, for example, is a Chardonnay made in Burgundy, France. In the United States the wine is simply labeled *Chardonnay*.

White grape varieties Applied to grapes, *white* has a specialized meaning. White grapes are any light-skinned grape and may range from pale green to gold. White wines differ from red wines because they lack anthocyanins and pigmented tannins from the skins and sometimes the stems and pips of black grapes. White wines can also be fermented from black grapes if the juice does not come in extended contact with the skins. There are white and red Zinfandel wines, for example, but both are made from the same black grape.

Chardonnay Growers are particularly fond of the Chardonnay grape because it is so malleable and adaptable to different climates. The classic Old World model is used for white Burgundies such as Chablis, Montrachet, Meursault, and Pouilly-Fuissé. These wines have good acidity, dryness with apple or melon aromas, and vanilla and buttery notes when aged in oak. The wines can develop enormous complexity with bottle age.

In the New World, wines made from Chardonnay tend towards higher alcohol levels and flavors with hints of sweetness; more peach and tropical nuances; more oak-derived notes such as coconut; and lower acidity, which may result in a somewhat reduced ability to age.

Sauvignon Blanc, the principal white grape of Bordeaux and the eastern Loire Valley, makes a clean, dry, intense, aromatic white wine with a herbaceous, mineral-like character. In fact, the name *Sauvignon* comes from the French word *sauvage*, or "wild." Sauvignons from South Africa often have similar characters to Old World grapes. Sauvignon Blancs are frequently blended with Sémillons to mellow the tart, herbal character of Sauvignon Blanc—a practice that is common in Bordeaux, France, as well as in other locations such as California and Australia.

In New Zealand, Sauvignon Blancs have their grapefruit acidity balanced by the richness of higher alcohol, but they retain their intense herbaceous flavors balanced by tropical guava notes. In California, wine produced from Sauvignon Blanc is often referred to as Fumé Blanc, although the wines do not have a smoky character. California Sauvignon wines are more often aged in oak and often have a softer fig or melon character than is produced from grapes from other regions. Most are, however, rather high in alcohol content—about 13%.

Some Chilean wine labeled *Sauvignon Blanc* may actually be made from Sauvignon Vert grapes, a variety that is less herbal and unrelated to Sauvignon Blanc. Many Chilean vineyards are now being replanted with Sauvignon Blanc, however.

Riesling, often identified as the most noble of the white grapes, produces wines with searing acidity balanced by residual sweetness, delicate rose aromas, and notes of peaches, apricots, and melons. These qualities, coupled with Riesling's often low alcohol content when made into wine, are responsible for this grape's reputation for light body, delicacy, and transparency. From classic regions of Germany such as the Mosel, Riesling can develop mineral or earthy notes balanced by delicate sweetness. Rieslings from the Alsace region of France, Germany, northern Austria, and New York are light-bodied and complex, perhaps because Rieslings adapt well to the cooler growing sites these locations offer.

The Rieslings grown in warmer regions in Australia and California and those from Washington state and Oregon are generally softer and slightly fuller, sometimes with more diffuse flavors.

Chenin Blanc Old World wines made from Chenin Blanc are vibrant, complex, long-lived, and shimmering in their acidity. The wines include such great wines coming from Vouvrays, Savennières, Anjou, and Saumur. In the Loire Valley in France, these grapes are fermented to varying degrees of sweetness, from bone-dry to lusciously sweet, balancing their high acidity.

In California, Chenin Blanc was once the most widely planted classic grape variety, but it has now been supplanted by Chardonnay. Chenin Blanc is used mostly in bulk wines in North America. In South Africa, where it is also known as *Steen*, Chenin Blanc makes up 30% of the country's grape harvest. When compared with Chenin Blancs made from grapes grown in the Loire Valley in France, wine from both of these areas is characterized by crispness but otherwise considered to be rather bland because of overcropping.

Gewürztraminer, a pink-skinned native grape of Germany and Alsace, produces particularly aromatic and full-bodied white wines. The name perfectly describes the character of the grape. *Gewürz* in German is "spiced," or, in the context of wine, "perfumed." *Traminer* identifies the older grape variety from which the Gewürztraminer mutated. Wine tasters use such words as lychee nuts, gingerbread, honey, and musk to describe the flavors of wines made from these grapes, but it is their scents of jasmine and roses that make them some of the most recognized wines in the world.

The very best Gewürztraminers grow in the Alsace, where the region's fine, crisp autumns produce late-picked grapes that make wines with low acidity and a mouth-filling viscous quality. Germany also produces delicious examples. One of only a few white wines with a slightly bitter finish, Gewürztraminer can be dry as produced in Austria, or off-dry as produced in Germany, California, and Washington state. Although it is at times underappreciated, Gewürztraminer is one of the most versatile wines for pairing with food, complementing foods as diverse as Alsatian cuisine and spicy Asian dishes.

Sémillon, a golden grape variety from southwest France, is one of the principal varieties produced in Bordeaux's sweet wine-producing communes. This grape plays two roles in winemaking—one as the star and one as an understudy. For Sauternes—those rich, complex dessert wines counted among the world's most long-lasting unfortified wines—Sémillon is the star. It produces luscious, richly honeyed wines with perfectly balanced sweetness, acidity, and alcohol, partly because its thin skin makes it particularly susceptible to *Botrytis cinerea*, or "noble rot."

In its supporting role, Sémillon is blended with Sauvignon Blanc, especially in Bordeaux and in California, and sometimes, as in Australia, with Chardonnay, to improve the balance of both varieties.

Sémillon plays quite another role in Australia, however, especially in the Lower Hunter Valley. Hunter Valley Sémillon wines are light, acidic, dry, and unoaked, but they age very well. After about five years, this variety develops into rich wines with an intensely honeyed bouquet and an almost orange color.

Pinot Gris A natural mutation of Pinot Noir, Pinot Gris grapes come in colors as varied as the strikingly different flavors of the wines made from them. Pinot Gris (gray pinot) grapes can be bluish to silver, mauve-pink, or a grayed or ashy yellow. Depending on where they are grown, they produce very different wines mainly because of different levels of alcohol and acidity. In Italy the grapes are called Pinot Grigio, and the wine is generally crisp and light. By contrast, the Pinot Gris of Alsace, once known as Tokay-Pinot Gris, produces rich, somewhat spicy and fuller-bodied wines. In Germany, the variety is called *Grauburgunder* or *Ruländer*, and the wines have a broader flavor.

The Pinot Gris of the New World, particularly in Oregon, produces wines with flavors some tasters compare to spice cake and pears.

Viognier originated in the Rhône Valley of France, and although close to obscurity until recently, it found its best expression in the appellations of Condrieu and Château Grillet. It is planted in many different AVAs in California and has found impressive expressions in Virginia. Viognier has many characteristics of Chardonnay in that it is somewhat full-bodied, has good acidity,

and is malleable. Wines produced from this variety are described as elegant and exotic, with hints of honeysuckle or musky fruit and a smooth texture. Without oak, it has distinctive floral and peach aromas with a nutty almond finish.

Muscat is the many-hued grape that Pliny the Elder once called "the grape of the bees" for its attractive aroma. With several branches on its family tree, the variety has grown around the Mediterranean Sea for centuries. Most Muscats thrive in relatively hot climates—Greece, Morocco, Sicily, and Sardinia—where they are made into sweet or semi-sweet wines with generally low alcohol content and a pronounced taste of the grape. In Italy, Muscat is the grape of choice for sparkling Asti.

In Alsace, however, the Muscat Blanc à Petits Grains and Muscat Ottonel branches of the family tree produce fresh and fruity wines that are always fermented to dryness. In Australia, the Muscat Gordo Blanco (sometimes called the Muscat of Alexandria) is used to make "liqueur Muscats." Californian Andrew Quady produces a number of Muscat-based dessert wines, particularly in the fortified style of a French *Vin Doux Naturel* such as Beaumes-de-Venise.

GEWÜRZTRAMINER   CHARDONNAY   RIESLING

PINOT NOIR   CABERNET SAUVIGNON   SYRAH

Palomino grapes yield a neutral-tasting wine that oxidizes easily because of its low acidity. The variety grows prolifically in hot climates and is the grape used to make sherry in Spain.

Ugni Blanc or Trebbiano originated in Italy and is the most widely-planted white grape in both France and Italy. It is the basis for Cognac and Armagnac in France, as well as for balsamic vinegar in Italy.

Muscadet Although the variety is technically called Melon de Bourgogne, it derives its name from the region of the Loire Valley closest to the Atlantic where it thrives—an area called Muscadet de Sèvre-et-Maine. When allowed to remain on the *lees,* sediment that forms during fermentation, until bottling, the wine made from Muscadet develops a more defined and refreshing character with a lively spritz. Such a wine would be labeled *sur lie* (on the lees) and is particularly suitable to serving with seafood.

Albariño (Alvarinho) is a thick-skinned grape variety that is particularly adapted to damp climates. Some versions of the wines made from Albariño, principally those grown in northwest Spain (Riax Baixas) and Portugal, are characterized by delicate floral aromas and high acidity. In some other versions, though, the wines are fuller bodied and more alcoholic. Albariño makes one of the few Spanish wines produced as a varietal.

Grüner Veltliner is Austria's most planted wine grape. The variety has also spread to other areas of Eastern Europe. Although some wines produced from this grape are quite simple, those from the best growing regions are complex with tropical fruit notes, high acidity balancing high alcohol.

Pinot Blanc, derived from Pinot Noir, has characteristics similar to those of Chardonnay, although the wines made from this variety are not as complex in flavor, aroma, or texture.

Black grape varieties Just as "white" grape varieties are not really white, but rather pink, green, or yellow, "black" grape varieties are not really black. Their colors may range from red to purple to deep blue violet, but they do share one important characteristic: black grapes are necessary to produce red wines because these wines derive their color from macerating with the skins.

Pinot Noir is a difficult grape to grow successfully in the necessary cool growing regions, but it is responsible for France's fine red Burgundies and Champagne. Many connoisseurs believe that Pinot Noir produces the finest red wines in the world. The wines are more delicate and have lower tannins and higher acidity than varieties such as Cabernet Sauvignon. Burgundies have aromas of cherries, raspberries, mint, and herbs, but New World Pinot Noirs have warmer baked cherry and floral aromas. With bottle aging, the wines develop distinct earthy bouquets of leather, mushrooms, and game.

The legendary silky quality of Pinot Noir has also made it a world traveler. In the late 1980s, growers in the Russian River Valley, Carneros, and Santa Barbara, California, took advantage of cool growing areas to produce Pinot Noir that began to produce notable wines. By the 1990s, New Zealand growers were also planting Pinot Noir, and by 1997 the variety overtook Cabernet as the region's most-planted black grape. Much of the harvest from these plantings is destined for sparkling wines.

Cabernet Sauvignon, a tiny dark purple grape that Sotheby's describes as "the noblest variety of Bordeaux," produces satiny, rich, and complex wines with proper barrel and bottle aging. Proper aging is important because the fruit's small size gives Cabernet a high ratio of skin to pulp and therefore produces a very astringent young wine. With aging, however, Cabernet's acidity allows it to mature into complex wines with blackberry, black currant, cassis, plum, mint, violet, roasted bell pepper, eucalyptus, and cedar bouquets. When less fully ripe, Cabernet Sauvignon makes wines with a more vegetable-like character.

The most notable Cabernet Sauvignon-based wines in the Old World come from the Médoc growers of Margaux, St.-Julien, Pauillac, and St.-Estèphe in Bordeaux. In the New World, California growers, particularly in Napa and Sonoma, are producing world-class Cabernets. Today Cabernet Sauvignon is widely grown in Italy, Spain, California, Washington state, Chile, and Australia. In the Médoc region of France, Cabernet is frequently blended with Merlot and Cabernet Franc for mellowing. Similar blends in California are sometimes called

Meritage, although the need for blending is not as great.

Merlot—the name means "little blackbird"—is a deep blue cousin to Cabernet Sauvignon. Merlot is the predominant variety grown in the Bordeaux region of France, especially in St. Émilion and Pomerol. Merlot, when fully ripe, produces textures that are softer and smoother than Cabernet, with plum and blackberry character. The bouquets are more buttery and creamy, and the wine has cocoa and sometimes truffle flavors. Merlot is frequently blended with Cabernet to moderate Cabernet's astringency, particular in Bordeaux. Because of Merlot's ripe and less tannic profile, it became a fad variety in the 1990s and is frequently present in restaurants by the glass. Merlot responds well to heavier soils and is easier to ripen in cooler climates, so the variety has also become popular in Long Island's North Fork and in the southeastern part of Washington state, where it produces some exceptional wines. Chile also makes exceptional Merlot, especially with grapes from the Rapel Valley, although much of the wine labeled Merlot may be made from a closely related variety called Carmenère, which gives the wine a different taste profile.

Cabernet Franc, a parent plant of Cabernet Sauvignon, is the most-planted grape in the Anjou-Touraine region of the Loire Valley and is also found to a lesser extent in Bordeaux, especially on the right bank of the Gironde River. It is particularly suited to cooler, inland climates and ripens about a week earlier than Cabernet Sauvignon.

The Cabernet Franc variety produces wines that are generally lighter in color, lower in tannins, and slightly more aromatic, with hints of violets, blackberries, and licorice, than its Sauvignon offspring. As New World winemakers follow the Bordeaux recipe for blending with Cabernet Sauvignon, Cabernet Franc is being planted in limited numbers in Australia and New Zealand.

Syrah (Shiraz), an old, black variety, produces rich, tannic fruits in the northern Rhône region of France. The smaller-berried fruits generally contain more phenolics, which, along with anthocyanins, make Syrah a wine that benefits from long aging in oak and in the bottle.

The best French Syrah wines are Hermitage or Côte Rôtie.

Richly aromatic, with hints of black pepper, green olive, violets, and black currants, Syrah also forms the basis for Australia's finest red wines and has been Australia's most-planted variety, perhaps because the variety can do well in warmer climates. Recently, Australian winemakers have blended Shiraz with Cabernet Sauvignon.

Because of its recent surge in popularity, many vintners are producing Syrah in the cool Santa Rita Hills of Santa Barbara and in the Napa Valley, as well as in the warmer regions of Mendocino and Sonoma. Washington state is also developing a potential for fine Syrah wines.

Gamay, a plump grape with a characteristic cherry and raspberry aroma, is grown principally in the southern Burgundy region of Beaujolais. Simple and fruity, wines made from the Gamay grape tend to be light and fresh, especially when vinified with carbonic maceration, which gives the wine fruity, almost bubble gum, banana, and mint aromas. The wines are generally at their best when they are young.

Grenache (Garnacha) is grown primarily in the southern Rhône Valley of France. The basis for many of the renowned Châteauneuf-du-Pape wines, it is also one of the principal varieties used in Spain's Rioja wines.

Grenache earned much of its reputation as the primary grape in the high alcohol, dry Tavel rosé wines. Grenache has a floral and white pepper profile along with olive and licorice aromas. Grenache is also found in southeastern Australia and in Monterey County in California, where it is frequently blended with other varieties.

Tempranillo is the key varietal in many of Spain's wines. It has good color, attractive cherry and strawberry flavors, good acidity, and silky tannins, and it derives a vanilla bouquet from its adaptability to long-term American oak barrel aging.

Zinfandel, according to DNA testing, originated from the Croatian Crljenak (pronounced sirl-yen-knock) and is the same variety as the Italian *Primitivo,* which may itself have been imported from the United States. In the United States, Zinfandel was first grown on the East Coast and then traveled to California. Wine made from this grape was hailed as California's claret. Like Syrah in Australia, Zinfandels became one of California's most planted grapes.

The variety produces its best fruits if the growing season is warm, not hot, and the vines are not allowed to overproduce. Still, producing wines from Zinfandels is not easy. The compact bunches ripen unevenly, leaving a narrow window for harvesting. The best red Zinfandels are dry, acidic, and alcoholic wines balanced by ripe sweet- or dried-fruit character with fresh tobacco and spice notes. They are ideal accompaniments to barbecues and roast turkey. In California, white Zinfandels became a useful outlet for this formerly predominantly grown variety.

Sangiovese is Italy's most famous grape, so ancient that its name translates to "blood of Jove." It is responsible for Italy's noted Tuscan wines—Chianti, Vino Nobile de Montepulciano, and Brunello di Montalcino. Although the variety's quality varies from year to year because of fluctuations in the weather and its slow, late ripening, Sangiovese has good acidity and makes a good food wine.

Italian immigrants brought Sangiovese to the New World, but it wasn't until the 1980s and 1990s that Italy's reputation for high quality developed. Italy's wines became a ubiquitous presence on restaurant wine lists in the United States, prompting a sudden increase in the number of acres planted in this variety California. In the Napa Valley, but also in Sonoma County, San Luis Obispo County, and the Sierra foothills, growers planted Sangiovese and began making excellent wines in the Californian, rather than the Tuscan, styles.

Nebbiolo, the king of Italian grapes, grows almost exclusively in the Piedmont region in northwestern Italy. Wines made from this pale purple grape are tannic, austere, and highly alcoholic, but they mature into remarkably fine, elegant wines. Their aromas are floral, and the bouquets have an earthy, truffle-like character.

Hybridized grapes Although many hybridized grapes were developed in response to *Phylloxera,* some hybrids occurred by chance, such as Catawba, which became the basis of Ohio's sparkling wine industry in the mid-1800s. Other hybrids, such as Chancellor and Baco Noir, are used in winemaking in New England, New York, and Canada, where they better withstand the cold winters. For the most part, however, hybrids have not been as successful as wine grapes as developers originally hoped.

Climate

Climate depends to a certain degree on latitude, but several other factors are also important in determining a location's general or prevailing weather patterns. Temperatures, an important component of climate, can be modified by proximity to bodies of water, prevailing wind patterns, precipitation, altitude, and the amount of sunshine in a given location. See Figure 36-3.

Latitude Latitude is a significant indicator of a climate's suitability for viticulture. Tropical areas are generally too hot for growing grapes; the high latitudes are too cold. Most successful vineyards are located between 30° and 50° north latitude and south latitude. Because latitude affects the

FIGURE 36-3

Mild, damp winters and warm, dry summers with cool nights and misty mornings are ideal conditions for viticulture in California.

FIGURE 36-4

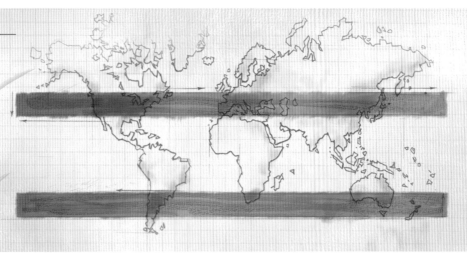

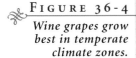

length of days and the relative coolness of nights in a region, different varieties of grapes are often suited to different locations in a relatively small area. In cool climates, low solar exposure associated with higher latitudes or altitudes produces the compounds that are responsible for the grape's distinctive aromas. See Figure 36-4.

Temperature The amount of sugar and acidity that a grape variety develops as it ripens depends on the growing season of the area where it is planted. Research by Maynard Amerine and Albert Winkler at the University of California-Davis School of Oenology demonstrated that different grape varieties need to be grown in specific climatic zones to ripen fully. To conduct their research, Amerine and Winkler developed a model using Heat Summation Areas. The method is based on the fact that vines lie dormant when aggregate temperatures remain below 50°F. For any day that the temperature averaged above 50°F, Amerine and Winkler assigned degrees based on the difference between the average temperature for that day and 50° F. For example, if the average temperature is 69°F on April 1, that day is a 19-degree day. The Heat Summation (the sum of all the degree days between April 1 and October 31) determines the classification.

Here are the five classifications:

Region I	Fewer than 2500°F accrued degrees
Region II	2501°F–3000°F accrued degrees
Region III	3001°F–3500°F accrued degrees
Region IV	3501°F–4000°F accrued degrees
Region V	4001°F–4500°F accrued degrees

In the Northern Hemisphere, the growing season begins about April 1, when the average temperature is high enough (above 50°F) for new shoots to develop from the dormant buds (bud-break). Flowering occurs from mid-May to June, and tiny berries appear and develop, but remain green, until mid-July. The onset of ripening is called *veraison* (French for "true season"), when the berries develop color and begin to soften. Harvest generally begins in mid-September but varies from region to region with weather conditions in the location and the grape variety.

Temperatures are very important to grape development. Higher temperatures elevate the sugar content in the grape and cause acidity to decline more rapidly. See Figure 36-5 on page 876. This inverse relationship is important to the winemaker, who hopes to balance the alcohol and acidity in wine, but varietal characteristics are also important in this process. Usually the winemaker and the vineyard manager work together to harvest the grapes at their optimum quality. In parts of France, such as Burgundy, the grape may physiologically ripen before sufficient sugars have developed to make a wine with the proper balance between alcohol and acidity. Winemakers may then rectify the condition with sugar. In warmer parts of coastal California, on the other hand, grapes may develop too much sugar before the grapes are physiologically ripe. Such grapes produce an unbalanced wine with too much alcohol.

Early Romans first recognized the correlations between fine wines and cooler climates when they discovered that although grapes grown in cool areas produced

smaller quantities, the fruit's quality was higher. In cooler environments, flavors and colors have a longer time to develop and the grapes retain good acidity. Acidity is the component in wine that makes it refreshing and is one of the reasons that the world's best wines are produced from grapes that grow in cool regions.

Bodies of water Bodies of water have a profound influence on climate. Large, deep masses of water, such as an ocean, a large lake, or a river, moderate both summer and winter temperatures. Temperatures warm later in the spring and fall frosts generally come later in the season.

Wind In locations where strong winds cause sudden temperature fluctuations (called wind stress), growers often plant tall shrubs or fast-growing trees to act as windbreaks. Winds can damage ripening vines and decrease final yields by bringing about changes to the vine's ability to transpire.

Rainfall and humidity Few crops are as sensitive to rainfall or humidity as the grape. Excessive rain during the growing season can cause rot and fungal diseases in the fruit. During the summer, too much rain leads to excessive plant growth rather than to good fruit development. At harvest time, too much rain can bloat the grapes and dilute their sugar content. In winter, on the other hand, plentiful rainfall is beneficial because it provides the necessary water table for deep roots of vines to extract needed moisture and trace minerals throughout the summer growing season.

Frost For grape growers, late and early frosts are a disaster. A late spring frost can seriously diminish a vine's production

FIGURE 36-5

potential, and an early autumn frost can damage the harvest's quality and yield.

Sunlight The process of photosynthesis (the formation of sugars from carbon dioxide and a source of hydrogen—such as water—in the chlorophyll-containing tissues of plants exposed to light) is essential to plant growth and development. The amount of direct sunlight the plants receive, therefore, affects not only the health of the vines but also the sweetness of the grapes, and, ultimately, the alcohol content of the wines made from them.

Viticulture

Viticulture, or the science of growing grapevines, encompasses all major fruit-growing conditions.

Terroir Terroir is a French term that is sometime loosely translated as "territory," but in viticulture, terroir encompasses much more than a land location. It includes all the elements that comprise growing conditions—soil, climate, topography, geology, and hydrology.

Soil French wines have long been named according to the region where the grapes are grown because many French winemakers believe that grapes derive flavor and quality from the soil as well as from other regional growing conditions. American and other New World winemakers, until recently, maintained that the soil is merely a support for the vine and a reservoir for water and nutrients.

Climate, they said, plays the largest part in determining grape flavor and quality. Regardless of nationality, however, viticulturists agree that grapevines grow best in well-drained soils on bench lands or slopes that encourage deep root growth. Fertility, too, is important to vine growth, although growers are wary of overly fertile soil that might encourage overgrowth of vines or overproduction of insipid grapes.

Irrigation Irrigation is not allowed in Europe's quality wine regions after the vine is mature enough to produce yields for appellation designation (usually the fourth year). The result is significant variation from vintage to vintage in grape quality. In other wine producing regions, drip irrigation produces consistently high-quality yields.

Vintage Vintage, from the French word *vendange*, means "harvest," but it also designates the year in which a wine was made. Ideal weather may bring a great vintage year, but early or late frosts, hail, or heavy rains might be disastrous. Great vintage years are usually the exception rather than the rule in the cool wine-growing regions of Europe—and even great growing years require a skilled winemaker to take full advantage of an exceptional grape harvest's flavor development and balance.

Some wines may not have a vintage label because they contain blends of grapes of different vintages. Nonvintage champagnes, for example, are such blends and do not necessarily reflect lower quality. Table wines in the European Union are forbidden to state a vintage, but in the United States, "jug" wines generally lack vintage designation.

Viticultural practices Although nature plays a pivotal role in the grape's flavor and composition, nurturing the vines is also critically important. First, the selection of rootstock and clone will affect the grapes, as will the age of the vines. Vines do not provide fruit of high quality in sufficient quantity to make wine until at least their fourth year, and many vines do not attain peak quality until their eighth to tenth year. Although some areas have vines that are 100 years old, most vines are economically productive for 25 to 40 years.

Growers also manipulate the size and shape of the vines by training, trellising, pruning, and a process called canopy management. The canopy is made up of the grape leaves that absorb sunlight for photosynthesis. New World growers, principally those in the United States and Australia, encourage leaf growth to limit yields. They also prune the vines to determine how the vine will grow and how many buds it will have. The number of buds affects the number of clusters of grapes, or the vines' yields. The correlation between high vine density and good quality is a matter of controversy among growers. In Europe, appellation laws limit vine density, but in New World vineyards, there are no set limits—although grapevines tend to be far less densely planted than in, for example, Burgundy.

Yield management How growers manage yields is important to the quality of wine that is produced from grapes. Different varieties yield different quantities of grapes. High-yielding varieties such as Colombard or Carignan generally produce undistinguished wines—called table wines in Europe—because the warm areas where they thrive encourage large yields, higher alcohol, lower acidity, and less well-defined flavors.

Growers know that smaller yields and longer "hang time" on the vine generally produce harvests with better balance. In the European Union, quality wine regions have specific limits placed on yields. Fine wine varieties are manipulated to reduce yields through pruning and crop thinning, a process called *vendange vert* (green harvest). The resulting wines tend to be much more expensive but are of considerably higher quality because up to half the crop may be thinned and discarded.

Harvesting The decision of when to harvest the grapes is so important to the quality of wine produced that the decision is made jointly by the vineyard manager and the winemaker (when the fall weather does not dictate the timing for them). Growers use a refractometer to determine the Brix measurement, the name given to the scale used to measure sugar density. (In many of California's regions, grapes tend to develop too much sugar; in many of the European Union's wine regions, the opposite is true.)

The method of harvesting is also significant. Because technology has improved dramatically and because the labor shortage of agricultural workers continues to rise, more grapes are mechanically harvested than ever before. Mechanical harvesting does not necessarily have a negative impact on the quality of the juice.

Sustainable agriculture Sustainable agriculture is perhaps one of the most important issues facing all agricultural producers. Increasingly, growers have become aware of the long-term environmental effects of using chemical pesticides, herbicides, and fungicides. Sprays may drift to neighboring properties, and their residues can contaminate aquifers and impact wildlife habitats. As growers look for alternatives to chemicals, they are adopting more organic methods of sustainable agriculture. By investigating pest species—their life cycles, their activities, and their predators—growers are finding new ways to control pests. Birds of prey, such as owls, or more sophisticated technological solutions, such as pheromone strips that disrupt the mating cycles of some pests, are replacing chemical sprays. Vineyard managers are also moving away from the monoculture of the vine. Planting cover crops such as mustard greens between the rows of vines, for example, attracts pests away from the vines and also helps reduce soil impaction. Physical barriers such as nets, which do not have a negative impact on the environment, can protect the crops from flocks of migratory birds that could otherwise consume the harvest in minutes.

Vinification

Among winemakers, there is an often-repeated adage: It is easy to make a bad wine from good grapes, but you cannot make a good wine from bad grapes.

Winemakers produce wine on the basis of the quality of grapes they are able to grow. Over the past decades, science has enhanced traditional viticulture, and grape quality has generally improved with new horticultural methods. See Figure 36-7 on page 881. Critics, however, have charged that better science has also been accompanied by a sameness in the international varieties used in winemaking. Although modern wines are clean and generally consistent, critics say, they also have less individualistic taste profiles. Over the past decade, that concern has sparked a philosophical shift among some winemakers. Minimum treatment or intervention is becoming more standard. Although technology has provided winemakers with tools their predecessors did not have, many have come to believe that the costs exceed the benefits. A strictly scientific approach based on chemistry alone may have led to the homogenization trend that has produced wines with less typicity and fewer subtle differences due to site and terroir. See Figure 36-6.

Classification of Wines

Wines generally are organized into five classifications: table wine, dessert wine, sparkling wine, fortified wine, and aromatized wine. Part of the winemaker's art involves deciding which class of wine is most suited to the grapes at hand, much as a chef decides on the type and quality of ingredients.

Table Wine

The term "table wine" is applied differently in the United States and the European Union. In the United States, the term is used to distinguish table wines from sparkling or fortified wines. Table wines generally contain from 6.5% to 14.5% alcohol, but the normal range is from 10% to 12% alcohol. Table wines may be fermented to dryness or to off-dryness. Depending on how they are made, the wines may be white or red and range in color from pale white to amber, crimson to tile brick red, or a shade of salmony pink for rosé or blush wines.

FIGURE 36-6

Terroir is defined in part by different soils, such as the chalky soil of Champagne, the Terra Rossa of South Australia, the gravelly soil of Azzoyo Secco, Monterey, and the slate of Germany. (Shown left to right.)

Making White Wines

destemming ➡ crushing ➡ sulfiting ➡ skin contact ➡ pressing ➡ adjusting ➡ fermentation ➡ racking ➡ [malolactic fermentation]* ➡ blending and aging ➡ fining and adjusting ➡ finishing and bottling

*Note: Only a few white wines, such as Chardonnay, undergo malolactic fermentation.

Making Red Wines

destemming and crushing ➡ sulfiting ➡ maceration and fermentation ➡ pressing ➡ racking ➡ malolactic fermentation ➡ blending and aging ➡ fining and adjusting ➡ finishing and bottling

Destemming After grapes are harvested, the stalks and stems are generally removed by a crusher/destemmer in the winery. White wines are pressed and strained by various kinds of presses. The extracted juice, with minimal fragments of stems, seeds, or skins, is called the *must*. Some black grapes that will be made into red wines may not have all stems and pips removed from the must if the wine will require the tannins they produce.

Crushing and pressing Crushing is a misleading term because the process is quite gentle. Its objective is to split the skins of grapes to release free-run juice. Crushing is quite distinct from pressing, during which the juice is squeezed from the pulp that is closer to the skins of the grapes. The juice of white wine may then be kept in skin contact for several hours and up to two days at low temperatures to extract greater flavor. Grapes for white wines, including Champagne, are pressed gently before fermentation, but grapes used for red wines are pressed after fermentation.

The key point is that the greater the pressure, the greater the tannin levels in the must. When winemakers make white wines, they try to maximize the amount of must without extracting the tannins and bitter oils contained in the pips. The first pressing extracts about 75% of the juice and is used for better-quality wine. Subsequent pressings have more tannin and may be fermented and blended later into the wine or used to produce vinegar or

an inexpensive brandy called marc, grappa, or, in the United States, pomace brandy.

Grapes for red wine are crushed and then fermented before being pressed so that maceration extracts the color and tannins from the grapes' skins and pips. The pressing need not be gentle because the release of tannins is desirable in red wines.

Must adjustments Winemakers can make adjustments to the must before it is fermented, including chaptalization or must enrichment, SO_2 treatment, settling, and acidification or deacidification.

Chaptalization is the process of adding beet sugar to the must to increase the potential alcoholic content of a wine. Increasing the alcohol in the wine gives it a rounder, softer texture because alcohol counterbalances acidity. However, must is more commonly enriched using rectified concentrated grape must, a colorless and tasteless concentrate of grape sugars: glucose and fructose. Enrichment of the must is common in the wine regions of northern Europe, especially in parts of France, where it is carefully regulated. This practice is also followed in Canada and the northeastern United States, where cool climates may prevent grapes from having enough sugar for developing sufficient alcohol to give the wine the necessary balance.

Musts are also commonly treated with sulfur dioxide to prevent oxidation, to control the growth of bacteria, and to eliminate any undesirable wild yeasts that may have been present on the grapes. If winemakers use cultured yeasts to ferment the must, they may be added at this time.

Winemakers also may need to adjust the pH of their must. In warm climates where grapes fail to develop sufficient acids to ensure good balance in the finished wine, winemakers may acidify the wine by adding tartaric acid. In cooler areas, it is sometimes necessary to deacidify the wine by adding calcium bicarbonate.

Maceration By definition, maceration involves soaking a material in liquid to separate softened parts of the material from the harder ones. When making red wines, winemakers use this process to extract the phenolics, including tannins, coloring materials, anthocyanins, and other glycosides, including flavor precursors and compounds from the grape skins and sometimes pips or stems, into the must.

Left untreated, the must would normally begin to ferment during maceration because the sugar and yeasts needed for this process are already present in the grapes. To macerate without fermentation, winemakers need to keep the must cold—below 48°F, at which point yeast growth is retarded. Cold maceration may last for two or three days. It is not uncommon for high-quality red wines to undergo extended maceration (including fermentation) of up to 36 days to create longer chain tannins that will feel less astringent and taste less bitter. If the winemaker is making a blush or rosé wine, the maceration period is a few hours.

Fermentation During fermentation, yeasts in the must convert sugar to ethyl alcohol and carbon dioxide as part of their metabolic cycle and release heat as a by-product. Violent fermentation can raise temperatures to more than 100°F if left uncontrolled. At that temperature, the yeast dies. Conversely, if temperatures are allowed to fall below 48°F, in a wintertime, unheated structure, for example, the yeast will stop growing. Northern Europe's fermenting rooms (cuverie) were often warmed; those in parts of California and Australia may require cooling.

Fermenting white wine Although fermentation creates both white wines and red wines, each type of wine requires different fermentation conditions. One important variable in fermenting white wine is temperature. Today's winemakers control temperatures precisely by using stainless steel vats with cooling jackets, although some winemakers still use small wooden barrels (**barriques**) for certain wines such as Chardonnay, whose character can be more adapted to oak flavors.

Winemakers ferment white wines between 50°F and 65°F for 1–3 weeks, and at those temperatures and durations, the wine is refreshing, fruity, and faster to mature. At higher temperatures, fermentation is quicker, but for most wines, quality suffers. Chardonnays can be an exception. They are fermented in oak barrels at 68°F and higher to gain complexity and longevity.

Fermenting red wine Black grapes are fermented with their skins and pips in vats. Most vats are made of wood, but there are also concrete, stainless steel, or glass-lined plastic vats. For red wines, fermentation occurs 68°F–88°F (20°C–32°C). At higher

Following the Steps from Grapes to Wine

From first pressing to final racking and finishing, winemaking has not changed essentially for thousands of years, although today's winemakers are rigorously scientific about the process.

Steps in vinification are as follows:

Mechanical or hand harvesting brings the grapes to the winery.

White grapes are pressed before fermentation to extract the must. Black grapes are pressed after fermentation to extract the wine.

Fermentation can take place in large open vats.

For more delicate red wines, the "punch down" method is preferred.

Racking siphons the wine from one vat or container into another, leaving the sediment behind.

Wine acquires additional flavors from toasted oak barrels used for storage and aging.

Fining helps clarify the wine more quickly than natural processes.

Thieving allows the winemaker to maintain quality control during aging.

temperatures, the wine's fruitiness and delicacy may diminish. Fermented at cooler temperatures, red wines contain greater fruit flavors.

Because the grape skins are left in the must, red wines also require additional attention during fermentation. Carbon dioxide and heat force skins and any remaining stems to the surface of the must, forming a cap. Winemakers need to submerge this cap to prevent excessive heat buildup beneath it. Punching down the cap also prevents prolonged exposure to oxygen (allowing actobacter to turn the wine into vinegar) and creates a more uniform maceration and fermentation. Modern winemakers use several processes to ensure that the cap is submerged, including punch down for more delicate reds and pumping over the cap for more hardy reds. Fermentation ends naturally when all the fermentable sugars in the must are converted or when the alcohol level generally reaches 14% (in rare cases over 15%). At that level, alcohol is toxic to the yeast, and it dies.

Several other conditions can also cause fermentation to stop prematurely. Some of these are accidental, and others are deliberately created by the winemaker.

1. Temperatures above 105°F will kill the yeast, and a "stuck fermentation" occurs.
2. Adding brandy or a neutral spirit to the wine raises the alcohol level above the maximum that the yeast will tolerate, and fermentation stops. Winemakers add alcohol when they wish to leave residual sugar in the wine for sweetness.
3. Pasteurizing, or flash-heating wine to 185°F for one minute, stops fermentation. Although pasteurization also neutralizes harmful bacteria, many believe that it also strips the wine of some flavor components. Pasteurization, therefore, is not suited to wines requiring bottle aging.
4. To stop fermentation before all of the sugar is metabolized, winemakers may also add sulfur compounds.
5. Some winemakers use a centrifuge and filtration to remove yeasts from the wine. A rough filter followed by a sterile filtration prevents harmful bacteria or yeast from remaining in the wine, especially during clarification and final bottling stages.

Racking After fermentation has occurred and the lees have precipitated to the bottom of the vessel, winemakers generally siphon the wine into a clean vat, cask, or barrel, leaving the lees behind. Each time wine is racked into a new container, 2%–3% of its volume is lost. All fine wines are racked at least twice, and the finest are racked four times the first year and twice more in the second. *Racking* not only clarifies the wine but also aerates it, a process that gives controlled exposure to air so that the limited contact with oxygen can help the wines mature.

Malolactic fermentation After the primary (or alcohol) fermentation is complete, almost all red wines, Chardonnay, and a very few other white wines undergo a malolactic fermentation. Unlike the original fermentation, malolactic fermentation is not caused by yeasts, but by lactobacteria that convert harsher malic acid in the wine to softer lactic acid. This fermentation has advantages and disadvantages. It can give cool-climate, acidic wines a softer, more buttery character, but it can also leach out or mask the wine's fruit flavors. For this reason, some winemakers prevent malolactic fermentation by centrifuging or filtering the wine and storing it in a sanitized vessel.

Lees and bâtonnage Lees is the term for the sediment containing dead yeast and other solids that collects in the bottom of the wine tank or barrel following fermentation. Most wines are racked off the lees as part of the winemaking process. However, some wines fermented in barrels are left on the lees, which are stirred back into the wine in a process called bâtonnage. This process contributes to autolysis, or breakdown of yeast cells, releasing agents throughout the wine that reduce bitterness from wood tannins and add a creamy quality and complexity to the wine.

Blending and aging Many wines develop greater complexity and better balance if they are blended with other wines. Generally speaking, wines that need blending are fermented separately and then blended before aging. Wine may also develop complexity over time in a process called aging—a process that generally takes place in wood. Not all wines benefit from oak aging. Winemakers age their wines in oak because the wood is tightly grained enough to store the liquid and yet sufficiently porous to allow slow and minute interaction with oxygen. Oak's flavors should support rather than overwhelm the flavors in the wine.

The source of the oak—its treatment, age, and size—all affect how the wood interacts with the wine. Oak from different regions of France—Limousin, Tronçais, Allier, Nevers, and Vosges—generally has tighter grain than American oak. (More porous American oak also gives wines distinct vanillin, coconut, and tannic flavors.) French oaks, however, may cost 3–4 times as much as American oak varieties.

Making the oak barrels is complex; therefore, producers called cooperages make barrels using carefully controlled processes. The degree to which the oak barrel is toasted affects the amount of toastiness in the wine's taste. The smaller the barrel, the more contact it has with the wine and the more it affects the flavor. Newer oak contributes more oak flavors than older oak. After four years of use, however, old oak barrels contribute little to the wine's flavor.

During the first few months of aging, some of the wine evaporates and some is absorbed by the wood, creating an airspace, called ullage, in the barrel. If the airspace is allowed to remain, the wine will oxidize, so winemakers fill the space with additional wine of the same kind, a process called topping off. At the point where topping off is occurring, wine casks are loosely sealed with glass bungs (stoppers), which are later replaced with wooden bungs. During aging, impurities sink to the bottom of the cask, so the wine is racked into another cask, leaving the accumulated impurities behind.

Because many wines cannot stand up to 100% oak aging, a winemaker may blend different lots of wine from the same vintage and vineyard; for example, the first may be 100% oak aged in new casks; a second aged in older wood, and a third aged in stainless steel.

Fining *Fining* is a process used for clarification to give the wines brilliance. Although the wine will eventually clarify itself, fining saves time and the expense of waiting for the wine to finish. Fining agents include gelatin, egg whites, casein, isinglass, or bentonite clay. In addition to removing cloudiness, fining agents also remove some tannin and phenolics to achieve a more balanced wine. Most commercial wines are either fined or filtered.

Finishing and bottling Before bottling, many wines are either centrifuged or filtered twice—the first is a rough filtration used soon after fermentation, and the second is a sterile filtration done immediately before bottling. Although some winemakers do centrifuge the wines, the process can dilute the flavors. Consequently, the process is not used for fine wines.

Although filtration is controversial, it is used mainly for white wines, especially those with residual sugar or those that do not undergo malolactic fermentation.

Fine red wines, however, are not filtered because the filtration process may also cause the wine to be stripped of some flavor components and complexity. These wines are sold as unfiltered and may not be as brilliant as other red wines.

Winemakers can also correct a wine's balance by finishing or adjusting its acidity by adding ascorbic acid. Balancing wine with ascorbic acid is most common in warmer climates, where wines often lack acidity.

Cold stabilization Wine is bottled in sterilized bottles. After the bottle has been filled, the neck may be flushed with nitrogen or carbon dioxide to prevent oxidation. The bottle is then corked, and the wine is stored upside down to keep the cork moist. Moisture swells the cork and ensures a tight seal to prevent oxidation of the wine. Wine is not usually shipped for release until it is allowed to rest for several weeks because of what is termed bottle shock.

Cork Cork is the bark taken from a species of oak tree prevalent in Portugal and Spain. When the oak reaches 20–25 years of age, the cork bark is stripped manually from the tree; cork can be reharvested from the same tree every 9–15 years. Cork provides an excellent seal because it is resistant to liquids and provides an efficient barrier to oxygen. However, as much as 5% of all cork used is tainted by the organic compound TCA (trichloranisole), which gives off a distinctive dank fungal smell and ruins the potential enjoyment of the wine. Although the screw cap is the perfect barrier to oxygen, its image is too closely associated with inexpensive jug wines to meet with general acceptance. The use of syn-

thetic corks, however, is increasing, and further changes are likely to occur.

Cellar and bottle aging Almost all wines are best consumed within 1–3 years and do not improve with age. The tiny minority (1%) that does benefit from bottle aging undergoes revealing changes with time.

Wines mature at different rates on the basis of individual vintage characteristics, their appellation, and vinification. The higher the level of acidity, the greater the potential for aging. Although residual sugar and tannins act as preservatives, they are also key to the evolution of flavors and balance. Without acidity, the wine's balance disintegrates. White wines generally have higher acid levels but few tannins. Fine Riesling and Loire Chenin Blanc wines evolve more slowly than most Chardonnays. Red wines from Bordeaux that are Cabernet-based have not only the tannins but also the acidity to make them long-lived.

Storage conditions also affect the rate of aging. As a rule, warmer storage conditions accelerate aging; cooler storage retards it. Longer aging in cooler conditions, however, gives the wine greater complexity and more

FIGURE 36-7

Science has helped modern winemakers create a more consistent product.

pleasing bouquet. Bottle size also affects aging times, with smaller bottles aging faster than larger ones.

Special Winemaking Methods

Various methods for creating distinctive wines have evolved over the centuries.

Carbonic Maceration

Carbonic maceration is a red winemaking method prevalent in, but not limited to, the Beaujolais region of Burgundy, France. Carbonic maceration extracts a fruity, light-bodied, aromatic wine such as Beaujolais Nouveau from whole grapes. In this process, bunches of uncrushed grapes are placed in a carbon dioxide-filled vat. When the grapes are sealed inside, they begin to ferment. The sealed grape bunches undergo an intracellular enzymatic fermentation that produces no more than 3% alcohol. After 1–3 weeks, the grapes are crushed, and the must is macerated and fermented in the traditional way. Red wines made using carbonic macerations are ready to drink without long periods of aging because the process results in wine with little tannin and increased fruity and mentholated aromas. The wines,

in fact, do not age well. The process is generally not suitable for white wines.

Dessert Winemaking

Technically, dessert wines are one of two categories designated by the Federal Standards of Identity as fortified wines. Not all dessert wines are fortified, however. Some are made using special viticultural or vinification practices. There are five primary methods for making a dessert wine.

Late harvest Late harvest wines are made from grapes that have been allowed to continue ripening for at least one week after the regular harvest. Extended ripening produces intensely sweet grapes, but waiting to harvest them is risky because the grapes are vulnerable to pests or sudden changes in weather.

Botrytis cinerea *Botrytis cinerea* is a mold that causes infected grapes to dehydrate, which proportionately increases their sugar and glycerol content. See Figure 36-8. *Botrytis* is common in sites that are near bodies of water where considerable humidity is created in the mornings and then burned off by the midday sun. The best-known botrytised wines are from Sauternes, in Bordeaux, France; Trockenbeerenausleses

from Germany and the Neusiedlersee in Austria; and Tokay wines from Hungary. These wines are also made in Australia and the United States as Special Select Late Harvest wines.

Raisined grape wines Many famous wines are made from intentionally raisined grapes, including Vin Santo of Tuscany, Umbria or Pedro Ximénez from Spain, or some of the Muscats from Samos or other Greek isles.

Ice wine Ice wine, or eiswein as it is known in Germany, where it originated, is produced from grapes that have been allowed to freeze naturally on the vine before being harvested and pressed. The result is a high concentration of sugar in the must, producing an intensely sweet wine. Canada's most famous wines are its ice wines, but many "ice wines" in the United States are made by artificially freezing late-harvest grapes.

Mutage Mutage is generally the adding of alcohol or, rarely, sulfur dioxide to prevent the yeast from continuing to convert sugar into alcohol. Wine referred to as *Vin Doux Naturel* from France and Port wines are examples. (See also fortification.)

FIGURE 36-8

By increasing the sugar content of the grapes, winemakers can produce complex, sophisticated dessert wines.

Sparkling Wines

Although many people use the term champagne as a synonym for sparkling wine, champagne is only one of many sparkling wines. Champagne takes its name from the region in France where it is produced. Five basic methods are used to create sparkling wines.

- *classic method (or traditional method, formally called champagne method or méthode champenoise)*
- *transfer method*
- *dioise method*
- *bulk or charmat method*
- *carbonation or injection method*

Classic or Traditional Method

True champagne is produced only in the Champagne region of France, though other winemakers may adapt the classic method, or *méthode champenois*. See Figure 36-9 on page 884. The European Union does not allow the term on labeling for non-champagne wines.

Champagnes are made from one, or a blend of up to three, grape varieties: Chardonnay, Pinot Noir, and Pinot Meunier. Other classic method wines may use other varieties. The grapes are hand harvested and carefully pressed to avoid contact with skin and pips. The free run of juice is called the *tête de cuvée* and is reserved for prestige wines such as Dom Pérignon. The juice from the first pressing is called the *cuvée,* and the second pressing is called the *premières tailles*, which may be used by some producers. The total yield of juice is strictly enforced by the *Comité Interprofessionnel du Vin de Champagne* (CIVC) to 2550 liters for each marc or 4000 kg/8800 lbs. of grapes. The must settles and ferments in steel tanks or old oak vats. Then most, but not all wines undergo malolactic fermentation.

The wine is then blended according to the style desired by the winemaker, and 20% is held in reserve for future years. Next, a solution composed of sugar and yeast, known as *liqueur de tirage*, is added to the wine, which is then bottled and capped. The carbon dioxide produced in the bottle during the second fermentation, or *prise de mousse*, causes champagne's characteristic effervescence. The pressure caused by trapped carbon dioxide is between five and six bars or 90 pounds per square inch, which translates to 50–70 million bubbles per bottle. After the wine finishes the second fermentation in 3–4 weeks, the bottle is aged on its side for a minimum of one year *en tirage* or on the lees (from January 1 following the vintage) to qualify for nonvintage champagne. (The minimum requirement is nine months in the United States.) The lees or yeast cells are partially absorbed in a process called autolysis, which lends added flavor and complexity to the wine.

The next stage in the classic method is to move the lees stuck to the side of the wine bottle down to the neck. The bottle is angled neck down at 45°, shaken, and turned by hand or by machines (gyropalettes) in a process called riddling, or *rémuage,* that may last several weeks. After the lees are in the bottle's neck, the bottle may age further upside down *(sur pointe)* or have its lees expelled through a process known as disgorgement, or *dégorgement*, in which the neck of the bottle is placed upside down in a solution to freeze the top inch or two of wine and trapped lees. When the cap is removed, the gas expels the frozen plug. Then the bottle is topped off with identical wine called a *liqueur d'exposition*, which may have a dosage of varying degrees of cane sugar solution dictating the level of sweetness. The levels are as follows:

Champagne and sparkling wines come in a variety of bottle sizes:

Heavy glass bottles have a punt, or indentation, at their bottoms; a mushroom-shaped cork; and a wire cage or muzzle to keep the cork in place.

Transfer Method

Similar to the classic champagne method, the transfer method produces a pleasantly carbonated sparkling wine. In this method, the wine is aged on the lees but is then filtered and dosed in bulk before being rebottled. The wine will tend to have a coarser texture than champagne because of the resulting loss of carbonation.

Dioise Method

This method is primarily used for Asti, in which the wine undergoes a single fermentation in a sealed vat. The fermentation is then interrupted so that the wine is low in alcohol and has residual sugar. The wine is then centrifuged, filtered, and bottled.

Bulk/Charmat Method

In the charmat method, wine is twice fermented in bulk and then bottled. Cheaper and faster than either the transfer or classic champagne method, the bulk method produces a lower-quality wine.

Carbonation/Injection Method

The least expensive and lowest-quality sparkling wines are made by the carbonation/injection method, in which carbon dioxide is injected into the wine vat and the wine is then bottled under pressure, much as a soft drink is produced. Because the resulting wine is coarse and the effervescence dissipates rapidly, only about 10% of sparkling wines are prepared in this way.

FIGURE 36-9

Producing classic champagne is a painstaking process that blends high technology with age-old traditional wisdom.

Fortified Wines

Fortified wines are those that have had neutral spirits or brandy added to fermenting or fermented wine, a process that generally raises the level of alcohol from 16% to 22%. When fermentation stops and the wine retains sweetness, the process is called mutage. Winemakers also fortify wines to ensure their stability. The most common fortified wines are Port, Sherry, Madeira, Marsala, and Vin Doux Naturel.

Port

Port, which originated in the Douro Valley of northern Portugal, begins its transformation to a fortified wine with grape must fermented to the 6%–9% alcohol stage. Then the winemaker mixes in aguardiente brandy (77% alcohol) so that the wine is about 20% brandy and 80% grape wine. The Port is then aged in old wooden barrels called *pipes* for varying lengths of time, depending on the type of Port desired.

Two basic types of Port are wood and vintage. Wood Port is aged in wood and is ready to be consumed shortly after it is bottled. Of the wood Ports, tawny and ruby are the most significant styles. Ruby Port is aged for 2–3 years, and tawny Port is aged for at least six but up to 40 years. The more Ports age in wood, the more they lose their hard tannins and color. Ruby Ports, named for their deep red color, have a very sweet fruit flavor and are one of very few wines that can stand up to dark chocolate without being overwhelmed.

Vintage Port, made from the best available grapes from a single vintage year, are aged 2–3 years in wood and then require at least 10–15 years in the bottle. Some vintage Ports may be aged for 50 or more years. With so much bottle aging, vintage Ports require decanting to separate the wine from its thick sediment. Extensive sediment is so prevalent that Port aficionados say the wine is "throwing a crust."

Recently, a hybrid style of Port has been developed in response to the high cost of vintage Port. Called Late Bottled Vintage (LBV) Port, it is made from a specific vintage, traditionally aged 4–6 years in wood, and then bottle aged for another four years. It can continue to improve before being consumed. Unlike vintage Ports, both tawny and LBVs can be kept for several weeks after opening.

Sherry

Sherry, produced in the southern region of Spain known as Andalusia, is made from grapes grown in the chalky soils, called albariza, around the town of Jerez de la Frontera. (Sherry is the English corruption of Jerez). Although similar fortified wines have been called sherry, the name has now been restricted to sherries produced there, at least in Europe, by the European Union. The Palomino makes up 95% of the grapes grown in that region. Pedro Ximénez, or PX, grapes make a very sweet wine for blending, and it is an added component for making sweet cream sherry.

Unlike Port wines, sherry is fortified after fermentation. The Palomino grapes are hand harvested, gently pressed to form must, fermented, and then fortified. Two fundamental processes make sherry unique: partial oxidation through yeast flor development and fractional blending through the solera system.

There are two basic types of sherries: fino and oloroso. Fino sherry is light with a very distinctive nose, stemming from the partial oxidation and development of acetaldehydes. To produce a fino or its lightest style manzanilla, winemakers use the best free run juice. The wine is fortified to 15.5% alcohol, placed in American oak casks until they are five-sixths full, and inoculated with yeast flor. (Yeast flor can also occur naturally.) The yeast flor feed on oxygen, alcohol, and glycerin in the wine. These components need to be replenished by blending new wine into the older wine—a process called "tipping the scales"—during its five years of aging. Amontillados are finos aged for a minimum of ten years. Finos and manzanillas look like white wines and are light bodied, dry, and consumed upon release. Once opened, they deteriorate as quickly as a white still wine.

Oloroso sherry, which never develops a flor, is fortified to 18% alcohol. The wines are oxidized and fuller bodied than finos and lack the distinctive nose. When blended with PX, Oloroso becomes a sweet cream sherry.

Madeira

Madeira wines, named after the Portuguese island of Madeira, once functioned as ballast in ships that used the island as a revictualing station on the voyage from England to the American colonies. It was soon discovered that hot aging in the hold of the ships improved these fortified wines. In fact, Madeira was used by the colonists to toast the signing of the Declaration of Independence.

Madeiras are fortified after fermenting for dry styles, but during fermentation for sweeter styles. They undergo a unique baking process called the estufagem system. The best wines are those that are baked naturally in lofts or attics by the heat of the sun. Those of lesser quality are stored for a minimum of three months in a steampipe heated room (estufa) at 40°C–50°C or heated directly by heating coils running in the wine vats. The purpose is to caramelize the sugars and promote oxidation, making the wines virtually indestructible. A few wines may also go through a sherry-like solera process. The best Madeiras are special reserve, extra reserve, and vintage. Special reserves are blends at least ten years old. Extra reserves are at least 15 years old, and vintage Madeiras must be from a single vintage and aged a minimum of 20 years in the barrel and two years in the bottle. Since the formation of the European Union, producers cannot label their wines varietally unless they contain 85% of that variety. Previously, much of the wine sold as Madeira had little of the varieties that originally made Madeiras famous. There are, however, four varietally labeled Madeiras.

Sercial	Dry and tart
Verdelho	Medium dry and smoky
Bual	Medium sweet, aromatic, and reminiscent of nuts and prunes
Malmsey	An English corruption of Malvasia, the sweetest Madeira, but balanced by high acidity with great, dark, and rich dried-fruit aromas

Marsala

Originally named for the city of Marsala, Sicily, Marsala was originally produced in 1770 by an English merchant named John Woodhouse. Fortified by alcohol and sweetened by concentrated grape must, Marsala has an alcohol content of 17%–19%. Marsala wines may be golden, amber, or ruby-colored, and the sugar level in each color can vary from secco (dry) to semi-secco (semi-dry) to dolce (sweet). Most Marsalas labeled fine are aged one year, but a number of quality Marsalas labeled *Superiore Riserva* (aged four years), *Vergina* (aged five years) and *Stravecchio* (aged ten years) make for delightful sipping.

Vin Doux Naturel

French for "naturally sweet wine," *Vin Doux Naturel* is actually the product of mutage. A majority of these wines are made from Muscat grapes. Especially satisfying as dessert wines, these French sweet wines are best if balanced by acidity. The most famous come from the village of Beaumes-de-Venise in the Rhône Valley. The other famous appellation for VDN is Rasteau and Banyuls, using the red Grenache grape. These Port-like wines are deliberately exposed to air and topped off with new wine every six months to help develop the quality of rancio, also found in old cognacs.

Aromatized Wines

Aromatized, or apéritif, wines are best served before a meal because their bitter and aromatic ingredients are appetite stimulants. Any number of aromatic ingredients may be infused into an apéritif, including herbs, spices, flowers, and barks. Aromatized wines such as Vermouth, Dubonnet, Lillet, and Kir have an alcohol content of at least 15%.

Vermouth Vermouth stems from the German term *vermut,* meaning "wormwood," an herb that was once used frequently in beverages. Both dry white and sweet red Vermouth are made in France and in Italy. Dry Vermouth is the result of a white wine fermented to dryness, infused with aromatics, and fortified with brandy to an alcohol content of 19%. After it is bottled, it is aged for 3 1/2–4 years. Dry Vermouth is served chilled and is sometimes substituted for dry white wine in cooking.

Sweet Vermouth uses sweeter white grape varietals fortified to 17% alcohol and infused with aromatics and quinine. After sugar and caramel coloring are added, sweet Vermouth is aged for two years. Sweet Vermouth is usually served on the rocks with soda. Both dry and sweet vermouths are often used in cocktails such as Martinis and Manhattans.

Dubonnet French Dubonnet is available in dry white and sweet red varieties. It is best served chilled or on the rocks with a twist of lemon.

Lillet Infused with citrus flavors, Lillet may be red or white, dry or off-dry. It is best served chilled or on the rocks with a twist of lemon or orange.

Kir Kir is made by blending the acidic Aligoté white grape wine with Crème de Cassis, a black currant liqueur.

Wine Purchasing and Tasting

Most restaurants and other establishments purchase wine from distributors who, in turn, purchase from importers or from merchants known as *négociants*. In most states, it is illegal for an establishment to purchase wine directly from a vineyard. Factors to consider when purchasing wine include the brand name; place of origin; variety; the reputation of the distributor, négociant, and importer; and finally, the cost of the wine. See Figure 36-10.

✤ FIGURE 36-10
Wine labels provide a variety of important information to consumers.

Wine Purchasing

Several factors influence the purchasing decisions for wines.

Brand name Wines may be purchased solely on the basis of the brand name and the reputation of the producer. Such names as Château Lafite Rothschild®, Robert Mondavi®, or Opus One® are often the only guarantee of quality a purchaser needs.

Place of origin In Europe, the appellation or place of origin reflects the most significant differences in aroma and taste of wines. Generally speaking, the more delimited an area, the better the quality. Appellations are becoming increasingly important as consumers' awareness evolves. Quality wine producers in the United States and the New World are marketing their wines by stressing increasingly recognized appellations such as Napa or Sonoma. There are now more than 140 American Viticultural Areas in the United States.

Varietal labeling The marketing of wines by varietal labeling, such as Chardonnay, is a fairly recent phenomenon. In response to the less distinctive wines sold under generic labels such as California burgundy, producers began differentiating their better wines by labeling them with the variety. Many consumers make the varietal the primary factor in their purchasing decision.

Reputation of the _négociant_, importer, and distributor Many _négociants_, importers, and distributors have built reputations for their expertise by either producing or selecting, storing, and transporting wines and then delivering them in optimum condition.

Cost Cost is a factor in any purchasing decision. For a food and beverage establishment, the cost of the wine purchased must fall within the budget parameters of the menu. A casual-dining restaurant, for example, would not offer a wine list featuring rare and expensive vintages.

In general, an establishment in the United States looks for a return of 100% or more on the cost of the wine. Volume purchases usually result in significant savings.

Decoding the Wine Label

Knowing how to read a wine label can provide a wealth of information. Unfortunately, no standard, universal method or legal requirements for labeling exist. Today, however, all European wines conform to one set of standards. The information of greatest concern to the purchaser is the place of origin, the quality level, the vintage year, and the varietal or proprietary labeling.

Place of Origin

The place of origin is determined and guaranteed by the official state or regulatory agency of each country. The entire appellation system is based on the primacy of the concept of place of origin. The wine may be labeled primarily for the location in which the grapes were grown, especially for some quality French and Italian wines. In Europe, if a label identifies a geographic area, 100% of the grapes must have been grown in that area. In Australia, however, the requirement is that 80% of the grapes have to have been grown in that area, and in the United States, 85%.

When determining the place of origin, the purchaser must examine the geographic level given on the label. In general, the more defined the area, the higher the quality of the wine. Five levels, from the broadest to the narrowest geographically defined areas, are listed in Figure 36-11.

Quality Level

Although much of the world shares similar standards, they are by no means uniform. Members of the European Union must meet hierarchic criteria.

Each country has a governmental or regulatory agency to oversee viticultural and winemaking practices. These agencies qualify the level of each wine on the basis of place of origin, which determines viticultural practices and winemaking processes. There are three general quality levels: Quality Wines Produced in a Specified Region (QWPSR); Table Wine with a Specified Region; and Table Wine, the lowest category. In countries with less clearly defined appellation-based or hierarchic systems than those of the European Union, there is greater freedom to experiment.

The United States also has a federal regulatory agency, the Bureau of Alcohol, Tobacco, and Firearms (ATF), as well as state regulatory agencies to oversee the wine industry.

The brand name or name of a producer may be as significant as the quality rating given by a regulatory agency. For example, Angelo Gaja in Italy produces unconventional wines of the highest quality—such as Chardonnay, which is nontraditional in Piedmont—that have not been designated by the Italian regulatory agency as the highest quality rating of DOCG. In addition, the purchaser should be aware of the reputation of the _négociant_, wine merchant, or importer (Frederick Wildman and Sons, Neal Rosenthal, or Kobrand Corporations, for example).

Vintage

Vintages are a reflection of the weather for a particular year. Thanks to scientific developments, vintages matter less today than in the past. Although winemakers are able to manipulate wines to extract the most flavors possible, there are limits to what they can achieve. Winemakers can make a good wine in an "off year," but not a great one. A great vintage will indicate the potential for a quality wine to develop greater complexity and aging potential than wines from a mediocre or poor vintage. In disastrous vintages, the producer may decide not to sell the wine under his primary label in order to protect the label's integrity. In Europe, vintages cannot appear on the label for table wine.

Varietal, Generic, or Proprietary

Wines can be labeled with varietal, generic, or proprietary names. Australian and European varietal wines must contain a minimum of 85% of the grape variety stated on the label. In the United States, varietal wines must contain a minimum of

FIGURE 36-11

Area Levels	COUNTRY	France	U.S.A.
	REGION	Bordeaux	California
	DISTRICT	Médoc	Napa/Sonoma
	COMMUNE/VILLAGE	Pauillac	Oakville/Dry Creek
	VINEYARD	Château Latour	To-Kalon/Stefani Ranch

75% of the stated variety, except in Oregon, where a 90% minimum is required.

Lower-quality American wines are often semi-generically labeled—for example, as California Chablis, Claret, or Madeira. These wines can be any blend of any variety of grapes and typically bear little or no resemblance to their European namesakes. The United States has 14 acceptable semi-generic labels:

Burgundy	Chablis	Champagne
Chianti	Claret	Hock
Madeira	Malaga	Moselle
Port	Rhine	Sauterne
Sherry	Tokay	

Many wines are also marketed under an exclusive proprietary or brand name such as Opus One® from the United States. Those wines do not reflect any single quality. Some proprietary labels, such as Blue Nun® from Germany, represent European table wines, and others, such as Sassicaia® from Italy, represent the best quality.

United States Labeling Laws

United States law requires the following information on wine labels (see Figure 36-12):

1. **Brand Name:** Either the name of the producer or the proprietary name
2. **Type of Wine:** Semi-generic, table (red, white or rosé), or sparkling
3. **Name and Address of the Bottler**
4. **Alcohol Content:** For table or still wines, a variance of 1.5% is allowed; for sparkling wines < 1%
5. **Net Contents of the Bottle**
6. **Sulfite Statement:** States whether or not the wine contains sulfites (most do)
7. **Health Warning:** To advise pregnant women and heavy machinery operators against consuming alcoholic beverages

Accepted labeling terms in the United States follow:

Vocabulary
U.S. Labeling Terms

Vintage	*95% of grapes must be from that vintage year*
Estate Bottled	*100% grown, made, and bottled at the winery*
Produced by	*75% or more crushed, made, and bottled at the winery*
Cellared and Bottled by	*10% or less crushed, made at the winery*
Vineyard name	*95% or more grown at the particular vineyard*

❦ FIGURE 36-12
U.S. wine labels are the source of important information about the wine.

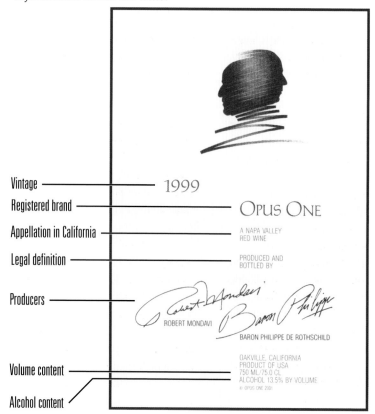

Vintage — 1999
Registered brand — OPUS ONE
Appellation in California — A NAPA VALLEY RED WINE
Legal definition — PRODUCED AND BOTTLED BY
Producers — ROBERT MONDAVI / BARON PHILIPPE DE ROTHSCHILD
Volume content — OAKVILLE, CALIFORNIA PRODUCT OF USA 750 ML/75.0 CL
Alcohol content — ALCOHOL 13.5% BY VOLUME
© OPUS ONE 2001

❦ FIGURE 36-13
The Label Integrity Program regulates wine labeling in Australia.

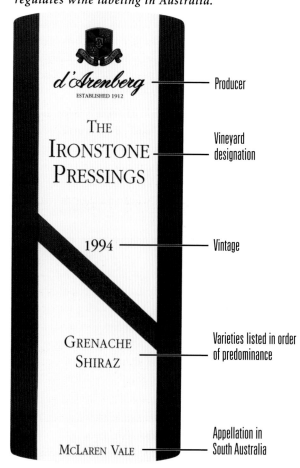

d'Arenberg ESTABLISHED 1912 — Producer
THE IRONSTONE PRESSINGS — Vineyard designation
1994 — Vintage
GRENACHE SHIRAZ — Varieties listed in order of predominance
McLAREN VALE — Appellation in South Australia

Australian Labeling Laws

Australia's Wine and Brandy Corporation is the regulatory agency that enforces labeling laws through an annual audit of the Label Integrity Program. See Figure 36-13 on page 890. The LIP enforces regulations that include the following:

1. A minimum 85% of the wine is made from the stated varietal.
2. A minimum of 85% of the wine comes from the stated region.
3. If a wine is composed of more than one variety, the varieties must be named in descending order. For example, a wine labeled Cabernet Shiraz would contain more Cabernet Sauvignon than Shiraz.
4. Semi-generic labels that are named for European appellations, such as champagne, have been or are being phased out.
5. If the term "reserve bin" or "bin number" is listed, the wine must indicate distinctiveness and higher quality.
6. If the term "show reserve" is used, the wine must have won a medal at a wine-tasting competition, an event that is taken very seriously by wine makers.
7. Geographic indications are an official description of Australian wine zones, regions, or subregions. They are increasingly important, just as American Viticultural Areas are in the United States. Sixty-five different regions have now been classified.

European Union Labeling Requirements and System of Quality

All European wines must meet the standards and be labeled in accordance with and approved by the European Union **Office International du Vin (OIV)**. See Figure 36-14. The philosophical basis of labeling reflects the primacy of typicity of style coming from a specific region as a result of a basic belief in *terroir*.

The European Union identifies five different categories for still wines and four categories of sparkling wines.

Quality Wine Produced in a Specified Region (QWPSR) This level refers to wines produced in recognized EU appellations. Many countries have two levels of

Registered trademark

Country of origin

FIGURE 36-14
The European Union requires specific quality designations on its labels.

QWPSR region as registered with EU

Name and address of bottler

Alcohol content

Volume content

Importer

QWPSR wine, such as Italy's DOCG and DOC or France's AC and VDQS. These regions must be registered with the European Union, and each defined region is governed by regulations established by EU criteria and legislated within the respective member countries in the following categories:

1. Grape varieties recommended or authorized
2. Viticultural practices
3. Maximum yields
4. Winemaking practices
5. Minimum alcoholic content
6. Analysis of the finished wine

Table Wine with Geographic Description The second level, Table Wine with Geographical Description, translates as a wine produced from a specific European, but nonquality wine, appellation. The wine may have a vintage and include up to two varieties on the label including:

France	*Vin de Pays*
Italy	*Indicazione Geografica Tipica*
Spain	*Vino de la Tierra*
Portugal	*Vinho Regional*
Germany	*Landwein, Deutscher Tafelwein*

Table Wine The third level is Table Wine and can refer only to European-produced wines. The label may not include either the variety or vintage.

Non-EU Wine with Geographical Description The fourth level, Wine with Geographical Description, refers to wines produced from specific recognized wine regions outside the European Union.

Non-EU Table Wine The fifth level is for non-EU wines of lower quality that cannot include either a vintage or a variety on the label. The U.S. healthwarning requirement is forbidden in the European Union.

France

The **Institute National des Appellations d'Origine (INAO)** is France's regulatory agency governing wine production and labeling and its enforcement arm of the *Service de Répression des Fraudes*, which enforces the law and punishes fraud.

French wines are categorized into four broad classifications (see Figure 36-15 on page 892):

Appellation d'Origine Contrôlée (AOC or AC) is the highest classification, representing 57% of all wines produced in France. The wines fall under the classification of QWPSR and are governed by the same criteria. Different classifications are unique to each AC region, but most have a tiered system that is defined by the geographic boundaries. In sequence of quality, from highest to lowest, they are as follows:

Grand cru classé—generally a single vineyard site

Premier cru classé—single vineyard

Village

District

Region

Vin Delimité de Qualité Supérieure (VDQS), representing less than 1%, are superior quality wines from regions that aspire to be AC wines and are subject to AC regulations.

Vin de Pays is country wine, created to upgrade wine-growing regions from table wine production. There has been explosive growth because of the dominance of international varieties (aka French varieties) being grown and marketed worldwide.

Vin de table is ordinary table wine, equivalent to U.S. jug wines.

Vocabulary
French Labeling Terms

Vendange/Récolte	Vintage/harvest
Mis en bouteille au château	Estate bottled
Cru	"Growth," indicating a specific vineyard of high quality and often a classification level
Cuvée	Blend
Clos	Walled vineyard
Sec	Dry
Moelleux	Sweet

FIGURE 36-15

French wines are categorized into four broad classifications, which appear on their labels.

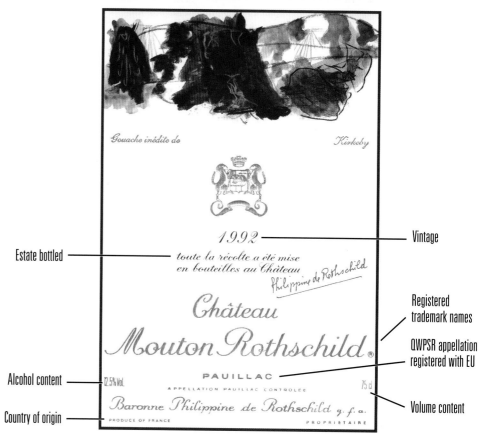

Estate bottled

Alcohol content

Country of origin

Vintage

Registered trademark names

QWPSR appellation registered with EU

Volume content

Italy

Italy and France are the largest producers and have the highest consumption per capita of wine (15 gallons per person per year). It was the wine laws of 1963, creating the **Denominazione di Origine Controllata (DOC)** and patterned after France's AOC, that spurred Italian wine industry toward modernization and quality. However, less than 15% of Italy's total wine production is classified DOC or DOCG, and within that category more than 900 types of wines are produced in more than 320 appellations.

Because of the very stringent DOC and DOCG regulations, many producers refused to abide by them and were therefore excluded, even though they were producing some of Italy's finest quality and most expensive wines. This anomaly precipitated changes with the Goria laws of 1992, creating the new category of IGT. It is no wonder that Italian wine labeling is difficult to understand. See Figure 36-16. Generally, the wines are labeled in the following four ways:

Name of the village, district, or region	Barolo
Name of the variety	Pinot Grigio
Name of a variety and the region	Moscato d'Asti
Proprietary names	such as Summus® or Ornellaia®

FIGURE 36-16

Italian wines are labeled according to variety; variety and the region; the appellation; or proprietary names.

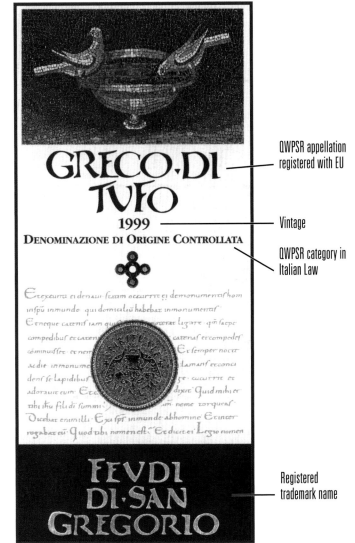

QWPSR appellation registered with EU

Vintage

QWPSR category in Italian Law

Registered trademark name

As with the other EU members, Italy has four wine classifications:

Denominazione di Origine Controllata e Garantita (DOCG) The highest and most stringent category, it requires the producer not only to follow the requirements of the DOC but also to guarantee what is stated on the label. There are currently 24 DOCG wines.

Denominazione di Origine Controllata (DOC) Equivalent to the French AOC designation and governed by the same kinds of regulations, this classification has more than 320 wines.

Indicazione Geographica Tipica (IGT) A relatively new classification, similar to Vin de Pays, IGT is meant to upgrade 40% of Italy's table wines. Producers must apply for this status, and currently more than 100 have done so.

Vino da Tavola (VDT) Table wine, by far the largest category, encompasses 85% of Italy's total wine production. Neither the variety nor the vintage may appear on the label.

Germany

German wine labels are the most detailed but are also at times among the most unintelligible. See Figure 36-17. In accordance with the EU standards, German wines are divided into the two categories of *Qualitätswein* (quality wine) and *Tafelwein* (table wine). Wines in Germany are classified according to the ripeness of the grapes at the time of harvest. *Tafelwein* is divided into three sub-categories of *Tafelwein*, *Deutscher Tafelwein* and *Deutscher Landwein*, the latter of better quality and mirroring *Vin de Pays*. Consumers in the

Vocabulary

Italian Labeling Terms

Vendemmia	*Vintage*
Azienda agricola, fattoria, tenuta	*Estate (each)*
Imbottigliato all' castelo	*Estate bottled*
Imbottigliato all' Origine	*Estate bottled*
Classico	*From the center of a DOC wine region*
Riserva	*A DOC(G) wine with additional aging*
Superiore	*A DOC(G) wine with 0.5% or more alcohol than is required*
Bianco	*White*
Rosso	*Red*
Nero	*Dark red*
Rosato	*Pink*
Secco	*Dry*
Abboccato	*Semi-dry*
Dolce	*Sweet*
Spumante	*Sparkling*
Frizzante	*Sparkling*
Cantina Sociale	*Vine-growers cooperative*
Marchio Nazionale	*Appears on a red seal on the neck of a wine bottle, indicating compliance with government controls for wines exported to the United States*

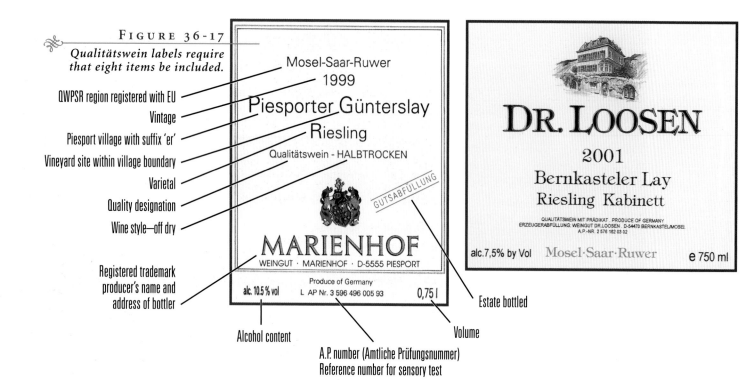

FIGURE 36-17
Qualitätswein labels require that eight items be included.

QWPSR region registered with EU

Vintage

Piesport village with suffix 'er'

Vineyard site within village boundary

Varietal

Quality designation

Wine style—off dry

Registered trademark producer's name and address of bottler

Alcohol content

A.P. number (Amtliche Prüfungsnummer) Reference number for sensory test

Mosel-Saar-Ruwer
1999
Piesporter Günterslay
Riesling
Qualitätswein - HALBTROCKEN
GUTSABFÜLLUNG
MARIENHOF
WEINGUT · MARIENHOF · D-5555 PIESPORT
alc. 10.5 % vol   Produce of Germany   L AP Nr. 3 596 496 005 93   0,75 l

Estate bottled

Volume

DR. LOOSEN
2001
Bernkasteler Lay
Riesling Kabinett
QUALITÄTSWEIN MIT PRÄDIKAT · PRODUCE OF GERMANY
ERZEUGERABFÜLLUNG: WEINGUT DR.LOOSEN · D-54470 BERNKASTEL/MOSEL
A.P.-NR. 2 576 182 03 02
alc. 7,5% by Vol   Mosel·Saar·Ruwer   e 750 ml

United States are concerned with *Qualitätswein*, the quality wines, which are divided into two subclassifications.

Qualitätswein bestimmter Anbaugebiete (QbA) (quality wines from one of the 13 specified wine regions) is the largest category of German wines. The wines tend to be light, fresh, and fruity and are allowed to be enriched with süss reserve, or sweet reserve made of sterile unfermented must.

Qualitätswein mit Prädikat (QmP) (quality wine with special distinction) is the best of Germany's wines, which are further classified into six categories with special attributes in ascending order of ripeness at harvest.

Kabinett—Normal harvest time; lightest of *Prädikat* wines

Spätlese—Late harvest with more intensity and richness; not necessarily sweet

Auslese—Hand-selected grapes; intensely flavored, but may have been affected by *botrytis* and not usually sweet

Beerenauslese (BA)—Overripe berries that are individually selected; a rare sweet wine that is rich and flavorful

Eiswein—Literally means "ice wine;" has the ripeness of BA and is harvested and pressed while frozen; remarkable acidity balancing sweetness

Trockenbeerenauslese (TBA)—Grapes that are affected by *botrytis* and individually picked, making a very rich, sweet, honeylike wine

Consumers also see the term *trocken* and *halbtrocken* on labels, indicating dry or semi-dry styles of wine.

In addition to this classification, vintage 2000 marked the start of "Classic" and "Selection" terms. "Classic" wines will be the equivalent of above-average quality *QbA* wines, made with traditional varieties. "Selection" wines must be hand harvested from a single vineyard, and thus present German wine producers the opportunity to develop a French "cru" system. The elements for a classification system based on *terroir* are already in place—13 regions (*anbaugebiete*), 39 districts (*bereiche*), 165 collective vineyard sites (*grosslagen*), and 2,643 individual vineyard sites (*einzellagen*).

Finally, German wine bottles may have seals and awards placed on them, indicating that the wine has qualified as exceeding the standards for a particular classification.

Vocabulary

German Labeling Terms

Rotwein	Red wine
Weissherbst	Rosé QbA or QmP wine made from a single variety of black grapes
Rotling	Rosé made from a blend
Schillerwein	QbA or QmP rosé wine from Württenberg
Perlwein	A red or white wine with a light sparkle, usually by carbon dioxide injection
Deutscher Sekt	A quality sparkling wine with less alcohol than champagne
Trocken	Dry
Halbtrocken	Semi-dry
Erzeugerabfüllung	Estate bottled
Gutsabfüllung	Estate bottled
Winzergenossenschaft	Wine growers' cooperative

A gold seal on the neck indicates a dry wine, a green seal indicates an off-dry wine, and a red seal indicates that the wine is sweet.

Spain

Although Spain has an ancient history of winemaking, only recently has it adopted a modern regulatory system with the establishment of the **Instituto de Denominaciones de Origen (INDO)** in 1972. See Figure 36-18 on page 896. The INDO works in tandem with the local or regional *Consejo Regulador* to maintain and certify that the regulations and standards are applied.

Spanish wines are grouped under five classifications:

Denominación de Origen Calificada (DOCa) The highest standard, it is comparable to an Italian DOCG wine. Only Rioja is designated DOC, although several appellations will soon join this rank.

Denominación de Origen (DO) Equivalent to the AC designation in French wines; there are 53 DO appellations.

Vino de la Tierra (VdlT) Equivalent to the French *Vin de Pays*, these wines have a regional character and are striving for DO status.

Vino Comarcal (VC) This classification indicates one of 23 regional appellations for wines that are outside the bounds of a DO.

Vocabulary

Spanish Labeling Terms

Vino Joven	Intended for immediate drinking upon release, in the spring following the vintage
Vino de Crianza	Aged a minimum of 6 months in oak and 2 years in the bottle; Rioja and Ribera del Duero wines are aged 1 year in oak
Reserva (white)	Aged 6 months in oak and released after 3 years
Reserva (red)	Aged 1 year in oak and released in the fourth year
Gran Reserva	Only from exceptional vintages; whites are aged 6 months in oak and released in the fourth year; reds are aged 2 years in oak and 3 more in the bottle

Vocabulary

Other Spanish Terms

Fino	A light, dry type of sherry
Manzanilla	The lightest sherry, similar to fino
Amontillado	A type of aged fino sherry
Oloroso	A type of oxidized sherry
Cava	Sparkling wine, classic method
Cosecha	Vintage
Mistela	A blend of grape juice and alcohol

Vino de Mesa (VdM) is table wine, the lowest classification.

In addition to following the EU regulations, Spain's DOCa and DO follow aging criteria.

Portugal

Portugal has one of the earliest protected appellations, *Oporto,* dating back to 1756. However, it is only since joining the European Union that Portugal's regulatory system, through the **Instituto da Vinha e Vinho (IVV)**, has established a comparable tiered system. See Figure 36-19 on page 897.

FIGURE 36-18

Spain adopted a modern regulatory system for wines in 1972, and labels reflect the new system.

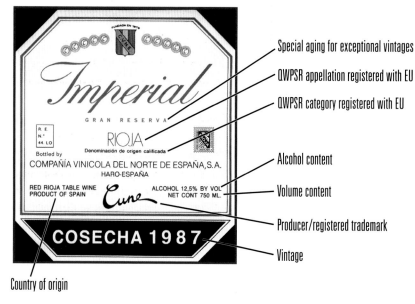

Special aging for exceptional vintages

QWPSR appellation registered with EU

QWPSR category registered with EU

Alcohol content

Volume content

Producer/registered trademark

Vintage

Country of origin

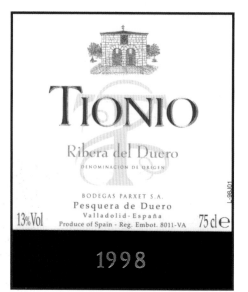

FIGURE 36-19

Classifications for Portuguese wines are reflected on their labels.

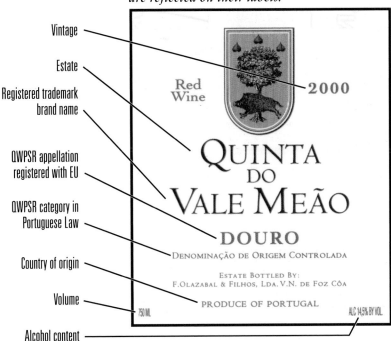

Vintage
Estate
Registered trademark brand name
QWPSR appellation registered with EU
QWPSR category in Portuguese Law
Country of origin
Volume
Alcohol content

Portuguese wines are similarly classified:

Denominação de Origem Controlada (DOC) This classification is similar to a French AC or Italian DOC wine; there are currently about 40 DOC regions.

Indicação de Proveniência Regulamentada (IPR) This classification ompares to the French VDQS, although in 1999 most were promoted to DOC status. Both DOC and IPR are required to have a paper seal, the *Selo de Origem,* that goes over the cork but under the capsule.

Vinho Regional This classification compares to France's Vin de Pays.

Vinho de Mesa Table wine is the lowest classification, where neither variety nor vintage can be mentioned on the label.

Storing Wine

Because wine is a living entity, it can either suffer or thrive, depending on how it is treated. See Figure 36-20. When storing wine, five important factors must be controlled: temperature, humidity, light, position, and stability.

In addition, the organization of the wine cellar is important to food service establishments that purchase wine in volume. Because most wines are made to be consumed within two to three years, it is important to keep track of when the wine was purchased. An efficient inventory system will also keep careful records with the name, vintage, price, amount purchased, distributor, shipper, and numbered bins.

Temperature Wine should be stored at a constant temperature of 50°F–55°F, although temperature stability is more important than the actual temperature level because some bacteria become active as temperature fluctuates. However, the lower the temperature (down to 50°F), the slower the maturation of the wine. Wines should not be refrigerated for any length of time because refrigeration can cause the cork to dry out, allowing oxygen to enter the bottle.

Humidity Wine should be stored in a well-ventilated space with a relative humidity of 60%–75% to prevent the corks from drying out.

Light Avoid storing wine in direct light, whether natural or artificial. Too much light causes heat and, therefore, deterioration.

Position Wine bottles should be stored on their sides, keeping the corks moist, thus inhibiting oxidation.

Vibrations Wine should be stored in a place that is free of agitation or vibration, conditions that can cause rapid deterioration.

Wine Tasting

Wine tasting can be both simple and complex. It is simple to quaff wine and enjoy its attributes without contemplating its subtleties. Fuller appreciation comes with learning to distinguish the subtle characteristics of color, aroma, bouquet, flavor, texture, intensity, balance, and length of the

FIGURE 36-20

To retain its quality, wine must be stored properly.

finish. For a professional wine taster, all of these characteristics must be recognized, identified, and recorded. See Figure 36-21. For others—the novice and the appreciative amateur—part of the enjoyment of tasting wine comes from exploring and learning about a world of subtle sensations.

Types of Tastings

There are four basic types of wine tastings. See Figure 36-22.

General tastings General tastings are often conducted by retailers or distributors, special event organizers of food and wine expositions, or fund-raisers. Tasters try a variety of wines in an arranged sequence, typically beginning with dry white wines and ending with fortified wines.

Copyright American Society for Oenology and Viticulture. Noble, A. C. et al. Am J Enol Vitic 38:143–146, 1987.

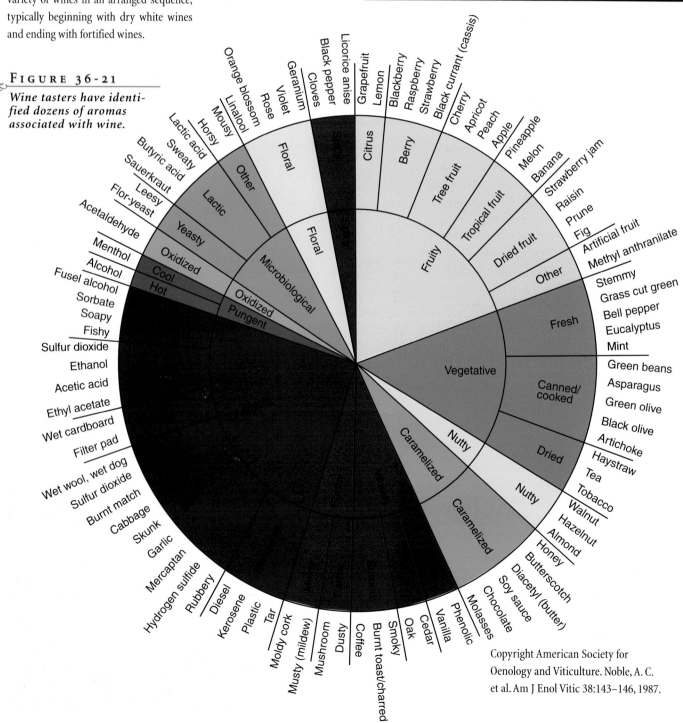

FIGURE 36-22
Wine tasting is both simple and complex.

FIGURE 36-21
Wine tasters have identified dozens of aromas associated with wine.

Horizontal tastings Horizontal tastings are for evaluating wines of a particular region or vintage. Horizontal tastings allow the taster to evaluate the differences among wines produced by several winemakers from the same region, or within the same parameters of varieties and vintage.

Vertical tastings Vertical tastings evaluate wines of different vintages, usually from a limited number of producers. The taster focuses on the wine's maturation and the factors that differentiate the vintages.

Blind tastings Blind tastings are the most complex in that the tasters have no prior information about the wines. The wines are generally chosen from the same varietals or vintage. A blind tasting allows tasters to sharpen their skills at differentiating subtleties among wines.

Set-Up and Requirements

An appropriate atmosphere is key to a professional wine-tasting event: The room should be well lit, ideally with natural daylight or nonfluorescent lighting to allow for accurate color evaluation. Glassware should be clean and free of any lingering odor of detergent. The room should be free of any extraneous scents such as flowers or air freshener. Tasters should not wear cologne or other heavy scents that would interfere with accurate sensory evaluation.

Glasses should be the appropriate size and shape for the wines being tasted. They should be placed on a white background so that tasters can discern a wine's color and intensity accurately.

Water should be served to cleanse the palate; no foods other than bread or flavorless water biscuits should be served. Spittoons should be provided.

Each taster should have an evaluation sheet and a pen or pencil for making observations and for evaluating each wine. The room should be silent throughout the tasting exercise so that tasters are not distracted.

During wine tastings, wine is served in 1.5- to 2-ounce portions and grouped in *flights,* or groupings of similar vintages, varietals, or other comparable factors. Groupings allow the taster to evaluate the wines against one another and to prevent dissimilar wines from interfering with the subtle tastes of other wines.

When different styles of wine are being evaluated, the sequence in which they are tasted is significant to the taster's ability to discern the subtleties—light-bodied wines before full-bodied wines; dry wines before off-dry or sweet wines; and generally whites before reds.

The Six Ss of Wine Tasting

The six Ss of wine tasting are see, swirl, sniff, sip, swallow or spit, and savor.

See Although sight is the least accurate of the senses with which to evaluate wine, it provides clues to and anticipation of what is to come. First, examine the upper surface of the wine, known as the *disc.* The edge of the disc may appear colorless. The variation of color or hue between the rim and the core of the wine will indicate possible aging, origin, and vinification to an experienced taster. Note that the disc is not flat, but rather forms a concave curve, called the *meniscus,* as the wine extends a short way up the sides of the wine glass.

The color or hue of the wine is called the *robe.* The robe gives important clues about the wine. A white wine with little or no color will indicate that the fruit was immature, for example; the wine will probably lack aroma and flavor. Pale and light-colored wine often comes from cooler climates. Most white wines tend to range from straw green-yellow to light yellow. As white wine barrel or bottle ages, it develops more color. Medium yellow and light gold wines tend to be sweet dessert wines. If the wine is brown, it has either been fortified or it has oxidized.

A red wine with a blue or purple rim indicates immaturity. Light reds indicate varietals such as Pinot Noir. The majority of red wines are medium cherry red, but they may develop a red tile or brick hue with age. Red wines lose color with age, so examining the color gives clues to the wine's age.

Swirl Swirling the wine lightly coats the upper level of the glass, aerating the wine and allowing it to "breathe" and open. As the wine evaporates off the side of the glass, flavor components are released. The residual wine that clings to the glass is called *legs,* tears, or arches. Legs are caused by alcohol and glycerol levels in the wine. The more alcohol, the denser and more pronounced the legs.

Sniff Smell is the most important sense for wine tasting. The olfactory sense allows tasters to discern hundreds of smells. The taster differentiates between aromas and bouquets. Aroma descriptors include such terms as fruity, spicy, floral, or vegetative. Bouquet descriptors include nutty, caramelized, woody, earthy, and petroleum. Some wines may have off odors as a result of faulty winemaking or storage. When sniffing wine, the taster should sniff once and then swirl the wine and tilt the glass toward himself or herself, so that his or her nose is directly in the glass, and sniff again.

Taking short sniffs without inhaling deeply, the taster notes an initial impression, often called the attack, or first nose. After 30 seconds or so, the wine is sniffed again for second impressions, called second nose. After a short interval, the sniffing process is repeated to verify or add to the earlier impressions. Too-frequent sniffing will result in palate adaption, in which the taster will be unable to discern any differences at all.

Sip Using the mouth alone, humans are able to distinguish only five tastes: sweet, sour, salty, bitter, and umami, the best example of which is the taste of monosodium glutamate (MSG). Research has shown that although most taste buds are concentrated on the tip and sides of the tongue, they are also located on the roof and back of the mouth. That is why it is important to roll the wine on and around the tongue to coat these taste buds. Saltiness is not a typical component of a wine's taste, and bitterness is only slightly less so.

Tasters describe the degree of sweetness in a wine as dry, off-dry or mildly sweet, sweet, and very sweet. Although most wines lack bitterness, if present they are described as slightly bitter, moderately bitter, and very bitter. Sourness or acidity can be described as flatness if the wine is not sufficiently acidic, fruitiness if it is normally acidic, and acidulous for excessive acidity.

Wine tasting also involves tactility—the texture or "mouth feel" of the wine, which is a function of tannins, glycerol, and alcohol. Astringency is the "drying out" effect or rough feeling a taster perceives from tannins. Tannic wines may be described as slightly astringent or chalky, moderately tannic, or astringent.

Alcohol gives the taster the perception of sweetness and a tactile sensation of heat. Glycerol, like alcohol, gives a perception of richness and weight on the palate.

Swallow or Spit A taster cannot remain alert and assess a wine accurately if he or she is consuming it. Spitting between tastes is necessary for proper assessment.

Savor Savoring wine involves the taster's appreciation and evaluation of the wine by focusing on the way it lingers in the mouth. The key to tasting is to determine the balance of the wine between the acidity and tannins on the one hand and the sweetness and alcohol on the other. The combined sensations of taste, smell, texture, balance, and length, or how quickly or slowly those perceptions remain on the palate, determine the evaluation of the wine's *finish.*

The best wines have a balanced finish integrated into a satisfying whole. If one element predominates, the wine is unbalanced. Wines are described as having a short, medium, or long finish, depending on how long sensations linger. Wines with short finishes leave lingering flavors for less than 15 seconds. Great wines, on the other hand, have finishes that linger from one to several minutes.

Wine-Tasting Terms

In the past, winetasters tended toward the poetic when they described the taste of wine because it is difficult to communicate abstract and subjective sensations like taste. To help improve communications among wine tasters, Professor Anne Noble at the University of California-Davis developed the aroma wheel (see Figure 36-20) in an attempt to make the adjectives that describe wines more uniform and scientific. The following terms have also become accepted within the wine trade:

Vocabulary
Wine-Tasting Terms

Term	Definition	Term	Definition
Austere	Unyielding, possibly too young	Long	A lingering finish
Baked	Lacks freshness and acidity	Mouth-filling	Richly textured
Big/Full	Full-bodied and full-flavored	Pétillant	Spritzy, slight carbonation
Buttery	Soft, round whites with bouquet of malolactic fermentation	Robust	Full-bodied
		Rough	Coarse; unpolished
Coarse	Lacking complexity or finesse	Sharp	High acid
Complex	Multilayered and multifaceted	Short	Lacking finish
Creamy	Denoting richness	Silky	Smooth; mature tannins
Crisp	Good acidity	Simple	Lacking distinction
Dense	Intensely flavorful and colorful	Smooth	Mature tannins
Dried-out	Fruit flavors have dissipated	Soft	Mellow flavors
Earthy	Aromas reminiscent of soil or minerals	Sour	Overly acidic; vinegary
Elegant	Great finesse and balance	Spritz	Prickly from carbon dioxide
Fat	Full-bodied but lacking acidity	Stalky/stemmy	Bitter vegetal taste
Firm	Structure backed by tannins, acid	Steely	Good acidity
Flabby	Lacks acidity; or "flat"	Supple	Sensuously smooth
Fragrant	Flowery	Thin	Lacks body
Green	A young wine or wine made from unripe grapes	Vegetal	Vegetable aroma (e.g., bell pepper)
		Velvety	Rich silkiness
Hard	Tannic; too young	Watery	Weak and thin
Heavy	Overly alcoholic	Woody	Odors of old casks
Herbaceous	Aromas of grass; herbs	Zesty	Crisp and fresh
Jammy	Overly ripe fruit		
Lean	Limited flavor; high acidity		

The following terms are used for wines that are spoiled:

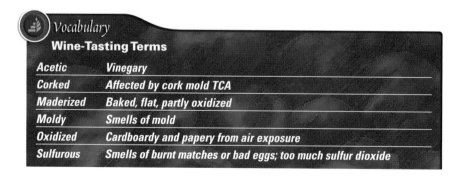

Vocabulary
Wine-Tasting Terms

Acetic	Vinegary
Corked	Affected by cork mold TCA
Maderized	Baked, flat, partly oxidized
Moldy	Smells of mold
Oxidized	Cardboardy and papery from air exposure
Sulfurous	Smells of burnt matches or bad eggs; too much sulfur dioxide

 **PROCESS**

The Six Ss of Wine Tasting

Professional wine tasters have trained their senses to make subtle comparisons and judgments.

Use the following steps for full appreciation of wine:

1 **Examine the color of the wine against a white background.**

SEE

2 **Swirl the wine to release its aroma.**

SWIRL

3 **Sniff the wine to form a first impression; then sniff again to enjoy the wine's subtle aroma and bouquet.**

SNIFF

4 **Sip the wine, and roll it around in the mouth so that it touches all the taste buds.**

SIP

5 **Spit the wine into a cup or sink, and cleanse the palate with water or plain crackers or wafers.**

SPIT/SWALLOW

6 **Savor the finish, or aftertaste, of the wine, and take notes of your impressions before tasting the next sample.**

SAVOR

Food and Wine Pairing

Pairing wine with food used to be a straightforward, if not rigid, matter of following the French tradition of specific wines with specific dishes. See Figure 36-23 on page 903. The classic dictum held that red wine was always served with red meats and white wine was served with fish and poultry.

Over the past several decades, however, Western cuisine has expanded and incorporated many cultural ingredients and techniques. As a result, Western society needed to become much more adventurous with wine pairings. There do remain, however, some common sense guidelines for matching wine to food.

Guidelines

The following guidelines apply to food-wine pairings: Match the intensity of flavors in both food and wine. A full-bodied red wine would overpower poached sole; a grilled steak would overwhelm a light white wine.

Match or contrast components of both food and wine. Having similarities in components (sweet, sour, salty, bitter) may be safe, but not necessarily interesting. For example, sweet food with sweet wines match perfectly as long as the wine is sweeter than the food, but a sweet Sauternes is perhaps more interesting with salty Roquefort cheese.

Think about the acidity. Acidic foods need to be accompanied by acidic wines like Sauvignon Blanc and cool-climate Chardonnays. Highly acid foods will wash out low-acid wines. Acidic wines also pair well with salty and oily foods. The effect is similar to pairing citrus with fish.

Modify bitterness. Bitter food and bitter wine reinforce bitterness, but sweetness or acidity can modify it. A mixed green salad with grilled chicken, for example, might be paired with a white wine such as white Zinfandel or Chenin Blanc.

Match or contrast dominant flavors of both food and wine. Herbs, spices, seasonings, and cooking techniques can enhance flavors in wine. For example, thyme or basil in a dish will bring out the herbaceous character of a Sauvignon Blanc. Grilled foods such as salmon will match the spiciness and toastiness of Pinot Noir. Contrasting smoky and floral flavors can also be interesting, such as serving smoked salmon with a floral Riesling.

Match the intensity of textures to make sure that one does not overpower the other. Lightly textured foods pair well with light-bodied wines and rich foods with full-bodied wines—a California Cabernet with grilled sirloin steak, for example.

Remember that tannins bind with fat. For example, a hard tannic Cabernet Sauvignon will not taste astringent if accompanied by fatty beef, duck, cheese, or rich sauces.

Accompany a fine older wine with simpler food that acts as a foil. Use good, drinkable-quality wine for cooking.

Use the same style wine in cooking as will be served with the meal for better harmony.

Be aware of interactions of food and wine: artichokes compete with acidity in wine. Foods high in umami, such as anchovy, soy sauce, bonito, or smoked salmon, react badly to tannins and leave a metallic flavor on the palate. Corn is difficult to pair with very dry wine because of its high starch and sugar content.

Be aware that mixed green salads, especially those with vinaigrette, will ruin the taste of wine. If possible, avoid using vinegar, and substitute citrus juice; then serve with a slightly off-dry wine with good acidity, such as Chenin Blanc. Be alert to the difficulty of pairing egg dishes, especially those without other taste components, with wine. Poached eggs, for example, will coat the tongue and palate and limit the perception of the wine. A Western-style omelet, however, has taste and flavor components such as onions, tomatoes, peppers, and cheese—all of which enhance compatibility with wine.

Consider the intensity of chocolate; it is difficult to pair if it is very sweet or bitter. It is less of a problem if it is merely a component of a dessert.

If possible, avoid serving wine with very spicy foods, which will not only overwhelm a wine's flavors but also enhance the perception of tannins if present. Remember that the best wine is the wine that the taster most enjoys and that many psychological factors are involved in a consumer's wine choice that have little to do with the gustatory senses.

- Seasonality—Most people enjoy light and white wines in warm seasons and full-bodied red ones in cold weather.
- Prestige—Consumers often want to pair fine quality food with expensive wines, regardless of the wine's suitability.
- Ethnicity—Consumers enjoy pairing regional wines with cuisines of the same region.
- Occasionality—Some wines, like champagne, are associated with celebrations.
- The company—Sharing a bottle of wine may make an experience most memorable.

When serving more than one wine with dinner, here are a few general guidelines:

- Serve dry wine before sweet wine.
- Serve light-bodied wines before full-bodied ones.
- Serve whites before reds.
- Serve young wines before older ones.

As the ancient Greek philosopher Socrates noted, "Wine moistens and tempers the spirit, lulls the cares of the mind to rest; it revives our joys and is oil to the dying flame of life. If we drink temperately and smell drafts at a time, the wine distills into our lungs like the sweetest morning dew. It is then the wine commits no rape upon our reason, but pleasantly invites us to agreeable mirth."

Figure 36-23

Where white wine might be lost against the rich flavor of salmon, Pinot Noir is an elegant complement to this dish because of its acidity and light body.

APPENDIX A

Common Measurement Conversions

U.S. Standard	Metric
WEIGHT	
0.035 ounce	1 gram
1 ounce	28.35 grams
16 ounces (or 1 pound)	454 grams
2.2 pounds	1 kilogram
VOLUME (LIQUID)	
0.034 ounce	1 milliliter
1 ounce	29.57 milliliters
8 ounces (or 1 cup)	237 ml
16 ounces (or 1 pint)	474 milliliters (or .47 liter)
2 pints (or 1 quart)	946 milliliters (or .95 liter)
33.8 ounces (or 1.06 quarts)	1,000 milliliters or 1 liter
4 quarts (or 1 gallon)	3.79 liters
VOLUME (DRY)	
1 pint	.55 liter
0.91 quart	1 liter
2 pints (or 1 quart)	1.1 liters
8 quarts (or 1 peck)	8.81 liters
4 pecks (or 1 bushel)	35.24 liters
LENGTH	
0.39 inches	1 centimeter
1 inch	2.54 centimeters
39.4 inches	1 meter

Common Conversion Factors

Weight	To convert:	Multiply by:
	ounces to grams	28.35
	grams to ounces	.03527
	kilograms to pounds	2.2046

Volume	To convert:	Multiply by:
	quarts to liters	.946
	pints to liters	.473
	quarts to milliliters	946
	milliliters to ounces	.0338
	liters to quarts	1.05625
	liters to pints	2.1125
	liters to ounces	33.8

Length	To convert:	Multiply by:
	inches to millimeters	25.4
	inches to centimeters	2.54
	millimeters to inches	.03937
	centimeters to inches	.3937
	meters to inches	39.3701

Common Temperature Conversions

Degrees Fahrenheit	Degrees Celsius
32°F	0°C
41°F	5°C
140°F	60°C
150°F	66°C
160°F	71°C
166°F	74°C
180°F	82°C
212°F	100°C
300°F	149°C
325°F	163°C
350°F	177°C
375°F	191°C
400°F	204°C
425°F	218°C
450°F	232°C
475°F	246°C
500°F	260°C

Temperature Conversion Factors

To convert Fahrenheit to Celsius:
Subtract 32, multiply by 5, and then divide by 9.

To convert Celsius to Fahrenheit:
Multiply by 9, divide by 5, and then add 32.

APPENDIX B

Wine Pronunciation Guide

Aloxe-Corton *ah lohs kor tohn*

Alsace *ahl sahss*

Amontillado *ah mohn te YAH doh*

Anjou *ahn zhoo*

Armagnac *ar mah nyahk*

Asti Spumante *ahs tee spoo MAHN tee*

Aurora *oh ROHR uh*

Baden *bah din*

Banyul *ban yul*

Barbera *bar BEH rah*

Bardolino *bar doh LEEN oh*

Barsac *bar sahk*

Beaujolais *boh zhoh lay*

Beaune *bone*

Beaumes de Venise *bohme duh vuh nees*

Bergerac *behr zhe rahk*

Bernkastel *BEHRN kahs tel*

Blanc de Blancs *blahnk duh blahnk*

Bordeaux *bor doh*

Cabernet Sauvignon *kah behr nay soh vee nyohn*

Cahors *KAH or*

Calvados *kahl vah dohs*

Catawba *kuh TAW bah*

Chablis *shah blee*

  Les Clos *lay kloh*

  Valmur *vahl moor*

Chambertin, Le *luh shahm behr tahn*

Château *shah toh*

  Cheval Blanc *sheh vahl blahnk*

  d'Yquem *dee kem*

  Grilet *gree yay*

  Haut-Brion *oh bree ohn*

  Latour *lah toor*

  Margaux *mahr goh*

  Mouton-Phillippe *moo tawn fee leep*

Chateâuneuf du Pape *shah toh nuf doo pahp*

Chenin Blanc *sheh neen blahnk*

Chevalier-Montrachet *shey vahl yay mohn trah shay*

Chianti *kee AHN tee*

Clos *cloh*

Corton-Clos du Roi *kor tohn kloh doo rwah*

Corvo *kohr voh*

Côte de Nuits *koht duh nwee*

Côte Chalonnaise *koht shah loh nayse*

Côte d'Or *koht dohr*

Côte-Rôtie *koht roh tee*

Crianza *kree AHN zah*

Criolla *kree OH ya*

Cru *kroo*

Cynar *CHEE nar*

Dolcetto *dohl CHET toh*

Dão *dow*

Dubonnet *doo boh nay*

Fino *FEE noh*

Fleurie *fluh ree*

Frascati *frahs KAH tee*

Gevrey *zhev ray*

Gewürztraminer *geh VURTZ tra meen er*

Graves *grahv*

Griotte *gree ut*

Grumello *groo MEL oh*

Haut-Médoc *oh may dohk*

Hessiche Bergstrasse *HES sih shuh BEHRG shtrah suh*

Johannisberg Riesling *yoh HAHN is behrk REES ling*

Jura *joo rah*

Juracon *joo rah sohn*

Lacryma Christi *lah creem ah KREES tee*

Lambrusco *lahm BROOS coh*

Liebfraumilch *LEEB frow milkh*

  Lillet *lee lay*

Mâcon *mah cohn*

Maconnais *ma koh nay*

Madeira *mah DEER ah*

Madiran *ma DEE rahn*

Malaga *MAH lah gah*

Malmsey *MALM zee*

Marsala *mahr SAH lah*

Médoc *may dohk*

Mercurey *mehr kyu ray*

Meursault *mer soh*

Midi *mee dee*

Mittelrhein *MIT el rine*

Montrachet, Le *luh mohn trah shay*

Moscato *mohs KAH toh*

Mosel *MOH zel*

Mosel-Saar-Ruwer *mo zell sahr rooer*

Moulin-à-Vent *moo lan ah vahn*

Moulis *moo lee*

Muscadet *moos kah day*

Musigny, Les *lay moo see nyee*

Nebbiolo *neb bee OH loh*

Nuit St. Georges *nwee san jor jeh*

Oloroso *oh loh ROH soh*

Orvieto *ohr vee EHT oh*

Pais *pah eess*

Pauillac *poy yak*

Pessac-Léognan *pay sak lay oh nyahn*

Pfalz *fahltz*

Pinot Blanc *pee noh blahnk*

Pinot Noir *pee noh nwahr*

Pomerol *pah meh rol*

Pommard *poh mahr*

Pouilly-Fuissé *pwee yee fwee say*

Pouilly Fumé *pwee yee foo may*

Puligny-Montrachet *poo lee nyee mohn trah shay*

Qualitätswein *kval ih tats vine*

Recioto *reh chee OH toe*

Rheingau *RINE gow*

Rheinhessen *RINE hes sen*

Riesling *REES ling*

Romanée, La *lah roh mah nay*

Saint-Amour *sahn tah moor*

Saint-Émilion *sahn tay meel yohn*

Sancerre *sahn sehr*

Saumur *soh mur*

Sauternes *soh tehrn*

Savoie *sa vwah*

Sekt *zehkt*

Sémillon *seh mee yohn*

Soave *SWAH veh*

St. Estèphe *sahnt es tef*

Tavel *tah vel*

Trimoulet *tree moo lay*

Valpolicella *vahl poh lee CHEH lah*

Verdelho *vehr DEL yo*

Verdicchio *vehr DEE kee oh*

Vernaccia *vehr NAH chah*

Volnay *vuhl nay*

Vosne Romanée *vohn roh mah nay*

Vougeot *voo zhoe*

Vouvray *voo vreh*

Württemberg *VUR tem behrg*

Würzburger *VURTZ behr gehr*

Zinfandel *TZIN fahn dehl*

BIBLIOGRAPHY

Books

Amendola, Joseph, and Donald Lundberg. *Understanding Baking.* 2nd ed. New York: John Wiley & Sons, Inc., 1992.

American Red Cross. *Responding to Emergencies.* 2nd ed. St. Louis: Mosby Lifeline, 1996.

Anderson, Burton, and Stuart Pigott. *Wine Atlas of Italy.* UK: Antique Collector's Club, 1997.

Anderson, Jean. *The American Century Cookbook.* New York: Clarkson Potter, 1997.

Barker, William. *The Modern Pâtissier.* London: Northwood Publications Ltd., 1978.

Beard, James. *James Beard's American Cookery.* N.p.: Little, Brown & Co, 1972.

Cass, Bruce, and Jancis Robinson, eds. *Oxford Companion to Wines of North America.* Oxford: Oxford University Press, 2000.

Chalmers, Irena. *The Great Food Almanac.* San Francisco: Collins Publishers San Francisco, 1994.

Clarke, Oz. *Wine Atlas.* London: Webster's International Publishers, 2002.

Connelly, Paul, and Malcolm Pittam. *Practical Bakery.* London: Hodder & Stoughton, 1997.

Cracknell, H. L., and R. J. Kaufmann. *The Illustrated Escoffier.* London: Octopus Books Ltd., 1987.

Davidson, Alan. *The Oxford Companion to Food.* Oxford: Oxford University Press, 1999.

Dornenburg, Andrew, and Karen Page. *Becoming a Chef.* New York: John Wiley & Sons, Inc., 1995.

Ellmer, Bruno H., C.M.C. *Classical and Contemporary Italian Cooking for Professionals.* New York: Van Nostrand Reinhold, 1990.

Escoffier, A., D. Hervé, and J. M. Pouradier. *Special and Decorative Breads.* New York: Van Nostrand Reinhold, 1987.

Flandrin, J. L., and M. Montanari, eds. *Food: A Culinary History.* New York: Columbia University Press, 1996.

France, W. J. *The Student's Manual of Breadmaking and Flour Confectionery.* London: Routledge, 1966.

Friberg, Bo. *The Professional Pastry Chef.* 3rd ed. New York: John Wiley & Sons, Inc., 1996.

Gisslen, Wayne. *Professional Cooking.* 4th ed. New York: John Wiley & Sons, Inc., 1999.

Halliday, James. *Australia and New Zealand Wine Companion.* Australia: HarperCollins Publishers, 2001.

Herbst, Sharon Tyler. *The New Food Lover's Companion: Comprehensive Definitions of Nearly 6,000 Food, Drink, and Culinary Terms.* 3rd ed. Hauppauge, N.Y.: Barron's Educational Series, 2001.

Jamieson, Ian. *German Wine.* UK: Faber & Faber, 1991.

Johnson & Wales University. *Culinary Fundamentals.* Dubuque: Kendall/Hunt Publishing Co., 2001.

Johnson & Wales University. *Culinary Service.* Dubuque: Kendall/Hunt Publishing Co., 2001.

Johnson & Wales University. *Johnson & Wales Student Handbook 2001–2002.* Providence: Johnson & Wales University, 2001.

Johnson, Hugh, and Jancis Robinson. *World Atlas of Wine.* UK: Mitchell Beazley, 2001.

Kafka, B. *Soup: A Way of Life.* New York: Artisan, 1998.

Kiple, Kenneth F., and Kriemhild Coneè Ornelas, eds. *The Cambridge History of Food, Vol. 1.* Cambridge: Cambridge University Press, 2000.

Kittler, P. G., and K. P. Sucher. *Cultural Foods: Traditions and Trends.* Belmont, CA: Wadworth/Thomson, 2000.

Labensky, Sarah R., and Alan M. Hause. *On Cooking: A Textbook of Culinary Fundamentals.* 2nd ed. Upper Saddle River, NJ: Prentice-Hall, Inc., 1999.

Larousse Gastonomique. New York: Clarkson Potter/Publishers, 2001.

MacNeil, Karen. *The Wine Bible.* New York: Workman Publishing, 2001.

Matz, Samuel A. *Technology of the Materials of Baking.* Essex: Elsevier Science Publishers Ltd., 1989.

McGee, Harold. *On Food and Cooking: The Science and Lore of the Kitchen.* New York: Scribner, 1984.

McIlhenny, Paul, and Barbara Hunter. *The Tabasco Cookbook.* New York: Clarkston/Potter Publishers, 1993.

McIntosh, E. N. *American Food Habits in Historical Perspective.* Westport, CT: Praeger, 1995.

McVety, Paul J., Susan Desmond Marshall, and Bradley J. Ware. *The Menu and the Cycle of Cost Control.* 2nd ed. Dubuque: Kendall/Hunt Publishing Company, 2001.

McWilliams, Margaret. *Foods: Experimental Perspectives.* 3rd ed. Upper Saddle River, NJ: Prentice-Hall, Inc., 1997.

Miller, Mark, and John Harrisson. *The Great Chile Book.* Berkeley: Ten Speed Press, 1991.

Molt, Mary. *Food For Fifty.* 10th ed. Upper Saddle River, NJ: Prentice-Hall, Inc., 1997.

NAMP. *The Meat Buyers Guide.* Reston: NAMP, 1997.

NAMP. *The Poultry Buyers Guide.* Reston: NAMP, 1997.

National Restaurant Association Educational Foundation. *Principles of Food, Beverage, and Labor Cost Control.* 6th ed. New York: John Wiley & Sons, Inc., 1999.

National Restaurant Association Educational Foundation. *ServSafe Coursebook.* N.p.: National Restaurant Association Educational Foundation, 1999.

Newman, David, and Christine Thompson. *Feeding the Hungry: A Guide for Foodservice Professionals.* Providence: Johnson & Wales University, 2001.

Nicolello, I., and R. Foote. *Complete Confectionery Techniques.* London: Hodder & Stoughton, 1994.

Paston-Williams, Sara. *The Art of Dining: A History of Cooking & Eating.* London: The National Trust, 1993.

Pauli, Philip. *Classical Cooking The Modern Way: Methods and Techniques.* Translated by Hannelore Dawson-Holt. 3rd ed. New York: John Wiley & Sons, Inc., 1999.

Peterson, James. *Fish & Shellfish.* New York: William Morrow and Company, Inc., 1996.

Peterson, James. *Sauces: Classical and Contemporary Sauce Making.* New York: John Wiley & Sons, Inc., 1998.

Piras, Claudia, and Eugenio Medagliani, eds. *Culinaria Italy.* N.p.: Könemann, 2000.

Quantum Books, Ltd. *Nuts, a Cookbook.* New Jersey: Chartwell Books, 1993.

Reinhard, Peter. *The Bread Baker's Apprentice.* Berkeley: Ten Speed Press, 2001.

Rombauer, Irma. *Joy of Cooking.* New York: Scribner, 1997.

Senn, C. Herman, O.B.E., F.R.H.S. *The Menu Book: A Menu Compiler and Register of Dishes.* 8th ed. London and Melbourne: Ward, Lock & Co., Limited, n.d.

Simon, Joanna. *Wine with Food.* New York: Simon & Schuster, 1996.

Sizer, Frances Sienkiewicz, and Eleanor Noss Whitney. *Nutrition Concepts and Controversies.* 8th ed. Belmont, CA: Wadsworth/ Thomson Learning, 2000.

Stevenson, Tom. *The New Southeby's Wine Encyclopedia.* New York: Dorling Kindersley, 2001.

Sultan, William J. *Practical Baking.* 5th ed. New York: Van Nostrand Reinhold, 1990.

Toussaint-Samat, Maguelonne. *A History of Food.* Translated by Anthea Bell. Cambridge: Blackwell Publishers, 1992.

Trager, James. *The Food Chronology: A Food Lover's Compendium of Events and Anecdotes, from Prehistory to the Present.* New York: Henry Holt and Company, 1995.

Webster's New World Dictionary of Culinary Arts. Upper Saddle River, NJ: Prentice-Hall, Inc., 1997.

Williams, Chuck, ed. *Williams-Sonoma Kitchen Companion: The A to Z Guide to Everyday Cooking, Equipment & Ingredients.* San Francisco: Weldon Owen Inc. and Williams-Sonoma, 2000.

Yena, Donna J. *Career Directions.* 3rd ed. New York: Glencoe/McGraw-Hill, 1997.

Periodicals

Hatchwell, Leora C. "Overcoming Flavor Challenges in Low-Fat Frozen Desserts." *Food Technology* (February 1994): 98–102.

IFIC Foundation. "Experiments in Good Taste." *Food Insight: Current Topics in Food Safety and Nutrition* (March/April 1995): 1–8.

Lewis, Ricki. "When Smell and Taste Go Awry." *FDA Consumer* (November 1991): 29–33.

Mangels, Reed. "Vegetarian Journal's Guide to Tofu and Tempeh." *Vegetarian Journal* (March/April 1999).

Mattes, R. D. "The Taste of Fat Elevates Postprandial Triacylglycerol." *Physiology & Behavior* 74 (2001), Purdue Agricultural Communications.

Mela, David J., and Richard D. Mattes. "The Chemical Senses and Nutrition: Part 1." *Nutrition Today* (March/April 1988): 4–9.

Nussinow, Jill. "Seitan—The Vegetarian Wheat Meat." *The Vegetarian Journal* (March/April 1996).

Nussinow, Jill. "Moove Over Milk." *The Vegetarian Journal.* (January/February 1996).

Stauffer, Clyde E. "Balance and Impact." *Baking & Snack* (September 1995): 24–30.

Stone, Judith. "Like Chips in the Night." *Discover* (February 1994): 88–91.

Tibbott, Seth. "Adventures in Tempehland." *The Vegetarian Journal* (May/June 1999).

United States Department of Agriculture. "How to Buy Butter." *Home and Garden Bulletin* 148 (1995), Agricultural Marketing Service.

Web Sources

"Alcohol and Health: Weighing the Benefits and Risks of Drinking." Mayo Foundation of Medical Education and Research. 14 July 2002 <http://www.mayoclinic.com/invoke.cfm?id=SC00024>.

Alden, Lori. *The Cook's Thesaurus.* 13 June 2002 <http://www.foodsubs.com>.

"Alfredo." Cooking Light Online. 19 April 2002 <http://www.cookinglight.com/special/1025_alfredo.asp>.

"All About Champagne Grapes." Zupan's Market. May 2002 <http://www.zupans.com/cookbook/all_about_champagne_grapes.html>.

"Americans Eat Nearly 15 Pounds of Seafood a Year." *CNN Interactive.* 29 March 2002 <http://www.cnn.com/FOOD/news/9907/13/eating.fish/>.

"Antioxidant Vitamins for Optimal Health." American Dietetic Association. 19 April 2002 <http://www.eatright.org/nfs/nfs84.html>.

Azar, Beth. "What Predicts Which Foods We Eat?" *American Psychological Association (APA) Monitor.* Volume 29, Number 1 (January 1998). March 2002 <http://www.apa.org/monitor/jan98/food.html>.

"Bacillus cereus." *Bacteriological Analytical Manual Online.* U.S. Food & Drug Administration Center for Food Safety & Applied Nutrition (January 2001). 19 April 2002 <http://vm.cfsan.fda.gov/~ebam/bam-14.html>.

"Barging in for Mussels." *Commerce Success Stories.* Maine Science & Technology Foundation (2002). 4 April 2002 <http://www.mainescience.org/commerce_success.01.Mumbles.html>.

Bartoshuk, L. M. "Comparing Sensory Experiences Across Individuals: Recent Psychophysical Advances Illuminate Genetic Variation in Taste Perception." *Chem. Senses* 25 (2000): 447–460. <http://www.tastelab.org/supertaster-inc.php3>.

"Blue Mussel." University of Delaware Sea Grant. 4 April 2002 <http://www.ocean/udel.edu/mas/seafood/bluemussel.html>.

Cancer Facts & Figures 2002. American Cancer Society. <http://www.cancer.org/downloads/STT/CancerFacts&Figures 2002TM.pdf>.

Cancer Prevention & Early Detection: Facts & Figures 2002. American Cancer Society (2002). <http://www.cancer.org/downloads/STT/CPED2002.pdf>.

"The Chill Factor." *The Environmental Enquirer.* Guilford County Department of Public Health. 9 May 2002 <http://www.co.guilford.nc.us/ehindex.html>.

"Coffee Chemistry—Aroma." Coffee Research Institute. March 2002 <http://www.coffeeresearch.org/science/aromamain.htm>.

"Control of Food Structure and Organoleptic Properties (CoFSOP)." Biotechnology and Biological Sciences Research Council. March 2002 <http://www.bbsrc.ac.uk/science/areas/af/priorities/cofsop.html>.

Corriher, Shirley. "Choosing Fruit That's Truly Ripe." *Fine Cooking Magazine* (April, 2002). <http://www.taunton.com/finecooking/pages/c00019.asp>.

"The Cultivation of Molluscs." *Aquascope.* Tjärnö Marine Biological Laboratory, Strömstad, Sweden (2000). <http://www.vattenkikaren.gu.se/fakta/ovrigt/vattenbr/vabr07e.html>.

Davis, Carole, and Etta Saltos. "Dietary Recommendations and How They Have Changed Over Time." Economic Research Service, U.S. Department of Agriculture. 14 July 2002 <http://www.ers.usda.gov/publications/aib750/aib750b.pdf>.

"Definitions: Fluid Milk and Milk Products." International Dairy Foods Association. 13 March 2002 <http://www.idfa.org/facts/milk/milkfact/pg7-8.pdf>.

"Definitions: Lecithin." *Food Allergy News* Vol. 2, No. 1. 29 April 2002 <www.foodallergy.org/topics_archives/ lecithin.htm>.

"Definitions: Lecithin." *Lecithin Applications.* Riceland Foods, Inc. 29 April 2002 <www.lecithin.com/applications/p.35.html>.

"Definitions: Silpats and Flexipats." E-chefs by Demarle. 25 April 2002 <www.e-chefs.net/flexipan.htm>.

"Diet and Disease." National Library of Medicine. 19 April 2002 <http://www.nlm.nih.gov/medlineplus/ency/article/002096.htm>.

"The Early Days." *Raytheon History.* The Raytheon Company (2001). 9 May 2002 <http://www.raytheon.com/about/early.htm>.

Escobar, Alyson. "Are All Food Pyramids Created Equal?" *Nutrition Insights* (April 1997). 14 July 2002 <http://www.usda.gov/cnpp/FENR/fenrv12n4/fenrv12n4p75.PDF>.

Fabricant, Florence. "Del Monte Foods: History of Canning." *New York Times* (Feb. 28, 1996). April 2002 <http://www.delmonte.com/News/cans1/body.htm>.

"FDA Announces Advisory on Methyl Mercury in Fish." U.S. Food and Drug Administration, Office of Public Affairs (January 12, 2001). 7 April 2002 <http://www.fda.gov/bbs/topics/ANSWERS/2001/ANS01065.html>.

"Federal Inspection Marks for Fishery Products." U.S. Department of Commerce. 3 March 2002 <http://www.st.nmfs.gov/stl/fus/fus98/fim-fp98.pdf>.

"Feijoa Fruit Facts." May 2002 <http://www.crfg.org/pubs/ff/feijoa.html>.

"Fish Facts & Fancies." North American Precis Syndicate. 29 March 2002 <http://www.napsnet.com/food/52269.html>.

"Florida Citrus News Release: Cultivating an Industry." May 2002 <http://www.floridajuice.com/floridacitrus/aninfo/news13.htm>.

"Florida Farm Facts." *Planet Ag.* May 2002 <http://www.fl-ag.com/PlanetAg/citrus.htm>.

Food and Nutrition Digest: Extension Foods and Nutrition. Cooperative Service, Kansas State University (March/April 1996). April 2002 <http://www.oznet.ksu.edu/ext_f&n/_fndigest/1996/marapr96/htm>.

"Food Consumption: Overview" U.S. Department of Agriculture, Economic Research Service. 29 March 2002 <http://www.ers.usda.gov/briefing/consumption/overview.htm>.

"Food Editors Prefer Umami Taste Sensation." Family Haven. March 2002 <http://www.familyhaven.com/health/umami.html>.

"Food Processing." U.S. Department of Health and Human Services. 1 April 2002 <http://www.cfsan.fda.gov/~dms/fcannex6.html>.

"Focus on Shell Eggs." United States Department of Agriculture, Food Safety and Inspection Service (Updated June 2001). 7 March 2002 <http://www.fsis.usda.gov/OA/pubs/shelleggs.htm>.

"Food Pyramids: What Should You Really Eat?" Harvard School of Public Health. 14 July 2002 <http://www.hsph.harvard.edu/nutritionsource/pyramids.html>.

"Freshness, Not Fat, Makes Best Butter." *Cooks Illustrated.* Boston Common Press. 7 March 2002 <http://www.cooksillustrated.com/show_printdocument.asp?iDocumentID=787>.

"Fruit and Tree Nuts: Questions and Answers." *Briefing Room* (May 2002). Economic Research Service, U.S. Department of Agriculture. <http://www.ers.usda.gov/Briefing/FruitAndTreeNuts/Questions/>.

Gentry, Karen. "Phytonutrients in Apples Help Reduce Levels of Bad Cholesterol." *The Fruit Growers News.* April 2002 <http://www.virtualorchard.net/glfgn/october99/applenutrition.html>.

"Geography of Production: United States." International Rice Institute. 19 April 2002 <http://www.riceweb.org/countries/usa.htm>.

Gerrior, S. and L. Bente. "Nutrient Content of the U.S. Food Supply, 1909–99: A Summary Report." U.S. Department of Agriculture. 10 July 2002 <http://www.usda.gov/cnpp/Pubs/Food%20Supply/food-supply09_99.pdf>.

Givens, David B. "Glutamate." Center for Nonverbal Studies. March 2002. <http://members.aol.com/nonverbal3/glutamt.htm>.

"Glutamate in Foods." International Glutamate Information Service. March 2002. <http://www.glutamate.org/media/ginfoods.htm>.

Graber, Karen Hursh. "Mexico Connect: Adding Zest to Summer's Bounty: Part 1: Salsa de Fruta." April 2002 <http://www.mexconnect.com/mex_recipes/puebla/kgsalsas1.html>.

"Grades of Frozen Salmon Steaks." U.S. Department of Commerce, Seafood Inspection Program. 30 March 2002 <http://seafood.nmfs.noaa.gov/262SubpartC.htm>.

Harper, Charles R., M.D. "The Fats of Life: The Role of Omega-3 Fatty Acids in the Prevention of Coronary Heart Disease." *Archives of Internal Medicine,* Vol. 161, No. 18 (October 8, 2001). 29 March 2002 <http://archinte.amaassn.org/issues/v161n18/abs/ira00082.html>.

Hicks, Doris. "Consumers: Know the Facts About Eating Raw Shellfish." University of Delaware Sea Grant. 3 April 2002 <http://www.ocean.udel.edu/mas/masnotes/rawshellfish.html>.

Huskey, Robert J. "Vitamin C and Scurvy." September 1998. April 2002 <http://www.people.virginia.edu/~rjh9u/vitac.html>.

"Keeping Your Cool About Food Temperatures." *Food Talk.* Pike & Fischer, Inc. 9 May 2002 <http://www.pf.com/pdf/ft.pdf>.

Kurtzweil, Paula. "Critical Steps Toward Safer Seafood." U.S. Food and Drug Administration (November–December 1997, revised February 1998 and February 1999). 3 March 2002 <http://www.cfsan.fda.gov/~dms/fdsafe3.html>.

Larsen, Joanne, MS, RD, LD. "Ask the Dietician: Food Guide Pyramid." May 2002 <http://www.dietitian.com/foodguid.html>.

Lorenzini, Beth. "Special Report: The Hot Sheet on Reach-In Blast Chillers." *Foodservice Equipment Reports* (November 2000, updated March 2001). 9 May 2002 <http://www.fermag.com/sr/v4i11_sr.htm>.

"Lychee Fruit Facts." May 2002 <http://www.crfg.org/pubs/ff/lychee.html>.

"Managing Your Diabetes." Nutrition.gov. 6 June 2002 <http://www.nutrition.gov/home/index.php3>.

Mattes, R. D. "Fatty Food Triggers Taste Buds, New Research Finds." March 2002. <http://www.cosmiverse.com/science12040103.html>.

"The McDonald's Story." The McDonald's Corporation. 21 March 2002 <http://www.mcdonalds.com/corporate/info/history/history3/history3.html>.

"Mercury in Fish Threatens Unborn: A 20/20 Investigation." abcNEWS.com. 7 April 2002 <http://www.abcnews.go.com/sections/2020/2020/2020_010112.toxicfish_feature.html>.

"Milestones." *Raytheon History.* The Raytheon Company (2001). 9 May 2002 <http://www.raytheon.com/about/milestone.htm>.

"Milestones in Milk History in the U.S." International Dairy Foods Association. 13 March 2002 <http://www.idfa.org/facts/milk/milkfact/pg4.pdf>.

"Miracle of Rice." *NOVA Online.* 17 April 2002 <http://www.pbs.org/wgbh/nova/satoyama/rice.html>.

Moffitt, Christine M. "Reflections on Eating Fish." *President's Hook.* The American Fisheries Society. 29 March 2002 <http://www.fisheries.org/fisheries/hook/hook_Jan_00.htm>.

Morton, Julia F. Cherimoya. "In Fruits of Warm Climates." May 2002 <http://www.hort.purdue.edu/newcrop/morton/cherimoya.html>.

Nussinow, Jill. "Seitan—The Vegetarian Wheat Meat." The Vegetarian Resource Group (1996). 26 March 2002 <http://www.vrg.org/recipes/vjseitan.htm>.

"Nutrition: Guiding Food Aid for Development." World Health Organization (March 13, 2002). 10 July 2002 <www.who.int/nut/aid.htm>.

"Oldways Healthy Diet Pyramids." Oldways Preservation & Exchange Trust (December 5, 2001). 14 July 2002 <http://www.oldwayspt.org/html/pyramid.htm>.

"Percy Spencer." *The Invention Dimension.* Massachusetts Institute of Technology School of Engineering (May 1996). 9 May 2002 <http://web.mit.edu/invent/index.html>.

"Phytochemicals in Produce, Part 2 of 2." Colorado State University Cooperative Extension. 14 July 2002 <http://www.ext.colostate.edu/pubs/columnnn/nn980826.html>.

"Phytochemicals—Vitamins of the Future?" Ohio State University Extension Fact Sheet. 14 July 2002 <http:ohioline.osu.edu/hyg-fact/5000/5050.html>.

Putnam, Judy and Shirley Gerrior. *Trends in the U.S. Food Supply, 1970–97.* Economic Research Service, U.S. Department of Agriculture. 29 March 2002 <http://www.ers.usda.gov/publications/aib750/>.

"Purchasing Seafood Is Easy." U.S. Department of Commerce Seafood Inspection Program. 3 March 2002 <http://seafood.nmfs.noaa.gov/consumer.htm>.

"Report: Fish-Mercury Risk Underestimated." CNN.com (April 12, 2001). 7 April 2002 <http://www.cnn.com/2001/HEALTH/parenting/04/12/fish.pregnant?related.>.

Roth, Dennis. "America's Fascination with Nutrition." *Food Review.* Volume 23, Issue 1 (January–April 2000). 10 July 2002 <http://www.ers.usda.gov/publications/foodreview/jan2000/frjan2000f.pdf>.

"Safe Handling of Cheese." Clemson Extension, Home & Garden Information Center. 13 March 2002 <http://hgic.clemson.edu/factsheets/HGIC3506.htm>.

"A Taste of the 20th Century." *Food Review,* Vol. 23, Issue 1 (January–April 2000). 14 July 2002 <http://www.ers.usda.gov/publications/foodreview/jan2000/frjan2000e.pdf>.

"Technology Leadership." *Raytheon History.* The Raytheon Company (2001). 9 May 2002 <http://www.raytheon.com/about/tech.htm>.

"Tempeh." Indiana Soybean Board (1996). 26 March 2002 <http://www.soyfoods.com/soyfoodsdescriptions/Tempeh.html>.

The 2002 Soyfoods Guide: Helpful Tips and Information for Using Soyfoods. Soy Protein Partners. 13 June 2002 <http://www.soyfoods.com/SFG2002.pdf>.

"The Waffle House Story." Waffle House, Inc. 21 March 2002 <http://www.wafflehouse.com/story.htm>.

Zander, Ann. "The Scoop on Salsa." Colorado State University Cooperative Extension (July 21, 2000). April 2002 <http://www.ext.colostate.edu/pubs/columncc/cc000721.html>.

Selected Web Resources

American Culinary Federation <http://www.acfchefs.org >

American Dietetic Association <http://www.eatright.org>

American Disabilities Act Information <http://www.usdoj.gov/crt/ada>

American Institute of Wine and Food <www.aiwf.org>

Bureau of Labor Statistics <http://www.bls.gov >

ChefNet <www.chefnet.com>

Chefs de Cuisine Association <chefsdecuisine-acfla.org>

Cook's Thesaurus <http://www.foodsubs.com>

Epicurious <http://www.epicurious.com>

Food Network: <http://www.foodtv.com>

Food Reference <http://www.foodreference.com>

Green Restaurant Association <http://www.dinegreen.com>

Hunger Information <http://www.secondharvest.org> and <http://www.strength.org>

International Council on Hotel, Restaurant, and Institutional Education <www.chrie.org>

Internet Wine Guide <http://www.internetwineguide.com>

The James Beard Foundation <www.jamesbeard.org>

Johnson & Wales University <http://www.jwu.edu >

Les Dames d'Escoffier <www.ldei.org>

National Restaurant Association <http://www.restaurant.org>

Recipe Archives <http://recipes.alastra.com >

U.S. Department of Agriculture <http://www.ers.usda.gov>

U.S. Department of Health and Human Services <http://www.hhs.gov>

U.S. Department of Labor <http://www.oalj.dol.gov>

U.S. Environmental Protection Agency <http://www.epa.gov>

U.S. Equal Employment Opportunity Commission <http://www.eeoc.gov>

U.S. Food Safety and Inspection Service <http://www.fsis.usda.gov>

U.S. Small Business Administration <http://www.sba.gov>

GLOSSARY

Subject

A

à la carte menu A bill of fare listing a variety of food items, each priced separately.

aboyeur/announcer One who gives the order to the correct chef.

abrasion Scrape or minor cut.

achenes Minute black seeds that cover strawberries.

acidulate To dip, cut, or peel fruit in citrus juice, vinegar, or water to prevent browning.

additive Substance placed in food to improve certain characteristics such as flavor or texture.

adjuncts Ingredients, other than barley, used to produce a lighter, smoother beer.

aerobic Needing oxygen to survive.

aftertaste Final flavor that remains in the mouth after food is swallowed.

agar-agar Vegetable or seaweed alternative to gelatin used to prepare meatless aspic.

aging Process by which naturally occurring enzymes tenderize meat.

al dente To the bite.

albumin Protein.

alcohol Volatile, colorless liquid obtained through the fermentation of a liquid containing sugar.

alcoholic beverage Any potable liquid containing from 0.05% to 75.5% ethyl alcohol by volume.

alcoholic distillation Process by which alcohol from a fermented liquid is evaporated, captured, and cooled to liquid form.

ale Top-fermented beer.

allumette Match-size cut.

amino acids Building blocks of protein.

amuse-bouche Complimentary small, bite-sized sampler.

anaerobic Ability to survive without oxygen.

anglais (à l') English style, plainly cooked food.

antioxidant Chemical substance that prevents or repairs damage to cells caused by exposure to oxidizing agents.

AP weight Weight of the product when purchased.

apéritif Liqueur consumed before dinner.

Appellation Contrôlée System used in France for the production of wine.

apprentice One who works under the guidance of a skilled chef in order to learn a particular skill.

arabica Highest-quality coffee.

aroma Fragrance.

aromatics Herbs, spices, and flavorings.

aromatized wine Wine served before a meal to stimulate the appetite; also called an apéritif.

arrowroot Fine powder made from the roots of the arrowroot plant; purified starch.

as purchased (AP) Price per unit paid to wholesalers.

aspic Clear jelly made from concentrated liquid in which meat, poultry, or fish was cooked.

assumptive selling Sales technique whereby servers guide the guest's choices by asking open-ended questions.

ATF Bureau of Alcohol, Tobacco, and Firearms.

autolysis Process in which sucrose is extracted from wheat, giving bread a sweeter and nuttier taste.

AVA American Viticultural Area.

avulsion Partially or completely removed portion of skin.

B

bacteria Tiny, single-celled microorganisms; leading cause of food-borne illness.

bain-marie Double-boiler insert used for slow cooking; also used as a steam table in which smaller pans and their contents are kept hot.

baked Alaska Ice cream covered with merigue quickly baked in the oven.

baker's percentage Percentage of each ingredient in relationship to the weight of flour in the final baked product.

baking Dry cooking technique that uses dry, hot air to cook food in a closed environment.

balance scale Two-platform scale used in bakeshops.

ballotine Stuffed boneless game or domestic bird served hot or cold.

banquet Style of service in which all guests are served at the same time and the meal is predetermined.

banquette Type of seating arrangement in which guests are seated facing the dining room with their backs against a wall or partition.

barbecueing Dry cooking technique in which food is slowly roasted over burning wood or hot wood coals.

barding Wrapping lean meats with fat.

barquette Small boat-shaped pastry or mold.

base Powdered or concentrated form of stock; foundation of an hors d'oeuvre.

base notes (background notes) Aromas with the largest, heaviest molecules, which do not evaporate.

batch cooking Process of preparing small amounts of food several times a day.

batonnet Long, rectangular cut similar to the julienne.

batter Semiliquid mixture that combines a liquid such as milk with a starch such as flour; liquid dough thin enough to pour.

béchamel Basic white sauce.

beignets Fritters.

benching Period when dough rests, allowing the gluten to relax; also called intermediate proof.

beurre blanc White butter.

beurre manié Kneaded butter, or uncooked thickening agent, used for thickening sauces.

beurre noir Black butter.

beurre noisette Brown butter.

beverage cost Total dollar amount spent by a foodservice operation to purchase the ingredients needed to produce a beverage item.

biga Firm mixture of water, flour, and yeast giving bread a closed crumb structure.

binder Ingredients, such as panadas and egg whites, added to forcemeat to provide greater shape and smoothness.

biological hazards Disease-causing microorganisms such as bacteria and viruses.

biscuit method Quick bread mixing method in which fat is cut or rubbed into flour, creating a mixture with the consistency of cornmeal.

bisque Thick cream soup made from shellfish.

bitter Very bitter, or bittersweet, liquid distilled from various herbs and roots.

bivalve Mollusk with two shells hinged together; oysters, clams.

black tea Strongly flavored tea with an amber or coppery brown color; varieties include Earl Grey and English breakfast.

blanching Moist cooking technique used to partially cook food before using another cooking method to finish the cooking process.

blanquette White stew.

blast chiller Special refrigeration unit designed to quickly chill prepared foods by drawing hot air away from the food and forcing cold air across it.

blazer pans Used to prepare oval, rectangular, or round food items, such as crêpes, tableside.

blending method Mixing quickbread dry ingredients, except sugar, and then combining them with wet ingredients and the sugar.

blind baking Baking an unfilled pie crust.

block frozen Fish or fish pieces frozen together in a block for shipping.

bloom Dusty white coating on grapes indicating that they have been recently harvested.

blueprint Drawing that shows what a platter will look like with food displayed.

bob veal Youngest veal calves marketed, aged several days to four weeks.

body mass index (BMI) Measure of a person's weight in relation to height.

boiling Moist cooking technique that transfers heat to food through convection, using a greater amount of liquid and with greater agitation than poaching or simmering.

bolster Metal point on the knife where the blade and handle meet; also called a shank.

bombe Several layers of molded ice cream served with meringue.

boneless fish Fish with cartilage instead of bones, such as sharks and rays.

bouchée Small edible container made of puff pastry.

boucher/butcher One who cuts or butchers meats and poultry.

bouillabaisse Fish stew, a speciality of southern France.

boulanger/baker One who bakes.

bound salad Salad made with mayonnaise or other dressing that binds the ingredients together; tuna salad, chicken salad, potato salad.

bouquet Fragrance that results from fermentation and aging.

bouquet garni Aromatics tied together in a sachet bag, consisting of thyme leaves, bay leaves, whole black peppercorns, and parsley stems.

bracelet Primal rack of lamb with the adjoining breast pieces intact.

braisière Braising pan or stewing pan with lid.

braising Combination cooking technique in which food is cooked in a small amount of liquid over low heat.

bran Outer protective covering of a grain kernel.

brassica Quick-growing, cool-weather vegetable used for its head, flower, or leaves.

breading Process of coating food with bread crumbs in preparation for frying.

brigade System that identifies the professional staff duties in a kitchen operation.

brine Mixture of water, salt, and sometimes seasonings.

broiling Dry cooking technique that uses radiant heat from above to cook food.

broth Liquid that results from simmering meat, poultry, or fish with vegetables and aromatics to produce a clear soup.

brunoise Very fine dice cut.

bruschetta Italian bread slathered with olive oil, chopped tomatoes, herbs, and pecorino romano cheese.

buffet service Style of service in which guests serve themselves, choosing from a variety of food items located in a central zone or buffet area; includes simple, modified deluxe, and deluxe service.

buffetier One who maintains the buffet; part of the garde-manger brigade system.

bulbs Category of vegetables used mostly for flavoring and seasoning other food.

butler service Similar to Russian service except that the guest, not the server, serves the food item from the platter, tureen, or casserole dish.

butterflied Dressed and cut so that the two sides lie open and attached.

buttermilk Liquid left after butter has been churned from cream.

C

cake Sweet, baked mixture of flour, liquid, eggs, and other ingredients; three basic types of cake: sponge, layer, and pound.

calf Veal calves 20 weeks or older.

calibrated Adjusted to standard.

calorie Food energy measured in units of heat.

Canadian bacon Boneless pork loin, trimmed and then brine-cured and smoked.

canapé Small, open-faced sandwich made of toasted bread, garnished and served as an appetizer or snack.

candling Process of holding an egg up to a light to check the shell for cracks and tiny holes.

cannoli Cylinders of sweet, crispy pastry filled with a variety of fillings, from sweet ricotta cheese to pastry-cream with dried fruit and nuts.

capers Pickled flower buds.

carbohydrate Compound made up of sugar units; classified as simple or complex.

carbon dioxide Gas formed during periods of fermentation caused by the action of yeast or chemical leaveners, baking powder, or baking soda.

carcass Whole animal after slaughter, minus the head, feet, hide, and entrails.

caramelization Process of heating sugar above its melting point until the sugar units break down.

carré Large dice cut.

carryover cooking Continued cooking that occurs even after food is removed from the heat source.

casein Primary protein in milk.

cayenne Very hot red pepper.

cephalopod Mollusk with a thin internal shell but no outer protection; octopus, squid.

certified milk Milk that has met strict sanitary conditions.

chafing dish Holds hotel pans filled with food for service.

chain restaurant Foodservice operation in which the atmosphere, service, menu, and quality of food are established by a parent company.

chalaza Twisted white cord that holds the yolk in place within the shell.

chambréing Process of bringing wine to room temperature for service.

charcuterie Cooking of flesh, especially that of pig.

charcutier One who makes all sausage and smoked items; part of the garde-manger brigade system.

chaud-froid Food coated with cold white sauce.

chauffe plats Heat-retaining panels used to keep food warm during tableside plating.

chef de cuisine Chef in charge or executive chef.

chef de rang/captain One who explains the menu to the guests, takes the order, and prepares food tableside.

chef de sale/dining room manager Person responsible for service in the dining room.

chemical hazards Substances such as cleaning supplies and pesticides that may cause food contamination.

chévre Cheese made from goat's milk.

chiffonnade Cut used on leaf vegetables producing shredded or thinly cut ribbons.

chinois Cone-shaped fine strainer or sieve; also called a china cap.

cholesterol Waxy substance in the body cells of all animals, found only in foods of animal origin; needed by humans to produce hormones, cell membranes, bile, and vitamin D.

chowder Specialty soup made with shellfish or fish and vegetables.

churning Mixing, as when making butter or ice cream.

ciabatta Classic Italian bread.

classic cuisine Escoffier's version of grande cuisine, observing the basic principles of classical French cooking without complicated procedures.

clarified butter Pure butterfat; also called drawn butter.

cleaning Removing all visible dirt and grime.

cleanup Mixing stage when the dough's ingredients have been properly hydrated and the dough has a cohesive consistency, forming a ball.

clearmeat Collection of ingredients used to clarify consommé.

clip-on Printed menu, fastened to the inside of the main menu, that draws attention to seasonal offerings and specials.

coagulate To change from a liquid or semiliquid state to a solid state.

coarse chopping Process of cutting food into imprecise but relatively uniform sizes.

cocktail Short drink made by mixing liquor or wine with fruit juices, eggs, and/or bitters.

cold closed sandwich Made with a split roll or two pieces of bread encasing a cold filling.

cold open-faced sandwich Bite-sized sandwich usually served as hors d'oeuvre.

cold-pack cheese Mixture of one or more varieties of cheeses, ground together; also called club cheese.

cold paddles Paddles filled with water, frozen, and placed in food such as soup to chill it quickly.

cold smoking Process of imparting flavor to food without cooking it; also called slow smoking.

cold triple-decker sandwich Similar to the hot variety; made with cold fillings and served cold.

collagen Soft, white connective tissue; breaks down into water and gelatin when cooked slowly with moist heat.

combination cooking Transferring heat via both moist and dry techniques.

commercial operation Fast-food chain or restaurant in business to make a profit.

commis Apprentice in the kitchen or dining room.

commis de barrasseur/busser One who clears and grooms the table.

commis de suite/back waiter One who places and picks up orders from the kitchen.

commis de rang/front waiter One who serves food and beverages to guests.

common chemical sense Sensory system made up of nerve endings that perceive feeling factors.

communard One who prepares food for the staff.

comparative buying Purchasing from two or more vendors to study the differences between them.

competitors' pricing method Pricing menu items in relation to those of a restaurant's competitors.

complementary proteins Combination of amino acids from separate foods by the body.

complete proteins Proteins that contain all essential amino acids.

complex carbohydrates Composed of starch and fiber units; maintain the body's digestive system.

composed hors d'oeuvre Appetizer that contains two or more food elements; canapé, bouchée.

compound butter Butter with one or more ingredients added to change its color or flavor; can be simple or complex.

compound sauce Any of the leading sauce derivatives.

conching Process by which huge granite rollers slowly combine heated chocolate liquor, eliminating water and unstable acids.

condensed milk Milk that has been evaporated and condensed, with sugar added as a preservative.

condiment Flavored sauce served as an accompaniment to food; relishes, pickles, mustards, ketchup.

conditioning Storing beer in vats for a specified length of time after fermentation.

conduction Direct exchange of heat by physical contact with another item.

confit Meat cooked and preserved in fat; fruit preserved in sugar or liquor.

congener Flavoring agent.

connective tissue Web of proteins that covers individual muscle fibers, bundles the fibers together, and attaches them to the bones; the amount present determines the texture of meat.

consommé Clarified, fortified soup made from broth or stock and additional ingredients.

contamination To make impure through contact or mixture.

continental breakfast Quick meal consisting of coffee, a bread or pastry, and fruit.

convection Direct exchange of heat through a liquid or gas.

conversion factor Number that results from dividing the desired yield by the existing standard yield.

cook-chill system Cooking and chilling large quantities of food for reheating at a later time.

cookie Small cakes; three basic types are crisp, chewy, and soft; cookie varieties include bagged, bar, dropped, icebox, molded, rolled, sheet, and wafer.

cooking Process of transferring energy from a heat source to food.

cooking line Arrangement of the kitchen equipment.

cooking loss test Performed on products that must be cooked before the edible yield weight is determined.

coral Lobster eggs or ovaries.

cordial Sweet alcoholic beverage.

cornstarch One of the most easily digested starch foods; cooks transparent.

cost Amount of money paid out by a foodservice operation to produce food and to serve its customers.

cost of sales Combination of both food and beverage costs spent by a foodservice operation.

coulis Dessert sauce made from fresh, canned, or frozen fruit.

coupe Ice cream served in a dessert glass with fruit or sauce.

court-bouillon Aromatic short-broth used to poach fish, sweetbread, and so on.

couscous Granular semolina flour resembling yellow pellets.

couverture High-quality dark, milk, and white chocolate.

cover letter Letter that accompanies and introduces the résumé and includes a brief summary of qualifications.

cream puff Light, delicate hollow puff served as a dessert with whipped cream or custard filling.

creaming method Blending softened fat or butter with sugar and gradually adding the remaining ingredients.

crema Emulsified coffee oils that float on the surface of freshly brewed espresso.

crème anglaise Mixture of milk, heavy cream, sugar, and eggs or egg yolks cooked over a water bath.

crème brûlée Thicker custard made with heavy cream, eggs, and additional egg yolks.

crème caramel Custard baked over caramelized sugar.

crème fraîche Heavy, cultured cream that resembles a thinner, richer version of sour cream.

crêpe Thin pancake prepared from an egg-rich batter; a quick bread.

critical control point Last point in the flow of food where a potential hazard can be prevented.

cross-contamination To transfer microorganisms or harmful bacteria from one source to another.

croûtons Fried or toasted pieces of bread of various sizes and shapes served as accompaniments to soups or used as a socle.

crumb crust Pie crust made from finely ground cookies or graham crackers.

crumbing To clear the table of crumbs and other food particles between courses.

crunch Decorative cookie that offers textural contrast to the main plated dessert item.

crustaceans Shellfish with jointed exterior skeletons.

cuisine minceur Cookery of slimness that reduces calories without sacrificing flavor.

curdle To separate and congeal, as egg solids do when overcooked.

curds Coagulated milk solids.

curing Process of preserving food with salt or by drying or aging; includes dry curing and wet curing.

custard Combination of eggs, sugar, and milk or cream that thickens as the egg proteins coagulate during baking.

cutlery Knives.

cuvée Juice from the first pressing of grapes.

cycle menu Menu that changes daily for a set period of time.

D

daily production report Form that helps control and manage costs and show how much product was prepared, how much was sold, and how much was not used.

daily values Amount of nutrients a person needs every day on the basis of a 2000-calorie diet.

dairy product Usually associated with products that are derived from milk; this category has been extended to include eggs, cheese, and margarine.

darne Thick cross-section of fish.

death phase Period in which more bacteria are dying than growing; a population decline.

débarrasser/busser One who clears the table.

decanting To pour wine from its bottle into a decanter in order to separate the wine from sediments and to accelerate its exposure to oxygen.

deep-frying Dry cooking technique that cooks food by completely submersing it in hot fat.

deglazing Dissolving cooked food particles in a pan with wine or a stock.

Delmonico steak Tender strip of boneless top loin.

demi-glace Half glaze; brown sauce.

demitasse Half cup used to serve espresso; also a small cup of black coffee.

denaturation Breakdown of protein by acid.

dépouillage Process of removing fat and impurities from the surface of liquid during cooking.

descriptive copy Text that describes each food item on the menu.

desired dough temperature (DDT) Unique temperature to each type of dough.

détrempe Mixture of flour and water.

diatase Enzyme that converts starches into sugars; essential in yeast breads.

digestif Liqueur consumed after dinner.

direct contamination Occurs when raw foods or the plants and animals from which they come are exposed to toxins in their natural environment.

disc Upper surface of wine.

discrimination Unfair treatment based on age, gender, race, ethnicity, religion, physical appearance, disability, or other attributes.

docking Making small holes in the surface of dough.

domestic game Animals and birds bred and raised in a farmlike environment.

drawn fish Whole fish with the internal organs removed.

dredge To coat lightly, usually with seasoned flour or sugar.

dress To kill, bleed, and defeather poultry.

dressed fish Fish with internal organs, gills, fins, and scales removed.

drip loss Loss of moisture that occurs as fish thaws.

drupe Stone fruit.

dry aging Process of hanging large, unpacked cuts of meat in a controlled environment for a period of six weeks.

dry cooking Transfer of heat by hot metal, hot air, hot fat, or radiation.

dry curing Drying a food product in granular salt.

dry milk solids (DMS) Most concentrated form of milk, containing no more than 5% moisture.

dry-rendered leaf lard Made from the internal fat of a pig.

dry slow baking Technique of baking slowly at low heat allowing the moisture in a food product to evaporate.

dues Regular fees required for membership in a professional organization.

E

eclair Rich, finger-shaped pastry filled with cream.

economies of scale Price breaks for purchasing in larger quantities.

edible portion (E.P.) Cost of a usable portion of the product, incorporating loss from trimming, shrinkage, and packaging.

edible yield Usable portion of the food product after it has been trimmed.

edible yield portion Percentage of a food product left after trim and/or shrinkage.

egg wash Mixture of egg and milk or water.

elastin Hard, yellow connective tissue that does not break down during cooking; prevalent in older animals.

emulsification Method of thickening sauces.

emulsifier Substance that allows two or more liquids that usually do not mix to form a stable mixture or emulsion.

en papillote Moist cooking technique that bakes food in sealed parchment paper with aromatics and liquid.

enchilada Rolled flour tortilla filled with a mixture containing meats or cheeses and covered with a spicy sauce.

endosperm Main part of the seed from which flour or meal is made; innermost portion.

enriched soft/medium dough Most popular type of yeast-raised product, producing a soft crust and crumb.

entrails Internal organs.

entremetier/vegetable chef One who prepares all hot appetizers, vegetables, soups, pasta, and egg dishes.

entrepreneur Self-motivated individual who creates and operates a business, putting forth all the risk but reaping all the rewards.

enzymes Class of protein substances produced by living cells; act as catalysts in metabolism.

espresso Thick, dark, intensely fragrant beverage; espresso-based drinks include americano, caffe latte, and cappuccino.

essence Significantly reduced liquid with a dominant prevailing flavor.

ethylene gas Colorless, odorless gas given off by fruit as it ripens.

evaporate To escape in the air, as in moisture.

extract Concentrated substance made by infusing alcohol with natural ingredients such as vanilla.

extractor Used to liquefy fruits and vegetables.

extrude To force dough through a pierced disk or plate.

espagnole Basic brown sauce.

evaporated milk Canned concentrated milk.

eviscerate To remove an animal's entrails.

F

fabricated cut Smallest portion of meat taken from the subprimal cut.

facultative Ability to survive with or without oxygen.

family-style service Style of service in which all food is prepared in the kitchen and served on platters or in casseroles and tureens placed in the center of the guests' table for self-service.

fan Ratite thigh meat.

fanning Decorative cut used to spread vegetables into a fan shape.

fast aging Aging meat via the use of ultraviolet light.

fat Lipid that is solid at room temperature.

fat cap Layer of fat that surrounds the muscle tissue.

fat compound Combination of 20% rendered animal fat and 80% hydrogenated vegetable oil.

feathered game Large and small animals including woodcock and ostrich.

fermentation Chemical reaction in a yeast-raised dough or other mixture brought about by carbon dioxide gas.

fermented dairy product Product with the addition of a starter bacterial culture; also called cultured dairy product.

fermenting solution Liquid flavored and seasoned with herbs and spices to impart flavor to a base vegetable.

fillet Thin cut of meat, poultry, and so on; the skinless flesh of fish removed from bone.

filtered Aged liquid; process used to dispel the harshness of a spirit.

finger sandwich Thinly sliced bread cut into shapes with the crust removed; bite-sized.

fining Process used to clarify wine.

first aid Assisting an injured person until professional medical help arrives.

first in, first out (FIFO) Method of rotation of goods whereby older items are moved to the front and used before newer ones.

fixed menu Menu that offers the same dishes every day for an extended period of time.

flambé To flame.

flaming swords Used for flambé service.

flat fish Fish with a flat body and backbone that runs horizontally through the center of its body.

flat-top range Solid plate of metal that conceals the burners below; also called a French-top range.

flatware Generic term referring to all dining utensils.

flavor Blend of taste, aroma, and feeling factor sensations.

flavor enhancer Added to food to increase the perception of taste without altering the food's flavor.

flavor profile Description of a product's flavor from the time it is first smelled until after it is swallowed.

flavoring Substance commonly added to food to change and strengthen flavor.

flow of food Process by which food items move through a foodservice operation, beginning with receiving and ending with reheating.

fluting Decorative cut used to prepare vegetables such as mushrooms; method of finishing a pie crust by making pleats or folds in the dough.

focaccia Italian flat bread.

foie gras Fattened duck or goose liver.

folded dough Dough to which a fat has been added and folded in numerous times.

folding in Using the hand or a rubber spatula when combining two or more mixtures without the loss of air.

food allergy Reaction by the body's immune system to proteins found in some foods.

food cost Total dollar amount spent by a foodservice operation to purchase food and beverages for resale.

food intolerance Side affects and problems that result from consuming certain foods; not an allergic reaction.

forcemeat Uncooked ground meat, poultry, fish, shellfish, and vegetables that are seasoned and emulsified with fat; four types: straight, country-style, gratin, and mousseline.

forequarter Front portion of a split carcass.

foresaddle Front portion of a calf.

formula Standardized recipe used in baking.

fraise des bois Small alpine strawberry.

frangipane Almond pastry cream.

freeze Frozen drink.

freezer burn Light-colored spots that appear on frozen food indicating that surface drying has occurred.

French service Elaborate style of service in which food is prepared tableside and served to the guests.

frenching Cutting away from lamb the excess fat from the eye muscle and trimming meat and connective tissue from the ribs on a rack or chops.

fricassé White stew.

friturier/fry chef One who cooks fried foods.

fruit-vegetable Any vegetable that develops from the ovary of a flowering plant and contains one or more seeds.

fumet Concentrated stock made from vegetables, fowl, poultry, game, or fish.

functional food Food that provides health benefits beyond basic nutrients.

fungi Microorganisms found in plants, animals, soil, water, and the air, also responsible for some types of foodborne illnesses.

furred game Large and small animals including deer, elk, moose, rabbit, and squirrel.

fusion cuisine Combination of culinary elements from the United States, France, Spain, Italy, China, and Thailand.

G

galantine Boned poultry or game stuffed and rolled, poached in its own skin, and served cold.

game Wild species of animals and birds.

garde-manger/pantry chef Literally translated, means "keeper of food to be eaten"; cold-kitchen chef who prepares cold food items such as appetizers, pâtés, mousses, and galantines.

garnish Optional, decorative, edible accompaniment that is placed on food to improve visual appeal.

gaufrette Waffle cut.

gelatin Obtained from the cartilage in skin and bones of animals; gives stock its body.

gelato Italian-style ice cream with a dense texture.

genetically modified organisms (GMO) Foods that have undergone a change in their genes.

germ Embryo that produces a new plant; gives wheat its nutty taste.

germinate To grow.

glace White or brown stock reduced 85%–90% through simmering.

glaze Thin coating applied to baked goods to add color, shine, and flavor, and to preserve moisture.

gliadin Component that provides dough with elasticity.

glucose Single sugar that makes up half of sucrose (table sugar).

gluten Protein found in wheat flour; serves as the structure in yeast dough.

glutenin Component that gives dough strength and structure and the ability to retain the gases given off by the yeast.

gnocchi Italian dumplings made of semolina, flour, or potatoes.

goujonette Finger-sized strip of fish cut from the fillet.

gourds Vegetables with large, complex root systems, trailing vines, and large leaves.

grading Measuring the quality of foods; may be mandatory or voluntary, depending on the food product.

grains Seeds from edible cereal plants.

grande cuisine Elaborate cuisine consisting of many courses following strict cooking rules.

granita Italian ice made with puréed fruit, sugar syrup, and sometimes fruit juice or alcohol.

gravlax Cured, uncooked salmon.

green shrimp Fresh or frozen headless shrimp.

green tea Unfermented, yellowish-green tea with a slightly bitter flavor.

griddling Dry cooking technique that involves cooking food on a solid metal surface over a gas or electric heat source.

grillardin/grill chef One who produces all grilled foods.

grilled sandwich Sandwich that is hot from the inside out.

grilling Dry cooking technique that uses radiant heat from below to cook food on an open grid.

grist Coarse meal made from barley.

grits Hominy that has been coarsely ground into meal.

grosse pièce Centerpiece with a large, uncut portion of the main food item.

guéridon Portable work table used for all tableside preparation.

H

halal Following or in accordance with Muslim dietary laws.

hand tool Any handheld tool used in the preparation, cooking, baking, or service of food.

hash Finely chopped roast or corned beef combined with cubed potatoes.

Hazard Analysis Critical Control Point (HACCP) System used to monitor the flow of food.

heat transfer Efficiency with which heat passes from one object to another; can be accomplished by conduction, convection, or radiation.

herbs Fragrant leaves, stems, buds, or flowers from aromatic perennial or annual plants.

high-density lipoproteins (HDL) Good cholesterol; carries excess cholestrol in the blood to the liver where it leaves the body.

high-ratio shortening Vegetable shortening with mono- and diglycerides added to improve emulsifying properties.

high tea Light, midday meal that bridges the gap between early-morning breakfasts and late-evening dinners; also called afternoon tea.

highball Drink consisting of a carbonated mixer, water, or juice and liquor.

highlighting Sales technique whereby the server draws the guest's attention to particular menu items as an order is placed.

hindquarter Rear portion of a split carcass.

hindsaddle Rear portion of a calf.

holding cabinet Large, wheeled, metal container used to hold sheet pans of food.

holding equipment Allows prepared foods or ingredients to be held at the proper temperature.

hollandaise Basic warm butter sauce.

hollowware Service pieces such as water pitchers, teapots, sauce boats, and cake plates.

hominy Dried corn kernel with the hull and germ removed.

homogenization Process of breaking down fat globules by forcing warm milk through a very fine nozzle.

hop Cone-shaped flower; preserves beer and imparts aroma and bitterness.

hors d'oeuvre Appetizer served hot or cold at the beginning of a meal.

hors d'oeuvre variés Assortment of light, tasty items plated on a platter or cart.

hors d'oeuvrier One who creates and prepares all hors d'oeuvre; part of the garde-manger brigade.

hot closed sandwich Sandwich with a hot filling between two slices of bread or split roll.

hot open-faced sandwich Made with a hot filling stacked on a slice of bread and often covered with a sauce.

hot smoking Process of smoking and cooking food at the same time; also called fast smoking.

huevos rancheros Classic Mexican egg sandwich.

hydrogenated fat Shortening processed from a vegetable oil by the addition of hydrogen to improve color, melting point, firmness, and emulsification.

hydrogenation Process that forces hydrogen into fat and oil.

I

icing Decorative, sweet coating for cake and other baked goods; types include fudge, boiled, fondant, flat, royal, and buttercream.

improved mix method Most common method of mixing and kneading dough items.

incomplete proteins Proteins missing one or more essential amino acid.

independent restaurant Foodservice operation that is not affiliated with any theme or brand.

independent sauce Any sauce that does not rely on another sauce or stock for preparation, such as applesauce or curry sauce.

infection Result of pathogens growing in the intestines of a person who consumed contaminated food.

infusion Process of steeping flavoring agents in water.

insoluble fiber Fiber that absorbs water.

intensive mix method Requires dough mixture to be mixed for an extended amount of time.

intermezzo service Pause or intermission between two courses during which a sorbet, sherbet, or granita is served to cleanse the palate.

intoxication Occurs when pathogens produce toxins that cannot be seen, tasted, or smelled, such as in the case of botulism; drunkenness.

invoice List of the products that are being delivered, including amount, description, weight or count per package, unit price, and extension, as well as terms of payment and total cost to the operation, including taxes and transportation costs.

invoice cost per unit Cost to purchase an ingredient in a specified unit.

IQF Individually quick frozen packaging of meat and fish.

irradiation Process of exposing food to radiant energy in a controlled environment in an efffort to kill harmful bacteria, insects, and fungi, or to slow ripening.

isinglass Gelatin obtained from fish and used as aspic.

isoflavones Phytochemicals.

J

jigger Legal measure of 1.5 ounces (45 ml) of liquid.

jugging Preserving game by cooking and storing it in fat.

julienne Matchstick cut.

jus Natural juice of meat, vegetable, or fruit.

K

kashruth Jewish dietary laws.

kataifi Shredded phyllo dough.

keywords Significant words, such as foodservice, included in one's résumé that indicate a match between background and qualifications and the job requirements.

kiln To dry.

L

labor cost Cost of paying employees wages, salaries, and benefits.

laceration Deep cut or tear in the skin.

lacto vegetarian One who eats dairy products but not eggs, meat, poultry, or fish.

lacto-ovo vegetarian One who eats dairy and egg products but not meat, poultry, or fish.

lag phase Period of time when bacteria adjust to their new environment.

lager Bottom-fermented beer.

lagering Process of fermenting stubborn sugars during the conditioning of beer.

laminated dough/rolled-in fat dough Dough with many layers of dough and fat, adding to the final product's flavor, tenderness, and flakiness.

lard Fat obtained from the fatty tissue of pigs.

larding Inserting long, thin strips of fat with a larding needle into lean meat.

lattice crust Interwoven strips of dough placed across the top of a pie.

leach To dissolve in water.

leading sauces Basic sauces from which all other sauces are derived; brown sauces, white sauces, tomato sauces, warm butter sauces, and oil-based sauces; also called mother sauces.

leafy vegetables Tender, green vegetables cooked or served raw.

lean/hard dough Made with four basic ingredients; contains no or little sugar; produces a crispy crust and chewy crumb.

leavening agent Substance that causes a baked good to rise.

lecithin Natural emulsifier found in egg yolks.

lees Sediment containing dead yeast and other solids that collects in the bottom of a wine tank after fermentation.

legs Residual wine that clings to the glass.

legumes Seeds from plants; sometimes split when ripe.

letter of request Letter asking a potential employer for an application form or request for an interview.

liaison Thickening or binding agent consisting of cream and egg yolks; used in the preparation of a sauce.

liner Optional ingredient used on sandwiches or hors d'oeuvre to add texture and visual appeal.

lipid Organic compound that is insoluble in water but can be used by the body; fats and oils.

liquid smoking Process of using a smoke-flavored liquid to impart flavor to food without subjecting it to the smoking process.

log phase Period of accelerated bacterial growth.

low-density lipoprotein (LDL) Bad cholesterol; carries cholesterol to tissues, where it slowly builds up as a thick, hard, deposit.

lowboy Under the counter refrigerator unit that may also serve as a counter.

M

macédoine 1/4-inch (6-mm) square dice cut.

Maillard browning Process of heating the sugars in food above their melting point until the sugar units break down and browning occurs.

maître d'hôtel One who is in charge of all front-of-house operations.

malting Brewing process with three essential steps: steeping, germinating, and kilning.

maltose Grain sugar.

mandoline Specialized cutting tool used to make gaufrette or julienne slices.

mantle Edible, hollow body-tube of squid.

marbling Fat within the muscle tissue.

margarine Often referred to as a butter substitute; made from blending animal or vegetable fats with additives for color, flavor, and absorption.

marinade Blend of liquids and flavorings used for soaking a main ingredient, such as meat.

market form Purchase form for poultry such as fresh, frozen, and fully cooked.

marmite Stockpot.

masa harina Flour made from finely ground hominy.

mash Combination of grain meal and water.

mash tun Large container where grist is mashed with hot water.

mass Amount of matter, or the weight of an object.

material safety data sheets (MSDS) List of chemicals that pose a possible hazard and advice on ways to avoid these hazards.

mayonnaise Sauce made with oil and egg yolks.

measurement Amount of an ingredient that is included in the baker's formula or chef's recipe.

mechanical convection Distribution of heat by mechanical means.

menu Bill of fare listing the dishes offered by the foodservice operation.

menu board Handwritten menu printed on a chalkboard, white board, or easel.

meringue Delicate, fluffy mixture of stiffly whipped egg whites plus sugar; used as an icing, ingredient, or dried pastry item; three basic types include common, Swiss, and Italian.

metric system System of measurement that is commonly used worldwide.

middle notes Aromas with large molecules that slowly evaporate, thereby providing satisfying staying power to food.

milling Process of breaking down grain into finer particles or of grinding barley into grist.

mincing Process of cutting food into very fine pieces.

minerals Essential elements needed by the body in very small amounts; classified as major minerals and trace minerals.

mirepoix Roughly chopped vegetables and herbs sautéed in fat and used to add flavor.

mise en place Literally, put in place; the kitchen expression for being prepared for cooking or for service.

mixed drink Tall drink, served over ice; combination of liquor and mixer.

mixology The study of cocktails, mixed drinks, and their ingredients.

modified atmosphere packaging (MAP) Packaging system that replaces air with gas such as carbon dioxide or nitrogen.

modified straight dough method Combines the straight dough method with the creaming method to ensure an even distribution of fat and sugar.

moist cooking Transferring heat through a liquid other than oil.

mollusks Various types of unjointed shellfish with shells that protect their soft bodies; includes univalves, bivalves, and cephalopods.

monosodium glutamate (MSG) Sodium salt of glutamic acid occuring naturally in a number of foods.

monounsaturated fat Fat that is liquid at room temperature.

monte au beurre To enrich a sauce or reduction by dropping in small pieces of butter and tossing to blend.

mooshi sandwich Stir-fried vegetables and meats or fish wrapped in thin pancakes.

mousse Sweet or savory forcemeat mixture of poultry, fish, vegetables, or fruit and whipped cream or beaten eggs prepared in molds; dessert mixture of whipped cream, whipped egg whites or egg yolks, and flavorings.

muffaletta Regional sandwich originating in New Orleans.

mushrooms Members of the fungi family that have no seeds, stems, or flowers.

must Extracted juice of grapes with minimal fragments of stems, seeds, or skin.

mutage Process in which the fermentation of wine stops and sweetness is retained.

mutual supplementation Strategy of eating two protein-rich foods that, when combined, contain all the essential amino acids.

mycoprotein Fermented fungi.

myoglobin Primary substance that gives meat its red color.

N

napoleons Pastry docked heavily before it is baked, cut into rectangles, and filled with a pastry cream.

natural convection Distribution of heat by the continuous, natural movement of a liquid or gas.

neapolitan Three-layer ice cream "cake."

Neolithic period New Stone Age.

networking To make use of personal contacts to achieve one's career goals.

noncommercial operation Foodservice operation such as a government facility, school, hospital, or the armed forces that aims to cover daily expenses.

nonedibles Nonfood products.

nonfat dry milk Whole milk in dry form after the fat has been removed.

nonperishable Food item with a long shelf life, whose quality is unaffected when stored for up to one year.

notice Letter or memo informing your current employer of your intent to leave your current position.

nourishing element Most important element of a stock; provides flavor, nutrients, and color.

nouvelle cuisine New cooking that moved away from rich sauces, intricate garnishes, and traditional accompaniments for lighter, fresher food that is simple yet elegant.

nut butter Smooth spread made from whole nuts and used in dough, frostings, fillings, and ice cream.

nutrients Chemical compounds that make up food and perform one or more functions: supply energy, build and repair tissue, or regulate body processes; includes macronutrients and micronutrients.

nutrition Process by which food is taken in and used.

O

oblique Cut that creates a wedge-shaped piece with two diagonal sides.

off-site catering Foodservice operation that prepares food in a centralized kitchen and delivers it to the customer's event or location.

oil A lipid that is liquid at room temperature.

on-site catering Foodservice operation that caters special events at the customer's locations.

oolong tea Flavored tea with the characteristics of both green and black teas; varieties include black dragon and pouchong.

opacity Degree or quality of opaqueness.

open market Common system of buying that requires a restaurateur to secure price quotes for identical items from several sources of supply.

open-spit roasting Roasting foods over an open fire.

operating expenses Combination of labor and overhead expenses.

outside contractor Independent business contracted to provide a specific service.

oven spring Rapid expansion of dough caused by the yeast's reaction to the heat of the oven.

overhead cost All expenses an organization incurs except food, labor, and profit.

overrun Increase in volume to ice cream as a result of the incorporation of air.

ovo vegetarian One who eats eggs, but no meat, poultry, fish, or dairy.

oxidative rancidity To become rancid when exposed to oxygen.

P

pale malt The most common type of beer; light in color.

Paleolithic period Old Stone Age.

pan gravy Sauce that incorporates pan drippings.

pan smoking Smoking food in a covered pan under high heat; also called roast smoking.

panada Binding agent, usually for forcemeats or stuffing.

panning Matching the dough weight to the pan size, ensuring even distribution of heat.

papain Enzyme in papayas that serves as an excellent meat tenderizer.

par Inventory system that establishes the range of minimum to maximum desirable amount of product on hand.

parasites Tiny organisms that must live on a host to survive, and are also responsible for foodborne illnesses.

parmentier 1/2-inch (12-mm) square dice cut.

pasteurization Processing of milk and other liquids to prevent spoilage.

parstock Amount of a product kept on hand between deliveries.

pastry cream Egg custard thickened with cornstarch and/or flour.

pâté Rich, ground forcemeat enclosed in a layer of fat and then baked; paste or pastry.

pâte à bombe Mixture of whipped egg yolks and hot sugar syrup.

pâte à choux Paste composed of bread flour, water or milk, fat, eggs, and salt; used to prepare many desserts, including éclairs and cream-puff shells.

pâté en croûte Rich, ground forcemeat baked in pastry dough.

pâté en terrine Ground forcemeat enclosed in a layer of fat and then baked in a mold with a thin layer of fat.

pâté fermenté Piece of overfermented dough that contains the same ingredients as new dough; one of the oldest forms of bread making.

pathogens Disease-producing bacteria responsible for 95% of all foodborne illnesses.

patissier/pastry chef One who produces all baked goods, desserts, and pastries.

paupiette Thin, flattened slices of meat or fish, stuffed and rolled.

paysanne Triangular-shaped vegetable cut.

periodic ordering method Establishes how much product will be used for a given period of time.

perishable Food product that has a relatively short shelf life.

perpetual inventory Sophisticated inventory system used to maintain constant records of expensive and highly perishable inventory items.

pesco vegetarian One who eats fish but no meat or poultry.

phyllo dough Paper-thin pastry dough.

physical hazards Foreign particles such as glass, toothpicks, and keys that contaminate food.

phytochemicals Nonnutritive chemicals made by plants that may help guard against disease.

pickup Mixing stage when the ingredients are first incorporated and the dough starts to form.

pico de gallo Sauce made from a variety of fresh ingredients such as cilantro, tomatoes, and chilies.

pièce montée Centerpiece on a platter or buffet.

pigment Matter in cells and tissues of plants and animals that provides color.

pilaf Rice dish with or without meat.

pilferage Theft in small quantities.

pips Grape seeds.

pith Bitter white section of citrus fruit that lies beneath the zest.

plate cost Amount of a menu item.

poaching Moist cooking technique that cooks food gently in a small amount of flavorful liquid.

point-of-sale system Computerized system used to place orders with kitchen staff.

poissonier/fish chef One who is responsible for all fish preparations and their sauces.

polenta Type of porridge that becomes solid when cold.

pollo vegetarian One who eats poultry but no meat or fish.

polyunsaturated fats Fats that are liquid at room temperature.

pome Tree fruit with a central core, such as an apple.

poolish Mixture of equal parts of flour and water with a small amount of yeast; used to break down some of the starches in flour, converting them to sugar.

portfolio Collection that highlights one's accomplishments.

portion Amount of a menu item that is served to the customer.

portion control (PC) cuts Meat cut to specification.

portion cost Cost of one portion of a standardized recipe.

potentially hazardous foods Foods that present more of a risk for harboring miccroorganisms that cause foodborne illnesses.

poultry Large domestic birds such as chicken, turkey, duck, and goose.

poussin Young, small chicken weighing less than one pound.

prawns Freshwater shrimp.

prefermented dough Yeast-raised dough in which the gluten has overdeveloped or the dough has overfermented; also called old dough.

preliminary selling price Lowest suggested selling price listed on the menu.

Prepared and Perishable Food Programs (PPFP) Recovery programs that redistribute small quantities of freshly prepared foods and perishables.

presalé Lamb or mutton raised on salty grass on the French seacoast; a high quality of meat.

price factor method Method of setting menu item prices by comparing food cost to desired food cost percentages and the amount of money the operation wants to achieve.

primal cut Large, primary piece of meat; a wholesale cut.

prime steam lard Fat that is stripped from the internal organs of an animal at the time of slaughter.

prix fixe Menu that charges a set price for the entire meal.

processed cheese Pasteurized product that combines melted ripened and fresh cheeses with flavorings and emulsifiers.

processed eggs Shell eggs that have been frozen or dried.

product specification Describes the quality and quantity of each standardized recipe ingredient.

progressive grinding Grinding with successively smaller plates; a standard method for grinding forcemeat.

proof Percentage of alcohol.

proofing cabinet Enclosed cabinet capable of producing heat and moisture for proofing of bread, rolls, and other yeast-raised items.

protein One of a class of complex compounds that are an essential part of living matter.

protein alternative Plant-based protein.

psychological pricing method Determining menu item prices by considering what guests will pay for any given item.

pulses Dried seeds such as lentils.

punching down Method used to collapse dough's cell structure, allowing the carbon dioxide gas to escape; redistributes yeast; promotes continued growth.

purchase order Form that communicates to the purveyor the items to be purchased.

purchasing Functions of planning, obtaining quotes, ordering, receiving, storage, and issuance of product for an establishment.

purée Mashed or sieved potatoes, vegetables, fruit, and so on.

purveyor Vendor.

putrefactive Describes undesirable bacteria that cause food to spoil.

pyrolysis Process of roasting coffee beans until the oils emerge.

Q

Q factor Price charged to recover the cost of all the ingredients that are too small to calculate.

quarter To divide or cut into quarters.

quenelle Fine forcement mixture that is poached.

quiche Open tart filled with a baked egg custard to which other fillings have been added; for example, quiche lorraine.

quick breads Items that have a breadlike texture but contain no yeast products.

R

racking Process of clarifying and aerating wine.

radiation Energy (heat) transmitted through space by the propagation of a wave through any form of matter; can be in the form of infrared or microwave cooking.

radura symbol International sign applied to irradiated food.

raft Coagulated protein formation that floats on a stock and acts as a clarifying agent.

ragù Any meat- or poultry-based pasta sauce prepared by stewing or braising.

ramekin Earthenware dish in which food is baked and served.

rancio Refers to the nutty, fatty richness of brandy.

random garnish Ingredient such as nuts or olives folded into forcemeat.

ratite Small-winged bird that does not fly.

ravioli Stuffed pasta made from small squares or circular envelopes of egg and flour dough.

receiving Process by which products are accepted from the purveyor.

recipe conversion To change a recipe to produce a new amount or yield.

recipe cost Total cost to prepare a recipe.

recipe cost per unit Ingredient cost per recipe unit.

reamer Used to extract juice from citrus fruits.

ready to cook (RTC) Poultry that is dressed with head, feet, and internal organs removed.

réchaud Portable stove used for cooking and flambéing food tableside.

recovery time Time it takes for the fat in a deep-fat fryer to return to the required cooking temperature after the food has been submerged.

reduction Simmering a liquid for increasing lengths of time to produce a stock rich in flavor.

references Names of people who can confirm one's job skills or qualifications.

regional cuisine Foods, ingredients, and cooking methods characteristic of a given part of the country.

relative humidity Percentage of moisture or water vapor contained in air at any definite temperature.

remouillage Weak stock made with solid ingredients left after straining stock.

requisition Form that allows management to track the physical movement of inventory items and costs internally.

résumé Summary of one's work history, experience, qualifications, and education.

retarder/proofer Refrigerating unit designed to slow down the fermentation of dough.

rice The seeds of a grassy aquatic plant; varieties include short-grain, medium-grain, long-grain, brown, white, enriched, converted, instant, and specialty.

rigor mortis Condition that sets into the body of a dead animal, stiffening muscles; it is caused by chemical changes in the flesh.

rillette Preserved meat.

rind Skin or outer coat that may be peeled, grated, or taken off certain citrus fruits, such as the lemon or orange.

ripening Stage in the cheese-making process in which bacteria or molds begin to work on the fresh curds.

risotto Italian rice dish.

rivet Flat piece of metal that holds the tang in a knife's handle.

roasting Dry cooking technique in which food is cooked on a rack or mirepoix in a closed environment using dry, hot air.

robe Color or hue of wine.

robusta Hardier type of coffee with a heavy, earthy aroma.

rondelle Round cut made to a cylindrical vegetable.

roots Deep taproots of plants that are edible.

rotisserie Used to cook meats and other foods as they turn slowly on a spit in front of a heat source.

rôtisseur/roast chef One who roasts, braises, and stews foods and produces their sauces.

rotissoire Roasting pan.

roulade Boned poultry or game stuffed in cheesecloth or plastic wrap instead of skin.

round fish Fish with a round or oval compressed body and a backbone that runs across the top of its body.

rounding Shaping divided pieces of dough into smooth, round balls, allowing them to seal; also called preshaping.

roux Thickening agent made of flour and clarified butter or other fat used to thicken soups and sauces.

russe Saucepan with a long handle and straight sides.

Russian service Style of service in which the server spoons or plates portions of the meal directly on the plate in front of guests; may include tureen, platter, or casserole service; also called English or Silver service.

S

salamander Top-fired grill used for glazing or browning of food.

sales Amount of money brought into a foodservice operation by customers.

sanitation Knowledge of healthy and clean conditions; application of methods to remove disease-causing bacteria.

sanitizing To reduce the number of pathogenic microorganisms to a safe level through the use of chemicals and/or moist heat.

satiety Feeling of fullness.

saturated fats Fats that are solid at room temperature.

sauce Flavored, thickened liquid served with entrées, accompaniments, and desserts.

saucier/sauce chef One who prepares sautéed foods and their sauces.

sautéing Dry cooking technique in which food is quickly tossed in a sauté pan in a small amount of hot fat.

sauteuse Sauté pan with sloped sides.

sautoir Shallow sauté pan with with straight sides.

scaling Term used in weighing bakeshop ingredients.

scone Quick bread that resembles a biscuit but has a richer flavor.

seafood Any edible animal that lives in water.

searing Browning the exterior of food prior to putting it in the oven; can be done either manually or in the oven.

seasonings Blend of herbs, spices, or salts used to enhance the flavor of foods.

seitan Protein alternative cooked from wheat gluten; has a chewy, meatlike texture.

semi à la carte Menu that presents some dishes priced and served together and others separately.

semiperishable Treated with preservatives to extend shelf life.

semolina flour High-protein flour ground from hard durum wheat.

sensory evaluation Systematic tasting of food to determine its objective qualities and consumer appeal.

sensory perception Ability of the sensory organs to detect and evaluate sensory stimuli such as sights, sounds, odors, tastes, and textures.

serrated Having saw-toothed edges, as in a serrated knife.

service set Large fork and spoon used as pincers by servers for tableside service.

seviche Raw scallops marinated in lime juice and tossed with chilies and other seasonings.

sexual harassment Any unwelcome behavior of a sexual nature.

shallow-frying Dry cooking technique that transfers heat to food with a moderate amount of oil; also called pan-frying.

shallow poaching Cooking technique that combines poaching with steaming.

shatter pack Packaging that includes poly sheets between frozen food before it is block frozen.

sherbet Sugar-syrup base with the addition of fruit, fruit juice, and sometimes alcohol; not a solid.

shirred eggs Eggs baked in individual ramekins or casserole dishes.

shocking Plunging blanched food immediately into cold water or an ice bath; stops the cooking process.

shoots Plant stems with a high percentage of cellulose fiber; also called stalks.

shortening Fat used in the bakeshop because of its ability to shorten gluten strands.

short dough Mixture of butter, sugar, pastry flour, and eggs.

short-mix method Creates a light gluten development and soft dough consistency.

shot Measure of liquid served straight up.

shrinkage Percentage of food lost during cooking; loss of moisture as a result of oxidation, which occurs during storage or aging, from high cooking temperatures, or from cooking too long.

shucked Removed from the shell.

side of beef Partial carcass or a quarter of beef.

side work Behind-the-scenes work required to prepare for service.

sieve Implement used in the bakeshop to sift or make fine in texture.

silken tofu Soft tofu with the consistency of flan or custard.

simmering Moist cooking technique that cooks food by means of mild convection in a flavorful liquid.

simple carbohydrate Made up of single sugars and pairs of sugars linked together; helps retain moisture.

singer Process of dusting a pan with flour to absorb the fat.

single-source buying Linking of a foodservice establishment with one purveyor for most of the products that will be bought.

skirting Specialized linen used for draping tables; three basic types include sheer, accordion, and box.

slurry Uncooked thickening agent made by diluting pure starch in cold water.

smallwares Small, nonmechanical kitchen equipment.

smoking Processing method in which food is exposed to the smoke of fragrant hardwoods to enhance flavor.

smoking point Maximum temperature to which a fat or oil can be taken before it begins to burn.

socle Platform to elevate a product to improve presentation and appearance.

soft dough Dough with a thick, pliable consistency ideal for rolling and cutting into shapes before baking; somewhat sticky.

soluble fiber Fiber which dissolves in water.

sommelier/wine steward One in charge of all aspects of wine service.

sorbet Water ice served between meals to stimulate appetite.

soufflé Light spongelike food, either sweet or savory; made to order.

soup Liquid, savory food made with meat, fish, or vegetable stock as a base.

sour Drink made with a sour base, such as lemon juice.

sourdough starter Simple mixture of flour, water, sugar, and sometimes yeast, added as a leavener to ensure consistency and reliability.

sous chef Assistant to the chief cook.

sous cloche Food served under a large, domed plate cover that is removed in front of the guest for added theater of dining.

sous vide Slightly cooked or raw food packaged in airtight pouches.

soy-based analog Soy product formulated to simulate the taste, texture, and cooking characteristics of an animal product.

spätzle Tiny dumplings made from flour, eggs, milk, and seasonings.

specification Written description of each product to be procured; commonly referred to as a spec.

spices Fruits, flowers, bark, seeds, and roots of plants and trees.

spirit Highly alcoholic beverage produced by both fermentation and distillation.

spoken menu One that is recited to customers by the server announcing daily specials.

sponge method Mixing method that allows dough to ferment and develop gas and flavor before it is mixed with other ingredients; used to develop heightened flavor and a lighter, airy texture.

spread Seasoned, easily applied mixture that adheres to a base or foundation.

squashes Fleshy fruits of the gourd family with a center cavity containing seeds.

staling Change in texture and aroma of baked goods as moisture is lost; occurs as soon as product is removed from the oven.

standard Rules or measures used for making comparisons and judgments.

standard breading procedure Sequence of steps in which food is coated alternately with wet and dry ingredients.

standard of quality Degree of excellence of a raw or finished product.

standard of quantity Measurement of weight, count, or volume.

standard portion Amount of food that is served for each order.

standard transport plate (STP) Small plate used by servers to carry flatware to and from a table; also called a serviette.

standard yield Consistent amount of product produced by a standardized recipe.

standardized recipe Written set of directions customized to meet the needs of the foodservice operation and produce the same quality item again and again.

staples Nonfood items, such as cleaning materials, paper goods, and smallwares.

starch Form in which plants store carbohydrates.

stationary growth phase Period in which bacteria grow and die at the same rate.

steaming Moist cooking technique that cooks food in a closed environment via the use of steam.

steam-jacketed kettle Double-walled stainless steel kettle that allows steam pressure to build between the kettle walls.

steep To soak.

stewing Combination cooking technique in which smaller pieces of food are cooked in liquid after browning or blanching.

still Appartus used to recondense vaporized alcohol.

stippling Decorative cuts made on the top of certain types of bread and rolls.

stir-frying Dry cooking technique using a large pan with sloping sides to cook food over high heat in a small amount of oil.

stock Gelatinous, flavorful liquid used in the preparation of sauces and soups.

storage Two-way function in which goods are received and issued from the storeroom.

straight-dough method Simple mixing method in which all ingredients are mixed in one operation; also called bulk fermentation.

streusel Crumb mixture of sugar, shortening, flour, spices, and flavorings; used as a topping.

strudel dough Dough that has been stretched paper-thin and sprinkled with butter for added flavor and flakiness.

style Refers to the amount of cleaning and processing of poultry prior to receiving it.

submersion poaching Cooking technique that completely covers food, such a fish, with liquid.

subprimal cut Basic cut of meat made from the primal cut.

suet Animal fat obtained from the area around the kidneys and loins of beef and sheep.

suggestive selling Sales technique in which the server encourages guests to add items to original orders.

supertasters People who have significantly more than the average number of fungiform papillae.

supreme Citrus segment.

surimi Formed fish; processed with various fish and flavorings to mimic shellfish.

sushi Cooked or raw fish served with rice.

sweating Combination cooking technique that uses a food's natural moisture to cook slowly without browning.

sweet/rich dough Used in most breakfast pastries and breads; can contain more than 25% sugar and fat.

sweetbread Calf's thymus gland; served as a variety meat.

sweetened condensed milk Whole milk that has had 60% of its water removed and a large amount of sugar added.

symposium Consumption of wine after a lavish, Greek dinner.

T

table d'hôte Set menu for the day at a fixed price.

table tent Folded menu placed on the table featuring specials, seasonal offerings, specialty drinks, and desserts.

tang Portion of the knife's blade that extends into the handle.

tannin Chemical component found in the stems, skin, and seeds of grapes.

tapenade Spread made with anchovies, capers, black olives, olive oil, and lemon juice.

tare weight Counterweight of a balance scale.

target market Group of people a foodservice operation will serve or attract.

tart European version of the American pie.

tartlet Small edible container made of puff pastry; shaped like a round pie.

taste Perception of dissolved substances by taste buds.

tempeh Protein alternative made from fermented whole soy beans that have been formed into a cake; has a nutty flavor.

temperature danger zone (TDZ) Temperature range between 41°F–140°F/5°C–60°C, in which bacteria may thrive.

tempering Process of equalizing the temperatures of two liquids before mixing them together.

template Pattern for a design, as in an ice sculpture.

terrine Ground forcemeat mixture baked in an earthenware casserole; served cold.

terroir Wine-growing territory referring to the region's ecosystem: soil, climate, topography, geology, and hydrology.

textured soy protein Bland-tasting, processed, dehydrated soy bean protein made from soy bean flour or soy protein concentrate.

theme Central concept or motif of a buffet.

thermal death point (TDP) Temperature at which yeast is no longer active; 138°F–140°F (59°C–60°C).

thermometers Bimetallic stem and digital types used to take the internal temperature of foods at various points in the flow of food.

tincture Basis of a liqueur.

tisane Herbal tea.

tofu Soy bean curd with a soft cheeselike texture.

tomalley Lobster liver.

tomato concassée Peeled, seeded, and diced or chopped tomato.

top notes Aromas with the smallest and lightest molecules that are quick to evaporate but provide instant impact.

topping Nourishing element of an hors d'oeuvre.

total temperature factor Result of the desired dough temperature multiplied by three.

tourant/swing chef One who works every station in the absence of the regular chef.

tourné Cut used to trim and shape vegetables into a football shape.

toxin Poison produced in organic matter.

toxin-mediated infection Foodborne illness that occurs when one consumes contaminated food.

Traditional Food Banks Organizations that distribute large quantities of nonperishable food.

tranche Slice of fish made by cutting through a fillet at an angle.

trans-fatty acids Result of hydrogenated and hardened polyunsaturated oils.

tray stands Collapsible frames on which servers may rest trays of food; also called jacks.

triglyceride Class of chemicals that includes fats and oils.

trim Percentage of food lost during the preparation of the food product.

trim loss By-product material trimmed from the food item.

triple-decker sandwich Sandwich made with three pieces of bread sliced into three layers.

trueing Process in which steel is used to keep the blade of a knife straight and smooth; it does not sharpen the knife.

truffles Pungent fungi that grow underground in northern Italy and France.

trunnion kettle Specially designed steam-jacketed kettle that can be emptied easily.

trussing Process of tying meat or a whole bird's wings and legs against its body to form a compact whole; allows for even cooking.

truth in menu Federal law mandating that all menu information be factual.

tubers Fat, underground stem vegetables.

tunneling Formation of holes within a baked good.

U

ultra high temperature (UHT) processing Combination of ultrapasteurization with special packaging.

ultrapasteurization Process of subjecting dairy products to much higher temperatures for shorter periods of time, killing nearly all bacteria in order to extend the product's shelf life.

umami Savoriness.

univalve Mollusk with a single, one-piece shell that covers the body; whelk, conch.

upselling Sales technique used by servers to increase a guest's order by suggesting larger portions or more expensive items.

V

vacuum-pack Airtight, moisture-proof packaging.

vacuum-packed aging Process of storing smaller cuts of meat for six weeks in airtight and moisture proof pouches that prevent the growth of bacteria and mold; also called Cryovac® aging.

variety meat Internal organs and other meat removed from the carcass during processing.

veal Tender, lean meat with delicate flavor; from calves.

vealer Veal from a calf ranging in age from 4 to 18 weeks.

vegan Strict vegetarian; one who consumes no meat or animal products.

vegetable Plant or parts of a plant that form part of the human diet.

vegetable shortening Lipid used for frying or baking.

vegetarian One who does not consume meat but may eat other animal products.

velouté Thick-textured white soup or sauce.

vendor One who supplies food or nonfood products to a foodservice operation.

venison Meat from various game animals such as deer, elk, and antelope.

vertical cutter mixer (VCM) Preparation equipment used to prepare large volumes of food quickly.

vinaigrette Temporary emulsion of oil and vinegar.

vinification Process of winemaking.

viruses Smallest known forms of life, also responsible for foodborne illnesses.

viscosity Appropriate degree of thickness.

vitamins Essential nutrients needed by the body in very small amounts. There are two classes of vitamins: fat soluble and water soluble.

viticulture Science of growing grapevines; growing condition for grapevines.

Vitis vinifera Grape species used to produce most wine.

volatile To evaporate when heated.

vol-au-vent Puff-pastry shell.

volume Amount of space an ingredient takes up.

W

wagon cart Used for carving large cuts of meat tableside; also called a slicing cart.

waiter's friend Simple, T-shaped corkscrew; the most common corkscrew in the foodservice industry.

water activity (a_w) Moisture needed for bacteria to survive.

water-packed tofu Firm or extra-firm tofu.

weight Heaviness of ingredients.

Weiner schnitzel Veal cutlet prepared Viennese style.

wet cure Curing food products in brine.

wet slow baking Technique of insulating the food item in a water bath during baking to protect the delicate ingredients and promote even baking.

wheat Main ingredient of breads.

whetstone Stone used to sharpen knives.

whey The part of milk that does not coagulate.

whipping method Quick bread method in which eggs and sugar are whipped together to create a foam before the remaining ingredients are added.

whole fish Entire fish with organs intact.

whole grains Seed kernels that have not been ground.

wild game Animals and birds that grow and live in their native environment; for personal consumption only.

window Thin membrane that forms when stretching dough; an indication of a dough's elasticity.

wine Fermented juice of grapes.

work section Related work stations that may share the same equipment and similar tasks grouped together for efficiency.

work simplification Technique used to perform mise en place most efficiently.

work station Area that contains all the tools and equipment needed to prepare a certain type of food.

wort Sweet, brown liquid extracted from the mash bed.

wrap Soft flat bread wrapped around a filling.

Y

yeast Microscopic plant used for fermentation.

yield test Procedure used to determine the edible yield percentage.

young dough Yeast-raised dough in which the gluten has not properly developed; underfermented.

Z

zest Outer, colored rind of citrus fruit used for flavoring.

zone Buffet area.

Recipe

A

al dente To the bite.

à la minute Cooked to order.

B

bain-marie Hot water bath.

baste To brush food as it cooks with melted butter or other fat, meat drippings, or liquid.

batonnet Small stick measuring 1/4″ × 1/4″ × 3″ (6 mm × 6 mm × 7.62 cm).

batonnette 1/4″ × 1/4″ × 3″ (6 mm × 6 mm × 7.62 cm) strip.

batons Sticklike cuts.

baumé scale A scale used to measure the specific gravity of liquids.

blanch To parcook.

blind baking To bake a pastry shell before it is filled.

bouquet garni Bouquet of herbs and spices.

brunoise 1/8″ (3 mm) dice.

C

caramelize To heat sugar in food until it reduces to a clear syrup ranging in color from golden to dark brown.

chiffonade Ribbons of leafy greens.

chinois Cone-shaped strainer.

chinois mousseline Fine-mesh cone strainer.

clouté Studded with cloves.

concassé Peeled, seeded, and roughly chopped.

cornstarch slurry The result of adding water to cornstarch before it is used, whipping it to eliminate any lumps.

couverture Professional quality coating, creating chocolate that is extremely glossy.

D

deglaze To add liquid to a hot pan.

dépouille Skim off impurities or grease.

diffuse To spread and disseminate.

dredge To coat with flour.

duchesse potatoes Puréed potatoes with egg yolks, salt, pepper, and nutmeg.

E

emulsify To bind two ingredients together that do not normally mix.

F

farce Forcemeat stuffing.

flambé French for "flamed."

flexipan Silicone sheet that can be molded to hold mousse.

fork-tender Without resistance.

fortified butter Clarified butter to which another fat has been added.

G

galantine Term commonly used for a boned and stuffed bird.

I

ice bath A container with ice and cold water used to rapidly cool foods.

instant starch Precooked starch that requires no heating to enable it to absorb water and gelatinize.

J

julienne 1/8″ × 1/8″ × 1″–2″ strips (3 mm × 3 mm × 2.5–5 cm strips).

jus A flavorful sauce of unthickened natural meat juices.

K

kirschwasser A clear, distilled cherry liqueur.

M

macédoine 1/4″ (6 mm) dice.

malt diastase A group of enzymes found in wheat flour that break down some of the starch and sugars.

mandoline Double-bladed slicing tool.

marmite Stockpot.

mirepoix Carrots, onion, celery, and sometimes leeks—rough-cut.

monter au beurre To whisk a piece of butter into a hot liquid.

N

nappé Coated or to coat.

O

onion clouté Onion studded with cloves.

osmosis Spreading of fluid through a membrane until there is an equal concentration of fluid on both sides of the membrane.

P

paillard A veal scallop or thin slice of beef that is quickly grilled or sautéed.

panada A thick paste made by mixing bread crumbs, flour, rice, and so on, with a liquid such as water, stock, or milk.

panko Coarse bread crumbs sold in Asian markets.

papillon Food baked inside a wrapping of greased parchment paper.

parmentier 1/2″ (1.27 cm) dice.

pastry cloth Large, lightweight canvas cloth on which pastry dough is rolled out.

paupiette Rolled meat or fish.

plaque à rôtir Roasting pan.

R

ragù Meat sauce typically served with pasta.

ramekin A single serving dish.

reduction Evaporation of liquid by boiling.

render To melt fat.

ricer Kitchen utensil used to mash or rice cooked foods.

rondeau Braising/stewing pan.

roulade A rolled slice of meat or fish filled with savory stuffing.

S

sake Rice wine.

salamander A small broiler unit used to quickly brown the tops of foods.

scant Slightly less than.

score To cut into fat in a diamond pattern.

sear To brown quickly.

shingle To overlap.

shock To submerge in ice water.

silpat A silicone baking sheet that will not stick to the sheet pan.

singe To dust with flour.

skimmer Long-handled, round, perforated tool.

soufflé dish Round baking dish with straight sides.

sweat To extract moisture using low heat and a cover.

T

temper To equalize products with two extreme temperatures or textures.

tournéed Trimmed to a large olive shape.

truss To tie or secure.

V

velouté Velvety-textured sauce or soup.

INDEXES

Subject

Page references in *italics* refer to graphics, illustrations, sidebars, or italicized text.

All recipes are listed in a separate index titled "Recipes."

Indexes

959

Recipes

CREDITS

A Adam Woolfitt/CORBIS, **831**; Advance Tabco, **106 (n)**; American Library Color Slide Co., Inc., **4**; American Metal Craft, Inc., **100 (o)**; American Society for Oenology and Viticulture/Anne Noble, **898 (b)**; Amy Neunsinger/Stone/Getty Images, **43**; Andre Jenny/Focus Group/PictureQuest, **837 (b)**; Ann Garvin, **41 (a–g)**; Ateco, **101 (y)**, **493 (l)**, **653 (k, m)**; **B** Baronne Philippine de Rothschild, **892 (b)**; Baxter, **650 (d)**; Becky Luigart-Stayner/CORBIS, **742**; Boyd's Coffee Company, **82 (d, e)**, **823, 825**; British Beer and Pub Association, **832**; Buddy Mays/CORBIS, **400 (d)**, **421 (d)**; Burke/Triolo Productions/FoodPix/Getty Images, **631 (d)**, **834 (c)**; Buzzard's Bay Brewing, **833 (e)**; **C** Candlelamp Company, **82 (c)**; Carlisle FoodService Products, **652 (g)**, **653 (l)**, **654 (q, w)**, **81 (b)**, **82 (a, b)**, **83**, **99 (a, c)**, **100 (g, j)**, **100 (r)**, **102 (aa, dd, ee, gg)**, **103 (d)**, **104 (e–h)**, **105 (a, b, c, e, g)**, **106 (o)**; Carpigiani/Cold Delite, **651 (c)**; Casa Solar Plata, **896 (a)**; Castello Banfi, **893 (a, c)**; Cat Gwynn/Stone/Getty Images, **38**; Catherine Karnow/CORBIS, **11**; Catherine Karnow/Woodfin Camp/PictureQuest, **838**; Charles O'Rear/CORBIS, **872 (e)**, **879 (c–f)**, **882**; Christina Peters/FoodPix/Getty Images, **436 (a)**; Cleveland Range, **77 (l, j, m)**; CookShack, **77 (l)**, **492 (a)**; Coors, **830 (a)**, **833 (d)**; Cragganmore, **839 (d)**; Cune, **896 (b)**; **D** d'Arenberg Wines, **890 (b)**; Dalwhinnie, **839 (a)**; David W. Hamilton/The Image Bank/Getty Images, **400 (c)**; Delamain, **840 (c)**; Demarle, Inc. USA, **654 (z)**; Denis Waugh/Stone/Getty Images, **827 (b)**; Detecto, **75 (h)**, **103 (a–c)**, **646**; Dinkel Acker, **833 (a)**; Don Stevenson/Index Stock Imagery/PictureQuest, **837 (a)**; Dr. Loosen, **894 (b)**; **E** Eising FoodPhotography/StockFood America, **Back cover**, **422 (e)**; Erika Records LLC, **651 (a)**; **F** F. Dick Corporation, **86 (a–h)**, **100 (f)**, **381 (a, b)**, **492 (c)**, **493 (c)**; Firestone Vineyard, **888 (c)**; Firestone, **833 (h)**; Foodcollection/StockFood America, **421 (h)**; FoodPix, **2–3**, **174, 294, 420 (c)**, **421 (f, i)**, **422 (a, b, c)**, **438 (a)**, **439 (f)**, **621 (d, f)**, **632 (e)**, **690–691, 846–847**; Fortant De France, **892 (a)**; Franziskaner, **833 (b)**; **G** Gallo Vineyards, **874, 879 (h)**; Garland Commercial Industries, Inc., **76 (a, d)**, **78 (p)**, **650 (a)**; George Killian's, **833 (c)**; Glenkinchie, **839 (b)**; Greco Di Tufo, **893 (b)**; **H** Harpoon, **833 (f)**; Harry Bischof/StockFood Munich/StockFood America, **421 (c)**; Hatco Corporation, **81 (c, d, e)**, **649 (d)**; Hennessy, **840 (a, b)**; Herb Segars, **420 (b)**; Hobart Corporation, **74 (a, b, d)**, **78 (q, s)**, **80 (b)**, **492 (b)**, **649 (a, e)**, **650 (b)**; Hunter/StockFood America, **421 (g)**; **I** InterMetro Industries, Inc., **75 (i)**, **82 (f)**; **J** JB Prince Company, **493 (j)**, **652 (c, h)**, **653 (j, n)**, **654 (s, u, v, x)**; John Boos & Co., **651 (d)**; Joseph Phelps, **888 (e)**; **K** Kelly-Mooney Photography/CORBIS, **897 (c)**; Keren Su/CORBIS, **828 (b)**; Kindra Clineff Photography, **10**; Kobrand, **888 (d)**; **L** Lagavulin, **839 (c)**; Lance Nelson/CORBIS, **872 (f)**; Le Muscadet De Barre, **891**; Lori Alden/Cook's Thesaurus, **420 (d)**, **421 (k)**, **429, 438 (b)**, **439 (a, c)**, **620 (d)**, **625 (b, d)**; Luis Pato, **897 (b)**;